Applied Welfare Economics

The International Library of Critical Writings in Economics

Series Editor: Mark Blaug

> *Professor Emeritus, University of London, UK*
> *Professor Emeritus, University of Buckingham, UK*
> *Visiting Professor, University of Amsterdam, The Netherlands*

This series is an essential reference source for students, researchers and lecturers in economics. It presents by theme a selection of the most important articles across the entire spectrum of economics. Each volume has been prepared by a leading specialist who has written an authoritative introduction to the literature included.

A full list of published and future titles in this series is printed at the end of this volume.

Wherever possible, the articles in these volumes have been reproduced as originally published using facsimile reproduction, inclusive of footnotes and pagination to facilitate ease of reference.

For a list of all Edward Elgar published titles visit our site on the World Wide Web at
www.e-elgar.com

Applied Welfare Economics

Edited by

Richard E. Just

Distinguished University Professor
University of Maryland, USA

Darrell L. Hueth

Professor
University of Maryland, USA

and

Andrew Schmitz

Professor and Ben Hill Griffin, Jr. Endowed Chair, University of Florida, USA
Research Professor, University of California, USA
and Adjunct Professor, University of Saskatchewan, Canada

THE INTERNATIONAL LIBRARY OF CRITICAL WRITINGS IN ECONOMICS

An Elgar Reference Collection
Cheltenham, UK • Northampton, MA, USA

Published by
Edward Elgar Publishing Limited
Glensanda House
Montpellier Parade
Cheltenham
Glos GL50 1UA
UK

Edward Elgar Publishing, Inc.
William Pratt House
9 Dewey Court
Northampton
Massachusetts 01060
USA

A catalogue record for this book is available from the British Library

Library of Congress Control Number: 2007937485

ISBN 978 1 84720 577 3

Printed and bound in Great Britain by MPG Books Ltd, Bodmin, Cornwall

Contents

Acknowledgements

The editors and publishers wish to thank the authors and the following publishers who have kindly given permission for the use of copyright material.

American Economic Association for articles: E. J. Mishan (1959), 'Rent as a Measure of Welfare Change', *American Economic Review*, **49** (3), June, 386–94; Kenneth J. Arrow and Robert C. Lind (1970), 'Uncertainty and the Evaluation of Public Investment Decisions', *American Economic Review*, **60** (3), June, 364–78; Arnold C. Harberger (1971), 'Three Basic Postulates for Applied Welfare Economics: An Interpretive Essay', *Journal of Economic Literature*, **9** (3), September, 785–97; Eugene Silberberg (1972), 'Duality and the Many Consumer's Surpluses', *American Economic Review*, **62** (5), December, 942–52; Robert D. Willig (1976), 'Consumer's Surplus Without Apology', *American Economic Review*, **66** (4), September, 589–97; Richard E. Just, Andrew Schmitz and David Zilberman (1979), 'Price Controls and Optimal Export Policies under Alternative Market Structures', *American Economic Review*, **69** (4), September, 706–14; Richard E. Just and Darrell L. Hueth (1979), 'Welfare Measures in a Multimarket Framework', *American Economic Review*, **69** (5), December, 947–54; Alan Randall and John R. Stoll (1980), 'Consumer's Surplus in Commodity Space', *American Economic Review*, **70** (3), June, 449–55; Jerry A. Hausman (1981), 'Exact Consumer's Surplus and Deadweight Loss', *American Economic Review*, **71** (4), September, 662–76; Daniel A. Graham (1981), 'Cost-Benefit Analysis under Uncertainty', *American Economic Review*, **71** (4), September, 715–25; Nancy E. Bockstael and Kenneth E. McConnell (1983), 'Welfare Measurement in the Household Production Framework', *American Economic Review*, **73** (4), September, 806–14.

Kenneth J. Arrow for his own excerpt: (1970), 'The Organization of Economic Activity: Issues Pertinent to the Choice of Market versus Nonmarket Allocation', in Julius Margolis and Robert H. Haveman (eds), *Public Expenditures and Policy Analysis*, Chapter 2, 59–73.

Blackwell Publishing Ltd for articles: Nicholas Kaldor (1939), 'Welfare Propositions of Economics and Interpersonal Comparisons of Utility', *Economic Journal*, **XLIX** (195), September, 549–52; J. R. Hicks (1939), 'The Foundations of Welfare Economics', *Economic Journal*, **XLIX** (196), December, 696–712; T. de Scitovszky (1941), 'A Note on Welfare Propositions in Economics', *Review of Economic Studies*, **9** (1), November, 77–88; J. R. Hicks (1943), 'The Four Consumer's Surpluses', *Review of Economic Studies*, **11** (1), Winter, 31–41; Otto A. Davis and Andrew B. Whinston (1965), 'Welfare Economics and the Theory of Second Best', *Review of Economic Studies*, **32** (1), January, 1–14; Andrew Schmitz and David Seckler (1970), 'Mechanized Agriculture and Social Welfare: The Case of the Tomato Harvester', *American Journal of Agricultural Economics*, **52** (4), November, 569–77; Karl-Göran Mäler (1971), 'A Method of Estimating Social Benefits from Pollution Control', *Swedish Journal of*

Volume One, Chapter 6, 153–80. (A revised version of an article originally published in *Review of Economic Studies*, **XXIV**, 1956, 11–32.)

MIT Press Journals for articles: Paul A. Samuelson (1954), 'The Pure Theory of Public Expenditure', *Review of Economics and Statistics*, **36** (4), November, 387–9; Francis M. Bator (1958), 'The Anatomy of Market Failure', *Quarterly Journal of Economics*, **LXXII** (3), August, 351–79; Benton F. Massell (1969), 'Price Stabilization and Welfare', *Quarterly Journal of Economics*, **83** (2), May, 284–98; Gary S. Becker and Kevin M. Murphy (1993), 'A Simple Theory of Advertising as a Good or Bad', *Quarterly Journal of Economics*, **108** (4), November, 941–64.

Oxford University Press for article: Paul A. Samuelson (1950), 'Evaluation of Real National Income', *Oxford Economic Papers*, **2** (1), New Series, January, 1–29.

Springer Science and Business Media for article: Richard G. Lipsey (2007), 'Reflections on the General Theory of Second Best at its Golden Jubilee', *International Tax and Public Finance*, **14** (4), August, 349–64.

Scandinavian University Press for excerpt: W. Michael Hanemann (1992), 'Preface', in Ståle Navrud (ed.), *Pricing the European Environment*, 9–35.

University of Chicago Press for excerpt: Paul A. Samuelson (1942), 'Constancy of the Marginal Utility of Income', in Oscar Lange, Francis McIntyre and Theodore O. Yntema (eds), *Studies in Mathematical Economics and Econometrics: In Memory of Henry Schultz*, 75–91.

University of Wisconsin and Board of Regents of the University of Wisconsin System for article: Timothy J. Bartik (1988), 'Measuring the Benefits of Amenity Improvements in Hedonic Price Models', *Land Economics*, **64** (2), May, 172–83.

In addition the publishers wish to thank the Library at the University of Warwick, UK, and the Library of Indiana University at Bloomington, USA, for their assistance in obtaining these articles.

Introduction

Introduction

Richard E. Just, Darrell L. Hueth, and Andrew Schmitz

Applied welfare economic practices extend deeply into the classic papers in the field. In many cases, the intuitive insights provided by the innovative scholars transcend much of the mathematical sophistry and plethora of critical social issues of a much later time. Perhaps, more importantly, the practicality of these insights still drives much of current practice in applied analysis of the economic welfare implications of public policies.

With the intent of providing current students and scholars with a convenient single source for some of the most basic foundations of applied welfare economics, we offer this book of readings. While many other attempts have been made to collect the essential readings in welfare economics, past efforts are either now old and out of date, focused on theoretical ends, include few exemplary papers on application, and/or cover the waterfront so broadly that many volumes are required. We offer this volume as an alternative for practitioners of applied welfare economics. We have collected in one volume the most important papers that serve as a foundation for applied welfare economic practices, the major papers that develop the methodology of applied economic welfare measurement, and some of the most exemplary applications in the major fields of applied work. These papers complement well and serve as a supplementary reference book for our textbook, *The Welfare Economics of Public Policy: A Practical Approach to Project and Policy Evaluation* (Northampton, MA: Edward Elgar, 2004).

We provide in the remainder of this introduction some historical perspective and description of the relationship of significant contributions to current practices in applied welfare economics. These descriptions are arranged according to the overall outline of this volume. The first group of five papers provides the primary justification for government intervention that gives rise to the need for economic welfare analysis of public policies and projects. The primary motivation is market failure, but results on the theory of second best make clear that certain conditions must hold before elimination of market failures is valid at the individual market level.

The second group of nine papers provides the theoretical foundations for applied welfare economics. Four of these papers provide the historical roots of what remain valid measures of individual welfare, as well as historical and practical explanations of why consumer surplus has remained such a widely used concept for more than a century. The remaining five papers provide the historical roots of the compensation principle, sometimes called the potential Pareto principle, that remains as the primary principle for evaluating public projects and policies that have both losers and gainers.

The third group of six papers provides the methodological foundations for modern applied welfare economics. They demonstrate the problems of nonuniqueness and path dependence that eliminate consumer surplus as an underlying principle for consumer welfare evaluation for an individual. However, they demonstrate the abilities of consumer surplus to approximate willingness-to-pay measures that have validity both in their uniqueness and path independence as well as in their direct applicability in applying the compensation criterion.

The remaining papers in this volume focus on a variety of generalizations and applications of economic welfare analysis. Because the issue of whether to pay compensation remains a value judgment, most modern economic welfare practices focus on identifying the distributional effects of policies and projects as well as their overall social efficiency as determined according to the compensation criterion. Because distributional issues cut across virtually all interesting fields of application, we include a short section, consisting of two papers, intended to emphasize the importance of illuminating distributional considerations in practical applications to policy analysis.

The remaining sections on applications provide perspective on the extension of classical welfare economic practices to noncompetitive behavior (two papers), multimarket issues and the case where distortions in other markets cannot be ignored (four papers), stochastic settings with risk and uncertainty (four papers), incorporating the role of information in modern economic welfare analysis (three papers), and welfare measurement in cases of externalities and nonmarket goods such as environmental amenities (eight papers). In each of these areas, generalizations of the classical foundations of welfare economics have been required. But the collective set of these generalizations now represents a rather complete foundation for practitioners of applied welfare economics.

We conclude with three thoughtful reflections that have been offered by some of the prominent practitioners of applied welfare economics in forums that have called for retrospective assessments (at 12–15 year intervals from 1980 to the present).

The justification for public intervention

Any practitioner of applied welfare economics must understand well the justification for public intervention in order to determine the merit and efficiency of intervention. The economist A.C. Pigou (1952), first published in 1920, was one of the first to provide a justification for public intervention in markets. In his classical and lengthy book (876 pages), *The Economics of Welfare*, he argued that subsidies and taxes could be used to correct for externalities, which he called divergences between social and private product. Samuelson (1954, Chapter 1, this volume) later generalized the concept of externalities to the case of public goods which can be regarded as symmetrical consumer-consumer externalities for non-rival, non-excludible goods. He also developed the necessary conditions for the optimal provision of these goods and provided a diagrammatic exposition of these conditions. It was Bator (1958, Chapter 2, this volume), however, who first provided a rigorous analytic exposition of the general theory of externalities including the distinctions between pecuniary and technological externalities, positive and negative externalities, public goods and other cases that lead to market failure such as increasing returns in the large and indivisibilities. Later Arrow (1970, Chapter 3, this volume) added critical clarification to the interrelationships between the concepts of (1) competitive equilibrium, (2) externalities, (3) convexity of consumption sets and input requirement sets and (4) the existence of universal markets. Arrow showed that as long as markets exist for 'external' effects, competitive equilibrium will be Pareto efficient and that the key role of convexity has to do with the existence of competitive equilibrium rather than externalities. These core studies define market failure as the justification for public intervention. Accordingly, the measurement of welfare effects of market failures and policies designed to correct them is a primary purpose of the study of applied welfare economics.

Until Lipsey and Lancaster (1956–57, Chapter 4, this volume) wrote their classical article on the theory of the second best, most practitioners of welfare economics assumed implicitly that the appropriate government intervention in cases of externalities and other forms of market failure was to recommend elimination of distortions wherever they existed, independent of conditions in other markets. Lipsey and Lancaster showed, however, that if distortions exist in related markets that cannot be eliminated, then the optimal intervention is not to eliminate entirely the distortion in the market of interest. Or, stated another way, if a distortion cannot be removed in one market, then distortions must also exist in other markets to attain social optimality. In this work, the term 'distortion' refers to any non-zero difference between the marginal social value and marginal social cost of a good.

While the work of Lipsey and Lancaster suggested that the common practice of considering economic welfare analysis for a single market as in Marshall's classical approach was not appropriate, because some markets are distorted, Davis and Whinston (1965, Chapter 5, this volume) were able to provide some rehabilitation for partial (single-market) welfare analysis. Almost a decade later, they were able to relax this rather unsettling conclusion by showing that, if the uncorrectable distortion was in a market sufficiently removed from the market of interest (for example, by a zero elasticity in some intervening market), then efficiency would imply elimination of the distortion in the market of interest.

Prior to the development of this literature on market failure, market-oriented economists believed that the only justifiable government intervention was lump sum income redistribution. Motivated at least in part by these foundations of applied welfare economics, a surge of government intervention has occurred over the last 50 years with efforts to correct non-competitive market structure, reduce environmental externalities, and provide public goods. Many of these core issues lie at the root of public intervention today, but modern times have brought about a realization and concern that government intervention, even when warranted, does not necessarily bring about a social optimum due to political power of non-competitive market interests, unanticipated risk, information and measurement failures, and a failure of Davis and Whinston's assumption required to make other distortions irrelevant.

Theoretical foundations of welfare measurement

From the time of Dupuit (1844) through Marshall (1890), engineers and economists used changes in the area below the demand curve and above the price line as a measure of the change in benefits for consumers. Likewise, the area above the supply curve and below the price line was used as a measure of producer benefits. These consumer and producer surplus areas, however, were not strongly tied to ordinal utility theory or given willingness-to-pay interpretations until the pioneering work of Hicks (1943, Chapter 6, this volume). He demonstrated that four different consumer surplus areas were candidates for measuring the welfare effect of a change in price for the consumer. Two of these apply to the case where the consumer is free to adjust the consumption quantity to the price change, which he called compensating and equivalent variation, and two apply to the case where the consumer is not free to adjust, which he called compensating and equivalent surplus. Moreover, he showed that the appropriate area for measuring these concepts of welfare change is not the area below an ordinary demand (and above the price line) that holds income constant as suggested by Marshall, but is rather the area below a compensated demand that holds utility constant. Hick's measures are commonly called willingness-to-pay measures (although equivalent variation and equivalent surplus measure willingness-to-accept). While these willingness-to-pay measures have a more formal basis in economic theory, the classical concept of consumer surplus continued to be used in many studies because of its perceived convenience.

Similarly, Mishan (1959, Chapter 7, this volume) rigorously established the relationship of the producer surplus area (above the supply curve and below the price line) to the neoclassical theory of the firm. He showed that producer surplus can be given an interpretation as the rent accruing to fixed factors, which is not equal to the profit of the producing firm, but rather is equal to the sum of the firms profit and fixed costs of production. This difference accounts for the fact that the firm loses not only its profit but also incurs a loss equal to its fixed cost in the event of a shutdown. In this early Mishan framework, the firm was assumed to be a price taker in both input and output markets.

Although largely unlike producer surplus, the term *consumer surplus* has been at the center of controversy almost since its first use. After decades of common use by practitioners of applied welfare economics because of its simplicity, amidst rather constant criticisms by economic theoreticians, two important papers served as major rehabilitating forces for the decades that have followed. Currie, Murphy, and Schmitz (1971, Chapter 8, this volume) presented an important survey paper that clarified the issues in this controversy and set the stage for a number of subsequent studies that rigorously resolved them. Along a much different track, Harberger (1971, Chapter 9, this volume) presented his famous 'three basic postulates' under which he presented compelling arguments for consumer surplus as a useful and practical basis for applied welfare economic analysis regardless of the various criticisms. These three basic postulates were adopted at least in spirit by the applied economic policy evaluation literature in subsequent decades as evidenced by the dominant use of consumer surplus.

While the theoretical foundations of applied welfare measurement for an individual have been centered in the use of producer and consumer surplus as modified by Hicks, perhaps the greatest controversies have related to interpersonal comparisons and compensation criteria which can justify intervention which make some individuals worse off in order to make other individuals better off. Harold Hotelling's (1938, Chapter 10, this volume) paper evaluating railway financing by taxation and utility rate regulation provided amazing foresight and rigor as a foundation for compensation criteria. His work provides the justification for aggregating surplus gains among individuals and comparing to aggregate project costs to measure the now common concept of *deadweight loss*, which he called *dead loss* (p. 254), as an aggregate economic measure of the costs of market failure.

At almost the same time, Kaldor (1939, Chapter 11, this volume) and Hicks (1939, Chapter 12, this volume) were addressing the question of whether consumer surplus measures of utility could be meaningfully aggregated without welfare weights, given Pareto's (1896) criticism that any policy that makes at least one person worse off cannot be supported on objective grounds. Their work introduced the now widely used Kaldor-Hicks compensation principle whereby a policy is desirable if the gainers' willingness to pay exceeds the losers' willingness to accept. Under their principle, while compensation is at least potentially possible, it is not necessarily paid. While this principle significantly widened the set of policy issues for which applied welfare economists could offer useful advice, the issue of whether actual compensation was required remained controversial. For example, Scitovsky (1941, Chapter 13, this volume) further complicated this debate by showing that cases can exist where the gainers can compensate the losers but, once implemented, those who lost can also compensate those who gained to return to the original state. However, this is only possible if compensation is not actually paid. Although not included in this volume, Gorman (1955) also showed for essentially the same reason that social preferences according to the Kaldor-Hicks compensation criterion can be intransitive if compensation is not actually paid. In contrast, Samuelson (1950, Chapter 14, this volume), using utility possibilities frontiers, demonstrated the inadequacy of the potential utility criterion even if the underlying consumer utilities could be measured accurately, because potential utility comparisons order few alternatives. Prior to the development of willingness-to-pay measures, consumer surplus was regarded as a money measure of utility that was comparable among consumers for purposes of interpersonal welfare comparisons. These results further strengthened the use of the Kaldor-Hicks compensation criterion because it was not motivated by an attempt to measure utility, but simply willingness to pay.

Methodological foundations of welfare measurement

Generalization of the Marshallian concept of consumer surplus to the case where a consumer is simultaneously affected by changes in multiple markets brought a very different controversy to the forefront. Samuelson (1942, Chapter 15, this volume) presented an insightful demonstration that consumer surplus is not well defined in this case. Specifically, he showed that consumer surplus cannot be a unique money measure of utility and that its nonuniqueness can imply contradictions depending on the use of data by the practitioner.

Much later, Silberberg (1972, Chapter 16, this volume) demonstrated clearly the path dependence of the line integral that defines consumer surplus in the multiple-market case. His work set the stage for the typical modern mathematical treatment of concepts of consumer welfare measurement. Further, while invalidating consumer surplus as a useful measure of welfare on its own merits, he showed that the Hicksian willingness-to-pay measures are well defined by the same standards. Henceforth, this work ascribed prime validity to willingness-to-pay measures as the underlying basis for applied welfare economics, although the issue of whether to pay compensation remained.

After Silberberg's work seemed to leave consumer surplus without basis, Willig (1976, Chapter 17, this volume) provided a rehabilitation by deriving the relationship of consumer surplus to Hicks' willingness-to-pay measures in terms of income elasticities and deriving error bounds on consumer surplus as a measure of the Hicksian concepts of compensating and equivalent variation. Not many years later, Randall and Stoll (1980, Chapter 18, this volume) followed with a similar analysis for the Hicksian concepts of compensating and equivalent surplus. These results showed that consumer surplus was unlikely to err by more than 5 percent as measures of the Hicksian willingness-to-pay concepts (much less with small income elasticities), which again gave the common practitioner of applied welfare economics a justification for using consumer surplus that many conventional practitioners preferred.

Further technical developments in the following decade, however, made compensating and equivalent variation almost as easy or even easier to measure than consumer surplus depending on the estimation approach. Following the same spirit as initial work by Hause (1975), Hausman (1981, Chapter 19, this volume) showed how the differential relationship between the indirect utility function and ordinary Marshallian demands given by Roy's identity could be used to find Hicksian demands from estimates of ordinary demands for an individual consumer. This simply required solving a differential equation. Vartia (1983, Chapter 20, this volume) further developed a simple algorithm that amounted essentially to a numerical approach for solving Hausman's differential equation problem for the multiple price change case. As a result, estimates of willingness to pay can be found directly from estimates of ordinary demands, eliminating the need to rely upon consumer surplus, even if the second-order flexible forms of duality that provide analytical forms for calculation of willingness-to-pay are not used in estimation (see Section 6.F of Just, Hueth, and Schmitz, 2004).

In spite of these results, consumer surplus measurements are still found in some of the literature. One reason is that applied practitioners of welfare economics often have a limited basis for choosing between compensating and equivalent variation, whereas the change in consumer surplus is spanned in typical applications by the two Hicksian variation measures, and approximates both based on Willig results.

Income distributional considerations in welfare measurement

With virtually all applications of welfare economics, income distribution is an issue. We offer two papers that illustrate the cross-cutting importance of whether compensation is actually paid. Both are exemplary applications highlighting the distributional consequences of policies that have been the subject of considerable public debate. One of the early and exemplary papers was Schmitz and Seckler's (1970, Chapter 21, this volume) ex post study of the mechanical tomato harvester. Their work drew wide attention to public financing of agricultural research, because the benefits of this technological innovation (developed with university involvement) to consumers, processors, farmers and landowners came at the expense of displacement of migrant California agricultural labor, the poorest of these groups. Schmitz and Seckler demonstrated the practical consequences of whether compensation was paid. Gardner's (1983, Chapter 22, this volume) paper presents an interesting prospective distributional analysis of choices available to policy makers regarding controversial agricultural subsidies that are so often stumbling blocks in industrialized countries' trade negotiations. He develops and estimates the insightful concept of a surplus possibilities frontiers to illustrate the tradeoffs among major societal groups of farmers and consumers presented by policy choices in the event that compensation is not paid.

Dimensions of public policy evaluation

In other areas of public policy evaluation, the social welfare effects of unchecked monopoly power is a major concern. After the implementation of anticompetitive prohibitions such as the Sherman Antitrust Act in the United States in response to unchecked monopolization in the late nineteenth century, concern remained regarding social inefficiency because some firms were able to operate below the radar of antitrust legislation. While Harberger (1954) presented an early estimate of the remaining inefficiency from monopoly in the US, suggesting that it was insignificant, several studies criticized his methodology. Subsequently, Cowling and Mueller (1978, Chapter 23, this volume) presented a study of a number of individual industries correcting major objections to Harberger's methodology and showing that the social costs of monopoly are substantial, particularly in some industries. Just, Schmitz, and Zilberman (1979, Chapter 24, this volume) demonstrate similar issues of inefficiency caused by market power in international trade and arising from the use of export taxes, producer cartels, and the like, depending on international market structures.

Traditional concepts of consumer and producer surplus were developed in a partial equilibrium framework that focused on a single market. An important and growing area of concern in applied welfare economics relates to cases where equilibrium responses in related markets invalidate the use of surplus concepts associated with partial equilibrium supplies and demands as an overall measure of welfare effects. While a few early studies attempted to derive the implications of changes in an input (output) price for output (input) market surpluses, Just and Hueth (1979, Chapter 25, this volume) were the first to introduce the concept of multimarket welfare measurement where introduction or elimination of a distortion in one market affect many markets. Thurman and Easley (1992, Chapter 26, this volume) and Brännlund and Kriström (1996, Chapter 27, this volume) offer applications of this methodology as extended in our earlier text (Just, Hueth, and Schmitz, 1982). One of the most important recent findings about the necessity to recognize general equilibrium relationships has been in the literature on the 'double' dividend. Intially it was argued that, if environmental taxes were substituted for labor taxation, then society could obtain a double dividend by not only eliminating the deadweight loss in the leisure-labor market, but also by reducing environmental externalities (the deadweight loss in in the market causing environmental damage). Parry (1995, Chapter 28, this volume) and others, however, showed that under reasonable cross-elasticities of demand between leisure and the good associated with environmental damage, this result would not hold. The literature on the double dividend along with the equilibrium material in our text addresses cases where the early Davis and Whinston (1965) approach to distortions in other markets fails because the distorted markets are not remote.

The classical concepts of welfare economics were developed under assumptions of certainty. Practical applications, however, encountered the realities of risk and uncertainty and the related need to evaluate welfare implications for individuals whose benefits were determined by different circumstances than those anticipated at the time of decision making. In this case, the observed quantities and prices could not be taken as a direct reflection of preferences, as is necessary to evaluate willingness to pay. In response to earlier papers by Waugh (1944) and Oi (1961) that seemed to show that both consumers and producers benefit from instability, Massell (1969, Chapter 29, this volume) showed that consumers and producers could not gain simultaneously in a market context because the counterpart of the gainer is worse off with instability. However, all of these early papers applied traditional welfare concepts with the implicit assumption that decision makers could instantaneously adjust to changing prices, essentially as if one could make decisions with perfect foresight. In reality, due to production lags, producers may have to make production decisions before prices are known while consumers may be able to make short-run consumption choices after observing prices with certainty. Graham (1981, Chapter 30, this volume) presented the early and insightful conceptual foundations for economic welfare analysis of decisions made under risk. Pope, Chavas, and Just (1983, Chapter 31, this volume) along with our earlier text (Just, Hueth, and Schmitz, 1982) presented the first approaches for using estimates of firm and market supplies to infer compensating and equivalent variation associated with changes in risk distributions. We also include the work of Arrow and Lind (1970, Chapter 32, this volume) in this section, which presents a very different public perspective in considering whether the government can eliminate the social inefficiencies of risk by acting as a risk-neutral facilitator of arbitrage.

A dominating theme of economic thinking that began with the Nobel prize-winning work of Joseph Stiglitz has been the role of information. While all the issues of asymmetric information, moral hazard, adverse selection, and the like, are beyond the scope of this volume, we include some of the basic papers that illustrate how issues of information can be incorporated in applied economic welfare analysis. Stiglitz (1985, Chapter 33, this volume) provides a useful overview and perspective on how issues of information affect economic analysis and economic well-being in general. Foster and Just (1989, Chapter 34, this volume) present a framework and welfare analysis where withholding information about a food contamination problem adversely affected consumers not only because of the contamination problem itself, but also because of consumption choices made in ignorance before information was revealed. Similar issues arise in product advertising regarding whether advertising is socially optimal. Becker and Murphy (1993, Chapter 35, this volume) present a household production approach that permits evaluation of the benefits of advertising on the basis of consistent preferences unlike the early advertising literature based on Dixit and Norman (1978). As we show in our text (Just, Hueth, and Schmitz, 2004), combining the concepts in Foster and Just (1989) and Becker and Murphy (1993) permits evaluation of false and misleading advertising as well as informative advertising.

In his classic 1920 book on welfare economics, A.C. Pigou (1952, p. 11) restricted the purview of economists to the area he called 'economic welfare' defined as 'that part of social welfare that can be brought directly or indirectly into relation with the measuring-rod of money'. This suggested that applied welfare economics was restricted to analysis of impacts on goods and services that had prices and quantities and for which methods had been developed to estimate supply curves, demand curves and elasticities. It was not until 1947, when Harold Hotelling sent his well-known letter regarding valuation of recreational services to the Director of the National Park Service (1947, Chapter 36, this volume), that the process of recovering nonmarket goods and services and nonmarket welfare measurement began. The Hanemann paper in the Reflections section of this book provides a complete story of this development.

Although Hotelling had laid out the general approach of using round-trip travel expenditures to estimate a demand curve for recreational service flows from a National Park and, subsequently, using this demand curve to infer the value of the Park itself, the method was not widely applied until the late 1960s and early 1970s. Most of the early studies used the zonal approach to estimate travel cost demand curves and focused on a single site. Based on statistical considerations, standard practice shifted to estimation based on individual observations. In 1971, Burt and Brewer (Chapter 37, this volume) extended travel cost methodology to the case of multiple sites, thus allowing for estimation of policy impacts on substitute sites and allowing for site valuation interdependence. In this study, Burt and Brewer were also the first to apply the line integral suggested by Hotelling (1938) to insure path independence of the integral of the demand equations.

Karl-Göran Mäler (1971, Chapter 38, this volume) investigated the conditions under which the change in the area between compensated demand curves could be regarded as a measure of willingness to pay for a change in environmental quality at a site. He introduced the concept of 'weak-complementarity' and explained that, if a market good could be identified that was weakly complementary with the environmental nonmarket good, then the change in the area between the demand curves could be regarded a valid welfare measure. Weak complementarity requires the existence of a 'choke' price where none of the good would be purchased and that utility is not affected by the environmental quality when purchases are zero. Bockstael and McConnell (1983, Chapter 39, this volume) later used the concept of weak complementarity in the household production model to show that welfare effects of non-market goods entering or produced with household technology could be measured by market data for essential goods. Bockstael and Kling (1988, Chapter 40, this volume) extended the concept of weak complementarity to the case where environmental quality is complementary with a set of market goods rather than a single good. During the 1970s and 1980s, a number of other approaches were developed to exploit complementary as well as substitute (Courant and Porter, 1981) relationships between market and nonmarket goods to measure effects of both marginal and discrete changes. Further, the hedonic approach (Bartik, 1988, Chapter 41, this volume) viewed the utility function as dependent on a set of characteristics of a market good including environmental characteristics. This approach works well for marginal changes but not so well for discrete changes.

During the last 30 years, willingness-to-pay for non-use or passive use values of natural resources has attracted increasing attention. However, relating these values to the measuring rod of money suggested by Pigou is difficult. Contingent valuation surveys of willingness-to-pay have generally been used to elicit the stated-preference values of persons or households (Randall, Ives and Eastman, 1974, Chapter 42, this volume). While initial surveys asked open-ended valuation questions subject to various forms of bias, referendum (discreet choice) models have resolved many of those problems (Hanemann, 1999, Chapter 43, this volume). This approach combines discrete choice theory, welfare theory and econometric methodology in a complete approach considered to best mimic a normal market. The result is a total valuation methodology.

Reflections

After many decades of development, we close this volume with three broad perspectives on applied welfare economics. Krutilla (1981, Chapter 44, this volume) reviews 30 years of theoretical attacks on applied welfare economics and asks 'how have applied welfare economists ... responded?' His answer (p. 4) is that they acted as though 'they were innocent of the controversy'. Decision makers continued to demand quantitative assessment of proposed policies and projects, but before various subsequent generalizations, applied welfare practitioners continued to provide their assessments using the best theory and methods available. Hanemann (1992, Chapter 45, this volume) reviews the development of nonmarket valuation techniques and surrounding controversies. He points out that well-known economists were strongly opposed to early nonmarket methods such as travel cost valuation when these were first presented. He suggests that, just as opposition subsided with improvements in travel cost methods, the opposition to contingent valuation methodology will also diminish as advances are made. Finally, Lipsey (2007, Chapter 46, this volume) revisits the theorem of the second best after 50 years and finds that it is still fully applicable. Piecemeal policy recommendations based on first-best solutions are almost always inappropriate. He argues (p. 5) that useful policy advice requires not only formal modeling but also 'appreciative theorizing, empirical knowledge and a good dose of good judgment'.

References

Courant, P.N. and Porter, R. (1981), 'Averting expenditure and the cost of pollution', *Journal of Environmental Economics and Management* **8** (4), 321–329.

Dixit, A.K. and Norman, V.D. (1978), 'Advertising and welfare', *Bell Journal of Economics*, **9** (1), 1–17.

Dupuit, J. (1844), 'On the measurement of utility of public works', *Annals des Ponts et Chaussées*, Second Series, **8**.

Just, R.E., Hueth, D.L. and Schmitz, A. (1982). *Applied Welfare Economics and Public Policy*, Englewood Cliffs, NJ: Prentice-Hall.

Just, R.E., Hueth, D.L. and Schmitz, A. (2004). *The Welfare Economics of Public Policy: A Practical Approach to Project and Policy Evaluation*, Northampton, MA: Edward Elgar.

Gorman, W.M. (1995), 'The intransitivity of certain criteria used in welfare economics', *Oxford Economic Papers, New Series*, **7** (1), 25–35.

Harberger, A.C. (1954), 'Monopoly and resource allocation', *American Economic Review*, Proceedings, **44** (2), 77–87.

Oi, W.Y. (1961), 'The desirability of price instability under perfect competition', *Econometrica*, **27** (1), 58–64.

Pareto, V. (1896), *Cours d'Economie Politique*, 2, Lausanne: F. Rouge.

Pigou, A.C. (1952), *The Economics of Welfare*, 4th edn, London: Macmillan & Company Ltd.

Waugh, F.V. (1944), 'Does the consumer benefit from price instability?', *Quarterly Journal of Economics*, **58** (4), 602–14.

Part I
The Justification for
Public Intervention

A
Market Failure

[1]

THE PURE THEORY OF PUBLIC EXPENDITURE

Paul A. Samuelson

1. *Assumptions.* Except for Sax, Wicksell, Lindahl, Musgrave, and Bowen, economists have rather neglected the theory of optimal public expenditure, spending most of their energy on the theory of taxation. Therefore, I explicitly assume two categories of goods: ordinary *private consumption goods* $(X_1, \cdots, X_n)$ which can be parcelled out among different individuals $(1, 2, \cdots, i, \cdots, s)$ according to the relations $X_j = \overset{s}{\underset{1}{\Sigma}} X^i_j$; and *collective consumption goods* $(X_{n+1}, \cdots, X_{n+m})$ which all enjoy in common in the sense that each individual's consumption of such a good leads to no subtraction from any other individual's consumption of that good, so that $X_{n+j} = X^i_{n+j}$ simultaneously for each and every ith individual and each collective consumptive good. I assume no mystical collective mind that enjoys collective consumption goods; instead I assume each individual has a consistent set of *ordinal preferences* with respect to his consumption of all goods (collective as well as private) which can be summarized by a regularly smooth and convex utility index $u^i = u^i(X^i_1, \cdots, X^i_{n+m})$ (any monotonic stretching of the utility index is of course also an admissible cardinal index of preference). I shall throughout follow the convention of writing the partial derivative of any function with respect to its jth argument by a j subscript, so that $u^i_j = \partial u^i / \partial X^i_j$, etc. Provided economic quantities can be divided into two groups, (1) *outputs* or goods which everyone always wants to maximize and (2) *inputs* or factors which everyone always wants to minimize, we are free to change the algebraic signs of the latter category and from then on to work only with "goods," knowing that the case of factor inputs is covered as well. Hence by this convention we are sure that $u^i_j > 0$ always.

To keep production assumptions at the minimum level of simplicity, I assume a regularly convex and smooth production-possibility schedule relating totals of all outputs, private and collective; or $F(X_1, \cdots, X_{n+m}) = 0$, with $F_j > 0$ and ratios F_j/F_n determinate and subject to the generalized laws of diminishing returns.

Feasibility considerations disregarded, there is a *maximal* (ordinal) *utility frontier* representing the Pareto-optimal points — of which there are an $(s - 1)$ fold infinity — with the property that from such a frontier point you can make one person better off only by making some other person worse off. If we wish to make normative judgments concerning the relative ethical desirability of different configurations involving some individuals being on a higher level of indifference and some on a lower, we must be presented with a set of ordinal interpersonal norms or with a *social welfare function* representing a consistent set of ethical preferences among all the possible states of the system. It is not a "scientific" task of the economist to "deduce" the form of this function; this can have as many forms as there are possible ethical views; for the present purpose, the only restriction placed on the social welfare function is that it shall always increase or decrease when any one person's ordinal preference increases or decreases, all others staying on their same indifference levels: mathematically, we narrow it to the class that any one of its indexes can be written $U = U(u^1, \cdots, u^s)$ with $U_i > 0$.

2. *Optimal Conditions.* In terms of these norms, there is a "best state of the world" which is defined mathematically in simple regular cases by the marginal conditions

$$\frac{u^i_j}{u^i_r} = \frac{F_j}{F_r} \qquad \begin{matrix} (i = 1, 2, \cdots, s; \ r, j = 1, \cdots, n) \text{ or} \\ (i = 1, 2, \cdots, s; \ r = 1; \ j = 2, \cdots, n) \end{matrix} \qquad (1)$$

$$\sum_{i=1}^{s} \frac{u^i_{n+j}}{u^i_r} = \frac{F_{n+j}}{F_r} \qquad \begin{matrix} (j = 1, \cdots, m; \ r = 1, \cdots, n) \text{ or} \\ (j = 1, \cdots, m; \ r = 1) \end{matrix} \qquad (2)$$

$$\frac{U_q u^i_k}{U_q u^q_k} = 1 \qquad \begin{matrix} (i, q = 1, \cdots, s; \ k = 1, \cdots, n) \text{ or} \\ (q = 1; \ i = 2, \cdots, s; \ k = 1). \end{matrix} \qquad (3)$$

Equations (1) and (3) are essentially those given in the chapter on welfare economics in my *Foundations of Economic Analysis*. They constitute my version of the "new welfare economics." Alone (1) represents that subset of relations which defines the Pareto-optimal utility frontier and which by itself represents what I regard as the unnecessarily narrow version of what once was called the "new welfare economics."

The new element added here is the set (2), which constitutes a pure theory of government expenditure on collective consumption goods. By themselves (1) and (2) define the $(s-1)$-fold infinity of utility frontier points; only when a set of interpersonal normative conditions equivalent to (3) is supplied are we able to define an unambiguously "best" state.

Since formulating the conditions (2) some years ago, I have learned from the published and unpublished writings of Richard Musgrave that their essential logic is contained in the "voluntary-exchange" theories of public finance of the Sax-Wicksell-Lindahl-Musgrave type, and I have also noted Howard Bowen's independent discovery of them in Bowen's writings of a decade ago. A graphical interpretation of these conditions in terms of *vertical* rather than *horizontal* addition of different individuals' marginal-rate-of-substitution schedules can be given; but what I must emphasize is that there is a different such schedule for each individual at each of the $(s-1)$ fold infinity of different distributions of relative welfare along the utility frontier.

3. *Impossibility of decentralized spontaneous solution.* So much for the involved optimizing equations that an omniscient calculating machine could theoretically solve if fed the postulated functions. No such machine now exists. But it is well known that an "analogue calculating machine" can be provided by competitive market pricing, (a) so long as the production functions satisfy the neoclassical assumptions of constant returns to scale and generalized diminishing returns and (b) so long as the individuals' indifference contours have regular convexity and, we may add, (c) so long as all goods are private. We can then insert between the right- and left-

hand sides of (1) the equality with uniform market prices p_j/p_r, and adjoin the budget equations for each individual

$$p_1 X^i_1 + p_2 X^i_2 + \cdots + p_n X^i_n = L^i$$
$$(i = 1, 2, \cdots, s), \qquad (1)'$$

where L^i is a lump-sum tax for each individual so selected in algebraic value as to lead to the "best" state of the world. Now note, if there were no collective consumption goods, then (1) and (1)' can have their solution enormously simplified. Why? Because on the one hand perfect competition among productive enterprises would ensure that goods are produced at minimum costs and are sold at proper marginal costs, with all factors receiving their proper marginal productivities; and on the other hand, each individual, in seeking as a competitive buyer to get to the highest level of indifference subject to given prices and tax, would be led as if by an Invisible Hand to the grand solution of the social maximum position. Of course the institutional framework of competition would have to be maintained, and political decision-making would still be necessary, but of a computationally minimum type. namely, algebraic taxes and transfers $(L^1, \ldots L^s)$ would have to be varied until society is swung to the ethical observer's optimum. The servant of the ethical observer would not have to make explicit decisions about each person's detailed consumption and work; he need only decide about generalized purchasing power, knowing that each person can be counted on to allocate it optimally. In terms of communication theory and game terminology, each person is motivated to do the signalling of his tastes needed to define and reach the attainable-bliss point.

Now all of the above remains valid even if collective consumption is not zero but is instead *explicitly set* at its optimum values as determined by (1), (2), and (3). *However no decentralized pricing system can serve to determine optimally these levels of collective consumption.* Other kinds of "voting" or "signalling" would have to be tried. But, and this is the point sensed by Wicksell but perhaps not fully appreciated by Lindahl, now it is in the selfish interest of each person to give *false* signals, to pretend to have less interest in a given collective consumption activity than he

THE PURE THEORY OF PUBLIC EXPENDITURE

really has, etc. I must emphasize this: taxing according to a benefit theory of taxation can not at all solve the computational problem in the decentralized manner possible for the first category of "private" goods to which the ordinary market pricing applies and which do not have the "external effects" basic to the very notion of collective consumption goods. Of course, utopian voting and signalling schemes can be imagined. ("Scandinavian consensus," Kant's "categorical imperative," and other devices meaningful only under conditions of "symmetry," etc.) The failure of market catallactics in no way denies the following truth: given sufficient knowledge the optimal decisions can always be found by scanning over all the attainable states of the world and selecting the one which according to the postulated ethical welfare function is best. The solution "exists"; the problem is how to "find" it.

One could imagine every person in the community being indoctrinated to behave like a "parametric decentralized bureaucrat" who *reveals* his preferences by signalling in response to price parameters or Lagrangean multipliers, to questionnaires, or to other devices. But there is still this fundamental technical difference going to the heart of the whole problem of *social* economy: by departing from his indoctrinated rules, any one person can hope to snatch some selfish benefit in a way not possible under the self-policing competitive pricing of private goods; and the "external economies" or "jointness of demand" intrinsic to the very concept of collective goods and governmental activities makes it impossible for the grand ensemble of optimizing equations to have that special pattern of zeros which makes *laissez-faire* competition even *theoretically* possible as an analogue computer.

4. *Conclusion.* To explore further the problem raised by public expenditure would take us into the mathematical domain of "sociology" or "welfare politics," which Arrow, Duncan Black, and others have just begun to investigate. Political economy can be regarded as one special sector of this general domain, and it may turn out to be pure luck that within the general domain there happened to be a subsector with the "simple" properties of traditional economics.

[2]

REPRINTED FROM
THE QUARTERLY JOURNAL OF ECONOMICS
VOL. LXXII, AUGUST, 1958

THE ANATOMY OF MARKET FAILURE

By FRANCIS M. BATOR*

Introduction, 351. — I. The conditions of market efficiency, 353. — II. Neoclassical external economies: a digression, 356. — III. Statical externalities: an ordering, 363. — IV. Comments, 371. — V. Efficiency, markets and choice of institutions, 377.

What is it we mean by "market failure"? Typically, at least in allocation theory, we mean the failure of a more or less idealized system of price-market institutions to sustain "desirable" activities or to estop "undesirable" activities.[1] The desirability of an activity, in turn, is evaluated relative to the solution values of some explicit or implied maximum-welfare problem.

It is the central theorem of modern welfare economics that under certain strong assumptions about technology, tastes, and producers' motivations, the equilibrium conditions which characterize a system of competitive markets will exactly correspond to the requirements of Paretian efficiency.[2] Further, if competitively imputed incomes are continuously redistributed in costless lump-sum fashion so as to achieve the income-distribution implied by a social welfare function, then the competitive market solution will correspond to the one electronically calculated Pareto-efficient solution which maximizes, subject only to tastes, technology and initial endowments, that particular welfare function.[3]

* Center for International Studies and Department of Economics, Massachusetts Institute of Technology.

I am much indebted to R. S. Eckaus and R. M. Solow for detailed comment and discussion.

1. "Activities" broadly defined, to cover consumption as well as production.

2. I.e., to the conditions which define the attainable frontier of maximal utility combinations with given preference functions, resource endowments and technology. A community is on its Paretian frontier if it is impossible to make anyone better off (in terms of his own ordinal preference function) without making someone else worse off. Associated with the utility possibility frontier, in turn, is a production possibility frontier denoting maximal alternative output combinations. (Cf. my "Simple Analytics of Welfare Maximization," *American Economic Review*, XLVII (Mar. 1957), 22–59, and references therein.)

3. In other words, given the "right" lump-sum taxes, markets will match the allocation called for by the point of tangency of the relevant W-function with the utility-possibility frontier, i.e., by the "bliss point." The W-function need not, of course, be explicit — it could be implicit in the political power-configuration which characterizes a community. On the other hand, it cannot be just any kind of function. It has to have some special characteristics which reflect a number of ethic-loaded restrictions, e.g., that individuals' preference functions are to count, and to count positively (cf., *ibid.*, and Section V below).

Many things in the real world violate such correspondence: imperfect information, inertia and resistance to change, the infeasibility of costless lump-sum taxes, businessmen's desire for a "quiet life," uncertainty and inconsistent expectations, the vagaries of aggregate demand, etc. With most of these I am not here concerned: they have to do with the efficiency of "real life" market institutions operated by "real life" people in a nonstationary world of uncertainty, miscalculation, etc.

What follows is an attempt, rather, to explore and order those phenomena which cause even errorless profit- and preference-maximizing calculation in a stationary context of perfect (though limited) information and foresight to fail to sustain Pareto-efficient allocation. I am concerned, in other words, with the decentralizing efficiency of that regime of signals, rules and built-in sanctions which defines a price-market system.[4]

Specifically, Section I sets out the necessary conditions for efficiency of decentralized price-profit calculations both in a "laissez-faire" and in a "socialist" setting of Lange-Lerner civil servants. Section II is a brief digression on an often discussed mode of failure in these conditions: neoclassical external economies. It is concluded that the modern formulation of the doctrine, in terms of "direct interaction," begs more questions than it answers; further, that the usual emphasis on "divorce of scarcity from effective ownership" is misplaced. Section III, then, suggests a comprehensive ordering of types of market failure, with generalized indivisibility, public goods, and, last and least, nonappropriability as the villains of the piece. Section IV consists of some comments on the Meade and Scitovsky classifications of external economies; on the analytical link between indivisibility and public goods; on the significance of "exclusion"; on organizational arrangements designed to offset externality; and on blends of the various types of market failure. Section V concludes with some cautionary notes on the relevance of market-efficiency for choice of institutions.

4. In most of what follows, I shall assume that individual preferences, though not necessarily sensitive only to own-consumption, are representable by strictly convex indifference surfaces (i.e., by an ordering (one for each individual) such that all points on a straight line connecting two equivalent points x and y are preferred to x (hence to y)). But convexity is too restrictive. It excludes not only such characteristics of man's psyche as violate the "usual" regularities — these I do want to exclude — but also such physical and topographical facts as lumpy consumption-goods. Rather than attempt a specification of preferences with convex-like properties where choice must be made among discrete bundles, I dodge the problem by attributing lumpiness only to inputs (including, however, inputs that are intermediate outputs).

I. THE CONDITIONS OF MARKET EFFICIENCY

The central theorem of modern welfare economics, the so-called *duality theorem*, asserts a correspondence between Pareto efficiency and market performance. Its analytical essence lies in the remarkable fact that with all-round convexity, independence of tastes, etc., the technocratically formulated, institutionally neutral, Paretian maximum-of-welfare problem has embedded within it a set of constants: "duals," Lagrangean multipliers, shadow-prices, which have all the analytical characteristics of prices, wages, rents, interest rates.[5] Correspondence between Pareto-efficiency and market performance implies, at the least, that decentralized decisions in response to these "prices" by atomistic profit- and satisfaction-maximizers sustain just that constellation of inputs, outputs and commodity-distribution, that the maximum of the specified social welfare function calls for. It implies, in other words, that decentralized market calculations correctly account for all "economic" costs and benefits to which the relevant W-function is sensitive.[6]

Duality can fail in many ways. Specifically, and in a statical and "laissez-faire" context:[7]

(1) Duality will fail unless the Pareto-efficient (a) input-output points (production) and (b) associated commodity distribution points (exchange) which associate with the maximum of the welfare function in hand are characterized by a complete set of marginal-rate-of-substitution (MRS) equalities (or limiting inequalities) which, in

5. The theorem holds for the statical steady-state flow model of the Walrasian sort where the solution values are stationary time-rates; it holds, also, for dynamical systems involving capital formation (given, still, convexity throughout). For these last, the solution values are time paths of inputs, outputs, prices, etc. (A set of points is convex if, and only if, the straight lines connecting all possible pairs do not anywhere pass outside the set. The set of feasible output points bounded by a production possibility curve is convex, for instance, if the curve itself is concave-to-the-origin or a straight line. On all this, see Section V of "Simple Analytics," *ibid.*)

6. Given, again, optimal lump-sum redistribution of as-imputed incomes. While I make use of the lump-sum transfer device throughout this paper to abstract from the income distribution problem and permit exclusive attention to Pareto efficiency, it is well to note that this involves a measure of sleight-of-hand. No decentralized price-market type "game" can reveal the pattern of taxes and transfers that would maximize a particular welfare function. "Central" calculation — implicit if not explicit — is unavoidable. Moreover, since distribution (hence correct redistribution) of numeraire-incomes interdepends with allocation in production and exchange, the supposedly automatic, nonpolitical character of market mediation is a myth on the strictest neoclassical assumptions. This is not to say, even on our stratospheric levels of abstraction, that markets are "useless." Where they do compute well we are saved an awful lot of calculation.

7. With optimal redistribution.

turn, yield a set of price-like constants. Where no such constants exist, reference will be to *failure of existence*.[8]

(2) Should such an associated set of Lagrangean parameters exist, duality would nevertheless fail, specifically in production, unless the bliss configuration of inputs and outputs, evaluated in terms of these price parameters, will yield: (a) a local profit-maximum position for each producer, rather than, as possible, a profit minimum; (b) non-negative profits for all producers from whom production is required; (c) maximum profits-in-the-large for each producer. Failure on counts (a) and (c) will be labeled *failure by signal*, that on count (b) *failure by incentive*.[9]

(3) Even if all efficient production configurations, or the one which maximizes a particular welfare-function, coincide with points of maximum and non-negative producers' profits, market mediation may fail in production. If prices are determined by market forces, they will not correspond to a Paretian maximum unless self-policing perfect competition obtains in all markets. Self-policing competition requires "very many" producers in every market.[1] If, then, for whatever reason, some markets are saturated by a few firms of "efficient" scale, the full welfare-maximum solution of inputs, outputs *and prices* will not be sustained. There will be *failure by structure*.

(4) Finally, even if all above is satisfied, market performance could still fail, and fail in a statical sense, due to arbitrary legal and organizational "imperfections," or feasibility limitations on "keeping book," such as leave some inputs or outputs "hidden," or preclude their explicit allocation or capture by market processes (e.g., the restriction, unless I go into baseball, on the sale of the capitalized value of my lifetime services). Failure is *by enforcement*.

8. We could consider, instead, the configuration which associates with the initial pattern of ownership of endowment. Or we could play it safe and extend the conditions to cover each and every Pareto efficient configuration. But this would be overly strict, since many efficient situations have no relevance either to any interesting *W*-functions or in terms of the initial distribution of scarcities.

It may be worth noting, incidentally, that "existence," as used above, is not the same as existence in the sense of, e.g., Arrow and Debreu (in "Existence of an Equilibrium for a Competitive Economy," *Econometrica*, Vol. 22 (July 1954), pp. 265–90). They use the term to denote the complete set of conditions which defines competitive equilibrium, and this includes, in addition to all that is implied by (1) above, conditions akin to my conditions (2), and some analogous conditions on consumers.

9. This is slightly misleading: as we shall see, failure on count (c) leads both to signaling and to incentive troubles. Anyway, the labels are only for expository convenience.

1. Or at least the potentiality of very many producers, ready and able to "enter the fray" instantaneously. This may be sufficient in the constant-cost case, where the equilibrium number of firms per industry is indeterminate.

All the above are germane to duality in its usual sense, to the statical Pareto-efficiency of laissez-faire markets with genuine profit- and satisfaction-seekers.[2] Conditions (1), (2) and (4) are relevant, also, to the decentralizing efficiency of a Lange-Lerner type organizational scheme. In its "capitalist" version, with profit-motivated operation of privately-owned means of production where it is simply an anti-monopoly device to assure parametric take-prices-as-given behavior, conditions (1), (2) and (4) are all necessary for efficiency. Of course condition (3): self-policing competition, no longer matters.

In its true socialist version, a Lange-Lerner system can afford to "fail" also "by incentive," (2b). Socialist civil servants, under injunction to maximize profit (in the small) in terms of fixed centrally-quoted prices, care or should care not at all about absolute profitability. By assumption the scheme can dispense with the built-in incentive of positive profit: the lure of bureaucratic advancement, the image of Siberia, or the old school tie presumably substitute for the urge to get rich. But if prices and the injunction to maximize profit are to be used to decentralize, condition (1): existence, and (2a) and (2c): correct and unambiguous signals, remain crucial.[3] So does condition (4): the solution of quantities and prices need not be profitable and self-enforcing, but it does have to be enforceable. If the nectar in apple blossoms is scarce and carries a positive shadow price, it must be possible to make every beekeeper pay for his charges' meals.

It warrants repetition that this has to do with whether a decentralized price-market game will or will not *sustain* a Pareto-efficient configuration. The word sustain is critical. There exists a host of further considerations which bear on dynamical questions of adjustment, of "how the system gets there." (E.g., will some "natural" price-market type computational routine of price-quantity responses with a meaningful institutional counterpart tend to track the solution?) These are not here at issue. We shall be concerned only with the prior problem of whether a price-market system which finds itself

2. The mathematically minded will object that (3) and (4), at least, do not really violate "duality" in its strict mathematical sense; the dual minimum problem still yields Lagrangean constants. True, yet I think it suggestive to use "duality" rather more loosely as a label for the general welfare theorem, particularly as this does not lead, in this context, to any ambiguity.

3. It is tempting, but wrong, to suggest that in a true Lange-Lerner world totals do not matter and only margins count. It is true that the non-negativeness of profits is immaterial. Where there is any sharing of shadow-price sets by two or more production points, however, totals necessarily become a part of the signaling system and if 2(c) does not hold they may lead down the garden path.

at the maximum-welfare point will or will not tend to remain there.[4]

The relevant literature is rich but confusing. It abounds in mutually reinforcing and overlapping descriptions and explanations of market failure: external economies, indivisibility, nonappropriability, direct interaction, public goods, atmosphere, etc. In a sense, our problem is simply to sort out the relations among these. In doing so, it is appropriate and useful to begin with a brief review of the neoclassical doctrine of external economies and of its modern formulation in terms of "direct interaction."

II. Neoclassical External Economies: A Digression

By Way of Some History

Marshall, as has often been pointed out, proposed the external economy argument to explain, without resort to dynamics, the phenomenon of a negatively sloped ("forward falling") long-run industry supply curve in terms consistent with a horizontal or rising marginal cost curve (MC) in the "representative" firm. The device permits — in logic, if not in fact — long-run competitive equilibrium of many firms within an industry, each producing at its profit-maximum price-equal-to-a-rising-MC position, without foreclosing the possibility of a falling supply price with rising industry output.[5]

The mechanism is simple. It is postulated that an expansion in the output of the industry as a whole brings into play economies which cause a downward shift of the cost curves of all the component

---

4. More precisely, whether the point of maximum welfare is or is not a point of self-policing and "enforceable" market equilibrium, where, following common usage, equilibrium is defined to subsume both the first-order and the second-order inequalities for a maximum. A firm, for instance, is taken to be in equilibrium only at a point of maximum profit. This way of defining equilibrium does bring in issues of stability, hence some implicit dynamics. In particular, the word "sustain" is taken to imply some scanning or reconnaissance by producers and consumers at least in the neighborhood of equilibrium. But I do not think it does any harm to subsume this much stability in the equilibrium notion. The possibility of a firm in *unstable* "equilibrium," i.e., in equilibrium at a point of minimum profit, is hardly likely to be of import.

On the other hand, correspondence between Pareto-efficiency and the equilibrium state of perfectly competitive markets is not sufficient to insure market efficiency. It is the burden of "failure by structure" that markets may fail to be competitive, and of "failure by enforcement" that legal or institutional constraints may prevent competitive markets from allocating efficiently, even though there does exist a competitive equilibrium for each Pareto-efficient configuration. "Existence" in the sense of Arrow and Debreu (*op. cit.*) is necessary but not sufficient for market-efficiency in the present context.

5. This refers to a so-called Marshallian supply curve. It has nothing whatever to do with the Walrasian "maximum quantity supplied at a given price" type schedule.

THE ANATOMY OF MARKET FAILURE   357

firms. These economies, however, are not subject to exploitation by any one of the myriad of tiny atomized firms. Their own MC curves, at $p = MC$, rise both before and after the shift, due, presumably, to internal diseconomies associated with the entrepreneurial function which defines the firm. Even the modern formulation is not entirely without ambiguity — institutional ambiguity is intrinsic to the device of parametrization: how many firms does it take for the demand curve of each to be perfectly horizontal? — but it does provide a means for "saving" the competitive model, of ducking the monopoly problem.

Marshall, and also Professor Pigou, "preferred," as it were, the other horn of what they perhaps saw as a dilemma. The external economy device, while saving competition, implies a flaw in the efficacy of the "invisible hand" in guiding production.[6] "Price equal to MC" is saved, but wrong. Market forces, they argued, will not give enough output by industries enjoying external economies and will cause industries with rising supply curves to overexpand. Hence the Marshall-Pigou prescription: to harmonize private production decisions with public welfare, tax the latter set of industries and subsidize the former.

It took the better part of thirty years, and the cumulative powers of Allyn Young, and Messrs. Robertson, Knight, Sraffa, and Viner, to unravel the threads of truth and error which run through the Marshall-Pigou argument.[7] The crucial distinction, which provides the key to it all, is between what Viner labeled technological external economies, on the one hand, and pecuniary external economies on the other. The latter, if dominant, cause the long-run supply curve of an industry, say A, to decline because the price of an input, B, falls in response to an increase in A's demand for it. The technological variety, on the other hand, though also a reversible function of industry output, consists in organizational or other improvements in efficiency which do not show up in input prices.[8]

6. That there are difficulties also with income distribution was by that time generally recognized.

7. The strategic articles, with the exception of Young's ("Pigou's *Wealth and Welfare*," this *Journal*, XXVII (1913), 672–86), as well as Ellis and Fellner's 1943 treatment, have all been reprinted in American Economic Association, *Readings in Price Theory*, ed. Stigler & Boulding. For an excellent modern discussion, see R. L. Bishop, *Economic Theory* (to appear).

8. Note, however, that there need be nothing about an organizational improvement to make it obvious in advance whether it will turn out to be technological or, through "internalization," pecuniary. Many trade-association type services which are justified by the scale of an industry could as well be provided commercially, and vice versa.

As regards pecuniary external economies, Robertson and Sraffa made it clear that in a sense both the Marshall-Pigou conclusions were wrong. For one thing, no subsidy is called for. The implied gains in efficiency are adequately signaled by the input price, and profit-maximizing output levels by the A-firms are socially efficient. Second, monopoly troubles may be with us, via, as it were, the back door. For what causes the price of B to drop in response to increased demand? We are back where we started: a declining long-run supply curve.

In the end, then, if *internal* technological economies of scale are ruled out, we are left with only *technological* external economies. All pecuniary external economies must be due to technological economies somewhere in the system.[9] It is true — and this is what remains of the original Marshall-Pigou proposition — that technological externalities are not correctly accounted for by prices, that they violate the efficiency of decentralized market calculation.

The Modern Formulation[1]

In its modern version, the notion of external economies — external economies proper that is: Viner's technological variety — belongs to a more general doctrine of "direct interaction." Such interaction, whether it involves producer-producer, consumer-consumer, producer-consumer, or employer-employee relations, consists in interdependences that are external to the price system, hence unaccounted for by market valuations. Analytically, it implies the nonindependence of various preference and production functions. Its effect is to cause divergence between private and social cost-benefit calculation.

That this is so, is easily demonstrated by means of a simplified variant of a production model suggested by J. E. Meade.[2] Assume a world of all-round perfect competition where a single purchasable and inelastically supplied input, labor $(\overline{L})$, is used to produce two homogeneous and divisible goods, apples (A) and honey (H), at nonincreasing returns to scale. But while the output of A is dependent only on $L_A : A = A(L_A)$, honey production is sensitive also to the level of apple output: $H = H(L_H, A(L_A))$. (Professor Meade

9. Pecuniary diseconomies, in contrast, need have no technological counterpart. Finite-elastic supplies of unproduced inputs are a sufficient cause. Recall, incidentally, that only narrowly statical reversible phenomena are admissible here.

1. While this section makes some slight use of elementary calculus, the reader uninterested in technicalities may avoid, without loss of continuity, all but some simple notation.

2. *Economic Journal*, LXII (Mar. 1952). Meade uses a two factor model and, while he does not explicitly solve the Paretian maximum problem, shows that market imputed rates of remuneration will not match marginal social product.

THE ANATOMY OF MARKET FAILURE   359

makes pleasurable the thought of apple blossoms making for honey abundance.)[3]

By solving the usual constrained maximum problem for the production-possibility curve, it can be shown that Paretian production efficiency implies

$$p_H \frac{\partial H}{\partial L_H} = w \tag{1}$$

$$p_A \frac{dA}{dL_A} + p_H \frac{\partial H}{\partial A} \frac{dA}{dL_A} = w \tag{2}$$

where p_H, p_A, and w represent the prices, respectively, of honey, apples and labor.[4] Equation (1) is familiar enough and consistent with profit maximizing. Each competitive honey producer will do for profit what he must for efficiency: hire labor until the value of its social as well as private marginal product equals the wage rate. Not so the apple producers; unless $\frac{\partial H}{\partial A} = 0$ — unless the cross effect of apples on honey is zero — their profit-maximizing production decisions will be nonefficient. Specifically, if apples have a positive external effect on honey output, market-determined L_A will be less than is socially desirable.[5]

A different way to see this is to examine the relations of private to social marginal cost. The marginal money cost of apples to the com-

---

3. Both functions are assumed homogeneous of degree one. Moreover, apple blossoms (or the nectar therein) are exhaustible, rationable "private" goods: more nectar to one bee means less to another. On the need for this assumption, see Section III-3 below.

4. Assuming internal tangencies and all-round convexity (the last is implicit in constant returns to L: the A-effect on H reinforces convexity), as well as nonsatiation and nonredundancy ($\overline{L} = L_A + L_H$), the maximization of $p_A A + p_H H$, subject to the production functions and the supply of labor, is equivalent to finding a critical value for the Lagrangean expression, $F = p_A A(L_A) + p_H H[L_H; A(L_A)] + w(\overline{L} - L_A - L_H)$. To do so, differentiate F with respect to L_A and L_H, treating p_A, p_H and w as arbitrary constants and set the resulting first order partial derivatives equal to zero. This will give exactly (1) and (2). (Needless to say, the value weights can be varied at will, or taken as given.)

5. To see this, rewrite (2) to read $\dfrac{dA}{dL_A} = \dfrac{w}{p_A + p_H \dfrac{\partial H}{\partial A}}$ and match it against

the profit-maximizing rule, $\dfrac{dA}{dL_A} = \dfrac{w}{p_A}$. Clearly, $\dfrac{\partial H}{\partial A} \lessgtr 0 \longrightarrow$

$$\left(\frac{dA}{dL_A}\right)_{\text{Private}} \gtrless \left(\frac{dA}{dL_A}\right)_{\text{Social}}$$

petitive apple producer is $\dfrac{w}{dA/dL_A}$; that of honey to the beekeeper,

$\dfrac{w}{\partial H/\partial L_H}$. It is the ratio of the two: $\dfrac{\partial H/\partial L_H}{dA/dL_A}$, that competitive market-mediation brings into equality with the equilibrating configuration of relative prices. Markets will be efficient if, and only if, this *private* marginal cost ratio reflects the true marginal cost to society of an extra apple in terms of foregone honey: the marginal rate of transformation between H and A.

What is MRT in the model? Differentiating (totally) the two production functions and dividing the value of one derivative into the other, we get, in absolute (cost) terms:

$$MRT \equiv \left| \frac{dH}{dA} \right| = \frac{\partial H/\partial L_H}{dA/dL_A} - \frac{\partial H}{\partial A}.$$

If, then, $\dfrac{\partial H}{\partial A} > 0$, the true marginal *social* cost of an "extra"

apple, in terms of honey foregone, is less than the market-indicated private cost. It is less precisely by the amount of positive "feedback" on honey output due the "extra" apple.

By combining (1) and (2), eliminating w, and dividing through

by p_H and $\dfrac{dA}{dL_A}$, we get the condition for Pareto efficiency in terms of

private MC's:
$$\frac{\partial H/\partial L_H}{dA/dL_A} = \frac{p_A}{p_H} + \frac{\partial H}{\partial A}.$$

Clearly, price equal to private marginal cost will not do. Further, if prices are market-determined, they will diverge from true, *social* marginal cost.

Any number of variations on the model suggest themselves. As Meade pointed out, interactions can be mutual and need not be associated with the outputs. Even in the above case, it is perhaps more suggestive to think of L_A as producing some social value-product both in the A industry and the H industry. In the most general formulation, one can simply think of each production function as containing all the other variables of the system, some perhaps with zero weight. Moreover, by introducing two or more nonproduced inputs one can, as Meade does, work out the consequences for income distribution and input proportions.[6]

6. The question of whether technological external economies involve shifts of each other's production functions, or mutually induced movements along such functions, is purely definitional. If one chooses so to define each producer's

THE ANATOMY OF MARKET FAILURE   361

Some Queries

The modern formulation of the doctrine of external economies, in terms of direct interaction, is not only internally consistent: it also yields insight. Yet one may well retain about it some dissatisfaction. There is no doubt that the Robertson-Sraffa-Viner distinction between the technological and the pecuniary sort gets to the nub of what is the matter with the original Marshallian analysis. It cuts right through the confusion which led Marshall and Pigou to conclude that the price mechanism is faulty in situations where in truth it is at its best: in allocating inputs in less than infinitely elastic supply between alternative productive uses. It also facilitates unambiguous formulation of the more difficult "falling supply price" case. But in a sense it only begs the fundamental question: what is it that gives rise to "direct interaction," to short circuit, as it were, of the signaling system?

Most modern writers have let matters rest with the Ellis-Fellner type explanation: "the divorce of scarcity from effective ownership."[7] Does nonappropriability then explain all direct interaction? In a sense it does, yet by directing attention to institutional and feasibility considerations which make it impracticable for "real life" market-institutions to mimic a price-profit-preference computation, it diverts attention from some deeper issues. Surely the word "ownership" serves to illuminate but poorly the phenomenon of a temperance leaguer's reaction to a hard-drinking neighbor's (sound insulated and solitary) Saturday night, or the reason why a price system, if efficient, will not permit full "compensation," in an age of electronic scramblers, for an advertisement-less radio program, or for the "services" of a bridge.[8]

function as to give axes only to inputs and outputs that are purchased and sold, or at least "controlled," and the effects of everything else impinging on production (e.g., of humidity, apple blossoms, etc.) are built into the curvature of the function, then it follows that externalities will consist in shifts of some functions in response to movements along others. On the other hand, if, as in our apple-honey case, it seems useful to think of the production function for H as having an A-axis, then, clearly, induced movement along the function is a signal of externality.

7. *Op. cit.*

8. Moreover, in the one sense in which nonappropriability fits all cases of direct interaction, it explains none. If all it denotes is the failure of a price-market game properly to account for (to appropriate) all relevant costs and benefits, then it is simply a synonym for market failure (for generalized externality), and cannot be used to explain what causes any particular instance of such failure. I use it in a much narrower sense, to mean the inability of a producer of a good or service physically to exclude users, or to control the rationing of his produce among them. In my sense not only bridges but also, say, television programs are fully appropriable: it is always possible to use scramblers.

It may be argued, of course, that at least the two latter examples are out of order, that radio programs and bridges do not involve "direct," i.e., non-price, interaction. But is this really so? Does not the introduction of a new program directly affect my and your consumption possibilities, in ways other than by a change in relative prices? Does not a bridge, or a road, have a direct effect on the production possibilities of neighboring producers, in precisely the sense in which apples affect the possibilities of beekeepers?[9]

True, perhaps bridges and roads are unfair: they violate the neoclassical assumption of perfect divisibility and nonincreasing returns to scale. But they surely do involve non-price interaction. In fact, lumpiness and increasing returns are perhaps the most important causes of such interaction. Are they to be denied status as externalities? More generally, are we to exclude from the class of externalities any direct interaction not due to difficulties with "effective ownership," any failures other than "by enforcement"?

It would be, of course, perfectly legitimate to do so — tastes are various. But I think it more natural and useful to broaden rather than restrict, to let "externality" denote any situation where some Paretian costs and benefits remain *external to* decentralized cost-revenue calculations in terms of prices.[1] If, however, we do so, then clearly nonappropriability[2] will not do as a complete explanation. Its concern with the inability of decentralized markets to sustain the solution-prices and quantities called for by a price-profit-preference type calculation, as computed by a team of mathematicians working with IBM machines, tends to mask the possibility that such machine-

---

9. It is possible, of course, to interpret these examples as involving very large changes in price: from infinity to zero. But it does not help to do so. The shared characteristic of bridges and programs is that there is no price which will efficiently mediate both supply and demand.

I have puzzled over ways of limiting the notion of "direct interaction" to something less than all instances where there is some interaction not adequately signaled by price. Robert Solow has suggested to me that this might be done by distinguishing situations where something is not subject to a market test at all from instances where no single price constitutes a correct test for both sides of a transaction (e.g., where the correct ration price for the services of an expensive facility is zero). I am inclined, rather, to drop the attempt to use "direct interaction" as an explanation of market failure; it is best used, if at all, as yet another synonym for such failure.

1. Recall that it is the existence of such "externality," of residue, at the bliss-point, of Pigouvian "uncompensated services" and "incidental uncharged disservices" that defines market failure. It may be objected that to generalize the externality notion in this way is to rob it of all but descriptive significance. But surely there is not much to rob; even in its strictest neoclassical formulation it begs more than it answers. In its generalized sense it at least has the virtue of suggesting the right questions.

2. As defined in fn. 8, p. 361 above.

calculated solution q's may well be nonefficient.[3] It explains failure "by enforcement," but leaves hidden the empirically more important phenomena which cause failure by "nonexistence," "signal," and "incentive." Section III is designed to bring these deeper causes of generalized externality into the foreground.

III. STATICAL EXTERNALITIES: AN ORDERING

If nonappropriability is, by itself, too flimsy a base for a doctrine of generalized (statical) externality, what broader foundation is there? Section I's hierarchy of possible modes of market failure suggests a fivefold classification. If, however, one looks for an organizing principle not to modes of failure but to causes, there appear to be three polar types: (1) Ownership Externalities, (2) Technical Externalities,[4] and (3) Public Good Externalities. These are not mutually exclusive: most externality phenomena are in fact blends. Yet there emerges a sufficient three-cornered clustering to warrant consolidation.[5]

Type (1): Ownership Externalities

Imagine a world which exhibits generalized technological and taste convexity, where the electronically calculated solution of a Paretian maximum-of-welfare problem yields not only a unique set of inputs, outputs and commodity-distribution, but where initial endowments plus lump-sum transfers render income distribution optimal in terms of the community's social welfare function. Assume, further, that everything that matters is divisible, conventionally rationable, and either available in inelastic total supply,[6] or producible at constant returns to scale; also that tastes are sensitive only to own-consumption. We know, then, from the duality theorem, that

3. Or that the algorism may break down for lack of a consistent set of p's.
4. I should much prefer "technological," but since this would necessarily confuse my Type (2) with Professor Viner's "technological" I fixed on "technical."
5. In effect, we end up with a five-by-three ordering of types of "failure": five "modes" vs. three "causes." Its relation to Meade's categories (*op. cit.*) and to Tibor Scitovsky's classification (in "Two Concepts of External Economies," *Journal of Political Economy*, LXII, April 1954) is discussed in Section IV below. I have had the benefit of reading, also, William Fellner's "Individual Investment Projects in Growing Economies," *Investment Criteria and Economic Growth* (Proceedings of a Conference, Center for International Studies, Massachusetts Institute of Technology, 1955) and an unpublished paper by Svend Laursen, "External Economies and Economic Growth."
6. The supply of such nonproduced scarcities need not, of course, remain constant. On the other hand, their ownership distribution must not be so concentrated as to preclude competitive rationing. There must exist no "indivisible" lake full of fish, etc., such as might be subject to monopolization, but thousands of lakes, all perfect substitutes.

the bliss point implies a unique[7] set of prices, wages and rents, such as would cause atomistic profit- and preference-maximizers to do exactly what is necessary for bliss. In particular, all required production points give maximum and non-negative producer's profits.

This is an Adam Smith dream world. Yet it is possible that due to more or less arbitrary and accidental circumstances of institutions, laws, customs, or feasibility, competitive markets would not be Pareto-efficient. Take, for instance, the Meade example of apples and honey. Apple blossoms are "produced" at constant returns to scale and are (we assumed) an ordinary, private, exhaustible good: the more nectar for one bee, the less for another. It is easy to show that if apple blossoms have a positive effect on honey production (and abstracting from possible satiation and redundancy) a maximum-of-welfare solution, or any Pareto-efficient solution, will associate with apple blossoms a positive Lagrangean shadow-price.[8] If, then, apple producers are unable to protect their equity in apple-nectar and markets do not impute to apple blossoms their correct shadow value, profit-maximizing decisions will fail correctly to allocate resources (e.g., L) at the margin. There will be failure "by enforcement."

This is what I would call an *ownership* externality. It is essentially Meade's "unpaid factor" case. Nonappropriation, divorce of scarcity from effective ownership, is *the* binding consideration. Certain "goods" (or "bads") with determinate non-zero shadow-values are simply not attributed. It is irrelevant here whether this is because the lake where people fish happens to be in the public domain, or because "keeping book" on who produces, and who gets what, may be impossible, clumsy, or costly in terms of resources.[9] For whatever legal or feasibility reasons, certain variables which have positive or negative shadow value are not "assigned" axes. The beekeeper thinks only in terms of labor, the orchard-owner only in terms of apples.

The important point is that the difficulties reside in institutional arrangements, the feasibility of keeping tab, etc. The scarcities at issue are rationable and finely divisible and there are no difficulties with "total conditions": at the bliss-configuration every activity would pay for itself. Apple nectar has a positive shadow price, which

7. Or, where there are corners, only inessentially indeterminate.
8. Set up a variant of the Apple-Honey model of Part II, introducing apple blossoms, B, explicitly. Add a production function, $B = B(L_A)$, and substitute $B(L_A)$ for $A(L_A)$ as the second input in honey production. The solution will give out a positive Lagrangean shadow price for B, and profit-maximizing producers of the joint products: A and B, will push L_A to the socially desirable margin.
9. Though on this last, see Section IV, first paragraph.

THE ANATOMY OF MARKET FAILURE   365

would, if only payment were enforceable, cause nectar production in precisely the right amount and even distribution would be correctly rationed. The difficulty is due exclusively to the difficulty of keeping accounts on the nectar-take of Capulet bees as against Montague bees.[1]

Many of the few examples of interproducer external economies of the reversible technological variety are of this type: "shared deposits" of fish, water, etc.[2] Much more important, so are certain irreversible dynamical examples associated with investment. For instance, many of Pigou's first category of externalities: those that arise in connection with owner-tenant relationships where durable investments are involved, have a primarily organizational quality.[3] Perhaps the most important instance is the training of nonslave labor to skills — as distinct from education in a broader sense (which partakes more of Type (3)). In the end, however, and in particular if restricted to reversible statical cases, it is not easy to think of many significant "ownership externalities" pure and simple. Yet it turns out that only this type of externality is really due to nonappropriability.

Type (2): Technical Externalities

Assume, again, that all goods and services are rationable, exhaustible, scarcities, that individual ordinal indifference maps are convex and sensitive only to own-consumption and that there exist no ownership "defects" of Type (1). If, then, the technology exhibits indivisibility or smooth increasing returns to scale in the relevant range of output, these give rise to a second and much more important type of market failure: "technical externality."[4]

---

1. More generally, it could as well be due to difficulty in knowing who "produced" the "benefit" — oil wells drawing on the same pool are an example. The owner cannot protect his own; in fact it is difficult to know what one means by "his own." Moreover, in the case of *dis*economies, at least, it may be that both the source and the recipient of the "bad" are identified: one factory producing soot and nothing but one laundry in the neighborhood, yet it is difficult to see how a price can be brought to bear on the situation. Presumably the laundry can pay for negative units of smoke.

2. Though indivisibility elements enter into some of these. Why can't somebody "own" part of a lakeful of fish?

3. When not simply due, in a world of uncertainty, to inconsistent expectations.

4. Again, this is not the same as Viner's "technological." Note, incidentally, that the above formulation unabashedly begs the question of whether smooth increasing returns to scale could or could not arise without indivisibility somewhere. The issue is entirely definitional: it is conceptually impossible to disprove either view by reference to empirical evidence. (Cf. "Simple Analytics," *loc. cit.*, fn. 37 and references.) (*Continued on page 366.*)

The essential analytical consequence of indivisibility,[5] whether in inputs, outputs or processes, as well as of smooth increasing returns to scale, is to render the set of feasible points in production (input-output space) nonconvex. A connecting straight line between some pairs of feasible points will pass outside the feasible set. Nonconvexity, in turn, has a devastating effect on duality.[6]

In situations of pure "technical externality" there does, of course, still exist a maximal production possibility frontier (*FF*); and with a Samuelson-type social indifference map (*SS*) — i.e., a map "corrected" for income distribution which provides a ranking for the community as a whole of all conceivable output combinations[7] — it is possible, in concept, to define a bliss point(s).[8] Also, where indivisibility is exhibited by outputs, and only outputs, or, stronger, where smoothly increasing returns to scale is the only variety of nonconvexity — isoquants for one, are properly convex — the locus of efficient output combinations can be defined in terms of conditions on marginal-rates-of-input-substitution.[9] Moreover, bliss could possibly occur at a point where *SS* is internally tangent to *FF*, perhaps to a convex *FF*. But even in the least "pathological," most neoclassi-

---

The pioneer work on decreasing cost situations is Jules Dupuit's remarkable 1844 essay, "On the Measurement of Utility of Public Works," translated in *International Economic Papers*, No. 2, ed. A. T. Peacock, *et al.* Harold Hotelling's "The General Welfare in Relation to Problems of Taxation and of Railway and Utility Rates," in the July 1938 issue of *Econometrica*, is the originating modern formulation. Cf., also, references to work by R. Frisch, J. E. Meade, W. A. Lewis and others in Nancy Ruggles' excellent survey articles on marginal cost pricing (*Review of Economic Studies*, XVII (1949–50), 29–46, and 107–26).

5. Indivisibility means lumpiness "in scale" and not the kind of indivisibility-in-time we call durability. (Durability, as such, does not violate convexity.) Lumpiness has to do with the impossibility to vary continuously, e.g., the capacity service-yield per unit time of such things as bridges.

6. The best known and perhaps most important variety of nonconvexity occurs where isoquants are properly convex, but returns to scale are increasing, hence the full set of feasible input-output points is nonconvex. (In a two-input, one-output situation, slices by (vertical) planes through the origin perpendicular to the input plane will cut the production surface in such a way as to give a nonconvex boundary.) A production point lying in an "increasing returns" region of a production function implies that (1) the associated average cost curve (*AC*) is downward sloping at that level of output; (2) the associated marginal cost curve (*MC*), while it may be rising, could as well be falling and will certainly lie below *AC*; and (3) the production possibility curve of the community may be nonconvex. On all this, see Part V of "Simple Analytics," *loc. cit.*

7. Cf. P. A. Samuelson, "Social Indifference Curves," this *Journal*, LXX (Feb. 1956), 1–22. Such a function presumes that *numeraire*-incomes are continuously redistributed so as to maximize in utility space over the community's operative social welfare function.

8. This is saying very little, of course, except on the level of metaphysics.

9. Inequalities due to kinks and corners are as good as equalities where all is smooth.

cally well-behaved case, where there exists a meaningfully defined set of shadow prices associated with the bliss point, genuinely profit-seeking competitive producers, responding to that set of prices, would fail to sustain optimal production. At best, even if at the bliss-configuration all MC's are rising, some producers would have to make continuing losses, hence would go out of business; market calculations would necessarily fail "by incentive." If, in turn, prices are not centrally quoted but permitted to set themselves, monopoly behavior will result. There will be failure "by structure."

Further, bliss may require production at levels of output where losses are not only positive, but at a constrained maximum;[1] $p = MC$ may be correct, though MC at that point is falling. If so, the embedded Lagrangean constants may still retain meaning as marginal rates of transformation, but they will fail to sustain efficient production even by Lange-Lerner civil servants who care only about margins and not about absolute totals. There will be failure "by signal": producers under injunction to maximize profit (in the small) will not remain where they ought to be.

If, moreover, we drop the assumption of smooth increasing returns to scale and permit indivisibilities such as give scallop-like effects and kinks in cost curves and in the production-possibility curve, things get even more complicated. Bliss could require production at points of positive but locally minimum profit, where MC exceeds AC but is falling. Worse, even if bliss should occur at points where production functions are locally convex and MC (greater than AC) is rising, prequoted prices may still not sustain the solution unless production functions are in fact convex throughout. Though positive and at a local maximum, profits may not be at their maximum-maximorum: other hills with higher peaks may induce producers with vision at a distance to rush away from bliss. Alternatively, if prices are not administered, competition may not be self-policing and markets could fail "by structure."[2]

1. Subject to the requirement that total cost for that level of output be a minimum, i.e., that each producer be on his least-cost expansion path.

2. Where sharp indivisibility gives a nonconvex production possibility curve with corners and kinks, duality may fail even if there exists a price vector in terms of which decentralized producer-calculations would sustain the bliss-point output mix. The existence of such a vector does not assure that it will coincide with the price-vector which would efficiently ration that bill of goods among consumers. The point is that there may not exist a *single* set of prices which will at the same time keep both consumers and producers from rushing away from where they ought to be. The prices which will effectively mediate production may cause consumers' calculations to go wrong and vice versa.

It should be noted, incidentally, that none of the above takes space and distance considerations into account. For some interesting effects of plant-indivisi-

On the other hand, given our assumptions, the Paretian contract locus of maximal (ordinal) utility combinations which is associated with any one particular output point is defined, as in the trouble-free neoclassical model, by the usual subjective, taste-determined, marginal-rate-of-substitution equalities (or, at corners, inequalities). These *MRS* equalities, in turn, imply a set of shadow-prices which, if centrally quoted, would efficiently ration among consumers the associated (fixed) totals of goods. In the sphere of exchange, then, a decentralized price system works without flaw.

In what sense do these Type (2) situations exhibit "externality"? In the (generalized) sense that some social costs and benefits remain external to decentralized profitability calculations. With Type (1) externalities, though it is not feasible to police the bliss values of all quantities and prices, there exists embedded in the solution a set of prices whose use for purposes of decentralized signaling would sustain, if only appropriation or exclusion were feasible, both itself and the maximum welfare configuration of inputs, outputs, and distribution. This is not the case here. In Type (1) situations, at the bliss point there is complete correspondence between social and private pay-off, both at the margin and in totals.[3] Profits are at their maxima and non-negative throughout. Here there is no such correspondence; there may well be divergence, either at the margin: bliss-profits may be at a "minimum," or in *totals*. The private totals in terms of which producers in an (idealized) market calculate — total revenue minus total cost — will not reliably signal the social costs and benefits implied by the relevant social indifference curves.[4] Hence at the set of prices which would correctly ration the bliss point bill of goods, that bill of goods may not be produced by profit seekers, or even by Lange-Lerner civil servants.[5]

bility where there are interplant flows and transport takes resources, see T. C. Koopmans and M. Beckmann, "Assignment Problems and the Location of Economic Activities," *Econometrica*, Vol. 25 (Jan. 1957).

3. More correctly, there would be such correspondence, if only the *p*'s could be policed.

4. This is particularly awkward since the very nonconvexities which cause a divergence between private and social total conditions render output-mix calculations based on margins alone wholly inadequate. Even if bliss gives all local profit maxima, there may be several such open to any one producer, hence he must make total calculations in order to choose.

5. There is one qualification to be made to the above. It may be that the bliss configuration gives unique and positive profit maxima throughout, though some production functions exhibit nonconvexities at a distance. It was to exclude this case that we assumed that increasing returns or indivisibility obtain in the "relevant ranges." Should this happen, no "externality" divergence of social and private calculation will occur, at least in a statical context. But unless all

THE ANATOMY OF MARKET FAILURE   369

A point to note, in all this, is that in relation to "technical externalities" the nonappropriability notion, as generally conceived, tends to miss the point. Strictly speaking, it is, of course, true that price mediation, if efficient, cannot be counted on to "appropriate" the full social benefits of activities showing increasing returns to scale or othe types of indivisibility to those engaged in them. But the existence of such "uncompensated services" has in this case nothing whatever to do with "divorce of scarcity from ownership," with feasibility limitations on "exclusion." It is entirely feasible to own a bridge and profitably ration crossings; indeed, a private owner would do so. The point is, rather, that such profitable rationing, such "compensation" for services rendered, would inefficiently misallocate the "output" of bridge crossings. If in terms of scarce resource inputs the marginal cost of an additional crossing is zero, any positive toll will, in general, have the usual monopolistic effect: the resulting output configuration will not be efficient.[6]

This, incidentally, is where most pecuniary external economies lead: a supplier is required to produce in a range of declining AC due to internal technological economies of scale and hence cannot make "ends meet" at the socially correct price. The crucial associated difficulty at the level of social organization is monopoly.

Can we leave matters at that? Not quite. There is a third kind of externality, recently emphasized by Professor Samuelson, caused by so-called "public goods."

Type (3): Public Good Externalities

In some recent writings on public expenditure theory, Samuelson has reintroduced the notion of the collective or public good. The defining quality of a pure public good is that "each individual's consumption of such a good leads to no subtractions from any other individual's consumption of that good . . .",[7] hence, "it differs from a private consumption good in that each man's consumption of it, X_2^1 and X_2^2 respectively, is related to the total X_2 by a condition of

---

is convex throughout, the existence of such a locally stable tangency cannot be taken as evidence that the point is in fact the bliss-point — a difficulty of considerable significance for dynamical efficiency.

6. Of course, if at bliss the bridge were to be used "to capacity," it is possible that the Lagrangean ration price (now positive) would make commercial operation profitable. If so, an administered price setup would efficiently mediate the demand and supply of crossings. But while a Lange-Lerner system would work fine, laissez-faire markets would fail "by structure."

7. P. A. Samuelson, *Review of Economics and Statistics*, XXXVI (Nov. 1954), 387.

equality rather than of summation. Thus, by definition, $X_2^1 = X_2$ and $X_2^2 = X_2$."[8]

As Samuelson has shown, the form of the marginal rate of substitution conditions which define the Pareto-efficient utility possibility frontier in a world where such public goods exist, or at least where there are outputs with important "public" qualities, renders any kind of price-market routine virtually useless for the computation of output-mix and of distribution, hence, also, for organizational decentralization. Where some restraints in the maximum problem take the form: total production of X *equals* consumption by Crusoe of X *equals* consumption of X by Friday, Pareto efficiency requires that the marginal rate of transformation in production between X and Y equal not the (equalized) MRS of each separate consumer, but rather the algebraic *sum* of such MRS's. This holds, of course, in what in other respects is a conventionally neoclassical world: preference and production functions are of well-behaved curvature, all is convex.

If, then, at the bliss point, with Y as numeraire, Px is equated to the marginal Y-cost of X in production (as is required to get optimal production), and X is offered for sale at that p_x, preference-maximizing consumers adjusting their purchases so as to equate their individual MRS's to p_x will necessarily under-use X. Moreover, a pricing game will not induce consumers truthfully to reveal their preferences. It pays each consumer to understate his desire for X relative to Y, since his enjoyment of X is a function only of total X, rather than, as is true of a pure private good, just of that fraction of X he pays for.

The two Samuelson articles[9] explore both the analytics and the general implications of "public goods." Here the notion is of relevance because much externality is due precisely to the "public" qualities of a great many activities. For example, the externality associated with the generation of ideas, knowledge, etc., is due in good part to the public character of these "commodities." Many interconsumer externalities are of this sort: my party is my neighbor's disturbance, your nice garden is any passerby's nice view, my children's education is your children's good company, my Strategic Air Command is your Strategic Air Command, etc. The same consumption item enters, positively or negatively, both our preference func-

8. P. A. Samuelson, *Review of Economics and Statistics*, XXXVII (Nov. 1955), 350.

9. And a third unpublished paper, which was read at the 1955 American Economic Association meetings and to a copy of which I came to have access while this paper was being written. For earlier writings on public goods, by Wicksell, Lindahl, Musgrave, Bowen and others see references in the above cited Samuelson articles.

tions. The consumptions involved are intrinsically and essentially joint.

This kind of externality is distinct from either of the other two pure types. Here technological nonconvexities need in no way be involved. In fact the $MRT = \Sigma MRS$ condition is certain to hold true precisely where production takes place at constant or non-increasing returns, and hence where the production possibility set is necessarily convex. Further, there are no decentralized organizational rearrangements, no private bookkeeping devices, which would, if only feasibility were not at issue, eliminate the difficulty. It is the central implication of the Samuelson model that where public good phenomena are present, there does not exist a set of prices associated with the (perfectly definable) bliss point, which would sustain the bliss configuration. The set of prices which would induce profit-seeking competitors to produce the optimal bill of goods, would be necessarily inefficient in allocating that bill of goods. Moreover, even abstracting from production, no single set of relative prices will efficiently ration any fixed bill of goods so as to place the system on its contract locus, except in the singular case where at that output and income-distribution MRS's of every individual are identically the same (or zero for all but one). There is failure "by existence."

IV. COMMENTS

Type (1). In a sense, Type (1) is not symmetrical with the other two categories. One can think of some nontrivial instances where the institutional element does appear to be "binding": skill-training of people, for example. But even there, it could be argued that the crucial elements are durability, uncertainty, and the fact that slavery as a mode of organization is itself in the nature of a public good which enters people's preference functions, or the implicit social welfare function, inseparably from the narrowly "economic" variables. In those instances, in turn, where bookkeeping feasibility appears to be the cause of the trouble, the question arises why bookkeeping is less feasible than where it is in fact being done. In the end, it may be that much of what appears to partake of Type (1) is really a compound of Types (2) and (3), with dynamical durability and uncertainty elements thrown in. At any rate, a deeper analysis of this category may cause it substantially to shrink.

Nonproduced scarcities. One particular instance where what appears like Type (1) is really Type (2) warrants special mention. Public ownership of nonproduced resources, e.g., the lakes and mountains of national parks, may make it appear that externality is due to statutory barriers to private ownership and commercial rental. But this is missing the point. Take, for instance, a community which has available a single source of fresh water of fixed capacity. Assume that the bliss solution gives out a positive ration-price per gallon such as would make sale of the water commercially profitable. Yet a laissez-faire system would fail, "by structure," to sustain bliss. A private owner of the single indivisible well, if given his head, would take advantage of the tilt in the demand curve. The real cause of externality is not the arbitrary rapaciousness of public authority but the indivisibility of the source of supply. This case, by the way, is akin to where indivisibility or increasing returns to scale within a range allow profitable scope for one or a few efficient producers, but for no more. At the bliss price all will do the right thing, but if prices are not administered, oligopoly or monopoly will result. A capitalist Lange-Lerner system with private ownership but administered prices would work fine, but laissez-faire markets would fail.

Meade's "atmosphere." The relation of my tri-cornered ordering to Meade's polar categories is of interest.[1] His first category, "unpaid factors," is identical to my Type (1). But his second, labeled "atmosphere," is a rather curious composite. Meade's qualitative characterization of "atmosphere": e.g., of afforestation-induced rainfall, comes very close to the public good notion.[2] He links this, however, as necessarily bound up with increasing returns to scale in production to society at large, hence a J. B. Clark-like overexhaustion, adding-up problem.[3]

If, following Meade, one abstracts from shared water-table phenomena (let rain-caused water input be rigidly proportional to area) then Farmer Jones' rain is Farmer Smith's rain and we have my Type (3). But nothing in this situation requires that either farmer's full production function (with an axis for rain) need show increasing returns to scale. It may be that returns to additional bundles of non-rain inputs, with given constant rainfall, diminish sharply, and that it takes proportional increases of land, labor *and rain* to get a proportional effect on output. If so, Meade's overexhaustion problem

1. *Op. cit.* (This and the next section can be omitted without loss of continuity.)
2. See esp. bottom of p. 61 and top of p. 62, *op. cit.*
3. Since his argument is restricted to competitive situations, hence necessarily excludes increasing-returns-to-paid-factors such as would require production at a loss, Meade specifies constant returns to proportional variation of labor and land in wheat farming, though the full production function for wheat, including the atmosphere input (rain), exhibits increasing returns to scale. But the individual farmer does not pay for rain, hence his factor payments just match his sales revenue, by the Euler Theorem.

THE ANATOMY OF MARKET FAILURE   373

will not arise. But all would not be well: the public good quality of rainfall would cause an independent difficulty, one that Meade, if I understand him correctly, does not take into account, i.e., that rain ought to be "produced" by timber growers until its MC is equal to the sum of all the affected farmers MRS's for rain as an input, whatever may be the curvature of the latter's production functions.[4]

On the other hand, Meade's formal mathematical treatment of "atmosphere," as distinct from his verbal characterization and his example, suggests that it is a nonappropriable, and therefore unpaid, factor which gives rise to increasing returns to scale to society though not to the individual producer. At least this is all he needs for the effect he is looking for: a self-policing though nonoptimal competitive situation, where, because the full production functions (i.e., with an axis for rain) are of greater than first degree, the correction of externality via subsidies to promote the creation of favorable atmosphere requires net additions to society's fiscal burden. If this is the crucial consequence of "atmosphere," then it need have no "public" quality. All this would happen even though Smith and Jones were "competing" for the water from the shared water-table under their subsoil, just like bees competing for nectar.

Scitovsky's "two concepts."[5] Professor Scitovsky, in turn, in his suggestive 1954 article, distinguishes between the statical direct interactions of equilibrium theory and the kinds of pecuniary external economies emphasized in the economic development literature. He classifies the former as consumer-consumer, producer-consumer, and producer-producer interactions, labels the last as external economies and asserts that they are rare and, on the whole, unimportant.

While Scitovsky does not raise the question of what gives rise to such producer-producer interactions, both his examples, and his conclusion that they are of little significance, suggest that he is thinking

---

4. Formally, Meade denotes "atmosphere" as a situation where the production function, e.g., of farmers takes the form $X_1 = H_1(L_1, C_1) A_1(X_2)$, with L as labor, C as capital and A the atmosphere effect on X_1 of X_2. The full function exhibits increasing returns to scale but the H function alone, with A constant, is homogeneous of first degree. But why can't this be put in terms of Meade's unpaid factor type function where $X_1 = H_1(L_1, C_1, X_2)$? Example: $X_1 = L_1^a C_1^{1-a} X_2$. All this has nothing to do with whether $A = A_1 + A_2$ or rather $A = A_1 = A_2$. Unfortunately, the example itself tends to mislead. The fact that exclusion of rain-users (farmers) by producers (timber-growers) is hardly feasible, i.e., that rain is like Type (1), distracts attention from the important point that *if* rain is, as Meade tells us, a public good, then rationing it by price would be inefficient even if it were feasible. (It should be said that Meade concludes his article: "But, in fact, of course, external economies or diseconomies may not fall into either of these precise divisions and may contain features of both of them.")

5. *Op. cit.*

primarily of Type (1): nonappropriability. But this is to ignore public goods — surely a more important cause of interaction. Moreover, by taking full account of these, Scitovsky's "fifth and important case, which, however, does not quite fit into . . . (his) . . . classification . . . , where society provides social services through communal action and makes these available free of charge to all persons and firms," can be made nicely to fall into place.[6]

Samuelson on Types (2) and (3). While the public good model helps to sort out the phenomena Meade lumped under "atmosphere," Samuelson himself emphasizes the analytical bond between indivisibility and public good situations. In both an explicit "summing in" is required of "all direct and indirect utilities and costs in all social decisions."[7] In Type (2) situations it is the intramarginal consumer's and producer's surpluses associated with various all or nothing decisions "in-the-lump" that have to be properly (interpersonally) weighted and summed, while in Type (3) it is only utilities and costs at the margin that require adding. But, and this is the crucial shared quality of the two categories, both make it necessary to sum utilities over many people.[8]

Exclusion. One more comment may be warranted on the significance, in a public good type situation, of nonappropriability. "Exclusion" is almost never impossible. A recluse can build a wall around his garden, Jones can keep his educated children away from those of

6. *Ibid.*, fn. 3, p. 144. Scitovsky, following Meade, restricts his "first concept" of external economies to phenomena consistent with competitive equilibrium. He treats indivisibilities and increasing returns to scale as belonging to his "second concept" which has to do with disequilibrium, investment decisions, and growth. It is, of course, entirely legitimate to restrict analysis to competitive situations. But the Scitovsky treatment must not be taken to imply that lumpiness is irrelevant to statical analysis of stationary solution points. If one is interested in the statical efficiency of decentralized price calculations, they are crucial. But this is carping. Scitovsky's important contribution lies in emphasizing and clarifying the point first hinted at by P. N. Rosenstein-Rodan that in a world of disequilibrium dynamics pecuniary external economies may play an independent role — one distinct, that is, from simply being an unreliable signal of monopoly troubles (*Economic Journal*, LIII, 1943, 202–11).

7. *Ibid.*, p. 9.

8. There is one qualification to be made: if all public good and increasing returns to scale industries produce only intermediate products, all externalities may cancel out in intra-business-sector transactions. If so, only total revenues and total costs have to be summed. Incidentally, the exposition may misleadingly suggest another symmetry between Types (2) and (3). In a pure Type (3) situation, *if* there are no public producers' goods, then while prices cannot be used to ration the bliss point output-mix, they can be used efficiently to mediate production. In Type (2), on the other hand, *if* all final consumables are divisible, price calculations, while failing in production, will work in exchange. This symmetry breaks down, of course, as soon as one violates, as does the real world, the two "if's."

THE ANATOMY OF MARKET FAILURE   375

Smith, etc. But if thereby some people (e.g., the recluse) are made happier and some (e.g., the passers-by) less happy, any decision about whether to "exclude" or not implies an algebraic summing of the somehow-weighted utilities of the people involved. And if the wall requires scarce resources, the final utility sum must be matched against the cost of the wall. When Type (3) blends with indivisibility in production, as it does in the case of the wall, or in the case of a lighthouse, the comparison has to be made between intramarginal totals. Where no lumpiness is involved (e.g., the decibels at which I play my radio) only MRS and perhaps MC calculations are called for. But the really crucial decision may well be about how much perfectly feasible appropriation and exclusion is desirable.

Arrangements to offset. It is of interest to speculate what, if any, organizational rearrangements could offset the three categories of externality and avoid the need for centrally calculated tax-subsidy schemes.[9] In concept, Type (1) can be offset by rearrangements of ownership and by "proper" bookkeeping, such as need not violate the structural requirements of decentralized competition. Further, no resort to nonmarket tests would be required.[1]

Types (2) and (3) are not so amenable to correction consistent with decentralized institutions. The easiest possible case occurs where increasing returns obtain on the level of single producers'-good plants, much of whose production can be absorbed by a single user firm. Here vertical integration takes care of the problem. Not every process inside a well-run firm is expected to cover its cost in terms of the correct set of internal accounting (shadow) prices. Total profits are the only criterion, and it may pay a firm to build a private bridge between its two installations on opposite sides of a river yet charge a zero accounting price for its use by the various decentralized manufacturing and administrative divisions; the bridge would make accounting losses, yet total company profits will have increased. As long, then, as such integration is consistent with the many-firms requirement for competition, no extra-market tests are required.[2] The private total conditions: TR less TC, correctly account for social gain.

9. For illustrative derivation of the formulas for corrective taxes and subsidies in Type (1) situations, see Meade (*op. cit.*).

1. The Emancipation Proclamation could constitute, of course, a substantial barrier.

2. If, however, the "break even" scale of operation of the integrated firm (i.e., where MC cuts AC from below) is much greater than if the river had not been there to span, or could be spanned by some means of a lower fixed-cost-to-variable-cost ratio, the monopoly problem may simply be "pushed forward" to consumer markets.

Where a producers'-good firm, required to produce at a stage of falling AC, sells to many customer firms and industries, an adding up of all the associated TR's and TC's at the precalculated "as if" competitive prices associated with the bliss point would again effectively "mop up" all social costs and benefits.[3] But the institutional reorganization required to get correct decentralized calculation involves horizontal and vertical integration, and the monopoly or oligopoly problem looms large indeed. The Type (3) case of a pure *producers'* public good belongs here: only input MRS's along production functions require summing.

In the general case of a mixed producer-consumer good (or of a pure consumer good) which is "public" or is produced under conditions of increasing returns to scale, it is impossible to avoid comparison of multiperson utility totals. Explicit administrative consideration must be given, if you like, to consumer's and producer's surpluses for which no market-institution tests exist short of that provided by a perfectly discriminating monopolist. But to invoke perfect discrimination is to beg the question. It implies knowledge of all preference functions, while as Samuelson has emphasized,[4] the crucial game-theoretical quality of the situation is that consumers will not correctly reveal their preferences: it will pay them to "cheat."

Blends. Examination is needed of various blends of Types (2) and (3), such as Sidgwick's lighthouse;[5] or, for that matter, and as suggested by Samuelson, of blends of public and private goods even where all production functions are fully convex. There are many puzzling cases. Do bridge crossings differ in kind from radio programs? Both involve indivisibility and, where variable cost is zero for the bridge, zero MC's. The correct price for an extra stroller, as for an extra listener, is clearly zero. Yet bridge crossings have a distinctly private quality: bridges get congested, physical capacity is finite. This is not true of a broadcast. There is no finite limit to the number

---

3. Assuming that all consumer goods are finely divisible and require no lumpy decisions by consumers.

4. Cf. any of the three "Public Expenditure" articles (*supra*).

5. Sidgwick, by the way, as also Pigou, thought of a lighthouse as of Type (1). It is, of course, "inconvenient" to levy tolls on ships, but it is hardly impossible to "exclude," for instance by means of "scrambling" devices (though poor Sidgwick could hardly have known about such things). The point is, rather, that it would be inefficient to do so: the marginal cost to society of an additional ship taking directional guidance from the beacon atop the Statue of Liberty is zero, *ipso* price should be zero. In the case of a lighthouse this is twice true: because the beacon is in the nature of a public good: more for the Queen Mary means no less for the Liberté; and because a lighthouse is virtually an all-fixed-cost, zero variable-cost facility.

of sets that can costlessly tune in.[6] Radio programs, then, have a
public dimension. Yet, in a sense, so do bridges. While your bridge
crossing is not my bridge crossing, in fact could limit my crossings,
your bridge is my bridge. What is involved here is that most things
are multidimensional and more than one dimension may matter.

V. Efficiency, Markets and Choice of Institutions

All the above has to do with the statical efficiency of price-
directed allocation in more or less idealized market situations. Relevance to choice of institutions depends, of course, on the prevalence
of the phenomena which cause externality and on the importance to
be attached to statical efficiency. Space precludes extensive discussion of these important issues, but a few casual comments, in the
form of *dicta*, are perhaps warranted.

How important are nonappropriability, nonconvexity and public
goods? I would be inclined to argue that while nonappropriability
is of small import,[7] the same cannot be said of the other two. True
enough, it is difficult to think of many examples of pure public goods.
Most things — even battleships, and certainly open air concerts and
schools (though not knowledge) — have an "if more for you then
less for me" quality. But this is of little comfort. As long as activities have even a trace of publicness, price calculations are inefficient.[8]
And it is surely hard to gainsay that some degree of public quality
pervades much of even narrowly "economic" activity.

Lumpiness, in turn, and nonlinearity of the increasing returns
sort, while in most instances a matter of degree, and, within limits, of
choice, are also in the nature of things. The universe is full of singu-
larities, thresholds and nonproportionalities: speed of light, gravita-
tional constant, the relation of circumference to area, etc. As economists we can cajole or bully engineers into designing processes and
installations that save on congealed inputs and give smaller maximal
service yields, especially when designing for low-income communities.
But the economically perhaps arbitrary, not completely physics-
imposed quality of indivisibilities associated with standard designs

---

6. Richard Eckaus has suggested to me that it is possible to exhaust the
space to which the broadcast is limited and that this makes the situation a little
more like that of a bridge. Neither of us is entirely satisfied, however.

7. Except for labor skills — and these would take us beyond the bounds
of reversible statics.

8. This is not to say that there exist other feasible modes of social calculation
and organization which are more efficient.

and ways of doing things should not blind. Nonlinearity and lumpiness are evident facts of nature.[9]

More important, at this level of discourse[1] — though perhaps it hardly need be said — is that statical market efficiency is neither sufficient nor necessary for market institutions to be the "preferred" mode of social organization. Quite apart from institutional considerations, Pareto efficiency as such may not be necessary for bliss.[2] If, e.g., people are sensitive not only to their own jobs but to other people's as well, or more generally, if such things as relative status, power, and the like, matter, the injunction to maximize output, to hug the production-possibility frontier, can hardly be assumed "neutral," and points on the utility frontier may associate with points inside the production frontier.[3] Furthermore, there is nothing preordained about welfare functions which are sensitive only to individual consumer's preferences. As a matter of fact, few people would take such preferences seriously enough to argue against any and all protection of individuals against their own mistakes (though no external effects be involved).

All this is true even when maximization is subject only to technological and resource limitations. Once we admit other side relations, which link input-output variables with "noneconomic" political and organizational values, matters become much more complicated. If markets be ends as well as means, their nonefficiency is hardly sufficient ground for rejection.[4] On the other hand, efficient markets may

9. Their quantitative significance is, of course, very sensitive to scale, to "size" of markets. This explains the particular emphasis on the role of "social overheads" in low income countries.

1. Where recourse to strategic considerations of feasibility, crucial though they be, is quite out of order.

2. That it is never sufficient is, of course, well known. Of the infinite Pareto-efficient configurations at best only one: that which gives the "right" distribution of income in terms of the W-function that is to count, has normative, prescriptive significance. Moreover, most interesting W-functions are likely to be sensitive to "noneconomic" factors, such as are, if not inconsistent, at least extraneous to Paretian considerations. Where such additional values of a political or social nature are separable from input-output values (i.e., where the two sets can be varied independently of each other) one "can" of course separate the overall W-function into a "political" and an "economic" component and maximize separately over each.

3. This is different from the usual case of consumer sensitivity to the input-output configuration of producers, e.g., factory soot or a functional but ugly plant spoiling the view. Such joint-product "bads" can be treated as inputs and treated in the usual Paretian fashion. It is a different matter that their public quality will violate duality, hence render market calculation inefficient.

4. This is too crude a formulation. It is not necessary that markets as such be an "ultimate" value. Political and social (non-output) values relating to the configuration of power, initiative, opportunity, etc., may be so much better served

THE ANATOMY OF MARKET FAILURE   379

not do, even though Pareto-efficiency is necessary for bliss. Even with utopian lump-sum redistribution, efficiency of the "invisible hand" does not preclude preference for other efficient modes of organization, if there be any.[5]

Yet when all is said, and despite the host of crucial feasibility considerations which render choice in the real world inevitably a problem in the strategy of "second best," it is surely interesting and useful to explore the implications of Paretian efficiency. Indeed, much remains to be done. There is need, in particular, for more systematic exploration of the inadequacies of market calculation in a setting of growth.[6]

by some form of nonefficient market institutions than by possible alternative modes of more efficient organization as to warrant choice of the former. The analytical point, in all this, is that the outcome of a maximization process and the significance of "efficiency" are as sensitive to the choice of side-conditions as to the welfare-function and that these need be "given" to the economist in the same sense that a welfare function has to be given.

5. The above is still strictly statical. For related dynamical problems, e.g., possible conflict between one-period and intertemporal efficiency, cf., "On Capital Productivity, Input Allocation and Growth," this *Journal*, LXXI (Feb. 1957).

6. The development literature on market failure, while full of suggestive insight, is in a state of considerable confusion. Much work is needed to exhaust and elucidate the seminal ideas of Young, Rosenstein-Rodan, Nurkse and others. For important beginnings, see Scitovsky (*op. cit.*), M. Fleming, "External Economies and the Doctrine of Balanced Growth," *Economic Journal*, LXV (June 1955), and Fellner (*op. cit.*).

The view that we should not turn social historian or what not, that the logic of economizing has some prescriptive significance, rests on the belief that narrowly "economic" efficiency is important in terms of many politically relevant *W*-functions, and consistent with a wide variety of power and status configurations and modes of social organization. On the other hand, some may feel that the very language of Paretian welfare economics: "welfare function," "utility-frontier," in relation to choice of social institutions, is grotesque. What is at stake, of course, is not the esthetics of language, on which I yield without demur, but abstraction and rigorous theorizing.

[3]

THE ORGANIZATION OF ECONOMIC ACTIVITY: ISSUES PERTINENT TO THE CHOICE OF MARKET VERSUS NONMARKET ALLOCATION

Kenneth J. Arrow

INTRODUCTION

The concept of public goods has been developed through a process of successive refinement over a long period of time. Yet surprisingly enough there does not seem to exist anywhere in the literature a clear general definition of this concept or the more general one of "externality." The accounts given are usually either very general and discursive, difficult of interpretation in specific contexts, or else they are rigorous accounts of very special situations. What exactly is the relation between externalities and such concepts as "appropriability" or "exclusion"?

Also, there is considerable ambiguity in the purpose of the analysis of externalities. The best developed part of the theory relates to only a single question: the statement of a set of conditions, as weak as possible, which insure that a competitive equilibrium exists and is Pareto efficient.[1] Then the denial of any of these hypotheses is presumably a sufficient condition for considering resort to non-market channels of resource allocation—usually thought of as government expenditures, taxes, and subsidies.

At a second level the analysis of externalities should lead to criteria for nonmarket allocation. We are tempted to set forth these criteria in terms analogous to the profit-and-loss statements of private business; in this form, we are led to benefit-cost analysis. There are, moreover, two possible aims for benefit-cost analysis; one, more ambitious but theoretically simpler, is specification of the nonmarket actions which will restore Pareto efficiency; the second involves the recognition that the instruments available to the government or other nonmarket forces are scarce resources for one reason or another, so that all that can be achieved is a "second-best."

Other concepts that seem to cluster closely to the concept of public

Kenneth J. Arrow is Professor of Economics at Harvard University and is associated with the Project on Efficiency of Decisionmaking in Economic Systems at that institution.

goods are those of "increasing returns" and "market failure." These are related to Pareto inefficiency on the one hand and to the existence and optimality of competitive equilibrium on the other; sometimes the discussions in the literature do not adequately distinguish these two aspects. I contend that market failure is a more general category than externality; and both differ from increasing returns in a basic sense, since market failures in general and externalities in particular are relative to the mode of economic organization, while increasing returns are essentially a technological phenomenon.

Current writing has helped bring out the point that market failure is not absolute; it is better to consider a broader category, that of transaction costs, which in general impede and in particular cases completely block the formation of markets. It is usually though not always emphasized that transaction costs are costs of running the economic system. An incentive for vertical integration is replacement of the costs of buying and selling on the market by the costs of intrafirm transfers; the existence of vertical integration may suggest that the costs of operating competitive markets are not zero, as is usually assumed in our theoretical analysis.

Monetary theory, unlike value theory, is heavily dependent on the assumption of positive transaction costs; the recurrent complaint about the difficulty of integrating these two branches of theory is certainly governed by the contradictory assumptions made about transaction costs. The creation of money is in many respects an example of a public good.

The identification of transaction costs in different contexts and under different systems of resource allocation should be a major item on the research agenda of the theory of public goods and indeed of the theory of resource allocation in general. Only the most rudimentary suggestions are made here. The "exclusion principle" is a limiting case of one kind of transaction cost, but another type, the costliness of the information needed to enter and participate in any market, has been little remarked. Information is closely related on the one hand to communication and on the other to uncertainty.

Given the existence of Pareto inefficiency in a free market equilibrium, there is a pressure in the market to overcome it by some sort of departure from the free market; i.e., some form of collective action. This need not be undertaken by the government. I suggest that in fact there is a wide variety of social institutions, in particular generally accepted social norms of behavior, which serve in some means as compensation for failure or limitation of the market, though each in turn involves transaction costs of its own. The question also arises how the behavior of individual economic agents in a social institution (especially in voting) is related to their behavior on the market. A good deal of theoretical literature has arisen in recent years which seeks to describe political behavior as analogous to economic, and we may hope for a general theory of socioeconomic equilibrium. But it must always be kept in mind that the contexts of choice are radically different, particularly when the hypotheses of perfectly costless action and information are relaxed. It is not accidental that economic analysis has been successful only in certain limited areas.

COMPETITIVE EQUILIBRIUM AND PARETO EFFICIENCY

A quick review of the familiar theorems on the role of perfectly competitive equilibrium in the efficient allocation of resources will be useful. Perfectly competitive equilbrium has its usual meaning: households, possessed of initial resources, including possibly claims to the profits of firms, choose consumption bundles to maximize utility at a given set of prices; firms choose production bundles so as to maximize profits at the same set of prices; the chosen production and consumption bundles must be consistent with each other in the sense that aggregate production plus initial resources must equal aggregate consumption. The key points in the definition are the parametric role[2] of the prices for each individual and the identity of prices for all individuals. Implicit are the assumptions that all prices can be known by all individuals and that the act of charging prices is not itself a consumer of resources.

A number of additional assumptions are made at different points in the theory of equilibrium, but most are clearly factually valid in the usual contexts and need not be mentioned. The two hypotheses frequently not valid are (C), the convexity of household indifference maps and firm production possibility sets,[3] and (M), the universality of markets. While the exact meaning of the last assumption will be explored later at some length, for the present purposes we mean that the consumption bundle which determines the utility of an individual is the same as that which he purchases at given prices subject to his budget constraint, and that the set of production bundles among which a firm chooses is a given range independent of decisions made by other agents in the economy.

The relations between Pareto efficiency and competitive equilibrium are set forth in the following two theorems:

1. *If (M) holds, a competitive equilibrium is Pareto-efficient.* This theorem is true even if (C) does not hold.

2. *If (C) and (M) hold, then any Pareto-efficient allocation can be achieved as a competitive equilibrium by a suitable reallocation of initial resources.*

When the assumptions of proposition 2 are valid, then the case for the competitive price system is strongest. Any complaints about its operation can be reduced to complaints about the distribution of income, which should then be rectified by lump-sum transfers. Of course, as Pareto already emphasized, the proposition provides no basis for accepting the results of the market in the absence of accepted levels of income equality.

The central role of competitive equilibrium both as a normative guide and as at least partially descriptive of the real world raises an analytically difficult question: does a competitive equilibrium necessarily exist?

3. *If* (C) *holds, then there exists a competitive equilibrium.* This theorem is true even if (M) does not hold.

If both (C) and (M) hold, we have a fairly complete and simple picture of the achievement of desirable goals, subject always to the major qualification of the achievement of a desirable income distribution. The price system itself determines the income distribution only in the sense of preserving the status quo. Even if costless lump-sum transfers are possible, there is needed a collective mechanism reallocating income if the status quo is not regarded as satisfactory.

Of course (C) is not a necessary condition for the existence of a competitive equilibrium, only a sufficient one. From proposition 1, it is possible to have an equilibrium and therefore efficient allocation without convexity (when (M) holds). However, in view of the central role of (C) in these theorems, the implications in relaxing this hypothesis have been examined intensively in recent years by Farrell (1959), Rothenberg (1960), Aumann (1966), and Starr (1969). Their conclusions may be summarized as follows: Let (C′) be the weakened convexity assumption that there are no indivisibilities large relative to the economy.

4. *Propositions 2 and 3 remain approximately true if* (C) *is replaced by* (C′).

Thus, the only nonconvexities that are important for the present purposes are increasing returns over a range large relative to the economy. In those circumstances, a competitive equilibrium cannot exist.

The price system, for all its virtues, is only one conceivable form of arranging trade, even in a system of private property. Bargaining can assume extremely general forms. Under the assumptions (C′) and (M), we are assured that not everyone can be made better off by a bargain not derived from the price system; but the question arises whether some members of the economy will not find it in their interest and within their power to depart from the perfectly competitive price system. For example, both Knight (1921, pp. 190–194) and Samuelson (1967, p. 120) have noted that it would pay all the firms in a given industry to form a monopoly. But in fact it can be argued that unrestricted bargaining can only settle down to a resource allocation which could also be achieved as a perfectly competitive equilibrium, at least if the bargaining itself is costless and each agent is small compared to the entire economy. This line of argument originated with Edgeworth (1881, pp. 20–43) and has been developed recently by Shubik (1959), Debreu and Scarf (1963), and Aumann (1964).

More precisely, it is easy to show:

5. *If (M) holds and a competitive equilibrium prevails, then no set of economic agents will find any resource allocation which they can accomplish by themselves (without trade with the other agents) which they will all prefer to that prevailing under the equilibrium.*

Proposition 5 holds for any number of agents. A deeper proposition is the following converse:

6. *If (C′) and (M) hold, and if the resources of any economic agent are small compared with the total of the economy, then, given any allocation not approximately achievable as a competitive equilibrium, there will be some set of agents and some resource allocation they can achieve without any trade with others which each one will prefer to the given allocation.*

These two propositions, taken together, strongly suggest that when all the relevant hypotheses hold, (*a*) a competitive equilibrium, if achieved, will not be upset by bargaining even if permitted, and (*b*) for any bargain not achievable by a competitive equilibrium there is a set of agents who would benefit by change to another bargain which they have the full power to enforce.

The argument that a set of firms can form a monopoly overlooks the possibility that the consumers can also form a coalition, threaten not to buy, and seek mutually advantageous deals with a subset of the firms; such deals are possible since the monopoly allocation violates some marginal equivalences.

In real life, monopolizing cartels are possible for a reason not so far introduced into the analysis: bargaining costs between producers and consumers are high, those among producers low—a point made most emphatically by Adam Smith (1937, p. 128); "People of the same trade seldom meet together, even for merriment or diversion, but the conversation ends in a conspiracy against the public, or in some contrivance to raise prices." *It is not the presence of bargaining costs per se but their bias that is relevant.* If all bargaining costs are high, but competitive pricing and the markets are cheap, then we expect the perfectly competitive equilibrium to obtain, yielding an allocation identical with that under costless bargaining. But if bargaining costs are biased, then some bargains other than the competitive equilibrium can be arrived at which will not be upset by still other bargains if the latter but not the former are costly.

Finally, in this review of the elements of competitive equilibrium theory, let me repeat the obvious and well-known fact that in a world where time is relevant, the commodities which enter into the equilibrium system include those with future dates. In fact, the bulk of meaningful future transactions cannot be carried out on any existing present market, so that assumption (M), the universality of markets, is not valid.

EXTERNALITIES ILLUSTRATED

After this long[4] excursus into the present state of the theory of equilibrium and optimality, it is time to discuss some of the standard concepts of externality, market failure, and public goods generally. The clarification of these concepts is a long historical process, not yet concluded, in which the classic contributions of Knight (1924), Young (1913, pp. 676–684), and Robertson (1924) have in more recent times been enriched by those of Meade (1952), Scitovsky (1954), Coase (1960), Buchanan and Stubblebine (1962), and Demsetz (1966). The concept of externality and the extent to which it causes nonoptimal market behavior will be discussed here in terms of a simple model.

Consider a pure exchange economy. Let x_{ik} be the amount of the kth commodity consumed by the ith individual ($i = 1, \ldots, n; k = 1, \ldots, m$) and $\bar{x}_k$ be the amount of the kth commodity available. Suppose in general that the utility of the ith individual is a function of the consumption of all individuals (not all types of consumption for all individuals need actually enter into any given individual's utility function); the utility of the ith individual is $U_i(x_{11}, \ldots, x_{mn})$. We have the obvious constraints:

(1)
$$\sum x_{ik} \leq \bar{x}_k$$

Introduce the following definitions:

(2)
$$x_{jik} = x_{ik}.$$

With this notation a Pareto-efficient allocation is a vector maximum of the utility functions $U_j(x_{j11}, \ldots, x_{jmn})$, subject to the constraints (1) and (2). Because of the notation used, the variables appearing in the utility function relating to the jth individual are proper to him alone and appear in no one else's utility function. If we understand now that there are n^2m commodities, indexed by the triple subscript jik, then the Pareto-efficiency problem has a thoroughly classical form. There are n^2m prices, p_{jik}, attached to the constraints (2), plus m prices, q_k, corresponding to constraints (1). Following the maximization procedure formally, we see, much as in Samuelson (1954), that Pareto efficiency is characterized by the conditions:

(3) $$\lambda_j(\partial U_j/\partial x_{ik}) = p_{jik},$$

and

(4) $$\sum_j p_{jik} = q_k,$$

where λ_j is the reciprocal of the marginal utility of income for individual j. (These statements ignore corner conditions, which can easily be supplied.)

Condition (4) can be given the following economic interpretation: Imagine each individual i to be a producer with m production processes, indexed by the pair (i,k). Process (i,k). has one input, namely commodity k, and n outputs, indexed by the triple (j,i,k). In other words, what we ordinarily call individual i's consumption is regarded as the production of joint outputs, one for each individual whose utility is affected by individual i's consumption.

The point of this exercise is to show that by suitable and indeed not unnatural reinterpretation of the commodity space, externalities can be regarded as ordinary commodities, and all the formal theory of competitive equilibrium is valid, including its optimality.

It is not the mere fact that one man's consumption enters into another man's utility that causes the failure of the market to achieve efficiency. There are two relevant factors which cannot be discovered by inspection of the utility structures of the individual. One, much explored in the literature, is the appropriability of the commodities which represent the external repercussions; the other, less stressed, is the fact that markets for externalities usually involve small numbers of buyers and sellers.

The first point, Musgrave's "exclusion principle," (1959, p. 86) is so well known as to need little elaboration. Pricing demands the possibility of excluding nonbuyers from the use of the product, and this exclusion may be technically impossible or may require the use of considerable resources. Pollution is the key example; the supply of clean air or water to each individual would have to be treated as a separate commodity, and it would have to be possible in principle to supply to one and not the other (though the final equilibrium would involve equal supply to all). But this is technically impossible.

The second point comes out clearly in our case. Each commodity (j,i,k) has precisely one buyer and one seller. Even if a competitive equilibrium could be defined, there would be no force driving the system to it; we are in the realm of imperfectly competitive equilibrium.

In my view, the standard lighthouse example is best analyzed as a problem of small numbers rather than of the difficulty of exclusion, though both elements are present. To simplify matters, I will abstract from uncertainty so that the lighthouse keeper knows exactly when each ship will need its services, and also abstract from indivisibility (since the light is either on or off). Assume further that only one ship will be within range of the lighthouse at any moment. Then exclusion is perfectly possible; the lighthouse need only shut off its light when a nonpaying ship is coming into range. But there would be only one buyer and one seller and no competitive forces to drive the two into a competitive equilibrium. If in addition the costs of bargaining are high, then it may be most efficient to offer the service free.

If, as is typical, markets for the externalities do not exist, then the allocation from the point of view of the "buyer" is determined by a rationing process. We can determine a shadow price for the buyer; this will differ from the price, zero, received by the seller. Hence, formally, the failure of markets for externalities to exist can also be described as a difference of prices between buyer and seller.

In the example analyzed, the externalities related to particular named individuals; individual i's utility function depended on what a particular individual, j, possessed. The case where it is only the total amount of some commodity (e.g., handsome houses) in other people's hands that matters is a special case, which yields rather simpler results. In this case, $\partial U_j / \partial x_{ik}$ is independent of i for $i \neq j$, and hence, by (3), p_{jik} is independent of i for $i \neq j$. Let,

$$p_{iik} = p_{ik}, \; p_{jik} = \bar{p}_{jk} \text{ for } i \neq j.$$

Then (4) becomes,

$$p_{ik} + \sum_{j \neq i} \bar{p}_{jk} = q_k,$$

or,

$$(p_{ik} - \bar{p}_{ik}) + \sum_{j} \bar{p}_{jk} = q_k,$$

from which it follows that the difference, $p_{ik} - \bar{p}_{ik}$, is independent of i. There are two kinds of shadow prices, a price $\bar{p}_{ik}$, the price that individual i is willing to pay for an increase in the stock of commodity k in any other individual's hands, and the premium, $p_{ik} - \bar{p}_{ik}$, he is willing to pay to have the commodity in his possession rather than someone else's. At the optimum, this premium for private possession must be the same for all individuals.

Other types of externalities are associated with several commodities simultaneously and do not involve named individuals, as in the case of neighborhood effects, where an individual's utility depends both on others' behavior (e.g., esthetic, criminal) and on their location.

There is one deep problem in the intepretation of externalities which can only be signaled here. What aspects of others' behavior to we consider as affecting a utility function? If we take a hard-boiled revealed preference attitude, then if an individual expends resources in supporting legislation regulating another's behavior, it must be assumed that that behavior affects his utility. Yet in the cases that students of criminal law call "crimes without victims," such as homosexuality or drug-taking, there is no direct relation between the parties. Do we have to extend the concept of external-ity to all matters that an individual cares about? Or, in the spirit of John Stuart Mill, is there a second-order value judgment which excludes some of these preferences from the formation of social policy as being illegiti-mate infringements of individual freedom?

MARKET FAILURE

The problem of externalities is thus a special case of a more general phenomenon, the failure of markets to exist. Not all examples of market failure can fruitfully be described as externalities. Two very important examples have already been alluded to; markets for many forms of risk-bearing and for most future transactions do not exist and their absence is surely suggestive of inefficiency.

Previous discussion has suggested two possible causes for market failures: (1) inability to exclude; (2) lack of necessary information to permit market transactions to be concluded.

The failure of futures markets cannot be directly explained in these terms. Exclusion is no more a problem in the future than in the present. Any contract to be executed in the future is necessarily contingent on some events (for example, that the two agents are still both in business), but there must be many cases where no informational difficulty is presented. The absence of futures markets may be ascribed to a third possibility: (3) supply and demand are equated at zero; the highest price at which anyone would buy is below the lowest price at which anyone would sell.

This third case of market failure, unlike the first two, is by itself in no way presumptive of inefficiency. However, it may usually be assumed that its occurrence is the result of failures of the first two types on complementary markets. Specifically, the demand for future steel may be low because of uncertainties of all types; sales and technological uncertainty for the buyer's firm, prices and existence of competing goods, and the quality specification of the steel. If, however, adequate markets for risk-bearing existed, the uncertainties could be removed, and the demand for future steel would rise.

TRANSACTION COSTS

Market failure has been presented as absolute, but in fact the situation is more complex than this. A more general formulation is that of transaction costs, which are attached to any market and indeed to any mode of resource allocation. Market failure is the particular case where transaction costs are so high that the existence of the market is no longer worthwhile. The distinction between transaction costs and production costs is that the former can be varied by a chance in the mode of resource allocation, while the latter depend only on the technology and tastes, and would be the same in all economic systems.

The discussions in the preceding sections suggest two sources of transaction costs. (1) exclusion costs; (2) costs of communication and information, including both the supplying and the learning of the terms on which transactions can be carried out. An additional source is (3) the costs of disequlibrium; in any complex system, the market or authoritative allocation, even under perfect information, it takes time to compute the optimal allocation, and either transactions take place which are inconsistent with the final equilibrium or they are delayed until the computation are completed (see T. Marschak, 1959).

These costs vary from system to system; thus, one of the advantages of a price system over either bargaining or some form of authoritative allocation is usually stated to be the economy in costs of information and communication. But the costs of transmitting and especially of receiving a large number of price signals may be high; thus, there is a tendency not to differentiate prices as much as would be desirable from the efficiency viewpoint; for example, the same price is charged for peak and offpeak usage of transportation or electricity.

In a price system, transaction costs drive a wedge between buyer's and seller's prices and thereby give rise to welfare losses as in the usual analysis. Removal of these welfare losses by changing to another system (for example, governmental allocation on benefit-cost critera) must be weighed against any possible increase in transaction costs (for example, the need for elaborate and perhaps impossible studies to determine demand functions without the benefit of observing a market).

The welfare implications of transaction costs would exist even if they were proportional to the size of the transaction, but in fact they typically exhibit increasing returns. The cost of acquiring a piece of information, for example, a price, is independent of the scale of use to which it will be put.

COLLECTIVE ACTION: THE POLITICAL PROCESS

The state may frequently have a special role to play in resource allocation because, by its nature, it has a monopoly of coercive power, and coercive power can be used to economize on transaction costs. The most important use of coercion in the economic context is the collection of taxes; others are regulatory legislation and eminent domain proceedings.

The state is not an entity but rather a system of individual agents, a widely extensive system in the case of a democracy. It is appealing and fruitful to analyze its behavior in resource allocation in a manner analogous to that of the price system. Since the same agents appear in the two systems, it becomes equally natural to assume they have the same motives. Hotelling (1929, pp. 54–55) and Schumpeter (1942, ch. XXII) had sketched such politicoeconomic models, and von Neumann and Morgenstern's monumental work is certainly based on the idea that all social phenomena are governed by essentially the same motives as economics. The elaboration of more or less complete models of the political process along the lines of economic theory is more recent, the most prominent contributors being Black (1958), Downs (1957), Buchanan and Tullock (1962), and Rothenberg (1965).

I confine myself here to a few critical remarks on the possibilities of such theories. These are not intended to be negative but to suggest problems that have to be faced and are raised by some points in the preceding discussion.

1. If we take the allocative process to be governed by majority voting, then, as we well know, there are considerable possibilities of paradox. The possible intransitivity of majority voting was already pointed out by Condorcet (1785). If, instead of assuming that each individual votes according to his preferences it is assumed that they bargain freely before voting (vote-selling), the paradox appears in another form, a variant of the bargaining problems already noted in section 2. If a majority could do what it wanted, then it would be optimal to win with a bare majority and take everything; but any such bargain can always be broken up by another proposed majority.

Tullock (1967) has recently argued convincingly that if the distribution of opinions on social issues is fairly uniform and if the dimensionality of the space of social issues is much less than the number of individuals, then majority voting on a sincere basis will be transitive. The argument is not, however applicable to income distribution, for such a policy has as many dimensions as there are individuals, so that the dimensionality of the issue space is equal to the number of individuals.

This last observation raises an interesting question. Why, in fact, in democratic systems has there been so little demand for income redistribution? The current discussion of a negative income tax is the first serious attempt at a purely redistributive policy. Hagström (1938) presented a mathematical model predicting on the basis of a self-interest model for voters that democracy would inevitably lead to radical egalitarianism.

2. Political policy is not made by voters, not even in the sense that they choose the vector of political actions which best suits them. It is in fact made by representatives in one form or another. Political representation is an outstanding example of the principal-agent relation. This means that the link between individual utility functions and social action is tenuous, though by no means completely absent. Representatives are no more a random sample of their constituents than physicians are of their patients.

Indeed, the question can be raised: to what extent is the voter, when acting in that capacity, a principal or an agent? To some extent, certainly, the voter is cast in a role in which he feels some obligation to consider the social good, not just his own. It is in fact somewhat hard to explain otherwise why an individual votes at all in a large election, since the probability that his vote will be decisive is so negligible.

COLLECTIVE ACTION: SOCIAL NORMS

It is a mistake to limit collective action to State action; many other departures from the anonymous atomism of the price system are observed regularly. Indeed, firms of any complexity are illustrations of collective action, the internal allocation of their resources being directed by authoritative and hierarchical controls.

I want, however, to conclude by calling attention to a less visible form of social action: norms of social behavior, including ethical and moral codes. I suggest as one possible interpretation that they are reactions of society to compensate for market failures. It is useful for individuals to have some trust in each other's word. In the absence of trust, it would become very costly to arrange for alternative sanctions and guarantees, and many opportunities for mutually beneficial cooperation would have to be foregone. Banfield (1958) has argued that lack of trust is indeed one of the causes of economic underdevelopment.

It is difficult to conceive of buying trust in any direct way (though it can happen indirectly, for example, a trusted employee will be paid more as being more valuable); indeed, there seems to be some inconsistency in the very concept. Nonmarket action might take the form of a mutual agreement. But the arrangement of these agreements and especially their continued extension to new individuals entering the social fabric can be costly. As an alternative, society may proceed by internalization of these norms to the achievement of the desired agreement on an unconscious level.

There is a whole set of customs and norms which might be similarly interpreted as agreements to improve the efficiency of the economic system (in the broad sense of satisfaction of individual values) by providing commodities to which the price system is inapplicable.

These social conventions may be adaptive in their origins, but they can become retrogressive. An agreement is costly to reach and therefore costly to modify; and the costs of modification may be especially large for unconscious agreements. Thus, codes of professional ethics, which arise out of the principal-agent relation and afford protection to the principals, can serve also as a cloak for monopoly by the agents.

NOTES

[1] A competitive equilibrium is defined below. An allocation of resources through the workings of the economic system is said to be Pareto efficient if there is no other allocation which would make every individual in the economy better off.

[2] By "parametric role" is meant that each household and firm takes the market prices as given, not alterable by its consumption or production decisions.

[3] For households, "convexity" means that if we consider two different bundles of consumption, a third bundle defined by averaging the first two commodity by commodity is not inferior in the household's preferences to both of the first two. For a firm, "convexity" means that if we consider two different specifications of inputs and outputs, either of which is possible to the firm (in that the inputs suffice to produce the outputs), then a third specification defined by averaging the inputs and outputs of the first two is also possible for the firm to carry out.

[4] The extended version of this paper which appeared in the Compendium of the Joint Economic Committee contained sections on Imperfectly Competitive Equilibrium and Risk and Information.

REFERENCES

Aumann, R. J. 1964. Markets with a continuum of traders. *Econometrica* 32:39–50.

Aumann, R. J. 1966. The existence of competitive equilibria in markets with a continuum of traders. *Econometrica* 34:1–17.

Banfield, E. C. 1958. *The Moral Basis of a Backward Society.* The Free Press.

Black, D. 1958. *The Theory of Committees and Elections.* Cambridge, U.K.: Cambridge University Press.

Buchanan, J. and W. C. Stubblebine. 1962. Externality. *Economica* 29:371–384.

Buchanan, J. and G. Tullock. 1962. *The Calculus of Consent.* Ann Arbor, Michigan: University of Michigan Press.

Coase, R. H. 1960. The problem of social cost. *Journal of Law and Economics* 3:1–44.

Condorcet, Marquis de. 1785. *Essai sur l'application de l'analyse à la probabilitié des décisions rendues à la pluralité des voix.* Paris.

Demsetz, H. 1966. Some aspects of property rights. *Journal of Law Economics* 9:61–70.

Downs, A. 1957. *An Economic Theory of Democracy.* New York: Harper.

Hagström, K. G. 1938. A mathematical note on democracy. *Econometrica* 6:381–383.

Hotelling, H. 1929. Stability in competition. *Economic Journal* 39:41–57.

Knight, F. H. 1921. *Risk, Uncertainty, and Profit.* Boston and New York: Houghton-Mifflin. Reprinted by London School of Economics and Political Science, 1948.

Knight, F. H. 1924. Some fallacies in the interpretation of social cost. *Quarterly Journal of Economics* 38:582–606.

Marschak, T. 1959. Centralization and decentralization in economic organizations. *Econometrica* 27:399–430.

Meade, J. E. 1952. External economies and diseconomies in a competitive situation. *Economic Journal* 62:54–67.

Musgrave, R. A. 1959. *The Theory of Public Finance: A Study in Public Economy.* New York: McGraw-Hill Book Company.

von Neumann, J., and O. Morgenstern. 1944. *Theory of Games and Economic Behavior.* Princeton, N.J.: Princeton University Press. Second edition, 1947.

Robertson, D. H. 1924. Those empty boxes. *Economic Journal* 34:16–30.

Rothenberg, J. 1960. Non-convexity, aggregation, and Pareto optimality. *Journal of Political Economy* 68:435–468.

Rothenberg, J. 1965. A model of economic and political decision-making. In J. Margolis (ed.) *The Public Economy of Urban Communities.* Washington, D.C.: Resources for the Future.

Samuelson, P. A. 1954. The pure theory of public expenditures, *Review of Economic Statistics* 36:387–389.

Samuelson, P. A. 1967. The monopolistic competition revolution. In R. E. Kuenne (ed.) *Monopolistic Competition Theory: Studies in Impact.* New York, London, and Sydney: Wiley, pp. 105–138.

Schumpeter, J. 1942. *Capitalism, Socialism, and Democracy.* New York: Harper. Third Edition, 1950.

Scitovsky, T. 1954. Two concepts of external economies. *Journal of Political Economy* 62:143–151

Shapley, L. S., and M. Shubik. 1967. Ownership and the production function. *Quarterly Journal of Economics* 81:88–111.

Shubik, M. 1959. Edgeworth market games. In A. W. Tucker and R. D. Luce (eds.) *Contributions to the Theory of Games IV. Annals of Mathematics Study.* Princeton, New Jersey: Princeton University Press, 40:267–278.

Smith, A. 1937. *An Enquiry Concerning the Causes of the Wealth of Nations.* New York: Modern Library.

Starr, R. 1969. Quasi-equilibria in markets with nonconvex preferences. *Econometrica* 37:25–38.

Tullock, G. 1967. *Toward a Mathematics of Politics.* Ann Arbor, Michigan: University of Michigan Press.

Young, A. A. 1913. Pigou's Wealth and Welfare. *Quarterly Journal of Economics* 27:672–686.

B
Second Best

[4]

The general theory of second best[1]

There is an important basic similarity underlying a number of recent works in apparently widely separated fields of economic theory. Upon examination, it would appear that the authors have been rediscovering, in some of the many guises given it by various specific problems, a single general theorem. This theorem forms the core of what may be called *the general theory of second best*. Although the main principles of the theory of second best have undoubtedly gained wide acceptance, no general statement of them seems to exist. Furthermore, the principles often seem to be forgotten in the context of specific problems and, when they are rediscovered and stated in the form pertinent to some problem, this seems to evoke expressions of surprise and doubt rather than of immediate agreement and satisfaction at the discovery of yet another application of the already accepted generalizations.

In this paper, an attempt is made to develop a *general* theory of second best. The first section gives, by way of introduction, a verbal statement of the theory's main general theorem, together with two important negative corollaries. The second section outlines the scope of the general theory of second best. Next, a brief survey is given of some of the recent literature on the subject. This survey brings together a number of cases in which the general theory has been applied to various problems in theoretical economics. The implications of the general theory of second best for piecemeal policy recommendations, especially in welfare economics, are next considered. This general discussion is followed by two sections giving examples of the application of the theory in specific models. These examples lead up to the general statement and rigorous proof of the central theorem. A brief consideration of the existence of second-best solutions is followed by a classificatory discussion of the nature of these solutions. This taxonomy serves to illustrate some of the important negative corollaries of the theorem. The paper is concluded with a brief discussion of the difficult problem of multiple-layer second-best optima.

A general theorem in the theory of second best
It is well known that the attainment of a Paretian optimum requires the simultaneous fulfilment of all the optimum conditions. The general theorem for the second-best optimum states that if there is introduced into a general equilibrium system a constraint which prevents the attainment of one of the Paretian conditions, the other Paretian conditions, although still attainable, are, in general, no longer desirable. In other words, given that one of the Paretian optimum conditions cannot

be fulfilled, then an optimum situation can be achieved only by departing from all the other Paretian conditions. The optimum situation finally attained may be termed a second-best optimum because it is achieved subject to a constraint which, by definition, prevents the attainment of a Paretian optimum.

From this theorem there follows the important negative corollary that there is no *a priori* way to judge as between various situations in which some of the Paretian optimum conditions are fulfilled while others are not. Specifically, it is *not* true that a situation in which more, but not all, of the optimum conditions are fulfilled is necessarily, or is even likely to be, superior to a situation in which fewer are fulfilled. It follows, therefore, that in a situation in which there exist many constraints which prevent the fulfilment of the Paretian optimum conditions, the removal of any one constraint may affect welfare or efficiency either by raising it, by lowering it, or by leaving it unchanged.

The general theorem of the second best states that if one of the Paretian optimum conditions cannot be fulfilled a second-best optimum situation is achieved only by departing from all other optimum conditions. It is important to note that in general, nothing can be said about the direction or the magnitude of the secondary departures from optimum conditions made necessary by the original non-fulfilment of one condition. Consider, for example, a case in which the central authority levies a tax on the purchase of one commodity and returns the revenue to the purchasers in the form of a gift so that the sole effect of the tax is to distort relative prices. Then all that can be said in general is that given the existence and invariability of this tax, a second-best optimum can be achieved by levying some system of taxes and subsidies on all other commodities. The required tax on some commodities may exceed the given tax, on other commodities it may be less than the given tax, while on still others a subsidy, rather than a tax, may be required.

It follows from the above that there is no *a priori* way to judge as between various situations in which none of the Paretian optimum conditions are fulfilled. In particular, it is *not* true that a situation in which all departures from the optimum conditions are of the same direction and magnitude is necessarily superior to one in which the deviations vary in direction and magnitude. For example, there is no reason to believe that a situation in which there is the same degree of monopoly in all industries will necessarily be in any sense superior to a situation in which the degree of monopoly varies as between industries.

The scope of the theory of second best

Perhaps the best way to approach the problem of defining the scope of the theory of second best is to consider the role of constraints in economic theory. In the general economic problem of maximization a function is maximized subject to at least one constraint. For example, in the simplest welfare theory a welfare function is maximized subject to the constraint exercised by a transformation function. The theory of the Paretian optimum is concerned with the conditions that must be fulfilled in order to maximize some function subject to a set of constraints which are generally considered to be 'in the nature of things'. There are, of course, a whole host of possible constraints beyond those assumed to operate in the Paretian optimization problem. These further constraints vary from the 'nature-dictated' ones, such as indivisibilities and boundaries to production functions, to the obviously 'policy-created' ones such as taxes and subsidies. In general, there would seem to be no logical division between those constraints which occur in the Paretian optimum theory and those which occur only in the theory of second best. All that can be said is that, in the theory of the Paretian optimum, certain constraints are assumed to be operative and the conditions necessary for the maximization of some function subject to these constraints are examined. In the theory of second best there is admitted at least one constraint additional to the ones existing in Paretian optimum theory and it is in the nature of this constraint that it prevents the satisfaction of at least one of the Paretian optimum conditions. Consideration is then given to the nature of the conditions that must be satisfied in order to maximize some function subject to this new set of constraints.

It is important to note that even in a single general equilibrium system where there is only one Paretian optimum, there will be a multiplicity of second-best optimum positions. This is so because there are many possible combinations of constraints with a second-best solution for each combination. For this reason one may speak of the existence of *the* Paretian optimum but should, strictly speaking, refer to *a* second-best optimum.

It is possible to approach problems in the theory of second best from two quite different directions. On the one hand, the approach used in this paper is to assume the existence of one constraint additional to those in the Paretian optimum problem (e.g., one tax, one tariff, one subsidy, or one monopoly) and then to investigate the nature of the conditions that must be satisfied in order to achieve a second-best optimum and, where possible, to compare these conditions with those necessary for the attainment of a Paretian optimum. On the other hand, the approach used by Professor Meade is to assume the existence of a large number of taxes, tariffs, monopolies, and so on, and then to inquire into the effect of changing any one of them. Meade, therefore, deals with a system containing many constraints and investigates the optimum (second-best) level for one of them, assuming the invariability of all the others.[2] It would be futile to argue that one of these approaches was superior to the other. Meade's is probably the appropriate one when considering problems of actual policy in a world where many imperfections exist and only a few can be removed at any one time. On the other hand, the approach used in the present paper would seem to be the more appropriate one for a systematic study of the general principles of the theory of second best.

The theory of second best in the literature of economics
The theory of second best has been, in one form or another, a constantly
recurring theme in the post-war literature on the discriminatory reduction of trade
barriers. There can be no doubt that the theory of customs unions provides an
important case study in the application of the general theory of second best. Until
customs union theory was subjected to searching analysis, the 'free trader' often
seemed ready to argue that any reduction in tariffs would necessarily lead to
an improvement in world productive efficiency and welfare. In his path-breaking
work on the theory of customs unions[3] Professor Viner has shown that the removal
of tariffs from some imports may cause a decrease in the efficiency of world
production.
    One important reason for the shifts in the location of production which would
follow the creation of a customs union was described by Viner as follows:

> There will be commodities which one of the members of the customs union will
> now newly import from the other, whereas before the customs union it imported them
> from a third country, because that was the cheapest possible source of supply even
> after payment of the duty. The shift in the locus of production is now not as between
> the two member countries but as between a low-cost third country and the other, high-
> cost, member country.

Viner used the term 'trade diversion' to describe production shifts of this sort
and he took it as self-evident that they would reduce the efficiency of world
production. Since it is quite possible to conceive of a customs union having only
trade-diverting production effects, it follows, in Viner's analysis, that the discriminatory reduction of tariffs may reduce, rather than raise, the efficiency of
world production.
    Viner emphasized the production effects of customs unions,[4] directing his
attention to changes in the location. and hence the cost, of world production.
Recently Professor Meade has shown that a customs union has exactly parallel
effects on the location, and hence the 'utility' of world consumption.[5] Meade
isolates the 'consumption effects' of customs unions by considering an example
in which world production is fixed. In this case Viner's problem of the effects
of a union on the cost of world production cannot arise. Meade argues that, under
these circumstances, a customs union will tend to raise welfare by encouraging trade between the member countries but that, at the same time, it will tend
to lower welfare by discouraging the already hampered trade between the union
area and the rest of the world. In the final analysis a customs union will raise
welfare, lower it, or leave it unchanged, depending on the relative strength of
these two opposing tendencies. The Viner–Meade conclusions provide an application of the general theorem's negative corollary that nothing can be said *a
priori* about the welfare and efficiency effects of a change which permits the
satisfaction of some but not all of the Paretian optimum conditions.

Another application of second-best theory to the theory of tariffs has been provided by S.A. Ozga who has shown that a non-preferential reduction of tariffs by a single country may lead 'away from the free trade position'.[6] In other words, the adoption of a free-trade policy by one country, in a multi-country tariff-ridden world, may actually lower the real income of that country and of the world. Ozga demonstrates the existence of this possibility by assuming that all commodities are, in consumption, rigidly complementary, so that their production either increases or decreases simultaneously. He then shows that in a three-country world with tariffs all around, one country may adopt a policy of free trade and, as a result, the world production of all commodities may decrease. This is one way of demonstrating a result which follows directly from the general theory of second best.

In the field of public finance, the problems of second best seem to have found a particularly perplexing guise in the long controversy on the relative merits of direct *versus* indirect taxation. It would be tedious to review all the literature on the subject at this time. In his 1951 article, I.M.D. Little[7] has shown that because of the existence of the 'commodity' leisure, the price of which cannot be directly taxed, both direct and indirect taxes must prevent the satisfaction of some of the conditions necessary for the attainment of a Paretian optimum. An indirect tax on one good disturbs rates of substitution between that good and all others while an income tax disturbs rates of substitution between leisure and all other goods. Little then argues that there is no *a priori* way to judge as between these two positions where some Paretian optimum conditions are satisfied while others are not. This is undoubtedly correct. However, Little might have gone on to suggest that there is an *a priori* case in favor of raising a given amount of revenue by some system of *unequal indirect taxes* rather than by either an income tax or an indirect tax on only one commodity. This interesting conclusion was first stated by W.J. Corlett and D.C. Hague.[8] These authors have demonstrated that the optimum way to raise any given amount of revenue is by a system of unequal indirect taxes in which commodities 'most complementary' to leisure have the highest tax rates while commodities 'most competitive' with leisure have the lowest rates. The reason for this general arrangement of tax rates should be intuitively obvious. When an equal *ad valorem* rate of tax is placed on all goods the consumption of leisure will be too high while the consumption of all other goods will be too low. The consumption of untaxed leisure may be discouraged by placing especially high rates of tax on commodities which are complementary in consumption to leisure and by placing especially low rates of tax on commodities which are competitive in consumption with leisure.

Professor Meade has recently given an alternative analysis of the same problem.[9] His conclusions, however, support those of Corlett and Hague. In theory at least, the tables have been completely turned and the indirect tax is proved to be superior to the income tax, provided that the optimum system of indirect taxes is levied. This conclusion is but another example of an application of the general theorem that if one of the Paretian optimum conditions cannot be fulfilled then a second-best optimum situation can be obtained by departing from all the other optimum conditions.

What is perhaps not so obvious is that the problem of direct versus indirect taxes and that of the 'consumption effects' of customs unions are analytically identical. The Little analysis deals with a problem in which some commodities can be taxed at various rates while others must be taxed at a fixed rate. (It is not necessary that the fixed rate of tax should be zero.) In the theory of customs unions one is concerned with the welfare and efficiency effects of varying some tariff rates while leaving others unchanged. In Little's analysis there are three commodities, X, Y and Z, commodity Z being leisure. By renaming Z home goods and X and Y imports from two different countries one passes immediately to the theory of customs unions. An income tax in Little's analysis becomes a system of non-discriminatory import duties while a single indirect tax becomes the discriminatory tariff introduced after the formation of a customs union with the producers of the now untaxed import. A model of this sort is considered later in the paper.

An application of the general theory of second best to yet another field of economic theory is provided by A. Smithies in his article, 'The Boundaries of the Production and Utility Function'.[10] Smithies considers the case of a multi-input firm seeking to maximize its profits. This will be done when for each factor the firm equates marginal cost with marginal revenue productivity. Smithies then suggests that there may exist boundaries to the production function. These boundaries would take the form of irreducible minimum amounts of certain inputs, it being possible to employ more but not less than these minimum amounts. It might happen, however, that profit maximization called for the employment of an amount of one factor less than the minimum technically possible amount. In this case production would take place 'on the boundary' and the minimum possible amount of the input would be used. However, in the case of this input, marginal cost would no longer be equated with marginal productivity, the boundary conditions forcing its employment beyond the optimum level. Smithies then shows that given the constraint, marginal cost does not equal marginal productivity for this input, profits will be maximized only by departing from the condition marginal cost equals marginal productivity for all other inputs. Furthermore, there is no *a priori* reason for thinking that the nature of the inequality will be the same for all factors. Profit maximization may require that some factors be employed only to a point where marginal productivity exceeds marginal cost while other factors are used up to a point where marginal productivity falls below marginal cost.

Problems of the 'mixed economy' provide an application of second-best theory frequently encountered in popular discussion. Consider, for example, a case where one section of an economy is rigidly controlled by the central authority while another section is virtually uncontrolled. It is generally agreed that the economy is not functioning efficiently but there is disagreement as to the appropriate remedy. One faction argues that more control over the uncontrolled sector is needed, while another faction pleads for a relaxation of the degree of control exercised in the public sector. The principles of the general theory of second best suggest that *both sides* in the controversy may be advocating a policy appropriate to the desired ends. Given the high degree of control in one sector and the almost complete absence of control in another, it is unlikely that anything like a second-best optimum position has been reached. If this is so, then it follows that efficiency would be increased either by increasing the degree of control exercised over the uncontrolled sector or by relaxing the control exercised over the controlled sector. Both of these policies will move the economy in the direction of some second-best optimum position.

Finally, mention may be made of the problem of 'degrees of monopoly'. It is not intended to review the voluminous literature on this controversy. It may be mentioned in passing that, in all but the simplest models, a Paretian optimum requires that marginal costs *equal* prices throughout the entire economy. If this equality is not established in one firm, then the second-best conditions require that the equality be departed from in all other firms. However, as is usual in second-best cases there is no presumption in favor of the same degree of inequality in all firms. In general, the second-best position may well be one in which prices greatly exceed marginal costs in some firms, only slightly exceed marginal costs in others, while, in still other firms, prices actually fall short of marginal costs.

A similar problem is considered by Lionel W. McKenzie in his article 'Ideal output and the interdependence of firms'.[11] He deals with the problem of increasing the money value of output in situations in which marginal costs do not equal prices in all firms. The analysis is not conducted in a general equilibrium setting and many simplifying assumptions are made such as the one that resources can be shifted between occupations as desired without affecting their supplies. McKenzie shows that even in this partial equilibrium setting if allowance is made for inter-firm sales of intermediate products, the condition that marginal costs should bear the same relation to prices in all firms does not provide a sufficient condition for an increase in the value of output. Given that the optimum conditions marginal cost equals price for each commodity cannot be achieved, a second-best optimum would require a complex set of relations in which the ratio of marginal cost to price would vary as between firms. Although the analysis is not of a full general equilibrium, the conclusions follow the now familiar pattern: (1) if a Paretian optimum cannot be achieved a second-best optimum requires a general departure from all the Paretian optimum conditions and (2) there are unlikely to be any simple sufficient conditions for an *increase* when a *maximum* cannot be obtained.

The theory of second best and 'piecemeal' policy recommendations
It should be obvious from the discussion in the preceding sections that the principles of the general theory of second best show the futility of 'piecemeal welfare economics'. To apply to only a small part of an economy welfare rules which would lead to a Paretian optimum if they were applied everywhere, may move the economy away from, not toward, a second-best optimum position. A nationalized industry conducting its price–output policy according to the Lerner–Lange 'Rule' in an imperfectly competitive economy may well diminish both the general productive efficiency of the economy and the welfare of its members.

The problem of sufficient conditions for an increase in welfare, as compared to necessary conditions for a welfare maximum, is obviously important if policy recommendations are to be made in the real world. Piecemeal welfare economics is often based on the belief that a study of the *necessary* conditions for a Paretian welfare optimum may lead to the discovery of *sufficient* conditions for an increase in welfare. In his *Critique of Welfare Economics*,[12] I.M.D. Little discusses the optimum conditions for exchange and production '... both as necessary conditions for a maximum, and as sufficient conditions for a desirable economic change'. Later on in his discussion Little says '... necessary conditions are not very interesting. It is *sufficient* conditions for improvements that we really want ....' But the theory of second best leads to the conclusion that there are in general no such sufficient conditions for an increase in welfare. There are necessary conditions for a Paretian optimum. In a simple situation there may exist a condition that is necessary and sufficient. But in a general equilibrium situation there will be no conditions which in general are sufficient for an increase in welfare without also being sufficient for a welfare maximum.

The preceding generalizations may be illustrated by considering the following optimum conditions for exchange: 'The marginal rate of substitution between any two "goods" must be the same for every individual who consumes them both.' Little concludes that this condition gives a sufficient condition for an increase in welfare provided only that when it is put into effect, '... the distribution of welfare is not thereby made worse'. However, the whole discussion of this optimum condition occurs only after Little has postulated '... a fixed stock of "goods" to be distributed between a number of "individuals"'. The optimum condition that all consumers should be faced with the same set of prices becomes in this case a sufficient condition for an increase in welfare, because the problem at hand is merely how to distribute efficiently a fixed stock of goods. But in this case the condition is a necessary and sufficient condition for a

Paretian optimum. As soon as variations in output are admitted, the condition is no longer sufficient for a welfare maximum and it is also no longer sufficient for an increase in welfare.

The above conclusion may be illustrated by a simple example. Consider a community of two individuals having different taste patterns. The 'government' of the community desires to raise a certain sum which it will give away to a foreign country. The community has made its value judgement about the distribution of income by deciding that each individual must contribute half of the required revenue. It has also been decided that the funds are to be raised by means of indirect taxes. It follows from the Corlett and Hague analysis that the best way to raise the revenue is by a system of *unequal* indirect taxes in which commodities 'most complementary' to leisure are taxed at the highest rates while commodities 'most substitutable' for leisure are taxed at the lowest rates. But the two individuals have different tastes so that commodity X is substitutable for leisure for individual I and complementary to leisure for individual II, while commodity Y and leisure are complementary for individual I and substitutes for II. The optimum way to raise the revenue, therefore, is to tax commodity X at a low rate when it is sold to individual I and at a high rate when it is sold to individual II, while Y is taxed at a high rate when sold to I but a low rate when sold to II. A second-best optimum thus requires that the two individuals be faced with different sets of relative prices.

Assume that the optimum tax rates are charged. The government then changes the tax system to make it non-discriminatory as between persons while adjusting the rates to keep revenue unchanged. Now the Paretian optimum exchange condition is fulfilled, but welfare has been decreased, for both individuals have been moved to lower indifference curves. Therefore, in the assumed circumstances, this Paretian optimum condition is a sufficient condition for a *decrease* in welfare.

A problem in the theory of tariffs
In this section the simple type of model used in the analysis of direct *versus* indirect taxes is applied to a problem in the theory of tariffs. In the Little–Meade–Corlett and Hague analysis it is assumed that the government raises a fixed amount of revenue which it spends in some specified manner. The optimum way of raising this revenue is then investigated. A somewhat different problem is created by changing this assumption about the disposition of the tax revenue. In the present analysis it is assumed that the government returns the tax revenue to the consumers in the form of a gift so that the only effect of the tax is to change relative prices.[13]

A simple three-commodity model is used, there being one domestic commodity and two imports. It is assumed that the domestic commodity is untaxed and that a fixed rate of tariff is levied on one of the imports. The optimum level for the

162   Microeconomics, Growth and Political Economy

tariff on the other import is then investigated. This is an obvious problem in
the theory of second best. Also it is interesting to note that the conclusions reached
have immediate applications to the theory of customs unions. In the second part
of this section the conclusions of the first part are applied to the problem of the
welfare effects of a customs union which causes neither trade creation nor
trade diversion, but only the expansion and contraction of the volumes of
already existing trade.

Second-best optimum tariff systems with fixed terms of trade
The conditions of the model are as follows: country A is a small country spe-
cializing in the production of one commodity (Z). Some of Z is consumed at
home and the remainder is exported in return for two imports, X from country
B and Y from country C. The prices of X and Y in terms of Z are unaffected by
any taxes or tariffs levied in country A. It is further assumed that none of the
tariffs actually levied by A are high enough to protect domestic industries
producing either X or Y, that country B does not produce commodity Y and that
country C does not produce commodity X. The welfare of country A is defined
by a community welfare function which is of the same form as the welfare
functions of the identical individuals who inhabit A.

It is assumed that A levies some fixed tariff on imports of commodity Y and
that commodity Z is not taxed. It is then asked: what tariff (≤ 0) on imports of
commodity X will maximize welfare in country A? This tariff will be termed
the optimum X tariff.

The model may be set out as follows: let there be three commodities, X, Y
and Z. Let p_x and p_y be the prices of X and Y in terms of Z. Let the rate of *ad
valorem* tariff charged on X and Y be $t_x - 1$ and $t_y - 1$.

$$u = u(x, y, z) \tag{1}$$

$$\frac{\partial u}{\partial x} = \frac{\partial u}{\partial z} p_x t_x \tag{2a}$$

$$\frac{\partial u}{\partial y} = \frac{\partial u}{\partial z} p_y t_y \tag{2b}$$

$$Xp_x + Yp_y + Z = C \tag{3}$$

Equation (1) expresses country A's community welfare function. Equations (2a
and b) are the demand equilibrium conditions. Equation (3) gives the condition
that A's international payments be in balance.

These equations will yield a solution in general for any t_x and t_y, in X, Y and
Z. Hence, for given p_x, p_y, C and whatever parameters enter into (1):

$$X = f(t_x, t_y) \tag{4a}$$
$$Y = g(t_x, t_y) \tag{4b}$$
$$Z = h(t_x, t_y) \tag{4c}$$

Attention is directed to the sign of the change in U when t_x changes with t_y > 1 kept constant. From equations (1) and (4):

$$\frac{\partial u}{\partial t_x} = \frac{\partial u}{\partial x} \cdot \frac{\partial x}{\partial t_x} + \frac{\partial u}{\partial y} \cdot \frac{\partial y}{\partial t_x} + \frac{\partial u}{\partial z} \cdot \frac{\partial z}{\partial t_x} \tag{5}$$

Substitute (2a and b) into (5):

$$\frac{\partial u}{\partial t_x} = P_x t_x \frac{\partial u}{\partial z} \cdot \frac{\partial x}{\partial t_x} + P_y t_y \frac{\partial u}{\partial z} \cdot \frac{\partial y}{\partial t_x} + \frac{\partial u}{\partial z} \cdot \frac{\partial z}{\partial t_x}$$
$$= \frac{\partial u}{\partial z} \left(P_x t_x \frac{\partial x}{\partial t_x} + P_y t_y \frac{\partial y}{\partial t_x} + \frac{\partial z}{\partial t_x} \right) \tag{6}$$

Next, take the partial derivative of (3) with respect to t_x.

$$P_x \frac{\partial x}{\partial t_x} + P_y \frac{\partial y}{\partial t_x} + \frac{\partial z}{\partial t_x} = 0$$

or

$$P_x \frac{\partial x}{\partial t_x} + P_y \frac{\partial y}{\partial t_x} = -\frac{\partial z}{\partial t_x} \tag{7}$$

Substitute (7) into (6):

$$\frac{\partial u}{\partial t_x} = \frac{\partial u}{\partial z} \left(P_x t_x \frac{\partial x}{\partial t_x} + P_y t_y \frac{\partial y}{\partial t_x} - P_x \frac{\partial x}{\partial t_x} - P_y \frac{\partial y}{\partial t_x} \right)$$
$$= \frac{\partial u}{\partial z} \left[P_x \frac{\partial x}{\partial t_x} (t_x - 1) + P_y \frac{\partial y}{\partial t_x} (t_y - 1) \right] \tag{8}$$

164   Microeconomics, Growth and Political Economy

It is assumed, first, that some tariff is levied on Y but that X is imported duty free. Therefore, $t_x = 1$ and $t_y > 1$. Equation (8) reduces to:

$$\frac{\partial u}{\partial t_x} = \frac{\partial u}{\partial z}\left[p_y \frac{\partial y}{\partial t_x}(t_y - 1)\right]$$

(9)

In (9) $\partial u/\partial t_x$ takes the same sign as $\partial y/\partial t_x$. It follows that the introduction of a marginal tariff on X will raise welfare if it causes an increase in imports of commodity Y, will leave welfare unchanged if it causes no change in imports of Y and will lower welfare if it causes a decrease in imports of Y. Therefore, the optimum tariff on X is, in fact, a subsidy, if imports of Y fall when a tariff is placed on X, it is zero if the X tariff has no effect on imports of Y and it is positive if imports of Y rise when the tariff is placed on X.

It is now assumed that a uniform rate of tariff is charged on X and Y. Therefore, $t_x = t_y \equiv T$ and equation (8) becomes:

$$\frac{\partial u}{\partial t_x} = \frac{\partial u}{\partial z}(T-1)\left(p_x \frac{\partial x}{\partial T} + p_y \frac{\partial y}{\partial T}\right)$$

Substituting from (7):

$$\frac{\partial u}{\partial t_x} = -\left[\frac{\partial u}{\partial z}\cdot\frac{\partial z}{\partial t_x}(T-1)\right]$$

(10)

In (10) the sign of $\partial u/\partial t_x$ will be opposite to the sign of $\partial z/\partial t_x$. It follows that a marginal increase in the tariff on X will increase welfare if it causes a decrease in the consumption of Z, will leave welfare unchanged if it causes no change in the consumption of Z and will lower welfare if it causes an increase in the consumption of Z. It may be concluded, therefore, that the optimum tariff on X exceeds the given tariff on Y if an increase in the X tariff reduces the consumption of Z, that the optimum X tariff equals the given Y tariff if there is no relation between the X tariff and the consumption of Z and that the optimum X tariff is less than the given Y tariff if an increase in the X tariff causes an increase in consumption of Z.

In the case where an increase in the tariff on X causes an increase in the consumption of Y and of Z the optimum X tariff is greater than zero but less than the given tariff on Y.

Welfare effects of a customs union causing only trade expansion and trade contraction

It is assumed that country A initially charges a uniform *ad valorem* rate of tariff on imports of X and Y. A then forms a customs union with country B. Now X is imported duty-free while the pre-union tariff still applies to Y. What is the effect on A's welfare of such a customs union? Some answers follow immediately from the previous analysis:

Case 1: Any increase in the tariff on X causes a fall in the consumption of Y. The optimum tariff on X is, in fact, a subsidy. Therefore, the customs union must raise A's welfare.

Case 2: Variations in the tariff on X have no effect on consumption of Y. The optimum tariff on X is now zero. The customs union raises welfare in A. Furthermore, it raises it to a second-best optimum level (assuming that only the X tariff can be varied).

Case 3: Variations in the tariff on X have no effect on the purchases of Z. The optimum tariff on X is equal to the Y tariff. The customs union lowers A's welfare. Furthermore, the union disturbs an already achieved second-best optimum.

Case 4: An increase in the tariff on X causes a fall in the consumption of Z. In this case the optimum tariff on X exceeds the given Y tariff. Therefore, the customs union lowers A's welfare.

Case 5: An increase in the tariff on X causes an increase in the consumption of both Y and Z. The optimum X tariff is greater than zero but less than the given Y tariff. The effect of the customs union on welfare is not known. Assume, however, that the X tariff is removed by a series of stages. It follows that the initial stages of tariff reduction must raise welfare and that the final stages must lower it. Although nothing can be said about the welfare effect of a complete removal of the X tariff, another important conclusion is suggested. A small reduction in tariffs must raise welfare. A large reduction may raise or lower it. It follows, therefore, that a partial preferential reduction of tariffs is more likely to raise welfare than is a complete preferential elimination of tariffs. Of course, this conclusion depends upon the specific assumptions made in the present model but it does provide an interesting and suggestive hypothesis for further investigation.

Nationalized industry in an economy with monopoly: A simple model

An interesting, and not unlikely, situation in which a 'second-best' type of policy may have to be pursued is that of a mixed economy which includes both nationalized industries and industries which are subject to monopoly control.

The monopoly is assumed to be one of the data: for one reason or another this monopoly cannot be removed, and the task of the nationalized industry is to determine that pricing policy which is most in 'the public interest'.

When there is full employment of resources then, if the monopoly is exercising its power, it will be producing less of the monopolized product than is required to give an optimum (in the Paretian sense) allocation of resources. Since there is less than the optimum production of the monopolized good, there will be more than the optimum production of the non-monopolized goods as a group.

Suppose that one of the non-monopolized industries is now nationalized. What should be its price–output policy? If it behaves competitively then it will tend to produce more of its product, relative to the monopolized good, than the Paretian optimum would require. If, on the other hand, it behaves monopolistically itself, then it will cut down the excess of its own production relative to that of the monopoly but will increase the excess of the remaining goods relative to both its own product and that of the monopolized industry. This is a typical 'second-best' situation: any policy will make some things worse and some better.

It is clear that no policy on the part of the nationalized industry can restore the Paretian optimum, for the existence of the monopoly prevents this. The nationalized industry must aim at a second-best policy, designed to achieve the best that still remains open to the economy. In purely generally terms it is impossible to be more definite than this, as will be shown in a later section. Intuitively, however, one might expect that, in some situations at least, the best policy for the nationalized industry would be to behave something like the monopoly, but to a lesser extent. In the case of the simple model to be presented in this section, one's intuitions would be correct.

There are assumed to be, in the present model, three industries producing goods x, y, z. Labor is the only input, costs are constant, and the total supply of labor is fixed. These assumptions define a unique linear transformation function relating the quantities of the three goods:

$$ax + by + cz = L \tag{11}$$

The production functions from which this is derived are:

$$x = \frac{1}{a}l_x, \ y = \frac{1}{b}l_y, \ z = \frac{1}{c}l_z; \ \ l_x + l_y + l_z = L \tag{12}$$

The marginal costs are constant and proportional to a, b, c.

The 'public interest' is assumed to be defined by a community preference function, which is of the same form as the preference functions of the identical individuals who make up the society. For simplicity, this preference function is assumed to take the logarithmic form:

$$U = x^\alpha y^\beta z^\gamma, \ \alpha, \ \beta, \ \gamma > 0 \tag{13}$$

The partial derivatives of this are:

$$\frac{\partial U}{\partial x} = \alpha \frac{U}{x}, \frac{\partial U}{\partial y} = \beta \frac{U}{y}, \frac{\partial U}{\partial z} = \gamma \frac{U}{z}$$

so that the marginal utilities of x, y, z are proportional, respectively to α/x, β/y, γ/z. For a utility function of this type, all goods are substitutes in both the Edgeworth–Pareto and Hicksian senses.

If there were no constraints in the economy (other than the transformation function itself), the Paretian optimum would be that found by maximizing the expression $U - \lambda(ax + by + cz - L)$, where λ is the Lagrangian multiplier. This would lead to the three equations:

$$\left.\begin{array}{l} \dfrac{\partial U}{\partial x} - \lambda a = 0 \\[2mm] \dfrac{\partial U}{\partial y} - \lambda b = 0 \\[2mm] \dfrac{\partial U}{\partial z} - \lambda c = 0 \end{array}\right\} \qquad (14)$$

which can be expressed in the proportional form:

$$\frac{a}{\alpha} x = \frac{b}{\beta} y = \frac{c}{\gamma} z \qquad (15)$$

These conditions are of the familiar Paretian type, namely that the marginal utilities (or prices which, assuming the ordinary consumer behavior equations, are proportional to them) are proportional to the marginal costs. There being no monetary conditions, and the supply of labor being fixed, equality between prices and marginal costs is not necessarily implied.

Suppose now that the industry producing x is a monopoly. The monopoly will set the price of x higher (in terms of some numeraire, which will be taken to be z) in relation to marginal cost than in the conditions of the Paretian optimum. A numeraire is necessary since money, and money prices, are not being considered.

For the present purposes, the exact margin between marginal cost and price in the monopolized industry (relative to the numeraire) does not matter. It is necessary only for the problem that the monopolist set the prices of x higher, relative to the price of z, than the ratio of the marginal cost of producing x to the marginal cost of producing z.

In other words, the monopolist's behavior can be expressed by:

$$\frac{p_x}{p_z} > \frac{mc_x}{mc_z}$$

Substituting for $\dfrac{p_x}{p_z}\left(=\dfrac{\partial U}{\partial x}\Big/\dfrac{\partial U}{\partial z}=\dfrac{\alpha z}{\gamma x}\right)$ and $\dfrac{mc_x}{mc_z}\left(=\dfrac{a}{c}\right)$, this gives:

$$\frac{\alpha z}{\gamma x} > \frac{a}{c}$$
$$c\alpha z > a\gamma x$$
$$= k a \gamma x \quad \text{where } k > 1 \tag{16}$$

The actual value of k (provided it is > 1) does not matter for the analysis. It is not necessary for the argument that k is constant as the monopolist faces the changes brought about by the policies of the nationalized industries, but it simplifies the algebra to assume this.

The behavior of the monopolist, assumed unalterable, becomes an additional constraint on the system. The best that can be done in the economy is to maximize U subject to two constraints, the transformation function (11) and the monopoly behavior condition (16). The conditions for attaining the second-best optimum (the Paretian optimum being no longer attainable) are found, therefore, as the conditions for the maximum of the function $U - \mu(c\alpha z - k\alpha\gamma x) - \lambda'(ax + by + cz - L)$, where there are now two Lagrangian multipliers μ, λ'. Neither of these multipliers can be identified with the multiplier λ in the equations (14).

The conditions for attaining the second best are, therefore:

$$\alpha \frac{U}{x} + \mu k a \gamma - \lambda' a = 0 \tag{17}$$

$$\beta \frac{U}{y} - \lambda' b = 0 \tag{18}$$

$$\gamma \frac{U}{z} - \mu c \alpha - \lambda' c = 0 \tag{19}$$

To appreciate these conditions, it is necessary to compute the ratio p_y/p_z, compare it with the ratio mc_y/mc_z, and relate the result to both the Paretian optimum conditions and the mode of behavior of the monopolist.

Although there are three equations (17), (18), (19) above, these involve the two Lagrangian multipliers, so that there is actually only one degree of freedom. Hence, the policy of the nationalized industry (that which produces *y*) is sufficient for attaining the second best. If the nationalized industry sets its price, relative to its marginal cost, so as to satisfy the above conditions, it will have done all that is within its power to further the public interest.

To complete the solution it is necessary to determine μ and λ'. From (17)

$$\mu k a \gamma x = -\alpha U + \lambda' a x \tag{20}$$

and from (19)

$$-\mu c \alpha z = \gamma U - \lambda' c z \tag{21}$$

Hence

$$\mu(k a \gamma x - c \alpha z) = -(\alpha + \gamma)U + \lambda'(a x + c z)$$

but, from (16),

$$k a \gamma x - c \alpha z = 0$$

so that

$$(\alpha + \gamma)U - \lambda'(a x + c z) = 0$$

$$\lambda' = \frac{(\alpha + \gamma)U}{a x + c z} \tag{22}$$

Substituting for λ' in (20)

$$\mu k a \gamma x = -\alpha U + \frac{(\alpha + \gamma)U}{a x + c z}$$
$$= \frac{\gamma a x - c \alpha x}{a x + c z} U$$

$$\mu = \frac{k-1}{k} \cdot \frac{-U}{a x + c z} \qquad [c \alpha z = k \gamma a x, \text{ from (16)}] \tag{23}$$

The correct pricing policy for the nationalized industry is given from the ratio p_y/p_z which is implicit in the equations (17), (18), (19).

$$\frac{p_y}{p_z} = \frac{\frac{\partial U}{\partial y}}{\frac{\partial U}{\partial z}}$$

$$= \frac{\beta \frac{U}{y}}{\gamma \frac{U}{z}}$$

$$= \frac{\lambda' b}{\mu c \alpha + \lambda' c} \qquad \text{[From (18), (19)]}$$

$$= \frac{b}{c + \frac{\mu}{\lambda'} c \alpha}$$

$$= \frac{\frac{b}{c}}{1 - \frac{k-1}{k} \cdot \frac{\alpha}{\alpha + \gamma}} \qquad \text{(From (22), (23))} \qquad (24)$$

Now $b/c = MC_y/MC_z$, from (12), so that:

$$\frac{p_y}{p_z} = \frac{MC_y}{MC_z} \cdot \left(\frac{1}{1 - \frac{k-1}{k} \cdot \frac{\alpha}{\alpha + \gamma}} \right) \qquad (25)$$

Consider the expression $((k-1)/k \cdot \alpha/(\alpha + \gamma))$. Since $k > 1$, $0 < (k-1)/k < 1$, and $\alpha/(\alpha + \gamma) < 1$ since $\gamma > 0$. Thus the bracketed expression on the right hand side of (25) is greater than unity.

In other words, $p_y/p_z > MC_y/MC_z$, so that, relative to the numeraire, the nationalized industry should set its price higher than its marginal cost and, to that extent, behave like the monopoly.

But now consider the relationship between the nationalized industry and the monopoly:

$$\frac{p_y}{px} = \frac{\beta\dfrac{U}{y}}{\alpha\dfrac{U}{x}}$$

$$= \frac{\dfrac{b}{a}}{\dfrac{\mu}{\lambda'}k\gamma + 1}$$

$$= \frac{\dfrac{b}{a}}{-\dfrac{k-1}{\alpha+\gamma}\cdot\gamma + 1}$$

$$= \frac{b}{a}\cdot\frac{\alpha+\gamma}{\alpha+k\gamma} \tag{26}$$

In this case, since $k > 1$, α, $\gamma > 0$, $(\alpha + \gamma)/(\alpha + k\gamma) < 1$. Since $b/a = MC_y/MC_x$, the nationalized industry should set its price less high, in relation to marginal cost, than the monopoly.

In short, in the particular model analyzed, the correct policy for the nationalized industry, with monopoly entrenched in one of the other industries, would be to take an intermediate path. On the one hand, it should set its price higher than marginal cost (relative to the numeraire) but, on the other hand, it should not set its price so far above marginal cost as is the case in the monopolized industry.

These conclusions refer, it should be emphasized, to the particular model which has been analyzed above. This model has many simplifying (and therefore special) features, including the existence of only one input, constant marginal costs and a special type of utility function. As is demonstrated later there can be no *a priori* expectations about the nature of a second-best solution in circumstances where a generalized utility function is all that can be specified.

A general theorem of the second best

Let there be some function $F(x_1 \ldots x_n)$ of the n variables $x_1 \ldots x_n$, which is to be maximized (minimized) subject to a constraint on the variables $\Phi(x_1 \ldots x_n) = 0$. This is a formalization of the typical choice situation in economic analysis.

Let the solution of this problem – the Paretian optimum – be the $n - 1$ conditions $\Omega^i(x_1 \ldots x_n) = 0$, $i = 1 \ldots n - 1$. Then the following theorem, the theorem of the second best, can be given.

If there is an additional constraint imposed of the type $\Omega^i \neq 0$ for $i = j$, then the maximum (minimum) of F subject to both the constraint Φ and the constraint $\Omega^i \neq 0$ will, in general, be such that none of the still attainable Paretian conditions $\Omega^i = 0$, $i \neq j$, will be satisfied.

Proof
In the absence of the second constraint, the solution of the original maximum (minimum) problem is both simple and familiar. Using the Lagrange method, the Paretian conditions are given by the n equations:

$$F_i - \lambda \Phi_i = 0 \qquad i = 1 \ldots n \tag{27}$$

Eliminating the multiplier, these reduce to the $n - 1$ proportionality conditions:

$$\frac{F_i}{F_n} = \frac{\Phi_i}{\Phi_n} \qquad i = 1 \ldots n - 1 \tag{28}$$

where the nth commodity is chosen as numeraire.
   The equations (28) are the first-order conditions for the attainment of the Paretian optimum. Now let there be a constraint imposed which prevents the attainment of one of the conditions (28). Such a constraint will be of the form (the numbering of the commodities is, of course, arbitrary):

$$\frac{F_1}{F_n} = k \frac{\Phi_1}{\Phi_n} \qquad k \neq 1 \tag{29}$$

It is not necessary that k be constant, but it is assumed to be so in the present analysis. There is now an additional constraint in the system so that, using the Lagrangean method, the function to be maximized (minimized) will be:

$$F - \lambda' \Phi - \mu \left(\frac{F_1}{F_n} - k \frac{\Phi_1}{\Phi_n} \right) \tag{30}$$

The multipliers λ', μ will both be different, in general, from the multiplier λ in (27).
   The conditions that the expression (30) shall be at a maximum (minimum) are as follows:

$$F_i - \lambda'\Phi_i - \mu\left\{\frac{F_n F_{1i} - F_1 F_{ni}}{F_n^2} - k\frac{\Phi_n\Phi_{1i} - \Phi_1\Phi_{ni}}{\Phi_n^2}\right\} = 0 \quad i = 1...n \quad (31)$$

If the expression $(F_n F_{1i} - F_1 F_{ni})/F_n^2$ is denoted by Q_i and the equivalent expression for the Φs by R_i, then the conditions (31) can be rewritten in the following form:

$$\frac{F_i}{F_n} = \frac{\Phi_i + \frac{\mu}{\lambda'}(Q_i - kR_i)}{\Phi_n + \frac{\mu}{\lambda'}(Q_n - kR_n)} \quad (32)$$

These are the conditions for the attainment of the second-best position, given the constraint (29), expressed in a form comparable with the Paretian conditions as set out in (28).

Clearly, any one of the conditions for the second best will be the same as the equivalent Paretian condition only if:

(i) $\mu = 0$
(ii) $\mu \neq 0$, but $Q_i - kR_i = Q_n - kR_n = 0$

The first of these cannot be true for, if it were, then, when $i = 1$, F_1/F_n would be equal to Φ_1/Φ_n, in contradiction with the constraint condition (29).

It is clear from the nature of the expressions Q_i, Q_n, R_i, R_n that nothing is known, in general, about their signs, let alone their magnitudes, and even the signs would not be sufficient to determine whether (ii) was satisfied or not.

Consider $Q_n = (F_n F_{1n} - F_1 F_{nn})/F_n^2$. If F were a utility function then it would be known that F_1, F_n were positive and F_{nn} negative, but the sign of F_{1n} may be either positive or negative. Even if the sign of F_{1n} were known to be negative, the sign of Q_n would still be indeterminate, since it would depend on whether the negative or the positive term in the expression was numerically the greater. In the case of Q_i, where $i \neq n$, the indeterminacy is even greater, since there are two expressions F_{i1} and F_{ni} for which the signs may be either positive or negative.

The same considerations as apply for the Qs also apply for the Rs of course. In general, therefore, the conditions for the second-best optimum, given the constraint (29), will all differ from the corresponding conditions for the attainment of the Paretian optimum. Conversely, given the constraint (29), the application of these rules of behavior of the Paretian type which are still attainable will not lead, in general, to the best position in the circumstances.

The general conditions for the achievement of the second-best optimum in the type of case with which this analysis is concerned will be of the type F_i/F_n = $k_i(\Phi_i/\Phi_n)$, where $k_i \neq k_j \neq 1$, so that $F_i/F_j = \Phi_i/\Phi_j$, $F_i/F_j \neq F_k/F_j$, $\Phi_i/\Phi_j \neq \Phi_k/\Phi_j$, and the usual Paretian rules will be broken all round.

The existence of a second-best solution

The essential condition that a true second-best solution to a given constrained situation should exist is that, if there is a Paretian optimum in which F has a maximum (minimum) when the constraint is removed, then the expression (30) must also have a true maximum (minimum). There is no reason why this should, in general, be the case.

For one thing, whereas well-behaved functions F and Φ will always have a solution which satisfies the comparatively simple first-order conditions for a Paretian optimum, it is by no means certain that the much more complex first-order conditions (31) for a second-best solution will be satisfied, since these conditions involve second-order derivatives whose behavior (subject only to convexity–concavity conditions of the functions) is unknown.

If the first-order conditions for the existence of second-best solutions present difficulties, the difficulties are quite insurmountable in the case of the second-order conditions. Let it be supposed, for concreteness, that the nature of the case is such that F is to be maximized. Then the existence of a second-best solution requires that the first-order conditions (31) shall give a maximum, not a minimum or a turning point. This requires that the second differential of the expression (30) shall be negative. But the second differential of (30) involves the *third*-order derivatives of F and Φ. Absolutely nothing is known about these in the general case, and their properties cannot be derived from the second-order condition that the Paretian optimum represents a true maximum for F.

The nature of second-best solutions

The extraordinary difficulty of making *a priori* judgements about the types of policy likely to be required in situations where the Paretian optimum is unattainable, and the second best must be aimed at, is well illustrated by examining the conditions (32) in the light of possible knowledge about the signs of some of the expressions involved.

In order to simplify the problem, and to render it less abstract, the function F will be supposed to be a utility function and Φ, which will be supposed to be a transformation function, will be assumed to be linear. The second derivatives of Φ disappear, so that $R_i = 0$ for all i, and attention can be concentrated on the expressions Q.

With the problem in this form, the derivatives F_i are proportional to the prices p_i, and the derivatives Φ_i are proportional to the marginal costs MC_i. As an additional simplification which assists verbal discussion but which does not affect the essentials of the model, it will be supposed that price equals marginal cost for the nth commodity, which will be referred to as the numeraire.

From (32), with these additional assumptions, therefore:

$$\frac{F_i}{F_n} = p_i = \frac{MC_i + \theta Q_i}{1 + \theta Q_n}$$

where $\theta = \mu/\lambda'$ so that

$$p_i - MC_i = \theta(Q_i - p_i Q_n) \tag{33}$$

Thus, for the ith commodity, price is above, equal to, or below, marginal cost according as Q_i/p_i is greater than, equal to, or less than, Q_n.

Since $Q_i = (F_n F_{1i} - F_1 F_{ni})/F_n^2$, the most we can expect to know is the sign of Q_i, unless a specific social utility function is given. From signs only, we can deduce only the following:

(i) if $\theta > 0$, $P > 1$ if $Q_i > 0$, $Q_n < 0$
$ P < 1$ if $Q_i < 0$, $Q_n > 0$ (34)
(ii) if $\theta < 0$, $P > 1$ if $Q_i < 0$, $Q_n > 0$
$\phantom{(ii) if \theta < 0,} P < 1$ if $Q_i > 0$, $Q_n < 0$

Nothing can be said about P if Q_i, Q_n are of the same signs.

Now consider Q_i. The denominator is always positive, and F_1, F_n are both positive, so that the determining factors are the signs of the mixed partial derivatives F_{1i} and F_{in}. It is assumed that goods are known to be substitutes ($F_{ij} < 0$) or complements ($F_{ij} > 0$) in the Edgeworth–Pareto sense. There are four possible cases:

(a) If $F_{1i} > 0$, $F_{ni} > 0$, then $Q_i \gtrless 0$
(b) If $F_{1i} < 0$, $F_{ni} < 0$, then $Q_i \gtrless 0$
(c) If $F_{1i} > 0$, $F_{ni} < 0$, then $Q_i > 0$
(d) If $F_{1i} < 0$, $F_{ni} > 0$, then $Q_i < 0$

In cases (c) and (d), but not in cases (a) and (b), therefore, the sign of Q_i is determinate.

To complete the picture the sign of θ is also needed. Where the sign of this can be found at all, it is found by putting $i = 1$ and substituting in the constraint condition (29). For concreteness, let k be > 1 (the first good will be referred to as the monopolized good). Then, since $(1 + \theta Q_1)/(1 + \theta Q_n) = k > 1$, it can be deduced that, if $Q_1 < 0$, $Q_n > 0$, then $\theta < 0$, and if $Q_1 > 0$, $Q_n < 0$, then $\theta < 0$. In all other cases the sign of θ is indeterminate.

For $Q_1 > Q_n$, it is known that F_{11}, $F_{nn} < 0$, and $F_{n1} = F_{1n}$ so that there are only two cases, $F_{n1} > 0$ and $F_{n1} < 0$. The information conveyed in each of the two cases is as follows:

I $F_{n1} > 0 : Q_1 < 0$, $Q_n > 0$, so that $\theta < 0$
II $F_{n1} < 0 : Q_1 \gtrless 0$, $Q_n \gtrless 0$, so that $\theta \gtrless 0$

The combination of cases I and II with the independently determined cases (a), (b), (c), (d) gives a total of eight cases. These are given in Table 12.1, showing the information which can be derived about the signs of Q_i, Q_n and θ, and the consequent information about P using the conditions (34).

Table 12.1   Determining relationship between price and marginal cost

Case		Q_i	Sign of Q_n	θ	Relationship of price to marginal cost for x_i
I $F_{ni} > 0$	(a) F_{ij}, $F_{ni} > 0$	?	+	−	?
	(b) F_{ij}, $F_{ni} < 0$	?	+	−	?
	(c) $F_{1i} > 0$, $F_{ni} < 0$	+	+	−	?
	(d) $F_{1i} < 0$, $F_{ni} > 0$	−	+	−	Price exceeds marginal cost
II $F_{ni} < 0$	(a) F_{1i}, $F_{ni} > 0$	?	?	?	?
	(b) F_{1i}, $F_{ni} < 0$	?	?	?	?
	(c) $F_{1i} > 0$, $F_{ni} < 0$	+	?	?	?
	(d) $F_{1i} < 0$, $F_{ni} > 0$	−	?	?	?

Of the eight cases tabulated, the signs of Q_i, Q_n and θ are simultaneously determinate in only two, I(c) and I(d), and in only one of these two, I(d), does this lead to a determinate relationship between price and marginal cost. This sole case leads to the only *a priori* statement that can be made about the nature of second-best solutions on the basis of the signs of the mixed second-order partial derivatives of the utility function.

If the monopolized commodity is complementary (in Edgeworth–Pareto sense) to the numeraire, and the *i*th commodity is also complementary to the numeraire, but a substitute for the monopolized good, then, in order to attain a second-best solution, the price of the *i*th commodity must be set higher than its marginal cost.

Since knowledge of the sign alone of the derivatives F_{ij} reveals only one determinate case, it would seem worthwhile to examine the situation if more heroic assumptions can be made about the knowledge of the utility function. The additional information which is assumed is that two commodities may be known to be 'weakly related', that is, that the derivative F_{ij} is either zero or of the second-order relative to other quantities.

In the expression $Q_i = (F_n F_{1i} - F_1 F_{ni})/F_n^2$, for example, if the ith commodity and the numeraire are weakly related in this sense, then the term $F_1 F_{ni}$ can be neglected relative to the term $F_n F_{1i}$, and the sign of Q_i is wholly determined by the sign of F_{1i}.

If the monopolized good and the numeraire are weakly related, then $Q_1 < 0$ and $Q_n > 0$. This is similar to the case I, in which the two goods were complements, leading to the same conclusions. There are now, however, four additional cases to add to (a), (b), (c), (d), for various combinations of weak relatedness with substitution and complementarity as between the ith commodity and the monopolized good and the numeraire. All the cases which can be given in terms of the three relationships (weakly related, complements, substitutes) are shown in Table 12.2. There are now three determinate cases, which can be summarized as follows.

Table 12.2   *Relationship between ith commodity, monopolized good and numeraire*

Relationship between monopolized good and numeraire	Relationship of ith good to:		Signs of Q_i Q_n θ			Price of ith good relative to marginal cost
	Monopolized good	Numeraire	Q_i	Q_n	θ	
Complements, or weak	Complements	Complements	?	+	−	?
	Substitutes	Substitutes	?	+	−	?
	Complements	Substitutes	+	+	−	?
	Substitutes	Complements	−	+	−	Higher
	Complements	Weak	+	+	−	?
	Substitutes	Weak	−	+	−	Higher
	Weak	Complements	−	+	−	Higher
	Weak	Substitutes	+	+	−	?
Substitutes	Any	Any	$\left.\begin{array}{c} + \\ - \\ ? \end{array}\right\}$?	?		?

If the monopolized good and the numeraire are either complements or only weakly related, then the second-best solution will certainly require the price of the ith good to be set above its marginal cost either if the good is a substitute for the monopolized good and either complementary or only weakly related to the numeraire, or if the good is weakly related to the monopolized good but complementary to the numeraire.

With any other combinations of relatedness among the goods, it cannot be determined, *a priori*, whether the second-best solution will require the price of any particular good to be above or below its marginal cost. In particular, if there is no complementarity between any pairs of goods, and the relationship between the monopolized commodity and the numeraire is not weak, then there are no determinate cases.

As a matter of interest it is possible to work out conditions that may be likely to bring about any particular result. For example, a possible case in which the price of a good might be set below its marginal cost would be that in which the monopolized good, the numeraire, and the other good were all substitutes, but the rate at which marginal utility diminished was small in the case of the monopolized good (so that Q_1, Q_n would both be positive, with Q_1 large compared with Q_n, giving a positive value for θ), and the relationship of the good under discussion was much stronger with the monopolized good than with the numeraire (so that Q_i might be negative). There can be few real cases, however, where such guesses about the magnitudes of the quantities involved could be made.

The problem of multiple-layer optima

In all the preceding analysis, the problems have been conceived in terms of a single-layer optimum. It has been assumed that the constraint which defined the Paretian optimum (the transformation function, for example) was a technically fixed datum, and was not, itself, the result of an optimization process at a lower level.

The characteristic of general economic systems is, however, that they usually involve several successive processes of optimization, of increasing generality. The transformation function, for example, may have been derived as the result of competitive firms maximizing their profits. Firms are assumed to have minimized their costs before proceeding to maximize their profits, and these costs are themselves derived from processes involving optimization by the owners of the various factors of production.

It is of the nature of the economic process, therefore, that optimization takes place at successive levels, and that the maximization of a welfare function subject to a transformation function is only the topmost of these. It is also of the nature of Paretian optima (due to the simple proportionality of the conditions) that the optimization at the different levels can be considered as independent problems.

In the case of a second-best solution, however, the neat proportionality of the Paretian conditions disappears: this immediately poses the question whether a second-best solution in the circumstances of a multiple-layer economic system will require a breaking of the Paretian conditions at lower levels of the system, as well as at the level at which the problem was initiated.

The present paper does not propose to examine the problem, for it is a subject that would seem to merit full-scale treatment of its own. There seems reason to suppose, however, that there may well be cases in which a breaking of the Paretian rules at lower levels of the process (moving off the transformation function, for example) may enable a higher level of welfare to be obtained than if the scope of policy is confined to one level only.

A two-dimensional geometric illustration that is suggestive, although not conclusive, is set out in Figure 12.1. *Ox, Oy* represent the quantities of two goods *x*, *y*. The line *AB* represents a transformation function (to be considered as a boundary condition) and *CD* a constraint condition. In the absence of the constraint *CD* the optimum position will be some point, such as *P*, lying on the transformation line at the point of its tangency with one of the contours of the welfare function.

If the constraint condition must be satisfied, only points along *CD* can be chosen, and the optimum point *P* is no longer attainable. A point on the transformation

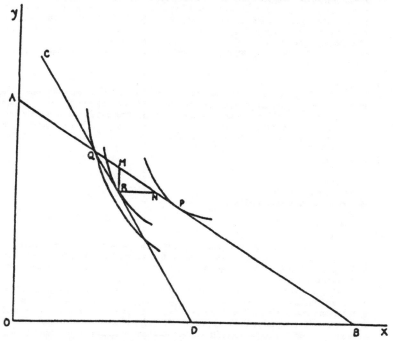

Figure 12.1   Determining the location of the second-best solution

line (Q) is still attainable. Will the second-best solution be at the point Q, or should the economy move off the transformation line? If the welfare contours and the constraint line are as shown in the diagram, then the second-best point will be at the point R, inside the transformation line.

It is obvious, of course, that the second best will never be at a point which is technically inefficient (has less of one commodity and no more of the other) relative to any attainable point. Although there are points (the segment MN) on the transformation line which are technically more efficient than R, these are not attainable. R is not technically inefficient relative to Q, even though R lies inside the transformation line.

If the line CD had a positive slope (as have the types of constraint which have been exemplified in the preceding analyses), the second best would always lie at its point of intersection with the transformation line, since all other points on CD would be technically inefficient relative to it.

Notes

1. Written with R.G. Lipsey and originally published in the *Review of Economic Studies*, 24 (1956), 11–32. At the suggestion of H.G. Johnson, then editor of the *Review*, independently written papers by the two authors, on the same topic but complementary in coverage, were combined into a single paper. The term 'second best' in this context was derived from Meade 1955b. In the original version, there was an algebraic error which affected two equations and a half page of text, but not the basic analysis, proof, or conclusions. A note was made of this when the paper was reprinted in Farrell, M.J. (ed.), *Readings in Welfare Economics*, London, Macmillan, 1973. Here the appropriate corrections have been made, affecting equations (32), (33) and some text.
2. Meade 1955b.
3. Viner 1950.
4. His neglect of the demand side allowed him to reach the erroneous conclusion that trade diversion necessarily led to a decrease in welfare. It is quite possible for an increase in welfare to follow from the formation of a customs union whose sole effect is to divert trade from lower- to higher-cost sources of supply. Furthermore this gain may be enjoyed by the country whose import trade is so diverted, by the customs union as an entity, and the world as a whole. See Lipsey 1957.
5. Meade 1955a.
6. Ozga 1955.
7. Little 1951.
8. Corlett and Hague 1953.
9. Meade 1955b, *Mathematica Appendix*.
10. Smithies 1936.
11. McKenzie 1951.
12. Little 1950.
13. If consumers have different utility functions then each consumer must receive from the government an amount equal to what he pays in taxes. However, if all consumers have identical homogeneous utility functions then all that is required is that all the tax revenue be returned to some consumer(s).
14. Obviously this is a problem in the theory of second best. The initial tariff on Y causes the consumption of Y to be too low relative to both X and Z. If the consumption of Y can be encouraged at the expense of X, welfare will be increased. However, if the consumption of Z is encouraged at the expense of X, welfare will be lowered. A tariff on X is likely to cause both sorts of consumption shift and the optimum X tariff will be one where, at the margin, the harmful effect of the shift from X to Z just balances the beneficial effect of the shift from X to Y.

[5]

Welfare Economics and the Theory of Second Best[*]

1. Introduction

The belief seems to be prevalent that the article by R. G. Lipsey and K. Lancaster, " The General Theory of Second Best " [6], has cast doubt upon the usefulness of the propositions of welfare economics in actual policy decisions. The main proposition of the theory of second best can be stated briefly. In the words of Lipsey and Lancaster:

> " The general theorem for the second best optimum states that if there is introduced into a general equilibrium system a constraint which prevents the attainment of one of the Paretian conditions, the other Paretian conditions, although still attainable, are, in general, no longer desirable. In other words, given that one of the Paretian optimum conditions cannot be fulfilled, then an optimum situation can be achieved only by departing from all the other Paretian conditions." [1]

Although Lipsey and Lancaster qualify their results by the inclusion of the term " in general " in the statement of their theorem, they give no hint as to when the Pareto conditions should or should not be satisfied. One of our purposes is to develop a method of analysis which will allow one to determine whether a specified violation of one or more Pareto conditions means that it is socially desirable that certain other of the Paretian conditions be violated.

2. The Lipsey-Lancaster Development

Suppose that there exists a real-valued differentiable function

(1.1) $$F(x_1, \ldots, x_n)$$

of n variables. F is to be maximized subject to the following constraint on the variables

(1.2) $$G(x_1, \ldots, x_n) = 0$$

where G is a real-valued and differentiable function. From this problem comes the familiar first-order conditions for a Pareto optimum.

(1.3) $$\frac{\partial F}{\partial x_i} - \lambda \frac{\partial G}{\partial x_i} = 0, \qquad i = 1, \ldots, n.$$

[*] This paper is a revision of Cowles Foundation Discussion Paper 146, July 1962, and it was presented at the December 1962 meeting of the Econometric Society. The research was jointly sponsored by the Cowles Commission for Research in Economics under Task NR—047—006 with the Office of Naval Research and by the Graduate School of Industrial Administration, Carnegie Institute of Technology. The authors are indebted to numerous persons for helpful comments and criticisms. Professor Francesco Forte, University of Torino, proposed this topic to us and gave assistance on various points. Professors T. C. Koopmans, Cowles Foundation, and Kelvin Lancaster, Johns Hopkins University, made numerous suggestions which resulted in alterations in the paper. Professors W. Brainard, E. Drandakis, and T. N. Srinivason of the Cowles Foundation made very helpful, constructive criticisms. Finally, the thoughtful comments of the referees provoked several improvements. Only the authors are responsible for errors.

[1] [6], p. 11.

1

2   REVIEW OF ECONOMIC STUDIES

By eliminating the Langrangean multiplier λ these conditions can be reduced to the following form:

(1.4)
$$\frac{\dfrac{\partial F}{\partial x_i}}{\dfrac{\partial F}{\partial x_n}} - \frac{\dfrac{\partial G}{\partial x_i}}{\dfrac{\partial G}{\partial x_n}} = 0, \qquad i = 1, \ldots, n-1.$$

These are the Pareto conditions as they are usually stated. Identifying (1.1) as a utility function and (1.2) as a transformation function, we have from (1.4) that the marginal rates of substitution in consumption must equal the marginal rates of substitution in production.

Lipsey and Lancaster construct a second best problem by introducing

(1.5)
$$\frac{\dfrac{\partial F}{\partial x_1}}{\dfrac{\partial F}{\partial x_n}} = k \frac{\dfrac{\partial G}{\partial x_1}}{\dfrac{\partial G}{\partial x_n}}, \qquad k \neq 1$$

as a constraint which represents a violation of a Pareto condition. The question is whether the introduction of (1.5) into the system causes an alteration in the form of the optimality conditions (1.3).[1] Suppose that both (1.1) and (1.2) are separable.[2] Now (1.1) is to be maximised subject to both (1.2) and (1.5). The conditions for a maximum are:

(1.6)
$$\frac{\partial F}{\partial x_i} - \lambda \frac{\partial G}{\partial x_i} - \mu \left[\frac{\dfrac{\partial F}{\partial x_n}\dfrac{\partial^2 F}{\partial x_1 \partial x_i} - \dfrac{\partial F}{\partial x_1}\dfrac{\partial^2 F}{\partial x_n \partial x_i}}{\left(\dfrac{\partial F}{\partial x_n}\right)^2} - k \frac{\dfrac{\partial G}{\partial x_n}\dfrac{\partial^2 G}{\partial x_1 \partial x_i} - \dfrac{\partial G}{\partial x_1}\dfrac{\partial^2 G}{\partial x_n \partial x_i}}{\left(\dfrac{\partial G}{\partial x_n}\right)^2} \right] = 0,$$

$i = 1, \ldots, n.$

This is expression (7.4) in the Lipsey-Lancaster proof of the general theorem of second best.[3] Note that, under the assumption of separability,

(1.7)
$$\frac{\partial^2 F}{\partial x_i \partial x_j} = \frac{\partial^2 G}{\partial x_i \partial x_j} = 0, \qquad i \neq j$$

so that we have immediately

(1.8)
$$\frac{\partial F}{\partial x_i} - \lambda \frac{\partial G}{\partial x_i} = 0, \qquad i = 2, \ldots, n-1.$$

Since the form of (1.8) is identical to that of (1.3), it appears that the Pareto conditions should be satisfied for the above commodities and that for a second best solution a violation is indicated only for the 1st and nth commodities, both of which appeared in the added constraint (1.5).[4]

Note that separability is a sufficient condition for the above results and even if the functions are non-separable the conclusion can remain unaltered by chance either if the

---

[1] M. McManus [8] has presented some criticisms of the use of (1.5) as an additional constraint. Lipsey and Lancaster [7] point out that this constraint need not reflect correctly the behavior of deviant units

[2] A function $f(x_1, \ldots, x_n)$ is separable if and only if $f(x_1, \ldots, x_n) = f_1(x_1) + f_2(x_2) + \ldots + f_n(x_n)$.

[3] [6], p. 26.

[4] Of course, it is true that the λ in (1.8) will not have the same value as the λ in (1.3), but this fact is of no consequence here since the optimality conditions refer only to the functional forms.

WELFARE ECONOMICS AND THE THEORY OF SECOND BEST   3

relevant cross-derivatives happen to be zero at the optimum or if they are non-zero but offsetting.[1] However, it should be emphasized that separability is not an unduly restrictive assumption. If there are no technological externalities in the system, there must be separability in terms of the decision units (consumers and producers) in the general equilibrium model. Since the model under consideration is defined in a manner which obscures this important fact, and since it is not constructed on the basis of the behavioral assumptions of participating units, we shall attempt to clarify the notion of second best on the basis of another general equilibrium model.

3. A Basic Model

The following definitions are used for the remainder of the paper:

u_i = the utility function of the ith individual. It is assumed that all u_i are concave.[2]

x_{ik} = the quantity of the kth good consumed by the ith individual.

$X_i = (x_{i1}, \ldots, x_{in})$, the " bundle " of goods consumed by the ith individual.

y_{rk} = the quantity of the kth good produced by the rth firm.

g_r = the transformation function which represents the technology of the rth firm by defining the outputs which can be produced with given inputs. It is assumed that all g_r are convex.

h_{rkj} = the quantity of the jth resource used by the rth firm in producing y_{rk} of the kth good.

H_j = the total available quantity of the jth resource.

Consider the following vector maximization problem:

$$(2.1) \quad \max \ [u_1(X_1), \ldots, u_m(X_m)]$$

subject to

(2)

$$(2.2) \quad \sum_{i=1}^{m} x_{ik} \leq \sum_{r=1}^{z} y_{rk}, \qquad\qquad k = 1, \ldots, n$$

$$(2.3) \quad g_r(y_{r1}, \ldots, y_{rn}, h_{r11}, \ldots, h_{rns}) \leq 0, \qquad r = 1, \ldots, z$$

$$(2.4) \quad \sum_{k=1}^{n} \sum_{r=1}^{z} h_{rkj} \leq H_j \qquad\qquad j = 1, \ldots, s$$

$$(2.5) \quad x_{ik}, y_{rk}, h_{rkj} \geq 0 \ \text{all} \ i, r, k, j.$$

This problem (2) is our basic model. In general, many solutions exist for problems of this type, but this point need not bother us here. Note that (2.1) is a vector composed of individual utility functions. Constraint (2.2) requires that the sum of the quantities of the kth good, ($k = 1, \ldots, n$), which are obtained by the m consumers, be less than or equal to the amount supplied by the z firms. Constraint (2.3) represents the given technologies. Note that by including only the firm's own inputs and outputs as arguments of g_r we rule out technological externalities. Constraint (2.4) states that the firms cannot use greater quantities of resources than are available in the society, and (2.5) states plausible non-negativity requirements.

---

[1] We are indebted to one of the referees for this point.

[2] A function $f(x)$ is convex if the domain of definition is convex, and if $(1 - \theta)f(x^*) + \theta f(x) \geq f((1 - \theta)x^* + \theta x)$ for $0 \leq \theta \leq 1$ and all x^* and x in the domain of definition of $f(x)$. Conversely, the function $f(x)$ is concave if $-f(x)$ is convex. We note that this assumption of concavity can be relaxed since convex indifference curves require only quasi-concave utility functions. See Arrow and Enthoven [1]. However, we prefer the stronger assumption in order to avoid the additional complications in the conditions for a maximum for the problem stated below in the paper.

Having presented the above model of an economic system, we note that if $X_1^*, \ldots, X_m^*$ is a solution to (2), then this implies that there do not exist feasible quantities $X_1', \ldots, X_m'$ such that $u_i(X_i') \geq u_i(X_i^*)$ for each i, $(i = 1, \ldots, m)$, with at least one $u_i(X_i') > u_i(X_i^*)$. Thus any solution to (2) satisfies the Pareto welfare criterion. No individual can be made better off without making some other individual worse off. This point makes clear the reason why the possible existence of many solutions to (2) is of no concern here. We are interested only in efficient solutions—i.e., Pareto optimal ones—and have no concern for problems of distribution.

For the purpose of deriving the general conditions for Pareto optimality, model (2) is not entirely satisfactory. It is necessary that we replace (2.1) by a scalar function. From the Kuhn-Tucker equivalence theorem [5] we know that any vector maximization problem can be represented by a problem which has as its criterion function a positively weighted sum of the vectors. Hence, it is legitimate to make our analysis under the presumption that

$$(3) \qquad max \sum_{i=1}^{m} \alpha_i u_i(X_i)$$

has been substituted for (2.1) in our basic model (2). Furthermore, Negishi [10] has pointed out that the weight α_i can be interpreted as the reciprocal of the ith consumer's marginal utility of income.

Granted the scalar criterion function (3), sufficient conditions for a solution to (2) are that there exist non-negative vectors $(\lambda_1, \ldots, \lambda_n)$, $(\mu_1, \ldots, \mu_z)$, and $(\rho_1, \ldots, \rho_s)$ which satisfy the conditions listed under (4) below.[1] Furthermore, the λ's will be identified with constraints (2.2), the μ's with (2.3) and the ρ's with (2.4). It is well-known that multipliers measure the " cost " of constraints and can be interpreted as prices.[2] While we do not explicitly discuss the dynamic adjustment of a market mechanism here, it is worth pointing out that the differential (or difference) equations of the gradient method for solving non-linear programming problems similar to the one under consideration here have often been taken as representing the functioning of a tâtonnement market.[3] Since we have no interest here in discussing paths to an equilibrium, we merely interpret the λ's and ρ's as prices of goods and resources respectively, and the μ's as the implicit costs of the technology constraints. In each instance we presume that equilibrium values of the multipliers (the λ's and ρ's) are generated by markets and are available to the participants.

Turning to the Pareto optimum conditions, we consider first those which refer to the theory of consumer demand.

$$(4.1) \qquad \alpha_i \frac{\partial u_i}{\partial x_{ik}} - \lambda_k \left\{ {\leq \atop =} \right\} 0 \text{ if } x_{ik} \left\{ {= \atop >} \right\} 0, \quad {k = 1, \ldots, n \atop i = 1, \ldots, m}$$

Condition (4.1) states that the ith individual's marginal utility of the kth good, weighed by α_i, must be less than or equal to the price λ_k if the good is *not* purchased and equal if it is acquired.

The Pareto requirements for goods are:

$$(4.2) \qquad \sum_{i=1}^{m} x_{ik} - \sum_{r=1}^{z} y_{rk} \left\{ {\leq \atop =} \right\} 0 \text{ if } \lambda_k \left\{ {= \atop >} \right\} 0, k = 1, \ldots, n.$$

This states that if the price λ_k is positive the quantity demanded must equal the quantity supplied.

[1] Kuhn and Tucker [5] derive these conditions.
[2] See Samuelson [11], p. 231, for a discussion of this interpretation of multipliers.
[3] See, e.g., Arrow and Hurwicz [2] and Uzawa [12] [13].

WELFARE ECONOMICS AND THE THEORY OF SECOND BEST 5

For the production sector the Pareto optimum conditions are:

(4.3)
$$\lambda_k - \mu_r \frac{\partial g_r}{\partial y_{rk}} \begin{Bmatrix} \leq \\ = \end{Bmatrix} 0 \text{ if } y_{rk} \begin{Bmatrix} = \\ > \end{Bmatrix} 0, \quad \begin{matrix} k = 1, \ldots, n \\ r = 1, \ldots, z \end{matrix}$$

(4.4)
$$-\mu_r \frac{\partial g_r}{\partial h_{rkj}} - \rho_j \begin{Bmatrix} \leq \\ = \end{Bmatrix} 0 \text{ if } h_{rkj} \begin{Bmatrix} = \\ > \end{Bmatrix} 0, \begin{matrix} j = 1, \ldots, s \\ k = 1, \ldots, n \\ r = 1, \ldots, z \end{matrix}$$

(4.5)
$$g_r(y_{r1}, \ldots, y_{rn}; h_{r11}, \ldots, h_{rns}) \begin{Bmatrix} \leq \\ = \end{Bmatrix} 0 \text{ if } \mu_r \begin{Bmatrix} = \\ > \end{Bmatrix} 0, r = 1, \ldots, z.$$

These conditions will be interpreted presently.

The final conditions are:

(4.6)
$$\sum_r \sum_k h_{rkj} - H_j \begin{Bmatrix} \leq \\ = \end{Bmatrix} 0 \text{ if } \rho_j \begin{Bmatrix} = \\ > \end{Bmatrix} 0, \quad j = 1, \ldots, s$$

which states that if the factor price ρ_j is to be positive all the available quantity H_j of the resource must be used.

We turn now to two related questions. First, in what sense is this model based upon behavioral assumptions? Consider the following utility maximization problem for the ith consumer, $(i = 1, \ldots, m)$:

(5.1) $max \; u_i(X_i)$

subject to

(5)

(5.2) $\sum\limits_{k=1}^{n} \lambda_k x_{ik} \leq M_i$

where M_i represents a given income and the λ_k are prices. Letting $\hat{a}_i$ represent the multiplier associated with (5.2) and defining $\alpha_i = 1/\hat{a}_i$, we note that the conditions for a maximum to (5) are given by (4.1).[1] Similarly, consider the rth firm's maximization problem, $(r = 1, \ldots, z)$:

(6.1) $max \sum\limits_{k=1}^{n} \lambda_k y_{rk} - \sum\limits_{k=1}^{n} \sum\limits_{j=1}^{s} \rho_j h_{rkj}$

(6) subject to

(6.2) $g_r(y_{r1}, \ldots, y_{rn}, h_{r11}, \ldots, h_{rns}) \leq 0$

(6.3) $y_{rk}, h_{rkj} \geq 0$ $\qquad \begin{matrix} k = 1, \ldots, n \\ j = 1, \ldots, s \end{matrix}$

where the λ_k and ρ_j represent the prices of goods and inputs respectively so that (6.1) represents profits and (6.2) is the previously defined technological constraint. Noting that μ_r is identically the multiplier associated with (6.2), we observe that the conditions for a maximum to (6) are given by (4.3), (4.4), and (4.5). It is apparent that model (2) is compatible with the behavioral assumptions of utility and profit maximization.

Second, we note that only variables directly under the consumer's or firm's control enter in (5) and (6). Thus technological externalities are not present in the system and it follows that model (2) is separable in terms of the decision units.

[1] Of course, we assume all $\hat{a}_i > 0$.

6   REVIEW OF ECONOMIC STUDIES

4. *Decision Rules, Pareto and Second Best Problems*

In order to distinguish between Pareto and second best problems, we now consider more carefully the relationship between behavioral assumptions and this model. Accordingly, let

$$(7.1) \qquad\qquad x_{ik} = B_{ik}(\lambda_k; \ldots), \qquad\qquad \begin{matrix} k = 1, \ldots, n \\ i = 1, \ldots, m \end{matrix}$$

$$(7.2) \qquad\qquad y_{rk} = D_{rk}(\lambda_k, \rho_1, \ldots, \rho_s; \ldots), \qquad\qquad \begin{matrix} k = 1, \ldots, n \\ r = 1, \ldots, z \end{matrix}$$

represent respectively the behavioral rules of the ith consumer and the rth producer in the choice of quantities of the kth good. The dots after the semicolons are intended to represent other variables, if any, which the decision-making units might consider in making their choices.

Suppose that there exists an omniscient, beneficent, and all-powerful dictator whose task is to specify to each and every decision maker the form of his decision rule (7.1) or (7.2). Suppose further that this dictator is interested in efficient solutions, the vector maximum of $[u_1(X_1), \ldots, u_m(X_m)]$. It is obvious that different choices of the functional forms of (7.1) and (7.2) can produce different results. Thus the problem is to choose those B_{ik}, D_{rk} for which the solution is at least as great a utility vector as for any other $\hat{B}_{ik}$, $\hat{D}_{rk}$ which could be chosen. We present a heuristic method for determining the desired functional forms.

First, we assert that under Pareto type considerations the best that the dictator can do is to specify to the ith consumer ($i = 1, \ldots, m$) and the rth firm ($r = 1, \ldots, z$) that (5) and (6) respectively are to be solved and the implicit form of the decision rules for the selection of quantities are the respective conditions for a maximum of these problems. In order to justify this assertion we note again that the conditions for a maximum of (5) and (6) are conditions (4.1) and (4.3), (4.4) and (4.5) respectively. As these decision rules (in their implicit forms) can be viewed as being derived from (2), there is no issue of their being satisfied at a solution to (2). Since we assume that all λ_k and ρ_j are equilibrium prices, (4.2) and (4.6) are satisfied. It follows that there is an exact correspondence between the solution values of this set of problems (5 and 6) and the solution values of (2). Furthermore, if any other behavioral (decision) rules are indicated, then these must become additional constraints to (2) in order to insure that equilibrium (solution) values can satisfy these alternative decision rules. Since additional constraints cannot increase the value of a functional, no behavioral rules can be better in the Pareto sense than the ones specified above.[1] Hence, we assert that the conditions for a maximum can be given a normative, behavioral interpretation.

Definition: A Pareto optimum problem is one in which, given the market clearing conditions and the technology of the economy, all normative behavioral rules can be determined so that the solutions of the system achieve a vector maximum of $[u_1(X_1), \ldots, u_m(X_m)]$.

Definition: A second best optimum problem is one in which, given the market clearing conditions and the technology of the economy, at least one of the behavioral rules is non-trivially specified, cannot be changed, and neither can the behavior of the deviant(s) be altered by any policy, and the remainder of the normative behavioral rules are to be chosen so as to achieve a vector maximum of $[u_1(X_1), \ldots, u_m(X_m)]$.

---

[1] Of course, the same values of the α_i have to be specified in each instance. As was noted earlier, the α_i are interpreted as the reciprocals of the marginal utilities of income, so that we must presume that some omniscient observer arranges the appropriate lump-sum transfers to maintain the equality of the α_i for any two sets of decision rules.

WELFARE ECONOMICS AND THE THEORY OF SECOND BEST 7

Note that this latter definition, at least as it is stated here, leads to a general class of problems since (i) at least one decision rule is specified in a non-trivial manner—i.e., as different from that which would be chosen in a Pareto problem—and (ii) all alternative policies aimed at achieving a Pareto optimal solution—e.g. taxes and subsidies—are ruled out.[1] Thus the second best problem is to determine a new set of decision rules, given the behavioral rules of one or more deviants, which will best compensate for the effect of the deviant(s) upon welfare.

Before developing two examples of second best problems, it is appropriate to indicate our method of analysis so that the points at issue can be clearly determined. Accordingly, suppose that the decision rules

$$(8) \qquad x_{\tau k} = B_{\tau k}[\lambda_k; \ldots] \qquad\qquad k = 1, \ldots, n$$

are specified. Then the problem is to find those behavioral rules for all other choices which, given (8), will result in a maximum of the vector $[u_1(X_1), \ldots, u_m(X_m)]$.

Let (8) be considered as additional constraints for (2) along with the requirements that the multipliers appearing in (8) are the same as the respective multipliers of the second best problem.[2] Then the implicit forms of the desired behavioral rules (conditions for a maximum of the second best problem) for consumers are:

$$(9.1) \qquad \alpha_i \frac{\partial u_i}{\partial x_{ik}} - \lambda_k - \sum_{q=1}^{n} \gamma_q \frac{\partial B_{\tau q}}{\partial x_{ik}} \begin{Bmatrix} \leq \\ = \end{Bmatrix} 0 \text{ if } x_{ik} \begin{Bmatrix} = \\ > \end{Bmatrix} 0,$$

$$k = 1, \ldots, n$$
$$i = 1, \ldots, \tau - 1, \tau + 1, \ldots, m$$

where the γ_q represent the multipliers associated with (8). Note that if $\partial B_{\tau q}/\partial x_{ik} = 0$ for all q and k—as is the case, for example, when x_{ik} does not appear to the right of the semi-colon in (8)—then (9.1) is of the same form as (4.1) so that the Pareto and second best conditions and behavioral rules are the same. In this instance, the consumer's maximization problem is again given by (5). Only if $\partial B_{\tau q}/\partial x_{ik} \neq 0$ for some q and k—i.e., only if the ith consumer's choice of x_{ik} has some effect upon the behavior of individual τ—will the second best and Pareto decision rules differ in form. If such is the case, then the consumer's maximization problem must be altered by attaching (8) as constraints to (5) along with the requirements that the multipliers associated with (8) be equal to the γ_q obtained in the second best problem formed above. Only if this is done will the conditions for a maximum to the consumer's problem (the actual behavioral rules) be the same as the normative decision rules (9.1) for second best behavior.

Similarly, the implicit forms of the desired behavioral rules for producers are:

$$(9.2) \qquad \lambda_k - \mu_r \frac{\partial g_r}{\partial y_{rk}} - \sum_{q=1}^{n} \gamma_q \frac{\partial B_{\tau q}}{\partial y_{rk}} \begin{Bmatrix} \leq \\ = \end{Bmatrix} 0 \text{ if } y_{rk} \begin{Bmatrix} = \\ > \end{Bmatrix} 0, \qquad \begin{matrix} k=1, \ldots, n \\ r=1, \ldots, z \end{matrix}$$

$$(9.3) \qquad -\mu_r \frac{\partial g_r}{\partial h_{rkj}} - p_j - \sum_{q=1}^{n} \gamma_q \frac{\partial B_{\tau q}}{\partial h_{rkj}} \begin{Bmatrix} \leq \\ = \end{Bmatrix} 0 \text{ if } h_{rkj} \begin{Bmatrix} = \\ > \end{Bmatrix} 0, \qquad \begin{matrix} j=1, \ldots, s \\ k=1, \ldots, n \\ r=1, \ldots, z \end{matrix}$$

along with conditions (4.5). Again, if for all q, k, and j $\partial B_{\tau q}/\partial y_{rk} = 0$ and $\partial B_{\tau q}/\partial h_{rkj} = 0$, then (9.2) and (9.3) are of the same form as (4.3) and (4.4) respectively so that the Pareto

---

[1] McManus [8] objects to this specification of a second best problem since, at least in a great number of cases, alternative policies can achieve a Pareto optimum. See, however, Davis and Whinston [3] for illustrations of situations where the tax-subsidy policy cannot be expected to work. In addition there may be many reasons for not seeking a Pareto optimal solution in some specific situation.

[2] See the appendix for a discussion of a mathematical problem which has multipliers included in the constraints.

8   REVIEW OF ECONOMIC STUDIES

and second best behavioral rules and conditions are the same and the firm's maximization problem is given by (6). Only if for some q, k, and j $\partial B_{\tau q}/\partial y_{rk} \neq 0$ or $\partial B_{\tau q}/\partial h_{rkj} \neq 0$ will the corresponding second best and Pareto decision rules differ in form, and the producer's maximization problem must be altered by attaching (8) as constraints to (6) along with the requirements that the multipliers associated with (8) be equal to the γ_q obtained in the second best problem formed above.

In order to justify the asserted optimality of the above behavioral rules we observe that these rules are conditions for a maximum of the second best problem. Hence, provided that the appropriate consumer and producer maximization problems are specified as was indicated above, there is no issue of these decision rules being satisfied at a solution. However, decision rules chosen in some other manner require that additional constraints be added to (2) in order to insure that equilibrium values can satisfy these alternative rules and, for the same values of the α_i, a problem formed in such a fashion would have an optimal solution which cannot be higher and will generally be lower than the optimal solution to the above problem. Finally, observe also that for the same α_i the value of the equilibrium solution to the second best allocation problem cannot be greater and will generally be less than the solution value of the Pareto problem.

5. Two Examples of Pareto and Second Best Problems

Having defined both Pareto and second best problems and having outlined our approach, it is appropriate to consider two examples which are designed to demonstrate our method of determining whether second best conditions and normative behavioral rules differ from Pareto ones. Before proceeding, however, it should be noted that an alteration in the structure of basic model (2) can result in a change in the form of some of the optimality conditions (4) and, by implication, the normative Pareto behavioral rules for consumers and producers. Indeed, this is the case in our second example when externalities are introduced. However, we shall utilize basic model (2) in the interest of brevity and simply indicate the change in structure, the Pareto conditions, and the corresponding behavioral rules where this is required in the second example. Furthermore, the second example is designed to illustrate an instance in which, except for the deviant, Pareto and second best conditions and behavioral rules are of the same form. The first example illustrates a case in which, aside from the deviant, one second best condition (decision rule) differs in form from the corresponding Pareto condition (decision rule).

Example I: Monopoly with Interdependent Demand

Granted the well-known difficulties of characterizing a monopoly in a general equilibrium system (especially when the purpose of the problem is to find normative behavioral rules), our approach is to designate the 1st firm as the sole producer of the 1st good and assume that the 2nd good, which is produced only by the governmentally owned or controlled 2nd firm, is so " closely related " to the 1st good that output of the second good directly affects the demand curve of the 1st good.[1] Thus we presume that the monopolist perceives a demand curve of the form.

$$(10) \qquad\qquad \lambda_1 = f(y_{11}, y_{22}).$$

Both the 1st and 2nd firm are assumed to produce only one good each. Note first that (10) represents a " perceived " demand curve which is presumed to be equivalent to the actual demand curve at an equilibrium.[2] Second, observe that model (2) is appropriate as

---

[1] Presumably, this implies certain restrictions on utility functions concerning substitutes and complements. In addition, we avoid other side issues by assuming that it is technologically impossible for other firms to produce the 1st good for any relevant range of prices, and that it is possible for the 1st firm to produce that good even if prices are set at competitive levels. Similar assumptions are made in regard to the 2nd firm.

[2] See Negishi [9] for a general equilibrium analysis which uses the notion of a perceived demand curve.

WELFARE ECONOMICS AND THE THEORY OF SECOND BEST   9

it stands (with proper modifications to permit the 1st and 2nd firms to produce only the 1st and 2nd goods respectively—see (11.2) and (14.2) below) for the Pareto problem so that the optimality conditions and the implicit forms of the Pareto behavioral rules are given by (4).

In order to formulate a second best problem we presume that the monopolist desires to take advantage of the perceived demand curve. Thus the monopolist's profit maximization problem is:

$$\text{(11.1)} \quad max\, f(y_{11},\, y_{22})y_{11} - \sum_{j=1}^{s} p_j h_{11j}$$

subject to

(11)   (11.2) $g_1(y_{11},\, h_{111},\, \ldots,\, h_{11s}) \leq 0$

(11.3) $y_{11},\, h_{11j} \geq 0,\, j = 1,\, \ldots,\, s.$

The conditions for a maximum to (11) are:

$$\text{(12.1)} \quad \frac{\partial f}{\partial y_{11}} y_{11} + f(y_{11},\, y_{22}) - \mu_1 \frac{\partial g_1}{\partial y_{11}} \begin{Bmatrix} \leq \\ = \end{Bmatrix} 0 \text{ if } y_{11} \begin{Bmatrix} = \\ > \end{Bmatrix} 0$$

(12) $$\text{(12.2)} \quad -p_j - \mu_1 \frac{\partial g_1}{\partial h_{11j}} \begin{Bmatrix} \leq \\ = \end{Bmatrix} 0 \text{ if } h_{11j} \begin{Bmatrix} = \\ > \end{Bmatrix} 0, \qquad j=1,\, \ldots,\, s$$

$$\text{(12.3)} \quad g_1(y_{11},\, h_{111},\, \ldots,\, h_{11s}) \begin{Bmatrix} \leq \\ = \end{Bmatrix} 0 \text{ if } \mu_1 \begin{Bmatrix} = \\ > \end{Bmatrix} 0.$$

These conditions (12) are the implicit forms of the given behavioral rules of the monopolist.[1] By the definition of a second best problem these decision rules are taken as given, no policies can be undertaken to alter the monopolist's behavior, and our task is to determine the second best conditions and behavioral rules for the remainder of the decision units in the system.

Accordingly, let (12) be considered additional constraints for (2) along with the requirements that the multipliers in (12) are to be the same as the multipliers associated with the respective constraints in (2). Then, noting that only the variables y_{11}, y_{22}, and h_{11j}, $(j = 1,\, \ldots,\, s)$, appear in (12), we have immediately that the second best conditions for consumers are given by (4.1); those for all firms except the 1st and 2nd $(r = 3,\, \ldots,\, z)$ by (4.3), (4.4), and (4.5); and conditions (4.2) and (4.6) also obtain. Thus for all decision units except the 1st and 2nd firms, the second best and Pareto conditions and behavioral rules are of the same form. All consumers are to solve problems (5) and the rth firm $(r = 3,\, \ldots,\, z)$ is to solve (6).

For the governmentally owned or controlled 2nd firm the second best behavioral rules (conditions) are

$$\text{(13.1)} \quad \lambda_2 - \mu_2 \frac{\partial g_2}{\partial y_{22}} - \gamma \left[\frac{\partial^2 f}{\partial y_{11} \partial y_{22}} y_{11} + \frac{\partial f}{\partial y_{22}} \right] \begin{Bmatrix} \leq \\ = \end{Bmatrix} 0 \text{ if } y_{22} \begin{Bmatrix} = \\ > \end{Bmatrix} 0$$

(13) $$\text{(13.2)} \quad -\mu_2 \frac{\partial g_2}{\partial h_{22j}} - p_j \begin{Bmatrix} \leq \\ = \end{Bmatrix} 0 \text{ if } h_{22j} \begin{Bmatrix} = \\ > \end{Bmatrix} 0, \qquad j=1,\, \ldots,\, s$$

$$\text{(13.3)} \quad g_2(y_{22},\, h_{221},\, \ldots,\, h_{22s}) \begin{Bmatrix} \leq \\ = \end{Bmatrix} 0 \text{ if } \mu_2 \begin{Bmatrix} = \\ > \end{Bmatrix} 0$$

[1] For the sake of convenience, we deal only with implicit forms in this example.

10   REVIEW OF ECONOMIC STUDIES

where the γ in (13.1) is the multiplier associated with constraint (12.1) in the second best problem. Note, first, that (13.1) differs from condition (4.3) of the Pareto problem. Second, observe that these conditions (13) mean that the governmentally owned 2nd firm cannot be given prices λ_2, p_j and told to maximize profits if the second best solution is to be achieved. Instead, the 2nd firm must exert its influence upon the 1st firm via the interdependence introduced into the demand curve (10). This is easily seen from the entries inside the brackets in (13.1). Thus the 2nd firm must be instructed to solve a problem (14) which, in addition to the usual technological constraint (14.2), has the decision rules of the 1st firm (12) as additional constraints along with the requirements that the multipliers associated with (12) be equal to the corresponding multipliers of the second best problem.

Suppose that the governmental authority mistakenly instructed the 2nd firm to act as follows:

(14.1) $max \ \lambda_2 y_{22} - \sum\limits_{j=1}^{s} p_j h_{22j}$

(14)   subject to

(14.2) $g_2(y_{22}, h_{221}, \ldots, h_{22s}) \leq 0$

(14.3) $y_{22}, h_{22j} \geq 0,$ $j = 1, \ldots, s$

and omitted the additional constraints (12) and the requirements on the multipliers, both of which are necessary if the above second best solution is to be achieved. Then it is clear that a new second best problem can be formulated by attaching, in addition to the decision rules (13) for the monopolist, the conditions for a maximum of (14) as constraints for (2). Furthermore, since it is clear that only variables y_{11}, y_{22}, h_{11j} and h_{22j}, $(j = 1, \ldots, s)$, enter this new set of constraints, the second best conditions and behavioral rules for all decision making units except for the 1st and 2nd firms are given by (4). Also, since additional constraints cannot increase the value of a functional, this second best problem would have a value which could not exceed, and would generally be less than, the value of the above second best problem.

Example II: An Interdependent Utility Function

Suppose that the utility of the 2nd consumer depends not only upon his own consumption but also upon the 1st individual's consumption x_{11} of the 1st good. In other words, we have $u_2(X_2, x_{11})$ instead of $u_2(X_2)$, and the utility functions of all other individuals and all other assumptions are as in model (2) so that we have here one external effect in consumption. Therefore, in formulating a general equilibrium model which incorporates this new feature we have as a criterion function

(15) $max \ \alpha_1 u_1(X_1) + \alpha_2 u_2(X_2, x_{11}) + \sum\limits_{i=3}^{m} \alpha_i u_i(X_i)$

which can be substituted for (2.1) of model (2) since all other assumptions and constraints remain unchanged.

Turning our attention to the derivation of the Pareto optimum conditions for this model, we obviously find that the requirements for the two markets are given by (4.2) and (4.6), and those for the production sector are stated by (4.3), (4.4) and (4.5). For the consumption sector (4.1) gives these conditions except that the 1st consumer's choice x_{11} of the 1st good must be omitted. For that particular choice the Pareto optimum conditions are:

(16) $\alpha_1 \dfrac{\partial u_1}{\partial x_{11}} + \alpha_2 \dfrac{\partial u_2}{\partial x_{11}} - \lambda_1 \begin{Bmatrix} \leq \\ = \end{Bmatrix} 0 \ \text{if} \ x_{11} \begin{Bmatrix} = \\ > \end{Bmatrix} 0$

so that optimality requires that the 1st consumer take into account the effect of his choice x_{11} of the 1st good on the well-being of the 2nd individual if that good is purchased.

WELFARE ECONOMICS AND THE THEORY OF SECOND BEST   11

While it is obvious that the usual problems—(5) and (6)—are appropriate for all decision making units except the 1st consumer, (16) clearly indicates that, in the absence of bargaining between the 1st and 2nd individuals or other corrective policy measures, the 1st consumer cannot maximize his individual utility if a Pareto optimum is to be attained. Presuming that the 1st consumer insists upon maximizing his individual utility without regard for the 2nd individual, we use the conditions for a maximum to (5) when $i = 1$ in order to express the 1st consumer's behavioral rules in the explicit form

(17) $$x_{1k} = B_{1k}(\lambda_k), \qquad\qquad k = 1, \ldots, n$$

The second best problem is formulated by again substituting (15) for (2.1) and attaching (17) as additional constraints to (2) along with the requirements that the λ_k in (17) be set equal to the respective multipliers associated with (2.2).

Derivation of the second best conditions reveals that (4.3), (4.4), and (4.5) hold for the production sector, (4.2) and (4.6) are the conditions for the goods and factor markets respectively, and with the exception of the 1st consumer (4.1) expresses the conditions for the consumption sector. Hence, except for the given violation expressed by (17), the second best and Pareto conditions and behavioral rules have the same form.

In order to make the nature of a second best problem completely clear we present here an overly simplified numerical example of an economy involving two consumers (1 and 2), two units of one divisible good, and no production. Furthermore, we assume $\alpha_1 = \alpha_2 = 1$ always and ignore problems associated with given incomes. Then letting

$$u_1(x_1, x_2) = 6x_1 - 2x_1^2 + 2x_1x_2$$
$$u_2(x_2) = -2x_2^2 + 10$$

be the utility functions of the 1st and 2nd individuals as indicated by the relevant subscripts where x_1 represents the consumption of the good by the 1st person and x_2 the consumption by the 2nd person, we note that we have one externality in consumption. Under these assumptions the Pareto problem is

(18.1)   *max* $6x_1 - 2x_1^2 + 2x_1x_2 - 2x_2^2 + 10$

        subject to

(18)   (18.2) $x_1 + x_2 \leq 2$

        (18.3) $x_1, x_2 \geq 0$

and the solution is $x_1 = \frac{2}{3}$, $x_2 = \frac{1}{3}$, and $\lambda = 1$. The number λ can be interpreted as the implicit price of the good. Note that, at a Pareto optimum, the 2nd individual is required to purchase some of the good even though it decreases his utility level.

In order to formulate a second best problem we presume that the 2nd individual acts in an individualistically rational manner and ignores the fact that purchases of the good benefit the 1st consumer. (No bargaining or other policies to attain the Pareto optimum are allowed.) Presuming that money is no problem, the 2nd individual solves, for a given λ,

(19)   *max* $-2x_2^2 + 10 - \lambda x_2$
            $x_2 \geq 0$

which has for behavioral rules (conditions)

(20.1) $-4x_2 \leq \lambda$

(20.2) $-4x_2^2 = \lambda x_2.$

Thus the second best problem is

(21.1) $max\ 6x_1 - 2x_1^2 + 2x_1x_2 - 2x_2^2 + 10$

subject to

(21.2) $x_1 + x_2 \leq 2$

(21.3) $-4x_2 \leq \lambda$

(21.4) $-4x_2^2 = \lambda x_2$

(21.5) $x_1, x_2 \geq 0.$

It is easily seen that the solution to this problem is $x_1 = \frac{3}{2}$, $x_2 = 0$, $\lambda = 0$.

6. *Concluding Comments*

The fundamental proposition of modern welfare economics is that given independent preference orderings for consumers, independent technologies for producers, and certain conditions on the shapes of these functions, then, if consumers maximize utility subject to given income and price parameters, and if producers maximize profits subject to these price parameters, there is a set of prices such that a social maximum is achieved where no individual can be made better off without making some other individual worse off.[1] Furthermore, granted certain assumptions, this Pareto welfare maximum can be achieved via a pricing mechanism and decentralized decisions.

In this paper we have been primarily concerned with situations where at least one individual actor has a preference ordering, a criterion function, or a technology other than the one specified for the above theorem. Then, granted the behavior of the deviant, we have attempted to determine the behavioral rules for the other actors which would best compensate for the deviant's behavior. Of special interest was whether the optimal behavioral rules for a Pareto problem differed in form from those of a second best problem.

We have analyzed second best problems by attaching as constraint(s) the given explicit or implicit form of the behavorial rule(s) of the deviant to a model from which the Pareto conditions were derived. When the additional constraint(s) contained only variables subject to the choice of the deviant, then, except for the deviant, all Pareto conditions and behavorial rules were of the same form as those for the second best problem. When the additional constraint(s) contained variables whose values depended upon the choices of other units, then only for the deviant and those units whose variables entered into the additional constraint(s) did the Pareto conditions and behavioral rules differ from those of the second best problem.

The results of this analysis have certain implications for economic policy. The classical maxim that " everything depends upon everything else " is well known. However, the pricing mechanism takes into account that interconnectedness caused by scarcity; and whenever there is deviant (non-Pareto) behavior in a situation where only prices and the variables under the deviant's control enter into his decision rule, then the market takes that behavior into account. In such situations " piecemeal policy " is all that is required. However, whenever subsets of economic units are functionally interconnected, either by externalities or by other means which cause non-price variables not directly under the individual unit's control to be in his behavioral rule, the policy maker must consider the entire functionally interconnected subset of units in order to avoid undesirable consequences.

[1] See, e.g., the first essay in [4].

WELFARE ECONOMICS AND THE THEORY OF SECOND BEST   13

Finally, it is appropriate to stress the limitations of the above analysis in the concluding paragraph. We have not considered questions concerning the existence of second best solutions, whether a market mechanism can achieve such solutions, or whether solutions via markets are stable.[1] These topics are themselves large enough to be subjects of papers.

APPENDIX

In the discussion of this paper the following type of maximization problem was encountered.

$$max\ F(x)$$

$$s.\ t.\ G_j(x, \hat{\lambda}) \leq 0, \qquad\qquad j = 1, \ldots, m$$

$$x' \geq 0$$

$$x = (x_1, \ldots, x_n) \qquad\qquad \hat{\lambda} = (\hat{\lambda}_1, \ldots, \hat{\lambda}_k).$$

Here, x represents a vector of variables which are restricted to be non-negative and λ is a vector of parameters. Let x^* be a solution to the maximization problem for given values of the parameters $\hat{\lambda}^*$. Also associated with x^* is a vector of multipliers $\lambda^* = (\lambda_1^*, \ldots, \lambda_m^*)$. If a maximizing solution exists for a specified value of $\hat{\lambda}$, then we obtain a vector of values (x^*, λ^*). Thus the maximization problem determines a mapping from a subset of E^k to a subset of $E^n \times E^m$. We are interested in solutions which have the property that $\hat{\lambda}_i^* = \lambda_i^*$ where $i \in I$, and I is an index set.

In order to clarify the above discussion we present the following example:

minimize $x^2 + y^2 + z^2$

subject to: (1) $x + y + z = 1$

(2) $3x + 3y - \lambda = 0.$

Letting λ be the Langrangean multiplier for (1) and μ for (2), we obtain:

$$2x - \lambda - 3\mu = 0$$

$$2y - \lambda - 3\mu = 0$$

$$2z - \lambda = 0$$

$$x + y + z = 1$$

$$3x + 3y - \hat{\lambda} = 0.$$

Adding the constraint $\hat{\lambda} = \lambda$ and solving the entire system we obtain:

$$(x^*, y^*, z^*, \mu^*, \lambda^*, \lambda^*) = (\tfrac{1}{3}, \tfrac{1}{3}, \tfrac{1}{3}, -\tfrac{4}{15}, \tfrac{2}{3}, \tfrac{2}{3})$$

and a minimum of $\frac{11}{24}$. This may be contrasted with a solution to the same example excluding constraint (2) of $(x^*, y^*, z^*, \lambda^*) = (\tfrac{1}{3}, \tfrac{1}{3}, \tfrac{1}{3}, \tfrac{2}{3})$ and a minimum of $\frac{1}{3}$ which is less than $\frac{11}{24}$.

Carnegie Institute of Technology.   OTTO A. DAVIS.

University of Virginia.   ANDREW B. WHINSTON.

[1] Note, for example, that the possibility of non-convexity of the specified behavioral rules in second best problems can cause difficulties which can be accommodated, to an extent, by the results of K. J. Arrow and L. Hurwicz [2].

14   REVIEW OF ECONOMIC STUDIES

REFERENCES

[1] K. J. Arrow and A. C. Enthoven. " Quasi-Concave Programming ", *Econometrica*,
     Vol. 29 (1961), pp. 779-800.

[2] K. J. Arrow and L. Hurwicz. " Decentralization and Computation in Resource
     Allocation ", in R. W. Pfouts, ed., *Essays in Economics and Econometrics*, Chapel
     Hill: University of North Carolina Press, 1960, pp. 34-104.

[3] O. A. Davis and A. Whinston. " Externalities, Welfare and the Theory of Games ",
     Journal of Political Economy, Vol. 70 (1962), pp. 241-262.

[4] T. C. Koopmans. *Three Essays on the State of Economic Science*, New York:
     McGraw-Hill, 1960.

[5] H. Kuhn and A. Tucker. " Nonlinear Programming ", in J. Neymon, ed., *Pro-
     ceedings of the Second Berkeley Symposium on Mathematical Statistics and Probability*,
     Berkeley: University of California Press, 1951, pp. 481-492.

[6] R. G. Lipsey and K. Lancaster. " The General Theory of Second Best ", *Review
     of Economic Studies*, Vol. 24 (1956-57), pp. 11-32.

[7] R. G. Lipsey and K. Lancaster. " McManus on Second Best ", *Review of Economic
     Studies*, Vol. 26 (1958-59), pp. 225-226.

[8] M. McManus. " Comments on the General Theory of Second Best ", *Review of
     Economic Studies*, Vol. 26 (1958-59), pp. 209-224.

[9] T. Negishi. " Monopolistic Competition and General Equilibrium ", *Review of
     Economic Studies*, Vol. 28 (1960-61), pp. 196-201.

[10] T. Negishi. " Welfare Economics and Existence of an Equilibrium for a Com-
     petitive Economy ", *Metroeconomica*, Vol. 11 (1960), pp. 92-97.

[11] P. A. Samuelson. *Foundations of Economic Analysis*, Cambridge: Harvard University
     Press, 1947.

[12] H. Uzawa. " Market Mechanisms and Mathematical Programming ", *Econometrica*,
     Vol. 28 (1960), pp. 872-881.

[13] H. Uzawa. " Walras' Tatonnement in the Theory of Exchange ", *Review of Economic
     Studies*, Vol. 27 (1959-60), pp. 182-194.

Part II
Theoretical Foundations
of Welfare Measurement

A
Economic Surplus

[6]

The Four Consumer's Surpluses.

1. In present circumstances the problems of pure theory can only, at the best, receive very intermittent attention ; I must, therefore, beg pardon of my readers if my studies in Consumers' Surplus[1] are becoming something of a serial. In my last article[2] I reached some very simple and pleasing conclusions about the relations between the corrected measures of Consumer's Surplus and the Marshallian measure, in cases where income effects cannot be neglected ; but the proof which was given, though very general, was nasty, complicated and algebraic. Now simple conclusions can nearly always be established in a simple way, though the simple way may take some discovering ; I have since been looking for some more simple way of proving my propositions. I think I have found it, at least so far as the ordinary case of a change in the price of a single commodity is concerned ; I propose to set it out in this paper. As usually happens, when one discovers a simpler method of proof, the whole argument can be better understood and appreciated in the new way ; and things which were not clear to me before have in the process been considerably clarified.

2. I need as background a device which has a certain intrinsic interest of its own— a somewhat simplified way of presenting the now familiar analysis of consumers' demand. This presentation is inferior to the indifference curve presentation, for purpose of general (equilibrium or optimum) theory ; but for purposes of partial analysis it is considerably more convenient. From the pedagogic point of view, it has the decided advantage that it reduces the purely geometrical difficulties to a minimum. The student's interest is, therefore, concentrated on the economic problems, not on the geometrical properties which sometimes provide a rather competing interest.

The first step in the analysis is the redefinition of Marshall's " marginal utility curve " in such a way as to allow for income effects and to eliminate any reference to " measurable " utility. Let us suppose that we are considering a consumer with a given money income, who is confronted by given market prices of $n - 1$ commodities. If he had to confine his purchases to these $n - 1$ commodities, he would lay out his expenditure in such and such a way. Now suppose that another commodity is made available ; suppose that in the first place one unit only of this nth commodity is offered. Will he be willing to purchase this one unit ? Clearly it will depend upon the price. If the price is too high he will not purchase ; if it is very low he will purchase with alacrity. There will be some price which will separate the high prices, at which he will not purchase, from the low prices at which he will purchase—the price at which he is just *on the edge* of purchasing. I shall call this price his *marginal valuation* of the unit. (Evidently it is the same thing as Marshall's " marginal utility in terms of money ".)

With given wants, given income, and given prices of the other goods, the marginal valuation of the first unit is a perfectly determinate magnitude. If the actual price is less than the marginal valuation, the unit will be purchased ; if it is greater, the unit will not be purchased. But (and this is what the traditional presentation does not bring out so clearly) the marginal valuation of a second unit is not necessarily determinate in the same way. The marginal valuation of the second unit depends upon the price which has been paid for the first. If the first unit has been acquired very cheaply, the consumer will be better off (he will have more to spend) than he would have been if he had been made to pay through the nose for the first unit.

[1] *Value and Capital*, pp. 38–41 ; the Rehabilitation of Consumers' Surplus (R.E.S., February, 1941) ; Consumers' Surplus and Index Numbers (R.E.S., Summer, 1942). I shall refer to these latter articles as " Rehabilitation " and " Index-Numbers " respectively.

[2] " Index-Numbers," p. 134.

On the other hand, once the price which has to be paid for the first unit is given, the marginal valuation of the second is determined. Once the actual price of the second is given, the marginal valuation of the third is determined ; and so on. Thus, if we suppose that the commodity has a given market price, the marginal valuations of all units are determined. But the marginal valuations depend upon the given market price.

We can now draw out the situation on a diagram of the familiar type (Fig. 1) with quantities on the horizontal axis, prices on the vertical. If OH is the given market price, valid for any number of units, AV will be the determinate marginal valuation curve. As long as the marginal valuation of any unit is greater than the price OH, that unit will be purchased. The amount purchased will, therefore, equal HP, where P is the intersection of AV with the horizontal line through H.

The downward slope of the marginal valuation curve at the point P is a necessary condition of stability. We may retain the convention of drawing it falling throughout, though there is, in fact, nothing to exclude the possibility that it might rise a little before it starts to fall.

Now what happens if there is a change in price ? Suppose that the market price (still valid for any number of units) falls from OH to Oh. This will make no difference to the marginal valuation of the first unit, but it may make a difference to the marginal valuation of the subsequent units, since the consumer now has a little more to spend when he comes to buy those units. This is an *income effect* ; an increase in spending power (other things being equal) usually makes the consumer more willing to purchase a particular unit—thus it raises the marginal valuation. But occasionally it may make him less willing (the case of an *inferior* good).

Excepting in the case of an *inferior* good, a fall in price will thus tend to move the marginal valuation curve slightly *upwards* ; it will pivot upon its left flank, since the marginal valuation of the first unit cannot be affected. I have drawn the new position as Av (Fig. 1), greatly exaggerating the probable amount of the shift, for convenience in drawing. The point of equilibrium at the price Oh is therfore at p, where Av intersects the horizontal line through h. Thus the fall in price moves the point of equilibrium from P to p ; there is a movement along the curve AV (or Av) and also a shift from one curve to the other.

Since movement along a marginal valuation curve is not the same thing as movement along an indifference curve (the consumer gets better off as he moves down the marginal valuation curve), this distinction is not exactly the same as the distinction between substitution and income effects which was made in *Value and Capital*. But

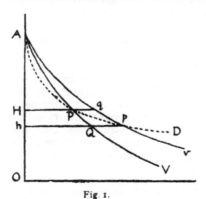

Fig. 1.

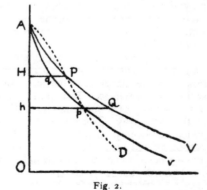

Fig. 2.

THE FOUR CONSUMER'S SURPLUSES

the difference does not seem to be important for most purposes.[1] We shall rarely be led astray if we identify the movement along the marginal valuation curve with the substitution effect, and the movement from one curve to another with the income effect.

The main propositions about the two effects come out at once on the diagram. In the ordinary case (Fig. 1) the two effects work in the same direction ; but in the case of an inferior good (Fig. 2) they may work in opposite directions.

The consumer's *demand* curve is got (without any manipulation) by tracing out the locus of P as the price varies. Since at a price OA one unit will just be purchased, the demand curve will start from A, just as all the marginal valuation curves do. (It is shown by the dotted curve AD in each figure). It is obvious, as it should be, that in the ordinary case the demand curve is more elastic than the marginal valuation curves it intersects ; but in the case of an inferior good it is less elastic.

3. We have now seen how to make a distinction between substitution and income effects, in what seems an adequate way, without using anything but Marshallian geometry. Can we use the same sort of construction for the case of consumer's surplus ?

The matter needs to be approached a little cautiously. It has become apparent in our earlier enquiries[2] that when we take account of income effects, consumer's surplus turns out to be, not one idea, but several. We shall have to take these different definitions one by one. We shall see that they can all be distinguished on our diagram.

I shall begin with the definition of an increment of consumer's surplus which I introduced in *Value and Capital*, and called the " Compensating Variation." The price falls from OH to Oh ; we ask what is " the loss of income which would just offset the fall in price, leaving the consumer no better off than before." That is to say, we seek to discover the loss of income which, if experienced while the price is at Oh, would make him as badly off as he is with his actual income while the price is at OH. It can be assessed in the following way.

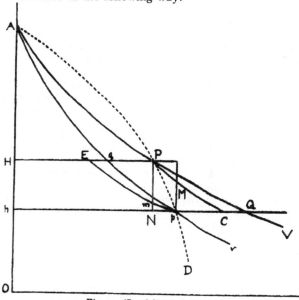

Suppose that successive units of the commodity are supplied to the consumer on the following plan. First of all, he is allowed to acquire HP units at the price OH. At this price he would buy no more units, so in order to induce him to purchase the next unit the price is dropped, but no more than is necessary to induce him to buy that next unit. Then in order to induce him to purchase the unit after that the price is dropped again, but again no more than is necessary. And so on, until the price has been dropped to Oh, after which there are no further reductions.

Fig 4. (See following page.)

[1] See below, p. 36 note.
[2] See particularly "Index-Numbers" ; also A. Henderson. "Consumers' Surplus and the Compensating Variation" (R.E.S., February, 1941).

Under this treatment, the path which will be followed will be *HPC* (Fig. 3) *C* must lie between *Q* and *p*, since at *C* the consumer is better off than he would have been if he had been compelled to purchase the extra units at the higher price *OH* (notice that he would not have done so unless he had been subjected to some form of compulsion), but worse off than if he had been allowed to purchase all units at the price *Oh*. The curve *PC* must, therefore, lie between the marginal valuation curve *PV* and the demand curve *Pp*. Consequently *C* must lie between *Q* and *p*.

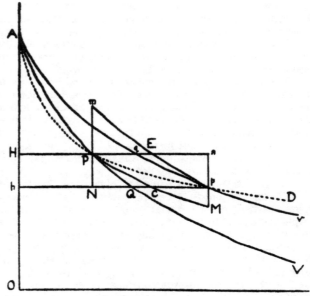

Fig. 3.

There will be the same " betweenness " in the case of an *inferior* good (Fig. 4) ; but in this case *QCp* will be in the reverse order.

Now consider the position of the consumer at *C*, when he has reached it by this peculiar route. He is exactly as well off as he was at *P*, since each subsequent unit purchased has made him neither better nor worse off. He is able to purchase a marginal unit at the price *Oh*, but for each of the earlier units he has paid an excess price above *Oh*, these excess prices being measured by the ordinates of the figure *HPCh*. He is thus in identically the same position as if the price had been at *Oh* throughout, but he had lost an amount of money income equal to the area of this figure. Consequently this area *HPCh* measures the Compensating Variation—the amount of income he would have to lose in order to offset the gain due to the fall in price.

If, instead of considering a fall in price from *OH* to *Oh*, we had considered a rise in price from *Oh* to *OH*, we should have got a different expression for the compensating variation. For the compensating variations in the two directions are not the same thing. The one is a loss of income, experienced when the price is *Oh*, the other is a gain in income experienced when the price is at *OH*. The gain and loss are equal in terms of " utility " ; but they are not equal in terms of money, because the value of money in terms of goods is different in the two cases. Thus we have to distinguish between the Compensating Variation for an upward and a downward movement in price.

As I have pointed out on an earlier occasion,[1] the " upward " Compensating Variation remains an interesting magnitude even when the actual change in price which we are analysing is a fall, not a rise. For when we are considering a fall in price, the " upward " variation can be defined as " the gain in income which, if experienced without the price falling, would make the consumer as much better off as he is made

[1] " Index-numbers." p. 128

THE FOUR CONSUMER'S SURPLUSES 35

by the fall in price without a change in money income." It is for this reason that I have named this second measure the "Equivalent Variation." It is an Equivalent Variation when we are considering a fall in price from *OH* to *Oh*, but it becomes a Compensating Variation when we are considering a rise in price from *Oh* to *OH*. When we turn over to a rise in price, the two "variations" change places. The Equivalent Variation becomes the Compensating, and the Compensating becomes the Equivalent.

The Equivalent Variation (for a fall in price) is measured on Fig. 3 in the following way. Starting from *p*, where *hp* units have been acquired at a price *Oh*, we enquire into the *minimum* prices which the consumer would exact for a diminution in his consumption below that point, by a first, second, third . . ., units. In this way we trace out a curve *pE*. At *E* (on the horizontal line through *H*) he is exactly as well off as at *p* ; but the valuation of the marginal unit retained is now *OH*. He has, however, acquired his *HE* units at a total cost much lower than he would have acquired them if he had paid a price *OH* for each unit. The difference in his net expenditure, as a result of the peculiar method of acquisition, is measured by the area *HEph*. He is thus in the same position as if he had purchased *HE* units at the higher price, but had experienced a gain in income equal to this area. Thus it is this area which measures the Equivalent Variation.

We have seen that the point *C* must lie between *Q* and *p* ; it is, however, not the case that *E* lies between *P* and *q*. For, compare the position of the consumer at *E* with his position as it would be if he had acquired the same number of units by proceeding along the marginal valuation curve *Apv*. At *E* he is as well off as he is at *p* ; but at the point on *Av* vertically below *E* he is less well off than at *p* (he gets better off as he proceeds downwards towards *p* along the marginal valuation curve). Consequently his marginal valuation of the same number of units must be lower (excepting in the case of an inferior good); we have, therefore, drawn the curve *pE* correctly in Fig 3 when we have placed it above *pq*.

Thus, with the equivalent variation, *q* must lie *between* *P* and *E* ; this relation also holds in the case of an inferior good, but once again *PqE* are in the reverse order (Fig. 4).

4. Another advantage of the apparatus I am using in this paper is that it throws considerable light upon the point which was made by Mr. Henderson in his contribution to this discussion.[1] If we turn back to the compensating variation, it will be noticed that at the point *C* the consumer is, in fact, buying less of the commodity than at *p* ; he must do so, if there is a positive income effect, and it is appreciable. Thus the compensating variation, as we have defined it, does not measure the extra price which the consumer would be willing to pay for the extra units of the commodity which he gets when the price falls to *Oh*, and his income is unchanged. What the compensating variation measures is the change in income required to offset the fall in price, not the change in income required to offset the rise in quantity acquired. It becomes apparent that these are not the same thing.

We must, therefore, distinguish between what I may now call the "price-compensating variation" (with which we have hitherto been concerned) and the "quantity-compensating variation" (to which we must now turn our attention). It is very probable (as Mr. Henderson has shown) that it was the quantity-compensating variation which was uppermost in Marshall's mind, rather than the price-compensating variation. But it is evident that he had not really bothered to distinguish.

In order to represent on our diagram (Fig. 3) the quantity-compensating variation, we must continue onwards the line *PC* (supposing that the price goes on being reduced just enough to induce the purchase of each extra unit). We must continue it until

---

[1] Henderson, op. cit.

it intersects the ordinate through p at M. At M the consumer is just as well off as he was at P, although he has the same quantity of this commodity as at p. But as compared with his p situation he has lost an amount of income equal to the price-compensating variation $HPCh$ minus the triangle CMp. Thus it is this difference which measures the quantity-compensating variation.

Just as there was a " quantity " variation corresponding to the compensating, so there will be a " quantity " variation corresponding to the equivalent. (It will be got, for instance, if we turn to consider a rise in price instead of a fall.) In order to measure the quantity-equivalent variation, we must similarly continue onwards the curve pE (supposing that the price goes on being raised just enough to induce the sacrifice of each extra unit) until this curve intersects the ordinate through P at m. At m he is as well off as he was at p, although he has no more units of this commodity than at P ; but as compared with his position at P he has gained an amount of spending power equal to the price-equivalent variation $HEph$ *plus* the triangle EmP. Thus it is the sum of these areas which measures the quantity-equivalent variation.

It will be noticed, if the argument is worked through on Fig. 4, that exactly the same conclusions hold in the case of an inferior good. It is still true that the quantity-compensating variation is *less* than the price-compensating variation by a triangle CMp ; and that the quantity-equivalent is greater than the price-equivalent by a triangle EmP.

5. Having now identified our four definitions of Consumer's Surplus, let us proceed to see what can be deduced from our diagram about the arithmetical relations between their magnitudes. It is fairly obvious that in what is likely to be the most common case, where the income effect is positive but relatively small, the quantity-compensating variation, the price-compensating variation, the price-equivalent variation, and the quantity-equivalent variation will be in ascending order and they will all lie between the " inner " and " outer " rectangles $HPNh$, $Hnph$. But it is already apparent from Fig. 4 that these inequalities will not hold in all cases. Can we make the matter more precise ?

If we confine our attention to a small change in price, assuming that H and h are near together, the matter can be made much more precise. For the differences between the various variations can then be readily identified.

If the change in price which we are considering is a small one, we get the following simplifications. (1) All the curves between P and p (or corresponding points) can be treated as straight lines. (2) The lines PQ, PC coincide with one another, and so do pq, pE. For the difference between PQ and PC depends on a difference in the prices charged for marginal units only. Thus if the whole distance between the two valuation curves is *small*, although it depends upon the change in price of the whole quantity purchased, the distances QC, qE, which only depend upon changes in the price of marginal units, must be of the second order of small quantities.[1] (3) Similarly the difference between the distances Pq and Qp, each of which are of the first order, must be of the second order of small quantities. $PQpq$ can, therefore, be treated as a parallelogram, and it coincides with $PCpE$, which in consequence can also be treated as a parallelogram. Whence the triangles PNC, pnE can be treated as equal ; and the triangles PCp, pEP can be treated as equal.

I shall denote the area of the triangle PNC by $\frac{1}{2}S$; S is necessarily positive, since the curve PC must slope downwards to the right. The magnitude of S depends

---

[1] Thus PC, PQ should *touch* at P ; and pE, pq at p. I am sorry that this does not come out very well on the diagrams as drawn. This is the justification for treating the movement along the marginal valuation curve as a substitution effect. For small changes in price, the marginal valuation curve has the same properties as the curve PC, which is a *marginal* indifference curve.

THE FOUR CONSUMER'S SURPLUSES

upon the magnitude of the substitution effect. We have just proved that for a small change in price, the area of the triangle pnE can also be taken as $\frac{1}{2}S$.

I shall denote the area of the triangle PCp by $\frac{1}{2}I$; I is dependent on the income effect. It is positive if the income effect is positive (Fig. 3) but negative if the income effect is negative (Fig. 4). We have just proved that for a small change in price, the area of the triangle pEP can also be taken as $\frac{1}{2}I$.

Now what about the area of the triangle CMp, which measures the difference between the price-compensating and the quantity-compensating variations? For a small change in price, we can treat PCM (or, in Fig. 4, PMC) as a straight line. Thus PCN, MCp are similar triangles. Now the areas of similar triangles are to one another as the *squares* of the lengths of corresponding sides; but the ratio of the corresponding sides NC, Cp is the same as the ratio of the areas PNC, PCp (for the altitudes of these latter triangles are the same). Now the ratio of these latter areas is $S : I$; consequently the ratio of the areas PCN, MCp is $S^2 : I^2$. But the area of the triangle PCN has been defined as $\frac{1}{2}S$; consequently the area of the triangle MCp is:

$$\frac{1}{2}\frac{I^2}{S}$$

Similarly we prove that, for a small change in price, the area of the triangle EmP is:

$$\frac{1}{2}\frac{I^2}{S}$$

Since S is always positive, this magnitude is always positive (as has otherwise been shown).

We are now in a position to write down formulae for the magnitudes of all our variations. If we write r for the area of the *inner rectangle HPNh*, and R for the area of the *outer rectangle Hnph*,[1] while we express the four variations by the following notation.

Quantity-compensating	..	..	..	C_q
Price-compensating	..	..	..	C_p
Price-equivalent	..	..	..	E_p
Quantity-equivalent	..	..	..	E_q

the formulae can be expressed as follows:

$$R = r + I + S$$

$$C_q = r + \tfrac{1}{2}S - \tfrac{1}{2}\frac{I^2}{S} \quad = R - \tfrac{1}{2}S - I - \tfrac{1}{2}\frac{I^2}{S}$$

$$C_p = r + \tfrac{1}{2}S \quad = R - \tfrac{1}{2}S - I$$

$$E_p = r + \tfrac{1}{2}S + I \quad = R - \tfrac{1}{2}S$$

$$E_q = r + \tfrac{1}{2}S + I + \tfrac{1}{2}\frac{I^2}{S} = R - \tfrac{1}{2}S + \tfrac{1}{2}\frac{I^2}{S}$$

Marshall's measure (the increment in the triangle under the demand curve) is:

$$r + \tfrac{1}{2}I + \tfrac{1}{2}S = R - \tfrac{1}{2}I - \tfrac{1}{2}S.$$

It is thus exactly half-way between the two price-variations, half-way between the two quantity-variations, and (of course) half-way between the inner and outer rectangles.

[1] In " Index-Numbers " (as seemed appropriate for the more general case there considered) I called these the Laspeyre and Paasche variations. As will be noticed, our present geometrical method enables us to get the formulae for the price-variations by a simpler route, and also to add the formulae for the quantity-variations, which can, however, be verified by the other method.

It will be noticed that $C_q = R - \frac{1}{2}\frac{(I+S)^2}{S}$, $E_q = r + \frac{1}{2}\frac{(I+S)^2}{S}$ so that C_q is always less than R, E_q always greater than r, as, indeed, is otherwise evident. (At M, for instance, the consumer has the same amount of the commodity as at p, but he is worse off than at p; therefore he must have paid more for it).

The relations between our six magnitudes are best shown on a diagram, but a diagram of quite a different type. Let us take S (the substitution effect) as given, and measure all the " variations " and " rectangles " from a base half-way between all the pairs—that is to say, from Marshall's measure. The difference between each " variation " or " rectangle " from the Marshall measure then becomes a function of I and can be plotted as a function of I. This is done on Fig. 5.

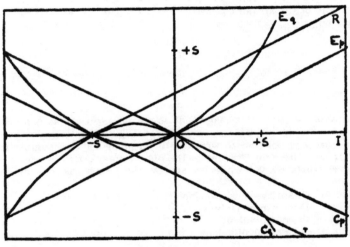

Fig. 5.

It will be seen that if I/S is small and positive, all the four " consumer's surpluses " lie within the inner and outer rectangles ; the equivalent variations are greater than the compensating variations ; the price-variations are intermediate between the quantity-variations. This we may call the orthodox case ; it will be far and away the most common. If I is zero, then, of course, all the " variations " coincide.

There are, however, a whole galaxy of " queer " possibilities. One will occur even with positive income effects. If I is large ($I > S$), the four consumer's surpluses are still in their orthodox order, but the quantity-variations have shot outside the rectangles.

In cases of inferior goods all sorts of things may happen. In the commonest case, when the inferiority is slight, the four consumer's surpluses are still inside the rectangles, but the price-variations are now outside the quantity-variations, and the compensatings and equivalents have changed places. As inferiority becomes greater, the first thing to happen is that the price-variations run outside the rectangles. At $I = -S$, the demand curve turns backwards, and so the two rectangles change places. As the rectangles have turned inside out, the quantity-variations are bound to go outside

THE FOUR CONSUMER'S SURPLUSES

them. Finally, at $I = -2S$ (but this is altogether at the back of beyond), the quantity-variations overtake the price-variations.

6. This appears to complete the theory of the increment (or decrement) of consumer's surplus which results from a *small* change in price. If the change in price under consideration is a large one, then it is no longer possible to assume that the lines PC, pE (Fig. 3) will be parallel, so that the exact symmetry between compensating and equivalent variations will disappear. Further, it is no longer safe to assume that the demand curve will be linear, so that the Marshall measure ceases to lie exactly midway between the two " rectangles."

Nevertheless, even when the change of price is a large one, the three inequalities must still hold :

$$(\text{I}) \quad E_q > E_p \text{ and } C_q < C_p$$
$$(2) \quad E_q > r \quad \text{ and } C_q < R$$
$$(3) \quad E_p < R \text{ and } C_p > r$$

All of these follow from Figs. 3 and 4, without any restriction on the size of the change in price. It would seem to follow that although the other relations shown in Fig. 5 will not work out very exactly (the diagram will, as it were, have worked a little loose and have been given a shake), the general effect will be broadly similar.

One of the most important cases of a large change in price will be such that at the higher price the article will not be purchased at all ; what we are then concerned with is the " total " consumer's surplus which accrues as a result of being able to acquire the commodity at a reasonable price, instead of lacking it altogether. Even for this case, our four definitions still need to be distinguished, though some are evidently more important than others. In particular, if the article is not merely outside the reach of this particular consumer, but is actually not being produced at all in one of the situations which are being compared, E_p ceases to be an important magnitude. For E_p (measured by the area $HEph$) depends upon the particular level at which we suppose the prohibitive " price " to be fixed, and that, although we know it to be greater than OA, is otherwise completely arbitrary. E_q, on the other hand (measured by the triangle hpm, since m is now on the vertical axis), is an interesting magnitude. It is the amount of extra income which the consumer would need to get if he were to be as well off without the commodity as he is when he can get it at a price Oh.

It was very largely the consideration of this case which made me realise that it is necessary to have a theory of quantity-variations—the theory I have tried to provide in this paper. For although in other cases it is probably the price-variations which are the more important, we do need to consider this case, when the article disappears altogether (it is a very important case in Welfare Economics[1]), and here we must have recourse to quantity-variations.

One of the propositions which we have established about quantity-variations seems to be particularly interesting in this connection. It will be noticed that for all cases where income-effects are positive (Fig. 3), the curve pEm lies above the marginal valuation curve Apv ; thus when m is on the vertical axis it will be above A. Further, we have learned that in cases where I is large relatively to S, it is perfectly possible for pEm to intersect the vertical axis far above A, so much so that the triangle mhp (with m on the vertical axis) may have a larger area than that of the whole outer rectangle (which has now become the outer rectangle of the whole demand curve— the rectangle on Ap as diagonal). This possibility—it is, of course, an extreme possibility—throws interesting light on one of the most famous of the " paradoxes " of consumers' surplus.

[1] See, for example, " Rehabilitation," pp. 115–6.

Suppose that we are dealing with a commodity which is an absolute necessity—say food in general. We may take as our unit of " food " the minimum necessary to maintain life over the period to which the curves refer. If the price of food rose sufficiently high, it might happen—in an extreme case—that the whole of income was devoted to the purchase of this one unit of food. We may regard this as the highest point to which the demand curve can rise—it gives us our point A. The outer rectangle of the demand curve may by then have become very large, but it is still a finite quantity. The quantity-equivalent variation, on the other hand, will not be a finite quantity, since there is no addition to income, which, in the absence of sufficient food to maintain life, will make the consumer as well off as he is when he has sufficient food. This is an extreme case, of course ; but it ought to fit into our theory, and it will be seen that it does fit. The substitution effect, along the curve pEm, ultimately becomes zero, for as we follow the curve upwards, it ultimately becomes parallel to the vertical axis. The " triangle " under that curve is therefore infinitely large.

7. When, in an earlier paper, I first envisaged the possibility of the sort of analysis I have carried through in this article, I dismissed it as " a fiddling business, not likely to be of much importance."[1] And that still holds. Nevertheless, I am glad that I have brought myself to carry it through. For the potentialities of the Consumers' Surplus technique are so large, both in the exposition and in the future development of economic theory, that anything which can be done to firm in its foundations seems well worth doing. The foundations have proved to be tricky, but this does not in the least make the concept of consumers' surplus unusable. In the first place, the distinctions we have been making will, in the vast majority of cases, be of very little importance. No theory of economic policy will want to discuss the desirability of measures which would involve the deliberate withdrawal from production of things which are absolute necessaries, or even of things which are anywhere near being absolute necessaries. Even when we are interested in *total* consumer's surplus, so that we do want to consider the total withdrawal of an article (or the introduction of a new article), it will nearly always be something for which good substitutes are available, so that the income effect must be small relatively to the substitution effect. In all such cases it is evident that Marshall's technique will involve little danger of error. But it is something to have satisfied ourselves on that point.

In the second place, even if a problem does arise (as will sometimes happen) in which our distinctions are relevant, even then they will not give much trouble. For the problem itself will decide whether we are concerned with price-variations or quantity-variations. In the case of a tax, for instance, it is obviously the price-variation which has to be considered ; in a case of rationing, the quantity-variation. The question of compensating *versus* equivalent variations may cause more difficulty. It has been pointed out by Mr. Scitovszky in another connection[2] (but it is really the same point) that we can only say definitely that a group of consumers are made better off by a particular change in their circumstances if both the compensating and equivalent variations (summed up for the total change in circumstances and over all the consumers) show a gain ; they are definitely worse off only if both variations show a loss. It is possible (for a group, but not for an individual) that one might show a gain and the other a loss—in which case it would not be possible to regard the change as a distinct improvement or a distinct disimprovement. Consequently, if there is any reason to suspect that the two variations may differ appreciably, we ought to be prepared to make a double reckoning. But since in practice we are unlikely to work

---

[1] " Rehabilitation," p. 109.
[2] "A Reconsideration of the Theory of Tariffs" (R.E.S., Summer, 1942), pp. 91–2.

THE FOUR CONSUMER'S SURPLUSES   4I

up any enthusiasm for "improvements" which offer an unequivocally positive, but only small, gain, it will not perturb us much to discover that changes in the economic situation are conceivable which are theoretically, not just practically, neutral.

The most important thing which emerges from our investigation, so it seems to me, is of a different character. It has already become apparent that the most serious error in the older conception of consumers' surplus (how far Marshall shared this error I shall not presume to discuss) lay in treating it as an absolute magnitude, in making statements such as that a consumer, just because he is in such and such a position, is getting so and so much consumer's surplus. The newer conception is quite different from this. Consumers' surplus is relative, not absolute. We are always considering the *movement* from one defined situation to another defined situation ; we are asking what is the gain (or loss) of money income which would measure the gain (or loss) of economic welfare resulting from the movement. This gain or loss of income must itself always refer to one or other of the two situations ; otherwise it is meaningless. We have now seen that even in this restricted sense consumers' surplus is not an unambiguous magnitude ; but we have now cleared up the ambiguities (so far as can be seen at present) and they are not after all so very formidable. Consumers' surplus remains a usable instrument of analysis—as usable as it ever was ; and we ought now to be enabled to use it with more security and greater confidence.

I hope, in yet another article, to employ my present technique to clear up the parallel ambiguities in the concept of producers' surplus.

Manchester.   J. R. HICKS.

[7]

Rent as a Measure of Welfare Change

The definitions of economic rent in current use fall easily into two categories: (1) a payment in excess of that necessary to maintain a resource in its current occupation. Thus, Frederick Benham [1, p. 227] tells us that rents are ". . . the sums paid to the factors which need not be paid in order to retain the factors *in the industry.*" While to Kenneth Boulding [2, p. 230] it is the payment to a factor ". . . in excess of the minimum amount necessary to keep that factor in its present occupation." (2) The difference between the current earnings of a resource and its transfer earnings[1]—the latter term signifying its earnings in the next best alternative use [1, p. 328]. For instance, Paul Samuelson [6, p. 593] says, ". . . we should term the excess of his income above the alternative wage he could earn elsewhere as *a pure rent.*" Similarly, for George Stigler [7, p. 99] the rent of a factor is ". . . the excess of its return in the best use over its possible return in other uses? . . ."[2]

While the first type of definition is, as we shall see, unavoidably ambiguous, the second type is yet more inadequate. Among other things it would require that, in the choice of occupation, men were motivated solely by pecuniary considerations.

I. *A Measure of Rent as an Economic Surplus*

For the purpose of revealing ambiguities in the existing definitions of economic rent and of demonstrating the logic of the proposed definition, we shall find it no less convenient and a good deal more suggestive to take our bearings from a more generalized version of the traditional theory of consumer's choice.

Rather than maximizing the utility function $W\{u(x_1, \ldots, x_n)\}$, over the range in which $\dfrac{\partial W}{\partial x_r} > O$ for all x_r, subject to the usual constraint $\Sigma b_r x_r = Y$, where Y is the individual's income [cf. 3, p. 305], we require our individual, in possession of given resources, or assets, to maximize such a function subject to $\Sigma p_r x_r = O$. At least one of the x's is negative in order to indicate a quantity supplied per period by the individual of a good or service and, of course, at least one of the x's is positive to indicate a quantity demanded per

---

[1] To impart precision to this measure of economic rent the period of adjustment should be specified, as should, also, the area of comparison—within the industry, region, country, or within the world as a whole. But since the inadequacy of this definition of rent prevails irrespective of these distinctions, I shall make no further mention of them in this paper.

[2] In all these cases the writers appear to be using "factor" in the sense in which I shall use the term "resource." And though, generally, I prefer to reserve the term factor for the productive service of the resource, it will avoid possible confusion if instead I adhere to the term productive service.

period of a good or service. The suggested constraint expresses nothing more than the proposition that, in all circumstances, the individual's current earnings are equal to the current value of his expenditure.[3] It is a significant amendment, however, because it brings to the fore the notion of simultaneous determination of the individual's allocation of his productive services and of his earnings in response to a given pattern of prices: an obvious point perhaps, but one frequently ignored in the analysis of the individual's demand and supply curves.

Maximizing the utility function subject to our new constraint, we derive the well-known equilibrium condition $\dfrac{\partial W}{\partial x_r} = \lambda p_r$ (λ being identified as the marginal utility of income) for all goods and services whether their magnitudes are positive or negative—whether, that is, they are demanded or supplied by the individual.[4] Or, dispensing with utility, we can write $\dfrac{\partial x_i}{\partial x_j} = \dfrac{p_j}{p_i}$ for any i and j.

It should be apparent that, although the substitution effect may be defined in the customary way, there can be no income effect, $\dfrac{\partial x_r}{\partial Y}$, since there is no necessary correspondence, using our new constraint, between changes in the individual's welfare and changes in his income, real or money. For with the new constraint, money income, Y, is no longer held constant; it is determined along with all the other variables. It may increase, remain unchanged, or diminish, with an improvement in the individual's welfare. In its place, therefore, we derive a *welfare* effect, $\dfrac{\partial x_r}{\partial W}$. In consequence, the effect on the quantity bought or sold of any chosen good or service of a given change in the set of prices is divided into a substitution effect and a welfare effect.

The implications of this less-restricted formulation, though straightforward enough, are worth recording. A change in the price of any good or service—whether it is supplied or demanded by the individual—changes, in general, the quantities of all goods and services which the individual buys and sells. Consequently it changes the value of his earnings and expenditure. A search for a useful definition of an "incentive good" might begin with the implication that a fall in the price of any consumed good will, *inter alia*, increase or reduce the amount of work done by the individual as a result of the operation of the welfare effect. But this will not be pursued here.

[3] Strictly speaking his spending is equal to current earnings *less* current saving *plus* current dissaving. This could easily be allowed for without any modification of our conclusions. Over time, if his assets grow, his demand for goods and his disposal of productive services will, of course, alter. This problem is, however, common to all such static analysis.

[4] Since we restrict ourselves to the range in which the marginal utilities of all goods and services are positive, the acquisition of goods or services adds to the individual's total utility while the supply of goods and services from the individual's assets or resources subtracts from his total utility. Corresponding to the equilibrium conditions for goods purchased, the marginal utilities of the productive services supplied to the market are proportional to their corresponding supply prices.

Having extended the customary confines of the theory of consumer's choice
we may now develop the argument largely in terms of two or three goods or
services, but deriving from our hypothesis a more symmetrical construction
of the individual indifference map. Since $\Sigma p_r x_r = 0$, the price hyperplane
passes through the origin of an n-dimensional indifference map and is nega-

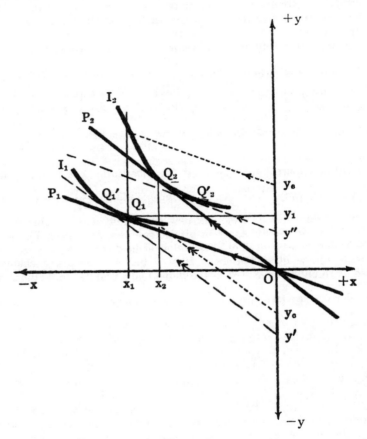

FIGURE 1

tive in slope with respect to all the axes. This means that in order to acquire
(surrender) more of one good or service, other goods or services must be
surrendered (or acquired).

A two-dimensional cross section of this indifference map is represented in
Figure 1. Any distance Ox to the right of the origin measures amount per
unit period of x acquired by the individual. Any distance Ox to the left of the
origin measures the amount of x per period given up by the individual. Similarly, Oy above the origin measures the quantity of y taken, and Oy below the
origin, the quantity of y given up. Inasmuch as rent partakes of the nature of

COMMUNICATIONS

a surplus, and is to be measured in exactly the same way as consumer's surplus is measured, it is advantageous to consider in some detail the simple problem of the individual supplying x, say a single type of productive service, "labor," to the market in return for which y is demanded. Thus, we operate in the north-west quadrant of the figure. And though we may not do so in an n-dimensional treatment of the problem, confined as we are to two dimensions we may find it convenient to regard y as all other goods at fixed prices, the only price which alters being the price of x, labor.[5] We now seek a precise measure of the difference in welfare resulting from alternative supply prices of labor.

If we construct a price line P_1 passing through the origin and tangent to Q_1 on the indifference curve I_1, the individual is represented as in equilibrium, giving up Ox_1 of labor and acquiring in exchange Oy_1 of income y. We now perform the familiar Hicksian experiment in order to have the supply effects on all fours with those of demand. The price of x is now increased from p_1 to p_2, the individual's new equilibrium being at Q_2 on the indifference curve I_2. The change in equilibrium positions consequent upon the change in the price of labor may be divided into the substitution effect, Q_1 to Q_1', and the welfare effect, Q_1' to Q_2 (or alternatively the welfare effect Q_1 to Q_2' and the substitution effect Q_2' to Q_2). Although the welfare effect can, of course, go either way, it should be noticed that a positive welfare effect on x, implying an increase in the *demand* for x, constitutes a reduction in its supply, which is to say that a positive or "normal" welfare effect of a rise in the supply price of labor, or in the supply price of any good or service, is that of a reduction in the quantity supplied by the individual. The "backward-bending" supply curve of labor is, then, the outcome of a strong positive, or normal, welfare effect, and not a negative, or perverse, welfare effect.

Suppose we are now to measure the increase in welfare following a rise in the price of x to p_2, we may follow Hicks' practice [4, pp. 69-82] and distinguish between two preliminary measures: the compensating variation (CV), and the equivalent variation (EV). The CV is the amount of y which, following a change in the price of x, has to be given to or taken from the individual in order that his initial welfare—indicated by the indifference curve I_1 in Figure 1—remain unchanged. In this instance, the individual's welfare being

[5] This construction, and its later elaboration, are, I believe, to be preferred to the more common leisure-income diagram apart from the fact that the present diagram is derived directly from the more general condition in which the individual chooses to supply a combination of various goods and productive services to the market in amounts which depend upon the current set of prices: (1) Giving up leisure, a homogeneous good, does not have the same connotation as providing various kinds of services each of which requires a different skill and entails a different degree of hardship for the individual. (2) We need not evoke the artifice of a fixed amount of the good, leisure, say 24 hours a day, with the rather awkward result that an improvement in welfare may be represented along one axis as equivalent to more than 24 hours of leisure a day. In the construction used here, the shape of the indifference curves acts to limit the supply of any productive service furnished to the market, and our measure of welfare changes is in terms only of the good, y. Finally (3) the indifference map used here is the correct prior construction to that useful textbook diagram in which a downward-sloping line crosses the price-axis, to the right of which is represented the demand schedule and to the left, the supply schedule.

improved as a result of the price change, Oy' measures the CV. For if Oy' were taken from his income he could still maintain his initial welfare position on I_1, given that the higher supply price P_2 is available to him. The EV, on the other hand, is the amount of y which has to be given to, or taken from, the individual to ensure that he reaches the new level of welfare when the change in price does not apply to him. Since in this instance the increment in welfare is positive he is to receive a money equivalent. If he receives Oy'' he can just reach I_2, the new level of welfare, with the old price P_1.

The concept of rent as an economic surplus, it is suggested here, should be measured as a CV or an EV in a manner symmetrical in all respects with the concept of consumer's surplus. In the example above, it arises as the difference in welfare experienced by the individual from the rise in the supply price to P_2, P_1 being regarded as the most preferred alternative open to him.[6] The rent obiviously becomes larger the lower the initial supply price P_1. In the limiting case, P_1 will be a no-transactions price tangent to an indifference curve at the point where it crosses the vertical axis.

Since the current definitions treat rent as a surplus which may be appropriated without any effects on the supply of the individual's productive services in his current occupation, it is important to observe that in all cases in which the individual is made to pay or to receive compensation equal to the measures of rent suggested, the amount of the productive service he will then offer will differ from that which he originally supplied at the current price. For example, if, having reached Q_2 in Figure 1, he is made to pay the full CV, equal to Oy', he will no longer continue to supply Ox_2 of labor. Instead he will supply the amount indicated by the equilibrium point Q_1'—a larger amount than before if x is normal.

Finally it may be instructive to remove the restriction of a single occupation in our analysis and to consider briefly the case of the supply of productive services to two alternative occupations, A and B, in which, although the individual might choose to work part-time in each if that were feasible, he is obliged, owing to institutional arrangements, to work entirely in the one occupation or the other.

In Figure 2, a three-dimensional indifference map with a vertical y-axis and two horizontal axes, a and b, crossing at right angles, we cut a vertical slice along the negative ay plane and along the negative by plane as far as the

---

[6] Though we are working with a single productive service, labor, the notion and the definition of economic rent may, just as in the analysis of consumer's surplus, be extended to several services with obvious modifications. If, for example, the individual is providing two services, x_1 and x_2, then a rise in the supply price of both services yields a CV rent which is the maximum he is willing to pay—prices of all goods and services other than those of x_1 and x_2 remaining unchanged—rather than forego these higher prices. This measure remains the same, as we might expect, if we measure each in turn and add them: the rent when the price of x_1 rises, all other prices, including that of x_2, being constant, *plus* the additional rent when now the price of x_2 rises, all other prices remaining constant with x_1 unchanged at its new price.

This argument is symmetrical with that of Hicks on consumer's surplus [4, pp. 178-79], but the generalization in the conclusion of this paper goes further than Hicks'.

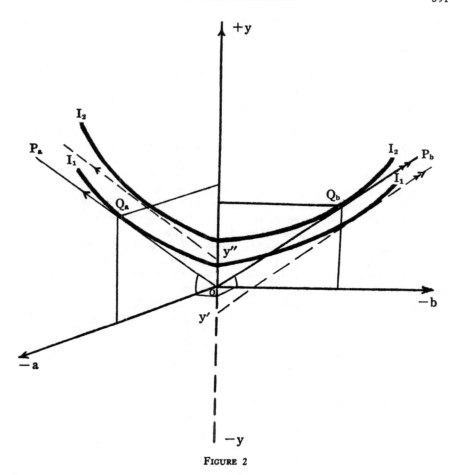

FIGURE 2

y-axis and remove the segment. Hence, if we imagine our figure divided vertically into four quarters, we shall be looking into the space left after the removal of the vertical quarter in which *a* and *b* are both negative. The upper part of what meets the eye is represented in Figure 2. By removing the vertical quarter referred to, we have removed the possibility of combining employment A and B.

Despite the fact that both the rate of pay and the resultant earnings are higher in A than in B, the individual chooses to supply his services to B, his equilibrium there being at Q_b on the indifference surface I_2 compared with the alternative equilibrium position Q_a on I_1. Nonetheless, he enjoys a positive economic rent in the lower-paid occupation B which can be measured by the CV, Oy'—the maximum he is prepared to pay to remain in B when A, at the existing wage-rate, is the only alternative open to him. It can also be measured by the *EV, Oy"*—the minimum the individual must be paid in order to induce him to transfer his services from B to A.[7]

II. *Comparison with the Marshallian Concept*

Let us now compare our results with Marshall's concept of rent. Though the *Principles* do not contain a formal definition of rent, the sense of most of Marshall's dicta on the subject points to a definition of rent as a surplus above that necessary to elicit the productive services of a resource.[8] This Marshallian definition, essentially that of category (1), suffers from the same imprecision as his definition of consumer's surplus.[9] For one thing, the surplus was treated as if it could be taxed away without affecting the supply of the productive service, which is manifestly false on our analysis. Once this is granted the difficulties are easily perceived. In order to persist with the Marshallian definition we have to interpret it to have reference to some unchanged amount of the productive service; either (a) the amount supplied in the equilibrium position resulting from the price change (Ox_2 in Figure 1), or (b) that supplied in the original equilibrium position (Ox_1 in Figure 1). In either case we are saddled with an improbable and cumbersome measure inasmuch as we have to compel the individual to supply an amount of the productive service other than that which he would freely choose. For instance, if we adopt (a) we derive what may be called, for convenience, the Marshallian *CV*, equal to Oy_c. It represents the maximum amount of money the individual would surrender in order to retain P_2 if at the same time he were constrained to provide no more than Ox_2 of productive service—Ox_2 being the amount supplied at P_2 when he is free to choose. As we should expect, the restriction on his choice of quantity reduces the maximum he is prepared to pay for the privilege of the P_2 price. In a like manner, if we adopt (b), the Marshallian *EV*, we are left with a measure Oy_e. It is larger than the *EV* proper, *Oy"* since the minimum payment to him must be greater if he is now

[7] In all cases in which institutional arrangements preclude a combination of occupations —the individual having the choice only of putting the services of his resources entirely in A or in B—the coincidence of the four definitions and the Marshallian measure of rent no longer follow from a zero welfare elasticity, for the *EV* and the *CV* now arise from different cross-sections of the individual indifference map.

[8] In particular see pp. 155-62, and pp. 427-30 [5]. Elsewhere in the *Principles* Marshall talks of the additional earnings resulting from superior abilities as a surplus or rent [5, pp. 577-79 and 623-27]. What part of the additional earnings might be regarded as rent on the definition attributed to Marshall cannot be known without determining first what part of the additional earnings is necessary to attract the resource into that occupation. From the point of view of the firm, however, the additional payments for superior abilities must appear as efficiency payments.

[9] [5, p. 124] Marshall was, of course, aware of the slippery nature of his consumer's surplus (though not, apparently, of his economic rent) and tried to cover himself by specifying a change in the demand price for a particular good whose real-income effect was so small in relation to the individual's budget that the marginal utility of money income could be taken, for all practical purposes, as constant. The trouble with this is that it is double-edged: ambiguity is reduced by reducing the significance of what is being measured. Ambiguity disappears entirely only when the price change under consideration becomes zero and there is nothing left to measure.

COMMUNICATIONS   393

compelled to provide the original quantity of productive services Ox_1 at the original price P_1 when his welfare is increased from I_1 to I_2. There is obviously nothing strictly illogical about such definitions, but on the grounds of plausibility and convenience they are to be rejected in favor of the CV and EV proper.

If, on the other hand, a Marshallian *measure* of economic rent is taken to be the area above the supply curve of the services of the individual's resource[10] —a measure which seems to correspond with the category (2) definition if the individual's supply curve represents maximum earnings of successive increments of productive services in alternative uses—for this measure to be of any use requires (i) an upward-sloping supply curve, and (ii) exclusion of nonpecuniary considerations. Clearly this Marshallian measure, which is popular in textbooks, is inadequate since it represents no more than a first derivative of the locus of price-quantity equilibria of an indifference map. Nor is this derivative necessarily upward-sloping; it may be backward-bending in contrast to the *marginal* indifference curves which will always be upward-sloping. It appears yet more unsatisfactory if the restriction to pecuniary considerations is removed. We may then discover that differences between the earnings of the resource in its current occupation and those of the relevant alternative occupation are negative, a tribute to the individual's preference for his present occupation.

Hicks has done some admirable work in tracing the relationships between Marshall's definition of consumer's surplus, Marshall's way of measuring consumer's surplus (the area under the individual's demand curve), and the two precise measures CV and EV which were initially suggested by his indifference curve analysis. Important as these contributions were in clarifying our ideas on this tangled subject, it can be held that the tracing of these precise relationships assumes a far greater importance on the neglected supply side. For it is surely just there that we cannot reasonably suppose that a change in price has negligible effects on the welfare of the individual inasmuch as the supply of any one of his productive services enters significantly into his budget. To the extent it does so, the area above the individual's supply curve, especially in the case of only one productive service, is a much less reliable index of the surplus welfare than the area under his demand curve for any one good.

In the special case in which the welfare elasticity of the supply of x is zero there is a coincidence of the CV, EV, Marshallian CV, Marshallian EV, and the Marshallian measure, the area above the supply curve. (This same coincidence obtains when the rent is reckoned as between the current and alternative occupations in the case in which the choice between occupations rests on a purely pecuniary basis.) While in general, a zero elasticity of supply with

[10] [5, p. 811.] Here Marshall graphically illustrates consumer's surplus and producer's surplus for an *industry*. But even if we interpret the industry's supply curve as a marginal curve, the producer's surplus could be identified with the rent of resources in that industry only under restricted conditions. On the other hand, it would hardly be inconsistent with Marshall's view of things to interpret the measurement of the individual's rent in a manner symmetrical with his suggested measurement of the individual's consumer's surplus [5, pp. 125-27] as the area under the individual's demand curve.

respect to price does not entail a zero welfare elasticity, in the particular case in which the former derives from a zero substitutibility *plus a zero welfare elasticity*, these four definitions and the Marshallian measure all come to the same thing. The zero substitutability implies no alternative uses and therefore a set of vertical *marginal* indifference curves. The zero welfare elasticity implies that all the marginal indifference curves will coincide. Ricardian land is a favorite example of a zero elasticity of supply of this sort. Its characteristic is that it has only one use, say wheat production. As a consequence of this characteristic (i) it cannot move elsewhere in response to changes in relative prices (zero substitution effect), and therefore (ii) *all* of a given acreage of land of uniform quality is brought into wheat production in response to any positive price per acre (zero welfare effect).[11]

III. *Conclusion*

Little further reflection is required to recognize that consumer's surplus and economic rent are both measures of the change in the individual's welfare when the set of prices facing him are changed or the constraints imposed upon him are altered. Any distinction between them is one of convenience only: consumer's surpluses have reference to demand prices, economic rent to supply prices. Furthermore, no consideration of logic precludes our measuring the individual's gain—in terms either of the *CV* or the *EV*—from, say, a simultaneous fall in the price of a good bought and a rise in the price of a service provided.

Indeed, in general, if any one, several, or even all prices change for the individual, some demand prices and some supply prices rising, others falling, the resulting change in the individual's welfare can, in principle, be measured by either of our definitions. The *CV* is an exact measure of the transfer, to or from the individual, following a change in the set of all prices, in order to maintain his initial level of welfare. In this case the amount transferred is measured in terms of any one good, in combinations of various goods, or in a combination of all goods dealt in, always using the *new* set of prices. This is quite possible since, given a set of prices, the amount of any one good is equivalent in value to various combinations of some particular goods or of all goods. More usefully, an amount of money calculated at the given set of prices will suffice to measure the *CV*.

On the other hand, the *EV* is an exact measure of the transfer necessary to bring the individual's level of welfare into equality with what it would have been if he were not, as he is, debarred from the new set of prices. The amount of the transfer is now calculated at the *old* prices, and may be expressed in money or in any combination of goods at these prices.

E. J. MISHAN*

[11] The indifference curves in this special case would all be horizontal (signifying zero elasticity of substitution) up to a distance representing the maximum supply of productive service from the given resource. At this distance they would all become vertical and, hence, coincide. Rent however measured would, on this vertical limit, be equal to the vertical distance between the two price lines in question.

*The author is assistant lecturer at the London School of Economics. He wishes to acknowledge his indebtedness to S. A. Ozga for valuable criticisms and suggestions.

[8]

THE ECONOMIC JOURNAL

DECEMBER 1971

THE CONCEPT OF ECONOMIC SURPLUS AND ITS USE IN ECONOMIC ANALYSIS [1]

THE concept of economic surplus occupies a controversial but important place in economic theory. At times it has lapsed into relative obscurity; at other times it has been the subject of heated debate. Some eminent economists have argued that it is one of the most vital concepts in economic theory; others have lamented the enormous attention devoted to it. In 1953 Pfouts [116, p. 315] wrote about consumer's surplus: " Probably no single concept in the annals of economic theory has aroused so many emphatic expressions of opinion as has consumer's surplus; indeed even today the biting winds of scholarly sarcasm howl around this venerable storm centre." Some years earlier Hicks [55, p. 116] concluded:

> " But enough has been said to show that consumer's surplus is not a mere economic plaything, a *curiosum*. It is the foundation of an important branch of Economics, a branch cultivated with superb success by Marshall, Edgeworth, and Pigou, shockingly neglected in recent years, but urgently needing reconstruction on a broader basis. Beyond all doubt it is still capable of much further development; if economists are to play their part in shaping the canons of economic policy fit for a new age, they will have to build on the foundations of consumer's surplus."

Disagreeing with Hicks, Samuelson [137, p. 195] dismissed the concept as being of " historical and doctrinal interest with a limited amount of appeal as a purely mathematical puzzle; " and Little [86, p. 180] described it as a " totally useless theoretical toy." Recently, controversy over the concepts of producer's surplus and economic rent has also arisen [103, 177, 105, 144]. [2]

[1] The authors would like to express their gratitude to the Giannini Foundation for financial support while this article was being written. They are also grateful to J. Bieri, P. Helmberger, S. S. Hoos, H. G. Johnson, A. P. Lerner, W. Peters, A. J. Rayner, J. A. Seagraves, E. Sadan, S. Soznick and, particularly, the ECONOMIC JOURNAL referee for their valuable comments on earlier drafts. The authors are, of course, responsible for all errors and omissions.

[2] Regarding some of the practical applications of the concept of economic surplus, Mundell has recently remarked that " . . . there have appeared in recent years studies purporting to demonstrate that the welfare loss due to monopoly is small, that the welfare importance of efficiency and production is exaggerated, and that gains from trade and the welfare gains from tariff reduction are almost negligible. Unless there is a thorough theoretical re-examination of the validity of the tools on which these studies are founded, and especially of the revitalized concepts of producers' and consumers' surplus, some one inevitably will draw the conclusion that economics has ceased to be important! " [108, p. 622].

The debate over the usefulness of the concept of economic surplus is not simply academic. Indeed, the extent to which the " old " or " new " welfare economics can contribute to actual policy decisions seems to depend greatly on the validity and usefulness of this concept.

Over the years considerable discussion, sometimes of a highly abstract nature, has been directed towards making the concept as precise as possible. The first part of this paper summarises the major theoretical developments that have taken place since the concept was first suggested. We discuss, in turn, consumer's surplus, producer's surplus and economic rent, and outline the most important theoretical considerations underlying these concepts.

The major impetus for the theoretical refinement of the concept of economic surplus has been the hope that it might provide a powerful tool for practical application. Indeed, it has been applied to a wide variety of problems. The second part of this paper considers some of the more significant applications of the concept of economic surplus. Although the coverage is not exhaustive, we hope that it will provide a useful survey for those interested in pursuing this type of approach further. Finally, we discuss why there has been so much controversy surrounding the concept (and doubtless let our own feelings show through).

I. The Concept of Economic Surplus

For expository convenience we will distinguish between surpluses which accrue to buyers and surpluses which accrue to sellers. This distinction facilitates the discussion of the historical development of the concept of economic surplus for such a division is firmly embedded in the literature. However, we hope that the essential symmetry between surpluses on the demand and supply side will emerge from our discussion.

In the ensuing discussion, unless there is an explicit statement to the contrary, we will assume that a buyer can purchase as much as he likes at a given price and that a seller can sell as much as he likes at a given price.

Consumer's Surplus.

Dupuit and Marshall. The concept of consumer's surplus dates back to Dupuit [34] who, in 1844, in his classic paper on the utility of public works, claimed that a buyer may receive a surplus from a transaction. He defined this surplus as " the difference between the sacrifice which the purchaser would be willing to make in order to get it and the purchase price he has to pay in exchange " [34, p. 29]. He proposed that this surplus can be measured by the triangle-like area below the demand curve and above the price line.

The concept of consumer's surplus was popularised by Marshall [94]. His approach differed in one significant respect from Dupuit's. Dupuit was satisfied with a monetary measure of the consumer's surplus. He acknowledged that the maximum payment a consumer is prepared to make " is not, in the last analysis, a rigorous measure of the quality which things have *of being able to satisfy men's needs* " [34, p. 28]. However, he argued that " political economy, being concerned only with wealth, can take account of the intensity of a wish only through its monetary expression."

Marshall, on the other hand, was concerned with emphasising that a consumer derives a surplus *utility* from being able to buy a commodity at a particular price [12]. His basic (but unwritten) definition of consumer's surplus would *seem* to be the excess of the total utility afforded by his consumption of the commodity over the utility he foregoes on other commodities by buying that commodity [153, 46, 154]. He used " the excess of the price (*i.e.*, total expenditure) which he would be willing to pay for the thing rather than go without it, over that which he actually does pay " [94, p. 124]— henceforth referred to as " extra expenditure "—and the Dupuit triangle as economic *measures* of this " true " surplus. A common tendency in the literature has been to regard " extra expenditure " as Marshall's basic *definition* and to treat the triangle as a measure of this [55, 44]. This interpretation is certainly plausible, particularly as Marshall's somewhat confusing presentation of this subject is open to more than one interpretation. However, as Bishop's [12] penetrating analysis of Marshall's treatment of consumer's surplus shows, if extra expenditure and the triangle are regarded as alternative measures of the " true surplus," Marshall's analysis becomes much more comprehensible.

To justify the use of extra expenditure and the triangle as economic measures of the true surplus, Marshall assumed that the marginal utility of money (M.U.M.) is *approximately* constant. According to Bishop, Marshall needed this assumption for two reasons: [1]

1. It permits the use of money as an acceptable cardinal index of utility. In this event the maximum *extra* amount the consumer would have been prepared to pay for something provides an acceptable measure of the surplus utility from the transaction.[2] In fact, for Marshall, as far as this extra expenditure measure is concerned, the M.U.M. would never be exactly constant because if the consumer were to spend more for a certain quantity of the commodity than he actually does spend, he would have to spend less on other commodities. Assuming, as he did, diminishing marginal utilities of all commodities, this retrenchment would raise the marginal utilities of the other goods so that the M.U.M. would necessarily rise. Marshall, recognising this, restricted his attention to a commodity on which expenditure is a small fraction of total expenditure since the quantities bought of the

[1] What Marshall meant by this assumption has been basic to the long debate over the nature of his demand curve [2, 3, 44, 114, 149].

[2] Bishop, in fact, demonstrates a special case in which extra expenditure exactly measures the true surplus even if the M.U.M. changes.

other commodities (and thus their marginal utilities) would be less likely to be appreciably affected.[1]

2. If the M.U.M. remains approximately constant *for movements along the consumer's demand curve*, the area below this curve would provide an acceptable measure of the total utility from the commodity and the Dupuit triangle would approximate the true surplus. The M.U.M. will be *exactly* constant with respect to changes in the price of the good if the price elasticity of demand for that commodity is unity and if the marginal utilities of the other goods are unaffected by changes in the consumption of that commodity.[2] Thus, assuming, as he did, independent marginal utilities, the acceptability of using the triangle as an approximate measure of the true surplus will depend on the nearness to unitary price elasticity and on the effects of any resulting change in expenditure elsewhere on the M.U.M. (and, thus, on the importance of the commodity in the overall budget).[3]

Bishop has shown that, when the M.U.M. is not constant, either extra expenditure or the triangle may provide the better measure of the true surplus, depending on the circumstances. He concluded that " for small consumer's surpluses, extra expenditure may be superior but that for large consumer's surpluses the demand method is to be preferred " [12, p. 435].[4]

[1] Marshall wrote: " Strictly speaking we ought to take account of the fact that if he spent less on tea, the marginal utility of money would be less than it is, and he would get an element of consumers' surplus from buying other things which now yield him no such rent. But these changes of consumers' rent (being of the second order of smallness) may be neglected, on the assumption, which underlies our whole reasoning, that his expenditure on any one thing, as, for instance tea, is only a small part of his total expenditure " [94, p. 842].

[2] A rational consumer will allocate his expenditure on N commodities so that

$$\frac{MU_1}{P_1} = \frac{MU_2}{P_2} = \ldots = \frac{MU_N}{P_N} = \text{M.U.M.}$$

For the area below the demand curve of, say, the first commodity to provide an exact cardinal index of the total utility of that commodity, the M.U.M. must be constant with respect to changes in P_1. Given the assumptions of independent and diminishing marginal utilities, this requires that expenditures on all other commodities must be unaffected by changes in P_1.

[3] The evident confusion about the rigorous implications of a constant M.U.M. prompted Samuelson [133] to clarify the issue. It should be emphasised that the M.U.M. cannot be independent of all prices and of income. Indeed, the M.U.M. is homogeneous of degree minus one in all prices and income. Of the possible interpretations of " constancy " which Samuelson distinguished, the one of interest here is the one he termed the " pure Marshallian case "; namely that the M.U.M. is independent of all prices but *not* of income. He showed that, assuming an additive utility function, constancy in this sense implies a unitary income elasticity of demand for each good, a unitary own-price elasticity of demand for each good, and zero cross-price elasticities of demand.

We might mention at this point that Samuelson [133, p. 90] also showed that in the " pure " Marshallian case, where utilities are independent and the M.U.M. is independent of price changes, consumer's surplus is infinite! Marshall [94, p. 841] had suggested that, if a certain amount of a commodity is vital for existence, one should " take life for granted and estimate separately the total utility of that part of the supply of the commodity which is in excess of absolute necessaries." In fact, Samuelson showed that, in the " pure " case, there does not exist a unique minimum or subsistence level.

[4] One reason extra expenditure is unsatisfactory for large consumer's surpluses is that it is necessarily constrained by the level of income. The recognition of this may have led some writers, who took extra expenditure as the basic Marshallian definition, to reject the concept of consumer's surplus. For example, Young rejected it because " its sum, for any one consumer, comes precisely to zero " [188, p. 149]. We consider the question of the surplus on all commodities later in the article.

He also demonstrated how, conceptually at least, a cardinal measure of the true surplus utility can be obtained without Marshall's apologetic assumption that the M.U.M. be approximately constant.[1]

Hicks and Henderson. Following the development of ordinal utility analysis, the concept of consumer's surplus was largely forgotten until, in the 1940s, Hicks [55, 57] redefined the concept, using an ordinal system of indifference curves. He defined consumer's surplus as the amount of income variation that would leave the consumer on his original indifference curve following the introduction of the commodity at the particular price. Subsequently, Henderson [53] demonstrated a fundamental difference between the Dupuit–Marshallian extra-expenditure measure and the Hicksian measure— the former constrains the consumer to buy a certain quantity of the commodity, whereas the latter does not. Moreover, Henderson pointed out that, in general, the relevant compensating variation in income would depend on whether the consumer had to pay for the privilege of buying the new good or whether he was to be paid for not being able to buy the good.[2]

[1] Bishop achieved this by *making* the M.U.M. exactly constant. He proposed a " marginal utility demand curve " of the form

$$X_1 = F(P_1; \ \bar{P}_2, \bar{P}_3, \ldots, \bar{P}_N; \ \bar{X}_2, \bar{X}_3, \ldots, \bar{X}_N)$$

where income is allowed to vary in order to keep $\bar{X}_2, \bar{X}_3, \ldots, \bar{X}_N$ constant. Since these quantities are held constant and since their prices do not alter, then, assuming their marginal utilities are independent of the quantity of X_1, the M.U.M. is unaffected by changes in P_1. The area below this marginal utility demand curve provides an exact measure of the total utility of that commodity.

[2] Consider the introduction of a commodity X at a price given by the slope of P. At that price the consumer, with income OA, would buy OK units of X, paying BC for them. The maximum amount the consumer would be prepared to pay for OK units of X is given by BD. Thus, the Dupuit–Marshallian extra-expenditure measure of his surplus is CD.

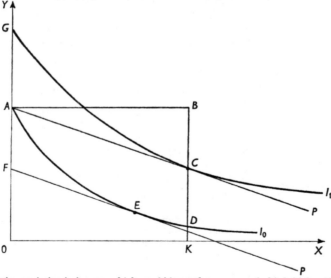

The Hicksian variation in income which would leave the consumer in his initial welfare position following the introduction of the commodity at price P is given by AF. If this amount were sub-

In response, Hicks [56, 58, 60] defined four measures of the change in a consumer's welfare resulting from an actual or proposed price change. Using the terminology ultimately adopted by Hicks in his *Revision of Demand Theory* [p. 99]:

1. " Compensating variation " is the amount of compensation, paid or received, that will leave the consumer in his *initial* welfare position *following the change in price* if he is free to buy any quantity of the commodity at the new price.

2. " Compensating surplus " is the amount of compensation, paid or received, that will leave the consumer in his *initial* welfare position *following the change in price* if he is constrained to buy at the new price the quantity he would have bought at that price in the absence of compensation.

3. " Equivalent variation " is the amount of compensation, paid or received, that will leave the consumer in his *subsequent* welfare position *in the absence of the price change* if he is free to buy any quantity of the commodity at the old price.

4. " Equivalent surplus " is the amount of compensation, paid or received, that will leave him in his *subsequent* welfare position *in the absence of the price change* if he is constrained to buy at the old price the quantity he would have bought at that price in the absence of compensation.[1]

These four measures are illustrated in Fig. 1 for the case of a price fall. Consider a consumer with income OY_0. The initial price for commodity X is given by the slope of P_0 and falls to P_1. Compensating variation—that is, the maximum sum of money the consumer would be prepared to pay for the privilege of buying the commodity at the lower price in whatever quantity he wished—is Y_0Y_1. Compensating surplus—that is, the maximum sum of money he would be willing to pay for the privilege of buying at the lower price that quantity he would have bought at this price in the absence

---

tracted from his income, he could still reach indifference curve I_0 at E. Note that, in this case, there is no constraint on the quantity the consumer buys whereas, in the Dupuit–Marshallian measure, the consumer is constrained to buy OK units. However, note that there is another plausible measure of the benefit to the consumer of being able to buy X. AG represents the minimum payment the consumer would be prepared to accept to relinquish the privilege of being able to buy X at price P. With this compensation he would still reach indifference curve I_1. (See Patinkin [114, Appendix A] for evidence that Marshall, himself, may have been thinking more along the lines of AG than CD. CD has always been considered in the literature to be the basic Marshallian measure.)

Much of the early discussion concentrated on the introduction of a new commodity. Later treatments have tended to consider this as a special case of a change in price.

[1] Hicks originally called these four measures the *price* compensating variation, the *quantity* compensating variation, the *price* equivalent (or equilibrating) variation and the *quantity* equivalent (or equilibrating) variation respectively. This terminology was challenged by Little [86, p. 170] who insisted on calling them the price equilibrating variation, the quantity equilibrating variation, the price compensating variation and the quantity compensating variation respectively!

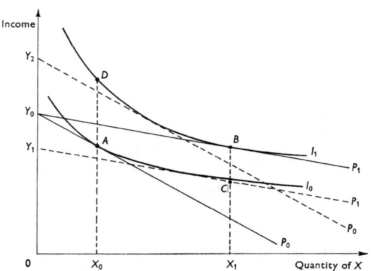

Fig. 1.   Alternative measures of the welfare effect of a price change.

of any compensating loss in income—is BC.   Equivalent variation—that is, the minimum sum of money he would be prepared to accept to relinquish the privilege of buying any quantity desired at the new price—is Y_0Y_2. Equivalent surplus—that is, the minimum sum of money he would accept as compensation to forego the lower price if he has to buy the quantity he would have bought at the original price in the absence of compensation—is AD.

At first sight it might seem strange that there are various alternative measures of the welfare effect of a given price change.[1]   However, as Henderson stressed, for any specific question only one of these measures will usually be relevant. Mishan [99] has argued that, " in all plausible circumstances," only compensating variation and equivalent variation should be considered.   According to Patinkin [114, p. 93], Mishan's contention is correct provided only perfectly competitive equilibrium situations are considered but ceases to be correct if the analysis is broadened to other types of situation (such as a consumer faced by a perfectly discriminating monopolist).

Hicksian Compensated Demand Curve.   A significant contribution to the theory of consumer's surplus has been the development of the Hicksian compensated demand curve (H.C.D.C.).   Whereas the ordinary demand curve (O.D.C.) gives the quantity that a utility maximising consumer with a given income level will demand at each price, the H.C.D.C. shows the quantity a consumer will demand at each price, assuming his income is

----

[1] Knight [74] suggested a fifth measure.   For discussions of this, see [99, 116].   According to Patinkin [114, p. 83], " in principle it would seem possible to define a set of circumstances that would enable us to interpret as consumer's surplus any of the infinite ways there are of measuring the ' distance ' between two indifference curves."

Applied Welfare Economics

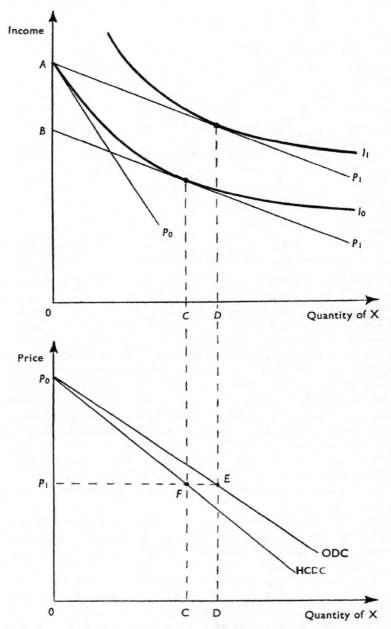

Fɪɢ. 2.   Derivation of the ordinary and compensated demand curves.

adjusted so that he remains on his original indifference curve. The H.C.D.C. also represents the maximum price the consumer would be prepared to pay for an additional unit, assuming that he has already paid the respective maximum prices for each preceding unit [114].

A graphical derivation of the ordinary and compensated demand curves for a " normal " good is presented in Fig. 2. A consumer with income OA will consume none of the commodity at (or above) price P_0 and will be on indifference curve I_0 (that is, P_0 is tangent to indifference curve I_0 at A). At a price P_1 the consumer will purchase OD, yielding point E on his ordinary demand curve. If, however, following the change in price from P_0 to P_1 his income is adjusted by an amount AB so as to keep him on his original indifference curve I_0, with the remaining income OB he will purchase quantity OC. This gives a point F on his compensated demand curve. In this way, by varying price, the O.D.C. can be derived; and if for each price change income is adjusted so as to keep the consumer on I_0, the H.C.D.C. can be derived.

Hicks [60] and Patinkin [114] have demonstrated that the triangle-like area below the H.C.D.C. and above the price line provides an exact measure of the compensating variation in income that would leave the consumer just as well off being able to buy the commodity at the specified price as he would be if he were unable to buy it at all. Thus, area $P_0 P_1 F$ is equal to AB. Thus, the H.C.D.C. can be used to show the effect on the consumer's welfare of introducing a commodity at a particular price. To establish the welfare effect of a change in price, it is necessary to construct a compensated demand curve based on the indifference curve the consumer was on prior to the price change. The appropriate measure would then be the area between the two price lines and the compensated demand curve.[1] To find the

---

[1] $AP_0 B$ is the maximum amount the consumer would be prepared to pay for the privilege of being able to buy the commodity at price P_0 rather than not being able to buy it at all. $AP_1 D$ is the maximum amount he would pay for being able to buy at price P_1 rather than not being able

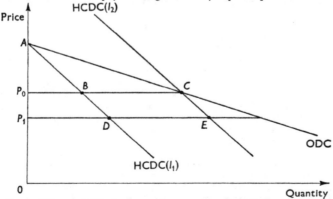

to buy it at all. $P_0 BDP_1$ would be the appropriate measure of the welfare effect of the change in price from P_0 to P_1 if he had already paid compensation and was consuming at B. If, however,

equivalent variation associated with the introduction of a new commodity or with a price change, it would be necessary to use a compensated demand curve based on the indifference curve the consumer would reach following the change.

An important consideration is that the O.D.C. and the H.C.D.C. (based on any indifference level) coincide if the " income effect " is zero. This is because, whereas the H.C.D.C. indicates the substitution effect of a price change, the O.D.C. reflects both the substitution and income effects. Graphically, a zero income effect implies parallel indifference curves at any quantity of the commodity. As a result, all four Hicksian measures and the Dupuit–Marshallian triangle coincide. This is of great practical importance. Hicks, in summing up his exhaustive analysis of consumer's surplus in *A Revision of Demand Theory*, states [60, p. 177]:

> " What in the light of this approach, we have been trying to do is to establish, more precisely than Marshall thought necessary, the conditions needed for the Marshall measure (*i.e.*, the relevant area below the ordinary demand curve) to be a good measure. And so considered, the result of our inquiry is very simple. In order that the Marshall measure of consumer's surplus should be a good measure, one thing alone is needful—that the income effect should be small."

If the income effect is not zero, the sign of the income effect will determine the direction of the bias from using the relevant area below the ordinary demand curve. For falls in the price of a " normal " good, the H.C.D.C. (based on the initial welfare position) will lie to the left of the O.D.C. (as in Fig. 2) and the Dupuit–Marshallian area below the ordinary demand curve will exceed compensating variation. For falls in the price of an " inferior " good, the H.C.D.C. will lie to the right of the O.D.C. and the Dupuit–Marshallian measure will understate compensating variation. The opposite relationships will, of course, hold for equivalent variation.[1]

---

he had not paid any compensation and was consuming at C on his ordinary demand curve, then it is necessary to derive a new compensated demand curve for indifference curve I_2. The appropriate measure of the welfare effect of the price fall would, thus, be P_0CEP_1.

  [1] We might at this point mention that Winch [184] has recently attempted to rehabilitate the Dupuit–Marshallian measure (*i.e.* the relevant area below the ordinary demand curve) in the case of a *non zero* income effect. His argument would *seem* to run as follows (except that we have supplied the hypothetical numbers to simplify the matter.) Suppose that, as a result of a price fall, we could extract from the consumer a sum of five pounds (i.e. compensating variation) so that he is now just as well off (with the new price and five pounds less) as he was originally. If we actually take five pounds from him everything is fine. However, if we do not extract the five pounds from him, these five pounds are now worth, say, six pounds, because of the increase in the purchasing power of money accompanying the price fall. Thus, six pounds represents the " consumer's gain." Thus compensating variation understates the " gain " to the consumer. We are unable to understand this, probably because we think of a " gain " as something the loss of which would leave us where we started. In addition, we are unable to see how Winch would argue the case of an " inferior " good where compensating variation for a price fall exceeds the area below the ordinary demand curve. Presumably he would argue that if the five pounds were not taken away, they would be worth, say, three pounds. Yet the purchasing power of money has surely not fallen.

A Digression on the Relationship Between a Zero Income Effect and a Constant Marginal Utility of Money. A source of some confusion in the literature has been the relationship between a zero income effect and a constant M.U.M. Several authors have treated these as equivalent. In fact, a constant M.U.M. is neither necessary nor sufficient for a zero income effect. It is not necessary since a zero income effect merely implies a constant marginal rate of substitution between the commodity and money at any given quantity of the commodity. A zero income effect is thus consistent with an increasing, constant or decreasing M.U.M. A constant M.U.M. is not sufficient to ensure a zero income effect because, in addition, the marginal utilities would have to be independent and the marginal utility of the commodity would have to be changing.[1]

Aggregation over Commodities

So far the discussion has been confined to a single commodity with the assumption that the prices of all other commodities remain constant. The extension of consumer's surplus to more than one commodity raises additional considerations.

Marshall discussed the possibility of aggregating consumer's surplus over *all* commodities. He realised that it would be impossible to use the extra-expenditure method because a consumer cannot spend increased amounts on all commodities simultaneously. He also recognised that it would be impossible to maintain the assumption of an approximately constant M.U.M. He did propose, as a theoretical possibility, using the relevant area below some aggregate demand curve " if we could find a plan for grouping together in one common demand curve all those things which satisfy the same wants, and are rivals; and also for every group of things of which the services are

---

[1] In order to see this, consider

$$\frac{\partial X}{\partial I} = \begin{vmatrix} 0 & 1 & UY \\ UX & 0 & UXY \\ UY & 0 & UYY \end{vmatrix} \bigg/ \begin{vmatrix} 0 & UX & UY \\ UX & UXX & UXY \\ UY & UXY & UYY \end{vmatrix}$$

where X is the commodity, I is income and Y is " money " [57, p. 307]. First, the numerator may equal zero, even if $UYY \neq 0$, provided that $UX/UY = UXY/UYY$ [13, p. 858]. Secondly, $UYY = 0$ does not ensure that the numerator is zero. The additional requirement is $UXY = 0$. Moreover, if $UXY = UYY = 0$, then for the income effect to be determinate (that is, a non-zero denominator), $UXX \neq 0$ [114, p. 10].

We should emphasise that we are using Y as " money " in the Hicksian sense of a *numéraire*. A constant M.U.M. here means that the marginal utility of the *numéraire* is unaffected by changes in the quantity of the *numéraire* (*i.e.*, $UYY = 0$). It is not assumed here that the marginal utility of the *numéraire* is independent of income and of all prices, other than its own, as Samuelson [133] assumed in discussing one possible interpretation of the constancy of the M.U.M. This later assumption does ensure a zero income effect for every commodity other than the *numéraire*. We might also note that Samuelson's " pure Marshallian case," in which the M.U.M. is independent of all prices but not of income, implies unitary income elasticities of demand for each good and is thus incompatible with a zero income effect for any good. Thus the relationship between a " constant M.U.M." and a zero income effect depends on how the former is interpreted. Our own interpretation would seem to be the one most commonly used in the literature on consumer's surplus. Any reader, who is confused by this necessarily brief discussion, is referred to the excellent article of Patinkin [114].

complementary " [94, p. 842]. However, he fully acknowledged the practical impossibility of doing this (with perhaps less regret than some of his contemporaries [16, 188] thought he should have).

A more practically significant problem for Marshall was the aggregation of consumer's surplus over only a few of the many commodities consumed if their utilities are interdependent. He wrote: " The loss that people would suffer from being deprived both of tea and coffee would be greater than the sum of their losses from being deprived of either alone " [94, p. 131]. He suggested that " this difficulty can be theoretically evaded by grouping the two ' rival ' commodities together under a common demand schedule." However, there is no obvious way of grouping competitive or complementary commodities together under a common demand schedule unless their prices always move proportionally.

Conceptually, compensating and equivalent variations can easily be generalised to the case of a simultaneous change in several prices by the use of index numbers [59, 116] or the " expenditure function " [57, 191]. Given a vector of prices P and a certain utility level U one can minimise expenditure $M = P \cdot X$ subject to the utility constraint $U(X) \geq U$. The functional relationship $M = M(U,P)$ is called the " expenditure function." Suppose that the consumer is originally able to reach utility level U^0 when prices are P^0 and following a change in prices to P^1 is able to reach utility level U^1. Then:

$$\text{Compensating variation} = M(U^0,P^1) - M(U^0,P^0)$$
$$\text{Equivalent variation} \quad = M(U^1,P^0) - M(U^1,P^1)$$

The important question, however, is whether it is possible to obtain, say, aggregate compensating variation from demand curves for the various commodities. As Hicks concludes in his *Revision of Demand Theory* [p. 178], conceptually this is also easy. Consider a simultaneous change in the prices of two commodities X and Y. It is clearly legitimate to obtain aggregate compensating variation by summing the compensating variation associated with the change in the price of X, assuming that the price of Y is fixed at its *initial level*, and the compensating variation associated with the change in the price of Y, assuming that the price of X is held at its *new* level.[1] However, as Hicks [60, p. 179] stresses, the more commodities whose prices are changing the less likely are the income effects to be negligible and the greater the likelihood of errors from using the relevant areas below ordinary demand curves.

    [1] As Patinkin has stressed [114, p. 100], in the general case of interdependent marginal utilities, it would be meaningless to attempt to partition this aggregate compensating variation into " that part due to the change in the price of X " and " that part due to the change in the price of Y." But, as he emphasises, " it is difficult to conceive of policy questions for which such a disentanglement would be of interest. For what concerns us in practice is the total surplus generated by any particular action. The abstract accounting imputation of this total to particular commodities is of no operational significance " [p. 101].

Aggregation over Individuals

So far only a single consumer has been considered. When considering the effects of price changes on all actual and potential consumers of the commodities, additional conceptual problems arise.

Marshall conceded that a problem does exist in that " a pound's worth of satisfaction to an ordinary poor man is a much greater thing than a pound's worth of satisfaction to an ordinary rich man " [94, p. 130]. However, he still felt justified in equating the triangle under the market demand curve for a commodity with collective consumer's surplus on the grounds that " by far the greater number of events with which economics deals, affect in about equal proportions all the different classes of society " [p. 131]. However, Hicks [55] denied the necessity for such a questionable assumption. He claimed that the amount of money which consumers would have to lose in order to make each of them as badly off as prior to the introduction of a commodity has a clear meaning, even though it says nothing about how this loss would be distributed among individual consumers.

Suppose compensating variation for the rth individual is

$$CV_r = M_r (U_r^0, P^1) - M_r (U_r^0, P^0)$$

Then, assuming independent utilities among individuals, aggregate compensating variation is

$$CV_A = \sum_r [M_r (U_r^0, P^1) - M_r (U_r^0, P^0)]$$

If the price of one good only is changing then aggregate compensating variation would be given by the relevant area below the aggregate compensated demand curve (derived for the initial utility level of each individual and obtained by horizontally summing the individual compensated demand curves). A sufficient but not necessary condition for the aggregate compensated demand curve to coincide with the market demand curve is clearly that each individual have a zero income elasticity of demand for the commodity.[1]

Producer's Surplus

Marshall [94] introduced the concept of producer's surplus to formalise the notion that a seller as well as a buyer may receive some sort of surplus from a transaction. When he makes a sale, an individual generally receives

[1] In certain circumstances it may be theoretically possible to find an aggregate utility function such that one could derive the compensated demand function from it by a process equivalent to that used to derive an individual's compensated demand function. Gorman [47] has shown that a suitably behaved aggregate utility function can be constructed if individual utility indices are such that, at any given price ratio, all income consumption curves are parallel straight lines. Eisenberg [38] has demonstrated that an aggregate utility function can be constructed for all prices if individual utility indices are homogeneous (though not necessarily identical) and if each individual's share of the total income remains constant (i.e., $M_r = K_r M$ where K_r is a constant).

something which has a greater direct or indirect utility to him than the utility of the thing he gives up. To this extent he receives a surplus. Marshall presumably used the term " producer's surplus " to stress the close symmetry of this concept with consumer's surplus.[1] This terminology may, in retrospect, have been unfortunate, for the literature on this topic suffers from a somewhat spurious separation of the concepts of producer's surplus and economic rent, both of which relate to the same phenomenon. The situation is exacerbated by the apparent existence of some confusion over what exactly " producer's surplus " refers to. Indeed, Mishan has recently argued that the term " producer's surplus " is " misleading and otiose " and should be " struck from the economist's vocabulary " [103, p. 1279] in favour of the more general concept of economic rent. We will now discuss these two concepts and, in so doing, attempt to show why Mishan came to this conclusion.

Meaning. Whereas on the demand side consumers may be considered as a relatively homogeneous group, the situation on the supply side is complicated by the existence of diverse groups of sellers. There are, for example, sellers of final products (that is, firms) and sellers of the services of land, entrepreneurial ability, labour and capital. All of these groups may receive surpluses of some sort. One source of confusion over the concept of producer's surplus is to whom the term " producers " refers. There are two possible interpretations which have not been carefully distinguished in the literature. The first interpretation is that the term refers solely to the owners of firms. The second is that it refers to the owners of factors of production.

The first interpretation is plausible for it is the one perhaps suggested by the term itself. Moreover, on one occasion Marshall did define producer's surplus as " the excess of the gross receipts which a producer gets for any of his commodities over their prime cost—that is, over that extra cost which he incurs in order to produce those things and which he could have escaped if he had not produced them " [92, p. 495].

The second interpretation is much more comprehensive and seems to be the one implied by most authors. Marshall himself seems to have meant this interpretation for he generally used the term to encompass the surpluses of all factors of production. For example, he wrote, " *Producer's surplus* is a convenient name for the genus of which the rent of land is the leading species " [92, p. 495]. Moreover, when he considered the surplus enjoyed by a worker, he wrote [94, p. 141]:

> " So if the price paid to him for doing any work is an adequate
> reward for that part which he does most unwillingly; and if as generally

[1] In order to stress the very close relationship between these two surpluses, Marshall wrote [94, p. 831]: " These two sets of surpluses are not independent, and it would be easy to reckon them up so as to count the same thing twice. For when we have reckoned the producer's surplus at the value of the general purchasing power which he derives from his labour or saving, we have reckoned implicitly his consumer's surplus too, provided his character and the circumstances of his environment are given."

happens the same payment is given for that part of the work which he does less unwillingly and at less real cost to himself, then from that part he obtains a producer's surplus."

Measurement. A second source of confusion closely related to the meaning of the concept has arisen over its measurement. The traditional measure of producer's surplus is the area above the product supply curve and below the price line.[1] An important consideration, therefore, is what this area actually measures.

In the short run, the area above a competitive firm's short-run supply curve and below the price line provides a measure of the " excess of gross receipts over prime costs " since the firm's short-run supply curve coincides with its short-run marginal cost curve.[2] This surplus, formally equivalent to " quasirent," is attributable to the short-run fixity of some factor(s) of production.[3] For a perfectly competitive industry in the short run, the area above the industry supply curve and below the price line is a measure of the aggregate surplus accruing to the owners of firms provided that the prices of all variable factors of production are fixed—that is, assuming their supplies are perfectly elastic to the industry in question.[4] In this case the traditional

---

[1] A *caveat* may be in order here. Marshall drew an industry " supply curve " and attached meaning to the area above it [94, p. 811]. However, he stressed that this was not a normal supply curve but rather a " particular expenses curve." This curve, obtained by placing firms in order of

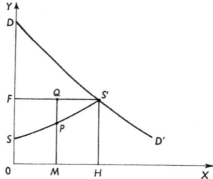

diminishing efficiency, is drawn with reference to a specific industry output and represents a particular phase in the industry. All firms are assumed to have access to the internal and external economies pertaining to this output. In the figure SS' is the particular expenses curve drawn with reference to industry output, OH; DD' is the demand curve; and $S'H$ is the equilibrium price per unit. The producer of the OHth unit has no differential advantage, but the producer of the OMth unit has a differential advantage QP. The excess of price over particular expenses—that is, QP—is his producer's surplus or rent. The area SFS' thus provides a measure of the aggregate surplus enjoyed by non-marginal firms.

[2] For simplicity in exposition, it is assumed that the minimum of the average variable cost curve occurs at a very small output.

[3] This, at least, is the usual definition of quasirent, that is, " the excess of receipts over total variable costs " [150, p. 193]. For a different definition of quasirent, see Davis [30, p. 247].

[4] If the price of a necessary factor increases as industry use of the factor expands, then this area will overstate the aggregate surplus to owners. In the figure, at price P_1 industry output is Q_1,

measure is, in a sense, consistent with the first interpretation of producer's surplus, as a surplus which accrues to the owners of firms in their production and sale of the product. However, it should be stressed that this surplus results from the ownership by the firms in the industry of the fixed factors of production.

For a perfectly competitive industry in the long run, the supply curve is, according to traditional theory, a locus of minimum average costs for the industry. Competitive forces ensure that in equilibrium each firm produces at the minimum of its long-run average costs curve and that this minimum is the same for all firms. For each firm, total revenue equals total cost and there are no excess profits. This is true even if the long-run industry supply curve is positively sloped. Thus, the area above such a curve and below the price line says nothing about the welfare of owners of firms.[1] Consequently, using this area as a measure of producers' surplus is inconsistent with the narrower interpretation of the concept. Thus, if producer's surplus refers solely to something gained by the owner of a firm, then in a perfectly competitive situation it only has relevance to the short run and is then formally equivalent to a quasirent attributable to the firm's ownership of fixed factors.

But what about the wider interpretation of producer's surplus? Does the relevant area above a rising long-run industry supply curve have any rela-

and owners' surplus is AP_1B. ΣMC_1 represents the sum of what individual firms think they would

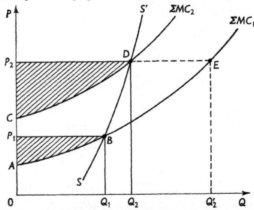

supply at various product prices, given prevailing factor prices. If product price rises to P_2 and the prices of factors remain constant, supply would rise to Q_2' and the surplus would be AEP_2. However, if the additional demand for a necessary factor leads to a rise in its price, there will be an upward shift in marginal costs. Actual output rises to Q_2, and the surplus accruing to the owners of the firms (as a result of their ownership of the fixed factors of production) is CDP_2. Thus the area above the actual supply curve, SS', does *not* reflect the welfare of the owners of the firms in the industry, in any sense.

[1] It may, of course, to some degree reflect rent to the superior entrepreneurial ability of certain owners. However, since they would still receive this if they were employed by other firms in the industry, this surplus is traditionally considered an opportunity cost for that particular firm.

tion to the welfare of the owners of the factors of production? This clearly depends on the nature of the supply curve in question. The literature on the long-run supply curve of a perfectly competitive industry is vast [127, 164, 73, 124], and only a few summary remarks can be made here. There is widespread agreement that it does represent the average costs of each firm in the industry. However, these costs may include payments to factors which are in the nature of rents or surpluses—that is, loosely speaking, payments in excess of the minimum amounts necessary to elicit their services.[1] While these are costs from the point of view of the firms, they are not real costs to society. The inevitable question is whether the relevant area above a competitive industry's supply curve represents these rents. The answer is " yes, if the supply curve, as well as being an *average cost curve including rents*, is also a *marginal cost curve excluding rents*."

One case in which this condition is met is that of Ricardian rent to a fixed supply of land. Consider an industry with a fixed supply of land and with all other factors available at constant prices. The long-run industry supply curve slopes upward because of diminishing returns in the application of these other factors to the absolutely limited factor. The supply curve is then a long-run average cost curve including rent to land and a long-run marginal cost curve excluding rent to land [164, pp. 207–10]. The area above this curve provides an unambiguous measure of the Ricardian rent to land [103, p. 1275].

Another suggested case is where one necessary factor of production has some inelasticity of supply so that the industry can buy greater quantities of it only at higher prices. If all other factors are perfectly elastic in supply, then in the absence of technological external economies or diseconomies, the industry long-run product supply curve will be a marginal cost curve excluding rents as well as an average cost curve including rents. The relevant area above the product supply curve will reflect the rents received by the owners of this particular factor, that is, excess payments made for intramarginal units of the factor [128, p. 134].

Recently Mishan [103] has argued that, for an industry using two variable inputs, neither of which is perfectly elastic in supply, the area above the long-run supply curve cannot be associated with a net gain by both factors taken together.[2] He wrote [103, p. 1277]:

" The industry supply curve is, admittedly, an average cost curve *including* rents—the rents of both factors in fact, since these alter as the

[1] We will discuss more precisely the definition of economic rent later in the paper.
[2] Recently Shepherd [144] has challenged Mishan's conclusion. He asserts that the area above the long-run industry supply curve does measure the rent to intramarginal factors of production, *i.e.*, the excess earnings of those factors over the amount necessary to keep them in the industry. He argues that, in the case of constant returns to scale and input prices that vary directly with the industry output, then the supply curve—as well as being an average cost curve including rents—is also a marginal cost curve excluding intramarginal increments of factor rents [144, p. 209]. However, Shepherd does not really seem to get at the heart of Mishan's analysis. Rather, invoking

industry's equilibrium output expands. But it is *not* also a marginal curve *excluding* rent (as in the Ricardian average cost curve). An average curve including rent, equal to a marginal curve excluding rent, can be derived only in those cases in which rent accrues to a single fixed factor, all other factors being infinitely elastic. In the more general case, however, where the changes in rents of all factors are fully taken account of in the average curve, including of course the rental of capital (but no Knightian profit), the area above the rising industry supply curve carries no economic significance."

So far we have considered only a perfectly competitive industry. In an imperfectly competitive industry, firms may receive a surplus in the long run as well as in the short run, for there is no inevitable force ensuring zero excess profits in the long run. Such a surplus results from some degree of market power. In the case of monopoly, it is essentially a rent from being the only seller in the market.

By way of a summary, Mishan's contention that the term producer's surplus could safely be dispensed with is most convincing. It is more satisfactory to think in terms of economic rent—rent to a short-run fixity of some factor of production, rent to land, rent to entrepreneurial ability, rent to market power and so on. This has the very important added advantage of directing explicit attention to the markets for factors of production.

Economic Rent

Having rejected the term producer's surplus in favour of the term economic rent, we find that there is also some disagreement over the appropriate definition and measurement of the latter.[1] The concept of economic rent dates back to Ricardo [121]. Since land is a " free gift of nature," he considered all the earnings of land to be a surplus or rent. Subsequently, the term economic rent was also used to designate part of the earnings of labour, capital and entrepreneurial ability. The classical definition of economic rent came to be the payment to a factor of production over and above the minimum necessary to induce it to do its work. For example, according to Joan Robinson, " the minimum payment necessary to induce a labourer to continue to work with any given intensity is the real income which will maintain his physiological efficiency at an adequate level," while " the necessary minimum for an entrepreneur is the level of earnings which is sufficient to prevent him from relapsing into the ranks of employed labour " [128, p. 103].

A somewhat different definition of economic rent which has been traced back to the writings of Pareto [113] is the excess payment to a factor over and

---

the analysis of Ellis and Fellner, [39] he *states* that the average cost of the industry is also the cost of the marginal unit of industry output, *taken by itself*, that is, exclusive of intramarginal increments of factor rents [p. 209]. But this seems to be the very assertion that Mishan is questioning.

[1] For example, see the debate between Wessel [177] and Mishan [105].

above the minimum amount necessary to keep it in its " present occupation." Whereas the former definition revolves around whether or not the factor is supplied to the *economy*, this latter definition is applicable to questions as to whether or not the factor is supplied to a particular industry or to a particular firm (depending on the definition of " present occupation ").[1] Some economists restrict this latter conception of economic rent further by defining it as the excess of a factor's current earnings over its earnings in its next best alternative use. For example, according to Samuelson [135, p. 543], " we should term the excess of his income above the alternative wage he could earn elsewhere as a pure rent." This definition ignores all the nonpecuniary rewards a factor owner may receive from his work.

The measure of economic rent that is traditionally suggested is the area above the supply curve of a factor and below the price line. Depending on the definition of rent, the supply curve would be derived from the factor owner's indifference map or from his maximum earnings elsewhere.

Mishan on Economic Rent. In 1959 Mishan [100] rejected all these various definitions of economic rent on the ground that they treat rent as a surplus which may be appropriated without any effects on the supply of the factor. He attacked the definition involving the excess of payments over maximum earnings elsewhere because of its complete neglect of nonpecuniary considerations. Moreover, he questioned the use of the area above the supply curve of a factor as a measure of rent. He demonstrated that, in fact, economic rent is symmetrical with consumer's surplus in that they are " both measures of the change in the individual's welfare when the set of prices facing him are altered or the constraints upon him are altered. Any distinction between them is one of convenience only; consumer's surpluses have reference to demand prices, economic rents to supply prices " [100, p. 394].

Accordingly, he defined four measures of a change in economic rent

---

[1] For a discussion of the relative merits of these alternative definitions, see, for example, Worcester [185], Wessel [178], and Shepherd [144]. Much of the discussion has revolved around the usefulness of economic rent for explaining the distributive shares of the various factors [70]. This is outside the scope of this paper and will not be alluded to further (even though Ricardo considered this the " principal problem in Political Economy "). As for the comparison between the Ricardian and Paretian concepts, Shepherd wrote [144, p. 211]: " But of what analytical value is it to know that most factor income is in excess of the amount that will deter the factor from complete economic inactivity? . . . The reason for this sterility is that the price that will trigger a decision to do *anything* rather than *nothing* does not imply enough information about either the menu of society's wants or the economy's production possibilities. Paretian opportunity costs, on the other hand, give society's valuation of alternatives foregone and imply thereby an extensive matrix of product and factor supply and demand relationships. In short, propositions about economic welfare involve factor allocation among industries (occupations and commodities), not simply factor allocation between idleness on the one hand and *any* socially useful activity on the other." If a choice *has* to be made between the Paretian and Ricardian concepts, Shepherd's argument is convincing. But it is by no means clear why such a choice must be made on general grounds. In any specific situation the choice would be apparent. *As Lerner has stressed, the relevant rent concept would depend on the demarcated area of the economy under consideration, which, in turn, would depend on both spatial and temporal considerations* [81, Ch. 18].

resulting from an actual or proposed price change. Using the same terminology as we did on the demand side:

1. " Compensating variation " is the amount of compensation, paid or received, that will leave the factor owner in his *initial* welfare position following the change in price if he is free to supply any quantity after compensation.

2. " Compensating surplus " is the amount of compensation, paid or received, that will leave the factor owner in his *initial* welfare position following the change in price if he is constrained to supply the quantity he would have supplied at the new price in the absence of compensation.

3. " Equivalent variation " is the amount of compensation, paid or received, that will leave the factor owner in his *subsequent* welfare position in the absence of the price change if he is free to supply any quantity after compensation.

4. " Equivalent surplus " is the amount of compensation, paid or received, that will leave the factor owner in his *subsequent* welfare position in the absence of the price change if he is constrained to supply at the old price the quantity he would have supplied at that price in the absence of compensation.

These four measures are illustrated for the case of a rise in price in Fig. 3 where Y represents income, X is the quantity supplied and the slope of OP represents the price (or wage) per unit of the factor. Suppose the price of the factor shifts from OP_1 to OP_2. The supplier moves from equilibrium point Q_1 to equilibrium point Q_2. Compensating variation is OY_C, equivalent variation is OY_E, compensating surplus is Q_2A, and equivalent surplus is Q_1B. Mishan argued that the most useful measures of the welfare effect of a price change are likely to be compensating and equivalent variations. He claimed that the traditional conception of economic rent is unsatisfactory because it implies a constraint on the quantity supplied as in the compensating and equivalent surpluses.

Ordinary and Compensated Supply Curves. From the individual's preference map, it is possible to derive his ordinary supply curve (O.S.C.) showing the quantities he will supply at various prices. In Fig. 4, Y is income, X is quantity supplied, and P is price. He will supply quantity X_1 at price P_1, quantity X_2 at price P_2, and quantity X_3 at price P_3. These give three points on his O.S.C. By varying price continuously, the O.S.C. can be obtained. It is also possible to derive his compensated supply curve (C.S.C.) for any initial position. Suppose that the individual is initially supplying quantity X_1 at price P_1. If price rises to P_2 and if a lump sum tax is imposed on him so as to keep him on indifference curve I_1, he will supply X_2' at the new price. Similarly, if price rises to P_3 and if a compensating variation in income keeps him on indifference curve I_1, he will supply X_3'. In this way his C.S.C. can be drawn. There is, of course, a C.S.C. corresponding to any initial position.

Whereas the O.S.C. may be backward bending at certain prices, reflecting an increased desire for leisure, the C.S.C. can never be negatively sloped. The C.S.C. could theoretically be used to find the effect on the welfare of the factor owner of raising the price. Thus, P_1ABP_2 would represent the maximum lump sum payment he would be prepared to pay for the privilege of facing P_2 rather than P_1.[1] Similarly, P_1AEP_3 would be the maximum amount he would be prepared to pay for facing P_3 rather than P_1.[2]

[1] By construction, the individual is indifferent between, on the one hand, receiving price P_1 and, on the other hand, receiving price P_2 and, at the same time, paying compensating variation CV_y. Clearly, $CV_y \geq P_1ADP_2$; for if he gives up P_1ADP_2, he is still as well off supplying $P_2D = P_1A$ at price P_2. The individual is also indifferent between, on the one hand, receiving price P_1 and the same compensating variation CV_y and, on the other hand, receiving price P_2. Clearly, $CV_y \leq P_1CBP_2$; for if he receives P_1CBP_2, he is just as well off supplying $P_1C = P_2B$ at price P_1 as he is receiving P_2. Thus, compensating variation CV_y cannot be less than rectangle P_1ADP_2 nor exceed rectangle P_1CBP_2.

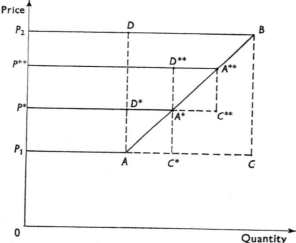

Suppose that, instead of an abrupt change in price from P_1 to P_2, there is a series of smaller price increases. At each step, there is a compensating variation in income. By similar reasoning, the compensating variation for a price rise from P_1 to P^* lies between rectangles $P_1AD^*P^*$ and $P_1C^*A^*P^*$. Likewise, the compensating variation for a price rise from P^* to P^{**} lies between rectangles $P^*A^*D^{**}P^{**}$ and $P^*C^{**}A^{**}P^{**}$. (Since, by assumption, the individual is indifferent between positions A, A^*, and A^{**}, compensating variation from P_1 to P^{**} is the sum of those from P_1 to P^* and P^* to P^{**}.) In this way, it is theoretically possible to reduce the limits between which CV_y must lie. If price is assumed to vary continuously from OP_1 to OP_2, supply expands continuously along curve AB, and the limits of both sums of rectangles become equal to P_1ABP_2. This proof is exactly analogous to that used by Hicks [60, pp. 72–74] in the case of the compensated demand curve.

[2] Note that area P_2BEP_3 will only give the effect on the welfare of the factor owner of a change in price from P_2 to P_3, provided that he had previously paid a lump-sum tax of P_1ABP_2 and was still on indifference curve I_1. If such compensating variation had not been paid, it would be necessary to derive a compensated supply curve corresponding to point F.

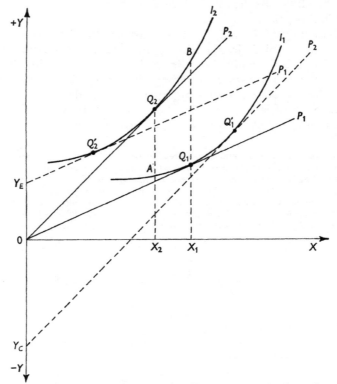

FIG. 3. Alternative measures of the welfare effect on a seller of a change in price.

The sufficient condition for Mishan's four measures to be equal and for the O.S.C. and C.S.C. to coincide is that the indifference curves be parallel at any given quantity of X.[1]

[1] Parallel indifference curves correspond to Mishan's condition of a zero " welfare effect." In Fig. 3 the movement from Q_1 to Q_1' is the substitution effect, and the movement from Q_1' to Q_2 is the " welfare effect." Whereas the substitution effect will always lead to the substitution of income for leisure as price rises (i.e. to an increase in the supply of X) the " welfare effect " may work in any direction. In Fig. 3, the " welfare effect " reflects an increased desire for leisure sufficient to outweigh the substitution effect and to lead to a fall in quantity supplied as price rises from P_1 to P_2.

Mishan called this the " welfare effect " rather than the income effect because income is endogenous. At many points in this paper, we refer to the " welfare effect of a price change " by which we mean the total effect on the welfare of the individual of a price change. This differs, of course, from Mishan's " welfare effect." We might mention at this time that our presentation of Mishan's four measures differs in some significant respects from his own. Whereas we have considered the supply side without mentioning the factor owner's demand for commodities, Mishan considered both simultaneously. He assumed that the individual, in possession of given resources, will maximise the utility function $W [U(X_1, X_2, \ldots, X_N)]$, subject to the constraint $\sum_{i=1}^{n} P_i X_i = 0$, where a subset of the X's will be negative in the optimal solution, indicating that the individual will supply at least one good or service. In this way he was able to demonstrate the symmetry between consumer's surplus and economic rent.

The Mishan measures of economic rent and the notion of a compensated supply curve are applicable to all factors of production. In general, the shape of the indifference curves will depend on the type of the factor. For example, if the analysis concerns the daily work supply of a labourer, the indifference curves are likely to become vertical at some level of work (say, 18 hours a day). On the other hand, a landowner who has no alternative use for land would have horizontal indifference curves up to his endowment of land.

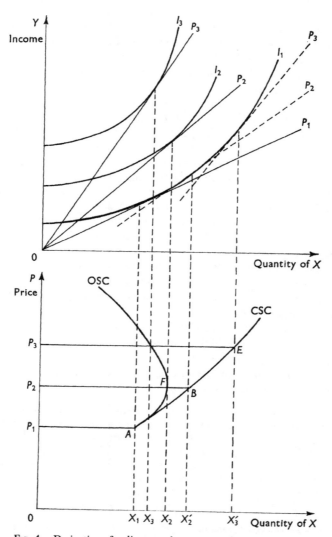

Fig. 4. Derivation of ordinary and compensated supply curves.

The extension of the Mishan formulation of economic rent to more than one outlet for the factor owner's service and to more than one individual is symmetrical to the demand side.[1]

Some Concluding Remarks

The traditional conception of economic surplus is that in a transaction an individual generally gives up something which has a (direct or indirect) utility in exchange for something which has at least as great a (direct or indirect) utility. To the extent that the latter is greater, he receives an " economic surplus " from this transaction. Given that " utils " are not measurable, the most meaningful measure of this surplus is in terms of the usual medium of exchange, money, even though money itself affords only indirect utility. While the monetary measure of this surplus which appeals most to experience is, for a buyer, the extra amount he would have been prepared to pay for something and, for a seller, the difference between what he actually receives for a sale and the minimum amount he would have been prepared to accept, the more operational monetary measure is the relevant area below the demand curve or above the supply line.

The more recent Hicksian notions of compensating and equivalent variations look at the concept of economic surplus from a slightly different viewpoint. Any change in the trading possibilities facing an individual is likely to affect his welfare. A meaningful measure of the effect on his welfare is the lump sum transfer which would offset this change where the measure is defined in such a way that, following the transfer, the individual is free to decide what quantities he wishes to buy or sell (and, thus, to satisfy the marginal conditions of welfare maximisation). Conceptually, compensating or equivalent variations for a single price change may be measured exactly by the relevant area below or above the appropriate compensated demand or supply curve.

An inevitable question is what the extensive theoretical discussion of the concept of economic surplus has achieved. Much of the debate has been of a highly abstract nature and divorced from any foreseeable practical application. The participants in the debate clearly appreciated this. For example, Mishan wrote [99, p. 27]:

> " Since the rehabilitation of consumer's surplus by Professor Hicks several attempts have appeared to establish the most appropriate money measures of this concept, attempts accompanied by apologies for introducing into the concept refinements which are apparently of little practical significance. Consequently, it is with some misgivings that I find myself fiddling about with this somewhat fragile notion of consumer's surplus, albeit not without hope that the result of the fiddling about will be to cause it to shed a little of its ostensible complexity."

[1] Mishan provides a useful graphical presentation of the case of a factor owner with two outlets for his services [100, pp. 206–8].

Yet, as the participants also realised, precision is of the utmost importance in any discipline. Certainly, the contributions of Hicks, Henderson, Mishan, Patinkin, Bishop and many others have given greater precision to the concept of economic surplus as formulated initially by Ricardo, Dupuit and Marshall.

II. Uses of the Concept of Economic Surplus

We now present some of the applications of the concept of economic surplus. We discuss in turn two broad areas: (1) the misallocation of resources in a closed economy and (2) international trade. Finally we briefly discuss some studies pertaining to price instability and the welfare effects of investment. Our general approach is to trace the historical development of the concept's uses in these areas. We intend to be illustrative rather than exhaustive in our coverage. Moreover, we emphasise the methods of analysis and the questions addressed without reiterating the theoretical considerations discussed in the previous section.[1]

Misallocation of Resources in a Closed Economy

Implicit in most of the studies which attempt to identify and measure the welfare effects of resource misallocation is the traditional belief that the competitive equilibrium represents an optimum. As Samuelson observed, " at least from the time of the physiocrats and Adam Smith there has never been absent from the main body of economic literature the feeling that in some sense perfect competition represented an optimal solution " [137, p. 203]. Lerner also stressed that " the importance of the competitive position lies in its implications of being a position which in some way or another is better than other positions. It is the position in which the ' Invisible Hand ' has exerted its beneficial influences to the utmost. It has become the symbol for the social optimum " [79, p. 12]. A discussion of the reasons why the competitive equilibrium has been considered optimal would take us beyond the scope of this paper. In any case, the concept of economic surplus is not necessary, nor has it been found useful, for defining an optimum. In contrast, it has been considered by many to be particularly useful for measuring the welfare effects of deviations from an optimum [55, p. 112; 82]. It is to this purpose that the majority of its applications are directed.

Dupuit and Marshall. This type of application can be traced back to Dupuit's analysis of the welfare effects of the imposition of an excise tax [34]. In Fig. 5, as a result of the imposition of a per unit tax, *AB*, price rises from

---

[1] In particular, the reader should keep in mind the conditions which are necessary if the area above a product supply curve is to have any welfare meaning. Throughout this section we will follow the authors' interpretations of such areas (and their use of the term " producer's surplus ") without discussing in each case whether these interpretations are justified. As Mishan [103] has pointed out, many authors who have used the concept of producer's surplus have failed to state explicitly the nature of their supply curves.

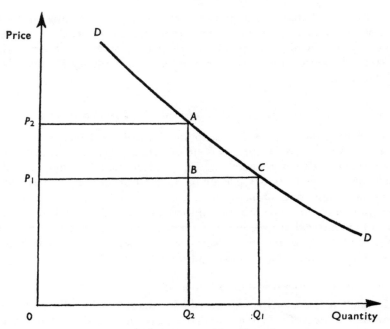

Fɪɢ. 5.   Dupuit's analysis of the effects of a tax.

P_1 to P_2. The loss in consumers' surplus is P_1P_2AC; the gain in tax revenue is P_1P_2AB. Thus, the *net* social loss is represented by the area of ABC. From this, Dupuit derived his famous theorem that the net social loss is (approximately) proportional to the square of the tax.[1] Dupuit justified cancelling out area P_1P_2AB on the grounds that it represents " merely a change in the distribution of wealth " [34, p. 36]. This one-to-one weighting characterises most of the later studies based on the concept of economic surplus.[2]

Dupuit's analysis was extended by Marshall to incorporate producers. Marshall used the diagram reproduced in Fig. 6 " to represent roughly the leading features of the problem " [94, p. 473]. If SS' is the original " supply curve," then the imposition of a per unit tax Ea $(= AT = Ss)$ will vertically shift this curve to ss'.[3] The loss in consumers' surplus is $caAC$; the loss to

---

[1] Assuming that the demand curve is linear in the relevant region, the net social loss is given by

$$\text{NSL} = \tfrac{1}{2}(P_2 - P_1)(Q_1 - Q_2)$$

Given the linearity assumption

$$Q_1 - Q_2 = K(P_2 - P_1) \text{ where } K \text{ is a constant.}$$

Therefore,

$$\text{NSL} = \frac{K}{2}(P_2 - P_1)^2$$

where $P_2 - P_1$ equals the tax.

[2] We will briefly return to this aspect in the concluding section.

[3] See the discussion above on Marshall's " particular expenses curve".

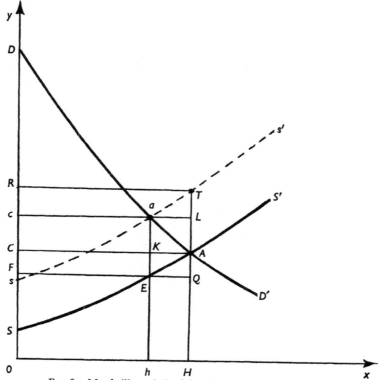

FIG. 6.   Marshall's analysis of the effects of a tax and subsidy.

producers is $CAEF$; and the tax revenue is $caEF$. Thus, the net social loss is aAE. Using the same diagram, Marshall demonstrated the effect of a per unit subsidy. Suppose in this case the initial supply curve is ss'. With the payment of a subsidy of aE per unit of output, the supply curve becomes SS'. The cost to taxpayers, $RTAC$, exceeds the sum of the gain to consumers, $caAC$, and the gain to producers, $RTac$. Thus, the net loss is given by the area of TAa.

Nerlove and Wallace. This type of analysis has been used by Nerlove [110] and Wallace [166] to evaluate a number of government domestic programmes for agriculture. Nerlove considered three alternative types of support programmes: (I) the government sets a support price above the equilibrium price and purchases and destroys all the excess; (II) the government sets a support price in excess of the equilibrium, and the resultant output is sold on the open market with the government making up the difference between the support price and the market price by means of a per unit subsidy; and (III) the desired price is achieved by directly restricting output.[1] These

[1] For the ensuing analysis, it is necessary that the production quotas be perfectly divisible and transferable thus ensuring they will be optimally allocated among the individual firms.

three programmes are illustrated in Fig. 7.   He assumes that SS' represents
the marginal social cost of the resources used to produce the commodity,
and DD' reflects the marginal value of the commodity to the community.
It is also assumed that each programme is designed to achieve a price OM.
The net losses of the three programmes are given by the areas of $ANJPC$,
JPE and NJI, respectively.   Nerlove pointed out that, assuming a given

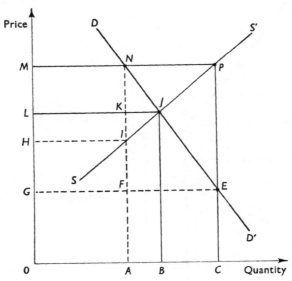

FIG. 7.   Nerlove's analysis of alternative government programmes.

support price, the first type of programme will never involve a lower net
social loss than the other programmes.   Wallace demonstrated that, for a
given support price,

$$NSL \text{ (III)} \gtreqless NSL \text{ (II)}$$
$$\text{as } \eta \gtreqless \epsilon$$

where NSL (III) and NSL (II) are the net social losses associated with
programmes of type III and type II, respectively, and η and ϵ are the absolute values of the price elasticities of demand and supply, respectively.[1]

Wallace also analysed the effects of output restriction through controlling
the input of a particular factor of production (for example, through acreage
control).   In Fig. 8 the effect of the programme is to shift the marginal
social cost curve from CS to CS' as a result of the less efficient use of other
inputs with the limited input.   The net social loss is given by the area of
ABC.   Of this loss, ABD may be associated with the reduction in output
(as in type III above), while ADC may be attributed to the inefficient use of

[1] In addition, Nerlove and Wallace briefly compared these programmes on the assumption that
they are designed to achieve a given gain to producers.

other resources with the limited input. For a given price increase, this programme will, therefore, entail a higher net social loss than the programme of type III. This framework of analysis was employed by Johnson [67] to estimate the net social cost of the United States tobacco programme. He extended the analysis to take into account the strong monopoly power which the United States holds in the world market for flue-cured tobacco. The

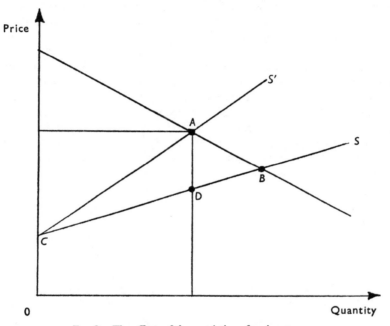

FIG. 8. The effects of the restriction of an input.

resulting monopoly rent represents a gain which he set against the losses from the output restriction and from the less efficient use of other factors with the limited acreage.[1]

Monopoly and Economic Welfare. In recent years there has been a growing interest in the use of the concept of economic surplus to analyse the welfare effects of monopolies. In fact, Dupuit suggested that his analysis of the effects of an excise tax could be applied to the case of a monopolist who restricts output. Marshall also applied the concept of economic surplus to monopolies. He considered the case of a " benevolent " monopolist faced with decreasing costs [94]. If the monopolist were to " weight " consumers' surplus and his own profits equally and to maximise their sum, he would

[1] We might also mention that Welch [173] has studied supply controls with marketable quotas and, unlike previous authors, introduced uncertainty into the analysis. He demonstrated that supply control under conditions of uncertainty results in greater social costs than under certainty. In addition, Hushak [63] has very recently studied the welfare effects of the United States voluntary corn diversion programme.

produce at the point where price equals marginal cost. Thus, he would (with a decreasing average cost curve) take a loss on his operation. The output level would decline as less weight was attached to consumers' surplus. In the extreme case where he disregarded entirely the effects on consumers, he would set output so as to maximise profits.

In 1934, Lerner [79] presented an interesting study of the welfare effects of monopoly. In Fig. 9, AR is the average revenue or demand curve; MR is the marginal revenue curve; AC represents average costs including rents to intra-marginal factors (and marginal costs excluding rents); and MC represents marginal costs including rents to factor owners. P' is the competitive point where output is OM' and price is $M'P'$. A profit-maximising monopolist would produce output OM and receive a price MP. The loss in consumers' surplus under monopoly is $SPP'T$. The gain in monopoly profit (or rent) is $RQPS$. The loss in rents to factors of production is given by $RQP'T$. Thus, the net social loss is PQP'. Lerner differentiated between that part of monopoly rent which essentially results from the monopolist's exploitation of consumers and that part which results from his monopsonistic exploitation of the owners of factors of production. He argued

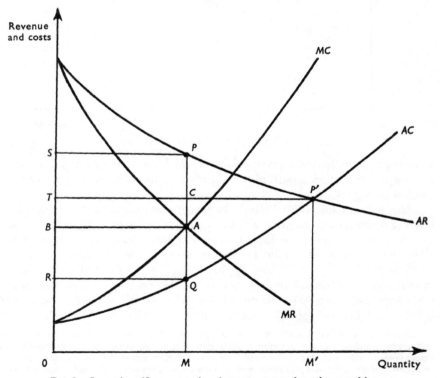

Fig. 9. Lerner's welfare comparison between monopoly and competition.

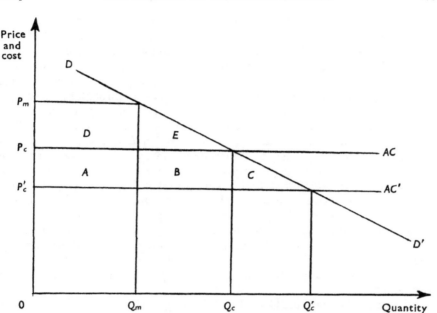

FIG. 10.   Welfare comparison between monopoly and competition.

that the former is properly measured by *SPAB* and the latter by *BAQR*. From this he concluded that " the mark of the absence of monopoly is the equality of price or *average* receipts to *marginal* costs, and the mark of the absence of monopsony is the equality of *average* costs to *marginal* receipts " [79, p. 11].[1]

Harberger [51] seems to have been the first to use the concept of economic surplus to quantify the welfare effects of monopolies.   Suppose that, in Fig. 10, *AC* represents constant per unit costs under *both* monopoly and competition.   Then area *E* represents what he called a " dead weight loss " to society.[2]   Tullock [160] argued that the assumption of identical unit costs under monopoly and competition leads to an underestimate of the loss from monopoly.   He maintained that investments designed to secure

---

[1] Lerner went on to suggest his famous index of monopoly power for the case of horizontal costs,

$$\text{Monopoly Power} = (P - MC)/P.$$

He stressed that this index cannot be applied to the whole economy.   To measure the " social " degree of monopoly, he proposed modifications necessary for taking into account more than one product and monopolistic practices in industries producing raw materials.

[2] Harberger estimated the welfare loss from monopolies in the United States to be less than 0·10% of national income.   Schwartzman [140, 141, 142], using the same framework, and Worcester [186], using a similar framework, also estimated the welfare losses to be quite small.   However, Kamerschen [71] suggested that the welfare loss to American society is significantly higher—roughly 6% of the average national income.   Stigler [151, p. 34], in commenting on Harberger's study, wrote: " If this estimate is correct, economists might serve a more useful purpose if they fought fires or termites instead of monopoly."   (In fact, Stigler argued that this estimate may well be too low because of Harberger's method of estimating monopoly profit, his assumption of unitary elasticity of demand, and his neglect of rents to factors of production employed by the monopolist.)

and defend a monopoly position are often of significant magnitude and are socially undesirable so that social costs under monopoly are higher than under competition. Recently, Bell [8] and Comanor and Leibenstein [21] have also argued that unit costs are likely to be higher under monopoly. Bell attributed the higher unit costs to the willingness of firms enjoying monopoly profits to share gains with their employees through higher wages. His analysis may also be illustrated in Fig. 10. Suppose unit costs are AC under monopoly and AC' under competition. He asserts that the welfare loss from the monopoly is $E + B + C$, of which E is due to " monopoly profit " and $B + C$ is due to " monopoly wages." (Area A represents a " transfer " from monopoly profit to employees' wages.)[1] Comanor and Leibenstein attributed their assumption of higher unit costs under monopoly to " X-inefficiency "—that is, to the failure of the monopolist to minimise costs because of the absence of the " competitive stick." Their analysis may also be demonstrated in Fig. 10. Again, unit costs are AC under monopoly and AC' under competition. They assert that the welfare loss from monopoly is given by $C + E + B + A$. They call A the " X-inefficiency component " and $E + B + C$ the " allocative inefficiency component." [2]

Recently, Williamson [180, 181, 182] suggested that in certain circumstances unit costs may be *lower* under monopoly than under competition. Assume that in Fig. 10 AC' is now the unit cost curve under monopoly and AC represents unit costs under competition. Then, from an efficiency standpoint, monopoly is at least as good as competition if $A \geqslant E$. Williamson argued that only small decreases in costs may be needed to offset large increases in price resulting from monopoly power. Thus, there is a possibility that monopolies may be desirable on efficiency grounds. However, this conclusion has been challenged by De Prano and Nugent [32], who contended that the cost reductions needed under monopolies to offset the higher prices are very unlikely to be realised in practice. Koo [75] has argued that, where costs are lower under monopoly than under competition, the comparison of the monopoly position (P_m, Q_m) with the competitive position (P_c, Q_c) understates the social loss attributable to monopoly. He maintained that the comparison should be between the actual monopoly position (P_m, Q_m) and the situation under a " benevolent " monopoly (P_c', Q_c'). The gain to consumers $(A + B + C + D + E)$ from moving to Q_c' would exceed the minimum sum of money $(A + D)$ necessary to bribe the monopolist to produce that output.

Increasing- and Decreasing-cost Industries. As mentioned earlier, many

---

[1] He estimated that the gain from eliminating monopoly profits and monopoly wages in the United States would be 0·08% and 0·604% of total revenue in manufacturing, respectively.

[2] Comanor and Leibenstein assert that " X-inefficiency is, of course, likely to be largest of all " [21, p. 30]. At least in the case of a linear demand curve this conclusion does not hold if, as is traditional, the monopolist is assumed to maximise profits. In this case, A would equal B in Fig. 10 so that allocative inefficiency would necessarily exceed X-inefficiency.

economists have believed that the competitive equilibrium represents a social optimum.   Marshall, one of the earliest economists to question the general validity of this belief, suggested that intervention in the workings of the competitive system *might* be socially desirable.   Specifically, he suggested that " . . . it might even be for the advantage of the community that the government should levy taxes on commodities which obey the law of diminishing return, and devote part of the proceeds to bounties on commodities which obey the law of increasing return " [94, p. 475].   In essence, he suggested that the loss in consumers' surplus from raising a certain revenue by taxing decreasing-returns industries *may* be less than the gain in consumers' surplus from using that revenue to subsidise increasing-returns industries.   Marshall proposed this with some reservation, acknowledging that, as well as certain " semi-ethical " questions, the effects of the taxes and subsidies on producers' surplus should be considered before deciding on such a course of action.   There has been a tendency to overlook this qualification, to elevate his hypothesis to the status of a theorem, and then to deny its general validity on the grounds that he ignored producers' surplus!   In addition, some authors [39, p. 242; 137, p. 207] may have misinterpreted Marshall's proposition to mean that he believed that decreasing-returns industries produce beyond their social optimum and should be taxed even if there are no increasing-returns industries to subsidise.   Certainly the analysis of footnote 2, page 468, of his *Principles* might be interpreted in this light since it does not consider producers' surplus.   However, in footnote 1, page 473, Marshall did incorporate producers' surplus into the analysis (our Fig. 6) and, as a result, the imposition of a tax on a decreasing-returns industry was shown to entail a net social loss.

In contrast to Marshall, Pigou [117] did initially suggest that the output of an increasing-cost industry may exceed the optimum.   Briefly, his analysis (which did not entail the concept of economic surplus) ran as follows: In Fig. 11, S_1 is the usual industry supply curve—that is, a locus of minimum long-run average costs for the industry.   Pigou called S_2 " a curve of marginal supply prices "—that is, it represents the increase in industry aggregate costs necessary to produce the marginal unit (thus, S_2 is marginal to S_1).   Pigou initially held that I rather than C (the competitive output) represents the ideal output.   This assertion led to considerable controversy over the nature of the long-run industry supply curve [73, 145, 148, 124, 127, 37].   Several economists, notably Young [187], pointed out that Pigou had mistakenly treated rents as social costs and argued that, if the supply curve slopes upward solely because of rising transfer costs or diminishing returns, then S_1 represents industry marginal costs *excluding rents* (as well as average costs including rents) so that the competitive output C represents the optimum [39].[1]   As a result, Pigou drastically modified his position and

---

[1] Since this article was written, a full discussion of this topic by Mishan has been published in the *Journal of Economic Literature*, March 1971.

adopted the limited proposition that the competitive output exceeds the
ideal where the industry employs imported factors which are not perfectly
elastic in supply on the assumption that rents to the foreign owners of intramarginal units of these factors should be considered costs to the community
[118, pp. 802–7].

However, Pigou still argued that, in general, it is to the advantage of

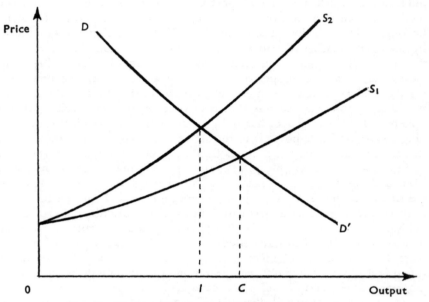

FIG. 11. Ideal output under increasing industry supply price.

society to subsidise decreasing-cost industries. In its final form, his tax-
bounty thesis was that " . . . while, with rare exceptions, simple competition always causes too little investment to be made in industries of decreasing
supply price (*simpliciter*), it does not always, or even generally, cause too
much to be made in industries of increasing supply price (*simpliciter*) "
[118, p. 223]. The argument in favour of subsidising decreasing-cost
industries is based on treating declines in intramarginal costs from the realisa-
tion of external economies as a gain to society. Ellis and Fellner [39], who
discussed the tax-bounty thesis in some depth, concluded that if the economies are " reversible " an argument may be made for a permanent bounty
but that if they are " irreversible " the bounty should at best be temporary.

Pricing of Public Utilities. In the 1930s the idea that price should equal
marginal cost (excluding rent) appeared in explicit form in the literature and
subsequently was the subject of considerable controversy.[1] Although the

---

[1] For discussions of the marginal cost pricing debate, the reader is referred to Ruggles [131,
132], Little [86, Ch. 11], Vickrey [163], and Coase [20]. For a discussion of the contribution of the
French economists to the theory and practice of marginal cost pricing, see Drèze [33, Part I].

classic work of Hotelling [61] took as its starting point the analysis of taxes by Dupuit, most of the subsequent debate involved only indirectly the concept of economic surplus. Rather, it was concerned with the specification of the conditions necessary for the optimal allocation of the resources of the economy. Of particular practical concern was the case of a decreasing-cost public utility where marginal cost pricing would require a subsidy to cover the resulting loss. This raised the question of how such a scheme of subsidisation should be financed. *Ideally*, the required revenue should be raised by lump-sum taxes. According to Ruggles, " A true lump-sum tax is by definition one which falls on either producers' or consumers' surplus and therefore does not violate the marginal conditions " [132, p. 32]. However, where such taxes are imposed outside the industry under consideration, this procedure involves a redistribution of income in favour of the consumers of the subsidised product. Some economists, notably Coase [19, 20], have argued that this is generally not acceptable and that consumers should cover the full costs of production and have, accordingly, advocated charges independent of consumption to cover costs not included in marginal costs. The justification for multipart tariffs is, by now, well established. Recently, Williamson [179], in an attempt to supply the welfare motivation he found lacking in earlier studies, applied the concept of economic surplus to the peak-load pricing problem and derived a solution for the optimal adjustment of capacity and for the optimal pricing of peak and off-peak loads.

Foster [43] also considered the pricing of transport facilities according to the concept of economic surplus. Assuming that the nationalised industries are directed to serve the " public interest," he argues in favour of a practicable price policy which maximises consumers' surplus subject to the constraint that total revenue equals total costs. For the increasing-cost case represented in Fig. 12, the strict application of this criterion would result in output OQ_1 being sold at price OP_1. Because this solution would be unstable unless some form of rationing was used, Foster proposed as a practical solution that price and output should be determined by the intersection of the average revenue and average cost curves.[1]

International Trade

Most, if not all, countries engage in some form of international trade. There is a presumption that in some sense a country " gains " from trading with other countries. The possibility of measuring this gain has appealed to many economists. An obvious approach is to treat it as an economic surplus arising from the opportunity to exchange goods with other countries. Over the years various suggestions have been made as to how gains from trade might be defined and measured in this way. We will now briefly describe some of these suggestions. Following that we will discuss several

---

[1] For a discussion of the practical problems involved in the application of Foster's criterion, see Tipping [157].

776   THE ECONOMIC JOURNAL   [DEC.

studies concerned with the welfare effects of government intervention in
trade.   These latter studies are generally of a partial nature, concentrating
on a specific product.

Measuring the Gains From Trade.   In 1923 Marshall [93, pp. 161–3]
suggested as a measure of a country's " net benefit " from foreign trade, the
excess of the maximum number of " representative bales " that it would be

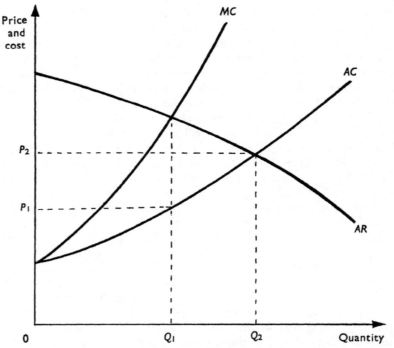

Fɪɢ. 12.   Foster's " consumers' surplus maximisation " price policy.

prepared to give up for the quantity of bales it imports over the amount it
actually hands over at the equilibrium " rate of interchange." [1]   He
developed an ingenious graphical technique for measuring the net benefit
from trade [93, Appendix J].   His method essentially entailed using the
country's reciprocal demand curve to derive a triangle-like area which he
then used to measure the net benefit.   However, Viner [165, p. 570]

---

[1] Marshall's use of " representative bales " is significant for three reasons:

    1. As Viner has observed, representative bales have a direct utility of their own " so it
cannot be said of them, as it can of money, that their utility is merely a reflection of the utility
of what can be obtained in exchange for them " [165, p. 575].

    2. Conceptually, the use of representative bales reflects an attempt at a general equilibrium
analysis instead of the partial analysis implied by his earlier use of specific products [91].

    3. Marshall is able to move from representative bales to " unit products of labour and
capital " and then to aggregate the surpluses of different countries [93, p. 163].

discovered a basic flaw in this procedure. Marshall implicitly assumed that the country's offer curve is the same whether the country pays the equilibrium price (in terms of exportables) for its intramarginal units of imports or whether it pays the maximum price for each unit. Viner argued that because a given number of imported bales will cost more in the latter case the marginal utility of exportables will be greater. The country will thus be willing to give up fewer bales of exports for a marginal import bale if it has paid the maximum price for previous import bales than if it had bought them at the equilibrium price. Thus, he argued, Marshall's measure will overestimate the country's net benefit from trade. In order to measure the surplus correctly, Viner suggested deriving from the country's utility function an offer curve showing the maximum price it would be prepared to pay in terms of exports for each successive bale of imports. He then used the same technique as Marshall to find an accurate measure of the net benefit from trade.

In 1923 Edgeworth [36] applied the notion of an indifference curve, or what he called a " no gain from trade " curve, to the surplus analysis of Marshall. It is indeed remarkable that as early as 1889 Edgeworth [35] had developed the concept of a " no gain from trade " curve and had measured a country's gain from trade as the distance between this curve and the country's reciprocal demand curve. It was inevitable that, following Hicks' rehabilitation of consumer's surplus, the idea of using indifference curves to measure gains from trade would be taken up again.[1]

The most comprehensive discussion of the application of the Hicksian measures of consumer's surplus to a country's gain from trade is presented by Bhagwati and Johnson [11]. They suggested that a country's gain can be measured by compensating (or Marshallian) surplus, compensating variation or equivalent variation, and that each of these can be measured in terms of either the export commodity or the import commodity. Thus, for a single country there are six alternative measures.[2] These are illustrated in Fig. 13. Suppose country A exports good X and country B exports good Y. The no-trade indifference curves are OU_0^A and OU_0^B, respectively. With free trade, the indifference curves are OU_1^A and OU_1^B, and P' represents the free-trade equilibrium point with equilibrium terms of trade given by the slope of OP.[3] For country A, the six possible measures of its gain from trade are S_x, S_y, C_x, C_y, E_x, and E_y. Compensating surplus, measured in

---

[1] See the discussions of Meier [97] and Das Gupta [29].

[2] More generally, for a change in the terms of trade (as opposed to the introduction of trade) there would be *eight* possible measures in all; that is, the usual four Hicksian measures either in terms of the export good or the import good.

[3] Each trade indifference curve is a locus of trading situations between which the country concerned is indifferent. For example, country A is indifferent between no trade and all combinations of exports of X and imports of Y lying on U^A_0. (The origin refers to a situation of no trade.) For the derivation of these trade indifference curves from a country's consumption indifference curves and its production possibility set, see J. E. Meade, *A Geometry of International Trade* (London 1952).

terms of its export good—that is, the amount of X that could be extracted
from country A at the free-trade equilibrium without making it worse off
than it would be in the absence of trade—is given by S_x. Compensating
variation, in terms of its export good—that is, the amount of X that could be
extracted from A without making it worse off than it would be in the absence
of trade if, after the loss of that quantity of X, it is free to trade at the

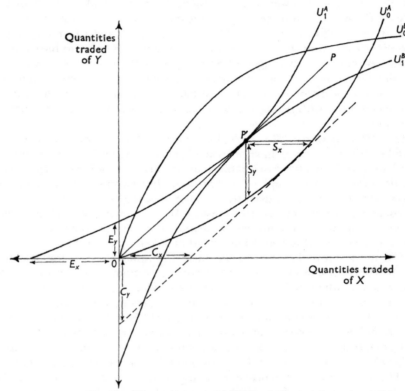

FIG. 13. Alternative measures of the gain from trade.

equilibrium terms of trade—is given by C_x. Equivalent variation, measured
in terms of its export good—that is, the amount of X which would have to
be given to country A to make it as well off without trade as it would be
when free to trade at the equilibrium terms of trade—is given by E_x.
Compensating surplus, compensating variation and equivalent variation,
measured in terms of the import commodity Y, are given by S_y, C_y, and E_y,
respectively.[1]

  [1] When Bhagwati and Johnson use the import good to measure the gain from trade, they
refer to it as a " consumer's gain " and as a " producer's gain " when measuring the gain in terms
of exportables. As they recognise, this terminology may be confusing. In fact, Marshall, himself,
never used this terminology. As Viner argued: " Marshall here uses the terms ' surplus ' or ' net

As Bhagwati and Johnson pointed out, if the quantity of the relevant good which measures the gain were actually extracted from the country, the equilibrium volume and terms of trade would differ from their initial equilibrium values. To avoid this inconsistency, the gain would have to be measured by the quantities of the two goods which, if extracted, would leave the international trade equilibrium unchanged [11, p. 89].

Partial Welfare Analyses in International Trade. A general equilibrium approach may be conceptually useful for defining precisely alternative measures of a country's gain from trade. However, any attempt to estimate the actual gain of a country from foreign trade would lead to highly dubious results. As Marshall acknowledged, " there is seldom much to be gained from speculations as to the results of conditions far removed from those which have already been experienced " [93, p. 165]. Yet, important classes of problems in international trade do not necessarily involve changes of such unmanageable dimensions. The imposition of a tariff on an imported commodity, the implementation of an import quota, or the introduction of subsidies on an export good are typical cases where a partial analysis, based on the concept of economic surplus, might be of considerable practical usefulness. Meier [97] has even urged the rewriting of much of trade and welfare theory in terms of such partial analyses.

The use of partial analyses in international trade has a long history. One widely used analytical framework, which dates back at least to Barone [7], is based on the famous back-to-back diagram represented in Fig. 14.[1] The demand and supply curves for the particular commodity under consideration are expressed in terms of money in a common currency. In the absence of trade in the commodity, its price would be $P_A Q_A$ in country A and $P_B Q_B$ in country B. If trade is opened up, country A will import the commodity from country B. Equilibrium will be established when CE, country A's imports, is equal to FG, country B's exports. The corresponding prices will be CH in country A and FK in country B (so that the price differential is equal to transportation costs $O_A O_B$). According to Barone, both countries gain from the trade. In country A, the gain to consumers, $MNCP_A$, exceeds the loss to producers, $MNEP_A$. In country B the gain to producers of $NGP_B R$ exceeds the loss to consumers of $NFP_B R$. The net gain to country A is $CP_A E$; the net gain to country B is FGP_B.

In passing, we might mention the considerable attention devoted to formulating this basic spatial model in a programming framework which

---

benefit ' instead of ' consumer's surplus,' perhaps because his procedure in his international trade analysis is supposed to account for ' producer's surplus ' as well as for ' consumer's surplus ' " [165, p. 570]. In a recent paper Mishan [103] has also argued that one cannot meaningfully distinguish between producer's and consumer's surplus, in the case of international trade. See the resulting discussion [77, 107].

[1] Marshall used this framework for domestic regional trade. It seems to have first been applied to international trade by Cunynghame [24]. However, Barone appears to have been the first to attach welfare connotations to this analysis.

can then be solved, given data on supply and demand curves and transportation costs. The spatial model was formulated by Samuelson [136] as a mathematical programming problem. Samuelson specified as the objective function a "net social payoff function" defined as the area between the excess demand and excess supply curves (represented in Fig. 14 by ED_A and ES_B, respectively). The net social payoff function is maximised when the

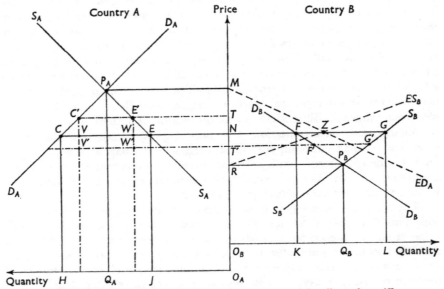

Fig. 14. Partial analysis of the gain from trade and of the effects of a tariff.

volume of trade is NZ. This procedure is equivalent to maximising the net welfare gains to both countries from trade according to the concept of economic surplus (since $MZN = EP_AC$ and $NZR = FGP_B$). Samuelson realised this but used the term "net social payoff function" to avoid the "strange connotations" associated with consumers' surplus.[1]

Clearly, in the foregoing case, if country A imposed a *prohibitive tariff* on the import of the commodity, *both* countries would be worse off than under free trade. The imposition by country A of a tariff which is not prohibitive provides an interesting and widely discussed case. Suppose in Fig. 14 that initially free trade exists between countries A and B and that country A imposes a per unit tariff of TT' on the import of the commodity. The new equilibrium is where A's imports, $C'E'$, equals B's exports, $F'G'$ (so that the price differential is equal to the tariff rate plus the unit transport cost). For country A the loss to consumers is given by $TC'CN$, the gain to producers by $TE'EN$, and the gain in government revenue by $E'C'V'W'$. The net gain to country A is thus $VWW'V' - (CC'V + EE'W)$. This may

[1] For a survey of spatial price equilibrium models, see Weinschenck *et al.* [172].

be positive or negative, depending on the size of the per unit tariff. The net loss to country B is given by $FF'G'G$. Whereas country A may gain from the imposition of the tariff, the two countries taken together must necessarily lose (since $FF'G'G$ must exceed $VWW'V'$).[1]

It is interesting to note that, as Enke [40, p. 238] pointed out, Barone, himself, incorrectly concluded that a country could not gain from the imposition of a tariff because he ignored the revenue obtained from the tariff and considered only the effects on consumers and producers. Recognising that a country may gain as a result of a tariff if it is confronted by a positively sloped foreign product supply curve, Enke demonstrated how the country might maximise "the algebraic sum of its nationals' suppliers' and consumers' surpluses plus its own revenue from duties" [40, p. 230]. The level of this "optimum tariff" must be such that the marginal cost to the country of the imported good is equal to the equilibrium domestic demand and supply price.[2]

The previous analysis explicitly allows for any change in the terms of trade following the imposition of the tariff. A less sophisticated but widely used version of Barone's basic model assumes that there are *no* effects on the terms of trade as a result of the imposition of a tariff by the country under consideration. It appears that Corden [22] was the first to use this framework. The basic model is presented in Fig. 15. At the free trade price P_f, the country imports Q_1Q_4 of the commodity. If a tariff of P_fP_t is imposed, imports will only be Q_2Q_3. The loss to consumers is given by the area of P_tBFP_f, the gain to producers by the area of P_tAEP_f, and the gain in government revenue by $ABDC$. Thus, the net welfare loss from the tariff is given by $AEC + BDF$. Area AEC is referred to in the literature as the "production cost" because it represents the loss imposed by the distortion of production from the optimal pattern corresponding to the international price ratio. Area BDF is referred to as the "consumption cost" since it represents the loss resulting from the distortion of consumption from the optimal pattern corresponding to the international price ratio. The case of an export subsidy is illustrated in the upper half of Fig. 15. Suppose P_f' is the world price. Then the payment of a per unit export subsidy of $P_f'P_t'$ results in a net welfare loss of $HGJ + KLM$.[3]

---

[1] In recent years the framework discussed above has formed the basis of several empirical studies. Dean and Collins [31] and Zusman, Melamed and Katzir [191] have used this type of model to consider the welfare effects of the European Common Market's trade policy with regard to oranges. Johnson [64] has applied this type of analysis to the welfare effects of discriminatory tariff reductions and the formation of a customs union.

[2] We might at this point refer the reader back to Pigou's contention that if an industry employs imported factors which are not perfectly elastic in supply the competitive output exceeds the ideal output and some form of government intervention may be justified on nationalistic grounds.

[3] The Corden type of model outlined above has been used by Dardis [26] to estimate the welfare costs of grain protection in the United Kingdom, by Wemelsfelder [174] to estimate the short-term effects of lowering import duties in Germany, and by Johnson [65] to estimate the gains to England from free trade with the E.E.C. countries.

In 1960 Johnson [66] provided an impressive demonstration of the potential usefulness of the concept of economic surplus in the formulation of trade policies. As we have seen, tariffs may well entail a net welfare cost in terms of economic surplus. However, they may still have results which are considered beneficial by society. If the costs and benefits of the tariffs can be specified in a clearly defined and measurable objective function, then

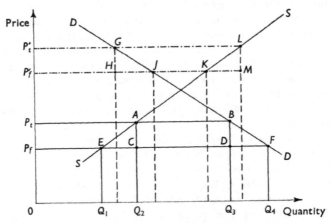

Fig. 15. The effects of a tariff and subsidy.

the choice of the " scientific tariff " is straightforward—namely, the selection of the " general level of protection at which marginal benefit from protection equals marginal cost of protection " [66, p. 341]. In the first part of his paper, Johnson considered the cost of protection. He initially assumed no terms of trade effects, using as his basic model a variant of Fig. 15. Extending the analysis to many commodities, he derived mathematical expressions for the aggregate production costs and consumption costs of the tariffs.[1] He argued that these costs, expressed as a proportion of national expenditure, are, in general, likely to be low, particularly when allowance is made for any beneficial effects on the terms of trade.[2] He then turned to the problem of quantifying the benefits of protection. Since many of the objectives of tariffs are vague, he suggested how these might be translated into precise objectives. For example, he suggested that the objective of " national self-sufficiency and independence " may be measured by the " value of imports excluded " and that the " promotion of industrialisation " may be measured either by the " increase in the quantity of desired production " or by the

[1] These are the " production " and " consumption " costs referred to earlier with respect to Fig. 15.

[2] He draws from this the general implication that " if the cost of protection is a small proportion of the level of national income at any point in time and if protectionists happen to be correct in their claim that protection increases an economy's rate of growth, the increase does not have to be very great for its effect in raising national income to counterbalance the reduction due to the cost of protection within relatively few years " [66, p. 339].

" increase in income earned in the relevant industries." Once this translation of objectives is made and given the knowledge of the costs of protection, the scientific tariff structure is easily derived, if one attributes a " value " to each unit of the other objectives which is achieved.

A particularly interesting development has been the attempt to incorporate in one model both intermediate and final goods. Representative of these studies is the analysis by Dardis and Dennisson [27] of alternative methods of protecting raw wool in the United States. In their analysis they assume that there exists a tariff and a deficiency payment in the raw wool market and a tariff on the final wool product (part of which is a compensatory tariff to offset the effect on producers of the final product of the tariff on raw wool). Of the three alternative policies they analyse, the only one which would represent a net gain to society would be the removal of both the tariff on raw wool and the compensatory tariff combined with an increase in deficiency payments on raw wool such that producers of raw wool would be unaffected.[1]

Price Instability and Investment

In 1944 Waugh [169] demonstrated, using consumer's surplus, that consumers may benefit from price instability generated by fluctuating shifts in supply. Almost 20 years later, Oi [111] showed that producers may benefit from price instability resulting from fluctuating shifts in the demand curve. More recently, Massell [95, 96] has argued that, no matter whether instability is caused by shifts in supply or demand, the actual payment of compensation would mean that both producers and consumers would prefer price stability.[2]

The case of a shifting supply curve is shown in Fig. 16. The corresponding prices are P_1 and P_2. A crucial assumption is that each price occurs with 0·5 probability. Alternatively, price P_a which equals $\frac{1}{2}(P_1 + P_2)$ can

---

[1] A similar analysis, dealing with both final and intermediate products, has been employed by Dardis and Learn [28] to estimate the welfare cost of protecting agriculture in Canada, Denmark, France, Italy, the Netherlands, the United Kingdom, the United States and West Germany. This approach has also been used by Snape [146, 147] to examine the welfare effects of imposing tariffs on both raw wool and refined sugar. Josling [68] also uses an intermediate-final goods model in analysing the welfare effects of various agricultural schemes which might be implemented in the United Kingdom.

Two other papers may be mentioned briefly: Ffrench and Davis [41] considered the effect of export quotas on allocative efficiency under conditions of market instability. They demonstrated that there may be a possible justification for the use of export quotas when there exists price instability and it originates in foreign markets. Corden [22], also using a partial equilibrium analysis, examined the effects of imports on a domestic monopolist which experiences increasing returns. A major conclusion is that a tariff should not be used in the case of a monopolised industry with falling costs in order to achieve a social optimum. He demonstrated that for this purpose a tariff is either bad or useless. Consequently, unless a social optimum is brought about by international trade, the only means of achieving this state is through a lump-sum subsidy or a subsidy per unit of output.

[2] Some comments pertinent to these studies are contained in Tisdell [158], Oi [112], Zucker [190], and Nelson [109].

be established by a buffer stock (with no storage costs.)   If the price is increased from P_1 to P_a producers gain $(c + d + e)$ and consumers lose $(c + d)$ resulting in a net gain of area e.   Similarly reducing the price from P_2 to P_a results in a net gain of b.   Thus, stabilising price at P_a leads to a net loss to consumers of $(c + d) - (a + b)$ (that is, the Waugh result) but a net gain of $(b + e)$ to consumers and producers jointly (that is, the Massell result).   Thus producers are able to compensate consumers so as to leave

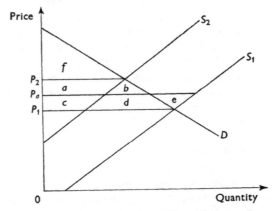

FIG. 16.   Effects of price stabilisation with a shifting supply curve.

both groups better off from price stability.   If price fluctuations are caused by shifts in demand, producers will lose from price stabilisation (as Oi has shown) but the gain to consumers will be sufficiently large for them to " over-compensate " the producers (as Massell has shown).

Recently Hueth and Schmitz [62] have shown that when dealing with internationally traded products, the above conclusions depend on whether or not a region experiences price instability because of domestic shifts in supply or demand or whether instability is generated from abroad such that domestic price changes come about via quantity changes along given supply and demand schedules.   In the latter case, the Waugh and Oi conclusions hold for domestic consumers and producers.   Both groups prefer price instability, and hence no compensation is needed for the result to hold since it is Pareto superior.

The concept of economic surplus has also been used to evaluate the welfare effects of public and private investments.   The basic type of model is given in Fig. 17.   Suppose prior to some technological innovation equilibrium price and quantity is P_0 and Q_0.   Following the development of a new technique, production costs are lowered, shifting the supply curve from S to S'.   The net social gain is $B + C + E + F$, since the change in producer's surplus is $(E + F) - A$, while the gain in consumer's surplus is $A + B + C$.   If the initial supply curve were perfectly elastic, the gain to society would be the gain in consumers' surplus $A + B + C$, which results from the shift in the supply curve from $P_0 S_1$ to $P_1 S_1'$. The first case is representative of the model used by Peterson, [115] to evaluate the effects of poultry research. The latter was used by Griliches [49] to estimate the rate of return on investment in hybrid corn research. Recently, Schmitz and Seckler [138] used the basic framework outlined above to compute the

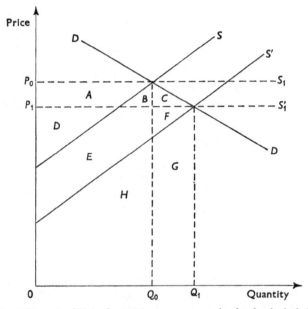

Fig. 17.   Effects of a shift in the supply curve as a result of technological change.

rate of return on investment in the development of a recent labour-saving technological innovation—the mechanical tomato harvester. They computed both the gross and net social rate of return and concluded that sufficient savings were generated from the use of the harvester so that compensation could have been paid to the displaced workers, and the users of the machine would still have preferred it to handpicking methods.

In addition, various economists have suggested the use of consumer's surplus to evaluate investment in a variety of public projects, such as, water resource development [89, 90], transport projects [42, 43, 167], and the provision of recreational facilities [17, 18, 15, 84, 159, 161, 50, 98, 175, 176]. However, a discussion of the broader technique of cost-benefit analysis and its application would take us beyond the scope of this article and into the field so thoroughly surveyed by Prest and Turvey [120].

III. CONCLUDING OBSERVATIONS

So far we have discussed the theoretical foundations of the concept of economic surplus and some of its theoretical and empirical applications without directly considering why there has been so much controversy over its usefulness. There does seem to be widespread agreement that the concept is, at least, heuristically useful. Little, who has questioned the practical usefulness of the concept of consumer's surplus, did admit [86, p. 180]:

> " It is, in fact, to a limited extent, useful as a heuristic device— so long as its limitations, as such, are understood. It is also, admittedly, a useful phrase for referring to the fact that a person may be willing to pay more for something than he has to; and also for pointing out the fact that the amount someone pays for something cannot be taken as a measure of the satisfaction it gives him, and that the price of a good cannot be taken as a measure of its importance."

Lerner also argued [80, p. 80]:

> " Consumer's surplus nevertheless seems to me to be of very great use not only as a heuristic device for showing students of economics the benefits from an increase in the freedom of trade, but also for indicating where one should look for indications and estimates of the social benefits or damages from many an important governmental or other policy decision."

For Samuelson, however [137, p. 197]:

> " . . . my ideal *Principles* would not include consumer's surplus in the chapter on welfare economics except possibly in a footnote, although in my perfect *Primer* the concept might have a limited place, provided its antidote and the alternatives were included close at hand."

In fact, Samuelson mounted the most fundamental attack on the concept of consumer's surplus. In arguing that the concept is superfluous, he wrote [137, p. 210]:

> " Even if consumer's surplus did give a cardinal measure of the change in utility from a given change, it is hard to see what use this could serve. Only in the contemplation of alternative movements which begin or end in the same point could this cardinal measure have any significance and then only because it is an indicator of ordinal preference."

The supporters of the concept would surely argue that the maximum sum of money an individual would be prepared to pay for the benefits of some change is a useful cardinal magnitude; whether it is obtained from an ordinal preference map is immaterial. In the simple case of a consumer who buys exactly the same quantity of a commodity before and after a price change, the change in his expenditure on the good certainly has more than an ordinal meaning.

Samuelson also argued [137, p. 197]:

> " Should discriminating prices be allowed if a uniform price will not keep an activity in business?   Should the number of firms producing differentiated products be reduced, and in what way?   Should a particular small industry be expanded or contracted by means of a tax or subsidy? etc., etc.   Aside from their extraneous interpersonal aspects, all of these questions can more conveniently (and more honestly!) be answered in terms of the consumer's ordinal preference field."

If, indeed, one knows the consumer's ordinal preference field, what could be more convenient (and more honest?) than finding the appropriate Hicksian measure?   Even accepting Samuelson's claim, this, as Little observed, is a " rather surprising passage " [86, p. 181] since Samuelson chose to attack the concept at a purely theoretical level on the assumption that everyone's preference field is known, while the main appeal of the concept of consumer's surplus actually lies in its relationship with the demand curve.   Given that the economist does not have a copy of everyone's preference map filed away, it does not really diminish the practical significance of the concept to argue that " it is a tool which can be used only by one who can get along without its use and not by all such " [137, p. 209] as if such knowledge of preferences were available.

In order to evaluate the practical usefulness of the concept, it is important to review what actually has been claimed for it.   We presented earlier several of the suggested or actual applications of the concept.   Most of these studies are concerned with the effects of deviations from the " optimum " organisation of production.   In regard to the general usefulness of consumer's surplus for this purpose, Hicks wrote [55, p. 112]:

> " The idea of consumer's surplus enables us to study in detail the effects of deviations from the optimum in a particular market.   It is not merely a convenient way of showing when there will be a deviation (consumer's surplus is not necessary for that purpose, since the basic optimum conditions . . . show us at once when there will be a deviation); it also offers us a way of measuring the size of the deviation. This, if we are right in our general viewpoint, is a most important service."

A main consideration, therefore, is how reliable measures of deviations from an optimum will be.   We will now discuss some of the more important reasons why such measures may, in practice, be suspect.

Partial Welfare Analysis

Most of the applied studies surveyed in this article are of a " partial " nature.   This is virtually inevitable, for the economist's limited knowledge

of the complex interrelationships characterising any economic system precludes any possibility of allowing for all the ramifications generally associated
with a change in one particular industry. Although Hicks realised the
possible significance of repercussions elsewhere, he nevertheless claimed that
this type of partial analysis may be most useful. He wrote [55, p. 110]:

> " There is one whole branch of economic theory which is absolutely
> dependent upon the idea of Consumer's Surplus; a very important
> branch it is too, though naturally enough it has been far too much
> neglected in recent years. It is the branch which may be called Partial
> Welfare Analysis, since it occupies the same place in General Welfare
> Analysis as the study of Partial Equilibrium does in positive economics.
> There are few branches of economic theory which have greater practical
> use."

Little [86, pp. 166–184], on the other hand, has seriously questioned the
validity of partial welfare analyses. Indeed, this was one of the main reasons
why he dismissed consumer's surplus as a useless toy. According to Little,
an important consideration in deciding whether a partial analysis may be
legitimate is whether the optimality conditions are fulfilled elsewhere. If
prices equal marginal costs in the rest of the economy, then, assuming no
external economies or diseconomies, the prices of factors used in the industry
under consideration will reflect their value to society elsewhere. If, however, prices exceed marginal costs elsewhere, the private costs of expanding
the output of this industry will understate the real costs to society. Hicks,
recognising this, suggested that in this event it would be appropriate to
raise the marginal cost curve of the commodity in question in order to allow
for the divergence between private and social costs [55]. As Mishan [101,
p. 75] has argued, this simple technique falls down when prices depart from
marginal costs in different degrees in different industries.

The absence of optimal conditions elsewhere, in fact, means that attempting to fulfil the usual optimal conditions in this industry alone is not necessarily the best procedure. For example, if all other industries are monopolised, it will not necessarily be desirable to ensure that price equals marginal
cost in this industry. Moreover, it is not even necessarily true that some
degree of output restriction will also be desirable in this industry. This is,
of course, a special case of the more general " theory of second best " as put
forward by Lipsey and Lancaster [85].

Even if prices do equal marginal costs elsewhere, repercussions in the
rest of the economy may still be significant if adjustments in other industries
are not " marginal." If the commodity in question has close substitutes or
complements on the demand or supply side, a partial analysis is not likely
to be adequate [86]. For example, if a commodity A has a close substitute,
B, on the demand side, then a change in the price of A will shift the demand
curve for B. If the price of B is unaffected—that is, if the supply curve for

B is horizontal over the relevant range—then the relevant area below the compensated demand curve for A will reflect the effect of the price change on the welfare of consumers. However, if the market price of B changes, then producers of B will be affected. This ought to be taken into account. In addition, the demand curve for A, constructed on the assumption that the price of B is given, will also shift. If this leads to a further change in the price of A, the demand curve for B will shift once again and so on until equilibrium is restored. We saw earlier that conceptually it is possible to determine the welfare effect of changes in the prices of two (or more) commodities. One could find the compensating variation associated with the change in the price of A, holding the price of B at its initial level, and then find the compensating variation associated with the change in the price of B, holding the price of A at its new level.[1]

Some Further Considerations

Because people's preferences are unknown, the economist generally has to rely on recorded market behaviour. Thus he can at best hope to have reliable estimates of ordinary curves. As we have seen, even if these curves are known exactly, certain assumptions are necessary: (*a*) For the relevant area below the ordinary demand curve to represent exactly compensating variation (or any of the other three Hicksian measures), the income effect must be zero. Where the income effect is close to zero, one may still obtain a reasonable measure. For the income effect to be negligible, the income elasticity of demand for the commodity must be small or expenditure on the commodity must constitute a small proportion of total expenditure. (*b*) For the relevant area above the ordinary supply curve of a factor to measure exactly compensating variation, the O.S.C. and the C.S.C. must coincide. As Mishan [100, p. 393] pointed out, however, whereas the assumption of a zero income effect on the demand side may be tenable, the assumption that the four measures of rent and the relevant area above the ordinary supply curve coincide is seldom likely to be met. (*c*) For the area above the product supply curve to reflect the welfare of owners of firms, the supply curve must coincide with the industry private marginal cost curve. For the area above the product supply curve to reflect the rents of all factors of production, the supply curve must be a marginal cost curve *excluding* rents.

A further problem is that since most data are of an aggregate nature, some grouping of the members of society is inevitable. The most common

---

[1] For a discussion of an alternative way of allowing for interdependence between products, see Berry [9].

Conceptually, if it is possible to take into account *every* repercussion on each individual (as factor supplier and consumer) the question of whether optimality conditions are fulfilled elsewhere ceases to be relevant. Such optimality conditions are significant if a product supply curve is to be taken as a reflection of social costs. However, if one concentrates on the factor markets, as Mishan has recommended, such an assumption would no longer be necessary.

grouping is "consumers," "producers" and "taxpayers." The corresponding assumption is that a pound gain to one consumer is considered of equal value as a pound gain to another consumer (and similarly for producers and taxpayers). In some circumstances, this assumption may be reasonable. However, to the extent that we are primarily concerned with the welfare of *individuals* and not groups, this assumption in many instances may be unsatisfactory. For example, in evaluating the welfare effects of a government programme, the welfare differences between poor consumers and wealthy consumers and between poor producers and wealthy producers may be more significant than the difference between producers as a group and consumers as a group.

Even if it were permissible to assume equality within groups the direct aggregation of economic surpluses *between* groups, which is so prevalent in the studies cited in section II, is of questionable validity. It may, on the one hand, imply equal "weighting" of the welfare of the different groups involved. This procedure, which may be a reflection of the scale of social values held by the particular economist, would appear to be implicit in the work of Marshall, Pigou and other early economists [54]. On the other hand, it may reflect an implicit acceptance of the principle of hypothetical compensation first put forward by Kaldor [69] and Hicks [55]. Neither of these approaches is acceptable as a general solution to the problem of interpersonal comparisons of utility.[1] However, the usefulness of the concept of economic surplus does not critically depend on the validity of either approach. Describing the effects of an economic change on the individual groups is logically distinct from evaluating the overall desirability of the change. If the concept of economic surplus can be used to describe the effects of a change, it has made a major contribution. Presumably, it is the responsibility of the "decision-maker" to decide whether, on balance, the change is "desirable."

A Final Comment

In recent years, an increasing number of economists have undertaken studies based on the concept of economic surplus. As Bhagwati [10, p. 213] has stressed, the measurement of losses and gains from changes in policy has resulted from pressure on economists to provide such measures.

> "Policies are maintained or changed largely for non-economic reasons; and the (economic) 'cost' involved is a magnitude that is commonly demanded and bandied about in discussions of public policy. Whether we like it or not, this is what the policy makers do want; and the trade theorist, in consonance with the best traditions in the profession, has begun to meet this need in an attempt to bring economic analysis closer to fulfilling the objective that provides its ultimate *raison*

[1] For discussions of the problem of interpersonal comparisons of utility and the compensation principle see [61, 72, 86, 102, 106, 125, 129, 132, 134, 143].

d'être. The result has been a definite and significant trend, in the welfare analysis of pure theory, towards measurement of welfare change."

While it is easy to raise objections to the use of the concept of economic surplus for providing answers for policy formulation, it is difficult to find any workable alternative.

JOHN MARTIN CURRIE

University of Manchester.

JOHN A. MURPHY

University College, Dublin.

ANDREW SCHMITZ

University of California, Berkeley.

REFERENCES

1. M. Ahmed, " The Development of the Concept of Consumer's Surplus in Economic Theory and Policy," *Indian Economic Journal*, Vol. 13, April–June 1966.

2. R. F. G. Alford, " Marshall's Demand Curve," *Economica* (NS), Vol. XXIII, February 1956.

3. Martin J. Bailey, " The Marshallian Demand Curve," *Journal of Political Economy*, Vol. LXII, June 1954.

4. Enrico Barone, " Sulla ' Consumer's Rent,' " *Giornale degli Economisti*, Vol. 16, September 1894.

5. Enrico Barone, *Principi di Economia Politica* (Rome, 1913).

6. Enrico Barone, " Related Costs in the Economics of Transport," *International Economic Papers* (1921).

7. Enrico Barone, *Grundzüge der Theoretischen Nationalökonomie* (Bonn, 1927); translated from original Italian edition (1908).

8. Frederick W. Bell, " The Effect of Monopoly Profits and Wages on Prices and Consumers' Surplus in U.S. Manufacturing," *Western Economic Journal*, Vol. 6, June 1968.

9. R. Albert Berry, " A Note on Welfare Comparisons Between Monopoly and Pure Competition," *The Manchester School of Economic and Social Studies*, No. 1, March 1969.

10. Jagdish Bhagwati, " The Pure Theory of International Trade: A Survey," American Economic Association and Royal Economic Society, *Surveys of Economic Theory*, Vol. 2 (New York, 1965).

11. J. Bhagwati and H. G. Johnson, " Notes on Some Controversies in the Theory of International Trade," ECONOMIC JOURNAL, Vol. LXX, March 1960.

12. Robert L. Bishop, " Consumer's Surplus and Cardinal Utility," *Quarterly Journal of Economics*, Vol. LVIII, May 1943.

13. K. E. Boulding, " The Concept of Economic Surplus," *American Economic Review*, Vol. XXXV, December 1945.

14. A. L. Bowley, " Does Mathematical Analysis Explain? A Note on Consumer's Surplus," *Economica* (OS), Vol. 11, June 1924.

15. Wayne Boyet and George Tolley, " Recreation Projection Based on Demand Analysis," *Journal of Farm Economics*, Vol. 48, November 1966.

16. E. Cannan, " ' Total Utility ' and ' Consumer's Surplus,' " *Economica* (OS), No. 10, February 1924.

17. Omer L. Carey, " The Economics of Recreation: Progress and Problems," *Western Economic Journal*, Vol. 3, Spring 1965.

18. Omer L. Carey, " Reply," *Western Economic Journal*, Vol. 4, Spring 1966.

19. R. H. Coase, " The Marginal Cost Controversy," *Economica* (NS), Vol. XIII, August 1946.

20. R. H. Coase, " The Theory of Public Utility Pricing and its Application," *The Bell Journal of Economics and Management Science*, Vol. 1, Spring 1970.

21. W. S. Comanor and Harvey Leibenstein, " Allocative Efficiency, X-Efficiency, and the Measurement of Welfare Losses," *Economica*, Vol. 36, August 1969.

22. W. M. Corden, " The Calculation of the Cost of Protection," *Economic Record*, Vol. 33, May 1957.

23. W. M. Corden, " Monopoly, Tariffs, and Subsidies," *Economica*, Vol. 34, February 1967.

24. H. H. S. Cunynghame, *A Geometrical Political Economy* (Oxford, 1904).

25. Rachel Dardis, " The Welfare Cost of Grain Protection in the United Kingdom," *Journal of Farm Economics*, Vol. 49, August 1967.

26. Rachel Dardis, " Intermediate Goods and the Gain from Trade," *Review of Economics and Statistics*, Vol. 49, November 1967.

27. R. Dardis and J. Dennisson, " The Welfare Cost of Alternative Methods of Protecting Raw Wool in the United States," *American Journal of Agricultural Economics*, Vol. 51, May 1969.

28. Rachel Dardis and Elmer W. Learn, *Measures of the Degree and Cost of Economic Protection of Agriculture in Selected Countries*. U.S. Department of Agriculture, Economic Research Service. Technical Bulletin 1384, 1967.

29. A. K. Das Gupta, " Marshall's Measure of ' Net Benefit ' from Foreign Trade," *The Indian Economic Review*, Vol. 2, August 1954.

30. Richard M. Davis, " The Current State of Profit Theory," *American Economic Review*, Vol. XLII, June 1952.

31. Gerald W. Dean and Norman R. Collins, *World Trade in Fresh Oranges: An Analysis of the Effect of European Economic Community Tariff Policies*. University of California, Berkeley, Giannini Foundation Monograph 18, 1967.

32. Michael E. De Prano and Jeffrey B. Nugent, " Economies as an Antitrust Defense: Comment," *American Economic Review*, Vol. 59, December 1969.

33. J. Drèze, " Some Postwar Contributions of French Economists to Theory and Public Policy," *American Economic Review*, Vol. 54, June 1964.

34. J. Dupuit, " On the Measurement of the Utility of Public Works," *Annales des Ponts et Chaussees*, Second Series, Vol. 8, 1844; translation reprinted in D. Munby, *Transport*, 1968.

35. F. Y. Edgeworth, " On the Application of Mathematics to Political Economy," *Journal of the Royal Statistical Society*, Vol. 52, 1889.

36. F. Y. Edgeworth, Review of " Money, Credit and Commerce " by Alfred Marshall, ECONOMIC JOURNAL, Vol. XXXIII, June 1923.

37. F. Y. Edgeworth, " The Revised Doctrine of Marginal Social Product," ECONOMIC JOURNAL, Vol. XXXV, March 1925.

38. E. Eisenberg, " Aggregation of Utility Functions," *Management Science*, Vol. 7, July 1961.

39. H. S. Ellis and W. Fellner, " External Economies and Diseconomies," *American Economic Review*, Vol. XXXIII, September 1943. Reprinted in Stigler and Boulding (eds.), *A.E.A. Readings in Price Theory*, Vol. VI (Chicago, 1952).

40. Stephen Enke, " The Monopsony Case for Tariffs," *Quarterly Journal of Economics*, Vol. 58, February 1944.

41. Ricardo F. Ffrench and M. Davis, " Export Quotas and Allocative Efficiency Under Market Instability," *American Journal of Agricultural Economics*, Vol. 50, August 1968.

42. C. D. Foster, " Surplus Criteria for Investment," *Oxford Institute Statistical Bulletin 22*, No. 4, 1960.

43. C. D. Foster, *The Transport Problem* (London, 1963).

44. M. Friedman, " The Marshallian Demand Curve," *Journal of Political Economy*, Vol. LVII, December 1949.

45. M. Friedman, *Price Theory* (Chicago, 1962).

46. M. H. Gopal, " Consumer's Surplus: A Reply," *Indian Journal of Economics*, Vol. XXI, October 1939.

47. W. M. Gorman, " Community Preference Fields," *Econometrica*, Vol. 21, January 1953.

48. R. O. Goss, " Towards an Economic Approval of Port Investments," *Journal of Transport Economics and Policy*, Vol. 1, 1967. Reprinted in Denys Munby (ed.), *Transport* (1968).

49. Zvi Griliches, " Research Costs and Social Returns: Hybrid Corn and Related Innovations," *Journal of Political Economy*, Vol. 66, October 1958.

50. H. W. Grubb and J. T. Goodwin, " Economic Evaluation of Water-Oriented Recreation in the Texas Water Plan," Texas Water Development Board (Austin, 1966). Reported in Samuel B. Chase, Jr. (ed.), *Problems in Public Expenditure Analysis* (Washington, 1968) by Allen V. Kneese.

51. A. C. Harberger, " Monopoly and Resource Allocation," *American Economic Review*, Vol. 44, May 1954.

52. A. C. Harberger, " Using the Resources at Hand More Effectively," *American Economic Review*, Vol. 49, May 1959.

53. A. Henderson, " Consumer's Surplus and the Compensating Variation," *Review of Economic Studies*, Vol. 8, February 1940–41.

54. J. R. Hicks, " Foundations of Welfare Economics," ECONOMIC JOURNAL, Vol. XLIX, December 1939.

55. J. R. Hicks, " The Rehabilitation of Consumers' Surplus," *Review of Economic Studies*, Vol. 8, February 1940–41.

56. J. R. Hicks, " The Four Consumers' Surpluses," *Review of Economic Studies*, Vol. 11, Winter 1943.

57. J. R. Hicks, *Value and Capital: An Inquiry Into Some Fundamental Principles of Economic Theory*, 2d ed. (Oxford, 1946).

58. J. R. Hicks, " The Generalized Theory of Consumer's Surplus," *Review of Economic Studies*, Vol. 13, 1945–46.

59. J. R. Hicks, " Consumers' Surplus and Index Numbers," *Review of Economic Studies*, Vol. 9, Summer 1942.

60. J. R. Hicks, *A Revision of Demand Theory* (London, 1956).

61. H. Hotelling, " The General Welfare in Relation to Problems of Taxation and of Railway and Utility Rates," *Econometrica*, Vol. 6, July 1938.

62. D. Hueth and Andrew Schmitz, " International Trade in Intermediate and Final Goods: Some Welfare Implications of Destabilizing Prices," *Quarterly Journal of Economics*, forthcoming.

63. L. J. Hushak, " A Welfare Analysis of the Voluntary Corn Diversion Pro-Program, 1961 to 1966," *American Journal of Agricultural Economics*, Vol. 53, No. 2, May 1971.

64. Harry G. Johnson, " Discriminating Tariff Reduction: A Marshallian Analysis," *Indian Journal of Economics*, Vol. 38, July 1957.

65. Harry G. Johnson, " The Gains from Freer Trade with Europe: An Estimate," *The Manchester School of Economics and Social Studies*, Vol. 26, September 1958.

66. Harry G. Johnson, " The Cost of Protection and the Scientific Tariff," *Journal of Political Economy*, Vol. 68, August 1960.

67. Paul R. Johnson, " The Social Cost of the Tobacco Program," *Journal of Farm Economics*, Vol. 47, May 1965.

68. T. Josling, " A Formal Approach to Agricultural Policy," *Journal of Agricultural Economics*, Vol. XX, May 1969.

69. N. Kaldor, " Welfare Propositions in Economics," ECONOMIC JOURNAL, Vol. XLIX, September 1939.

70. N. Kaldor, " Alternative Theories of Distribution," *Review of Economic Studies*, Vol. XXIII, 1955–56.

71. David R. Kamerschen, " An Estimation of the ' Welfare Losses ' from Monopoly in the American Economy," *Western Economic Journal*, Vol. 4, Summer 1966.

72. C. M. Kennedy, " Welfare Criteria—A Further Note," ECONOMIC JOURNAL, Vol. 73, June 1963.

73. F. H. Knight, " Some Fallacies in the Interpretation of Social Cost," *Quarterly Journal of Economics*, Vol. 38, August 1924.

74. Frank Knight, " Realism and Relevance in the Theory of Demand," *Journal of Political Economy*, Vol. LII, December 1944.

75. Shou-Eng Koo, " A Note on the Social Welfare Loss Due to Monopoly," *Southern Economic Journal*, Vol. XXXVII, October 1970.

76. Adolf Kozlik, " Conditions for Demand Curves Whose Curves of Total Revenue, Consumer's Surplus, Total Benefit and Compromise Benefit are Convex," *Econometrica*, 1940.

77. M. Kraus and D. M. Winch, " Mishan on the Gains from Trade: Comment," *American Economic Review*, Vol. LXI, No. 1, March 1971.

78. Harvey Leibenstein, " Allocative Efficiency vs. X-Efficiency," *American Economic Review*, Vol. 56, June 1966.

79. Abba P. Lerner, " The Concept of Monopoly and the Measurement of Monopoly Power," *Review of Economic Studies*, Vol. 1, June 1934. Reprinted in Lerner, *Essays in Economic Analysis* (London, 1953).

80. Abba P. Lerner, " Statics and Dynamics in Socialist Economics," ECONOMIC

JOURNAL, Vol. XLVII, June 1937. Reprinted in Lerner, *Essays in Economic Analysis* (London, 1953).

81. Abba P. Lerner, *The Economics of Control* (New York, 1944).
82. Abba P. Lerner, " Consumer's Surplus and Micro-Macro," *Journal of Political Economy*, Vol. 71, February 1963.
83. Abba P. Lerner, " Consumer's Surplus and Micro-Macro: A Reply," *Journal of Political Economy*, Vol. 78, January–February 1970.
84. Lionel Lerner, " Quantitative Indices of Recreational Values," *Water Resources and Economic Development of the West: Economics in Outdoor Recreation Policy*, Report No. 11, 1962.
85. R. G. Lipsey and K. Lancaster, " The General Theory of Second Best," *Review of Economic Studies*, Vol. 24, February 1956–57.
86. I. M. D. Little, *A Critique of Welfare Economics* (Oxford, 1960).
87. S. C. Littlechild, " Marginal Cost Pricing with Joint Costs," ECONOMIC JOURNAL, Vol. LXXX, June 1970.
88. D. M. MacGregor, " ' Total Utility ' and ' Consumer's Surplus ': Reply," *Economica* (OS), Vol. 14, June 1924.
89. Stephen A. Marglin, " Objectives of Water Resource Development: A General Statement," in Arthur Maass *et al.*, *Design of Water Resource Systems: New Techniques for Relating Economic Objectives, Engineering Analysis, and Governmental Planning* (Cambridge, 1962).
90. S. A. Marglin, *Public Investment Criteria* (London, 1967).
91. Alfred Marshall, *Pure Theory of Foreign Trade*.
92. Alfred Marshall, " On Rent," ECONOMIC JOURNAL, Vol. III, March 1893.
93. Alfred Marshall, *Money, Credit and Commerce* (London, 1923).
94. Alfred Marshall, *Principles of Economics* (London, 1930).
95. Benton F. Massell, " Price Stabilization and Welfare," *Quarterly Journal of Economics*, Vol. LXXXIII, May 1969.
96. Benton F. Massell, " Some Welfare Implications of International Price Stabilization," *Journal of Political Economy*, Vol. 78, March–April 1970.
97. G. M. Meier, " The Theory of Comparative Costs Reconsidered," *Oxford Economic Papers*, Vol. 1, June 1949.
98. Leonard Merewitz, " Recreational Benefits of Water-Resource Development," *Water Resources Research*, Vol. 2, Fourth Quarter 1966.
99. E. J. Mishan, " Realism and Relevance in Consumer's Surplus," *Review of Economic Studies*, Vol. 15, 1947–48.
100. E. J. Mishan, " Rent as a Measure of Welfare Change," *American Economic Review*, Vol. 49, June 1959.
101. E. J. Mishan, " A Survey of Welfare Economics, 1939–59," ECONOMIC JOURNAL, Vol. LXX, June 1960.
102. E. J. Mishan, " Welfare Criteria: Are Compensation Tests Necessary? " ECONOMIC JOURNAL, Vol. LXXIII, June 1963.
103. E. J. Mishan, " What is Producer's Surplus? " *American Economic Review*, Vol. 58, December 1968.
104. E. J. Mishan, " A Note on the Costs of Tariffs, Monopolies and Thefts," *Western Economic Journal*, Vol. 7, September 1969.
105. E. J. Mishan, " Rent and Producer's Surplus: Reply," *American Economic Journal*, Vol. 59, September 1969.

106. E. J. Mishan, *Welfare Economics: An Assessment* (Amsterdam and London, 1969).
107. E. J. Mishan, " Mishan on the Gains from Trade: Reply," *American Economic Review*, Vol. LXI, No. 1, March 1971.
108. R. A. Mundell, Review of " Free Trade, Protection, and Customs Union," by L. H. Janssen, *American Economic Review*, Vol. 52, June 1962.
109. Richard R. Nelson, " Uncertainty, Production and Competitive Equilibrium," *Quarterly Journal of Economics*, Vol. LXXV, February 1961.
110. Marc Nerlove, *Dynamics of Supply* (Baltimore, 1958).
111. Walter W. Oi, " The Desirability of Price Instability Under Perfect Competition," *Econometrica*, Vol. 29, January 1961.
112. Walter W. Oi, " Rejoinder," *Econometrica*, Vol. 31, January–April 1963.
113. V. Pareto, *Cours d'Économie Politique*, Vol. 2 (Lausanne, 1896).
114. Don Patinkin, " Demand Curves and Consumer's Surplus," in Carl Christ *et al.*, *Measurement in Economics: Studies in Mathematical Economics and Econometrics in Memory of Yehuda Grunfeld* (Stanford, 1963).
115. W. L. Peterson, " Return to Poultry Research in the United States, "*Journal of Farm Economics*, Vol. 49, August 1967.
116. R. W. Pfouts, " A Critique of Some Recent Contributions to the Theory of Consumer's Surplus," *Southern Economic Journal*, Vol. 19, 1953.
117. A. C. Pigou, *Wealth and Welfare* (London, 1912).
118. A. C. Pigou, *The Economics of Welfare* (London, 1948).
119. Robert Piron, " Consumer's Surplus and Micro-Macro: Comment," *Journal of Political Economy*, Vol. 78, January–February 1970.
120. A. R. Prest and R. Turvey, " Cost Benefit Analysis: A Survey," American Economic Association and Royal Economic Society, *Surveys of Economic Theory*, Vol. 3 (New York, 1965).
121. David Ricardo, *The Principles of Political Economy and Taxation* (London, 1829).
122. Christopher Ritson, " The Use of Home Resources to Save Inputs: A New Look," *Journal of Agricultural Economics*, Vol. 21, January 1970.
123. L. C. Robbins, *The Theory of Economic Policy in English Classical Political Economy* (London, 1952).
124. D. H. Robertson, " Those Empty Boxes," ECONOMIC JOURNAL, Vol. XXXIV, March 1924.
125. Dennis Robertson, " Utility and All What? " ECONOMIC JOURNAL, Vol. LXIV, December 1954.
126. Herbert W. Robinson, " Consumer's Surplus and Taxation: Ex-Ante or Ex-Post? " *South African Journal of Economics*, Vol. 7, September 1939.
127. J. Robinson, " Rising Supply Price," *Economica* (NS), Vol. VIII, February 1941.
128. Joan Robinson, *Economics of Imperfect Competition* (London, 1948).
129. Joan Robinson, *Economic Philosophy* (Chicago, 1962).
130. Peter Ross, " Economies as an Antitrust Defence: Comment," *American Economic Review*, Vol. 58, December 1968.
131. Nancy Ruggles, " The Welfare Basis of the Marginal Cost Pricing Principle," *Review of Economic Studies*, Vol. 17, 1949–50.
132. Nancy Ruggles, " Recent Developments in the Theory of Marginal Cost Pricing," *Review of Economic Studies*, Vol. 17, 1949–50.

133. Paul A. Samuelson, " Constancy of the Marginal Utility of Income," in Oscar Lange *et al.*, *Studies in Mathematical Economics and Econometrics: In Memory of Henry Schultz* (Chicago, 1942).

134. P. A. Samuelson, " Evaluation of Real National Income," *Oxford Economic Papers*, N.S., Vol. 2, January 1950.

135. Paul A. Samuelson, *Economics* (New York, 1951).

136. P. A. Samuelson, " Spatial Price Equilibrium and Linear Programming," *American Economic Review*, Vol. XLII, June 1952.

137. Paul A. Samuelson, *Foundations of Economic Analysis* (New York, 1967).

138. Andrew Schmitz and David Seckler, " Mechanized Agriculture and Social Welfare: The Case of the Tomato Harvester," *American Journal of Agricultural Economics*, Vol. 52, November 1970.

139. Henry Schultz, " Measures of Determining Tariff Effectiveness," *Journal of Farm Economics*, Vol. 17, November 1935.

140. David Schwartzman, " The Effects of Monopoly on Price," *Journal of Political Economy*, Vol. LXVII, August 1959.

141. David Schwartzman, " Monopoly and Wages," *Canadian Journal of Economics and Political Science*, Vol. 61, August 1960.

142. David Schwartzman, " The Burden of Monopoly," *Journal of Political Economy*, Vol. 68, December 1960.

143. Tibor Scitovsky, " A Note on Welfare Propositions in Economics," *Review of Economic Studies*, Vol. 9, November 1941.

144. A. Ross Shepherd, " Economic Rent and the Industry Supply Curve," *Southern Economic Journal*, Vol. XXXVII, October 1970.

145. G. F. Shove, " Varying Costs and Marginal Net Products," ECONOMIC JOURNAL, Vol. XXXVIII, June 1928.

146. R. H. Snape, " Some Effects of Protection in the World Sugar Industry," *Economica*, Vol. 30, June 1963.

147. R. H. Snape, " Sugar: Costs of Protection and Taxation," *Economica*, Vol. 36, February 1969.

148. P. Sraffa, " The Laws of Returns Under Competitive Conditions," ECONOMIC JOURNAL, Vol. XXVI, December 1926.

149. George J. Stigler, " The Development of Utility Theory," *Journal of Political Economy*, Vol. LVIII, October 1950.

150. George J. Stigler, *The Theory of Price* (New York, 1952).

151. George J. Stigler, " The Statistics of Monopoly and Merger," *Journal of Political Economy*, Vol. LXIV, February 1956.

152. L. G. Telser, " On the Regulation of Industry: A Note," *Journal of Political Economy*, Vol. 77, November–December 1969.

153. K. J. M. Tharakan, " The Theory of Consumer's Surplus: A Defense," *Indian Journal of Economics*, Vol. XIX, January 1939.

154. K. J. M. Tharakan, " A Rejoinder," *Indian Journal of Economics*, Vol. XXI, January 1941.

155. J. M. Thomson, " Some Aspects of Evaluating Road Improvements in Congested Areas," *Econometrica*, Vol. 38, March 1970.

156. G. Tintner and M. Patel, " The Evaluation of Indian Fertilizer Projects— An Application of Consumer's and Producer's Surplus," *Journal of Farm Economics*, Vol. 48, August 1966.

157. David G. Tipping, " Consumers' Surplus in Public Enterprise," *The Manchester School of Economics and Social Studies*, Vol. XXXIV, September 1966.

158. Clem Tisdell, " Uncertainty, Instability, Expected Profit," *Econometrica*, Vol. 31, January–April 1963.

159. Andrew H. Trice and Samuel E. Wood. " Measurement of Recreation Benefits," *Land Economics*, Vol. XXXIV, August 1958.

160. Gordon Tullock, " The Welfare Costs of Tariffs, Monopolies and Theft," *Western Economic Journal*, Vol. 5, June 1967.

161. Edward T. Ullman, Ronald R. Boyce, and Donald J. Volk, *The Meramec Basin, Report of the Meramec Basin Research Project to the Meramec Basin Corporation. Vol. II, Economy and Character of the Basin* (St. Louis, 1961).

162. Edward T. Ullman and Donald J. Volk, " An Operational Model for Predicting Reservoir Attendance and Benefits," Papers on the Michigan Academy of Science, Arts and Letters, 1962.

163. W. Vickrey, " Some Objections to Marginal-Cost Pricing," *Journal of Political Economy*, Vol. LVI, June 1948.

164. J. Viner, " Cost Curves and Supply Curves," *Zeitschrift für Nationalökonomie*, Vol. III, 1931–32.

165. Jacob Viner, *Studies in the Theory of International Trade* (New York, 1937).

166. T. D. Wallace, " Measures of Social Costs of Agricultural Programs," *Journal of Farm Economics*, Vol. 44, May 1962.

167. A. A. Walters, " The Theory and Measurement of Private and Social Cost of Highway Congestion," *Econometrica*, Vol. 29, May 1961.

168. H. Y. Wan, " Maximum Bonus—An Alternative Measure for Trading Gains," *Review of Economic Studies*, Vol. 32, January 1965.

169. Frederick V. Waugh, " Does the Consumer Benefit from Price Instability? " *Quarterly Journal of Economics*, Vol. 58, August 1944.

170. Frederick V. Waugh, " Reply," *Quarterly Journal of Economics*, Vol. 59, February 1945.

171. Frederick V. Waugh, " Consumer Aspects of Price Instability," *Econometrica*, Vol. 34, April 1966.

172. G. Weinschenck, W. Henricksmeyer, and F. Aldinger, " The Theory of Spatial Equilibrium and Optimal Location in Agriculture: A Survey," *Review of Marketing and Agricultural Economics*, Vol. 37, March 1969.

173. Finis Welch, " Supply Control with Marketable Quotas: The Cost of Uncertainty," *Journal of Farm Economics*, Vol. 49, August 1967.

174. J. Wemelsfelder, " The Short-Term Effect of the Lowering of Import Duties in Germany," ECONOMIC JOURNAL, Vol. LXX, March 1960.

175. E. Boyd Wennergren, *Value of Water for Boating Recreation*. Utah State University, Logan, Agricultural Experiment Station Bulletin 453, 1965.

176. E. Boyd Wennergren and Gardner B. Delworth, " The Economics of Recreation: Progress and Problems—Comment," *Western Economic Journal*, Vol. 4, Spring 1966.

177. Robert H. Wessel, " What is Producer's Surplus?—Comment," *American Economic Review*, Vol. 59, September 1969.

178. Robert H. Wessel, " A Note on Economic Rent," *American Economic Review*, Vol. 57, December 1967.

179. Oliver E. Williamson, " Peak-Load Pricing and Optimal Capacity Under Indivisible Constraints," *American Economic Review*, Vol. 56, September 1966.

180. Oliver E. Williamson, " Economies as an Antitrust Defense: The Welfare Tradeoffs," *American Economic Review*, Vol. 58, March 1968.

181. Oliver E. Williamson, " Economies as an Antitrust Defense: Correction and Reply," *American Economic Review*, Vol. 58, December 1968.

182. Oliver E. Williamson, " Economies as an Antitrust Defense: Reply," *American Economic Review*, Vol. 59, December 1969.

183. T. Wilson, " Price and Output Policy of State Enterprise: A Comment," ECONOMIC JOURNAL, Vol. LV, December 1945.

184. D. M. Winch, " Consumer's Surplus and the Compensation Principle," *American Economic Review*, Vol. 55, June 1965.

185. Dean A. Worcester, " A Reconsideration of the Theory of Rent," *American Economic Review*, Vol. XXXVI, June 1946.

186. Dean A. Worcester, Jr., " Innovations in the Calculation of Welfare Loss to Monopoly," *Western Economic Journal*, Vol. VII, September 1969.

187. Allyn A. Young, " Pigou's Wealth and Welfare," *Quarterly Journal of Economics*, Vol. 27, August 1913.

188. Allyn A. Young, " Marshall on Consumers' Surplus in International Trade," *Quarterly Journal of Economics*, Vol. 39, November 1924.

189. Allyn A. Young, " Increasing Returns and Economic Progress," ECONOMIC JOURNAL, Vol. XXXVIII, December 1928.

190. Albert Zucker, " On the Desirability of Price Instability: An Extension of the Discussion," *Econometrica*, Vol. 33, April 1965.

191. Pinhas Zusman, A. Melamed, and I. Katzir, *Possible Trade and Welfare Effects of EEC and ' Reference Price ' Policy on the European-Mediterranean Market for Winter Oranges*. University of California, Berkeley, Giannini Foundation Monograph 24, 1969.

Three Basic Postulates for Applied Welfare Economics: An Interpretive Essay

By Arnold C. Harberger

University of Chicago

I would like to extend my thanks to my colleague, Harry G. Johnson, for his helpful comments, to Daniel Wisecarver, for help extending well beyond the normal call of duty for a research assistant, and to Rudiger Dornbusch and Robert Gordon for valuable suggestions given after the first draft of this paper was completed. Needless to add, they do not bear any responsibility for such flaws or deficiencies as may remain in this paper.

THIS PAPER is intended not as a scientific study, nor as a review of the literature, but rather as a tract—an open letter to the profession, as it were—pleading that three basic postulates be accepted as providing a conventional framework for applied welfare economics. The postulates are:

a) the competitive demand price for a given unit measures the value of that unit to the demander;

b) the competitive supply price for a given unit measures the value of that unit to the supplier;

c) when evaluating the net benefits or costs of a given action (project, program, or policy), the costs and benefits accruing to each member of the relevant group (*e.g.*, a nation) should normally be added without regard to the individual(s) to whom they accrue.

In an era when literally thousands of studies involving cost-benefit analysis or other types of applied welfare economics are underway at any given moment, the need for an accepted set of professional standards for this type of study should be obvious. In proffering postulates *a–c* as the basis for such a set of standards, I do not want to overstate their benefits. Just as the road-construction standards that a team of highway engineers must meet can be checked by other highway engineers, so the exercise in applied welfare economics carried out by one team of economists should be subject to check by others. But while the highway engineers can apply professional standards to characteristics such as thickness of base, load-carrying capacity, drainage characteristics, and the like, characteristics such as scenic beauty are beyond their competence as professional engineers. In the same way, any program or project that is subjected to applied-welfare-economic analysis is likely to have characteristics upon which the economist as such is not professionally qualified to pronounce, and about which one economist is not professionally qualified to check the opinion of another. These elements—which surely include the income-distributional and national-defense aspects of any project or program, and probably its natural-beauty aspects as well—may be exceedingly important, perhaps even the dominant factors governing any policy decision, but they are not a part of that package of expertise that distinguishes the professional economist from the rest of humanity. And that is why we cannot expect to reach a professional consensus concerning them. If we are to take a (hopefully justified) professional pride in our work, we also must have the modesty and honesty not to claim for our profession more than we are particularly qualified to deliver. But this does not mean that we need be silent on matters that lie outside the range of our professional expertise; economists should probably participate more rather than less in the public discussion of such matters, but hopefully in a context that recognizes the extra-professional nature of their intervention.

Some readers will undoubtedly recognize that postulates *a-c* underlie most analyses that use the concepts of consumer and producer surplus. That being the case, one might ask, what is the need for a tract on the subject? My answer stems from the fact that, as an inveterate practitioner of applied welfare economics along many different lines, I encounter with considerable regularity colleagues who are skeptical of consumer surplus on one or more of several alleged grounds:

(*i*) Consumer-surplus analysis is valid only when the marginal utility of real income is constant.

(*ii*) Consumer-surplus analysis does not take account of changes in income distribution caused by the action(s) being analyzed.

(*iii*) Consumer-surplus analysis is partial-equilibrium in nature, and does not take account of the general-equilibrium consequences of the actions whose effects are being studied.

(*iv*) Consumer-surplus analysis, though valid for small changes, is not so for large changes.

(*v*) The concept of consumer surplus has been rendered obsolete by revealed-preference analysis.

While I do not have the impression that the skeptics dominate professional opinion in this area, they are sufficiently numerous (and a number of them sufficiently prestigious) that we surely cannot be said to have achieved a high degree of professional consensus on the subject. Yet I feel, precisely because of the power and wide applicability of the consumer-surplus concept, that a recognizable degree of consensus concerning it would increase, to society's general benefit, the influence on public policy of good economic analysis. Moreover, I think that there is a fair chance of convincing a goodly share of the skeptics that postulates *a* to *c* constitute the most reasonable basis on which to seek professional consensus in the area of applied welfare economics. The merit of attaining something like a consensus, and the possibility of helping to induce some movement toward that end, provide the motivation for this tract.

II

Ordinarily, I would consider it quixotic to expect much to result from any such effort. But in this case my hopes are buoyed by the fact that it is easily possible for many skeptics to join the consensus without really changing their minds on any fundamental issues. How can this happen? Because *i*) we already have a reasonably well-established consensus on the basic methodology of national-income measurement, *ii*) it is easy to show that postulates *a-c* incorporate a greater degree of subtlety of economic analysis than does national-income methodology, and *iii*) most of the "objections" to consumer-surplus analysis hold *a fortiori* with respect to the measurement of national income. If we are prepared to more-or-less agree on national-income methodology (while being mindful of its defects), why should we resist approaching an agreement on a methodology for applied welfare economics (also keeping its defects in mind, but aware at the same time that they are much less serious than those applying to national income)?

Let us consider specifically objections (*i*), (*ii*) and (*v*) above, comparing in each case the force with which the objection applies to consumer-surplus analysis on the one hand, and to the use of national income as an indication of welfare on the other—objections (*iii*) and (*iv*) are dealt with in section III below.

Objection (i). I will later show that the assumption of constancy of the marginal utility of real income is not essential for the validity of consumer-surplus measures of welfare. Here, however, I shall only note that the benefits and costs treated in most applications of consumer-surplus analysis (*e.g.*, measures of the efficiency costs of a tax or an agricultural program, cost-benefit analyses of highway or irrigation projects, etc.) involve only a small fraction of a normal year's growth in GNP. Far more vulnerable to the objection that the marginal utility of real income might have changed are observations like "Real GNP doubled between 1950 and 1970," or even "National income will grow by $60 billion next year."

Objection (ii). By the same token, the changes in income distribution resulting from a particular measure being subjected to cost-benefit or consumer-surplus analysis are likely to be minimal by comparison with those that occur from decade to decade, or even from year to year, as a consequence of all causes. If, then, it is felt that "distributional weights" should be applied in the former case, before judgments can be made, it is even more important that they should be incorporated in the latter case.

Objection (v). Consider the case of the coal miner who, racked with silicosis, voluntarily quits a $7-an-hour job in the mine to take a newly-available $2-an-hour job clerking in a grocery store. National income goes down, but welfare in all likelihood goes up. In this case consumer-surplus analysis accords with revealed preference, while the movement of national income is in the opposite direction from the change in welfare. The same is true for the textbook case of the housekeeper who marries her employer.

Of course, economists do not truly believe that real NNP or national income is a complete measure of welfare. But it is equally true that in most of the contexts in which changes in these magnitudes, or comparisons of them across regions or countries are dealt with, the discussion carries strong welfare connotations, often to the point where it would be meaningless if those connotations were denied. National income and NNP are, in a very real sense, measures of welfare under certain assumptions, but only to a first order of approximation. No one would deny that many other factors are important—the strength of the social fabric, the quality of life, and certainly the issue of to whom the income accrues—but it is not feasible to build these into a national-income measure. Hypothetically, one might contemplate a national income measure incorporating "distributional weights," but two obstacles stand in its way: first, the impossibility of achieving a consensus with regard to the weights, and second, the fact that most of the data from which the national accounts are built are aggregates in the first place, and do not distinguish the individuals or groups whose dollars they represent. Giving equal weight to all dollars of income is mathematically the simplest rule, and our data come that way in any event. In a sense, the second obstacle imposes, rather arbitrarily to be sure, a solution to the perplexing difficulties posed by the first. This solution is obviously a far-from-perfect measure of national welfare—indeed it is surprising how little dissatisfaction has been expressed (until quite recently) with its use as such. But even its firmest detractors would probably not deny the usefulness of the national accounts and the necessity for them to be built on the basis of rules or conventions reflecting some degree of professional consensus.

An easy way to see the relationship between national income and the consumer-surplus concept is to consider the first two terms of the Taylor expansion of a utility function

$$(1) \qquad U = U(X_1, X_2 \cdots X_n)$$

788   *Journal of Economic Literature*

$$\Delta U = \sum_i U_i \Delta X_i$$

(2)

$$+ \frac{1}{2} \sum_i \sum_j U_{ij} \Delta X_i \Delta X_j.$$

Since U_i is a function solely of $(X_1, X_2 \cdots X_n)$, we can write $\sum_j U_{ij} \Delta X_j = \Delta U_i$; with this (2) simplifies to

(3) $$\Delta U = \sum_i U_i \Delta X_i + \frac{1}{2} \sum_i \Delta U_i \Delta X_i.$$

Now, assuming utility maximization in the face of market prices $(P_1 \cdots P_n)$ we have $U_i = \lambda P_i$, where λ represents the marginal utility of income, and

(4) $$\Delta U_i = \lambda^0 \Delta P_i + P_i{}^0 \Delta \lambda + \Delta P_i \Delta \lambda.$$

Substituting from (4) into (3) we obtain

(5)

$$\frac{\Delta U}{\left(\lambda^0 + \frac{1}{2}\,\Delta\lambda\right)} = \sum P_i{}^0 \Delta X_i$$

$$+ \frac{1}{2} \sum \Delta P_i \Delta X_i + \frac{1}{4}\,\frac{\Delta\lambda \sum \Delta P_i \Delta X_i}{\left(\lambda^0 + \frac{1}{2}\,\Delta\lambda\right)}.$$

Neglecting third order terms, this yields

(5′)

$$\frac{\Delta U}{\lambda^0 + \frac{1}{2}\,\Delta\lambda} \approx \sum P_i{}^0 \Delta X_i$$

$$+ \frac{1}{2} \sum \Delta P_i \Delta X_i.$$

The first term on the right-hand side of (5′) measures the first-order change in utility, and can be identified with the change in national income (or, more properly, net national product) expressed in constant prices. The second term measures the second-order change in utility, and can be identified with the change in consumer surplus.[1] The fact

[1] This is strictly true only when the point of departure is one of full, undisturbed equilibrium. When the starting point is one where distortions are already present, some of the change in consumer surplus is incorporated in the first term. This point will be treated in more detail below.

that the consumer-surplus concept is associated with a higher-order term in the Taylor expansion of the utility function is simply the mathematical counterpart of the statement made earlier that "postulates *a–c* incorporate a greater degree of subtlety of economic analysis than does national income methodology."

Note, too, that (5) in effect converts the change in utility into monetary terms by dividing it by the marginal utility of income. There is obviously no problem when the latter is not changing, but when it does change as a consequence of the action(s) being analyzed, the conversion of utility into money is implicitly carried out at the midpoint of the beginning and ending marginal utilities of income. The criticism[2] that consumer-sur-

[2] The origin of this criticism is probably the thought that changes in consumer surplus ought directly to measure changes in utility. That this would be a fruitless pursuit should be obvious—among other things consumer surplus would not be invariant to monotonic transformations of the utility function. However, the measure $\frac{1}{2}\sum \Delta X_i \Delta P_i$ is invariant, with the change in ΔU stemming from a monotonic transformation being offset by the change in $(\lambda + \frac{1}{2}\Delta\lambda)$ in the denominator of the left-hand side of (5). The following way of stating the same argument avoids the approximation implicit in a two-term Taylor expansion: the change in utility stemming from the change in a policy variable from z_0 to z^* is

$$\Delta U = \int_{z_0}^{z^*} \sum_i U_i(z)\,\frac{\partial X_i}{\partial z}\,dz.$$

This, being expressed in utils, is not invariant to a monotonic transformation. However, transforming utility into money continuously through the integration process, always at the marginal utility of money prevailing at that point, we have

$$\Delta W = \int_{z_0}^{z^*} \sum_i \frac{U_i(z)}{\lambda(z)}\,\frac{\partial X_i}{\partial z}\,dz$$

$$= \int_{z_0}^{z^*} \sum_i P_i(z)\,\frac{\partial X_i}{\partial z}\,dz.$$

This obviously is invariant under any transformation of the original utility function which leaves unchanged the relevant behavioral reactions to changes in z.

An issue arises in connection with the comparability of measures of welfare loss, when one is comparing moves on two different paths (say T_1 and T_2) away from the undistorted equilibrium. If the marginal utility of the numeraire (here real income) is constant, there is no issue in this regard. However, comparability does not

plus concepts have validity only when the
marginal utility of income is constant must
therefore be rejected.

The conversion of utility into money also
greatly eases the aggregation problem.
Clearly both the first-order and the second-
order terms on the right-hand side of (5) can
be aggregated over individuals without difficulty.

III

In this section I shall discuss objections
(*iii*) and (*iv*), which were left aside in the
comparison between consumer surplus and
national income methodologies in the preceding section. Objection (*iii*), that consumer-
surplus analysis is partial-equilibrium in nature, and fails to take account of general-
equilibrium considerations, is totally invalid
on a theoretical level, but can fairly be levied
against some practical applications.

Taking the theoretical issue first, one need
only note that rigorous general-equilibrium
formulations of consumer-surplus measurement have long since been a part of the corpus of economic theory. Hotelling [10, 1938],
Hicks [7, 1941; 8, 1946; 9, 1956], and Meade
[18, 1955, esp. Vol. II] all have derived, in a
general-equilibrium framework, measures of
welfare change that are consistent with
postulates *a-c*, and many others have followed in their train.[3]

The key to understanding the general-
equilibrium nature of the consumer-surplus
concept is the following simple measure of
welfare change:

$$(6) \qquad \Delta W = \int_{z=0}^{z^*} \sum_i D_i(z) \frac{\partial X_i}{\partial z} dz.$$

---

require constancy of the marginal utility of real income,
but only "well-behavedness." By this I mean that when
real income falls by ΔY as a consequence of the imposition of T_2, its marginal utility should change by the
same amount as occurs when real income falls by ΔY as
a consequence of a tax T_1.

[3] See Corlett and Hague [1, 1953]; Harberger [3, 1964;
4, 1964]; Johnson [11, 1960; 12, 1962]; Lange [14,
1942]; Lipsey and Lancaster [15, 1956–57]; Lipsey
[16, 1970]; and McKenzie [17, 1951].

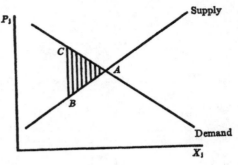

Figure 1.

Here D_i represents the excess of marginal
social benefit over marginal social cost per
unit level of activity i, X_i represents the
number of units of activity i, and z is the
policy variable, the effects of a change in
which we are interested in measuring. The
D_i (distortions) can take many forms—about
which more will be said below—but here, for
simplicity of exposition, I shall assume that
all the D_i take the form of taxes. A tax quite
obviously drives a wedge between demand
price (which under postulate *a* measures the
value of the marginal unit to the demander)
and supply price (which under postulate *b*
measures the value of the marginal unit to
the supplier), and this fits most naturally
into the framework of this paper.

If a tax is placed on a single good j in the
absence of any other distortions, (6) becomes

$$(7) \qquad \Delta W = \int_{T_j=0}^{T_j^*} T_j \frac{\partial X_j}{\partial T_j} dT_j,$$

which is equal to the familiar welfare-cost
triangle (*ABC* in Figure 1). Though the
demand and supply functions of other goods
may shift as a consequence of placing a tax
on good j, the measure of welfare change is unaffected by such shifts since the distortions
D_i in all other markets are, by assumption in
this case, zero. However, if taxes on other
goods already exist when T_j^* is imposed, the
effects of its imposition are given by:

$$(8) \quad \Delta W = \int_{T_j=0}^{T_j^*} T_j \frac{\partial X_j}{\partial T_j} dT_j$$

$$+ \int_{T_j=0}^{T_j^*} \sum_{i \neq j} T_i \frac{\partial X_i}{\partial T_j} dT_j.$$

This is equal to the triangle ABC in Figure 1 (which generates a negative contribution to welfare) plus, with constant T_is, the expression $\sum_{i \neq j} T_i \Delta_i$, where ΔX_i measures the change in the equilibrium quantity of X_i occasioned by the imposition of T_j^*. Any of the terms in this summation, which is what makes the difference between partial- and general-equilibrium approaches when other distortions are present, can be either positive or negative—when the distortion itself is positive (*e.g.*, a tax), a positive contribution is made to the change in welfare if, as a consequence of a new disturbance (in this case the imposition of T_j^*), X_i increases, and a negative contribution if X_i decreases. When the distortion itself is negative (*e.g.*, a subsidy), the contribution to welfare associated with activity i as a consequence of T_j^* is negative if $\partial X_i / \partial T_j > 0$ and positive if $\partial X_i / \partial T_j < 0$. This case is illustrated in Figure 2, where it is assumed that both the demand and supply curves of X_k shift as a consequence of the imposition of T_j^*. If the shift is from the solid demand and supply curves (when $T_j = 0$) to the broken ones (when $T_j = T_j^*$), the area $EFGH$ ($= T_k \Delta X_k$) is an added loss; if the shift is in the other direction it is an added benefit helping to offset (and possibly actually outweighing) the triangle ABC in Figure 1.

This is a convenient place to point out the relationship between the general expression (8) for welfare change and the approximation (5'). Define $C_i + T_i = P_i$, and assume constant costs of production C_i, with the resource constraint $\sum C_i X_i = Y$, a constant.[4] When a tax is imposed on X_j in the presence of pre-existing taxes on other goods $i \neq j$, we have, substituting $C_i + T_i = P_i^0$ for $i \neq j$, $C_j = P_j^0$ and $T_j^* = \Delta P_j$ into (5'),

$$P_i^0 \Delta X_i + \frac{1}{2} \sum \Delta P_i \Delta X_i = \sum C_i \Delta X_i$$

$$(5'') \qquad + \sum T_i \Delta X_i + \frac{1}{2} \sum \Delta C_i \Delta X_i$$

$$+ \frac{1}{2} T_j^* \Delta X_j.$$

Since $\sum C_i \Delta X_i = \sum \Delta C_i \Delta X_i = 0$ under our assumptions, we have

$$\sum P_i^0 \Delta X_i + \frac{1}{2} \sum \Delta P_i \Delta X_i$$

$$(5''') \qquad = \sum T_i \Delta X_i + \frac{1}{2} T_j^* \Delta X_j$$

as a measure of the change in welfare stemming from the imposition of T_j^*.[5] This is

----

[4] These assumptions are consistent with a situation in which the tax revenues received by the government are redistributed to the private sector *via* neutral transfers. For a more detailed treatment see Harberger [3, 1964].

[5] Where no pre-existing distortions are present, and a vector of distortions $T^* = (T_1^*, T_2^* \cdots T_n^*)$ is introduced, (6) becomes, for linear demand and supply curves, $\Delta W = \frac{1}{2} \sum T_i \Delta X_i$, where

$$\Delta X_i = \int_{\mu=0}^{1} \left(\frac{\partial X_i}{\partial T} \right)' T^* \mu d\mu.$$

That is to say, if the final set of taxes is (.5, .2, .1), one can imagine the process of integration taking place through steps like (.05, .02, .01), (.10, .04, .02), (.15, .06, .03), etc. The locus of points traced out by this exercise will define the set of triangles $\frac{1}{2} T_i \Delta X_i$. As this exercise can in principle be performed for any set of distortions (not just taxes), it is quite general. One must note, however, that the triangles traced out here are not triangles between stable demand and supply curves but rather triangles defined by the loci of marginal social benefit (demand price) and marginal social cost (supply

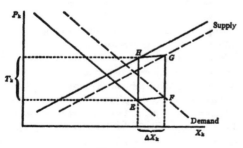

Figure 2.

Harberger: Postulates for Applied Welfare Economics

precisely what emerges from (8) in the case where the demand and supply curves for X_j are linear. It also shows how, when there are pre-existing distortions, elements of consumer surplus are present in the expression $\Sigma P_i^0 \Delta X_i$, representing the first-order approximation to welfare change.

Let us return to the discussion of objection (*iii*), that consumer-surplus analysis neglects general-equilibrium considerations. While it is clear that no theoretical obstacle stands in the way of taking such considerations into account, it is in fact rarely done in studies involving applied welfare economics. I do not want to appear to defend this neglect—indeed, the sooner it is rectified, the better—but at the same time I want to try to dispel any thoughts that the job of incorporating general-equilibrium aspects is so big as to be effectively hopeless. All that job entails is adding to the standard partial-equilibrium welfare analysis (of the tax T_j^* in our example), an expression $\Sigma_{i \neq j} D_i \Delta X_i$. That may look like a formidable task but it need not be. The set of activities with significant distortions is a subset of the set of all activities; the set of activities whose levels are significantly affected by the action under study (*e.g.*, T_j^*) is another subset of the set of all activities. Only their intersection (see Figure 3) is important for the analysis of the effects of the specific policy action in question, and it is to be hoped that in most cases the number of elements in it will be of manageable size.[6]

Objection (*iv*) can be dealt with on several levels. In the first place, there is the issue

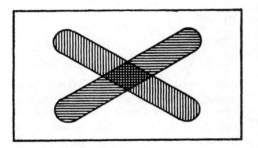

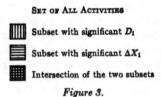

SET OF ALL ACTIVITIES

|||| Subset with significant D_i

≡ Subset with significant ΔX_i

⊞ Intersection of the two subsets

Figure 3.

of the exactness of (5); when the basic utility functions are quadratic, the first two terms of the Taylor expansion are all that are needed to describe the function fully; but when the basic utility functions are not linear or quadratic, (5) will be an approximation. And (5′) is vulnerable even when the utility function is quadratic, because of its neglect of the third term of (5). But while (5) and (5′) thus may contain errors of approximation which will be smaller, the smaller are the changes being studied, (6) is not subject to the same charge. The integrals set out there can be taken for curved as well as linear demand and supply curves, or, more properly stated, for curved or linear loci of demand prices and supply prices.

At another level entirely, one might interpret the large-versus-small-changes issue as raising up the old consumer-surplus conundrums about the value attaching to the first units of liquid or the first units of food, etc. I prefer to sidestep this issue on the ground that the problems arising in applied welfare economics typically do not involve carrying people to or from the zero point in their demand curves for food or for liquids, and where they do (as, for example in famine relief programs), it appears more appropriate

---

price) as μ goes from zero to one. On this result see Hotelling's equation 19 and the subsequent discussion [10, 1938].

[6] Certain distortions, such as the property tax or the corporation income tax, which apply to a large subset of activities, can be taken into account through the use of shadow prices—*e.g.*, in this case the social opportunity cost of capital. See Harberger [5, 1968 and 6, 1969]. Once the "general" distortions have been dealt with in this way, the remaining ones, it is to be hoped, will be sufficiently small in number so as to keep the problem manageable.

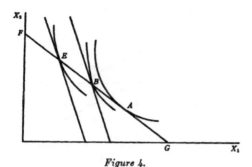

Figure 4.

to approach the problem through assigning a monetary value to the human lives saved or lost, a task which necessarily carries us beyond the narrow confines of consumer-surplus analysis.

At still another level, when large changes are involved, the well-behavedness of functions is less easily guaranteed than when only small changes are present. For example, it is easy to show that the Hicks-Slutsky substitution properties apply to demand functions defined by movements constrained to a locus of the form $\Sigma C_i X_i = Y$, a constant (FG in Figure 4) so long as one is concerned with small changes in the neighborhood of the undistorted equilibrium (*e.g.*, in the neighborhood of A). However, this cannot be shown to be generally true for large changes. For example, Figure 4 is so constructed that at both B and E the indifference curves intersecting FG have the same slope. This means that a demand function constrained to the locus FG (with real income being held constant in this sense) will have two quantities associated with the same relative price. Except in the case where the income expansion path at that price coincided with the segment EB between these two quantities, there would have to be some range(s) in that quantity interval in which the own-price elasticity of each good was positive, thus violating one of the Hicks-Slutsky conditions.[7]

[7] For a further elaboration of this point see Foster and Sonnenschein [2, 1970].

There are at least two ways in which analyses based on postulates *a* to *c* can be justified in the face of this possible criticism. At the strictly theoretical level, while some results of some exercises in applied welfare economics may derive directly from the Hicks-Slutsky properties, the validity of equation (6) does not depend on the existence of well-behavedness in this sense. Alternatively one may simply take it as a matter of convention that, just as measurements of real national income in a sense are built on a linear approximation of the utility function, so we shall base consumer-surplus and cost-benefit analyses upon a quadratic approximation of that function, incorporating the Hicks-Slutsky properties. This more "pragmatic" approach would presumably be based on the unlikelihood of our encountering cases in which empirical evidence can be mustered showing that such an approximation yields seriously biased numerical estimates of welfare costs and/or benefits.

A final variant of the large-versus-small-changes question concerns the normalization of measures of welfare change to correct for changes in the general price level. Consider the case of a two-good economy with $X_1 C_1 + X_2 C_2 = Y$, a constant. In this context one can analyze the effects of imposing, say, a 100 percent tax on X_1, with no distortion on X_2, or alternatively granting a 50 percent subsidy to X_2 with no distortion in the market for X_1. Assuming that the tax proceeds are returned to the public via neutral transfers and that the money for the subsidy is raised by neutral taxes, we should expect the same real equilibrium to be achieved in both of the alternative situations being compared. We should also, presumably, arrive at the same measure for ΔW. If we set $C_1 = C_2 = 1$, which is simply a question of choice of units and entails no loss of generality, with the 100 percent tax on X_1, the measure of welfare change is $\Delta W = \frac{1}{2}\Sigma \Delta X_1 \Delta P_1 = \frac{1}{2}\Delta X_1$. Alternatively, with a 50 percent subsidy to X_2, the welfare change measure is

$-\frac{1}{4}\Delta X_2$, which is equal to $\frac{1}{4}\Delta X_1$, since under our assumptions $\Delta X_2 = -\Delta X_1$. This ambiguity can readily be resolved through the appropriate choice of a numeraire. When X_1 is the numeraire, the 100 percent tax on it is reflected in the price vector changing from $(1, 1)$ to $(1, \frac{1}{2})$, which is exactly what happens when a 50 percent subsidy to X_2 is introduced, so long as X_1 is the numeraire. Likewise, when X_2 is the numeraire, the 50 percent subsidy to it produces the same price vector $(2, 1)$ as is generated by the 100 percent tax on X_1. My own preference as to a conventional way of correcting for changes in the absolute price level is to normalize on net national product = national income. This entails setting $\Sigma P_i X_i = \Sigma C_i X_i = Y$, a constant, which in turn implies, since $C_i + T_i = P_i$, that $\Sigma T_i X_i = 0$. This normalization automatically calls attention to the fact that most problems of applied welfare economics are "substitution-effect-only" problems, a point to which we shall turn in the next section.

IV

In this section I shall discuss some of the complexities that may arise in applications of the analytical approach represented by postulates *a–c*. Let us first consider in more detail the close relation of the postulates to "revealed preference." Essentially, postulates *a* and *b* state that when demanders (suppliers) pay (get) their demand (supply) price for each marginal unit, the balance of their indifference as between demanding (supplying) that unit and undertaking the relevant available alternative activities has just barely been tipped. In effect, demand and supply prices are measures of the alternative benefits that demanders and suppliers forego when they do what they decide to do.

Equation (6) appears to capture all effects of an exogenous policy change, z, that are relevant to our three postulates—and indeed it does except when the exogenous change z in itself alters the resources available to the

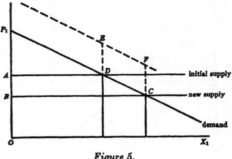

Figure 5.

economy in question, the technological possibilities under which it operates, or the trading conditions that it faces in external markets. So long as the exogenous change does not alter any of these things, all that it entails is the reshuffling of available resources among activities. It is in this sense that "substitution effects only" are involved in expression (6) in such cases.

To see that (6) does not capture the "income effects" of changes in resources, technology, or trading conditions, let us consider them in turn. Suppose, for example, that the exogenous change is that emigrant remittances, which were previously outlawed under foreign countries' exchange controls, are now permitted. The country receiving the remittances clearly gains, even if no distortions whatsoever are present in its economy. Hence (6) fails to capture the direct benefit associated with the remittances, even though in the presence of distortions it would capture the welfare "repercussions" that the receipt of the remittances might engender.

When technological advance occurs, the resources thus freed are enabled to increase total welfare, again even if no distortions are present. In Figure 5, the benefit from a technological advance that reduced unit costs from OA to OB would be given by the area $ABCD$ in the absence of other distortions, and by that area plus expression (6) in their presence. Expression (6) would of course include the area $CDEF$ if a unit tax equal to ED were already in existence on X_1. The exogenous force z in (6) would in this case be the reduction in unit cost (price) of producing X_1 and the terms in $\partial X_i/\partial z$ would include movements due to both the income and the substitution effects of this price change.

An exactly similar analysis applies in the case of an improvement in trading conditions in external markets. Here again a measure of the contribution to welfare that would be entailed in the absence of distortions must be added to (6), and the $\partial X_i/\partial z$ in (6) reinterpreted as above.

I believe that the three cases mentioned—new resources (gifts from outside), new technology (gifts of science and nature), and improved trading terms—or their respective negatives, are the only ones for which estimated first-order income effects must be added to expression (6). It is very important to note that such effects are not generated by price changes taking place within the economy under study in the absence of technical change. In this case, unless there are distortions, the benefits to demanders of a fall in price are cancelled by the costs to suppliers, and *vice versa* in the case of a rise in price. And when distortions are present, (6) captures their effect. Likewise it is important to recognize that no additional term should be added to (6) in cases where production moves from a point on the true (outer) production frontier to some interior point as a consequence of the introduction of a new distortion (such as a tax on the employment of a factor in some lines of industry but not in others).

This brings to mind a second subtlety involved in (6): it is essential to recognize that the X_i refer to activities, not just products. In the case just mentioned the tax would be on the activity of using, *e.g.*, capital in a certain subset of industries—say the corporate sector. D_i would here be the tax per unit of corporate capital, and X_i its amount.

The activities of producing and consuming a given good should be kept analytically separate whenever the distortions affecting them differ;[8] likewise, a given type of activity which is affected by different distortions in different regions should be broken down into as many separate activities as there are different distortions. Perhaps the best guide that can be given in this matter is "identify the relevant distortions and let them define the relevant set of activities."

We now turn to a brief listing of the various types of distortion. (1) Taxes have probably been given sufficient attention already; let me only add that all kinds of taxes (income, excise, property, sales, consumption, production, value-added, etc.) fit easily into the framework presented here. (2) Monopoly profits, in the sense of any return (above the normal earnings of capital) that is obtained as a consequence of artificially restricting sales to a point where price exceeds marginal cost should also clearly be included. Note that for a great many analytical purposes monopoly profits can be treated as a privately-imposed and privately-collected tax. (3) The excess of price over marginal revenue in any external market in which the society in question has monopoly power is another case. This is a negative distortion which can be offset by an optimal export tax or by the implicit tax imposed by a private export monopoly. Categories (4) and (5) are simply the counterparts of (2) and (3) for the case of monopsony, the distortion in (4) stemming from monopsony profits, and that in (5) from the excess of marginal cost over price in any external market in which the society in question has monopsony power. (6) Externalities of all kinds represent distortions, positive or negative. Pollution of air or water is a negative distortion, which could, under postulates *a–c*, be offset by a tax per unit of pollutant equal to what people

[8] Except in the trivial case of a closed economy or of non-traded goods, where production and consumption are necessarily the same.

would be willing to pay not to have it, or what they require as compensation in order to put up with it. The congestion of highways and streets represents another negative distortion, which could in principle be offset by an optimum congestion toll reflecting the extra cost (in terms of time, fuel, wear and tear, etc.) imposed upon others as a consequence of the presence of the marginal driver on the road.

Some readers may be inclined to question my classifying all taxes (and all monopoly profits) as distortions, only to go on to point out cases where they can be used to offset other distortions. Why not make special categories for cases like the optimum tariff, optimum export tax, optimum pollution charge, and optimum congestion toll? My answer is twofold. First, it is overwhelmingly simpler to avoid the special categories, and its cost—if any—is only the acceptance of the idea that distortions can offset each other. But this idea is needed in any event for activities where more than one distortion is present; different distortions applying to a given activity can either reinforce, or wholly or partially offset each other. Second, by avoiding special categories we highlight the fact that we are very unlikely to find optimal taxes and tolls in any real-world context.

V

This brings me back to my main theme: to plead for the "conventionalization" of postulates *a–c*. Arguing in favor of them are the facts that they are both simple and robust and that they underlie a long tradition in applied welfare economics. They are simple both in the sense that their use entails no more than the standard techniques of received economic theory, and in the sense that the data that their use requires are more likely to be available than those required by alternative sets of postulates (in particular any that involve the full-blown use of "distributional weights").

The robustness of the postulates is another attribute of special importance. They can readily be used to define a set of policies that characterizes a full optimum. This entails no more than introducing taxes, subsidies, or other policies to neutralize distortions (*e.g.*, monopoly, pollution) that would otherwise exist, so that the consolidated D_i affecting each activity are all zero, and raising government revenue by taxes that are truly neutral (lump-sum or head taxes),[9] or (cheating only slightly) by almost-neutral taxes such as Kaldor's progressive consumption-expenditure tax [13, 1955]. The postulates can also, in principle, be used to solve second-best problems such as finding the excise tax rates T_i on a subset of commodities $X_1, X_2 \cdots X_k$ that entails the minimum cost of distortions while still raising a given amount of revenue. But these problems, taken from the theoretical literature, are likely to remain textbook problems. The practitioner of applied welfare economics knows full well that his clients do not come to him in search of full optima or elegant suboptima. He is more likely to be asked which of two alternative agricultural programs is better, or what resource-allocation costs a given tax increase involves, or whether a certain bridge is worth its cost. And to be relevant, his answer must recognize the existence of many distortions in the economy, over whose presence neither he nor his client have control. Most applied welfare economics thus answers questions like "Does this action help or hurt, and by approximately how much?" or "Which of two or three alternative actions helps most or hurts least, and by approximately how much?"—all this in a context in which most (if not all) existing distortions have to be taken as given. It is the fact that the three postulates are able to handle these kinds of questions, as well as more elegant optimization problems, that gives them the robustness to which I refer.

[9] The best definition of a head tax is one which must be paid either with money or with the taxpayer's head!

While it is true that there is no complete correspondence between what is traditional and what is right, some weight must be given to the fact that no alternative set of basic assumptions comes nearly as close as postulates *a–c* to distilling the fundamental assumptions of applied welfare economics as we know it. These postulates are reflected not only in the general-equilibrium literature referred to in footnotes 5 and 6, but also in the standard practice of down-to-earth cost-benefit analyses [see, for example: 20, U. S. Inter-Agency Committee on Water Resources, 1958]. And it is here, really, that the need for a consensus is greatest. In the United States, cost-benefit (and its counterpart, "cost-effectiveness") analysis received a major boost when the PPB (Planning-Programming-Budgeting) concept was endorsed by President Lyndon Johnson and decreed as official policy by the Bureau of the Budget. And at the state and local level, investment projects and programs are also being scrutinized with an unprecedented degree of care, largely owing to the increasing concern that people have for environmental issues. Moreover, not just the United States is involved in this movement; the concerns about the environment, the worries about "what we are doing to ourselves," the recognition that our resources are too scarce to be wasted on bad programs, have no national limits. There is, indeed, a worldwide trend in which, country by country, an increasing fraction of the key decision-making posts are occupied by economists, and in which increasing efforts are applied to provide a sound economic justification for the projects that governments undertake. Finally, we have seen in the last decade a growing involvement of international organizations in the issues to which this paper is addressed: three regional development banks newly formed for Africa, Asia, and Latin America; increasing resources are devoted by the United Nations Development Programme to project identification and

development, and by the World Bank to project financing. The OECD [19, 1968, 1969] has also shown increasing concern in this area.

The developments described above simply highlight the need for a set of standards, of "rules of the game" by which our professional work in applied welfare economics can be guided and judged. The three basic postulates that have been the subject of this essay provide a *de minimis* answer to this need: their simplicity, their robustness, and the long tradition that they represent all argue for them as the most probable common denominator on which a professional consensus on procedures for applied welfare economics can be based.

And so, having made my plea, let me salute the profession with what might well have been the title of this paper, with what is certainly the key that points to the solution of most problems in applied welfare economics, with what surely should be the motto of any society that we applied welfare economists might form, and what probably, if only we could learn to pronounce it, should be our password:

$$" \int_{z=0}^{z^*} \sum_i D_i(z) \, \frac{\partial X_i}{\partial z} \, dz. "$$

REFERENCES

1. CORLETT, W. J. and HAGUE, D. C. "Complementarity and the Excess Burden of Taxation," *Rev. Econ. Stud.*, 1953, *21*(1), pp. 21–30.

2. FOSTER, E. and SONNENSCHEIN, H. "Price Distortion and Economic Welfare," *Econometrica*, March 1970, *38*(2), pp. 281–97.

3. HARBERGER, A. C. "Taxation, Resource Allocation and Welfare" in NATIONAL BUREAU OF ECONOMIC RESEARCH AND THE BROOKINGS INSTITUTION, *The role of direct and indirect taxes in the federal revenue system.* Princeton: Princeton

University Press, 1964, pp. 25–75. See esp. pp. 30–33.

4. ———, "The Measurement of Waste," *Amer. Econ. Assoc. Pap. and Proc.*, May 1964, *54*, pp. 58–76.

5. ———, "On Measuring the Social Opportunity Cost of Public Funds" in *The discount rate in public investment evaluation* (Conference Proceedings of the Committee on the Economics of Water Resources Development, Western Agricultural Economics Research Council, Report No. 17, Denver, Colorado, Dec. 17–18, 1968). Pp. 1–24.

6. ———, "Professor Arrow on the Social Discount Rate" in *Cost-benefit analysis of manpower policies*, edited by G. G. SOMERS and W. D. WOOD. Kingston, Ontario: Industrial Relations Centre, Queen's University, 1969, pp. 76–88.

7. HICKS, J. R. "The Rehabilitation of Consumers' Surplus," *Rev. Econ. Stud.*, Feb. 1941, pp. 108–16. Reprinted in AMERICAN ECONOMIC ASSOCIATION, *Readings in welfare economics*. Homewood, Ill.: Richard D. Irwin, Inc., 1969, pp. 325–35.

8. HICKS, J. R. *Value and capital.* Second Edition. Oxford: The Clarendon Press, 1946.

9. ———, *A revision of demand theory.* London: Oxford University Press, 1956. Chapters X and XVIII.

10. HOTELLING, H. "The General Welfare in Relation to Problems of Railway and Utility Rates," *Econometrica*, July 1938, *6*(3). Reprinted in AMERICAN ECONOMIC ASSOCIATION, *Readings in welfare economics*. Homewood, Ill.: Richard D. Irwin, Inc., 1969.

11. JOHNSON, H. G. "The Cost of Protection and the Scientific Tariff," *J. Polit. Econ.*, August 1960, *68*(4), pp. 327–45.

12. ———, "The Economic Theory of Customs Unions" in *Money, trade and economic growth*. London: George Allen and Unwin, 1962, pp. 48 ff.

13. KALDOR, N. *An expenditure tax.* London: George Allen and Unwin, 1955.

14. LANGE, O. "The Foundations of Welfare Economics," *Econometrica*, July–Oct. 1942, *10*, pp. 215–28. Reprinted in AMERICAN ECONOMIC ASSOCIATION, *Readings in welfare economics*. Homewood, Ill.: Richard D. Irwin, Inc., 1969, pp. 26–38.

15. LIPSEY, R. G. and LANCASTER, K. "The General Theory of Second Best," *Rev. Econ. Stud.*, 1956–57, *25*(63), pp. 11–32.

16. LIPSEY, R. G. *The theory of customs unions: A general equilibrium analysis.* London: Weidenfeld and Nicholson, 1970.

17. McKENZIE, L. W. "Ideal Output and the Interdependence of Firms," *Econ. J.*, Dec. 1951, *61*, pp. 785–803.

18. MEADE, J. E. *Trade and welfare,* Vol. II, Mathematical Supplement. London: Oxford University Press, 1955.

19. ORGANIZATION FOR ECONOMIC COOPERATION AND DEVELOPMENT. *Manual of industrial project analysis in developing countries.* Paris, Vol. I, 1968; Vol. II (by I. M. D. LITTLE and J. A. MIRRLEES), 1969.

20. UNITED STATES INTER-AGENCY COMMITTEE ON WATER RESOURCES. *Proposed practices for economic analysis of river basin projects.* Washington: Government Printing Office, 1958.

B
Compensation Criteria

[10]

THE GENERAL WELFARE IN RELATION TO PROBLEMS OF TAXATION AND OF RAILWAY AND UTILITY RATES*

By Harold Hotelling

IN THIS PAPER we shall bring down to date in revised form an argument due essentially to the engineer Jules Dupuit, to the effect that the optimum of the general welfare corresponds to the sale of everything at marginal cost. This means that toll bridges, which have recently been reintroduced around New York, are inefficient reversions; that all taxes on commodities, including sales taxes, are more objectionable than taxes on incomes, inheritances, and the site value of land; and that the latter taxes might well be applied to cover the fixed costs of electric power plants, waterworks, railroads, and other industries in which the fixed costs are large, so as to reduce to the level of marginal cost the prices charged for the services and products of these industries. The common assumption, so often accepted uncritically as a basis of arguments on important public questions, that "every tub must stand on its own bottom," and that therefore the products of every industry must be sold at prices so high as to cover not only marginal costs but also all the fixed costs, including interest on irrevocable and often hypothetical investments, will thus be seen to be inconsistent with the maximum of social efficiency. A method of measuring the loss of satisfactions resulting from the current scheme of pricing, a loss which appears to be extremely large, will emerge from the analysis. It will appear also that the inefficient plan of requiring that all costs, including fixed overhead, of an industry shall be paid out of the prices of its products is responsible for an important part of the instability which leads to cyclical fluctuations and unemployment of labor and other resources.

A railway rate is of essentially the same nature as a tax. Authorized and enforced by the government, it shares with taxes a considerable degree of arbitrariness. Rate differentials have, like protective tariffs and other taxes, been used for purposes other than to raise revenue. Indeed, the difference between rail freight rates between the same points, according as the commodity is or is not moving in international transport, has been used in effect to nullify the protective tariff. While it has not generally been perceived that the problems of taxation and those of railway rate making are closely connected, so that two independent bodies of economic literature have grown up, nevertheless the underlying unity is such that the considerations applicable to

* Presented at the meeting of the Econometric Society at Atlantic City, December 28, 1937, by the retiring president.

242

taxation are very nearly identical with those involved in proper rate making. This essential unity extends itself also to other rates, such as those charged by electric, gas, and water concerns, and to the prices of the products of all industries having large fixed costs independent of the volume of output.

I. THE CLASSICAL ARGUMENT

Dupuit's work of 1844 and the following years[1] laid the foundation for the use of the diagram of Figure 1 by Marshall and other econo-

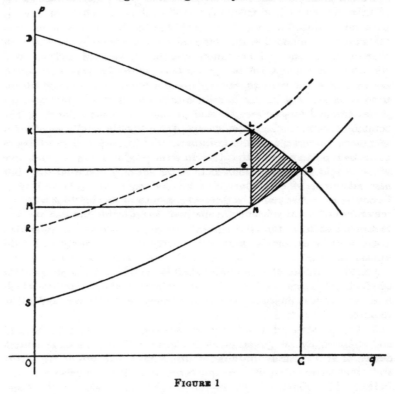

FIGURE 1

mists. A rising supply curve SB is used, and is sometimes regarded as coinciding with the marginal-cost curve. Such a coincidence would arise if there were free competition among producers, in the sense that each would regard the price as fixed beyond his control, and adjust

[1] Collected and reprinted with comments by Mario di Bernardi and Luigi Einaudi. "De l'Utilité et de sa Mesure," *La Riforma Sosiale*, Turin, 1932.

244   HAROLD HOTELLING

his production so as to obtain maximum net profits. This condition is approximated, for example, in most agriculture. *DB* is a declining demand curve. The buyers are presumed to compete freely with each other. The actual quantity and price are the co-ordinates of the intersection *B*. Then it is supposed that a tax *t* per unit is imposed upon the sellers. Since this is a uniform increment to marginal cost, the marginal-cost curve *SB* is lifted bodily to the new position *RL*, at height $t = SR = NL$ above its former position.

Three conclusions have been derived with the help of this figure, all of which must be reviewed to take account of the interrelations of the particular commodity in question with others. One of these arguments has almost universally been accepted, but must be rejected when account is taken of related commodities. A second has been accepted, and is actually true. The third has been condemned and attacked by a long line of prominent economists, but in the light of the more thorough analysis made possible by modern mathematical methods must now in its essence be accepted. The first is the proposition that since the point *L* of intersection of the demand curve with the supply curve *RL* is higher by *GL*, a fraction of the tax rate *NL*, than the intersection *B* with the tax-free curve *SB*, therefore the price is increased as a result of the tax, by an amount less than the tax. That this conclusion is not necessarily true when account is taken of related commodities I have shown in an earlier paper.[1] The second proposition—whose conclusion remains valid under certain plausible assumptions[1a]—is that, since *L* is to the left of *B*, the quantity of the taxed commodity will diminish. With this diminution is associated an approximately measurable net social loss.

The third argument is based on Dupuit's, and is of primary concern here. Dupuit sought a criterion of the value to society of roads, canals, bridges, and waterworks. He pointed out the weakness of calling the value of a thing only what is paid for it, since many users would if

[1] "Edgeworth's Taxation Paradox and the Nature of Demand and Supply Functions," *Journal of Political Economy*, Vol. 40, 1932, pp. 577–616. Edgeworth had discovered, and maintained against the opposition of leading economists, that a monopolist controlling two products may after the imposition of a tax on one of them find it profitable to reduce both prices, besides paying the tax. However he regarded this as a "mere curiosum," unlikely in fact to occur, and peculiar to monopoly. But it is shown in the paper cited that the phenomenon is also possible with free competition, and is quite likely to occur in many cases, either under monopoly or under competition.

[1a] On p. 600 of the paper just cited the conclusion is reached that it is reasonable to regard the matrix of the quantities h_{ij} as negative definite. From this and equation (19) of that page it follows that a positive increment in the tax t_j on the *j*th commodity causes a negative increment in the quantity of this commodity.

necessary pay more than they actually do pay. The total benefit he measured by the aggregate of the maximum prices that would be paid for the individual small units of the commodity (a term used here to include services, e.g., of canals) corresponding to the costs of alternatives to the various uses. If $p=f(q)$ is the cost of the best alternative to the use of an additional small unit of the commodity when q units are already used, then, if q_0 units are used altogether,

(1) $$\int_0^{q_0} f(q)dq$$

is the total benefit, which Dupuit called *utilité*, resulting from the existence of the canal or other such facility making possible the commodity (service) in question. Since $p=f(q)$ is the ordinate of the demand curve DB in Figure 1, this total benefit is the total area under the arc DB. To obtain what is now called the *consumers' surplus* we must subtract the amount paid by consumers, namely the product of the price by the quantity, represented by the rectangle $OCBA$. Thus the consumers' surplus is represented by the curvilinear triangle ABD. There is also a *producers' surplus* represented by the lower curvilinear triangle SBA; this is the excess of the money received by producers (the area of the rectangle $OCBA$) over the aggregate of the marginal costs, which is represented by the curvilinear figure $OCBS$. The total net benefit, representing the value to society of the commodity, and therefore the maximum worth spending from the public funds to obtain it, is the sum of consumers' and producers' surpluses, and is represented by the large curvilinear triangle SBD. It is the difference between the integral (1) of the demand function and the integral between the same limits of the marginal-cost function.

Imposition of the tax, by raising the price to the level of KL, appears to reduce the consumers' surplus to the curvilinear area KLD. The new producers' surplus is the area RLK, which equals SNM. There is also a benefit on account of the government revenue, which is the product of the new quantity MN by the tax rate NL, and is therefore measured by the area of the rectangle $MNLK$. The sum of these three benefits is $SNLD$. It falls short of the original sum of producers' and consumers' surpluses by the shaded triangular area NBL.

This shaded area represents the net social loss due to the tax, and was discovered by Dupuit. If the tax is small enough, the arcs BL and NB may be treated as straight lines, and the area of the triangle is, to a sufficient approximation, half the product of the base NL by the altitude GB. Since GB is the decrement in the quantity produced and consumed because of the tax, and NL is the tax rate, we may say that the net loss resulting from the tax is half the product of the tax rate by the decrement in quantity. But since the decrement in quantity is, for small taxes, proportional to the tax rate, it then follows that the net loss is proportional to the *square* of the tax rate. This fact also was remarked upon by Dupuit.

This remarkable conclusion has frequently been ignored in discussions in which it should, if correct, be the controlling consideration. The open attacks upon it seem all to be based on an excessive emphasis on the shortcomings of consumers' and producers' surpluses as measures of benefits. These objections are four in number: (1) Since the demand curve for a necessity might for very small quantities rise to infinity, the integral under the curve might also be infinite. This difficulty can be avoided by measuring from some selected value of q greater than zero. Since in the foregoing argument it is only *differences* in the values of the surpluses that are essentially involved, it is not necessary to assign exact values. The situation is the same as in the physical theory of the potential, which involves an arbitrary additive constant and so may be measured from any convenient point, since only its differences are important. (2) Pleasure is essentially nonmeasurable and so, it is said, cannot be represented by consumers' surplus or any other numerical magnitude. We shall meet this objection by establishing a generalized form of Dupuit's conclusion on the basis of a ranking only, without measurement, of satisfactions, in the way represented graphically by indifference curves. The same analysis will dispose also of the objections (3) that the consumers' surpluses arising from different commodities are not independent and cannot be added to each other, and (4) that the surpluses of different persons cannot be added.

In connection with the last two points, it will be observed that if we have a set of n related commodities whose demand functions are

$$p_i = f_i(q_1, q_2, \cdots, q_n), \qquad (i = 1, 2, \cdots, n),$$

then the natural generalization of the integral representing total benefit, of which consumers' surplus is a part, is the line integral

(2)
$$\int (f_1 dq_1 + f_2 dq_2 + \cdots + f_n dq_n),$$

taken from an arbitrary set of values of the q's to a set corresponding to the actual quantities consumed. The net benefit is obtained by subtracting from (2) a similar line integral in which the demand functions $f_1, f_2, \cdots, f_n$ are replaced by the marginal-cost functions

$$g_i(q_1, q_2, \cdots, q_n), \qquad (i = 1, 2, \cdots, n).$$

If we put

$$h_i = f_i - g_i,$$

the total net benefit is then measured by the line integral

(3) $$w = \int \sum h_i dq_i.$$

Such indeterminacy as exists in this measure of benefit is only that which arises with variation of the value of the integral when the path of integration between the same end points is varied. The condition that all these paths of integration shall give the same value is that the integrability conditions

$$\frac{\partial h_i}{\partial q_j} = \frac{\partial h_j}{\partial q_i}$$

be satisfied. In the paper on "Edgeworth's Taxation Paradox" already referred to, and more explicitly in a later note,[3] I have shown that there is a good reason to expect these integrability conditions to be satisfied, at least to a close approximation, in an extensive class of cases. If they are satisfied, the surpluses arising from different commodities, and also the surpluses belonging to different persons, may be added to give a meaningful measure of social value. This breaks down if the variations under consideration are too large a part of the total economy of the person or the society in question; but for moderately small variations, with a stable price level and stable conditions associated with commodities not in the group, the line integral w seems to be a very satisfactory measure of benefits. It is invariant under changes in units of measure of the various commodities, and also under a more general type of change of our way of specifying the commodities, such as replacing "bread" and "beef" by two different kinds of "sandwiches." For these reasons the total of all values of w seems to be the best measure of welfare that can be obtained without considering the proportions in which the total of purchasing power is subdivided among individuals, or the general level of money incomes. The change in w that will result from a proposed new public enterprise, such as building a bridge, may fairly be set against the cost of the bridge to decide whether the enterprise should be undertaken. It is certainly a better criterion of social value than the aggregate $\sum p_i q_i$ of tolls that can be collected on various classes of traffic, as Dupuit pointed out for the case of a single commodity or service. The actual calculation of w in such a case would be a matter of estimation of vehicular and pedestrian traffic originating and terminating in particular zones, with a comparison of distances by alternative routes in each case, and an evaluation

[3] "Demand Functions with Limited Budgets," *Econometrica*, Vol. 3, 1935, pp. 66–78. A different proof is given by Henry Schultz in the *Journal of Political Economy*, Vol. 41, 1933, p. 478.

of the savings in each class of movement. Determination whether to build the bridge by calculation merely of the revenue $\sum p_i q_i$ obtainable from tolls is always too conservative a criterion. Such public works will frequently be of great social value even though there is no possible system of charging for their services that will meet the cost.

II. THE FUNDAMENTAL THEOREM

But without depending in any way on consumers' or producers' surpluses, even in the form of these line integrals, we shall establish a generalization of Dupuit's result. We take our stand on the firm ground of a system of preferences expressible by a function

$$\Phi = \Phi(q_1, q_2, \cdots, q_n)$$

of the quantities $q_1, q_2, \cdots, q_n$ of goods or services consumed by an individual per unit of time. If the function Φ, Pareto's *ophélimité*, has the same value for one set of q's as for another, then the one combination of quantities is as satisfactory to the individual in question as the other. For two commodities, Φ is constant along each of a set of "indifference curves"; and likewise for n commodities, we may think of a system of hypersurfaces of which one passes through each point of a space of n dimensions, whose Cartesian co-ordinates are the quantities of the various goods. These hypersurfaces we shall refer to as *indifference loci*.

It is to be emphasized that the indifference loci, unlike measures of pleasure, are objective and capable of empirical determination. One interesting experimental attack on this problem was made by L. L. Thurstone, who by means of questionnaires succeeded in mapping out in a tentative manner the indifference loci of a group of girls for hats, shoes, and coats.[4] Quite a different method, involving the study of actual family budgets, also appears promising.[5] The function Φ, on the other hand, is not completely determinable from observations alone, unless we are prepared to make some additional postulate about independence of commodities, as was done by Irving Fisher in defining utility,[6] and by Ragnar Frisch.[7] The present argument does not depend on any such assumption, and therefore allows the replacement of Φ by

[4] "The Indifference Function," *Journal of Social Psychology*, Vol. 2, 1931, pp. 139–167, esp. pp. 151 ff.

[5] R. G. D. Allen and A. L. Bowley, *Family Expenditure*, London, 1935.

[6] *Mathematical Investigations in the Theory of Value and Prices*, New Haven, 1892.

[7] *New Methods of Measuring Marginal Utility*, Tübingen, 1932. Dr. Frisch also considered the possibility of substitute commodities in his *Confluence Analysis*, and in collaboration with Dr. F. V. Waugh made an attempt to handle this situation statistically.

an arbitrary increasing function Ψ of Φ, such as sinh Φ, or $\Phi + \Phi^2$. The statements we shall make about Φ will apply equally to every such function Ψ. Negative values of the q's are the quantities of labor, or of goods or services, produced by the individual. It is with the understanding that this kind of indeterminacy exists that we shall sometimes refer to Φ and Ψ as utility functions.

Consider now a state in which income and inheritance taxes are used to pay for the construction of bridges, roads, railroads, waterworks, electric power plants, and like facilities, together with other fixed costs of industry; and in which the facilities may be used, or the products of industry consumed, by anyone upon payment of the additional net cost occasioned by the particular use or consumption involved in each case. This additional net cost, or marginal cost, will include the cost of the additional labor and other resources required for the particular item of service or product involved, beyond what would be required without the production of that particular item. Where facilities are not adequate to meet all demands, they are made so either by enlargement, or by checking the demand through inclusion in the price of a rental charge for the facilities, adjusted so as to equate demand to supply. Such a rental cost, of which the site rental of land is an example, is an additional source of revenue to the state; it must not be confused with carrying charges on invested capital, or with overhead cost. Some such charge is necessary to discriminate economically among would-be users of the facilities. Another example is that of water in a dry country; if demand exceeds supply, and no enlargement of supply is possible, a charge must be made for the water sufficient to reduce the demand to the supply. Such a charge is an element of marginal cost as here defined.

The individual retains, after payment of taxes, a money income m. At prices $p_1, p_2, \cdots, p_n$ determined in the foregoing manner, he can buy or sell such quantities $q_1, q_2, \cdots, q_n$ as he pleases, subject to the condition that

$$(4) \qquad\qquad \sum p_i q_i = m.$$

The combination he chooses will be such as to make his indifference function Φ a maximum, subject to the condition (4). We may put aside as infinitely improbable—having probability zero, though not impossible—the contingency that two different sets of values of the q's satisfying (4) will give the same degree of satisfaction. We therefore have that, if $q_1, \cdots, q_n$ are the quantities chosen under these conditions, and if $q_1', \cdots, q_n'$ are any other set of quantities satisfying (4), so that

$$(5) \qquad\qquad \sum p_i q_i' = m,$$

then

$$\Phi = \Phi(q_1, \cdots, q_n) > \Phi(q_1', \cdots, q_n') = \Phi + \delta\Phi,$$

say. Hence, putting $q_i' = q_i + \delta q_i$ in (5) and subtracting (4), we find that any set of values of $\delta q_1, \cdots, \delta q_n$ satisfying

$$(6) \qquad \sum p_i \delta q_i = 0,$$

and not all zero, must have the property that

$$(7) \quad \delta\Phi = \Phi(q_1 + \delta q_1, \cdots, q_n + \delta q_n) - \Phi(q_1, \cdots, q_n) < 0.$$

Let us now consider an alteration of the system by the imposition of excise taxes and reduction of income taxes. Some of the taxes may be negative; that is, they may be bounties or subsidies to particular industries; or, instead of being called taxes, they may be called tolls, or charges for services or the use of facilities over and above marginal cost. There ensues a redistribution of production and consumption. Let p_i, q_i, and m be replaced respectively by

$$(8) \qquad p_i' = p_i + \delta p_i, \quad q_i' = q_i + \delta q_i, \quad m' = m + \delta m,$$

where the various increments δp_i, δq_i are not constrained to be either positive or negative; some may have one sign and some the other. The yield of the new excise taxes will be the sum, over all individuals, of the quantity which for the particular individual we are considering is $\sum q_i' \delta p_i$. (We use the sign $\sum$ to denote summation over all commodities, including services.) Since this person's income tax is reduced by δm, the net increment of government revenue

$$(9) \qquad \delta r = \sum q_i' \delta p_i - \delta m$$

may be imputed to him, in the sense that summation of δr over all persons gives the total increment of government revenue.[8] We neglect changes in administrative costs and the like.

The individual's budgetary limitation now takes the form $\sum p_i' q_i' = m'$, which may also be written

$$(10) \qquad \sum (p_i + \delta p_i)(q_i + \delta q_i) = m + \delta m.$$

[8] A friendly critic writes. "It is not clear to me why δp_i should be the exact per-unit revenue of the state from an excise tax which raises the price by δp_i from its old level. . . . I should expect (referring to Figure 1) an increase in price of GL, and a revenue to the state of NL." The answer to this is that the summation of δr over all persons includes the sellers as well as the buyers, and that the government revenue per unit of the commodity is derived in part from each— though it must be understood that the contribution of either or both may be negative. In the classical case represented by Figure 1, the buyers' δp is the height GL, while the sellers' is NG in magnitude and is negative. Since q' is positive for the buyer and negative for the seller, the product $q' \delta p$ is in each case positive. The aggregate of these positive terms is the total tax revenue from the commodity.

Subtracting the budget equation (4) corresponding to the former system and using (8) we find that

(11) $$\delta m = \sum q_i' \delta p_i + \sum p_i \delta q_i.$$

Substituting this in (9) we find that

(12) $$\delta r = - \sum p_i \delta q_i.$$

Suppose that, to avoid disturbing the existing distribution of wealth, the excise taxes paid by each individual (in the sense of incidence just defined; not in the sense of handing over the money to the government in person) are exactly offset by the decrement in his income tax. Then $\delta r = 0$. From (12) it then follows that (6) is satisfied. Except in the highly improbable case of all the δq's coming out exactly zero, it would then follow from (7) that this man's new state is worse than his old. The change from income to excise taxes has resulted in a net loss of satisfactions. Conversely, if we start from a system of excise taxes, or any system in which sales are not at marginal cost, this argument shows that there is a possible distribution of personal income taxes such that everyone will be better satisfied to change to the system of income taxes with sales at marginal cost. The problem of the distribution of wealth and income among persons or classes is not involved in this proposition.

This argument may be expressed in geometrical language as follows: Let $q_1, \cdots, q_n$ be Cartesian coordinates in a space of n dimensions. Through each point of this space passes a hypersurface whose equation may be written $\Phi(q_1, \cdots, q_n) = $ constant. The individual's satisfaction is enhanced by moving from one to another of these hypersurfaces if the value of the constant on the right side of the equation is thereby increased; this will usually correspond to moving in a direction along which some or all of the q's increase. The point representing the individual's combination of goods is however constrained in the first instance to lie in the hyperplane whose equation is (4). In this equation the p's and m are to be regarded as constant coefficients, while the q's vary over the hyperplane. A certain point Q on this hyperplane will be selected, corresponding to the maximum taken by the function Φ, subject to the limitation (4). If the functions involved are analytic, Q will be the point of tangency of the hyperplane with one of the "indifference loci." The change in the tax system means that the individual must find a point Q' in the new hyperplane whose equation is $\sum p_i' q_i = m'$. If we denote the coordinates of Q' by $q_1', \cdots, q_n'$, we have, upon substituting them in the equation of this new hyperplane, $\sum p_i' q_i' = m'$. If the changes in prices and m are such as to leave the government revenue unchanged, (12) must vanish; that is,

$$\sum p_i q_i' = \sum p_i q_i.$$

Since $\sum p_i q_i = m$, this shows that $\sum p_i q_i' = m$; that is, that Q' lies on the same hyperplane to which Q was confined in the first place. But since Q was chosen among all the points on this hyperplane as the one lying on the outermost possible indifference locus, for which Φ is a maximum, and since we are putting aside the infinitely improbable case of there being other points on the hyperplane having this maximizing property, it follows that Q' must lie on some other indifference locus, and that this will correspond to a lesser degree of satisfaction.

The fundamental theorem thus established is that *if a person must pay a certain sum of money in taxes, his satisfaction will be greater if the levy is made directly on him as a fixed amount than if it is made through a system of excise taxes which he can to some extent avoid by rearranging his production and consumption.* In the latter case, the excise taxes must be at rates sufficiently high to yield the required revenue *after* the person's rearrangement of his budget. The redistribution of his production and consumption then represents a loss to him without any corresponding gain to the treasury. This conclusion is not new. What we have done is to establish it in a rigorous manner free from the fallacious methods of reasoning about one commodity at a time which have led to false conclusions in other associated discussions.

The conclusion that a fixed levy such as an income or land tax is better for an individual than a system of excise taxes may be extended to the whole aggregate of individuals. In making this extension it is necessary to neglect certain interactions among the individuals that may be called "social" in character, and are separate and distinct from the interactions through the economic mechanisms of price and exchange. An example of such "social" interactions is the case of the drunkard who, after adjusting his consumption of whisky to what he considers his own maximum of satisfaction, beats his wife, and makes his automobile a public menace on the highway. The restrictive taxation and regulation of alcoholic liquors and certain other commodities do not fall under the purview of our theorems because of these social interactions which are not economic in the strict sense. With this qualification, and neglecting also certain possibilities whose total probability is zero, we have:

If government revenue is produced by any system of excise taxes, there exists a possible distribution of personal levies among the individuals of the community such that the abolition of the excise taxes and their replacement by these levies will yield the same revenue while leaving each person in a state more satisfactory to himself than before.

It is in the sense of this theorem that we shall in later sections speak of "the maximum of total satisfactions" or "the maximum of general welfare" or "the maximum national dividend" requiring as a necessary, though not sufficient, condition that the sale of goods shall be without additions to price in the nature of excise taxes. These looser expressions are in common use, and are convenient; when used in this paper, they refer to the proposition above, which depends only on rank ordering of satisfactions; there is no connotation of adding utility functions of different persons.

The inefficiency of an economic system in which there are excise taxes or bounties, or in which overhead or other charges are paid by excesses of price over marginal cost, admits of an approximate measure when the deviations from the optimum system described above are not great, if, as is customary in this and other kinds of applied mathematics, we assume continuity of the indifference function and its derivatives. Putting for brevity

$$\Phi_i = \frac{\partial \Phi}{\partial q_i}, \qquad \Phi_{ij} = \frac{\partial^2 \Phi}{\partial q_i \partial q_j},$$

we observe that the maximum of Φ, subject to the budget equation (4), requires that

$$(13) \qquad \Phi_i = \lambda p_i, \qquad (i = 1, 2, \cdots, n),$$

where the Lagrange multiplier λ is the marginal utility of money. Differentiating this equation gives

$$(14) \qquad \Phi_{ij} = \lambda \frac{\partial p_i}{\partial q_j} + p_i \frac{\partial \lambda}{\partial q_j} .$$

Expanding the change in the utility or indifference function we obtain, with the help of (13), (12), and (14),

$$(15) \qquad \delta \Phi = \sum \Phi_i \delta q_i + \tfrac{1}{2} \sum \sum \Phi_{ij} \delta q_i \delta q_j + \cdots$$

$$= - \lambda \delta r + \tfrac{1}{2} \lambda \sum \sum \frac{\partial p_i}{\partial q_j} \delta q_i \delta q_j - \tfrac{1}{2} \delta r \sum \frac{\partial \lambda}{\partial q_j} \delta q_j + \cdots$$

where the terms omitted are of third and higher order, and are therefore on our assumptions negligible. Their omission corresponds to Dupuit's deliberate neglect of curvilinearity of the sides of the shaded triangle in Figure 1. With accuracy of this order we have further,

$$\delta p_i = \sum_j \frac{\partial p_i}{\partial q_j} \delta q_j, \qquad \delta \lambda = \sum_j \frac{\partial \lambda}{\partial q_j} \delta q_j.$$

Upon substituting for these expressions, (15) reduces to

$$(16) \qquad \delta \Phi = - \lambda \delta r + \tfrac{1}{2} \lambda \sum \delta p_i \delta q_i - \tfrac{1}{2} \delta r \delta \lambda + \cdots .$$

If the readjustment from the original state of selling only at marginal cost, with income taxes to pay overhead, is such as to leave $\delta r = 0$ as above, (16) reduces to

$$(17) \qquad \delta \Phi = \tfrac{1}{2}\lambda \sum \delta p_i \delta q_i + \cdots,$$

where the terms omitted are of higher order.

As another possibility we may consider a substitution of excise for income tax so arranged as to leave this person's degree of satisfaction unchanged. Upon putting $\delta \Phi = 0$ in (16) and solving for δr we have, apart from terms of higher order,

$$(18) \qquad \delta r = \tfrac{1}{2} \sum \delta p_i \delta q_i + \cdots.$$

This is the net loss to the state in terms of money, so far as this one individual is concerned. The net loss in terms of satisfactions is merely the product of (18) by the marginal utility of money λ, that is, (17), if we neglect terms of higher order than those written. The total net loss of state revenue resulting from abandonment of the system of charging only marginal costs, and uncompensated by any gain to any individual, is the sum of (18) over all individuals. If the prices are the same for all, this sum is of exactly the same form as the right-hand member of (18), with δq_i now denoting the increment (positive or negative) of the total quantity of the ith commodity.

The approximate net loss

$$(19) \qquad \tfrac{1}{2} \sum \delta p_i \delta q_i$$

may be regarded as the sum of the areas of the shaded triangles in the older graphic demonstration. It should however be remembered that the readjustment of prices caused by excise taxes is not necessarily in the direction formerly supposed, that some of the quantities and some of the prices may increase and some decrease, and that some of the terms of the foregoing sum may be positive and some negative. But the aggregate of all these varying terms is seen by the foregoing argument to represent a dead loss, and never a gain, as a result of a change from income to excise taxes, or away from a system of sales at marginal cost. Any inaccuracy of the measure (19) is of only the same order as the error involved in replacing the short arcs LB and NB in Figure 1 by straight segments, and can never affect the sign.

It is remarkable, and may appear paradoxical, that without assuming any particular measure of utility or any means of comparison of one person's utility with another's, we have been able to arrive at (19) as a valid approximation measuring in money a total loss of satisfactions to many persons. That the result depends only on the conception of ranking, without measurement, of satisfactions by each person is readily apparent from the foregoing demonstration; or we may for any person replace Φ by another function Ψ as an index of the same system of ranks among satisfactions. If we do this in such a way that the derivatives are continuous, we shall have $\Psi = F(\Phi)$, where F is an increasing function with continuous derivatives. Upon writing the expressions for the first and second derivatives of Ψ in terms of those of F and Φ it may be seen that the foregoing formulae involving Φ are necessary and sufficient conditions for the truth of the same equations with Ψ written in place of Φ. The result (18) is independent of which system of indicating ranks is used. The fundamental fact here is that *arbitrary* analytic transformations, even of very complicated functional forms, always induce *homogeneous linear* transformations of differentials.

Not only the approximation (19) but also the whole expression indicated by (18) are absolutely invariant under all analytic transformations of the utility functions of all the persons involved. These expressions depend only on the demand and supply functions, which are capable of operational determination. They represent simply the money cost to the state of the inefficiency of the system of excise taxation, when this is arranged in such a way as to leave unchanged the satisfactions derived from his private income by each person.

The arguments based on Figure 1 have been repeated with various degrees of hesitation, or rediscovered independently, by numerous writers including Jevons, Fisher, Colson, Marshall, and Taussig. Marshall considered variations of the figure involving downward-sloping cost curves and multiple solutions, and was led to the proposal (less definite than that embodied in the criterion established by our theorem) that incomes and increasing-cost industries be taxed to subsidize decreasing-cost ones. He observed the difficulty of defining demand curves and consumers' surplus in view of the interdependence of demand for various commodities. These difficulties are indeed such that it now seems better to stop talking about demand *curves*, and to substitute demand *functions*, which will in general involve many variables, and are not susceptible of graphic representation in two or three dimensions. Marshall was one of those misled by Figure 1 into thinking that a tax of so much per unit imposed on producers of a commodity leads necessarily to an increase of price by something less than the tax.

Though the marginal-cost curve in Figure 1 slopes upward, no such assumption is involved in the present argument. It is perfectly possible that an industry may be operated by the state under conditions of diminishing marginal cost. The criterion for a small increase in production is still that its cost shall not exceed what buyers are willing to pay for it; that is, the general welfare is promoted by offering it for sale at its marginal cost. It may be that demand will grow as prices decline until marginal cost is pushed to a very low level, far below the average cost of all the units produced. In such a case the higher cost of the first units produced is of the same character as fixed costs, and is best carried by the public treasury without attempting to assess it against the users of the particular commodity as such. Our argument likewise makes no exception of cases in which more than one equilibrium is possible. Where there are multiple solutions we have that sales at marginal cost are a necessary, though not a sufficient, condition for the optimum of general welfare.

The confusion between marginal and average cost must be avoided. This confusion enters into many of the arguments for laissez-faire policies. It is frequently associated with the calm assumption, as a self-evident axiom, that the whole costs of every enterprise must be paid out of the prices of its products. This fallacious assumption appears, for example, in recent writings on government ownership of railroads. It has become so ingrained by endless repetition that it is not even stated in connection with many of the arguments it underlies.

III. TAX SYSTEMS MINIMIZING DEAD LOSS

The magnitude of the dead loss varies greatly according to the objects taxed. While graphic arguments are of suggestive value only, it may be observed from Figure 1 that the ratio of the dead loss NBL to the revenue $MNLK$ depends greatly on the slopes of the demand and supply curves in the neighborhood of the equilibrium point B. It appears that if either the demand or the supply curve is very steep in this neighborhood, the dead loss will be slight. For a tax on the site rental value of land, whose supply curve is vertical, the dead loss drops to zero. A tax on site values is therefore one of the very best of all possible taxes from the standpoint of the maximum of the total national dividend. It is not difficult to substantiate this argument in dealing with related commodities; for the δq_i's corresponding to such a tax are zero. Since the incidence is on the owner of the land and cannot be shifted by any readjustment of production, it has the same advantages as an income tax from the standpoint of maximizing the national dividend. The fact that such a land tax cannot be shifted seems to account for the bitterness of the opposition to it. The proposition that there is no ethical objection to the confiscation of the site value of land by taxation, if and when the nonlandowning classes can get the power to do so, has been ably defended by H. G. Brown.[9]

Land is the most obviously important, but not by any means the only good, whose quantity is nearly or quite unresponsive to changes

[9] *The Theory of Earned and Unearned Incomes*, Columbia, Missouri, 1918.

in price, and which is not available in such quantities as to satisfy all demands. Holiday travel sometimes leads to such a demand for the use of railroad cars as to bring about excessive and uncomfortable crowding. If the total demand the year around is not sufficiently great to lead to the construction of enough more cars to relieve the crowding, the limited space in the existing cars acquires a rental value similar to that of land. Instead of selling tickets to the first in a queue, or selling so many as to bring about an excessive crowding that would neutralize the pleasure of the holiday, the economic way to handle this situation would be to charge a sufficiently high price to limit the demand. The revenue thus obtained, like the site value of land, may properly be taken by the state. The fact that it helps to fill the treasury from which funds are drawn to pay for replacement of the cars when they wear out, and to cover interest on their cost in the meantime, does not at all mean that any attempt should be made to equate the revenue from car-space rental to the cost of having the cars in existence.

Another thing of limited quantity for which the demand exceeds the supply is the attention of people. Attention is desired for a variety of commercial, political, and other purposes, and is obtained with the help of billboards, newspaper, radio, and other advertising. Expropriation of the attention of the general public and its commercial sale and exploitation constitute a lucrative business. From some aspects this business appears to be of a similar character to that of the medieval robber barons, and therefore to be an appropriate subject for prohibition by a state democratically controlled by those from whom their attention is stolen. But attention attracting of some kinds and in some degree is bound to persist; and where it does, it may appropriately be taxed as a utilization of a limited resource. Taxation of advertising on this basis would be in addition to any taxation imposed for the purpose of diminishing its quantity with a view to restoring the property of attention to its rightful owners.

If for some reason of political expediency or civil disorders it is impossible to raise sufficient revenue by income and inheritance taxes, taxes on site values, and similar taxes which do not entail a dead loss of the kind just demonstrated, excise taxes may have to be resorted to. The problem then arises of so arranging the rates on the various commodities as to raise the required sum while making the total dead loss a minimum. A solution of this theoretical question, taking account of the interrelations among commodities, is given on p. 607 of the study of Edgeworth's taxation paradox previously referred to.

IV. EFFECT ON DISTRIBUTION OF WEALTH

We have seen that, if society should put into effect a system of sales at marginal cost, with overhead paid out of taxes on incomes, inheritances, and the site value of land, there would exist a possible system of compensations and collections such that everyone would be better off than before. As a practical matter, however, it can be argued in particular cases that such adjustments would not in fact be made; that the general well-being would be purchased at the expense of sacrifices by some; and that it is unjust that some should gain at the expense of others, even when the gain is great and the cost small. For example, it appears that the United States Government can by introducing cheap hydroelectric power into the Tennessee Valley raise the whole level of economic existence, and so of culture and intelligence, in that region, and that the benefits enjoyed by the local population will be such as to exceed greatly in money value the cost of the development, taking account of interest. But if the government demands for the electricity generated a price sufficiently high to repay the investment, or even the interest on it, the benefits will be reduced to an extent far exceeding the revenue thus obtained by the government. It is even possible that no system of rates can be found that will pay the interest on the investment; yet the benefits may at the same time greatly exceed this interest in value. It appears to be good public policy to make the investment, and to sell the electric energy at marginal cost, which is extremely small. But this will mean that the cost will have to be paid in part by residents of other parts of the country, in the form of higher income and inheritance taxes. Those who are insistent on avoiding a change in the distribution of wealth at all costs will object.

One answer to this objection is that the benefits from such a development are not by any means confined to the persons and the region most immediately affected. Cheap power leads for example to production of cheap nitrates, which cut down the farmers' costs even in distant regions, and may benefit city dwellers in other distant regions. A host of other industries brought into being by cheap hydroelectric power have similar effects in diffusing general well-being. There is also the benefit to persons who on account of the new industrial development find that they can better themselves by moving into the Tennessee Valley, or by investing their funds there. Furthermore, the nation at large has a stake in eradicating poverty, with its accompaniments of contagious diseases, crime, and political corruption, wherever these may occur.

A further answer to the objection that benefits may be paid for by those who do not receive them when such a development as that of the Tennessee Valley is undertaken is that no such enterprise stands alone. A government willing to undertake such an enterprise is, for the same reasons, ready to build other dams in other and widely scattered places, and to construct a great variety of public works. Each of these entails benefits which are diffused widely among all classes. A rough randomness in distribution should be ample to ensure such a distribution of benefits that most persons in every part of the country would be better off by reason of the program as a whole.

If new electric-power, railroad, highway, bridge, and other developments are widely undertaken at public expense, always on the basis of the criterion of maximizing total benefits, the geographical distribution of the benefits, and also the distribution among different occupational, racial, age, and sex groups, would seem pretty clearly to be such that every such large group would on the whole be benefited by the program. There are, however, two groups that might with some reason expect not to benefit. One of these consists of the very wealthy. Income and inheritance taxes are likely to be graduated in such a way that increases in government spending will be paid for, both directly and ultimately, by those possessed of great wealth, more than in the proportion that the number of such persons bears to the whole population. It would not be surprising if the benefits received by such persons as a result of the program of maximum total benefit should fall short of the cost to them.

The other class that might expect not to benefit from such a program consists of land speculators. If we consider for example a bridge, it is evident that the public as a whole must pay a certain cost of construction, whether the bridge be paid for by tolls or by taxes on the site value of land in the vicinity. There will be much more use of the bridge if there are no tolls, so that the public as a whole will get more for its money if it pays in the form of land taxes. But it will not in general be possible to devise a system of land taxes that will leave everyone, without exception, in a position as good as or better than as if the bridge had not been built and the taxes had not been levied. Landowners argue that the benefits of the bridge go to others, not to them; and even in cases in which land values have been heightened materially as a result of a new bridge, the landowners have been known to be vociferous in favor of a toll system. Payment for the bridge by tolls (when this is possible) has the advantage that no one seems to be injured, since each one who pays to cross the bridge has the option of not using it, and is in that case as well off as if the bridge did not exist. This reasoning is not strictly sound, since the bridge may have put out of business a ferry which for some users was more convenient and economical. Nevertheless, it retains enough cogency to stiffen the resistance of real-estate interests to the more economical system of paying for the bridge by land taxes.

Attempts at excessive accuracy in assessing costs of public enterprises according to benefits received tend strongly to reduce the total of those benefits, as in the case of the bridge. The welfare of all is promoted rather by a generous support of projects for communal spending in ways beneficial to the public at large, without attempting to recover from each enterprise its cost by charges for services rendered by that enterprise. The notion that public projects should be "self-liquidating," on which President Hoover based his inadequate program for combating the oncoming depression, while attractive to the wealthier taxpayers, is not consistent with the nation's getting the maximum of satisfactions for its expenditure.

V. DISTINCTION OF OPTIMUM FROM COMPETITIVE CONDITIONS

The idea that all will be for the best if only competition exists is a heritage from the economic theory of Adam Smith, built up at a time when agriculture was still the dominant economic activity. The typical agricultural situation is one of rising marginal costs. Free competition, of the type that has usually existed in agriculture, leads to sales at marginal cost, if we now abstract the effects of weather and other uncertainty, which are irrelevant to our problem. Since we have seen that sales at marginal cost are a condition of maximum general welfare, this situation is a satisfactory one so far as it goes. But the free competition associated with agriculture, or with unorganized labor, is not characteristic of enterprises such as railroads, electric-power plants, bridges, and heavy industry. It is true that a toll bridge may be in competition with other bridges and ferries; but it is a very different kind of competition, more in the nature of duopoly. To rely on such competition for the efficient conduct of an economic system is to use a theorem without observing that its premises do not apply. Free competition among toll-bridge owners, of the kind necessary to make the conclusion applicable, would require that each bridge be parallelled by an infinite number of others immediately adjacent to it, all the owners being permanently engaged in cutthroat competition. If the marginal cost of letting a vehicle go over a bridge is neglected, it is clear that under such conditions the tolls would quickly drop to zero and the owners would retire in disgust to allow anyone who pleased to cross free.

The efficient way to operate a bridge—and the same applies to a railroad or a factory, if we neglect the small cost of an additional unit of product or of transportation—is to make it free to the public, so long at least as the use of it does not increase to a state of overcrowding. A free bridge costs no more to construct than a toll bridge, and costs less to operate; but society, which must pay the cost in some way or other, gets far more benefit from the bridge if it is free, since in this case it will be more used. Charging a toll, however small, causes some people to waste time and money in going around by longer but cheaper ways, and prevents others from crossing. The higher the toll, the greater is the damage done in this way; to a first approximation, for small tolls, the damage is proportional to the square of the toll rate, as Dupuit showed. There is no such damage if the bridge is paid for by income, inheritance, and land taxes, or for example by a tax on the

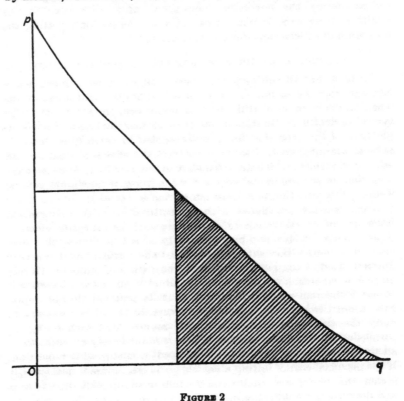

FIGURE 2

real estate benefited, with exemption of new improvements from taxation, so as not to interfere with the use of the land. The *distribution* of wealth among members of the community is affected by the mode of payment adopted for the bridge, but not the total wealth, except that it is diminished by bridge tolls and other similar forms of excise. This is such plain common sense that toll bridges have now largely disappeared from civilized communities. But New York City's bridge and tunnels across the Hudson are still operated on a toll basis, because of the pressure of real estate interests anxious to shift the tax burden to wayfarers, and the possibility of collecting considerable sums from persons who do not vote in the city.

If we ignore the interrelations of the services of a bridge with other goods, and also the slight wear and tear on the bridge due to its use, we may with Dupuit represent the demand for these services by a curve such as that in Figure 2. The total benefit from the bridge is then represented by the whole area enclosed between the demand curve and the axes, provided the bridge is free. All this benefit goes to users of the bridge. But if a toll is charged, of magnitude corresponding to the height of the horizontal line, the recipients of the toll are benefited to an extent represented by the area of the rectangle, whose base is the number of crossings and whose height is the charge for each crossing. But the number of crossings has diminished, the benefit to bridge users has shrunk to the small triangular area at the top, and the total benefit has decreased by the area of the shaded triangle at the right. This triangle represents the net loss to society due to the faulty method of paying for the bridge. If, for example, the demand curve is a straight line, and if the owners set the toll so as to bring them a maximum return, the net loss of benefit is 25 per cent of the total.

These are the pertinent considerations if the bridge is already in existence, or its construction definitely decided. But if we examine the general question of the circumstances in which bridges ought to be built, a further inefficiency is disclosed in the scheme of paying for bridges out of tolls. For society, it is beneficial to build the bridge if the total area in the figure exceeds the interest, amortization, and maintenance costs. But if the bridge must be paid for by tolls, it will not be built unless it is expected that these costs will be exceeded by the rectangular area alone. This area cannot, for our example of a linear demand function, be greater than half the total. We may in this case say that the toll system has 75 per cent efficiency in use, but only 50 per cent efficiency in providing new bridges. In each case the efficiency will be further diminished by reason of the cost of collecting and accounting for the tolls.

The argument about bridges applies equally to railroads, except that in the latter case there is some slight additional cost resulting from an extra passenger or an extra shipment of freight. My weight is such that when I ride on the train, more coal has to be burned in the locomotive, and I wear down the station platform by walking across it. What is more serious, I may help to overcrowd the train, diminishing the comfort of other travelers and helping to create a situation in which additional trains should be run, but often are not. The trivial nature of the extra costs of marginal use of the railroads has from the first been realized by the railroad managements themselves; indeed, it is implied in the amazingly complex rate structures they build up in the attempt to squeeze the last possible bit of revenue from freight and passenger traffic. If in a rational economic system the railroads were operated for the benefit of the people as a whole, it is plain that if people were to be induced by low rates to travel in one season rather than another, the season selected should be one in which travel would otherwise be light, leaving the cars nearly empty, and not a season in which they are normally overcrowded. Actually, our railroads run trains about the country in winter with few passengers, while crowding multitudes of travelers into their cars in summer. The rates are made high in winter, lower in summer, on the ground that the summer demand is more elastic than that of the winter travelers, who are usually on business rather than pleasure, and thus decide the question of a trip with less sensitiveness to the cost.

VI. COMPLEXITY OF ACTUAL RAILWAY RATES AND REMOTENESS FROM MARGINAL COST

The extreme and uneconomic complexity of railway freight and passenger rate structures is seldom realized by those not closely in touch with them. A few random examples will illustrate the remoteness of actual rates from what may be presumed to be marginal costs, which railway managements will find it profitable to cover even by the lowest rates. Prior to the last enforced reduction of American passenger rates the regular round-trip fare between New York City and Wilkesbarre, Pa. was $11.04. But at various times between 1932 and 1935 round-trip tickets good for limited periods were sold at $2.50, $6.00, $6.10, and $6.15. Between New York and Chicago the round-trip fare in the same period varied between $33 and $65 for identical accommodations. Between New York and Washington the ordinary round-trip fare was $18.00, but an "excursion rate" of $3.50 was applied spasmodically.

The lumber and logging activities of the country, which have been at a standstill for several years, are suffering from freight rates which in many important cases nearly equal, and even exceed, the mill price of the lumber. Thus from the large sawmills at and near Baker, Oregon, which produce lumber for the New York market, the freight amounts to $16.50 per thousand board feet. For No. 3 Common Ponderosa Pine, the grade shipped in largest quantities, the price of one-by-four inch boards ranged in the autumn of 1933 from $14.50 to $15.50 at the mill. Thus the New York wholesale buyer must pay more than double the mill price, solely on account of freight. The freight even to Chicago approximated the mill price. For No. 4 Common, also an important grade, the price was $12.50 per thousand board feet at the mill, but the New York buyer had to pay $29.00. A few months earlier, the prices were about $8 per thousand board feet less than those just given, so that the railroads received far more than the mill operators. It is hard to escape the conclusion that these high freight rates interfered seriously with the sale of lumber.

One advantage of the system of charging only marginal cost would be a great simplification of the rate structure. This is a great desideratum. It must not be assumed too readily that every purchaser distributes his budget accurately to obtain the maximum of satisfactions, or the most efficient methods of production, when the determination of the optimum requires the study of an encyclopedic railroad tariff, together with complicated trial-and-error calculations. Neither, from the standpoint of a railroad, can it be assumed that the enormously complex rate differentials have been determined at all accurately for the purposes for which they were designed. These complicated rate structures further contravene the public interest in that they enhance artificially the advantages of large over small concerns. When immense calculations are required to determine the optimum combinations of transportation with other factors of production, the large concerns are in a distinctly better position to carry out the calculations and obtain the needed information.

VII. MARGINAL COST DEPENDS ON EXTENT OF UNUSED CAPACITY

In the determination of marginal cost there are, to be sure, certain complications. When a train is completely filled, and has all the cars it can haul, the marginal cost of carrying an extra passenger is the cost of running another train. On the other hand, in the more normal situation in which the equipment does not carry more than a small part of its capacity load, the marginal cost is virtually nothing. To avoid a sharp increase in rates at the time the train is filled, an averaging process is needed in the computation of rates, based on the probability of having to run an extra train. Further, in cases in which the available equipment is actually used to capacity, and it is not feasible or is of doubtful wisdom to increase the amount of equipment, something in the nature of a rental charge for the use of the facilities should, as indicated above, be levied to discriminate among different users in such a way that those willing to pay the most, and therefore in accordance with the usual assumptions deriving the most benefit, would be the ones obtaining the limited facilities which many desire. This rental charge for equipment, which for passenger travel would largely take the place of fares, should never be so high as to limit travel to fewer persons than can comfortably be accommodated, except for unpredictable fluctuations. The proceeds from the charge could be added to the funds derived from income, inheritance, and land taxes, and used to pay a part of the overhead costs. But there should be no attempt to pay all the overhead from such rental charges alone.

Except in the most congested regions, there would, however, be no such charge for the use of track and stations until the volume of traffic comes to exceed enormously the current levels. An example is the great under-utilization of the expensive Pennsylvania Station, in New York City, whose capacity was demonstrated during the war by bringing into the city the trains of the Erie and the Baltimore and Ohio railroads. These trains are now required to stop on the New Jersey shore, constituting a wasteful nuisance which had existed before government operation, which was replaced by the more efficient procedure by the government, but which was resumed when the lines were handed back to their private owners.

VIII. THE ATTEMPT TO PAY FIXED COSTS FROM RATES AND PRICES CONTRIBUTES TO RIGIDITY AND SO TO INSTABILITY

One of the evil consequences of the attempt to pay overhead out of operating revenue is the instability which it contributes to the economic system as a whole. This is illustrated by the events leading to the depression. The immense and accelerating progress of science and technology led to the creation of new industries and the introduction of wonderfully efficient new methods. The savings from the new methods were so great that corporate profits and real incomes surged upwards. So large were the profits and so satisfactory the dividends that the operating officials of great industries did not feel under compulsion to push up the selling prices of their products to the levels corresponding to maximum monopoly profit. Because they kept their prices low, while paying relatively high wages, the physical volume of goods produced and transferred became enormous. The impulse to produce, with possibly some altruistic motives besides, tempered the desire for profits in many concerns. But under a profit system this could not last. As the prices of corporate shares rose, pressure developed to pay dividends equivalent to interest on the higher prices. This pressure would probably have led presently to gradual increases in the money prices of manufactured products, if the general level of prices had remained stationary. Such however was not the case. The general level of prices was declining.

And decline it must, according to the equation of exchange, when there was such a great new flood of goods to be sold. The vast increase in physical volume of goods, created by the new technology, called for a greater use of money, if the price level was to be maintained. This need was met for a time by increases in bank loans and deposits, and in the velocity of circulation. But neither bank loans nor velocities could continue to increase as fast as goods, and prices had to fall. The fall was not uniform. Corporations under increasing pressure to cover their overhead and pay high dividends out of earnings were strongly averse to reducing the selling prices of their products, when these selling prices were already below the points which would yield maximum profit. For several years prior to the crash, the prices of manufactured products stuck fast, while the proportion of national expenditure paid for these products continued to increase. This left a shrinking volume of money payments to be made for the remaining commodities, and these, including particularly the agricultural, had to come down in price. If, as the general price level fell, railroad, utility, and manufacturing concerns had reduced their selling prices proportionately, the prosperity of the years 1922 to 1928 might have continued. But such reductions in selling prices were not possible when an increasing volume of overhead charges had to be paid out of earnings. The intensified efforts to do this resulted in a pushing up of "real" prices of manufactured products—that is, of the ratios of their prices to the general price level—and of "real" transportation rates. Indeed, with a rapidly falling general price level, railroad freight rates, measured in money, were actually increased in 1931. This increase of 15 per cent on a large range of commodities, like the subsequent increases in suburban commuters' passenger rates, was obtained on the ground that the railroads needed the money to cover their overhead costs, though their operating costs had declined. Of course the effect was to make the depression worse, by stopping traffic which would have flowed at the lower rates. On the theory that bond interest and other such items must be paid out of operating revenues, the railroads were "entitled" to the higher rates, for their business had fallen off. But economic equilibrium calls for a rising rather than a declining supply curve; if demand falls off, the offer price must be reduced in order to have the offered services taken. This antithesis of rising railway rates, when general prices and the ability to pay are falling, well illustrates the disequilibrating consequences of the idea that overhead costs must be paid from operating revenues. There now seems to be a possibility of a repetition of the disastrous 15 per cent freight-rate increase in a time of decline.[16]

This explanation of the contrast of the prosperity of 1928 with the cessation of production in the following years rests upon the contrast of the system of prices which results from the whole-hearted devotion

[16] Since this was written the Interstate Commerce Commission has allowed a part of this proposed increase and postponed consideration of a request for a passenger fare rise.

of different concerns to their own respective profits, with the system of prices best for the economic organism as a whole. Under free competition, with no overhead, these two systems of prices tend to become identical. Where there are overhead costs, competition of the ideally free type is not permanently possible. Monopoly prices develop; and a system of monopoly prices is not a system which can serve human needs with maximum advantage.

IX. CRITERION AS TO WHAT INVESTMENTS ARE SOCIALLY WORTH WHILE

When a decision whether or not to construct a railway is left to the profit motive of private investors, the criterion used is that the total revenue $\sum p_i q_i$, being the sum of the products of the rates for the various services by the quantities sold, shall exceed the sum of operating costs and carrying charges on the cost of the enterprise. If no one thinks that there will be a positive excess of revenue, the construction will not be undertaken. We have seen in Section V that this rule is, from the standpoint of the general welfare, excessively conservative. What, then, should society adopt to replace it?

A less conservative criterion than that of a sufficient revenue for total costs is that *if some distribution of the burden is possible such that everyone concerned is better off than without the new investment, then there is a prima facie case for making the investment.* This leaves aside the question whether such a distribution is *practicable.* It may often be good social policy to undertake new enterprises even though some persons are put in a worse position than before, provided that the benefits to others are sufficiently great and widespread. It is on this ground that new inventions are permitted to crowd out less efficient industries. To hold otherwise would be to take the side of the hand weavers who tried to wreck the power looms that threatened their employment. But the rule must not be applied too harshly. Where losses involve serious hardship to individuals, there must be compensation, or at least relief to cover subsistence. Where there are many improvements, the law of averages may be trusted to equalize the benefits to some extent, but never completely. It will always be necessary to provide for those individuals upon whom progress inflicts special hardship; if it were not possible to do this, we should have to reconcile ourselves to greater delays in the progress of industrial efficiency.

Subject to this qualification of avoiding excessive hardship to individuals, we may adopt the criterion stated. In applying it there will be the problem of selecting a limited number of proposed investments, corresponding to the available capital, from among a larger number of possibilities. The optimum solution corresponds to application of our criterion to discriminate between each pair of combinations. The total amount of calculation and exercise of judgment required will not, however, be so great as might be suggested by the number of pairs of combinations, which is immense. Numerous means are available to shorten this labor. One of these is by the application of the line integral (3), namely

$$w = \int \sum h_i dq_i,$$

which provides a measure of value corresponding to the sum of consumers' and producers' surpluses. The part of w constituting the generalized consumers' surplus is (2); the validity of this line integral as a measure of an individual's increment of satisfaction corresponding to sufficiently small changes in the q's may be seen merely by replacing p_i in (13) by f_i, and noticing that for small changes the marginal utility of money λ changes little, so that f_i is very nearly proportional to the derivative of the utility function Φ. Hence the increment in Φ is proportional to the sum of the integrals of the f's, apart from terms of higher order; and the factor of proportionality λ is such as to measure this increment in money so as to be comparable to an increase in income. Similar considerations apply to the part of w corresponding to producers' surplus.

Defenders of the current theory that the overhead costs of an industry must be met out of the sale of its products or services hold that this is necessary in order to find out whether the creation of the industry was a wise social policy. Nothing could be more absurd. Whether it was wise for the government to subsidize and its backers to construct the Union Pacific Railroad after the Civil War is an interesting historical question which would make a good subject for a dissertation, but it would be better, if necessary, to leave it unsolved than to ruin the country the Union Pacific was designed to serve by charging enormous freight rates and claiming that their sum constitutes a measure of the value to the country of the investment. Such an experimental solution of a historical question is too costly. In addition, it is as likely as not to give the wrong answer. The sum of the freight and passenger rates received, minus operating costs, is not the line integral $w = \int \sum h_i dq_i$, which with some accuracy measures the value to society of the investment, but is more closely related to the misleading measure of value $\sum p_i q_i$. In other words, the revenue resembles the area of the rectangle in Figure 2, while the possible benefit corresponds to the much larger triangular area. The revenue is the thing that appeals to an investor bent on his own profit, but as a cri-

terion of whether construction ought in the public interest to be undertaken, it is biased in the direction of being too conservative.

Regardless of their own history, the fact is that we now have the
railroads, and in the main are likely to have them with us for a considerable time in the future. It will be better to operate the railroads
for the benefit of living human beings, while letting dead men and dead
investments rest quietly in their graves, and to establish a system
of rates and services calculated to assure the most efficient operation.
When the question arises of building new railroads, or new major industries of any kind, or of scrapping the old, we shall face, not a historical, but a mathematical and economic problem. The question then
will be whether the aggregate of the generalized surpluses of the form
(3) is likely to be great enough to cover the anticipated cost of the new
investment. This will call for a study of demand and cost functions
by economists, statisticians, and engineers, and perhaps for a certain
amount of large-scale experimentation for the sake of gaining information about these functions. The amount of such experiment and
research which could easily be paid for out of the savings resulting
from operation of industry in the public interest is very large indeed.
Perhaps this is the way in which we shall ultimately get the materials
for a scientific economics.

Columbia University
New York, N. Y.

MANAGING EDITOR'S NOTE: Professor Frisch has written a brief criticism of
Professor Hotelling's argument, but because of limitations of space it has had to
be held over for publication in a later issue.—D. H. L.

[11]

WELFARE PROPOSITIONS OF ECONOMICS AND INTER-PERSONAL COMPARISONS OF UTILITY

IN the December 1938 issue of the ECONOMIC JOURNAL Professor Robbins returns to the question of the status of inter-personal comparisons of utility.[1] It is not the purpose of this note to question Professor Robbins' view regarding the scientific status of such comparisons; with this the present writer is in entire agreement. Its purpose is rather to examine the relevance of this whole question to what is commonly called " welfare economics." In previous discussions of this problem it has been rather too readily assumed, on both sides, that the scientific justification of such comparisons determines whether " economics as a science can say anything by way of prescription." The disputants have been concerned only with the status of the comparisons; they were—apparently—agreed that the status of prescriptions necessarily depends on the status of the comparisons.

This is clearly Mr. Harrod's view. He says : [2] " Consider the Repeal of the Corn Laws. This tended to reduce the value of a specific factor of production—land. It can no doubt be shown that the gain to the community as a whole exceeded the loss to the landlords—*but only if individuals are treated in some sense as equal.* Otherwise how can the loss to some—and that there was a loss can hardly be denied—be compared with the general gain ? If the incomparability of utility to different individuals is strictly pressed, not only are the prescriptions of the welfare school ruled out, but all prescriptions whatever. The economist as an adviser is completely stultified, and unless his speculations be regarded as of paramount aesthetic value, he had better be suppressed completely." This view is endorsed by Professor Robbins : [3] " All that I proposed to do was to make clear that the statement that social wealth was increased [by free trade] itself involved an arbitrary element—that the proposition should run, *if* equal capacity for satisfaction on the part of the economic subjects be assumed, *then* social wealth can be said to be increased. Objective analysis of the effects of the repeal of duties only showed that consumers gained and landlords lost. That such an arbitrary element was

[1] " Interpersonal Comparisons of Utility : A Comment," ECONOMIC JOURNAL, December 1938, pp. 635–691.

[2] " Scope and Method of Economics," *ibid.*, September 1938, pp. 396–397. (Italics mine.)

[3] *Loc. cit.*, p. 638.

involved was plain. It seemed no less plain, therefore, that, here as elsewhere, it should be explicitly recognised."

It can be demonstrated, however, that in the classical argument for free trade no such arbitrary element is involved at all. The effects of the repeal of the Corn Laws could be summarised as follows : (i) it results in a reduction in the price of corn, so that the *same* money income will now represent a higher real income ; (ii) it leads to a shift in the distribution of income, so that some people's (*i.e.*, the landlord's) incomes (at any rate in money terms) will be lower than before, and other people's incomes (presumably those of other producers) will be higher. Since aggregate money income can be assumed to be unchanged, if the landlords' income is reduced, the income of other people must be correspondingly increased. It is only as a result of this consequential change in the distribution of income that there can be any loss of satisfactions to certain individuals, and hence any need to compare the gains of some with the losses of others. But it is always possible for the Government to ensure that the previous income-distribution should be maintained intact : by compensating the " landlords " for any loss of income and by providing the funds for such compensation by an extra tax on those whose incomes have been augmented. In this way, everybody is left as well off as before in his capacity as an income recipient ; while everybody is better off than before in his capacity as a consumer. For there still remains the benefit of lower corn prices as a result of the repeal of the duty.

In all cases, therefore, where a certain policy leads to an increase in physical productivity, and thus of aggregate real income, the economist's case for the policy is quite unaffected by the question of the comparability of individual satisfactions ; since in all such cases it is *possible* to make everybody better off than before, or at any rate to make some people better off without making anybody worse off. There is no need for the economist to prove—as indeed he never could prove—that as a result of the adoption of a certain measure nobody in the community is going to suffer. In order to establish his case, it is quite sufficient for him to show that even if all those who suffer as a result are fully compensated for their loss, the rest of the community will still be better off than before. Whether the landlords, in the free-trade case, should in fact be given compensation or not, is a political question on which the economist, *qua* economist, could hardly pronounce an opinion. The important fact is that, in the argument in favour of free trade, the fate of the landlords is wholly irrelevant : since the benefits of free trade are by no means destroyed even if the landlords are fully reimbursed for their losses.[1]

This argument lends justification to the procedure, adopted by Professor Pigou in *The Economics of Welfare*, of dividing " welfare economics " into two parts : the first relating to production, and the second to distribution. The first, and far the more important part, should include all those propositions for increasing social welfare which relate to the increase in aggregate production ; all questions concerning the stimulation of employment, the equalisation of social net products, and the equalisation of prices with marginal costs, would fall under this heading. Here the economist is on sure ground ; the scientific status of his prescriptions is unquestionable, provided that the basic postulate of economics, that each individual prefers more to less, a greater satisfaction to a lesser one, is granted. In the second part, concerning distribution, the economist should not be concerned with " prescriptions " at all, but with the relative advantages of different ways of carrying out certain political ends. For it is quite impossible to decide on economic grounds what particular pattern of income-distribution maximises social welfare. If the postulate of equal capacity for satisfaction is employed as a criterion, the conclusion inescapably follows that welfare is necessarily greatest when there is complete equality ; yet one certainly cannot exclude the possibility of everybody being happier when there is some degree of inequality than under a régime of necessary and complete equality. (Here I am not thinking so much of differences in the capacity for satisfactions between different individuals, but of the satisfactions that are derived from the prospect of improving one's income by one's own efforts—a prospect which is necessarily excluded when a régime of complete equality prevails.) And short of complete equality, how can the

---

[1] This principle, as the reader will observe, simply amounts to saying that there is no interpersonal comparison of satisfactions involved in judging any policy designed to increase the sum total of wealth just because any such policy *could* be carried out in a way as to secure unanimous consent. An increase in the money value of the national income (given prices) is not, however, necessarily a sufficient indication of this condition being fulfilled : for individuals might, as a result of a certain political action, sustain losses of a non-pecuniary kind—*e.g.*, if workers derive satisfaction from their particular kind of work, and are obliged to change their employment, something more than their previous level of money income will be necessary to secure their previous level of enjoyment; and the same applies in cases where individuals feel that the carrying out of the policy involves an interference with their individual freedom. Only if the increase in total income is sufficient to compensate for such losses, and still leaves something over to the rest of the community, can it be said to be " justified " without resort to interpersonal comparisons.

economist decide precisely how much inequality is desirable—*i.e.*, how much secures the maximum total satisfaction? All that economics can, and should, do in this field, is to show, given the pattern of income-distribution desired, which is the most convenient way of bringing it about.

NICHOLAS KALDOR

London School of Economics.

[12]

THE FOUNDATIONS OF WELFARE ECONOMICS [1]

1. THE subject of this paper is a matter of very fundamental importance, both for economic theory and for the proper attitude of economists towards economic policy. That being so, it is not surprising that it should have been a matter of controversy, controversy which has even tended to widen into a profound difference of opinion. During the nineteenth century, it was generally considered to be the business of an economist, not only to explain the economic world as it is and as it has been, not only to make prognostications (so far as he was able) about the future course of economic events, but also to lay down principles of economic policy, to say what policies are likely to be conducive to social welfare, and what policies are likely to lead to waste and impoverishment. To-day, there is one school of writers which continues to claim that economics can fulfil this second function, but there is another which (formally at least) desires to reject it. According to their view the economics of welfare, the economics of economic policy, is too unscientific in character to be a part of economic *science*. So long as economics is concerned with explanation, it can hope to reach conclusions which will command universal acceptance as soon as they are properly understood; but once it goes beyond that point, and endeavours to prescribe principles of policy, then (so they hold) its conclusions must depend upon the scale of social values held by the particular investigator. Such conclusions can possess no validity for any-one who lives outside the circle in which these values find acceptance. Positive economics can be, and ought to be, the same for all men; one's welfare economics will inevitably be different according as one is a liberal or a socialist, a nationalist or an internationalist, a christian or a pagan.

It cannot be denied that this latter view is in fact widely accepted. If it is intellectually valid, then of course it ought to be accepted; and I must admit that I should have subscribed to it myself not so long ago. But it is rather a dreadful thing to have to accept. No one will question the activity of some of our " positivists " in the criticism of current institutions; but it can hardly be denied that their authority to advance such

[1] Based on a paper read to the Economic Society of Stockholm, May 1939.

criticism *qua* economists is diminished by their abnegation, so that in other hands economic positivism might easily become an excuse for the shirking of live issues, very conducive to the euthanasia of our science.

Fortunately there is no need for us to accept it. The way is open for a theory of economic policy which is immune from the objections brought against previously existing theories.

The standard representative of these existing theories is of course Professor Pigou's *Economics of Welfare*. It is such, not only in its own right, but as the culmination of a great line of economic thought. A whole series of economists, among whom Dupuit, Walras, Marshall and Edgeworth deserve particular mention, had sought to find in utility theory a sure basis for prescriptions of economic policy. In those of its aspects which particularly concern us, the *Economics of Welfare* is essentially a systematisation of this tradition.

I am not so much concerned in this paper with Professor Pigou's conclusions (most of which are very readily acceptable, and are abandoned with reluctance even by the positivists), as with the grounds on which those conclusions are based. It is not surprising that these grounds should have caused so much trouble. Professor Pigou derives his prescriptions from the postulate that the aim of economic policy is to maximise the real value of the social income. In order to arrive at such a *real value*, the quantities of the various commodities produced must be weighted by a *given* set of prices—and the prices actually selected are those ruling on the market in the actual circumstances considered. In order to justify this procedure, a long argument is needed, which occupies most of Part I of the book. There are three steps in this argument which cause difficulty. The first is at the very outset, when the reader is asked to accept a direct correlation between economic welfare and social welfare in general (whatever that may be). This is not easy to swallow; in any case it is open to the positivist objection that it reflects a particular social outlook, held by certain classes at certain times, and never likely to be acceptable universally. At the next step, we have to admit the possibility of comparing the satisfactions derived from their wealth by different individuals. (This is where Professor Robbins parts company; for my own part, I go with him.) And then further, even if these things are admitted, a third jump has to be taken.[1] Strictly speaking, the quantity to be maximised is the sum of the consumers' surpluses derived

[1] *Economics of Welfare*, 4th edition, p. 57.

from the various commodities in the social dividend. This is too awkward to handle, so it is replaced by the real value of the dividend—which is not the same thing at all.

I do not think that anyone can be blamed for declining to entrust himself to a chain containing three links as weak as these. If there were no alternative foundations for the theory of economic welfare, it would be nothing more than the development of an interesting ethical postulate—the status Professor Robbins allows. Alternative foundations are, however, available. A way round the first difficulty has been shown by Mr. Harrod; [1] round the second by Mr. Kaldor; [2] while Professor Hotelling, in a most valuable and suggestive paper covering the whole subject, has provided a mathematical analysis in which all these difficulties are in fact overcome. [3]

Therefore my own task is mainly one of synthesis. I propose to set out briefly and simply the main lines of the new welfare economics. It will appear that the main propositions can be established quickly and easily, and at the same time their significance can be made perfectly clear.

2. The *positive* theory of economics exhibits a system in which people co-operate with one another in order to satisfy their wants. We assume each individual (each free economic unit [4]) to have a certain scale of preferences, and to regulate his activities in such a way as best to satisfy those preferences. As Pareto put it, in his famous masterpiece of generalisation, the economic problem consists in an opposition of " tastes " and " obstacles," each individual endeavouring to satisfy his tastes as far as is possible in view of the obstacles to satisfaction which confront him. Looking at society as a whole, the obstacles are technical obstacles—the limited amount of productive power available, and the technical limits to the amount of production this productive power will yield. Looking at a single individual, the obstacles which prevent him from attaining a fuller satisfaction of his wants are not only technical obstacles but also the wants or tastes of other people. He is prevented from being better off than he is, not only because total production is limited, but also because so much

---

[1] " Scope and Method of Economics," ECONOMIC JOURNAL, Sept. 1938, pp. 389–395.

[2] " Welfare Propositions and Inter-personal Comparisons of Utility," ECONOMIC JOURNAL, Sept. 1939, pp. 549–52. See also Viner, *Studies in the Theory of International Trade*, pp. 553–4.

[3] " The General Welfare in Relation to Problems of Taxation and of Railway and Utility Rates," *Econometrica*, July 1938.

[4] It would appear from Mr. Harrod's analysis that we ought to be prepared, on occasion, to reckon public and semi-public bodies among our " individuals."

of total production is at the disposal of persons other than himself. The same thing holds, of course, for any group or society of individuals, so long as that group is less than the totality of a closed community.

Now as soon as the economic problem is conceived in this way (and it is in some such way that all modern economists regard it), we are really obliged to go on and to consider as part of our business not only the objective consequences of this pursuit of satisfactions (the quantities of goods produced and exchanged, and the prices at which they are exchanged—the problems of positive economics) but also a further problem. We ought to examine how far these activities are effective in achieving the ends for which they are designed, to be able to examine the efficiency of any particular economic system as a means of adjusting means to ends. We are obliged to go so far, because the subject-matter of our study is something which is defined relatively to its purpose. We are not like geologists, comparing rocks laid down by natural forces; we are like archæologists, comparing flint implements made by man for a purpose, one of whose functions must be to compare the relative efficiency of these implements, and by tracing the ups and downs of that efficiency, to trace out the tortuous course of human evolution.

The task of examining the efficiency—in this sense—of any given economic organisation is thus one which we should like to regard as an integral part of economics. But before we can accept it as such, we have to face the second difficulty which lies in our way, the difficulty of inter-personal comparisons. Although the economic system can be regarded as a mechanism for adjusting means to ends, the ends in question are ordinarily not a single system of ends, but as many independent systems as there are "individuals" in the community. This appears to introduce a hopeless arbitrariness into the testing of efficiency. You cannot take a temperature when you have to use, not one thermometer, but an immense number of different thermometers, working on different principles, and with no necessary correlation between their registrations. How is this difficulty to be overcome?

We may list three possible ways of dealing with it, two of which have to be rejected as unsatisfactory. One is to replace the given thermometers (the scales of preference of the individuals) by a new thermometer of one's own. The investigator himself decides what he thinks to be good for society, and praises or condemns the system he is studying by that test. This is the method which is rightly condemned as unscientific. It is the way of the prophet and the social reformer, not of the economist.

Secondly, one may seek for some way of aggregating the reports of the different thermometers. This is the traditional method of Marshall, Edgeworth and Pigou. The fundamental reason why it cannot be accepted is that it is impossible to arrive at an aggregate without " weighting " the component parts; and in this case there is no relevant reason why we should choose one system of weights rather than another. (The equal weights, 1, 1, 1, . . . are just one possible system of weights like the rest.) As a matter of fact, when they are composing their aggregate, Marshall and Pigou pay no attention to variations of the marginal utility of money between rich and poor—a point which, on their own principles, ought plausibly to be taken into account.[1] Thus although their method can produce results, the significance of those results remains quite uncertain.

The third method is Mr. Kaldor's. It consists in concentrating attention upon those cases which have been admitted, even by some of the positivists,[2] to be an exception to their general rule that the impossibility of inter-personal comparisons prevents any estimation of the general efficiency of the economic system. Mr. Kaldor's contribution is to have shown that these cases are not the mere trifling exception they appear to be at first sight, but that they do actually offer a sufficient foundation for at least the more important part of welfare economics.

3. Let us go back to the Paretian scheme referred to a little while ago. For society as a whole, the only *obstacles* to satisfaction are the limited quantity of physical resources, and the limited quantities of products which can be got from those resources. For the individual, however, the wants of other people have to be reckoned among the obstacles which limit the satisfaction of his wants. There are usually some ways in which he can improve his position without damaging the satisfactions of other people; there are other ways in which an improvement in his position (an upward movement on his scale of preferences) involves a downward movement for other people on their scales. Now these latter movements, which make some people better off and some people worse off, cannot be reckoned as involving an increase in " social satisfaction " unless we have some means of reducing the satisfactions of different individuals to a common

[1] Cf. Kahn, " Notes on Ideal Output," ECONOMIC JOURNAL, 1935, p. 2.

[2] Cf., for example, G. Myrdal, *Das politische Element in der nationalökonomischen Doktrinbildung*, p. 288.

measure—and no unambiguous means for such reduction seems to exist.   But the former movements, which benefit some people without damaging others, stand in another category.   From any point of view, they do represent an increase in economic welfare— or better, an increase in the efficiency of the system as a means of satisfying wants, that is to say, in the efficiency of the system *tout court*.

Let us then define an *optimum* organisation of the economic system as one in which every individual is as well off as he can be made, subject to the condition that no reorganisation permitted shall make any individual worse off.   This is not an unambiguous definition of an optimum organisation; it does not enable us to say that with given resources and given scales of preference, there will be one optimum position and one only.   That is not so; there will be an indefinite number of different possible optima, distinguished from one another by differences in the *distribution* of social wealth.[1]   In spite of this, we are able to lay down the conditions which must be fulfilled in order that a particular organisation should be optimum, and so we can test whether an actual organisation is optimum or not.   If it is not optimum, then there is a definite sense in which its efficiency can be increased. Some at least of the individuals in the system can have their wants satisfied better, without anyone having to make a sacrifice in order to achieve that end.

The significance of this definition may be illustrated by taking the familiar case of comparative costs in inter-regional trade. Suppose that the supplies of two commodities are each derived from two regions, each region producing each commodity. Suppose that each commodity, in each region, is produced under diminishing returns, and that no migration of factors between the regions is possible.   Then, as is well known, the technical possibilities of production in each region can be represented by a *substitution curve*.[2]   The abscissa of each point on this curve represents a certain quantity of the one commodity, and the corresponding ordinate represents the maximum amount of the

---

[1] If we start from a given organisation which is not optimum, there will be several different optima which can be reached subject to the condition of no one being damaged, since the " increment of wealth " can be divided in different ways.   In addition to these there will be many other optima which cannot be reached from the initial position, since they involve some people being worse off than they were initially.   These are optimum positions all the same, although they could only be reached by a " permitted reorganisation " if we begin from some other starting-point.

[2] Haberler, *Theory of International Trade*, p. 176.

other whose production is consistent with the production of that amount of the first. A and B (Fig. 1) represent the substitution curves of the two regions. Under the assumed diminishing returns, each substitution curve will be concave to the origin.

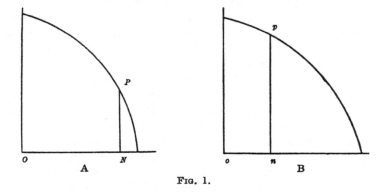

FIG. 1.

Suppose we start with a case where the quantities of the goods produced in the two regions are *ON*, *PN* and *on*, *pn*. Then, taking the two regions together, the total amounts produced of

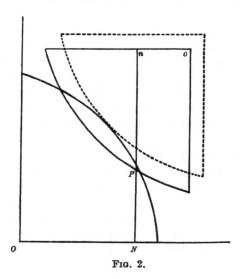

FIG. 2.

the two commodities are *ON* + *on*, *PN* + *pn*. These total amounts might be plotted on a third diagram, but a more instructive method of compounding is to " sit " the one curve on the other, keeping the axes parallel, as in Fig. 2. It will be observed that the curve B is reversed before being superposed,[1] so that it is the co-ordinates of o with respect to the A-axes which represent the total amounts produced. This reversal has a definite advantage, since it shows us at once what condition must be fulfilled in order for the distribution of production between the regions to be optimum. If, when the diagrams are superposed, the curves intersect, a reorganisation of production will enable the outputs of both products (in the two areas taken together) to be increased. It is only when the curves touch (as in the dotted position) that an optimum organisation is realised.

When two curves touch, their slopes are the same; and the slope of a substitution curve measures the ratio between the marginal costs of the two products. It is thus a condition of optimum organisation that the marginal costs of the two commodities should be in the same ratio in the two regions. If this condition is not satisfied, the position is not an optimum; for the production of both commodities can be increased by a suitable re-arrangement.

An exactly similar construction can be used for the case of exchange between two individuals. Here again we can construct a substitution curve (an indifference curve, as it is more commonly called), showing the various quantities of two commodities which would yield a particular individual the same amount of satisfaction. His whole scale of preferences can be represented by a series of such curves. Now if the first individual only moves from one position on his scale to another position by exchanging goods with the second, every movement of the first individual implies a movement of the second in the opposite direction. We can then draw the second individual's indifference map upon the same diagram as the first's, but his curves will naturally all turn the other way.[2]

Once again, if the amounts possessed by the two parties are such that their indifference curves through that point intersect, the position cannot be an optimum. For it will be possible for either party to reach a preferred position (a position on a higher indifference curve) while the other party remains on the same indifference curve as before. One party can be made better off without the other being worse off, so the position is not an optimum position. The position will only be an optimum if the curves touch—in this case, if the ratio of the marginal utilities of the two commodities is the same for both parties.

---

[1] I owe this device to Mr. Kaldor.

[2] Bowley, *Mathematical Groundwork of Economics*, fig. 1.

4. The general conditions for the attainment of an optimum organisation may now be set out in a formal manner.[1]

The first set of conditions are *marginal* conditions. They state—in the terminology I prefer—that the marginal rate of substitution [2] between any two commodities must be the same for every individual (who consumes them both) and for every producing unit (which produces them both) in the whole economy. In the older terminology, the ratio of the marginal utilities of the two commodities must be the same for every individual; the ratio of the marginal costs must be the same for every producing unit; and these ratios must be equal. Exactly similar conditions must hold between factor and product, and factor and factor, as between product and product. Thus the marginal product of labour in terms of a particular product must equal the marginal disutility of labour in terms of that product. And so on.

If these conditions are not fulfilled, some " tightening-up " (of the kind illustrated in our diagrams) will always be possible.

The second set of conditions are *stability* conditions. Their rôle is to ensure that the position established is one of maximum, not minimum, satisfaction. They can be defined in terms of the curvature of the substitution curves; but it does not seem necessary to elaborate them here, because their importance for the theory of the optimum is largely eclipsed by that of the third set of conditions—which we may call the *total* conditions.[3]

The function of the total conditions is to ensure that no improvement can be brought about by the complete abandonment of the production or consumption of some one commodity, either in one producing or consuming unit, or generally; and that no improvement can be secured by the introduction of new commodities, which could have been produced or consumed, but were not being produced or consumed, either partially or generally, in the initial situation, Similar conditions must hold for factors— thus conditions referring to the mobility of labour (occupational or local) arise in the form of total conditions.

[1] It should be observed that it is not at all necessary to raise the awkward problems about the definition of real income, which gave so much trouble to Professor Pigou. We can *proceed directly* to the analysis of the optimum. This is, of course, not to deny that a definition of real social income is wanted for other (statistical) purposes, and that the issues raised in the search for that definition are very cognate to those in question here. In my ideal *Principles of Economics* the theory of economic welfare and the theory of the social income would be the subjects of consecutive chapters—but they would not get into the same chapter.

[2] See my *Value and Capital*, pp. 20, 86.

[3] Compare the triple classification of the conditions of equilibrium in positive economics, given in *Value and Capital*, chap. 6.

The working of both these latter sets of conditions can be readily understood by reference to our diagrams. In Fig. 2 (the inter-regional trade case) both the stability condition and the

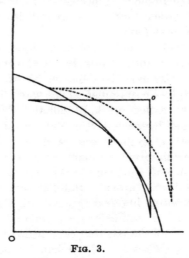

FIG. 3.

total condition were in fact assumed to be satisfied—as a consequence of the assumption of diminishing returns. Complications arise from increasing returns. In Fig. 3 the marginal

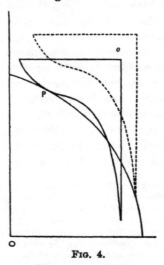

FIG. 4.

condition is satisfied, but neither of the other conditions. In Fig. 4 we have both the marginal condition and the stability condition, but not the total condition. In both these cases, it is only possible for an optimum position to be reached if production of one commodity is abandoned in one of the regions. (Optimum positions are such as those indicated by the dotted curves.) There must be specialisation in the inter-regional case; more generally, there must be a change in the kinds of goods produced or consumed somewhere.

5. These are the general conditions for optimum organisation; they are universally valid, being applicable to every conceivable type of society. No economic system has ever existed, nor (we may be sure) will any ever exist, to which they are irrelevant.[1] But for us the most interesting application which they offer still lies in their use as a means of criticising or testing the efficiency of production by private enterprise.[2] It is this which I shall take as my topic for the remainder of this paper.

When we are dealing with the system of private enterprise, there is one point which requires special attention, although it is (in a sense) nothing but the practical aspect of that theoretical difficulty which has concerned us all along. Under private enterprise, any ordinary change in economic policy involves a change in the price-system, and any change in prices benefits those on one side of the market, and damages those on the other. Thus no simple economic reform can be a permitted reorganisation in our sense, because it always inflicts a loss of some sort upon some people. Nevertheless, this does not prevent us from applying our criteria to the case of private enterprise, because we can always suppose that special measures are taken through the public revenue to compensate those people who are damaged. A " permitted reorganisation " must thus be taken from now on to mean a reorganisation which will allow of compensation being paid, and which will yet show a net advantage. The position is not optimum so long as such reorganisation is possible.

The critique of private enterprise naturally begins by pointing out the one conceivable case in which an optimum position may be attained by perfect *laisser-faire*. This occurs when competition

---

[1] Most of them are still relevant even if there is only *one* free economic unit.

[2] Another important application of Welfare Economics, which should perhaps be distinguished from this, is the application to Public Finance. Welfare Economics, defined as we have defined it, cannot lay down what is *the* optimum method of raising a given revenue—the " least sacrifice " method, as taxation theorists would call it. That is impossible without inter-personal comparisons. It can, however, distinguish between those methods of raising revenue which are consistent with optimum production and those which are not. In practice, this would seem to be a quite sufficient achievement.

On these questions of optimum taxation Professor Hotelling (*op. cit.*) has thrown particular light.

is *perfect* in all industries, so that every producer and every consumer takes for granted the prices of all those things he buys or sells, and contents himself with adjusting quantities to these (for him) given prices. If these conditions are realised, the *perfection* of the consumers' market ensures that each individual consumer equalises his marginal rate of substitution between every pair of goods to the ratio of their market prices; and the *perfection* of the producers' market ensures that each producer makes the marginal cost of every article he sells equal to its price. Thus the marginal conditions for the optimum must be satisfied. The fact that such universal perfect competition is only possible under universal diminishing returns [1] ensures that the stability and total conditions for the optimum must be satisfied too. Thus, so it appears, an optimum position must be reached.

There are, however, certain reasons why an optimum position may not be attained, even in these favourable circumstances of universal perfect competition and universal *laisser-faire*. The first is one which has been rightly emphasised by Professor Pigou.[2] It is of enormous importance that only some of the ways by which human beings affect one another's prosperity are controlled through the mechanism of the price-system. We are all of us affected by the economic activities of other people in ways for which we do not pay, or are not paid. Thus it is not necessarily to the social advantage (even in the narrow sense in which we are using that term) that a person should be able to acquire a particular product so long as he is willing to pay a price equal to the marginal cost of that product. This condition ensures that he can acquire it without making anyone else worse off because that person has to bear a part of the ordinary costs of production of that commodity; but there are other ways in which other people may be injured (or benefited). The ultimate implications of this exception are indeed very large. Hidden under this heading are some of the gravest philosophical issues about the relationship between the individual and society.

This qualification is generally admitted; but there are other qualifications, of a more dynamic character, whose place in the

---

[1] Since these particular technical conditions are necessary in order for universal perfect competition to be a possible state of affairs, the true basis for the criticism of monopolistic output is always to compare it with optimum output. not with competitive output (which may easily be a meaningless term in the state of affairs assumed). Whatever the technical conditions, an optimum output always exists.

[2] *Op. cit.*, pp. 172 ff.

theory is less generally appreciated. When they are taken strictly, the optimum conditions can only be interpreted *ex post*; it is only *after the event* that we can say whether an optimum organisation has in fact been achieved. Now even under perfect competition, producers only equate prices to marginal costs *ex ante*; it is anticipated marginal costs which are made equal to anticipated prices, so that if any of these anticipations are wrong, actual prices will not equal actual marginal costs, and the position achieved, though planned to be an optimum, will not turn out as such in fact. Of course, the utmost which can be done by wise economic policy is to secure equality *ex ante*—the planned optimum, but it is as well to remind ourselves that this does not necessarily imply a realised optimum, in order that we should be quite clear about the part played by foresight in economic efficiency.

Nor is this all; if the optimum conditions are interpreted *ex post*, they can make no allowance for risk, since risk is a phenomenon due to uncertainty of the *future*. On the other hand, the policy of the individual producer, being *ex ante*, is greatly influenced by risk; consequently prices always tend to exceed the relevant marginal costs by a risk-premium. Consequently production is carried less far in the more risky industries than is theoretically desirable.

If foresight is very bad, there may be little harm in this; for the refusal to embark resources in risky enterprises may prevent much mal-investment and waste. Indeed, so long as it confines itself to deflecting resources from more risky to less risky sorts of *production*, wo may not need to have much quarrel with the risk factor in practice, the trouble is that it may go beyond this. Liquidity-preference is only a form of risk-aversion; and the effect of liquidity-preference on the general activity of industry is well known. When liquidity-preference manifests itself in a large amount of "involuntary unemployment," a monetary policy directed to the reduction of interest rates, and even a public works policy which calculates the profitability of public enterprise at an "artificially" low rate of interest, may be measures which promote movement in the direction of the optimum as we have defined it.[1]

[1] In spite of the close dependence of actual interest rates upon risk factors (expressed by Mr. Keynes in his liquidity-preference theory), it must not be supposed that the payment of interest is itself inconsistent with optimum organisation. For a convincing demonstration of this, see Lindahl, "The Place of Capital in the Theory of Price" (*Ekonomisk Tidskrift*, 1929, appearing in English as Part III of his *Studies in the Theory of Money and Capital*). The

6. I do not propose to say very much in this paper about the welfare economics of monopoly and imperfect competition, for this is altogether too large a subject to be capable of useful treatment on the scale here available. A very large part of the established theory of imperfect competition falls under the head of welfare economics, and it is actually much the strongest part of the theory which does so. Considered as a branch of positive economics, the theory of imperfect competition is even now not very convincing; the assumption that the individual producer has a clear idea of the demand curve confronting him has been justifiably questioned, and the presence of intractable elements of oligopoly in most markets has been justifiably suspected.[1] When it is considered as a branch of welfare economics, the theory of imperfect competition has a much clearer status. Oligopoly and monopolistic competition fall into their places as reasons for the inequality between price and marginal cost, whose consequences are then a most fertile field for study along welfare lines.

It is perhaps rather to be regretted that modern theories of imperfect competition have not been cast more overtly into this form; for the general apparatus of welfare economics would have made it possible to state some of the most important propositions in a more guarded way than usual. Take, for example, the very important question of the optimum number of firms in an imperfectly competitive industry, which is so near the centre of modern discussion. Since (*ex hypothesi*) the different firms are producing products which are economically distinguishable, the question is one of those which falls under the heading of our *third* set of optimum conditions—the *total* conditions; we have to ask whether a reduction in the number of products would be conducive to a movement towards the optimum.

Suppose then that a particular firm is closed down. The loss involved in its cessation is measured by the compensation which would have to be given to consumers to make up for their loss of the opportunity to consume the missing product, *plus* the compensation which would have to be given to producers to make up for the excess of their earnings in this use over what they could

---

economy with perfect foresight and perfect competition, elaborately analysed by Professor Lindahl, is automatically an economy with optimum organisation and yet it has a rate of interest (of course a pure time-preference rate). The time-preference element in interest is that element which is consistent with the optimum, the liquidity-preference element is that which is not.

[1] Cf. Hall and Hitch, *Price Theory and Business Behaviour*, Oxford Economic Papers, Number 2.

earn in other uses. The loss is therefore measured by Marshall's *Surplus* (Consumers' Surplus [1] *plus* Producers' Surplus). Under conditions of perfect competition, this loss is a net loss. For when the factors are transferred to other uses, they will have to be scattered about at the margins of those uses; and (since the earnings of a factor equal the value of its marginal product) the additional production made possible by the use of the factors in these new places is equal in value to the earnings of the factors (already accounted for). Under perfect competition, the marginal productivity law ensures that there is no producers' surplus generated at the new margins; while, since the marginal unit of any commodity is worth no more than what is paid for it, there can be no consumers' surplus either. Thus there is nothing to set against the initial loss; there cannot be a movement towards the optimum if the number of products is reduced.

But if competition is imperfect, there is something to set on the other side. The earnings of a factor are now less than the value of its marginal product by an amount which varies with the degree of monopolistic exploitation; and therefore the increment to production which can be secured by using the factors at other margins is worth more than the earnings of the factors. There is a producers' surplus, even at the margin, and this producers' surplus may outweigh the initial loss. The general condition for a particular firm to be such that its existence is compatible with the optimum is that the sum of the consumers' and producers' surpluses generated by its activities must be greater than the producers' surplus which would be generated by employing its factors (and exploiting them) elsewhere.

The rule usually given is a special case of this general rule. If entry to the industry is "free," price equals average cost, and the producers' surplus generated by the firm as a whole can be neglected. If the products of the different firms are very close substitutes, or merely distinguished by "irrational preferences," consumers' surplus can perhaps be neglected as well. With these simplifications, the number of firms in an imperfectly

---

[1] This use of Consumers' Surplus is not open to any of the objections which have been brought against Marshall's concept; it does not involve either interpersonal comparisons or the measurement of utility. Consumers' surplus is the measure of the compensation which consumers would need in order to maintain them at the same level of satisfaction as before, after the supply of the commodity had been withdrawn. It is, however, not exactly equal to the area under the ordinary demand curve (see my *Value and Capital*, Appendix to Chapter II). This inequality (usually only a slight inequality) was responsible for the difficulties about the aggregation of consumers' surpluses which troubled Professor Pigou.

competitive industry is always excessive, so long as price is greater than marginal cost anywhere in the industry. (Or, if we can retain the identity of price with average cost, the number of firms is excessive until average cost is reduced to a minimum.)

These, however, are simplifications; it is not always true that the number of firms in an imperfectly competitive industry is excessive, though very often it may be. Before recommending in practice a policy of shutting down redundant firms, we ought to be sure that the full condition is satisfied; and we ought to be very sure that the discarded factors will in fact be transferred to more productive uses. In a world where the most the economist can hope for is that he will be listened to occasionally, that is not always so certain.

7. By adopting the line of analysis set out in this paper, it is possible to put welfare economics on a secure basis, and to render it immune from positivist criticism. That is a great gain in itself; but, as often happens in such cases, other gains are secured with it. The main practical advantage of our line of approach is that it fixes attention upon the question of compensation. Every simple economic reform inflicts a loss upon some people; the reforms we have studied are marked out by the characteristic that they will allow of compensation to balance that loss, and they will still show a net advantage. Yet when such reforms have been carried through in historical fact, the advance has usually been made amid the clash of opposing interests, so that compensation has not been given, and economic progress has accumulated a roll of victims, sufficient to give all sound policy a bad name.

I do not contend that there is any ground for saying that compensation ought always to be given; whether or not compensation should be given in any particular case is a question of distribution, upon which there cannot be identity of interest, and so there cannot be any generally acceptable principle. This being so, it will often happen in some particular case that the economist will find himself not at all anxious for compensation to be given [1]; but his personal feeling in that direction will be based either upon the non-economic ground that the persons damaged

[1] The typical hard-boiled attitude is, of course, to reject all compensation on the ground that such risks *ought* to have been allowed for. In view of the importance of foresight for economic efficiency, there is something in this; when applied to ordinary changes in data which promote productivity (such as inventions) it is probably a decisive consideration; nevertheless, if it is always regarded as decisive, the case for an active pursuit of economic efficiency in other ways is seriously weakened.

do not deserve much consideration, or upon the only quasi-economic ground that the loss inflicted on them is nothing but the materialisation of a risk they may be expected to have allowed for. Nevertheless we must expect that there will be many other cases where the redistribution, resulting from a sound measure carried through without compensation, would be regarded by him as deplorable; and then, if he considers the measure in isolation from the question of compensation, he will pay no more than lip-service to its productive efficiency, and probably reject it in practice. From this it is only a step to the state of mind which judges measures solely by reference to their distributive justice, without reference to their bearing on efficiency. If measures making for efficiency are to have a fair chance, it is extremely desirable that they should be freed from distributive complications as much as possible.

We can make this separation in our own minds if we accustom ourselves, whenever we can, to thinking of every economic reform in close conjunction with some measure of compensation, designed to render it approximately innocuous from the distributive point of view. Since almost every conceivable kind of compensation (re-arrangement of taxation, for example) must itself be expected to have some influence on production, the task of the welfare economist is not completed until he has envisaged the total effects of both sides of the proposed reform; he should not give his blessing to the reform until he has considered these total effects and judged them to be good. If, as will often happen, the best methods of compensation feasible involve some loss in productive efficiency, this loss will have to be taken into account. In practice, it is not unlikely that we shall have to reject on these grounds many measures which would be approved of by the traditional analysis, but which would only be reckoned by that analysis as offering a small gain. (It is not very surprising to find that some of the fine points in welfare theory are nothing but snares.)

Further investigations of such matters would lead us far beyond the " Foundations " which have been the subject of this paper. I have accomplished my end if I have demonstrated the right of Welfare Economics—the " Utilitarian Calculus " of Edgeworth—to be considered as an integral part of economic theory, capable of the same logical precision and the same significant elaboration as its twin brother, Positive Economics, the " Economical Calculus."

J. R. HICKS

[13]

A Note on Welfare Propositions in Economics

Modern economic theory draws a sharp distinction between positive economics, which explains the working of the economic system, and welfare economics, which prescribes policy. In the domain of welfare economics the impossibility of interpersonal utility comparisons has for a long time been believed to impose strict limitations on the economist, which kept this branch of economic theory in the background. Recently, however, there has been a reawakening of interest in welfare problems, following assertions that these limitations are less restrictive than they were hitherto supposed to be.[1] The present note attempts to analyse the problem in detail.

I

The aim of welfare economics is to test the efficiency of economic institutions in making use of the productive resources of a community. For analytical and historical reasons it is useful to distinguish between welfare propositions based on the assumption of a fixed quantity of employed resources and those that regard that quantity as a variable.

The former are concerned with the allocating efficiency of the system ;[2] i.e. with its ability of best allocating a given quantity of utilised resources among their various uses in consumption and production. They can be conceived of as criteria for judging institutions and policy in a closed community whose potential resources are fixed and can be trusted to be fully employed, either because of the automatism of the system or because of the existence of a governmental policy aiming at full employment.

The latter, which may be called welfare propositions in the wider sense, are in addition to the above problems concerned also with the total quantity of resources available to an open group and the degree of utilisation of those resources. They are therefore relevant, first of all, to problems of international trade from the point of view of a single country ; and secondly, to the general problem of employment.

II

All the welfare propositions of the classical economists—viz., perfect competition, free trade, and direct taxation—belong in the first category ; a fact which has not always been realised. They are all based on the principle that

---

[1] Cf. N. Kaldor : " Welfare Propositions of Economics and Interpersonal Comparisons of Utility," *Economic Journal*, vol. 49 (1939), p. 549 ; J. R. Hicks : " Foundations of Welfare Economics," *Economic Journal*, vol. 49 (1939), p. 696. See also N. Kaldor " A Note on Tariffs and the Terms of Trade," *Economica* (N.S.), vol. 7 (1940), p. 377 ; and J. R. Hicks : " The Rehabilitation of Consumers' Surplus," *Review of Economic Studies*, vol. 8 (1941), p. 108. The present note is a criticism of the principle enunciated in Mr. Kaldor's first-quoted article and underlying the argument of the others. It is not presented in polemic form, in order to enable the reader not acquainted with the articles here quoted to follow its argument.

[2] This expression was suggested to me by Mr. George Jaszi to whom I am also indebted for reading the manuscript and making valuable suggestions.

given the total quantity of utilised resources, they will be best distributed among different uses if their rates of substitution are everywhere and for every person equal ; for only in such a situation will each person's satisfaction be carried to that maximum beyond which it cannot be increased without diminishing someone else's. Perfect competition, free trade, and direct taxation are one (probably the simplest) among the many ways of achieving this aim.

By limiting our universe of discourse to two commodities and two persons, we can illustrate this principle on a simple diagram. Let us draw the indifference maps of the two individuals superposed on each other, one of them reversed, with the axes parallel and in such a position that their intersection gives the quantities of the two goods jointly possessed by the two people. Every point of the rectangle enclosed by the axes corresponds to a given distribution of the two goods between the two persons, and the two indifference curves going through that point show their respective welfare positions. At some points, indifference curves do not cut but are tangential one to another. At these points the rate of substitution of the two goods is equal for the two persons, and they represent optimum situations, because once such a point has been reached no redistribution of the two goods can increase the welfare of either person without diminishing that of the other. The locus of all optimum points gives the contract curve.

We judge the allocating efficiency of economic institutions by the criterion whether or not they enable people so to redistribute goods and services among themselves (irrespective of their initial position) as to arrive on the contract curve. That perfect competition or, from the point of view of the universe, free trade are efficient in the above sense can be proved by showing that all pairs of offer (reciprocal demand) curves drawn from any point within the rectangle intersect on the contract curve. Similarly, excise taxes and, from the point of view of the universe, import and export duties are inefficient, because they can be represented as distortions of offer curves that make them intersect outside the contract curve. The arguments based on this diagram can be generalised for any number of persons and commodities.[1] It implies only one limitation : the quantities of goods available to the community as a whole must be fixed ; for they determine the points of intersection of the axes and the position of the contract curve. This shows that the propositions illustrated by the diagram are allocative welfare propositions ; and it also appears to limit their applicability to the problem of the exchange of goods whose quantities coming onto the market are given. It can be proved, however, that our arguments are equally valid when instead of these quantities those of the factors utilised in their production are considered to be fixed. For the formal proof of the geometrical arguments and their generalisations the reader is referred to the original sources and to textbooks dealing with the subject.[2]

[1] This also holds good for all arguments based on other diagrams in this note.
[2] Cf. F. Y. Edgeworth : *Mathematical Psychics*, London, 1881, and " The Pure Theory of International Trade," *Economic Journal*, vol. 4 (1894) ; Alfred Marshall : *The Pure Theory of Foreign Trade* (1879), London School reprint, 1930 ; and his *Principles of Economics*, Bk. V, Chap. II. Note on Barter and Mathematical Note XII ; A. P. Lerner ; " The Symmetry between Export and Import Taxes," *Economica* (N.S.), vol. 3 (1936) ; J. R. Hicks : *Value and Capital*, Oxford, 1939, etc. For the best analysis of the nature of this kind of diagram see A. L. Bowley ; *The Mathematical Groundwork of Economics*, Oxford, 1924.

A NOTE ON WELFARE PROPOSITIONS IN ECONOMICS 79

III

We have seen above that allocative welfare propositions are based on the criterion of economic efficiency. They state that of alternative situations, brought about by different institutions or courses of policy, one is superior to the other in the sense that it would make everybody better off for every distribution of welfare, *if* that were the same in the two situations. This is different from saying that one situation is actually better than the other from everybody's point of view, because a change in institutions or policy almost always redistributes welfare sufficiently not to have a uniform effect on everybody but to favour some people and prejudice others. It follows from this that economic welfare propositions cannot as a rule be made independently of interpersonal comparisons of utility.

It would hardly be satisfactory, however, to confine the economist's value judgments to cases where one situation is superior to the other from the point of view of everybody affected. It is doubtful if in practice any choice comes within this category ; besides, there would not be much point in soliciting the economist's expert opinion when everybody is unanimous, except in order to enlighten people as to their true interest.

Favouring an improvement in the organisation of production and exchange *only* when it is accompanied by a corrective redistribution of income fully compensating those prejudiced by it might seem to be a way out of the difficulty, because such a change would make some people better off without making anyone worse off. For instance, it might be argued that the abolition of the Corn Laws should not have been advocated by economists in their capacity of pure economists without advocating at the same time the full compensation of landowners out of taxes levied on those favoured by the cheapening of corn. Yet, in a sense, and regarded from a long-run point of view, such propositions are not independent of value judgments between alternative income distributions either. For, going out of their way to preserve the existing distribution of income, they imply a preference for the *status quo*.

There seem to be two solutions of the problem. First of all, in addition to admitting his inability to compare different people's satisfaction, the economist may postulate that such comparisons are impossible, and that therefore there is nothing to choose between one distribution of income and another. He may then make value judgments on the sole criterion of efficiency without bothering about concomitant shifts in the distribution of income, since he considers one income distribution as good as any other.[1] In this case, however, he cannot claim that his value judgments are independent of interpersonal utility comparisons, because they depend on the assumption of their impossibility.

Secondly, the economist may put forward his welfare propositions with due

---

[1] This, I think, was the attitude of the classical economists ; at least of those who did not, like Bastiat, impute ethical values to the distribution of income under perfect competition. It seems to be the correct interpretation of that fairly representative statement of Cairnes' : " . . . standards of abstract justice . . . are inefficacious as means of solving the actual problems of . . . distribution. . . . If our present system of industry (perfect competition) is to be justified, it must . . . find its justification . . . in the fact that it secures for the mass of mankind a greater amount of material and moral well-being, and provides more effectively for its progress in civilisation than any other plan."

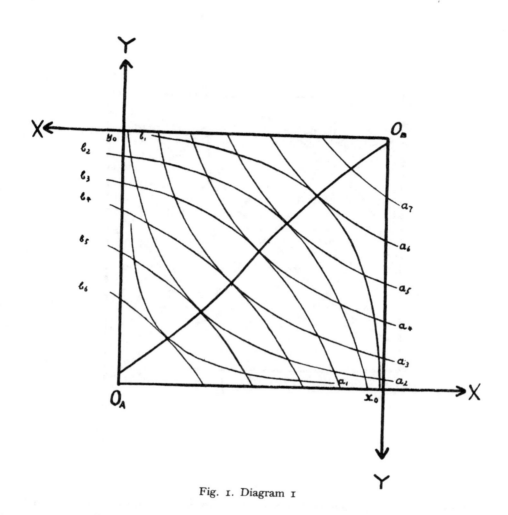

Fig. 1. Diagram 1

emphasis on their limitations, as being based on the sole criterion of efficiency.
He may then point out the nature of eventual redistributions of income likely
to accompany a given change, and stress the necessity of basing economic
policy on considerations both of economic efficiency and of social justice.[1] Such
an attitude, which I think is the only correct one, may diminish the force of the

[1] Or, of course, he may also renounce his claim to purity and base his own recommendations
on both criteria.

A NOTE ON WELFARE PROPOSITIONS IN ECONOMICS   81

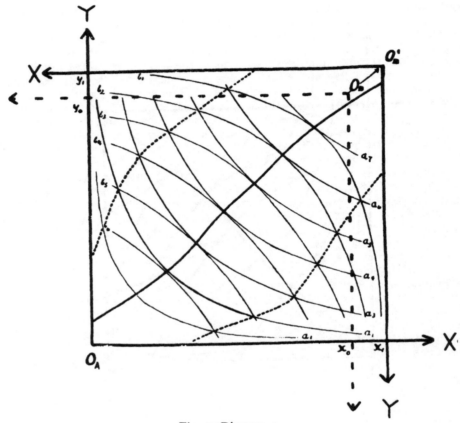

Fig. 1, Diagram 2

economist's welfare propositions but does not make them less useful. The above considerations qualify also the welfare propositions to be discussed below.

IV

When we come to the problem of welfare propositions in the wider sense, we can no longer illustrate a change in economic institutions or policy on a single diagram. For such a change will no longer mean a mere redistribution of income and alteration of the rules of production and exchange ; but may also involve a change both in the total quantity of resources available to the community, and in their degree of utilisation. The former may be due to the imposition of a duty on international trade, which from the point of view of an individual country alters the quantities of imports and retained exports available for home consumption ; while the latter may be caused by this or any other change, if it affects the propensity to save or the inducement to invest and thereby changes employment. Analytically there is no difference between the two cases. In both, the quantities of resources available for consumption are changed, hence the relative position of the indifference maps is altered ; whence it follows that welfare propositions in the wider sense must involve the comparison of two diagrams. Since these are constructed from the identical two indifference maps and differ only in the latter's relative position to each other, such comparisons are not the hopeless task they might seem at first sight. For we can represent some (not all) welfare positions on both diagrams ; and it is possible to represent on one diagram the welfare positions corresponding to all those points of the other diagram's contract curve that are inferior to its " own " contract curve. This follows from the fact that our diagrams admit the representation of all welfare situations that are inferior (worse from the point of view of at least one of the two persons) to their contract curve, while welfare positions superior to the contract curve cannot be represented on them.

Our welfare propositions may necessitate the comparison of points on the contract curves of the two diagrams, or of points suboptimal to them, or of a point on one contract curve with a point suboptimal to the other contract curve. The first case is that where the system's allocating efficiency is at an optimum both before and after the given change ; the second, where it is suboptimal both before and after the change ; the third, where the change affects allocating efficiency. Taking an example from the theory of inter-national trade, the first case may be illustrated by the imposition of an import duty by a country in which taxation is direct and domestic markets are per-fectly competitive ;[1] the second case can be represented by a duty imposed in a monopolistic world ; and the third by a duty which favours the formation of monopolies or is linked with an excise tax on the home production of import substitutes.

V

Let us draw two diagrams (Fig. 1), both consisting of the superposed indifference maps of individuals A and B, but with the difference that in the second, B's map has been shifted by $o_B o_B$; so that the joint possessions of A and B have increased by $x_0 x_1$ of X and $y_0 y_1$ of Y compared with what they were in the first. This shift will bring into a position of tangency indifference curves that in the first diagram have neither touched nor intersected, and will thus make the second diagram's contract curve superior to that of the first diagram throughout its range. This follows from that fundamental postulate of economic

---

[1] A tariff on foreign trade is not incompatible with the tariff imposing country's domestic trade and production being of optimum allocating efficiency. The reader must not let himself be confused by the fact that similar diagrams have been used for illustrating the waste caused by tariffs from the point of view of the universe as a whole. We are here solely concerned with the effects of a tariff on the welfare of a single country, consequently the indifference maps that constitute our diagrams belong to inhabitants of the same country.

A NOTE ON WELFARE PROPOSITIONS IN ECONOMICS 83

theory that indifference curves can never have a positive slope, and it will be the case whenever the shift in the relative position of the indifference maps represents an increase in the quantity of at least one of the two commodities without a diminution in that of the other. From the fact that the second diagram's contract curve is superior to that of the first, it follows that the latter can be represented on the second diagram by tracing the locus of the points of intersection of all the indifference curves that in the first diagram are tangential to each other. This will give us a curve on each side of the second diagram's contract curve, and the area between them represents welfare positions that are superior to the first diagram's contract curve. Hence, a change that brings the welfare of our groups from a point of the first diagram's contract curve onto a point of the second diagram's contract curve (or at least within the area between the broken lines), can be said to be desirable with the same generality and significance with which perfect competition or direct taxation are said to be desirable on the ground of their allocating efficiency. In other words, while it need not actually improve everybody's position, it would do so for every possible distribution of welfare if the change were to leave that distribution unaffected.

The above argument is an explicit formulation of the statement that getting more of some (or all) commodities at no cost of foregoing others is a good thing. This may be considered as overpedantic, since that statement seems to be obvious ; on the other hand, it is subject to the same limitations that qualify allocative welfare propositions (cf. section 3 above) ; and besides, it is not even always true. Increased plenty is a good thing only if it is not linked with a redistribution of welfare, too retrogressive from the point of view of social justice ; and if it does not lead to a serious deterioration of the allocating efficiency of the economic system. For the former there exists no objective criterion, but there is a simple test for the latter. To test whether a diminution in allocating efficiency has not obviated the advantages of increased plenty, we must see if after the change, it is possible fully to compensate people prejudiced by it out of funds levied on those favoured by the change, without thereby completely eliminating the latter's gain. From the geometrical argument above it follows that if this test is fulfilled for one initial income distribution, it will be fulfilled for all possible initial income distributions, and *vice versa*. Our test is completely general also in the sense that it is applicable whether or not the initial situation is of optimum allocating efficiency. (I.e. whether or not it lies on the contract curve).

VI

The kind of change contemplated above, where the quantity of some or all goods is increased without a diminution in others, is likely to occur as a result of increased employment, capital accumulation, technical progress, better utilisation of strategic advantages in international trade (by putting a duty on the export of goods for which foreign demand is inelastic), and the like. Another kind of change, especially important in international trade, is that where the quantity of some resources is increased and that of others diminished.[1] In

[1] This is the effect of import and export duties whenever the foreigners' reciprocal demand for exports is not inelastic and employment is given.

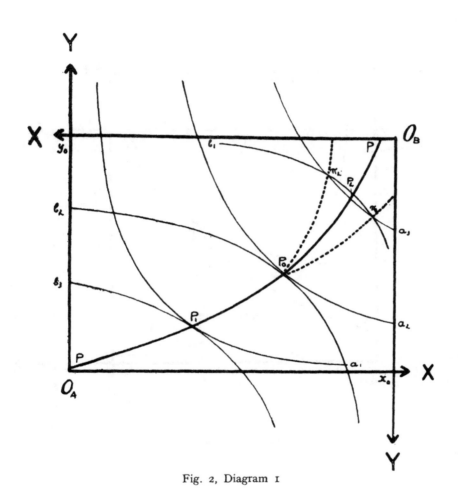

Fig. 2, Diagram I

Fig. 2 this is represented by a parallel displacement of one of the two indifference maps in the negative direction ; so that the quantity of X is diminished
by x_0x_1 and that of Y increased by y_0y_1. Nothing general can be said about the
relationship of the two contract curves in this case without detailed knowledge
of the shape of the indifference maps. It is possible that the change will result
in superior welfare positions throughout the whole range of the contract curve,
in the same way as was depicted in Fig. I. This is especially likely to happen
when the increase is large and the diminution small.   When on the other hand,

A NOTE ON WELFARE PROPOSITIONS IN ECONOMICS   85

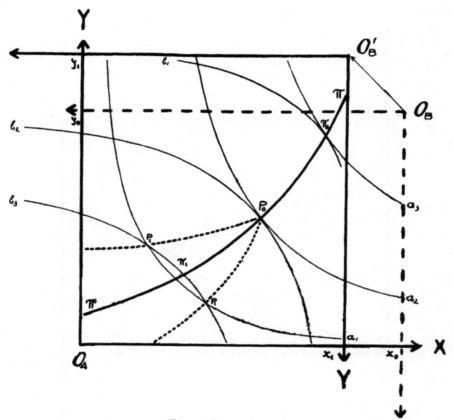

Fig. 2, Diagram 2

the diminution is large and the increase small, the change may result in inferior positions throughout the contract curve ; a situation which can be visualised by thinking of diagram 2 (Fig. 1) as showing the initial, and diagram 1 the new, position. Between these two extremes lies the more general case in which some sectors of the new contract curve are superior to the old one, while others are inferior to it. Its simplest example is illustrated in Fig. 2, where P_0 is a common point of the two contract curves, to the left of which the new contract curve, $\pi\pi$, represents welfare positions superior to the corresponding welfare positions of the old contract curve, PP ; while to the right of P_0, the old contract curve is superior to the new one. In each diagram the broken lines show the welfare positions corresponding to the other diagram's contract curve wherever that is inferior to the diagram's own contract curve.

The economic meaning of this is that the identical change in the composition of the national income would improve general welfare for some hypothetical welfare distributions and worsen it for others. Imagine members of a community divided into two groups according to their preference for goods Y and X respectively.[1] Then assume a change that increases the quantity of Y and diminishes that of X, but leaves the distribution of money income between our two groups unaffected. From the point of view of individuals, the change will appear as a shift in relative prices ; which, given the distribution of income, will be likely to make those with a special preference for Y better off, and those with a liking for X worse off, than they were before. Assume next that the members of our first group are rich and those of the second poor. Then the gain of the first group expressed in money (or in terms of any single commodity) will be greater than the money equivalent of the loss suffered by the second group. Therefore, if we so redistributed income as to restore approximately the initial distribution of welfare, there would be a net gain, making members of both groups better off than they were before. Conversely, if the people favoured by the change were poor, and those prejudiced by it were rich, the money equivalent of the former's gain would be insufficient fully to compensate the latter's loss, so that a redistribution of income tending to restore the initial distribution of welfare would result in a net loss of satisfaction for everybody.

What significance are we to attach to this case ? To refrain altogether, as the classical economists did, from making welfare propositions relating to it, seems unduly restrictive. It is true that as we have seen such a change would improve general welfare for some welfare distributions and worsen it for others ; on the other hand, we are not interested in all possible welfare distributions. There are only two distributions of welfare that really matter. Those actually obtaining immediately before and after the change contemplated.[2] It seems therefore sufficient to concentrate on these and to investigate how the change would affect general welfare if it were to leave the distribution of welfare unaffected and if that were both before and after it, first what it actually is before, secondly what it actually is after, the change. Whenever these two comparisons yield identical results, we can make welfare propositions of almost the same generality and significance as the allocative welfare propositions of the classical economists ; especially since the identical results for the two welfare distributions imply a strong presumption in favour of the same result holding for all intermediate welfare distributions as well.

We propose, therefore, to make welfare propositions on the following principle. We must first see whether it is possible in the new situation so to redistribute income as to make everybody better off than he was in the initial situation ; secondly, we must see whether starting from the initial situation it

[1] The term " preference " is used in a loose sense. It denotes the whole shape of indifference surfaces and not only their slope at the relevant point, which in equilibrium conditions is the same for everybody.

[2] The reader's attention is called to the fact that in reality the distribution of income is not *given* as we have assumed in the argument above. As a rule, the change will affect the distribution of welfare not only by shifting relative prices but also by boosting some industries and depressing others, and thereby redistributing money income.

A NOTE ON WELFARE PROPOSITIONS IN ECONOMICS   87

is not possible by a mere redistribution of income to reach a position superior to the new situation, again from everybody's point of view. If the first is possible and the second impossible, we shall say that the new situation is better than the old was. If the first is impossible but the second possible, we shall say that the new situation is worse ; whereas if both are possible or both are impossible, we shall refrain from making a welfare proposition.[1]

We can illustrate this procedure in Fig. 2 for the special case when allocating efficiency is at its optimum both before and after the change. Each situation can then be represented by a point on its respective contract curve and compared with the corresponding point on the other contract curve. If both points lie to the left of P_0 on their respective contract curves, the change will increase general welfare, because starting from the new situation on the second diagram's contract curve it is always possible to travel along that curve by redistributing income and arrive at a point which is superior to the initial situation from everybody's point of view ; whereas starting from the initial situation on the first diagram's contract curve, it is impossible by travelling along that curve to reach a position superior to the new situation. If on the other hand, both points lie to the right of the common point P_0, the change can be said to diminish general welfare on the same reasoning ; while if one point lies to the left and the other to the right, we can make no welfare propositions relative to our group.

VII

Our two criteria for making welfare propositions bear a close resemblance to Paasche's and Laspeyre's formulae in the theory of cost of living index numbers. There, just as here, the difficulty lies in comparing averages whose weighting is different ;[2] and the solution is sought in comparing the two real situations not one with another, but each with a hypothetical situation, which resembles it in weighting but is otherwise identical with the other real situation. In the theory of index numbers, budgets of different dates or places are compared each with the cost of the identical bundle of commodities at the prices of the other date or place ; and these two comparisons, expressed as ratios (Paasche's and Laspeyre's formulae), are the limits within which the true difference in the cost of living must lie.[3] In welfare problems, of course, we can aim neither at a " true " answer nor at its quantitative expression without measuring satisfaction and comparing different people's. But our two criteria are exactly analogous to Paasche's and Laspeyre's formulae. For we compare the first welfare situation with what general welfare would be if the satisfaction, yielded by the physical income of the second situation were distributed as it was in the first ; and contrast the second situation with the welfare that the first situation's physical income would yield to each person if it were so distri-

---

[1] It need hardly be recalled that in the situation discussed in section 5—that is, when the quantities of goods and services all change in the same direction—this last case can never occur, and we can always make welfare propositions.

[2] Because the general welfare can be conceived of as average welfare.

[3] Cf. Henry Schultz : " A Misunderstanding in Index Number Theory," *Econometrica*, vol. 7 (1939), p. 1 ; and A. A. Konüs : " The Problem of the True Index of the Cost of Living," *Econometrica*, vol. 7 (1939), p. 10.

buted as to make the distribution of welfare similar to that of the second situation.[1]

VIII

Mr. Kaldor and Professor Hicks have asserted that it is *always* possible to tell whether a given change improves general welfare, even if not all people gain by it and some lose. The test suggested by them : to see whether it is possible after the change fully to compensate the losers at a cost to those favoured that falls short of their total gain, is fundamentally identical with the first of our two criteria. The objection to using this criterion by itself is that it is asymmetrical, because it attributes undue importance to the particular distribution of welfare obtaining before the contemplated change. If the government had a special attachment to the *status quo* before the change and would actually undertake to reproduce that welfare distribution by differential taxation after the change, then Mr. Kaldor's test would be sufficient. For then, the economist could regard that particular welfare distribution as the only relevant one and would be entitled to use it as his sole standard of reference. But in the absence of such a governmental policy there can be no justification in attaching greater importance to the welfare distribution as it was before than as it is after the change.

To illustrate the pitfalls of this one-sided criterion, imagine a change, say the imposition of a duty on imports, that brings the welfare of A and B from P_1 (Fig. 2) on the contract curve of diagram 1 onto π_2 on the contract curve of diagram 2. According to Mr. Kaldor's test this change is desirable, because by redistributing income we could travel from π_2 along the $\pi\pi$ curve to π_1, which is superior to P_1. But once the tariff has been imposed and situation π_2 established, it will be free trade and the resulting (original) situation P_1 that will appear preferable *by the same test*, because starting from P_1, income could be so redistributed (travelling along the PP curve in the first diagram this time) as to reach P_2, which is superior to π_2. So the two situations can be shown each to be preferable to the other by the identical criterion : an absurd result, which can only be avoided by using our double criterion.

Washington, D.C.

T. DE SCITOVSZKY.

---

[1] We say that the distribution of welfare is similar in two situations if every member of the community prefers the same situation. A more exact definition would be unnecessary for our purposes ; besides, it is also impossible, since welfare cannot be measured.

[14]

EVALUATION OF REAL NATIONAL INCOME

By PAUL A. SAMUELSON

Introduction

1. Improved measurement of national income has been one of the out-standing features of recent progress in economics. But the theoretical interpretation of such aggregate data has been sadly neglected, so that we hardly know how to define real income even in simple cases where statistical data are perfect and where problems of capital formation and government expenditure do not arise.

In 1940 J. R. Hicks made an important advance over the earlier work of Professor Pigou. This has given rise to recent discussions between Kuznets, Hicks, and Little, but the last word on the subject will not be uttered for a long time. I have tried to treat the problem somewhat exhaustively in this paper, relating it to the modern theories of welfare economics of Pareto–Lerner–Bergson type. The result is not easy reading even to the author—but without such a careful survey I doubt that even the classical writings of Pigou can be adequately gauged.[1]

2. In Fig. 1, the point A represents observed consumption data for a single consumer in equilibrium at the indicated price-slope line through A. All the other points are each to be regarded as alternative to A and have nothing to do with each other. The following statements are immediate consequences of the modern theory of a single consumer's behaviour and are based on $\sum pq$ data such as the national income statistician might be able to measure:

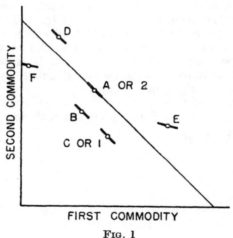

FIG. 1

(*a*) We can immediately infer that B is on a lower indifference curve than A.

[1] The principal references are to J. R. Hicks, 'The Valuation of the Social Income', *Economica*, 1940, pp. 105–24; Simon Kuznets, 'On the Valuation of Social Income—Reflections on Professor Hicks' Article', *Economica*, Feb. 1948, pp. 1–16, and May 1948, pp. 116–31; J. R. Hicks, 'The Valuation of the Social Income—A Comment on Professor Kuznets' Reflections', *Economica*, Aug. 1948, pp. 163–72; I. M. D. Little, 'The Valuation of the Social Income', *Economica*, Feb. 1949, pp. 11–26; A. C. Pigou, *Economics of Welfare*, 4th ed. (1932), Part I, especially chaps. ii, iii, v, vi; P. A. Samuelson, *Foundations of Economic Analysis* (1948), chap. viii. Since writing this article I have benefited from reading two

2   EVALUATION OF REAL NATIONAL INCOME

(*b*) Less directly, but with equal certainty, C reveals itself to be inferior
to A.

(*c*) The point D reveals itself to be superior to A.

(*d*) The points E and A reveal nothing about their order in the consumer's taste-pattern.

(*e*) The point F is inconsistent with A. The consumer has changed his
tastes, or he is not in equilibrium at the indicated points.

Problems of Inference from Group Market Data

3. Let us now regard Fig. 1 as applying to market data for two or more
individuals, so that each quantity, q, represents the total of two or more
individuals' consumption, $q'+q''+,\dots$, &c. The slope through A or any
other point represents the market-price ratio of the first and second goods,
the only commodities in our simplified world.

What can we now say about our points? Advances in the theory of
welfare economics since 1940—many of them growing out of Hicks's own
researches—suggest that certain of the definitions and propositions then
laid down need to be modified. I resurrect these matters only because
most people who have seen the recent discussion between Kuznets, Hicks,
and Little must find their heads swimming, and must be in considerable
doubt as to what the proper status of this vital matter is.

4. First we may clear up one misunderstanding, in itself unimportant,
but giving an initial clue that we cannot make any very sweeping inferences from aggregate price-quantity data. In 1940 it was held that a
situation like that of A and F is quite impossible on the assumption that
individuals preserve the same well-defined tastes and are in true equilibrium in competitive markets.[1] It was held that, for national totals,

$$\sum p_2 q_2 > \sum p_2 q_1 \quad \text{implies} \quad \sum p_1 q_1 < \sum p_1 q_2.$$

As stated earlier, for a single individual this would be a correct assertion;
but it is definitely false for group data involving two or more individuals.
Examples to show this can be given *ad lib*. No recourse need be made to
the Kuznets case of necessaries and luxuries (understanding by the latter,
goods which some individuals do not choose to buy at all)—but, of course,
there is no reason why such examples should not also be used. Perhaps
the very simplest example to illustrate the possibility of a contradiction
would be one in which we keep the exact national totals of the point A,
but reallocate goods between the individuals so that they come into final
equilibrium with a new and different price ratio. Then already we are on

further papers by Little and from corresponding with him. See I. M. D. Little, 'The
Foundations of Welfare Economics', *O.E.P.*, June 1949, and an addendum to his *Economica*
article 'A Note on the Significance of Index Numbers'.
   [1] See *Economica*, May 1940, pp. 112–13.

P. A. SAMUELSON   3

the borderline of a contradiction, and by making a slight change in the totals we can obviously get a strong outright contradiction.

Already we are warned that $\sum p_2 q_2 > \sum p_2 q_1$ cannot imply that the second situation represents an 'increase in social real income' over that of the first—since this implication would leave us with the real possibility that each situation is better than the other!

This should also warn us against thinking that we can save such a definition by applying it only where there is no such outright contradiction. For suppose that we consider a case which just escapes *revealing* itself to be contradictory; being so close to a nonsense situation, such a case can in no wise escape being subject to the same *fundamental* (as yet undiagnosed) difficulty, even though it may not be advertising the fact to us.

Inadmissibility of the 1940 Definition of Increased Real Income

5. This tells us already that either there is something inadequate about the 1940 definition of an 'increase in society's real income' or else there is something faulty about the logical proof that the index-number criterion $\sum p_2 q_2 > \sum p_2 q_1$ implies such a defined increase in real income.

The 1940 passage in question is so compact that one must be careful in interpreting it. In my judgement the root of the trouble lies more in the inadequacy of the definition enunciated than in the logic of the demonstration that the stated index-number criterion does imply an increase in defined real income. Although it has already been extensively requoted, the relevant 1940 passage is so brief that it can be given completely here.

'... What does it signify if $\sum p_2 q_2 > \sum p_2 q_1$?

'It should first of all be noticed that since this condition refers only to the total quantities acquired, it can tell us nothing about the distribution of wealth among the members of the group. There may be a drastic redistribution of wealth among the members and the aggregates will remain exactly the same. Thus what the condition $\sum p_2 q_2 > \sum p_2 q_1$ tells us is that there is *some* distribution of the q_1's which would make every member of the group less well off than he actually is in the II situation. For if the corresponding inequality were to hold for every individual separately, it would hold for the group as a whole.

'As compared with this particular distribution, every other distribution of the q_1's would make some people better off and some worse off. Consequently, if there is one distribution of the q_1's in which every member of the group is worse off than he actually is in the II situation, there can be no distribution in which everyone is better off, or even as well off. Thus if we start from any actual distribution of wealth in the I situation, what the condition $\sum p_2 q_2 > \sum p_2 q_1$ tells us is that it is impossible to reach, by redistribution, a position in which everyone is as well off as he is in the II situation.

'This would seem to be quite acceptable as a definition of increase in real social income. Let us say that the real income of society is higher in Situation II than in Situation I, if it is impossible to make everyone as well off as he is in Situation II by any redistribution of the actual quantities acquired in Situation I. If this definition is accepted, our criteria can be applied to it without change.'[1]

[1] J. R. Hicks, 'The Valuation of the Social Income', *Economica*, May 1940, p. 111.

4   EVALUATION OF REAL NATIONAL INCOME

6. A diagram that we shall place major reliance on in the later discussion can be used to illustrate exactly what is involved in this definition of an 'increase in social real income'. On the axes in Fig. 2 there is laid out the ordinal utility of each of two individuals: the exact scale of U'' or U' is of no consequence, only the north–south and east–west orderings being important. Corresponding to the point A or 2 in Fig. 1, there will actually be some allocation of the total of goods between our individuals, and hence some determined level of well-being for each. Let the point labelled 2 in Fig. 2 represent that actual level of ordinal well-being. Now consider the other situation that was labelled C or 1 in our earlier figure. Behind the

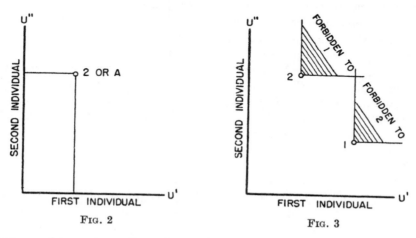

FIG. 2   FIG. 3

scenes, unknown to us from the totals, there is again an actual allocation of the goods to the individuals and again a new point in Fig. 2. If we knew where it was, we could write it in and label it 1. We do not know where this new point will fall: it may be south-west of point 2 so that all individuals are worse off, or south-east so that one individual is better off and the other worse off, and so forth.

Hicks's 1940 definition of an increase in real income from the point 1 to 2 consists of this: if we can be sure that neither point 1 nor any reallocation of its quantities among individuals lies north-east of point 2 (with both individuals better off in 1 than in 2), then point 2 is defined to represent an increase in real income over point 1.

How acceptable is this definition, leaving aside for the moment the question of whether the index-number criteria does permit us to place such a restriction on the admissible position of point 1? Upon reflection, we will all agree, I think, that such a definition is not very satisfactory. By means of it a point 1 may be both better and worse than another point 2. This is shown in Fig. 3. Also the definition has small claims on

P. A. SAMUELSON 5

our affections in terms of our common-sense intuitions. Its last disadvantage is a subtle but important one: correctly stated, the new welfare
economics is a body of doctrines which attempts to go as far as possible
in preparing the way for the final a-scientific step involving ethical judgements; it should never, therefore, prejudice the final step, but only make
statements which are uniformly valid for a wide class of ethical systems.
Suppose now that we have given to us in Fig. 2 a set of social indifference
curves (the contours of a Bergson social welfare function). It is more than
possible that a 'point' or 'situation' (they are not quite the same thing)
judged by the 1940 criterion to be the superior one may actually be the
'inferior' one in terms of the wider ethical judgements.

7. Instinctively Hicks was reaching out, I believe, for a rather different
definition than the one he actually enunciated. The simpler problem of
comparing A and B in Fig. 1 will bring this out and at the same time
require no intricate index-number reasoning. As before, corresponding
to the point A in Fig. 1 there is in Fig. 2 a point 2 representing the
ordinal well-being of all individuals. Now with less of *all* goods available
to society as shown by B, there will be a new point of individuals'
well-being in Fig. 2. Where will the new point lie with respect to the
former point 2?

We would have to give the unsatisfactory answer 'anywhere' were it
not for one important assumption. We have assumed that behind the
scenes of A all individuals are in competitive equilibrium facing the same
price ratio. This assures us that all marginal rates of substitution are
equal and that there exists no reallocation of the goods of A between them
which will permit them both to be better off. (In technical parlance the
competitive solution lies somewhere on the *Edgeworth contract locus*.) A
fortiori, for a point like B, which involves smaller totals for *every* commodity, there is *no* reallocation of goods that could possibly make all individuals better off than they were in A. Without introducing price or index
numbers, we know therefore that the point B is forbidden to be north-
east of the point A—and we know that B corresponds to a decrease in
real income over A according to the old 1940 definition.

But that is not really saying much. It is possible that one individual
may be worse off even though the other individual is better off. And we
must still entertain the darkest suspicions of a possible contradiction. But
this simple case turns out to have at least one surprising feature: if we try
to reallocate goods in either of the two situations—always letting the
individuals come ultimately into competitive equilibrium—it turns out
that we shall *never* find a case where on the 1940 definition the situation
B turns out to be 'better' (as well as 'worse') than A. I have not yet
proved this in my discussion; but, accepting this fact as true, we find

6   EVALUATION OF REAL NATIONAL INCOME

ourselves on the trail of a better way of defining an increase in real income
—or more accurately, an increase in *potential* real income.

The Crucially Important 'Utility-Possibility Function'

8. Let us consider all possible reallocations between individuals of the
consumption totals corresponding to A or 2. For each way of allocating
the goods there will be a given level of well-being for each and every
individual—as can be indicated by a point on the $U'-U''$ diagram. The
totality of all such possible points obviously cannot go indefinitely far in
the north-east direction; equally obviously there is a frontier curve or
envelope giving, for each amount of one person's utility, the maximum
possible amount of the other person's utility. This frontier is the important
'utility-possibility function' corresponding to A.

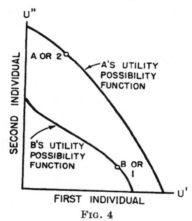

FIG. 4

The point 2 happens to lie on the frontier because at 2 all individuals
are known to be in competitive equilibrium. Corresponding to the smaller
totals of point B, there is also a utility-possibility function. We can now
state the sense in which A or 2 is *potentially* better than B.

The total of all goods being greater in A than in B, the utility-possibility
function of A is uniformly outside and beyond the utility-possibility function of B. (This is shown in Fig. 4.) The reason for this statement is
intuitively obvious and can be expressed in the language of a currently
popular song: A can do everything B can do—(and) better.

9. This, then, is the sense in which we can, without introducing detailed
ethical assumptions, define an 'increase in society's potential real income
in going from point B to point A'. Such an increase means a uniform outward shift in society's utility-possibility function.

Let us now return to the index-number problem. Can we infer that A
is superior to C in terms of our new definition of potential real income?

P. A. SAMUELSON   7

If we can, then with minor modifications the 1940 analysis can be accepted. But, unfortunately for economic theory, we cannot make any such inference about potential superiority from the index-number analysis of aggregate price-quantity data.[1]

Any single counter-example will prove the falsity of the index-number criteria as applied to more than one individual. Perhaps the simplest such example would be one in which the first individual cares only for so-called necessaries. If less of total necessaries are available in A, then A's utility-possibility curve must cut inside of B's when we get in the region of the U''–U' quadrant favouring the necessary-loving individual; and hence A cannot represent an unequivocal increase in potential real income. Simple as this example is, it is open to the objection that it seems to involve the case where the individuals consume nothing of some commodity. Actually this is an irrelevant feature of the example.

But, in any case, greater insight into the nature of the problem can be had if we examine the steps in the reasoning linking up the index-number criterion and the 1940 definition of an increase in real income.

10. If we have between the points A and C, or 2 and 1,

$$\sum p_2(q_2' + q_2'' + \ldots) > \sum p_2(q_1' + q_1'' + \ldots),$$

then according to the 1940 argument we can find some redistribution of the quantities in C or 1, so that the new quantities of every good going to each individual, which we may call

$$q_3' + q_3'' + \ldots = q_1' + q_1'' + \ldots,$$

are such as to make the crucial index-number criteria hold for each and every individual; namely,

$$\sum p_2 q_2' > \sum p_2 q_3', \qquad \sum p_2 q_2'' > \sum p_2 q_3'', \ldots.$$

Hence there exists a new situation resulting from the reallocation of the q_1's which is worse for *every* individual than is situation 2.

A missing step in the 1940 logic must be filled in at this point. The fact that we can reallocate the q_1's to get a new point q_3 which makes both individuals worse off than they are in 2 is taken to mean that the utility-possibility curve of 1 must be south-west of the point 2. But nothing has been said to show that q_3 is a frontier point on the utility-possibility function of point 1. Fortunately, it can be easily proved that there does exist at least one (and actually an infinite number) reallocation of the q_2's that

---

[1] Simple logic tells us that this negative answer must be forthcoming in a comparison of A and F since each of two curves cannot both lie uniformly outside of each other; and already we have seen reason to believe that the A and F comparison does not differ materially from that of A and C.

8   EVALUATION OF REAL NATIONAL INCOME

(*a*) lies on the utility-possibility function of 1, and (*b*) causes our index-number criteria to hold for each and every individual.[1]

With the above provision, we may accept the 1940 demonstration that when aggregate data satisfy the index-number criterion, the 1940 definition of superiority is definitely realized.[2] But there is nothing in this demonstration that tells us whether the utility-possibility function of 2 lies above (or below) the point 1 ;[3] all we know is that 1's utility-possibility function lies somewhere south-west of the point 2.

---

[1] Fig. 5 shows all this. An Edgeworth–Bowley box has been drawn up with the dimensions of the quantities in the q_1 situation. From the south-west corner of the box we measure off the consumption of the first individual, U'. From the north-east corner we measure downward and to the left the consumption of the U'' individual. Any point in the box represents a possible allocation of the total q_1 quantities, with the point marked q_1 being the one actually observed.

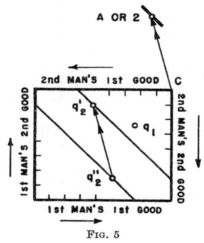

Fɪɢ. 5

On this same diagram we may also show the actual quantities consumed by the individuals in the q_2 situation. But now it takes two points in the box, as far apart from each other as C is from A. They are marked q_2' and q_2'' respectively, and the price-lines through their points are drawn in with the slope of the p_2 situation.

As the picture stands q_1 does not satisfy the index-number criteria for the U' individual since q_1 does *not* lie inside the crucial triangle of the point q_2'. Hicks's statement is that there is some reallocation which will move the point q_1 to a new point q_3 which lies between the two parallel lines. For any such point our index-number criteria are satisfied for both individuals. The missing step is to show that there exist points in this strip which are also on the Edgeworth contract curve. Since the contract curve must go from one corner of the box to the other and pass through all levels of U' and U'', it must obviously somewhere pass through the intervening strip between the parallel lines. This supplies the missing step. Readers of Kuznets should note that it is the totals of q_1, not of q_2, that are reallocated so as to lead to Hicks's conclusion.

[2] This is apparently what Little means when he concludes that the 1940 definition is 'immune from Professor Kuznets conditions' (loc. cit., p. 13).

[3] In any case, no one should think that the condition

$$\Sigma\, p_1\, q_2 > \Sigma\, p_1\, q_1$$

which is satisfied in C (but not in F) helps to rule out a contradiction.

P. A. SAMUELSON   9

11. Our final conclusions may be summarized briefly. The index-number criterion

$$\sum p_2(q'_2+q''_2+\ldots) > \sum p_2(q'_1+q''_1+\ldots)$$

tells us that the utility-possibility function of 2 does lie outside of that of 1 *in the neighbourhood* of the actual observed point 2—but that is all it tells us. The curve may intersect and cross elsewhere—as shown in the later Fig. 6.

The Hicks–Kaldor–Scitovsky Version of New Welfare Economics

12. Having failed to relate the stronger definition of potential superiority to index-number criteria, we must reconsider whether, after all, the 1940 definition of superiority may not be tolerably acceptable. If we examine this definition, we find that it is in all essentials the same one as that earlier suggested by N. Kaldor and by Hicks in his earlier article on the 'Foundations of Welfare Economics'.[1] It will be recalled that these two writers had ruled that situation X is better than situation Y if there exists a reallocation of the goods in X which makes everybody better off than he was in Y. Except that the 1940 definition applied to a *decrease* in well-being between 2 and 1, this is identical with the earlier 1939 definition.

Dissatisfaction early developed over the 1939 definition. In particular T. Scitovsky[2] came forward with the objection that it seemed to assume that there was something right (ethically) about the distribution of income in the *status quo ante* of the Y situation. To get around this he suggested (in effect) that a *double* test be applied.

To say that 'X is better than Y' we must be sure that (a) there exists a reallocation of the X goods that could make everybody better off than he actually was in Y; and (b) we must make sure there exists a reallocation of the goods in Y that could make everybody worse off than he actually was in X.

Or, in our terminology, the Scitovsky definition of superiority requires the utility-possibility curve of one situation to be beyond that of the other in the neighbourhood of *both* actual observed points.

13. In his criticism of the 1940 definition Kuznets can be generously interpreted to be trying (presumably independently) in effect to reiterate the Scitovsky double criterion. Kuznets says at one point that we must

---

[1] N. Kaldor, 'Welfare Propositions in Economics', *Economic Journal*, xlix, 1939, pp. 549–52; J. R. Hicks, 'Foundations of Welfare Economics', *Economic Journal*, xlix, 1939, pp. 696–712.

[2] T. Scitovsky, 'A Note on Welfare Propositions in Economics', *Review of Economic Studies*, 1941, pp. 77–88, and 'A Reconsideration of the Theory of Tariffs', *Review of Economic Studies*, 1942, pp. 89–110. To be precise Hicks is in 1940 riding the Scitovsky and Kuznets the Kaldor horse.

10   EVALUATION OF REAL NATIONAL INCOME

supplement the Hicks condition [that there must be a reallocation of the
q_1's that makes everyone worse off than he actually was in the q_2 situation]
by the further condition that '[it must be] impossible to make *everyone* as
well off as he is in situation I by any redistribution of the actual quantities
acquired in situation II' (*Economica*, 1948, p. 4).

Kaldor has explicitly accepted the Scitovsky correction, and as far as I
know so has Hicks. Therefore they would both presumably have no quarrel
with this Kuznets reversibility condition.[1] But both Kuznets and Hicks do
not seem to realize that the difficulty is basic and has nothing to do with
the question of substitutability of necessaries or luxuries. On the Scitovsky-
amended definition, the whole demonstration of superiority of one position
over another by aggregate index-number criteria breaks down completely.[2]

14. Our whole theory of arriving at a measure of real income by aggregative price-quantity data has broken down. But the worst is still to come.
The Scitovsky conditions are themselves very definitely unsatisfactory.
It is not enough to double the 1939 conditions—we must increase them
infinitely. Instead of a two-point test we need an infinitely large number
of tests—that is to say, we must be sure that one of the utility-possibility
functions *everywhere* lies outside the other. Without this test at an infinite
number of points, no acceptable definition of an increase in potential real
income can be devised at the non-ethical level of the new welfare economics.

Just as Scitovsky has criticized Kaldor and 'compensationists' for
assuming the correctness of the *status quo ante*, so we must criticize him for

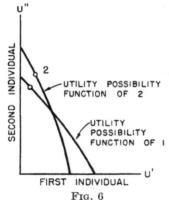

FIRST INDIVIDUAL

Fig. 6

assuming in some sense the correctness of the
status quo ante and/or the *status quo post*.

Suppose, for example, we have *everybody
actually* better off in situation 2 than in 1.
Kaldor and Hicks will be satisfied to call 2
better than 1. So will Scitovsky. But the
utility-possibility curves might very well
cross as in Fig. 6, so that according to many
ethical welfare functions both Scitovsky and
the others would be rendering false statements.

What Scitovsky should have done was to
free all of his comparisons from any depend-

---

[1] Little has argued (*Economica*, 1949, pp. 12–16) that there is a confusion in Kuznets on
the point of reversibility. Perhaps I am setting down what Kuznets should have meant
rather than what he meant to say.

[2] The best that we can say is the following. Imagine the change from point 2 to point 1
to be a continuous one. So long as the two points are sufficiently (!) close together, then the
condition $\Sigma p_2 q_2 > \Sigma p_2 q_1$ assures us that 2 is better than 1 in the Scitovsky sense. For
changes of any size $\Sigma p_2 q_2 > \Sigma p_2 q_1$ tells us that 1 *cannot* be superior to 2 in Scitovsky
or in my sense, and that is all it tells.

ence upon either *actually observed* $U''-U'$ situation. He should, instead, have made the comparison depend upon the totality of all *possible* positions in each situation. This would have led to the definition of potential real income earlier proposed, which seems to be the only satisfactory, self-consistent definition within the sphere of the 'new' (relatively *wert-frei*) welfare economics. Aggregate index numbers can tell us little about this except in a negative way. Even this definition is not—by itself—worth very much of anything for policy purposes, as will be shown.

Inadequacies for Policy of the New Welfare Economics

15. We have seen that the new welfare economics is able to define an increase in potential real income which is unambiguous, consistent, and which will not turn out to contradict a wide class of ethical social welfare functions that must later be introduced into any problem. The new welfare economics does not go all the way in settling the problems of normative policy: taken by itself, and without supplementation, it goes virtually none of the way; but taken in conjunction with later ethical assumptions, it attempts to clear the way of all issues that can be disposed of in a non-controversial (relatively) ethical-free fashion. This is the solid kernel of usefulness in the new approach begun by Pareto, and this should not be lost sight of in the welter of exaggerated claims for the new welfare economics.

The inadequacy for actual policy decisions—even in the most idealized, simplified world—of all of the discussed measures of 'real income' can be illustrated by numerous examples. Consider the very best case where we can establish the fact that situation 2 is *potentially* better than 1 (in the sense of having a uniformly farther-out utility-possibility function). Would a good fairy given the chance to throw a switch from 1 to 2 be able to justify doing so? Upon reflection we must, I am afraid, answer *no*. Potentialities are not actualities—and unless she can give a justification of her act that will satisfy all reasonably defined social welfare functions, she cannot know whether or not to pull the switch.

A few negative remarks are possible: for any ethical system with the property that an increase in one individual's well-being is, others' being equal, a good thing[1]—for all such systems a final optimum position must necessarily be on 2 and not on 1. That we can certainly say. But without going into the realm of (modern, streamlined) 'old' welfare economics, we cannot say more or get conclusive advice on this problem of policy. The attempt to divide the problem into two parts so that one can say 'a change from 1 to 2 is *economically* desirable in the sense of objectively increasing

---

[1] i.e. for all social welfare propositions W, with the property $W = F(u', u'',...)$ and $\dfrac{\partial W}{\partial u'} > 0 < \dfrac{\partial W}{\partial u''}, ...$.

12 EVALUATION OF REAL NATIONAL INCOME

production or wealth, whether or not the actual resulting situation will be ethically superior', only gets one into a semantic snarl and glosses over the intrinsic difficulties of the problem.

How much more severe are the policy limitations of some of the modern even weaker 'compensationist' definitions. Following them, the good fairy might do perpetual and irremediable harm. Suppose, for example, that our two *actually observed* points, 1 and 2, both lie above the intersection of the two schedules in Fig. 6, but with the point 1 being south-east of point 2, so as to represent an increase in well-being of one individual and a decrease for the other. The Kaldor condition would be satisfied and so would the Scitovsky condition. Suppose that once the angel has thrown the switch, she can never again reverse it (e.g. capital sunk into a mine may be irrecoverable). Let her now follow the counsel of the compensationists and throw the switch from 1 to 2. According to any ethical view that considers individual U' to be of the elect (or relatively so) and U'' to be relatively undeserving of consideration, the good life lies in a rather easterly direction. For ever and ever 'society' is condemned to 'unhappiness' because of the premature decision based on the Kaldor–Hicks–Scitovsky rules.[1]

Production Possibilities and Group Inferences

16. This completes the problem of making group inferences from simple index-number comparisons. At the non-philosophical level there are still two more grave difficulties to be faced. Up till now I have always spoken of the utility-possibility function of *point A*, not of situation A. But the totals of goods at A or 2 do not fall from heaven in fixed amounts. Obviously other total quantities might instead have been produced. Therefore, the true utility-possibility function corresponding to situation A is really wider and out farther than the one defined for point A. At best, if all markets are perfect and there are no external effects or government distortions, the utility-possibility function for point A may just touch that of situation A at the actual observed point, elsewhere being inside it. The wider schedule is the envelope of a family of schedules corresponding to each *possible* point of total consumption goods. (See Fig. 8.)

Obviously it is the wider possibility function of a 'situation' rather than of a 'point' with which we should be concerned, and before we go throwing

---

[1] If both individuals are better off in the observed 2 point than in the observed 1 point, how reasonable it seems to counsel that the switch be pulled. And if the only alternative were these two situations, almost all old welfare economists might agree. But this need not be our choice of alternatives at all. Realistically, the choice may be between these two points and a third ethically superior point that lies on 1's locus. As a matter of tactics and *realpolitik*, one will sometimes want to follow such simple criteria *and* actually give compensation, or perhaps fail to compensate. But tactics aside, these rules are in principle incomplete.

any switches or making policy decisions we must make sure how alternative production possibilities affect the problem. A few truths continue to remain self-evident, but, generally speaking, this new element makes the problem of definite inference even more difficult—an important but sad fact.

Let us consider an example. Up till now the one unshaken truth that remained was this: If more of every good is observed in point A than in point B, then A represents an increase in potential real national income over B. Even this is no longer necessarily valid! Suppose we draw up production-possibility curves showing how much of each good can be produced in total when the total of the other good is specified. Such a chart might look like Fig. 6 except that now the two outputs rather than utilities are on the axes. In Fig. 7 our observed point A lies north-east of the observed point B, and yet it is obvious that the production-possibility curves can still cross; and it is also obvious, upon reflection, that depend-

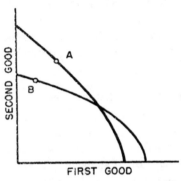
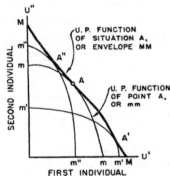

Figs. 7 and 8

ing upon how much people like one good as compared to another, the *corresponding utility-possibility curve can most definitely cross*—making no unambiguous inference about an increase in potential real income possible.

17. So long as commodities are really economic rather than free goods, this much can be said: *If the production-possibility function of one situation lies uniformly outside that of a second situation, then the utility-possibility function of the one will also be outside that of the other.* In the limiting case where one or both individuals do not care at all for one of the goods, the schedules might just be touching at one or more points. Also it is to be understood that if the total of resources (land, labour, &c.) is not the same in the two situations, these resources are to be treated just like negative commodities, and it is in this sense that one production-possibility function must lie uniformly outside the other.

Hicks attempted in 1940 to explore the relationship between index-number criteria based on price-quantity data and productivity as measured

14 EVALUATION OF REAL NATIONAL INCOME

by the position of the production-possibility function of society. His treatment was brief and much of it he had abandoned prior to Kuznets's 1948 criticisms. But even after the recent exchange of views I do not feel the subject is left in its proper state. To analyse the problem in its entirety would be too lengthy a task, but a number of observations are relevant to our discussion. In all that follows I shall assume that there are no excise taxes, so that the irrelevant distinction between income-at-factor-prices and income-at-market-prices can be disregarded.

Under this last assumption, would the same $\sum pq$ tests relevant to indicating a (1940-defined) increase in welfare also serve to indicate a shift in productivity? One is almost tempted to read such a belief into the following passage:

'If competition were perfect, and if state activities were so designed as not to disturb the *optimum* organization of production, marginal utilities and prices and marginal costs would all be proportional, so that the same valuation which would give us the social income as a measure of economic welfare would also give us the social income as a measure of productivity.'[1]

Kuznets objected to all this on the grounds that production-possibility curves, unlike indifference curves, can intersect and can be of variable curvature. His instinct that something is rotten in Denmark may be a sound one, but the precise trouble has not really been isolated, nor a worse difficulty brought to light.

In the first place, there is no need for an individual's indifference curves always to be concave: he need only be assumed to be in equilibrium at the observed points. In the second place, it is untrue that collectively defined indifference curves (*à la* Scitovsky or otherwise) are forbidden to intersect and cross. Our earlier discussion of the points A and F may be referred to in this connexion. Neither of these two reasons can serve to isolate the basic difficulties of making production inferences.[2]

---

[1] *Economica*, 1940, p. 122. Hicks goes on to say, parenthetically: 'It would not be very reliable as a measure of productivity, but it might usually satisfy the productivity tests for small displacements, over which the substitution curves might not differ very much from straight lines.' To make the only comparisons between different situations that are valid, this last linearity assumption can be shown to be unnecessary; but it foreshadows Hicks's later desire for an approximate representation of the production-possibility function in the neighbourhood of an observed optimal point. A straight line gives, under the assumed conditions, an upper (rather than a conservative, lower) bound as to what is producible.

[2] Kuznets has a third objection which has little or nothing to do with the problem here discussed. Working by analogy with the consumption problem, he makes the strange and unnecessary assumption that a perfect price system is in some sense maximizing 'producers' surpluses', and he raises the question whether specificity of some resources may not make it impossible for every producer to be as well off as previously. Both Hicks and I would consider producers and consumers to be the same units, who buy goods and also sell services; all such services can be treated as negative goods and all ordinal disutilities treated along with ordinal utilities. Firms (corporations) provide the place where producers work but themselves have no welfare feelings, although their owners' welfare is important. The problem at hand is what we can or cannot say about the production-possibility functions *of society* in two situations.

In the production or firm field we have an institutional difficulty absent from the household markets: few families act like monopsonists, but many, if not most, firms sell in markets which are less than perfectly competitive. Let us waive this difficulty for the moment and assume that technological and market conditions are most suitable to perfect competition: namely, constant-returns-to-scale prevails and there is 'free entry'. In this case, any observed point of total output—such as A or 2 in Fig. 1—would represent a *maximum* of $\sum p_2 q$ subject to all the production possibilities of the situation. Geometrically the straight line running through A can never be inside the true production-possibility schedule.

Does this mean that the criterion $\sum p_2 q_2 > \sum p_1 q_1$ in Fig. 1 assures us of *both* of the following: that 2 is better than 1 *in welfare*, and 2 is better *in a production-possibility sense* than 1 ? It must *not* be so interpreted. The production problem involves a certain *maximum* condition, the consumption case a related *minimum* condition. The same index-number calculation can never serve as a crucial indicator for the two problems: if it is a reliable criterion for welfare, it tells us nothing about production; if it has unambiguous production implications, then welfare inferences are impossible.

There are essentially only four possible cases that have to be considered: a comparison of A and C in Fig. 1, of A and D, of A and F, and the almost trivial case of A and B. In this last case, where the A situation has more of every good than the B, we know immediately that the production-possibility function of A lies outside that of B in the neighbourhood of both observed points, and we also know that A's utility-possibility function (defined narrowly for the points rather than broadly for the situations) lies everywhere outside of that of B. All this is obvious, so we can concentrate our attention on the three other possible comparisons. To keep the notation simple we can always give the point A the number 2 and give all other compared points the number 1. Our cases, then, are as follows:

	Concerning 1940 def. of welfare	*Concerning position of production-possibility function (p.p.f.)*
Case A (or 2) and C (or 1):		
$\sum p_2 q_2 > \sum p_2 q_1$ tells us	2 better than 1	nothing
$\sum p_1 q_2 > \sum p_1 q_1$ tells us	nothing	p.p.f. of 1 outside of p.p.f. of 2 near point 2
Case A (or 2) and D (or 1):		
$\sum p_2 q_2 < \sum p_2 q_1$ tells us	nothing	p.p.f. of 1 outside of p.p.f. of 2 near point 1
$\sum p_1 q_2 > \sum p_1 q_1$ tells us	nothing	p.p.f. of 2 outside of p.p.f. of 1 near point 2
Case A (or 2) and F (or 1):		
$\sum p_2 q_2 > \sum p_2 q_1$ tells us	2 better than 1	nothing
$\sum p_1 q_1 > \sum p_1 q_2$ tells us	1 better than 2	nothing

Under the present assumptions we can make inferences about the shifting of production-possibility functions that are no less strong than those about welfare. We can never hope to infer from index-number tests that one production-possibility curve has shifted *uniformly* with respect to another—but then we have earlier seen that we can never hope to make such welfare inferences either. It will be noted from the table that where light is thrown on productivity it is withheld from welfare, and vice versa. This might almost seem to offer comfort: we seem always to be able to say *something* about any situation. But, alas, this is an illusion.

The Impossibility of Unequivocal Inferences

18. Even that which we have in the field of welfare indicators is to be taken away from us now that we have enlarged our alternatives to all the production possibilities of each situation rather than to the single observed points. *We shall never be able to infer a genuine change in potential real income as I have earlier defined the term*—no, not even in the simplest comparison of *A* which shows more of every good than the point *B*. (This was already shown in Fig. 7.) Unsatisfactory as the 1940 definitions of welfare were, we are tempted to beat a hasty retreat back to them. But to no good purpose: even these fragile reeds are blown down by the new winds.

Specifically, the observation $\sum p_2 q_2 > \sum p_2 q_1$ no longer implies that the utility-possibility function of *situation* 1 lies inside that of *A* even in the neighbourhood of the point 2, or anywhere at all for that matter! The whole 1940 proof by Hicks—as supplemented in my earlier lengthy footnote concerning the box-diagram—breaks down completely. The demonstration fails, the argument no longer leads logically to the desired conclusion. By itself this does not show that there may not be found some different proof. However, the theorem can be proved to be false, so that no valid alternative proof exists.

A single example provides a decisive exception to the theorem (that we can infer a local shift in the utility-possibility function). The point *F* in Fig. 1 has a utility-possibility curve which may be almost anywhere with respect to that of *A*, as far as anything we know. There is no reason why it could not always lie outside of *A*'s; there is also no reason why the point *F* should not lie on *C*'s production-possibility curve; there is also no reason why the utility-possibility function of the general situation *C* should not be close to or identical with the utility-possibility function of the point *F* (except possibly at the observed point *C* itself). It follows that we can easily imagine the utility-possibility function of the situation *C* to lie *above and beyond* the observed point *A*—which contradicts the Hicks-like theorem that situation *C*'s curve must lie somewhere south-west of the *A* point. This example shows that the Hicks's proof remains no longer

P. A. SAMUELSON   17

valid when it ceases to be simply a question of reallocating a given fixed total in the 1 situation.

The Interrelation between Production and Utility-Possibility Functions

19. Production possibilities as such have no normative connotations. We are interested in them for the light they throw on utility possibilities. This is why economists have wanted to include such wasteful output as war goods in their calculations of national product; presumably they serve as some kind of an index of the useful things that might be produced in better times. Our last hope to make welfare statements lies in spelling out the welfare implications of any recognizable shifts in production possibilities.

A uniform outward shift in the production-possibility function—such as can never be revealed by index-number comparisons—must certainly shift the utility-possibility schedule outward. The converse is not true. An outward shift in the utility-possibility function may have occurred as the result of a *twist* of the production-possibility curve. This is because people's tastes for different goods may be such that the points on the new production schedule that lie inward may be points that would never be observed in any optimal competitive market. An 'observable' point is one which, as the result of some allocation of initial resources or so-called 'distribution of income', would lead to one of the points on the utility-possibility frontier.

In the typical case where $\sum p_1 q_1 < \sum p_1 q_2$, so that we know that the production-possibility function of 2 is outside of that of 1 somewhere near the observed point 2, we should like to be able to say that 2's utility-possibility function lies outside that of 1 in the neighbourhood of the observed point 2. But we cannot. The utility-possibility functions of situation 2 and of point 2 both lie outside the utility-possibility function of the points which are known to lie south-west of the observed point 2 on the production-possibilities diagram. But all such points might turn out to be non-observable ones. Only if an observable point 2 is known to give more of all goods than an *observable* point of the situation 1 can we even infer that situation 2 is superior to 1 in the weak 1940 sense. Index-number data are never enough to provide us with knowledge of two such observable points except in the trivial case (like A and B) where one point is better in respect to every good, and where index-number calculations are unnecessary to establish the only fact that can be established: namely, the production-possibility function of A must lie outside that of B near the observed points and the same must be true about the related utility-possibility function.

Under the best conditions of the purest of competition very little indeed

4520.3   C

of welfare significance can ever be revealed by price-quantity data alone. Needless to say, with the actual statistical problems in a world of imperfect competition and decreasing costs, observed prices have even less significance as indicators of the shape of society's true production-possibility curve.

Political Feasibility as a Crucial Condition in Welfare Economics

20. The last limitation on the applicability to policy of the new welfare economics concepts is in practice one of the most important of all. It hinges around the practical unattainability of the production-possibility and utility-possibility function earlier discussed. It is not simply that imperfections of competitions are so widespread as to keep society from reaching its optimal production frontier; or that government interferences inevitably cause distortions; or that external diseconomies and economies can never be recognized and computed. All these are true enough.[1]

The essential point now to be stressed is that we could move people to different points on the utility-possibility function only *by an ideally perfect and unattainable system of absolutely lump-sum taxes or subsidies*. In point of fact, suppose that, in the simplest case, competitive *laissez-faire* puts us at one point on the utility-possibility function. Then we can only seek to change the distribution of income by a system of *feasible* legislation: e.g. progressive income tax, rationing, &c. All such policies involve a distortion of marginal decisions, some involving great distortions but in every case some distortion. They move us then *inside* the utility-possibility curve. We can pick policies which strive to minimize the harmful effects of redistribution, but in practice we cannot reduce such effects to zero. A 'feasible utility function' can conceptually be drawn up which lies more or less far inside the utility-possibility function, depending upon how Utopian were our assumptions about legislation, public opinion, &c.

All this is shown in Fig. 9. The point *L* represents the imputation resulting from a situation of relatively *laissez-faire*. It is made to lie on the heavy-line utility-possibility function—which it would only do in a very perfect competitive world.

Let us suppose that the tastes and abilities of the two individuals are identical so that we can use similar indicators of their ordinal preferences. But let them differ in their ownership of resources (say land) so that the

[1] They can be thought of as forces keeping us from reaching the true possibility frontier; or if we are in a non-perfectionist mood and willing to compromise with evil, they may be thought of as defining a not-so-far-out but pragmatically obtainable frontier. If the latter interpretation is made, we must be careful to realize that the slopes of the defined frontiers need have little correspondence with market prices, marginal costs of production, &c. As I have earlier pointed out (*Foundations*, p. 221), the constraints under which society is conceived as working are arbitrary and must be given by non-economic assumptions. England's production possibilities would be different if the laws of physics could be disregarded or if we could assume that all workers would do their 'best', or . . . or.

P. A. SAMUELSON

income of U'' is much greater than that of U', as indicated by the position of L relative to the 45°-line of 'equal income'. In a Utopia there might be some way of redistributing wealth or income that would move us along the outside curve from L to the point of complete equality, E, or even beyond. But in practice the only feasible path that Congress or Parliament could follow would be along the light-line utility-feasibility curve.[1]

Space does not permit me to work out the far-reaching implications of this point of view. It is enough to point out here that situation A may have a uniformly better production-possibility function than B, and also a uniformly better utility-possibility function. But a change from B to A might so alter the distribution of market-imputed income away from the 'worthy' and towards the 'unworthy' as to make it an undesirable move from many ethical viewpoints. The *utility-feasibility function* of A may very well cross that of B, so that no statement about potentialities, much less about actualities, can be validly made.

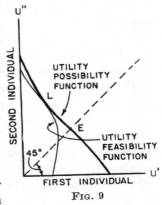

FIG. 9

By all means let us pray that feasibilities and possibilities be brought closer and closer. But let us not indulge in the illusion that our prayers have been answered and that we can issue new-welfare-economics prescriptions accordingly.[2]

Final Summary

21. This has been a long and closely reasoned essay. A brief summary may pull the threads together.

1. Certain $\sum pq$ calculations tell us when a single individual has improved himself.

2. The only consistent and ethics-free definition of an increase in potential

---

[1] A strong ethical equalitarian would have to reckon with this fact; and unless his social welfare functions had complete L-shaped corners along the 45° line, or even bent back *à la* Veblen and like the dog-in-the-manger, he would find his feasible optimum at some distance from equality of incomes. All this has a bearing, I believe, on the debate between Meade and Kahn as to whether rationing and food subsidies ought necessarily to be rejected by rational equalitarians in favour of greater reliance on income taxes or other more orthodox devices.

[2] A few comments on the cited Little article on 'Foundations' are perhaps in order. There is much I agree with in this paper, and much I do not yet understand. His semantic jousts with the post-Kaldor school falls under the first heading; his analysis of the meaning of a *social or economic welfare function* under the second. The part of his paper that is most relevant to the present technical discussion is his proposed 'foundations' for a 'system' of welfare economics. In my present understanding of it—still admittedly vague—Little has stated a few theorems of one type. These are understandable in terms of the language of a welfare function, and are more in the nature of one arch or wing of a structure than its foundations. The technical content of the theorems is discussed in the last footnote of the appended Pigou note.

20   EVALUATION OF REAL NATIONAL INCOME

real income of a group is that based upon a uniform shift of the utility-possibility function for the group. $\sum pq$ calculations based on aggregate data never permit us to make such inferences about uniform shifts.

3. The condition $\sum p_2 q_2 > \sum p_2 q_1$ does tell us that the utility-possibility function of the *point* 2 is outside the utility-possibility function of the *point* 1 somewhere near 2. It is not acceptable to define this as an increase in real income for a number of reasons, not the least being that we may end up with 2 defined to be both 'better' and 'worse' than 1.

4. Scitovsky and later Kuznets have suggested a partial strengthening of the earlier definitions of superiority so as to rule out certain revealed inconsistencies. But even these two-sided requirements are not stringent enough; when made infinite-sided, as they must be to avoid inconsistency or implicit ethics, they become equivalent to the definition based upon a uniform shift of the utility-possibility schedule. And even when this rigid definition is realized, we cannot properly prescribe complete policy prescriptions without bringing in ethics.

5. When we come to make inferences about two *situations*, each of which involves a whole *set* of production possibilities rather than about just the observed *points*, even the limited welfare inferences of point 3 break down completely. Under the most perfect conditions suitable for pure competition (where the production-possibility curve can never be concave) a few inferences concerning the local shifts of the production-possibility schedules are possible: e.g. $\sum p_2 q_2 < \sum p_2 q_1$ implies that 1's production-possibility function is outside 2's in the neighbourhood of the observed 2 point.

6. The inferred shifts of production-possibility functions are not enough to permit similar inferences about the utility-possibility functions. This is because that portion of a production-possibility curve which has clearly been revealed to be inside another or 'inferior' may (for all we know) consist entirely of 'unobservable points' that have no correspondence with the truly observable points along the related utility-possibility frontier.

7. The utility-possibility functions defined above are not really possible or available to society; they would be so only in a Utopian world of 'perfect' lump-sum taxes and other ideal conditions. Depending upon how optimistic our assumptions are, we must think of society as being contained within a *utility-feasibility function* which lies inside the *utility-possibility function*. At best these are close together in the neighbourhood of the 'points of relative *laissez-faire*'. Other things being equal, redistribution of income will usually involve 'costs', which have to be weighed against the ethically defined 'advantages' of such policies.

8. All this being true, we come to the paradoxical conclusion that a policy which seems to make possible greater production of all goods and

a uniformly better utility-possibility function for society may result in so great (and ethically undesirable) a change in the imputation of different individuals' incomes, that we may have to judge such a policy 'bad'. Such a judgement sounds as if it necessarily involves ethics, but it may be reworded so as to be relatively free of value judgements by being given the following interpretation: A policy that shifts society's utility-possibility function uniformly outward may not at the same time shift the utility-feasibility function uniformly outward, instead causing it to twist inward in some places. One last warning is in order: to define what is feasible involves many arbitrary assumptions, some of them of an ethical nature.

The above analysis enables us to appraise critically Pigou's important definitions of real income; this has been reserved for a separate appendix, which—except for a few cross-references—is self-contained.

MASSACHUSETTS INSTITUTE
    OF TECHNOLOGY.

A NOTE ON PIGOU'S TREATMENT OF INCOME

1. Despite the vast efforts of government agencies and bureaux in the last 20 years, Pigou's *Economics of Welfare* remains the classic discussion of the definition of real national income. Our previous analysis permits us to make a rapid critique of his masterly analysis. Even if I am right that certain of his formulations need minor amendation, his conclusions for welfare economics remain untouched. Pigou's principal theorem—that each resource should have equal marginal (social) productivity in every use, with price everywhere equal to marginal (social) cost—does not depend for its demonstration upon the elaborate discussion of the national dividend in Part I. In these days, when the national income approach is all the rage as a pedagogic device for coating the pill of elementary economics, it is worth noting that Pigou had seized upon this method of exposition more than a quarter of a century ago. Whether it would have been possible for him to have side-stepped completely the introductory discussion of real national income is irrelevant, since by choosing not to do so Pigou was led to make substantial contributions to the modern theory of economic index numbers (of the Könus, Bowley, Haberler, Staehle type).

2. According to Pigou, economic welfare is 'that part of social welfare that can be brought directly or indirectly into relation with the measuring-rod of money'. The national dividend or real national income is 'the objective counterpart of economic welfare'. Pigou would like to adopt the intuitive position that the dividend should be a function of objective quantities of goods alone, and not depend on 'the state of people's tastes'. But since (a) there is not a single commodity, and (b) all commodities do not move in the same proportion, or (c) even all in the same general direction, Pigou reluctantly considers such an objective definition not feasible, and settles for a more subjective definition according to which *the real income of any person is said to be higher for batch of goods II than for I if II is higher up on his indifference or preference map.*

These are not his words but my interpretation of them, expressed so as to be theoretically independent of any relationship with money or market-price behaviour. Pigou's exact statement for the case of a single individual is as follows:

'Considering a single individual whose tastes are taken as fixed, we say that his

EVALUATION OF REAL NATIONAL INCOME

dividend in period II. is greater than in period I. if the items that are added to it in period II. are items that he wants more than the items that are taken away from it in period II.' (*Economics of Welfare*, 4th ed., p. 51.)

The wording is cast in a comparative form to pave the way for consideration of the more complex case of many individuals where it may be especially difficult to ask people about their wants and desires and theoretically difficult to define what is meant by the *wants* of the *group*. Pigou extends his definition further:

'Passing to a group of persons (of given numbers), whose tastes are taken as fixed and among whom the distribution of purchasing power is also taken as fixed, we say that the dividend in period II. is greater than in period I. if the items that are added to it in period II. are items *to conserve which they would be willing to give more money than they would be willing to give to conserve the items that are taken away from it in period II.*' (Ibid., pp. 51–2.)

For the moment let us accept the assumption of constant tastes and 'distribution of purchasing power' and the assumption that people know their own minds and correctly identify *ex ante* desire with *ex post* satisfaction. Pigou then gives another verbal reformulation of his definition, saying that the dividend is higher in period II than in I if 'the economic satisfaction (as measured in money) due to the items added in period II is greater than the economic satisfaction (as measured in money) due to the items taken away in period II' (p. 54). Under the assumptions stated, Pigou believes this method of definition to be 'the natural and obvious one to adopt' (p. 52).

3. I wonder. One can sympathize with the attempt to introduce into the definition something that a statistician might sink his punch-cards into, but has the introduction of money left the problem unambiguous? I have repeated the definition to myself aloud again and again; and yet even in the case of a single consistent individual about whom unlimited data were available, I would still not be sure how to proceed.

Pigou himself, according to my interpretation of his various writings, is also put in an ambivalent mood by his definition. In the next chapter he proceeds to work with index-number expressions of the form $\sum pq$ where the p's and q's are observed market data. To my mind this is a perfectly valid procedure in the case of a single individual (and it can be given a measure of validity for the case of a group along the lines indicated in my present article). But it is not at all clear that Pigou regards his own procedure as really valid. Again and again he states that the proper procedure is to measure the monetary strength of people's desires not by the marginal price data observed but rather by some kind of consumers-surplus type of construction indicating how much they could be made to pay rather than do without the thing altogether.[1]

Pigou's definition has for the moment betrayed him, and I am willing to defend his practice against his precept. I suspect that what happened is something like the following: instead of continuing to look for an ordinal indicator of utility, Pigou suddenly caught a glimpse of the butterfly of cardinal utility and set out in hot

---

[1] Ibid., pp. 57, 59. In his 1945 introductory work, *Income*, p. 13, Pigou still shows a desire to use some measure of consumers' surplus (or total utility) rather than market values. In the 1949 *Veil of Money* he is even more explicit in insisting that the relative weight of goods should in principle depend upon 'how much of their money income people *would have been willing* to spend . . . [rather than on] how much money they *actually do spend*. . . . Weighting by reference to this entails, other things being equal, giving a smaller weight to changes in items of inelastic and a larger weight to changes in items of elastic demand than "ought" to be assigned to them if our object is, as I have suggested it might be, to measure importance by reference to impact on economic satisfaction, given that tastes are constant. Thus at the very basis of any structure we may erect there is an incorrigible flaw. At the best, we shall have to content ourselves with a makeshift measure, what exactly in the last resort it is measuring being ill-defined and blurred' (pp. 60–1). Cf. J. R. Hicks, 'Foundation of Welfare Economics', *Economic Journal*, xlix, 1939, p. 697, for a related criticism of Pigou's treatment of marginal and intra-marginal concepts.

P. A. SAMUELSON   23

pursuit. But he realized that the difficulties of this approach were more than statistical, necessarily involving all the familiar difficulties of Marshallian consumers' surplus. Whether or not the butterfly is obtainable or of any use once caught, we must take care not to belittle the solid fruits of index-number theory that are in our grasp.

4. What Pigou does establish—on pp. 62–3—is that

$$\sum p_2 q_2 > \sum p_2 q_1$$

means that II is better than I for any consistent individual. The reasoning is exactly that of the A and C comparison in my Fig. 1. Likewise

$$\sum p_1 q_1 > \sum p_1 q_2$$

would have meant that I was better than II. Pigou prefers to make the comparisons in the more usual Laspeyre and Paasche index-number ratios[1]

$$P = \frac{\sum p_2 q_2}{\sum p_2 q_1} \gtreqless 1 \quad \text{and} \quad L = \frac{\sum p_1 q_2}{\sum p_1 q_1} \gtreqless 1.$$

If we treat work and other efforts as negative commodities, our analysis becomes slightly more general.[2] But our $\sum pq$ expressions may then be zero or negative, so that the method of ratios may be inapplicable even though the proper comparisons can be made in non-ratio form. As we shall see, the use of such ratios has the further disadvantage that it tempts people to attach *cardinal* significance, in an exact or probalistic sense, to the numerical value of the $\sum pq$ ratios.

5. If both P and L are greater than unity, II is clearly better than I. If both are less than unity, then I is better than II. If they are numerically almost equal—and Pigou seems to think they often will be—then the measurement of welfare is thought to be fairly definite. When they differ numerically, Pigou would often measure welfare by some kind of intermediate mean between them: because the geometric mean—which is the Irving Fisher so-called 'Ideal-Index'—has certain convenient properties, Pigou accepts it 'as the measure of change most satisfactory for our purpose' (p. 69).

I cannot persuade myself to follow Pigou's use of the numerical value of the P and L ratios. In the first place, he—along with Kuznets and many others—treats the measures much too symmetrically. When $P > 1$, we already know that II is better than I. If we learn in addition that $L > 1$, we cannot regard this as further corroboration that II is superior to I; at best it serves as corroboration of the fact that we are dealing with a consistent individual.

The case is much different when you tell us that $L > 1$, and nothing else. We have no right to presume that II is definitely better than I. If now you volunteer to us the second bit of information that $P > 1$ also, we cannot regard this as corroboration of an earlier presumption or certainty yielded by the first bit of information. *In its own right* the second fact, that $P > 1$, tells us all we want to know.

With respect to the opposite case, of recognizing when I is better than II, we must attach crucial importance to $L < 1$; and once again the behaviour of P is corroboration of nothing, except of the presence of inconsistency and changed tastes.

---

[1] Pigou lets x, y, z,... stand for q's and a, b, c,... for p's and writes these expressions in the form

$$P = \frac{I_2}{I_1} \frac{x_1 a_1 + y_1 b_1 + \ldots}{x_1 a_2 + y_1 b_2 + \ldots} \quad \text{or} \quad \frac{\sum p_2 q_2}{\sum p_1 q_1} \frac{\sum p_1 q_1}{\sum p_2 q_1} = \frac{\sum p_2 q_2}{\sum p_2 q_1},$$

$$L = \frac{I_2}{I_1} \frac{x_2 a_1 + y_2 b_1 + \ldots}{x_2 a_2 + y_2 b_2 + \ldots} \quad \text{or} \quad \frac{\sum p_2 q_2}{\sum p_1 q_1} \frac{\sum p_1 q_2}{\sum p_2 q_2} = \frac{\sum p_1 q_2}{\sum p_1 q_1}.$$

[2] Pigou's difficulty concerning an increase in the dividend at the expense of leisure, p. 87, n. 1, could then have been avoided.

24   EVALUATION OF REAL NATIONAL INCOME

6. Looking into Pigou's probability argument, we will find one difficulty that stems from his treating of P and L as symmetrical indicators of welfare. Suppose $P = 3 > 1$ and $L = 0.99 < 1$, and these measurements are known to be perfectly accurate, statistically speaking. Then the testimony of the two measures is contradictory, one being greater and the other less than unity. But P exceeds unity by a greater ratio than L falls short of unity, so that $\sqrt{PL}$, the ideal-index, is much greater than unity. Pigou would conclude—according to my interpretation of pp. 65–6— that II is *probably* greater than I.

My conclusion would be different. I would say that either the individual's tastes have definitely changed between the periods or that he was not in equilibrium in both situations. This is because $P > 1$ tells me that II is higher on his indifference curves than is I, and $L < 1$ tells me the exact opposite, and that is the end of it. There is no sense that I can see in believing that, because P is much greater than 1, its testimony is in a loud enough voice to shout down the whisper of $L < 1$.

7. Actually all is not lost as far as exact inference from such a case is concerned. We can validly state: $P > 1$ implies that the batch of goods II is higher *on the indifference curves that prevailed in period II* than *is* the batch of goods I; and $L < 1$ implies that the first batch of goods is higher than batch II *on the indifference curves that prevailed in period I*.

It would be tempting to argue that P always measures welfare from the II period's tastes and L always measures welfare from the I period's tastes. This would be quite wrong, as Pigou is clearly aware. If $P = 0.99$ and $L = 3.0$, we most certainly cannot state the reverse of the previous paragraph's conclusions. We cannot even infer anything about inconsistency. By its nature P can only give definite evidence concerning batch II's superiority over I, and L can only give definite evidence concerning batch I's superiority over II.[1]

8. The case where $P < 1$ and $L > 1$ is the only one to which Pigou explicitly applies his probability reasoning. As in Fig. 1's comparison of A and E, no certain inference is possible. The unknown indifference curve through A could pass above or below the point E. Now the closer is E to the budget-line through A, or what is the same thing the closer is P to 1, then, 'other things being equal', we should expect that the chance of A's indifference curve's passing above E would be increased. The same chance would be increased, the more L is reduced towards unity, 'other things being equal'. This is the basis for Pigou's common-sense view that the degree to which $\sqrt{(PL)} \gtrless 1$ determines the likelihood of II's being better or worse than I. Between 1928 and 1932 Pigou felt compelled to abandon an argument based upon 'the principle of sufficient reason' that attempted to establish this common-sense conclusion. His reason for abandoning it was not because of any impregnation with the modern tendency among statisticians and philosophers to question arguments based on ignorance or on the 'equal-probability of the unknown', but because of technical difficulties previously unnoticed. I think that some of these difficulties could be side-stepped, but since Pigou is content to abandon his old view, and since I am not enamoured of the principle of sufficient reason, I shall confine my attention to the exact inferences possible.

Consider a point A on an individual's indifference map. Consider the region of all alternative points in comparison with A, A being regarded as II and each of these

---

[1] In § 5, chap. vi, p. 58, Pigou leans over backward too far on the issue of the inferences possible when tastes have changed. He believes that the best we can hope for is to devise measures giving the correct results *when tastes have not changed*. This is because he thinks that to make the inference that the batch II is better than the batch I on the basis of the indifference curves of II, we must know what the batch I *would have been* if the indifference curves of II (rather than the actual indifference curves of I) had then prevailed. This is incorrect, as can be noted from the above discussion and from the fact that in my earlier Fig. 1 the inference about A and C was independent of the actual indifference-ratio slope *through C*.

points as I. Consider the contour lines of any symmetric mean of P and L, such as $\sqrt{(PL)}$ = constants. Also consider the contour lines of P = constants and L = constants.

Then this much is true: the contour lines $P = 1$, $L = 1$, and $\sqrt{(PL)} = 1$ all go through A and are tangent to the indifference curve through A. Suppose we use any of the three measures $P \gtrless 1$, $L \gtrless 1$, or $\sqrt{(PL)} \gtrless 1$ to decide whether A is better or worse than the other point tested. Then the 'percentage of points' for which we get wrong answers by these methods goes to zero as we confine ourselves to smaller and smaller regions around A. Also the probability will approach one, as we confine ourselves to ever closer regions around A, that all three methods will give the same testimony. In the limit as the region around A shrinks, the use of the P criterion in those rare cases when it disagrees with the L criterion will lead to a biased estimate —in that all points under such conditions of contradiction will in the limit be declared to be worse than A, including those points which are really better than A. Exclusive reliance on L in case of contradiction will result in an opposite bias towards declaring all doubtful points better than A. In the limit as the second point is constrained to lie in ever closer regions to A, the use of $\sqrt{(PL)} \gtrless 1$ criterion will lead to a percentage of wrong decisions that approaches ever closer to zero.[1] These are exact statements about limits.

9. Besides Pigou, other writers such as Kuznets and Little have seen fit to attach significance to the numerical values of the P and L ratios. (Readers not interested in technicalities can skip this section.) Kuznets argues as follows:

> Suppose as we go from I to II, both P and L are greater than they are when we go from I to III. Then II is 'generally' better than III, provided that the shift in prices from II to III has effects on the ratios of certain identical quantity aggregates of an [allegedly] usual sort.[2]

It will be noted that Kuznets is attempting to use certain numerical or cardinal comparisons for the sole purpose of arriving at a purely *ordinal* comparison. There is nothing methodologically objectionable about this; but none the less the Kuznets result is a self-contained truism that does not permit us to make any general inferences of certain validity in any empirical situation.

First an example may illustrate the loopholes in Kuznets's results. Back in my Fig. 1, let us consider the three points A, B, C. Kuznets will find that P and L computed for A and B are *exactly* the same as for A and C. According to his theorem, C and B should be equally satisfactory or approximately so. Actually the indifference curve through C passes above that of B, and if there were any sense in speaking of 'well above' we might use this stronger expression. More than that, by moving C south-west a little or B north-east a little, we could arrive at the even falser presumption that B is better than C.

There is nothing faulty about Kuznets's arithmetic or the truism he derives from his substitution. He would have to say in this connexion: 'My proviso about price-quantity correlation has been violated in the example.' And why should it not be ? When Kuznets says that P is 'in general' less than L, he does not mean by the words 'in general' what a mathematician means when he says that the two sides of a triangle are 'generally' greater than the third. Kuznets means, I think it is clear, that *usually* the price-quantity correlation will be such as to make P less than L. (Actually a long line of writers in index-number theory fell into the actual error of thinking that $P \leqslant L$ and between them lies some 'true' value; an almost equally

---

[1] Mathematically, the indifference curve through A is tangential to the $P = 1$ and $L = 1$ contours, lying 'half-way' between them. The contour $\sqrt{(PL)} = 1$ also has their mean curvature and is an osculating tangent to the indifference curve, differing only in its third and higher derivatives. See my *Foundations*, p. 148.

[2] This is my brief transcription of Kuznets's Appendix, *Economica*, 1949, pp. 124–31 and his remarks on p. 5.

26   EVALUATION OF REAL NATIONAL INCOME

long line of writers have pointed out the falsity of this relation.) I venture the conjecture that Kuznets formed his belief concerning the usual or normal numerical dominance of L over P from considering the special case where there are no real income changes and where any increase in the price of a good (or set of goods) is followed by a necessary decrease in its quantity. But it is precisely when we are trying to arrive at an estimate of whether II is better or worse than III that we must not beg the question by assuming that they are on the same indifference locus.

Even in a loose probability sense, it would be dangerous to say that P is usually less than L. If all goods had an income elasticity of exactly one—so that a pure income change resulted in proportionate changes in every item of consumption—then this would be a certainty. But so long as the well-attested Engel's laws and observed budgetary patterns hold, we must *certainly* have a reversal of the P–L relations throughout the area between the income-expenditure curve through A and the straight line joining A to the origin. This shows that my ABC example is not an isolated case, but is typical of what will always be true in some region.[1]

10. So far I have discussed only the single-individual aspects of Pigou's treatment of real income. All these pages of the Appendix were necessary to cover what took scarcely more than a page of my main text. But now I must consider Pigou's analysis of national income in its group-welfare aspects. Because this problem was treated so fully in the main text, my treatment here may be rather brief.

It will be recalled that Pigou regards his inferences as being valid if the members of the group always have 'a fixed distribution of income' (and, of course, unchanging tastes). When we subject his book to microscopic examination, two questions immediately come to mind. (1) Exactly what is meant by 'a fixed distribution of income' between two situations? And (2) even after this by-no-means-simple question has been adequately disposed of, what is it that Pigou thinks is true of the group or of the individuals in the group as we go from one situation to another? Is there a group-mind that registers more utility? Or is it the algebraic sum of utility that has gone up for the group? Or is it that every single member of the group is now better off than before?

11. One must read between the lines to answer these questions—at least, I have not been able to find their explicit answers. I suspect that Pigou does not have any place in his philosophy for any group-mind. But his technical argument seems to come very close to the following Wieser construction:

> 'The theory of the "simple economy" ... begins with the idealizing assumption that the subject is a single person. However, we do not have in mind here the meagre economy of an isolated Robinson Crusoe ... [but] the activities of an entire nation. At the same time millions of people are regarded as a massed unit.'[2]

We may read elements of this general line of reasoning in Pigou's concern with the question of whether market prices can be considered as given to society in the way that they can be assumed to be prescribed for a single small competitive individual. If Fig. 10 applied to a single individual, he could legitimately regard the straight line NN through A as being open to him. But if the chart holds for society, there could be shown on it the true (but possibly unknown) production-possibility or opportunity-cost curve of type MM or of some other shape.

Pigou is uneasy about applying the argument to the group as a whole. 'But, when it is the whole of a group, or, if we prefer it, a representative man who shifts his consumption in this way, it is no longer certain that prices would be unaffected' (p. 61). For a moment, Pigou seems to lapse into the assumption that the representa-

[1] Little gives a probability interpretation of the significance of the cardinal size of P on pp. 46–7, *Economica*, 1949. He has in mind a closely related, but distinct, group inference from that discussed in this paper. He also relies on our rough empirical knowledge of preference patterns in evaluating his probabilities.

[2] F. v. Wieser, *Social Economics* (1927), pp. 9–10.

P. A. SAMUELSON   27

tive man knows that he is an image of the group and therefore acts collusively as if
a group decision were being made. The group mind knows that the only choice
really open to it is along MM; therefore in the initial A situation it does not think
that C is obtainable; consequently we cannot infer that A has been revealed to be
better than C by a deliberate act of choosing A over C. Something like this Pigou
must have believed for the moment, else he would not have felt the need to add a
'certain assumption' of paragraph 8, ruling out the possibility that the production-
possibility curve of society is like MM, but instead requiring it to show constant
slope like NN. It is fortunate that Pigou's argument can be salvaged without making
this extraneous assumption—fortunate because I cannot agree with his appraisal
of the *a priori* probabilities: 'In real life, with a large number of commodities, it is
reasonable to suppose that the upward price movements caused by shifts of con-

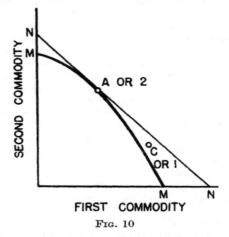

FIG. 10

sumption would roughly balance the downward movements' (p. 62). That is to say,
concave or convex curves are equally likely, so we may assume the curve to be a
straight line. Rather, I would think that in the conditions most suited to healthy
competition—where external economies either balance external diseconomies or
both are negligible and where tendencies towards increasing or decreasing returns
to scale are absent or just balancing—we would still be left with the good old law of
diminishing returns in the classical (qualitative and quantitative) senses, so that
convex production-possibility schedules are the 'normal' case.

Actually, if Pigou is concerned to make normative statements about points like
A and C that hold valid for groups, it does not matter that the true production-
possibility curve is something other than NN.[1] We have seen in Hicks's paper and
in the text what these valid inferences are. Another way of looking at the problem
is by means of the 'collective indifference curves' that Professor Scitovsky has
taught us to use in the second of his cited papers.

12. But first we must settle what is meant by Pigou's 'fixed distribution of
income'. How tempting to think of money as being concrete and the distribution
of income to be fixed if everybody's money income changes proportionately. But
money itself means nothing. If two men each have the same money income and if
one likes meat and the other cheese and the terms of trade between meat and cheese

---

[1] Pigou does not stand alone. 'Unless the groups considered are small in relation to
the whole, market prices cannot be considered as constant, and therefore the condition
$\Sigma\, p_2\, q_2 > \Sigma\, p_2\, q_1$ would no longer indicate that goods of situation I were rejected in favour
of those of situation II' (*Economica*, 1949, p. 17).

28   EVALUATION OF REAL NATIONAL INCOME

change, then would Pigou consider the distribution of income to have remained fixed? Probably not. Moreover, if we follow the convenient practice of treating the services of labour and property that people supply as negative commodities, then in the absence of government taxes we might say that everybody has a zero (net) income *always*.

Probably in the beginning Pigou had in mind the simple case of identical individuals, any one of whom is representative, and where they all fare alike. Then when situation II is better than I, it is also true that both individuals are better off. When we leave the case of perfect symmetry, it becomes difficult to say that the extra welfare of one man is always to be some fixed multiple of the increment of welfare of another since this involves ethical inter-personal comparisons that Pigou is trying to avoid in these chapters dealing with the relatively objective aspects of welfare and the national dividend. But for his purposes Pigou needs only to assume that the ordinal well-being of all individuals are required to move always *in the same direction* according to some prescribed relationship. [Some complicated monetary shifts must be assumed to take place to bring this about.]

If I am right in this interpretation, then the comparison of A or 2 and C or 1 in terms of

$$\sum p_2 q_2 > \sum p_2 q_1$$

is immediately obvious and independent of the shape of MM or of any assumptions of group-consciousness. The fortunes of all being linked, any one person reflects the fate of all. Now, obviously, for some one person we must have

$$\sum p_2 q_2 > \sum p_2 q_1,$$

because if the opposite were true for each and every person, how could the totals show this relation? But if at least one has been made worse off in I than in II, then the 'fixed distribution of income assumption' means that they must all have been made worse off. Q.E.D.

In terms of Scitovsky indifference curves, the story runs as follows: For a prescribed amount of both people's ordinal utility, U' and U'', we can draw up a collective indifference curve. For any prescribed distribution linking U' and U'' in a monotonic fashion we can draw up a family of collective indifference curves. If each person has concave indifference curves, the collective curves will also be concave. But regardless of concavity, the collective curve through A is never permitted to cross below the NN line. This will be obvious to every reader in the case of concave curves; and the same can be shown to be true in general by simple mathematical argument. It follows that C lies on a lower collective indifference curve than A— *regardless of the true shape of society's production-possibility curve MM.*

13. Pigou's argument has been removed from any dependence on constant (opportunity) cost assumptions. But a worse restriction remains. For him to make any inference, *everybody* in the community must have been made better or worse off. The wind scarcely ever blows that brings good to absolutely everyone. Lucky it is that the remaining fifty-odd chapters of the *Economics of Welfare* do not depend in an essential way upon the results of the early chapters of Part I dealing with the national dividend. Fortunately, too—just as was seen to be true when tastes change —we can make some valid inferences when the distribution of income is known *not* to remain fixed. From our earlier analysis we know that $\sum p_2 q_2 > \sum p_2 q_1$ implies that the II's utility-possibility curve lies outside of I's at least in the neighbourhood of the actual observed situation II.

14. One last case not yet considered by any of the writers. Suppose we have given to us certain well-defined ethical notions concerning inter-personal well-being. In the simplest case they can be summarized in a Bergson social welfare function, $W = W(U', U'',\ldots)$, with the usual property that anything that helps one man without hurting anyone else will mean an increase in W.

P. A. SAMUELSON 29

As before, let us observe prices, p, and total quantities for all society, q. And finally, suppose that *the distribution of income is ethically optimal both in situation 1 or C and 2 or A*. What can we now infer from the condition $\sum p_2 q_2 > \sum p_2 q_1$? The answer is that situation A lies higher on the ethical social welfare function than does C.[1]

The logical proof of this result is not so easy as I at first thought it would be. This is because our move from C to the better position A need not represent an improvement for all individuals. U' may go down provided U'' goes up relatively more, as measured, of course, by the W function. Hence, when cost conditions change in such a way as to make it optimal to alter the relative 'distribution of income', our earlier argument cannot apply.

To prove that $W(A) > W(C)$, we can use 'social indifference curves'. But they are not the arbitrary ones of the Scitovsky new-welfare-economics type. They are a unique old-welfare-economics set of curves showing the combinations of total goods capable of giving (when all optimal arrangements have been made) equal levels of W. In the 'normal' case, where playing the game of competition can be depended to follow the invisible hand to bliss, these social indifference curves will be concave. It follows that whenever C lies inside the straight line NN going through A, it must also lie inside the social indifference curve (of equal W) going through A. This proves our result.[2]

---

[1] This is related to Bergson's interesting interpretation of Pigou in infinitesimal terms. Bergson, 'Reformulation of Certain Aspects of Welfare Economics', *Q.J.E.*, lii (1938), p. 331.

[2] In the last two of his cited papers Little has stated theorems a little bit like the one above. There are two or three different versions, but the typical Little theorem shows that a certain point A is better than another point C because we can imagine going from C to A in two steps: one of these involves an improved distribution of real income (somehow defined) and the other an improvement in each and every person's well-being. I give an abbreviated interpretation of one of the variants discussed in *O.E.P.*, pp. 235–7.

1. Suppose we have a W function as defined above, with $\partial W / \partial U' > 0$, &c., and start at a point C and end up at a point A.
2. The point A is assumed to lie out and beyond the utility-possibility locus of the point C; e.g. there is a point C' on the latter locus that is south-west of the point A in the U'–U'' plane. Thus the Scitovsky test is satisfied.
3. Now make the assumption that in terms of W 'the distribution of real income is better' at C' than in C. (Thus, ideally, we should not have been in C in the first place.)
4. Then it follows that A is higher on the assumed welfare function than is C. (This conclusion does not depend upon whether the Hicks–Kaldor test is satisfied.)
5. It does not follow that a little angel, given the choice of throwing a switch that moves society from C to A, ought to throw that switch. There may be an infinity of points on C's locus still better than A. Little's policy conclusion is to be qualified, therefore, by the following statement that he has been kind enough to send to me in private correspondence: 'The shift from C to A ought to be made if the shift does not prejudice any other move which might result in a position still more favourable than A.'

The chain of reasoning involved in 1–4 is simple once we pin down what is meant by 'the distribution of real income being better'. This means $W(C') > W(C)$. Since the Scitovsky test implies $W(A) > W(C')$, the Little result $W(A) > W(C)$ immediately follows. Just as Little talks prose, he can be said to be using a *welfare* function whenever he talks welfare economics. But like the new welfare economists, he wants to see what results he can get with an *incompletely* defined welfare function—a commendable effort, perhaps useful for an important class of policy decisions, but necessarily not complete for all policy situations.

MASSACHUSETTS INSTITUTE

OF TECHNOLOGY.

Part III
Methodological Foundations
of Welfare Measurement

[15]

CONSTANCY OF THE MARGINAL UTILITY OF INCOME

PAUL A. SAMUELSON

Massachusetts Institute of Technology

I N THE theoretical and empirical literature on the theory of consumer's demand behavior one repeatedly encounters the hypothesis that the marginal utility of income or money can be assumed to be constant, or at least "sensibly" so.[1] As a result, many of the conclusions derived are of restricted validity; indeed, outright contradictions often emerge from this seemingly innocent assumption. It is proposed here to examine briefly, but exhaustively, the rigorous implications of the constancy of the marginal utility of income.

According to a well-known condition of equilibrium in the theory of consumer's behavior, a consumer with a given monetary income, I, confronted with respective prices, $(p_1, \cdots, p_n)$, of n goods, $(x_1, \cdots, x_n)$, will purchase each good up to the point where its marginal (degree of) utility is proportional to its price. Thus, in equilibrium

$$\phi_i(x_1, \cdots, x_n) = m_\phi p_i, \tag{1}$$

where ϕ_i represents the partial derivative with respect to the ith good of the cardinal index of utility, $\phi(x_1, \cdots, x_n)$, and m_ϕ is a factor of proportionality. This relation may be rewritten in the form

$$m_\phi = \frac{\phi_1(x_1, \cdots, x_n)}{p_1} = \frac{\phi_2(x_1, \cdots, x_n)}{p_2} = \cdots$$
$$= \frac{\phi_n(x_1, \cdots, x_n)}{p_n}. \tag{2}$$

This proposition is often translated to mean that in equilibrium the utility of the last dollar spent in every use must be equal; the value of this magnitude is m_ϕ and will be known hereafter as the

[1] Alfred Marshall, *Principles of Economics* (8th ed.; London, 1930); Vilfredo Pareto, *Manuel d'économie politique* (Paris, 1909), Appendix; Henry Schultz, *The Theory and Measurement of Demand* (Chicago: University of Chicago Press, 1938), chap. xviii; Milton Friedman, "Professor Pigou's Method for Measuring Elasticities of Demand from Budgetary Data," *Quarterly Journal of Economics*, L(1935), 151–63; A. C. Pigou, Milton Friedman, and N. Georgescu-Roegen, "Marginal Utility of Money and Elasticities of Demand," *Quarterly Journal of Economics*, L (1935), 532–39; E. B. Wilson, "Pareto versus Marshall," *Quarterly Journal of Economics*, LIII (1939), 645–49.

76 MATHEMATICAL ECONOMICS AND ECONOMETRICS

marginal utility of income for the cardinal utility index, ϕ. The subscript ϕ is appended in order to emphasize its dependence upon the particular choice of utility index. It will further depend upon the equilibrium position attained by the consumer; i.e., on the set of prices and income with which he is confronted. Given such prices and income, the consumer will select a given amount of each and every good. His demand functions can be written in the form

$$x_i = h^i (p_1, \cdots, p_n, I) , \qquad (i = 1, \cdots, n) \qquad (3)$$

where

$$\sum_{i\,1}^{n} p_i x_i = I . \qquad (4)$$

One feature of these demand functions should be noted. A simultaneous doubling of all prices and income will leave the individual with the same choice as between commodities and hence will leave unaffected the amount demanded of each good. More generally,

$$h^i (\lambda p_1, \cdots, \lambda p_n, \lambda I) = h^i (p_1, \cdots, p_n, I) , \qquad (i = 1, \cdots, n) \qquad (5)$$

where λ is any positive constant. Mathematically, the demand functions are homogeneous of order zero.

Thus, the marginal utility of income, as well as depending upon the particular cardinal index of utility selected, is also a function of all prices and income:

$$m_\phi = \frac{\phi_i [h^1 (p_1, \cdots, p_n, I) , h^2 (p_1, \cdots, p_n, I) , \cdots]}{p_i} ,$$

$$= m_\phi (p_1, \cdots, p_n, I) . \qquad (6)$$

DEPENDENCE UPON THE CHOICE OF UTILITY INDEX

It is well known that the demand functions or schedules of the consumer remain unaltered under any change of utility index. One may write the conditions of equilibrium so that they are independent of the choice of utility index, or even by the use of indifference varieties so that no index is employed. The last approach introduces the minor inconvenience of a notational asymmetry, but this is a small price to pay for the clarity of thought which the method often imparts.

The marginal utility of income does not possess this invariance. Let us consider a transformation of the utility index of the form

$$F = F[\phi(x_1, \cdots, x_n)] = F(x_1, \cdots, x_n) , \qquad (7)$$

where $F'(\phi) > 0$, and

CONSTANCY OF THE MARGINAL UTILITY OF INCOME 77

$$F_i = F'\phi_i$$

$$F_{ij} = F'\phi_{ij} + F''\phi_i\phi_j .$$ (8)

Obviously,

$$m_F = \frac{F_i}{p_i} = \frac{F'(\phi)\phi_i}{p_i} = F'(\phi)m_\phi$$

$$= m_F(p_1, \cdots, p_n, I) .$$ (9)

In general, the change in this magnitude with respect to any parameter, say α, is also dependent upon the choice of utility index since

$$\frac{dm_F}{d\alpha} = \frac{d}{d\alpha}(F'm_\phi) = F'\frac{dm_\phi}{d\alpha} + F''m_\phi\frac{d\phi}{d\alpha} .$$ (10)

In our transformation of any utility index, no restriction can be placed upon $F''(\phi)$. Therefore, provided that $d\phi/d\alpha$ does not vanish, by an appropriate selection of utility index the rate of change in the marginal utility of income with respect to any parameter can be made to be of any arbitrary magnitude and sign. Thus, the change in the marginal utility of income with respect to a change in income, prices being constant, cannot be said to be unambiguously of any given sign. There exists an infinity of indexes for which it is of either algebraic sign at any position of equilibrium; at such a point an index can be found for which the value of this derivative is zero.

Care must be taken not to misinterpret these remarks. There need not, and in general there will not, exist any utility index for which this derivative vanishes at *every* level of income and all levels of prices. Moreover, in general there will not exist an index for which the marginal utility is constant with respect to two different parameters simultaneously. The force of these remarks will appear in the course of the argument.

There exists one particular compound change in price and income which does present an interesting invariance. Scrutiny of equation (10) reveals that

$$\frac{1}{m_F}\frac{dm_F}{d\alpha} = \frac{1}{m_\phi}\frac{dm_\phi}{d\alpha} = \frac{d\log m}{d\alpha} ,$$ (11)

provided that $d\phi/d\alpha = 0$. That is, *the logarithmic derivative of the marginal utility of income with respect to any parameter which leaves the level of utility unchanged is invariant under any transformation of utility index.* A compound change in any single price, p_i, accompanied by a change in I sufficiently great to leave the consumer at the

78 MATHEMATICAL ECONOMICS AND ECONOMETRICS

same level of utility must necessarily fulfil this requirement. We should expect, therefore, to find the above coefficient invariant under such a "compensated price change."[2] This compensated price change can be written

$$\frac{1}{m_\phi} \frac{dm_\phi}{da} = \frac{1}{m_\phi} \left(\frac{\partial m_\phi}{\partial p_i} + x_i \frac{\partial m_\phi}{\partial I} \right). \tag{12}$$

Actually, by simple differentiation of equation (1), one can verify the following equivalence,[3]

$$\frac{1}{m_\phi} \left(\frac{\partial m_\phi}{\partial p_i} + x_i \frac{\partial m_\phi}{\partial I} \right) = - \frac{\partial x_i}{\partial I}. \qquad (i = 1, 2, \cdots, n) \tag{13}$$

The right-hand term, being a property of the demand functions, is independent of the choice of utility index so that our invariance is verified.

This also confirms the previous assertion that we cannot arbitrarily fix the sign of the change in the marginal utility of income with respect to both income and a given price, since these two must add up in a certain way (as given in eq. [13]) to a given number. Similarly, the change in the marginal utility of income with respect to each of two prices cannot be arbitrarily preassigned, since we can deduce from equation (13) the relation

$$\frac{1}{m_\phi} \left(\frac{\partial m_\phi}{\partial p_i} x_j - \frac{\partial m_\phi}{\partial p_j} x_i \right) = - \left(\frac{\partial x_i}{\partial I} x_j - \frac{\partial x_j}{\partial I} x_i \right). \tag{14}$$

The right-hand side of this equation cannot be altered by a transformation of the utility index.

In what follows reference will be made repeatedly to equation (13). It must be emphasized that it holds regardless of any assumptions of independence of utility, etc.

ALTERNATIVE INTERPRETATIONS OF CONSTANCY

The statement that the marginal utility of income is assumed to be constant is ambiguous.[4] With respect to what is it assumed to be constant? With respect to price changes? Income change? Or with respect to all of these?

[2] See Schultz, *op. cit.*, pp. 41–46.
[3] *Ibid.*, p. 40, eq. (3.15).
[4] One must be on guard against a superficial error. The fact that the marginal utility of income changes but slightly with respect to *small* changes in the variables under consideration does not imply that the *rate* of change of marginal utility with respect to these variables is small. The former proposition is a consequence simply of continuity and differentiability and holds for all functions possessing these properties.

CONSTANCY OF THE MARGINAL UTILITY OF INCOME 79

Actually, it can be shown by simple mathematical argument that the latter cannot possibly hold. Recall that

$$m_\phi = m_\phi(p_1, p_2, \cdots, p_n, I) = \frac{\phi_i(x_1, x_2, \cdots; x_n)}{p_i}. \qquad (15)$$

Consider a simultaneous doubling of all prices and income. This will leave the quantities of all goods unchanged and hence will not affect the numerator of the right-hand member. However, the denominator will be doubled. The total effect is to halve the marginal utility of income. Mathematically, m_ϕ is a homogeneous function of order minus one in the prices and income. As a consequence,

$$m_\phi(p_1, p_2, \cdots, p_n, I) = \lambda m_\phi(\lambda p_1, \lambda p_2, \cdots, \lambda p_n, \lambda I), \qquad (16)$$

where λ is any positive constant. Applying Euler's theorem on homogeneous functions, we have the following identity:

$$-m_\phi \equiv \frac{\partial m_\phi}{\partial p_1} p_1 + \frac{\partial m_\phi}{\partial p_2} p_2 + \cdots + \frac{\partial m_\phi}{\partial p_n} p_n + \frac{\partial m_\phi}{\partial I} I. \qquad (17)$$

Of course, m_ϕ, $p_1, \cdots, p_n$, I, all are positive quantities. Therefore, we cannot have simultaneously

$$\frac{\partial m_\phi}{\partial p_i} \equiv 0 \qquad (i = 1, 2, \cdots, n) \qquad (18)$$

$$\frac{\partial m_\phi}{\partial I} \equiv 0,$$

else the right-hand sign of equation (17) would not add up to a negative quantity. This becomes even more clear if we divide (17) by m_ϕ to get the following expression involving dimensionless elasticity coefficients:

$$-1 \equiv \left(\frac{\partial m_\phi}{\partial p_1} \frac{p_1}{m_\phi}\right) + \cdots + \left(\frac{\partial m_\phi}{\partial p_n} \frac{p_n}{m_\phi}\right) + \left(\frac{\partial m_\phi}{\partial I} \frac{I}{m_\phi}\right) \qquad (19)$$

The right-hand terms cannot all vanish and still add up to a -1.

How then shall we interpret constancy of the marginal utility of income? Knowingly or unknowingly, economists have formulated two distinct and alternative hypotheses under this heading. The first one involves the assumption that there exists an index of utility for which the marginal utility of income becomes independent of a change in any price, or

$$\frac{\partial m_\phi}{\partial p_i} \equiv 0. \qquad (i = 1, 2, \cdots, n) \qquad (20)$$

80 MATHEMATICAL ECONOMICS AND ECONOMETRICS

As we have seen, this cannot possibly imply that the marginal utility of income is also constant with respect to income.

In introducing the second hypothesis attention is drawn to the fact that throughout I have repeatedly employed the term "marginal utility of *income*" rather than the "marginal utility of *money*." The latter is perhaps the term most commonly met in the literature. Not the least of its disadvantages is the fact that it suggests to the literally minded the second interpretation we are about to give.

As a preliminary it must be remembered that all demand functions and conditions of equilibrium depend upon *relative* prices and income. Very often writers arbitrarily equate the price of one good to unity, employing it as *numéraire,* or unit of reckoning, and referring to it as "money." It was only natural for such writers to conclude that constancy of the marginal utility of "money" meant constancy of the marginal utility of the good selected as *numéraire.*

Although Marshall does employ the term "marginal utility of money," there is no evidence that he had in mind this last interpretation.[5] In the first place, he rarely, if ever, employed the concept of a *numéraire.* Furthermore, he repeatedly states that the marginal utility of money decreases with income, which I shall later show to rule out the second hypothesis. He also insists that the marginal utility of money is to be associated with a flow of income rather than a stock of a commodity. This insistence is not conclusive proof but may be significant.

FIRST HYPOTHESIS

I turn then to the first or Marshallian hypothesis that the marginal utility of income is independent of price changes as expressed in equation (20). Obviously,

$$\frac{\partial m_\phi}{\partial p_i} \frac{p_i}{m_\phi} \equiv 0 . \qquad (i = 1, 2, \cdots, n) \tag{21}$$

Therefore, substituting into equation (19), we have

$$\frac{\partial m_\phi}{\partial I} \frac{I}{m_\phi} \equiv -1 . \tag{22}$$

[5] The only passages in the *Principles* which do suggest this interpretation are to be found in the Mathematical Appendix, Note XII. This argument, however, is borrowed from Edgeworth and other writers in order to establish the conclusion that market price is determinate. Against this may be cited pp. 95, 134–35, Mathematical Appendix, Note II, etc. In interpreting Marshall, it must be remembered that he regarded the constancy of the marginal utility of income as only "approximate." I shall follow out the rigorous implications of assuming this exactly; the closer is Marshall's approximation, the more nearly will the results coincide.

CONSTANCY OF THE MARGINAL UTILITY OF INCOME 81

*This says that the income elasticity of the marginal utility of income
must be identically equal to minus unity.* Therefore, we have

$$m_\phi = \frac{a}{I} , \tag{23}$$

where a is a constant. Mathematically, (23) is the only form that a
homogeneous function of order -1 in a single variable can take.
Equation (13) now becomes

$$\frac{\partial x_i}{\partial I} \frac{I}{x_i} \equiv - \frac{\partial m_\phi}{\partial I} \frac{I}{m_\phi} \equiv 1 . \qquad (i = 1, 2, \cdots, n) \tag{24}$$

In words, *the seemingly innocent assumption that there exists a
utility index for which the marginal utility of income is constant with
respect to price changes results in the empirical restriction of unitary
income elasticities of demand, or that the consumption of each and
every good is exactly proportional to income.* In this case the demand
functions take the special form

$$x_i = I \psi^i (p_1 , \cdots , p_n) \equiv I \lambda \psi^i (\lambda p_1 , \cdots , \lambda p_n) . \tag{25}$$
$$(i = 1, 2, \cdots, n)$$

There is a vast amount of budgetary statistical data relating to
income variations in consumption. As far as I know, every investigation contradicts flatly this basic assumption. Moreover, these relations
do not hold approximately even in the neighborhood of a single point.[6]

Let us go still further and investigate the strict implications of
imposing an additional Marshallian assumption, namely, that there
exists a utility index which is the sum of the independent utilities of
each good:

$$\phi(x_1 , \cdots , x_n) = f_1(x_1) + f_2(x_2) + \cdots + f_n(x_n) . \tag{26}$$
Then

$$\frac{f'_i(x_i)}{p_i} = \frac{a}{I} . \tag{27}$$

[6] It is only in the empirically unimportant case of expenditure proportionality
that the correct integrability conditions

$$\frac{\partial x_i}{\partial p_j} + x_j \frac{\partial x_i}{\partial I} \equiv \frac{\partial x_j}{\partial p_i} + x_i \frac{\partial x_j}{\partial I} \tag{1}$$

can be replaced by the special relations

$$\frac{\partial x_i}{\partial p_j} \equiv \frac{\partial x_j}{\partial p_i} . \tag{2}$$

82   MATHEMATICAL ECONOMICS AND ECONOMETRICS

Since the right-hand side of (27) does not contain $p_j (\neq p_i)$, the quantity demanded of the ith good must depend only upon its own price and income. Differentiating partially the budget equation with respect to p_j, we find

$$\frac{\partial I}{\partial p_j} = 0 = \sum_{i=1}^{n} p_i \frac{\partial x_i}{\partial p_j} + x_j \ . \tag{28}$$

Under the present independence of demand we derive

$$\frac{\partial x_j}{\partial p_j} \frac{p_j}{x_j} \equiv -1 \ . \qquad (j = 1, 2, \cdots, n) \tag{29}$$

In words, *the combined assumptions of constancy of the marginal utility of income and independence of utility imply that the elasticity of demand be always unity.* This together with the assumption that all demand functions be homogeneous of order zero requires that the demand functions take the special form

$$x_i = k_i \frac{I}{p_i} \ , \qquad (i = 1, 2, \cdots, n) \tag{30}$$

where the k's are constants equal to the fraction of income spent on each commodity.

Equation (27) can be rewritten

$$f'_i (k_i \frac{I}{p_i}) = a \frac{p_i}{I} \ . \tag{31}$$

Therefore,

$$f'_i (v) = \frac{a k_i}{v} \ , \tag{32}$$

or

$$f'_i (x_i) = \frac{a k_i}{x_i} \ . \qquad (i = 1, 2, \cdots, n) \tag{33}$$

Hence,

$$\phi = b + a (k_1 \log x_1 + k_2 \log x_2 + \cdots + k_n \log x_n) \ . \tag{34}$$

This result could also have been derived with the aid of the generalized form of Burk's theorem that expenditure proportionality plus independence of utilities restricts severely the indifference surfaces and utility indexes.[7]

As an illustration of the lack of invariance of the marginal utility

[7] A. Burk, "Real Income, Expenditure Proportionality, and Frisch's 'New Methods of Measuring Marginal Utility,'" *Review of Economic Studies*, IV, No. 1 (1936), 33–52.

of income the reader is invited to compute this magnitude for the transformed, equivalent utility index

$$F = B + A x_1^{k_1} x_2^{k_2} \cdots x_n^{k_n} . \tag{35}$$

It need hardly be said that no empirical observations justify the imposition of such a definite form upon the utility indexes of indifference surfaces and demand functions.

SUFFICIENCY CONDITIONS FOR CONSTANCY IN THE FIRST SENSE

The introduction of the assumption of independence of utilities was in the nature of a digression designed to show the damage that may result from the addition of seemingly harmless and plausible hypotheses. I return now to the hypothesis of constancy of the marginal utility of income. We have seen that it implies (income) *expenditure proportionality*. Is this all? Are there perhaps still further hidden restrictions which more thorough investigation might reveal?

It is desirable to be able to answer definitely such questions. Fortunately, it can be proved that no further restrictions are implied by this hypothesis. This can be done once and for all by proving that the necessary conditions of equation (25) are also sufficient to insure the existence of a utility index in terms of which the marginal utility of income is constant with respect to price changes. The proof consists of a specification of the steps by means of which such an index can be constructed.

If expenditure proportionality holds, the indifference surface can be written in the following special form:

$$\frac{F'(\phi)\phi_i}{F'(\phi)\phi_j} = {}^jR^i(x_1 , x_2 , \cdots , x_n) = {}^jR^i(\lambda x_1 , \lambda x_2 , \cdots , \lambda x_n) ; \tag{36}$$

i.e., the slope functions are homogeneous of order zero. This being the case, a utility index can be found which is homogeneous of the first order in the quantities of goods,

$$\Phi = \Phi(x_1 , x_2 , \cdots , x_n) = \frac{1}{\lambda} \Phi(\lambda x_1 , \lambda x_2 , \cdots , \lambda x_n) . \tag{37}$$

In fact, the indifference surfaces can be "numbered" according to their respective distances from the origin along an arbitrary "spoke" going through the origin, and we will have such an index. In terms of this index the conditions of equilibrium can be written

$$\Phi_i = m_\bullet p_i . \quad (i = 1, 2, \cdots, n) \tag{38}$$

84 MATHEMATICAL ECONOMICS AND ECONOMETRICS

Multiplying each equation by x_i, respectively, and adding, we have

$$\sum_{i=1}^{n} \Phi_i x_i = m_* \sum_{i=1}^{n} p_i x_i . \tag{39}$$

Because of the budget equation (4) and the fact that Φ obeys Euler's theorem for homogeneous functions of the first order, this can be written

$$m_* = \frac{\Phi}{I} . \tag{40}$$

Consider the utility index, ϕ, defined as

$$\phi = b + a \log \Phi . \tag{41}$$

From equation (9) we find

$$m_\phi = \frac{a}{\Phi} m_* = \frac{a}{I} , \tag{42}$$

which is identically equation (23). Hence, expenditure proportionality implies that a utility index can always be found for which the marginal utility of income is independent of prices. This completes the sufficiency proof and guarantees that there are no hidden additional implications of the assumption of constancy of the marginal utility of income in the Marshallian sense.

CONSTANCY OF THE MARGINAL UTILITY OF "MONEY"

I now turn to a brief analysis of the empirical implications of the second possible interpretation of constancy of the marginal utility of income.[8] According to this point of view, the marginal utility of some one good, which can be designated as *numéraire*, is constant with respect to changes in all *other* prices and income. Designating the *numéraire* as the first good, we have

$$\frac{\partial m_\phi}{\partial p_i} \equiv 0 , \quad (i = 2, 3, \cdots, n)$$

$$\frac{\partial m_\phi}{\partial I} \equiv 0 . \tag{43}$$

Because m_ϕ is homogeneous of order -1 in all prices and income, we have

[8] See Wilson, *op. cit.*; J. R. Hicks, *Value and Capital* (Oxford: Clarendon Press, 1939), pp. 38–41.

CONSTANCY OF THE MARGINAL UTILITY OF INCOME 85

$$m_\phi \equiv \frac{a}{p_1}. \tag{44}$$

Substituting equations (43) into equation (13), we have

$$\frac{\partial x_i}{\partial I} \equiv 0, \quad (i=2,3,\cdots,n)$$

$$\frac{\partial x_1}{\partial I} \equiv -\frac{\partial m_\phi}{\partial p_1}\frac{1}{m_\phi} \equiv \frac{1}{p_1}. \tag{45}$$

The demand functions must take the special form[9]

$$x_i = G^i(p_1,\cdots,p_n) = G^i(\lambda p_1,\cdots,\lambda p_n), \quad (i=2,3,\cdots,n)$$

$$x_1 = \frac{I}{p_1} - \sum_{i=2}^{n}\frac{p_i}{p_1}G^i(p_1,\cdots,p_n). \tag{46}$$

This means that any increase in income is spent completely on one commodity. It need hardly be said that all empirical budgetary studies show this hypothesis to be absurd.

As with the first hypothesis, I shall now prove the sufficiency of the necessary conditions of equations (46). Because of the homogeneity condition on the G's, the first $(n-1)$ equations can be solved to give the prices, $(p_2/p_1, p_3/p_1,\cdots,p_n/p_1)$ in terms of the goods, $(x_2, x_3,\cdots,x_n)$. These price ratios are independent of x_1, so the indifference curves take the special form

$$\frac{p_i}{p_1} = R^i(x_2,x_3,\cdots,x_n). \quad (i=2,3,\cdots,n) \tag{47}$$

The linear differential expression

$$adx_1 + \sum_{i=2}^{n} aR^i dx_i, \tag{48}$$

is an exact differential because the existence of at least one utility index implies

$$R_j{}^i - R_i{}^j \equiv R^j R_1{}^i - R^i R_1{}^j \equiv 0. \tag{49}$$

Hence, a utility index exists of the form

$$\phi = b + ax_1 + a\sum_{i=2}^{n}\int_{c_i}^{x_i} R^i(x_2,\cdots,x_n)dx_i. \tag{50}$$

---

[9] Pigou appears to be in error in his belief that constancy of the marginal utility of income with respect to income implies infinite elasticity of demand. Equations (46) reveal no such implication.

86 MATHEMATICAL ECONOMICS AND ECONOMETRICS

For this index,

$$m_\phi = \frac{a}{p_1} \; ,$$

which is identically equal to equation (44). This proves the sufficiency of the conditions of equation (46).

As with the previous case, it is of interest to consider the simultaneous effects of the assumption of independence of utilities and constancy of the marginal utility of income. In this case, a utility index exists of the following form

$$\phi = b + ax_1 + f_2(x_2) + f_3(x_3) + \cdots + f_n(x_n) \; . \tag{51}$$

Hence,

$$m_\phi = \frac{f'_i(x_i)}{p_i} = \frac{a}{p_1} \; . \tag{52}$$

But

$$x_i = G^i\left(1 \, , \frac{p_2}{p_1} , \frac{p_3}{p_1} , \cdots , \frac{p_n}{p_1}\right) \tag{53}$$

so that

$$f'_i\left[\, G^i \left(1 \, , \frac{p_2}{p_1} , \frac{p_3}{p_1} , \cdots , \frac{p_n}{p_1}\right)\right] = a\frac{p_i}{p_1} \; . \tag{54}$$

Since the right-hand side does not involve (p_j/p_1) $(\neq p_i/p_1)$, neither can the left, requiring our demand curves to take the special form

$$x_i = G^i\left(\frac{p_i}{p_1}\right), \qquad (i = 2, 3, \cdots, n)$$

$$x_1 = \frac{I}{p_1} - \sum_{i=2}^{n} \frac{p_i}{p_1} G^i\left(\frac{p_i}{p_1}\right). \tag{55}$$

This does *not* imply unitary elasticity of demand, as some earlier writers have thought. In fact, unitary elasticity would lead to a contradiction. Of course, the restrictions imposed by the combined assumptions are even more incompatible with the facts of economic life.

CONSUMER'S SURPLUS AND ALLIED CONCEPTS

We have seen the empirical implications of the various hypotheses with respect to the strict constancy of the marginal utility of income and noted their incompatibility with statistical observations. It is desirable before concluding to indicate the effects of this analysis upon various constructions which depend for their validity upon the constancy of the marginal utility of income.

CONSTANCY OF THE MARGINAL UTILITY OF INCOME 87

The first of these is Marshallian consumer's surplus. Before examining it in detail, let us consider the uses to which it is put. Among other things it is proposed as a measure of the gain (loss) of utility that results from a decrease (increase) in price of a single good. An attempt also has been made to apply it to the analysis of the burden involved in commodity taxation. It has been used to determine the maximum amount of revenue that a perfectly discriminating monopolist might exact from the consumer for a given amount of the good in question.

Since only an ordinal preference field is assumed in the theory of consumer's behavior, there is really little importance to be attached to any numerical measure of the gains from a price change. In particular, one cannot fruitfully compare the gain derived from a movement between two given price situations with the gain between two other price situations.[10] Moreover, all valid theorems relating to the burden of taxation can be stated independently of any numerical measure of utility change. We should not be greatly perturbed, therefore, if the concept of consumer's surplus should be found to be inadmissible. Its only advantage seems to lie in its easy two-dimensional representation.

Consider an initial price and income situation, $(p_1{}^a, \cdots, p_n{}^a, I^a)$, and the corresponding amount of goods purchased, $(x_1{}^a, \cdots, x_n{}^a)$. For any selected utility index, ϕ, there will also be a given amount of utility, $\phi(X^a)$. Suppose that a change is made in but one price, p_i, and income is left unchanged. There will be new amounts of every commodity, $(x_1{}^b, \cdots, x_n{}^b)$, and of utility, $\phi(X^b)$, corresponding to the new prices and income, $(p_1{}^b, \cdots, p_n{}^b, I^b)$, or $(p_1{}^a, p_2{}^a, \cdots, p_i{}^b, \cdots, p_n{}^a, I^a)$.

We are interested in the following magnitudes:

1. The gain (loss) in utility resulting from the price change, or $\phi(X^b) - \phi(X^a)$.

2. The area between the demand curve of the ith good and the p_i axis within the range of the price movement, or

$$- \int_{p_i{}^a}^{p_i{}^b} x_i \, dp_i .$$

3. The amount by which the expenditure on the ith good in the new situation is exceeded by the maximum amount of money which

[10] One can, however, compare the gains derived from a change in the basic price situation with an alternative price change from the *same* basic situation, since this resolves itself into an *ordinal* comparison of the alternative new situations. The initial situation "cancels out" so to speak.

88   MATHEMATICAL ECONOMICS AND ECONOMETRICS

the consumer would be willing to pay for $x_i{}^b$ in preference to trading at the old set of prices. (This may be negative if we are dealing with a price increase rather than a decrease.) Call this E_{ab}.

   4.   The change in income which will make trading at the new set of prices as attractive as trading at the old set of prices with the initial income. Call this ΔI_{ab}.

   5.   The change in income which will make trading at the old set of prices as attractive as trading at the new set of prices with the initial income. Call this $\Delta I'_{ab}$. [11]

   According to the Marshallian doctrine of consumer's surplus, all five of these magnitudes are equal except for dimensional constants. We are explicitly warned, however, that this doctrine holds unqualifiedly only when the marginal utility of income is constant, and only if utilities are independent. I shall now examine the value of each of these magnitudes in four cases: (*a*) in the general unrestricted case of stable demand; (*b*) under the first interpretation of constancy of the marginal utility of income; (*c*) under the second hypothesis when the *i*th good is not the *numéraire*; and (*d*) under the second hypothesis when the *i*th good itself has constant marginal utility of income. Only the most sketchy proofs will be indicated.

   In the general case we have the following relations:

$$\phi(X^b) - \phi(X^a) = \int_{p_i{}^a}^{p_i{}^b}\left(\frac{d\phi}{dp_i}\right)dp_i = \int_{p_i{}^a}^{p_i{}^b}\sum_{j=1}^{n}\left(\frac{\partial\phi}{\partial x_j}\frac{\partial x_j}{\partial p_i}\right)dp_i$$

$$= \int_{p_i{}^a}^{p_i{}^b} m_\phi \sum_{j=1}^{n}\left(p_j\frac{\partial x_j}{\partial p_i}\right)dp_i = -\int_{p_i{}^a}^{p_i{}^b} m_\phi\, x_i\, dp_i . \tag{56}$$

$$\Delta I_{ab} = \max\left(\sum_{j=1}^{n} p_j{}^b x_j{}^b - \sum_{j=1}^{n} p_j{}^b x_j\right), \quad \text{where } \phi(X) = \phi(X^a), \tag{57}$$

$$\geqq \sum_{j=1}^{n} p_j{}^b(x_j{}^b - x_j{}^a), \tag{58}$$

$$\geqq \sum_{j=1}^{n} (p_j{}^a - p_j{}^b) x_j{}^a . \tag{59}$$

If only the *i*th price changes, this becomes

$$\Delta I_{ab} \geqq (p_i{}^a - p_i{}^b) x_i{}^a . \tag{60}$$

Similarly,

$$\Delta I'_{ab} \leqq \sum_{j=1}^{n} p_j{}^a(x_j{}^b - x_j{}^a) \tag{61}$$

[11] Note that $\Delta I_{ab} = -\Delta I'_{ba}$; $\Delta I'_{ab}$, but not ΔI_{ab} nor E_{ab}, can exceed I.

CONSTANCY OF THE MARGINAL UTILITY OF INCOME 89

$$\leq \sum_{j=1}^{n} (p_j{}^a - p_j{}^b) x_j{}^b \tag{62}$$

and

$$\Delta I'_{ab} \leq (p_i{}^a - p_i{}^b) x_i{}^b . \tag{63}$$

It is impossible in the general case[12] to determine the relative magnitude of ΔI_{ab} and $\Delta I'_{ab}$. Hence,

$$\Delta I_{ab} \gtreqless \Delta I'_{ab} . \tag{64}$$

It can be shown that

$$E_{ab} = - \int_{p_i{}^a}^{p_i{}^b} x_i dp_i + \int_{p_i{}^a}^{p_i{}^b} (\bar{p}_i - p_i) \frac{\partial x_i}{\partial p_i} dp_i , \tag{65}$$

where $\bar{p}_i$ is the price which would have to prevail for the consumer *freely* to select the batch of goods which he actually does consume when presented with an "all-or-none" offer by the perfectly discriminating monopolist. The first term on the right-hand side of equation (65) is the area under the demand curve. The second "correction" term may be of either sign.[13] It also follows from the definition of ΔI_{ab} that

$$\Delta I_{ab} \geq E_{ab} . \tag{66}$$

In case (*b*) we find

$$E_{ab} < \Delta I_{ab} < \Delta I'_{ab} , \tag{67}$$

and

$$\frac{\phi(X^b) - \phi(X^a)}{m_\phi} = - \int_{p_i{}^a}^{p_i{}^b} x_i dp_i > E_{ab} . \text{[14]} \tag{68}$$

The following relations must be satisfied in case (*c*):

$$\frac{\phi(X^b) - \phi(X^a)}{m_\phi} = - \int_{p_i{}^a}^{p_i{}^b} x_i dp_i = E_{ab} = \Delta I_{ab} = \Delta I'_{ab} . \ (i \neq 1) \tag{69}$$

[12] If we rule out the inferior good phenomenon so that demand is "normal,"

$$\Delta I_{ab} < \Delta I'_{ab} . \tag{1}$$

Actually,

$$\Delta I_{ab} - \Delta I'_{ab} = \int_{p_i{}^a}^{p_i{}^b} \{ x_i (p_1{}^a, \cdot p_2{}^a, \dots, p_i, \dots p_n{}^a, \phi^b)$$

$$- x_i (p_1{}^a, p_2{}^a, \dots, p_i, \dots, p_n{}^a, \phi^a) \} dp_i .$$

[13] In the "normal" two-dimensional case it will be of negative sign; i.e., a perfectly discriminating monopolist will be able to exact less than the area under the demand curve from the consumer.

[14] The last of these inequalities will certainly hold in the two good case. I have not developed a satisfactory proof that it holds for the *n*-dimensional case.

90   MATHEMATICAL ECONOMICS AND ECONOMETRICS

Although this is not the Marshallian interpretation, consumer's surplus seems to be most justified in this case. However, the above equalities cannot hold simultaneously for every good.[15]

For case (d) we have the same relations as case (b) ; i.e., equations (67) and (68) must hold with the possible exception of the inequality referred to in a previous footnote.[16]

[15] Case (c) is *sufficient* to insure the equalities of eq. (69). Some of them may hold in other cases.

[16] It is of some interest to calculate these magnitudes in the *purest Marshallian case* when utilities are independent and the marginal utility of income is independent of price changes. Here we have for consumer's surplus

$$\frac{\phi(X^b) - \phi(X^a)}{m_\phi} = - \int_{p_i^a}^{p_i^b} x_i \, dp_i ,$$

$$= k_i I \log \frac{p_i^a}{p_i^b} > 0 , \quad p_i^a > p_i^b . \tag{1}$$

If we compute consumer's surplus from the origin, i.e., from the price at which the consumption of x_i is equal to zero, we find that consumer's surplus is infinite! That is

$$\lim_{p_i^a \to \infty} \log \frac{p_i^a}{p_i^b} = \infty . \tag{2}$$

Some writers regard consumer's surplus as being infinite but suggest that it may be made finite if measured from some minimum or subsistence level of the commodity in question. In the purest Marshallian case since the demand curve approaches the price axis asymptotically in such a way that the integral or area under the curve is divergent, there exists no such unique minimum level.

Also

$$E_{ab} = I \left\{ 1 - \left(\frac{p_i^b}{p_i^a} \right)^{k_i/(1-k_i)} \right\} \leq I , \tag{3}$$

$$\Delta I_{ab} = I \left\{ 1 - \left(\frac{p_i^b}{p_i^a} \right)^{k_i} \right\} \leq I , \tag{4}$$

$$\Delta I'_{ab} = I \left\{ \left(\frac{p_i^a}{p_i^b} \right)^{k_i} - 1 \right\} > \Delta I_{ab} . \tag{5}$$

In the limit as p_i^a goes to infinity we have

$$E_{ab} = I = \Delta I_{ab} , \tag{6}$$

$$\Delta I'_{ab} = \infty . \tag{7}$$

When the Marshallian assumptions are met perfectly, the area under the demand curve is not equal to the amount that a perfectly discriminating monopolist could exact from the consumer by an all or none offer—even though the marginal utility of income is constant!

CONSTANCY OF THE MARGINAL UTILITY OF INCOME 91

HISTORICAL SUMMARY

In concluding I should like to touch briefly on the history of the discussion of the marginal utility of income. As cited earlier, Marshall assumed constancy in the first sense as a basis for his doctrine of consumer's surplus. He also employed constancy in the second sense to show that market price is determinate. It is amusing in this connection to notice that he did not feel it necessary to point out that the accidental determinateness of final price in this case is accompanied by complete indeterminateness in the quantity of one of the goods.

Pareto disliked the constancy of the marginal utility of income, although it is not possible to infer unambiguously from his *Manuel* in which sense he interpreted this. He clearly considers it to be constant with respect to $(n - 1)$ prices; since he does not differentiate with respect to the price of the *numéraire* good, either interpretation might hold. Throughout he deals only with the case of independent utilities. An incomplete derivation of the theorem of unitary price elasticity of demand for each good under these conditions suggests that it would be necessary to adopt the first interpretation.

Assuming marginal utility of income to be constant, utilities to be independent, and the proportion spent on each good to be small relative to the income elasticities of demand, Pigou suggested that the ratio of the price elasticities of demand of two goods is equal to the ratio of their respective income elasticities of demand.[17] The latter can be computed from budgetary studies. By the use of a theorem established by Friedman[18] it can be shown that this same conclusion follows from the second and third of these assumptions and is independent of the assumption of constancy of the marginal utility of income. It still seems to depend upon independence of utilities, the empirical implication of which I deal with in a forthcoming paper.

Aside from its use in connection with consumer's surplus, the main concern of writers has been to derive the negative slope of the demand curve by means of the assumption of constancy. For it is only when marginal utility of income is constant and utilities are independent that the slope of the demand curve can be derived from the behavior of the curve of marginal utility. In this case, the alleged law of diminishing marginal utility implies negatively sloping demand curves. We have seen here that the rigorous assumption of this relation for every good implies something much more definite; namely, unitary price and income elasticity of demand and vanishing cross-elasticities of demand.

[17] A. C. Pigou, *Economics of Welfare* (London, 1920), Appen. II.
[18] *Op. cit.*

[16]

Duality and the Many Consumer's Surpluses

By Eugene Silberberg*

The concepts of duality and indirect utility functions have received renewed interest in recent years owing, in part, to a series of articles by Hendrik Houthakker (1960, 1965) and Paul Samuelson (1965). These discussions stemmed largely from the econometric problem of specifying demand relations. It will be shown that the above concepts provide an interesting and informative way of reformulating the consumer's surplus (or, more aptly, the consumer's surpluses) problem. It is my contention that despite the enormous literature in this area, including extensive analyses by Samuelson (1942, 1947) and John Hicks (1946, 1959), the basic nature of the problem has never been adequately delineated.[1]

The principal reason for the substantial and protracted interest in the concept of a consumer's surplus seems to be the desire to associate changes in monetary (i.e., money income) values with changes in the level of utility, to permit welfare judgments concerning alternative economic equilibria. But a constant source of frustration is that such "welfare" measures are, at best, ambiguous

and normative. This has led to a proliferation of consumer's surpluses, each designed to answer specific questions about the consumer's indifference map. Despite this profusion, one still finds in the literature the single phrase "welfare loss" applied to monopolies, taxes, and so on.[2]

The purpose of this paper is to present a unifying treatment of the many consumer's surpluses. In the older welfare theories, debate about value judgments disguised the importance of distinguishing between two fundamentally different concepts. One is the gain in money income attributable to a change in utility; following Hicks, we call this *equivalent variations* in money income. The other concept, which we label *compensating variations* (again following Hicks), is designed to measure offsetting changes in the budget plane that would leave the individual on the same utility level after a change in one or more of the prices faced by him. We shall show that all consumer's surpluses are variations on these two themes, and differences among them may be directly traced to what variables are being held fixed.

A welfare loss (WL) function as constructed and extensively used, for example, by Harberger (1954, 1964) must, if it is to have the meaning generally ascribed to it, be some sort of equivalent variation in income expressed as a function of the price distortions. For example, if $t_1, \ldots, t_n$ represent excise taxes on the n commodities $x_1, \ldots, x_n$, and if, in the absence of such taxes, the commodities were sold at prices equal to their respective marginal costs, then we would write $WL = f(t_1, \ldots, t_n)$. It will be conclu-

* University of Washington. I have benefited from discussions with J. Allan Hynes, Stephen N. S. Cheung and Yoram Barzel. All remaining errors are of course my own. I am indebted to Professor Yoshihiro Maruyama of Kyoto University, Japan, for providing me with a copy of M. Sono's Japanese paper on consumer's surplus, and to Kenji Kise for his help in translating that paper.

[1] No attempt has been made to provide an exhaustive bibliography on the consumer's surplus problem, nor will original sources necessarily be cited. Instead, the reader is referred to well-known summary treatments like Patinkin, Hicks (1959), and James Morgan (whose treatment of the problem is excellent) for references to the classical literature. A rather complete bibliography of literature on the consumer's surplus before 1960 can be found in E. J. Mishan.

[2] See Robert Bishop, Arnold Harberger (1964), David Schwartzman, to cite just a few examples.

sively demonstrated that such a construct is impossible, by showing the path dependence of WL, i.e., the dependence of WL upon the pattern of adjustment to the tax structure.

All the equivalent variations will be shown to be derivable from a single expression, a line integral, whose value will, in general, depend upon the particular path of price or excise tax changes. The condition under which a function such as WL is definable (i.e., the condition under which the line integral generating the equivalent variations is path-independent) will be shown to be that of constant marginal utility of money income. A precise interpretation and analysis of the "Marshallian Triangle," i.e., the area to the left of the demand curve, will be given, and its noncommensurability with the classical equivalent and compensating variations in income will be explained. After a discussion of the compensating variations, an example will be used to reveal the extent of money values that can be associated with a given utility gain experienced by a consumer when prices change. A final section relates these findings to welfare theory.

I. The "Equivalent Variations"

In analyzing the case of a single utility-maximizing consumer the appropriate Lagrangian function is

$$L = U(x_1, \cdots, x_n) + \lambda \left(M - \sum_{i=1}^{n} p_i x_i \right)$$

producing the usual first-order conditions

$$(1) \qquad U_i - \lambda p_i = 0, \qquad i = 1, \ldots, n$$

$$(2) \qquad M - \sum_{i=1}^{n} p_i x_i = 0$$

where $U_i = \partial U / \partial x_i$. The utility function is assumed to be strictly increasing and quasi-concave in x_i, and the Jacobian associated with equations (1) and (2) is assumed nonzero. Under these conditions these relations may be solved (in principle) for the "ordinary" (uncompensated) demand functions

$$(3) \qquad \begin{aligned} x_i^* &= h_i(p_1, \ldots, p_n, M), \\ & \qquad\qquad i = 1, \cdots, n, \end{aligned}$$

the $*$ denoting optimal (equilibrium) values. Also produced is the equilibrium λ^*. The x_i^* can be substituted into U, giving

$$(4) \qquad \begin{aligned} U^* &= U(x_1^*, \ldots, x_n^*) \\ &= V(p_1, \ldots, p_n, M) = V \end{aligned}$$

The indirect utility function, V, gives the maximum value of utility associated with a given price-income vector $(P, M) = (p_1, \ldots, p_n, M)$.

Consider now the following *line integral*:

$$(5) \qquad \Phi = \int_C \sum_{i=1}^{n} p_i dx_i^*$$

where C is some path of prices and income between initial and final price-income vectors $(P^0, M^0) = (p_1^0, \ldots, p_n^0, M^0)$ and $(P^1, M^1) = (p_1^1, \ldots, p_n^1, M^1)$, respectively.[3] Φ can be thought of as a generalization of the area under a demand curve, although there is more to it than that, as will be seen shortly. The adjustment process can be visualized as the gradual changing of prices and income or the changing of excise and income taxes (ignoring the destination of those tax revenues), with the consumer continuously and instantaneously adjusting to the new equilibria.[4] Hence the demand relations (3) hold along each point of the path of integration. To save notational clutter, the asterisks will be dropped from the variables. All values will be presumed to be in consumption equilibrium.

It is now possible to give Φ an economic interpretation, using the first-order relations (1):

$$(6) \qquad \begin{aligned} \Phi &= \int_C \sum p_i dx_i = \int_C 1/\lambda \sum U_i dx_i \\ &= \int_C 1/\lambda dU = \int_C 1/\lambda dV \end{aligned}$$

---

[3] A similar expression is used in the construction of Divisia price indices. Many of the results cited in the paper have analogous formulations in terms of such indices. See, for example, Herman Wold, William Gorman.

[4] A partial equilibrium approach to this problem is maintained for expositional ease. A more general approach would, of course, consider these price changes as

The Lagrange multiplier λ has the interpretation of the marginal utility of income. Its reciprocal, $1/\lambda$, can be regarded as the marginal cost of utility. It is the Lagrange multiplier associated with the cost-minimization problem,

Minimize $\qquad M = \sum_{i=1}^{n} x_i p_i$

subject to $\qquad U(x_1, \ldots, x_n) = U^0$

More precisely, $1/\lambda$ is the imputed marginal rent associated with the level of utility at a point along C. Hence the integral (6) can be regarded as the limit of a sum of marginal (dollar) rents associated with a given movement through the parameter space, and Φ is thus the total change in dollar rent associated with a change in utility *along a specified path.* It must be emphasized that Φ gives an imputed rent, or "shadow price," of utility changes and not an actual realized money income change. In general no shift in the budget plane can be uniquely associated with a given value of Φ. The term "rent" is appropriate to the partial equilibrium framework used here in that the consumer experiences an increase in real income with the same nominal income.

The central problem of the many consumer's surpluses can now be stated in terms of a fundamental mathematical property of line integrals: Integrals such as (5) above are generally not independent of the path of integration. We must, therefore, expect to find different dollar evaluations of the same gain in utility when price and income changes follow different paths, *even though the terminal price-income vectors are identical.* This path-dependency is the *raison d'être* of the many consumer surpluses. The restriction to single price changes (perhaps for graphical expediency) has formerly completely hidden from view the fundamental nature of the problem.[5]

changes in the marginal costs of producing the commodities due to, say, technological innovation or some such resource-saving device. Even that would not be completely satisfactory, since presumably resources are expended in producing technological change.

[5] Although Samuelson (1947) and Harold Hotelling refer to this generalization to line integrals, they seem

One can visualize the path dependence of Φ by noting that if, say, p_i changes, the demand curves for the other commodities begin to shift at the rate $(\partial x_j/\partial p_i)$, $j \neq i$. If, however, some other price p_j changes, the demand for commodity i shifts at the rate $\partial x_i/\partial p_j$. Since these rates are not in general equal, the way in which p_i and p_j are changed —for example, first p_i then p_j or vice versa— will affect the areas under the demand curves $\int p_i dx_i$ and hence the value of $\Phi = \int \sum p_i dx_i$. As it turns out, the condition $\partial x_i/\partial p_j = \partial x_j/\partial p_i$, $i, j = 1, \ldots, n$ is precisely the condition for path-independence.[6] This will be discussed in greater detail in the next section.

Integrating by parts yields

(7)
$$\Phi = \int_C 1/\lambda \, dV = \int_C \sum p_i dx_i$$
$$= \sum p_i^1 x_i^1 - \sum p_i^0 x_i^0 - \int_C \sum x_i dp_i$$

Hence the rent imputed to a movement through the parameter space has two components: the actual change in money income (independent of the path and not properly called a surplus since it involves an actual increase in money income) and a line integral which relates to price changes only and measures the consumer's imputed gain or loss due to changes in prices.

Some well-known equivalent variations in income will now be derived from the integral Φ and analyzed.[7] Suppose consumer equilibrium is at $X^0 = (x_1^0, \ldots, x_n^0)$ with prices $(P^0, M^0) = (p_1^0, \ldots, p_n^0 M^0)$ on an indifference

not to regard it as crucial. Samuelson is particularly cryptic here. He states that "In general, line integrals will replace simple integrals with the path of integration of the former a matter of no consequence" (1947, p. 202n). This cannot be true as it stands. Don Patinkin, on the other hand, does mention the path dependency of consumer's surplus, although no explicit presentation of that idea is offered.

[6] See any advanced calculus text; for example, Angus Taylor.

[7] That the Hicksian consumer's surpluses are derivable from Φ and the conditions under which the above expression is path independent, was apparently first shown by the mathematician Masuzo Sono in an article published in Japanese during World War II.

level U^0. Suppose that p_1 is lowered to p_1^1, producing a new equilibrium $X^1 = (x_1^1, \ldots, x_n^1)$ on indifference level U^1 where, of necessity, $U^1 > U^0$. What is the rent imputed to this gain in utility?

1. If p_1 is lowered from p_1^0 to p_1^1 (for example, an excise tax is lowered on Commodity 1, ignoring the destination of those tax revenues) such that the consumer continuously and instantaneously adjusts to this price movement, then from equation (7) the imputed value of the utility gain along this path is

$$\Phi = -\int_{p_1^0}^{p_1^1} x_1 dp_1,$$

or the area to the left of the ordinary demand curve. Thus we see that this famous Marshallian area does have an unambiguous interpretation. However, *it is only one of many shadow prices* associated with the utility increase $U^1 - U^0$, and, indeed, only one of many shadow prices associated with this particular price change. If the path of price changes involves changes in $p_2, \ldots, p_n$, even though the final price vector is $(p_1^1, p_2^0, \ldots, p_n^0)$, the consumer will impute a dollar gain to the new equilibrium different from the triangular geometrical area to the left of the demand curve. An example of this situation is given in Section IV below.

2. Suppose now that, with the original prices, money income M is raised from M^0 to, say, M^A, where the budget line is tangent to U^1 at the old prices. Then, clearly, Φ equals this change in money income. (The line integral $-\int \sum x_i dp_i$ is zero since prices are constant.) To make the terminal point the same as in paragraph 1 above, after the budget shift decrease M and all prices by the same proportion, returning M to M^0, then change relative prices so as to move the consumer along U^1 to the point X^1 at price-income vector $(p_1^1, p_2^0, \ldots, p_n^0, M^0)$. Since U is constant, $dU = 0$; hence Φ is zero for these latter operations. Thus Φ gives the classical equivalent variation in income associated with a rise in a price as defined by Hicks (1959). The classical equivalent variation in income for a price decrease (see Hicks (1959)) is yielded by a

similar procedure whereby relative prices are changed first so as to move the consumer along U^0 until the prices are proportional to the new prices $(p_1^1, p_2^0, \ldots, p_n^0)$ and then M is increased.[8] There is, of course, no reason why this second equivalent variation should equal the first one; indeed, they generally differ. Both represent imputed dollar rents associated with the utility gain $U^1 - U^0$, but for different paths of achieving that gain.

Clearly, an infinite number of consumer's surpluses can be generated, most of them uninteresting. Relative and absolute prices can be changed so as to hold x_1 fixed until U^1 is reached and then changed relatively so as to move the consumer along U^1 to X^1. Alternatively, $x_2, \ldots, x_n$ can be held constant. These paths generate values of Φ which correspond to (but are not exactly equal to) Marshall's surpluses in which quantities are held constant. There is no way in general to relate the magnitude of these surpluses to other values of Φ.

It is necessary now to show that the equivalent variations described in paragraph 2 above cannot meaningfully be compared with the area to the left of the demand curve. Since $1/\lambda = M / \sum U_i x_i$ and a proportional change in prices and income leaves the denominator unchanged, it is clear that $1/\lambda$ is homogeneous of degree 1 in prices and income (Samuelson (1942)). Therefore, the integral $\Phi = \int 1/\lambda dU$ is not invariant with respect to proportional changes in prices and income. With nonnormalized prices (i.e., with M allowed to vary) no unique value of Φ can be associated with a path *in the commodity space*—say, the price-consumption or income-consumption paths. Consider now the following "equivalent variation": Starting at point X^0 at (P^0, M^0), hold M constant at M^0 and slowly deflate all prices proportionally until the budget line is tangent to U^1. Evaluated on this path, Φ is less than the corresponding equivalent variation in paragraph 2 above when M was increased. The reason is that at every point along the income-consumption path between U^0 and U^1 beyond

---

[8] This is equivalent to the derivation of Laspeyres and Paasche indices from a Divisia index. See, for example, Wold.

X^0 at the original price ratios, $1/\lambda$ for the price-deflating case is less than $1/\lambda$ for the M increasing case. This is easily seen from the above definition of $1/\lambda$. While the same bundle may be purchased, an extra dollar represents more purchasing power if prices have been deflated than if M had increased. Hence the marginal utility of money income is greater, or the imputed rent to an extra utile is less when prices have deflated rather than when income has increased. Clearly, then, it makes no sense to compare a consumer's surplus where M has been held fixed (say, the area to the left of the demand curve as in paragraph 1 above) with one in which M has varied. The dollar amounts in the two cases are not commensurable, since the imputed rents are based on differing dollar bases.

It is therefore apparent that the values of Φ derived from the removal of excise taxes or tariffs or the removal of monopolistic pricing policies can in no way be used as a conceptual basis in constructing a welfare loss function for the community or in applying a compensation principle. This is so for two major reasons. First, the very value of Φ is in general dependent upon the adjustment path from one equilibrium to the next; no equivalent variation is a function solely of the terminal price-quantity coordinates. Second, the value of equivalent variations derived when money income is held constant is not commensurate with a value derived when money income has varied, as in the case of an actual income transfer.

II. The Constancy of the Marginal Utility of Income

We now inquire as to the conditions under which these surpluses have a common value. Since λ varies when all prices and income change in the same proportion, this question is meaningful only if M is held constant. We are then seeking to find out when

$$\Phi = \int \sum p_i dx_i = - \int \sum x_i dp_i$$

is independent of the path of integration. This integrability holds if $\partial x_i / \partial p_j = \partial x_j / \partial p_i$,

$i, j, = 1, \ldots, n$. As is well known (see Samuelson (1942, 1947); Laurence Lau), this condition implies that the utility function is homothetic (i.e., the income-consumption paths are rays emanating from the origin) or that the income elasticities are all unity.[9]

Geometrically, the relation between exactness of Φ and homotheticity is as follows. Suppose the utility function is homothetic and the consumer is at point X^0 at prices P^0 on utility level U^0. Now decrease prices or increase M by some proportion. The consumer will now attain some higher utility level U^1. Suppose now that he had started at some other point along U^0, say $X^{0'}$ at prices $P^{0'}$. Suppose these prices are lowered, or M increased, by the same proportion as before. Then, since the indifference curves are radial blow-ups of each other, the consumer must achieve a point again on U^1. Thus in this case of homothetic utility functions there is a unique correspondence between utility gains and proportions of income gains, no matter where the consumer starts on U^0; i.e., no matter what price vector he faces initially. This suggests that for homothetic indifference maps, λ, the marginal utility of income, is independent of prices. Indeed, this is the case. As Lau showed, $1/\lambda = 1/\lambda(U) = 1/\lambda(V)$ if, and only if, the utility function U (and hence the indirect utility function V) is homothetic. If $1/\lambda = 1/\lambda(V)$ then

$$\Phi = \int_{V^0}^{V^1} 1/\lambda(V) dV$$

is an ordinary definite integral, dependent only on the initial and final utility levels and not on the path of adjustment.

This analysis can be approached from another direction. From equation (7), λ is seen to be an integrating factor for $d\Phi = \sum x_i dp_i$.

[9] Using the Slutsky equation

$$\frac{\partial x_i}{\partial p_j} = \left(\frac{\partial x_i}{\partial p_j}\right)_U - x_j \frac{\partial x_i}{\partial M},$$

and noting that

$$\left(\frac{\partial x_i}{\partial p_j}\right)_U = \left(\frac{\partial x_j}{\partial p_i}\right)_U$$

always, it immediately follows that all the income elasticities must be unitary.

In other words, the "reciprocity" relation $\partial(\lambda x_i)/\partial p_j = \partial(\lambda x_j)/\partial p_i$, $i, j = 1, \ldots, n$ holds for all utility functions; hence $\lambda d\Phi$ is always an exact differential.[10] If λ is constant, i.e., independent of prices, it can be removed from the integral sign, yielding

$$
\begin{aligned}
[\Phi(P^1) - \Phi(P^0)] &= (1/\lambda) \int \sum \lambda x_i dp_i \\
&= \left(1/\lambda \int dV\right) \\
&= (1/\lambda)(V^1 - V^0)
\end{aligned}
$$

(8)

Hence, in this case the imputed dollar gain is proportional to the utility gain.

To sum up, all the equivalent variations in income are equal when, and only when, the utility function is homothetic. Empirically, alas, this case is unimportant;[11] but in it the line integral generating the shadow prices of utility changes is independent of the adjustment path. When the utility function is not homothetic, literally an infinity of imputed rents can be associated with any given utility change.

III. The Compensating Variations

We now come to the second major class of "consumer's surpluses," the compensating

[10] This can also be proved by direct differentiation:

$$
\frac{\partial(\lambda x_i)}{\partial p_j} = \frac{1}{D} (\lambda^2 D_{ij} + x_j D_{n+1.i} + x_i D_{n+1.j}
$$

$$
+ x_i x_j D_{n+1.n+1}) = \frac{\partial(\lambda x_j)}{\partial p_i}.
$$

where D is the determinant of the bordered Hesian matrix associated with the first-order equations (1) and (2), with D_{ij} the cofactor of the element in the ith row and jth column.

Using an example of Samuelson's (1942), if U is the particular homothetic function $U = \log W$, where W is homogeneous of degree 1, then

$$
\lambda = \sum U_i x_i / M = 1/M \cdot 1/W \sum W_i x_i = 1/M
$$

Hence λ is constant with respect to prices. Since all homothetic utility functions can be expressed as a monotonic transformation of a function of the type above ($U = \log W$), say, $Z = F(U)$, $\lambda_Z = F' \cdot \lambda_U$ is similarly independent of prices.

[11] There are, however, important special cases where homotheticity may hold—specifically, in intertemporal analysis. See, for example, Milton Friedman's analysis of the consumption function.

variations, defined as the change in money income needed to exactly offset the gain (loss) in utility due to a fall (rise) in one or more prices. In the context of the present analysis the concept is an attempt to avoid the path-depending problems associated with the equivalent variations. Differentiating the budget constraint totally,

$$
dM = \sum x_i dp_i + \sum p_i dx_i
$$

Since the individual remains on the same indifference level,

$$
dU = dV = \lambda \sum p_i dx_i = 0
$$

Hence,

$$
(10) \quad M^0 - M^1 = - \int_{p^0}^{p^1} \sum x_i dp_i
$$

independently of the path of integration. Alternatively, since U is constant, the symmetry of the substitution matrix yields $\partial x_i/\partial p_j = \partial x_j/\partial p_i$; hence when income-compensated demands are used, $\sum x_i dp_i$ is an exact differential. When only one price changes, say p_1, then the compensating change in income equals the area to the left of the compensated demand curve, or

$$
- \int_{p_1^0}^{p_1^1} x_1 dp_1
$$

This measure is not, in general, invariant with respect to the utility level the consumer is held to; only in the case of vertically parallel indifference curves will this special property occur.[12]

The significance of the path independence of the compensating variations is that it is possible to associate a unique money income change with any change in prices, as long as

[12] $\dfrac{\partial(M^0 - M^1)}{\partial U^0}$

$$
= - \int_{p_1^0}^{p_1^1} \frac{\partial x_1}{\partial U^0} dp_1 \gtrless 0 \quad as \quad \frac{\partial x_1}{\partial U^0} \gtrless 0
$$

i.e., as x_1 is a superior or inferior good. The intermediate case (invariance with respect to the level of utility of the compensating variation) is a vertical income-consumption path. See, for example, Patinkin.

the consumer remains on the same indifference level. The only data needed to calculate the compensating changes in income are the terminal price vectors. No attention need be given to the adjustment path; hence, it is possible to meaningfully formulate questions such as, "How much will an individual pay for the privilege of purchasing a commodity at a lower price?" or "How much compensation is needed for an individual to voluntarily accept a higher price?" or "How much in addition to what a consumer now pays for the amount x of good X would the consumer be willing to pay for x rather than go without any X?" These questions, which relate to changes in money income needed to hold utility constant, have meaningful, unique answers because of the path-independence property of compensating variations.

This path independence, though not generally recognized as such, has led economists to attempt to substitute the compensating variations for the equivalent variations in income, as a welfare measure. These efforts are futile, as we now demonstrate for the particular case of a fall in one price.

The ordinary demand curve lies to the right of the compensated demand curve in the case of a "normal" good as price is lowered; hence the dollar gain imputed to a lowering of, say, p_1

$$\Phi = -\int_{p_1^0}^{p_1^1} x_1 dp_1$$

is greater than the corresponding compensating variation, or vice versa in the case of an inferior good. However, in the light of the discussion relating to the meaning of equivalent variations when money income changed, it is apparent that these equivalent and compensating variations cannot meaningfully be compared. As Hicks (1959) showed, the compensating variation above, where $U = U^0$, equals the equivalent variation for a fall in price, as described in Section I, paragraph 2 above. As shown there, this equivalent variation is not commensurate with the area to the left of the uncompensated demand curve. It is true that for "small" variations in price (i.e., if the price change causes small changes

in utility) the two areas approximate each other. But equivalent variations and compensating variations are clearly two different concepts. The former imputes a dollar evaluation to a change in utility levels for a particular path of price changes, while the latter derives dollar values necessary to hold utility constant when prices change, over any path of adjustment. There is no reason to expect these values to be comparable in any way.

Consider again the area to the left of the uncompensated demand curve. Graphical analyses of this area made by Harberger (1964) and by David Winch agree with the approach presented in this paper insofar as explicit attention is given to the adjustment path. Winch correctly derives the "Marshallian Triangle" as the limit of a sum of compensating variations in income that a consumer would be willing to pay for the privilege of consuming at a slightly lower price, always assuming, however, that he never actually pays those amounts. Winch did not show, however, that all of the equivalent variations can be so derived. If a different adjustment path of prices were specified, the limit of the sum of the compensating variations the consumer would be *willing* to pay (not actually pay) along this new path would, in general, differ from the original sum, even though the initial and final price vectors were not changed. This crucial point alone invalidates the assertion that the Marshallian area is *the* consumer's gain.

If the consumer actually makes payment at each point along the adjustment path he would no longer be on his ordinary demand curve but rather on his compensated curve. In noting this aspect of the Marshallian area, Winch described it as the "consumer's gain." A characteristic of this gain, or shadow price as it is called here, is that it can be captured only by the consumer. A perfectly discriminating monopolist having sufficient information could capture an amount equal to the area to the left of the compensated demand curve (which for noninferior goods is less than the consumer's gain). This case, in which any attempt to manipulate the experiment fundamentally changes the phenomenon being observed, further indicates the futility of using equivalent variations as welfare measures.

Harberger (1964) is less precise about the areas involved, and eventually he returns to the compensated curves. His analysis, dealing explicitly with the shifting of demand curves for the commodities whose prices have not changed, is precisely the evaluation of the line integral

$$\Phi = \int \sum p_i dx_i$$

for a single price change, his rectangles being $p_i^0(x_i^0 - x_i^1)$, $i = 2, \ldots, n$.[13] However, both Harberger (1964) and Winch ignored the natural generalization of their analyses presented in this paper and therefore did not explore the path-dependency aspects of their results.[14] Their analyses mistakenly imply that the derived welfare gains or losses are unique with respect to the terminal price coordinates. As we have shown, and will perhaps clarify in an example below, an infinity of such shadow gains is associated with the simple act of lowering even one price.

IV. Extreme Values of Φ: An Important Example

Returning now to the general unrestricted case of stable ordinary demand curves, we inquire whether such a path may exist between (P^0, M^0) and (P^1, M^0) that the line integral Φ has an interior extremum. This can be formulated as:

$$(12) \quad \max - \int_{p^0}^{p^1} \sum x_i dp_i \quad \text{or}$$

$$\min \int_{p^0}^{p^1} \sum x_i dp_i$$

The necessary conditions for these two problems are the same; we consider only the maximum case. Parameterizing this as $p_i = p_i(t)$, $p_i^0 = p_i(t^0)$, $p_i^1 = p_i(t^1)$, one gets

[13] Harberger deals with "tax revenue constant" demand curves, hence his resulting area does not correspond exactly to that presented in this paper.

[14] In an earlier article, Harberger (1954) mentions the path dependency of his results but chooses to assume away the problem.

$$(13) \quad \max - \int_{T^0}^{T^1} \left(\sum x_i \dot{p}_i \right) dt$$

Since this is a fixed end-point problem, the Euler-Lagrange conditions of control theory can be applied. They yield the matrix equation

$$(14) \quad (x_{ij} - x_{ji})(\dot{p}_i) = (0),$$

where

$$x_{ij} = \frac{\partial x_i}{\partial p_j}$$

Nontrivial solutions can appear only if the matrix $(x_{ij} - x_{ji})$ is singular. Since this is not the case in general, Φ will not have an interior maximum or minimum. A special case where (14) is satisfied is when $\partial x_i / \partial p_j = \partial x_j / \partial p_i$. Under these conditions, all paths generate the same value of Φ, hence a trivial extremum. The linearity in $\dot{p}_i$ of the integrand in (13) is clearly the reason why no interior extremum can exist.

As an example of the possibilities for identifying money income changes with given utility changes, consider the utility function $U = (\log x_1) + x_2$.[15] (See Figure 1.) Since M is

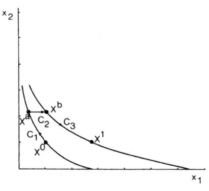

FIGURE 1

[15] The indifference curves here are vertically parallel, and the price consumption path for x_1 is horizontal. These properties make the arithmetic easier but in no way destroy the meaning of the results, since these properties are irrelevant to equivalent variations.

to be held constant, let $M = 1$. The associated demand curves are

$$x_1 = p_2/p_1, \; x_2 = 1/p_2 - 1, \; p_2 < 1$$

Let the consumer be initially at $X^0 = (1, 1)$ at prices $P^0 = (1/2, 1/2)$ with $U^0 = 1$. Suppose p_1 is lowered to $1/2e$, yielding the terminal point $X^1 = (e, 1)$, $P^1 = (1/2e, 1/2)$; $U^1 = 2$. What dollar values can the consumer impute to this change in utility?

Let us evaluate $\Phi = \int_C 1/\lambda \, dV$ over the following path. Starting at P^0, change relative prices so as to move the consumer along U^0 to some point X^a at (p_1^a, p_2^a). (Call this branch C_1.) Now lower p_1, moving the consumer out to X^b on U^1 at prices (p_1^b, p_2^a). (Call this path C_2.) Now change relative prices to move the consumer along U^1 to X^1 at P^1 above (path C_3). Along C_1 and C_3 Φ is zero. Along C_2, since p_2 is constant,

$$\Phi = - \int_{p_1}^{p_1^b} x_1 dp_1 = - \int_{p_1^a}^{p_1^b} \frac{p_2^a}{p_1} \, dp_1$$

$$(12) \qquad = - p_2^a \log p_1 \Big|_{p_1^a}^{p_1^b}$$

$$= p_2^a(\log p_1^a - \log p_2^a)$$

The indirect utility function is $V = \log p_2 - \log p_1 + 1/p_2 - 1$. Hence, the change in utility in moving from X^a to X^b is

$$V^b - V^a = \left(\log p_2^a - \log p_1^b + \frac{1}{p_2^a} - 1 \right)$$

$$(13) \qquad - \left(\log p_2^a - \log p_1^a + \frac{1}{p_2^a} - 1 \right)$$

$$= \log p_1^a - \log p_1^b$$

Substituting this into Φ yields

$$(14) \qquad \Phi = p_2^a(V^b - V^a)$$

In this example $V^b - V^a = U^1 - U^0 = 1$, and $0 < p_2^a < 1$. Hence the imputed value of the one unit gain in utility can be any real number between zero and one! No reason appears why an example could not be constructed yielding any real number as an imputed value of a finite utility gain. The upper bound on Φ in this example is produced by the intersection of the indifference curves with the horizontal axis.

V. Concluding Remarks: Are the Eqivalent and Compensating Variations in Income of Any Use in Economic Analysis?

The above analysis and example demonstrate the arbitrary nature of the assignment of dollar values to utility changes. If the price change is abrupt and discontinuous in nature, then simply no dollar value can be associated with the resulting equilibrium change.

Suppose a dam is constructed which lowers the marginal costs of electricity, local recreation, and irrigation. In evaluating what benefit consumers would place on this project, some assumption must be made about the price adjustment path. Curiously paradoxical is the fact that a given consumer will impute a different shadow price to the project if first the price of electricity is lowered, then that of irrigation, and then of recreation, than if prices were lowered in some other sequence; yet the nagging truth remains that nothing can be done to correct such an inconsistency. It is therefore time, at long last, for economists to abandon the term "welfare loss" in their discussions of monopolies, tariffs, etc. If the term were merely ambiguous, the analysis could be narrowed and at some cost the term could be meaningfully applied. However, the phrase simply has no meaning at all. It is impossible to construct the function depicted in the introduction to this paper which designates welfare loss as a function of a set of price distortions.

Where, then, are we to turn? Are economists doomed to making strictly ordinal comparisons of alternative equilibria? Not quite, I think. The compensating variations in income are not path dependent and are, hence, well defined. However, to merely substitute the compensating variations for the equivalent variations as a measure of welfare loss or

COMMUNICATIONS 951

gain (as Harberger (1954, 1964) and others do) is to use the inappropriate to measure the undefinable.[16] The following alternative, however, is within the realm of positive economics: statistically estimated ordinary demand curves, together, perhaps, with estimates of income elasticities can be used to obtain approximations to the compensating variations in income. When a public-policy decision implies that some will be net losers, the compensating variations give well-defined measures of how much money income would have to be transferred to those individuals to restore them to a just-as-preferred position. Similarly, estimates can be derived as to the amounts which could be extracted from the net gainers and still leave them at just-as-preferred positions. Data of this sort can be provided; however, this is all that the economist, *qua* economist can provide.[17]

It is now generally recognized that where a public policy will result in both losers and gainers, value judgments are involved in the decisions whether to implement the policy at all and, if so, whether to make compensations. These decisions are necessarily made via the political process; however, by providing knowledge of the relevant compensating variations associated with policy decisions, economists may contribute information useful in the formulating of means of payment and the policing of benefits.

Scientific objectivity requires that areas to the left of empirical demand curves be regarded as estimates of compensating variations in money income and not some vague idea of consumers' gains from utility changes. In this context, consumer's surplus may be a

useful policy tool. It would be nice if there were always a unique one-to-one correspondence between utility changes and money-income changes. Much of welfare economics would be drastically simplified. However, it simply is not so.

REFERENCES

R. C. Bishop, "The Effects of Specific and Ad Valorum Taxes," *Quart. J. Econ.*, May 1968, *82*, 198–218.

M. Friedman, *A Theory of the Consumption Function*, Princeton 1957.

W. M. Gorman, "Notes on Divisia Indices," unpublished.

A. C. Harberger, "Monopoly and Resource Allocation," *Amer. Econ. Rev. Proc.*, May 1954, *44*, 77–87.

———, "Taxation, Resource Allocation, and Welfare," in *The Role of Direct and Indirect Taxes in the Federal Revenue System*, Princeton 1964.

J. R. Hicks, *A Revision of Demand Theory*, Oxford 1959.

———, *Value and Capital*, Oxford 1946.

H. Hotelling, "The General Welfare in Relation to Problems of Taxation and of Railway and Utility Rates," *Econometrica*, 1938, *6*, 242–269; reprinted in *Readings in Welfare Economics*, Homewood 1969.

H. S. Houthakker, "Additive Preferences," *Econometrica*, Apr. 1960, *28*, 244–57.

———, "A Note on Self Dual Preferences," *Econometrica*, Oct. 1965, *33*, 797–801.

L. J. Lau, "Duality and the Structure of Utility Functions," *J. Econ. Theor.*, Dec. 1969, *1*, 374–95.

E. J. Mishan, "A Survey of Welfare Economics, 1939–59," *Econ. J.*, June 1960, *70*, 197–256.

J. N. Morgan, "The Measurement of Gains and Losses," *Quart. J. Econ.*, Feb. 1948, *62*, 287–308.

D. Patinkin, "Demand Curves and Consumer's Surplus," in C. F. Christ et al., eds., *Measurement in Economics*, Stanford 1963.

P. A. Samuelson, "The Constancy of the Marginal Utility of Income," in O. Lange et al., eds., *Studies in Mathematical Economics and Econometrics in Memory of Henry Schultz,*

---

[16] It seems strange, at best, to use as a measure of consumer's benefits a construct which explicitly assumes that individuals remain at the same level of utility.

[17] The above analysis should not be construed to mean that the concept of a consumer's surplus as a compensating variation is not a useful construction in positive economic analysis. The test for its usefulness lies in the refutable hypothesis it generates. I feel that such a consumer's surplus concept is probably of substantial use in the analysis of such problems as monopolistic price discrimination, price controls, and theories of political behavior, to mention just a few.

Chicago 1942; reprinted in *The Collected Scientific Papers of Paul A. Samuelson*, Cambridge 1965.

——, *Foundations of Economic Analysis*, Cambridge 1947.

——, "Using Full Duality to Show that Simultaneously Additive Direct and Indirect Utilities Implies Unitary Price Elasticity of Demand," *Econometrica*, Oct. 1965, *33*, 781–96.

D. Schwartzman, "The Burden of Monopoly," *J. Polit. Econ.*, Dec. 1960, *68*, 627–30.

M. Sono, "Relative Effects of Output from Choice Theory," *Keizai Ronso*, 1943, *6*, 57.

A. E. Taylor, *Advanced Calculus*, New York 1955.

D. M. Winch, "Consumers Surplus and the Compensation Principle," *Amer. Econ. Rev.*, June 1965, *55*, 395–423.

H. Wold, *Demand Analysis*, New York 1953.

[17]

Consumer's Surplus Without Apology

By ROBERT D. WILLIG*

The purpose of this paper is to settle the controversy surrounding consumer's surplus[1] and, by so doing, to validate its use as a tool of welfare economics. I will show that observed consumer's surplus can be rigorously utilized to estimate the unobservable compensating and equivalent variations—the correct theoretical measures of the welfare impact of changes in prices and income on an individual.

I derive precise upper and lower bounds on the percentage errors of approximating the compensating and equivalent variations with consumer's surplus. These bounds can be explicitly calculated from observable demand data, and it is clear

* Economic Research Department, Bell Laboratories. This paper is drawn from doctoral research done at Stanford University under the guidance of Jim Rosse. I am grateful for his support and for the standards of professional excellence he tried to teach me. I would also like to thank Megina Jack for considerable editorial assistance.

[1] Throughout, the term consumer's surplus is used to refer to the area to the left of an individual's fixed-income (Marshallian) demand curve and between the relevant price horizontals. The concept of consumer's surplus originated in 1844 (see Jules Dupuit) and has been controversial ever since. Alfred Marshall, who popularized the tool, stipulated that for it to be validly used the marginal utility of money must be constant (Marshall, p. 842 or David Katzner, p. 152). However, Harold Hotelling wrote that consumer's surpluses "give a meaningful measure of social value. This breaks down if the variations under consideration are too large a part of the total economy of the person . . ." (p. 289). John Hicks too, stated only a gentle caution: "In order that the Marshallian measure of consumer's surplus should be a good measure, one thing alone is needful—that the income effect should be small" (p. 177). More recently, though, Paul Samuelson (pp. 194–95) concluded that consumer's surplus is a worse than useless concept (because it confuses), and I.M.D. Little (p. 180) agreed, calling it no more than a "theoretical toy." Nonetheless, theorists and cost-benefit analysts have persisted in their use of the tool. For justification they resort (see E. J. Mishan, pp. 337–38, for example), with no formal theoretical support, to statements similar to those quoted above from Hotelling and Hicks.

that in most applications the error of approximation will be very small. In fact, the error will often be overshadowed by the errors involved in estimating the demand curve. The results in no way depend upon arguments about the constancy of the marginal utility of income.

Consequently, this paper supplies specific empirical criteria which can replace the apologetic caveats frequently employed by those who presently apply consumer's surplus. Moreover, the results imply that consumer's surplus is usually a very good approximation to the appropriate welfare measures.

To preview, below I establish the validity of these rules of thumb: For a single[2] price change, if $|\bar{\eta}A/2m^0| \leq .05$, $|\underline{\eta}A/2m^0| \leq .05$, and if $|A/m^0| \leq .9$, then

$$(1) \qquad \frac{\underline{\eta}|A|}{2m^0} \leq \frac{C-A}{|A|} \leq \frac{\bar{\eta}|A|}{2m^0}$$

and

$$(2) \qquad \frac{\underline{\eta}|A|}{2m^0} \leq \frac{A-E}{|A|} \leq \frac{\bar{\eta}|A|}{2m^0}$$

Here, A = consumer's surplus area under the demand curve and between the two prices (positive for a price increase and negative for a price decrease)

C = compensating variation corresponding to the price change

E = equivalent variation corresponding to the price change

m^0 = consumer's base income

$\bar{\eta}$ and $\underline{\eta}$ = respectively the largest and smallest values of the income

[2] While I restrict attention to single price changes here, analogous, but more complex formulae are derived for multiple price changes in my papers (1973a, b).

elasticity of demand in the region under consideration.

The formulae place observable bounds on the percentage errors of approximating the C or E conceptual measures with observable A. For example, if the consumer's measured income elasticity of demand is 0.8 and if the surplus area under the demand curve between the old and new prices is 5 percent of income, then the compensating variation is within 2 percent of the measured consumer's surplus.

The ratio $|A|/m^0$ can be interpreted as a measure of the proportional change in real income due to the price change.[3] In most applications, the ratio will be very small. Measured income elasticities of demand tend to cluster closely about 1.0, with only rare outliers. Thus it can be expected that $\bar{\eta}|A|/2m^0$, the most important of the terms in (1) and (2), will usually be small enough to permit conscious and unapologetic substitution of A for C or E in studies of individual welfare.[4]

Should $\eta|A|/2m^0$ be large, A would not be close to C and E. For such rare cases, formulae are provided below in Section IV which enable the estimation of C and E from the observable $\bar{\eta}$, η, m^0, and A.

I. The Compensating and Equivalent Variations

In this section, I present definitions of conceptual tools to measure the costs or benefits of price changes to an individual consumer. While these theoretical measures are not directly observable, the analysis that follows in succeeding sections will show that they can be empirically estimated with consumer's surplus.

Throughout I will be assuming that the consumer behaves as though he were

choosing his consumption bundle $X = X^1$, $X^2, \ldots, X^n$ to maximize an increasing strictly quasi-concave ordinal utility function $U(X)$ subject to the budget constraint $\sum p_i X^i = m$. The resulting demand functions, denoted $X^i(p, m)$, are assumed to be differentiable. The indirect utility function, defined by

$$l(p, m) \equiv$$

$$U[X^1(p, m), X^2(p, m), \ldots, X^n(p, m)]$$

relates the price and income parameters to the maximum level of utility the consumer can achieve under the resulting budget constraint. Clearly, by nonsatiation, $l(p, m)$ is monotone increasing in income m, and decreasing in prices p.

The indirect utility function can be used to make statements about individual welfare. Let the base, initial situation be characterized by prices p^0 and income m^0, while an alternative situation can be summarized by p', m'. The economic well-being of the consumer in the different situations can be compared by means of the ordinal ranking of the numbers $l(p^0, m^0)$ and $l(p', m')$.

Another way to effect this welfare test is to compare the income change $m' - m^0$ to the smallest income adjustment needed to make the consumer indifferent to the change in prices from p^0 to p'. If $m' - m^0$ is larger, then welfare is greater in the new situation, and inversely.

This test level of income adjustment is called the compensating income variation, denoted by C below. Symbolically,

$$(3) \qquad l(p^0, m^0) = l(p', m^0 + C)$$

The welfare test above

$$(4) \quad l(p', m') \gtreqless l(p^0, m^0) \quad \text{as} \quad m' - m^0 \gtreqless C$$

follows immediately from (3) by nonsatiation. Thus the compensating variation is an individual's cost-benefit concept which makes price changes perfectly commensurable with changes in

[3] Or the ratio can be interpreted using the words of Hotelling quoted in fn. 1 as the relative size of the variation.

[4] Formulae (1) and (2) reflect the cautions (see fn. 1) of both Hotelling and Hicks.

income.

Similarly, the equivalent variation in income (E) can be defined[5] by

(5) $\qquad l(p^0, m^0 - E) = l(p', m^0)$

In words, $-E$ is the income change which has the same welfare impact on the consumer in the base situation as have the changes in prices from p^0 to p'. It reduces the impacts of different price changes down to the single dimension of income. As such, the equivalent variation concept can be used to rank the consumer's levels of well-being under various sets of prices. With the definitions $l(p^0, m^0 - E') = l(p', m^0)$ and $l(p^0, m^0 - E'') = l(p'', m^0)$, these welfare tests, too, follow from nonsatiation:

(6) $\quad l(p', m^0) \gtreqless l(p'', m^0)$ as $E'' \gtreqless E'$

$\quad l(p', m^0) \gtreqless l(p^0, m') \quad$ as $\quad m^0 - E \gtreqless m'$

The welfare tests (4) and (6) show that the compensating and equivalent variations are cost-benefit concepts which can be used to evaluate the impact of microeconomic policy on an individual.[6] These concepts derive practical importance from the fact that they can be estimated from observable consumer's surplus.

II. Consumer's Surplus

The compensating and equivalent variations can be most incisively studied and related to consumer's surplus by means of the income compensation function.[7] This is denoted by $\mu(p \mid p^0, m^0)$ and is defined to be the least income required by the consumer when he faces prices p to achieve the same utility level he could enjoy (by

maximizing behavior) under the parameters p^0, m^0. Thus, by definition,

(7) $\qquad l[p, \mu(p \mid p^0, m^0)] = l(p^0, m^0)$

Trivially, we have

(8) $\qquad \mu(p^0 \mid p^0, m^0) = m^0$

Now, we can see that the compensating and equivalent variations can be expressed or redefined in terms of the income compensation function. From (3), $m^0 + C = \mu(p' \mid p^0, m^0)$, or combining with (8),

(9) $\quad C = \mu(p' \mid p^0, m^0) - \mu(p^0 \mid p^0, m^0)$

Similarly, from (5), $m^0 - E = \mu(p^0 \mid p', m^0)$, or

(10) $\quad E = \mu(p' \mid p', m^0) - \mu(p^0 \mid p', m^0)$

These relationships serve as the bridge to consumer's surplus.

It is well known[8] that

(11) $\quad \dfrac{\partial \mu(p \mid p^0, m^0)}{\partial p_i} = X^i(p, \mu(p \mid p^0, m^0))$

This system of partial differential equations, together with the boundary condition (8), is the heart of analytical welfare economics.[9] The compensating and equivalent variations, or any measure of individual welfare that accepts the individual's own consumption preferences, can be calculated from the complete demand functions via (11) and (8).

Restricting attention to changes in a single price, p_1, let $p^0 = (p_1^0, p_2^0, \ldots, p_n^0)$ and $p' = (p_1', p_2^0, \ldots, p_n^0)$. Use the Fundamental Theorem of Calculus and (11) to rewrite (9) and (10) as

---

[5] The definitions (3) and (5) correspond to those of Hicks, p. 177, and Samuelson, p. 199.

[6] They also can serve as building blocks for methodologies to make social welfare judgments. The Compensation Principle is a well-known example (see Tibor Scitovsky).

[7] This theoretical tool was introduced by Lionel McKenzie, and definitively studied by Leonid Hurwicz and Hirofumi Uzawa.

[8] See Hurwicz and Uzawa for a state-of-the-art derivation. Heuristically, (11) says that the first-order income change, $d\mu$, required to compensate for the price increase, dp_1, is just the augmentation needed to buy the old consumption bundle, $X(p, \mu, (p \mid p^0, m^0))$, at the new prices $p_1 + dp_1, p_2, \ldots, p_n$, rather than at the old prices p. The irrelevance to this calculation of the concomitant substitution effects is the result of the envelope theorem.

[9] This point of view was taken by Herbert Mohring.

(12) $C = \int_{p_1^0}^{p_1'} X^1(p_1, p_2^0, \ldots, p_n^0,$

$\mu(p_1, p_2^0, \ldots, p_n^0 | p_1^0, p_2^0, \ldots, p_n^0, m^0))dp_1$

(13) $E = \int_{p_1^0}^{p_1'} X^1(p_1, p_2^0, \ldots, p_n^0,$

$\mu(p_1, p_2^0, \ldots, p_n^0 | p_1', p_2^0, \ldots, p_n^0, m^0))dp_1$

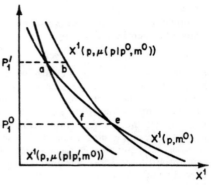

FIGURE 1

These formulae express the compensating and equivalent variations as areas under demand curves, between the old and new price horizontals. The demand curves are not Marshallian in that the income parameters are not constant. Instead, they are Hicksian compensated demand curves, because the income parameters include compensation which varies with the price to keep the consumer at a constant level of utility. The only distinction between C and E in (12) and (13) is the level of utility the compensation is designed to reach.

Referring to Figure 1, C is the area $p_1^0 p_1' b e$ under the demand curve compensated to $l(p^0, m^0)$. This curve crosses the Marshallian curve $X^1(p, m^0)$ at p_1^0, since $\mu(p^0 | p^0, m^0) = m^0$. With $p_1' > p_1^0$, if X^1 is noninferior $(\partial X^1/\partial m \geq 0)$ this compensated curve lies above the Marshallian one for $p_1 > p_1^0$, since $\mu(p_1, p_2^0, \ldots, p_n^0 | p^0, m^0) \geq m^0$ whenever $p_1 > p_1^0$. Similarly, E is the area $p_1^0 p_1' a f$ under the demand curve compensated to $l(p', m^0)$. This Hicksian curve crosses the Marshallian one at p_1', and lies below it for $p_1 < p_1'$. The area usually called consumer's surplus is $p_1^0 p_1' a e$, defined by the observable Marshallian demand curve. Denoting this area by A, we have, then, $C \geq A \geq E$, for noninferior X^1 (the inequalities reverse for X^1 inferior). Of course, it also follows immediately that if there is no income effect $(\partial X^1/\partial m \equiv 0)$, $C = A = E$.

These qualitative results may be useful for some cost-benefit analyses. For example, suppose a policy would raise both an individual's income and the price of a noninferior good. If the observable consumer's surplus area A were greater than the income boost, it could be inferred from the inequality that C also would be greater. Then, from the welfare test (4), an analyst could conclude that the policy would be injurious to the consumer.

However, usually more information than this is needed about C and E. What is required is a methodology to estimate the welfare measures from observable data. In the next section I show how C and E can be explicitly calculated from observables when the income elasticity of demand is constant.

III. Constant Income Elasticity

Constant income elasticity of demand for X^1 means that

$$\frac{\partial X^1(p, m)}{\partial m} \cdot \frac{m}{X^1(p, m)} \equiv \eta$$

Then, we have the simple differential equation $dX^1/X^1 = \eta(dm/m)$ which can be integrated from $X^1(p, m^0)$ to yield

$$X^1(p, m) = X^1(p, m^0)\left[\frac{m}{m^0}\right]^\eta$$

The entire income compensation function can be derived by substituting this expression into (11) and solving the resulting differential equation with boundary condition (8). We have, suppressing unchanging arguments,

$$\frac{d\mu}{dp_1} = X^1(p_1, \mu) = X^1(p_1, m^0)\left[\frac{\mu}{m^0}\right]^\eta$$

or

$$\mu^{-\eta}d\mu = (m^0)^{-\eta}X^1(p_1, m^0)dp_1$$

Then, integration between p_1^0 and p_1', remembering that $\mu(p_1^0) = m^0$, yields

$$(14) \quad \frac{[\mu(p_1')]^{1-\eta} - [m^0]^{1-\eta}}{1-\eta} =$$

$$(m^0)^{-\eta}\int_{p_1^0}^{p_1'} X^1(p_1, m^0)dp_1$$

for $\eta \neq 1$, and for $\eta = 1$,

$$\ln \mu(p_1') - \ln m^0 = \frac{1}{m^0}\int_{p_1^0}^{p_1'} X^1(p_1, m^0)dp_1$$

Hence, after rearranging we have these explicit expressions for the income compensation function:

$$(15) \quad \mu(p_1'|p_1^0, m^0) =$$

$$m^0\left[1 + \left(\frac{1-\eta}{m^0}\right)\int_{p_1^0}^{p_1'} X^1(p_1, m^0)dp_1\right]^{1/1-\eta}$$

$$\eta \neq 1$$

$$(16) \quad \mu(p_1'|p_1^0, m^0) =$$

$$(m^0)\exp\left[\frac{1}{m^0}\int_{p_1^0}^{p_1'} X^1(p_1, m^0)dp_1\right]$$

$$\eta = 1$$

These give the welfare measure μ in terms of the potentially observable constant income elasticity of demand and the consumer's surplus area under the Marshallian demand curve. Let us denote this area by

$$(17) \quad A \equiv \int_{p_1^0}^{p_1'} X^1(p_1, m^0)dp_1$$

From (15), we see that if $\eta = 0$, $\mu(p_1'|p_1^0, m^0) = m^0 + A$. However, from (16)

we see that if preferences are homothetic, the consequent unitary η does not imply any equalities among C, E, and A. Below, for expositional convenience, I ignore the case $\eta = 1$.

Recalling the definitions of C and E, (9) and (10), and loosely applying to (15) this Taylor approximation,

$$(1 + t)^{1/1-\eta} \approx 1 + \frac{t}{1-\eta} + \frac{\eta t^2}{2(1-\eta)^2}$$

(where $\approx$ means "approximately equal to"), we get:

$$C \approx A + \frac{\eta A^2}{2m^0}, \qquad E \approx A - \frac{\eta A^2}{2m^0}$$

$$\frac{C-A}{A} \approx \frac{\eta A}{2m^0} \quad \text{and} \quad \frac{A-E}{A} \approx \frac{\eta A}{2m^0}$$

This was the striking result on the percentage error of approximating C with A which was previewed in the introduction. The next section will establish this formula rigorously for nonconstant income elasticity of demand.

IV. Estimation Results

Assume that in the region of price-income space under consideration,[10] $\bar{\eta}$ and η are upper and lower bounds, respectively, on $(\partial X^1(p, m)/\partial m)(m/X^1(p, m))$, with neither equal to 1.[11] It follows from the Mean Value Theorem that

$$(18) \quad \left(\frac{m_2}{m_1}\right)^{\underline{\eta}} \leq \frac{X^1(p, m_2)}{X^1(p, m_1)} \leq \left(\frac{m_2}{m_1}\right)^{\bar{\eta}}$$

$$\text{for } m_2 \geq m_1$$

Let us consider the welfare impact of a price increase from p_1^0 to p_1'. Since $\mu(p_1|p^0, m^0) \geq \mu(p_1'|p^0, m^0)$ for $p_1 \geq p_1^0$, we can set $m_2 = \mu(p_1)$ and $m_1 = \mu(p_1^0) = m^0$ in (18):

---

[10] This region is $\{(p, m): p_1 = \alpha p_1^0 + (1-\alpha)p_1', 0 \leq \alpha \leq 1; p_i = p_i^0, i \neq 1; m = \gamma m^0 + (1-\gamma)\mu(p|p^0, m^0), 0 \leq \gamma \leq 1;$ and $X^1(p, m) > 0\}$.

[11] Either $\bar{\eta}$ or $\underline{\eta}$ can be arbitrarily close to 1.

$$\left[\frac{\mu(p_1)}{m^0}\right]^{\eta} \leq \frac{X^1(p_1, \mu(p_1))}{X^1(p_1, m^0)} \leq \left[\frac{\mu(p_1)}{m^0}\right]^{\bar{\eta}}$$

Rearranging, and substituting from (11) yields

$$0 \leq X^1(p, m^0)^{-\eta} \leq \frac{\partial \mu(p)}{\partial p_1}[\mu(p)]^{-\eta} =$$

$$\partial\left[\frac{\mu(p)^{1-\eta}}{1-\eta}\right] \Big/ \partial p_1$$

and

$$0 \leq \partial\left[\frac{\mu(p)^{1-\bar{\eta}}}{1-\bar{\eta}}\right] \Big/ \partial p_1 = \frac{\partial\mu(p)}{\partial p_1}\mu(p)^{-\bar{\eta}}$$

$$\leq X^1(p, m^0)(m^0)^{-\bar{\eta}}$$

Integrating these relationships with respect to p_1 between p_1^0 and p_1' (as in (14)) preserves the inequalities. Rearrangement of the resulting relationships yields these bounds:

$$(19) \quad m^0\left[1 + (1-\eta)\frac{A}{m^0}\right]^{1/1-\eta}$$

$$\leq \mu(p' \mid p^0, m^0)$$

$$\leq m^0\left[1 + (1-\bar{\eta})\frac{A}{m^0}\right]^{1/1-\bar{\eta}}$$

provided $\eta, \bar{\eta} \neq 1$, $1 + (1-\eta)\dfrac{A}{m^0} > 0$

and $\quad 1 + (1-\bar{\eta})\dfrac{A}{m^0} > 0$

For the case of a price decrease from p_1^0 to p_1', since $\mu(p_1 \mid p_1^0, m^0) \leq m^0$ for $p_1 \leq p_1^0$, we can set $m_2 = m^0$ and $m_1 = \mu(p_1)$ in (18), and then follow the same sequence of steps. Once again, (19) emerges, but reference to (17) shows that here A is negative.

Invoking the definition (9), (19) can be rewritten as

$$(20) \quad \frac{\left[1 + (1-\eta)\dfrac{A}{m^0}\right]^{1/1-\eta} - 1 - \dfrac{A}{m^0}}{|A|/m^0}$$

$$\leq \frac{C - A}{|A|}$$

$$\leq \frac{\left[1 + (1-\bar{\eta})\dfrac{A}{m^0}\right]^{1/1-\bar{\eta}} - 1 - \dfrac{A}{m^0}}{|A|/m^0}$$

Also, using (10) and reversing the roles of p' and p^0 in (19) (but not in the definition of A) gives

$$(21) \quad \frac{\left[1 - (1-\eta)\dfrac{A}{m^0}\right]^{1/1-\eta} - 1 + \dfrac{A}{m^0}}{|A|/m^0}$$

$$\leq \frac{A - E}{|A|}$$

$$\leq \frac{\left[1 - (1-\bar{\eta})\dfrac{A}{m^0}\right]^{1/1-\bar{\eta}} - 1 + \dfrac{A}{m^0}}{|A|/m^0}$$

The measures of a consumer's welfare can be tightly estimated from observables via (19)–(21), regardless of the size of A/m^0, if $1 \pm (1-\eta)A/m^0 > 0$, $1 \pm (1-\bar{\eta})A/m^0 > 0$, and if η, and $\bar{\eta}$ are sufficiently close in value.[12] Of course, in the limit, as η approaches $\bar{\eta}$, (19) reduces to the constant elasticity formula (15). Moreover, we shall see that if the absolute values of $\eta A/2m^0$ and $\bar{\eta}A/2m^0$ are small, then (20) and (21) reduce to elegant rules of thumb.

Table 1 displays the numerical values of the following coefficients for selected choices of η and a:

[12] The most plausible cause of the negation of these conditions is $(\partial X^1/\partial m)(m/X^1) \to \infty$. However, regions in which X^1 is identically zero can be ignored, since there both μ and A are unchanging. To handle the case in which $X^1 = 0$ and $\partial X^1/\partial m \neq 0$ near the boundary of the relevant region, bounds on μ can be derived from bounds on $\partial X^1/\partial m$. Because these are generally more gross than (19), the best approach is to take this tack only in the vicinity of the singularity, use (19) on the rest of the path of integration, and splice the sets of inequalities together. The formulae for such procedures can be found in my 1973a, b papers. An explicit solution for μ when $\partial X^1/\partial m$ is independent of m is also reported there.

TABLE 1[a]

η	.001	.005	.010	.020	.030	.040	.050	.075	.100	.150	.200	.250
-2.00	-.001	-.005	-.010	-.020	-.030	-.040	-.050	-.075	-.100	-.150	-.200	-.250
	-.001	-.005	-.010	-.019	-.029	-.038	-.046	-.067	-.086	-.121	-.152	-.180
	-.001	-.005	-.010	-.021	-.032	-.043	-.054	-.086	-.121	-.205	-.316	-.480
-1.01	-.001	-.003	-.005	-.010	-.015	-.020	-.025	-.038	-.051	-.076	-.101	-.126
	-.001	-.003	-.005	-.010	-.015	-.019	-.024	-.035	-.046	-.066	-.085	-.102
	-.001	-.003	-.005	-.010	-.016	-.021	-.027	-.041	-.056	-.090	-.129	-.174
.30	.000	.001	.002	.003	.005	.006	.008	.011	.015	.023	.030	.038
	.000	.001	.002	.003	.005	.006	.008	.011	.015	.023	.029	.036
	.000	.001	.002	.003	.005	.006	.008	.011	.015	.023	.031	.039
.50	.000	.001	.003	.005	.008	.010	.013	.019	.025	.038	.050	.063
	.000	.001	.003	.005	.008	.010	.013	.019	.025	.038	.050	.063
	.000	.001	.003	.005	.008	.010	.013	.019	.025	.038	.050	.063
.70	.000	.002	.004	.007	.011	.014	.018	.026	.035	.053	.070	.088
	.000	.002	.004	.007	.011	.014	.018	.027	.035	.054	.072	.090
	.000	.002	.004	.007	.010	.014	.017	.026	.035	.051	.068	.085
.90	.000	.002	.005	.009	.014	.018	.023	.034	.045	.068	.090	.113
	.000	.002	.005	.009	.014	.018	.023	.034	.046	.070	.095	.120
	.000	.002	.004	.009	.013	.018	.022	.033	.044	.065	.085	.105
1.01	.001	.003	.005	.010	.015	.020	.025	.038	.051	.076	.101	.126
	.001	.003	.005	.010	.015	.020	.026	.039	.052	.080	.108	.138
	.001	.003	.005	.010	.015	.020	.025	.037	.049	.072	.094	.116
1.10	.001	.003	.006	.011	.017	.022	.028	.041	.055	.083	.110	.138
	.001	.003	.006	.011	.017	.022	.028	.043	.057	.088	.119	.152
	.001	.003	.006	.011	.016	.022	.027	.040	.053	.078	.102	.125
1.20	.001	.003	.006	.012	.018	.024	.030	.045	.060	.090	.120	.150
	.001	.003	.006	.012	.018	.024	.031	.047	.063	.097	.132	.169
	.001	.003	.006	.012	.018	.024	.029	.043	.057	.084	.110	.134
1.50	.001	.004	.008	.015	.023	.030	.038	.056	.075	.113	.150	.188
	.001	.004	.008	.015	.023	.031	.039	.059	.080	.125	.173	.224
	.001	.004	.007	.015	.022	.029	.036	.054	.070	.102	.132	.160
2.00	.001	.005	.010	.020	.030	.040	.050	.075	.100	.150	.200	.250
	.001	.005	.010	.020	.031	.042	.053	.081	.111	.176	.250	.333
	.001	.005	.010	.020	.029	.038	.048	.070	.091	.130	.167	.200
3.00	.002	.008	.015	.030	.045	.060	.075	.113	.150	.225	.300	.375
	.002	.008	.015	.031	.047	.064	.082	.129	.180	.302	.455	.657
	.002	.008	.015	.029	.043	.056	.069	.100	.129	.180	.226	.266
5.00	.003	.013	.025	.050	.075	.100	.125	.188	.250	.375	.500	.625
	.003	.013	.026	.053	.082	.114	.147	.244	.362	.716	1.477	
	.002	.012	.024	.047	.069	.089	.109	.154	.193	.261	.317	.364
10.00	.005	.025	.050	.100	.150	.200	.250	.375	.500	.750	1.000	1.250
	.005	.026	.053	.115	.186	.271	.374	.774	1.916	**	**	**
	.005	.024	.047	.089	.126	.160	.191	.257	.312	.396	.460	.509

[a] Each group of three numbers includes, from the top, $\eta a/2$, $[(1+(1-\eta)a)^{1/1-\eta}-1-a]/a$, and $[(1-(1-\eta)a)^{1/1-\eta}-1+a]/a$. The entry ** indicates that $(1+(1-\eta)a)<0$.

$$\frac{\eta a}{2}, \qquad \frac{[1 + (1 - \eta)a]^{1/1-\eta} - 1 - a}{a}$$

and

$$\frac{[1 - (1 - \eta)a]^{1/1-\eta} - 1 + a}{a}$$

The latter two expressions encompass the forms of the bounds in (20) and (21), when a is interpreted as $|A|/m^0$.[13] It can

[13] For example, the value of the lower bound in (20) when $\eta = 2$ and $A/m^0 = -.05$ is .048. This can be found in Table 1 as the value of $[(1-(1-\eta)a)^{1/1-\eta}-1+a]/|a|$ when $\eta = 2$ and $a = .05$.

be readily seen from the table that for the ranges of parameter values studied,[14] when $|\eta a/2|$ is small (say less than .05), $\eta a/2$ is close enough (within .005) to the actual bounds for most practical purposes. This numerical observation corroborates the loose application to (15) of the Taylor Series expansion in Section III. More importantly, it establishes the rules of thumb previewed in (1) and (2).[15]

Addition of (1) and (2) yields a check on the numerical proximity of C and E: when $|\eta A/2m^0| \leq .05$, $|\bar{\eta} A/2m^0| \leq .05$, and $|A/m^0| \leq .9$,

$$(23) \qquad \frac{\eta |A|}{m^0} \leq \frac{C - E}{|A|} \leq \frac{\bar{\eta} |A|}{m^0}$$

So, the analysis hinges on the magnitudes of η and A/m^0. As discussed in the introduction, in most practical applications $|\eta A/2m^0|$ and $|A/m^0|$ are likely to be small enough for the rules of thumb to apply. If not, equations (19)–(21) and Table 1 will be useful. Even if the calculated error bounds are too large to be ignored, the compensating and equivalent variations may still be usefully estimated from the data via the formulae.

V. Individual Welfare and Consumer's Surplus

With the approximation results in hand, let us return to the question of how to make statements about individual welfare, based on observable data. Remember from (4) that $l(p', m') \gtreqless l(p^0, m^0)$ as $m' - m^0 \lesseqgtr C$. With the empirical information that $\underline{C} \leq C \leq \bar{C}$, where $\underline{C}$ and $\bar{C}$ can be calculated from (20) or (22), it can be concluded that

$$(24) \quad l(p', m') > l(p^0, m^0), \quad \text{if } m' - m^0 > \bar{C}$$
$$l(p', m') < l(p^0, m^0), \quad \text{if } m' - m^0 < \underline{C}$$

If $\underline{C}$ and $\bar{C}$ are close in value, (24) provides a welfare test of considerable power.[16] If $|\bar{\eta} A/2m^0|$ and $|\eta A/2m^0|$ are small enough, both $\underline{C}$ and $\bar{C}$ can be safely replaced in (24) by A. Otherwise, they can be calculated from η, $\bar{\eta}$, A, and m^0.

To conclude, at the level of the individual consumer, cost-benefit welfare analysis can be performed rigorously and unapologetically by means of consumer's surplus.

[14] These seem to include most values that would be found for these parameters in actual applications.

[15] When $|\eta A/2m^0| \leq .05$ and $|\bar{\eta} A/2m^0| \leq .05$, it suffices for $1 \pm (1-\underline{\eta})A/m^0 > 0$ and $1 \pm (1-\bar{\eta})A/m^0 > 0$ that $|A/m^0| < .9$.

[16] Another welfare comparison (which may be useful for an analysis of social welfare with a Bergsonian social welfare function) is made possible by the fact (see Hurwicz and Uzawa) that $\mu(p^0 | p, m)$, viewed as a function of p and m, is a proper indirect utility function.

$$\mu(p^0 | p, m) = E + m$$

where E is the equivalent variation associated with a change from p^0 to p. Hence this particular ordinal indirect utility function can be exactly expressed by areas under compensated demand curves, as in (13), or it can be estimated from consumer's surplus via (19), (21), or (2).

REFERENCES

K. J. Arrow and T. Scitovsky, *Readings in Welfare Economics*, vol. 12, Homewood 1969.

J. Dupuit, "On the Measurement of the Utility of Public Works," (1844), translated and reprinted in K. J. Arrow and T. Scitovsky, eds., *Readings in Welfare Economics*, vol. 12, Homewood 1969, 255–83.

J. R. Hicks, *A Revision of Demand Theory*, London 1956.

H. Hotelling, "The General Welfare in Relation to Problems of Taxation and of Railway and Utility Rates," reprinted in K. J. Arrow and T. Scitovsky, eds., *Readings in Welfare Economics*, vol. 12, Homewood 1969.

L. Hurwicz and H. Uzawa, "On the Integrability of Demand Functions," in J. S. Chipman et al., eds., *Preferences, Utility, and Demand*, New York 1971, 114–48.

D. Katzner, *Static Demand Theory*, New York 1970.

I. M. D. Little, *A Critique of Welfare Economics*, London 1957.

A. Marshall, *Principles of Economics*, 9th ed., New York 1961.

L. W. McKenzie, "Demand Theory without a Utility Index," *Rev. Econ. Stud.*, June 1957, *24*, 185–89.

E. J. Mishan, *Cost-Benefit Analysis: An Introduction*, New York 1971.

H. Mohring, "Alternative Welfare Gain and Loss Measures," *Western Econ. J.*, Dec. 1971, *9*, 349–68.

P. A. Samuelson, *Foundations of Economic Analysis*, Cambridge 1947.

T. Scitovsky, "A Note on Welfare Propositions in Economics," reprinted in K. J. Arrow and T. Scitovsky, eds., *Readings in Welfare Economics*, vol. 12, Homewood 1969.

R. Willig, (1973a) "Consumer's Surplus: A Rigorous Cookbook," tech. rep. no. 98, Economics Series, Inst. for Mathemat. Stud. in the Soc. Sci., Stanford Univ. 1973.

———, (1973b) "Welfare Analysis of Policies Affecting Prices and Products," memo. no. 153, Center for Research in Econ. Growth, Stanford Univ. 1973.

[18]

Consumer's Surplus in Commodity Space

By ALAN RANDALL AND JOHN R. STOLL*

In an article which is already widely quoted, Robert Willig demonstrated that observed Marshallian consumer's surplus can be rigorously utilized to estimate the (theoretically correct) Hicksian compensating and equivalent variations. Willig's analysis was confined to price space, and thus finds its application in the use of consumer's surplus to evaluate the welfare impacts of price changes.

There is another important area of empirical research in which consumer's surplus finds application: the evaluation of the benefits and costs of proposed projects and programs.[1] In benefit-cost analysis, the economist is often concerned not so much with the welfare impacts of price changes as with the welfare impacts of changes in the bundle of goods, services, and amenities possessed, used, or consumed by individuals. Proposed projects and programs may remove some goods from individual opportunity sets, while introducing new goods; and may decrease the quantities of some goods while increasing the quantities of others. Typically, these changes in individually held bundles of specific goods are not accompanied by directly related and commensurate changes in income (or the value of "all other goods").

The goods affected by proposed projects and programs may include divisible, exclusive goods whose competitive prices can be observed in well-functioning markets. They may also include recreational and environmental amenities, the existence of unique environments and endangered species, and increases or decreases in expected human mortality or morbidity, etc.: goods which

may be in varying degrees indivisible, non-exclusive, and unpriced.

The concern which motivated Willig's article, in particular, that observable consumer's surplus data are usually not in the theoretically correct form, apply to an even greater extent to the estimation of the welfare impacts of changes in the bundle of goods. In the case of priced goods, only Marshallian consumer's surplus is directly observable; for unpriced goods, value data may, depending on the estimation technique used, be in the form of Marshallian consumer's surplus, the Hicksian compensating measure, the Hicksian equivalent measure, or the expenditure function. This paper identifies the conditions under which Willig's conclusion that consumer's surplus data may be rigorously used "without apology" is adaptable to situations in which it is bundles of goods, rather than prices, which are changed.

Our findings, in broad outline, are as follows. (a) For goods which are perfectly divisible and exchanged at zero transactions costs in infinitely large markets, the Hicksian compensating and equivalent variation measures of consumer's surplus are equal in absolute value and are equal to the price multiplied by the quantity change. (b) For goods which are indivisible or lumpy, the Hicksian compensating measure of welfare loss (gain) is larger (smaller) in absolute value than the Marshallian consumer's surplus measure, which in turn is larger (smaller) than the Hicksian equivalent measure.[2] Given information on the price flexibility of income for the good in question, the individual's income and the proportion of that income which is spent on the good, bounds on the difference between the

*University of Kentucky and Texas A&M University, respectively. This paper (no. 79-1-3) is published with the approval of the Director of the Kentucky Agricultural Experiment Station. We appreciate helpful comments from an anonymous reviewer.

[1]See E. J. Mishan for example.

[2]This finding is in contrast to that of Karl-Göran Mäler (pp. 131-40) which has been cited without question by such authors as Charles Cicchetti, Anthony Fisher, and V. Kerry Smith.

compensating and equivalent measures can be rigorously calculated. (c) For divisible goods traded in costly markets (i.e., those where transactions costs are positive), the difference between the compensating and equivalent measures of welfare change will lie in the range identified in the first two cases. The result of case (a) is predicated upon costless postchange adjustments in holdings while that of case (b) is predicated on the impossibility of postchange adjustments.[3] Positive transactions costs impede adjustments in holdings, whereas either prohibitive transactions costs or indivisibility is sufficient to preclude such adjustments.

In pragmatic benefit-cost analysis terms, these findings may be interpreted as follows. When one is dealing with changes in any one individual's holdings of a divisible good which is traded in reasonably competitive and reasonably low-cost markets, the error inherent in using price multiplied by the quantity change is most likely overshadowed by inaccuracies in the estimation of, for example, the technical productivity coefficients which underlie the quantity change projections.[4] For changes in the quantities of indivisible or lumpy goods where the price flexibility of income falls in the typical range and the proportion of total budget spent on the good is small, the

bounds within which the Hicksian compensating and equivalent measures must fall can be rigorously calculated from estimates of Marshallian consumer's surplus; and these bounds will be quite narrow. Thus, the theoretically correct measure can be obtained from the estimates of more readily available value indicators.

However, the analyst is on occasion confronted with the task of evaluating lumpy changes in quantities of specific goods, services, or amenities, where one or more of the following holds: the change is large; the good is highly valued; and the price flexibility of income for the good is high and rises with income. In such cases,[5] our findings offer less comfort. The compensating measure of welfare loss (gain) is likely to be much larger (smaller) in absolute value than the equivalent measure, since the latter (former) is strictly limited by individual budget constraints while the former (latter) is not. While the rigorous bounds derived below remain valid, the information needed to estimate the correct (i.e., compensating, if the welfare criterion is the potential Pareto improvement)[6] measure from other measures more readily available to the analyst is less likely to be obtainable. Thus, in such cases, there may be no good substitute for methods capable of accurately estimating the compensating measure of welfare loss.

In short, the cases that competent benefit-cost analysts consider relatively hazard free are, in fact, relatively hazard free. On the other hand, there are cases (discussed in the preceding paragraph) which, as some benefit-cost analysts have suspected, pose the threat of significant error from the use of Marshallian consumer's surplus and, at the same time, present empirical difficulties to those who seek to estimate the correct measure of welfare change from other more readily available

---

[3]The impossibility of postchange adjustments along a quantity continuum, which may be called indivisibility or lumpiness from the perspective of the individual, may arise from any of several sources: 1) the Samuelsonian public good and congestible public good situations in which the individual consumer cannot continuously adjust his holdings of the good independently of all other individuals; 2) indivisibility in production, such that the good may be produced in one or more discrete quantities and the concept of a parametric unit price is meaningless (the argument of David Bradford is helpful); 3) nonexclusiveness, such that exchange in order to effect postchange adjustment is infeasible; 4) prohibitive transactions costs; and 5) institutional restrictions upon quantity per capita, for example, in the case of hunting where regulations such as bag limitations and hunting seasons prohibit quantity adjustments following changes in these kinds of regulations.

[4]This claim is analogous to Willig's claim (p. 589) that the errors from using Marshallian consumer's surplus will often be overshadowed by errors in estimation of the demand curve.

[5]Proposed projects or programs which have the potential to significantly modify unique environments, endangered species, threatened cultures, or the life and health expectancies of human beings may, under certain circumstances, provide examples.

[6]See Mishan.

measures. Our contribution will be to demonstrate in a rigorous manner that the intuitions of many benefit-cost analysts are in fact valid, and to show that, in those cases which we have indicated are relatively simple, consumer's surplus may be used "without" apology.

I. A Diagrammatic Exposition

Our conclusions are perhaps most readily grasped, at the intuitive level, from a diagrammatic exposition. Let us consider a normal good x, which, depending on the program alternatives chosen, may be provided in two different quantities, Q' and Q'', where Q'' is greater and *ceteris paribus* preferred. The traditional pragmatic measures of value of these two bundles of goods are willingness to pay (WTP) and willingness to accept (WTA). In a market exchange situation, these correspond, respectively, to the buyer's best offer and the seller's reservation price; in a nonmarket situation, they correspond to willingness-to-pay and willingness-to-accept compensation.

If the program alternative under evaluation would reduce the quantity of x from Q'' to Q', the compensating measure of welfare loss is WTA^C, the compensation which would keep the loser at his initial welfare level; and the equivalent measure is WTP^E, the loser's willingness to pay to avoid the quantity reduction from Q'' to Q' which, if paid, would place the loser at his subsequent welfare level. If the proposed program would increase the quantity of x from Q' to Q'', the compensating measure of welfare gain is WTP^C which, if paid, would keep the gainer at his initial welfare level; and the equivalent measure is WTA^E, the compensation which would be needed to bring the potential gainer to his subsequent welfare level in the event that the proposed program is not implemented. At this point, let us emphasize that WTA is not always the compensating measure and WTP is not always the equivalent measure.

Assume x is a perfectly divisible good, traded in infinitely large markets at zero transactions costs at the unit price p. Con-

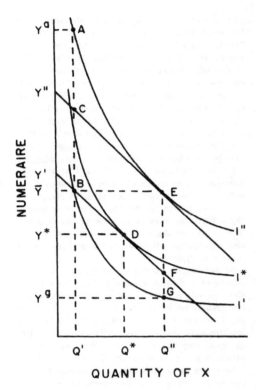

FIGURE 1. THE WELFARE IMPACT OF A CHANGE IN THE QUANTITY OF A GOOD X FROM Q'' TO Q'

sider a proposed program which if implemented would reduce an affected individual's holdings of x from Q'' to Q' while leaving his holdings of Y, a numeraire or a composite of "all other goods," at $\bar{Y}$. In Figure 1, the program would bump the individual from point E to B, lowering his welfare level from I'' to I'. However, there is no good reason for the individual to remain at B. Instead, frictionless markets will permit him to trade along his new budget line until he reaches D and achieves the welfare level I^*. Given this frictionless adjustment, his WTP^E is EF, which is equal to $Y''Y'$ while his WTA^C is BC, which is equal to $Y'Y''$. Thus, WTP^E is equal to WTA^C and both are equal to $p(Q'' - Q')$.

This conclusion can be grasped intuitively by considering that a good traded in infinitely large markets at a constant unit price with zero transactions costs has all the important characteristics of money (i.e., currency). Thus, the well-known result, that *WTA* compensation and permit imposition of a lump sum tax is equal to *WTP* to avoid the same tax and both are equal to the tax itself, applies to this quite restrictive case.

Now, assume that x is a lumpy good and can be held only in the amounts Q'' and Q'. Observe immediately that in the case of indivisible or lumpy goods, since intermediate adjustments in commodity holdings are not permissible, the Hicksian compensating and equivalent measures in commodity space are analogous to the Hicksian surpluses, not the variations, defined over price changes.

In this case and returning to Figure 1, the price lines become meaningless. WTP^E is EG which is equal to Y^gY, and WTA^C is BA, which is equal to $\overline{Y}Y^a$, and larger in absolute value than WTP^E. Note that this finding contrasts vividly with that of Mäler (pp. 131–140), but that Mäler's analysis is valid only if one assumes, trivially, that the individual is indifferent as to whether he holds the indivisible good or not, when its price is zero.

II. Bounds on the Difference between Compensating and Equivalent Measures, Defined in Commodity Space

Now, we derive rigorously the bounds on $WTA - WTP$ for indivisible or lumpy goods, using a formulation which proves, as a special case, that for perfectly divisible goods traded in frictionless markets, $WTA = WTP$. For the convenience of readers and to permit an otherwise unattainable brevity, our analysis at this point follows Willig. The necessary departures from Willig's treatment are explicitly highlighted and explained, while some intermediate steps analogous to those used by Willig are omitted.

Postulating the existence of the utility function $U [P(Q, Y)]$, implicit in prices p, and defined over the numeraire Y, and quantities Q of the good x, we define the following indirect utility function

$$(1) \qquad z(Q, Y) = U[P(Q, Y)]$$

Consider an individual with $\overline{Y}$ units of the numeraire (i.e., the value of "all other goods and endowments"), who is confronted with a change in his bundle of the good x from Q'' to Q', where Q'' represents a greater quantity than Q'. His WTP^E to avoid a change from Q'' to Q' is defined by

$$(2) \qquad z(Q', \overline{Y}) = z(Q'', \overline{Y} - WTP)$$

while his WTA^C to accept a change from Q'' to Q' is defined by

$$(3) \qquad z(Q', \overline{Y} + WTA) = z(Q'', \overline{Y})$$

Using the income compensation function, $\mu(Q|Q'', \overline{Y})$ which represents the least amount of income the individual would require with quantity Q to achieve the same utility level enjoyed with quantity Q'' and $\overline{Y}$, the individual's initial income is

$$(4) \qquad \mu(Q''|Q'', \overline{Y}) = \overline{Y}$$

The *WTP* and *WTA* measures defined in (2) and (3) can be expressed

$$(5) \qquad WTP = \mu(Q'|Q', \overline{Y}) - \mu(Q''|Q', \overline{Y})$$

$$(6) \qquad WTA = \mu(Q'|Q'', \overline{Y}) - \mu(Q''|Q'', \overline{Y})$$

Now the following partial differential equation may be derived (since, although we later define x as a lumpy good, preferences are continuous over Q):

$$(7) \qquad \frac{\partial \mu(Q|Q'', Y)}{\partial Q} = P[Q, \mu(Q|Q'', \overline{Y})]$$

Equation (7) may be treated as a system of equations when x is a vector of goods.

Considering only a change in the quantity of a single good and using the fundamental theorem of calculus,

$$(8) \qquad WTP = \int_{Q'}^{Q''} P[Q, \mu(Q \mid Q', \overline{Y})] dQ$$

$$(9) \qquad WTA = \int_{Q'}^{Q''} P[Q, \mu(Q \mid Q'', \overline{Y})] dQ$$

These equations express WTP and WTA as areas under compensated demand curves. The price axis consists of a range of implicit prices which corresponds to the domain of quantities being considered.

To arrive at bounds for the difference between the Marshallian measure of welfare change, and WTP and WTA, respectively, for a quantity change which permits no subsequent adjustments in the quantity of x, we assume constant price flexibility of income, ζ, for x such that

$$(\partial P(Q,Y)/\partial Y)(Y/P(Q,Y)) \equiv \zeta$$

and follow a procedure similar to Willig's to derive the income compensation function, which is

$$(10) \quad \mu(Q'|Q'',\overline{Y})$$

$$= \overline{Y}\left[1 + \frac{(1-\zeta)}{\overline{Y}} \int_{Q'}^{Q''} P(Q,\overline{Y})dQ\right]^{1/(1-\zeta)}$$

The expression $\int_{Q'}^{Q''} P(Q,\overline{Y})dQ$ can be interpreted as the area under an implicit Marshallian demand curve for the good x. Denoting this expression by M, it is apparent that when $\zeta = 0$ the welfare change measures will be equal to M.

Again following procedures similar to those used by Willig, we obtain

$$(11) \quad \frac{M-WTP}{M} \simeq \frac{\zeta M}{2\overline{Y}}$$

$$(12) \quad \frac{WTA-M}{M} \simeq \frac{\zeta M}{2\overline{Y}}$$

Thus,

$$(13) \quad WTA - WTP \simeq \frac{\zeta M^2}{\overline{Y}}$$

Dropping the assumption of constant price flexibility of income (see Willig, who dropped the assumption of constant income elasticity of demand) the following approximate bounds are appropriate when $\zeta M/2\overline{Y}$ is small (say, $< .05$), and are obtained for WTP and WTA for changes in the bundle of goods:

$$(14) \quad \frac{\xi^L M}{2\overline{Y}} < \frac{M-WTP}{M} < \frac{\xi^u M}{2\overline{Y}}$$

$$(15) \quad \frac{\xi^L M}{2\overline{Y}} < \frac{WTA-M}{M} < \frac{\xi^u M}{2\overline{Y}}$$

where ξ^L and ξ^u are the lower and upper bounds, respectively, on price flexibility of income for the good x. Rigorous bounds, applicable for all values of $\zeta M/2\overline{Y}$, are

$$(16) \quad \frac{\left[1-(1-\xi^L)\dfrac{M}{\overline{Y}}\right]^{1/(1-\xi^L)} - 1 + \dfrac{M}{\overline{Y}}}{M/\overline{Y}}$$

$$< \frac{M-WTP}{M}$$

$$< \frac{\left[1-(1-\xi^u)\dfrac{M}{\overline{Y}}\right]^{1/(1-\xi^u)} - 1 + \dfrac{M}{\overline{Y}}}{M/\overline{Y}}$$

$$(17) \quad \frac{\left[1+(1-\xi^L)\dfrac{M}{\overline{Y}}\right]^{1/(1-\xi^L)} - 1 - \dfrac{M}{\overline{Y}}}{M/\overline{Y}}$$

$$< \frac{WTA-M}{M}$$

$$< \frac{\left[1+(1-\xi^u)\dfrac{M}{\overline{Y}}\right]^{1/(1-\xi^L)} - 1 - \dfrac{M}{\overline{Y}}}{M/\overline{Y}}$$

The critical differences between these bounds for quantity changes and Willig's bounds for price changes are M and ζ in our bounds, and A and η in Willig's. The term A is Marshallian consumer's surplus measured as the area under a demand curve between two alternative prices for x, while M is the area under a demand curve between two quantities of x. Our ζ is the price flexibility of income for x, while Willig's η is the income elasticity of demand for x. An additional difference is that Willig's m is total income, while our $\overline{Y}$ is the amount of the numeraire held by the consumer.

Returning now to the case of a perfectly divisible good traded in frictionless markets, the expressions $P[Q, \mu(Q|Q', \bar{Y})]dQ$ (in equation (8)) and $P[Q, \mu(Q|Q'', \bar{Y})]dQ$ (in equation (9)) can both be replaced with the market price p of the good x. Thus

$$(18) \qquad WTP = \int_{Q'}^{Q''} pdQ = WTA$$

and it is shown that WTP and WTA are equal in value and both equal to $p(Q'' - Q')$.

For completeness, it is appropriate to note that for goods which are exchangeable and divisible, the difference between WTA and WTP becomes nonzero when transactions costs become positive and grows as transactions costs increase. It will, however, reach an upper limit at the point where transactions costs are just sufficiently great to preclude postchange quantity adjustments and will at that point be identical to the difference observed in the case of lumpy goods.[7]

III. Empirical Estimates of the Bounds

Willig presents empirical estimates of the parameters necessary to calculate the bounds on the difference between compensating, equivalent, and Marshallian consumer's surplus measures of the welfare

[7]In order to demonstrate this diagrammatically, it is possible to modify Figure 1 by introducing transactions costs, in the manner of Jürg Neihans, via a kinked budget constraint which touches the zero transactions costs budget constraint at the point denoting the individual's current holdings of x and moves progressively further away from it, always on the low side, as the quantity adjustment becomes larger. In a working paper available upon request from the authors, this diagrammatic analysis is provided, along with a method for approximating, subject to some restrictive assumptions, the bounds on the difference between WTA and WTP when transactions costs are positive but not sufficiently large to preclude any quantity adjustment. For example, if $M/\bar{Y} = 0.02$, the income elasticity of demand for the good x is 0.9 and transactions costs amount to 10 percent of p, the difference between WTA and WTP will be less than 0.36 percent of $p(Q'' - Q')$.

effects of price changes (his Table 1). That table can be adapted to permit calculation of these bounds for measures of the welfare effects of changes in the bundle of goods. If one substitutes $M/\bar{Y}$ for Willig's a in each column heading and ζ for η in each row title, the first entry in each cell of Willig's table becomes an estimate of $\zeta M/2\bar{Y}$ and may be used in empirical application of equations (11)–(13).

Making these adaptations and comparing the first entry in each cell with the second and third entries, it becomes clear that the rule of thumb for approximating WTA, M, or WTP from empirical estimates of any one of them (i.e., equations (11)–(13)) generates quite accurate results when $M/\bar{Y}$ is small, even in cases where ζ is substantially greater than 1. However, as $M/\bar{Y}$ becomes large, the error from using the rule of thumb grows; it becomes very large when both $M/\bar{Y}$ and ζ are large. In the case of a good which is indivisible and highly valued (i.e., $M/\bar{Y}$ is large) and for which the price flexibility of income rises with income, M provides only poor estimates of WTA and WTP, and the rule of thumb (equations (11)–(13)) is unreliable. The rigorous bounds, however, remain valid.

Some comment on ζ, the price flexibility of income, is appropriate. For the case of changes in the quantity of a good for which postchange quantity adjustments are impossible, ζ is the appropriate concept of income elasticity. The relevent concept is not η, which addresses the question of how changes in income affect the quantity of the good purchased at some parametric unit price, but ζ, which addresses the question of how changes in income affect the amount the consumer would spend to enjoy a given unit of the good.[8] For normal goods, $\zeta > 0$. For an especially treasured good, ζ may substantially exceed 1.

[8]The relationship of price flexibility of income, $\zeta = (\partial P(Q, Y)/\partial Y)(Y/P(Q, Y))$, to income elasticity of total value, $(\partial V/\partial Y)\cdot(Y/V)$, is obvious when one considers that $V = \int_0^Q P(Q, Y)dQ$.

REFERENCES

D. F. Bradford, "Benefit-Cost Analysis and Demand Curves for Public Goods," *Kyklos*, No. 4, 1970, *23*, 775 – 91.

C. J. Cicchetti, A. C. Fisher, and V. K. Smith, "An Econometric Evaluation of a Generalized Consumer's Surplus Measure: The Mineral King Controversy," *Econometrica*, Nov. 1976, *44*, 1259 – 76.

Karl-Göran Mäler, *Environmental Economics: A Theoretical Inquiry*, Baltimore 1974.

E. J. Mishan, *Cost-Benefit Analysis*, London 1971.

J. Neihans, "Money and Barter in General Equilibrium with Transactions Costs," *Amer. Econ. Rev.*, Dec. 1971, *61*, 773–83.

R. D. Willig, "Consumer's Surplus Without Apology," *Amer. Econ. Rev.*, Sept. 1976, *66*, 587–97.

[19]

Exact Consumer's Surplus and Deadweight Loss

By Jerry A. Hausman*

Consumer's surplus is a widely used tool in applied welfare economics. Both economic theorists and cost benefit analysis often use consumer's surplus despite its somewhat dubious reputation. The basic idea is to evaluate the value to a consumer or his "willingness to pay" for a change in price of a good from say price p^0 to price p^1. Because price changes affect consumer welfare, an evaluation of this effect is often a key input to public policy decisions. Yet consumer's surplus is probably the most controversial of widely used economic concepts. Both Paul Samuelson and Ian Little conclude that the economics profession would be better off without it.

It is my feeling of the situation that substantial agreement exists on the correct quantities to be measured: the amount the consumer would pay or would need to be paid to be just as well off after the price change as he was before the price change. The quantities correspond to John Hicks' compensating variation measures. An alternative measure which takes *ex post* price change utility as the basis of comparison is Hicks' equivalent variation.[1] The controversy arises in the measurement of these quantities. The usual measurement procedure is to use the area to the left of the Marshallian (market) demand curve between two price levels. Jules Dupuit originated this measure of welfare change, and Alfred Marshall and Hicks derived appropriate conditions for its use. The primary condition for the area to the left of the demand curve to correspond

to the compensating variation is to have constant marginal utility of income. Marshall gave this condition, and if it holds, the same quantity will be derived as the area to the left of the compensated (Hicksian) demand curve. This area to the left of the compensated demand curve is exactly what the compensating variation and equivalent variation measure. Thus the constant marginal utility of income is a sufficient condition for Marshallian consumer's surplus to be equal to Hicks' consumer's surplus. In this case Arnold Harberger's plea to use the welfare triangle as one-half times the product of the price change times the quantity change to measure deadweight loss corresponds to the correct theoretical amount of welfare change.

In a recent paper, Robert Willig derives bounds for the percentage difference between the correct measure of either the compensating or equivalent variation and the Marshallian measure derived form the market demand curve. His bounds, which depend on the income elasticity of demand for the single good in the region of price change being considered as well as the proportion of the consumer's income spent on the good, demonstrate that the Marshallian consumer's surplus is often a good approximation to Hicks' consumer's surplus. The fact that the proportion of the consumer's income spent matters as well as the income elasticity was first pointed out by Harold Hotelling. Willig contends that the approximation error will be less than the errors involved in estimating the demand curve. Thus he hopes to remove the need for apology that applied economists often need to give to theorists who remark on the inappropriateness of using Marshallian consumer's surplus to measure welfare change.

However, in this paper I show that for the case primarily considered by Willig of a single price change, which is also the situation in which consumer's surplus is often used in applied work, no approximation is necessary.

*Professor of economics, Massachusetts Institute of Technology, and research associate, National Bureau of Economic Research. I would like to thank Peter Diamond, Erwin Diewert, Daniel McFadden, Robert Merton, Robert Solow, Hal Varian, Joel Yellin, and the referees for help and comments. Research support from the National Science Foundation is acknowledged.

[1] The reason that we still have two, rather than one, of Samuelson's six measures of consumer's surplus arises from an index number problem of the correct basis for the welfare comparison. I will give both measures but plan to concentrate on the compensating variation.

From an estimate of the demand curve, we can derive a measure of the *exact* consumer's surplus, whether it is the compensating variation, equivalent variation, or some measure of utility change. No approximation is involved. While this result has been known for a long time by economic theorists, applied economists have only a limited awareness of its application. Furthermore, for the majority of cases the calculations are simple enough for a hand calculator. It seems preferable to remove completely any approximation argument from so important a matter as consumer's surplus. Also, my exact formulae allow calculation of the precision of our estimated consumer's surplus in terms of a standard error of estimation. Since unknown parameters for the demand curve will usually be estimated by econometric procedures, standard error formulae allow construction of confidence regions for the estimated compensated variation. These confidence regions might well be an important input to policy decisions. In most empirical applications we would like to account for the error in estimating the demand curve rather than including it in the approximation error as Willig implicitly does. Lastly, for some important uses of consumer's surplus, Willig's approximation argument is not useful. For instance, in assessing the welfare loss from taxation of labor income or capital income the proportion of total income can become so large that the Marshallian measure could differ markedly form the Hicks' measure of compensating variation or equivalent variation.[2]

However, a more important shortcoming of the use of the Marshallian measure (and Willig's approximation argument) arises in measuring deadweight loss. Here we are not interested in the complete compensating variation, which is a trapezoid to the left of the appropriate demand curve, but rather the triangle which corresponds to the excess of the compensating variation over the tax reve-

nue collected from an individual. This triangle corresponds to the welfare measure that Harberger has used in his many studies of the effect of taxation on the U.S. economy. Even in cases where Willig's approximations hold for the complete compensating variation, the Marshallian deadweight loss can be a very poor approximation for the theoretically correct Hicksian measure of deadweight loss based on the compensated demand curve. Thus the Marshallian measure of deadweight loss is not accurate for the important measurements often undertaken in applied welfare economics and public finance studies. But, again, given an estimate of the uncompensated demand curve we can derive the exact measure of deadweight loss. As the example in the concluding section of the paper shows, the traditional measurement of the welfare triangle can lead to badly biased estimates of the true deadweight loss even when the conditions for Willig's approximation argument hold true for measurement of consumer's surplus.

The basic idea used in deriving the exact measure of consumer's surplus is to use the *observed* market demand curve to derive the *unobserved* compensated demand curve. It is this latter demand curve which leads to the compensating variation and equivalent variation.[3] In the two-good case using modern duality theory, I begin with the market demand curve and derive the corresponding indirect utility function. These two functions permit exact calculation of the compensating variation, equivalent variation and deadweight loss. In the many-good case when a single price changes, I derive the "quasi" indirect utility function and the "quasi" expenditure function. I denote the appropriate functions as quasi since they do not corre-

---

[2] For recent uses of consumer's surplus in these situations, see Michael Boskin and Martin Feldstein. Many important applications in public finance have the feature that a large proportion of an individual's income is involved.

[3] Hal Varian derives the compensating variation as the area under the Hicksian compensated demand curve. He then remarks that "unfortunately, since the Hicksian demand curves are unobservable these expressions do not appear to be useful" (p. 210). Herbert Mohring considers the properties of different welfare measures and uses a technique similar to mine to derive the compensating variation for the Cobb-Douglas case. G. W. McKenzie and I. F. Pearce and Y. O. Vartia use somewhat similar approaches but use different methods of analysis.

spond exactly to the individual's indirect utility function and expenditure function. To derive these functions, one would require estimates of the complete system of demand equations. The complete demand system usually cannot be estimated due to lack of data. Instead, I use Hicks' aggregation theorem to demonstrate that the quasi functions which correspond to the assumption of a two-good world would give exactly the same measure of consumer's surplus as the actual functions for a single price change. Thus, the estimates of the uncompensated demand curve are all that is required to produce estimates which correspond to the correct theoretical magnitude.

My approach differs from much recent work in that I begin with the observed market demand curve and then derive the unobserved indirect utility function and expenditure function. The more common approach is to start from a specification of the utility function, for example, Stone-Geary or translog, and then estimate the unknown parameters from the derived market demand functions. The method used here seems preferable on two grounds. First, the only observable data are the market demand data so good econometric practice would indicate finding a function that fits the data well. Thus, different specifications of the demand curve, not the utility function, would be fit with the best-fitting demand equation chosen to base the applied welfare analysis on. Second, specifications such as the translog functions force all the demand curves to have the same functional form which are often difficult to fit econometrically. Since here I consider only partial-equilibrium welfare analysis, I need only estimate a single demand function. Again, alternative specifications of the demand curve allow consideration of the robustness of the results to the chosen specification. The demand curve approach offers considerably more flexibility than does the utility function approach in obtaining good econometric results given the available market data.

In the next section, I derive the indirect utility function and expenditure function for the two-good case. It is shown how the use of

these functions leads to correct measure of the compensating variation and equivalent variation. Section II then extends the analysis to the many-good case when only one price changes. There I show that the two-good analysis can be applied with only slight modifications. The functions for the case of a general quadratic demand curve are also derived. Lastly, in Section III, I provide an example of labor supply where the Marshallian approximation is inaccurate for the true compensating variation. I also provide an example of the calculation of deadweight loss to demonstrate that even when the Marshallian measure of the compensating variation is reasonably accurate, the Marshallian measure of deadweight loss can be incorrect by a relatively large amount. Section IV provides a brief conclusion to the paper.

I. The Compensating Variation and Equivalent Variation in the Two-Good Case

The basic tools which I will use in the analysis emerge from the dual approach to consumer behavior. The conventional treatment of consumer behavior considers the maximization of a strictly quasi-concave utility function defined over n goods, $x = (x_1, \ldots, x_n)$, subject to a budget constraint.

$$(1) \quad \max_{x} u(x) \text{ subject to } \sum_{i=1}^{n} p_i x_i = p \cdot x \leq y$$

where p_i are prices and y is (nonlabor) income.[4] The dual approach to the problem is to consider the associated minimization problem which defines the expenditure function

$$(2) \quad e(p, \bar{u}) \equiv \min_{x} p \cdot x \text{ subject to } u(x) \geq \bar{u}$$

The expenditure function was introduced into the literature by Lionel McKenzie; for recent

[4] Local nonsatiation will be assumed throughout the analysis so that the budget constraint will hold as an equality.

analysis and applications see Leo Hurwicz and Hirofumi Uzawa and Peter Diamond and Daniel McFadden. Charles Blackorby and W. Erwin Diewert have recently studied local properties of the expenditure function. The important property of the expenditure function which we will find extremely useful is that the partial derivative with respect to the jth price gives the Hicksian compensated demand curves.[5]

$$(3) \qquad \frac{\partial e(p,\bar{u})}{\partial p_j} = h_j(p,\bar{u})$$

These unobservable Hicksian demand curves should be distinguished from the observable market uncompensated demand curves $x(p,y)$. At an optimum solution to equations (1) and (2) the demands coincide at maximum utility u^*, $h(p,u^*) = x(p,y)$.

The other function we will use which connects the utility function of equation (1) and the expenditure function of equation (2) is the indirect utility function which is the solution to the maximization problem

$$(4) \qquad v(p,y) \equiv \max \left[u(x) : p \cdot x \leq y \right]$$

Properties of the indirect utility function are derived in Diewert. An important property of the indirect utility function which we will use is René Roy's identity which yields the observed market demand curves as partial derivatives of $v(p,y)$.

(5)

$$x_j(p,y) = -\partial v(p,y)/\partial p_j / \partial v(p,y)/\partial y$$

It is the difference between equation (3) for the compensated demand curve and equation (5) for the uncompensated demand curve that induces the difference between Marshallian consumer's surplus and exact Hicks'

consumer's surplus when a price change occurs. Since the indirect utility function of equation (4) is monotonically increasing in income while the expenditure function of equation (2) is monotonically increasing in utility, either function can be inverted to derive the other corresponding function.

Let us now consider a change in the price vector from p^0 to p^1 and formally define the exact measures of consumer's surplus, the compensating variation, and equivalent variation, using the expenditure function.[6] Holding nonlabor income constant at y^0, the compensating variation $CV(p^0, p^1, y^0)$ is the minimum quantity required to keep the consumer as well off as he was in the initial state characterized by (p^0, y^0) as he is in the new state $(p^1, y^0 + CV)$. In terms of the expenditure function

$$(6) \quad CV(p^0, p^1, y^0) = e(p^1, u^0) - e(p^0, u^0)$$

$$= e(p^1, u^0) - y^0$$

where $u^0 = v(p^0, y^0)$ from the indirect utility function. Equivalently the compensating variation can be defined through the indirect utility function as $v(p^1, y^0 + CV) = v(p^0, y^0)$. An alternative measure of welfare change is the equivalent variation, $EV(p^0, p^1, y^0)$, which uses utility after the price change as the basis of comparison:[7]

$$(7) \quad EV(p^0, p^1, y^0) = e(p^1, u^1) - e(p^0, u^1)$$

Using either the compensating variation or equivalent variation, it can be shown that the area under the compensated Hicksian demand curve corresponds to consumer's surplus.

---

[5]The other useful property of the expenditure function which will be utilized in subsequent analysis is that the second derivatives of the expenditure function yield the elements of the Slutsky matrix $S_{ij} = \partial^2 e(p,\bar{u})/\partial p_i \partial p_j = \partial h_j(p,\bar{u})/\partial p_i$.

[6]Willig and Avinash Dixit and P. A. Weller do a similar derivation.

[7]The compensating variation and equivalent variation always have the same sign because of the monotonicity of $e(p,u)$ in prices so long as the net demands do not change sign. Except for the single price change case, no inequality relationship holds in general.

Let us consider the case when only the first price changes from p_1^0 to p_1^1 with all other prices held constant. Equation (3) gives the compensated demand curve, and integrating it between the two price levels gives

(8) $CV(p^0, p^1, y^0) = e(p^1, u^0) - e(p^0, u^0)$

$$= \int_{p_1^0}^{p_1^1} h_1(p, u^0)\, dp_1 = \int_{p_1^0}^{p_1^1} \frac{\partial e(p, u^0)}{\partial p_1}\, dp_1$$

The equivalent variation is derived in an identical manner where u^0 is replaced by u^1.[8]

Let us now compare this measure of welfare change with the traditional measure of Marshallian consumer's surplus as the area under the uncompensated demand curve of equation (5).[9] The integral has the form

(9) $A(p^0, p^1, y^0) = \int_{p_1^0}^{p_1^1} x_1(p, y^0)\, dp_1$

$$= -\int_{p_1^0}^{p_1^1} \frac{\partial v(p, y^0)/\partial p_1}{\partial v(p, y^0)/\partial y}\, dp_1$$

This integral in general differs from the integral for the compensating variation in equation (8). To keep the individual on the same indifference curve, y^0 which enters both the numerator and denominator of equation (9) must be constantly adjusted along the path of the price change. Since y^0 is kept constant, this produces the difference between the uncompensated market demand curve with its Marshallian measure of consumer's surplus and the compensated demand curve with its measure of the compensating variation.

It is the supposed constancy or near constancy of the marginal utility of income which has often served as a basis for using Marshal-

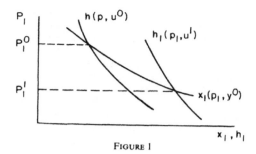

lian consumer's surplus as a measure of welfare change. However, equations (6) and (9) in general do not give the same measure. The difference between the compensated Hicksian demand curve which forms the basis for equation (6) and the uncompensated Marshallian demand curve which forms the basis for equation (9) follows from Slutsky's equation

(10)

$$\frac{\partial h_1(p, u^0)}{\partial p_1} - \frac{\partial x_1(p, y^0)}{\partial p_1} = x_1 \cdot \frac{\partial x_1(p, y^0)}{\partial y}$$

A sufficient condition for equation (10) to equal zero is that both $\partial^2 v(p, y^0)/\partial y \partial p$ and $\partial^2 v(p, y^0)/\partial y^2$ equal zero. These conditions correspond to the case of constant marginal utility of income. For the case of a normal good, the compensated demand curve has steeper slope than the market demand curve so Figure 1 demonstrates the inequalities for a single price change $EV(p^0, p^1, y^0) \leqslant A(p^0, p^1, y^0) \leqslant CV(p^0, p^1, y^0)$, an inequality found in Willig. His paper shows that even when the marginal utility of income is not constant that the percentage difference, $(CV - A)/A$, is not large under certain conditions.

Let us now turn to the empirical application of consumer's surplus. It turns out that for many applications no approximation is needed since equation (6) or (7) can be computed exactly. I begin with the simplest case, two goods only with prices $p^0 = (p^0, 1)$. Thus I use the second good as numeraire and consider a price change to p_1^1. Both the price of the first good and income are normalized with respect to the price of the second good,

---

[8]An alternative but equivalent method of interpreting our procedure is to use equation (3) to write $\partial e/\partial p_j = h_j(p, \bar{u}) = x_j(p, e(p, \bar{u}))$. In principle this implicit equation can always be numerically integrated from p^0 to p^1 to find the exact compensating variation. Vartia gives a computer algorithm for the numerical integration method. My technique to find closed-form solutions uses Roy's identity to derive a differential equation which can be explicitly solved in many cases.

[9]Varian (pp. 209 ff.) does a similar analysis.

which does not change. While this case is very simple, it is not totally unrealistic. It is often used in empirical analysis, especially when a separability assumption between the good whose price changes and the other goods is appropriate. A very general treatment of separability is contained in Blackorby, Primont, and Russell, but for use herein, a simple interpretation of separability which allows us to write the utility function of equation (1) as $u(x_1, \ldots, x_n) = u(x_1, g(x_2, \ldots, x_n))$ is adequate. The appropriate price index which corresponds to the structure of $u(\cdot)$ provides the numeraire good. Separability of the indirect utility function is defined in an analogous manner, $v(p_1, k(p_2, \ldots, p_n))$ where $k(\cdot)$ provides the price index. In general separability of $u(\cdot)$ does not imply separability of $v(\cdot)$ or vice versa.

Separability utility functions justify specification and estimation of demand curves that have only a single price in them. An important example often used in empirical studies is the linear labor supply relationship

$$(11) \quad x_j = \alpha w_j + \delta y_j + z_j \gamma + \varepsilon_j; \quad j = 1, \ldots, J$$

estimated over a sample of J individuals where w_j is the commodity price deflated (net after tax) wage, y_j is the commodity price deflated nonlabor income, Z_j is a vector of socioeconomic characteristics, and ε_j is a stochastic disturbance. Numerous other commodity demand equations are specified in this form where the wage is replaced by the price of the commodity.

To derive the exact compensating variation is straightforward and provides an exact welfare measure. The basic idea is to take the *observed* market demand curve and to use Roy's identity from equation (5) to integrate and derive the indirect utility function.[10] Inversion of the indirect utility gives the expenditure function which allows calculation of the compensating variation. Equivalently, using equation (3) we can derive the *unobservable* compensated demand curve.

And equation (8) shows that the area under the compensated demand curve yields the exact consumer's surplus.

In principle we can always perform this integration for a well-specified demand function. This statement is the essence of the famous integrability problem in consumer demand.[11] So long as the derivatives of the *compensated* demand functions satisfy the properties of symmetry and negative semidefiniteness of the Slutsky matrix and the adding-up condition, the indirect utility function can be recovered by integration.[12] In practice, many commonly used demand functions in empirical work yield explicit solutions so that exact welfare analysis is easily done.

Returning to the two-good example, consider the nonstochastic demand function (where both p_1 and y are deflated by the price of the other good, p_2):[13]

$$(12) \quad x_1 = \alpha p_1 + \delta y + z\gamma$$

$$= -\partial v(p_1, y)/\partial p_1 / \partial v(p_1, y)/\partial y$$

I solve this linear partial differential equation by applying the method of characteristic curves which assures a unique solution, given an initial condition.[14] To make welfare comparisons we will want to be on a given indifference curve. As the price changes I will use the equation $v(p_1(t), y(t)) = u_0$ for some u_0; for example, initial utility in the compensat-

---

[10] This technique has been used in estimating demand with nonlinear budget constraints by Gary Burtless and myself, and in my earlier article.

[11] See Samuelson and Hurwicz and Uzawa.

[12] In addition a regularity condition is needed. A Lipschitz-type condition is given by Hurwicz and Uzawa. A stronger sufficient condition that often holds is for the demand function to be continuously differentiable.

[13] It has been pointed out to me by Diewert that this demand specification corresponds to a flexible functional form for the underlying preferences as discussed in Blackorby and Diewert. Basically, three independent parameters are needed for the demand function in the two-good case, which equation (12) has, so that the value of demand, the uncompensated price derivative, and the income derivative can attain arbitrary values.

[14] See Fritz John or Richard Courant and David Hilbert. Given that along an initial curve (here an indifference curve), the initial values are continuously differentiable then a unique solution to the partial differential equation exists.

ing variation case. Along a path of price change to stay on the indifference curve, we have

(13)
$$\frac{\partial v(p_1(t), y(t))}{\partial p_1(t)} \frac{dp_1(t)}{dt}$$

$$+ \frac{\partial v(p_1(t), y(t))}{\partial y(t)} \frac{dy(t)}{dt} = 0$$

Then, using the implicit function theorem and Roy's identity from equation (12),

(14)
$$\frac{dy(p_1)}{dp_1} = \alpha p_1 + \delta y + z\gamma$$

I have now expressed y as a function of p_1 and can solve the ordinary differential equation (14) to find

(15) $\quad y(p_1) = c e^{\delta p_1} - \frac{1}{\delta}\left(\alpha p_1 + \frac{\alpha}{\delta} + z\gamma\right)$

where c, the constant of integration, depends on the initial utility level u_0. In fact, I simply choose $c = u_0$ as our cardinal utility index. Therefore, solving equation (15), we find the indirect utility function[15]

(16)

$$v(p_1, y) = c = e^{-\delta p_1}\left[y + \frac{1}{\delta}\left(\alpha p_1 + \frac{\alpha}{\delta} + z\gamma\right)\right]$$

Then the corresponding expenditure function (again normalized by the price of the second good) follows simply from equation (16) by interchanging the utility level with the income variable

(17) $\quad e(p_1, \bar{u}) = e^{\delta p_1}\bar{u} - \frac{1}{\delta}\left(\alpha p_1 + \frac{\alpha}{\delta} + z\gamma\right)$

It is important to note that this procedure yields a *local solution* to the differential equation over some domain in price space. It is

[15]Any monotonic transformation of this equation will of course satisfy the differential equation since ordinal utility is determined only up to a monotonic transformation. The only change would be in c, the constant of integration.

not always the case that there exists a global solution to equation (12) which satisfies the integrability conditions. However, we need only a local solution to make the welfare calculations that we are interested in. That is, we only want to compute a welfare measure at two price points, sat p_1^0 and p_1^1, which equations (16) and (17) permit us to do.

We now have a solution to Roy's identity, but we need to check whether we have a valid indirect utility function which arises from consumer maximization.[16] The indirect utility function of equation (16) is continuous and homogeneous of degree zero in prices and income by my normalization condition using p_2 as numeraire. It is also decreasing in prices if $\alpha \leqslant 0$ and increasing in income if $\delta \geqslant 0$. The other condition $v(p_1, y)$ must satisfy is quasi concavity which is equivalent to the Slutsky condition

(18) $\quad s_{11} = \frac{\partial h_1(p_1, \bar{u})}{\partial p_1}$

$$= \alpha + \delta(\alpha p_1 + \delta y + z\gamma) \leqslant 0$$

where the compensated demand curve $h_1(p_1, \bar{u})$ follows from the expenditure function of equation (17) by differentiation with respect to p_1. So long as the sign conditions are satisfied by the demand function we can calculate exact consumer's surplus and deadweight loss using the expenditure function of equation (17) and indirect utility function of equation (16).

To compute the compensating variation we use equation (17) and equation (6) to find

(19) $\quad CV(p_1^0, p_1^1, y_0)$

$$= e^{\delta(p_1^1 - p_1^0)}\left[y_0 + \frac{1}{\delta}\left(z\gamma + \frac{\alpha}{\delta} + \alpha p_1^0\right)\right]$$

$$- \frac{1}{\delta}\left(z\gamma + \frac{\alpha}{\delta} + \alpha p_1^1\right) - y^0$$

$$= \frac{1}{\delta} e^{\delta(p_1^1 - p_1^0)}\left[x_1^0(p_1^0 \cdot y_0) + \frac{\alpha}{\delta}\right]$$

$$- \frac{1}{\delta}\left[x_1^1(p_1^1 \cdot y^0) + \frac{\alpha}{\delta}\right]$$

[16]Diewert discusses the appropriate conditions.

This expression for the compensating variation, while certainly more complicated than the Marshallian triangle formula, is still straightforward to calculate. The corresponding equivalent variation would be calculated from equation (7). Furthermore, since the parameters for equation (17) are presumably estimated by econometric methods, well-known methods allow calculation of the large sample standard error for the compensating variation in equation (19) (for example, see Rao, p. 323). Note, also that the compensating variation now varies across individuals by their socioeconomic characteristics and their income levels while the corresponding Marshallian expressions neglects these factors in its approximation. Use of the compensating variation or equivalent variation ends all arguments about the appropriateness of the Marshallian approximation since they give the exact measure of welfare change.

Another commonly used demand curve specification in the two-good case is the constant elasticity specification[17]

$$(20) \quad x_1 = e^{z\gamma} p_1^\alpha y^\delta$$

$$= -\partial v(p_1, y)/\partial p_1 / \partial v(p_1, y)/\partial y$$

$$\delta \neq 1$$

which is often estimated in *log*-linear form as $\log x_{1j} = z_j \gamma + \alpha \log p_{1j} + \delta \log y_j + \varepsilon_j$ for $j = 1, \ldots, J$.[18] To find the indirect utility function we use the technique of separation of variables and integrate to find

$$(21) \quad v(p_1, y) = c = -e^{z\gamma} \cdot \frac{p_1^{1+\alpha}}{1+\alpha} + \frac{y^{1-\delta}}{1-\delta}$$

where c, the constant of integration, has again been set at the initial utility level. The Slutsky condition is $s_{11} = x_1(\alpha/p_1 + \delta x_1/y)$. The expenditure function (again normalized by

p_2) is

$$(22)$$

$$e(p_1, \bar{u}) = \left[(1-\delta) \left(\bar{u} + e^{z\gamma} \frac{p_1^{1+\alpha}}{1+\alpha} \right) \right]^{1/1-\delta}$$

so that the compensating variation for a change in price from p_1^0 to p_1^1 is the quantity

$$(23) \quad CV(p_1^0, p_1^1, y^0) = \left\{ (1-\delta) \left[\frac{e^{z\gamma}}{1+\alpha} \right. \right.$$

$$\left. \left(p_1^{1\ 1+\alpha} - p_1^{0\ 1+\alpha} \right) \right] + y^{0(1-\delta)} \right\}^{1/1-\delta} - y^0$$

$$= \left\{ \frac{(1-\delta)}{(1+\alpha)y^{0\delta}} \left[p_1^1 x_1^1(p_1^1, y^0) \right. \right.$$

$$\left. \left. - p_1^0 x_1^0(p_1^0, y^0) \right] + y^{0(1-\delta)} \right\}^{1/1-\delta} - y^0$$

Again an exact formula for the compensating variation is derived for which a standard error could be straightforwardly calculated given a covariance matrix for the estimated parameters. No approximation argument is required in using the compensating variation as a measure of welfare change. It is interesting to note that while the denominator of equation (9) is constant for the demand specification of equation (20) so that in this case the Marshallian area also gives an exact measure of welfare change, it is not equal to either the compensating variation or the equivalent variation. The income effect from equation (10) is not zero so that the compensated demand derivative and uncompensated demand derivative differ by a positive amount. Thus, use of the Marshallian measure still involves an error of approximation if either the compensating variation or the equivalent variation are the desired measure.

II. The Many-Good Case and More General Demand Specifications

The welfare measures developed at the beginning of Section I were all fully general in the sense that they considered n different

---

[17]Again this demand curve provides a flexible functional form for the underlying preferences.

[18]Willig considers a constant income elasticity demand specification in deriving his approximations. For $\delta = 1$ the indirect utility function has the same form as equation (19) except that the last term is replaced by *log y*.

goods and allowed all n prices to change. In particular, the compensating variation of equation (6) and the equivalent variation of equation (7) used the expenditure function whose arguments are the complete price vector and the appropriate utility level. In this section I generalize the methods of calculating the compensating variation to the many-good case but continue to consider only one price change.[19] While we cannot recover the complete expenditure function as before, we can still recover the quasi-expenditure function whose derivative yields the appropriate compensated demand curve. Thus again the compensating variation and equivalent variation can be estimated exactly given information on the market demand curve for the good whose price has changed.

A complete specification of a system of demand equations would have the general form

$$(24) \quad x_i = x(p, y, z, \varepsilon_i); \qquad i = 1, \ldots, N$$

where p is the price vector, z is a vector of socioeconomic characteristics, and ε_i is a stochastic disturbance. So long as the estimated coefficients of the demand system have the property that the Slutsky matrix is symmetric and negative semidefinite and that the function $x(\cdot)$ is regular in p and y, then in principle the system can be integrated and the expenditure functions derived. However, the usual case is that we do not have information on all quantity demands at the individual level. But suppose we do have information on demand for, say, the first good whose price is expected to change as a result of the public policy measure being considered. A first-order Taylor expansion of equation (24) would lead to the econometric specification[20]

$$(25) \quad x_1(p, y) = z\gamma + \sum_{i=2}^{N} \frac{\delta_i y}{p_i} + \sum_{i=2}^{N} \frac{\alpha_i p_1}{p_i} + \varepsilon_1$$

The important point to note about equation (25) is that by assumption only p_1 will change due to the contemplated policy measure, while z, y, and $p_2, \ldots, p_n$ will remain constant. Thus, all prices except the first can be written as a scalar multiple of a price index, $p_2 = \lambda_2 q, \ldots, p_N = \lambda_N q$ where $\lambda_2, \ldots, \lambda_N$ are known fixed positive constants. We can now apply Hicks' composite commodity theorem.[21] Rewrite equation (25) as

$$(26) \quad x_1(p_1, q, y)$$

$$= z\gamma + \left(\sum_{i=2}^{N} \frac{\delta_i}{\lambda_i} \right) \frac{y}{q} + \left(\sum_{i=2}^{N} \frac{\alpha_i}{\lambda_i} \right) \frac{p_1}{q}$$

$$= z\gamma + \delta \frac{y}{q} + \alpha \frac{p_1}{q}$$

where $\quad \delta = \sum_{i=2}^{N} \delta_i / \lambda_i$ and $\alpha = \sum_{i=2}^{N} \alpha_i / \lambda_i$

Since equation (26) is the same as equation (12) except that the composite price q has replaced p_2, I can repeat the analysis of the last section with the welfare analysis based on equations (16) and (17). Note that the resulting functions might best be referred to as a quasi-indirect utility function and a quasi-expenditure function. We have not recovered the complete indirect utility function or expenditure function, but the "quasi" functions lead to exact welfare measures when all other prices are constant. But they cannot be used to analyze the welfare change when more than one price changes (except proportionately) without further analysis.

Let us now briefly consider some extensions of our techniques to more general cases. First, we can generalize the *log*-linear demand specification of equation (20) to the many good consumer

$$(27) \quad x_1(p, y) = e^{z\gamma} \prod_{i=2}^{N} \left(\frac{p_1}{p_i} \right)^{\alpha_i} \prod_{i=2}^{N} \left(\frac{y}{p_i} \right)^{\delta_i}$$

---

[19] The one-price-change situation is the case considered by Willig.

[20] I am indebted to Diewert for help in improving this section of the paper from an earlier version.

[21] For other references and developments of this theorem, see Terrance Gorman and Blackorby et al. and Diewert.

Again, if only the first price changes, we can obtain the quasi-expenditure function corresponding to equation (22) by the application of Hicks' composite commodity theorem to obtain

$$(28) \quad x_1(p_1, q, y) = e^{zy} \left(\frac{p_1}{q} \right)^{\sum\limits_{i=2}^{N} a_i} \left(\frac{y}{q} \right)^{\sum\limits_{i=2}^{N} \delta_i}$$

Use of the quasi-expenditure function allows exact welfare measures to be calculated.

I now return to the two-good case to present some generalizations of the demand specification with the observation that they can be expanded to the N good case by the techniques which lead to equations (26) and (28). Thus, I again normalize by the second price so that p_1 and y are divided by p_2. I return to the linear demand specification of equation (12) but allow the price and income coefficients of the demand specification, as well as the intercept, to depend on individual socioeconomic characteristics. Let $\delta = zd$ and $\alpha = za$ which leads to the demand specification[22]

$$(29) \quad x_1(p_1, y) = zy + zdy + zap_1 + \varepsilon_1$$

Calculation of the welfare measures proceeds in the same way except that δ and α vary across individuals. Perhaps a more important generalization is to allow interactions among the price terms to move away from the linear demand curve specification. A demand function quadratic in prices is

$$(30) \quad x_1(p_1, y) = zy + \delta y + \beta_1 p_1 + \beta_2 p_1^2 + \varepsilon_1$$

so long as the Slutsky term is negative we can integrate the corresponding differential equation by parts to find the indirect utility function

$$(31) \quad v(p_1, y) = e^{-\delta p_1} \left[y + a_1 p_1 + a_2 p_1^2 + a_3 \right]$$

where $a_1 = \beta_1/\delta + 2\beta_2/\delta^2$, $a_2 = \beta_2/\delta$, and a_3

[22]Stochastic terms can be added of the type $\delta = Zd + v$, which lead to a random coefficients specification. The resulting heteroscedasticity can be accounted for in the estimation procedure. This type of demand function is estimated in my article with Burtless.

$= zy/\delta + 2\beta_2/\delta^3$. With equation (31) exact welfare analysis is again straightforward since the expenditure function, compensating variation, and equivalent variation all follow from equation (31).

The last and most general demand curve that is considered is fully quadratic in both prices and income. The demand function is

$$(32) \quad x_1 = \beta_0 + \beta_1 y + \beta_2 p_1 + \beta_3 y^2$$
$$+ \beta_4 p_1^2 + \beta_5 p_1 y + \varepsilon_1$$

where $\beta_0 = zy$. Using Roy's identity we have the nonlinear differential equation

$$(33) \quad \frac{dy}{dp_1} + Qy + Ry^2 + S = 0$$

where $R = -\beta_3$, $Q = -(\beta_1 + \beta_5 p_1)$ and $S = -(\beta_0 + \beta_2 p_1 + \beta_4 p_1^2)$. It turns out that this equation can be transformed by changes of variables to the famous Schrodinger wave equation of physics. I give the derivation in the Appendix where the indirect utility function is found to have the form

$$(34) \quad v(p, y) = (h\tilde{W}_1 - \tilde{W}_1^1)/(\tilde{W}_2^1 - h\tilde{W}_2)$$

where $h = -\beta_3 y + (\beta_5/2)(\beta_1 + \beta_5 p)^2$ and $\tilde{W}_1$ and $\tilde{W}_2$, functions of the β parameters of equation (32) and prices, which are straightforward to calculate. Their exact form is given in the Appendix. Again, the expenditure function and exact welfare measures follow directly from equation (34). Thus, we have a very general demand specification with associated exact welfare measures. In fact, the demand function may well provide a third-order flexible function form in the sense of Blackorby and Diewert.

III. Calculation of the Compensating Variation and of the Deadweight Loss

In the previous section, I have given formulae for calculating the exact welfare change by deriving the unobservable compensated demand curve given market information. Here I consider two examples to demonstrate use of the formulae. I can also assess how accurate the Marshallian approximations are for the exact welfare measures. The first example of labor supply shows that the approximation may be quite poor for goods which form a large proportion of total expenditure. Since Willig showed that the approximation might not do well in this case, the finding is not surprising. However, the second example raises severe doubt about the use of uncompensated market demand for a commodity which is only a small proportion of the budget when we calculate the deadweight loss from the imposition of a tax. Even though the conditions for an accurate approximation to the compensating variation hold, the approximation to the deadweight loss is very inaccurate. In fact, this finding seems to hold in general. While the Marshallian approximation is adequate in certain situations for the compensating variation, it is often *not* accurate under these conditions for measurement of the deadweight loss. Since measurement of the deadweight loss is often the goal in applied welfare economics, this finding strongly recommends use of the exact measure deadweight rather than the Marshallian approximation.

The first example used, is a linear labor supply function of the form of equation (11). The estimates used are taken from a study of wives' labor supply functions in my forthcoming paper. The estimated values used for the jth individual are

$$(35) \quad h_j = 495.1 w_j - .1250 y_j + 765.1$$

The left-hand side variable is hours per year of work, w_j is market wage which has a mean of \$4.15 per hour, y_j is after tax income of the husband which has a mean of \$8,236, and the constant takes account of demographic factors such as age and children.

Here I calculate the required compensating variation after the imposition of a 20 percent proportional tax on labor earnings. Compared to a no-tax situation, the expenditure takes the form

$$(36) \quad e(w, \bar{u}) = e^{-\delta w} \bar{u} - \frac{\alpha}{\delta} w + \frac{\alpha}{\delta^2} - \frac{z\gamma}{\delta}$$

Calculating u^0 from the corresponding indi-

rect utility function and using it in equation (36) leads to a required expenditure of \$9485 per year. I find that the compensating variation is \$2,056. Using the formula for distribution of a nonlinear function, I find one standard error for the compensating variation to be plus or minus \$481. Then to find the aggregate compensating variation for the complete population, a sample enumeration would be done allowing the wages, husband's income, and socioeconomic variables to differ across individuals.

Calculations of the Marshallian approximation is straightforward since we use the estimates of equation (35) and measure the area to the left of the labor supply curve between the initial and final net wages of \$4.15 per hour and \$3.32 per hour. The Marshallian approximation is \$1,315 per year so that the two measures differ by 44.6 percent. Thus, the Marshallian measure provides a very poor approximation to the exact measure of welfare change. That the Marshallian measure provides a poor approximation in this case is in line with Willig's results since the Marshallian area is large with respect to base income. Hence, the Taylor approximation which provides Willig's bounds demonstrates that the derivation between the two measures can be substantial. It is worth emphasizing again that the exact welfare change is easily calculated from the indirect utility function and the expenditure function. Then no worry about the accuracy of the approximation is needed.

The last example I consider is the more important one, since it involves a quite common use of consumer's surplus in applied welfare economics. I consider the deadweight loss from imposition of a commodity tax.

Consider the compensated demand curve $h(p, u_0)$ shown in Figure 2. The compensating variation is the area to the left of the demand curve between the initial price p^0 and the final, post tax, price p^1. But we are often *more* interested in the welfare triangle which measures the efficiency loss from the use of distorting taxes. This triangle corresponds to the Harberger measure. Therefore, I define the deadweight loss to be the difference of the compensating variation minus

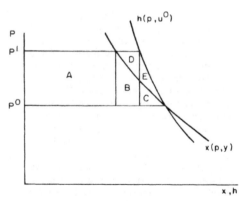

FIGURE 2

the tax revenue collected. The rectangle in Figure 2 thus has only distributional consequences while the triangle is the deadweight burden which cannot be undone. Optimal tax policy typically tries to minimize the sum of the deadweight losses to achieve a second best optimum, for example, see Diamond and Mirrlees.

The particular example I consider is meant to approximate the long-run demand for gasoline, although the numbers used are hypothetical. The demand function is

$$(37) \quad q_j = -14.22p + .082y_j + 4.95$$

Choosing income for the mean person to be $720 per month and initial price to be $.75 per gallon, the price elasticity is .2 with an income elasticity of 1.1. Both elasticities are similar to elasticities which have been found in empirical studies. Let us now consider imposition of a tax which raises the price of gasoline to $1.50 per gallon. Using equation (17) we find that the compensating variation equals $37.17 per month. The Marshallian approximation equals $35.99 per month, so that the two measures differ by only 3.2 percent. Thus, the Willig results are confirmed since demand for gasoline is only a small part of the total budget for the individual.

However, when we compare the two measures of deadweight loss we find a substantial difference. The compensated measure of

the deadweight loss is $2.88 while the Marshallian measure is $3.96. The two measures differ by 31.7 percent, even though the approximation is good for the compensating variation. Why can the approximation be so poor for the deadweight loss? Using order arguments somewhat loosely, the compensating variation is composed of two pieces, the rectangle which is a first-order quantity of demand times change in price while the deadweight loss is a second-order quantity of one-half the changes in demand times the change in price. While the Marshallian approximation does reasonably well for the first-order part of the compensating variation under certain conditions given by Willig, its performance on the second order part may still be quite bad.

In Figure 2 we see that both measures of the compensating variation have rectangle A in common, which is a large part of the whole. In measuring the first-order effect they differ only by triangle D, which is small compared to the whole. However, in measuring the deadweight loss, the percentage difference will depend on the difference of area B and triangle E compared to the area of triangle C. Figure 2 shows that this difference can often be substantial. Thus, the Marshallian approximation is not accurate for measurement of the deadweight loss. Instead, the exact Hicksian measure should be used. While the Willig results will hold for the compensating variation, if the goal of the calculation is deadweight loss, the Marshallian approximation should not be used. In many cases it is a very inaccurate measure of the true deadweight loss.

IV. Conclusion

In empirical situations where a measure of either the compensating variation, equivalent variation, or deadweight loss is needed, economists often work with relatively simple demand specifications. For these types of specifications we have developed the exact measures of welfare change. While it has been known that use of the compensated demand curves lead to the appropriate welfare measures, it has not been generally recognized how straightforward it is to derive the compensated demand curves from observed market demand curves. I derived methods which are easily applied to the two-good case. These methods are then extended to the many-good case with one price change. The quasi-indirect utility function and expenditure function provide the appropriate compensated demand curve and thus the appropriate welfare measure. While our measures tell us the appropriate compensation, they, of course, do not necessarily give the correct measurement of the loss in social welfare if no compensation is paid.

Through two examples I attempt to assess the accuracy of the Marshallian approximation. For a good which forms a small part of the total budget, the Marshallian area is reasonably accurate as proven by Willig. But if the good forms a large part of the budget, the approximation may be quite inaccurate as our labor supply example shows. A more important finding is the high level of inaccuracy when the deadweight loss, or welfare triangle, is measured. For deadweight loss, the Marshallian area can often be quite far off even though it is reasonably accurate for the compensating variation in the same situation. The gasoline example shows that the deadweight loss measures differ by 32 percent even though the compensating variation measures differ by 3.2 percent. Thus, it seems *inappropriate* to measure deadweight loss by using the market demand curve. But since the exact deadweight loss measure can be often calculated by use of the compensated demand curve, no special problem arises. The formulae given in this paper permit exact calculation of both the compensating variation and of the deadweight loss.

APPENDIX

Let us consider derivation of the indirect utility function and expenditure function which corresponds to the fully quadratic demand curve of Section II.[23]

The demand function that I consider is

$$x_1 = \beta_0 + \beta_1 y + \beta_2 p_1 + \beta_3 y^2 + \beta_4 p_1^2$$
$$+ \beta_5 p_1 y + \varepsilon_1$$

where $\beta_0 = Z\gamma$. Using Roy's identity this demand equation may be written as the non-linear differential equation

$$y' + Qy + Ry^2 + S = 0$$

where $R = -\beta_3$, $Q = -(\beta_1 + \beta_5 p_1)$ and $S = -(\beta_0 + \beta_2 p_1 + \beta_4 p_1^2)$. I do one change of dependent variable $y = (1/R)(u'/u)$ and one change of independent variable $t = \beta_1 + \beta_5 p_1$ calling the resulting function $\phi(t)$ to find

$$\phi'' + \beta_5 t \phi' + q\phi = 0$$

where $q = \beta_5^2 SR$. Thus, I have transformed the nonlinear equation, a Ricatti equation, to a second-order differential equation of the form studied by physicists. I then transform by $W = \phi e^{\beta_5 t^2/4}$ to put the equation in parabolic cylinder form $W'' + WM = 0$ where $M = \delta_0 + \delta_1 t + \delta_2 t^2$ and the δ_i's are easily calculated functions of the β_i's. I have thus transformed the original equation into the famous Schrodinger wave equation. One last change of independent variable $x^2 = 4(\delta_1 t + \delta_2 t^2)$ and we have the final form

$$W'' + W\big(\delta_0 + (x^2/4)\big) = 0.$$

Define the functions $W_1 = 1 + \delta_0(x^2/2) + (\delta_0^2 - (1/2)(x^4/4!) + \dots$ and $W_2 = x + \delta_0(x^3/3!) + (\delta_0^2 - 3/2)(x^5/5!) + \dots$, which converge quickly for values likely to be encountered in economics.[24] Now define $\gamma_0 = \delta_1\beta_1 + \delta_2\beta_1^2$, $\gamma_2 = \delta_1\beta_5 + 2\delta_2\beta_1\beta_5$, and $\gamma_3 = \delta_2\beta_5^2$ and we have the W_i function in terms of prices $\bar{W}_1 = 1 + 2\delta_0(\gamma_1 + \gamma_2 p_1 + \gamma_3 p_1^2) + (2/3)(\delta_0^2 - 1/2)(\gamma_1 + \gamma_2 p_1 + \gamma_3 p_1^2)^2 + \dots$ and $W_2 = 2\delta_0(\gamma_2 + 2\gamma_3 p_1) + (1/3)(\delta_0^2 - 1/2)(\gamma_1 + \gamma_2 p_1 + \gamma_3 p_1^2)(\gamma_2 + 2\gamma_3 p_1) + \dots$ which again converge

---

[23] Generalization to the many-good case is straightforward. Only a sketch of the derivation is provided here. Further details may be obtained by writing the author.

[24] Description and analysis of the parabolic cylinder functions is found in Milton Abramowitz and Irene Stegum (ch. 19). The successive coefficients of the expansion have a simple recursive formula which eases calculation.

quickly. The indirect utility function thus takes the form

$$(A1) \qquad v(p, y) = \frac{h\tilde{W}_1 - \tilde{W}_1'}{\tilde{W}_2' - h\tilde{W}_2}$$

where $h = -\beta_3 y + \beta_5 t^2/2$. The expenditure function also takes a simple form in terms of the W functions

$$(A2) \qquad e(p_1, \bar{u}) = \frac{t\beta_5^2}{2\beta_3} - \frac{1}{\beta_3}\left(\frac{\tilde{W}_1' + \bar{u}\tilde{W}_2'}{\tilde{W}_1 + \bar{u}\tilde{W}_2}\right)$$

Then equation (A1) is used to compute utility at original prices p_1^0 and equation (A2) is used to compute $e(p_1^1, \bar{u})$ so that after subtracting off y_0 we find the compensating variation. The W functions are straightforward to calculate and both tables and computer routines exist to do the calculation.

I might note that it is straightforward to generate demand functions and corresponding indirect utility functions and expenditure functions that are closed form and contain quadratic terms in both prices and incomes. But I have not yet found demand functions of this type which can be estimated using linear regression techniques. The specification leading to (A1) and (A2) has this advantage although specialized computer routines then become necessary to evaluate the consumer's surplus and deadweight loss measures.

REFERENCES

Milton Abramowitz and Irene Stegum, *Handbook of Mathematical Functions*, Washington 1964.

Charles Blackorby and W. E. Diewert, "Expenditure Functions, Local Duality, and Second Order Approximations," *Econometrica*, May 1979, 47, 579–601.

_____, Daniel Primont, and Robert Russell, *Duality Separability and Functional Structure*, New York 1978.

M. J. Boskin, "Taxation, Saving and the Rate of Interest," *J. Polit. Econ.*, Apr. 1978, 86, S3–S28.

G. Burtless and J. Hausman, "The Effect of Taxation on Labor Supply," *J. Polit. Econ.*, Feb. 1978, 86, 1103–30.

Richard Courant and David Hilbert, *Methods of Mathematical Physics*, *II.*, New York 1962.

P. Diamond and D. McFadden, "Some Uses of the Expenditure Function in Public Finance," *J. Public Econ.*, Feb. 1974, 3, 3–21.

_____ and J. Mirrlees, "Optimal Taxation and Public Production," *Amer. Econ. Rev.*, Mar. 1971, 61, 8–27.

W. E. Diewert, "Applications of Duality Theory" in Michael. D. Intriligator and David A. Kendrick, eds., *Frontiers of Quantitative Economics*, *II*, Amsterdam 1974.

_____, "Hicks Aggregation Theorem and the Existence of a Real Value Added Function," mimeo, 1976.

A. Dixit and P. A. Weller, "The Three Consumer's Surpluses," *Economica*, May 1979, 46, 125–35.

J. Dupuit, "On the Measurement of the Utility of Public Works," in Kenneth Arrow and Tibor Scitovsky, eds., *Readings in Welfare Economics*, Homewood 1969.

M. Feldstein, "The Welfare Cost of Capital Income Taxation," *J. Polit. Econ.*, Apr. 1978, 86, S29–S52.

W. M. Gorman, "Community Preference Fields," *Econometrica*, Jan. 1953, 21, 63–80.

A. Harberger, "Three Basic Postulates for Applied Welfare Economics: An Interpretive Essay," *J. Econ. Lit.*, Sept. 1971, 9, 785–97.

J. A. Hausman, "The Effect of Wages, Taxes, and Fixed Costs on Women's Labor Force Participation," *J. Public Econ.*, Oct. 1980, 14, 161–94.

_____, "The Effects of Taxes on Labor Supply," in Henry Aaron and Joseph Pechman, *How do Taxes Affect Economic Behavior*, forthcoming 1981.

J. R. Hicks, *Value and Capital*, Oxford 1939.

_____, *A Revision of Demand Theory*, London 1956.

H. Hotelling, "The General Welfare in Relation to Problems of Taxation and of Railway and Utility Rates," *Econometrica*, July 1938, 6, 242–69.

J. Hurwicz and H. Uzawa, "On the Integrability of Demand Functions," in John S. Chipman, ed., *Preferences, Utility and Demand*, New York 1971.

Fritz John, *Partial Differential Equations*, New

York 1978.

I. M. D. Little, *A Critique of Welfare Economics*, London 1957.

G. McKenzie and I. Pearce, "Exact Measures of Welfare and the Cost of Living," *Rev. Econ. Stud.*, Oct. 1976, *43*, 465–68.

L. W. McKenzie, "Demand Theory Without a Utility Index," *Rev. Econ. Stud.*, June 1957, *24*, 185–89.

Alfred Marshall, *Principles of Economics*, New York 1961.

H. Mohring, "Alternative Welfare Gain and Loss Measures," *Western Econ. J.*, Dec. 1971, *9*, 349–68.

C. R. Rao, *Linear Statistical Inference*, New York 1973.

R. Roy, "La Distribution du revenue entre les divers biens," *Econometrica*, July 1947, *15*, 205–25.

Paul A. Samuelson, *Foundations of Economic Analysis*, Cambridge, Mass. 1947.

_____, "The Problem of Integrability in Utility Theory," *Economica*, Nov. 1950, *17*, 355–85.

Hal Varian, *Microeconomic Analysis*, New York 1978.

Y. O. Vartia, "Efficient Methods of Measuring Welfare Change and Compensated Income," mimeo., 1978.

R. Willig, "Consumer's Surplus without Apology," *Amer. Econ. Rev.*, Sept. 1976, *66*, 589–97.

[20]

Econometrica, Vol. 51, No. 1 (January, 1983)

EFFICIENT METHODS OF MEASURING WELFARE CHANGE AND COMPENSATED INCOME IN TERMS OF ORDINARY DEMAND FUNCTIONS

By Yrjö O. Vartia[1]

A utility maximizing consumer with a completely known system of ordinary demand functions $q = h(p, C)$ is considered. Let (p^0, q^0) and (p^1, q^1) be two arbitrary equilibrium situations; the problem is to evaluate in which of the situations the utility is higher without knowing the utility function. Revealed preference theory tells that the ordinary demand functions (which are in principle observable) contain enough information to solve the problem. Remaining difficulties are therefore mainly computational.

We present how the compensated income $\bar{C}^1 = \bar{C}(p^1, q^0)$ and the compensated demand $\bar{q}^1 = h(p^1, \bar{C}^1)$ are calculated with arbitrary accuracy using only the ordinary demand system. Our two efficient algorithms also have interesting interpretations in terms of index numbers and consumer surplus measures.

1. INTRODUCTION

A UTILITY MAXIMIZING CONSUMER is considered. Our consumer chooses a bundle of goods $q = (q_1, \ldots, q_n)$ as if he were maximizing a well-behaved ordinal utility function $u(q)$ under a budget constraint $p \cdot q = \sum p_i q_i \leq C$, where $p = (p_1, \ldots, p_n)$ and $C > 0$ denote exogenous positive prices and expenditure. We denote the ordinary demand system of our consumer by $h(p, C)$. Let $q^0 = h(p^0, C^0)$ and $q^1 = h(p^1, C^1)$ be two equilibrium demands corresponding to price-expenditure situations (p^0, C^0) and (p^1, C^1). Our problem is to find out whether the welfare change from q^0 to q^1 is positive ($q^0 \prec q^1$), negative ($q^0 \succ q^1$), or zero ($q^0 \sim q^1$). If $u(q)$ or its strictly increasing transform is known there is no problem. Let us suppose therefore that the utility function is not known and consider what must be known in order to solve the problem.

If we do not know the demand functions, $q_i = h^i(p, C)$ $(i = 1, \ldots, n)$, the problem cannot in general be solved. All we can infer if we know only two equilibrium points (p^0, q^0) and (p^1, q^1) is presented in the following revealed

	$Q^{Pa} < 1$	$Q^{Pa} = 1$	$Q^{Pa} > 1$
$Q^{La} < 1$	$q^1 < q^0$	Inconsistent preferences	Inconsistent preferences
$Q^{La} = 1$	$q^1 \precsim q^0$	$q^1 \sim q^0$	Inconsistent preferences
$Q^{La} > 1$	Zone of Indeterminacy	$q^1 \succsim q^0$	$q^1 > q^0$

[1] I am indebted to Professor Leo Törnqvist and Dr. Pentti Vartia for valuable discussions and advice and to Mr. Heikki Vajanne for programming the Main Algorithm. Valuable comments of Professor Angus Deaton and of two anonymous referees are also gratefully acknowledged.

80   YRJÖ O. VARTIA

preference table (see Vartia [39], Afriat [1, p. 20, 2, pp. 64–78], and Vartia and Weymark [42]).

Here $Q^{Pa} = Q^{Pa}(q^1, q^0, p^1, p^0) = p^1 \cdot q^1 / p^1 \cdot q^0$ and $Q^{La} = Q^{La}(q^1, q^0, p^1, p^0) = p^0 \cdot q^1 / p^0 \cdot q^0$ are Paasche's and Laspeyres' quantity indices. Instead of "inconsistent preferences" we perhaps should write "impossible under utility hypothesis." Note that if $Q^{Pa} = p^1 \cdot q^1 / p^1 \cdot q^0 > 1$, then $q^1 > q^0$, and if $Q^{La} = p^0 \cdot q^1 / p^0 \cdot q^0 < 1$, then $q^1 < q^0$ necessarily.

In the zone of indeterminacy any two equilibrium points (p^0, q^0) and (p^1, q^1) giving $Q^{Pa} < 1 < Q^{La}$ could be generated by numerous alternative preferences some of which order q^0 and q^1 differently. This was demonstrated already by Samuelson [26].

This revealed preference table is based on a continuous, strictly increasing, quasi-concave preference ordering $\succeq$. Its indifference surfaces may contain flat regions. For a strictly quasi-concave preference ordering there exist no flat regions and somewhat more may be inferred if either Q^{Pa} or Q^{La} equals 1 (see Vartia and Weymark [42], who also correct a slight slip of Diewert [13]).

In order to solve our problem in any situation something more must be known. We assume that the ordinary demand system $h(p, C) = (h^1(p, C), \ldots, h^n(p, C))$ of the utility maximizing consumer is known to us although his utility function is not. This assumption has also empirical relevance because it is possible (at least in principle) to estimate or work with a demand system $h(p, C)$ without knowing the utility function corresponding to it. Although the known $h(p, C)$ describes completely the market behavior of our consumer, it is still difficult to evaluate when his satisfaction or utility has increased and when it has remained constant. These difficulties are however mainly of a computational nature. Revealed preference and integrability theory show that demand functions give all the information needed to determine the indifference surfaces and thus the utility function (see [35] and [8], especially [20]). The over- and undercompensated 'demand curves' used in revealed preference arguments approximate the indifference surface from above and below, respectively, and converge therefore slowly towards it, as demonstrated by our Algorithms 1 and 2. Our Main Algorithm generates sequences of quantity vectors that approximate the indifference surface more accurately and converge quickly towards it. Although the principle of our algorithms has been stated, e.g., by Bergson [4, p. 39], a practical algorithm has been lacking as concluded recently by Chipman and Moore [10, p. 948].

The approximation of economic index numbers or measurement of consumer surpluses is complicated mainly because of this kind of computational difficulty, as is clearly demonstrated by McKenzie and Pearce [24]. Their theoretically elegant solution to this same problem is based on high order derivatives of the demand functions and its applicability depends on their existence and how easily these can be evaluated (see also G. McKenzie [23]). Therefore their solution is as such unsuitable for computer simulation.

Willig [43] also considers essentially the same problem. In brief, the differences of our approaches are the following: Willig allows only a single component of the p-vector to change while we allow changes in the whole price vector; Willig gives exact bounds for the compensating variation and thus for the compensated income while our algorithms determine its value with arbitrary accuracy.

Our algorithms have interesting connections with the theory of Divisia–Törnqvist chain indices, consumer surplus measures, and numerical methods of solving differential equations, and are fully comprehensible even to the computer.

2. CONCEPTUAL BACKGROUND

Let $\Omega = \mathbb{R}_+^{n+1}$ be the nonnegative quadrant of $(n + 1)$ dimensional Euclidean vector space and Ω^* its subset. Consider functions $h : \Omega^* \to \mathbb{R}_+^n$ assigning to any price-expenditure pair (p, C) in Ω^* one and only one quantity vector $q = h(p, C)$ in $\mathbb{R}_+^n$. We are liberal and call $h : \Omega^* \to \mathbb{R}_+^n$ a *demand function* (*or system*) if $h(p, C)$ is an element of the budget set $B(p, C) = \{ q \mid p \cdot q \leq C \}$, i.e. if h satisfies BC:

BC. BUDGET CONDITION: $\forall(p, C) \in \Omega^* : p \cdot h(p, C) \leq C.$

We do not consider here demand correspondences or more general choice functions where $h(p, C)$ may denote a set of q's (see Richter [25]). The name 'demand function' is often used only for h's that satisfy B and H:

B. BALANCE: $\forall(p, C) \in \Omega^* : p \cdot h(p, C) = C.$

H. HOMOGENEITY OF DEGREE ZERO:

$$\forall(p, C) \in \Omega^* : \forall \lambda > 0: \qquad h(\lambda p, \lambda C) = h(p, C) = h(p/C, 1).$$

As we said we are more liberal here.

A demand function $h(p, C)$ may or may not correspond to some (utility) function $u : \mathbb{R}_+^n \to \mathbb{R}$. We say that a utility function $u : \mathbb{R}_+^n \to \mathbb{R}$ *represents* a given demand function $h : \Omega^* \to \mathbb{R}_+^n$ if $h(p, C)$ is the unique u-maximal element in any budget set $B(p, C)$: For all $(p, C) \in \Omega^* : \forall q \in B(p, C) : q \neq h(p, C) \Rightarrow u(q) < u(h(p, C))$. Sometimes such a $u(q)$ is said to rationalize $h(p, C)$. We try to apply here Richter's [25] terminology, where 'rationalize' is used only in connection with (preference) relations R and is therefore more general.

A demand function may satisfy the following (rather weak) utility hypothesis.

WUH: WEAK UTILITY HYPOTHESIS: *The demand function $h : \Omega^* \to \mathbb{R}_+^n$ is representable by some utility function, i.e., there exists a function $u : \mathbb{R}_+^n \to \mathbb{R}$ representing the given demand function.*

Note that if $u(q)$ represents $h(p, C)$ and $g : \mathbb{R} \to \mathbb{R}$ is strictly increasing, then also $\bar{u}(q) = g(u(q))$ represents $h(p, C)$. If $h(p, C)$ satisfies WUH then H is true, but e.g. B may well be untrue.

82   YRJÖ O. VARTIA

A standard practice in demand theory to derive demand systems using a Lagrangean $F(q,\lambda) = u(q) - \lambda(p \cdot q - C)$ imposes additional regularity to $u(q)$. Following this classical line of thinking gives rise to the following (rather strong) utility hypothesis:

SUH: STANDARD UTILITY HYPOTHESIS: *The demand function* $h : \Omega^* \to \mathbb{R}^n_+$ *is representable by a standard (i.e. twice continuously differentiable, strictly increasing and strictly quasi-concave) utility function* $u : \mathbb{R}^n_+ \to \mathbb{R}$.

If SUH holds for a $h(p, C)$ then it satisfies B and H, is continuous and differentiable and has many other nice properties. For example, its *Slutsky matrix* $A(p, C)$, an $(n \times n)$-matrix consisting of substitution terms $a^i_j(p, C)$ $= h^i_j(p, C) + h^j(p, C)h^i_{n+1}(p, C)$, is *symmetric* (S) and *negatively semidefinite* (NSD) for all $(p, C) \in \Omega^*$. Conditions S and NSD are just the economic integrability conditions considered by Hurwicz [19] (see also [21, 34, 9, pp. 79 and 111]). It is shown in [9] that if a continuously differentiable $h(p, C)$ satisfies B, H, S, and NSD, then there exists a twice differentiable *indirect* utility function $V(p, C)$ representing $h(p, C)$. Hurwicz and Uzawa [20] show that if a merely differentiable $h(p, C)$ satisfies in addition a *Lipschitz condition*, then there exists an increasing and strictly quasi-concave *direct* utility function $u(q)$ representing $h(p, C)$ in its range. Their Lipschitz condition is a weak condition that all income derivatives $\partial h^i(p, C)/\partial C$ exist and are uniformly bounded by a constant. We call this condition BID (bounded income derivatives). Because the existence of a well-behaved direct utility function is required here we suppose that $h(p, C)$ satisfies DUH:

DUH: DIRECT UTILITY HYPOTHESIS: *The demand function* $h : \Omega^* \to \mathbb{R}^n_+$ *is differentiable (D) and satisfies B, H, S, NSD, and BID.*
   Note that BID holds if $h(p, C)$ *is continuously differentiable.*

It is in principle straightforward to check whether the conditions D, B, H, S, NSD, and BID hold for some $h(p, C)$. If they do, then we know that a well-behaved utility function $u(q)$ exists although its form may be very complicated and unknown to us.

As demonstrated first by Hicks [18] and Samuelson [26] and shown later by Shephard [31, 32], L. McKenzie [22], Diewert [12], Afriat [1, 2] and others, it is possible to define the *minimum expenditure (or cost) function*

$$C(p, q) = \min\{ C \mid C = p \cdot \tilde{q} \ \& \ u(\tilde{q}) = u(q)\} = \min_{\tilde{q} \sim q} p \cdot \tilde{q}$$

under fairly general conditions on $u(q)$. $C(p, q)$ is the minimum expenditure needed to buy the well-being determined by q (i.e. some $\tilde{q}$ indifferent to q) when prices are p. For any given p the function $C(p, q)$ of q is a utility function, in particular $q \sim \tilde{q} \Leftrightarrow C(p, q) = C(p, \tilde{q})$ (see, e.g., Afriat [1, p. 17 and 36]). If

WELFARE CHANGE   83

$q = h(p, C)$ or (p, q) is an equilibrium pair, then $C = p \cdot q = C(p, q)$. We will use $C(p, q)$ freely in our later operations.

3. COMPENSATED INCOME AND COMPENSATED DEMAND

The problem is further specified as follows. Choose any price-expenditure pair (p^0, C^0) and let $q^0 = h(p^0, C^0)$ be the corresponding unique market demand, where $h(p, C)$ is supposed to be known. Change prices $p^0 \to p^1$ and determine the *compensated income* (or rather compensating expenditure[2])

$$(1) \qquad \bar{C}^1 = C(p^1, q^0) = \min_{q \sim q^0} p^1 \cdot q$$

$$= \min\{ C \mid C = p^1 \cdot q \, \& \, u(q) = u(q^0) \}$$

and the *Hicksian (or compensated) demand*

$$(2) \qquad \bar{q}^1 = H(p^1, q^0) = h(p^1, C(p^1, q^0))$$

for any given price vector p^1. Of course one of $\bar{q}^1$ and $\bar{C}^1$ determines the other because $\bar{q}^1 = h(p^1, \bar{C}^1)$ and $\bar{C}^1 = p^1 \cdot \bar{q}^1$. Here $\bar{q}^1$ is the cheapest bundle of goods under prices p^1, which gives the same satisfaction as q^0 and $\bar{C}^1$ is the least expenditure needed to attain the satisfaction given by q^0, when prices have changed to p^1. As our $h(p, C)$ is supposed to satisfy DUH, a direct utility function $u(q)$ exists but is not known. The compensated income (1) should be determined using only the ordinary demand system $h(p, C)$.

The compensated income (1) allows us to compute, e.g., *the (Laspeyres type) economic price index*

$$(3) \qquad P(p^1, p^0; q^0) = C(p^1, q^0) / C(p^0, q^0)$$

$$= \bar{C}^1 / C^0$$

and the *(Paasche type) economic quantity index*

$$(4) \qquad Q(q^1, q^0; p^1) = C(p^1, q^1) / C(p^1, q^0)$$

$$= C^1 / \bar{C}^1$$

$$= (C^1 / C^0) / P(p^1, p^0; q^0)$$

---

[2]To fix ideas, think that prices increase. Then more income is needed to attain the previous level of living or to *compensate* for the price change: $\bar{C}^1 > C^0$. Here $\bar{C}^1 - C^0$ is the *compensation* (or needed extra income) in monetary units, $100(\bar{C}^1 - C^0)/C^0$ in per cent and $100\ln(\bar{C}^1/C^0)$ in log per cent, and $\bar{C}^1$ is the *compensated* income, which includes the compensation. Terminology is rather unsettled here.

84 YRJÖ O. VARTIA

corresponding to any two equilibrium situations (p^0, q^0) and (p^1, q^1), where $q^t = h(p^t, C^t)$, $t = 0, 1$. Because $Q(q^1, q^0; p^1)$ is for fixed q^0 and p^1 and for arbitrary variable q^1 a utility function,[3] it solves e.g. our original problem:

(5) $Q(q^1, q^0; p^1) > 1 \Leftrightarrow C^1 > \bar{C}^1 \Leftrightarrow q^1 \succ q^0,$

$Q(q^1, q^0; p^1) = 1 \Leftrightarrow C^1 = \bar{C}^1 \Leftrightarrow q^1 \sim q^0,$

$Q(q^1, q^0; p^1) < 1 \Leftrightarrow C^1 < \bar{C}^1 \Leftrightarrow q^1 \prec q^0.$

Or verbally: if the actual income $C^1 = p^1 \cdot q^1$ *exceeds* (falls short of) the income $\bar{C}^1$ just compensating for the price change $p^0 \to p^1$, then the welfare change from q^0 to q^1 is *positive* (negative). If $\bar{C}^1 = C^1$, the welfare has remained the same. Our problem is reduced to the calculation of the compensated income $\bar{C}^1$ in terms of the ordinary demand system $h(p, C)$, which is still a rather complicated task. Next we give some differential expressions stating necessary conditions for movements on the same indifference surface.

4. CONDITIONS FOR MOVEMENTS ON THE SAME INDIFFERENCE SURFACE

Let t denote an auxiliary variable such that $0 \leq t \leq 1$ and let $p(t)$ be a differentiable curve in the price space connecting $p^0 = p(0)$ to $p^1 = p(1)$. $C(t)$ is any expenditure development starting from $C^0 = C(0)$. If $u(q)$ is a possible utility function, then $V(p, C) = u(h(p, C))$ is the corresponding indirect utility function. Differentiate $V(t) = V(p(t), C(t))$ with respect to t to get

(6) $$\frac{dV(t)}{dt} = \sum_{i=1}^{n} \frac{\partial V(p(t), C(t))}{\partial p_i(t)} \frac{dp_i(t)}{dt} + \frac{\partial V(p(t), C(t))}{\partial C(t)} \frac{dC(t)}{dt}.$$

This gives the rate of change in the utility at every point t when prices $p(t)$ and expenditure $C(t)$ change in an arbitrary way. Using Roy's theorem[4] we get

(7) $$\frac{dV(p(t), C(t))}{dt} = \lambda(p(t), C(t)) \left[\frac{dC(t)}{dt} - \sum h^i(p(t), C(t)) \frac{dp_i(t)}{dt} \right].$$

Because $V(p, C)$ is strictly increasing in C, $\lambda(p, C) > 0$. Thus a necessary and sufficient condition for $h(p(t), C(t))$ moving on the same indifference surface is that the rate of change in utility equals zero for every $t \in [0, 1]$, which leads to the

---

[3] That is $Q(q^1, q^0; p^1) = Q(q^2, q^0; p^1)$ if and only if $q^1 \sim q^2$, and $Q(q^1, q^0; p^1) > Q(q^2, q^0; p^1)$ if and only if $q^1 \succ q^2$. These types of general properties of (3) and (4) following from those of $C(p, q)$, are supposed to be known (see, e.g., Samuelson and Swamy [27], and Theil [37, pp. 112–144]).
[4] That is: $\partial V(p, C)/\partial p_i = -(\partial V(p, C)/\partial C)h^i(p, C) = -\lambda(p, C)h^i(p, C)$. For a short, elegant and very general proof, see Chipman and Moore [9, p. 74].

first order differential equation in $C(t)$:

(8) $$\frac{dC(t)}{dt} = \sum h^i(p(t), C(t)) \frac{dp_i(t)}{dt}.$$

This is the basic equation of our paper. Note that $p(t)$ and the derivatives $dp_i(t)/dt$ are here known functions and $C(t)$ is an unknown function to be solved. Integrating this we get an equivalent integral equation

(9) $$C(t) - C^0 = \sum \int_0^t h^i(p(t), C(t)) \frac{dp_i(t)}{dt} \, dt.$$

Let $p(t)$ be any differentiable price curve connecting p^0 to p^1. By the definition (1) of compensated income $C(t) = C(p(t), q^0)$ the compensated demand $H(p(t), q^0) = h(p(t), C(p(t), q^0))$ moves on the indifference surface determined by q^0 when $t \in [0, 1]$ changes. Therefore the compensated income $C(t) = C(p(t), q^0)$ is a solution of both (8) and (9) having the initial value $C(0) = C^0 = p^0 \cdot q^0 = p^0 \cdot h(p^0, C^0)$. Using the uniqueness property of first order differential equations (see e.g. [17, p. 264]), the compensated income $C(t) = C(p(t), q^0)$ is the only solution having this initial value. Therefore by solving (8) or (9) we get just the compensated income $C(p(t), q^0)$. Especially $C(p(1), q^0) = C(p^1, q^0) = \bar{C}^1$.

Equations (7) and (8) correspond to the usual but somewhat ambiguous total differential expressions $dV = \lambda(dC - \sum q_i \, dp_i)$ and $dC = \sum q_i \, dp_i$ (see, e.g., [6, 24, 33]). The gist of our basic equation (8) is the auxiliary variable t, which makes it a first order differential equation in $C(t)$.

By a simple transformation (8) may be expressed equivalently as

(10) $$\frac{d \log C(t)}{dt} = \sum w_i(p(t), C(t)) \frac{d \log p_i(t)}{dt},$$

where $w_i(p, C) = p_i h^i(p, C)/C$ is the ith value share. The integrated version is

(11) $$\log \frac{C(t)}{C^0} = \sum \int_0^t w_i(p(t), C(t)) \, d \log p_i(t).$$

The only solution $C(t)$ starting from $C(0) = C^0 = p^0 \cdot q^0$ is also here the compensated income $C(p(t), q^0)$ corresponding to the given price curve $p(t)$.

When equation (11) is solved its left hand side is the logarithm of the economic price index (3), $\log[C(t)/C^0] = \log[C(p(t), q^0)/C^0] = \log P(p(t), p^0; q^0)$, and its right hand side is the Divisia-Törnqvist integral representation of $\log P(p(t), p^0; q^0)$. The value shares in (11) are determined from demand $h(p(t), C(t))$ constrained on the same indifference surface.

Note that $\bar{C}^1 = C(p^1, q^0)$ equals the only solution $C(t)$ of equations (8)–(11) for $t = 1$ and for arbitrary price curve $p(t)$ connecting p^0 to p^1. This means that the same compensated income $\bar{C}^1$ results irrespective of the choice of an appropriate $p(t)$ curve. If the right hand sides of (9) and (11) are written as line integrals in the $(n + 1)$-dimensional (p, C)-space, these line integrals are independent of the path of integration, when $h(p(t), C(t))$ moves on the same indifference surface. This is shown and discussed, e.g., by Silberberg [33, pp. 947–948].

5. HOW TO MOVE ON THE SAME INDIFFERENCE SURFACE

Our Algorithms 1, 2, and 3 of calculating $\overline{C}^1 = C(p^1, q^0)$ are based on equations (8)–(9); almost as simple algorithms (e.g. our Algorithm 4) may be derived from (10)–(11).

Our basic equation (8) is a first order nonlinear differential equation of the form $C'(t) = f(t, C(t))$, where $f(t, C(t)) = \sum h^i(p(t), C(t))(dp_i(t)/dt)$ is a rather complicated function. Only the most simple first order differential equations can be solved explicitly; others must be solved numerically. Numerical solution of first order differential equations is shortly reviewed in Appendix 1. Here we only sketch the idea of our algorithms in intuitive terms.

Choosing $t_0, t_1, \ldots, t_N$ so that $0 = t_0 < t_1 < \cdots < t_N = 1$, we derive from (9) the following equation:

$$(12) \qquad \overline{C}^1 - C^0 = \sum_{k=1}^{N} \left[C(t_k) - C(t_{k-1}) \right] = \sum_{k=1}^{N} \left[\sum_i \int_{t_{k-1}}^{t_k} h^i(p(t), C(t)) \, dp_i(t) \right].$$

The terms in brackets are pairwise equal. Although the integration of $h^i(p(t), C(t))$ cannot be performed explicitly the integral can be approximated by different methods. In the simplest polygon method $h^i(p(t), C(t))$ is replaced by its value at the lower integration limit t_{k-1}, i.e. by the constant $h^i(p(t_{k-1}), C(t_{k-1}))$. This may be integrated explicitly and we get for $k = 1, 2, \ldots, N$,

$$(13) \qquad C(t_k) - C(t_{k-1}) \approx h(p(t_{k-1}), C(t_{k-1})) \cdot (p(t_k) - p(t_{k-1})).$$

Denote $p_k = p(t_k)$, any approximation of $C(t_k)$ by C_k, and the demand corresponding to price-expenditure situation (p_k, C_k) by $q_k = h(p_k, C_k)$. Replacing $C(t_k)$ and $C(t_{k-1})$ by their approximations C_k and C_{k-1}, (13) becomes our *Algorithm 1*:

$$(14) \qquad C_k - C_{k-1} = q_{k-1} \cdot (p_k - p_{k-1}).$$

Because $C_{k-1} = q_{-1} \cdot p_{k-1} = h(p_{k-1}, C_{k-1}) \cdot p_{k-1}$, (14) may be presented also by $C_k = q_{k-1} \cdot p_k$.

Algorithm 1 is started by setting $(p_0, q_0, C_0) = (p^0, q^0 = h(p^0, C^0), C^0)$. Because $C_k = q_k \cdot p_k = h(p_k, C_k) \cdot p_k$, still another representation of the Algorithm 1 is

$$(15) \qquad Q^{Pa}(q_k, q_{k-1}, p_k, p_{k-1}) = \frac{q_k \cdot p_k}{q_{k-1} \cdot p_k} = 1,$$

i.e. consecutive equilibrium pairs $(p_{k-1}, q_{k-1}), (p_k, q_k)$ are chosen so that the Paasche quantity index comparing the pairs equals unity.

Geometrically, the points q_{k-1} and q_k lie on the hyperplane being tangent to the indifference surface $S(q_k) = \{q \mid q \sim q_k\}$ at q_k. By the revealed preference table we infer that $q_k \succeq q_{k-1}$. In fact $q_k \succ q_{k-1}$ because the underlying unknown utility function was supposed to be strictly quasi-concave, which implies that its indifference surface $S(q_k)$ is totally above its tangent plane at q_k. Although $q^0 = q_0 \prec q_1 \prec \cdots \prec q_N$ and therefore for every $k \geq 1$, $q_k = h(p_k, C_k) \succ H(p_k, q^0) \sim q^0$ and $C_k > C(p_k, q^0)$, the approximation errors vanish gradually when all price steps $p_k - p_{k-1}$ approach zero: q_k approaches then $H(p_k, q^0)$ and C_k approaches $C(p_k, q^0)$ from above. Geometrically, the appropriate parts of the consecutive tangent planes envelope the indifference surface $S(q^0)$ along the curve $H(p(t), q^0)$, $0 \leq t \leq 1$. Especially $C_N \to C(p^1, q^0) = \overline{C}^1$ from above when $p_k - p_{k-1} \to 0$ for all k.

Replacing $h^i(p(t), C(t))$ in (12) by $h^i(p(t_k), C(t_k))$ we end up similarly to *Algorithm 2*:

(16) $C_k - C_{k-1} = q_k \cdot (p_k - p_{k-1})$,

where $q_k = h(p_k, C_k)$. This is an implicit equation for C_k which can be solved iteratively, e.g., from $C_k^{(m)} = C_{k-1} + h(p_k, C_k^{(m-1)}) \cdot (p_k - p_{k-1})$, $C_k^{(0)} = C_{k-1}$. Because $C_{k-1} = q_{k-1} \cdot p_{k-1}$ and $C_k = q_k \cdot p_k$, (16) may be reduced to $Q^{La}(q_k, q_{k-1}, p_k, p_{k-1}) = q_k \cdot p_{k-1} / q_{k-1} \cdot p_{k-1} = 1$, i.e., according to Algorithm 2 consecutive equilibrium pairs (p_{k-1}, q_{k-1}), (p_k, q_k) must be chosen so that the Laspeyres' quantity index comparing the pairs equals unity. Geometrically, the points q_{k-1} and q_k lie on the hyperplane being tangent now to the indifference surface $S(q_{k-1}) = \{q \mid q \sim q_{k-1}\}$ at q_{k-1}. Therefore $q_k \prec q_{k-1}$. Further we infer that $q^0 = q_0 \succ q_1 \succ \cdots \succ q_N$ which implies that $q_k = h(p_k, C_k) \prec H(p_k, q^0)$ and $C_k < C(p_k, q^0)$ for all $k \geq 1$. Especially $C_N < C(p^1, q^0) = \overline{C}^1$ here although it approaches it slowly from below when price steps $p_k - p_{k-1}$ approach zero.

These slowly converging algorithms were presented only in order to illustrate our basic idea. Using some average of the overcompensated and undercompensated expenditures generated by the Algorithms 1 and 2 respectively would speed up the convergence. However, a mathematically more elegant method is provided by approximating the integrands $h^i(p(t), C(t))$ of (12) by the average of their end point values, cf. Collatz [11, p. 53]. We get, for $k = 1, 2, \ldots, N$,

(17) $C(t_k) - C(t_{l-1}) \approx \sum \frac{1}{2} \left[h^i(p(t_k), C(t_k)) + h^i(p(t_{k-1}), C(t_{k-1})) \right]$

$$\times (p_i(t_k) - p_i(t_{k-1})).$$

Equation (17) forms the basis of our Main Algorithm, which is considerably more efficient than the previous algorithms, especially insofar as the C_k's generated by the Main Algorithm always lie between the over- and undercompensated expenditures generated above.

MAIN ALGORITHM (ALGORITHM 3): *Let $p(t) = p^0 + t(p^1 - p^0)$, $0 \leq t \leq 1$, be the linear price curve connecting p^0 to p^1. For a given integer N let $t_k = k/N$,*

88   YRJÖ O. VARTIA

$p_k = p(t_k)$, *and generate a sequence* $C_1, \ldots, C_N$ *so that*

(18) $C_k - C_{k-1} = \frac{1}{2}(q_k + q_{k-1}) \cdot (p_k - p_{k-1})$,

where $q_k = h(p_k, C_k)$, $k = 1, \ldots, N$, *and the starting values are* $(p_0, q_0, C_0) = (p^0,$
$q^0 = h(p^0, C^0), C^0)$.

The solution C_k of (18) is determined by iteration from[5]

(19) $C_k^{(m)} = C_{k-1} + \frac{1}{2}\left(h(p_k, C_k^{(m-1)}) + q_{k-1}\right) \cdot (p_k - p_{k-1})$,

where $C_k^{(0)} = C_{k-1}$, $k \geq 1$. When $|C_k^{(m)} - C_k^{(m-1)}|$ is negligible set $C_k = C_k^{(m)}$
and $q_k = q_k^{(m)}$ and start the calculation for the next k.

The Main Algorithm solves our original problem of calculating the compensated income (1) and Hicksian demand (2) efficiently. This is stated more accurately in the following theorem.

THEOREM 1: *Suppose that the ordinary demand system* $h(p, C)$ *satisfies the direct utility hypothesis* DUH. *Then the quantity* C_N *of our Main Algorithm converges to the compensated income* $\bar{C}^1 = C(p^1, q^0)$ *and the vector* $q_N = H(p_N, C_N)$ *converges to the compensated demand* $\bar{q}^1 = H(p^1, q^0) = h(p^1, \bar{C}^1)$ *as the number of steps N increases. The convergence is cubical, i.e. errors are asymptotically proportional to* $(1/N)^3$.

We have demonstrated in the text that if C_N converges, it converges to the compensated income $\bar{C}^1 = C(p^1, q^0)$. Therefore it remains to be shown that C_N converges. Theorem 1 and the convergence of (19) are proved in Appendices 1 and 2 using basic results from the numerical solution of differential equations.

6. INTERPRETATIONS AND GENERALIZATIONS

The idea of our Main Algorithm is to move by small steps along the indifference surface from q^0 to $\bar{q}^1$. Each q_k approximates $\bar{q}_k = H(p_k, q^0)$, the true compensated demand corresponding to p_k and q^0. Equation (18) is an accurate discrete analog for equation (8). Actually (18) requires that consecutive pairs (p_{k-1}, q_{k-1}) and (p_k, q_k) are equilibrium points, for which the Harberger welfare indicator (see [16, 14])

(20) $H(p_{k-1}, p_k, q_{k-1}, q_k) = p_{k-1} \cdot (q_k - q_{k-1}) + \frac{1}{2}(p_k - p_{k-1}) \cdot (q_k - q_{k-1})$

$= \frac{1}{2}(p_k + p_{k-1}) \cdot (q_k - q_{k-1})$

---

[5]Note that a practical way of writing (19) is

$C_k^{(m)} = \frac{1}{2}h(p_k, C_t^{(m-1)}) \cdot (p_k - p_{k-1}) + C^*$,

where $C^* = C_{k-1} + \frac{1}{2}q_{k-1} \cdot (p_k - p_{k-1})$ is independent of m.

is zero. To show this we only need to note that $H(p^1, p^2, q^1, q^2) = p^1 \cdot (q^2 - q^1) + \frac{1}{2}(p^2 - p^1) \cdot (q^2 - q^1) = \frac{1}{2}(p^2 + p^1) \cdot (q^2 - q^1)$ is zero if and only if

(21) $\qquad C^2 - C^1 = \frac{1}{2}(q^2 + q^1) \cdot (p^2 - p^1) = H(q^1, q^2, p^1, p^2)$

where $C^2 = p^2 \cdot q^2$ and $C^1 = p^1 \cdot q^1$. Equation (21) says approximately that the change in expenditure is required to compensate exactly for the price changes. Generally, the change in expenditure has a decomposition

(22) $\qquad C^2 - C^1 = \frac{1}{2}(p^2 + p^1) \cdot (q^2 - q^1) + \frac{1}{2}(q^2 + q^1) \cdot (p^2 - p^1)$

$\qquad\qquad = H(p^1, p^2, q^1, q^2) + H(q^1, q^2, p^1, p^2)$

into arithmetic contributions of quantity and price changes. Note that this is the finite change version of $dC = \sum p_i \, dq_i + \sum q_i \, dp_i$. Therefore $H(p^1, p^2, q^1, q^2) = 0$ if and only if (21) holds.

The decomposition (22) was the starting point of Stuvel [36] in the derivation of his remarkable price and quantity indices. Stuvel's quantity index has, e.g., the representation

(23) $\qquad Q^S(q^2, q^1, p^2, p^1) = A + \sqrt{A^2 + C^2/C^1}$, where

$$A = \frac{1}{2}\left(\frac{p^1 \cdot q^2}{p^1 \cdot q^1} - \frac{p^2 \cdot q^1}{p^1 \cdot q^1} \right) = \frac{1}{2}(Q^{La} - P^{La}) = \frac{1}{2}\left(Q^{La} - \frac{C^2/C^1}{Q^{Pa}} \right).$$

Stuvel's index satisfies the time and factor reversal tests, reacts correctly to extreme quantity or price changes, is consistent in aggregation, and has other remarkable properties (see Stuvel [36], van Yzeren [44], Banerjee [3], and Vartia [39, p. 140, 159–172]). Van Yzeren shows, e.g., that (23) and Edgeworth's quantity index $Q^E(q^2, q^1, p^2, p^1) = (p^2 + p^1) \cdot q^2/(p^2 + p^1) \cdot q^1$ equal one together. We see at once that this happens exactly if $H(p^1, p^2, q^1, q^2) = 0$ or equivalently if (21) holds. These expressions are beautifully symmetric and easy to work with. As a summary, our Main Algorithm tries to keep us on the indifference surface specified by q^0 by choosing its small steps $q_{k-1} \to q_k$ so that the following two conditions are satisfied for all $k = 1, \ldots, N$:

CONDITION C1: The quantity vector q_k is the demand corresponding to prices p_k and expenditure C_k:

$\qquad q_k = h(p_k, C_k) = h(p_k, p_k \cdot q_k).$

CONDITION C2: Stuvel's (or equivalently Edgeworth's) quantity index comparing consecutive pairs $(p_{k-1}, q_{k-1}), (p_k, q_k)$ remains equal to one:

$\qquad Q^S(q_k, q_{k-1}, p_k, p_{k-1}) = 1.$

Note that the economic or true quantity index (with reference prices p^*) $Q(q_k, q_{k-1}; p^*) = C(p^*, q_k)/C(p^*, q_{k-1})$ necessarily equals unity for all quantity vectors q_{k-1} and q_k on the same indifference surface.

Similar conditions using other index numbers and approximations of demand functions (or Engel curves) appear in approximating the economic or true price index, although notation sometimes hides the principles.[6] Banerjee [3, pp. 96–109] uses explicitly Stuvel's index in his "factorial approach" but demand functions do not appear explicitly. If pairs (p_k, q_k) are observations from "demand world" then Condition C1 holds automatically, which is not necessarily true if the researcher generates them.

In the chain of quantity indices of Condition C2 all the individual indices and therefore their product equals one. We have, approximately, followed a path of equilibrium points $(p(t), q(t))$, where the logarithm of the Divisia-Törnqvist quantity index (see Samuelson and Swamy [27] and Vartia [39]),

$$(24) \qquad \sum \int_0^t w_i(t)\, d\log q_i(t) = \sum_{i=1}^n \int_0^t w_i(p(t), C(t))\, d\log h^i(p(t), C(t))$$

has remained equal to zero. Because for all price-expenditure developments $(p(t), C(t))$ starting from (p^0, C^0) (24) is identical with

$$(25) \qquad \log\big(C(t)/C^0\big) - \sum \int_0^t w_i(t)\, d\log p_i(t)$$

$$= \log\big(C(t)/C^0\big) - \sum_{i=1}^n \int_0^t w_i(p(t), C(t))\, d\log p_i(t),$$

(24) and (25) are equal to zero simultaneously. The condition that (24) and (25) vanish for all t is *a necessary and sufficient condition* for movements on an indifference surface. This holds in the regular case when the marginal utility of expenditure $\lambda(p, C)$ is positive. Note that here is no trouble of the possible path dependency of the Divisia-Törnqvist line integral because for paths on the same indifference surface it is path-independent, i.e. only end points matter. Therefore any convenient price-path from p^0 to p^1 may be used.

These economic considerations led to the invention of our algorithm. Mathematically the algorithm happens to be a special case of Adams interpolation method for numerical solution of differential equations, which is used in proving that it works efficiently (see Appendix 1).

---

[6]The considerations are intimately connected with e.g. the concepts of consumer surplus, compensated and equivalent income variations, and different Divisia-Törnqvist line integrals, which provide alternative more or less different means to handle problems. But these are often used too freely (arguments are omitted, etc). Notable recent articles against or in favor of some use of these measures are, e.g., Bergson [4], Bruce [5], Burns [6, 7], Chipman and Moore [9, 10], Diewert [15], Harberger [16], G. McKenzie [23], McKenzie and Pearce [24], and Silberberg [33]. We think things would become clearer if the different measures were discussed in relation to economic price and quantity indices $P(p^1, p^0; q^*)$ and $Q(q^1, q^0; p^*)$, where q^* and p^* are some reference quantities and prices (see Samuelson and Swamy [27] and Vartia [39]). It is a sad fact that only in simple homothetic cases are these functions independent of q^* and p^*. This is one, but only one, source of confusion.

If the same method is used to solve the differential equation (10) in logarithms we get *Algorithm* 4, where (18) is replaced by

$$(26) \qquad \log(C_k/C_{k-1}) = \sum_{i=1}^{n} \frac{1}{2}(w_i(p_k, C_k) + w_i(p_{k-1}, C_{k-1}))\log(p_{k,i}/p_{k-1,i})$$

$$= \log P^T(p_k, p_{k-1}, q_k, q_{k-1}).$$

Here we have Törnqvist's price index for which

$$(27) \qquad \log P^T(p^1, p^0, q^1, q^0) = \sum \frac{1}{2}(w_i^1 + w_i^0)\log(p_i^1/p_i^0)$$

$$= \sum_{i=1}^{n} \frac{1}{2}\left(\frac{p_i^1 q_i^1}{p^1 \cdot q^1} + \frac{p_i^0 q_i^0}{p^0 \cdot q^0} \right)\log(p_i^1/p_i^0).$$

Algorithm 4 may work even better than the Main Algorithm, because value shares $w_i = w_i(p, C) = p_i h^i(p, C)/C$ are usually more slowly changing characteristics than quantities $q_i = h^i(p, C)$.

As in (18) iteration is also needed in (27) to solve for C_k. Theorem 1 renamed as Theorem 2 is proved similarly for Algorithm 4.

Using other price index number formulas instead of (27) we get other algorithms. The convergence properties would not be essentially altered if Törnqvist's index is replaced by the Sato–Vartia index:

$$(28) \qquad \log P^{SV}(p^1, p^0, q^1, q^0) = \sum_{i=1}^{n} \frac{L(w_i^1, w_i^0)}{\sum L(w_j^1, w_j^0)} \log(p_i^1/p_i^0),$$

where $L(x, y) = (x - y)/\log(x/y)$ is the logarithmic mean of positive x and y (see Vartia [**38, 39, 40**] and Sato [**29, 30**]). Evidently any quadratic approximation of (27) and (28) for small relative changes in p's and q's, such as Fisher's ideal index, Diewert–Sato quadratic mean of order r indices (see Diewert [**14, 15**], Sato [**28**], and Vartia [**41**]), Stuvel's or Edgeworth's indices, or just any good approximations of these indices, could be used to define a good "substitute" for Algorithm 4. Note that Laspeyres' or Paasche's indices are not sufficiently good approximations of these indices and using them instead of (27) will slow down the convergence. For example, if P^T in (26) is replaced by Laspeyres' price index $Q^{La}(p^1, p^0, q^1, q^0) = p^1 \cdot q^0/p^0 \cdot q^0$, Algorithm 4 reduces to our slowly converging Algorithm 1.

Note in particular that there is no need to use an exact index number formula for the demand system $h(p, C)$. If, however, the index number formula happened to be exact for $h(p, C)$, then any number N of prices steps (even $N = 1$) would give the same right results. Intuitively, the convergence is the faster the better an approximation is used for the exact index number formula.

Using other efficient numerical methods (which are numerous; see e.g., Collatz [**11**, p. 536]) to solve differential equations (8) or (10) leads to other efficient algorithms to calculate compensated income and compensated demand.

92   YRJÖ O. VARTIA

It is an easy task for a competent computer specialist to program the Main Algorithm for any computer.[7] Calculations in a few commodity case can be carried out even using only paper, pencil, and a functional pocket calculator as shown in Appendix 3.

7. CONCLUSIONS

We have considered a demand system $h(p, C)$ satisfying the direct utility hypothesis DUH, i.e. which is representable by some utility function $u(q)$. Two efficient algorithms have been presented to calculate the compensated income $C(p^1, q^0) = \min\{p^1 \cdot q \,|\, u(q) = u(q^0)\}$ and the compensated or Hicksian demand $H(p^1, q^0) = h(p^1, C(p^1, q^0))$ as accurately as one wishes using only the known ordinary demand system $h(p, C)$. A well-behaved utility function $u(q)$ exists by DUH but is not used nor needed in the calculation. Using the compensated income $C(p^1, q^0)$ we may compute the 'true' or 'economic' price index (of the Laspeyres type) $P(p^1, p^0; q^0) = C(p^1, q^0)/p^0 \cdot q^0$ and its pair, the 'economic' quantity index (of the Paasche type) $Q(q^1, q^0; p^1) = p^1 \cdot q^1/C(p^1, q^0)$ for any two equilibrium points (p^0, q^0) and (p^1, q^1). In fact the price index $P(p^1, p^0; q^0)$ may be calculated by our method for any p^1. But to determine $Q(q^1, q^0; p^1)$ for any quantity vector q^1 we have to find first some price vector p^1 satisfying $q^1 = h(p^1, p^1 \cdot q^1)$. Of course, if p^1 is a solution, also λp^1 is one for any $\lambda > 0$. This calls for the inverse demand function $r = \psi(q)$, where $r = p/C$ (see, e.g., Chipman and Moore [9, p. 104]). Alternatively we may use some numerical method to solve $q^1 = h(r^1, 1)$ for r^1 and put $p^1 = \lambda r^1$ for some $\lambda > 0$.

Computation of the compensated income $C(p^1, q^0)$ is all that is needed in making an exact welfare comparison between two equilibrium situations (p^0, q^0) and (p^1, q^1) (see equations (3)–(4)).

Starting from (p^1, q^1) instead of (p^0, q^0) and using the time inversal relations

(29) $P(p^0, p^1; q^1) = 1/P(p^1, p^0; q^1)$,

$Q(q^0, q^1; p^0) = 1/Q(q^1, q^0; p^0)$,

we may calculate similarly another pair of indices $P(p^1, p^0; q^1) = p^1 \cdot q^1/C(p^0, q^1)$, $Q(q^1, q^0; q^0) = C(p^0, q^1)/p^0 \cdot q^0$. Also these indices provide an exact welfare comparison between the two situations.

Our analysis allows us to get rid of an unnecessary assumption used in applied demand theory. The parametric families of demand systems used in applied work are usually restricted to families having a utility function (direct or indirect) of an *explicit parametric form*. Therefore, once the demand system is estimated, the utility function becomes completely known as well. However, our paper makes it possible to work with and estimate more general forms of demand functions, adjust the estimated functions to satisfy the integrability conditions of direct

---

[7] A program written by Mr. Heikki Vajanne in GE 635 FORTRAN IV is available upon request.

utility hypothesis (DUH) in the relevant region, and carry out arbitrary ordinal welfare comparisons in this region. Thus the assumption of explicit parametric form of the utility function can now be removed. Of course, this is only a beginning and the new approach contains many challenging research problems.

In short, we have provided an efficient and easily computerized method of welfare comparison between two arbitrary situations faced by a consumer, who has a completely known ordinary demand system corresponding to an arbitrary existing but unknown direct utility function.

University of Helsinki and the Research Institute of the Finnish Economy

Manuscript received December, 1978; final revision received December, 1981.

APPENDIX 1: Proof of Theorem 1

For the proof we need some results from the numerical solution of differential equations (see Collatz [11, pp. 48–114, 536] or Henrici [17, pp. 263–288]). Let $f(t, C)$ be a real valued function defined for $t \in [a, b]$ and for all real C and consider a first order differential equation

$$(1) \qquad C' = f(t, C).$$

Equation (1) symbolizes the following problem (see [17, p. 263]): Find a function $C = C(t)$, continuous and differentiable for all $t \in [a, b]$, such that

$$(2) \qquad C'(t) = f(t, C(t))$$

for all $t \in [a, b]$.

Let N be a positive integer and $t_k = a + k(b - a)/N$, so that $t_0 = a$ and $t_N = b$; $t_k - t_{k-1} = (b - a)/N$ is often called the step length or step and denoted by h. A simple but rather crude numerical method of solving (1) is the *"polygon method,"* where the exact solution $C(t)$ for points $t = t_0$, $t_1, \ldots, t_N$ is approximated by values $C_0, C_1, \ldots, C_N$ calculated by the formula

$$(3) \qquad C_k = C_{k-1} + \left(\frac{b - a}{N} \right) f_{k-1},$$

where $f_{k-1} = f(t_{k-1}, C_{k-1})$. Collatz [11, pp. 53–59] proves that if a Lipschitz condition (9) is satisfied, the error $C_k - C(t_k)$ tends to zero linearly, i.e. like $1/N$, as the step $(b - a)/N \to 0$.

We apply the polygon method for the differential equation (8) in the text:

$$(4) \qquad \frac{dC(t)}{dt} = \sum h'(p(t), C(t)) \frac{dp_i(t)}{dt},$$

where the price path connecting p^0 and p^1 is linear, $p(t) = p^0 + t(p^1 - p^0)$, $0 \le t \le 1$. We have $dp_i(t)/dt = (p_i^1 - p_i^0)$ so that for $p(t) = p^0 + t(p^1 - p^0)$

$$(5) \qquad f(t, C) = \sum h'(p(t), C)(p_i^1 - p_i^0)$$

$$= h(p(t), C) \cdot (p^1 - p^0).$$

The equation (3) becomes our Algorithm 1:

$$(6) \qquad C_k = C_{k-1} + \frac{1}{N} h(p_{k-1}, C_{k-1}) \cdot (p^1 - p^0)$$

$$= C_{k-1} + q_{k-1} \cdot (p_k - p_{k-1}) = q_{k-1} \cdot p_k$$

94 YRJÖ O. VARTIA

where $p_k = p(t_k)$ and $q_{k-1} = h(p_{k-1}, C_{k-1})$. Here C_k converges linearly to the solution $C(t_k)$ of (4), when the step $1/N$ and therefore the price steps $p_k - p_{k-1} = (p^1 - p^0)/N$ approach zero. As explained in the text the C_k's approach the compensated income curve $C(t) = C(p(t), q^0)$ from above.

A more efficient method for intergrating (1) is *Adams interpolation method* of order 1 which in the notation of Collatz [11, p. 85 and 536] is presented by

(7) $$y_{r+1} = y_r + h(f_{r+1} - \tfrac{1}{2}\nabla f_{r+1})$$

$$= y_r + h\left(\frac{f_{r+1} + f_r}{2}\right)$$

and in our notation by

(8) $$C_k = C_{k-1} + \left(\frac{b-a}{N}\right)\left(\frac{f_k + f_{k-1}}{2}\right).$$

It may be proved (see [17, pp. 280–3]), that the error $C_k - C(t_k)$ vanishes cubically, i.e. as $(1/N)^3$, as the step $(b-a)/N \to 0$. A sufficient condition for the convergence is that $f(t, C)$ satisfies the *Lipschitz condition* (see [17, p. 264]): There should exist a constant L such that for any y, z and all $t \in [a, b]$

(9) $$|f(t, y) - f(t, z)| \leq L|y - z|.$$

This is a very weak condition which is satisfied, e.g., if the derivative $\partial f(t, C)/\partial C$ exists and is bounded by L for all $t \in [a, b]$, because by mean value theorem $|f(t, y) - f(t, z)| = |(\partial f(t, \bar{C})/\partial C) \cdot (y - z)| \leq L|y - z|$.

Applying the Adams interpolation method (8) to equation (4) with $p(t) = p^0 + t(p^1 - p^0)$ leads to the following equation:

(10) $$C_k = C_{k-1} + \tfrac{1}{2}(q_k + q_{k-1}) \cdot (p_k - p_{k-1}),$$

where $p_k = p(k/N)$, $q_k = h(p_k, C_k)$, and $k = 1, \ldots, N$. While in equation (6) the price change $p_k - p_{k-1}$ was weighted by the "old basket" $q_{k-1} = h(p_{k-1}, C_{k-1})$, we have here the mean basket $\tfrac{1}{2}(q_k + q_{k-1})$. Equation (10) is equivalent to equation (18) of our Main Algorithm. The unknown C_k contained on both sides of the equation is determined by iteration as shown in (19), c.f. also [11, p. 86]. The convergence of the iteration is considered in Appendix 2.

We conclude that our Main Algorithm for solving (4) corresponds exactly to Adams interpolation method of order 1. Therefore Main Algorithm converges cubically, i.e. $C_k - C(t_k)$ vanishes like $(1/N)^3$, as $1/N$ and the price steps $p_k - p_{k-1} = (p^1 - p^0)/N$ approach zero. A sufficient condition for the convergence is that $f(t, C) = h(p(t), C) \cdot (p^1 - p^0)$ satisfies the Lipschitz condition (9), which holds, e.g., if the derivative

(11) $$\frac{\partial}{\partial C} f(t, C) = \sum \frac{\partial}{\partial C} h^i(p(t), C)(p_i^1 - p_i^0)$$

is bounded by some L for all $t \in [0, 1]$. We assumed that $h(p, C)$ satisfies DUH and therefore all its income derivatives are bounded by a positive constant K (condition BID). This gives

(12) $$\left|\frac{\partial}{\partial C} f(t, C)\right| \leq \left|\sum_{i=1}^{n} K(p_i^1 - p_i^0)\right|$$

$$\leq nKM,$$

where $M = \max|p_i^1 - p_i^0|$. Therefore $L = nKM$ works as a Lipschitz constant.

Especially our analysis in the text shows that for value $t_N = 1$ of our t-parameter C_N approaches $C(t_N) = C(1)$, the compensated income $\bar{C}^1 = C(p^1, q^0)$, and therefore $q_N = h(p^1, C_N) \to h(p^1, \bar{C}^1) = \bar{q}^1$, the compensated demand, when the number of steps $N \to \infty$. Theorem 1 is proved.

APPENDIX 2: CONVERGENCE OF THE ITERATION OVER m IN THE MAIN ALGORITHM

Iteration (19) over m is the ordinary cobweb iteration $x_m = f(x_{m-1})$, $m = 1, 2, \ldots$, where

(1) $\qquad f(x) = C_{k-1} + \frac{1}{2}(h(p_k, x) + q_{k-1}) \cdot (p_k - p_{k-1}).$

A sufficient condition for its convergence to a unique solution $x = f(x)$ for all starting values $x_0 \in [a, b]$, is that $f(x)$ is differentiable and

(2) $\qquad |f'(x)| \leq L \qquad$ for all $\quad x \in [a, b],$

where L is some constant smaller than 1 (see, e.g., [17, pp. 61–66]). Differentiating (1), we get

(3) $\qquad f'(x) = \frac{1}{2} \sum \frac{\partial}{\partial x} h^i(p_k, x)(p_{k,i} - p_{k-1,i}).$

By BID $|\partial h^i(p_k, x)/\partial x| \leq K$, and if $M = \max|p_i^1 - p_i^0|$, then $|p_{k,i} - p_{k,i-1}| \leq M/N$, which implies

(4) $\qquad |f'(x)| \leq \frac{1}{2}nKM/N.$

Therefore (2) holds when the number of steps N is great enough. For small price changes $p^0 \to p^1$ the iteration (19) converges even for $N = 1$.

APPENDIX 3: ILLUSTRATIVE CALCULATIONS

It is convenient to present the calculations in a table, where columns are reserved for vectors p_k and $q_k^{(m)}$ and for the scalar $C_k^{(m)}$. We illustrate the Main Algorithm using the simple example of McKenzie and Pearce [24], where $h(p, C) = ((p_2/p_1)(C/(p_1 + p_2)), (p_1/p_2)(C/(p_1 + p_2)))$. The demand system corresponds to the "unknown" indirect utility function $V(p, C) = (C/p_1) + (C/p_2)$, which we are not allowed to use here. The two equilibrium points are given in Table I.

Using the utility function it can checked that the change in satisfaction is zero, or q^0 and q^1 lie on the same indifference surface.

Starting from the initial situation (p^0, q^0, C^0), we try to move step by step on the indifference surface and approach the point of compensated demand $\bar{q}^1 = H(p^1, q^0)$, which here is equal to $q^1 = h(p^1, C^1) = (121.2119, 51.2125)$. We use first only 4 steps, i.e. $N = 4$.

The calculations run as follows: First calculate the linear price path $p^0 = p_0, p_1, p_2, p_3, p_4 = p^1$ given in Table II. The starting values $(p^0, q^0, C^0) = (p_0, q_0, C_0)$ are given in the first row $(k = 0)$. Using the demand system $q = h(p, C)$ calculate then for $(k, m) = (1, 1)$: $q_1^{(1)} = h(p_1, C^{(0)}) = h(p_1, C_0) = (140.0092, 39.7751)$. Next form the average $\frac{1}{2}(q_1^{(1)} + q_0)$ and take the inner product $\frac{1}{2}(q_1^{(1)} + q_0) \cdot (p_1 - p_0)$, which gives $C_1^{(1)} = 220.6433$. This is a new start and the next row is generated similarly: $q_1^{(2)} = h(p_1, C_1^{(1)})$, $C_1^{(2)} = C_0 + \frac{1}{2}(q_1^{(2)} + q_0) \cdot (p_1 - p_0)$. The iteration for $C_1^{(m)}$ converges quickly and after its convergence calculations for $k = 2$ proceed completely in the same way.

The five points $q^0 = q_0, q_1, q_2, q_3, q_4$ lie very near the same indifference surface and $q_4 = (121.2074, 51.2106)$ accurately approximates $\bar{q}^1 = H(p^1, q^0) = (121.2119, 51.2125)$. The economic price index $P(p^1, p^0; q^0) = \bar{C}^1/C^0$ (which equals 1 here) is estimated by $C_4/C^0 = 219.9917/220 = 0.99996$ and the economic quantity index $Q(q^1, q^0; p^1) = C^1/\bar{C}^1$ (which also equals 1 here) is estimated by $C^1/C_4 = 220/219.9917 = 1.00004$. Anyone who does not regard these estimates accurate enough may increase the accuracy without limits by increasing the number of steps from 4. It is

TABLE I
INITIAL AND FINAL VALUES

Variable	p		q		C
(0) Initial values	1.0000	2.0000[a]	146.6667	36.6667	220.0000
(1) Final values	1.1000	1.6923	121.2119	51.2125	220.0000

[a] McKenzie and Pearce [24] have a misprint here.

YRJÖ O. VARTIA

TABLE II

DEMAND SYSTEM: $q = h(p, C) = ((p_2/p_1)/(C/(p_1 + p_2)), (p_1/p_2)/(C/(p_1 + p_2)))$.
PRICE STEPS: $p_k - p_{k-1} = (0.025, -0.076925)$.

k	m	Price situation		Approximations for the compensated demand $q_k^{(m)}$		compensated income $C_k^{(m)}$
		p_k				
0		1.0000	2.0000	146.6667	36.6667	220.0000
1	1	1.0250	1.9231	140.0092	39.7751	220.6433
	2			140.4186	39.8915	220.6439
	3			140.4190	39.8916	220.6440
2	1	1.0500	1.8462	133.9518	43.3305	220.8727
	2			134.0907	43.3754	220.8727
3	1	1.0750	1.7692	127.8064	47.1849	220.6632
	2			127.6852	47.1402	220.6634
	3			127.6853	47.1402	220.6634
4	1	1.1000	1.6923	121.5774	51.3669	219.9904
	2			121.2066	51.2103	219.9918
	3			121.2074	51.2106	219.9917

convenient to half the price steps, or in some other way go through the previous price situations. This makes it possible to check the calculations and control the convergence.

Omitting the figures referring to the iteration steps and tabulating only the converged values we get for $N = 8$ steps Table III, where the economic price index $P(p_k, p^0; q^0) \approx C_k/C^0$ comparing the price situation p_k to the initial prices is also included.

All quantity vectors of Table III lie practically on the same indifference surface. Every second row of Table III corresponds to a row in Table II, which makes it possible, e.g., to control the convergence.

Four steps gave the approximation $H(p^1, q^0) \approx (121.2074, 51.2106)$ as 8 steps gave $H(p^1, q^0)$ $\approx (121.2106, 51.2119)$. The price steps are rather long even here, as for the second commodity they are about 2 per cent. However, the accuracy is sufficient for most purposes.

In computer simulations perhaps only the last row of Tables such as II or III corresponding to $H(p^1, q^0)$ deserves to be printed.

As a final illustration let $p^2 = (1.0500, 1.8462)$ and $C^2 = 221.0000$. The demand system gives the quantity vector $q^2 = h(p^2, C^2) = (134.1693, 43.3985)$, which the consumer would buy in this situation. Is the consumer better off in situation (2) than in situation (0) of Table I?

TABLE III

DEMAND SYSTEM: $q = h(p, C) = ((p_2/p_1)/(C/(p_1 + p_2)), (p_1/p_2)/(C/(p_1 + p_2)))$.
PRICE STEPS: $p_k - p_{k-1} = (0.0125, -0.0384625)$.

k	m	Price situation		Approximations for the compensated demand $q_k^{(m)} = q_k$		compensated income $C_k^{(m)} = C_k$	economic price index $P(p_k, p^0; q^0)$
		p_k					
0		1.0000	2.0000	146.6667	36.6667	220.0000	1.00000
1	3	1.0125	1.9615	143.5535	38.2482	220.3732	1.00170
2	3	1.0250	1.9231	140.4198	39.8918	220.6453	1.00293
3	2	1.0375	1.8846	237.2260	41.6002	220.8136	1.00370
4	2	1.0500	1.8462	134.0924	43.3759	220.8754	1.00398
5	2	1.0625	1.8077	130.8994	45.2219	220.8278	1.00376
6	3	1.0750	1.7692	127.6878	47.1412	220.6677	1.00304
7	3	1.0875	1.7308	124.4580	49.1367	220.3921	1.00178
8	3	1.1000	1.6923	121.2106	51.2119	219.9976	0.99999

WELFARE CHANGE   97

From Table III (row $k = 4$) we see that $P(p^2, p^0; q^0) \approx 1.0040$ or that 0.40 per cent more money is needed in situation (2) to compensate for the price changes. Expenditure has increased actually from 220 to 221 or 0.46 per cent. Hence real consumption has increased somewhat (about 0.06 per cent) and the consumer lies on a higher utility level. Table II gives the same results.

REFERENCES

[1] AFRIAT, S. N.: "The Theory of International Comparisons of Real Income and Prices," in *International Comparisons of Prices and Output*, NBER Studies in Income and Wealth, Vol. 37, ed. by D. J. Daly. New York: Columbia University Press, 1972, pp. 13–84.

[2] ———: *The Price Index*. Cambridge: Cambridge University Press, 1977.

[3] BANERJEE, K. S.: *Cost of Living Index Numbers, Practice, Precision, and Theory*. New York: Marcel Dekker, Inc., 1975.

[4] BERGSON, A.: "A Note on Consumer's Surplus," *Journal of Economic Literature*, 13(1975), 38–44.

[5] BRUCE, N.: "A Note on Consumer's Surplus, the Divisia Index, and the Measurement of Welfare Changes," *Econometrica*, 45(1977), 1033–1038.

[6] BURNS, M. E.: "A Note on the Concept and Measure of Consumer's Surplus," *American Economic Review*, 63(1973), 335–344.

[7] ———: "On the Uniqueness of Consumer's Surplus and the Invariance of Economic Index Numbers," *The Manchester School of Economic and Social Studies*, (1977), 41–61.

[8] CHIPMAN, J. S., L. HURWICZ, M. K. RICHTER, AND H. F. SONNENCHEIN (EDS): *Preferences, Utility and Demand Theory*. New York: Harcourt Brace Jovanovich, 1971.

[9] CHIPMAN, J. S., AND J. C. MOORE: "The Scope of Consumer's Surplus Arguments," in *Evolution, Welfare and Time in Economics, Essays in Honor of Nicholas Georgescu-Roegen*, ed. by A. M. Tang, et al. Lexington: Lexington Books, 1976.

[10] ———: "Compensating Variation, Consumer's Surplus, and Welfare," *The American Economic Review*, 70(1980), 933–949.

[11] COLLATZ, L.: *The Numerical Treatment of Differential Equations*. Berlin: Springer-Verlag; Heidelberg: Gottingen, 1960.

[12] DIEWERT, W. E.: "An Application of the Shephard Duality Theorem: A Generalized Leontief Production Function," *Journal of Political Economy*, 79(1971), 481–507.

[13] ———: "Harberger's Welfare Indicator and Revealed Preference Theory," *The American Economic Review*, 66(1976), 143–152.

[14] ———: "Exact and Superlative Index Numbers," *Journal of Econometrics*, 4(1976), 115–145.

[15] ———: "Superlative Index Numbers and Consistency in Aggregation," *Econometrica*, 46(1978), 883–900.

[16] HARBERGER, A. C.: "Three Postulates for Applied Welfare Economics: An Interpretive Essay," *Journal of Economic Literature*, 9(1971), 785–97.

[17] HENRICI, P.: *Element of Numerical Analysis*. New York: John Wiley & Sons, 1964.

[18] HICKS, J. R.: *Value and Capital*, 2nd ed. Oxford: Clarendon Press, 1946.

[19] HURWICZ, L.: "On the Problem of Integrability of Demand Functions," *Preferences, Utility and Demand Theory*, ed. by J. S. Chipman et al. New York: Harcourt Brace Jovanovich, 1971.

[20] HURWICZ, L., AND H. UZAWA: "On the Integrability of Demand Functions," *Preferences, Utility, and Demand Theory*, ed. by J. S. Chipman et al. New York: Harcourt Brace Jovanovich, 1971.

[21] KILSTROM, R., A. MAS-COLELL, AND H. SONNENSCHEIN: "The Demand Theory of the Weak Axiom of Revealed Preference," *Econometrica*, 44(1976) 971–978.

[22] McKENZIE, L.: "Demand Theory Without a Utility Index," *The Review of Economic Studies*, 65(1957), 185–189.

[23] McKENZIE, G.: "Measuring Gains and Losses," *Journal of Political Economy*, 84(1976), 641–646.

[24] McKENZIE, G. AND I. PEARCE: "Exact Measures of Welfare and the Cost of Living," *Review of Economic Studies*, 43(1976), 465–468.

[25] RICHTER, M. K.: "Invariance Axioms and Economic Indexes," *Econometrica*, 34(1966), 739–755.

[26] SAMUELSON, P. A.: *Foundations of Economic Analysis*. Cambridge, Massachusetts: Harvard University Press, 1947.

[27] SAMUELSON, P. A. AND S. SWAMY: "Invariant Economic Index Numbers and Canonical Quality: Survey and Synthesis," *The American Economic Review*, 64(1974), 566–593.

[28] SATO, K.: "Generalized Fisher's Ideal Index Numbers and Quadratic Utility Functions," Discussion Paper Number 297, State University of New York at Buffalo, Department of Economics, 1974.

98   YRJÖ O. VARTIA

[29] ——: "Ideal Index Numbers That Almost Satisfy Factor Reversal Test," *The Review of Economics and Statistics*, 56(1974), 549–552.

[30] ——: "The Ideal Log-Change Index Number," *The Review of Economics and Statistics*, 58(1976), 223–228.

[31] SHEPHARD, R. W.: *Cost and Production Functions*. Princeton: Princeton University Press, 1953.

[32] ——: *Theory of Cost and Production Functions*. Princeton: Princeton University Press, 1970.

[33] SILBERBERG, E.: "Duality and the Many Consumer's Surpluses," *American Economic Review*, 62(1972), 942–952.

[34] SONNENCHEIN, H. F.: "Demand Theory Without Transitive Preferences, With Applications to the Theory of Competitive Equilibrium," in *Preferences, Utility and Demand Theory*, ed. by J. S. Chipman et al. New York: Harcourt Brace Jovanovich, 1971.

[35] STIGUM, B. P.: "Revealed Preference—A Proof of Houthakker's Theorem," *Econometrica*, 41(1973), 411–423.

[36] STUVEL, G.: "A New Index Number Formula," *Econometrica*, 25(1957), 123–131.

[37] THEIL, H.: *Theory and Measurement of Consumer Demand*, Volume 1. Amsterdam: North Holland Publishing Company, 1975. Volume 2, 1976.

[38] VARTIA, Y.: "Relative Changes and Economic Indices," an unpublished licentiate thesis in Statistics, University of Helsinki, Department of Statistics, 1974.

[39] ——: *Relative Changes and Index Numbers*. Helsinki: Research Institute of the Finnish Economy, Series A4, 1976.

[40] ——: "Ideal Log-Change Index Numbers," *Scandinavian Journal of Statistics*, 3(1976), 121–126.

[41] ——: "Fisher's Five-Tined Fork and Other Quantum Theories of Index Numbers," in *Theory and Applications of Economic Indices*, ed. by W. Eichhorn, R. Henn, D. Opitz, and R. W. Shephard. Würzburg: Physica–Verlag, 1978.

[42] VARTIA, Y., AND J. WEYMARK: "Four Revealed Preference Tables," *Scandinavian Journal of Economics*, 83(1981), 408–418.

[43] WILLIG, R. D.: "Consumer's Surplus Without Apology," *American Economic Review*, 66(1976), 582–597.

[44] VAN YZEREN, J.: "A Note on the Useful Properties of Stuvel's Index Numbers," *Econometrica*, 26(1958), 429–439.

Part IV
Income Distributional Considerations in Welfare Measurement

[21]

Mechanized Agriculture and Social Welfare: The Case of the Tomato Harvester*

Andrew Schmitz and David Seckler

An integrated public-private approach to mechanical harvesting of tomatoes for canning has sharply reduced producers' labor requirements. Gross social returns to aggregate research and development expenditures are in the vicinity of 1,000 percent. Even if displaced labor had been compensated for wage loss, net social returns are still highly favorable. Since tomato pickers were unorganized, no compensation was demanded or paid. The analysis indicates a need for policies designed to distribute the benefits and costs of technological change more equitably. Social scientists could properly be concerned with developing institutional means of achieving this goal.

AT THE beginning of the industrial revolution in the 19th century gangs of workmen known as the Luddites roamed England, systematically destroying machinery. To their compatriots in the Netherlands we owe the word "sabotage," after "sabot," the heavy wooden shoe that Dutch workmen threw into the grinding gears of the new technology.

The other side of the coin is well illustrated by the lament of John M. Horner, one of the inventors of the wheat combine.[1] Writing to his friend, Colonel Warren, editor of the *California Farmer*, in July 1869 [11, p. 22], Horner said,

... we were brought more particularly to reflect upon our position by the burning of one of our machines.... We ask ourselves: Have we injured anyone so that personal vengeance is pursuing us, and this burning was done to gratify a revengeful feeling? No. We have had no misunderstanding with anyone, in fact, not an enemy in the world, a conscience void of offence to all men. We entered that neighborhood to perform honest labors, and harvested [1,600] acres in a good workmanlike manner to the entire satisfaction of our employers—so much so that most of them wanted us to consent to harvest their next crops.

Colonel Warren promptly responded with an editorial in his paper [11, p. 23]:

* Giannini Foundation Paper No. 310. We appreciate the data made available for this study by various departments at the University of California, Davis, and the University of Michigan. Ernie Blackwelder, Clarence Kelly, Philip Parsons, Gordon Rowe, Loy Sammet, and Ron Schuler also provided valuable information. We thank Roy Born for computational assistance and Bill Martin and Loren Ihnen for critical comments.
[1] We are indebted to Paul Barkley for this reference.

ANDREW SCHMITZ *is assistant professor of agricultural economics and* DAVID SECKLER *is acting associate professor of agricultural economics at the University of California, Berkeley.*

Such acts as the one named upon a man like Mr. Horner because he had invented a labor-saving machine should arouse the spirit of the lion among all good men and they should unite and hunt up the offenders and make them feel the heaviest penalties of the law for damages and then be driven from every civilized community.

The rhetoric of this ancient conflict has changed, but not its substance. "Technological displacement"—as it is now euphemistically called—remains the source of some of our greatest social problems. This is particularly true in agriculture. We point with justifiable pride to the fact that now only a small percentage of the total population produces our food needs. But we tend to forget the painful process of adjustment that accompanied the transition from a rural to an urban society. We have forgotten that for many people the transition was involuntary; that many people have been forced off the farm only into an economic and social limbo in rural towns and urban ghettos.

The overall purpose of this paper is to provide a means whereby the broad social costs of technological innovation can be mapped into the framework of economic analysis. It focuses specifically on a recent technological change affecting agriculture—the mechanical tomato harvester.

Development of the Tomato Harvester

The history of the development of the tomato harvester is a subject of interest in itself. It is an outstanding instance of the parallel development of innovations dovetailing into a viable system. As Rasmussen [26, pp. 532–533] states,

The invention of the mechanical tomato harvester contrasted decidedly with the development of the cotton picker. The tomato harvester resulted from the "system approach." A team made up of an engineering group and a horticultural group, with advice and assistance from agronomists and irrigation specialists, developed suitable plants and an efficient harvester at the same time. The necessary changes in planting, cultivation, and irrigating were developed concurrently. . . .

The systems approach was also followed in the development phase of the harvester. Manufacturers, scientists, and extension personnel worked closely with farmers, first in growing the new tomato varieties, then in getting the tomatoes harvested. Processors subsidized the first crops by lowering their purchasing standards on the new tomatoes and by adjusting their production techniques to accommodate the changed inputs. In the opinion of E. Blackwelder of the Blackwelder Manufacturing Company, which produced one of the first harvesters, it would have been virtually impossible to develop the harvester without an industry-wide integration of efforts. Thus, the harvester represents a social as well as a scientific and engineering success. Through coordinated efforts on many fronts, the industry was able to achieve results not economically available to any individual member.

The first 25 harvesters were used in California in 1961. By 1964, 75 were in use; a year later, 250. The number increased to 1,000 in 1967 [16], when approximately 80 percent of the California acreage was harvested by machines. However, in other tomato-producing states the harvester was adopted after this period.

Purpose and Framework of Analysis

Like the cotton harvester, the mechanical tomato harvester has created important production economies but has also undermined the livelihood of numerous agricultural laborers. In this paper we attempt to appraise both the heightened production efficiency and its effect on the welfare of workers. The pioneering work of Schultz [31] and Griliches [8] is carried one step further—into an appraisal of important social costs as well as social benefits.

Both gross and net social rates of return to the tomato harvester are computed; the difference is the wage loss of the displaced workers. To compute the gross social rate of return, we employ as a basis the framework used by Griliches [8] and Peterson [24] who estimated, respectively, the benefit to society from the introduction of hybrid corn and from poultry research.

Using the concepts of consumer's and producer's surplus, Griliches analyzed two polar cases. In Figure 1(a) supply is completely elastic and the original supply curve is S'; after the development of hybrid corn, the new supply curve is S. Since supply is completely elastic, producer surplus does not exist and the net gain, $E+F$, represents the addition to consumer surplus. In Figure 1(b) supply is perfectly inelastic; with the introduction of hybrid corn, supply shifts from S' to S. The gain in consumer surplus is $A+B$; the gain in producer surplus is $-A+D$; and the net gain to society is $A+B+(-A+D)=B+D$, from which is calculated the gross social rate of return.

Peterson, on the other hand, used the in-between case of a positive sloping supply curve. Thus, as demonstrated in Figure 2, the net benefit to society is $G+F+H+I$, that is, the area between the two supply curves and the demand curve, as in Figure 1(b). This is so since the net gain in consumer and producer

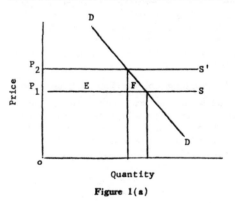

Figure 1(a)

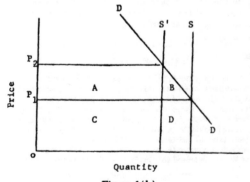

Figure 1(b)

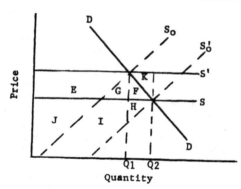

Figure 2

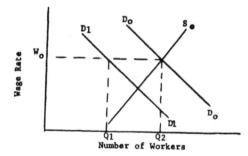

Figure 3

surplus is $E+G+F+(-E+H+I)$. As previously, the gross social rate of return is calculated from the area remaining after accounting for the changes in surpluses.

Various attempts at estimating the elasticities of demand and supply of processing tomatoes have met with little success.[2] Therefore, in computing the *gross* social returns from the harvester, we take the total production after the new equilibrium is achieved and multiply this by the ensuing cost savings per ton of tomatoes harvested. Thus, we are essentially measuring area $EGFK$ in Figure 2, where Q_1 is the equilibrium level of tomato production prior to the implementation of the harvester and Q_2 is the equilibrium level of production when the harvester is in use. Therefore, we would overestimate consumer surplus, and hence the gross social gain to society, by K if the demand for tomatoes were DD and supply were perfectly elastic. However, if the supply curve for tomatoes is not perfectly elastic, our calculations underestimate the gross social rates of return if the true demand and supply functions for tomatoes are approximately those represented by DD and S_0' (compare $EGFK$ and $GFHI$).[3]

To compute the *net* social rate of return from the development of the harvester, we explicitly took into account its effect on farm workers. With reference to Figure 3, prior to mechaniza-

tion the demand for tomato workers is D_0 and the supply is S_0, but subsequent to the harvester the demand becomes D_1. As one extreme, we computed $W_0 (Q_2-Q_1)$—the unemployment caused by the harvester—assuming no alternative employment possibilities and assuming that the remaining employed workers receive wages at least as high as those obtained prior to the implementation of the harvester. In addition, we calculated the net social rate of return assuming different levels of employment for farm workers in nonagricultural industries.

Gross Social Rate of Return

Gross social returns

We use "gross social returns" (GSR) to mean the value of the reduced costs of harvesting tomatoes by the mechanical harvester.[4] These returns differ from "net social returns" by the value of the costs incurred by workers displaced by the harvester.

Only for California have definitive studies been made of the comparative costs of hand and mechanical tomato harvesting methods [23, 36], and these data are used here for other tomato-producing states as well. According to the California studies, mechanical harvesting reduces costs by $5.41 to $7.47 per ton,[5] in-

---

[2] For consumer tomato demand, Babb et al. [1] estimated the price elasticity to be −.76, but this was statistically insignificant. They attributed their difficulty in estimation to data problems. For supply response of planted tomato acreage, they estimated the short- and long-run price elasticity to be 2.18 and 4.49 in Indiana; 1.05 and 2.65 in Ohio.

[3] Other configurations for supply could lead to an overestimate of the gross social rates of return.

[4] Some benefits of the harvester have been omitted from our estimates. We neglect benefits accruing to foreign countries (Germany, the U.S.S.R., and Israel, for example) that have imported these machines. Manufacturers' profits from the sale of the machines were not independently estimated, but enter our analysis as a cost of the machines. Royalties received by the University of California, which holds a patent on the most commonly used machines, were not included in our estimate of benefits; these amounted to $224,782 by 1969.

[5] These cost savings are not given explicitly in the studies; they were computed from Zobel's and Parsons' work [23, 36, 37]. Detailed calculations are available on request from the authors, as are the detailed calculations underlying the remainder of this paper.

Table 1. Rate of adoption of the tomato harvester, United States, 1965–1973[a]

Year	Percent of tomatoes harvested by machines		Total U.S. acreage of tomatoes harvested by machines
	California	Other states	
1965	25	0	48,302
1966	60	0	112,704
1967	80	0	144,905
1968	85	10	161,005
1969	90	20	193,206
1970	95	30	209,307
1971	95	40	225,405
1972	95	50	241,508
1973	95	60	257,608

[a] The rate of adoption was negligible before 1965 and is assumed to be zero for estimation purposes.

Sources: Adoption rates prior to 1968 were taken from Lynch [16]; succeeding adoption rates are the authors' projections (see footnote 7 of text). Estimated tomato acreage harvested by machine for 1965–1968 was derived by applying the above percentage rates of adoption to the acreage figures reported by the U. S. Department of Agriculture [33]. The equilibrium acreage in processing tomatoes was estimated to be 332,010, of which 257,608 are mechanically harvested.

cluding amortization and interest charges at 6 percent on the machine costs. The data apply only to tomatoes for processing since tomatoes for nonprocessing are still handpicked.

In order to estimate GSR from the harvester for the United States as a whole, it is necessary to estimate its rate of adoption. These estimates, presented in Table 1, are based on a total U. S. acreage of tomatoes for processing of 322,010, the average for 1966–1969.[6] We estimate that California will harvest 95 percent of its acreage by machine in 1973 and that the maximum rate of adoption by other states will be 60 percent. Webb [34, pp. 1–5] has estimated the total U. S. average rate of adoption to be 80 percent.[7]

Given these data and an estimated average yield of 22 tons of tomatoes per acre, we can now compute the GSR to the harvester for the

[6] Since this study was completed before 1969 acreage figures were available, total 1969 acreage was estimated to be 80 percent of the 1968 figure.

[7] Accurate estimates on the current rate of adoption do not exist. It appears, however, that for California at least 90 percent of the acreage is now mechanically harvested and could easily reach 95 percent by 1973. On the other hand, several people have expressed the opinion that our 60 percent adoption figure by 1973 for other states is too high. It may well be, however, that more processing tomatoes may be grown in California than the 55 percent of the acreage figure used. Therefore, we feel that the total acreage of 257,608 mechanically harvested of a possible estimated 322,010 acres is a conservative estimate.

Table 2. Gross social returns to the tomato harvester

Returns	Estimated cost reduction at	
	$5.41 per ton	$7.47 per ton
	dollars	
1. Cumulated GSR, 1965–1973	199,124,897	274,792,805
2. Annual value of cumulated GSR, 1973	11,947,494	16,487,568
3. Annual GSR, 1973	30,660,524	42,335,299
4. Total, 2 and 3	42,608,018	58,822,867

United States. All estimates have been carried to the year 1973 when, by assumption, tomato acreage attains a constant amount. Thus, the annual GSR for each year, 1965–1973, are calculated at 6 percent interest to 1973 and then converted to an annual perpetual sum.[8] This, together with the annual GSR in 1973 and thereafter, constitutes the annual value of GSR to the harvester. The results are shown in Table 2.

Research and development costs of the tomato harvester

Several universities and private firms contributed to research and development (R and D) of the tomato harvester. Reasonably good information is available on the costs incurred by two of the major parties to this invention— the University of California at Davis and Blackwelder Manufacturing Company of Rio Vista, California. The University of Michigan, the University of Florida, and the University of Maryland also have engaged in research and development; and some other firms, including H. D. Hume Company, Food Manufacturing Corporation, Massey-Ferguson, and Button Manufacturing Company, have incurred significant R and D costs in the development of tomato harvesters. Estimates of costs incurred by these universities and firms represent only an educated guess based on interviews with knowledgeable persons. Total R and D estimates compounded to 1967 are given in Table 3.[9]

[8] We cannot predict the ultimate impact of the harvester on wages, prices, and output; so, unless otherwise stated, we have assumed these to remain the same as in 1965–1969.

[9] Estimates include only direct R and D costs of developing the harvester. Costs to farmers and processors of transition to the new technique are not included, nor are the effects of the harvester on processing costs. R. Schuler of California Canners and Growers Association indicated that

Table 3. Research and development expenditures on the tomato harvester

	Expenditures[a]
Universities (to 1967)	
University of California, Davis	
Non-Extension activities	$ 588,000
Extension and related activities	100,000
Other universities (including Extension)	600,000
Total universities	$1,288,000
Private firms (to 1967)	
Blackwelder Manufacturing Company	$ 491,000
Other firms	1,473,000
Total firms	$1,964,000
Total 1967 value	$3,252,000
Total R and D costs: 1973 value (cumulated at 6 percent)	$4,585,320

[a] Figures rounded to the nearest thousand.

Rate of return

Given the above data on benefits accruing from the tomato harvester and the R and D costs to make the harvester a reality, it is possible to calculate the gross social rate of return (GSRR) to R and D costs as follows:

$$GSRR = \frac{\text{total annual value of gross social returns}}{\text{research and development costs}} (100).$$

Thus, assuming the low-cost saving of $5.41 per ton,

$$GSRR = \frac{\$42,608,018 \text{ (Table 2)}}{\$4,585,320 \text{ (Table 3)}} (100) = 929 \text{ percent.}$$

Similarly, for the cost saving of $7.47 per ton, the GSRR is 1,282 percent ($58,822,867 ÷ $4,585,320). Hence, the gross social rate of return may vary from 929 to 1,282 percent.

To this point we have followed traditional analysis to calculate the rates of return from an innovation in which the distributional effects are assumed to be zero. In the next section,

it is extremely difficult to determine whether the net effect on processing costs is positive or negative. Finally, we have not entered the discussion as to whether the new tomato grown for mechanical harvesting is of inferior quality than that grown prior to mechanization. If the new variety is inferior, which is debatable, then the costs incurred because of inferior quality are not accounted for.

this assumption is relaxed and the costs incurred by workers due to adoption of the tomato harvester are explicitly taken into account; but first we discuss welfare criteria relevant to this expanded view.[10]

Welfare Criteria

The concept of Pareto optimality implies that one cannot recommend a change from a state "*A*" to a state "*B*" unless everyone is better off in *B* than in *A*—that is, no one is worse off in *B* and at least one person is better off than in *A*.

A major problem arising is that Pareto optimality favors the status quo. But almost every conceivable change leaves someone worse off. Consequently, making recommendations on grounds other than "whatever is, is right" involves the inextricable difficulties of interpersonal comparisons of utility. If, for example, one is willing to recommend a change that will leave someone worse off than before, he is implying that he can cardinally evaluate the increase in welfare of the beneficiaries, subtract the decrease in welfare of the losers, and find a net increment in welfare. This is indeed a heroic presumption.

As a kind of halfway house between these extremes, the following "compensation" test has been proposed by Kaldor and Hicks. It is a necessary condition to recommending a change that the gainers shall be able to compensate the losers and still be better off. If the benefits of the change are not sufficient to pay its ordinary costs and compensation, it cannot be considered socially desirable. It should be noted, however, that it is not sufficient that compensation could be paid—it must actually be paid if a change from the status quo is to be recommended. Otherwise, the problem of interpersonal comparisons of utility still remains.

[10] We cannot go into all the complexities of welfare theory here. The interested reader is referred to Little [14] and Mishan [19].

The implications of this general analysis to the specific problem of the tomato harvester are clear. In order to determine the value of the harvester, we have to determine whether the gainers (producers, consumers, etc.) could compensate the losers (workers) and still be better off than before.[11]

Net Social Rate of Return

The tomato harvester displaced roughly 91 man-hours per acre of tomatoes harvested [23, pp. 1–9].[12] Using the acreage and adoption rates of Table 1, 478,637 man-hours were displaced in 1965; in 1973 and every year thereafter, 19,477,227 (see Appendix for calculations).[13] The average wage of harvest labor in California was approximately $1.65 per hour in 1967 [23]. With these figures, we computed the net social rate of return (NSRR) under varying assumptions of alternative employment opportunities and, hence, the amount of compensation (C) needed to offset the impact of technological change. The formula used is:

$$\text{NSRR} = \frac{\text{GSR} - \text{C}}{\text{R and D}} (100).$$

The results are given in Table 4. For the low-cost savings estimate of $5.47 per ton, NSRR

[11] The main losers from this particular technological change are farm workers. Undoubtedly there are other people who also lose, but these are not discussed in this paper. Furthermore, it becomes clear that cost-benefit studies must consider both allocative and distributional problems (see, for example, Prest and Turvey [25], Musgrave [21], and Knetch et al. [13]). Compensation is a necessary but not a sufficient condition for appraising an improvement. See Little [14, ch. 6] for a discussion of the Scitovsky reversal problem.

[12] The amount of the labor saved by the mechanical harvester is given in Parsons [23, p. 8]. The man-hours saved per acre vary from 29 for excellent workers to 178 for poor workers. The figure used, 91 man-hours, while substantially above that for poor workers, is only slightly below the man-hours displaced for good workers. However, it should be pointed out that Parsons' calculations are based on the specific type of harvester available in 1966 when approximately 20 good workers were needed per machine. A new tomato harvester will soon be made available which will require substantially less labor to operate; the use of an electronic sorting device can reduce the requirement to less than 8 workers per machine. In view of these recent developments, our estimates of labor displacement resulting from the harvester are probably conservative.

[13] When calculating the displacement by the tomato harvester, the analysis would become extremely complex if one attempted to distinguish between domestic workers and temporarily admitted aliens. In our analysis, we have assumed that had the tomato harvester not been invented the total workers employed would be the same as in the early 1960's.

Table 4. Net rates of social return to R and D on the tomato harvester

Percent of displaced wage bill paid in compensation	Annual 1973 amount of compensation	Net rate of social return to R and D Estimated cost savings at	
		$5.47 per ton	$7.51 per ton
	dollars	*percent*	
0	0	929	1,288
25	10,746,610	694	1,048
50	21,493,262	460	814
75	32,239,892	226	579
100	42,987,523	− 8	345

varies between 929 and −8 percent as the amount of compensation changes from 0 to 100 percent of the estimated displaced wage bill. For 100 percent compensation, it is assumed that displaced tomato workers have no alternative employment opportunities. For the cost savings of $7.51 per ton, NSRR varies between 1,288 and 345 percent.

We have not attempted to estimate the actual amount of unemployment created by the harvester, since this would require knowing all displaced workers' future employments.[14] The estimated wage loss from 1965 through 1972 has been compounded forward to 1973 and then converted to an annual flow. Thus, assuming a wage of $1.65 per hour, the cost to the workers is overestimated because, while the conversion to an annual flow makes it possible to calculate the NSRR, this assumes an infinite life for the displaced labor. This assumption is untenable unless one believes that there is a lasting effect on the workers' families in denied educational opportunities and the like resulting from unemployment caused by technological change.

Actual Payment of Compensation

We have shown that the rates of return to R and D expenditures on the tomato harvester were highly attractive when measured in the

[14] As Robinson [28, p. 2] points out, "Nearly four million workers were employed in 1957 in industries which did not exist or hardly existed in 1900. If we had been looking for jobs for those workers in 1900, we should never have foreseen the present number of workers in the motor industry and motor transport, in the making of gramophones, wireless or television sets, in electricity, or aviation. At any moment it is hard to foresee how those workers will ultimately be absorbed, for whose services in their former occupations there is likely to be less demand."

conventional way. More important, the rates of return remain attractive after deducting reasonable amounts of compensation for costs incurred by displaced workers. However, since compensation has not actually been paid, it cannot be concluded that society as a whole has benefited from the tomato harvester.

Our analysis has focused on unorganized workers confronted with technological displacement. Compensation was not paid because they lacked the organization to compel it. Contrast this situtaion with one in which workers were powerfully organized—the International Longshoremen's and Warehousemen's Union. Under the leadership of Harry Bridges, this union was able to mitigate the impact of technology on worker displacement through "featherbedding" provisions in its contracts, which it provided for many years. In the late 1950's, however, it became apparent that the momentum of technological development, particularly in the containerization of freight, would eventually overpower employment-preserving rules. Bridges recognized this in 1957 [9, p. 145]:

> I would say that we have resisted the impact of labor-saving machinery, mechanization, automation, whatever you want to call it, possibly with greater success than any other organization. It has been a combination of ways and means of going things and it has involved strikes, slow-downs, and what-not. However, we have reached the point possibly, and some of the demands that you are putting in (take this resolution, for example) and some other proposals for changes reflect the feeling that you have reached the point, where the battle against the machine for us has become a losing one. And we can continue to fight a losing battle, and we will lose in more ways than one, and finally after we have thrown away a lot of energy and a lot of bargaining power we will put on a showdown, last-stand fight, and we will lose that one, too.

Under Bridges' leadership, the union entered negotiations to trade its featherbedding prerogatives for job and income security and won a settlement of $5 million per year for 1961 through 1965; this, together with previous payments, totaled $29 million [9, p. 176]. In the union's view, $18 million of this, or approximately $3 million per year, was compensation for technological change or, as they put it, "the men's share of the machine" [9, p. 180].

The essence of the contract for the union was the principle of "sharing the machine." As Hartman [9, p. 344] says,

In the longshore experience, the older workers won a great deal; the retirement bonus was the equivalent of more than a year's pay. The younger workers were offered less but their prospects for promotion were enhanced by accelerated withdrawal of the older men. Further, they believed that the principle of 'sharing in the machine' had been established and would provide benefits to them in the years to come.

The longshoremen achieved a share in the machine of approximately $3 million per year on an estimated annual industry net savings (in 1965) of no more than and probably considerably less than $59.4 million [9, p. 332]. Thus, the settlement was certainly no less than 5 percent and probably no more than 10 percent of industry's benefits. While the two cases are perhaps noncomparable, it is interesting to observe that, had the tomato workers received a similar share in the machine, their compensation would have been between $2 and $4 million per year. On this basis, the conservatively estimated net social return to the harvester would still have exceeded 700 percent.

Concluding Observations

Our study of the development of the mechanical tomato harvester provides a microscopic look at a general social dilemma. The talents of science and industry combine to create enormously productive innovations, but the very success of these sectors of society creates consequences which bear unfavorably, as Fuller [7] has pointed out, on less organized and therefore more vulnerable sectors.

In order to illustrate this fact, we briefly examined the contrasting impacts of technological change on tomato workers and longshoremen. But labor unions are not the only means of protecting vulnerable sectors of society. Indeed, as Schultz [29] has stressed, it is the social scientist's task to devise a variety of institutional structures appropriate to the problems with which society is afflicted.

Thus, for compensation purposes, an alternative to unionization may be a form of state intervention in which a tax is imposed on units of output. The proceeds from this tax would then be used to finance retraining, relocative, and retirement programs. This solution is theoretically sound, but if extended through all sectors of the economy that are subject to technological displacement, it would be an organizational monstrosity. Before embarking on programs of this type, it would be wise to seek

576 / Andrew Schmitz and David Seckler

more general solutions to this general class of problems.[16] Specifically, we might explore whether there are any possibilities that general social programs could significantly reduce the need for compensation itself. We believe there are.

The process of adjustment is particularly painful for displaced tomato workers because they are highly immobile, mainly because of limited occupational versatility. If a fraction of the great economies generated by such tech-

[16] See, for example, H. G. Johnson [12].

nological innovations as the harvester could be allocated out of general taxes and applied to destroying the "vicious cycles of poverty" that afflict society, immobilities—and thus the social costs accompanying such innovations as the tomato harvester—would be substantially reduced. Interventions of this sort would allow social costs and benefits to fall more or less randomly on the population as a whole and thus, in a sense, cancel each other. If this were to occur, "everyone" would be better off with technological change. That is, to us, the moral of the tomato harvester.

Appendix

Total Man-Hour Displacement by the Tomato Harvester

The base acreage used prior to 1965 (that is, prior to the year when the harvester was used substantially) is 297,289, the average from 1958 to 1964. The base acreage used subsequently is 322,010, the average from 1966 to 1969. California is assumed to harvest approximately 55 percent of the processing tomatoes grown in the United States. Using the computations of Parsons [23], 163 man-hours were employed per acre prior to the harvester; with the harvester, this was cut to 72 man-hours.

Thus, prior to the harvester, 48,458,127 man-

hours were employed ($297,289 \times 163$). After the harvester was adopted, in 1965 for example, the number of man-hours employed dropped to 47,979,490, computed as follows: $322,010$ $[(163 \times .85) + (72 \times .15)]$. This represents a displacement of 478,637 man-hours ($48,458,127 - 47,979,490$).

It is estimated that in 1973 only 28,980,900 man-hours will be employed, computed as follows: $322,010[(163 \times .20) + (72 \times .80)]$. Total displacement will then be 19,477,227 man-hours ($48,458,127 - 28,980,900$).

References

[1] Babb, E. M., S. A. Belden, and C. R. Saathoff, "An Analysis of Cooperative Bargaining in the Processing Tomato Industry," *Am. J. Agr. Econ.* 51:13–25, Feb. 1969.

[2] Becket, J. W., "Labor Efficiency and Utilization," *California Citrograph* 52:318–327, June 1967.

[3] Bonnen, James T., "The Absence of Knowledge of Distributional Impacts: An Obstacle to Effective Program Analysis and Decisions," in U. S. Congress, Joint Economic Committee, *The Analysis and Evaluation of Public Expenditures: The PPB System*, 91st Cong., 1st Sess., 1969, vol. 1, pp. 419–449.

[4] Bowen, H. R., and G. L. Mangum, *Automation and Economic Progress*, Englewood Cliffs, New Jersey, Prentice-Hall, Inc., 1966.

[5] Diehl, W. D., "Farm-Nonfarm Migration in the Southeast: A Costs-Returns Analysis," *J. Farm Econ.* 48:1–11, Feb. 1966.

[6] Eckstein, Otto, *Water-Resource Development*, Cambridge, Harvard University Press, 1961.

[7] Fuller, Varden, "Political Pressures and Income Distribution in Agriculture," in *Agricultural Policy in an Affluent Society*, ed. V. W. Ruttan, A. D. Waldo, and J. P. Houck, New York, W. W. Norton & Company, Inc., pp. 255–263.

[8] Griliches, Zvi, "Research Costs and Social Returns: Hybrid Corn and Related Innovations," *J. Pol. Econ.* 66:419–431, Oct. 1958.

[9] Hartman, Paul Theodore, "Work Rules and Produc-

tivity in the Pacific Coast Longshore Industry," unpublished Ph.D. thesis, University of California, 1966.

[10] Heringer, Lester, "Need for Mechanization More Evident," *The California Tomato Grower*, 7:1–11, Jan. 1964.

[11] Higgins, F. Hal, "John M. Horner and the Development of the Combined Harvester," *Agr. Hist.* 32:14–24, Jan. 1958.

[12] Johnson, H. G., "The Social Policy of an Opulent Society," in *Money, Trade, and Economic Growth*, Cambridge, Harvard University Press, 1962, pp. 180–195.

[13] Knetch, J. L., R. H. Haveman, C. H. Howe, J. V. Krutilla, and M. F. Brewer, *Federal Natural Resources Development: Basic Issues in Benefit and Cost Measurement*, Natural Resources Policy Center, The George Washington University, 1969.

[14] Little, I. M. D., *A Critique of Welfare Economics*, Oxford, Clarendon Press, 1950.

[15] Lorenzen, C., and R. B. Fridley, "Mechanizing Specialized Crops," *Agr. Engineering* 47:336–337, June 1966.

[16] Lynch, Duke, "The Revolution of California Tomatoes," *Canner/Packer*, Western Edition, 137(4):10A–10F, April 1968.

[17] Mangum, G. L., "Contributions and Costs of Manpower Development and Training," *Policy Papers in Human Resources and Industrial Relations No. 5*, The Institute of Labor and Industrial Relations, University of Michigan, 1967.

[18] MEIJ, J. L., *Mechanization in Agriculture*, Amsterdam, North-Holland Publishing Company, 1960.

[19] MISHAN, E. J., "A Survey of Welfare Economics, 1939–1959," *Econ. J.* 70:197–264, June 1960.

[20] ———, *Welfare Economics: Ten Introductory Essays*, 2d ed., New York, Random House, Inc., 1969.

[21] MUSGRAVE, R. A., "Cost-Benefit Analysis and the Theory of Public Finance," *J. Econ. Lit.* 7:797–806, Sept. 1969.

[22] PADFIELD, HARLAND, and WILLIAM E. MARTIN, *Farmers, Workers and Machines*, Tucson, University of Arizona Press, 1965.

[23] PARSONS, PHILIP S., *Costs of Mechanical Tomato Harvesting Compared to Hand Harvesting*, California Agricultural Extension Service AXT-224, May 1966.

[24] PETERSON, WILLIS, "Return to Poultry Research in the United States," *J. Farm Econ.* 49:656–669, Aug. 1967.

[25] PREST, A. R., and R. TURVEY, "Cost-Benefit Analysis: A Survey," *Econ. J.* 75:683–736, Dec. 1965.

[26] RASMUSSEN, WAYNE D., "Advances in American Agriculture: The Mechanical Tomato Harvester as a Case Study," *Technology and Culture* 9:531–543, Oct. 1968.

[27] REES, A., "Economic Expansion and Persisting Unemployment: An Overview," in *Prosperity and Unemployment*, ed. R. A. Gordon and M. S. Gordon, New York, John Wiley and Sons, Inc., 1966, pp. 327–349.

[28] ROBINSON E. A. G., *The Structure of Competitive Industry*, Chicago, University of Chicago Press, 1958.

[29] SCHULTZ, T. W., "A Policy to Redistribute Losses from Economic Progress," *J. Farm Econ.* 43:554–565, Aug. 1961.

[30] ———, "Institutions and the Rising Value of Man," *Am. J. Agr. Econ.* 50:1113–1122, Dec. 1968.

[31] ———, *The Economic Organization of Agriculture*, New York, McGraw-Hill Book Company, 1953.

[32] SJAASTAD, L. A., "The Costs and Returns of Human Migration," *J. Pol. Econ.* 70:80–93, Oct. 1962.

[33] U. S. Department of Agriculture, Statistical Reporting Service, *Vegetables Processing—Annual Summary: Acreage, Production, and Value of Principal Commercial Crops by States with Comparisons, 1961–1968.*

[34] WEBB, RAYMON E., and W. M. BRUCE, "Redesigning the Tomato for Mechanized Production," in *Yearbook of Agriculture, 1968: Science for Better Living*, Washington, U. S. Department of Agriculture, pp. 103–107.

[35] YEAGER, L. B., and D. C. TUERCK, *Trade Policy and the Price System*, Scranton, Pennsylvania, International Textbook Company, 1969.

[36] ZOBEL, MELVIN P., and PHILIP S. PARSONS, "Tomato Costs, 1965: Hand Harvest, Yolo County," California Agricultural Extension Service, 1965, mimeo.

[37] ———, "Tomato Costs of Production: Yolo County— 1969," California Agricultural Extension Service, 1969, mimeo.

[22]

Efficient Redistribution through Commodity Markets

Bruce Gardner

Efficiency in redistribution is measured in terms of deadweight loss generated per dollar of economic surplus transferred between consumers and producers of a commodity by means of market intervention. The implications of supply and demand elasticities for efficiency in redistribution are examined with special attention to the comparison of production control and deficiency payment programs. The results may be used to aid in the evaluation of commodity programs and as a basis for consideration of the hypothesis that observed policies are efficient, given the political power of interest groups.

Key words: agricultural policy, income distribution.

Governmental intervention in farm commodity markets often has been evaluated using analytical procedures developed by Nerlove and Wallace to measure deadweight losses. These losses are the costs of obtaining various social and political objectives. The view in this paper is that the central purpose of intervention is to redistribute income to producers from consumers or taxpayers. In this context, the social cost of intervention is the deadweight loss per dollar transferred. This general view is not novel (Dardis, Josling). The purpose here is to treat it more systematically than previously.

The main innovation in this paper is to tie deadweight losses based on consumers' and producers' surpluses explicitly to surplus transfers. This can be important. Consider a particular example: a market with linear supply and demand curves of equal slope. In this situation, the standard approach holds that a production-control program to achieve price $\bar{P}$ (figure 1) at output Q_0 generates deadweight losses equal to area $b + c$. A deficiency-payment program that guaranteed producers price $\bar{P}$ would result in output Q_1, with dead-weight losses of area e. Since $e = b + c$, the deadweight losses are equal and there is no way to choose between them on efficiency grounds [Wallace, p. 585, eq. (4)]. However, the deadweight loss per dollar transferred to producers is quite different.

The amount transferred under the production control is the area a (price gain on output Q_0) minus c (rents lost on $Q_e - Q_0$). The amount transferred with the deficiency payment is area $a + b + d$. The deadweight loss per dollar transferred with production control is equal to $e/(a - c)$; for the payment program it is $e/(a + b + d)$. Since the latter denominator is larger, the ratio is smaller—the deadweight loss ratio is smaller for the payment program. Thus, payments are a more efficient redistributive mechanism even though the standard triangles are equal for both programs.

Quantifying Efficiency in Redistribution

It would be useful to have formulas analogous to those developed by Nerlove and Wallace, but specified to measure efficiency in redistribution. To visualize what is measured by such formulas, a graphical approach can illustrate the tradeoff between consumers' and producers' surpluses (Josling 1974). This surplus transformation curve is analogous to the economy-wide constraint on income redistribution which Bator calls the utility possibilities frontier.

The author is a professor in the Department of Agricultural and Resource economics, University of Maryland.

Scientific Article No. A-3323 of the Maryland Agricultural Experiment Station. The Center for the Study of the Economy and the State, University of Chicago, supported this research.

Parts of this material have been presented in seminars at the Universities of Chicago, Maryland, Purdue, Illinois, and Texas A&M.

The author is grateful for comments received from participants on these occasions, and from the *AJAE* reviewers.

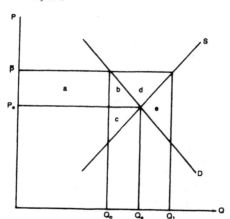

Figure 1.   Deadweight losses

Consider the inverse (price-dependent) demand and supply curves

(1) $P = D(Q)$,

(2) $P = S(Q)$.

Let redistribution from consumers to producers occur through production controls. Such intervention results in output $\hat{Q}$, which is less than or equal to the unregulated competitive output, Q_e.

The resulting consumer and producer surpluses (CS and PS, respectively) are defined as

(3) $CS = \int_0^{\hat{Q}} D(Q)dQ - D(\hat{Q})\hat{Q}$,

(4) $PS = D(\hat{Q})\hat{Q} - \int_0^{\hat{Q}} S(Q)dQ$.

The surplus transformation curve, T, is

(5) $T = T(CS, PS)$,

where the attainable CS, PS pairs are traced out by variations of the policy variable $\hat{Q}$. For example, consider linear demand and supply functions:

(6) $P = a_0 + a_1 Q; \ a_1 < 0$

(7) $P = b_0 + b_1 Q; \ b_1 > 0, \ 0 < b_0 < a_0$.

The surpluses with production controls are

(8) $CS = -\tfrac{1}{2} a_1 Q^2$

(9) $PS = (a_0 - b_0) Q + (a_1 - \tfrac{1}{2} b_1)Q^2$.

The surplus transformation curve is obtained by solving (8) for $\hat{Q}$ and substituting in (9), to obtain

(10)

$$PS = \sqrt{\frac{(a_0 - b_0)}{-a_1/2}} \sqrt{CS} + \frac{2a_1 - b_1}{-a_1} CS,$$

which is equation (5) for the linear case.

An example of equation (10) is shown in figure 2 as the solid curve to the left of point E, attained when $Q = Q_e$. It is analogous to Bator's endowment point. For given supply and demand curves, E results in the maximum sum of consumers' and producers' surpluses. At this point the marginal rate of transformation between PS and CS is -1.[1] Intervention that favors producers generates points to the left of E. The maximum producers' surplus is obtained at point M. This reflects monopoly production [confirm by differentiating (10) with respect to CS and equating it to zero]. Thus, intervention favoring producers yields points between E and M on the surplus transformation curve, such as R. At this point consumers lose ΔCS and producers gain ΔPS.

Efficiency at the margin is measured by the slope of the surplus transformation curve. If it is -1, then a dollar given up by consumers yields a dollar gained by producers. This could occur (theoretically) through a lump-sum transfer but not market intervention. The greater the slope's departure from -1, the less efficient the redistribution. The general expression for the slope is obtained from equations (3) and (4) as

(11) $\dfrac{dPS}{dCS} = \dfrac{dPS/dQ}{dCS/dQ}$

$$= \frac{D'(Q)\hat{Q} + D(\hat{Q}) - S(\hat{Q})}{-D'(Q)\hat{Q}}.$$

For an intuitive grasp of this slope's determinants, consider the cases of linear and constant-elasticity (log-linear) demand and supply curves. For the linear case, differentiate equation (10) with respect to PS using equation (8) to replace CS, and substitute $(a_0 - b_0) = Q_e(b_1 - a_1)$ to obtain

(12) $\dfrac{dPS}{dCS} = \dfrac{b_1 - a_1}{a_1}\left(1 - \dfrac{Q_e}{\hat{Q}}\right) - 1$.

The slope is negative for $\hat{Q}$ between Q_e and Q_m, the output that maximizes PS. It increases from -1 at Q_e to 0 at Q_m. Thus, the marginal efficiency of redistribution depends on the

---

[1] Derivations of these and following mathematical results are available from the author.

Gardner

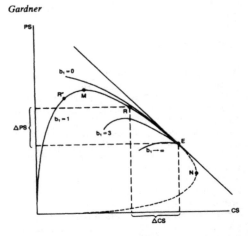

demand: P = 150 - 2Q
supply: P = b₀ + b₁Q

Figure 2. Surplus transformation curves: production control

supply and demand slopes and the extent of production cutback.

For log-linear supply and demand curves, the slope of the surplus transformation curve is

$$(13) \quad \frac{dPS}{dCS} = -\eta \left[1 - (\hat{Q}/Q_e)^A \right] - 1,$$

where $A = 1/\epsilon - 1/\eta$ with η the elasticity of demand (a negative number) and ϵ the elasticity of supply. The effect of an increase in ϵ is to make the first term of (13), which is always positive, smaller. Therefore, the slope of the surplus transformation curve, for any given restriction $\hat{Q}$, becomes closer to -1. This means that the marginal deadweight loss per dollar transferred (the "price of redistribution") is reduced. The effect of an absolute increase in η is to make the first term of (13) larger. Consequently, the marginal deadweight loss per dollar transferred is increased. Thus, the social cost of redistribution to producers is reduced by a lower demand elasticity or a higher supply elasticity.

Figure 2 shows the effect of a change in supply elasticity for the linear case from perfectly elastic ($b_1 = 0$) to perfectly inelastic ($b_1 \to \infty$). Equations (11) to (13) each imply that the slope is more sensitive to a change in supply elasticity, the more elastic is the demand function. Note that when $b_1 \to \infty$ (perfectly inelastic supply) in figure 2, it is impos-

sible to redistribute much surplus to producers. This occurs because *PS* is equal to total revenue and the elasticity of demand is only a little less than 1. For elastic demand curves at *E*, producers' surplus is reduced by output control when supply is perfectly inelastic. Fixed supply can generate corner solutions at *E*. The slope of the transformation curve at *E* is not -1 when $b_1 \to \infty$. Generally, there will be corners in the surplus transformation curve if output restriction is capable of driving supply price to zero.

These are the same qualitative results derived by Wallace. However, we can estimate more readily how sensitive marginal deadweight losses per dollar redistributed are to changes in supply and demand parameters. Note that by setting the derivatives of (11) or (12) with respect to $\hat{Q}$ equal to zero, the size of production cutback that maximizes *PS* can be found. This quantity (the output sold under pure monopoly) identifies the point at which further production control makes producers and consumers both worse off.

For a given finite change such as *E* to *R*, we can analyze the total redistribution, $\Delta PS/\Delta CS$. It is this trade-off, not the marginal redistributions, that is most directly comparable to deadweight losses analyzed by Nerlove and Wallace. Since $D = \Delta PS - \Delta CS$, where *D* is the deadweight loss, we can estimate $\Delta PS/\Delta CS$ if we have an estimate of ΔPS or ΔCS in addition to *D*. Rosine and Helmberger estimated that in 1970 \$4,829 million was distributed away from consumers and taxpayers in order to give farmers \$2,140 million. This implies that $\Delta PS/\Delta CS = .44$, but it does not provide an estimate of the marginal rate of substitution (dPS/dCS) at the restricted equilibrium point.

Analytically, the total redistribution to producers in the linear case is

$$(14) \quad \frac{\Delta PS}{\Delta CS} = \frac{(b_1/a_1)(1 - R) - 2}{1 + R},$$

where $R = Q_e/\hat{Q}$.

Total redistribution in the constant-elasticity case is

$$(15) \quad \frac{\Delta PS}{\Delta CS} = (1 + \eta) \left[\frac{1}{B} \left(\frac{1 - R^{-B}}{1 - R^{-C}} \right) - 1 \right],$$

$$(\eta \neq 1)$$

where $B = 1 + (1/\epsilon)$ and $C = 1 + (1/\eta)$.

228 *May 1983*

Amer. J. Agr. Econ.

An example will clarify these formulas and their relationship to the Nerlove/Wallace results. Suppose a commodity has (constant) elasticities of demand and supply of $\eta = -0.5$ and $\epsilon = 0.2$, respectively, and that a production-control program reduces output by 20% ($R = Q_e/\hat{Q} = 1.25$). Applying formula (11), $\Delta PS/\Delta CS = -0.75$. For simplicity let $P_e = 1$ and $Q_e = 1$ so that values redistributed are shares of equilibrium total revenue. The constant-elasticity assumption implies that $\hat{P}$ rises to 1.56 when $\hat{Q}$ falls to 0.8. Thus, $\Delta CS = -0.50$, $\Delta PS/\Delta CS = -0.75$, and $\Delta PS - 0.38$. The sum of ΔPS and ΔCS gives the deadweight loss, 0.12, or 12% of total revenue ($P_e Q_e$). The corresponding formula in Wallace (p. 582) gives the deadweight loss as $\frac{1}{2}(.5)(.45)^2 (1 + .5/.2) = 0.18$. The difference occurs because the Wallace formula is an approximation involving substantial error for large changes. The contribution of equation (15), besides being exact for constant elasticities, is that it ties deadweight losses explicitly to surplus redistribution. The contribution of equation (13), which has no parallel in the Nerlove/Wallace treatment, is to show the marginal costs of further redistribution. In the present example, $dPS/dCS = -.60$. Thus, at the margin, a dollar transferred from consumers results in a 60¢ gain for producers and a 40¢ deadweight loss. A marginal rate of surplus transformation less than the total gain in PS per dollar of CS lost is a quite general result. It follows from the convexity of the surplus transformation curve.

Redistribution toward Consumers

An extension of the surplus transformation curve to the right of point E involves intervention to redistribute income from producers to consumers. The mechanism could be a price ceiling below the unregulated market price. Then equations (3) and (4) become

$$(16) \quad CS = \int_0^{\hat{Q}} D(Q)dQ - S(\hat{Q})\hat{Q},$$

$$(17) \quad PS = S(\hat{Q})\hat{Q} - \int_0^{\hat{Q}} S(Q)dQ,$$

where $\hat{Q}$ is output forthcoming at the ceiling price, $S(\hat{Q})$. The surplus transformation curve for a linear example is to the right of point E in figure 2. It also has a slope of -1 at point E. The maximum consumers' surplus is at point N, the monopsony outcome. Equilib-

ria favoring consumers lie between points E and N.

The producer- and consumer-favoring surplus transformation curves meet with equal slope at point E. They form a continuous, smooth function describing all surplus-distributing possibilities available by ouput-restricting intervention. The vertical (or horizontal) difference between the surplus transformation curve and its tangent at point E measures the deadweight loss from redistribution. Note that the deadweight loss accelerates with the extent of intervention in either direction from E.

Deficiency Payments

There may be more efficient ways of redistributing surpluses than output restriction. In this context, "more efficient" means capable of generating a larger sum of surpluses for a given PS/CS ratio. An intervention mechanism that has been used for some agricultural commodities is to guarantee a "target" price to produce greater than P_e. Payments equal to the difference between the target price and the market-clearing price are made. This approach, equivalent to a subsidy, increases both producers' and consumers' surpluses. But it adds costs to taxpayers who provide the payments, creating a three-group redistribution that defeats graphics like figure 2. It also introduces deadweight losses from additional taxes.

Consider consumers/taxpayers as a single group. They are, of course, the same set of people, but individuals differ in their ratio of food expenditure to tax payments. So there may be significant redistribution within the group if intervention changes from production-control to deficiency payments. This is especially important because the ratio of tax payments to food expenditures changes across income classes, rising from near zero at the lowest incomes to well over one at higher incomes. In this paper, however, taxpayer costs will be subtracted from consumers' surplus to obtain a deficiency-payment income redistribution curve from consumers/taxpayers to producers. The relevant calculation of consumers' surplus plus taxpayers' costs, T, is obtained from equation (16). Producers' surplus comes from equation (17), except that $\hat{Q} > Q_e$ for a deficiency payment. The enforced maximum price has become a guaranteed minimum price. In the linear case, we have

(18)
$$CS - T = (a_0 - b_0)\hat{Q} + (\tfrac{1}{2}a_1 - b_1)\hat{Q}^2,$$

(19)
$$PS = \tfrac{1}{2}b_1\hat{Q}^2.$$

These imply the transformation curve,

(20)
$$CS - T = \sqrt{\frac{(a_0 - b_0)}{b_1/2}}\sqrt{PS} + \frac{(a_1 - b_1)}{b_1}PS.$$

Figure 3 compares the surplus transformation curve from figure 2 with that for equation (20), using the same supply and demand functions. The lower dotted curve running northwest from point E shows the trade-off between producers' surplus and consumers' surplus minus taxpayers costs. Between points E and F the production-control approach is relatively efficient, but to the left of F deficiency payments are more efficient. The dotted transformation curve could be extended rightward from point E to generate redistribution favoring consumers. This might involve an all-or-none offer to producers to produce output $Q'(>Q_e)$ to be sold at a regulated price

$P'(<P_e)$. This approach conceivably could be used to redistribute essentially all the producers' surplus to consumers, with relatively small deadweight loss. Stalinist delivery quotas at state-specified prices could approximate such a policy.

With constant elasticities, the slope of the transformation curve for a subsidy generating output $\hat{Q} > Q_e$ is

(21)
$$\frac{dPS}{dCS} = \frac{1}{-\epsilon\,[1 - (Q_e/\hat{Q})^A] - 1} - \tau.$$

Equation (21) is similar to (13) except for the parameter τ. This parameter is the deadweight loss associated with market distortion when taxes are imposed in order to raise funds for the deficiency payments. This loss is external to the regulated commodity market. It might be approximated by marginal deadweight losses per dollar of federal income tax. If this were negligible, then τ could be taken as zero. However, this loss is not negligible (Harberger, Layard). Moreover, even if the deadweight loss per dollar of additional taxes is no more than 15¢ at the margin, as suggested by Harberger, the cost per dollar transferred to producers is likely to be substantially greater. The reason is that part of the tax revenue is distributed back to consumers through lower prices. The net effectiveness of deficiency payments to producers depends on the supply and demand elasticities. (For a clear graphical analysis. see Wallace). The exact relationship, for the constant-elasticity case, is

(22)
$$\tau = D' / \left\{ 1 - \frac{1}{1 + \eta[1 - B(Q_e/\hat{Q})^{-A}]} \right\},$$

where D' is the deadweight loss per dollar of taxes raised. Note that if the distortion is very small, $Q_e/\hat{Q} \to 1$, and if ϵ and $-\eta$ are equal, then $\tau = 2D'$—0.30 if Harberger's estimate is correct. In this case, half the funds taxed are recycled to consumers and do not reach producers. This doubles the social cost of redistributing income.

Comparative Redistribution Efficiency—Production Controls versus Payments

Comparing equation (21) with (13) indicates that the relative size of the demand and supply elasticities determines whether a deficiency payment or production control is most efficient. But exact conditions for preferring one or the other are not obvious. Wallace's

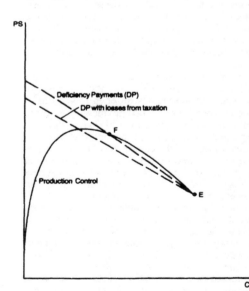

Figure 3. Surplus transformation curves for production control and subsidy

result that deadweight losses are the same when the supply and demand elasticities are equal does not hold. However, while the deadweight loss per dollar transferred is greater for the production control with equal elasticities, this advantage of deficiency payments may be offset by added social cost of raising taxes to finance the payments.[2]

A low demand elasticity or high supply elasticity tends to make production control the preferred alternative. Conversely, a low supply elasticity or a high demand elasticity favors deficiency payments. But the effect is not symmetrical, the demand elasticity being a more important determinant of efficiency for production controls and the supply elasticity more important for deficiency payments.

For linear supply and demand curves, it is even more obvious that there is no simple, general rule for tying supply and demand slopes to efficiency. This is illustrated by the crossing of the solid and dashed transformation curves in figure 3. Note also that in the limiting case in which supply is perfectly elastic, deficiency payment can generate no producers' surplus, so production control should always be chosen to aid producers. The transformation curve for deficiency payments is a horizontal line whose length measures the deadweight loss of taxpayer costs over consumers' surplus gains. If supply is perfectly inelastic a subsidy should be chosen, unless the deadweight loss per dollar raised in taxes exceeds $|\eta|$. The qualification is needed because if $\epsilon = 0$, the benefits of deficiency payments go entirely to producers. Therefore, $D' = \tau$ in equation (22), and $dPS/dCS = -1 + \tau$. For production controls we have $dPS/dCS = -(\eta + 1)$. Therefore, in order for production controls to be more efficient than the subsidy, $|\eta|$ must be less than τ (0.15 in the figure 3 example).

In general, the efficient form of intervention is determined by equations (13) and (21) for specific values of ϵ, η, τ, and $\dot{Q}/Q_e$.

Redistribution with International Trade

Consider the difference it makes for efficient redistribution if the product is exported. Assuming that foreigners have no political power

in the United States, their consumers' surplus is ignored. The surplus transformation curves of figure 4 are derived from linear supply and demand curves with own-price elasticities at free-market equilibrium of $-.88$ for domestic demand, -3.5 for export demand, and 1.75 for supply. E' is the market equilibrium without intervention. Production controls generate the solid surplus transformation curve northwest from E'. The sum of producers' surplus and domestic consumers' surplus is no longer maximized at market equilibrium, but at point R. Thus, production controls may be chosen to maximize the sum of surpluses, whereas this could only have been accomplished by laissez-faire in figure 2 or 3.

In the example shown, a deficiency payment program is less efficient in redistributing income, indicated by the upper dotted transformation curve, in figure 4. This is because the lower market prices resulting from payments transfer income to foreign consumers, while production controls transfer income away from them. However, if the demand for exports is sufficiently elastic, this result is reversed, with deficiency payments more efficient. In such cases there is no longer a gain in the sum of surpluses from intervention. The extreme case is the small-country case of perfectly elastic export demand at the world price. In this case, production controls leave price unchanged and reduce producers' surplus, while deficiency payments result in deadweight losses smaller than in figure 4.

Trade opens up possibilities for new forms

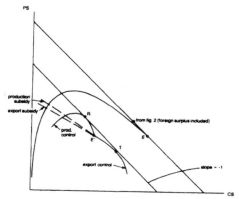

Figure 4. Surplus transformation curves (foreigners' surpluses excluded) under four forms of intervention

[2] A reviewer points out that there are administrative costs of production controls that should be taken into account; and there are also administrative costs of payment distribution, albeit probably smaller per dollar transferred than the administrative costs of production controls.

of intervention. Export quotas (or equivalent export taxes) redistribute income to consumers, shown in figure 4 by the solid surplus transformation curve southeast from E'. The sum of surpluses is increased by intervention, reaching a maximum at T, because there is redistribution away from foreign consumers. But the U.S. gainers are now consumers.[3] In such situations, production controls (favoring producers) and export controls (favoring consumers) could yield the same marginal rate of surplus transformation, with a sum of surpluses higher than the free-market equilibrium. Thus, it could be rational to switch, as in the 1970s, quite suddenly from controlling production via "set-asides" to export controls as supply/demand conditions change.

Export subsidies are harder to justify. The surplus transformation curve for an export subsidy is the lower dotted curve in figure 4. An export subsidy necessarily causes a greater domestic deadweight loss than a deficiency payment program, while the latter is less efficient than production controls. It is possible that, with domestic demand less elastic than export demand, price discrimination with export subsidies may be an efficient way to redistribute income to producers, but not as efficient as a domestic price floor plus deficiency payments.

Consider the most favorable circumstances for an export subsidy, a perfectly elastic demand function for exports, figure 5. Production controls are not useful because they reduce producers' surplus and leave price unchanged. However, a price floor for domestic consumption, or a tax on processors which is refunded to producers could be a relatively efficient transfer mechanism. A domestic price at P_d would redistribute $(P_d - P_w) \hat{Q}_d$ with the deadweight loss of the hatched triangle. An export subsidy of s per unit would redistribute an additional amount $s(\hat{Q}_s - \hat{Q}_d)$ to producers at the cost of the smaller shaded triangle. However, a deficiency payment program would transfer $s \hat{Q}_s$ to producers for the same deadweight loss. Efficiency in redistribution occurs at domestic price P_d and subsidy s at which the marginal rate of deadweight loss per dollar transferred is the same for both the domestic price floor and the production subsidy. (To be complete, the deadweight losses

[3] Export restraints could benefit both U.S. consumers and producers if total export demand were less elastic than domestic demand.

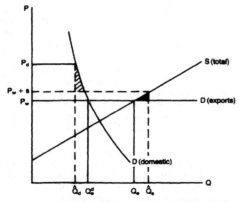

Figure 5. Inefficiency of export subsidy (world prices given)

of raising taxes to pay the subsidy must be added to the shaded triangle, but this cannot make an export subsidy more efficient than deficiency payments.)

If export demand is not perfectly elastic then the efficiency of export subsidies (and deficiency payments) is further reduced because transfers to foreign consumers will occur. The reason is shown in figure 6. Suppose we want producers to have rents attained at $\hat{P}$. This can be achieved with a deficiency payment of $\hat{P} - P_1$. Domestic and foreign consumers both pay P_1, and the deadweight loss is the shaded area. If the same producer price is achieved by an export subsidy, domestic consumers will pay $\hat{P}$. This reduces total demand at all (export) prices below $\hat{P}$ by the horizontal difference between the domestic demand curve and $\hat{Q}_d$, yielding the dashed total demand curve. Now it requires a larger subsidy

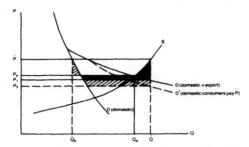

Figure 6. Export subsidy (world price influenced by exporter)

per bushel, $\hat{P} - P_2$, to boost total demand to $\hat{Q}$. The deadweight loss is increased by the hatched areas. In figure 5, with export demand perfectly elastic at the world price, deadweight losses below P_e disappear.

Export subsidies might be efficient in adjusting to past policy "mistakes." A commodity's support price may lead to an unanticipated buildup of stocks. The stocks may have sufficiently high storage costs that receiving even, say, half the support price for them would reduce taxpayers' costs. In these circumstances, an export subsidy may be efficient. However, domestic consumption subsidies and a move toward production controls also should occur, since these are more efficient adjustment mechanisms.

Use and Limitations

The formulas of this paper can be used in two related but distinct ways, one normative and one positive. The positive application is to explore whether policy variations over time and across commodities can be explained in terms of efficiency in redistribution. For example, does the move from production controls to direct payments in cotton and rice during the 1970s reflect changes in efficiency resulting from changes in supply or demand elasticities? Can the general absence of production-control programs for livestock products be explained in terms of efficiency with relatively high demand elasticities?

The normative application is to rank prospective programs for redistributing income. Suppose, for example, that it is the intention of Congress to increase peanut growers' incomes. How should this be accomplished, and what is the marginal cost of alternative redistribution levels? The best available analysis of alternative peanut programs is Nieuwoudt, Bullock, and Mathia. Their work implies an aggregate elasticity of demand for U.S. peanuts of -1.8 and an elasticity of supply of about 4.0. U.S. policy under the Food and Agriculture Act of 1977 involves marketing controls and acreage allotments and so is basically a production-control approach.[4] But there have been continuing proposals, most

recently by the Reagan administration early in 1981, to replace this program by a deficiency payment (subsidy) approach. Using the elasticities of -1.8 and $+4.0$, equations (13) and (21) imply a marginal rate of transformation of $-.74$ for a production-control and $-.27$ for a subsidy program, with a 20% quantity reduction or increase. This rough calculation indicates that it is relatively efficient to intervene with marketing controls and that the conclusion of Nieuwoudt, Bullock, and Mathia that "the target price plan would greatly reduce treasury and social costs" (p. 65) is wrong.

A serious limitation of the application just outlined, and of any use of the formulas developed, is that most commodity programs are not simply production-control or payment programs. Often they combine elements of each. However, complex schemes can be simulated for particular values of intervention variables given the values of key behavioral elasticities (or derivatives), and expectations of what such simulations would show can often be deduced from results in the simpler models. For example, the fact that inelastic demand makes production controls efficient relative to deficiency payments suggests that a higher price in the relatively inelastic fluid milk market is a means of reducing the deadweight loss per dollar transferred to dairy producers.[5]

Further limitations arise when commodity markets are interdependent. For example, the supply of soybeans, given the price of corn, is expected to be quite elastic. If intervention is to be undertaken to aid corn producers specifically (as it has been), because of the high supply elasticity, quantity controls should be more efficient than deficiency payments. The same would be true for soybeans. Yet, if we take corn and soybeans jointly, we have an aggregate commodity substantially less elastic in supply. This suggests that more efficient redistribution might result from intervention of the payment type for both products simultaneously. Indeed, extension of this reasoning suggests the most efficient method of redis-

---

[4] The two-tiered price supports, CCC stocks, and subsidies for crushing "excess" peanuts recently have been introduced. These complicate the program but production control remains the primary redistributive feature.

[5] CCC purchase for price-stabilizing storage between years, like the loan and FOR programs for grains, involves redistributional issues quite different from those discussed in this paper. The point about the dairy program is that it has recently involved simultaneous purchase and subsidized sales, making it equivalent to a subsidy program. In addition, as an *AJAE* reviewer points out, the subsidized consumer prices go to a particular subset of people. Therefore, in the absence of a costlessly functioning secondary resale market for subsidized dairy products, the deadweight losses are even greater than the usual triangle such as c in figure 1.

tributing income to farmers generally might be subsidies applicable to any crop.

Sector-wide intervention implies that the relevant interest group is farmers in total, not splintered commodity groups. Interaction between commodity markets has implications for the formation of political coalitions among commodity groups. The greater the cross elasticities of supply or demand between two commodities, the greater the difference between the partial and total elasticities of supply or demand, and the greater the efficiency gain in income redistribution from a program to protect both commodities jointly. Thus, apart from the political and economic factors that bear on producers' ability to form coalitions, one might expect that coalitions will be more prevalent among closely related commodities because the deadweight losses from intervention are reduced more by joint intervention under these circumstances.

In standard welfare economics the policy optimum is found with a social welfare function,

$$(23) \qquad W = W(UP, \ UC),$$

where UP and UC are the aggregate utilities of producers and consumers. Redistributional intervention in a commodity market involves changes in (23) via a regulatory variable, X, such as a level of controlled output, a price floor, or payment per bushel. Changes in UP and UC resulting from a change in X are taken to be changes in producer and consumer surpluses, following Harberger. Therefore, the policy optimum can be found by replacing UP and UC by PS and CS, then differentiating (23) with respect to X and equating to zero, which yields

$$(24) \qquad W_P \, \frac{dPS}{dX} + W_c \, \frac{dCS}{dX} = 0,$$

where W_p and W_c are the marginal contributions of producers' and consumers' surpluses to the social welfare function. The policy optimum is a point of tangency between a social welfare indifference curve and the highest attainable surplus transformation curve. With equal weights on the utilities of consumers and producers, the policy optimum is the market equilibrium.

The social welfare function is a normative concept. The comparable non-normative concept is a representation of how producers' and consumers' well-being is actually regarded in the political process. Political behavior may involve a bargaining game among interest groups (as in Zusman and Amiad) or a "policy preference function" (Rausser and Freebairn). Becker, in his analysis of the positive economics of redistribution, discusses in detail the properties of the behavioral function that replaces the social welfare function. In this context, W_c and W_p represent the (marginal) political power of consumers and producers. Thus, a point such as R in figure 2 is a political equilibrium in which the political power of producers exceeds that of consumers. The efficient redistribution hypothesis is that the political process places us at points like R, at which resources are used as efficiently as possible given the political preference function.

Concluding Remarks and Summary

The deadweight losses caused by governmental intervention in agricultural commodity markets do not tell the whole story about such intervention, nor is desire to redistribute income the sole reason for intervention. Under the assumption that it is an important reason, the deadweight losses can be viewed as a price paid to redistribute through market intervention. This paper develops models for estimating this price—the deadweight loss per dollar redistributed. It also derives for production-control and deficiency-payment programs the relationship between this price and its determinants—supply and demand elasticities, the extent of intervention, and the deadweight loss from raising general tax revenues. Qualitative results are also obtained for intervention when the export market is important.

In general, redistributive efficiency increases as either the supply or the demand function becomes less elastic. The efficient method of intervention depends on which function is less elastic. Inelastic demand favors production controls, and inelastic supply a deficiency payment approach. If demand is inelastic enough, less than about -0.15 in the cases considered in this paper, production controls are more efficient even than lump sum transfers to producers. This is because of deadweight losses associated with the taxes necessary for payments.

For intervention with an exported product, it is shown that deficiency payments are generally preferable to an export subsidy. Yet if the exporter is not a price taker in world markets, production controls may be more efficient than either type of subsidy. Moreover, under shifting economic conditions or political power, it may be efficient to shift between production controls (favoring producers) and export controls (favoring consumers).

The usefulness of the exact results generated by the formulas developed in the paper depends on having reliable estimates of supply and demand elasticities. These are often lacking. Nonetheless, it may still be of value to know exactly how much difference it makes for efficiency in distribution if the supply elasticity, say, is ½ or 1½. And the formulas can also be informative about the value of better information on elasticities. If costs of redistribution are sensitive to potential error in elasticities, it will be worthwhile to make the econometric effort necessary to sharpen our estimates. And if data do not permit accurate estimation, we can at least assess more exactly the range of likely errors in our redistributive analyses.

[Received October 1981; revision accepted
September 1982.]

References

Bator, Francis M. "The Simple Analytics of Welfare Maximization." *Amer. Econ. Rev.* 47(1957):22–29.

Becker, Gary S. "A Positive Theory of the Redistribution of Income and Political Behavior." CSES Work. Pap., University of Chicago, Oct. 1980.

Dardis, Rachel. "The Welfare Cost of Grain Protection in the United Kingdom." *J. Farm Econ.* 49(1967):597–609.

Harberger, A. C. "On the Use of Distributional Weights in Social Cost-Benefit Analysis." *J. Polit. Econ.* 86(1978):S87–S120.

Josling, T. E. "Agricultural Policies in Developed Countries: A Review." *J. Agr. Econ.* 25(1974):220–64.

———. "A Formal Approach to Agricultural Policy." *J. Agr. Econ.* 20(1969):175–91.

Layard, Richard. "On the Use of Distributional Weights in Cost-Benefit Analysis." *J. Polit. Econ.* 88(1980): 1041–47.

Nerlove, Marc. *The Dynamics of Supply.* Baltimore MD: Johns Hopkins University Press, 1958.

Nieuwoudt, W., J. B. Bullock, and G. Mathia. "Alternative Peanut Programs: An Economic Analysis." North Carolina Agr. Exp. Sta. Tech. Bull. No. 242, May 1976.

Rausser, G. C., and J. W. Freebairn. "Estimation of Policy Preference Functions: An Application to U.S. Beef Import Quotas." *Rev. Econ. and Statist.* 56(1974):437–49.

Rosine, J., and P. Helmberger. "A Neoclassical Analysis of the U.S. Farm Sector, 1948–1970." *Amer. J. Agr. Econ.* 56(1974):717–29.

Wallace, T. D. "Measures of Social Costs of Agricultural Programs." *J. Farm Econ.* 44(1962):580–94.

Zusman, P., and A. Amiad. "A Quantitative Investigation of a Political Economy—The Israeli Dairy Program." *Amer. J. Agr. Econ.* 59(1977):88–98.

Part V
Dimensions of
Public Policy Evaluation

A
Welfare Economics of Market Power

[23]

The Economic Journal, **88** (*December* 1978), 727–748
Printed in Great Britain

THE SOCIAL COSTS OF MONOPOLY POWER*

In 1954, Arnold Harberger estimated the welfare losses from monopoly for the United States at 0·1 of 1 % of GNP. Several studies have appeared since, reconfirming Harberger's early low estimates using different assumptions (e.g. Schwartzman, 1960; Scherer, 1970; Worcester, 1973). These papers have firmly established as part of the conventional wisdom the idea that welfare losses from monopoly are insignificant.

The Harberger position has been, almost from the start, subject to attack, however (e.g. Stigler, 1956); Kamerschen (1966) followed essentially the Harberger methodology, but assumed an elasticity of demand consistent with monopoly pricing behaviour at the industry level and obtained welfare loss estimates as high as 6 %. Posner (1975) made some rough estimates of the social costs of acquiring monopoly power, but, using Harberger's calculations, concluded that the real problem was the social cost imposed by regulation rather than of private market power.

The most sophisticated critique of Harberger's approach has been offered by Abram Bergson (1973). Bergson criticises the partial equilibrium framework employed by Harberger and all previous studies, and puts forward a general equilibrium model as an alternative. He then produces a series of hypothetical estimates of the welfare losses from monopoly, some of them quite large, for various combinations of the two key parameters in this model, the elasticity of substitution in consumption and the difference between monopoly and competitive price. Not surprisingly Bergson's estimates, suggesting as they do that monopoly can be a matter of some consequence, have induced a sharp reaction (see Carson, 1975; Worcester, 1975).[1]

The present paper levels several objections against the Harberger-type approach. It then calculates estimates of the welfare loss from monopoly using procedures derived to meet these objections, and obtains estimates significantly greater than those of previous studies. Although several of the objections we make have been made by other writers, none has systematically adjusted the basic Harberger technique to take them into account. Thus all previous estimates of monopoly welfare losses suffer in varying degrees from the same biases incorporated in Harberger's original estimates.

We do, however, employ a partial equilibrium framework as followed by Harberger and all subsequent empirical studies. Although a general equilibrium framework would be preferable, such an approach requires simplifying assump-

* This paper was started during the summer of 1975 when Keith Cowling visited the International Institute of Management and completed during the summer of 1976 when Dennis Mueller participated in the University of Warwick's Summer Workshop. Thanks are extended to both of these institutions for their support. In addition, special thanks are due to Gerald Nelson, who made the welfare loss calculations for the United States and Clive Hicks for making the estimates for the United Kingdom.

[1] In addition to the points Bergson (1975) raises in his own defence, we have serious objections to the arguments made by Carson (1975) and Worcester (1975). Some of these are presented below in our critique of previous studies.

tions which to our mind are just as restrictive as those needed to justify the partial equilibrium approach. For example, Bergson must assume that social welfare can be captured via a social indifference curve, and further that this indifference curve is the CES variety. The assumption that the elasticity of substitution (σ) is constant further implies, for a disaggregated analysis, that the elasticity of demand for each product (η_i) is the same, since $\eta_i \rightarrow \sigma$ as the share of the ith product in total output approaches zero. But the assumption that η_i is the same for all i is the same assumption made by Harberger and most other previous studies. It introduces a basic inconsistency between the observed variations in price cost margins and the assumed constant elasticities in demand, which the present study seeks to avoid. Given such problems, we have adopted the partial equilibrium framework, with all the necessary assumptions it requires (see Bergson, 1973). We present estimates for both the United States and the United Kingdom based on data gathered at the firm level.

I. THEORETICAL ANALYSIS

We have four substantive criticisms of the Harberger approach:

(1) In the partial equilibrium formula for welfare loss $\frac{1}{2}dp\,dq$, where dp is the change in price from competition to monopoly and dq is the change in quantity, dp and dq were considered to be independent of each other. Generally low values of dp were *observed* and low values of dq were *assumed*. In Harberger's case he assumed that price elasticities of demand in all industries were unitary. This must inevitably lead to small estimates of welfare loss.

(2) The competitive profit rate was identified with the mean profit rate and thus automatically incorporated an element of monopoly. In fact the underlying approach was a "constant degree of monopoly" – one in which distortions in output were associated with deviations of profit rate from the mean, rather than from the competitive return on capital.

(3) The use of industry profit rates introduces an immediate aggregation bias into the calculation by allowing the high monopoly profits of those firms with the most market power to be offset by the losses of other firms in the same industry. Given assumption (1), a further aggregation bias is introduced, which can easily be shown to result in additional downward bias in the estimates.

(4) The entire social loss due to monopoly was assumed to arise from the deviation of monopoly output from competitive levels. To this should be added the social cost of attempts to acquire monopoly positions, existing or potential.

We now seek to justify each of these four criticisms.

(A) *Interdependence of dp_i and dq_i*

Assuming profit maximising behaviour we can define the implied price elasticity of demand for a specific firm by observing the mark-up of price on marginal cost:

$$\hat{\eta}_i = p_i/(p_i - mc_i). \tag{1}$$

For a pure monopolist or perfectly colluding oligopolist $\hat{\eta}_i$ is the industry elasticity of demand. In other cases $\hat{\eta}_i$ reflects both the industry demand elas-

ticity and the degree of rivals' response to a change in price the ith firm perceives (Cubbin, 1975). Using (1) we shall obtain welfare loss estimates by
individual firms from their price/cost margins. These estimates indicate the
amount of welfare loss associated with a single firm's decision to set price above
marginal cost, given the change in its output implied by $\hat{\eta}_i$.[1] To the extent
other firms also charge higher prices, because firm i sets its price above marginal cost, the total welfare loss associated with firm i's market power exceeds
the welfare loss we estimate. To the extent that a simultaneous reduction to zero
of all price cost margins is contemplated, however, $\hat{\eta}_i$ overestimates the net
effect of the reduction in p_i on the ith firm's output. What the latter effect on
output and welfare would be is a matter for general equilibrium analysis and
is not the focus here. Rather, we attempt an estimate of the relative importance
of the distortions in individual firm outputs, on a firm by firm basis, on the
assumption that each does possess some monopoly power, as implied by the
price cost margin it chooses, and uses it.

This approach emphasising the interdependence of observed price distortions and changes in output contrasts with the methodology of Harberger
(1954), Schwartzman (1960), Worcester (1973) and Bergson (1973), who observe (or, in Bergson's case, assume) $(p_i - mc_i)/p_i$ and then *assume* a value of
η_i.[2] Harberger observed generally low values of dp_i and yet chose to assume
that $\eta_i = 1$, and therefore that dq_i was also very small. But, it is inconsistent
to observe low values of dp_i and infer low elasticities unless one has assumed
that the firm or industry cannot price as a monopolist, i.e. unless one has
already assumed the monopoly problem away.[3] Assuming interdependence we
obtain the following definition of welfare loss:

$$dW_i = \frac{1}{2}\frac{dp_i}{p_i}\frac{dq_i}{q_i}\,p_i q_i, \tag{2}$$

where

$$\frac{dp_i}{p_i} = \frac{1}{\hat{\eta}_i} \quad \text{and} \quad \frac{dq_i}{q_i} = \hat{\eta}_i\frac{dp_i}{p_i} = 1,[4]$$

therefore

$$dW_i = \frac{dp_i}{p_i}\frac{p_i q_i}{2}. \tag{3}$$

Assuming constant costs we can rewrite (3) in terms of profits:

$$dW_i = \frac{\Pi_i}{p_i q_i}\frac{p_i q_i}{2} = \frac{\Pi_i}{2}. \tag{4}$$

[1] We need here an assumption of perfect competition everywhere else, of course. We shall ignore
problems of the second best, along with the general equilibrium issue more generally, throughout the
paper.

[2] The Harberger and Schwartzman estimates are at the industry level.

[3] This position is questioned by Wenders (1967) and others who attempt to show how implausible
the implied η_i's are. However, their calculations are erroneous because they fail to recognise (a) that
the degree of collusion is a variable – we need not assume perfect joint profit maximisation and (b)
that entry is conditional on the same variables (plus others) that determine $(p_i - mc_i)/p_i$, for example η,
the degree of concentration and, for differentiated products, advertising also.

[4] This is true so long as the firm is in equilibrium, i.e. that the firms' expectations about the behaviour
of rivals are actually borne out. If this were not the case then the elasticity on which the pricing decision
was made would not correspond to the elasticity implied by the change in output. We assume firm
equilibrium in our calculations.

This formulation obviously contrasts sharply with Harberger's:

$$dW_i = \tfrac{1}{2}p_i q_i \eta_i t_i^2,$$ (5)

where

$$t_i = dp_i/p_i, \quad \eta_i = 1.$$

It is obvious that if t_i is small the welfare loss is going to be insignificant. If t_i were a price increase due to tariff or tax then it might be assumed to be independent of η_i,[1] and equation (5) would give a reasonable estimate of welfare loss. But where t_i is a firm decision variable, η_i and t_i must be interdependent, and formulae for calculating welfare losses should take this interdependence into account. Interesting here is the Worcester (1975) critique of Bergson for doing essentially this with his hypothetical general equilibrium calculations when Worcester himself followed the Harberger line without demure (Worcester, 1973).[2] In contrast to Harberger and Worcester, Bergson (1973) allowed himself to pick some combinations of t_i and η_i, which implied high values of welfare loss.

Harberger defended his choice of a demand elasticity of 1·0 across all products on the grounds that what was "envisage[d was] not the substitution of one industry's product against all other products, but rather the substitution of one great aggregate of products (those yielding high rates of return) for another aggregate (those yielding low rates of return)" (p. 79). Thus, the use of $\eta = 1·0$ was an attempt at compensating for the disadvantages of employing a partial equilibrium measure of welfare loss to examine a general equilibrium structural change. But certainly this is a very awkward way of handling the problem which neither answers the criticisms raised by Bergson (1973) against the partial equilibrium approach, nor those we have just presented. For this reason we have chosen to define the partial equilibrium methodology properly and obtain the best estimates we can with this approach, recognising that it leaves unanswered the issues raised by general equilibrium analysis and the theory of second best regarding the net effect of a simultaneous elimination of all monopoly power. We return to this point below in Subsection E.

(B) *The Measurement of Monopoly Profits*

The obvious measure of monopoly profit is the excess of actual profits over long-run competitive returns. For an economy in equilibrium, the competitive profit rate is the minimum profit rate compatible with long-run survival, after making appropriate allowances for risk. Monopoly profit is thus the difference between actual profits and profits consistent with this minimum rate.

Harberger (1954) and all subsequent studies have based their monopoly profit estimates on the size of the deviation between actual profit rates and the mean rate. To the extent that observed profits contain elements of monopoly

---

[1] But not necessarily so. Taxes and tariffs may be applied according to elasticity expectations.

[2] Worcester (1975) also offers some empirical support. His collection of industry price elasticities is either irrelevant (including many agricultural products and few manufacturing ones) or suspect (no allowance having been made in the studies quoted for quality change over time), and is certainly not comprehensive.

rent, the mean profit rate exceeds the minimum rate consistent with long-run survival. The deviations between profit rates above the mean and the mean rate underestimate the level of monopoly returns, and the estimate of monopoly welfare is biased downwards.[1] Indeed, if all firms and industries were in long-run equilibrium, all would earn profits equal to or greater than the minimum and the use of deviations from the mean would minimize the size of the measured monopoly profits.

It is unreasonable to assume that the time periods investigated in Harberger's study, the others which followed, or our own, are long enough or stable enough so that all firms and industries are in equilibrium. The presence of firms earning profits less than the competitive norm creates a methodological problem for a study of monopoly welfare losses. All studies to date have implicitly assumed that a monopolist's costs are the same as those of a firm in competitive equilibrium, and that all welfare loss is from the loss of consumers' surplus from a monopoly price above marginal cost. But, what is the appropriate assumption to make for a firm experiencing losses? It seems unrealistic to assume that its costs are at competitive levels and its prices below them. More reasonable seems the assumption that these firms are in disequilibrium, probably with costs currently above competitive levels. When calculating monopoly welfare losses, therefore, we simply drop all firms (or industries where relevant) with profits below the competitive return on capital, in effect assuming that they will eventually return to a position where they are earning normal profits or disappear. In either case, they represent no long-run loss to society. (It is possible that some of these losses represent expenditures by firms hoping to secure monopoly positions from other firms in the industry, as discussed below. These losses are then part of the social costs of monopoly. We attempt to account for them in one of our welfare loss formulae.)

Previous studies, to the extent we can ascertain, have followed Harberger and treated deviations in profits below and above the mean symmetrically. That is, an industry whose profit rate was 5 % below the mean profit rate was considered to have created as large a welfare loss as an industry whose profits are 5 % above the mean.[2] Thus, these studies have not actually estimated welfare loss under monopoly using perfect competition as the standard of comparison, but have effectively compared welfare loss under the present regime with that which would exist were the degree of monopoly equalised across all firms and industries. Under their procedures, a constant degree of monopoly power, however high, would result in no welfare loss. While such an approach has some theoretical support, it raises practical difficulties. How is this elusive concept of a constant degree of monopoly defined and measured? How is such a world created without an omniscient planner or regulator? In addition,

---

[1] Worcester (1973) makes some allowance for this bias by using 90 % of the median profit rate, but this adjustment is obviously rather *ad hoc*.

[2] One might believe that the losses by firms earning profits below the norm represent a form of *factor surplus loss* which must be added to the consumer surplus loss to obtain the full losses from monopoly. But, as Worcester (1973) has shown, these factor-surplus losses, if properly measured, are *an alternative way* of estimating the consumer surplus losses and should be used *instead of* the consumer surplus measure, rather than in addition to it, if used at all.

monopoly in product markets could be expected to induce distortions in factor markets. Finally, as developed below, the existence of monopoly power in product markets attracts resources to its acquisition and protection, which are part of the social cost of monopoly apart from the distortions in output accompanying it. For these reasons, and because it appears to be most directly in the spirit of the analysis, we have compared monopoly profits to competitive returns, and considered only deviations above the competitive rate when estimating welfare losses.

Following Harberger and other previous studies we have attempted to minimise the transitory component in our estimates by using averages of firm profits over several years.[1] Nevertheless, some of the companies earning profits above competitive levels in our samples are in temporary disequilibrium, and the welfare losses associated with these firms can be expected to disappear over time. Thus, our estimates of monopoly profits are a combination of both long-run monopoly profits and short-run disequilibrium profits. To the extent the time periods we have chosen are representative of the U.K. and U.S. economies under "normal" conditions, our calculations are accurate estimates of the annual losses from monopoly, both permanent and transitory, that can be expected in these countries. A further effort to eliminate the transitory monopoly components from the data would require a specification of what is meant by "permanent" and "transitory" monopolies. Many economists would take it for granted that in the "long run" all monopolies are dead and thus monopoly like unemployment is a "short run" phenomenon. As with unemployment, the question is how serious is the problem when it exists, and how long does it last. Our paper addresses the first of these questions. A full answer to the second question is clearly beyond the scope of our essentially cross-section analysis.

(C) *The Aggregation Biases from Using Industry Data*

Previous studies of monopoly welfare losses with the exception of Worcester (1973) used industry data at a fairly high level of aggregation. At any point in time some firms in an industry are likely to be earning profits below the competitive level. We have already discussed the methodological issues raised in a study of monopoly welfare losses by firms earning negative economic profits. If our interpretation of these firms as being in short-run disequilibrium is correct, then they should be dropped from an industry before calculating the industry's profit rate. Previous studies which have based their calculations solely on industry data have effectively combined the negative profits of some firms with the positive profits of others in estimating the welfare losses from monopoly. Thus they have implicitly assumed that the monopoly profits earned by the most profitable firms in the industry are somehow offset or mitigated by

---

[1] Harberger chose 5 years of "normal" business activity in the 1920s for his original study of the United States. Following his lead we have chosen 4 years in the 1960s for the U.S. estimates falling between a recession and the Vietnam War boom. The results reported below for the United Kingdom are for only two years, 1968/9. The U.K. results for 1970/4 indicate that averaging profits over five years does not change the nature of the outcome.

those experiencing transitory losses. But if there is a monopoly problem in an industry, it is represented by the positive rents earned by those firms with profits above the norm, and the losses of firms that are temporarily unable to compete successfully in no way alleviates the social costs arising from the monopoly positions of the other firms. The present study therefore measures monopoly welfare losses using firm level monopoly profit estimates.

A second aggregation bias is introduced into the estimates of all previous studies other than Kamerschen's (1966) through the assumption of a constant elasticity of demand across all industries. This results in the profit margin's appearance as a squared term in the welfare loss formula. The use of average firm profit margins (including firms with negative profits) implicit in the use of industry data, further biases the welfare loss estimates downwards. The extent of this bias is measured below.

(D) *Welfare Loss in the Acquisition of Monopoly Power*

Tullock (1967) and Posner (1975) have argued that previous studies under-state the social costs of monopoly by failing to recognise the costs involved in attempts to gain and retain monopoly power. These costs could take the form of investment in excess production capacity, excessive accumulation of adver-tising goodwill stocks, and excessive product differentiation through R and D.[1] Efforts to obtain tariff protection, patent protection and other types of pre-ferential government treatment through campaign contributions, lobbying or bribery are parts of the social costs of the existence of monopoly as defined by Tullock and Posner. To the extent that these expenditures enter reported costs in the form of higher payments to factor owners and legitimate business ex-penses, firm costs in the presence of monopoly exceed costs under perfect com-petition. Estimates of welfare loss based on those profits remaining *net* of these expenditures *under*estimate the social cost of monopoly in two ways: first, by understating monopoly rents they understate the distortions in output mono-poly produces; secondly, by failing to include these additional expenditures as part of the costs of monopoly.

Three adjustments to the usual welfare triangle measure of monopoly welfare loss are made to account for the additional expenditures to redistribute mono-poly rents, monopoly power induces. First, advertising is added to monopoly profit in calculating the welfare triangle loss to allow for the understatement of monopoly profit expenditures of this type produce. Second, all of advertising is added to the welfare loss. This takes the extreme view of advertising as merely an instrument for securing market power. To the extent advertising provides useful information to consumers, this measure overstates the cost of mono-poly.[2] Thirdly, all of measured, after-tax profits above the competitive cost of

---

[1] See Spence (1974). It is interesting to note that this type of activity generally dominates the entry-limiting pricing response. Entry-limiting pricing can be thought of as having extra capacity because of potential entry and actually using it to produce output. Thus the profits associated with restricting output are lost. From this viewpoint we cannot accept Posner's position that the elimination of entry regulation would eliminate waste. As the probability of entry increases so would the optimal degree of excess capacity. Monopoly pricing would be maintained but social waste would still occur.

[2] There will always be an inherent bias in the information provided given the interests of the agent

capital are used as the estimate of the expenditures incurred by others to obtain control of these monopoly rents. Obviously this estimate is but a first approximation. It is an underestimate, if the firm has incurred expenditures in the acquisition and maintenance of its monopoly position, which are included in current costs. It is an overstatement if actual and potential competitors can successfully collude to avoid these wasteful outlays. This type of argument can always be rebutted, however, by carrying the Tullock/Posner analysis one stage back and positing expenditures of resources to enter the potential competitor's position, and so on. The arguments that after-tax profits underestimate the additional costs associated with monopoly seem at least as reasonable as those suggesting overestimation.

(E) *An Objection and Alternative Estimating Technique*

The assumption that demand elasticity equals the reciprocal of the price–cost margin, equation (1), can give rise, when price–cost margins are small, to firm level elasticity estimates much greater than existing industry level estimates, and imply large increases in output from the elimination of monopoly. This has led several observers to criticise the use of the Lerner formula, and the underlying assumption that firms set price as if they possess and utilise market power. Worcester (1969) has made the argument most forcefully.

> Serious error...arise[s] if the "monopolist" is only an oligopolist who fears entry, unfavourable publicity, government regulation or a weaker position at the bargaining table should profits be too high, and for such reasons prices at P_0 (Fig. 1) and sells output Q_E in spite of the fact that the marginal revenue is far below zero at that point. [1969, p. 237, note that our Fig. 1 and Worcester's are drawn to scale.]

The elasticity of demand is lower at P_0 than at P_M, and the expansion in output following a reduction in price to competitive price P_c is obviously much smaller if we assume the "monopolist" sets price equal to P_0. Thus Worcester's depiction of the problem does meet the objections many have raised against the use of the Lerner formula to estimate demand elasticities. We observe only that if one assumes from the start that "monopolists" are so constrained in their behaviour that they must set price so low that marginal revenue is negative, it can be no surprise that calculations incorporating this assumption indicate insignificant welfare losses. But any estimates of welfare losses within a partial equilibrium framework, which impose demand elasticities significantly below those implied via the Lerner formula, must implicitly be assuming that firms set price in such an environment, if the data on price/cost margins are accepted at face value.

The latter assumption may not be valid, however, and its abandonment allows a reconciliation of existing profit-margin data with lower demand

---

doing the advertising so the argument for advertising as a provider of information should not be taken too seriously. Even if we base our welfare measures on post-advertising preferences it is still possible to demonstrate that monopolies (and *a fortiori* oligopolies) invest in too much advertising (see Dixit and Norman, 1975).

elasticity figures without also introducing the assumption that monopolists are either irrational or impotent. The preceding section discusses several business outlays that are made to maintain or preserve monopoly positions. Conceptually these are best treated as *investments* out of current profits made to secure future monopoly rents than as current production costs as is done for accounting purposes, and is carried through into the economist's calculations based on accounting data. A rational monopolist will not take these into account in making his short-run pricing decision. We can thus reconcile the monopoly pricing assumption with small demand elasticity estimates by assuming that average costs contain much investment-type expenditure and that marginal production costs are below these.

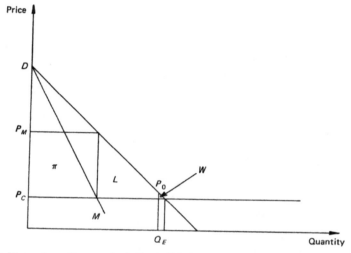

Fig. 1. π, Monopoly profit rectangle. *L*, Deadweight loss assuming firm exercises monopoly power. *W*, Worcester's proposed deadweight loss.

In Fig. 2 let C_0 be observed costs, including investment-type outlays, and P_0 observed price. For such price and cost figures to be consistent with monopoly pricing behaviour the firm's demand schedule would have to be D_0. Price P_0 would be consistent with a much more inelastic demand schedule, D_a say, if actual production costs were at C_a. Note that both profits (π), and the welfare triangle losses (*L*) are much larger under the more inelastic demand schedule assumption.

Thus, an alternative procedure for calculating the welfare losses from monopoly to the one described above would be to estimate price/cost margins from data on demand elasticities, where now we estimate demand elasticities from data on price/cost margins. We do not pursue these calculations here. First, because we do not have demand elasticity data applicable to firms, and the imposition of any constant η across all firms is obviously *ad hoc*. Secondly, the choice of any η in line with existing industry estimates would lead to welfare loss estimates far greater than those calculated here. The highest of the elasticities used in previous studies has been $\eta = 2 \cdot 0$. This implies a profit margin of 50 % and a welfare triangle loss equal to one-quarter of sales. These estimates exceed those reported here, whenever the firm's profits are *less* than one-half of sales. Since this is true for all our firms, our welfare loss estimates are all smaller than under the alternative procedure.

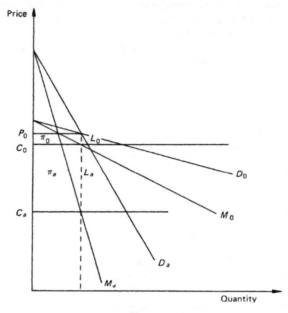

Fig. 2

We believe that reported costs do contain large amounts of investment-type expenditures beyond the advertising we allow for, that production costs are lower therefore, and that individual firm demand elasticities are typically lower than we implicitly estimate. We emphasise, however, that any attempt to take these costs into account, and adjust demand elasticities accordingly, while maintaining the assumption that companies do possess and exercise market power, will lead to larger estimates of welfare loss underlining again the conservative nature of our calculations.

II. EMPIRICAL ESTIMATES

Empirical estimates of the social cost of monopoly power were obtained for both the United States and United Kingdom. We provide two sets of estimates, one based on our assumptions (ΔW^k_{CM}), the other based on Harberger-type assumptions (ΔW^k_H), both measured at the firm-level. For each approach we give a range of four estimates defined in Table 1.

Thus for $k = 1$ we define two alternative estimates of the welfare triangle, the one (ΔW_{CM}^1) based on interdependence of dp_i and dq_i, the other (ΔW_H^1) based on the Harberger methodology. This latter estimate is included for comparison with previous results especially from the viewpoint of bias due to aggregation. For $k = 2$, the same calculations are performed but in calculating dp_i, advertising expenditure (A_i) is deducted from cost. For $k = 3$ we add in advertising expenditure as a social cost, and for $k = 4$ we also add in monopoly profits *after tax* as a further element of social cost. It should be noted at this point that in calculating dp_i the appropriate profit measure is *before tax*

Table 1

Alternative Definitions of Social Cost

k	ΔW_{CM}^k	ΔW_H^k
1	$\Pi/2$	$(R/2)\,(\Pi/R)^2$
2	$(\Pi+A)/2$	$(R/2)\,[(\Pi+A)/R]^2$
3	$A+(\Pi+A)/2$	$(R/2)\,[(\Pi+A)/R]^2+A$
4	$\Pi'+A+(\Pi+A)/2$	$(R/2)\,[(\Pi+A)/R]^2+A+\Pi'$

Π, before tax profit; Π', after tax profit; A, advertising; R, total revenue.

profit since the price and quantity choice of a monopolist should not be affected by a tax on profits. Thus, in contrast to most previous studies, we use before-tax profits to measure the distortion between price and costs under monopoly (the ΔW's for $k = 1, 2, 3$). However, it is *after-tax* monopoly profits which provide an inducement to additional expenditures to gain monopoly, and it is these that are added in to obtain our fourth measure of welfare loss.

To estimate monopoly profits an estimate of the return on capital of a firm in a competitive industry is needed. Any estimates based on actual returns earned in existing industries run the danger of including monopoly rents. The stock market might be regarded as coming fairly close to satisfying the free-entry and -exit requirement of a competitive industry, however. The returns on corporate stock will include monopoly rents to the extent that they become capitalised over the period for which the rate is estimated. The use of these returns for the United States is therefore equivalent to assuming that (1) all existing monopoly rents are fully capitalised at the beginning of the period, and (2) changes in monopoly rents over the period are accurately anticipated.

For the United States we use as our estimate of the competitive return on capital the Fisher–Lorie index of returns on a fully diversified portfolio of listed stocks for the same period for which our monopoly profit estimates are made (1963–6). This estimate was 12% which might be compared with the average return on capital earned by the firms in our sample of 14%.

For the United Kingdom we use the pre-tax real cost of capital as calculated by Flemming *et al.* (1976). These estimates avoid the newly capitalised monopoly rent problem mentioned above entirely. For the 1968/9 period they yield an estimate of the cost of capital of 8·15 %.[1]

[1] It may be argued that because of inflation we are undervaluing land or capital. This should not be a serious problem for the United States since our data follow a period of quite modest price increases.

The firms in our samples include companies operating in both intermediate and final goods markets. To justify the addition of triangular type measures of welfare loss for final and intermediate products, we must assume that the demand schedule for an intermediate product represents a derived demand schedule as in traditional Marshallian analysis. Under this assumption, triangular measures of welfare loss calculated from intermediate product demand schedules fully capture the loss in consumer welfare monopoly distortions in the intermediate markets cause, as Wisecarver (1974) has recently demonstrated. Assuming advertising and other efforts to obtain monopoly power are as wasteful when undertaken in intermediate markets as in final goods markets, the formulae presented in Table 1 can be applied for both intermediate and final good producers.

(A) *U.S. Estimates*

The range of welfare loss estimates for the United States are presented in Table 2. They refer to the 1963–6 period and the sample comprises the 734 firms on the COMPUSTAT tape with useable information.[1] The firms are ranked according to the size of welfare loss as measured by ΔW_{CM}^{A}. General Motors leads the list with an annual welfare loss of over $1¾ billion, which alone is over ¼ of 1 % of average GNP during the period, and exceeds Harberger's original welfare loss estimate for the entire economy. Most of the other members of the top 20 are names one also might have expected. One possible exception is AT & T. AT & T's gross profit rate was, in fact, less than our estimate of the cost of capital (≈ 0.12). Its advertising entry on the COMPUSTAT tape (and in this case we did have a COMPUSTAT figure, see appendix) was $¾ billion, and it is AT & T's advertising which leads to the high ΔW_{CM} estimate we have for it. Advertising also weighs heavily in the ΔW_{CM}^{A} estimates for Unilever, Proctor and Gamble, Sears Roebuck, Genesco, Colgate–Palmolive, Pan Am and Pacific Tel. At first sight this might seem surprising, particularly with respect to regulated firms like AT & T and Pacific Tel. But, as Posner (1975) has argued, this is precisely what one expects to find in industries with high market power, and, as Posner himself stresses, firms under regulatory constraint can be expected to engage, if anything, in more wasteful dissipation of their

---

Given that inflation in the United Kingdom in 1968/9 was substantial, although very much less than in the seventies, we have corrected our data at the company level. Using data from Walker (1974), we multiplied the profit figure derived from the company accounts by the ratio of the average rate of return at replacement cost to the average rate of return at historical cost and subtracted from this the estimated book value of assets times the cost of capital. The ratio of rates of return used was 9·4 : 13·4 in 1968 and 8·2 : 12·4 in 1969. We should in fact be using the ratio of the rate of return at replacement cost to the rate of return at book value but the latter rate was not available on a comparable basis (see Walker, 1974, table 3). This means that our measure of excess profits and therefore of welfare loss will tend to be biased down, given that (a) asset revaluations generally take place at merger, when acquired assets are given a current market valuation, and (b) revaluations, of land and buildings especially, do take place periodically, their frequency being related to the rate of inflation. The cost of capital measure used was the forward-looking, pre-tax measure which was estimated at 8·15 % for the period 1968/9 (Flemming *et al.* 1976).

[1] The COMPUSTAT tape contains data on a sample of large firms, mostly in manufacturing, listed on U.S. stock exchanges. The data definitions used in making the estimates are discussed in the appendix.

monopoly rents than non-regulated firms through expenditures like advertising. It is interesting to note in this regard that 6 of the 40 largest welfare losses are accounted for by regulated firms (3 telephone companies and 3 airlines) in which advertising made up all or most of the losses.

At the bottom of Table 2 the losses are summed over the firms with positive profit margins as defined for the ΔW^1 and ΔW^2 measures (see table notes), and then expressed as a proportion of our estimate of the Gross Corporate Product originating in the 734 firms in the sample. It should be stressed here, again, that the totals do not represent the estimated gains from the simultaneous elimination of all monopoly power. The answer to this question could be obtained only via a general equilibrium analysis. What we estimate via our partial equilibrium analysis is the relative cost of monopoly for each firm, and the column totals present average estimates of these costs for our sample of firms. Note, however, that the *additions* to our cost estimates that occur in moving from the W^2_{CM} to the W^3_{CM} and W^4_{CM} columns do sum across all firms, since these are estimates of the wasted expenditures made in pursuit of monopoly. If we see product market power as a ubiquitous characteristic of the economy, then it might be reasonable to assume that this estimate of monopoly welfare loss could be generalised to the entire economy. To the extent one believes monopoly power is more (e.g. see again Posner, 1975) or less pervasive in other sectors our estimates must be raised or lowered. Assuming the social costs of monopoly are the same across all sectors, we obtain estimates for our preferred model (ΔW^k_{CM}) ranging between 4 and 13 % of GCP. Thus, all losses are significant, but the range is considerable depending upon what components of social cost one includes. For the Harberger approach, the range is between 0·4 and 7 %. The lowest of these follows the Harberger assumptions most closely, but nevertheless we estimate a welfare loss four times as big as he did. This difference in large part is explained by the aggregation bias incorporated into the industry level estimates.

The extent of this bias can be seen by considering Table 3. Its entries are made by assigning each firm to an industry at the appropriate level of aggregation, and aggregating over the firms in each industry. Just as negative profit firms were excluded in calculating welfare losses at the firm level, negative profit industries are excluded in calculating welfare losses across industries. For the ΔW^k_{CM} measures aggregation bias is due simply to the inclusion of losses by some firms in the calculation of each industry's profits. Table 3 shows how this bias varies with the level of aggregation and with the choice of measure. Industry estimates are between 78 and 98 % of the firm level estimates in aggregate. For the ΔW^k_H estimates, a further cause of bias is introduced by the squared term, $(\Pi/R)^2$, in the formula. It can be seen from Table 3 that for the ΔW^1_H measures, the 2-digit industry estimates aggregate to only 40 % of the firm level estimates.[1] Note, however, that the biases are much smaller for the ΔW^3 and ΔW^4 measures and in the case of the ΔW^3_H measure at the

---

[1] Worcester (1973) plays down the extent of the bias by focusing on the *absolute* differences between the measures. Given that the absolute values of losses are small using ΔW^1_H, even very large relative biases result in small absolute distortions, as one would expect. For additional evidence on the importance of aggregation bias in previous studies, see Siegfried and Tiemann (1974).

Table 2

Monopoly Welfare Losses by Firm (yearly averages in $ millions): U.S. 1963/6

Company	$\Delta W_{\hat{C}M}^1$	$\Delta W_{\hat{C}M}^2$	$\Delta W_{\hat{C}M}^3$	$\Delta W_{\hat{C}M}^4$	ΔW_H^1	ΔW_H^2	ΔW_H^3	ΔW_H^4
1. General Motors	1,060·5	1,156·3	1,347·8	1,780·3	123·4	146·2	337·8	770·2
2. AT & T	0·0	257·3	1,025·0	1,025·0	0·0	13·4	781·1	781·1
3. Unilever	0·0	160·0	490·5	490·5	0·0	19·5	350·0	350·0
4. Procter & Gamble	56·7	180·1	427·0	427·0	3·3	33·0	279·9	279·2
5. Dupont	225·1	241·9	275·4	375·3	36·3	41·7	75·2	175·2
6. Ford Motor	160·4	217·5	331·7	331·7	5·2	9·3	123·5	123·5
7. IBM	251·7	264·0	288·7	319·8	36·8	40·5	65·2	96·3
8. Reynolds, R. J.	73·1	138·5	269·3	278·8	10·8	38·5	169·3	178·8
9. Sears Roebuck	36·2	115·0	272·5	272·5	0·5	4·4	162·0	162·0
10. Eastman Kodak	136·3	157·9	201·1	258·5	27·7	36·8	80·0	137·4
11. American Cyanamid Co.	27·6	98·7	240·8	240·8	1·9	23·6	165·8	165·8
12. Genesco, Inc.	0·0	67·5	202·6	292·6	0·0	14·9	150·0	150·0
13. Exxon Corp.	115·6	143·0	197·8	197·8	2·4	3·7	58·5	58·5
14. Colgate–Palmolive Co.	3·9	56·7	160·3	160·3	0·0	7·6	111·8	111·8
15. Chrysler Corp.	39·8	78·4	155·5	155·5	1·1	3·0	80·1	80·1
16. General Electric Co.	83·4	105·2	148·8	148·8	2·6	4·0	47·6	47·6
17. Pan Am Airways	1·1	49·8	147·2	147·2	0·1	7·5	104·9	104·9
18. Pacific Tel. & Tel.	0·0	18·4	138·1	138·1	0·0	0·8	128·5	128·5
19. Gillette Co.	27·8	56·0	112·3	129·2	4·7	18·9	75·3	92·2
20. Minnesota Mining & Mfg.	62·5	77·7	107·1	129·1	8·2	12·6	42·3	64·3
Totals all firms*	4,527·1	7,454·9	14,005·4	14,997·6†	448·2	897·8	7,448·3	8,440·1†
Total/GCP‡	0·0396	0·0652	0·1227	0·13137	0·0040	0·0079	0·0652	0·0739

* The ΔW^1's for all firms having monopoly profits (Π) less than zero were set equal to zero. The ΔW^2, ΔW^3, and ΔW^4's for all firms with ($\Pi+A$) < 0 were set equal to zero. The latter was based on the assumption that these firms would not survive in the long run and hence represent no *long run* welfare loss to society. There are 421 firms with Π > 0 and 525 firms with ($\Pi+A$) > 0 in the sample of 734 firms.

† When profits, after deducting taxes and the cost of capital (Π'), are less than zero, $\Delta W^4 = \Delta W^3$.

‡ The total welfare loss for all firms by each ΔW measure is first divided by the total sales of the 734 firms in the sample, and then multiplied by the ratio of corporate sales to gross corporate product over all industries (2·873) as given in Laffer (1969).

Table 3

Comparison of Firm and Industry Welfare Loss Estimates: U.S. 1963/6

	ΔW^1_{OM}	ΔW^2_{OM}	ΔW^3_{OM}	ΔW^4_{OM}	ΔW^1_{H}	ΔW^2_{H}	ΔW^3_{H}	ΔW^4_{H}
(1) Summation over firms	4,527·1	7,454·9	14,005·4	14,997·6	448·2	897·8	7,448·3	8,440·1
(2) Summation over 4 digit industries	3,767·8	6,902·5	13,752·6	14,052·8	276·9	628·8	7,478·9	7,790·2
(3) Summation over 3 digit industries	3,619·0	6,680·5	13,355·4	13,512·8	237·4	577·7	7,252·5	7,410·4
(4) Summation over 2 digit industries	3,515·2	6,634·5	13,262·7	13,287·9	178·9	485·3	7,113·5	7,148·8
(5) (2)/(1)	0·832	0·926	0·982	0·937	0·618	0·700	1·004	0·923
(6) (3)/(1)	0·799	0·896	0·954	0·901	0·530	0·643	0·974	0·878
(7) (4)/(1)	0·776	0·890	0·947	0·886	0·399	0·541	0·955	0·847

4-digit level the bias goes slightly the other way. This comes about because of the inclusion in the industry estimates of advertising for firms earning less

Table 4

Monopoly Welfare Losses by Firm (£ million): U.K. 1968/9

Company	ΔW^1_{OM}	ΔW^2_{OM}	ΔW^3_{OM}	ΔW^4_{OM}	ΔW^1_H	ΔW^2_H	ΔW^3_H	ΔW^4_H
1. British Petroleum	74·1	74·4	75·1	82·7	5·1	5·1	5·8	13·4
2. Shell Transport & Trading	49·4	50·8	53·6	53·6	2·2	2·3	5·1	5·1
3. British American Tobacco	26·8	27·0	27·5	49·1	1·0	1·1	1·6	23·1
4. Unilever	2·8	11·3	28·2	29·0	0·0	0·2	17·2	18·0
5. I.C.I.	17·6	18·8	21·1	27·9	0·5	0·5	2·9	9·6
6. Rank Xerox	13·9	14·0	14·2	27·5	3·4	3·4	3·5	16·9
7. I.B.M. (U.K.)	11·1	11·2	11·3	21·9	2·2	2·2	2·4	12·9
8. Great Universal Stores	9·6	10·0	11·0	21·6	0·5	0·5	1·5	12·1
9. Beecham	6·2	8·9	14·3	20·4	0·6	1·3	6·7	12·8
10. Imperial Group	2·8	8·6	20·1	20·1	0·0	0·1	11·7	11·7
11. Marks & Spencer	9·8	9·8	9·8	18·6	0·6	0·6	0·6	9·5
12. Ford	7·2	7·8	8·8	16·6	0·2	0·2	1·3	9·1
13. F. W. Woolworth	7·3	7·4	7·8	15·9	0·3	0·4	0·7	8·9
14. J. Lyon	0·0	0·7	2·8	14·2	0·0	0·0	2·1	13·4
15. Burmah	5·3	5·5	5·9	13·9	0·2	0·3	0·7	8·7
16. Distillers	5·6	6·1	7·1	13·4	0·2	0·2	1·2	7·5
17. Rank Organisation	11·5	11·7	12·1	12·5	1·2	1·2	1·7	2·1
18. Thorn	5·6	6·1	7·1	12·5	0·3	0·3	1·4	6·7
19. Cadbury Schweppes	1·8	5·0	11·4	12·3	0·0	0·3	6·7	7·6
20. Reckitt & Coleman	2·9	4·7	8·3	10·4	0·1	0·3	3·9	6·0
Total all firms (102)	385·8	435·0	537·4	719·3	21·4	24·2	118·8	304·4
Total ÷ GCP	0·0386	0·0436	0·0539	0·0720	0·0021	0·0024	0·0119	0·0305

No. of firms with $\Pi > 0 = 82$.
No. of firms with $\Pi + A > 0 = 86$.

than normal profits. Thus in future work along these lines, when data are limited to industry level observations, the ΔW^3 and ΔW^4 measures have an additional advantage over the other two measures.

(B) *U.K. Estimates*

These have been calculated on the same basis as the U.S. estimates, but since no convenient computer tape was available we contented ourselves with an analysis of the top 103 firms in the United Kingdom for the periods 1968/9 and 1970/4.[1] Over the periods in question these firms were responsible for roughly one-third of the GNP and were therefore proportionally more important than the 734 firms sample from the COMPUSTAT tape for the United States. The time-periods used have been dictated by the availability of data. The basic source has been EXTEL cards but advertising expenditure was estimated by aggregating up from the brand level, using estimates of press and TV

[1] The top 100 varies somewhat over time.

advertising contained in MEAL. We can therefore expect that our advertising expenditure figures will be biased down by the amount of non-media advertising, as is true also for the United States. Table 4 gives the results for 1968/9, with firms again being ranked by ΔW^4_{CM}. The two major oil companies, BP and Shell, dominate the table. The social cost associated with BP alone is roughly a quarter of 1 % of GNP. The other members of the Top Ten are industry leaders plus British–American Tobacco. Two interesting features of the Top Twenty are the high ranking of Rank Xerox despite its size (explained presumably by its U.K. patent rights) and, in contrast to the United States, the low ranking of motor-car manufacturers (absent from the Top Twenty in 1970/4). We have computed estimates of welfare loss for the 1970/4 period, but we have not reported these results here. It is well known that the early seventies was a period of very rapid inflation in the United Kingdom and this undoubtedly raises problems such as how to account for stock appreciation and the revaluation of capital adequately. Despite these problems, it is somewhat reassuring to note that the 1970–4 results look very much like the 1968/9 results except that the oil companies become even more dominant.[1]

The aggregate estimates of welfare loss for ΔW^k_{CM} range between 3·9 and 7·2 % of GCP for the 1968/9 period. The estimate for ΔW^1_{CM} is almost identical with that for the United States but in each of the other cases the value for the United Kingdom is well below that for the United States. The obvious and important difference between the two sets of results is the apparent greater expenditure on advertising in the United States. Taking direct account of advertising quadruples the welfare loss estimate for the United States but in the case of the United Kingdom welfare loss goes up by only about 40 % (compare ΔW^1_{CM} with ΔW^3_{CM}).[2] Using the Harberger approach estimates of welfare loss vary between 0·2 and 3 % of GCP for the United Kingdom in the same 1968/9 period.

Again, we must conclude that our evidence suggests significant welfare loss due to monopoly power. One other point is also brought out particularly by the U.K. results (e.g. in the case of the oil companies) and that is the international distribution of these social costs. Monopoly power held by U.K. companies in foreign markets may be advantageous to the U.K. economy whilst being disadvantageous in the global sense. Thus the issue is a distributional one and adds an international dimension to the distributional issues already implicit in our analysis. In any national evaluation of the social costs imposed by the actions of a particular company, the international distribution of these costs would presumably gain some prominence.

[1] Indeed, comparing the results for the two periods indicates the large extent to which oil companies have benefited from the recent "oil crisis". However, this inference has to be qualified by the problems raised for the measurement of profit by stock appreciation during a period of rapid inflation of oil prices.

[2] This does not of course mean that advertising implies no additional social costs, since profit-margins and the level of excess profits may both be partly determined by advertising in so far as elasticities of demand and entry barriers are influenced by the level of advertising in monopolistic industries. We should also note that in some cases our direct adjustment for advertising is very significant (e.g. Unilever, Imperial Group and Beecham Group).

III. IMPLICATIONS AND CONCLUSIONS

Previous studies of the social costs of monopoly have generally (and often unconsciously) assumed that "monopolies" set prices as if they did not possess market power, that the only important distortions in output are brought about through the deviations in one firm's market power from the average level of market power, that the losses of some firms (perhaps incurred in unsuccessful attempts to obtain monopoly power) legitimately offset the monopoly rents of others, and that all of the expenditures made in the creation and preservation of monopoly positions are part of the normal costs which would exist in a world without monopolies. With the problem so defined, it is not surprising that most of these studies have found the welfare losses from monopoly to be small.

Since we know from general equilibrium analysis that monopoly allocation distortions may be offsetting, the conclusion that partial equilibrium analysis yields small welfare loss estimates has seemed all the more impressive. Yet each of the studies that has come up with low estimates has done so in large part because it has made assumptions (e.g. demand elasticities equal to 1·0, monopoly profits are deviations from mean profits) that can be rationalised only as *ad hoc* attempts to answer the general equilibrium question. In contrast, the present study defines a procedure for estimating the costs of monopoly that is consistent with a partial equilibrium analysis that assumes market power does (or may) exist. Our results reveal that the costs of monopoly power, calculated on an individual firm basis, are on average large. The conclusion that "even" a partial equilibrium analysis of monopoly indicates that its costs are insignificant no longer seems warranted.

This conclusion has potentially important policy implications. Antitrust policy consists typically not of a frontal attack on all existing market power, but of selective assaults on the most flagrant offenders. Our partial equilibrium estimates of monopoly welfare losses indicate the most significant contributors to these losses. The tops of our lists of the largest welfare losses by firm are logical starting points for intensified enforcement of antitrust policy. Our figures and supporting analysis further demonstrate that "the monopoly problem" is broader than traditionally suggested. A large part of this problem lies not in the height of monopoly prices and profits *per se*, but in the resources wasted in their creation and protection. These costs of monopoly should be considered when selecting targets for antitrust enforcement.

One might argue that the high profits of some firms reflect economies of scale advantages, and, therefore, these firms should not be the victims of antitrust policy. This argument points to some form of regulatory or public enterprise solution to the monopoly problem. With respect to this type of policy, our estimates of the losses from monopoly represent a still further understatement of their potential magnitude. If a policy were adopted forcing the most efficient size or organisational structure upon the entire industry, the welfare loss under the existing structure would have to be calculated using the profit margin of the most efficient *firm and the output of the entire industry*, rather than the profit margins of the individual firms and their outputs.

These considerations suggest the difficulty in estimating the social gains from the elimination of all monopoly power, since one almost has to know what form of policy is to be used (antitrust, regulation), and what the underlying cause of monopoly power is, before answering this question. Nevertheless, this has been the question that has traditionally been asked in studies of monopoly welfare losses, and the reader who has persisted to this point can justifiably ask what light our figures cast on this question. By their very nature partial equilibrium calculations cannot give very *precise* estimates of these gains, but they may establish orders of magnitude. As stressed above, we regard the Harberger-type calculations based on uniform demand elasticities of $1\cdot0$ as essentially efforts to solve the general equilibrium problem inherent in this question. As such, we regard them as the most conservative estimates of what the elimination of all monopoly would produce. Thus, we would expect the elimination of all monopoly to yield gains at least as large as the 7 and 3 % of gross corporate product we estimate for the United States and United Kingdom, respectively, using ΔW_H^A. To the extent that firms sell differentiated products, and operate in separate markets, i.e. to the extent that they have and utilise market power, these gains are pushed in the direction of our ΔW_{CM}^A estimates of 13 and 7 %. Further upward pressure on these estimates is created by considering some of the other factors ignored in our calculations. We have already emphasised that reported profits understate true profits to the extent that firms compete for monopoly power by investing in excess plant capacity, advertising, patent lawyers, and so on. But much of the competition for *control* over monopoly rents may take place within the firm itself among the factor owners. Such competition will lead to an understatement of actual monopoly rents both through the inflation of costs that wasteful competition among factors owners brings about, and through the inclusion of part of the winning factor owners' shares of monopoly rents as reported costs. A large literature now exists on the variety of objectives managers have and the ways in which these objectives are satisfied through their discretionary control over company revenues. To the extent that managerial control over firm revenues is the reward for competing against other factor groups and potential managers successfully, reported profits understate the true profitability. By ignoring these possibilities we have erred in being conservative when estimating the social cost of monopoly. It is our reasoned guess that these additional costs would at least equal the "washing out" effect of the simultaneous elimination of all monopoly power on our partial equilibrium estimates and, therefore, that these latter figures are, if anything, underestimates of the true social costs of monopoly.

  In this respect, it is useful to note an alternative, aggregative approach to the question. Phillips, in an appendix to Baran and Sweezy (1966), isolated several categories of expenditure dependent on the existence of "Monopoly Capitalism" (e.g. advertising, corporate profits, lawyers' fees). Their sum came to over 50 % of U.S. GNP. Although the assumptions upon which these calculations were made are rather extreme, they do suggest both an alternative method of analysis and the potential magnitude of the problem. Here too it should be noted that our approach has been essentially micro-orientated and neoclassical in that we have taken the returns on corporate stocks as our cost of capital. From a more aggregative view it could be argued that profits are not required at all to generate the savings required to sustain a given rate of growth, since alternative macro policies are available. From this perspective, all profits are excess profits and our estimates of social cost are too conservative. Still further weight would be added against the position that monopoly power is unimportant if the link with the distribution of political power were considered.

Of course, any public policy has its own sets of costs and inefficiencies. For Tullock–Posner reasons a concerted effort to apply or strengthen the anti-trust laws induces large, defensive expenditures on the part of business. Price and profit regulation leads to efforts to change, influence, or circumvent the application of the rules. The public enterprise solution raises the same sort of problems, with members of the bureaucracy participating in the competition for monopoly rents. Thus it might be that any alternative for dealing with existing monopoly power would involve higher costs than the monopolies themselves create. The present study does not answer this question. What it does do is dispel the notion that it need not even be asked, since the costs of monopoly within the present environment are necessarily small. The question of what the costs and benefits from alternative antimonopoly policies are still seems worth asking.

Warwick University   KEITH COWLING

University of Maryland   DENNIS C. MUELLER

Date of receipt of final typescript: April 1978

REFERENCES

Baran, P. and Sweezy, P. (1966). *Monopoly Capital*. New York: Monthly Review Press.

Bergson, A. (1973). "On Monopoly Welfare Losses." *American Economic Review*, vol. 63 (December), pp. 853–70.

Carson, R. (1975). "On Monopoly Welfare Losses: Comment." *American Economic Review*, vol. 65 (December), pp. 1008–14.

Cubbin, J. (1975). "Apparent Collusion, Price–Cost Margins and Advertising in Oligopoly." Mimeo, University of Warwick.

Dixit, A. and Norman, V. (1978). "Advertising and Welfare." *Bell Journal of Economics* (June).

Flemming, J. S., Price, L. D. D. and Byers, S. A. (1976). "The Cost of Capital, Finance and Investment." *Bank of England Quarterly Bulletin*, vol. 16 (June), pp. 193–205.

Harberger, A. C. (1954). "Monopoly and Resource Allocation." *American Economic Review*, vol. 45 (May), pp. 77–87.

Kamerschen, D. R. (1966). "An Estimation of the Welfare Losses from Monopoly in the American Economy." *Western Economic Journal*, vol. 4 (Summer), pp. 221–36.

Laffer, A. B. (1965). "Vertical Integration by Corporations, 1929–65." *Review of Economics and Statistics*, vol. 51 (February), pp. 91–3.

Posner, R. A. (1975). "The Social Costs of Monopoly and Regulation." *Journal of Political Economy*, vol. 83 (August), pp. 807–27.

Scherer, F. M. (1970). *Industrial Market Structure and Market Performance*. Chicago: Rand McNally.

Schwartzman, D. (1960). "The Burden of Monopoly." *Journal of Political Economy*, vol. 68 (December), pp. 627–30.

Siegfried, J. J. and Tiemann, T. K. (1974). "The Welfare Cost of Monopoly: An Inter-Industry Analysis." *Economic Inquiry*, vol. 12 (June), pp. 190–202.

Spence, M. (1974). "Entry, Capacity, Investment and Oligopolistic Pricing." Technical Report 131, Institute for Mathematical Studies in the Social Sciences, Stanford University.

Stigler, G. J. (1956). "The Statistics of Monopoly and Merger." *Journal of Political Economy*, vol. 64 (February), pp. 33–40.

Tullock, G. (1967). "The Welfare Costs of Tariffs, Monopolies and Theft." *Western Economic Journal*, vol. 5 (June), pp. 224–32.

Walker, J. L. (1974). "Estimating Companies' Rate of Return on Capital Employed." *Economic Trends*, November, pp. xx–xxix.

Wenders, J. L. (1967). "Entry and Monopoly Pricing." *Journal of Political Economy*, vol. 75, pp. 755–60.

Wisecarver, D. (1974). "The Social Costs of Input-Market Distortions." *American Economic Review*, vol. 64 (June), pp. 359–72.

Worcester Jr., D. A. (1969). "Innovations in the calculations of welfare loss to monopoly." *Western, Economic Journal*, vol. 7 (September), pp. 234–43.

—— (1973). "New Estimates of the Welfare Loss to Monopoly: U.S. 1956–69." *Southern Economic Journal*, vol. 40 (October), pp. 234–46.

—— (1975). "On Monopoly Welfare Losses: Comment." *American Economic Review*, vol. 65 (December), pp. 1015–23.

APPENDIX

Data: Definitions and Sources

United States

All data on individual firms with one exception were taken from the COMPUSTAT tape of 1969, and all definitions conform therefore to those given in the COMPUSTAT manual. The numbers in brackets { } refer to the variable numbers assigned on the COMPUSTAT annual industrial file.

The competitive return on capital used in calculating monopoly profits was $0 \cdot 1197$, the geometric mean of the monthly Fisher–Lorie index of returns on the market portfolio between January 1963 to December 1967. The firm's capital was measured as Total Assets/Liabilities and Net Worth less Intangibles (goodwill, patents, etc.). The latter were deducted on the grounds that they largely represent capitalised monopoly rents (see Stigler, 1956; Kamerschen, 1966). Thus, the firm's opportunity cost of capital was estimated as:

$$CC = 0 \cdot 1197 \ (DATA\{6\} - DATA\{33\}).$$

Two estimates of monopoly profits were formed to compute the triangle-type measures. The first is gross profit flow (net income + interest expense + income taxes) less the cost of capital (CC).

$$\Pi = DATA\{18\} + DATA\{15\} + DATA\{16\} - CC.$$

The second is the first plus advertising ($A = DATA\{45\}$). For roughly 85 % of the sample firms the COMPUSTAT entry for advertising was missing, however. The product of the firm's Sales ($DATA\{12\}$) and the industry advertising to sales ratio for the firm's industry as given in *Advertising Age* (7 June 1965, pp. 101–3) was substituted for this entry in these cases.

To calculate the ΔW^4 measures, income taxes ($DATA\{16\}$) were subtracted from Π to obtain Π'.

United Kingdom

All the data on individual firms with the exception of advertising has its origin in the data tabulations of the Exchange Telegraph Statistics Service (EXTEL). Most of the relevant data in a summarised form was available in various issues of *The Times Review of Industry and Technology*. In the case of advertising the firm data had to be estimated via a process of aggregating estimates of press and TV advertising of the various products produced by each firm. These data were extracted from various issues of *MEAL* (*Advertisers' Annual Analysis of Media Expenditure*) and, in the case of 1968, from the *Statistical Review of Press and T.V. Advertising* (Legion Publishing Company). *Who Owns Whom* was used in the process of aggregation.

Each firm's capital was measured as total tangible assets less current liabilities (excluding bank loans, overdrafts and future tax). Profit was measured before interest and tax and then adjusted for the estimated cost of capital (taken from Flemming *et al.* 1976).

[24]

Price Controls and Optimal Export Policies under Alternative Market Structures

By Richard E. Just, Andrew Schmitz, and David Zilberman*

International trade is a transaction which takes place among institutions. Competitive producers rarely sell directly to competitive consumers in a world trading market! For example, a wheat producer in Kansas does not negotiate his wheat sales directly with Russian grain purchasers. It is common for private or semipublic institutions, such as international trading companies or marketing boards, to buy from producers and sell to consumers. In many exporting nations, marketing boards or organizations exist (for example, the Organization of Petroleum Exporting Countries, *OPEC*; Canadian and Australian Wheat Boards; Ghana Cocoa Board; Uganda Coffee Board) which are essentially producer boards that do the actual selling of the product both within and outside the country. In the United States, private grain traders who buy grain from thousands of *U.S.* farmers are the dominant sellers of *U.S.* grain domestically and to foreign markets.

The literature to date on optimal tariff policies does not treat explicitly the nature and role of firms engaged in international marketing. In the classical optimal tariff literature, there are essentially three sectors: competitive producers; competitive consumers; and the government. The latter uses its power to intervene in international trade to maximize domestic social welfare. Recently, alternative models have been constructed in which the government uses tariff policy to achieve other goals. For example, Harry Johnson (1951, 1968) and Trent Bertrand have developed the "optimum government revenue tariff." In their models the government plays the role of the marketing agency

using its monopoly and monopsony power to maximize the revenue it collects from international trade.

In this paper an international trade model for an exporting country is constructed in which international trading firms may exercise the type of market power Johnson (1951) and Bertrand attributed to the government sector; the government plays the traditional role of using tariff and other policies to maximize domestic social welfare.[1] The model thus consists of four sectors: 1) competitive producers; 2) competitive consumers; 3) the government; and 4) international trading institutions which are assumed to be noncompetitive. The welfare effects on society from the activities of two types of noncompetitive trading institutions are analyzed separately, and appropriate governmental actions for achieving maximum social welfare are suggested.[2] Explicitly, a marketing firm with both monopoly and monoposony power is considered where the firm operates independently from producers and consumers to maximize its own profits. This is an extension of results relating to the kind of firm introduced in Abba Lerner's classic paper on the measurement of monopoly power. A second case deals with international transactions carried out by producer cartels. Their activities are discussed both with and without government controls.

It is important to recognize that governmental controls are often imposed on interna-

---

*Department of agricultural and resource economics, University of California-Berkeley. We wish to thank an anonymous referee for useful comments on an earlier version of this paper. Giannini Foundation Paper No. 513.

[1] The models used are partial in nature in that only exporting firms are considered. Partial analysis is used because of simplicity and sharpness of results. Paul Samuelson (1971) developed conditions under which partial analysis leads to the same results as does the general equilibrium approach.

[2] The welfare sections of this paper are based on the classic concept of economic surplus. The limitations of this type of analysis, which have been discussed by John Currie, John Murphy, and Schmitz, should be borne in mind.

tional trading institutions. As examples, for the first time since World War II, the United States imposed export controls on grain shipments and required that export sales to the Soviet Union by the private trading companies be reported if the sales were over a certain volume, and the Canadian government imposed a ceiling on the price that millers in Canada pay for wheat, while the price for export sales is set by the Canadian Wheat Board (which has among its objectives the maximization of producer returns) for export sales.[3] The specific control examined in this paper is somewhat similar. The government in the exporting country permits the marketing institution to charge whatever price it can abroad but, internally, the price it charges domestic consumers must equal the (marginal) "costs" of production. Interestingly, this type of government regulation does not lead to maximum welfare for the exporting country as a whole. To attain welfare-efficient trade, an export *tax* is needed along with this type of control in the case where the export firm is a cartel or marketing board acting in the interest of producers (as shown in Section II); and an export *subsidy* is needed in the case where the export firm is a private monopoly-monopsony marketing firm (as shown in Section III). The conclusion that a subsidy is needed in the latter case simply states that the implicit export tax used in the firm's profit-maximizing calculations exceeds the implicit export tax that should be used if the firm were operating competitively.[4]

The debate over whether or not multinational marketing companies are competitive or not has occupied a large part of the economic literature and antitrust court cases. The results are inconclusive. However, in view of the recent behavior of such organizations as *OPEC* and other marketing boards and the description of firms presented by Jim Hightower, it seems worthwhile to consider, at

least theoretically, marketing firms which have market power. In addition, since the results from competition are well known, the analysis of alternative polar cases is of interest.

Readers familiar with the literature on market distortions (particularly factor-market imperfections) in the framework of international trade theory will recognize in this paper an application of the general principle that in order to achieve maximum welfare it is necessary to adopt a subsidy/tax scheme which offsets the domestic distortion, *plus* a tax aimed at taking advantage of the country's monopoly and/or monopsony power in trade. In this case an export tax is required for the latter purpose. Since a tax is equivalent to a subsidy to domestic consumers *and* a tax on domestic production, the optimum trade controls can be estimated by simply imposing taxes or subsidies on domestic concerns.

I. Optimal Trade for an Individual Country

In this section the optimal trade conditions for an individual country exporting a single good are reviewed. It can easily be shown that these conditions can be attained under competition by imposing an export tax. In subsequent sections, optimal policies under alternative noncompetitive institutional frameworks are determined in an analogous manner. In other words, controls are developed in each case which lead to the same pattern of trade as indicated by the optimal conditions derived in this section. This forms the basis for the optimization performed in succeeding sections.

Consider the two-country model in Figure 1: country A exports good x to country B. The domestic demand in country A is D_A, and B's demand for country A's exports is D_E.[5] The

---

[3]For a discussion of how the Canadian Wheat Board was established and the extent to which it serves producers' interests and enjoys producers' support, see Vernon Fowke.

[4]This result is similar to the proposition that maximum revenue (rather than maximum welfare) tariff exceeds the optimum tariff. On this, see Johnson (1951), Edward Tower, and W. M. Corden.

[5]If none of good x is produced in B, the demand schedule D_E is comparable to D_A in country A. However, if x is also produced in country B, the demand schedule D_E is an excess demand curve. In this case the results of the paper also hold since it is assumed that the marketing firm (either the board or the middleman) does not use its monopsony power against producers in B (i.e., the firm does not use the marginal outlay schedule to the supply schedule in B in calculating optimal conditions).

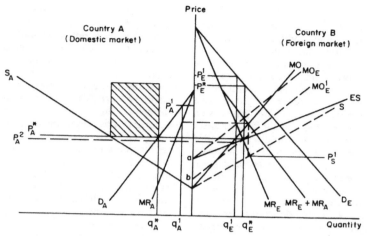

FIGURE 1. FIRM WITH MONOPOLISTIC AND MONOPSONISTIC POWER

supply function in A for the *competitive* industry producing x is S. Assume that A maximizes welfare from trade in x. Its welfare criterion is to maximize the sum of the social surpluses from consumption and exports minus the social cost of production. For competition in both production and demand, the exporting country must impose a tax or a quota on exports in order to achieve the optimum allocation of resources. The solution for the optimal export tax for country A can be determined by constructing an excess supply curve (ES) for country A and observing its intersection with the marginal revenue schedule MR_E which corresponds to demand D_E. In the optimal solution *the price to both consumers and producers in country A is the same, P_A^*, and the price in country B is P_E^*.*[6] The tax is given by $P_E^* - P_A^*$, and the tax revenue collected by country A on exports is represented by the crosshatched area. From the mathematical treatment in the Appendix, this tax can be calculated by $q_E^* D'(q_E^*)$ or, equivalently, $-P_E^*/\eta_E$, where η_E, is the elasticity of foreign excess demand.

---

[6] It is assumed that all demand curves are negatively sloped, all supply curves are positively sloped, and revenue functions are concave.

II. The Monopoly-Monopsony Model

Consider the monopoly-monopsony case where a single firm buys from competitive producers in country A and sells to competitive consumers in country B. Ignoring marketing costs, the optimization conditions for the monopoly-monopsony case are given in the Appendix and are illustrated geometrically in Figure 1.[7] To determine the optimum pricing policy that the marketing firm will use, a marginal outlay curve MO (i.e., the marginal cost schedule to the firm buying goods from competitive producers with supply schedule S) is constructed. Prices are determined where the MO schedule crosses the sum of the marginal revenue schedules, $MR_E + MR_A$. The firm will pay price P_S^1 to

---

[7] A marketing firm in reality incurs costs of transportation, etc.; but if these costs are constant at the margin, Samuelson (1952) has shown that conclusions in this kind of model are not substantially altered—one merely has to shift the axis of one country or the other by the amount of the marginal marketing cost. If marketing costs are not constant, then the results obtained herein will be altered; but often the changes will be minor. In many cases marketing costs are insignificant relative to the value of the good traded. For example, the Canadian Wheat Board charges less than 1 percent of the total value for marketing costs.

producers and charge price P_A^1 to consumers in A and price P_E^1 to consumers in B. Note that the consumer and producer prices are not identical in the exporting country.[8]

Even though large marketing firms may have market power, they are often regulated by government price controls imposed in the domestic market. In order to take price controls explicitly into account, the above model is modified. Since, in the Lerner solution and in the optimal tax situation under competition, producer and consumer prices in the domestic market are identical, and since the general welfare-maximization conditions for country A in Section I indicate domestic producer and consumer prices, the constraint of equality of domestic producer and consumer prices is explicitly considered.[9] Using such a policy, one might expect that domestic consumers are not being exploited when the marketing firm is free to choose its pricing policy abroad. But as shown below, even with this type of control, the marketing firm does not choose optimal export quantities which maximize social welfare in country A.

In the model in this section, the activities of the marketing firm are regulated so that the price charged domestic consumers has to be equal to the price paid to producers. Such a price control could thus be simply monitored by comparing observed market prices for producers and consumers. Since both producers and consumers operate competitively, this control in effect equates domestic consumer price with the marketing firm's average (purchasing) cost which is also equal to the producers' marginal cost (specified by the supply curve). Hence, the marketing firm cannot make profit in the domestic market; its only profit is obtained in the foreign market.

The solution (in Figure 1) is obtained by deriving the positive excess supply curve (the difference between domestic demand and supply at different prices labeled as ES) and determining where the marginal schedule (MO_E) to this curve crosses the excess marginal revenue curve (MR_E) of the importing country. As shown by Schmitz and Just under linearity and, assuming S_A intersects the vertical rather than the horizontal axis, the marginal outlay curve (MO_E) to the excess supply curve (ES) crosses the marginal revenue schedule of country B at the *same* level as the MO schedule crosses the sum of the marginal revenue schedules. Hence, exports may well be the same whether or not price controls are imposed domestically.

Although the consumer and producer prices in country A are identical with controls, the optimal allocation of resources is not achieved. The price P_A^2 is *below* the optimal domestic price P_A^* and, with the price constraint, the firm exports too little.[10] This happens because the firm with monopoly-monopsony power disregards the increase in domestic welfare (from increasing domestic production and consumption) when it operates according to the marginal outlay curve associated with the excess supply curve (which is used in country A's welfare maximization) rather than the excess supply curve itself.[11]

To achieve optimality, the government in A has to impose another control in addition to equating producer and consumer prices. One such policy would be to introduce an export *subsidy*. The exact subsidy which achieves optimality for country A can be computed mathematically (see the Appendix) or geometrically (see Figure 1). Geometrically, it is the distance ab since, with this subsidy, MO_E^1 (the marginal outlay after the subsidy) crosses the MR_E schedule at the optimal export level under competition.

---

[8]One way to reach the optimum for country A outlined in the previous section is to impose two subsidies, for example, one on domestic production and one on domestic consumption (the Appendix gives the specific subsidies).

[9]Other types of constraints not dealt with here could also be considered (for example, a regulation on the rate of return from goods sold in the domestic market); see Harvey Averch and Leland Johnson; William Baumol and Alvin Klevorick.

[10]Interestingly, however, it can be noted that consumers in the exporting country prefer the regulated monopoly-monopsony to both free trade with competition and social optimality from the standpoint of country A.

[11]This proof simply relies on the fact that the marginal excess supply curve always lies above the excess supply curve.

III. Producer Cartels (or Simple Monopoly)

Consider the alternative case where producers have monopolistic power both domestically and abroad and maximize producer profits from the production of good x. As indicated above, common institutions which can lead to this type of market power are producer cartels or producer marketing boards. As indicated in the Appendix (and Figure 2), the optimal solution for the marketing board is to equate S with the horizontal sum of MR_E and marginal revenue schedule MR_A in country A. The marketing board will restrict producer supply in country A to q^3. The board will charge price P_A^3 to consumers in country A and price P_E^3 to consumers in country B.[12] On the other hand, the optimal trade solution (from the perspective of country A) is determined where ES intersects MR_E. Total production under a marketing board is actually smaller than in the competitive optimal tax case because the horizontal sum of MR_E and MR_A is always below the horizontal sum of MR_E and D_A. Furthermore, exports with the marketing

board must be greater than is socially optimal for country A because $MR_E + MR_A$ intersects S_A at a lower price than $MR_E + D_A$; hence, more goods are exported at the lower foreign price corresponding to a lower point on the MR_E schedule. Also, note that domestic producer and consumer prices are not generally identical with the marketing board as under social optimality for country A.[13]

Suppose that, as in the monopoly-monopsony case, the government in A decides to protect local consumers by imposing a constraint similar to the one imposed in the previous case, namely, that the price the consumer pays must be equal to the marginal cost of domestic production. That is, the board can do whatever it wants in pricing the good abroad, but it is regulated in its domestic activities. The results in the Appendix clearly show that the regulated cartel/monopoly exports too much to achieve optimality.[14] This

---

[12]Of course, it is assumed that no controls are imposed by country B and that competition prevails within country B.

[13]In the absence of domestic demand, one can derive this result from Johnson's analysis (1968) that an export marketing board which maximizes returns to producers in the exporting country attains social optimality.

[14]Comparing the firm optimization conditions of the regulated cartel/monopoly with the social optimization conditions, this result is evident since the second right-hand term in the second condition for the former case is positive.

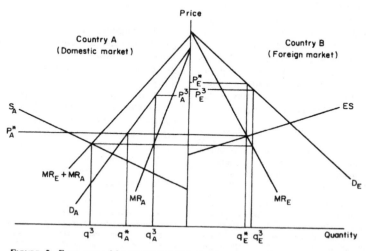

FIGURE 2. FIRM WITH MONOPOLISTIC POWER-MAXIMIZING PRODUCER RETURNS

is because the regulation prevents the board from exploiting domestic consumers; hence, compared to optimality, the board will sell less locally and will concentrate on exploiting foreign markets. Since the board exports too large a quantity, optimality for country A is achieved by imposing an export tax along with domestic price controls.

To see that an export tax is necessary in the producer's cartel case, suppose that the cartel is producing and exporting optimal quantities from the social point of view. If its marginal cost is upward sloping, when it produces one more unit, it can increase the price charged on domestic sales by the corresponding increase in its marginal cost and dump the extra unit produced plus the reduction in domestic consumption on the foreign market. This it will do unless it is stopped from exporting via the tax. Thus, the firm will always tend to produce and export too much unless stopped from so doing by an export tariff.

One must consider however, that an export tax may be difficult to impose. For example, the U.S. Constitution (Article I, Section 9, Paragraph 5) prohibits the United States from restricting trade by use of export taxes. A desirable alternative is to abolish price controls for monopolies and producer cartels when export taxes cannot be imposed; in this case social optimality can be attained by simply imposing a subsidy on domestic consumption (the Appendix gives the unregulated cartel/monopoly case). An advantage of this policy is that is may be less likely to lead to retaliation by trading partners since foreign trade policy is concealed in domestic controls. Explicit taxes and subsidies on exports may induce retaliation by other countries which reduce gains from international trade.[15]

[15]For similar reasons, it may also be advisable to conceal export subsidies for the monopoly-monopsony case. However, in this case it is somewhat more difficult to establish adequate alternative controls. For example, if one sets both domestic producer and consumer prices equal and at the appropriate absolute level, there is no guarantee or incentive for the monopoly-monopsony to satisfy domestic demand; it can make the same profit by merely buying domestically and selling abroad. Likewise, if marketing quotas are established, the monopoly-monopsony would have no incentive to use all of its domestic quotas, particularly if domestic prices are controlled. It seems that any adequate alternative

IV. Conclusions

A large part of international trading activities (i.e., buying the commodities in producing centers and making the goods available at consuming centers) is carried out by private trading firms and marketing boards. At the same time, federal governments are increasingly regulating the amounts of goods these firms can export and the prices they can charge consumers in the market where the export supply originates. This paper shows that, if the activities of international marketing institutions result in noncompetitive pricing, domestic price controls (where the government sets domestic prices equal to the marginal cost of production) do not result in the optimal allocation of resources even though some groups benefit from resource misallocation. Additional controls (export taxes or export subsidies) are needed along with this type of price control, and the type of fiscal policy depends on the type of marketing institution. With marketing boards, an export tax is suggested; and with the monopoly-monopsony case, an export subsidy is needed. Alternatively, with marketing boards, optimality can be achieved by eliminating price controls and using a simple domestic consumer subsidy.

Appendix A: Social Optimization

The Appendix develops the results of the paper mathematically. The first section examines conditions for social optimization independent of the marketing institutions. These results are then used to determine optimal controls for the monopoly-monopsony case (Appendices B and C) and, secondly, for the producer cartel case (Appendices D and E). In each case optimal controls are developed for situations where price controls are not used and then where price controls (equating domestic producer and consumer prices) are used.

controls would need to force the monopoly-monopsony to do at least some minimum level of business with domestic concerns (while also regulating domestic prices). The political and practical feasibility of the latter case may be considerably limited.

Consider an exporting country with inverse competitive supply $S(q)$ and inverse competitive demand $D_A(q_A)$ where q is quantity supplied and q_A is quantity consumed domestically. The importing country has inverse competitive demand $D_E(q_E)$ where q_E is the quantity traded ($q = q_A + q_E$). The social optimum for the exporting country is attained by maximizing the sum of domestic producer and consumer welfare,

$$\max_{q_A, q_E} \int_0^{q_A} D_A(x)\, dx$$

$$- \int_0^q S(x)\, dx + q_E D_E(q_E)$$

The resulting optimality conditions (assuming second-order conditions hold) are

(A1) $\qquad D_A(q_A^*) = S(q^*)$

(A2) $\qquad MR_E(q_E^*) = S(q^*)$

where * denotes optimal quantities and $MR_E(q_E)$ is the marginal revenue associated with the foreign demand for the export good,

$$MR_E(q_E) = D_E(q_E) + q_E D_E'(q_E)$$

If marketing is carried out under competition in equilibrium, the optimality conditions in (A1) and (A2) are attained, respectively, when $P_A^* = P_s^*$, and $P_E^*(1 + 1/\eta_E) = P_s^*$; where P_A^* is domestic consumer price and P_s^* is domestic producer price in the exporting country, P_E^* is consumer price in the importing country, and η_E the elasticity of demand in the importing country is defined as follows:

$$\eta_E = \frac{P_E}{q_E D_E'(q_E)}$$

Thus, the optimal export tax which attains optimality under competition is $-P_E^*/\eta_E$.

APPENDIX B: UNREGULATED MONOPOLY-MONOPSONY

Consider now the case of a profit-maximizing marketing firm which possesses both monopoly and monopsony power in both the exporting and importing countries; its objective is to

(A3) $\max_{q_A, q_E} q_A D_A(q_A) + q_E D_E(q_E) - q S(q)$

First-order conditions imply

(A4) $\qquad MR_A(q_A^1) = MO(q^1)$

(A5) $\qquad MR_E(q_E^1) = MO(q^1)$

where the superscript 1 denotes optimal quantities for the unregulated monopoly-monopsony case, $MR_A(q_A)$ represents marginal revenue from domestic demand

$$MR_A(q_A) = D_A(q_A) + q_A D_A'(q_A)$$

and $MO(q)$ represents the marketing firm's marginal outlay

$$MO(q) = S(q) + q\, S'(q)$$

The conditions in (A4) and (A5) can be translated into respective price conditions

$$P_A^1(1 + 1/\eta_A) = P_s^1(1 + 1/\eta_s)$$

$$P_E^1(1 + 1/\eta_E) = P_s^1(1 + 1/\eta_s)$$

where η_A and η_s are the elasticities of domestic demand and supply, respectively:

$$\eta_A = \frac{P_A}{q_A D_A'(q_A)} \qquad \eta_s = \frac{P_s}{q S'(q)}$$

To attain social optimality in this case, a production subsidy of p_s^1/η_s and a domestic consumption subsidy of $-P_A^1/\eta_A$ (note $\eta_A < 0$) can be established. In this case, the conditions in (A4) and (A5) become

(A6) $\quad MR_A(q_A^1) - \dfrac{P_A^1}{\eta_A} = MO(q^1) - \dfrac{P_s^1}{\eta_s}$

(A7) $\quad MR_E(q_E^1) = MO(q^1) - \dfrac{P_s^1}{\eta_s}$

since the domestic demand and supply curves are shifted by the amounts of the subsidies. Translating (A6) and (A7) into price terms, however, obtains price conditions $P_A^1 = P_s^1$, and $P_E^1(1 + 1/\eta_E) = P_s^1$, which corresponds to the social optimization conditions in Appendix A.

APPENDIX C: REGULATED MONOPOLY-MONOPSONY

Turn now to the case where a monopoly-monopsony marketing firms is regulated by a price control which forces him to equate domestic producer and consumer prices (in the exporting country). The firm's profit-maximization problem is thus the same as in (A3) except that the appropriate constraint is added

$$\max_{q_A, q_E} q_A D_A(q_A) + q_E D_E(q_E) - q\, S(q)$$

subject to $D_A(q_A) = S(q)$

Using a Lagrangian multipler approach, one obtains necessary conditions

(A8) $D_A(q_A^2) = S(q^2)$

(A9) $MR_E(q_E^2) = MO(q^2)$

$$- [q_A^2 D_A'(q_A^2) - q^2 S'(q^2)] S'(q^2)$$

$$\div [D_A'(q_A^2) - S'(q^2)]$$

where the superscript 2 denotes optimal quantities for the regulated monopoly-monopsony case. Equations (A8) and (A9) translate into respective price conditions $P_A^2 = P_s^2$, and

$$P_E^2 \left(1 + \frac{1}{\eta_E} \right) = P_s^2 \left(1 + \frac{q_E^2}{\eta_s q^2 - \eta_A q_A^2} \right)$$

Following the same approach as relating to equation (A6) and (A7), one can verify that imposition for an export subsidy of $P_s^2 q_E^2 / (\eta_s q^2 - \eta_A q_A^2)$ attains social optimality for the exporting country in this case.

APPENDIX D: THE UNREGULATED PRODUCER CARTEL

This section considers the case where the marketing institution selling to competitive consumers in both countries is a producer cartel acting on behalf of producers to maximize their just welfare (joint profits),

(A10) $\displaystyle \max_{q_A, q_E} q_A D_A(q_A) + q_E D_E(q_E)$

$$- \int_0^q S(x)\, dx$$

First-order conditions imply

(A11) $MR_A(q_A^3) = S(q^3)$

(A12) $MR_E(q_E^3) = S(q^3)$

where the superscript 3 denotes optimal quantities in the unregulated producer cartel case.

The conditions in (A11) and (A12) translate into respective price relationships

$$P_A^3(1 + 1/\eta_A) = P_s^3; \quad P_E^3(1 + 1/\eta_E) = P_s^3$$

Following the approach in the previous two sections, one can verify that imposition of a domestic consumption subsidy of $-P_A^3/\eta_A$ will cause the cartel to reach social optimality in this case.

APPENDIX E: THE REGULATED PRODUCER CARTEL

Finally, consider operation of a producer cartel under the regime of price controls forcing equality of domestic producer and consumer prices (in the exporting country). The maximization problem for the cartel is the same as in (A10) with the exception that the constraint must be added.

$$\max_{q_A, q_E} q_A D_A(q_A) + q_E D_E(q_E) - \int_0^q S(x)\, dx$$

subject to $D_A(q_A) = S(q)$

First-order conditions from the Lagrange constrained-maximization problem imply

$$D_A(q_A^4) = S(q^4)$$

$$MR_E(q_E^4) = S(q^4) - \frac{q_A^4 D_A'(q_A^4) S'(q^4)}{D_A'(q_A^4) - S_A'(q^4)}$$

which can be translated into respective price conditions $P_A^4 = P_s^4$, and

$$P_E^4 \left(1 + \frac{1}{\eta_E} \right) = P_s^4 \left(1 - \frac{q_A^4}{\eta_s q^4 - \eta_A q_A^4} \right)$$

where the superscript 4 denotes optimal quantities in the regulated producer cartel problem. Again, following the approach of the previous sections, one finds that an export tax of $q_A^4 P_s^4/(\eta_s q^4 - \eta_A q_A^4)$ will induce the regulated producer cartel to attain social optimality.

REFERENCES

H. Averch and L. L. Johnson, "Behavior of the Firm under Regulatory Constraint," *Amer.*

Econ. Rev., Dec. 1962, *52*, 1053–69.

W. J. **Baumol and A. K. Klevorick**, "Input Choices and Rate-of-Return Regulation: An Overview of the Discussion," *Bell J. Econ.*, Autumn 1970, *1*, 162–90.

T. J. **Bertrand**, "Optimal Tariff Policy Designed for Governmental Gain," *Can. J. Econ.*, May 1973, *6*, 257–60.

W. M. **Corden**, *Trade Policy and Economic Welfare*, New York 1974.

J. M. **Currie, J. A. Murphy, and A. Schmitz**, "The Concept of Economic Surplus and Its Use in Economic Analysis," *Econ. J.*, Dec. 1971, *81*, 741–99.

Vernon C. **Fowke**, *The National Policy and the Wheat Economy*, Toronto 1957.

Jim **Hightower**, *Eat Your Heart Out: Food Profiteering in America*, New York 1975.

H. G. **Johnson**, "Optimum Welfare and Maximum Revenue Tariffs," *Rev. Econ. Stud.*, Oct. 1951, *19*, 28–35.

⸻, "Alternative Maximization Policies for Developing Country Exports of Primary Products," *J. Polit. Econ.*, May/June 1968, *76*, 489–93.

A. P. **Lerner**, "The Concept of Monopoly and the Measurement of Monopoly Power," *Rev. Econ. Stud.*, June 1934, *1*, 157–75.

P. A. **Samuelson**, "Spatial Equilibrium and Linear Programming," *Amer. Econ. Rev.*, June 1952, *42*, 283–303.

⸻, "An Exact Hume-Ricardo-Marshall Model of International Trade," *J. Int. Econ.*, Feb. 1971, *1*, 1–18.

A. **Schmitz and R. E. Just**, "Semiprice Discrimination," *Econ. Rec.*, Dec. 1977, *53*, 559–74.

E. **Tower**, "Ranking the Optimum Tariff and the Maximum Revenue Tariff," *J. Int. Econ.*, Feb. 1977, *7*, 73–80.

B
Multimarket Equilibrium
Welfare Measurement

[25]

Welfare Measures in a Multimarket Framework

By Richard E. Just and Darrell L. Hueth*

E. J. Mishan (1968) has demonstrated the well-known partial equilibrium result that the area behind a competitive supply curve conditioned on fixed-input prices (producer's surplus) measures returns or quasi rents on fixed-production factors. It is also a simple matter to show that the area behind a derived demand for inputs (conditioned on fixity of other input and output prices) measures returns or quasi rents on fixed-production factors of the production process using the input.[1] These results suggest that when one estimates supply and demand in an intermediate market and calculates the associated producer's and consumer's surplus under the stated conditions, then the welfare quantities exactly measure quasi rents for the two groups of firms involved in selling and buying in that market, respectively. That is, when all other prices facing the selling and buying firms are uninfluenced by their (group) actions, the ordinary surplus quantities do not include effects on other groups, for example, final consumers (of which there would be none if all other prices were truly unaffected because of elastic supplies, etc.).

In contrast to this extremely partial approach, a number of other authors (see, for example, Harry Johnson; Melvin Krauss and David Winch) have attempted to approach welfare surpluses from a general equilibrium standpoint where all other prices in the economy are allowed to vary. These works have culminated in the recent paper by James Anderson (1974) which shows that welfare changes can be determined by comparing the change in income arising from production (the area behind the general equilibrium supply function) with the income effect of price changes in consumption (which, as Anderson critically notes, has been referred to as consumer's surplus).

Each of these approaches has serious and well-known shortcomings in applied welfare economics. In reality, the imposition of a quota, tax, etc. in an intermediate market, such as for wheat or crude oil, may have a substantial effect on final consumption prices

*Professor of agricultural and resource economics, University of California-Berkeley, and professor of economics, Brigham Young University; and associate professor of resource economics, University of Rhode Island, respectively. We would like to thank Andrew Schmitz, John M. Currie, and especially James Anderson for helpful comments. Giannini Foundation Paper No. 512; Rhode Island Agricultural Experiment Station Paper No. 1681.

[1]For example, consider a producer with variable inputs $x_1, \ldots, x_n$; output y; associated respective prices $\gamma_1, \ldots, \gamma_n, p$; and quasi-concave production function $f(x_1, \ldots, x_n)$ with

$$f(x_1, \ldots, x_{k-1}, 0, x_{k+1}, \ldots, x_n) = 0, \qquad k = 1, \ldots, n$$

Suppose that profit-maximizing levels of variable inputs and output are given by $x_k(\gamma, p)$, $k = 1, \ldots, n$, and $y(\gamma, p)$ where (γ, p) is considered a parametric vector for the competitive producer. Producer quasi rents are given by the restricted profit function,

$$\pi(\gamma, p) = p y(\gamma, p) - \sum_{k=1}^{n} \gamma_k x_k(\gamma, p)$$

where, by the envelope theorem,

$$\frac{\partial \pi}{\partial \gamma_k} = -x_k(\gamma, p), \qquad k = 1, \ldots, n.$$

Since $x_k(\gamma, p)$ may be interpreted as the derived demand for x_k when prices $\gamma_1, \ldots, \gamma_{k-1}, \gamma_{k+1}, \ldots, \gamma_n$ and p are considered fixed, the change in profits or quasi rents associated with an input price change from γ_k^0 to γ_k^* is

$$\Delta \pi_n = \int_{\gamma_k^0}^{\gamma_k^*} \frac{\partial \pi_n}{\partial \gamma_k} d\gamma_k$$

$$= \int_{\gamma_k^0}^{\gamma_k^*} -x_k^*(\gamma_1, \ldots, \gamma_{k-1}, \gamma_k, \gamma_{k+1}, \ldots, \gamma_n, p) d\gamma_k$$

and measures precisely the change in area behind the derived demand for x_k. In other words, *a producer's surplus as consumer of any one of his inputs is the same as his surplus as producer and supplier of his output in the fixed-price situation.*

947

and quantities, and conversely. Using partial methodology, these general equilibrium effects would be assumed away and thus ignored; in many interesting problems this practice is unacceptable. On the other hand, measurement with the general equilibrium approach "is far from our reach" (Anderson, 1974, p. 762) because of the intractability of practically estimating responses of all prices and quantities in an economy. Furthermore, general equilibrium measures only have "a satisfying and useful interpretation at the proper level of analysis, that of the economy" (Anderson, 1974, p. 761) which is at a too-aggregated level to answer many specific questions about proposed policy.

This paper is an attempt to fall somewhere between the above two cases in an effort to capture the essential generality of a class of important empirical problems while maintaining tractability. The framework considered involves a vertically structured competitive sector of an economy where each industry in the sector produces a single product using one major variable input produced within the sector, and a number of other variable inputs originating in other sectors of the economy. Any number of fixed-production factors may originate either from within or outside the sector. Assuming the sector is only one of many users of the other inputs, the prices in other sectors will be taken as fixed or uninfluenced by the sector in question. However, the actions of any individual industry in the sector may affect all other prices and quantities within the sector. In this context this paper examines the welfare significance of the classical triangles behind supply and demand as well as the possibilities of measuring both the direct and indirect effects of intervention.

Although the results may not be surprising for some practitioners of applied welfare economics (since on occasion some of the propositions of this paper have been used without proper examination), Daniel Wisecarver points out that considerable confusion has existed in the literature regarding these points. For this reason, Wisecarver, along with Richard Schmalensee (1971, 1976) and Anderson (1976), began to investigate the relationship of surplus measures in input

markets with those in output markets; but the cases considered thus far deal only with long-run equilibrium or infinitely elastic input supply which disregards the producer side of the problem. While the results due to Anderson (1974), noted above, strengthen these propositions from the standpoint of aggregate welfare analysis (since they suggest that the consumer and producer sides of the problem can be studied independently), it becomes clear in this paper that interpretation of the usual surplus triangles with respect to individual market groups changes with market level. In point of fact, in the framework of this paper it is possible to examine disaggregated welfare impacts on each affected market group. Nevertheless, the results here are consistent with Anderson (1974) and show that the overall impact of introducing a distortion in some intermediate market is reflected by the sum of areas behind the general equilibrium supply and demand functions in that market.

I. Consumer's Surplus in an Intermediate Market

This section considers the welfare significance of the triangle behind demand and above price in an intermediate market of a vertically structured sector. For notational convenience, assume that the industries in a sector are competitive and can be ordered so that each industry n producing y_n and facing output price p_n, $n = 1, \ldots, N$, uses as variable factor inputs the product y_{n-1} produced at the preceding industry level in the sector plus some subset of inputs $x = (x_1, \ldots, x_m)'$ with corresponding price vector γ produced in the rest of the economy. The restricted profit function for the industry is, thus,

$$\pi_n(\gamma, p) = p_n y_n^n(\gamma, p)$$
$$- p_{n-1} y_{n-1}^n(\gamma, p) - \gamma' x^n(\gamma, p)$$

where profit-maximizing levels of output and inputs at given prices are denoted by $y_n^n(\gamma, p)$, $n = 1, \ldots, N$, and $x^n(\gamma, p)$, respectively. Now suppose that prices in all industries in the sector are related through competition at the industry level so that, as price p_j is forcibly altered, the entire price vector changes (monotonically) following $p(p_j)$. All inputs purchased from other industries, however, are available in elastic supply from the standpoint of the sector.

As pointed out by Mishan (1968), evaluation of the welfare impact of such a distortion in this case requires looking beyond the buyers and sellers in market j. Consider first the effects on any industry n in the sector where $j < n$. By the envelope theorem, one finds

$$\frac{\partial \pi_n}{\partial p_j} = y_n^n \frac{\partial p_n}{\partial p_j} - y_{n-1}^n \frac{\partial p_{n-1}}{\partial p_j}$$

Integration for a specific change from, say, p_j^0 to p_j^* implies

$$(1) \qquad \Delta \pi_n = \int_{p_j^0}^{p_j^*} \frac{\partial \pi_n}{\partial p_j} dp_j$$

$$= \int_{p_j^0}^{p_j^*} y_n^n \frac{\partial p_n}{\partial p_j} dp_j$$

$$- \int_{p_j^0}^{p_j^*} y_{n-1}^n \frac{\partial p_{n-1}}{\partial p_j} dp_j$$

where $\Delta \pi_n$ denotes the change in quasi rents for industry n.

To interpret (1) when $j < n$, note that the first right-hand term is the change in area behind demand and above price in market n, denoted by ΔC_n,

$$(2) \qquad \Delta C_n = - \int_{p_j^0}^{p_j^*} y_n^n \frac{\partial p_n}{\partial p_j} dp_j$$

$$= - \int_{p_n(p_j^0)}^{p_n(p_j^*)} y_n^n dp_n$$

This is clear since, with $j < n$, integration in (1) is along equilibrium quantities in market n as the supply curve (influenced by p_j) is being shifted. It should be noted, however, that ΔC_n is not calculated with respect to the usual ordinary demand curve. It is, in fact, calculated according to the sector equilibrium demand curve (which is equivalent to a general equilibrium demand under the small-sector assumption of this paper) which accounts for adjustments in other industries in the sector.

To interpret the remaining right-hand term of (1) when $j < n$, note that integration is

along equilibrium quantities in market $n - 1$ as input supply (influenced or represented by p_j) is altered. Hence, the resulting integral represents the change in the area behind demand and above price in market $n - 1$,

$$(3) \qquad \Delta C_{n-1} = - \int_{p_j^0}^{p_j^*} y_{n-1}^n \frac{\partial p_{n-1}}{\partial p_j} dp_j$$

$$= - \int_{p_{n-1}(p_j^0)}^{p_{n-1}(p_j^*)} y_{n-1}^n dp_{n-1}$$

Again, one should bear in mind that the relevant demand curve for input y_{n-1} is a general equilibrium demand rather than an ordinary demand (in the same sense as above).

Using (2) and (3) in (1) implies that

$$(4) \quad \Delta \pi_n = \Delta C_{n-1} - \Delta C_n, \quad n = j + 1, \ldots, N$$

or, upon solving the difference equation for ΔC_j,

$$(5) \qquad \Delta C_j = \sum_{n=j+1}^{N} \Delta \pi_n + \Delta C_N$$

where ΔC_N represents the change in final consumer's surplus (associated with consumption of the sector's final product). Thus, the change in the "consumer's surplus" triangle in market j associated with an alteration in price p_j measures the sum of changes in final product consumer's surplus plus quasi rents for all industries (related by imperfectly elastic demands) involved in transforming the commodity traded in market j into final consumption form.

Of course, the welfare significance of $\Delta \pi_n$ is the same as in Mishan (1968). Also, if y_N is used as an input by some industry $N + 1$ facing elastic demand, then ΔC_N merely measures the change in quasi rents for that industry; and one need search no further (on the demand side) for welfare effects of changing p_j. On the other hand, if market N is a final goods market, then the term ΔC_N may hold welfare significance in the context of final consumption in one of several senses. That is, if ΔC_N is the Marshallian surplus calculated from an ordinary final goods demand, then the results of Robert Willig can be used to determine the closeness of approximation to the proper Hicksian concept. Thus, to the extent that his conditions apply in the final goods market, equation (5) holds welfare significance for market j measurements. Alternatively, one can interpret ΔC_N as a Hicksian surplus if the demand curve used in calculating ΔC_N and generating intermediate market demands is a compensated demand. In the latter case the measurement ΔC_j in (5) holds the proper Hicksian welfare significance without approximation.[2]

It is now clear that the Schmalensee (1976) and Anderson (1976) results hold only in a special case. Anderson's derivation, assuming long-run competitive equilibrium (in which case $\Delta \pi_N - 0$), shows that $\Delta C_{N-1} - \Delta C_N$ so that consumer's surplus can be measured in either the input or the output market. Schmalensee, on the other hand, assumed perfectly elastic input supply (i.e., $j - N - 1$) and found that $\Delta C_N + \Delta \pi_N - \Delta C_{N-1}$. Since this is the case where Mishan's (1968) results suggest that producer's surplus in market N measures quasi rents for industry N, equation (4) reduces to Schmalensee's result that the input market consumer's surplus is equivalent to the sum of producer's and consumer's surpluses in the output market.

II. Producer's Surplus in an Intermediate Market

To interpret ΔS_j, the change in the triangle area behind supply and below price in an intermediate market j, consider the effect of a similar change in p_j on market n where $j \geq n$. In this case, demand rather than supply in market n is affected by the change so that integration in (1) is along equilibrium quantities supplied as demand (or output price if $j - n$) is altered. Hence,

$$\Delta S_n - \int_{p_i^0}^{p_j^*} y_n^* \frac{\partial p_n}{\partial p_j} dp_j$$

$$- \int_{p_n(p_j^0)}^{p_n(p_j^*)} y_n^* dp_n$$

and similarly for ΔS_{n-1} which suggests that (1) can be rewritten as

$$(6) \qquad \Delta \pi_n - \Delta S_n - \Delta S_{n-1} \qquad n - 1, \ldots, j$$

Solving the difference equation in (6), one finds

$$(7) \qquad \Delta S_j - \Delta S_0 + \sum_{n-1}^{j} \Delta \pi_n$$

where ΔS_0 represents the change in initial resource supplier's surplus. Thus, the change in the "producer's surplus" triangle in market j associated with a change in p_j measures the sum of the change in initial resource supplier's surplus plus quasi rents for all industries (related by imperfectly elastic supplies) involved in transforming the raw resource into the commodity at market level j.[3]

Again, the welfare significance of $\Delta \pi_n$ is clear from Mishan (1968). The welfare significance of ΔS_0, on the other hand, is clear from Mishan (1959) in the case of a basic resource or from Mishan (1968) if there is an industry 0 facing perfectly elastic supply of *all* inputs. In the latter case, ΔS_0 simply measures the change in quasi rents for industry 0; and one need search no further (on the supply side) for welfare effects of changing p_j.

III. Market, Sector, and Economy-Wide Analysis

Summing the consumer's and producer's surplus measures in market j, one finds

$$(8) \qquad \Delta C_j + \Delta S_j - \Delta C_N + \Delta S_0 + \sum_{n-1}^{N} \Delta \pi_n$$

Hence, where market 0 is a resource market and market N is a final goods market (so that the related chain of markets, $n - 0, \ldots, N$, comprises an economic sector), it is found that the sum of changes in producer's and consumer's surpluses in the distorted market actually measures the change in total sector welfare (where no intervening supplies or

---

[2]Note that matters are more complicated if some other final goods price changes as a result of altering price in market j. Only the Hicksian version has the proper path independence of the line integral used to evaluate the change in the expenditure function; but this is well understood following Eugene Silberberg.

[3]It is noted here that Anderson (1974) corresponds to the special case of (7) in which $\Delta S_j - \Delta S_0$ and $\Delta \pi_1 - \ldots - \Delta \pi_j - 0$ since he assumed pure competition in long-run equilibrium with constant returns-to-scale technology.

demands are perfectly elastic). Furthermore, since other sectors are unaffected by this change, the change in welfare for the economy as a whole is also obtained.

Thus, it turns out that the restrictive perfect elasticity assumptions which have been made in applied classical welfare economics are unnecessary. Classical welfare measures defined with respect to sector (or, equivalently, general) equilibrium curves have validity regardless, at least in the restrictive (small-sector) economic framework employed in this paper. But, more importantly, it is found that the classical triangles provide an overall rather than a partial picture of welfare. Hence, the failure of perfect elasticity assumptions in a vertical market structure has no serious consequences so long as one is interested in aggregate welfare rather than the welfare of a particular set of producers or consumers.

On the other hand, if disaggregation of welfare effects into impacts on individual market groups is needed (as in many policy analyses), several possibilities exist. For example, general equilibrium curves in adjacent markets can be used to compute the change in quasi rents for a given industry using the difference equations in (4) or (6). Alternatively, one can use ordinary supply or demand curves directly to compute the change in surplus or quasi rent for a given industry (using the results of Mishan, 1968, on the supply side or those of fn. 1 on the demand side). Yet another alternative is provided at least in *ex post* analysis by using value-added data directly (noting that the change in value-added is simply the change in quasi rents or restricted profits) without estimating other supply and demand relationships. Using any of these three methods to determine intermediate industry effects, the change in resource owner's welfare and final consumer's welfare can be estimated following (7) and (5), respectively.

One may note that the results obtained here differ somewhat from earlier assertions by Arnold Harberger and others; that is, that the general equilibrium measure of a change in welfare is approximately equal to the sum of changes in national income plus final

consumer's surplus. Moreover, an exact relationship rather than an approximation is obtained here (in the case of Hicksian measurements). Indeed, one finds that the change in total welfare in the sector ($\Delta C_j + \Delta S_j$) is equal to the change in national income in the sector, $\Delta(p_N y_N)$, plus the change in final consumer's surplus (ΔC_N) only when initial resource supply is perfectly inelastic (in which case $S_0 = p_0 y_0$) since use of $\Delta \pi_j = \Delta(p_j y_j) - \Delta(p_{j-1} y_{j-1})$ in (8) thus implies

$$\Delta C_j + \Delta S_j = \Delta C_N + \Delta S_0 + \sum_{j-1}^{N} \Delta \pi_j$$

$$= \Delta C_N + \Delta(p_N y_N)$$

But when resource supply is not perfectly inelastic, as is the usual case with labor (for example, Mishan, 1959), the resource supplier's surplus is somewhat less than $p_0 y_0$ (supply is upward sloping) so that

$$\Delta S_0 + \sum_{j-1}^{N} \Delta \pi_j < \Delta(p_N y_N)$$

The amount by which the change in sector income overestimates ΔS_j is exactly the area under the resource supply curve.

IV. Empirical Implications and Considerations

The implications of the results in this paper for econometric welfare studies are several. First, it is clear that the definition of producer's surplus with imperfectly elastic input supply, etc. is not in terms of the usual competitive industry supply curve that is conditioned on fixed-input prices. Instead, ΔS_j is defined as the change in area behind the supply curve that takes account of general equilibrium price and quantity adjustments in markets $0, 1, \ldots, j - 1$. By contrast, if one calculates the area behind the supply curve which holds input price fixed, then one obtains rents to producers in that market only.

Thus, suppose one estimates a supply equation,

$$(9) \qquad p_j = b_0 + b_1 y_j + b_2 p_{j-1}$$

in an intermediate market j. It is clear from the results above that, if one calculates the "surplus" measure S_j^* using b_1 as the slope and holds input price p_{j-1} fixed, then the quantity one obtains, $S_j^* - (1/2) b_1 y_j^2$, is a measure of quasi rents only to producers selling in market j. That is, $S_j^* \neq S_j$ but, rather, $S_j^* - \pi_j < S_j$. To estimate S_j, it is necessary to use the competition-induced relationship between p_j and p_{j-1}. Suppose, for simplicity, this relationship is given by

(10) $p_j - a_0 + a_1 p_{j-1}$

Then, substituting (10) in (9), one obtains

(11) $p_j - \dfrac{a_1 b_0 - a_0 b_2}{a_1 - b_2} + \dfrac{a_1 b_1}{a_1 - b_2} y_j$

as the supply curve which takes account of varying input prices. The surplus measure associated with (11) is given by

(12) $S_j - \dfrac{a_1 b_1}{2(a_1 - b_2)} y_j^2$

which is greater than S_j^* and measures benefits for all producers in markets $n - 0, 1, 2, \dots, j$.

A problem which frequently arises in econometric work, however, is that input and output prices are highly correlated because of their theoretical relationship (which, indeed, leads to (10)). In practice, this condition usually prevents statistical identification of the parameters in (9) and thus leads to subsequent estimation of the equation,

(13) $p_j - b_0^* + b_1^* y_j$

where input price p_{j-1} is deleted. But, clearly, the interpretation of parameters and associated surpluses in (13) is different than in (9). Indeed, equation (13) is equivalent to (11); hence, an estimate of b_1^* in (13) is an estimate of $a_1 b_1 / (a_1 - b_2)$ in (11), and the surplus measure associated with (13), $1/2 \, b_1^* y_j^2$, is the same as S_j in (12).

It is also clear that symmetrical arguments can be made with respect to the area under estimated demand curves for intermediate goods. That is, replacing p_{j-1} by p_{j+1} and S_j by C_j, all of the derivation in (9)–(13) continues to hold.

The essence of this approach can be generalized to consider problems of econometric estimation and identification in the case where the relationships in (9)–(13) are changing because of varying prices (or determinants) imposed on the sector by the rest of the economy. That is, one can estimate a sector equilibrium supply curve in market j in the vertical sector case (encompassing endogenous adjustments of $p_0, \dots, p_{j-1}, p_{j+1}, \dots, p_N$) by regressing the quantity supplied y_j^s on market j price and all determinants γ_j^- affecting resource suppliers and industries $1, \dots, j$,

(14) $y_j^s - y_j^s(p_j, \gamma_j^-)$

Similarly, the market j sector equilibrium demand could be estimated in the form,

(15) $y_j^d - y_j^d(p_j, \gamma_j^+)$

where y_j^d is quantity demanded and γ_j^+ is a vector of all determinants associated with the rest of the economy affecting industries $j + 1, \dots, N$ and final consumer demand. If the small vertical sector assumption applies, then these sector equilibrium functions are indeed general equilibrium curves and can be used to estimate the overall welfare effects of a distortion.[4]

On the other hand, if one estimates (ordinary) supply and demand in the same intermediate market by considering prices in vertically related markets, that is, using a supply function of the form,

(16) $y_j^s - \tilde{y}_j^s(p_j, p_{j-1}, \gamma)$

and a demand function of the form,

(17) $y_j^d - \tilde{y}_j^d(p_j, p_{j+1}, \gamma)$

respectively, then one can obtain (assuming identifiability) partial equilibrium welfare measures, that is, measures of welfare for only the producers and consumers in the market in question by integrating only with respect to p_j as suggested above. Even when identification of (16) and (17) is not possible

---

[4] Note that econometric identification of the relations in (14) and (15) would be determined in the same manner as for simultaneous estimation of ordinary supply and demand except that the list of determinants is somewhat different.

because of multicollinearity, one can estimate price relationships,

$$p_{j-1} = p_{j-1}^s(p_j, \gamma) \tag{18}$$

$$p_{j+1} = p_{j+1}^d(p_j, \gamma) \tag{19}$$

which specify how prices in related markets change with respect to a distortion in market j for a given set of determinants outside the sector. If no other distortions exist in the sector, then satisfaction of the usual first- and second-order conditions for each industry in the sector implies that (18) and (19) are uniquely determined. Using (18) in (14) or (19) in (15), one can thus in principle solve for the ordinary functions in (16) or (17), respectively.[5] Hence, the ordinary surpluses pertaining only to industries j and $j + 1$, respectively, can be estimated. This approach can be expanded to determine quasi rents in other industries in the sector or, alternatively, the other approaches suggested above may be employed for this purpose.

V. Conclusions

This paper has studied welfare measures in a vertically structured sector. Given the usual conditions required for validity of consumer's surplus measures in the final goods market and producer's surplus measures in the initial resource market, the major results are as follows. The area behind a general equilibrium demand curve in an intermediate market does not measure benefits to buyers in that market alone, but rather measures the sum of rents to producers selling in all higher markets (assuming no intervening market has perfectly elastic demand) plus final consumer's surplus. Symmetrically, the area behind the general equilibrium supply curve in an intermediate market measures not only rents for producers selling in that market, but also rents for all producers selling in more basic markets (assuming no intervening market has perfectly elastic supply) plus initial resource

---

[5] For example, if one estimates equations (10) and (13), then one can use $b_1^* = a_1 b_1/(a_1 - b_2)$ and $b_0^* = (a_1 b_0 - a_0 b_2)/(a_1 - b_2)$ and equation (9) to solve for b_0, b_1, and b_2.

supplier's surplus. Where some markets exhibit perfect elasticity of supply (demand), then producer's (consumer's) surplus measures rents for producers (consumers) in all lower (higher) markets related by supplies (demands) which are not perfectly elastic. To attribute welfare effects to those involved directly in the market in question versus those in the rest of the economy (sector), one needs merely to compare the areas behind ordinary supply and demand with the areas behind general equilibrium supply and demand functions. A simple and practical approach to studying the distribution of welfare effects over all other market groups in a sector is thus to estimate areas behind general equilibrium supply and demand curves in the market of interest (the sum of which would provide a measure of welfare in the sector). Welfare effects on direct market participants are then separated out by subtracting areas behind ordinary supply and demand curves. If appropriate data exist, the distributional aspects for other industries can also be studied by separating out the respective values-added.

Fairly well-defined vertical market chains seem to exist in many cases where a basic commodity sequentially reaches higher stages of refinement as it passes through the marketing channel, for example, petroleum, minerals, fisheries, and agriculture. It seems that the results of this paper are of practical applicability in the subset of related problems where contemplated policies may lead to changes in prices within the sector but do not cause noticeable price variation outside the sector.

REFERENCES

J. E. Anderson, "A Note on Welfare Surpluses and Gains From Trade in General Equilibrium," *Amer. Econ. Rev.*, Sept. 1974, *64*, 758–62.

———, "The Social Cost of Input Distortions: A Comment and a Generalization," *Amer. Econ. Rev.*, Mar. 1976, *66*, 235–38.

A. C. Harberger, "Three Basic Postulates for Applied Welfare Economics: An Interpretive Essay," *J. Econ. Lit.*, Sept. 1971, *9*,

785–97.

H. G. Johnson, "The Cost of Protection and the Scientific Tariff," *J. Polit. Econ.*, Aug. 1960, *68*, 327–45.

M. Krauss and D. Winch, "Mishan on the Gains from Trade: Comment," *Amer. Econ. Rev.*, Mar. 1971, *61*, 199–200.

E. J. Mishan, "Rent as a Measure of Welfare Change," *Amer. Econ. Rev.*, June 1959, *49*, 386–95.

———, "What Is Producer's Surplus?," *Amer. Econ. Rev.*, Dec. 1968, *58*, 1269–82.

R. Schmalensee, "Consumer's Surplus and Producer's Goods," *Amer. Econ. Rev.*, Sept. 1971, *61*, 682–87.

———, "Another Look at the Social Valuation of Input Price Changes," *Amer. Econ. Rev.*, Mar. 1976, *66*, 239–43.

E. Silberberg, "Duality and the Many Consumer's Surpluses," *Amer. Econ. Rev.*, Dec. 1972, *62*, 942–52.

R. D. Willig, "Consumer's Surpluses Without Apology," *Amer. Econ. Rev.*, Sept. 1976, *66*, 589–97.

D. Wisecarver, "The Social Costs of Input-Market Distortions," *Amer. Econ. Rev.*, June 1974, *64*, 359–72.

[26]

JOURNAL OF ENVIRONMENTAL ECONOMICS AND MANAGEMENT 22, 226–240 (1992)

Valuing Changes in Commercial Fishery Harvests: A General Equilibrium Derived Demand Analysis

Walter N. Thurman and J. E. Easley, Jr.*

Department of Agricultural and Resource Economics, North Carolina State University,
P.O. Box 8110, Raleigh, North Carolina, 27695-8110

Received October 18, 1990; revised July 2, 1991

I. INTRODUCTION

When fishery stocks decline, regulators confront the problem of allocating diminished harvests between commercial and recreational fishermen. This has become a leading issue in the management of several fisheries.[1] In deciding to limit total catch, future users of the fishery are benefited through increases in the stock. As to the current costs of catch limits, there are those borne by recreational fishermen and those borne by participants in the commercial fishing industry: commercial fishermen, fish consumers, and cooperating factors in the production of fish meals for consumers.

To date, little empirical attention has been paid to the full costs of commercial catch restrictions. By full costs we mean to include the effects on consumers of higher seafood prices, the costs or benefits in related non-regulated fisheries, as well as the direct profit changes in the regulated fishery. In this paper we present a conceptual model for estimating surpluses from these related markets and present empirical estimates for the Gulf of Mexico red drum fishery. The conceptual model and empirical results employ general equilibrium derived demand functions. The general equilibrium derived demand for an input conceptually accounts (in a single market) for surpluses in related markets and economizes on data requirements in estimation.

The literature comprising models of commercial fishing historically has concentrated on solving for optimal harvest rates and stocks. Models have examined alternative policies for achieving efficient rates of harvests (e.g., Clark [8, 9]) under a variety of scenarios, such as biologically and technologically interdependent fisheries (Anderson [3]), congestion externalities (Brown [5]), and uncertainty (Smith [23]), to mention only a few. More recently, models have incorporated the self-interest theory of regulation with heterogeneity in harvesting groups to explain current management practices which may appear to be suboptimal (Johnson and

---

* We thank Richard Raulerson, NMFS, for helpful discussion and supplying us with a copy of the red drum plan, Doug Gregory, Gulf of Mexico Fishery Mgt. Council, for supplying red snapper data, and Lee Anderson, Doug Nychka, Ray Palmquist, Kerry Smith, Mike Wohlgenant, and two referees for helpful comments. This work represents continuation of a project originally supported by funding from The Gulf and South Atlantic Fisheries Development Foundation, and we gratefully acknowledge that support.

[1] For some recent examples, see Easley [12].

226

Libecap [17], Karpoff [20]) and avoidance and enforcement costs (Anderson and Lee [2], Sutinen and Andersen [24]). The major focus of these models is on the harvesting sector with the exception of the theoretical work of Clark and Munro [7], who incorporate the processing sector.

Allocation of harvests between recreational and commercial harvesters is examined in models by McConnell and Sutinen [21] and Bishop and Samples [4]. These models include a recreational harvesting sector but emphasize optimal stock and harvest rates and/or optimal effort (in contrast to models with a single, homogeneous commercial harvesting sector).

While economists acknowledge potential benefits or costs to ultimate fish consumers from regulations in the harvesting sector, little effort has been made to include explicitly consumer welfare in models of fishery regulation. This lack of attention to consumer markets may be due in part to the literature's focus on identifying stock-preserving optimal harvest rates, but it also may be due to a dearth of data from consumer markets. Similar arguments could be applied to the lack of attention to substitute species in the production of final consumer goods.

The empirical literature on demand for fish is relatively brief, and early works were largely motivated by desires to better understand relative effects of factors affecting seafood consumption. More recent work along these lines includes that of Cheng and Capps [6] on household at-home expenditure behavior for several species of shellfish, selected finfish, and aggregate commodities (selected earlier works on retail demand also are inventoried, see their Table 6). Tsoa *et al.* [26] estimated an inventory demand model for cod, flatfish and redfish fillets, and fish blocks using both monthly and annual data. These and earlier studies generally find inelastic own-price demand, which conflicts with Crutchfield's [10] findings of elastic own-price demand for three of the same species in fresh product form.

More recent work explicitly motivated by fishery regulations (minimum size limits) includes Wang and Kellogg [27], who predict the lobster price changes at the wholesale and vessel level that would result from changes in the size distribution of landings. These authors note that retail prices are generally not available and so focus on prices at wholesale and vessel levels.

A recent summary of eight selected New England groundfish demand studies is found in Emerson [14, Table 5.1]. These include estimates for demand at retail, wholesale, and vessel levels for selected species and product forms (primarily fresh and frozen fillets). Several of these studies, using various estimating techniques, incorporate price adjustment lags and interactions in price determination between several market levels. Substantial differences are reported—not unexpectedly—between own-price elasticities for fresh and frozen product forms of the same species.

Our model differs from earlier works in that we explicitly treat a given species as one input into final seafood commodities. This input faces a derived demand influenced both by characteristics of final consumer demand and by characteristics of the production function of the final consumer commodity and other input supplies. Thus we empirically acknowledge that catch restrictions in the harvesting sector may influence the welfare of firms elsewhere in the marketing chain for seafood commodities, the welfare of firms supplying other inputs (particularly substitute species), and the welfare of consumers. Further, by analyzing welfare effects with a single function at the vessel level, where catch restrictions are applied, we avoid two major problems: (i) Identifying final consumer products and estimating those demands, and (ii) making arbitrary assumptions about how a catch reduction would be distributed across retail markets.

II. A GENERAL EQUILIBRIUM DERIVED DEMAND FOR FISH

We view the commercial seafood sector as a series of vertically connected markets. The output of final retail seafood is produced with input fish, perhaps several species, and other marketing inputs. In this context the vessel-level demand for a given species is a derived demand. If this derived demand holds constant supply and demand schedules in related markets, rather than prices in those markets, then it is a general equilibrium demand curve. In a situation similar to this, Just and Hueth [18] demonstrate that one can use such a curve to measure in a single market the effects of a change in allowable harvest on various market levels. They show that (p. 953), "the area behind a general equilibrium demand curve in an intermediate market . . . measures the sum of rents to producers selling in all higher markets (assuming no intervening market has perfectly elastic demand) plus final consumer's surplus." Our context is somewhat different: the derived demand for fish is linked horizontally to other input markets as well as vertically to the consumer seafood market. But the same principle applies, as we demonstrate.

In the remainder of this section, we develop a model of a general equilibrium demand curve and establish its welfare significance. The derived demand model follows earlier work of Hicks [16], Diewert [11], and Gardner [15]. The welfare analysis is a special case of that found in Just, Hueth, and Schmitz [19, Appendix D].

We assume that the retail seafood industry is competitive in both its input and output markets and that it is composed of a large number of firms, each of which produces output using identical, two-input, constant-returns-to-scale production functions.[2] We further assume for simplicity that the two inputs are two species of fish, x_1 and x_2. Constant returns to scale imply that, for each firm, total cost can be written as

$$C^i(w_1, w_2, y^i) = c(w_1, w_2)y^i,$$

where w_1 and w_2 are the factor prices and y^i is the firm's output, defined as a composite retail fish commodity, and $c(w_1, w_2)$ is the unit cost function. For any one firm, output is indeterminate. For the industry, output is determined by demand and the competitive condition that output price equal marginal cost.

For a given level of output, an individual firm's demand for species one is given by Shepherd's lemma as

$$x_1^i(w_1, w_2, y) = \frac{\partial}{\partial w_1} C^i(w_1, w_2, y^i) = c_1(w_1, w_2)y^i,$$

[2] The assumption of constant returns to scale for each firm can be replaced with an assumption of a large number of firms with identical minimum average costs. The following argument only requires an industry supply curve that is horizontal for fixed factor prices.

where $c_1(\cdot)$ denotes the first partial derivative of $c(\cdot)$. Factor demand for the industry is given by the sum of the firms' factor demands,

$$x_1(w_1, w_2, y) = c_1(w_1, w_2)y, \tag{1}$$

where y is industry output. The industry demand for species one can be written to depend on output price by setting industry output, y, equal to retail demand, $D(p)$:

$$x_1(w_1, w_2, p) = c_1(w_1, w_2) \cdot D(p). \tag{2}$$

Expression (2) is a partial equilibrium demand for species one. It describes a relationship between x_1 and w_1, holding constant p and w_2. If w_1 were to exogenously change, however, p and w_2 would remain constant only if the supply of species two and the demand for output were perfectly elastic. In general, w_2 and p must change as w_1 is exogenously varied; they will change to maintain equilibrium in the x_2 and y markets. The two equilibrium conditions are that output price must equal unit cost and that the industry demand for species two must equal its supply. These two conditions are:

$$p = c(w_1, w_2) \tag{3}$$

and

$$c_2(w_1, w_2) \cdot D(p) = S_2(w_2). \tag{4}$$

The left-hand side of (4) is the industry demand for species two derived in the same way as the demand for species one. The right-hand side of (4) is the supply of species two as a function of its price.

For a given w_1, (3) and (4) implicitly define equilibrium values for p and w_2. They imply, first, that p is an increasing function of w_1: an increase in a factor price cannot lead to a decrease in output price. They imply, second, that w_2 is an increasing function of w_1 if the elasticity of substitution exceeds the absolute output demand elasticity (see Gardner [15]).[3]

Now consider the analysis of welfare changes due to an exogenous decrease in x_1, the catch of species one. Assume that the substitution effect dominates so that w_2 is bid up as a result. The situation is depicted in Fig. 1. There, the exogenous decrease in species one catch is from x_1^0 to x_1^1. The initial equilibrium price in that market is w_1^0, found by the intersection of x_1^0 and the partial equilibrium demand $D_1(p^0, w_2^0)$; p^0 and w_2^0 are the other-market equilibrium prices consistent with w_1^0 in the species one market. They are the solutions to (3) and (4) for $w_1 = w_1^0$.

---

[3]A rise in w_1 induces firms to substitute away from x_1 and toward x_2. This increase in demand for x_2 tends to increase w_2 as the industry moves along the supply curve for x_2. An offsetting effect on w_2 comes from the fact that a rise in w_1 will raise p and, therefore, reduce the quantity of output demanded. The reduction in output will tend to reduce the quantity demanded of x_2 and, therefore, lower w_2 by moving down the supply curve for x_2. In net, if the substitution effect dominates (the elasticity of substitution exceeds the output demand elasticity) then w_2 will be bid up. If not, then w_2 will be driven down.

230   THURMAN AND EASLEY

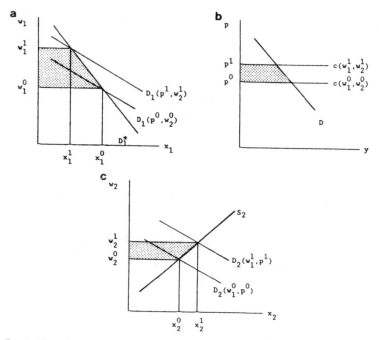

Fig. 1. General equilibrium derived demand applied to a species with substitution possibilities: (a) dockside market for species one subject to allocation; (b) retail market for y; and (c) dockside market for substitute species two.

When x_1 is exogenously reduced, this puts upward pressure on w_1, which shifts up the supply price of output and (we assume) shifts out the partial equilibrium demand for species two. The result is an increase in w_2 and p which shifts out the partial equilibrium demand for species one. The final equilibrium price in the species one market is found by the intersection of x_1^1 with the new demand curve. By connecting the two equilibrium points, (x_1^0, w_1^0) and (x_1^1, w_1^1), the D_1^* curve is a general equilibrium demand curve. Along it, p and w_2 vary so as to maintain equilibrium in the other two markets.

Because of the price changes in the three markets, there are three welfare effects from the catch decrease. First, there are profit changes to species one fishermen. They are represented by a supply relation in the species one market (not shown in Fig. 1). Second are the changes in the quasi-rents of species two suppliers (assumed positive due to the rightward shift in D_2). Third are the changes in consumer surplus of consumers of output. Because firms in the y industry earn no profits, there are no welfare effects that concern them directly. The question we next address is the relationship between the consumer surplus change measured behind D_1^* in the species one market and the welfare changes in the other two markets.

Begin the welfare analysis by measuring the change in quasi-rents in the species two market. That measure is given by

$$\Delta QR_2 = \int_{w_2^0}^{w_2^1} S_2(w_2)\, dw_2,$$ (5)

where $w_2^0 = w_2(w_1^0)$, $w_2^1 = w_2(w_1^1)$, and $w_2(w_1)$ denotes the equilibrium relationship between w_1 and w_2. The movement along S_2 depicted in panel (c) implies a shift in the derived demand for x_2. Equating the shift in that demand with the movement along S_2 gives

$$\Delta QR_2 = \int_{w_2^0}^{w_2^1} c_2[w_1(w_2), w_2]\, D\{p[w_1(w_2)]\}\, dw_2,$$ (6)

where $p(\cdot)$ denotes the equilibrium relationship between p and w_1, and $w_1(w_2)$ denotes the inverse of the relationship between w_2 and w_1. Changing the variable of integration from w_2 to w_1 gives

$$\Delta QR_2 = \int_{w_1^0}^{w_1^1} c_2[w_1, w_2(w_1)]\, D[p(w_1)]\left(\frac{dw_2}{dw_1}\right) dw_1,$$ (7)

where dw_2/dw_1 is the derivative of the equilibrium relationship $w_2(w_1)$.

Next calculate the change in consumer surplus in the output market,

$$\Delta CS = \int_{p^0}^{p^1} D(p)\, dp = \int_{w_1^0}^{w_1^1} D[p(w_1)]\left(\frac{dp}{dw_1}\right) dw_1,$$ (8)

where dp/dw_1 is an equilibrium derivative.

Combine (7) and (8) to calculate the net loss from the w_1 change,

$$\Delta CS - \Delta QR_2 = \int_{w_1^0}^{w_1^1} D[p(w)]\left\{\frac{dp}{dw_1} - c_2[w_1, w_2(w_1)]\frac{dw_2}{dw_1}\right\} dw_1.$$ (9)

The term in curly braces can be simplified. From the equilibrium relationships, we have

$$p(w_1) = c[w_1, w_2(w_1)],$$

which implies

$$\frac{dp}{dw_1} = c_1[w_1, w_2(w_1)] + c_2[w_1, w_2(w_1)]\frac{dw_2}{dw_1}.$$

The term in curly braces is, therefore, $c_1[w_1, w_2(w_1)]$. Substituting this into (9) yields

$$\Delta CS - \Delta QR_2 = \int_{w_1^0}^{w_1^1} D[p(w_1)]\, c_1[w_1, w_2(w_1)]\, dw_1$$

$$= \int_{w_1^0}^{w_1^1} D_1^*(w_1)\, dw_1.$$

In Fig. 1, the shaded area in panel (a) equals the difference between the shaded area in (b) and that in (c), or, the change in surplus measured behind the general equilibrium derived demand, D_1^*, equals the difference between the loss in consumer surplus in the retail market and the gain in quasi-rents in the market for the substitute species. Note that this result depends upon the identical firms assumption if it is to apply in long-run equilibrium; see Panzar and Willig [22]. When there are more than two inputs, D_1^* aggregates changes in quasi-rents in all other input markets.

Note that the derived demand welfare analysis does not include costs or benefits to producers in the restricted fishery. Those effects depend upon how the allowable harvest is distributed among fishing firms.[4] The effects on species two producers and retail consumers, on the other hand, depend only upon the restriction's effect on w_1. Once the allowed harvest of species one is landed, other markets are linked through the competitive price.

The important implication of the analysis is that we may be able to estimate in a single market the multi-market effects of changing allowable commercial harvests. In the following section, we provide an empirical example based on both partial and general equilibrium derived demands for red drum, a fishery of policy interest due to recent increased fishing pressure and declining stocks.

III. THE WELFARE EFFECTS OF RESTRICTIONS ON RED DRUM CATCH: EMPIRICAL ANALYSIS

In this section, an empirical counterpart to the derived demand model is estimated using annual data over the period 1970–1985. The model is used to analyze the welfare effects of a reduction in allowed commercial catch. The demand for red drum is considered to be derived from the consumer demand for retail seafood into which red drum is an input. Other inputs into retail seafood are considered to be two substitute species, red snapper and catfish, and non-fish inputs. The supplies of non-fish inputs are assumed to be perfectly elastic to the seafood industry, hence, there are no welfare effects in markets for those inputs.

An empirical implication of our general equilibrium model is that if quota restrictions on red drum cause welfare effects in markets for substitute species, then the red drum partial and general equilibrium demand slopes will differ. To investigate the difference in slopes, consider first a simple linear specification of the annual partial equilibrium demand curve for red drum,[5]

$$P_{dt} = a + b_1 Q_{dt} + b_2 P_{st} + b_3 P_{ct} + b_4 I_t + e_t, \tag{10}$$

---

[4]See for example, Anderson [1].

[5]Both price-dependent and quantity-dependent demands were estimated with small differences resulting in the point estimates of demand slopes and welfare costs. Note that the partial equilibrium demand in (10) excludes the price of the retail good, meals, but includes the prices of substitute species. The exclusion of retail prices is due to a lack of retail price data which itself provides motivation for exploring the general equilibrium derived demand.

where

$$P_{dt} = \text{price of red drum},$$
$$Q_{dt} = \text{per capita quantity of red drum consumed},$$
$$P_{st} = \text{price of red snapper},$$
$$P_{ct} = \text{price of catfish},$$
$$I_t = \text{per capita disposable income},$$
$$e_t = \text{a random demand disturbance}.$$

Prices and income are deflated by the Consumer Price Index.

To estimate (10) consistently requires consideration of the possible endogeneity of the right-hand side variables. Of the four, income is most clearly predetermined in the demand for red drum. In principle, the two substitute species' prices could be predetermined if their supply curves were horizontal: red drum price shocks would not induce rises in their prices. We will maintain, however, that only the supply of catfish is horizontal, while the supply of red snapper slopes up.

It seems unlikely that snapper supply is perfectly elastic, because it is caught in an open-water fishery; costs are likely to rise as the industry tries to harvest more fish at lower stock densities. Consistent with this, snapper price will be assumed endogenous. Catfish, on the other hand, are produced in replicable ponds and are more easily thought of as elastically supplied. Therefore, catfish price will be taken to be predetermined in (10). Finally, the quantity of drum consumed would be predetermined in (10) only if supply were vertical, an unlikely situation for annual data; Q_d is assumed endogenous.

Legitimate instruments for the two endogenous variables, Q_d and P_s, will be supply shifters. We use two: an index of the price of gasoline and a measure of the opportunity cost of labor in the Gulf states, the location of both the drum and snapper fisheries. We also use a linear time trend as an instrument to capture the effects on supply of declining fish stocks.

Consider next the general equilibrium demand for red drum. A general equilibrium specification must allow the prices of substitute inputs into retail seafood to change in response to parametric changes in the price of red drum. Of the substitutes considered here, snapper, catfish, and non-fish inputs, only snapper price is assumed to respond to changes in drum price. The previously discussed assumption of horizontal supply curves for catfish and non-fish inputs means that the prices of those inputs are predetermined in the general equilibrium demand. The price that is omitted from the GE demand curve is the price of red snapper, which *is* assumed to vary in response to changes in red drum price.

To complete the econometric specification of the GE demand curve, one must pay attention to possible sources of correlation between P_d and P_s that are not the GE sources. In particular, the historical correlation between P_d and P_s in the data will, in part, be due to the fact that drum and snapper production use many of the same inputs. The prices of both fish will rise and fall as the exogenous prices of these inputs rise and fall. So as not to confuse this source of correlation with the GE source due to the relatedness of drum and snapper in demand, the prices of these inputs are entered into the GE demand function (see Thurman and Wohlgenant [25]). The input prices we hold constant are those for gasoline and

234   THURMAN AND EASLEY

labor. The inverse GE demand curve becomes

$$P_{dt} = c + d_1 Q_{dt} + d_2 P_{ct} + d_3 I_t + d_4 P_{gt} + d_5 W_t + u_t, \qquad (11)$$

where

P_{gt} = index of the price of gasoline,

W_t = wage of Gulf state production workers: hourly compensation
for production workers in manufacturing, averaged for Florida
Louisiana, and Texas (BLS).

In Eq. (11) all right-hand side variables are taken to be predetermined except for
Q_d. The instruments for Eq. (11) are the same as for Eq. (10): the right-hand side
predetermined variables in (11) plus a linear time trend.

Notice that, in this instance, it is more difficult to identify the GE curve (11)
than the PE curve (10). Drum supply shifters cannot be used to identify the
empirical GE curve because they shift the GE curve and belong in it. One could
circumvent this problem if one had observations on variables that one was
confident shifted drum supply but not snapper supply. We are not confident that
gasoline price and the regional wage satisfy this condition. We *are* confident that
declines in stocks have, over time, shifted up the supply of drum. Therefore, we
use a time trend to represent these shifts and the GE demand curve is just-identi-
fied. We proceed assuming that time has not shifted consumer demand for drum
once one has taken account of changes in the prices of substitute species. The
reasonable results we get under this assumption are supportive, but the issue
warrants further investigation and testing.

Equations (10) and (11) are estimated as a system and the three-stage least
squares (3SLS) estimates are reported in Table I. The systems estimator is used
because PE and GE demand disturbances are highly correlated. Taking cross-
equation correlation into account increases estimation efficiency and allows accurate testing of equality of the PE and GE demand slopes. However, our time series
contains only 16 observations and the asymptotic distributions of 3SLS and its
associated test statistics are unlikely to represent the true finite sample distributions. For this reason, we present in Table I the standard t-ratios for tests of
hypotheses but p-values for those statistics derived from a parametric bootstrap
simulation. Our bootstrap procedure is described in detail in the Appendix. The
Table I column labeled "Bootstrap p-value" should be used as a data-based
alternative to the standard normal table. For each t-ratio, it gives the probability to
the right of that value (for a positive coefficient) in the bootstrap distribution.[6] As
it turns out, the bootstrap distributions for the t-ratios tend to be negatively
skewed and low variance relative to the standard normal distribution.

The last two columns of Table I display the price flexibilities (elasticities of drum
price with respect to the right-hand-side variables) and quantity elasticities evaluated at the sample means. The quantity elasticities are calculated by solving the
linear price-dependent equations for quantity and scaling the resulting partial
derivatives by sample means of the variables. We will discuss our results in terms
of the elasticities.

[6]See Efron and Tibshirani [13] for a discussion of the bootstrap method.

TABLE I

Three-Stage Least Squares Estimates: 1970–1985

Variable	Coefficient (*t*-ratio)	Bootstrap *p*-value (one-sided alternative)	P_d flexibility at means	Q_d elasticity at means
Partial equilibrium demand for red drum				
Per capita quantity of red drum (lb./person)	−3.015 (−1.955)	0.003	−0.214	−4.673
Real price of red snapper ($/lb.)	0.457 (3.744)	0	1.106	5.163
Real price of catfish ($/lb.)	0.288 (3.763)	0	0.379	1.769
Real p.c. disposable income ($1000's/person)	−0.0393 (−0.802)	0.283	−0.647	−3.021
General equilibrium demand for red drum				
Per capita quantity of red drum (lb./person)	−5.325 (−2.906)	0.002	−0.378	−2.644
Real price of catfish ($/lb.)	0.233 (2.269)	0.002	0.306	0.808
Real p.c. disposable income ($1000's/person)	0.102 (2.444)	0.006	1.671	4.418
Real price of gasoline ($/gallon)	0.269 (2.505)	0.008	0.388	1.026
Real wage ($/hour)	−0.0188 (−0.250)	0.441	−0.260	−0.686

Note. Dependent variable: real price ($/lb.) of red drum; endogenous variables: Prices of red drum and red snapper, quantity of red drum; predetermined variables: Prices of catfish and gasoline, income, wages, time trend. *System statistics*: Correlation between 3SLS residuals across equations = 0.811. T-test (*df* = 21) of equality between Q_d coefficient in partial equilibrium equation and Q_d coefficient in general equilibrium equation = 1.514 (bootstrap *p*-value for a one-sided alternative = 0.022). First-order autocorrelation coefficients of the 3SLS residuals are: partial equilibrium, −0.37 (asymptotic s.e. of 0.25); general equilibrium, −0.16 (asymptotic s.e. of 0.25).

TABLE II

Data Definitions and Sources

Variable	Source
P_s, Q_s	Gulf of Mexico Fishery Management Council (compiled from NMFS landings data).
P_d, Q_d	NMFS, "Final Secretarial Fishery Management Plan, Regulatory Impact Review, and Regulatory Flexibility Analysis for the Red Drum Fishery of the Gulf of Mexico," Dec. 1986.
P_c	USDA, Ag. Statistics Board, summary data, supplied by Mr. Jim Ayers, NMFS, Little Rock.
I	Bureau of Census, "Statistical Abstract of the U.S."
P_g	Gasoline price index from Bureau of Labor Statistics "Hotline" (personal communication).
W	BLS, Handbook of Labor Statistics, Bulletin 2217, various issues for years 1970–83; personal comm., 1984–85.
C.P.I.	Bureau of Census, "Statistical Abstract of the U.S."
Pop.	Bureau of Census, "Statistical Abstract of the U.S."

Conceptually, the partial equilibrium own-price elasticity of -4.673 measures the responsiveness of red drum demand to a parametric change in the price of red drum, holding constant the price of the substitute species catfish and red snapper (but allowing the price of retail seafood to vary; see Footnote 5). The general equilibrium own-price elasticity of -2.644 measures the responsiveness both to a change in the price of red drum and to the associated change in the price of red snapper. It can be shown that the general equilibrium response should be less elastic because it tempers the demand-reducing effect of the drum price increase with the demand-increasing effect of the associated snapper price increase. The estimates of these two elasticities bear out this relationship.

Further, just as the economic difference between an elasticity of -4.673 and one of -2.644 is large, the statistical evidence supports the hypothesis that the two price effects are different. The p-value of a test of the equality of the two coefficients is .022. The alternative hypothesis of this test is one-sided: that the PE slope exceeds in absolute value the GE slope. The evidence is also strong that both price coefficients are different from zero (t-statistics of -1.955 and -2.906 with bootstrap p-values of 0.003 and 0.002).

The economic significance of the Table I estimates can be conveyed through an illustrative welfare analysis. The case considered will be one of a 10% reduction in the allowed commercial red drum catch below the 1985 levels. The consumer surplus change will be measured with respect to the general equilibrium demand curve to measure both the change in surplus to final fish consumers and the gain to suppliers of the substitute species, red snapper. The welfare calculation is compared to what one would obtain from incorrectly using the partial equilibrium demand curve.

Taking 1985 as a base, a 10% catch reduction would have reduced red drum landings from 0.0265 pounds per capita to 0.0239 pounds per capita. The implied increase in real (1970 dollars) price using the general equilibrium demand slope is $0.0138 per pound. The consumer surplus loss per capita is a trapezoid: $(1/2)(\Delta P)(\Delta Q) + (\Delta P)(Q_0) = (1/2)(\$0.0138)(0.0026) + (\$0.0138)(0.0239) = (\$0.1794 \times 10^{-4}) + (\$3.2982 \times 10^{-4}) = \$3.4776 \times 10^{-4}$, where Q_0 is the new, smaller quantity. Multiplying by the 1985 civilian U.S. Population of 239.279 million gives a total demand-side surplus loss from the 10% catch reduction of $83,212 in 1970 dollars. In 1987 dollars, the surplus loss is $243,559. For comparison, the value of the 1985 catch was near $4.3 million in 1987 dollars; the estimated welfare loss from a 10% catch reduction equals 6% of the total value of the catch.

Because general equilibrium welfare analysis is uncommon, it is interesting to ask how the welfare calculation would have turned out had one used the more familiar partial equilibrium demand slope. Because the partial equilibrium curve is more elastic than the general equilibrium curve, the estimated welfare cost would necessarily be less than the previous calculation. In fact, because the expression for the welfare loss is linear in the demand slope parameter, the proportionate difference between the GE and PE welfare losses is the same as the proportionate difference between the GE and PE demand slopes.[7] As shown in Table I, the PE demand slope of -3.015 is 43.4% smaller in absolute value than the GE demand

---

[7] The expression for the trapezoid of welfare loss is $\alpha \beta Q^2 (2 - \alpha)/2$, where α is the proportionate reduction in catch, β is the absolute, price-dependent, demand slope, and Q is the base quantity from which the reduction is measured.

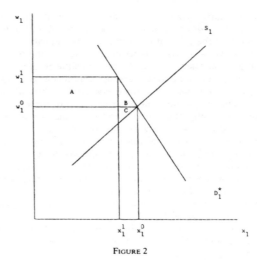

FIGURE 2

slope of -5.325. Therefore the PE, and incorrect, welfare calculation would give the welfare loss due to a 10% catch reduction in 1985 as \$137,902 1987 dollars instead of the GE value of \$243,559 1987 dollars.

The general equilibrium welfare analysis just described is not a complete accounting for the effects of a catch restriction. It *is* an accounting for the effects both on final consumers of fish and on suppliers of substitute fish species. In the main, what is left out of the derived demand analysis is the set of effects on red drum fishermen. To set our analysis in context, refer to the welfare analysis depicted in Fig. 2.

In that figure, the allowable catch is reduced from the equilibrium quantity of x_1^0 to x_1^1. This raises red drum price to w_1^1 along the GE demand curve D_1^*. The associated consumer surplus loss of area $A + B$ represents the loss to ultimate consumers net of the gain to suppliers of substitute species. This is the loss estimated in Table I. If the allowable catch is distributed at no charge through firm-level quotas, and done so efficiently, then the gain to red drum fishermen is the area $A - C$. This gain can be positive or negative. Because the demand for red drum is elastic (as estimated in Table I), total revenue is less at x_1^1 than at x_1^0. Total cost is, of course, also less at the lower quantity and the change in cost may be greater than or less than the change in revenue.

Aggregating across all direct and indirect participants in the red drum market, the net welfare cost is the triangle $B + C$. This places only a lower bound on the welfare cost because it assumes that the catch reduction is allocated efficiently. If the catch is distributed to firms such that their marginal costs differ, then the gain to fishermen is less than $A - C$, and the net welfare cost is larger than $B + C$. Further, if fishermen compete outside the market for the right to produce then there are rent-seeking and/or regulatory-avoidance costs[8] to be added in as well.

---

[8] For an interesting discussion of avoidance costs, see Anderson and Lee [2].

Finally, it must be recognized that the static analysis of Fig. 2 ignores the potential dynamic benefits of the catch reduction. We interpret area $B + C$ as the annual cost of implementing a program that may have future benefits through increases in fish stock levels. Similarly, our welfare measure does not include any dynamic externalities associated with increases in snapper catch. We do not speculate, as one referee suggests, on whether this improved valuation technique will lead to more or less conservative harvesting policies, with resulting effects on optimal stock. We believe this question requires incorporating the GE derived demand into a dynamic model—a logical extension of this paper. The results do suggest, however, that policies that shift harvests from the commercial sector to the recreational sector based on partial equilibrium derived demand estimates in the commercial sector will understate the costs of such a policy. This in turn may lead to overallocating harvests to the recreational sector, ceteris paribus. This is an important result to many fishery management debates taking place currently.

IV. CONCLUSIONS

This paper explores valuation procedures in the commercial fishing sector, being motivated by the recreational–commercial allocation issue. Conceptually, we argue that the general equilibrium derived demand is more appropriate than the traditional partial equilibrium derived demand for valuing the welfare effects of changes in allowable commercial harvest. Pragmatically, two factors make the general equilibrium approach all the more attractive. First, the dearth of retail-level data limits or rules out our ability to estimate consumer welfare effects directly in those markets. Second, our lack of understanding of which species substitute in production for a species subject to regulation limits our ability to estimate directly the welfare effects in horizontally related markets.

Welfare effects from a hypothetical reduction in harvest are contrasted using partial and general equilibrium price elasticies estimated for Gulf of Mexico red drum. The welfare effects estimated from the partial equilibrium price coefficient are 43% smaller than those estimated from the general equilibrium coefficient. Given the small sample, we view these results as illustrative. However we interpret them as evidence that consumer and other-market welfare effects can be significant and should not be ignored in fishery management decisions. We conclude that, in this instance, a sizable understatement of the costs of catch restrictions would result from ignoring their multi-market effects.

APPENDIX: THE PARAMETRIC BOOTSTRAP PROCEDURE

Write the system of partial and general equilibrium demand equations as:

$$\left. \begin{aligned} y_{1t} &= \beta_{12}y_{2t} + \beta_{13}y_{3t} + z'_{1t}\gamma_1 + \epsilon_{1t} \\ y_{1t} &= \beta_{22}y_{2t} + z'_{2t}\gamma_2 + \epsilon_{2t}, \end{aligned} \right\} \quad t = 1,\dots,16 \qquad \text{(A1)}$$

where

y_{1t} = drum price,

y_{2t} = drum quantity,

y_{3t} = snapper price,

z_{1t} = a vector of the predetermined variables in the first (partial equilibrium) equation,

z_{2t} = a vector of the predetermined variables in the second (general equilibrium) equation,

×

γ_1 and γ_2 are coefficient vectors conformable with z_1 and z_2.

Next write the reduced form equations for the three endogenous variables as

$$\left. \begin{array}{l} y_{1t} = z_t' \pi_1 + u_{1t} \\ y_{2t} = z_t' \pi_2 + u_{2t} \\ y_{3t} = z_t' \pi_3 + u_{3t}, \end{array} \right\} \quad t = 1, \ldots, 16 \quad (A2)$$

where z_t is the vector of all predetermined variables in the system (see Table I). Denote the 3SLS estimates of the structural parameters with tildes, e.g. $\tilde{\beta}_{12}$, and denote the OLS estimates of the reduced form parameters with hats, e.g. $\hat{\pi}_1$.

The bootstrap consists of 1000 simulations of (A2) to generate the endogenous variables and, for each simulated sample, calculation of the 3SLS estimates of the structural coefficients in (A1) and their covariance matrix. The simplest way to carry out the bootstrap would be, first, to estimate (A2) with OLS and then generate pseudo-samples by sampling with replacement from the calculated OLS residuals $(\hat{u}_{1t}, \hat{u}_{2t}, \hat{u}_{3t})$. Because there are only 16 observations, it was felt that more would be learned by using a parametric alternative. We assumed that (u_{1t}, u_{2t}, u_{3t}) was distributed normally with a covariance matrix equal to the estimated covariance matrix of the OLS reduced form residuals. This alternative views the trivariate normal distribution as a better approximation to the true (u_{1t}, u_{2t}, u_{3t}) distribution than the empirical distribution of $(\hat{u}_{1t}, \hat{u}_{2t}, \hat{u}_{3t})$, which may be unrepresentative due to the small sample size. The simulations do, however, preserve the covariance structure of the OLS residuals.

Once having generated a set of u_t's from the trivariate normal distribution, the endogenous variables are constructed using (A2) with the actual values of the z_t's, the actual OLS estimates of the π's, and the randomly generated u's. The z_t's are fixed from pseudo-sample to pseudo-sample. For each coefficient in each pseudo-sample a t-statistic is calculated. For example, letting $\tilde{\beta}_{12}$ be the 3SLS estimate of β_{12} from the original data, $\tilde{\beta}_{12}^{(i)}$ be the 3SLS estimate of β_{12} from the ith pseudo-sample, and $\tilde{s}_{12}^{(i)}$ be the 3SLS calculated standard error of $\tilde{\beta}_{12}^{(i)}$, the t-ratio $(\tilde{\beta}_{12}^{(i)} - \tilde{\beta}_{12})/\tilde{s}_{12}^{(i)}$ is calculated. A similar t-ratio is calculated for each of the 11 structural coefficients. A 12th t-ratio is calculated for the hypothesis of equality of the PE and GE demand slopes. It is $[(\tilde{\beta}_{12} - \tilde{\beta}_{22}) - (\tilde{\beta}_{12}^{(i)}) - \tilde{\beta}_{22}^{(i)})]/\tilde{s}_{12-22}^{(i)}$. This yields 1000 observations on each of the 12 t-ratios. The p-values in Table I report where, in the bootstrap distribution, the actual 3SLS t-statistics lie. For example, the first p-value of 0.003 means that out of the 1000 bootstrapped t-ratios for the GE quantity coefficient, three were less than the 3SLS t-ratio of -1.955 and 997 were greater. For comparison to the asymptotic standard normal approximation, 0.025 of the area under the standard normal p.d.f. lies to the left of -1.995.

REFERENCES

1. L. G. Anderson, Potential economic benefits from gear restrictions and license limitation in fisheries regulation, *Land Econom.* **61**, 409–418 (1985).
2. L. G. Anderson and D. R. Lee, Optimal governing instrument, operation level, and enforcement in natural resource regulation: The case of the fishery, *Amer. J. Agr. Econom.* **68**, 678–690 (1986).
3. L. G. Anderson, Analysis of open-access commercial exploitation and maximum economic yield in biologically and technologically interdependent fisheries, *J. Fish. Res. Board Canad.* **32**, 1825–1840 (1975).
4. R. C. Bishop and K. C. Samples, Sport and commercial fishing conflicts: A theoretical analysis, *J. Environ. Econom. Management* **7**, 220–233 (1980).
5. G. M. Brown, An optimal program for managing common property resources with congestion externalities, *J. Polit. Econom.* **82**, 163–73 (1974).
6. H. Cheng and O. Capps, Demand analysis of fresh and frozen finfish and shellfish in the United States, *Amer. J. Agr. Econom.* **70**, 533–542 (1988).
7. C. W. Clark and G. R. Munro, Fisheries and the processing sector: Some implications for management policy, *Bell J. Econom.* **11**, 603–616 (1980).
8. C. W. Clark, "Mathematical Bioeconomics: The Optimal Management of Renewable Resources," Wiley, New York (1976).
9. C. W. Clark, "Bioeconomic Modeling and Fisheries Management," Wiley, New York (1985).
10. S. R. Crutchfield, U.S. demand for selected groundfish products, 1967–80: Comment, *Amer. J. Agr. Econom.* **68**, 1018–1019 (1986).
11. W. E. Diewert, A note on the elasticity of derived demand in the *n*-factor case, *Economica* **38**, 192–198 (1971).
12. J. E. Easley, Selected issues in modeling allocation of fishery harvests, *Mar. Resource Econom.*, in press.
13. B. Efron and R. Tibshirani, Bootstrap methods for standard errors, confidence intervals, and other measures of statistical accuracy, *Statist. Sci.*, **1**, 54–77 (1986).
14. W. K. B. Emerson, "A Spatial Allocation Model for the New England Fisheries," unpublished Ph.D. dissertation, Department of Economics, Univ. of Rhode Island (1988).
15. B. L. Gardner, The farm-retail price spread in a competitive food industry, *Amer. J. Agr. Econom.* **57**, 399–409 (1975).
16. J. R. Hicks, "The Theory of Wages," Macmillan, London 1963).
17. R. N. Johnson and G. D. Libecap, Contracting problems and regulation: The case of the fishery, *Amer. Econom. Rev.* **72**, 1005–1022 (1982).
18. R. E. Just and D. L. Hueth, Welfare measures in a multimarket framework, *Amer. Econom. Rev.* **69**, 947–954 (1979).
19. R. E. Just, D. L. Hueth, and A. Schmitz, "Applied Welfare Economics and Public Policy," Prentice–Hall, Englewood Cliffs, NJ (1982).
20. J. M. Karpoff, Suboptimal controls in common resource management: The case of the fishery, *J. Polit. Econom.* **95**, 179–194 (1987).
21. K. E. McConnell and J. G. Sutinen, Bioeconomic models of marine recreational fishing, *J. Environ. Econom. Management* **6**, 127–139 (1979).
22. J. C. Panzar and R. D. Willig, On the comparative statics of a competitive industry with inframarginal firms, *Amer. Econom. Rev.* **68**, 474–478 (1978).
23. J. B. Smith, Replenishable resources management under uncertainty: A reexamination of the U.S. northern fishery, *J. Environ. Econom. Management* **7**, 209–219 (1980).
24. J. G. Sutinen and P. Andersen, The economics of fisheries law enforcement, *Land Econom.* **64**, 387–397 (1985).
25. W. N. Thurman and M. K. Wohlgenant, Consistent estimation of general equilibrium welfare effects, *Amer. J. Agr. Econom.* **71**, 1041–1045 (1989).
26. E. Tsoa, W. E. Schrank and N. Roy, U.S. demand for selected groundfish products, 1967–80, *Amer. J. Agr. Econom.* **63**, 483–489 (1982).
27. S. Wang and C. B. Kellogg, An econometric model for American lobster, *Mar. Resource Econom.* **5**, 61–70 (1988).

[27]

Welfare Measurement in Single and Multimarket Models: Theory and Application

Runar Brännlund and Bengt Kriström

In this paper we provide an analysis of tax reforms along the lines of the multimarket welfare measurement techniques suggested by Just, Hueth, and Schmitz. A key purpose of our analysis is to shed light on the approximating features of partial equilibrium models. We derive a result on the difference between single and multimarket welfare measurement, showing how the difference boils down to a set of key parameters. We use our approach to analyze a proposal put forward by the Swedish Commission of Environmental Charges regarding chlorine emissions from the Swedish pulp and paper industry.

Key words: environmental taxes, partial versus general equilibrium, policy reform, single and multimarket welfare measurement.

In this paper we provide an analysis of tax reforms along the lines of the multimarket welfare measurement techniques suggested by Just, Hueth, and Schmitz. The purpose of our analysis is to shed light on the approximating features of partial equilibrium models. In particular, we investigate how well a single-market model approximates consumer and producer surplus changes under multiple-market price changes. We derive a useful result on the difference between single-market and multimarket welfare measurement, showing how the difference boils down to a set of key parameters.

We also provide an empirical analysis of the distributional effects of taxes, focusing on issues such as the possibility of tax shifting backward or forward. Our empirical illustration covers the chlorine tax proposal put forward by the Swedish Commission on Environmental Charges (SOU 1989), where a (stiff) tax on chlorine effluents from bleaching processes in the pulp industry was proposed. Our model sheds light on issues that were considered vitally important in the discussion of this tax, e.g., the possibility for the forest industry to pass on some of the tax and its distributional impacts. We identify the winners and losers of the tax. We also estimate the environmental impact under different assumptions about price repercussions in several closely connected markets.

The Model

The analysis of tax incidence in general equilibrium models has a long history in economic analysis (e.g., Kotlikoff and Summers; Just, Hueth, and Schmitz). In recent years, the use of computable general equilibrium models has proved fruitful in evaluating the general equilibrium effects of economic instruments in environmental policy. Examples of such approaches include Johnson; Bergman; and Jørgensen and Wilcoxen. The work that comes closest to ours is Kokoski and Smith.

The model we analyze can be made perfectly general, along the lines suggested by Just, Hueth, and Schmitz. In order to make the model transparent and the results intuitive, consider the following set up. There are three separate but intimately related industries: pulp and paper, sawmills, and forestry. Given perfect competition in these industries, the short-run, or restricted, profit function for a representative

The authors are associate professor and professor in the Department of Economics at the University of Umeå, and in the Department of Forest Economics, Swedish University of Agricultural Sciences, respectively.

We acknowledge two anonymous referees for their very valuable comments, and a research grant from the Swedish Council for Agricultural and Forest Research, the Nordic Research Council, and the STORA Foundation.

158   *February 1996*   *Amer. J. Agr. Econ.*

pulp firm is defined as follows:

(1) $R\Pi^p = R\Pi^p(P_p, w_{pl}, w_{pe}, w_{pv}, w_{pc}; \bar{K}_p)$

where P_p is the price of the final product, pulp, and w_{pi} is the price of the input in the production of pulp. The subscripts l, e, v, c refer to inputs of labor, energy, pulpwood, and chlorine, respectively. Finally, $\bar{K}_p$ is the fixed capital stock. This implies that the model should be viewed as a short-run model. The pulp and paper industry is assumed to face an infinitely elastic demand curve for pulp; therefore, the tax cannot be shifted forward. In addition, we assume that chlorine, labor, and energy are supplied elastically.

Applying Hotelling's lemma to equation (1) gives us the supply of pulp, y, and the derived demand for the flexible factors of production, x, as

(2) $y(P_p, w_{pl}, w_{pe}, w_{pv}, w_{pc}; \bar{K}_p) = \dfrac{\partial R\Pi^p}{\partial P_p}$

(3) $x_{pi}(P_p, w_{pl}, w_{pe}, w_{pv}, w_{pc}; \bar{K}_p) = -\dfrac{\partial R\Pi^p}{\partial w_{pi}},$

$i = l, e, v, c.$

The specification of the forest owner's decision problem is conventional. We assume that a forest owner is supplying two different products: pulpwood, which is used as an input in the pulp industry, and sawtimber, which is used as an input in the sawmill industry. This is not a very strong assumption in our empirical illustration, since more than 90% of total harvested output is used by the pulp and sawmill industry in Sweden. To produce these two assortments, we assume that labor and the standing inventory of timber are used as inputs. Labor is viewed as a variable input while forest land is regarded as fixed, at least in the short run. The forest owners profit function is

(4) $R\Pi^f = R\Pi^f(w_{pv}, w_{sv}, w_{fl}; \bar{K}_f)$

where w_{sv} is the price of sawtimber, w_{fl} is the wage rate in forestry, and $\bar{K}_f$ is the fixed forest capital. Applying Hotelling's lemma to equation (4), we obtain the supply function of pulpwood and sawtimber as well as the demand function for labor in forestry; in the sequel, they will be denoted y_{pv}, y_{sv}, and x_{fl} respectively.

Finally, we assume that the sawmills supply one output, sawnwood, using labor, energy, sawtimber, and capital as inputs. Labor, energy, and sawtimber are assumed to be variable inputs, while capital is fixed. The profit function for a sawmill is defined as

(5) $R\Pi^s = R\Pi^s(P_s, w_{sl}, w_{se}, w_{sv}; \bar{K}_s)$

where P_s is the price of sawnwood and w_{si} is the input prices. The subscripts $i = l, e, v$ refer to labor, energy, and sawtimber, respectively. Finally, $\bar{K}_s$ is the fixed capital stock. The supply function (y_s) and the derived demand functions (x_{si}) for the sawmills can again be obtained via Hotelling's lemma.

Since more than 90% of the harvested timber volume is used by either the pulp industry or the sawmill industry, it is not likely that the equilibrium prices on pulpwood and sawtimber will remain unaffected by shifts in the demand curves for pulpwood and sawtimber. In order to take such factors into account, we proceed by defining market equilibrium conditions for pulpwood and sawtimber:

(6) $\displaystyle\sum_{i=1}^{m} x_{pv}^i(P_p; w_{pl}, w_{pe}, w_{pv}, w_{pc}, \bar{K}_p)$

$\displaystyle= \sum_{i=1}^{n} y_{pv}^i(w_{pv}, w_{sv}; w_{fl}, \bar{K}_f)$

(7) $\displaystyle\sum_{i=1}^{m_1} x_{sv}^i(P_s; w_{sl}, w_{se}, w_{sv}, \bar{K}_s)$

$\displaystyle= \sum_{i=1}^{n} y_{sv}^i(w_{pv}, w_{sv}; w_{fl}, \bar{K}_f)$

where m is the number of pulp-producing firms, n is the number of forest owners, and m_1 is the number of sawmills.

Solving equations (6) and (7) for w_{pv} and w_{sv}, respectively, gives the reduced form for the equilibrium prices of pulpwood and sawtimber as

(8) $w_{pv}^* = w_{pv}^*(P_p, P_s, \tilde{w}_p, \tilde{w}_s, w_{fl}, \bar{K})$

(9) $w_{sv}^* = w_{sv}^*(P_p, P_s, \tilde{w}_p, \tilde{w}_s, w_{fl}, \bar{K})$

where $\tilde{w}_p$ and $\tilde{w}_s$ are vectors of input prices, other than wood, referring to the pulp industry and sawmill industry, respectively, and $\bar{K}$ is a vector including capital stocks in each industry.

We can now define the industry, or aggregate, profit functions as

(10) $IR\Pi^p = IR\Pi^p(P_p; \tilde{w}_p, w_{pv}^*; \overline{K}_p)$

(11) $IR\Pi^j = IR\Pi^j(w_{pv}^*, w_{sv}^*; w_{fl}; \overline{K}_f)$

(12) $IR\Pi^s = IR\Pi^s(P_s; \tilde{w}_s, w_{sv}^*; \overline{K}_s)$.

These equations incorporate all the possible indirect effects that we allow for in this study.

The most straightforward way to derive the welfare impact of an increase in the price of chlorine is via the change in profits. Welfare measures are, of course, very simple in this case since there are no consumers in this model. If the price of chlorine (and no other price) changes, we may measure the change in profits at the relevant area bounded by the demand curve for chlorine. If an alteration in the price of chlorine induces price changes on other markets, we need to look beyond the change in profits for the pulp industry. For each industry we evaluate the changes in profits given the initial and final prices. Given the "equilibrium demand curve" for chlorine, it is sufficient to compute the area bounded by this curve since it incorporates the adjustments that take place in industries other than the one studied; i.e.,[1]

(13) $\Delta IR\Pi = \int_{w_{pc}}^{w_{pc}+t} -X_{pc}^* dw_{pc}$

where $\Delta IR\Pi = \Delta(IR\Pi^p + IR\Pi^j + IR\Pi^s)$ is the total change in profits and $X_{pc}^* = X_{pc}(\cdot, w_{pc}, w_{pv}^*)$ is the equilibrium demand curve for chlorine. The integral in equation (13) is then the area under the equilibrium demand curve for chlorine. This means that the repercussions from the roundwood markets are taken into account. Without any other price changes than for chlorine, equation (13) reduces to the conventional area under the demand function for chlorine. A formal proof of this result can be found in Brännlund and Kriström (1993). See also Just, Hueth, and Schmitz.

The usefulness of equation (13) in empirical

analysis is clear. In order to evaluate the change in total profits, it is not necessary to know all the parameters in all profit functions. In this specific case, all we need to know are the demand and supply functions in the roundwood markets and the chlorine demand function.

The main result of this paper is a quite transparent expression for the difference between partial and general equilibrium welfare measures (in this model). It is convenient to first define our measures of deadweight loss. For the single-market, or partial equilibrium case

(14) $DVL_p = \int_d X_{pc}(w_{pc} + s;)ds - tX_{pc}(w_{pc} + t;)$.

where d is the path $(0, t)$ and t denotes the tax on chlorine. Thus, the integral sums the change in profits, and we deduct tax revenue from this amount to obtain deadweight loss in the partial equilibrium model. By the definition of partial equilibrium, only the chlorine price changes. The corresponding measure for the multimarket version of our model is given by

(15)

$$DVL_g = \int_d X_{pc}\big[w_{pc} + s, w_{pv}(w_{pc} + s), \cdot\big]ds$$
$$- tX_{pc}\big[w_{pc} + t, w_{pv}(w_{pc} + t), \cdot\big].$$

The only difference is, of course, that this measure takes into account the repercussions in the pulpwood market.

PROPOSITION 1. *The difference between deadweight loss in the single and multimarket model is equal to*

$$\Delta DVL = DVL_p - DVL_g$$
$$= \int_d \frac{tX_{pc}/w_{pc}}{\varepsilon_v^s - \varepsilon_v^d} \left\{ \varepsilon_{cv}\varepsilon_{vc} + \left[\varepsilon_{cv}\varepsilon_{vs}^s\varepsilon_{sc}^*/(\varepsilon_s^s - \varepsilon_s^d) \right] \right\}$$

where $\varepsilon_{vc} = (\partial X_{pv}/\partial w_{pc})(w_{pc}/X_{pv})$ is the cross-price elasticity of pulpwood demand with respect to the chlorine price, ε_{cv} is the elasticity of chlorine demand with respect to the pulpwood price, ε_v^s and ε_v^d are the own-price supply and demand elasticity of pulpwood, respectively, ε_{vs}^s is the pulpwood supply elasticity with respect to the sawtimber price, ε_{sc}^* is the reduced form sawtimber supply elasticity with respect to the chlorine price, and, finally, ε_s^s and ε_s^d are the own-price sawtimber supply and demand elasticity, respectively.

---

[1] We focus here on tax distortions and the welfare impacts. Just, Hueth, and Schmitz (appendix D, p. 457–62) contains a detailed discussion about different types of distortions (e.g., quotas) and equilibrium welfare measurement. The general result—that we can measure all welfare impacts on one market—carries over.

Amer. J. Agr. Econ.

The proof of the proposition is available in Brännlund and Kriström (1994b). Briefly, one differentiates ΔDVL with respect to t and utilizes the equilibrium conditions on the pulpwood and sawtimber markets.

Several intuitively appealing properties follow directly from this result. First, note that $DVL_p - DVL_g \geq 0$ —a well-known result that is closely related to the Le Chatelier principle (Brännlund and Kriström 1994b). Second, the inequality does not depend on whether pulpwood and chlorine are substitutes or complements in production. Third, an infinitely elastic supply curve for pulpwood implies that there is no difference between single and multimarket welfare measures. This simply means that there will be no price repercussions in the pulpwood market when the chlorine tax is introduced if the supply curve for pulpwood is horizontal. A similar argument applies for the demand elasticity. Fourth, given estimates of the key parameters we can immediately see how "bad" a partial equilibrium model might be as an approximation to a more general case which includes repercussions in other markets. Fifth, the cross-price elasticity can be replaced by the product of chlorine's cost share and the elasticity of substitution between chlorine and pulp. Since the cost share for chlorine is low in this case, and the substitution possibilities are limited in the short run, we expect to find small differences in the empirical analysis between the partial and the "general" equilibrium setup.

The result in proposition 1 is perfectly general in the sense that the equilibrium demand curve for chlorine will tilt further clockwise if the pulp industry faces upward sloping supply curves on other inputs, or if it faces a downward sloping demand curve for the final product. Suppose, for example, that the industry faces a downward sloping demand curve for the final product. Then it can be shown that

$$(16) \quad \left.\frac{\partial \Delta DVL}{\partial t}\right|_{dP \neq 0} > \left.\frac{\partial \Delta DVL}{\partial t}\right|_{dP=0}$$

i.e., the difference in deadweight loss will increase. A crucial parameter to determine the importance of this latter result is, of course, the slope of the demand curve for pulp. Hultkrantz argues that -9.0 is a reasonable demand elasticity facing the Swedish pulp industry. In our case this means that it is very difficult to shift the tax burden forward.

Empirical Specification and Estimation Results

To estimate the parameters in the profit functions, we need to parameterize the model. This is done by assuming that the technology in each industry can be represented by a restricted Generalized Leontief (GL) profit function, which is a second-order differential approximation of any arbitrary profit function. This system is specified as follows:

$$(17) \quad R\Pi^p = \sum_i \sum_j \beta_{ij} w_i^{1/2} w_j^{1/2} + \sum_i \beta_{ik} w_i \bar{K}_p$$
$$+ \beta_{pp} P_p + \sum_i \beta_{ip} w_i^{1/2} P_p^{1/2} + \beta_{pk} P_p \bar{K}_p$$
$$i = pl, pv, pe, pc$$
$$j = pl, pv, pe, pc$$

$$(18) \quad R\Pi^f = \sum_i \sum_j \alpha_{ij} w_i^{1/2} w_j^{1/2} + \sum_i \alpha_{ik} w_i \bar{K}_f$$
$$i = pv, sv, fl, \bar{K}_f$$
$$j = pv, sv, fl, \bar{K}_f$$

$$(19) \quad R\Pi^s = \sum_i \sum_j \gamma_{ij} w_i^{1/2} w_j^{1/2} + \sum_i \gamma_{ik} w_i \bar{K}_s$$
$$+ \gamma_{ss} P_s + \sum_i \gamma_{is} w_i^{1/2} P_s^{1/2} + \gamma_{sk} P_s \bar{K}_s$$
$$i = sl, sv, se$$
$$j = sl, sv, se.$$

We impose symmetry by requiring $\beta_{ij} = \beta_{ji}$, $\alpha_{ij} = \alpha_{ji}$, and $\gamma_{ij} = \gamma_{ji}$ for all i and j. By applying Hotelling's lemma to equations (17), (18), and (19), we obtain the relevant demand and supply functions.

From equation (13) it is clear that we do not need, for our particular purpose, estimates of all parameters in each profit function. What we obviously need to estimate is the demand function for chlorine. However, in order to estimate the equilibrium demand curve for chlorine, X_{pc}^*, the equilibrium prices for pulpwood and sawtimber, equations (8) and (9), must be calculated. Since prices on pulpwood and sawtimber are determined by the equilibrium conditions on the pulpwood and sawtimber market, respectively, we need estimates of the demand and supply functions for both pulpwood and sawtimber. A minimum requirement to "close" our model, then, is estimates of five equations: chlorine demand, pulpwood demand and supply, and sawtimber demand and supply. Gains in efficiency (lower variance) would be obtained if all equations in the model were estimated simultaneously. However, because of lack of data, we have chosen to estimate the whole system of supply and demand equations only for the pulp industry. For forestry we estimate only the pulpwood supply and sawtimber supply equations, and for the sawmill industry, only the sawtimber demand equation.

The data we use are annual time-series data, collected from Swedish official statistics (mainly SOS Industry but also from the *Yearbook of Forest Statistics*). We have no time-series data on the capital stock in the pulp industry and sawmill industry. We use data available on production capacity in the pulp industry as a proxy for capital stock. We tried various approximations for the capital stock in the sawmill industry, including time and lagged production of sawed wood. The results, however, seem to be quite insensitive to whether we include such an approximation or not. Therefore, we have chosen to omit this variable.

We use two econometric approaches, an iterative SURE method with symmetry restrictions (IZEF) and 3SLS. The instruments used in 3SLS are all the exogenous variables in the model. The FIML method, in which both the pulpwood price and sawtimber price are endogenous, is problematic in this case, because the number of parameters exceeds the number of observations. The IZEF and 3SLS results are presented in table A1 in the appendix. We have chosen to present the t-ratios only, since the parameter values do not lend themselves to any intuitive interpretations. To estimate the model we have used the RATS program.

Since the estimation results are quite similar to those reported in Brännlund and Kriström (1993), we will only briefly comment upon them. The results for the pulp industry show that approximately 50% of the estimated parameters are significantly different from zero at the 10% probability level. The values of the Durbin-Watson (DW) statistic indicate that there are problems with serial correlation. As a consequence, the reported t-ratios may be overestimated. The low DW values seem to be connected to the assumption of symmetry. If we relax this assumption the DW values rise to acceptable levels (1.30 – 2.00). This indicates that the symmetry assumption is invalid. In fact, a chi-square test leads to a rejection of the symmetry hypothesis. A comparison between the

estimation methods, IZEF and 3SLS, shows that the differences are small. The DW values are about the same, and there is no clear evidence that the 3SLS estimates are more efficient, in terms of higher t-ratios, than the IZEF estimates.

For forestry, the DW values are higher, although they still lie in the inconclusive range. Most of the parameter estimates of the sawtimber demand equation are significantly different from zero, but, again, precision may be overestimated due to serial correlation. The results are similar across estimation methods.

Given these parameter estimates we derive the equilibrium demand curve for chlorine. This is done by solving for the equilibrium prices for pulpwood and sawtimber in terms of all exogenous variables, and then substituting back into the ordinary demand function for chlorine. However, from proposition 1 it is clear that the gain in calculating the equilibrium demand curve, in comparison to the ordinary demand curve, can be evaluated through the ordinary demand and supply elasticities. Thus, we will proceed with a presentation of the demand and supply elasticities in table 1. We have chosen to evaluate all elasticities at the mean values for all variables. As expected, for the pulp industry all own-price elasticities of demand are negative and all own-price elasticities of supply are positive. Another interesting result is the small magnitude, -0.01, of the cross-price elasticity of pulpwood demand with respect to the chlorine price (ε_{vc}). This implies that a change in the chlorine price has a very small effect on pulpwood demand.

To summarize, we have found that all output supply functions have positive own-price elasticities, and all input demand functions have negative own-price elasticities. The demand elasticities for the pulp industry are all less than one, implying that an increase in the price of a specific input will decrease the use of it while its cost share will increase.

Using proposition 1, we see that the difference between the partial and general equilibrium deadweight loss will be rather small. The reason is the small magnitudes of ε_{cv} and, especially, ε_{vc}. A small ε_{vc} implies that ε_{sc}^* is small because of the low elasticity of sawtimber demand. In general, however, the elasticities are not constant, which implies that the integral in proposition 1 becomes very complicated for large changes in the chlorine tax.

Standard procedures to calculate standard er-

162   *February 1996*

Amer. J. Agr. Econ.

Table 1. Output Supply and Input Demand Price Elasticities, Evaluated at the Mean Values of the Variables

| | Pulp Industry | | | | |
	Pulp	Wood	Labor	Energy	Chlorine
Pulp	0.19	−0.14	−0.03	−0.005	−0.008
Wood	0.42	−0.51	0.09	0.002	−0.01
Labor	0.35	0.36	−0.70	−0.004	−0.008
Energy	0.20	0.02	−0.01	−0.24	0.03
Chlorine	0.76	−0.41	−0.07	0.08	−0.35

| | Forestry | | |
	Pulpwood	Sawtimber	Labor
Pulpwood	0.26	−0.39	0.13
Sawtimber	−0.48	0.007	0.32

| | Sawmill Industry | | | |
	Lumber	Sawtimber	Labor	Energy
Sawtimber	0.56	−0.76	0.60	−0.39

rors for the elasticities do not apply, since the elasticities are functions of two endogenous right-hand side variables (w_{pv} and w_{sv}). Nevertheless, if the chlorine demand elasticity is significantly different from zero, it suggests that the prevailing regulations (per unit of output) on chlorine emissions are not binding. We expect that the regulatory constraint entering the profit function is highly correlated with production capacity. If chlorine demand is independent of the chlorine price, this implies that chlorine demand is determined solely by the constraint (capacity). To perform the test empirically, we compare the unrestricted model with the restricted one by using a chi-square statistic. The chi-square test statistics are 35.15 and 19.36 for the IZEF and 3SLS models, respectively. This implies that the hypothesis that the chlorine demand elasticity is zero can be rejected. This, in turn, is an indication that the regulations on chlorine emissions are not binding.

Impact of a Chlorine Tax on the Swedish Forest Sector

From the above discussion it should be clear that the difference between the single-market and multimarket welfare measure should be small. To test this proposition, we proceed in the following way. First, the estimated param-

eters are used to calculate the reduced form for the equilibrium pulpwood price which, in turn, is plugged into the demand equation for chlorine. The resulting equilibrium demand function for chlorine is then used to evaluate our welfare measure $\Delta IR\Pi$. The partial welfare measure is calculated using the ordinary demand curve. The change in profit is evaluated for 1988. The change of the tax is given by the 5 SEK/kg chlorine tax suggested by the Swedish Commission of Environmental Charges (SOU 1989). In this case, the quasi-rent loss is 412.5 million SEK for the pulp industry.

When we allow for repercussions in the roundwood market, the loss in the entire forest sector is approximately 418.9 million SEK. This confirms that the partial equilibrium estimate, in this case, is a good approximation to the "true" multimarket estimate. The similarity between the two measures implies that the ordinary demand curve and the equilibrium demand curve are very similar. An explanation of this result is, as pointed out earlier, the low magnitude of the cross-price elasticity of pulpwood demand with respect to the chlorine price, −0.01. The low elasticity can, in turn, be explained by a small cost share for the chlorine input, in combination with a small elasticity of substitution between wood and chlorine.

To obtain an estimate of the net loss for society, we subtract the revenue from the chlorine

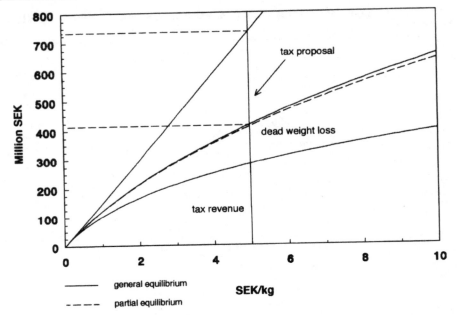

Figure 1. The loss function

tax, approximately 285 million SEK, which means that the deadweight loss is approximately 134 million SEK.

Equilibrium prices of pulpwood and sawtimber are both reduced, suggesting that the sawmills make slightly higher profits because they are able to pay a lower price for sawtimber. The equilibrium volumes of sawtimber rise, while the equilibrium volume of pulpwood falls. Thus, forest owners' profits will decrease due to the direct effect (the shift of the pulpwood demand curve), but will increase due to the indirect effect (the shift of the supply curves for pulpwood and sawtimber). It can be shown, using a revealed preference argument, that the net effect on the forest owners is negative, since the price of both pulpwood and sawtimber are lower after the introduction of a tax on chlorine. It should be pointed out, however, that this effect is very small due to the small changes in prices and volumes. Finally, we note, according to the model, that the tax would have reduced the consumption of chlorine input by 62%.

Our empirical findings suggest that the partial equilibrium model can serve as a useful approximation to the more general multimarket model. The partial model, therefore, can be

used to approximate the welfare effects of different environmental goals. To illustrate this, we define the following functions:

$$(26) \quad F(\tau) = \int_0^\tau X_{pc}\big[(w_{pc}^0 + s), \cdot\big] ds$$

$$(27) \quad T(\tau) = \tau \cdot \left\{ X_{pc}\big[(w_{pc}^0 + \tau), \cdot\big] \right\}.$$

The function F defines the loss in consumer surplus as a function of the tax rate, while T is the corresponding tax revenue function. In a similar way, we can define the corresponding multimarket functions $F^*(\tau)$ and $T^*(\tau)$. It is now easy to investigate how different tax rates affect the consumer surplus, the tax revenue, and the difference between these two, the dead weight loss. An illustration is provided in figure 1 which summarizes the deadweight loss, loss in profit, and tax revenue, as a function of the tax, for our two models. It also includes the loss in profit claimed by representatives of the pulp industry (henceforth denoted the industry measure, represented by the straight line in figure

164   *February 1996*

Amer. J. Agr. Econ.

1) see SOU (1989, p. 134). The latter is calculated as the tax times the pretax level of chlorine consumption; i.e., the calculations are
based on a vertical demand curve for chlorine.
Since figure 1 includes the welfare effects for a
large range of taxes, it may be useful for policy
purposes. For example, in the figure we can see
the well-known result that, for small changes in
the tax rate, the industry measure of the loss is
a good approximation of the "true" loss. However, for large changes the pulp industry will
substitute away from chlorine, making the industry measure a bad approximation. It is also
possible to include the effects on emissions by
adjoining a function that maps the emissions of
chlorine from different tax rates. The emission
functions, however, need to be estimated and
will be a focus for future research.

Conclusions

Economists often resort to partial equilibrium
analyses because they are much simpler analytically and empirically to handle. In this paper we give a constructive way to shed light on
the appropriateness of a partial equilibrium
model for a particular application. The suggested framework is particularly useful when it
is easy to identify a sector in the economy that
is more or less autonomous, i.e., when the price
repercussions will, to a large extent, stay within
the sector. The main contribution of the paper is
to develop a simple rule of thumb to evaluate
the welfare impact of taxes. If certain key parameters are small in magnitude, then a partial
equilibrium model is a good approximation of
the "true general equilibrium" model.

Our model can be improved in various directions. One such improvement is the introduction of dynamics into the model. For example,
it is not hard to believe that the substitution
possibilities are greater between chlorine and
capital than between chlorine and other inputs.
Thus, in the long run, when capital is variable,
one might expect elasticities which are considerably larger in magnitude. The suggested approach can be extended in a natural way to address the impacts of unilateral versus multilat-
eral environmental policy, competitiveness issues, and so on. These issues can be addressed
by adding, for example, the Finnish forest sector and a western European demand curve for
pulp to our model [compare equation (16)]. See
Brännlund and Kriström (1994a). We believe
that our approach can be a useful complement,

and sometimes a substitute, to a full general
equilibrium model. Because there are still exogenous prices in our model, we do not have a
full general equilibrium model. We pay the
price of realism in our model in order to gain
transparency. There are no "black boxes"; all
results are intuitively easy to explain. Perhaps
the most useful aspect of our analysis is that it
suggests when a partial equilibrium model is a
sufficiently good approximation. Thus, while
our application is specific to a particular policy
problem, the approach has wide applicability.

[Received May 1994;
final revision received October 1995.]

References

Bergman, L. "Tillväxt och miljö—en studie av
    målkonflikter" (Environment and growth, a
    study of conflicting goals). *Bilaga 9 till
    Långtidsutredningen* (Supplement number 9 to
    the Medium Term Survey of Sweden). Treasury
    of Sweden, 1990, in Swedish.
Berndt, E.R. *The Practice of Econometrics, Classic
    and Contemporary.* Reading MA: Addison-
    Wesley Publishing Company, 1990.
Brännlund, R. *The Swedish Roundwood Market; An
    Econometric Analysis.* The Swedish University
    of Agricultural Sciences, Department of Forest
    Economics Report 82, 1988.
Brännlund, R., and B. Kriström. "Assessing the Im-
    pact of Environmental Charges: A Partial Gen-
    eral Equilibrium Model of The Forest Sector."
    Resour. and Environ. Econ. 3(June 1993):297–
    312.
____. "Taxing Pollution in an Open Economy—An
    Empirical Analysis." Paper presented at confer-
    ence on "What is Determining Global Competi-
    tiveness in Pulp and Paper: Green Markets,
    Regulation, Technology or Resources?" Univer-
    sity of Washington, 12–14 September 1994a.
____. "Welfare Measurement in Single and
    Multimarket Models: Theory and Applications,"
    Working Paper #206, Swedish University of
    Agricultural Sciences, Department of Forest
    Economics, 1994b.
Hultkrantz, L. "The Cost of Edible Fish—Effects on
    the Swedish and Finnish Forest Industries from
    the Imposition of Effluent Charges on Chlorine
    Residuals in Sweden." *J. Environ. Manage.*
    32(March 1991):145–64.
Johnson, H.G. "The Cost of Protection and the Sci-
    entific Tariff." *J. Polit. Econ.* 68(August
    1960):327–45.

Jørgenson, D.W., and P.J. Wilcoxen. *Reducing U.S. Carbon Dioxide Emissions: The Cost of Different Goals.* Unpublished, Dept. of Econ., Harvard University, 1990.

Just, R.E., D.L. Hueth, and A. Schmitz. *Applied Welfare Economics and Public Policy.* New York: Prentice-Hall, 1982.

Kokoski, M.F., and V.K. Smith. "A General Equilibrium Analysis of Partial Equilibrium Welfare Measures: The Case of Climate Change." *Amer. Econ. Rev.* 77(June 1987):331–41.

Kotlikoff, L.J., and L.H. Summers. "Tax Incidence." *Handbook of Public Economics,* vol. 2. A.J.

Auerbach and M. Feldstein, eds. Amsterdam: North-Holland, 1987.

Mishan, E.J. "What is Producer Surplus?" *Amer. Econ. Rev.* 58(December 1968):1269–82.

Sweden, Kingdom of, Ministry of Environment (SOU). *Sätt värde på miljön! Miljöavgifter och andra ekonomiska styrmedel.* Report from the Environmental Charge Commission, Vol. 59, Stockholm, Sweden, 1990.

___. *Sätt värde på miljön! Miljöavgifter på svavel och klor. Betänkande av miljöavgiftsutredningen* Report from the Environmental Charge Commission, Vol. 21, Stockholm, Sweden, 1989.

Appendix

Estimation Results

Table A.1. Estimates of T-ratios for the Restricted Profit Functions

	Pulp	Wood	Labor	Energy	Chlorine	Capital	DW
			Pulp Industry				
Pulp	3.97	−4.74	−3.08	−2.55	−4.17	14.87	0.67
	(4.00)	(−4.59)	(−1.30)	(−3.10)	(−3.46)	(13.39)	(0.67)
Wood		1.60	4.60	0.39	−2.97	−1.56	1.17
		(1.10)	(5.17)	(−1.02)	(−2.88)	(−2.47)	(1.14)
Labor			−1.58	−0.17	−0.52	−1.15	0.27
			(−1.99)	(−0.66)	(−1.06)	(0.10)	(0.33)
Energy				−1.90	0.75	7.00	1.72
				(−1.28)	(1.18)	(6.23)	(1.77)
Chlorine					−0.53	2.30	0.28
					(−0.21)	(3.13)	(0.34)

	Pulpwood	Sawtimber	Labor	Capital	DW
		Forestry			
Pulpwood	1.52	−3.31	1.35	1.68	1.41
	(0.81)	(−1.08)	(0.16)	(1.35)	(1.23)
Sawtimber		1.17	4.49	1.78	1.00
		(1.48)	(5.23)	(4.04)	(0.81)

	Lumber	Sawtimber	Labor	Energy	DW	R^2
		Sawmill Industry				
Sawtimber	2.71	−1.92	6.07	−3.05	1.07	0.72
	(−0.32)	(2.55)	(4.88)	(0.05)	(0.75)	

Note: 3SLS estimates are in parenthesis.

[28]

JOURNAL OF ENVIRONMENTAL ECONOMICS AND MANAGEMENT **29**, S-64–S-77 (1995)

Pollution Taxes and Revenue Recycling*

IAN W. H. PARRY

Resources for the Future, 1616 P Street NW, Washington DC 20036

Received May 10, 1994; revised July 22, 1994

Discussions of environmental policy and the tax system have emphasized the value of pollution tax revenues, which can be used to reduce other tax distortions in the economy. However by raising private marginal production costs, environmental taxes also tend to reduce GDP and exacerbate the welfare costs of conventional taxes. For environmental taxes in consumption goods industries, the net welfare change from these two effects is negative unless this good is a relatively weak substitute for leisure. An estimate for the optimal pollution tax with full revenue recycling is 63 to 78% of marginal environmental damages. © 1995 Academic Press, Inc.

1. INTRODUCTION

This paper examines two important policy questions raised by the interaction of environmental taxes with the rest of the tax system. First, is the welfare gain and hence the case for introducing an environmental tax, greater or less than that implied by a partial equilibrium analysis? Second, what is the optimal level of environmental taxation in second-best economies?

To address these questions two effects need to be considered, which will be called the "revenue effect" (RE) and the "interdependency effect (IE). The RE refers to the welfare gain from using environmental tax revenues to cut distortionary taxes, relative to the case where revenues are returned lump-sum (and have no efficiency consequences).[1] Thus it has been claimed that allowing for interactions with the tax system raises the welfare gain from environmental taxes, the so-called "double dividend hypothesis" (see Oates [15]. Repetto *et al.* [19], Pearce, [18], Terkla [22]).[2] One implication is that environmental taxes would still be worthwhile, even if the environmental benefits were very small.

Furthermore, Lee and Misiolek [12] incorporated the RE in the familiar partial equilibrium analysis of externalities, and showed that the optimal pollution tax is greater (less) than marginal environmental damages (MED) when the pollution tax Laffer curve is upward- (downward-) sloping. Thus Nordhaus [14] calculated that the optimal tax on carbon in response to the possibility of future global warming

---

* I am grateful to Karen Palmer and two anonymous referees for very helpful comments.

[1] The cases when pollution tax revenues are used to finance additional public spending, or reduced borrowing, are not considered here.

[2] Two other meanings have been attached to the double dividend hypothesis, one weaker, the other stronger, than above. The weak form just asserts that there is a benefit from using revenues to cut other distortionary taxes, relative to lump-sum replacement, which is always valid. The strong form asserts that not only is there a net gain from interactions with the tax system, but that this exceeds the cost of pollution abatement. For a good discussion of these issues see Goulder [9].

0095-0696/95 $12.00

would rise from a modest $5 per ton to $59 per ton, when the value of tax revenues is taken into account—more than a tenfold increase!

The crucial problem with all of this is that the IE is ignored. This refers to the likely exacerbation of preexisting tax distortions caused by the environmental tax. There are large tax wedges in the labor and capital markets, and the efficiency and revenue raised from these markets is reduced, to the extent that environmental taxes discourage employment and investment. Determining the net effect of the RE and IE in the aggregate and at the margin answers the two questions above. The focus here will be on (permanent) environmental taxes in consumption goods industries, and therefore interactions with the capital market are not relevant.

The next section examines environmental taxes on final goods. When pollution taxes substitute for labor tax revenues, and the polluting commodity is an average substitute for leisure, then the benefit from the RE is a fraction of the cost from the IE, where this fraction is the ratio of the post to pretax level of output. Indeed the RE could only outweigh the IE and the double dividend hypothesis could only be correct when the polluting commodity is a sufficiently weaker than average substitute for leisure. However, the pollution tax is still potentially welfare-improving, and the optimal level is on the order of 63% of MED.

Section 3 extends this analysis to allow for taxes on polluting inputs. To the extent that there is substitution in production, both the IE and RE are relatively weaker. However the double dividend hypothesis is still likely to fail. A best estimate for the optimal pollution tax in this case is 63 to 78% of MED.

These theoretical results are consistent with contribution in the optimal commodity tax literature. Bovenberg and de Mooij [2, 3] have recently shown that the existence of a labor tax reduces the welfare gain from a pollution tax (on both final and intermediate goods) and that the optimal pollution tax is less than MED, given an exogenous revenue requirement.[3] However, I feel that the diagrammatic approach used below, and the decomposition of the RE and IE, provides a more simple and intuitive treatment of the issues (rather than lumping the RE and IE together in one optimization model). Moreover, the analysis in Bovenberg and de Mooij [2, 3] is a little restrictive, because they assume that output from the polluting sector is an average substitute for leisure, which guarantees that the IE exceeds the RE in the aggregate and at the margin. The empirical results below are similar to those from the computable general equilibrium model used by Bovenberg and Goulder [4], which incorporates a detailed treatment of the U.S. tax system. They found that the optimal tax on carbon is 68% of MED (for an environmental damage of $25 per ton), when carbon tax revenues are used to cut the rate of personal income tax.[4]

Section 4 concludes.

2. ENVIRONMENTAL TAXES ON FINAL COMMODITIES

This section examines environmental taxes on final commodities, allowing for interactions with the labor market. The polluting industry is assumed to produce a consumption good, and therefore taxes on this good will have no spillover effects in

---

[3] See also Sandmo [20], Ng [13], and Bovenberg and van der Ploeg [5].

[4] In some further analysis, Goulder [10] found that the welfare gains from recycling revenues are well below the costs (gross of environmental benefits) of taxes on carbon, gasoline, and fuels.

the capital market (so long as they are permanent rather than transitory), hence capital can be excluded from the analysis. Also, any effect the tax may have on environmental R & D is ignored.[5] The economy is assumed to produce $X_1 \ldots X_K$ market commodities, where the production of X_j $(1 \leq j \leq K)$ involves the discharge of waste emissions which harm the environment, while all other commodities are environmentally clean.[6] For simplicity the environmental damage function is given by cX_j, where $c > 0$, although allowing for convex damages would be straightforward, and there is no internalization of environmental damages in the absence of policy intervention.[7] Each market is assumed to be competitive, which seems reasonable from Oates and Strassmann [16], who suggested that allowing for imperfect competition is unlikely to have much empirical effect on environmental policy analysis, because the markup over competitive prices in industries with monopoly power is typically small. Also, distortions caused by nonlabor taxes are ignored, since they are relatively much less important.[8] Finally, marginal costs are assumed to be constant in each market—a conventional assumption in optimal tax exercises, which is less restrictive than it may sound.[9]

Without loss of generality, the units of each commodity and labor can be defined such that their pretax prices are unity. If there is a proportional tax of m on labor income, then the aggregate household budget constraint can be written[10]

$$\sum_{i=1}^{K} X_i + (1 - m)N = (1 - m)T + G, \qquad (1)$$

where N is leisure time, T is the household time endowment, or full income, and $T - N$ is labor supply. The labor tax is therefore equivalent to a tax on full income (which is not distortionary) plus a subsidy to leisure. G is an exogenous lump-sum transfer from the government, and for simplicity all revenues are assumed to be returned in such transfers, therefore $G = m(T - N)$.

The equilibrium in the only two distorted markets in the economy are shown in Fig. 1. In the upper panel, D_j and S_j are the demand and supply for X_j, and the initial output is X_j^0, where the demand and supply prices are equal. The marginal social cost curve is $S_j + c$. In the lower panel, D_N^0 and S_N are the demand and supply of leisure, which are, respectively, the mirror image of the supply of labor

[5] For a discussion of how pollution taxes might affect the incentive to invent cleaner technologies, see Parry [17].

[6] Obviously if there were important interactions between X_j and other polluting markets, these should be taken into account.

[7] This implies that (a) emitters do not bear any of the costs of their own pollution, (b) there is no scope for Coase–type [8] bargaining between polluters and victims, and (c) there is no altruism for the environment on behalf of consumers or producers. Alternatively, cX_j can be interpreted as that component of pollution damages which is not internalized by these factors.

[8] Revenues from excise taxes and customs duties are approximately 7% of Federal labor tax revenues (see "The Economic Report of the President" (1994)). State and local governments mainly rely on uniform sales taxes (which are approximately equivalent to labor taxes) and property taxes (which are a tax on capital).

[9] It would be straightforward to allow for upward-sloping marginal costs (see Harberger [11]). The Slutsky compensated price terms used below would be replaced by an analogous reduced-form coefficient, which shows how output in a particular market responds to changes in taxes, when there are potential interdependencies in the demand and supply for all goods.

[10] Allowing for nonproportional labor taxes would not affect the IE discussed below, or the amount of pollution tax revenues raised.

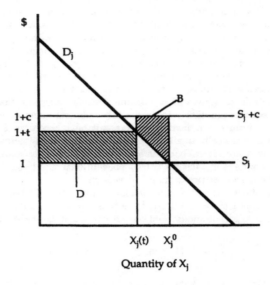

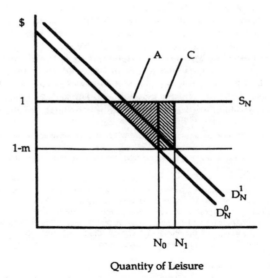

FIG. 1. The welfare effects of environmental taxes.

IAN W. H. PARRY

and the value marginal product of labor (ignore D_N^1 for the moment). The leisure subsidy drives a wedge of m between the supply and demand price of leisure, and the initial quantity of leisure is N_0. All the demand and supply curves in Fig. 1 are compensated, and the welfare cost of the leisure market distortion is therefore area A.

The Welfare Effects of Environmental Taxes

Suppose a specific tax of $t \le c$ is now imposed on X_j, and the additional revenues are used to reduce the labor tax, therefore disposable income is constant. The resulting welfare change consists of the following three components:

(i) The gain from the reduction in output to $X_j(t)$, trapezoid B in Fig. 1. Assuming the demand curve is linear over the relevant range (which is a reasonable approximation at least for modest levels of taxation), this equals a rectangle with area $(c - t)(X_j^0 - X_j(t))$, plus a triangle with area $t(X_j^0 - X_j(t))/2$, where $X_j^0 - X_j(t) = -(dX_j/dp_j)t$ (p_j is the price of X_j). This gives

$$tX_j^0 \eta_{jj}\left\{c - \frac{t}{2}\right\},\tag{2}$$

where $\eta_{jj} = -(dX_j/dp_j)/X_j^0$ is the (magnitude of the) compensated own-price elasticity of demand for X_j evaluated at X_j^0. If $t = c$, the expression in (2) is just the well-known Harberger triangle. For later, it is helpful to note that $t\eta_{jj} = (X_j^0 - X_j(t))/X_j^0$ or

$$t\eta_{jj} = 1 - \frac{X_j(t)}{X_j^0}.\tag{3}$$

(ii) The welfare loss from the exacerbation of the leisure market distortion, when X_j and leisure are substitutes (the IE). Imposing the pollution tax shifts up the private marginal cost and hence the demand price for X_j, and in general this will shift out the demand for leisure.[11] Put another way, the labor supply curve shifts up, since the bundle of goods that a given nominal wage can purchase is smaller. In the lower panel in Fig. 1 the new leisure demand curve is shown as D_N^1, and leisure increases by $N_1 - N_0 = (dN/dp_j)t$ (assuming the cross-price term dN/dp_j is constant over the relevant range). Since the marginal social cost exceeds marginal benefit by m for each of these units, the welfare loss from the increase in leisure, rectangle C, is[12]

$$m\frac{dN}{dp_j}t.\tag{4}$$

The formulas in (2) and (4) are just a straightforward application of the more general formula for the welfare effect of a set of market distortions derived in Harberger [11].

---

[11] It is possible that X_j and leisure are complements and the demand for leisure will shift the other way. However this is only applicable to a narrow range of goods (such as skis and video cassette recorders) and will be ignored below.

[12] Figure 1 is not drawn to scale. The area of B and C will typically be very small relative to that of A.

Rectangle C is also the reduction in labor tax revenues indirectly caused by the environmental tax. The efficiency value per dollar of changes in aggregate tax revenues will be denoted by V (which is defined below). From the Slutsky symmetry property,

$$\frac{dN}{dp_j} = \frac{dX_j}{dw} \tag{5}$$

that is, the effect on leisure from a unit increase in the price of X_j equals the effect on X_j from a unit increase in the price of leisure (where $w = 1 - m$ is the price of leisure or net of tax wage). Therefore, using (4) and (5), and multiplying and dividing by $(1 - m)X_j^0$, the total welfare loss from the IE (rectangle C multiplied by $(1 + V)$) is

$$(1 + V)\frac{m}{1 - m} tX_j^0 \eta_{jN}, \tag{6}$$

where $\eta_{jN} = (dX_j/dw)(1 - m)/X_j^0$ is the compensated elasticity of demand for X_j with respect to the price of leisure, evaluated at X_j^0.

(iii) The welfare gain from the pollution tax revenues raised (the RE). This is just the product of V and rectangle D in Fig. 1, which is

$$VtX_j(t). \tag{7}$$

Finally, when the price of leisure is increased, the demand for X_j will shift out. Since marginal social cost exceeds marginal benefit by $c - t$ in this market, this cause a welfare loss of

$$(c - t)\frac{dX_j}{dW} \Delta m, \tag{8}$$

where Δm is the reduction in labor tax. However, this feedback effect is relatively small so long as the proportionate reduction in labor tax is small (substituting (5) in (8) and comparing with (4)), and will be ignored in the analysis below.

When pollution tax revenues are used to reduce labor taxes, the appropriate formula for V is the "marginal welfare cost" of labor tax revenues. This is the addition to total welfare cost from a marginal increase in labor tax (or leisure subsidy), $-m(dN/dw)$, divided by the resulting increase in revenue, $(T - N) + m(dN/dw)$. Therefore

$$V = \frac{(m/1 - m)\epsilon}{1 - (m/1 - m)\epsilon}, \tag{9}$$

where $\epsilon = -(dN/dw)(1 - m)/(T - N)$ is the compensated labor supply elasticity, evaluated at the net of tax wage.[13] It is assumed that pollution tax revenues are small relative to aggregate labor tax revenues, hence the change in m and leisure are very small, and V can be taken as constant.

[13] This is essentially the same formula that was used by Browning [6] to estimate the marginal welfare cost of labor taxation. Browning [6] also suggests that allowing for a downward-sloping demand for labor (upward sloping supply of leisure) does not have much effect on estimates of V.

IAN W. H. PARRY

Rearranging (9) in terms of $m/(1-m)$ and substituting in (6), the cost of the IE can be expressed as

$$V t X_j^0 \frac{\eta_{jN}}{\epsilon}. \tag{10}$$

Unfortunately estimates of η_{jN} are not generally available for particular commodities, and therefore the IE cannot be calculated directly. However, a central estimate can be obtained when X_j is an average substitute for leisure at the pretax price. In this case

$$\eta_{jN} = \epsilon. \tag{11}$$

This follows because if labor supply increases by $\lambda\%$ in response to a compensated 1% increase in real wages, then aggregate consumption and hence average consumption must increase by $\lambda\%$.[15]

From (7) and (10), the benefit from the RE relative to the cost from the IE is simply

$$\frac{X_j(t)}{X_j^0} \frac{\epsilon}{\eta_{jN}}. \tag{12}$$

Therefore, when condition (11) holds, the benefit from the RE is a fraction of the cost of the IE, where this fraction is the ratio of the post- to pretax level of output. Only if X_j was a relatively weak substitute for leisure (that is, $\eta_{jN} < \epsilon(X_j(t)/X_j^0)$) could the RE exceed the IE and the double dividend hypothesis be correct.

The Optimal Environmental Tax

Differentiating (10) with respect to (the reduction in) X_j, the marginal cost from the IE is

$$MC_{IE} = \frac{V}{\eta_{hj}} \frac{\eta_{jN}}{\epsilon}, \tag{13}$$

[14] Deleted in proof.

[15] Differentiating the budget constraint in Eq. (1) with respect to the price of leisure, holding disposable income constant (which requires a compensation of N plus the recycling of extra tax revenues, $dG/dw = -m(dN/dw)$), gives

$$\sum_{i=1}^{K} \frac{dX_i}{dw} + \frac{dN}{dw} = 0.$$

Multiplying this equation by $(1-m)$ gives

$$\sum_{i=1}^{K} X_i \eta_{iN} = (T-N)\epsilon,$$

where $\eta_{iN} = (dX_i/dw)(1-m)/X_i$ is the compensated elasticity of demand for X_i with respect to the price of leisure. When all goods are equal substitutes for leisure, η_{iN} is constant across goods and equal to ϵ, since the aggregate value of consumption equals gross income.

(since $dX_j/dt = dX_j/dp_j$), which is a constant (all elasticities are defined at specific points). Differentiating (7) with respect to (the reduction in) X_j, the marginal benefit from the RE is

$$MB_{RE} = V\left\{\frac{1}{\eta_{jj}}\frac{X_j(t)}{X_j^0} - t\right\}. \tag{14}$$

This is the product of V and the marginal pollution tax revenue, which is declining because the tax base $(X_j(t))$ shrinks with abatement, and the revenue loss (t) from marginal reductions in X_j is increasing.

The upper panel in Fig. 2 shows the MC_{IE} and MB_{RE} curves as a function of $X_j^0 - X_j(t)$, when condition (11) holds, where each has the same intercept (substituting $t = 0$ in Eq. (14)). If X_j was a relatively strong (weak) substitute for leisure, the MC_{IE} curve would be higher (lower) and, ignoring the externality, it would be optimal to subsidize (tax) X_j relative to other goods.[16] In the lower panel of Fig. 2, the $D_j - S_j$ curve is the marginal cost of reducing X_j, ignoring interactions with the tax system, which is just the gap between D_j and S_j in Fig. 1, or t. The Pigouvian tax would be $t' = c$, and the optimal level of abatement $X_j^0 - X_j(t')$. Adding on the net marginal cost from the IE and RE reduces the optimal level of abatement to $X_j^0 - X_j(t^*)$, and the optimal tax t^* is defined by

$$c = t^* + MC_{IE} - MB_{RE}. \tag{15}$$

Substituting (13) and (14) into (15) and using (3) gives

$$\bar{t}^* = \frac{1 + (V/c\eta_{jj})\{1 - (\eta_{jN}/\epsilon)\}}{1 + 2V}, \tag{16a}$$

where $\bar{t}^* = t^*/c$ denotes the optimal tax as a proportion of MED. When condition (11) holds, this simplifies to

$$\bar{t}^* = \frac{1}{1 + 2V} \tag{16b}$$

in which case the optimal tax is less than MED.[17] Estimates of the economy-wide compensated labor supply elasticity typically lie within a range of 0.2 to 0.4, while the (marginal) rate of tax on labor income, which depends on the rate of personal income tax, social security tax, and benefit withdrawal as income rises, is around 0.38 to 0.48 (see Browning [6]). From Eq. (9), this gives a median estimate for V $(\epsilon = 0.3, m = 0.43)$ of 0.29, with lower and upper bounds of 0.14 and 0.59.[18]

---

[16] This is essentially the basic result from the optimal commodity tax literature (see, for example, Sandmo [21]).

[17] In Bovenberg and de Mooij [2, 3], environmental quality is treated as a public good which is separable from consumption and leisure in the utility function. The bottom line of this assumption is that a reduction in pollution leads to a negative income effect and a reduction in leisure, which dampens, though not overturns, their conclusion that the optimal environmental tax is less than MED. Whether it is appropriate to incorporate such income effects (usually they are excluded) is a difficult issue which has yet to be resolved.

[18] The above estimates are replicated from the second row in the lower half of Table 2 in Browning [6]. Results from computable general equilibrium models suggest that the marginal welfare cost of taxation lies between 10 and 60 cents per dollar (see for example Ballard *et al.* [1]).

IAN W. H. PARRY

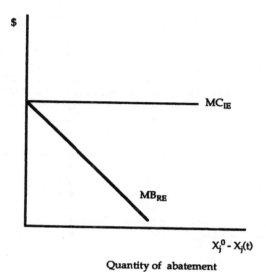

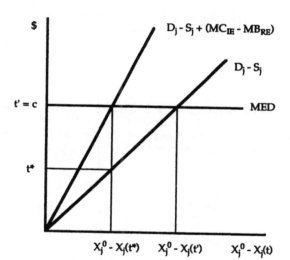

FIG. 2. The optimal environmental tax.

POLLUTION TAXES AND REVENUE RECYCLING   S-73

Table I shows simulations on the formulas in Eq. (16a) and (16b), under different assumptions about the degree of substitution with leisure, V, and $c\eta_{jj}$. This latter term is the proportionate reduction if X_j under a Pigouvian tax (substituting $t = c$ in Eq. (3)). The best estimate for the optimal pollution tax is 63% of MED, which is when X_j is an average substitute for leisure (condition (11) holds) and $V = 0.29$. This estimate is somewhat sensitive to V, and the lower and upper bounds are 46 and 78%, respectively (when (11) holds). The optimal tax is also sensitive to the degree of substitution with leisure and rises to 86–157% of MED if η_{jN} is 50% lower than average, and falls to 0–41% of MED when η_{jN} is 50% higher than average (assuming $V = 0.3$ and $c\eta_{jj}$ lies between 0.1 and 0.4).

3. ENVIRONMENTAL TAXES ON INTERMEDIATE GOODS

Sources of pollution are usually more directly related to inputs in the production process (such as chemicals and fuels) than final consumption goods. Therefore this section extends the previous analysis to allow for environmental taxes on an intermediate good. This good is denoted Z, is used in the production of X_j, and has a constant marginal production cost of unity. The environmental damage function is cZ. All other assumptions from the previous section are maintained, and there is no tax on X_j.

The Welfare Effects of Environmental Taxes on Intermediate Goods

The welfare change from imposing a specific tax of $u \leq c$ on Z consists of the following three components, which are analogous to those in (i) to (iii) above:
(i') The trapezoid gain in the Z market, which has area

$$uZ_0\eta_{ZZ}\left\{c - \frac{u}{2}\right\}, \tag{2'}$$

where $\eta_{ZZ} = -(dZ/dp_Z)/Z_0$ is the (magnitude of the) unconditional own-price elasticity of demand for Z, evaluated at Z_0 (p_Z is the price of Z). This elasticity reflects the fall in demand for Z from both the reduction in X_j (the output effect) and the substitution of other factors for Z in production (the substitution effect).

TABLE I

The Optimal Pollution Tax (as a Proportion of MED)

V	$c\eta_{jj}$	$\eta_j N/\epsilon$		
		0.5	1	1.5
0.14	0.1	1.33	0.78	0.23
	0.4	0.92	0.78	0.64
0.29	0.1	1.57	0.63	0
	0.4	0.86	0.63	0.41
0.59	0.1	1.79	0.46	0
	0.4	0.79	0.46	0.13

IAN W. H. PARRY

As before

$$u\eta_{ZZ} = 1 - \frac{Z(u)}{Z_0}. \tag{3'}$$

(ii') The welfare loss from the IE, when X_j and leisure are substitutes, which (including the value of reduced labor tax revenues) is given by

$$(1 + V)m\frac{\Delta N}{\Delta u}, \tag{17}$$

where $\Delta N/\Delta u$ is the increase in leisure induced by the tax. This can be broken down into

$$\frac{\Delta N}{\Delta u} = \frac{dN}{dp_j}\frac{\Delta p_j}{\Delta u} \tag{18}$$

where $\Delta p_j/\Delta u$ is the increase in price, or marginal cost, of X_j caused by the input tax. Substituting (5) and (18) into (17) and multiplying and dividing by $(1 - m)X_j^0$ gives

$$(1 + V)\frac{m}{1 - m}\frac{\Delta p_j}{\Delta u}X_j^0\eta_{jN}. \tag{6'}$$

(iii') The welfare gain from the RE, which is

$$VuZ(u). \tag{7'}$$

Using a second-order Taylor series expansion, the increase in price of X_j is the product of u and the average of the pre- and posttax ratio of Z to X_j, that is,

$$\frac{\Delta p_j}{\Delta u} = \frac{u}{2}\{R_0 + R(u)\}, \tag{19}$$

where the input to output ratio $R(u)$ is

$$R(u) = \frac{Z_0 + u(dZ^c/dp_Z)}{x_j^0} \tag{20}$$

and dZ^c/dp_Z is the slope of the conditional (output constant) factor demand curve.[19] Therefore, to the extent there is substitution in production ($dZ^c/dp_Z < 0$), R declines with the imposition of the environmental tax.

[19] From a second-order Taylor series expansion, the increase in total cost (C) of producing X_j following an increase of u in the price of input Z is

$$u\frac{dC}{dp_Z} + \frac{u^2}{2}\frac{d^2C}{dp_Z^2}.$$

Using Shephard's lemma, $dC/dp_Z = Z_0$ and $d^2C/dp_Z^2 = dZ^c/dp_Z$ (see Varian [23], Chapter 3), dividing by X_j^0 to convert to per unit or marginal production costs, and substituting from (20) gives the expression in (19).

From (6'), (9), and (19), the welfare loss from the IE can be expressed as

$$VuZ_0 \frac{\eta_{jN}}{\epsilon} \left\{ 1 - \frac{u\eta_{ZZ}^c}{2} \right\}, \tag{10'}$$

where $\eta_{ZZ}^c = -(dZ^c/dp_Z)/Z_0$ is the (magnitude of the) conditional (or output constant) own-price elasticity of demand for Z, evaluated at Z_0. Hence $u\eta_{ZZ}^c$ is the proportionate reduction in Z due to the substitution effect only. Clearly

$$0 \le \frac{\eta_{ZZ}^c}{\eta_{ZZ}} \le 1, \tag{21}$$

that is, the elasticity of demand for Z when X_j is held fixed cannot exceed that when X_j is variable.

Dividing (7') by (10'), the benefit from the RE relative to the cost of the IE is

$$\frac{Z(u)}{\{1 - (u\eta_{ZZ}^c/2)\}Z_0} \frac{\epsilon}{\eta_{jN}}. \tag{12'}$$

Therefore, when there is no substitution in production ($\eta_{ZZ}^c = 0$) and condition (11) holds, the benefit from the RE equals the cost from the IE multiplied by the ratio of the post- to pretax levels of output of the polluting good, which is the same result as before. For a given reduction in Z, the RE is the same regardless of the strength of the substitution effect relative to the output effect. However, the greater the relative size of the substitution effect (the greater the η_{ZZ}^c/η_{ZZ}), the weaker is the IE, because the impact on the price of X_j, and hence the leisure market spillover, is smaller. Nevertheless, this makes little difference. Using (3'), (21), and (12'), the IE clearly exceeds the RE (when (11) holds).

The Optimal Environmental Tax on an Intermediate Good

Differentiating (10') with respect to (the reduction in) Z gives

$$MC'_{IE} = \frac{V}{\eta_{ZZ}} \frac{\eta_{jN}}{\epsilon} \{1 - u\eta_{ZZ}^c\} \tag{13'}$$

(since $dZ/du = dZ/dp_Z$). Differentiating (8') with respect to (the reduction in) Z gives

$$MB'_{RE} = V \left\{ \frac{1}{\eta_{ZZ}} \frac{Z(u)}{Z_0} - u \right\}. \tag{14'}$$

Again, when condition (11) holds, the marginal cost from the IE and the marginal benefit from the RE, as a function of the reduction in Z, have the same intercept. The MC'_{IE} curve is now downward sloping, because substitution in production reduces the impact of successive increases in tax on the price of X_j (that is, $R(u)$ is declining in Eq. (19)).[20]

---

[20] However, it still lies above the MB'_{RE} curve. This is because the latter is declining due to both the output effect and the substitution effect.

IAN W. H. PARRY

Substituting (13') and (14') into (15), and setting $u = t$, gives the following formula for the optimal pollution tax, when X_j is an average substitute for leisure,

$$\bar{u}^* = \left\{ 1 + V\left(2 - \frac{\eta_{zz}^c}{\eta_{zz}}\right) \right\}^{-1}, \tag{16b'}$$

where $\bar{u} = u/c$. Using (21), the optimal tax lies between 63 and 78% of MED, when $V = 0.29$. Therefore, to the extent there is substitution in production, the optimal tax is higher than in the previous case, although the difference is not very substantial. These results are highly consistent with Bovenberg and Goulder [4], who estimated that the optimal tax on carbon, with full revenue recycling, is 68% of MED.[21]

4. CONCLUSION

This paper has emphasized that the gains from using pollution tax revenues to substitute for labor tax revenues tends to be more than offset by the cost of exacerbating the preexisting distortion in the labor market. Of course the opposite conclusions apply for subsidies which result in increasing the demand for labor. That is, the interdependency effect will tend to work against the revenue effect, hence reducing the welfare cost of financing subsidies. Thus economists may have been overly pessimistic about the cost of subsidies for environmentally cleaner goods, such as public transportation.[22]

REFERENCES

1. C. L. Ballard, J. B. Shoven, and J. Whalley, General equilibrium computations of the marginal welfare costs of taxes in the United States, *Amer. Econom. Rev.* **75**, 128–138 (1985).
2. A. L. Bovenberg and R. A. de Mooij, Environmental levies and distortionary taxation, *Amer. Econom. Rev.* **84**, 1085–1089 (1994).
3. A. L. Bovenberg and R. A. de Mooij, "Environmental Policy in a Small Open Economy with Distortionary Taxes: A General Equilibrium Analysis," Research Center for Economic Policy, Erasmus University, Rotterdam (1993).
4. A. L. Bovenberg and L. H. Goulder, Integrating Environmental and Distortionary Taxes: General Equilibrium Analyses, working paper, Stanford University (1994).
5. A. L. Bovenberg and F. van der Ploeg, Environmental policy, public finance and the labor market in a second best world, *J. Public Econom.* **55**, 349–390 (1994).
6. E. K. Browning, On the marginal welfare cost of taxation, *Amer. Econom. Rev.* **77**, 11–23 (1987).
7. E. K. Browning, Subsidies financed with distorting taxes, *Nat. Tax J.* **45**, 121–134 (1992).
8. R. H. Coase, The problem of social cost, *J. Law Econom.* **3**, 1–44 (1960).
9. L. H. Goulder, Environmental Taxation and the "Double Dividend": A Reader's Guide, working paper, Stanford University (1994).
10. L. H. Goulder, Effects of Carbon Taxes in an Economy with Prior Tax Distortions: An Intertemporal General Equilibrium Analysis, *J. Environ. Econom. Management* **29**, 271–297 (1995).
11. A. C. Harberger, The measurement of waste, *Amer. Econom. Rev.* **54**, 58–76 (1964).

[21] This assumes MED is $25 per ton (see Table 6 in Bovenberg and Goulder [4], the "optimized benchmark" column). The optimal tax rises to 85% of MED when MED is $100 per ton. This is reflecting the significant reduction in m and hence ϵ, when a large amount of carbon tax revenues are recycled, which reduces V and hence $\bar{u}$ in Eq. (16b').

[22] For example Browning [7] provides a thorough discussion of subsidies allowing for the revenue effect, but he ignored the interdependency effect.

POLLUTION TAXES AND REVENUE RECYCLING S-77

12. D. R. Lee and W. S. Misiolek, Substituting pollution taxation for general taxation: Some implications for efficiency in pollution taxation, *J. Environ. Econom. Management* **13**, 338–347 (1986).
13. Y. K. Ng, Optimal corrective taxes or subsidies when revenue raising imposes an excess burden, *Amer. Econom. Rev.* **70**, 744–751 (1980).
14. W. D. Nordhaus, Optimal greenhouse-gas reductions and tax policy in the "DICE" model, *Amer. Econom. Rev.* **83**, 313–317 (1993).
15. W. E. Oates, Pollution charges as a source of public revenues, *in* "Economic Progress and Environmental Concerns" (H. Giersch, Ed.), Springer-Verlag, Berlin (1993).
16. W. E. Oates and D. L. Strassmann, Effluent fees and market structure, *J. Public Econom.* **24**, 29–46 (1984).
17. I. W. H. Parry, Pollution taxes and endogenous technological progress, *Resour. Energy Econom.* **17**, 69–85 (1995).
18. D. W. Pearce, The role of carbon taxes in adjusting to global warming, *Econom. J.* **101**, 938–948 (1991).
19. R. Repetto, R. C. Dower, R. Jenkins, and J. Geoghegan, "Green Fees: How a Tax Shift Can Work for the Environment and the Economy," World Resources Institute, Washington, DC (1992).
20. A. Sandmo, Optimal taxation in the presence of externalities, *Swedish J. Econom.* **77**, 86–98 (1975).
21. A. Sandmo, Optimal taxation—an introduction to the literature, *J. Public Econom.* **6**, 37–54 (1976).
22. D. Terkla, The efficiency value of effluent tax revenues, *J. Environ. Econom. Management* **11**, 107–123 (1984).
23. H. R. Varian, "Microeconomic Analysis," Norton, New York (1984).

C
Welfare Measurement
with Risk and Uncertainty

[29]

PRICE STABILIZATION AND WELFARE [*]

BENTON F. MASSELL

I. INTRODUCTION

Some time ago Frederick Waugh demonstrated that, with a negatively sloped demand curve, assuming consumers to be price-takers, and starting from a given price, consumers gain more from a price decline than they lose from an equal price rise.[1] They thereby gain from price fluctuations, and accordingly lose from price stabilization. More recently, Walter Oi demonstrated that, with a positively sloped supply curve, and assuming producers to be price-takers, producers also gain from price fluctuations and hence lose from price stabilization.[2] Oi was apparently unaware of Waugh's much earlier work. But, having seen Oi's paper, Waugh restated his argument.[3] Unfortunately, in doing so, he stopped short of integrating the consumer and producer sides of the picture.

It is the purpose of the present paper to integrate the Waugh and Oi results and to consider the welfare effects of price stabilization in a model containing both producers and consumers. Following Waugh and Oi, we shall use as a measure of gain: (a) for producers, the expected value of producer surplus; and (b) for consumers, the expected value of consumer surplus. We thus ignore the effect of price stabilization on the variances of the variables involved. One interpretation of our model is that it assumes individuals to be indifferent to risk. A more palatable interpretation is that we assume the commodity under discussion to form a sufficiently small part of

[*] I am indebted to Professor R. M. Parish (University of New England, Armidale, Australia) for contributing actively to the formulation of some of the ideas contained in this paper and for stimulating comments on three earlier drafts. I also wish to thank the referee for helpful suggestions concerning the organization of the paper.

1. Frederick V. Waugh, "Does the Consumer Benefit from Price Instability?", this *Journal*, LVIII (Aug. 1944), 602–14.
2. Walter Oi, "The Desirability of Price Instability Under Perfect Competition," *Econometrica*, Vol. 29 (Jan. 1961), pp. 58–64.
3. Frederick V. Waugh, "Consumer Aspects of Price Instability," *Econometrica*, Vol. 34 (April 1966), pp. 504–8.

PRICE STABILIZATION AND WELFARE   **285**

total producer sales and consumer purchases that a change in its price leaves the marginal utility of money unchanged.

We begin, in the following section, with a review of the results obtained by Waugh and Oi. Then, in Section III, we consider a market consisting of producers and consumers, and examine the gains from price stabilization to each group individually and to society as a whole. It is assumed that the price fluctuations are due to parallel shifts in the demand or supply curves. Following Waugh and Oi, the analysis is presented geometrically, permitting the price to assume only a limited number of values. The assumption of costless storage, made in Section III, is relaxed in Section IV, and the results modified accordingly. In Section V we formulate the model algebraically, with price as a continuously distributed random variable, and consider the gains from price stabilization to producers and consumers jointly. Section VI continues with a discussion of the distribution of the gains between producers and consumers. Then, in Section VII, we extend the analysis to the case of an individual producer or consumer. Section VIII notes the relationship between price stabilization and quantity destabilization.

In Sections II–VIII, stabilization is referred to the arithmetic mean of the price; in Section IX, we indicate how the results can be modified to permit stabilization about a trend. Section X presents some concluding remarks.

II. The Waugh-Oi Results

Waugh's result can be seen in Figure I, where it is assumed that consumers are faced with either of two competitively determined prices: p_1 or p_2.[4] Each price occurs with .5 probability. Using a cardinal measure of utility, consumer surplus, C, can be written

$$(1) \qquad C = \begin{cases} a+b+c+d+f, & p=p_1 \\ f, & p=p_2 \end{cases}.$$

Then the expected value of consumer surplus, $E(C)$, is given by

$$(2) \qquad E(C) = f + \frac{1}{2}(a+b+c+d).$$

Now consider that consumers are given as an alternative a single price, $\mu = \frac{1}{2}(p_1+p_2)$, which obtains with certainty. At this price, the expected value of consumer surplus equals

4. Waugh, this *Journal*, op. cit.

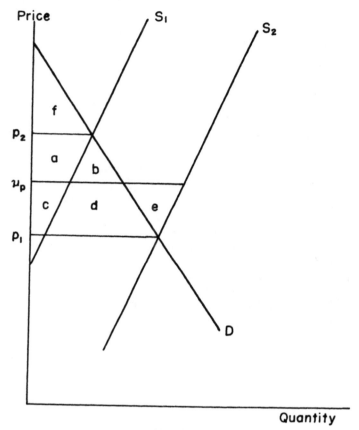

FIGURE I

$$(3) \qquad E(C) = a + b + f.$$

Compared with the prestabilization regime, the consumers stand to lose an amount equal to areas $c+d$ when the market price is p_1 and to gain $a+b$ when the price is p_2. Provided the demand curve is negatively sloped, and subject to the assumption that the marginal utility of money is constant with respect to a change in the price of the item, $c+d>a+b$, so that stabilization provides a net loss, measured in terms of consumer surplus; i.e., $E(C)$ is less in equation (3) than in equation (2).

Oi's argument is formally equivalent to the above.[5] In Figure II, producers are confronted with two prices, each with .5 probabil-

5. Oi, *op. cit.*

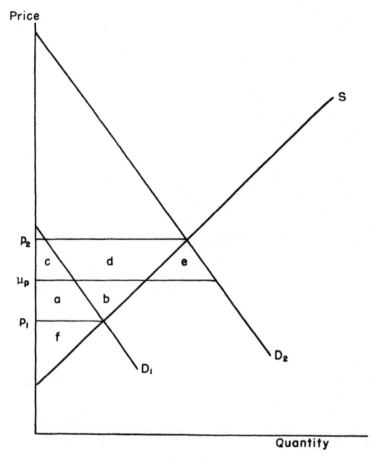

FIGURE II

ity. Producer surplus, F, is given by equation (1), and the expected value, $E(F)$ is given by (2). It can be seen that stabilization reduces the expected value of producer surplus by an amount equal to $\frac{1}{2}(c+d-a-b)$, as was the case above with consumer surplus. It is necessary to assume, as above, that the supply curve is positively sloped and that the marginal utility of money remains constant as producers move along this curve.[6]

6. For a further discussion of this point see: Clem Tisdell, "Uncertainty, Instability, Expected Profit," *Econometrica*, Vol. 31 (Jan.-Apr. 1963), pp. 243–47. Walter Oi, "Rejoinder," *Econometrica*, Vol. 31 (Jan.-Apr. 1963), p. 248.

In Waugh's analysis, consumers gain from a fluctuating price because they can adjust quantity purchased to the price. Thus they are able to buy more at a low than at a high price. If the price is stabilized not at μ_p but at a price p^*, defined

$$(4) \qquad p^* = \frac{q_1 p_1 + q_2 p_2}{q_1 + q_2}$$

where q_1 and q_2 are the quantities demanded at p_1 and p_2 respectively, then consumer welfare is not reduced through stabilization. A corresponding argument holds for producers.[7]

Oi's results depend on the assumption, not made explicit in his analysis, that there is a zero covariance between shifts in the supply curve and changes in the price. His analysis is based on a stationary supply curve, in which case the covariance is trivially zero. Thus, price changes are due solely to shifts in demand.

A similar condition holds for Waugh's results. His analysis implicitly assumes that the demand curve is stationary, so that price changes arise solely from shifts in supply. In this sense, the two sets of results cannot both hold simultaneously.

III. A Model with Producers and Consumers

Consider a market consisting of atomistic consumers and producers. In this market, price fluctuations can arise from shifts in either supply or demand or both. The case of a supply shift is depicted in Figure I and a demand shift in Figure II; in both cases, the curves are assumed to be linear and the shifts to be parallel.

In Figure I we have assumed that the price fluctuations are due to shifts in supply, with S_1 and S_2 each obtaining with .5 probability. The price μ_p is an alternative that can be achieved through a costless storage activity.[8] A buffer stock is set up, with a buying and

Albert Zucker, "On the Desirability of Price Instability: An Extension of the Discussion," *Econometrica*, Vol. 33 (April 1965), pp. 437–41. Oi's result was obtained independently, at about the same time, by Richard R. Nelson, "Uncertainty, Prediction, and Competitive Equilibrium," this *Journal*, LXXV (Feb. 1961), 41–62, in a slightly different context. Nelson's paper draws on this result to build an interesting model of the value of information to the firm. Oi's result was also obtained by H. G. Grubel. "Foreign Exchange Earnings and Price Stabilization Schemes," *American Economic Review*, LIV (June 1964), 378–85. A somewhat less sophisticated presentation of this point appeared earlier in Ragnar Nurkse, "Trade Fluctuations and Buffer Policies of Low-Income Countries," *Kyklos*, XI (Fasc. 2, 1958).

7. Zucker, *op. cit.*

8. In the discussion by Waugh and Oi it is unnecessary to specify how price stabilization is achieved. Here, however, it is necessary. We shall assume that stabilization is brought about by a buffer stock.

PRICE STABILIZATION AND WELFARE   **289**

selling price equal to μ_p, thereby establishing the market price at this level.

Raising the price from p_1 to μ_p involves a gain to producers of $c+d+e$, and a loss to consumers of $c+d$. If we subtract the consumers loss from the producers gain, there is a net gain equal to area e. Reducing the price from p_2 to μ_p benefits consumers by $a+b$ and costs producers only a; thus again there is a net gain of b. On balance, stabilizing the price at μ_p provides a net gain to producers of $c+d+e-a$, and a net loss to consumers of $c+d-(a+b)$, and therefore a net gain of $b+e$ to consumers and producers jointly. Although this analysis involves the addition of producer and consumer surplus,[9] and thus raises sticky welfare questions, one can argue that producers are able to compensate consumers so as to leave both groups better off. Given costless storage, the stabilization authority breaks even by buying and selling equal amounts at the same price, μ_p.[1]

In Figure II, price fluctuations are caused by shifts in the demand schedule, with D_1 and D_2 each obtaining with .5 probability. By an argument analogous to that above, it can be shown that there is a net gain to consumers of $c+d+e-a$, a net loss to producers of $c+d-(a+b)$, and a net gain to the two groups jointly of $b+e$.

The case considered by Waugh is that shown in Figure I, whereas Oi's results relate to the situation in Figure II. Waugh (Oi) is correct that price stabilization makes consumers (producers) worse off if the source of the instability is shifts in the supply (demand) schedule. However, this is only half of the story. If the instability is due to shifts in demand (supply), then consumers (producers) as a whole gain from a buffer stock scheme that stabilizes the price at μ_p. And the gain to consumers (producers) is sufficiently large to permit compensation, leaving both parties better off.[2]

---

9. This assumption is made by J. E. Meade "Degrees of Competitive Speculation," *Review of Economic Studies*, XVII (3), 1949–50, No. 44, 159–67, in his analysis of the welfare effects of speculation. Meade's gains from speculation are (not surprisingly) similar to our gains from stabilization.

1. An alternative would be to stabilize the price at $p^* = \dfrac{p_1 q_1 + p_2 q_2}{q_1 + q_2}$. In this case areas a and b would be larger and $c+d$ smaller, so that $a+b=c+d$. Consumers would then be indifferent to stabilization while producers would gain. However, the price p^* would not be an equilibrium price, as there would be on balance an excess demand providing pressure for the stabilization authority to raise the price.

2. Viewed differently, whereas the Waugh (Oi) results implicitly assume zero correlation between demand (supply) shifts and price changes, the analysis of the present section assumes perfect correlation.

IV. A POSITIVE STORAGE COST

A positive storage cost can easily be accommodated in the model. Figure III corresponds to Figure I, except that here the stabilization authority has set a buying price of $p_1' > p_1$ and a selling price of $p_2' < p_2$. As in Figure I producers and consumers jointly gain $e+b$ from stabilization, although these areas are smaller here than in Figure I. The stabilization authority makes a gross return of $p_2' - p_1'$ on each unit of the product handled. The pegged prices can be set so that $p_2' - p_1' = J$, the unit cost of storage. Stabilization will always afford a gain if $J < p_2 - p_1$.

V. THE GAINS FROM PRICE STABILIZATION: A MORE GENERAL ANALYSIS

This section presents a more general analysis of the gains from price stabilization. Here the supply and demand curves each have a shift factor that is a continuously distributed random variable. Consider a competitively priced commodity with supply and demand curves of the form

(5) $S = ap + x$ $(a \geq 0)$

(6) $D = -\beta p + y$ $(\beta \geq 0)$

where $S =$ quantity supplied, $D =$ quantity demanded, $p =$ price, a and β are constants, and x and y are jointly distributed random variables with means μ_x and μ_y, variances σ_{xx}, and σ_{yy} covariance $\sigma_{xy} = 0$.

By assuming that $\sigma_{xy} = 0$, we are in effect postulating a market in which shifts in demand and shifts in supply are influenced by different sets of forces. Shifts in demand may be related to changes in income and tastes, and in the prices of substitutes and complements; whereas shifts in supply may be related to changes in factor costs and technology. In the case of agricultural commodities, there are typically large shifts in supply because of factors related to the weather,[3] which are unrelated to the factors influencing demand.[4]

The equilibrium price and quantity traded are given by

(7) $p = \dfrac{y - x}{a + \beta}$

---

3. We are using "supply" here in an *ex post* sense, and not in the conventional *ex ante* sense. Thus the weather does not affect planting decisions (*ex ante* supply), but does affect the harvest (*ex post* supply).

4. If $\sigma_{xy} > 0$, the gains from stabilization are reduced but not eliminated.

(8) $q = \dfrac{ay + \beta x}{a + \beta}$

where $a + \beta > 0$, $p \geqslant 0$, and $q \geqslant 0$.

Consider that the mean price, μ_p, is known, and that a decision is made to eliminate price fluctuations by establishing a buffer stock authority that stands ready to buy or sell at μ_p. Stocks held by the authority are stored at zero cost. In any one year, producers gain

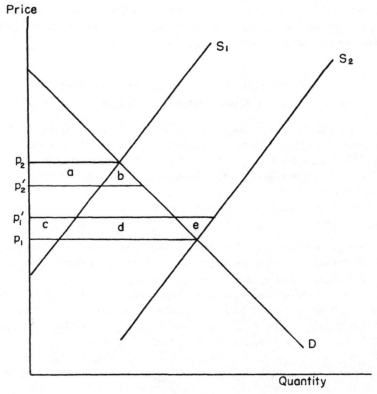

FIGURE III

an amount corresponding to $c + d + e$ in Figure I or $a + b$ in Figure II.[5] Algebraically, letting G_p = the gain to producers (i.e., the increase in producer surplus), we can write [6]

5. This amount may be negative.
6. Geometrically, this gain is the sum of the areas of a rectangle and a triangle. The area of the rectangle is given by the product $(\mu_p - p)[S(p)]$,

(9) $\qquad G_p = \frac{1}{2}(\mu_p - p)[S(p) + S(\mu_p)]$

where

(10) $\qquad \mu_p = \frac{\mu_y - \mu_x}{a + \beta}$.

Substituting (5), (7), and (10) into (9), and simplifying,

(11) $\qquad G_p = \frac{1}{2}\left[\frac{\mu_y - \mu_x - (y - x)}{a + \beta}\right]\left[2x + \frac{a(\mu_y - \mu_x + y - x)}{a + \beta}\right]$.

Integrating over x and y, the expected value of the gain can be written [7]

(12) $\qquad E(G_p) = \frac{(a + 2\beta)\sigma_{xx} - a\sigma_{yy}}{2(a + \beta)^2}$.

Next, consider the effect of price stabilization on consumer welfare, measured as the expected value of the change in consumer surplus. Denoting the gain from price stabilization by G_o, we can write [8]

(13) $\qquad E(G_o) = \frac{(2a + \beta)\sigma_{yy} - \beta\sigma_{xx}}{2(a + \beta)^2}$.

To derive the total gain, G, we add the gains to consumers and to producers:

(14) $\qquad G = G_p + G_o$.

Substituting (12) and (13) into (14), and simplifying,

(15) $\qquad E(G) = \frac{\sigma_{yy} + \sigma_{xx}}{2(a + \beta)}$

which is necessarily nonnegative and is positive if either σ_{yy} or σ_{xx} is. Thus those gaining from stabilization can compensate those losing, leaving everyone better off. This is then a generalization of the conclusions presented in Section III.

It can be seen that the price variance is given by

(16) $\qquad \sigma_{pp} = \frac{\sigma_{yy} + \sigma_{xx}}{(a + \beta)^2}$

thus

and the area of the triangle can be written $\frac{1}{2}(\mu_p - p)[S(\mu_p) - S(p)]$. Equation (9) is the sum of these two expressions.

7. Remember it is assumed that $\sigma_{xy} = 0$.

8. G_o is given by the areas $a + b$ in Figure I, $c + d + e$ in Figure II. The derivation of the algebraic expression for G_o is analogous to that for G_p, above.

(17) $E(G) = \left[\dfrac{a+\beta}{2}\right]\sigma_{pp}$.

It follows that the gains from price stabilization will tend to be greater the greater the degree of price instability. From (15) we see that $E(G)$ is greater the larger are the demand and supply variances and the steeper the two curves.

VI. The Distribution of Gains Among Producers and Consumers

In deriving expression (15) for the total gains, we obtained expressions for the gains to producers and consumers individually. Although there is necessarily a total net gain, it is possible for one group to gain at the expense of the other. It is correspondingly of interest to consider the conditions under which each group gains from stabilization.

From equation (12) we see that

(18) $E(G_p) > 0$ if $\dfrac{\sigma_{yy}}{\sigma_{xx}} < \dfrac{2\beta}{a} + 1$.

Producers are more likely to gain the larger the supply variance relative to the demand variance. Further, the likelihood of gain is greater the steeper the supply curve relative to the demand curve. In the limiting case of either a vertical supply curve or a zero demand variance, producers cannot lose from price stabilization.

The factors that influence the likelihood of a gain are nearly (but not exactly) the same as the factors that influence the magnitude of the gain. By differentiating (12) with respect to σ_{xx}, σ_{yy}, a, and β, we find that the magnitude of the gain to producers is a decreasing function of the demand variance and an increasing function of the supply variance and of the steepness of the supply curve. The relationship between $E(G_p)$ and the demand slope is more complex. It can be shown that

(19) $\dfrac{\partial E(G_p)}{\partial \beta} > 0$ if $\dfrac{\beta}{a} < \dfrac{\sigma_{yy}}{\sigma_{xx}}$.

Thus, beyond some point, further increases in the demand slope reduce the gain to producers. This results from the fact that the denominator of (12) increases faster than the numerator. In the limiting case of a horizontal demand curve, the price is stable even without a buffer stock, so the problem is irrelevant.[9]

9. In an important sense, this result is built into the model, by specifying

The gain to consumers was given by (13). A condition for this expression to be positive is

(22) $\qquad E(G_c) > 0$ if $\dfrac{\sigma_{ss}}{\sigma_{yy}} < \dfrac{2a}{\beta} + 1$.

This expression is analogous to that for producers. Consumers are more likely to gain, the larger the demand variance relative to the supply variance, and the steeper the demand curve relative to the supply curve. In the limiting case of a vertical demand curve, consumers cannot lose from price stabilization. Similarly, consumers cannot lose from stabilization if the supply variance is zero. The results of the present section can be viewed as an extension of the results obtained in Section III.

VII. Gains to Individual Producers and Consumers

Although producers as a whole may benefit from price stabilization, some producers may gain at the expense of others. It is of interest to consider the conditions under which the gains are positive to an individual producer — or a subset of producers. The notion of a subset of producers has particular real-world relevance if one wishes to consider whether an individual producing-country gains from an international buffer stock. For expository convenience we shall refer only to a single producer, but the analysis of this section can equally well apply to a subset of producers. We shall also discuss the gains to an individual consumer.

Consider an individual producer with supply curve

(23) $\qquad s = \gamma p + z \qquad (\gamma \geqslant 0)$

where $s = $ the firm's output and z is a random variable with mean and variance, μ_z and σ_{zz}. It is assumed that the producer is sufficiently small to be a price-taker. By the same method used in Section V, we may obtain the gain to the producer, g_p. Write

the demand shift as linear in the quantity (rather than price) variable. Strictly speaking, the demand curve shifts perpendicularly to the horizontal axis. The effect of a demand shift on the price diminishes as the demand curve becomes flatter, and becomes zero when the demand curve is horizontal. This assumption is acceptable if it is understood that one is discussing only demand curves that are fairly steep.

An alternative formulation would be to write

(20) $\qquad D = -\beta p + y[\lambda + \beta(1-\lambda)] \qquad (0 \leqslant \lambda \leqslant 1).$

Here, the demand curve shifts relative to both axes. The analysis can be generalized by substituting (20) for (6). It can be shown that, with this formulation,

(21) $\qquad \lim_{\beta \to \infty} \sigma_{pp} = \sigma_{yy}(1-\lambda)^2,$

which is positive if $\sigma_{yy} > 0$ and $\lambda < 1$.

PRICE STABILIZATION AND WELFARE   295

$$(24) \qquad g_p = \frac{1}{2}(\mu_p - p)\,[s(p) + s(\mu_p)]\,.$$

Substituting; integrating over x, y, and z; and simplifying, the expected value of the gain can be written

$$(25) \qquad E(g_p) = \frac{1}{a+\beta}\left[\sigma_{xz} - \frac{\gamma}{2(a+\beta)}(\sigma_{yy} + \sigma_{xx})\right]$$

where it is assumed that $\sigma_{yz} = 0$. It can be seen that

$$(26) \qquad E(g_p) > 0 \text{ if } \frac{2\sigma_{xz}}{\sigma_{yy} + \sigma_{xx}} > \frac{\gamma}{a+\beta}\,.$$

    If the individual producer's supply curve is influenced by some of the same forces that affect the industry's supply curve, then $\sigma_{xz} > 0$. Whether the producer gains from stabilization will then depend on the values of the parameters in inequality (26). He will be more likely to gain — and the gain will be greater — the larger is the covariance between his and the industry's supply curve, relative to the industry supply and demand variances. An intuitive interpretation of this result is that the industry will tend to be in a Section III rather than a Section II situation. He is also more likely to gain the steeper is his supply curve relative to the industry supply and demand curves. In the limiting case, where his supply curve is vertical (assuming $\sigma_{xz} \geqslant 0$), he cannot lose from stabilization.

    Consider next the effect of price stabilization on consumer welfare, measured as the expected value of the change in consumer surplus. Let the individual consumer's demand curve be written

$$(27) \qquad d = -\delta p + v \qquad (\delta \geqslant 0)\,.$$

Denoting by g_c the gain from price stabilization we can write

$$(28) \qquad E(g_c) = \frac{1}{a+\beta}\left[\sigma_{yv} - \frac{\delta}{2(a+\beta)}(\sigma_{yy} + \sigma_{xx})\right]$$

assuming $\sigma_{xv} = 0$. Thus

$$(29) \qquad E(g_c) > 0 \text{ if } \frac{2\sigma_{yv}}{\sigma_{yy} + \sigma_{xx}} > \frac{\delta}{a+\beta}\,.$$

The reader will note the similarity between (29) and (26). A consumer is most likely to gain if the covariance between his and the industry's demand curve is large relative to the industry demand and supply variances, and if his demand curve is steep relative to the industry demand and supply curves.[1]

    1. An interpretation of the Oi-Waugh results is that they relate not to producers (consumers) as a whole but to an individual producer (consumer). In the case considered by Oi, it is then implicitly assumed that $\sigma_{xx} = 0$, and $\gamma > 0$, so that (26) does not hold, and the producer loses from stabilization.

VIII. Quantity Destabilization

If producers benefit from price stabilization, a likely result is the destabilization of the quantity sold. Denote by $\sigma^*{}_{SS}$ and σ_{SS} the variance in producers' sales with and without price stabilization. Then let $\triangle\sigma_{SS}=\sigma^*{}_{SS}-\sigma_{SS}$. Now

$$(30) \quad \sigma_{SS}=E\left[a(p-\mu_p)+(x-\mu_x)\right]^2$$
$$=\frac{a\left[a\sigma_{yy}-(a+2\beta)\sigma_{xx}\right]}{(a+\beta)^2}+\sigma_{xx}$$

$$(31) \quad \sigma_{SS}{}^*=\sigma_{xx}.$$

Thus, subtracting (30) from (31), and substituting (12),

$$(32) \quad \triangle\sigma_{SS}=2aE(G_p).$$

Therefore, if $a>0$, then $\triangle\sigma_{SS}>0$ if and only if $E(G_p)>0$, establishing the link between producer gain and quantity destabilization.[2]

It is easy to show for consumers, as we did for producers, that if price stabilization increases consumer surplus, it must destabilize the quantity purchased, assuming the demand curve to be negatively sloped.

Assuming that neither the supply nor the demand curve is vertical, then either the quantity purchased by consumers or the quantity sold by producers must be destabilized. If consumer purchases are destabilized, then consumers gain; and if producer sales are destabilized, then producers gain. This suggests some scope for empirical research on particular stabilization schemes. In the absence of stabilization, $\sigma_{DD}=\sigma_{SS}$. Thus if $\sigma^*{}_{DD}>\sigma^*{}_{SS}$, it follows that $\triangle\sigma_{DD}>0$. Similarly, if $\sigma^*{}_{SS}>\sigma^*{}_{DD}$, then $\triangle\sigma_{SS}>0$. Therefore, if under stabilization, the variance in consumer purchase exceeds the variance in producer sales, then consumers have necessarily gained. Alternatively, if the variance in producer sales exceeds the

Similarly, with Waugh's implicit assumption that $\sigma_{yv}=0$ and $\delta>0$, (29) does not hold and the consumer also loses from stabilization. Although the Waugh and Oi results cannot both hold for consumers and producers as a whole, it is certainly possible for individual consumers and producers to lose from stabilization, if σ_{xx} and σ_{yv} are sufficiently small.

One can no doubt find the isolated producer whose *ex post* supply curve shifts in a way that is independent of shifts in the total supply curve for the product. This would be the case for a good whose supply curve shifts mainly in response to changes in the weather, and with respect to a producer situated in a climatically atypical area. However, it is a very special assumption, even for an individual producer and is less likely to hold for a group of producers. Similarly, the factors influencing shifts in demand are likely to affect large groups of consumers in roughly the same way. This is particularly the case for the derived demand by firms — for example, for materials for further processing.

2. If $a=0$, then $\triangle\sigma_{SS}=0$.

PRICE STABILIZATION AND WELFARE   **297**

variance in consumer purchases, producers have necessarily gained. This method permits us to determine that one group has gained. It does not permit us to say whether the other group has gained or lost. However, the more nearly equal are the two variances, and the more nearly equal are the slopes of the two curves, the greater the likelihood that both groups have gained.

IX. TIME TREND

Our analysis has proceeded thus far on the implicit assumption that there is no time trend in either demand or supply, and therefore in price or quantity traded. Clearly, if there is a trend, then stabilization of price about the mean would make little sense, and would produce some odd results.

Consider that both the demand and supply curves shift linearly to the right over time, not necessarily at the same rate. If the demand curve shifts faster (slower) than the supply curve, there will be an upward (downward) linear trend in price; only if the two curves shift at the same rate, will price contain no time trend. The reader can easily verify that the analysis of Sections V–VII holds if price is stabilized about the trend instead of about the mean. The stabilization authority is then assumed to know the expected value of price as a function of time.[3]

X. CONCLUSIONS

The present paper has tried to reconcile the analyses presented by Walter Oi and Frederick Waugh, concerning the gains to producers and consumers resulting from a stable as compared with a fluctuating price. Using the expected value of the change in producer and consumer surplus as a measure of gain, we have shown that price stabilization, brought about by a buffer stock, provides a net gain to producers and consumers taken together.

It is tempting to argue from this that a buffer stock is a desirable policy measure. However, one should bear in mind the simplifications underlying the analysis. First, we assumed storage to be costless. Taking the cost of storage into account would reduce the gains from price stabilization.

---

3. If storage operations stabilize price about a trend, the storage authority will no longer earn zero profits: instead, profits will be positive or negative depending on whether the price trend is rising or falling.

Second, we ignored the effect of price stabilization on the variance of producers' and consumers' incomes. This is particularly serious with respect to producers, because income from the commodity produced is likely to form a large part of total income. If price stabilization increased the expected value of producers' income but also increased the variance, then producers might on balance suffer a welfare decline. A more complete analysis would consider this aspect of the problem as well.

Third, we have assumed that μ_p was known so that the price could be stabilized at this level. It goes without saying that one of the chief difficulties of a price stabilization scheme is to predict the changes in the equilibrium market price.

FOOD RESEARCH INSTITUTE
STANFORD UNIVERSITY

[30]

Cost-Benefit Analysis under Uncertainty

By Daniel A. Graham*

The implications of uncertainty for cost-benefit analysis remain controversial. Two related problems are the subject of this analysis. First, for any given future period, a dollar magnitude must be identified which appropriately represents the value of the uncertain benefits (costs) to accrue in that year. Second, an appropriate discount rate for converting this future value into present value must be identified.

For illustrative purposes consider a simple problem. The construction of a dam is being considered. Potential benefits include flood control in wet years and the provision of irrigation water in dry years. A standard approach to determining the value of this dam employs the probabilities of wet and dry years together with the value of benefits to accrue under each circumstance to calculate the expected value (mathematical expectation) of benefits in each year. Thus, for example, if there were two possible states of nature within a given year—"wet" and "dry" with probabilities .7 and .3, respectively, and if a particular farmer were willing to pay up to $50 for the dam if a wet year were certain and up to $100 if a dry year were certain, then $65 would be counted as the value of benefits accruing to the farmer in the given year. Adding across affected individuals would then yield the total benefit for the year.

Having obtained a measure of the total value of the dam within each year, the standard approach then involves discounting these benefits to obtain the present value, with the discount rate to be selected so as to appropriately reflect the riskiness of the benefits. Needless to say, there has been considerable controversy regarding the appropriate discount rate.[1]

In addition to the debate regarding the discount rate, there has recently surfaced a second controversy regarding the use of expected value as a measure of benefit within a period. If the farmer in the example were willing to pay $50 for the dam contingent upon the occurrence of the state "wet" and $100 contingent upon "dry," what is the maximum sure payment that he would be willing to make in both states? Following Burton Weisbrod, the term "option price" has been used to describe this maximum sure payment. Millard Long asserted that option price is nothing more than the expected value of surplus of $65 in our example. Cotton Lindsay disagreed, the Charles J. Cicchetti and A. Myrick Freeman III and then John Krutilla et al. argued that option price should generally exceed the expected value of surplus so that in our example the farmer should be willing to pay more than $65 to insure the availability of the dam. More recently, Richard Schmalensee and Claude Henry have shown that option price depends upon individual preferences and may either exceed or be less than the expected value of surplus. This result is, of course, troublesome for the analyst wishing to employ cost-benefit analysis. Having available estimates of the expected value of surplus for the farmer as well as his option price, which number is to be used as a measure of his benefit for the period? To what extent does the answer to this question affect the choice of the appropriate discount rate?

In what follows, I provide a conceptually correct procedure for determining whether a risky project passes the "potential Pareto improvement" welfare criterion which forms

*Professor of economics, Duke University. Research for this paper was supported by a grant from the Robert Wood Johnson Foundation to the National Bureau of Economic Research.

[1]See, for example, the discussion in Kenneth Arrow and Robert Lind.

the normative basis of cost-benefit analysis. In this approach the role of secondary markets in providing opportunities for redistributing risk is made transparent and the modifications necessary when such markets do not exist are suggested. Some of the more interesting results include:

1) Option price is the appropriate measure of benefit in situations involving similar individuals and collective risk.

2) Expected value calculations are appropriate to situations involving similar individuals and individual risks.

3) Whether or not option price exceeds the expected value of surplus is largely irrelevant to the evaluation of risky projects.

4) In a wide range of circumstances, including incomplete markets, discounting for risky projects should be done at the riskless rate.

I. The Willingness-to-Pay Locus

To gain insight into the appropriate measure of uncertain benefits within a given period, I shall continue the example of the dam. To make matters more precise, suppose there are two goods, the first of which will be called "dollars" while the second is the proposed dam. As before there are two possible states of nature, wet and dry with probabilities .7 and .3, respectively. Following the state-preference approach of Arrow, let us suppose that the farmer is endowed with claims to the first good contingent upon which state occurs: e_W dollars to be received if wet occurs and e_D dollars if dry. Using the von Neumann-Morgenstern theorem as extended by Jack Hirschleifer, the farmer's utility function can be represented as

$$U = .7U_W(c_W, \delta) + .3U_D(c_D, \delta)$$

where c_W and c_D represent claims to dollars contingent upon wet and dry, respectively, and δ depicts the availability of the dam ($\delta = 1$ indicates that the services of the dam are available to the farmer under specified terms and $\delta = 0$ indicates that they are not).

The standard assumptions are made that

Nonsatiation: $\quad U_i'(c_i, \delta) \equiv \dfrac{\partial U_i}{\partial c_i} > 0$

$$i = W, D$$

Risk Aversion:[2] $\quad U_i''(c_i, \delta) \equiv \dfrac{\partial^2 U_i}{\partial c_i^2} < 0$

$$i = W, D$$

The terms "expected surplus" and "option price" may now be made precise. Define S_i, $i = W, D$ by the requirement

$$(1) \qquad U_i(e_i - S_i, 1) = U_i(e_i, 0); \quad i = W, D$$

Then the expected surplus is

$$(2) \qquad E(S_i) \equiv .7S_W + .3S_D$$

[2] There seems to be some confusion in the literature regarding the meaning of the term risk aversion; see, for example, Schmalensee, p. 815. The assumption as stated is sufficient to assure that the farmer would decline any fair, independent gamble. Suppose, for example, that given his endowment e_W, e_D he were given the chance to make any fair bet he wished on the toss of a (fair) coin. Supposing the outcome of the coin toss to be distributed independently of the states wet and dry, we have four states: "wet and heads," "wet and tails," etc. Let the bet pay x if heads and y if tails with $.5x + .5y = 0$, then the utility of accepting the gamble is

$$\hat{U} \equiv .7[.5U_W(e_W + x, \delta) + .5U_W(e_W + y, \delta)]$$
$$+ .3[.5U_D(e_D + x, \delta) + .5U_D(e_D + y, \delta)]$$

while the utility of declining the bet is

$$\bar{U} \equiv .7U_W(e_W, \delta) + .3U_D(e_D, \delta)$$

But risk aversion and $x, y \neq 0$ imply that

$$.5U_i(e_i + x, \delta) + .5U_i(e_i + y, \delta) < U_i(e_i, \delta); \quad i = W, D$$

Thus $\hat{U} < \bar{U}$ and the bet would be declined. On the other hand, gambles which are not independent of existing risks afford the individual an opportunity to buy insurance. It would surely be a misnomer to define risk aversion in a way that requires an individual to refuse the chance to buy fair insurance against an existing risk, and yet, this is the definition Schmalensee proposes.

Option price, on the other hand, is defined by the requirement:

(3)

$$.7U_W(e_W - OP, 1) + .3U_D(e_D - OP, 1) = \bar{U}$$

where $\quad \bar{U} \equiv .7U_W(e_W, 0) + .3U_D(e_D, 0)$

Option value is defined as the difference

(4) $\qquad OV \equiv OP - E[S_i]$

We may now introduce a concept which will prove crucial to subsequent analysis. The "willingness-to-pay locus" consists of ordered pairs (γ_W, γ_D) satisfying

(5)

$$.7U_W(e_W - \gamma_W, 1) + .3U_D(e_D - \gamma_D, 1) = \bar{U}$$

where $\bar{U}$ is defined in equation (3). By construction, the farmer would as soon make any of the contingent payments (γ_W, γ_D) for the dam as do without it. Notice, moreover, that the previously defined magnitudes S_W, S_D and OP correspond to particular points along this willingness to pay locus, that is,

$$(\gamma_W, \gamma_D) = (S_W, S_D) = (\$50, \$100)$$

is one point on the locus, and

$$(\gamma_W, \gamma_D) = (OP, OP)$$

is another. This is illustrated in Figure 1. The concavity which is illustrated for the locus follows directly from the assumption of risk aversion.

A further point along the locus which might be called the "certainty point" may be identified for expository purposes. Let (γ_W^*, γ_D^*) be that point on the locus satisfying

(6) $\quad U_W(e_W - \gamma_W^*, 1) = U_D(e_D - \gamma_D^*, 1)$

Were the farmer to contract for these contingent payments for the dam he would be indifferent as to which state of nature occurs. Put somewhat differently, he would have, in the process of contracting for these contin-

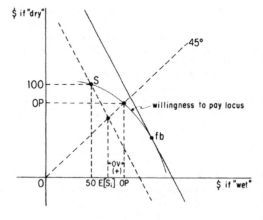

FIGURE 1

gent payments, simultaneously acquired a completely insured position against the uncertain state of nature.

Finally, let the "fair bet" point (γ_W', γ_D') be that point along the locus which has the largest expected value. While precise relationships among the surplus, certainty, and fair bet points can be developed, here it is sufficient to point out that they are, in general, distinct points along the willingness-to-pay locus.

II. Option Value

The willingness-to-pay locus can be used to indicate the factors determining whether option value (equation (4)) is positive or negative. One possibility is illustrated in Figure 1. Here the fair bet point lies to the right of the 45° line. Since the slope of the locus at this point gives the relative probability of wet versus dry, a parallel through the surplus point S yields all payment combinations with the same expected value as the surplus point. Where this line crosses the 45° line, payments are equal in both states and thus also equal to the expected value of surplus. Here option price necessarily exceeds the expected value of surplus and thus option value is positive.

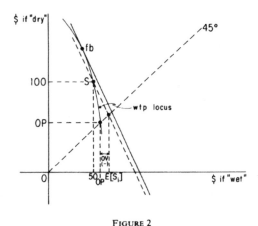

FIGURE 2

In Figure 2 the fair bet point lies to the left of the surplus point and a similar construction reveals that, in this case, the expected value of surplus must exceed option price yielding a negative option value.

A third possibility is that the fair bet point lies between the 45° line and the surplus point. Here there is ambiguity: option price may be greater or less than the expected value of surplus.

III. The Potential Pareto Improvement Test

Figures 1 and 2 not only summarize the considerations affecting the sign of option value, they also suggest that there may be little to recommend either option price or expected surplus for a role of prominence in cost-benefit analysis. They are, after all, only two arbitrarily selected points along the willingness-to-pay locus and have no obvious claim to preference over other points along the locus including the fair bet and certainty points. The question to be resolved ultimately is whether or not there exists payments for each individual which, when aggregated, yield sufficient resources to build the dam and which, when coupled with the provision of the dam, leave no individual worse off than he would otherwise have been. This question can be answered as follows. Having developed the idea of the willingness-to-pay locus for one individual, let us

suppose that there are N people in the society and that the willingness-to-pay locus of the ith person is given by

$$\gamma_D^i = f^i(\gamma_W^i) \qquad i = 1, \ldots, N$$

The method of aggregating these curves is illustrated for N equal to 2 in Figure 3 and will immediately be recognized as analogous to the "community indifference curve" construction from international trade theory. The curve labeled wtp_1 represents the willingness-to-pay locus of the first person. Similarly wtp_2 represents the locus of the second person.

The aggregate locus is obtained as the outer envelope of the set obtained by adding points from wtp_1 to points from wtp_2. Point C, for example, results from adding points A and B. Point C also represents the maximum sure payment that this "society" would be willing to make for the dam, and represents the magnitude that should be compared with a sure resource cost of building the dam. Should the cost of the dam itself be uncertain, no appreciable difficulty is added. If, for example, the cost is to be f_W in the state wet and f_D in the state dry, then the dam should be built on the potential Pareto improvement criterion since reference to Figure 3 indicates that society would be willing to sacrifice resources sufficient to cover actual costs in each possible state. (These are points on the aggregate locus to the northeast of F.) On the other hand, if resource costs are described by a point such as G which lies above the aggregate locus, then there does not exist a Pareto improving way of providing the dam.

It should be noted that if an aggregate payment such as C were actually collected with each person making a payment along his own willingness-to-pay locus, then a Pareto efficient distribution of risk would result. To see this, notice first that the slope of the aggregate locus at C is the same as the slope of each individual's locus at the implied payments points. But the slope of an individual's willingness-to-pay locus at a particular payments point is equal to his mar-

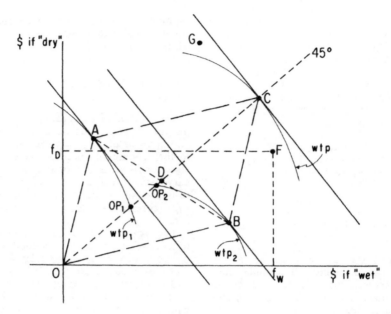

FIGURE 3

ginal rate of substitution between the two goods once the payments are contracted. Thus the marginal rates of substitution between "dollars if wet" and "dollars if dry" are equated for all individuals. Such a taxation scheme, therefore, is equivalent to establishing competitive markets for contingent dollar claims against the two states with relative prices equal to the common marginal rate of substitution.

This, then, is the general answer regarding which of the points along the individual's willingness-to-pay locus is relevant to cost-benefit analysis. For each possible pair of contingent claims prices for the two states, select that payment combination for each individual which has the greatest value at these prices. Adding these payments across individuals yields a point on the aggregate willingness-to-pay locus. Justification of the project hinges upon the question of whether or not contingent prices exist at which aggregate willingness to pay in each state exceeds the corresponding resource cost of the project. Should such prices exist, that point

from an individual's locus which has the greatest value at these prices is the one relevant for cost-benefit analysis, and the corresponding value at these prices is the appropriate measure of benefit.

IV. Special Cases

It remains to determine whether option price or expected value calculations have any potential relevance to cost-benefit analysis. Consider first a special case in which 1) the resource cost of the dam is certain and 2) all individuals are alike—same utility functions and same endowed claims. Here we are concerned with the intersection of the aggregate locus with the 45° line since this point represents the largest possible sure payment. But, with all individuals alike, this aggregate payment entails each individual making a payment corresponding to the intersection of his individual willingness-to-pay locus with the 45° line. This payment, moreover, is simply the individual's option price. With individuals alike, the initial distribution of risk is efficient and collecting the sure, option-price payment from each preserves this efficiency. Under these circumstances option price is the appropriate measure of benefit.

The second type of special case to be considered involves the concept of "individual risks" discussed by Edmond Malinvaud. The dam problem involves a "collective risk" since everyone will experience the state wet or everyone will experience the state dry. Consider an alternative situation based upon an example from Schmalensee. Here an individual can be in one of two "individual states." In the first he will have "a strong desire" to go to Yellowstone Park next summer. In the second he will have no desire to go. What is different about this situation is that it is possible for one person to experience "individual state 1" while another experiences "individual state 2."

It is possible, of course, to place this problem within the original framework by identifying states of nature according to the experience of each individual. Thus "state 1" might correspond to the situation in which each of the N members of society experiences individual state 1. Similarly, "state 2" might denote the case in which everyone except the Nth person experiences individual state 1 while the Nth experiences individual state 2. By expressing each person's willingness-to-pay locus in terms of contingent dollar claims against each of the 2^N possible states it is possible to proceed exactly as before.

A considerable simplification is possible, however, if we assume 1) again that individuals are alike and have the same endowments (the same individual state 1 and individual state 2 utility functions and the same endowed claims to dollars contingent upon these individual states), and 2) that the probability distribution of states takes a particular form. For simplicity, suppose that N is large and that the probability can be taken to be one that a total of $.3N$ individuals will be in individual state 1 in a given period and $.7N$ will be in individual state 2. While it is known with certainty what fractions of society will experience the alternative individual states, the fates of particular individuals are uncertain.[3] For any given person we simply suppose that the probability that he will be in individual state 1 is .3 while the probability of individual state 2 is .7. The willingness-to-pay locus of a representative individual is illustrated in Figure 4. The surplus point S indicates that the individual would be willing to pay up to \$100 above the costs of the trip for a visit to Yellowstone if he were certain of individual state 1 and nothing if individual state 2 were certain. This yields an expected surplus of \$30.

As previously mentioned, the discussion in Schmalensee focuses upon whether or not the individual's option price exceeds \$30. Here we will be concerned with the implications of individual risks. The fair bet point (labeled *fb* in Figure 4) represents that point where the slope of the locus equals (in absolute value) the odds of being in individual state 1. The tangent to the locus at this point, then, represents alternative payment combinations with the same expected value. Since individuals are alike each is willing to make payments of Oa "\$ if individual state 1" and Ob "\$ if individual state 2." The expected value of these payments is OV for each person. Moreover, since it is known that $.3N$ individuals will experience individual state 1 while $.7N$ will experience individual state 2 the aggregate payment resulting from these individual payments would be

$$.3N \cdot Oa + .7N \cdot Ob = (.3 \cdot Oa + .7 \cdot Ob)N$$

$$= OV \cdot N$$

Thus it is possible to collect an aggregate sure payment equal to N times the expected value of the fair bet point. Since no larger sure payment is possible, the fair bet point may, in these circumstances, be identified as the one appropriate to cost-benefit analysis. In this case, the expected value of the fair bet point is the appropriate measure of benefit.

This special case is an illustration of a more general proposition developed by

[3] This situation is analogous to knowing how many wrecks will occur on the fourth of July weekend without knowing who will have them.

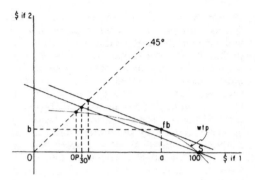

FIGURE 4

To restate, if individuals are alike, then option price measures benefit in cases of collective risk while expected willingness to pay (the expected value of the fair bet point) measures benefit in cases of individual insurable risks.

V. Second Best Considerations

The "hypothetical compensation test" of Kaldor, Hicks, and Scitovsky is the normative basis of cost-benefit analysis as it is normally applied. In this approach it is sufficient for the justification of a project that a set of payments be identified for a project which 1) individuals would willingly make for the project rather than do without it and 2) cover the actual costs of the project. It is not commonly required that a taxation scheme be identified which collects from each individual payments commensurate with his willingness to pay. Thus actual financing of a justifiable project may collect an amount exceeding benefits from some individuals and an amount less than benefits from others. In such cases it is simply argued that the winners could, in principle, compensate the losers.

The issue of the actual method of financing a project assumes a more crucial role in cases of uncertainty for reasons which will soon be apparent. Consider once again the situation illustrated in Figure 3. Here a society consisting of two people (who face a collective risk regarding the occurrence of state wet or state dry) is willing to make an aggregate sure payment corresponding to point C for a particular project. Suppose that actual financing of the project entails a sure collection of D from each $(C=2D)$. This yields a surprising situation in which both people are worse off than they would have been without the project since D exceeds the

Malinvaud which indicates circumstances in which equilibrium prices for contingent dollar claims against alternative states tend to be equal to the probabilities of the states. The simplified procedure followed in this case is made possible, in essence, by the knowledge that prices equal to the probabilities of the individual states will yield an efficient distribution of risk. Reference to Figure 4 indicates that this case is further characterized by the fact that the expected value of surplus, $30, is greater than option price and, therefore, option value is negative. It would obviously be easy to illustrate a case in which option value is positive simply by drawing the willingness-to-pay locus so that it crosses the 45° line above $30. The sign of option value is, however, irrelevant. If expected values are relevant at all, that is, if the situation involves individual-insurable risks, then the expected value of the fair bet point is the largest of all points along the locus and is, therefore, the appropriate measure of benefit. If the situation does not involve individual insurable risks then prices which support an efficient allocation of contingent claims will not in general be equal to probabilities and expected values have no bearing upon the appropriate "market price" value.[4]

[4]Estimates of option price and the expected value of surplus may, of course, be used as lower bounds for the expected value of the fair bet point. It should be noted in this regard that an estimate of consumer's surplus (the Hicksian compensating variation) derived from demand data for Yellowstone visitors would ideally estimate the expected value of surplus. To see this note that since .3N individuals visit the park each period with each having a surplus of $100, one would obtain 30N$, the aggregate expected value of surplus, from an ideal "area under the demand curve" type calculation. Since this measure is a lower bound for the true value, John Krutilla et al. were correct in their suspicion that expected surplus understates the true benefit.

option price of each person. The difficulty stems from the fact that being willing to make an aggregate payment of C is predicated upon achieving an efficient distribution of risk. Collecting payments corresponding to A and B, respectively, from the first and second people equates their marginal rates of substitution between "$ if state 1" and "$ if state 2" and is, therefore, consistent with efficiency. Collecting payments corresponding to D from each, on the other hand, does not equate marginal rates of substitution and is inconsistent with efficiency unless secondary markets are available in which the individuals can buy and sell contingent claims.

The case of independent risks poses similar problems. Looking back at Figure 4 we see that both expected willingness to pay, V, and expected surplus exceed option price. Should actual financing entail sure collections of either V or $30 from each individual, everyone would be a loser in that situation as well unless a secondary market for insurance exists.

It is implicit in the original discussions of the "hypothetical compensation test" that complete markets exist for all goods. One need not be concerned with the allocational efficiency of taxation schemes in such circumstances since trade in the perfect secondary markets assures ultimate allocational efficiency. However appropriate, this "complete markets" assumption was for the riskless world of these original debates, it is generally conceded that many of the contingent claims markets required for allocational efficiency in a risky world do not exist.[5] It is crucial in such circumstances that either 1) the particular method of financing the project be evaluated with respect to its implications for the distribution of risk, or 2) the analysis be modified in such a way as to avoid dependence on nonexisting markets.

---

[5]There are at least two important reasons why many types of contingent claims markets do not exist. The first is moral hazard: a person buying claims contingent upon a particular state may have incentives to alter his behavior in a way that is adverse to the seller. Second, such markets require complicated and specialized contracts which may be costly both to write and to enforce.

For these reasons option price may be regarded as a "second best" measure of benefit appropriate to situations in which 1) actual financing involves sure collections from individuals,[6] and 2) secondary contingent claims markets are not available.

VI. Generalizations

The approach to the illustrative cases examined thus far may easily be generalized to situations involving an arbitrary number of periods and states. Consider a general situation involving S states and $Q+1$ periods and suppose that markets exist in which individuals can exchange current sure (time zero) dollars for M different types of assets. Ownership of one unit of the ith asset entails claims to receipts of

$$a_{sq}^i \begin{cases} s=1,\ldots,S \\ q=1,\ldots,Q \\ i=1,\ldots,M \end{cases}$$

dollars at time q (the end of period q) if state s occurs. For notational convenience let current sure dollars be that asset indexed by zero. A portfolio, then, is an $M+1$ tuple, x, where the ith component x_i denotes the quantity of the ith asset, $i=0,\ldots,M$. Holding the portfolio x thus entitles the owner to x_0 current sure dollars and claims paying

$$\sum_{i=1}^{M} x_i a_{sq}^i \begin{cases} s=1,\cdots,S \\ q=1,\ldots,Q \end{cases}$$

dollars at time q if state s occurs. In vector

---

[6]It might be thought that state-dependent collections represent an unrealistic method of financing projects. This is not necessarily true, however. In the case of the dam, for example, a combination of sure taxes and water charges might produce exactly the combination of contingent payments required for allocational efficiency. Sure taxes and visitor charges might similarly be used in the case of Yellowstone Park. In Figure 4 a sure tax of Ob in both states plus a visitor charge of $Oa-Ob$ would produce exactly the desired result. In general, however, the same factors that prevent contingent claims markets from being privately organized would presumably inhibit the use of state-dependent collection schemes.

notation we have $c = Ax$ where

$$A \equiv \begin{bmatrix} 1 & 0 & 0 & \cdots & 0 \\ 0 & a_{11}^1 & a_{11}^2 & \cdots & a_{11}^M \\ 0 & a_{21}^1 & a_{21}^2 & \cdots & a_{21}^M \\ \vdots & & & & \\ 0 & a_{SQ}^1 & a_{SQ}^2 & \cdots & a_{SQ}^M \end{bmatrix}$$

and c is the $SQ+1$ vector of time-state dependent dollar claims associated with the portfolio x.

The utility function of the individual for consumption programs involving the $SQ+1$ possible types of time-state dependent claims $U(c)$ can be used to derive a utility function for portfolios by defining the utility of the portfolio to be equal to the utility of the associated vector of time-state dependent claims:[7] $u(x) \equiv U(Ax)$.

Similarly, if the list of goods is expanded to include the services to be derived from a proposed public project, then the notation $u(x, \delta)$ may be used to denote the utility of holding the portfolio x when the services are provided ($\delta = 1$), or when the services are not provided ($\delta = 0$). Supposing the individual to be endowed, following market trade, with the portfolio e the willingness-to-pay locus may be defined as consisting of those vectors γ which satisfy

$$\gamma = Ax; \quad u(e-x, 1) = u(e, 0)$$

By aggregating these loci across individuals in the manner suggested earlier, one obtains the aggregate willingness-to-pay locus. As before, the project is justifiable if the vector describing its resource costs lies below this aggregate surface. If, for example, all costs are to be incurred during the first period, then the relevant measure of benefit

[7]Notice that this general formulation requires only that an individual have a utility function ranking alternative consumption programs. This is less restrictive than the von Neuman-Morgenstern formulation and compatible with other approaches, for example, the certain equivalence formulation of Handa (1977).

is the intersection of the aggregate surface with the current sure dollar axis.

Turning now to the matter of risk discounting we suppose first that it is meaningful to discuss a "riskless" interest rate, that is, we assume that there exist portfolios x^t which satisfy

$$\sum_i x_i^t a_{sq}^i = \begin{cases} 1 & s = 1, \ldots, S \\ & q = t \\ 0 & \text{otherwise} \end{cases}$$

for $t = 1, \ldots, Q$. (Ownership of x^t returns a sure dollar at time t and nothing at other times.) The existence of these riskless portfolios establishes the riskless discount rates applicable to returns at time t as

$$1/(1+r_t) \equiv px^t; \quad t = 1, \ldots, Q$$

where $p \equiv (1, p_1, \ldots, p_M)$ is the vector of time zero sure dollar prices of the assets. Now suppose another portfolio, x, offers risky returns at time T, that is,

$$\sum_i x_i a_{sq}^i = \begin{cases} z_s & s = 1, \ldots, S \\ & q = T \\ 0 & \text{otherwise} \end{cases}$$

The current market price of this risky portfolio must be px. This present value may equivalently be determined by noting that the ratio px/px^T represents the price of the risky portfolio in terms of time T sure dollars. This is the future, time T, value of the risky portfolio. To determine its present value notice that

$$px/px^T = px(1+r_T)$$

or that $\quad px = 1/(1+r_T)\dfrac{px}{px^T}$

Thus the present value of the risky portfolio is obtained by discounting its future value at the riskless rate. This is the direct result of the existence of markets which afford opportunities for riskless investment.[8]

It should be noticed that this analysis supposes only that free competitive exchange is possible in the existing markets for assets. Although this is not equivalent to assuming the existence of complete contingent claims markets, it does include the case of complete markets as a possible special case. To see this notice first that the ability to buy and sell assets at prices $p = (1, p_1, \ldots, p_M)$ implies that an individual endowed with the portfolio e faces the "portfolio" budget constraint $px = pe$. Suppose now that the rank of A is equal to $SQ + 1$, that is, there are as many linearly independent assets as there are types of contingent dollar claims. Then we may write $x = A^{-1}c$ and the portfolio budget constraint is equivalent to the "contingent claim" budget constraint given by $Pc = PE$ where $E \equiv Ae$ and $P \equiv pA^{-1}$. Here the ability to buy and sell assets at prices p is equivalent to the ability to buy and sell contingent claims at prices P. This situation is therefore equivalent to one in which complete markets exist for trade in contingent claims. In general, however, the rank of A may be less than $SQ + 1$ in which case existing markets for assets do not provide opportunities for exchange of risk equivalent to those which would be afforded by a complete set of contingent claims markets.[9]

---

[8] The matter of discounting for risk may be clarified by a complete market example. Suppose there are S states with π_s denoting the objective probability of state s. Complete contingent claims markets exist with p_s the current price of a claim to one dollar in period two contingent upon the occurrence of s. The riskless discount rate is then $1/(1+r) \equiv \Sigma_s p_s$. Suppose now that ownership of an asset a entails claims to a_s dollars in period two if state s occurs, $s = 1, \ldots, S$. The current market price of this asset must be $V = \Sigma_s p_s a_s$. This market value may also be calculated by determining the value of the asset in period-two sure dollars $\Sigma_s (p_s / \Sigma_j p_j) a_s$ and then discounting at the riskless rate

$$V = 1/(1+r) \sum_s \left(p_s / \sum_j p_j \right) a_s$$

$$= \left(\sum_j p_j \right) \sum_s \left(p_s / \sum_j p_j \right) a_s = \sum_s p_s a_s$$

Now if one wished to discount the expected value of

REFERENCES

K. J. Arrow, "The Role of Securities in the Optimal Allocation of Riskbearing," *Rev. Econ. Stud.*, Apr. 1964, *31*, 91–96.

——— and R. C. Lind, "Uncertainty and the Evaluation of Public Investment Decisions," *Amer. Econ. Rev.*, June 1970, *60*, 364–78.

C. J. Cicchetti and A. M. Freeman, "Option Demand and Consumers Surplus: Further Comment," *Quart. J. Econ.*, Aug. 1971, *85*, 528–39.

P. J. Cook and D. A. Graham, "The Demand for Insurance and Protection: The Case of Irreplaceable Commodities," *Quart. J. Econ.*, Feb. 1977, *91*, 143–54.

C. Henry, "Option Values in the Economics of Irreplaceable Assets," *Rev. Econ. Stud.*, Symposium 1974, *64*, 89–104.

J. Handa, "Risk, Probabilities, and a New Theory of Cardinal Utility," *J. Polit. Econ.*, Feb. 1977, *85*, 97–122.

J. Hirschleifer, "Investment Decision under Uncertainty: Choice-Theoretic Approaches," *Quart. J. Econ.*, Nov. 1965, *79*, 509–36.

J. V. Krutilla et al., "Observations on the Economics of Irreplaceable Assets," in Allen V. Kneese and Blair T. Bower, eds., *Environmental Quality Analysis: Theory and Method in the Social Sciences*, Baltimore 1972.

C. M. Lindsay, "Option Demand and Consumer's Surplus," *Quart. J. Econ.*, May

---

period two claims rather than their true second-period market value then one would require the risky discount rate corresponding to

$$1/(1+\rho) \sum_s \pi_s a_s = \sum_s p_s a_s = V$$

If market prices were proportional to probabilities, $\pi_i / \pi_j = p_i / p_j$ for all i, j, then $\pi_s = p_s / \Sigma_j p_j$ and $\rho = r$. In general, however, market prices are not proportional to probabilities and $\rho \neq r$. In such circumstances the use of ρ represents nothing more than a correction factor for having used probabilities rather than prices to measure the future value of receipts.

[9] For a general discussion of the relationship of the rank of the assets matrix to the opportunities for achieving efficient distributions of risk, see Steven Ross.

J. Econ., Feb. 1976, *90*, 75–89.

M. F. Long, "Collective-Consumption Services of Individual-Consumption Goods: Comment," *Quart. J. Econ.*, May 1967, *81*, 351–52.

E. Malinvaud, "Markets for an Exchange Economy with Individual Risks," *Econometrica*, May 1973, *41*, 383–410.

S. A. Ross, "Options and Efficiency," *Quart.* 1969, *83*, 344–46.

R. Schmalensee, "Option Demand and Consumer's Surplus: Valuing Price Changes under Uncertainty," *Amer. Econ. Rev.*, Dec. 1972, *62*, 813–24.

B. A. Weisbrod, "Collective Consumption Services of Individual Consumption Goods," *Quart. J. Econ.*, Aug. 1964, *77*, 71–77.

Economic Welfare Evaluations for Producers under Uncertainty

Rulon Pope, Jean-Paul Chavas, and Richard Just

The validity of producer and consumer surplus measures of firm welfare under risk is examined. Under constant absolute risk aversion and output price uncertainty only, these measures are an exact measure of firm welfare as defined by compensating variation, equivalent variation or the change in the certainty equivalent. Under decreasing absolute risk aversion, qualitative comparisons of various measures are discussed. For example, producer's surplus as measured by the area above the uncompensated risk averse supply curve overstates the compensating variation of a change in expected price of output. Procedures for calculating firm welfare under production uncertainty and a variety of economic environments are proposed. Generally, these procedures are applicable only when absolute risk aversion is constant.

Key words: firm welfare, policy analysis, risk.

There is much literature on the use of surplus measures to evaluate agricultural welfare. Typically, average producer and consumer surpluses under certainty are used in the analysis (e.g., Akino and Hayami). This may be fairly realistic for food consumption. However, because of production lags and weather variability, farmers typically do not know with certainty the quantities they will produce or the price they will obtain when they make production decisions. Thus, uncertainty is typical for producer response. If producers respond to risk, then a riskless supply curve is inappropriate for measuring welfare.

Both theoretical and empirical stabilization studies (Massell; Turnovsky; Just et al.; Turnovsky, Shalit, Schmitz; Subotnik and Houck; Taylor and Talpaz; Burt, Koo, Dudley) evaluate welfare effects of price or quantity stabilization by considering varying prices and/or quantities. Expected producers' surplus at varying prices are compared to expected producer surplus at a stable price. In these cases, average supply responds along the riskless

supply curve as if price were certain. Prices vary, but there is no price uncertainty at the time decisions are made. Thus, distinguishing between price variability and price uncertainty is crucial. If supply decisions are not reflected by the riskless supply curve, Just (1975, 1978), Blandford and Currie, and others have pointed out that expected producer surplus from the riskless (or risk-neutral) supply curve cannot measure welfare properly. The purpose of this paper is to analyze the welfare significance of producers' surplus as measured with a risk-responsive supply (or expected supply) curve. Some practical issues about welfare measurement under uncertainty also are discussed. An extended discussion of these issues is contained in a lengthened version of this paper which includes an application. Upon request, it is available from the authors. Throughout, the behavioral model is kept simple by assuming that the firm maximizes expected utility of wealth. Risk aversion is maintained throughout, since the risk-neutral case is well-developed in this *Journal* and elsewhere. This investigation focuses on welfare measures for producers based on supply (or expected supply) and factor demand estimates rather than direct estimation of preferences. The analysis initially considers only price uncertainty but is then extended to consider production uncertainty.

Rulon Pope is an associate professor, Department of Economics. Brigham Young University; Jean-Paul Chavas is an associate professor, Department of Agricultural Economics, University of Wisconsin; and Richard E. Just is a professor, Department of Agricultural Economics, University of California, Berkeley. This work was done while Pope and Chavas were in the Department of Agricultural Economics, Texas A&M University.

The Firm Model

The model employed here uses a single-attribute utility function defined on wealth. Firms behave as expected utility maximizers following the axioms of rationality established by von Neumann and Morgenstern. If π denotes the random profit level as a function of control variables, $\mathbf{x} = (x_1, \ldots, x_n)$, a nonrandom parameter vector γ (including fixed input levels), and if U is the utility function and E is expectation, the firm maximizes $E[U(W_0 + \pi)]$ with respect to $\mathbf{x}$, given initial wealth, W_0. The expression $E[U(W_0 + \pi)]$ is assumed concave in $\mathbf{x}$ with $U' = dU/d\pi > 0$, $U'' = d^2U/d\pi^2 \leq 0$. The latter assumption, implying non-risk-loving behavior, has a broad empirical basis (Young et al.). The former assumption implies a technology sufficiently well-behaved so that a unique optimum exists.

Using Pratt's definition of the risk premium, expected utility can be expressed as $E[U(W_0 + \pi)] = U[W_0 + E(\pi) - R]$, where R is the risk premium. Thus, $R > 0$ with risk aversion and $R = 0$ with risk neutrality. In this context, the certainty equivalent of a risky situation,

$$L = W_0 + E(\pi) - R = U^{-1}\{E[U(W_0 + \pi)]\},$$

is useful as a measure of welfare because it is measured in money, and a change in L is equivalent to a change in wealth. Also, maximizing L with respect to $\mathbf{x}$ is equivalent to maximizing $E[U(W_0 + \pi)]$ with respect to $\mathbf{x}$, since $U' > 0$. Thus, let L^* denote the indirect certainty equivalent function obtained by evaluating L at x^*, where x^* is the optimal choice of $\mathbf{x}$ as a function of γ and W_0. Then, $U(L^*) = E[U(W_0 + \pi^*)]$, where

$$(1) \quad L^* (\gamma, W_0) = W_0 + E(\pi^*) - R^*$$
$$= U^{-1}\{E[U(W_0 + \pi^*)]\};$$

π^* and R^* are obtained by evaluating π and R at x^*, respectively. Thus, unless otherwise specified, functions will be evaluated at optimal values of the control variables.

Welfare change is analyzed with measures of willingness to pay (or accept payment), as is common in welfare economics literature. Using initial welfare as a reference point, willingness to pay is measured by the compensating variation, c, defined as

$$(2)$$
$$U[L^*(\gamma_1, W_0)] \equiv U[L^*(\gamma_2, W_0 - c)], \text{ or}$$
$$L^*(\gamma_1, W_0) \equiv L^*(\gamma_2, W_0 - c),$$

where γ_1 and γ_2 are the initial and subsequent parameter points, and inputs are free to adjust in each case. That is, c is the *ex ante* sum of money which, if paid in the subsequent situation, makes the firm indifferent to the change. Similarly, using the subsequent welfare situation as a reference point, willingness to pay is measured by the equivalent variation, e, defined as

$$(3) \quad L^*(\gamma_1, W_0 + e) \equiv L^*(\gamma_2, W_0),$$

with inputs free to adjust in each case. Thus, e is the *ex ante* sum of money which, when received in the initial situation, makes the firm indifferent to the change.[1]

As in consumer theory, an infinite number of other producer welfare measures also can be defined (Patinkin). However, the compensating and equivalent variations are of particular interest. They permit use of the Kaldor-Hicks compensation criterion (a change is desirable if gainers can compensate losers so that no one is worse off) and the Scitovsky reversal criterion (a change is desirable if losers cannot compensate gainers so that no one is worse off without the change). The Kaldor-Hicks criterion, with the initial situation as a reference point, calls for compensating variation. The Scitovsky reversal criterion, with the subsequent situation as a reference point, calls for equivalent variation.

The remainder of this paper focuses on these measures using the conventional calculations of areas above product supply curves and below derived demand curves. By differentiating and integrating (1), the ordinary compensated change in the certainty equivalent may be expressed as

$$(4) \quad \Delta L^* = \int_{\gamma_1}^{\gamma_2} \frac{\partial L^*}{\partial \gamma} \, d\gamma =$$
$$\int_{\gamma_1}^{\gamma_2} \left[\frac{\partial E(\pi^*)}{\partial \gamma} - \frac{\partial R^*}{\partial \gamma} \right] d\gamma$$
$$= \int_{\gamma_1}^{\gamma_2} (U^{-1})' \left[E(U') E\left(\frac{\partial \pi}{\partial \gamma} \right) \right.$$
$$\left. + \text{Cov}\left(U', \frac{\partial \pi}{\partial \gamma} \right) \right] d\gamma.$$

This formulation is of particular interest when it coincides with compensating or equivalent

---

[1] In Pratt's terminology, c is the maximum bid price for purchasing the subsequent situation, and e is the minimum selling price the firm would accept to give up the subsequent situation. Because of this equivalence, all of the results in this paper stated as compensating and equivalent variations also hold for bid and sell prices.

100 *February 1983*

Amer. J. Agr. Econ.

variations. However, ΔL^* is of practical interest on intuitive grounds. That is, the welfare measures, defined in (2)–(4), are analogous to the three popular welfare measures in consumer theory—the two Hicksian measures using compensated demands at initial and subsequent welfare levels and the Marshallian measures using ordinary, uncompensated demand functions. However, the ordinary change in the certainty equivalent of (4) does not exhibit path dependence, even with multiple parameter changes. It is a line integral of an exact differential of L^*.[2] Since none of the three measures in (2)–(4) suffers from path dependence, this paper generally considers only changes in a single coordinate of γ. Hence, the integral in (4) will be regarded as a standard univariate Riemann integral unless otherwise noted.

Calculation of Compensating and Equivalent Variation

The effect of initial wealth, W_0, on the certainty equivalent is important in risk analysis. Differentiating (1) with respect to W_0 and using the envelope theorem (Silberberg) yields:

$$(5) \quad \frac{\partial L^*}{\partial W_0} = U^{-1}(L)' \cdot E[U'(W_0 + \pi)]$$

$$\begin{cases} > 1 \text{ with decreasing absolute} \\ \quad \text{risk aversion [DARA]} \\ \\ = 1 \text{ with constant absolute risk} \\ \quad \text{aversion [CARA]} \end{cases}$$

The relationships on the right side of (5) are implied by Pratt and discussed explicitly in Pope and Paris. This result suggests that wealth increases imply that the risk premium is reduced (unaltered) as absolute risk aversion decreases (is constant).

The compensating and equivalent variations can be expressed as integrals upon differentiating (2) and (3) with respect to the changing parameter. For example,

$$(6) \quad L^*(\gamma, W_0 - c) = W_0 + E(\pi_c) - c - R_c$$
$$= U^{-1}\{E[U(W_0 + \pi_c - c)]\},$$

where c subscripts denote the optimum when

[2] Equation (4) can be regarded as a nontrivial line integral if $\partial L^*/\partial \gamma = (\partial L^*/\partial \gamma^1, \ldots, \partial L^*/\partial \gamma^k)$ and $d\gamma = (d\gamma^1, \ldots, d\gamma^k)'$, where $\gamma = (\gamma^1, \ldots, \gamma^k)'$. The key is symmetry of the demand or supply curves in parameters which are changing in the line integral. This yields a unique welfare measure (Silberberg).

appropriate compensation keeps welfare at the initial level. Differentiating (2) with respect to γ_2 (denoted by γ) and using the envelope theorem[3] (Silberberg) yields

$$(7) \quad \frac{\partial E(\pi_c)}{\partial \gamma} - \frac{\partial c}{\partial \gamma} - \frac{\partial R_c}{\partial \gamma} - \frac{\partial R_c}{\partial c}\frac{\partial c}{\partial \gamma}$$
$$= (U_c^{-1})'\left\{E(U'_c)\left[E\left(\frac{\partial \pi_c}{\partial \gamma}\right) - \frac{\partial c}{\partial \gamma}\right]\right.$$
$$\left. + \text{Cov}\left(U'_c, \frac{\partial \pi_c}{\partial \gamma}\right)\right\} = 0.$$

Note that c is an *ex ante*, nonstochastic payment. Similarly, from (3),

$$(8) \quad \frac{\partial E(\pi_e)}{\partial \gamma} + \frac{\partial e}{\partial \gamma} - \frac{\partial R_e}{\partial \gamma} - \frac{\partial R_e}{\partial e}\frac{\partial e}{\partial \gamma}$$
$$= (U_e^{-1})'\left\{E(U'_e)\left[E\left(\frac{\partial \pi_e}{\partial \gamma}\right) + \frac{\partial e}{\partial \gamma}\right]\right.$$
$$\left. + \text{Cov}\left(U'_e, \frac{\partial \pi_e}{\partial \gamma}\right)\right\} = 0,$$

where e subscripts denote the optimum when compensation keeps welfare at the subsequent level. The left-handed side of (2) and the right-hand side of (3) vanish since $L^*(\gamma_1, W_0)$ and $L^*(\gamma_2, W_0)$ are held constant. Using (7) and (8), one obtains two useful expressions for the compensating and equivalent variations:

$$(9) \quad c = \int_{\gamma_1}^{\gamma_2} \frac{\partial c}{\partial \gamma}\,d\gamma = \int_{\gamma_1}^{\gamma_2} \frac{\left(\frac{\partial E \pi_c}{\partial \gamma} - \frac{\partial R_c}{\partial \gamma}\right)}{\left(1 + \frac{\partial R_c}{\partial c}\right)}\,d\gamma$$

$$= \int_{\gamma_1}^{\gamma_2}\left[E\left(\frac{\partial \pi_c}{\partial \gamma}\right)\right.$$
$$\left. + \frac{\text{Cov}(U'_c, \partial\pi_c/\partial\gamma)}{E(U'_c)}\right]d\gamma, \text{ and}$$

$$(10) \quad e = \int_{\gamma_1}^{\gamma_2} \frac{\partial e}{\partial \gamma}\,d\gamma =$$
$$\int_{\gamma_1}^{\gamma_2} \frac{\left(\frac{\partial E(\pi_e)}{\partial \gamma} - \frac{\partial R_e}{\partial \gamma}\right)}{\left(1 - \frac{\partial R_e}{\partial e}\right)}\,d\gamma$$

$$= \int_{\gamma_1}^{\gamma_2}\left[E\left(\frac{\partial \pi_e}{\partial \gamma}\right)\right.$$
$$\left. + \frac{\text{Cov}(U'_e, \partial\pi_e/\partial\gamma)}{E(U'_e)}\right]d\gamma,$$

[3] The Envelope Theorem implies, for example, that $\partial L^*/\partial x^*$ $[\partial x^*/\partial\gamma + (\partial x^*/\partial c)(\partial c/\partial\gamma)] = 0$ from the first-order optimization conditions. This result holds even when the model is extended to include production constraints.

since $c = e = 0$ if $\gamma_1 = \gamma_2$. Equations (9) and (10) are obtained by solving (7) and (8) for $\partial c / \partial \gamma$ and $\partial e / \partial \gamma$, respectively, and then integrating.

Under risk neutrality, only the first term inside the brackets in (9) and (10) is relevant since R is identically zero.[4] Alternatively, under risk aversion if the risk premium is not altered by compensation, then $\partial R_c / \partial c$ and $\partial R_e / \partial e$ vanish, and $x^* = x_c = x_e$ (decisions do not depend on compensation) since maximizing $W_0 + E(\pi) - R$, $W_0 + E(\pi) - c - R$, or $W_0 + E(\pi) e - R$ is equivalent to maximizing $E(\pi) - R$. This implies that $\Delta L^* = c = e$. This is the case under constant absolute risk aversion since it is clear from (5) that compensation plays a role analogous to initial wealth. Hence, the Hicksian measures of compensating and equivalent variation and the certainty equivalent changes coincide with constant absolute risk aversion. In this case, from (4), (7), and (8),

$$(11) \quad \frac{\partial L^*}{\partial \gamma} = \frac{\partial c}{\partial \gamma} = \frac{\partial e}{\partial \gamma} = E\left(\frac{\partial \pi}{\partial \gamma}\right)$$

$$+ (U^{-1})' \, \text{Cov}\left(U', \frac{\partial \pi}{\partial \gamma}\right).$$

If the risk premium is not a function of either the parameter vector γ or the compensation, then

$$(12) \quad \Delta L^* = c = e = \int_{\gamma_1}^{\gamma_2} \frac{\partial E(\pi)}{\partial \gamma} d\gamma.$$

Ordinary Supply and Demand and Nonstochastic Production

Consider a single-product firm where x is a vector of input quantities, P is output price, y is output quantity, r_i is the price of input i (nonrandom), and the profit equation is $\pi = Py(x) - \sum_{i=1}^{n} r_i x_i$. Let $\bar{P}$ represent expected output price at decision-making time. Suppose also that all moments about $\bar{P}$ are constant. Then, assuming CARA and using (11), the envelope theorem implies

$$(13) \quad \frac{\partial L^*}{\partial \bar{P}} = \frac{\partial c}{\partial \bar{P}} \frac{\partial e}{\partial \bar{P}} = E(y)$$

$$+ (U^{-1})' \, \text{Cov}(U', y).$$

[4] However, $E(\pi^*)$ may be substantially altered when x^* reflects risk aversion rather than risk neutrality.

If production is nonstochastic (y is a non-stochastic function of x), then the covariance in (13) vanishes and

$$(14) \quad \Delta L^* = c = e = \int_{\bar{P}_1}^{\bar{P}_2} y \, d\bar{P}.$$

Thus, the change in the area above the ordinary product supply curve and below expected product price caused by a change in product price coincides with both compensating and equivalent variations. Furthermore, because the risk-averse supply curve is above the risk-neutral supply curve (Sandmo), the welfare change under the risk aversion is less than that under risk neutrality.

Compensation does not alter choices under constant absolute risk aversion because $x = x_c$, equation (5). However, under nonconstant absolute risk aversion, x_c is chosen to maximize $E[U(W_0 + \pi - c)]$ and, thus, $x_c = x_c(\gamma, W_0 - c)$. The value of c is chosen to keep the certainty equivalent at the reference level. Letting L_1 be this reference level, then $c(\gamma, W_0, L_1)$. Thus, the compensated choices can be written as $x_c = x^*[\gamma, W_0 - c(\gamma, W_0, L_1)]$. Differentiating x_c with respect to γ yields the Slutsky-Hicks type equation,

$$(15) \quad \frac{\partial x_c}{\partial \gamma} = \frac{\partial x}{\partial \gamma} - \frac{\partial x}{\partial W_0} \frac{\partial c}{\partial \gamma},$$

where at $c = 0$, $\partial x^* / \partial \gamma$ is the response of the uncompensated function. Expression (15) is of particular interest when $\gamma = \bar{P}$ or $\gamma = r$. In the former case ($\gamma = \bar{P}$), the left side of (15) is the slope of the compensated supply function. The first term on the right is the ordinary uncompensated supply function slope. Thus, the qualitative relationship between compensated and uncompensated supply functions can be obtained by knowing the sign of the last term in (15). When $\gamma = r$, a relationship between compensated and uncompensated input demand functions is obtained.

Let $\gamma = \bar{P}$ and consider output as a choice variable. It follows that $\partial c / \partial \gamma = y_c$ and equation (15) becomes

$$(16) \quad \frac{\partial y_c}{\partial \bar{P}} = \frac{\partial y}{\partial \bar{P}} - y \frac{\partial y}{\partial W_0}.$$

It can be shown that $\partial y / \partial W_0 > (=) 0$ as absolute risk aversion is decreasing (constant). Thus, (16) implies that the ordinary response exceeds the compensated response with decreasing absolute risk aversion. The two slopes are equal with constant absolute risk aversion. Similar results follow for y_e. Thus, Hicksian product supply curves intersect ordinary product supply curves from above (or are steeper than ordinary supply curves) under decreasing absolute risk aversion. Equation (17) summarizes the above discussion with respect to producer's surplus under decreasing absolute risk aversion.

$$(17) \quad \int_{\bar{P}_1}^{\bar{P}_2} \frac{\partial L^*}{\partial \bar{P}} \, d\bar{P} = \int_{\bar{P}_1}^{\bar{P}_2} T y \, d\bar{P} >$$

$$\int_{\bar{P}_1}^{\bar{P}_2} y \, d\bar{P} > \int_{\bar{P}_1}^{\bar{P}_2} y_c \, d\bar{P} = c,$$

where $\bar{P}_1$ is the initial situation with initial certainty equivalent L_1 and $T = E[U/(U^{-1})']$ > 1 under DARA [see (5)]. Similarly, $\partial y/\partial \bar{P} > \partial y_e/\partial \bar{P}$ implies

$$(18) \quad \Delta L^* = \int_{\bar{P}_1}^{\bar{P}_2} \frac{\partial L}{\partial \bar{P}} = \int_{\bar{P}_1}^{\bar{P}_2} T y \, d\bar{P}$$

$$> \int_{\bar{P}_1}^{\bar{P}_2} y \, d\bar{P} < \int_{\bar{P}_1}^{\bar{P}_2} y_e \, d\bar{P} = e,$$

where $\bar{P}_2$ is the subsequent situation with L_2 as the subsequent certainty equivalent. These results imply that the change in area above the ordinary product supply curve between two expected prices overestimates the compensating variation and underestimates the equivalent variation under DARA and nonstochastic production. In this case, the change in area above the ordinary product supply curve agrees in sign but underestimates the magnitude of the change in the ordinary certainty equivalent.

Figure 1 depicts an ordinary supply curve labeled y and compensated curves labeled y_e and y_c with $\bar{P}_1$ as the initial expected price. The welfare measure of a *ceteris paribus* rise in expected price from $\bar{P}_1$ to $\bar{P}_2$ is $\bar{P}_1\bar{P}_2\,a\,c$ for compensating variation and $\bar{P}_1\bar{P}_2 b\,d$ for equivalent variation. The Marshallian measure is $\bar{P}_1\bar{P}_2 b\,c$. For this single parameter change, compensating variation and $\bar{P}_1\bar{P}_2 b\,d$ for equivalent variation. The Marshallian measure is lent variation. Under constant risk aversion, all three coincide at $\bar{P}_1\bar{P}_2\,b\,c$ since $y_c = y_e = y$.

Equation (16) provides the intuition behind these results. Under constant absolute risk aversion, any change in the location of the distribution of wealth such as c or e does not alter risk aversion or choice. In such a case $\partial y/\partial W = 0$, and there is no wealth or compensation effect. With decreasing absolute risk aversion and for a rise in expected output

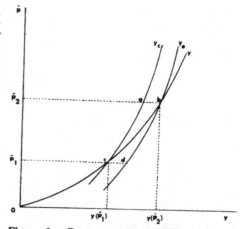

Figure 1. Compensated and ordinary supply curves under decreasing absolute risk aversion

price, compensating variation is positive, implying a reduction in wealth and a rise in absolute risk aversion. In such case, as the firm moves up the uncompensated supply curve, compensation becomes positive, reducing wealth and increasing risk aversion. This causes the compensated supply to fall [see (16)] so as to lie left of the ordinary curve. Thus, the ordinary curve has a greater supply elasticity than the compensated supply curve as shown in figure 1 (with expected price on the vertical axis). Similar reasoning applies to the cases of a fall in expected price or the calculation of equivalent variation.

Input price changes under DARA yield similar results. Analogous to (16) is the Slutsky-Hicks-type equation for a change in input price r_i on the ith input demand:

$$(19) \quad \frac{\partial x_{ic}}{\partial r_i} = \frac{\partial x_i}{\partial r_i} + x_i \frac{\partial x_i}{\partial W_0}.$$

Analogous to the output case, a key component in (19) is the wealth effects, $\partial x_i/\partial W_0$. It can be shown that $\partial x_i/\partial W_0 = 0$ if absolute risk aversion is constant. With DARA, the wealth effect is positive, $\partial x_i/\partial W_0 > 0$, if all factors of production exhibit Hicksian complementarity which is defined by $\partial^2 y/\partial x_i \partial x_j > 0$. (This is argued in more detail in Pope and Chavas.) Under these assumptions, $\partial x_i/\partial r_i < \partial x_{ic}/\partial r_i$, and

$$(20) \quad \Delta L^* = -\int_{r_{i1}}^{r_{i2}} x_i T \, dr_i < -\int_{r_{i1}}^{r_{i2}} x_i \, dr_i$$

$$> -\int_{r_{i1}}^{r_{i2}} x_{ic} \, dr_i = c,$$

where r_{i1} is the initial situation.

Similarly, $\partial x_1/\partial r_i < \partial x_{ie}/\partial r_i$ implies

$$(21) \quad \Delta L^* = -\int_{r_{i1}}^{r_{i2}} x_i \; T > dr_i < -\int_{r_{i1}}^{r_{i2}} x_i \; dr_i$$

$$< -\int_{r_{i1}}^{r_{i2}} x_{ie} \; dr_i = e,$$

where r_{i2} is the subsequent situation. These results imply that the absolute value of the change in the area below the ordinary derived demand curve and above input price underestimates the compensating variation and overestimates the equivalent variation (in absolute values) with DARA. Consider compensating variation. As r_i increases, wealth increases so that the compensated curve lies right of the ordinary curve. That is, the compensated factor demand elasticity is larger (the curve is steeper) than the ordinary factor demand elasticity. When there is no wealth effect (CARA), the ordinary and compensated curves coincide.

Stochastic Production

In several of the results above, simplifications occurred when the covariances in (4), (9), and (10) vanished. However, such may not occur when production is stochastic (e.g., where random weather conditions affect yields of crops in ways unanticipated at the decision-making time). To consider this case, suppose the production function $y(x)$ is stochastic [$y(x) = y(x, \epsilon)$ for some random variable ϵ]. In this case, (13) continues to hold under CARA where $y = y(x, \epsilon)$. It can be shown that $U'' < 0$ (risk aversion) implies that $cov(U', y) < 0$ assuming independence of P and y (the method of proof is found in Chavas and Pope), and

$$(22) \quad \Delta L^* = c = e = \int_{\bar{P}_1}^{\bar{P}_2} [E(y)$$

$$+ (U^{-1})' \; cov(U', y)] \; d\bar{P} < \int_{\bar{P}_1}^{\bar{P}_2} E(y)d\bar{P},$$

where the inequality in (22) is based on the presumption that $cov(U', y) < 0$—higher yields produce lower marginal utilities regardless of price. This is a strong presumption but occurs with independence of the distributions P and y.

Similar results hold for DARA, although ΔL^*, c, and e no longer coincide. With stochastic production, the area above the expected supply curve does not measure welfare

change except for risk neutrality, where $U'' = 0$ (U' is constant and the covariance vanishes). The area change above the expected supply curve overstates welfare change under CARA if product price is either nonstochastic or stochastically independent of production.

The results in (20) and (21) are not changed if x_i is chosen *ex ante* since the covariance terms in (4), (9), and (10) vanish even though ordinary factor demands depend on production uncertainty. Therefore, production uncertainty does not alter the earlier conclusion. With CARA, the change in the area below a factor demand measures the change in the ordinary certainty equivalent caused by an input price change. Alternatively, under DARA, this change does not reflect compensating or equivalent variations.

The Welfare Effects of Changes in Risk

Unfortunately, equations (4), (9), and (10) are not easily applied if γ is not a (mean) price. For example, if γ represents the spread of a price distribution holding the mean fixed (Sandmo), then the measure in (11) under CARA cannot be obtained with ordinary supply and demand functions alone and, in fact, cannot be obtained without further specification of preferences and the price distribution. For example, if output price is $\tilde{P} = \gamma(P - \bar{P}) + \bar{P}$, so that an increase in γ represents a mean-preserving spread, then with nonstochastic production (9) implies that

$$c = \int_{\gamma_1}^{\gamma_2} y_c \; \frac{Cov(U'_c, P)}{E(U'_c)} \; d\gamma.$$

Sandmo has shown that $Cov(U'_c, P) < 0$ under risk aversion. Hence, an increase in risk clearly reduces welfare. Unfortunately, c cannot be calculated from this equation without the moments of the joint distribution of U'_c and P, which require specific information on preferences, the price distribution, and/or technology.

However, some useful results can be obtained using the concept of shut-down prices to consider changes in risk and other nonprice parameters. First consider a change in the entire parameter vector from γ_1 to γ_2, where mean product price changes from $\bar{P}_1$ to $\bar{P}_2$. Then define the shut-down, mean product price in each case as

$$\bar{P}^\circ_j = max \; [\bar{P} \; such \; that \; y(\bar{P}, \bar{\gamma}^\circ_j, W_0)$$
$$= 0], \, j = 1, 2,$$

104 *February 1983*

Amer. J. Agr. Econ.

where γ°_j is given by γ_j except that $\bar{P}$ is omitted. Thus, at $\bar{P}^\circ_j$ production ceases. Viewing (4), (9), and (10) as line integrals with CARA yields

$$\Delta L^* = c = e = L^*(\gamma_2, W_0) - L^*(\gamma_1, W_0)$$
$$= L^*(\bar{P}_2, \gamma^\circ_2, W_0)$$
$$\quad - L^*(\bar{P}^\circ_2, \gamma^\circ_2, W_0)$$
$$\quad + L^*(\bar{P}^\circ_1, \gamma^\circ_1, W_0)$$
$$\quad - L^*(\bar{P}_1, \gamma^\circ_1, W_0)$$
$$= \Delta L^*_2 - \Delta L^*_1,$$

where, under nonstochastic production,

$$\Delta L_j^* = \int_{\bar{P}_j}^{\bar{P}_j} y(\bar{P}, \gamma^\circ_j, W_0) \, d\bar{P}, \quad j = 1, 2.$$

This result occurs since the certainty equivalent of a shut down, $L^*(\bar{P}^\circ_j, \gamma^\circ_j, W_0)$, is W_0 in both cases. Thus, with CARA and nonstochastic production, the change in the entire area above the product supply curve and below expected price, caused by a general change in any parameter (including risk), measures the compensating variation, equivalent variation, and ordinary change in certainty equivalent. In particular, with CARA and nonstochastic production, the area between supply curves measures the welfare change associated with a mean-preserving risk change. However, these results do not hold when either CARA or nonstochastic production assumptions are relaxed. Furthermore, this result does not generalize to a multiproduct firm unless the shut-down price ensures shutdown of all production activities (that is, if $\bar{P}^\circ_j$ implies y_j is zero, then all other production ceases as well) or that L is additive in outputs. In this latter case, one may isolate welfare for each production activity. This would be analogous to the nonjoint production case under certainty.

Consider a change in the entire parameter vector from γ_1 to γ_2, where the price of a necessary input i changes from r_{i1} to r_{i2}. Suppose the input is necessary in the sense that shut-down prices defined as

$$r^\circ_{ij} = \min \,[r_{ij} \text{ such that } x_i(r_{ij}, \bar{\gamma}^\circ_j, W_0) = 0]$$
$$= \min \,[r_{ij} \text{ such that } \pi^*(r_{ij}, \bar{\gamma}^\circ_j, W_0) = 0],$$
$$j = 1, 2,$$

exist where $\bar{\gamma}^\circ_j$ is given by γ_j, except that r_i is omitted. Again, viewing (4), (9), and (10) as line integrals and assuming CARA, so that the integrands coincide, gives

(23)

$$\Delta L^* = c = e = L^*(r_{i2}, \bar{\gamma}^\circ_2, W_0)$$
$$\quad - L^*(r^\circ_{i2}, \bar{\gamma}^\circ_2, W_0)$$
$$\quad + L^*(r^\circ_{i1}, \bar{\gamma}^\circ_1, Q_0)$$
$$\quad - L^*(r_{i1}, \bar{\gamma}^\circ_1, W_0)$$
$$= \Delta \bar{L}^*_2 - \Delta \bar{L}^*_1,$$

where

$$\Delta \bar{L}^*_j = \int_{r_{ij}}^{r^\circ_{ij}} x_i(r_i, \bar{\gamma}^\circ_j, W_0) \, dr_i; \quad j = 1, 2.$$

This result occurs because $L^*(r^\circ_{ij}, \gamma^\circ_j, W_0) = W_0$, $j = 1, 2$. Each represents a shutdown. Thus, with CARA, the change in the area below the derived demand curve for a necessary input and above the input price measures the compensating variation, equivalent variation, and ordinary change in the certainty equivalent whether or not production is stochastic. In particular, the area between derived demands associated with different levels of output price and/or production risk measures the change in welfare associated with the change in risk, *ceteris paribus*. Similar results do not hold if CARA is not assumed.

Suppose that input demands are $x_i = x_i(r, \bar{P}, \sigma, \alpha)$, where σ is the variance of output price, and α represents all other parameters. Consider a policy which stabilizes output price such that $\sigma_1 > \sigma_2$. For simplicity, assume that only r and σ vary. Let r°_{i1} and r°_{i2} be the shutdown input prices, given σ_1 and σ_2, respectively. This is illustrated in figure 2. Total firm

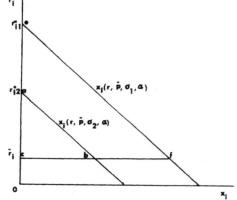

Figure 2. Demand surplus with constant absolute risk aversion and changing variance of output price

welfare, relative to a shutdown under CARA given σ_1 and input price $\bar{r}_i$, is (*cfe*). The change in welfare due to a reduction in price variance is (*abfe*).

This approach requires knowledge of factor demands in the shut-down neighborhood. Since there is likely to be little data for this neighborhood, caution must be used with this approach.

The necessary input (output) assumption can be relaxed if a set of (mean) price changes can be identified which cause the firm to shut down when all other parameters are at either their initial or subsequent levels. Then, the path of integration in (4), (9), or (10) involves changing all initial (mean) prices to shut down the initial situation. Then, the same operation is performed with the subsequent situation, producing $\Delta \bar{L}^*_2$ and $\Delta \bar{L}^*_1$ in (23). The welfare of both shut-down situations is W_0 so that the methodology of sections III and IV is sufficient to evaluate welfare changes along remaining segments of the path of integration, just as in (23). If production is stochastic, then this approach must generally reach a shut-down by changing only input prices since expected price changes do not conveniently generate welfare changes [see (22)]. With nonstochastic production, the shutdown may be reached by any combination of mean output price and input price changes.

Mean-Variance Analysis

This analysis shows that the CARA assumption facilitates welfare analysis with ordinary supply and demand curves. Since CARA is the most typical assumption for empirical research (Young et al.), a further exploration of Freund's additive expected utility function is of interest. It shows how further preference information can be used. In this case, denoting variance by V, we have

$$(24) \quad L(\gamma, W_0) = W_0 + E(\pi) - \frac{\psi}{2} V(\pi),$$

where ψ is the constant risk-aversion parameter. Suppose further that both P and y are stochastic and independent. Thus, (24) becomes

$$(25) \quad L(\gamma, W_0) = W_0 + \bar{P} \bar{y} - \sum_{i=1}^{n} r_i x_i$$

$$- \frac{\psi}{2} [\bar{y}^2 V(P) + \bar{P}^2 V(y) + V(P) V(y)],$$

where $\bar{y} = E(y)$.

Since risk aversion is constant, welfare can be measured by areas under derived demand curves. Suppose that information about derived demands is not available or is inaccurate. As shown in (23), the change in area above the expected supply curve is not a valid measure of welfare change when production is stochastic. In this case, noting that $\Delta L^* = c = e$ from (11), differentiating (25), integrating for an expected product price change from $\bar{P}_1$ to $\bar{P}_2$ gives

$$(26) \quad \Delta L^* = c = e = \int_{\bar{P}_1}^{\bar{P}_2} E(y)$$

$$[1 - \psi \bar{P} V(y)/E(y)] \, d\bar{P}.$$

Because the bracketed term gives the multiplicative bias of the area above the expected supply curve, (26) implies that the bias is negative under risk aversion. It increases with higher risk aversion, expected price, and production risk, *ceteris paribus*. It clearly disappears under production certainty, $[V(y) = 0]$. Furthermore, (26) shows how to estimate the correct compensating and equivalent variations using the change in area above the expected supply curve. That is, $\bar{P}$, $V(y)$, and $E(y)$ are estimable parameters or functions. If the coefficient of risk aversion is known or can be estimated, then one need merely subtract $\int_{\bar{P}_1}^{\bar{P}_2} \psi [\bar{P} V(y)] \, d\bar{P}$ from the change in area above the expected supply curve.

Consider a change in the price variance from σ_1 to σ_2. Note from (25) that

$$\Delta L^* = c = e = - \int_{\sigma_1}^{\sigma_2} \frac{\psi}{2} \{ [E(y)]^2 + V(y) \} \, d\sigma.$$

In this case, the appropriate welfare measure is a linear function of the change in area below the squared expected supply curve and change in area below the supply curve variance as functions of the price variance. These are also estimable functions and, with knowledge or estimation of the risk-aversion parameter, provide a way to estimate the welfare effects of change in price variance.

Conclusions

This paper has analyzed the validity of producer and consumer surplus for measuring producer welfare effects under risk aversion.

106   *February 1983*

Amer. J. Agr. Econ.

If traditional producer and consumer surplus triangles are based on expected prices and if supply and demand curves are appropriately conditioned on risk, they are valid measures under constant absolute risk aversion and nonstochastic production. Only the surplus in input markets is a valid measure under constant absolute risk aversion with stochastic production.

These results are disturbing for stochastic production and decreasing absolute risk aversion. The area above an expected supply curve of a product (often used in the agricultural stabilization literature) is an inappropriate welfare measure because agricultural production is risky. In this case, producer surplus associated with acreage supply curves is a valid measure of welfare change under constant absolute risk aversion regardless of the joint distribution of price and yields. Decreasing absolute risk aversion creates more serious problems. No ordinary supply or demand relationship permits welfare calculations in this case, although appropriate correction factors can in principle be estimated with restrictive assumptions.

Having summarized the results of this paper, it is clear that deviations from constant absolute risk aversion imply that compensated factor demands and product supplies (when nonstochastic) should be used for welfare measures under risk. There are two unanswered questions for future research. First, it may be that the wealth effect under DARA is quite small. This would indicate that the uncompensated curve is a good approximation to the compensated curve. Thus, the magnitude of error using the areas associated with observed, uncompensated curves for welfare measures may be small. This could be formalized by calculating bounds of error when using uncompensated curves, as Willig has done in the consumer case. Thus, use of uncompensated surplus measures could be accompanied by acknowledging quantitatively the corresponding error in welfare measurement.

A second approach, which is more cumbersome but has recently received some attention in the consumer case, consists of developing ways to obtain the Hicksian measures from ordinary curves. Such an approach was recently proposed by Hausman for the consumer case under separability using duality theory.

Until these approaches are developed, we would recommend that, when possible, surpluses using input demands or acreage supply functions be utilized for welfare measurement when a priori or empirical evidence suggests a small marginal impact of wealth changes on decisions.

[*Received October 1980; revision accepted June 1982.*]

References

Akino, M., and Y. Hayami. "Efficiency and Equity in Public Research: Rice Breeding in Japan's Economic Development." *Amer. J. Agr. Econ.* 57 (1975):1–10.

Blandford, D., and M. Currie. "Price Uncertainty—The Case for Government Intervention." *J. Agr. Econ.* 26(1975):37–51.

Burt, O. R., W. W. Koo, and N. J. Dudley. "Optimal Control of U.S. Wheat Stocks and Exports." *Amer. J. Agr. Econ.* 62(1980):172–87.

Chavas, J.-P., and R. D. Pope. "Welfare Measures of Production Activities under Risk Aversion." *S. Econ. J.* 48(1981):187–96.

Freund, R. J. "The Introduction of Risk into a Programming Model." *Econometrica* 24(1956):253–63.

Hausman, J. A. "Exact Consumer's Surplus and Deadweight Loss." *Amer. Econ. Rev.* 71(1981):662–76.

Just, R. "Risk Response Models and Their Use in Agricultural Policy Evaluation." *Amer. J. Agr. Econ.* 57(1975):836–43.

———. "The Welfare Economics of Agricultural Risk." *Market Risks in Agriculture: Concepts, Methods and Policy Issues.* Proceedings of Western Rgnl. Res. Proj. W-149, 1978.

Just, R., E. Lutz, A. Schmitz, and Stephen S. Turnovsky. "The Distribution of Welfare Gains from International Price Stabilization under Distortions." *Amer. J. Agr. Econ.* 59(1977):652–61.

Massell, B. F. "Price Stabilization and Welfare." *Quart. J. Econ.* 83(1969):285–97.

Patinkin, D. "Demand Curves and Consumer Surplus." *Measurement in Economics Studies in Mathematical Economics and Econometrics in Memory of Yehuda Grunfield,* ed. Earl Christ. Stanford CA: Stanford University Press, 1963.

Pope, R., and J.-P. Chavas. "Marshallian Surpluses and Ex Ante Welfare Evaluation of Agricultural Producers." Dep. Agr. Econ. Work. Pap., Texas A&M University, 1980.

Pope, R., and Q. Paris. "Long-Run Equilibrium of the Competitive Firm under Uncertainty." Dep. Agr. Econ. Work. Pap. No. 79-3, University of California, Davis, 1979.

Pratt, J. "Risk Aversion in the Small and in the Large." *Econometrica* 32(1964):122–36.

Sandmo, A. "On the Theory of the Competitive Firm under Price Uncertainty." *Amer. Econ. Rev.* 61(1971):65–73.

Silberberg, E. *The Structure of Economics: A Mathemati-*

Pope, Chavas, and Just

cal Analysis. New York: McGraw-Hill Book Co., 1978.

Subotnik, A., and J. P. Houck. "Welfare Implications of Stabilizing Consumption and Production." *Amer. J. Agr. Econ.* 58(1976):13–20.

Taylor, C. R., and H. Talpaz. "Approximately Optimal Carry-Over Levels for Wheat in the United States." *Amer. J. Agr. Econ.* 61(1979):32–40.

Turnovsky, S. "The Distribution of Welfare Gains from Price Stabilization: The Case of Multiplicative Disturbances." *Int. Econ. Rev.* 17(1976):133–48.

Turnovsky, S., H. Shalit, and A. Schmitz. "Consumer's Surplus, Price Instability, and Consumer Welfare." *Econometrica* 48(1980):135–52.

von Neumann, J., and O. Morgenstern. *Theory of Games and Economic Behavior.* Princeton: Princeton University Press, 1944.

Willig, R. D. "Consumer Surplus without Apology." *Amer. Econ. Rev.* 66(1976):589–97.

Young, D., W. Lin, R. Pope, L. Robinson, and R. Selley. "Risk Preferences of Agricultural Producers: Their Measurement and Use." *Risk Management in Agriculture: Behavioral, Managerial, and Policy Issues.* Proceedings of Western Rgnl. Proj. W-149, San Francisco, 1979.

[32]

Uncertainty and the Evaluation of Public Investment Decisions

By Kenneth J. Arrow and Robert C. Lind*

The implications of uncertainty for public investment decisions remain controversial. The essence of the controversy is as follows. It is widely accepted that individuals are not indifferent to uncertainty and will not, in general, value assets with uncertain returns at their expected values. Depending upon an individual's initial asset holdings and utility function, he will value an asset at more or less than its expected value. Therefore, in private capital markets, investors do not choose investments to maximize the present value of expected returns, but to maximize the present value of returns properly adjusted for risk. The issue is whether it is appropriate to discount public investments in the same way as private investments.

There are several positions on this issue. The first is that risk should be discounted in the same way for public investments as it is for private investments. It is argued that to treat risk differently in the public sector will result in overinvestment in this sector at the expense of private investments yielding higher returns. The leading proponent of this point of view is Jack Hirshleifer.[1] He argues that in perfect capital markets, investments are discounted with respect to both time and risk and that the discount rates obtaining in these markets should be used to evaluate public investment opportunities.

A second position is that the government can better cope with uncertainty than private investors and, therefore, government investments should not be evaluated by the same criterion used in private markets. More specifically, it is argued that the government should ignore uncertainty and behave as if indifferent to risk. The government should then evaluate investment opportunities according to their present value computed by discounting the expected value of net returns, using a rate of discount equal to the private rate appropriate for investments with certain returns. In support of this position it is argued that the government invests in a greater number of diverse projects and is able to pool risks to a much greater extent than private investors.[2] Another supporting line of argument is that many of the uncertainties which arise in private capital markets are related to what may be termed moral hazards. Individuals involved in a given transaction may hedge against the possibility of fraudulent behavior on the part of their associates. Many such risks are not present in the case of public investments and, therefore, it can be argued that it is not appropriate for the government to take these risks into account when choosing among public investments.

There is, in addition, a third position on the government's response to uncertainty. This position rejects the notion that indi-

* The authors are, respectively, professor of economics at Harvard University; and assistant professor of engineering-economic systems and, by courtesy, of economics at Stanford University. R. C. Lind's work has been supported by National Science Foundation grant NSF-GK-1683.
[1] J. Hirshleifer (1965, 1966) and Hirshleifer, J. C. De Haven, and J. W. Milliman (pp. 139–50).

[2] For this point of view, see P. A. Samuelson and W. Vickrey.

vidual preferences as revealed by market behavior are of normative significance for government investment decisions, and asserts that time and risk preferences relevant for government action should be established as a matter of national policy. In this case the correct rules for action would be those established by the appropriate authorities in accordance with their concept of national policy. The rate of discount and attitude toward risk would be specified by the appropriate authorities and the procedures for evaluation would incorporate these time and risk preferences. Two alternative lines of argument lead to this position. First, if one accepts the proposition that the state is more than a collection of individuals and has an existence and interests apart from those of its individual members, then it follows that government policy need not reflect individual preferences. A second position is that markets are so imperfect that the behavior observed in these markets yields no relevant information about the time and risk preferences of individuals. It follows that some policy as to time and risk preference must be established in accordance with other evidence of social objectives. One such procedure would be to set national objectives concerning the desired rate of growth and to infer from this the appropriate rate of discount.[3] If this rate were applied to the expected returns from all alternative investments, the government would in effect be behaving as if indifferent to risk.

The approach taken in this paper closely parallels the approach taken by Hirshleifer, although the results differ from his. By using the state-preference approach to market behavior under uncertainty, Hirshleifer demonstrates that investments will not, in general, be valued at the sum of the expected returns discounted at a rate

appropriate for investments with certain returns.[4] He then demonstrates that using this discount rate for public investments may lead to non-optimal results, for two reasons. First, pooling itself may not be desirable.[5] If the government has the opportunity to undertake only investments which pay off in states where the payoff is highly valued, to combine such investments with ones that pay off in other states may reduce the value of the total investment package. Hirshleifer argues that where investments can be undertaken separately they should be evaluated separately, and that returns should be discounted at rates determined in the market. Second, even if pooling were possible and desirable, Hirshleifer argues correctly that the use of a rate of discount for the public sector which is lower than rates in the private sector can lead to the displacement of private investments by public investments yielding lower expected returns.[6]

For the case where government pooling is effective and desirable, he argues that rather than evaluate public investments differently from private ones, the government should subsidize the more productive private investments. From this it follows that to treat risk differently for public as opposed to private investments would only be justified if it were impossible to transfer the advantages of government pooling to private investors. Therefore, at most, the argument for treating public risks differently than private ones in evaluating investments is an argument for the "second best."[7]

The first section of this paper addresses the problem of uncertainty, using the state-preference approach to market behavior. It demonstrates that if the returns

---

[3] For this point of view, see O. Eckstein and S. Marglin.

[4] Hirshleifer (1965 pp. 523–34); (1966, pp. 268–75).
[5] Hirshleifer (1966, pp. 270–75).
[6] Hirshleifer (1966, pp. 270–75).
[7] Hirshleifer (1966, p. 270).

from any particular investment are independent of other components of national income, then the present value of this investment equals the sum of expected returns discounted by a rate appropriate for investments yielding certain returns. This result holds for both private and public investments. Therefore, by adding one plausible assumption to Hirshleifer's formulation, the conclusion can be drawn that the government should behave as an expected-value decision maker and use a discount rate appropriate for investments with certain returns. This conclusion needs to be appropriately modified when one considers the case where there is a corporate income tax.

While this result is of theoretical interest, as a policy recommendation it suffers from a defect common to the conclusions drawn by Hirshleifer. The model of the economy upon which these recommendations are based presupposes the existence of perfect markets for claims contingent on states of the world. Put differently, it is assumed that there are perfect insurance markets through which individuals may individually pool risks. Given such markets, the distribution of risks among individuals will be Pareto optimal. The difficulty is that many of these markets for insurance do not exist, so even if the markets which do exist are perfect, the resulting equilibrium will be sub-optimal. In addition, given the strong evidence that the existing capital markets are not perfect, it is unlikely that the pattern of investment will be Pareto optimal. At the margin, different individuals will have different rates of time and risk preference, depending on their opportunities to borrow or to invest, including their opportunities to insure.

There are two reasons why markets for many types of insurance do not exist. The first is the existence of certain moral hazards.[8] In particular, the fact that someone has insurance may alter his behavior so that the observed outcome is adverse to the insurer. The second is that such markets would require complicated and specialized contracts which are costly. It may be that the cost of insuring in some cases is so high that individuals choose to bear risks rather than pay the transaction costs associated with insurance.

Given the absence of some markets for insurance and the resulting sub-optimal allocation of risks, the question remains: How should the government treat uncertainty in evaluating public investment decisions? The approach taken in this paper is that individual preferences are relevant for public investment decisions, and government decisions should reflect individual valuations of costs and benefits. It is demonstrated in the second section of this paper that when the risks associated with a public investment are publicly borne, the total cost of risk-bearing is insignificant and, therefore, the government should ignore uncertainty in evaluating public investments. Similarly, the choice of the rate of discount should in this case be independent of considerations of risk. This result is obtained not because the government is able to pool investments but because the government distributes the risk associated with any investment among a large number of people. It is the risk-spreading aspect of government investment that is essential to this result.

There remains the problem that private investments may be displaced by public ones yielding a lower return if this rule is followed, although given the absence of insurance markets this will represent a Hicks-Kaldor improvement over the initial situation. Again the question must be

[8] For a discussion of this problem see M. V. Pauly and Arrow (1968).

asked whether the superior position of the government with respect to risk can be made to serve private investors. This leads to a discussion of the government's role as a supplier of insurance, and of Hirshleifer's recommendation that private investment be subsidized in some cases.

Finally, the results obtained above apply to risks actually borne by the government. Many of the risks associated with public investments are borne by private individuals, and in such cases it is appropriate to discount for risk as would these individuals. This problem is discussed in the final section of the paper. In addition, a method of evaluating public investment decisions is developed that calls for different rates of discount applied to different classes of benefits and costs.

I. Markets for Contingent Claims and Time-Risk Preference[9]

For simplicity, consider an economy where there is one commodity and there are I individuals, S possible states of the world, and time is divided into Q periods of equal length. Further suppose that each individual acts on the basis of his subjective probability as to the states of nature; let π_{is} denote the subjective probability assigned to state s by individual i. Now suppose that each individual in the absence of trading owns claims for varying amounts of the one commodity at different points in time, given different states of the world. Let $\bar{x}_{isq}$ denote the initial claim to the commodity in period $q+1$ if state s occurs which is owned by individual i. Suppose further that all trading in these claims takes place at the beginning of the first period, and claims are bought and sold on dated commodity units contingent on a state of the world. All claims can be con-

structed from basic claims which pay one commodity unit in period $q+1$, given state s, and nothing in other states or at other times; there will be a corresponding price for this claim, p_{sq} ($s = 1, \ldots, S$; $q = 0, \ldots, Q-1$). After the trading, the individual will own claims x_{isq}, which he will exercise when the time comes to provide for his consumption. Let $V_i(x_{i1,0}, \ldots, x_{i1,Q-1}, x_{i2,0}, \ldots, x_{iS,Q-1})$ be the utility of individual i if he receives claims x_{isq} ($s = 1, \ldots, S$; $q = 0, \ldots, Q-1$). The standard assumptions are made that V_i is strictly quasi-concave ($i = 1, \ldots, I$).

Therefore each individual will attempt to maximize,

$$(1) \quad V_i(x_{i1,0}, \ldots, x_{i1,Q-1}, x_{i2,0}, \ldots, x_{iS,Q-1})$$

subject to the constraint

$$\sum_{q=0}^{Q-1} \sum_{s=1}^{S} p_{sq} x_{isq} = \sum_{q=0}^{Q-1} \sum_{s=1}^{S} p_{sq} \bar{x}_{isq}$$

Using the von Neumann-Morgenstern theorem and an extension by Hirshleifer,[10] functions U_{is} ($s = 1, \ldots, S$) can be found such that

$$
\begin{aligned}
(2) \quad & V_i(x_{i1,0}, \ldots, x_{iS,Q-1}) \\
& = \sum_{s=1}^{S} \pi_{is} U_{is}(x_{is0}, x_{is1}, \ldots, x_{iS,Q-1})
\end{aligned}
$$

In equation (2) an individual's utility, given any state of the world, is a function of his consumption at each point in time. The subscript s attached to the function U_{is} is in recognition of the fact that the value of a given stream of consumption may depend on the state of the world.

The conditions for equilibrium require that

$$
(3) \quad \pi_{is} \frac{\partial U_{is}}{\partial x_{isq}} = \lambda_i p_{sq} \quad (i = 1, \ldots, I;
$$

$$
s = 1, \ldots, S; q = 0, \ldots, Q-1)
$$

[9] For a basic statement of the state-preference approach, see Arrow (1964) and G. Debreu.

[10] J. von Neumann and O. Morgenstern, and Hirshleifer (1965, pp. 534–36).

where λ_i is a Lagrangian multiplier.

From (3) it follows that

(4) $\quad \dfrac{p_{sq}}{p_{rm}} = \dfrac{\pi_{is}\dfrac{\partial U_{is}}{\partial x_{isq}}}{\pi_{rm}\dfrac{\partial U_{ir}}{\partial x_{irm}}} \qquad (i = 1, \ldots, I;$

$r, s = 1, \ldots, S; m, q = 0, \ldots, Q - 1)$

Insight can be gained by analyzing the meaning of the prices in such an economy. Since trading takes place at time zero, p_{sq} represents the present value of a claim to one commodity unit at time q, given state s. Clearly,

$$\sum_{s=1}^{S} p_{s0} = 1$$

since someone holding one commodity unit at time zero has a claim on one commodity unit, given any state of the world. It follows that p_{sq} is the present value of one commodity at time q, given state s, in terms of a certain claim on one commodity unit at time zero. Therefore, the implicit rate of discount to time zero on returns at time q, given state s, is defined by $p_{sq} = 1/1 + r_{sq}$.

Now suppose one considers a certain claim to one commodity unit at time q; clearly, its value is

$$p_q = \sum_{s=1}^{S} p_{sq}$$

and the rate of discount appropriate for a certain return at time q is defined by

(5) $\quad \dfrac{1}{1 + r_q} = \sum_{s=1}^{S} \dfrac{1}{1 + r_{sq}} = \sum_{s=1}^{S} p_{sq}$

Given these observations, we can now analyze the appropriate procedure for evaluating government investments where there are perfect markets for claims contingent on states of the world.[11] Consider an investment where the overall effect on

[11] The following argument was sketched in Arrow (1966, pp. 28–30).

market prices can be assumed to be negligible, and suppose the net return from this investment for a given time and state is h_{sq} ($s = 1, \ldots, S; q = 0, \ldots, Q-1$). Then the investment should be undertaken if

(6) $\quad \displaystyle\sum_{q=0}^{Q-1} \sum_{s=1}^{S} h_{sq} p_{sq} > 0,$

and the sum on the left is an exact expression for the present value of the investment. Expressed differently, the investment should be adopted if

(7) $\quad \displaystyle\sum_{q=0}^{Q-1} \sum_{s=1}^{S} \dfrac{h_{sq}}{1 + r_{sq}} > 0$

The payoff in each time-state is discounted by the associated rate of discount. This is the essential result upon which Hirshleifer bases his policy conclusions.[12]

Now suppose that the net returns of the investment were (a) independent of the returns from previous investment, (b) independent of the individual utility functions, and (c) had an objective probability distribution, i.e., one agreed upon by everyone. More specifically, we assume that the set of all possible states of the world can be partitioned into a class of mutually exclusive and collectively exhaustive sets, E_t, indexed by the subscript t such that, for all s in any given E_t, all utility functions U_{is} are the same for any individual i ($i = 1, \cdots, I$), and such that all production conditions are the same. Put differently, for all s in E_t, U_{is} is the same for a given individual, but not necessarily for all individuals. At the same time there is another partition of the states of the world into sets, F_u, such that the return, h_{sq}, is the same for all s in F_u. Finally, we assume that the probability distribution of F_u is independent of E_t and is the same for all individuals.

Let E_{tu} be the set of all states of the world which lie in both E_t and F_u. For any given t and u, all states of the world in

[12] Hirshleifer (1965, pp. 523–34).

E_{tu} are indistinguishable for all purposes, so we may regard it as containing a single state. Equations (3) and (5) and the intervening discussion still hold if we then replace s everywhere by tu. However, $U_{is} = U_{itu}$ actually depends only on the subscript, t, and can be written U_{it}. From the assumptions it is obvious and can be proved rigorously that the allocation x_{isq} also depends only on t, i.e., is the same for all states in E_t for any given t, so it may be written x_{itq}. Finally, let π_{it} be the probability of E_t according to individual i, and let τ_u be the probability of F_u, assumed the same for all individuals. Then the assumption of statistical independence is written:

(8)
$$\pi_{itu} = \pi_{it}\tau_u$$

Then (3) can be written

(9)
$$\pi_{it}\tau_u \frac{\partial U_{it}}{\partial x_{itq}} = \lambda_i p_{tuq}$$

Since p_{tuq} and τ_u are independent of i, so must be

$$\left(\pi_{it} \frac{\partial U_{it}}{\partial x_{itq}} \right) \Big/ \lambda_i;$$

on the other hand, this expression is also independent of u and so can be written μ_{tq}. Therefore,

(10)
$$p_{tuq} = \mu_{tq}\tau_u$$

Since the new investment has the same return for all states s in F_u, the returns can be written h_{uq}. Then the left-hand side of (6) can, with the aid of (10), be written

(11)
$$\sum_{Q=0}^{Q-1} \sum_{s=1}^{S} h_{sq}p_{sq}$$
$$= \sum_{q=0}^{Q-1} \sum_{t} \sum_{u} h_{uq}p_{tuq}$$
$$= \sum_{q=0}^{Q-1} \left(\sum_{t} \mu_{tq} \right) \sum_{u} \tau_u h_{uq}$$

But from (10)

(12)
$$p_q = \sum_{s=1}^{S} p_{sq} = \sum_{t} \sum_{u} p_{tuq}$$
$$= \left(\sum_{t} \mu_{tq} \right)\left(\sum_{u} \tau_u \right) = \sum_{t} \mu_{tq},$$

since of course the sum of the probabilities of the F_u's must be 1. From (11),

(13)
$$\sum_{q=0}^{Q-1} \sum_{s=1}^{S} h_{sq}p_{sq} = \sum_{Q=0}^{Q-1} \frac{1}{1+r_q} \sum_{u} \tau_u h_{uq}$$

Equation (13) gives the rather startling result that the present value of any investment which meets the independence and objectivity conditions, equals the expected value of returns in each time period, discounted by the factor appropriate for a certain return at that time. This is true even though individuals may have had different probabilities for the events that governed the returns on earlier investments. It is also interesting to note that each individual will behave in this manner so that there will be no discrepancy between public and private procedures for choosing among investments.

The independence assumption applied to utility functions was required because the functions U_{is} are conditional on the states of the world. This assumption appears reasonable, and in the case where U_{is} is the same for all values of s, it is automatically satisfied. Then the independence condition is simply that the net returns from an investment be independent of the returns from previous investments.

The difficulty that arises if one bases policy conclusions on these results is that some markets do not exist, and individuals do not value assets at the expected value of returns discounted by a factor appropriate for certain returns. It is tempting to argue that while individuals do not behave as expected-value decision makers because of the nonexistence of certain markets for insurance, there is no reason why the government's behavior should not be consistent with the results derived above where the allocation of resources was Pareto optimal. There are two difficulties with this line of argument. First, if we are to measure benefits and costs in terms of individuals' willingness to pay, then we must treat risk in accordance with these individual valuations. Since individuals do not have the opportunities for insuring assumed in the state-preference model, they will not value uncertainty as they would if these markets did exist. Second, the theory of the second best demonstrates that if resources are not allocated in a Pareto optimal manner, the appropriate public policies may not be those consistent with Pareto efficiency in perfect markets. Therefore, some other approach must be found for ascertaining the appropriate government policy toward risk. In particular, such an approach must be valid, given the nonexistence of certain markets for insurance and imperfections in existing markets.

II. *The Public Cost of Risk-Bearing*

The critical question is: What is the cost of uncertainty in terms of costs to individuals? If one adopts the position that costs and benefits should be computed on the basis of individual willingness to pay, consistency demands that the public costs of risk-bearing be computed in this way too. This is the approach taken here.

In the discussion that follows it is assumed that an individual's utility is dependent only upon his consumption and not upon the state of nature in which that consumption takes place. This assumption simplifies the presentation of the major theorem, but it is not essential. Again the expected utility theorem is assumed to hold. The presentation to follow analyzes the cost of risk-bearing by comparing the expected value of returns with the certainty equivalent of these returns. In this way the analysis of time and risk preference can be separated, so we need only consider one time period.

Suppose that the government were to undertake an investment with a certain outcome; then the benefits and costs are measured in terms of willingness to pay for this outcome. If, however, the outcome is uncertain, then the benefits and costs actually realized depend on which outcome in fact occurs. If an individual is risk-averse, he will value the investment with the uncertain outcome at less than the expected value of its net return (benefit minus cost) to him. Therefore, in general the expected value of net benefits overstates willingness to pay by an amount equal to the cost of risk-bearing. It is clear that the social cost of risk-bearing will depend both upon which individuals receive the benefits and pay the costs and upon how large is each individual's share of these benefits and costs.

As a first step, suppose that the government were to undertake an investment and capture all benefits and pay all costs, i.e., the beneficiaries pay to the government an amount equal to the benefits received and the government pays all costs. Individuals who incur costs and those who receive benefits are therefore left indifferent to their pre-investment state. This assumption simply transfers all benefits and costs to the government, and the outcome of the investment will affect government disbursements and receipts. Given that the general taxpayer finances government expenditures, a public investment can be considered an investment in which each individual taxpayer has a very small share.

For precision, suppose that the government undertook an investment and that returns accrue to the government as previously described. In addition, suppose that in a given year the government were to have a balanced budget (or a planned deficit or surplus) and that taxes would be reduced by the amount of the net benefits if the returns are positive, and raised if returns are negative. Therefore, when the government undertakes an investment, each taxpayer has a small share of that investment with the returns being paid through changes in the level of taxes. By undertaking an investment the government adds to each individual's disposable income a random variable which is some fraction of the random variable representing the total net returns. The expected return to all taxpayers as a group equals expected net benefits.

Each taxpayer holds a small share of an asset with a random payoff, and the value of this asset to the individual is less than its expected return, assuming risk aversion. Stated differently, there is a cost of risk-bearing that must be subtracted from the expected return in order to compute the value of the investment to the individual taxpayer. Since each taxpayer will bear some of the cost of the risk associated with the investment, these costs must be summed over all taxpayers in order to arrive at the total cost of risk-bearing associated with a particular investment. These costs must be subtracted from the value of expected net benefits in order to obtain the correct measure for net benefits. The task is to assess these costs.

Suppose, as in the previous section, that there is one commodity, and that each individual's utility in a given year is a function of his income defined in terms of this commodity and is given by $U(Y)$. Further, suppose that U is bounded, continuous, strictly increasing, and differentiable. The assumptions that U is continuous and strictly increasing imply that U has a right and left derivative at every point and this is sufficient to prove the desired results; differentiability is assumed only to simplify presentation. Further suppose that U satisfies the conditions of the expected utility theorem.

Consider, for the moment, the case where all individuals are identical in that they have the same preferences, and their disposable incomes are identically distributed random variables represented by A. Sup-

pose that the government were to undertake an investment with returns represented by B, which are statistically independent of A. Now divide the effect of this investment into two parts: a certain part equal to expected returns and a random part, with mean zero, which incorporates risk. Let $\bar{B} = E[B]$, and define the random variable X by $X = B - \bar{B}$. Clearly, X is independent of A and $E[X] = 0$. The effect of this investment is to add an amount $\bar{B}$ to government receipts along with a random component represented by X. The income of each taxpayer will be affected through taxes and it is the level of these taxes that determines the fraction of the investment he effectively holds.

Consider a specific taxpayer and denote his fraction of this investment by s, $0 \leq s \leq 1$. This individual's disposable income, given the public investment, is equal to $A + sB = A + s\bar{B} + sX$. The addition of sB to his disposable income is valued by the individual at its expected value less the cost of bearing the risk associated with the random component sX. If we suppose that each taxpayer has the same tax rate and that there are n taxpayers, then $s = 1/n$, and the value of the investment taken over all individuals is simply $\bar{B}$ minus n times the cost of risk-bearing associated with the random variable $(1/n)X$. The central result of this section of the paper is that this total of the costs of risk-bearing goes to zero as n becomes large. Therefore, for large values of n the value of a public investment almost equals the expected value of that investment.

To demonstrate this, we introduce the function

$$W(s) = E[U(A + s\bar{B} + sX)],$$

(14)
$$0 \leq s \leq 1$$

In other words, given the random variables A and B representing his individual income before the investment and the income from the investment, respectively, his expected utility is a function of s which represents his share of B. From (14) and the assumption that U' exists, it follows that

(15) $W'(s) = E[U'(A + s\overline{B} + sX)(\overline{B} + X)]$

Since X is independent of A, it follows that $U'(A)$ and X are independent; therefore,

$$E[U'(A)X] = E[U'(A)]E[X] = 0$$

so that

(16) $\begin{aligned} W'(0) &= E[U'(A)(\overline{B} + X)] \\ &= \overline{B}E[U'(A)] \end{aligned}$

Equation (16) is equivalent to the statement

(17) $\displaystyle \lim_{s \to 0} \frac{E[U(A + s\overline{B} + sX) - U(A)]}{s}$

$$= \overline{B}E[U'(A)]$$

Now let $s = 1/n$, so that equation (17) becomes

(18) $\displaystyle \lim_{n \to \infty} nE\left[U\left(A + \frac{\overline{B} + X}{n}\right) - U(A)\right]$

$$= \overline{B}E[U'(A)]$$

If we assume that an individual whose preferences are represented by U is a risk-averter, then it is easily shown that there exists a unique number, $k(n) > 0$, for each value of n such that

(19) $\begin{aligned} &E\left[U\left(A + \frac{\overline{B} + X}{n}\right)\right] \\ &= E\left[U\left(A + \frac{\overline{B}}{n} - k(n)\right)\right], \end{aligned}$

or, in other words, an individual would be indifferent between paying an amount equal to $k(n)$ and accepting the risk represented by $(1/n)X$. Therefore, $k(n)$ can be said to be the cost of risk-bearing associated with the asset B. It can easily be demonstrated that $\lim_{n \to \infty} k(n) = 0$, i.e., the cost of holding the risky asset goes to zero as the amount of this asset held by the individual goes to zero. It should be noted that

the assumption of risk aversion is not essential to the argument but simply one of convenience. If U represented the utility function of a risk preferrer, then all the above statements would hold except $k(n) < 0$, i.e., an individual would be indifferent between being paid $-k(n)$ and accepting the risk $(1/n)X$ (net of the benefit $(1/n)\overline{B}$).

We wish to prove not merely that the risk-premium of the representative individual, $k(n)$, vanishes, but more strongly that the total of the risk-premiums for all individuals, $nk(n)$, approaches zero as n becomes large.

From (18) and (19) it follows that

(20) $\begin{aligned} &\lim_{n \to \infty} nE\left[U\left(A + \frac{\overline{B}}{n} - k(n)\right) \right. \\ &\left. - U(A)\right] = \overline{B}E[U'(A)] \end{aligned}$

In addition, $\overline{B}/n - k(n) \to 0$, when $n \to \infty$. It follows from the definition of a derivative that

(21) $\displaystyle \lim_{n \to \infty} \frac{E\left[U\left(A + \frac{\overline{B}}{n} - k(n)\right) - U(A)\right]}{\frac{\overline{B}}{n} - k(n)}$

$$= E[U'(A)] > 0$$

Dividing (20) by (21) yields

(22) $\displaystyle \lim_{n \to \infty} [\overline{B} - nk(n)] = \overline{B}$

or

(23) $\displaystyle \lim_{n \to \infty} nk(n) = 0$

The argument in (21) implies that $\overline{B}/n - k(n) \neq 0$. Suppose instead the equality held for infinitely many n. Substitution into the left-hand side of (20) shows that $\overline{B}$ must equal zero, so that $k(n) = 0$ for all such n, and hence $nk(n) = 0$ on that sequence, confirming (23).

Equation (23) states that the total of

the costs of risk-bearing goes to zero as the population of taxpayers becomes large. At the same time the monetary value of the investment to each taxpayer, neglecting the cost of risk, is $(1/n)\overline{B}$, and the total, summed over all individuals, is $\overline{B}$, the expected value of net benefits. Therefore, if n is large, the expected value of net benefits closely approximates the correct measure of net benefits defined in terms of willingness to pay for an asset with an uncertain return.

In the preceding analysis, it was assumed that all taxpayers were identical in that they had the same utility function, their incomes were represented by identically distributed variables, and they were subject to the same tax rates. These assumptions greatly simplify the presentation; however, they are not essential to the argument. Different individuals may have different preferences, incomes, and tax rates; and the basic theorem still holds, provided that as n becomes larger the share of the public investment borne by any individual becomes arbitrarily smaller.

The question necessarily arises as to how large n must be to justify proceeding as if the cost of publicly-borne risk is negligible. This question can be given no precise answer; however, there are circumstances under which it appears likely that the cost of risk-bearing will be small. If the size of the share borne by each taxpayer is a negligible component of his income, the cost of risk-bearing associated with holding it will be small. It appears reasonable to assume, under these conditions, that the total cost of risk-bearing is also small. This situation will exist where the investment is small with respect to the total wealth of the taxpayers. In the case of a federally sponsored investment, n is not only large but the investment is generally a very small fraction of national income even though the investment itself may be large in some absolute sense.

The results derived here and in the previous section depend on returns from a given public investment being independent of other components of national income. The government undertakes a wide range of public investments and it appears reasonable to assume that their returns are independent. Clearly, there are some government investments which are interdependent; however, where investments are interrelated they should be evaluated as a package. Even after such groupings are established, there will be a large number of essentially independent projects. It is sometimes argued that the returns from public investments are highly correlated with other components of national income through the business cycle. However, if we assume that stabilization policies are successful, then this difficulty does not arise. It should be noted that in most benefit-cost studies it is assumed that full employment will be maintained so that market prices can be used to measure benefits and costs. Consistency requires that this assumption be retained when considering risk as well. Further, if there is some positive correlation between the returns of an investment and other components of national income, the question remains as to whether this correlation is so high as to invalidate the previous result.

The main result is more general than the specific application to public investments. It has been demonstrated that if an individual or group holds an asset which is statistically independent of other assets, and if there is one or more individuals who do not share ownership, then the existing situation is not Pareto-efficient. By selling some share of the asset to one of the individuals not originally possessing a share, the cost of risk-bearing can be reduced while the expected returns remain unchanged. The reduction in the cost of risk-bearing can then be redistributed to bring about a Pareto improvement. This result is similar to a result derived by Karl Borch. He proved that a condition for Pareto optimality in reinsurance markets requires that every individual hold a share of every independent risk.

When the government undertakes an investment it, in effect, spreads the risk among all taxpayers. Even if one were to accept that the initial distribution of risk was Pareto-efficient, the new distribution of risk will not be efficient as the government does not discriminate among the taxpayers according to their risk preferences. What has been shown is that in the limit the situation where the risk of the investment is spread over all taxpayers is such that there is only a small deviation from optimality with regard to the distribution of that particular risk. The overall distribution of risk may be sub-optimal because of market imperfections and the absence of certain insurance markets. The great advantage of the results of this section is that they are not dependent on the existence of perfect markets for contingent claims.

This leads to an example which runs counter to the policy conclusions generally offered by economists. Suppose that an individual in the private sector of the economy were to undertake a given investment and, calculated on the basis of expected returns, the investment had a rate of return of 10 per cent. Because of the absence of perfect insurance markets, the investor subtracted from the expected return in each period a risk premium and, on the basis of returns adjusted for risk, his rate of return is 5 percent. Now suppose that the government could invest the same amount of money in an investment which, on the basis of expected returns, would yield 6 percent. Since the risk would be spread over all taxpayers, the cost of risk-bearing would be negligible, and the true rate of return would be 6 percent. Further, suppose that if the public investment were adopted it would displace the private investment. The question is: Should the public investment be undertaken? On the basis of the previous analysis, the answer is yes. The private investor is indifferent between the investment with the expected return of 10 percent, and certain rate of return of 5 percent. When the public investment is undertaken, it is equivalent to an investment with a certain rate of return of 6 percent. Therefore, by undertaking the public investment, the government could more than pay the opportunity cost to the private investor of 5 percent associated with the diversion of funds from private investment.

The previous example illustrates Hirshleifer's point that the case for evaluating public investments differently from private ones is an argument for the second best. Clearly, if the advantages of the more efficient distribution of risk could be achieved in connection with the private investment alternative, this would be superior to the public investment. The question then arises as to how the government can provide insurance for private investors and thereby transfer the risks from the private sector to the public at large. The same difficulties arise as before, moral hazards and transaction costs. It may not be possible for the government to provide such insurance, and in such cases second-best solutions are in order. Note that if the government could undertake any investment, then this difficulty would not arise. Perhaps one of the strongest criticisms of a system of freely competitive markets is that the inherent difficulty in establishing certain markets for insurance brings about a sub-optimal allocation of resources. If we consider an investment, as does Hirshleifer, as an exchange of certain present income for uncertain future income, then the misallocation will take the form of under-investment.

Now consider Hirshleifer's recommendation that, in cases such as the one above, a direct subsidy be used to induce more private investment rather than increase public investment. Suppose that a particular private investment were such that the benefits would be a marginal increase in the future supply of an existing commodity, i.e., this investment would neither introduce a new commodity nor affect future prices. Therefore, benefits can be measured at each point in time by the market value of this output, and can be fully captured through the sale of the commodity. Let $\overline{V}$ be the present value of expected net returns, and let V be the present value of net returns adjusted for risk where the certainty rate is used to discount both streams. Further, suppose there were a public investment, where the risks were publicly borne, for which the present value of expected net benefits was P. Since the risk is publicly borne, from the previous discussion it follows that P is the present value of net benefits adjusted for risk. Now suppose that $\overline{V} > P > V$. According to Hirshleifer, we should undertake the private investment rather than the public one, and pay a subsidy if necessary to induce private entrepreneurs to undertake this investment. Clearly, if there is a choice between one investment or the other, given the existing distribution of risk, the public investment is superior. The implication is that if a risky investment in the private sector is displaced by a public investment with a lower expected return but with a higher return when appropriate adjustments are made for risks, this represents a Hicks-Kaldor improvement. This is simply a restatement of the previous point that the government could more than pay the opportunity cost to the private entrepreneur.

Now consider the case for a direct subsidy to increase the level of private investment. One can only argue for direct subsidy of the private investment if $V < 0 < \overline{V}$. The minimum subsidy required is $|V|$.

Suppose the taxpayers were to pay this subsidy, which is a transfer of income from the public at large to the private investor, in order to cover the loss from the investment. The net benefits, including the cost of risk-bearing, remain negative because while the subsidy has partially offset the cost of risk-bearing to the individual investor, it has not reduced this cost. Therefore, a direct public subsidy in this case results in a less efficient allocation of resources.

We can summarize as follows: It is implied by Hirshleifer that it is better to undertake an investment with a higher expected return than one with a lower expected return. (See 1965, p. 270.) This proposition is not in general valid, as the distribution of risk-bearing is critical. This statement is true, however, when the costs of risk-bearing associated with both investments are the same. What has been shown is that when risks are publicly borne, the costs of risk-bearing are negligible; therefore, a public investment with an expected return which is less than that of a given private investment may nevertheless be superior to the private alternative. Therefore, the fact that public investments with lower expected return may replace private investment is not necessarily cause for concern. Furthermore, a program of providing direct subsidies to encourage more private investment does not alter the costs of risk-bearing and, therefore, will encourage investments which are inefficient when the costs of risk are considered. The program which produces the desired result is one to insure private investments.

One might raise the question as to whether risk-spreading is not associated with large corporations so that the same result would apply, and it is easily seen that the same reasoning does apply. This can be made more precise by assuming there were n stockholders who were identical in the sense that their utility functions were identical, their incomes were represented by identically distributed random variables, and they had the same share in the company. When the corporation undertakes an investment with a return in a given year represented by B, each stockholder's income is represented by $A + (1/n)B$. This assumes, of course, that a change in earnings was reflected in dividends, and that there were no business taxes. Clearly, this is identical to the situation previously described, and if n is large, the total cost of risk-bearing to the stockholders will be negligible. If the income or wealth of the stockholders were large with respect to the size of the investment, this result would be likely to hold. Note that whether or not the investment is a large one, with respect to the assets of the firm, is not relevant. While an investment may constitute a major part of a firm's assets if each stockholder's share in the firm is a small component of his income, the cost of risk-bearing to him will be very small. It then follows that if managers were acting in the interest of the firm's shareholders, they would essentially ignore risks and choose investments with the highest expected returns.

There are two important reasons why large corporations may behave as risk averters. First, in order to control the firm, some shareholder may hold a large block of stock which is a significant component of his wealth. If this were true, then, from his point of view, the costs of risk-bearing would not be negligible, and the firm should behave as a risk averter. Note in this case that the previous result does not hold because the cost of risk-bearing to each stockholder is not small, even though the number of stockholders is very large. Investment behavior in this case is essentially the same as the case of a single investor.

The second case is when, even though from the stockholder's point of view, risk should be ignored, it may not be in the interest of the corporate managers to neglect

risk. Their careers and income are intimately related to the firm's performance. From their point of view, variations in the outcome of some corporate action impose very real costs. In this case, given a degree of autonomy, the corporate managers, in considering prospective investments, may discount for risk when it is not in the interest of the stockholders to do so.

Suppose that this were the case and also suppose that the marginal rate of time preference for each individual in the economy was 5 percent. From the point of view of the stockholders, risk can be ignored and any investment with an expected return which is greater than 5 percent should be undertaken. However, suppose that corporate managers discount for risk so that only investments with expected rates of return that exceed 10 percent are undertaken. From the point of view of the stockholders, the rate of return on these investments, taking risk into account, is over 10 percent. Given a marginal rate of time preference of 5 percent, it follows that from the point of view of the individual stockholder there is too little investment. Now suppose further that the government were considering an investment with an expected rate of return of 6 percent. Since the cost of risk-bearing is negligible, this investment should be undertaken since the marginal rate of time preference is less than 6 percent. However, in this case, if the financing were such that a private investment with a 10 percent expected rate of return is displaced by the public investment, there is a loss because in both cases the risk is distributed so as to make the total cost of risk-bearing negligible. The public investment should be undertaken, but only at the expense of consumption.

III. *The Actual Allocation of Risk*

In the idealized public investment considered in the last section, all benefits and costs accrued to the government and were distributed among the taxpayers. In this sense, all uncertainty was borne collectively. Suppose instead that some benefits and costs of sizeable magnitudes accrued directly to individuals so that these individuals incurred the attendant costs of risk-bearing. In this case it is appropriate to discount for the risk, as would these individuals. Such a situation would arise in the case of a government irrigation project where the benefits accrued to farmers as increased income. The changes in farm income would be uncertain and, therefore, should be valued at more or less than their expected value, depending on the states in which they occur. If these increases were independent of other components of farm income, and if we assume that the farmer's utility were only a function of his income and not the state in which he receives that income, then he would value the investment project at less than the expected increase in his income, provided he is risk averse. If, however, the irrigation project paid out in periods of drought so that total farm income was not only increased but also stabilized, then the farmers would value the project at more than the expected increase in their incomes.

In general, some benefits and costs will accrue to the government and the uncertainties involved will be publicly borne; other benefits and costs will accrue to individuals and the attendant uncertainties will be borne privately. In the first case the cost of risk-bearing will be negligible; in the second case these costs may be significant. Therefore, in calculating the present value of returns from a public investment a distinction must be made between private and public benefits and costs. The present value of public benefits and costs should be evaluated by estimating the expected net benefits in each period and discounting them, using a discount factor appropriate for investments with certain returns. On the other hand, private benefits and costs must be discounted with respect to both time and risk in accordance with the preferences of the individuals to whom they accrue.

From the foregoing discussion it follows that different streams of benefits and costs should be treated in different ways with respect to uncertainty. One way to do this is to discount these streams of returns at different rates of discount ranging from the certainty rate for benefits and costs accruing to the government and using higher rates that reflect discounting for risk for returns accruing directly to individuals. Such a procedure raises some difficulties of identification, but this problem does not appear to be insurmountable. In general, costs are paid by the government, which receives some revenue, and the net stream should be discounted at a rate appropriate for certain returns. Benefits accruing directly to individuals should be discounted according to individual time and risk preferences. As a practical matter, Hirshleifer's suggestion of finding the marginal rate of return on assets with similar payoffs in the private sector, and using this as the rate of discount, appears reasonable for discounting those benefits and costs which accrue privately.

One problem arises with this latter procedure which has received little attention. In considering public investments, benefits and costs are aggregated and the discussion of uncertainty is carried out in terms of these aggregates. This obscures many of the uncertainties because benefits and costs do not in general accrue to the same individuals, and the attendant uncertainties should not be netted out when considering the totals. To make this clear, consider an investment where the benefits and costs varied greatly, depending on the state of nature, but where the difference between total benefits and total costs was constant for every state. Further, suppose that the benefits and costs accrued to different groups. While the investment is certain from a social point of view, there is considerable risk from a private point of view.

In the case of perfect markets for contingent claims, each individual will discount the stream of costs and benefits accruing to him at the appropriate rate for each time and state. However, suppose that such markets do not exist. Then risk-averse individuals will value the net benefits accruing to them at less than their expected value. Therefore, if net benefits accruing to this individual are positive, this requires discounting expected returns at a higher rate than that appropriate for certain returns. On the other hand, if net benefits to an individual are negative, this requires discounting expected returns at a rate lower than the certainty rate. Raising the rate of discount only reduces the present value of net benefits when they are positive. Therefore, the distinction must be made not only between benefits and costs which accrue to the public and those which accrue directly to individuals, but also between individuals whose net benefits are negative and those whose benefits are positive. If all benefits and costs accrued privately, and different individuals received the benefits and paid the costs, the appropriate procedure would be to discount the stream of expected benefits at a rate higher than the certainty rate, and costs at a rate lower than the certainty rate. This would hold even if the social totals were certain.

Fortunately, as a practical matter this may not be of great importance as most costs are borne publicly and, therefore, should be discounted using the certainty rate. Benefits often accrue to individuals, and where there are attendant uncertainties it is appropriate to discount the expected value of these benefits at higher rates, depending on the nature of the uncertainty and time-risk preferences of the individuals who receive these benefits. It is somewhat ironic that the practical impli-cation of this analysis is that for the typical case where costs are borne publicly and benefits accrue privately, this procedure will qualify fewer projects than the procedure of using a higher rate to discount both benefits and costs.

REFERENCES

K. J. Arrow, "The Role of Securities in the Optimal Allocation of Risk-Bearing," *Rev. Econ. Stud.*, Apr. 1964, *31*, 91–96.

——, "Discounting and Public Investment Criteria," in A. V. Kneese and S. C. Smith, eds., *Water Research*. Baltimore 1966.

——, "The Economics of Moral Hazard: Further Comment," *Amer. Econ. Rev.*, June 1968, *58*, 537–38.

K. Borch, "The Safety Loading of Reinsurance," *Skandinavisk Aktuarietid-skrift*, 1960, 163–84.

G. Debreu, *Theory of Value*. New York 1959.

O. Eckstein, "A Survey of the Theory of Public Expenditure," and "Reply," *Public Finances: Needs, Sources, and Utilization*, Nat. Bur. Econ. Res., Princeton 1961, 493–504.

J. Hirshleifer, "Investment Decision under Uncertainty: Choice-Theoretic Approaches," *Quart. J. Econ.*, Nov. 1965, *79*, 509–36.

——, "Investment Decision under Uncertainty: Applications of the State-Preference Approach," *Quart. J. Econ.*, May 1966, *80*, 252–77.

——, J. C. De Haven, and J. W. Milliman, *Water Supply: Economics, Technology, and Policy*, Chicago 1960.

S. Marglin, "The Social Rate of Discount and the Optimal Rate of Investment," *Quart. J. Econ.*, Feb. 1963, *77*, 95–111.

M. V. Pauly, "The Economics of Moral Hazard: Comment," *Amer. Econ. Rev.*, June 1968, *58*, 531–37.

P. A. Samuelson and W. Vickrey, "Discussion," *Amer. Econ. Rev. Proc.*, May 1964, *59*, 88–96.

J. von Neumann and O. Morgenstern, *Theory of Games and Economic Behavior*, 2d ed., New York 1964.

D
Welfare Effects of
Information and Advertising

[33]

INFORMATION AND ECONOMIC
ANALYSIS: A PERSPECTIVE*

Joseph E. Stiglitz

Ten years ago, I delivered a paper before this group with the title, 'Information and Economic Analysis.' I chose the title deliberately: I did not call the subject on which I was speaking the 'Economics of Information' because to do so would have been to suggest that my topic, like the economics of agriculture, or the economics of industry, or the economics of labour represented another branch of specialisation within economics. I wanted to suggest that informational considerations were, in fact, central to the analysis of a wide variety of phenomena, that they constituted a central part of the Foundations of Economic Analysis. At the time, though economists had long paid lip service to the importance of information, there was little formal literature. The last decade has seen a burgeoning of the literature. It has become to the late 70's and early 80's what growth theory was to the early 60's. And it has been greeted with some of the same scepticism. There seems to be a myriad of special cases and few general principles. The little examples are often contrasted unfavourably with the generality of general equilibrium theory. What have we learned? Have diminishing returns set in? Are there fruitful directions for future research, and if so, what are they? These are the questions which I wish to address here.

The work of the past decade has made, I think, a fundamental and lasting contribution to economic analysis. The contributions have been both negative and positive: we have learned that much of what we believed before is of only limited validity; that the traditional competitive equilibrium analysis, though having the superficial appearance of generality – in terms of superscripts and subscripts – is indeed not very general; the theory is not robust to slight alterations in the informational assumptions. It is but a special – and not very plausible – 'example' among the possible set of informational assumptions which can be employed to characterise an economy.

At the same time, the theory has been able to provide insights into phenomena about which the traditional model had nothing to say, or which seemed inconsistent or inexplicable within the competitive paradigm. It has provided some of the micro-foundations for macro-economics, it provided the basis of a New Theory of the Firm, of a New New Welfare Economics, and of a theory of Economic Organisation (including a Comparison of Economic

* Frank W. Paish lecture. Condensed version, full version available from the author. I am grateful to Ian Galt for research assistance.
Financial support from the National Science Foundation is gratefully acknowledged.

21

22 THE ECONOMIC JOURNAL

Systems which is of far more relevance than the misleading Lange-Lerner Taylor equivalency theorem).

Truth in advertising (itself a subject which can only be understood within an framework which focuses on imperfect information) requires, however, that I disclose some of what I shall not be able to do within this lecture. I have chosen to provide a general perspective, covering with broad strokes a vast area, leaving to the more technical surveys the task of filling in the details, specifying the specific assumptions under which the various assertions I make are valid. What I wish to show is how the "informational perspective" has altered both our views of how the economy functions and the approaches we take to the analysis of economic problems. But even with my broad strokes, there are important topics, including R & D and rational expectations, which I will not be able to mention, let alone do justice to.

Finally, let me admit a failure: I would have liked to have been able to announce at this lecture one or two general principles, under which all or most of the relevant literature of the past decade could be subsumed. Those of you not actively engaged in Information Economics could then walk away from this lecture, knowing all you would ever need to know on the subject. There is no single new Law of Economics. There are a few *themes*, a few techniques of analysis, a few fundamental insights. More than that, a new perspective, a new way of approaching Economic Analysis has been provided, and it is this which I wish to convey to you today.

I. THE FAILURE OF THE CONVENTIONAL (PERFECT INFORMATION) PARADIGM

Traditional economic analysis was predicated on three maxims. The first, due to Marshall, was that nature abhorred discontinuities. The second, due to Samuelson, was that nature abhorred non-convexities: not only could individual and firm behaviour be described as the solution to simple maximisation problems (in which an analysis of the second order conditions provides essential insights into the central comparative statics propositions), but the behaviour of the economy as a whole could be described as if it were the solution to some maximisation problem.

The third is the Law of Supply and Demand; it has played a central role in the traditional economist's tool kit. Indeed, there is a saying that you could teach a parrot to be an economist by simply teaching it to say. 'Supply must equal Demand'. It has played this central role in spite of ample evidence that there are circumstances where markets at least *seem* not to clear: massive unemployment of labour and extensive rationing of credit provide but two of the most important examples.

Recent work in the economics of information has cast doubt on all three maxims. The world is not convex; the behaviour of the economy cannot be described as if it were solving any (simple) maximisation problem; the law of demand and supply has been repealed. 'Unemployment and credit rationing are not phantasms'.[1] Indeed, in some circumstances, it may not even be possible to define demand independently of supply.[2]

Even the logic of the contention that individual and firm behaviour can be thought of as the solution to a maximisation problem has been questioned: for how is the individual to resolve the infinite regress of whether it is worthwhile to obtain information concerning whether it is worthwhile to obtain information... (See Winter (1964)).

Thus, Samuelson's contention that the analysis of maximisation behaviour provides the Foundations of Economics Analysis is at best a partial truth: it provides only one of the central building blocks.

Similarly the central insights of modern general equilibrium analysis – its stress on the interaction of markets and the role of prices in conveying information – though (at least partially) valid, are only a part of the story. In the standard competitive model, there is but a once and for all information problem; the economy does not confront the problem of repeatedly processing information (as it does in practice). What is meant by decentralisation is little more than a computer algorithm for the solution of a particularly complex problem. To ask, how information is processed and conveyed in the economy one must construct models in which information is continuously being collected and processed and in which decisions, based on that information, are continuously being made. Later in this lecture, I shall describe some ongoing work which is attempting to do just that. But even the work completed within the last decade has established that the interrelations among firms, individuals, and sectors are more complex than suggested by the traditional paradigm, that the notions of equilibrium embodied in that paradigm are special, and that prices are only one of the mechanisms by which information becomes conveyed in our economy.

A Taxonomy of Models

During the past decade, a large number of models examining economic behaviour in the presence of imperfect information have been constructed. Although I will not develop a complete taxonomy of that literature here, certain distinctions are worth noting: (a) while in models of *adverse selection*, there is imperfect information concerning the characteristics of what is being bought or sold in the market (labour, loans, or products), in *moral hazard* models there is imperfect information concerning the action which the individual undertakes; (b) models may be either static or dynamic; in adverse selection models, the uninformed party (the employer, the insurance firm, etc.) may learn about the characteristics of the individual over time; in moral hazard models if the relationship (between buyer and seller, employee and employer, bank and borrower) is long term, the payments (e.g. to or from the insurance company or to or from the employer) will be made contingent upon

---

[1] See Weiss and Stiglitz (1981).
[2] See Grossman and Stiglitz (1976).

observations made at earlier dates; (c) in adverse selection models, information may be conveyed either by 'examination' (individuals search for the lowest price store) or by self-selection, on the basis of inferences made by observing the actions of the individual. The 'action' which conveys information may be 'quantity-related' – the amount of education, the amount of insurance, etc. – or price related – the willingness of an individual to buy insurance at a given premium, the willingness of a worker to work at a given wage, the willingness of a borrower to borrow at a given interest rate; (d) In some cases, it is not the action of single individuals which conveys information, but action of groups of individuals. Thus, the set of prices in the market may convey information about the state of nature. In other cases, the information which is conveyed by a particular action is critically dependent on the behaviour of other individuals (the information conveyed by an individual applying for a job in a given labour market depends on the probability he has of obtaining the job, which depends on the number of other individuals who apply for the job; the information conveyed by an individual being in the 'used labour market' (individuals who have quit or been fired from some previous job) depends critically on the decisions of employees concerning quitting and employers concerning wage setting and firing); (e) Again, in the case of adverse selection models, it makes a difference whether the uninformed individuals move first (as in the insurance market, where the insurance firms are assumed not to know the characteristics of those applying for insurance, but offer a set of contracts to the market) or whether the informed individuals move first (individuals have to purchase a level of education before employers make job offers); (f) while most models to date have been characterised by one-sided imperfect information (the employee knows the characteristics of the firm, but the employer does not know characteristics of the individual; while there is a moral hazard problem on the part of the seller of the commodity, there is none on the part of the buyer) in some recent research models with two-sided imperfect information are being investigated; (g) while some models have investigated equilibrium in competitive markets, others have been concerned with monopolies or monopolistically competitive markets; (h) though there are general principles which apply to all markets, there are some natural parameterisations, some simplifications which seem more appropriate in some markets, while others seem more appropriate in other markets. Thus, imperfect information (of all the kinds we have described above) has been explored in capital, labour, and product markets; in less developed countries as well as in developed economies.

The Basic Propositions of Competitive Analysis

Existence. When I addressed this group ten years ago, I noted that in models with adverse selection, competitive equilibrium might not exist, using what I thought at the time – and still think – was the natural definition of competitive equilibrium: in the context of insurance markets, that there existed a set of insurance contracts, all of which at least broke even, such that there did not exist another insurance contract which, if offered, would make a profit. Since then, there have been several attempts to find alternative equilibrium concepts, under which competitive equilibrium could be assured to exist. In my judgment, all of these have failed. There are, of course, assumptions (definitions) under which equilibrium can be shown to exist; but these all entail a small firm taking into account a variety of (often peculiarly restricted) reactions to his entry, which seems to me inconsistent with competitive analysis.

I gave a second example of non-existence: in capital markets in which prices convey information, I argued that if no one obtains any information there is an incentive to obtain information, but if anybody does obtain information, the price will perfectly reflect the information – so that the individual who expends resources to obtain the information is no better off than the individual who does not. It is clear that an equilibrium does not exist. This problem of existence, unlike the previous one, is merely an artifact of the assumption that there is no noise in the economy; if changes in the market price reflect changes other than just the information which has been purchased, an uninformed individual cannot infer the information perfectly from looking at the price. This result – the importance of noise in the existence of equilibrium – appears repeatedly in the economics of information. (See Grossman and Stiglitz, 1976; 1980.)

I want to mention two other examples of non-existence among many that have been discovered in the last decade, both of which are of serious (academic) concern.

The first of these results (Stiglitz, 1979, Salop and Stiglitz, 1982) is associated with a non-convexity that arises from the discrete nature of search: there is a fixed cost associated with obtaining an additional sample, of visiting an additional store. If firms can impose non-linear price schedules, then they can in general extract all the consumer surplus out of the marginal individual, the one whose consumer surplus from entering the market is lowest given that he has arrived at the store; but this means that, taking into account the cost of going to the store, the individual's return to entering the market is negative; hence he will not enter the market. But if the marginal individual does not enter the market, no one does: the excessive greed of the petty store owners has caused a collapse of the market. This problem can be remedied by the presence of noise: if there are heterogeneous products sold in the markets, individuals differ in their tastes, and firms cannot tell who likes which commodities, then market equilibrium is restored.

The second example of a non-existence result parallels the Rothschild and Stiglitz (1976) and Wilson (1977) analysis for adverse selection. Arnott and Stiglitz (1984), using the same definition of equilibrium employed by Rothschild and Stiglitz, show that when there is moral hazard and the quantity of insurance purchased by any individual is not observable equilibrium may not exist. They show that equilibrium, when it exists, can be characterised as the point on the price (premia per unit of benefits) consumption locus inside (or on) the feasibility set which maximises consumer welfare. But this contract can be broken by an insurance contract providing more complete insurance, when there is a point on the income consumption locus with the price corresponding to that of the candidate market equilibrium which lies interior to the feasibility set and generates a higher level of utility. But this contract itself is not an equilibrium.

What can we learn from this plethora of existence results? First, it is clear that the standard paradigm is not very robust: many of the non-existence results arise from only slight perturbations in one of the assumptions of the analysis. The Salop-Stiglitz non-existence in product markets arises if there are any costs to going to a store (no matter how small); the Rothschild-Stiglitz non-existence result arises if there are only a few high risk individuals. Secondly there is no natural way of ruling out nonconvexities in the presence of imperfect information. Thirdly, some (but by no means all) of the problems arise from the fact that at least in many of the simplest models, an individual can obtain 'large' amounts of information from a single observation, so that they drastically revise their beliefs. The presence of noise eliminates many of these problems.

When, as in the Rothschild-Stiglitz model, we cannot restore equilibrium, either by the natural assumption of noise, or the use of a continuum of individuals, what are we to make of the non-existence of competitive equilibrium? What happens? The answer that I suggested a decade ago is still, I think, correct: markets are not perfectly competitive, though they may be monopolistically competitive. With perfect information and no nonconvexities, the postulates underlying perfect competition have a certain degree of plausibility, or should I say, at least internal consistency. The competitive paradigm is an artfully constructed structure: when one of the central pieces (the assumption of perfect information) is removed, the structure collapses. To construct a new paradigm several of the assumptions need to be replaced. This is the task to which I shall turn in the last part of this lecture.

Adam Smith's Palsied Hand

If there is one idea in economics that has attracted more attention than any other, it is Adam Smith's invisible hand: the notion that a competitive equilibrium would attain a Pareto efficient allocation. The results of the last decade have raised the possibility that Adam Smith's invisible hand may be something akin to the Emperor's New Clothes: The Invisible Hand may be invisible, because it simply is not there. But that, I think, underrates Smith's insight (and overrates the recent criticisms): I prefer to think of the Invisible Hand as being slightly palsied.

Information costs are no less real than production costs, and an evaluation of the efficiency of the economy must take these into account. (That is why I dislike the use of the term second best Pareto optimality or constrained Pareto optimality in analysing the optimality properties of economies with imperfect information: we do not use the term 'constrained' or second best optimality to refer to economies in which inputs are required to obtain outputs.) In traditional welfare analyses, we did not have to model the government very precisely: we established that no government, no matter how good, could do better than the private market. The results of the recent literature have established that that proposition is not correct: whenever there are information problems (whether of the adverse selection or moral hazard form) there are government interventions – taxes and subsidies levied on observable variables – which could make everyone better off.

These results can be looked at in several ways. One of the central results of traditional competitive analysis is the decentralisability of efficient resource allocations (without government taxes and subsidies). With imperfect information, there is a *fundamental non-decentralisability theorem*: efficient resource allocation cannot be efficiently decentralised without a whole set of subsidies and taxes.[1] To put it in a slightly different way, there are instruments available to the government which are not available to individual firms: the government can (in principle) monitor all purchases of goods and services; it can tax or subsidised these purchases. A single firm might (at best) subsidise its customers' purchases of some other commodity (by providing a coupon) but it cannot tell whether the individual has resold the commodity to another individual and it cannot tax its customers' consumption of that commodity.

The presence of these externalities provides an incentive for markets to attempt to internalise the externality, by *interlinking* the markets. In some cases, such as LDC's, these interlinkages are a central part of the economy. But to the extent that interlinkages incorporate more and more of the economy the competitive nature of the economy becomes undermined.

What I would like to do now is to attempt to provide a heuristic argument for the Fundamental Non-Decentralisability Theorem.[2]

In the case of moral hazard, the argument is simple: the provision of insurance affects the extent of care that individuals take to avoid the insured against events occurring; the insurance company cannot monitor the actions of the individual. But his actions may be affected by relative prices (and by the availability of insurance policies covering this as well as other risks). By imposing subsidies on complements to the non-monitorable accident avoidance activities and taxes on substitutes, the government can encourage accident avoidance. By subsidising, for instance, fire extinguishers and smoke alarms, losses associated with fires may be reduced.

A similar argument holds for the case of adverse selection. The self-selection constraints are affected by relative prices; changing relative prices may affect, for instance, the cost differential between low ability and high ability individuals in obtaining increased education. By changing the price structure (through taxes and subsidies) in such a way as to make sorting easier the losses associated with the self-selection constraints (the excessive purchase of education, the under-purchase of insurance, etc.) can be reduced.

Whenever there is imperfect information, individuals (or other objects) which are in fact different will be grouped together; in an economy with rational expectations, the price of this heterogeneous melange of individuals will reflect their average 'quality.'

Some time ago (Stiglitz, 1975), I suggested that one could view imperfect

[1] Even with taxes and subsidies, it may not be possible to decentralise competitively, because of important non-convexities, to which we have already alluded.

[2] See Greenwald and Stiglitz (1984) for a general proof of this result, and Arnott and Stiglitz (1983) for a proof for the case of moral hazard as well as an analysis of the structure of corrective taxation.

information like a tax (an ignorance tax). High ability individuals were taxed, while low ability individuals were subsidised. The distortions associated with this tax can be reduced by imposing other taxes, which encourage the supply of the taxed commodity (an increase in the supply of labour by high ability individuals) and a decrease in the supply of the subsidised commodity (a decrease in the supply of low ability workers).

Again, we need to ask ourselves, what are we to make of these results? What they show is how non-robust the Fundamental Theorem of Welfare Economics is. If one believes, as I do, that the problems of adverse selection and moral hazard are pervasive in the economy, then there is little ground for believing in the Pareto efficiency of the market economy. (The remarkable achievement of the Fundamental Theorem is to find that singular combination of assumptions for which Adam Smith's conjecture was correct.) Though recent analysis has identified the nature of the requisite interventions (the optimal corrective tax), and the empirical information is no greater (or less) than that entailed in the design of conventional optimal tax structures, I am not sanguine about government's ability to effect a welfare improvement.[1] As I noted before, when we could establish the efficiency of the market equilibrium, we did not need to model the government precisely: no government, no matter how well organised, could effect a Pareto improvement. Now, our analysis has established that there are interventions which are feasible (within the information structure) which would effect a Pareto improvement. But why should we believe that such improvements would evolve out of our political processes?

Repeal of the Law of Supply and Demand

We noted in our discussion of the existence of equilibrium the critical problems posed by the definition of equilibrium. Traditional theory takes market clearing and the assumption that there is a single price associated with any commodity as part of the definition of competitive equilibrium. The new theory has had to look for more primitive, more fundamental notions of equilibrium, notions for which, under the traditional assumptions of perfect information, it can be proved that equilibrium is characterised by market clearing and unique prices: the law of supply and demand and the law of the single price are theorems (albeit trivial theorems) for the special example investigated by Arrow and Debreu and the subsequent literature. In the presence of imperfect information, under reasonable definitions, equilibrium is not characterised by demand equalling supply or by the law of single price.

The first result obtains whenever prices convey information about quality, that is, whenever the productivity of the labour force increases with the wage paid, or when the probability of default on a loan increases with the rate of interest charged, or when the quality of the product sold by a firm may be affected by the price charged. Quality may be affected either because of selection effects (the mix of applicants changes as the wage changes) or because

---

[1] The information required for a welfare improvement may be even less.

of incentive effects (the effort expended by an individual increases with the wage paid, or the riskiness of the projects undertaken by an investor – and hence the probability of default – increases with the rate of interest charged).[1,2] In either case, the standard argument for why equilibrium should be characterised by market clearing no longer obtains. The standard arguments (it will be recalled) say that when supply exceeds demand, say for labour, the wage falls. An unemployed worker goes to a firm and offers to work for a wage less than it is currently paying its employees; but now the firm rejects this offer, since it believes that were it to hire this worker his productivity would be lower than that of current employees, lower enough that its total labour costs would actually increase. Similarly, if the demand for loans exceeds the supply, someone who does not obtain all the credit he would like goes to a bank and offers (in the traditional story) to pay a higher interest rate. But (in the new view) the bank believes that were it to lend at this higher interest rate, its expected returns would actually be lower.

In these situations, there exists a Walrasian equilibrium – a vector of wages and prices at which markets clear – but this is not the competitive equilibrium: there is nothing to stop a firm from raising its wage, when doing so increases its profits, or to stop a bank from lowering the interest rate it charges, when doing so increases its return.

Repeal of the Law of One Price

There have been three separate pieces of legislation repealing various parts of the Law of the Single Price. The first arose in the Rothschild-Stiglitz-Wilson analysis of competitive equilibrium with adverse selection: quantity variables (the amount of insurance purchased, the level of education, etc.) convey information; as a result, in market equilibrium the cost of insurance may not increase in proportion to the coverage or the interest charged may increase with the amount borrowed.

The second arises in the analysis of moral hazard, where quantity variables (the level of insurance purchased by an individual, the number of cigarettes he smokes, etc.) affect the individuals' accident avoidance activities or the effort he puts into a job. (See Arnott and Stiglitz 1984.)

The third arises when similar commodities are sold for different prices by different stores (or similar workers are paid different wages by different firms).

Though the facts that there are price distributions in the market, and that the existence of price distributions induces search, have long been recognised, the construction of equilibrium models of price distribution at first seemed a somewhat more difficult task: it must be optimal for firms to charge different prices or pay similar workers different wages. As it has turned out, there are

---

[1] Thus, the first effect arises in adverse selection models, the second in moral hazard models.

[2] There are other explanations for the dependence of quality on price. In the labour market, turnover may be affected by the wage. (Stiglitz, 1974). Akerlof (1984) has discussed sociological explanations of efficiency wages.

30   THE ECONOMIC JOURNAL

now a plethora of such models. They are of four sorts: (a) if firms differ, then the wage which it is optimal for them to pay similar workers may differ, or the price which it is optimal for them to charge may easily differ. Thus, in a model where workers may shirk, to avoid shirking, firms with higher monitoring costs will pay higher wages (see Stiglitz, 1974; Shapiro and Stiglitz, 1984); (b) if individuals differ, then price wage dispersions may be used as a discriminating device (See Salop (1977); Salop and Stiglitz (1977)); (c) if there is exogenous noise, (say affecting sub-markets) and arbitrage is costly, then equilibrium will be characterised by imperfect arbitrage across markets (Grossman and Stiglitz, 1976, 1980); (d) even if all individuals and all firms are identical, the profit function may have multiple peaks; the *only* equilibria may be characterised by price distributions. (See Stiglitz, 1974; Butters, 1977; and Salop and Stiglitz, 1982.) Thus, in the Salop and Stiglitz analysis, individuals can either purchase for current consumption only, or purchase in addition for future consumption, thus reducing future search costs. Under certain conditions, they show that there is no single price equilibrium: if all firms charged the same price, it would always pay a single firm to lower its price to induce customers that arrive at it to buy for future consumption. Notice in these models, the market *creates* noise; it is firms' attempt to take advantage of the fact that search is costly that leads to a wage or price dispersion.

Let me emphasise, in concluding this section, that I do not want to over-state my case: there may be situations, particular markets, in which information costs are low, and in which the traditional theory does apply: the Law of Supply and Demand and the Law of the Single Price remain valid. Our contention is only that there are many situations where information costs are significant, and where the nature of the market equilibrium is, as a result, significantly altered. To understand consumer and firm behaviour in these situations and to understand the consequences of various kinds of governmental intervention, requires an explicit analysis of how information affects the market equilibrium.

II. TOWARDS THE CONSTRUCTION OF A NEW PARADIGM

In the first part of this lecture, I spelled out the negative accomplishments of the recent work in the economics of information: How it has provided a fundamental criticism of the conventional competitive paradigm, showing that the existence, optimality, and characterisation results are not robust. I now want to discuss the more positive accomplishments: the insights it has provided into welfare economics, into the theory of the firm, into the nature of competition and the consequences of monopoly, into macro-economics, and finally into the theory of comparative economic systems.

The New New Welfare Economics

Shortly before and after the last World War, considerable attention was accorded to the New Welfare Economics. Its major accomplishment was that it dispensed with the interpersonal comparability of individuals (or at least attempted to distinguish among propositions which did and did not require interpersonal comparability). One resource allocation was 'better' than another if it Pareto dominated the other: some individuals were better off, and no one was worse off. Those who might be disadvantaged, for instance, by a new innovation were compensated by a lump sum transfer. The New Welfare Economics was predicated on the assumption that there was perfect information concerning individuals – e.g. it was known who was disadvantaged by the innovation. This assumption meant that lump sum transfers were feasible, which in turn had one important implication: the problems of economic efficiency and distribution could be separated. Every competitive equilibrium was Pareto efficient; if one did not like the distribution of welfare, one could simply engage in a set of lump sum redistributions. By engaging in different lump sum redistributions, one could trace out all Pareto efficient allocations.

The New New Welfare Economics is predicated on the assumption that the government does not have perfect information concerning different individuals; it cannot tell who is of high ability, who is of low ability, who is disadvantaged by some innovation, who is benefited by some public programme. It can *elicit* some information, but the processes by which this information is elicited affect resource allocations. Thus, the government cannot ask who is more able, who is less able, for individuals will not have an incentive to answer truthfully. The absence of this information means that lump sum redistributive taxes are in general not feasible; if the government wishes to redistribute income, it must do so through distortionary taxes. We can, however, characterise the set of *Pareto efficient taxes*. Assume that there are only two types of individuals in the economy, high ability and low ability. The government cannot, however, tell who is of which type; it cannot observe the leisure enjoyed by any individual, but can observe the income and consumption. While the New Welfare Economics characterised the utility possibilities schedules, the maximum level of utility that the less able could attain, given the level of utility of the more able, under the assumption that lump sum transfers were feasible, the New New Welfare Economics characterises the utility possibilities schedule under the assumption that lump sum transfers are not feasible. The government can impose a distortionary income (and commodity) tax structure, in which more able individuals are induced (by the choices which they face) to reveal who they are. But to induce individuals to reveal who they are (so that differential treatment is feasible) requires altering the set of choices facing individuals.

Whether moral hazard problems arise, and how they are best handled when they do arise, depends too on the distribution of wealth. Thus, the moral hazard problems associated with sharecropping arise partly from the fact that workers do not own the land upon which they work (and do not have the capital to buy it). Some of the moral hazard problems which arise in other aspects of the employment relation would be mitigated if individuals had the capital to post a bond. More generally a basic insight of the New New welfare economics is that whether the economy is or is not Pareto efficient may depend on the initial distribution of wealth (Shapiro and Stiglitz, 1984): the separation between equity and efficiency considerations is no longer generally valid.

The New Theory of the Firm

There has long been a feeling among many economists that the conventional text model of the profit maximising firm, while it might have been appropriate for the simple owner-managed firms of the nineteenth century, did not provide an adequate description of modern industrial enterprises. Several alternative versions of managerial firms (March and Simon, Marris, Baumol, etc.) have been put forward. Economic theorists have looked askance at these theories: the market imposes discipline on managers to ensure that they engage in value maximising activities, both through shareholder voting and through the take-over mechanism. Managers who simply satisficed would be replaced by managers who maximised.

The New Theory of the Firm has placed the older managerial theory of the firm on a solid grounding: it has shown why neither the voting nor the take over mechanism will work to ensure value maximisation, in the presence of costly information. If obtaining information concerning whether the managers of the firm are managing the firms' assets efficiently is costly, then it does not pay any small shareholder to obtain that information: the efficient management of a firm is a public good. Moreover, as Grossman and Hart (1980) have pointed out, it does not pay any shareholder to sell his shares to anyone who has the promise of managing the firms resources more efficiently: he would prefer to have the other shareholders sell their shares, while he himself reaps the gain in market value resulting from the improved management.

Closer examination of managerial firms has uncovered a large number of practices which appear to be clearly inefficient, or at least not in the best interests of the shareholders. Although in most circumstances, economists do not have the information required to judge whether the managers are undertaking value maximising strategies, there are a few instances, mainly involving tax strategy, where we can assess management practices. The extensive use of accounting practices which do not minimise present discounted value of tax liabilities provides one set of examples. The distribution of returns to shareholders via dividends (rather than buying back shares) – the so-called Dividend Paradox – is another. The use of stock options as a method of compensating executives is a third.

Other examples of firms not maximising the value of their firm include the decision of managers of closed end mutual funds selling at a discount not to disband.

The separation between ownership and control has had, in turn, several interesting implications. First, it necessitates the design of incentive devices to help motivate managers to act in the interests of shareholders (Ross, 1973; Stiglitz, 1974). This affects not only the form of managerial compensation, but also the financial structure of the firm. The debt equity ratio affects the likelihood of a firm going bankrupt (and this, in turn affects managerial incentives, both with respect to effort and risk-taking). (Weiss and Stiglitz, 1981.)

Asymmetries of information affect the financial structure of the firm in other ways as well. While managers control the disposition of retained earnings, to get control of funds beyond those generated directly by the firm, they must persuade others to turn over their capital to them. Thus, the cost to managers of increasing equity by retained earnings and by issuing new shares are markedly different (and one sees remarkably little of the latter).

Indeed, while in the traditional theory, it is the shareholders who control the managers, in the new theory, banks may hold greater leverage over managers than shareholders; their threat to restrict credit is clearly more effective than a shareholders threat to vote for an alternative management team. (The role of credit restrictions as an incentive device is explored in Stiglitz and Weiss, 1983).[1] It has long been noted that firms often seem to act in a risk averse manner. When managers are asked to evaluate projects, they are concerned with risk in the traditional use of that term, not just in the sense of the correlation of the return with the market. This behaviour seems hard to reconcile with the traditional theory of the firm: surely in the stock market, shareholders can sufficiently diversify themselves that they should be concerned only with the correlation with the return of the project with the market as a whole. Such risk averse behaviour is perfectly consistent with the new Theory of the Firm. Managers control the firm; their reward is dependent, in a significant way, on the performance of the firm. Asymmetries of information also mean that controlling shareholders often have a finite fraction of their wealth invested in the shares of a single firm, and that firms have limited access to the capital market (Stiglitz, 1982a).

Perfect Capital Markets

One of the more unpalatable assumptions of the conventional paradigm was that there were perfect capital markets. Individuals and firms are assumed to be able to borrow as much as they want at the prevailing rate of interest. Moreover, individuals should have widely diversified portfolios, and thus wish the firm to act in a risk neutral manner (paying attention only to the correlation of profits with the market). Capital markets are informationally efficient, with prices perfectly reflecting all the available information.

The perspective provided by information economics provides explanations for why these predictions of the conventional paradigm are incorrect and allows the construction of models of the capital market which seem more consistent with what is actually observed. Thus, we have already noted that in the presence of imperfect information, of either the adverse selection or moral hazard sort, there may be credit rationing; and that the issue of new equities may provide a signal which will depress the market value of outstanding shares and hence the effective marginal cost of issuing new equities may be very large. The cost of capital to a firm may rise as the original shareholders attempt to sell their shares, since doing so may be taken as a signal to the market. And even when it does not provide a signal, the debt equity ratio may affect managerial

---

[1] Thus the Modigliani-Miller theorem, which asserts the irrelevance of firms' financial structure, does not apply when there is imperfect information of the kind under consideration here.

34   THE ECONOMIC JOURNAL

incentives, and thus, again, the cost of capital will be dependent on the debt equity ratio.

Grossman and Stiglitz (1976, 1980) have, further, pointed out that prices will not, in general, perfectly reflect the information which is available to the participants in the market. Only in the absence of noise will this be the case; and then, the market will only reflect free information: when prices perfectly reflect the information which is available, no one has any incentive to invest in information. There is an equilibrium level of disequilibrium in the market. But this 'natural' level of noise has no optimality properties.

Theory of Competition

The new information economics has lead to a revision of our views of the functions of competition: while it may perform the functions for which it is given credit in the traditional paradigm less effectively than that paradigm suggests, it may play other roles, not discussed in the traditional theory.

As noted in the earlier discussion, a central consequence of imperfect information is that markets will not be characterised by perfect competition, in the sense that this is normally defined; product markets are more aptly described by models of imperfect competition, where slight changes in prices do not result in firms losing all of their customers; they perceive themselves facing downward sloping demand schedules.

Indeed, the relationship between the number of firms and the competitivity of the market may appear to be quite different than in the traditional theory. Markets with a limited number of firms may have much more effective competition than markets with a large number of firms; in the former case, for instance, if any firm lowers its price, it will not induce anybody to search, while in markets with a limited number of firms, if a firm lowers its price, it may induce considerable search. As a result, perceived demand curves may appear to be more elastic with a limited number of firms. (See Stiglitz, 1983).

On the other hand, competition provides a basis of comparison; it provides information which can be used in the design of reward schedules which allows a firm to provide greater incentives with lower risk than it could in the absence of this information, and it allows the adjustment of the reward to changes in the environment. (This is referred to as the property of *flexibility*, Nalebuff and Stiglitz, 1983*a*). Markets have the property that, like contests and relative performance compensation schemes, they reward firms and individuals on the basis of how well they do relative to others; they thus have the property that the reward is automatically adjusted to the difficulty of the task. Moreover, the presence of competition allows the design of managerial reward structures which provide better incentives while allowing the manager to bear less risk. (See Nalebuff and Stiglitz, 1983*b*.)

Theory of Monopoly

The New Information Economics has affected not only our views on how competition works, but also our views on monopolies. The older theory focused on two cases: monopolists who could charge a single price to all customers, and perfectly discriminating monopolists. In the new theory, the central case is that of the partially discriminating monopolist, the monopolist who would like to charge those who enjoy a greater consumer surplus from his product a higher fee, but cannot identify who these individuals are. (The analogy between the problem facing the government, which would like to impose a higher tax on the individual with the greater ability, but does not know who those individuals are, and the problem facing the monopolist should be clear.) There is a whole set of devices which the monopolist can use to discriminate among different categories of buyers. The major distortions associated with monopoly arise from these discrimination devices. Among the discrimination devices are non-linear price schedules, producing products of different qualities, randomising prices (which discriminates among individuals with different search costs), tie in sales, and queues. The theory thus provides an explanation for many practices which seem inexplicable in the traditional theory.

It has also lead to a re-examination of the arguments for (and the analysis of the consequences of) vertical integration. While the earlier literature simply assumed, for instance, that when two firms become integrated, their interests, which previously had been in conflict, now coincide, the new theory attempts to identify precisely in what way the set of available incentive structures might change by a change in ownership. (In the case of a merger, there is not even a change in ownership; what may be changed is the set of rules for the delegation of authority and decision making.) It asks, for instance, what can such a change accomplish that a set of contracts could not accomplish. These questions are closely related to the next set of topics which I wish to mention.

Finally, Salop (1979) has noted that the fact the price a monopolist charges conveys information about his costs can be used to develop a theory of limit pricing.

The Theory of Economic Organisation

The comparison of alternative economic systems has been a central concern of economics. In spite of its importance, the traditional theory gave us few insights. The Lange-Lerner Taylor Theorem suggested that market socialism and capitalism were equivalent. But neither the model of market socialism nor the model of modern capitalism on which this equivalence result was based remotely approximated the kinds of institutional structures found in the modern world. As I remarked earlier, the notions of decentralisation associated with neoclassical theory are more akin to a description of a computer algorithm – a description of how one might efficiently go about a complicated maximisation problem that one needs to solve once and for all – than of an institutional structure which is required to adapt and respond to a series of new and changing problems.

What I would like to do now is to describe briefly some work on which I am

36   THE ECONOMIC JOURNAL

currently engaged, which has the promise of providing a more meaningful basis of a comparison of economic systems. Problems of information gathering, communication, and decision making are central in this view. Individuals have finite capacities to gather and process information, while communication of information between individuals is both costly and imperfect. Information gathering and decision making takes real time, and both because of positive discounting and because the environment is constantly changing (so that information quickly becomes obsolete) there is a return to making decisions quickly. The consequences of these simple observations is that how individuals are organised to gather information, how information is communicated, and how decisions are made is critical to the performance of the economic system. We refer to the pattern of organisation of individuals in an economic system as its *architecture.*[1]

To see more clearly what I have in mind, let me consider two simple architectures: polyarchy versus hierarchy. Assume the problem facing the organisation is choosing among a large number of projects, some of which have a positive expected return, some of which have a negative expected return. In the polyarchy, each individual has the discretion to accept or reject the project; projects which are rejected are 'thrown' back into the pool of available projects, and may be considered by another individual in the polyarchy. In contrast, in the hierarchy, projects are taken from the available pool only once. Those which are approved by the lower level in the hierarchy are passed onto the next, which re-examines them. (In our analysis, we assume that there is very limited communication among the levels of the hierarchy: only a binary message can be sent, indicating approval or disapproval.) It is easy to show that (under the assumption that the probability of approval of a given project by a given individual within each organisational structure is the same) while a hierarchy rejects more good projects, a polyarchy accepts more bad projects. Thus, the overall performance of the two organisations is partially dependent on the distribution of projects, the ratio of good projects to bad projects. But under the plausible assumption that there are more bad projects than good projects – after all, it is easier to think up bad ideas than good ideas – polyarchy performs better than hierarchy. (Hierarchies reject too many of the scarce 'good' projects.) This result holds when the acceptance levels are determined rationally, on the basis of the information which is implicit within the organisational design, in each system. It should also be noted that the fact that the probabilities of projects with different characteristics differ between the organisations will affect incentives for innovators; thus one would expect the two systems to differ in the set of projects among which they must choose.

The different forms of organisation correspond to different sequential decision making rules. For instance, in a hierarchy, the rule is 'if A thinks well of the project, gather more information about it; if A does not think well of the project, reject it.' In a polyarchy, the rule is, 'if A thinks well of the project,

---

[1] The work described in this section is being done jointly with R. K. Sah. See Sah and Stiglitz (1984).

accept it; if *A* does not think well of the project, throw it back into the pool and give someone else a chance to take a look at it.'

The results I have just described represent just the beginning of an ambitious research programme attempting to investigate the consequences of different organisational designs. What are the consequences of different spans of control, different numbers of layers within the heirarchy, the use of committees, operating under different rules, for decision making? One aspect, to which I wish to call attention, arises from the fact that when individuals differ (in their abilities to gather information, or to make decisions, or in their willingness to undertake risks) then an important problem arises in allocating, say, the more able individuals to different slots within the organisation. Not only may an individual's marginal productivity be higher in one position within the organisation than in another, but the performance of some organisational structures may be more sensitive to how individuals are assigned. In most organisations, of course, decisions about who holds what position next period are made by those within the organisation this period, according to certain rules. That is, organisations are *self-perpetuating*. And among the central decisions which individuals in an organisation must make are decisions about who should be their successors. These decisions, like decisions concerning which projects should be undertaken, are made subject to error. The kinds of errors which will arise, and the sensitivity of the performance of the organisation to these errors, are both functions of the organisational architecture. In current work, we are investigating the resulting relative performance of some simple organisational forms.

Macro-economics

Macro-economics provides perhaps the area in which the New Information Economics has had some of its greatest successes and failures. It has provided models which can explain unemployment, price and wage rigidities, and credit rationing. The question is, how plausible are these models? How plausible are their informational (and other) assumptions? And do they have implications which seem inconsistent with the facts?

The subject is too broad for me to do justice to it here, so let me focus my remarks on only one aspect, theories of unemployment. The set of theories that I find most attractive are the *efficiency wage* theories, which I discussed earlier, in which productivity depends on the wage paid. These yield competitive equilibria in which there may exist an excess supply of workers. Firms do not cut wages, in spite of the excess supply, because they know that doing so will reduce the productivity of their labour force (either through selection effects or incentive effects), reduce it enough so that firm profits are lowered. In some versions, such as those in which unemployment is used as a worker discipline device, the only equilibria entail unemployment (see Shapiro and Stiglitz (1984).) At full employment, workers have no incentive to work: the worst that happens to them is that they are fired, but with full employment they are immediately rehired at the same wage. (In their model there is no uncertainty about the characteristics of workers.) To induce workers not to shirk, firms raise their wages. As they all increase their wages, their demand for labour decreases and unemployment develops. It is the unemployment which provides the discipline that ensures that workers do not shirk.

Furthermore, the efficiency wage theories provide an explanation for why firms adjust their wages slowly, and for why firms that fail to adjust their wages may lose relatively little; they provide, in other words, an explanation of wage stickiness. (Given the wage paid by other firms, it does not pay any firm to reduce its wage by much, even though a coordinated wage reduction might be profitable. And given that the wage was chosen optimally, to maximise expected profits, the failure to adjust wages to a small change in the environment results in a loss which is of a second order of smallness.)

Having noted one of the sets of theories which I find attractive, let me mention one set of theories which I find *unpersuasive*: the implicit contact theory with asymmetric information. Numerous versions of these models have been investigated. For a brief survey, see Azariadis and Stiglitz (1983) and Hart (1983). These are one period models in which the employees are assumed not to know the state of nature, but employers do know. In order to ensure that the firm is honest in its revelation of the state, the employment, the choices of the firm must be restricted. As in the other problems of adverse selection which we have discussed, a distortion must be introduced: here, either the firm must be compelled to employ more labourers than it would like in good states, or fewer labourers in bad states. The latter may be interpreted as generating involuntary unemployment.

Let me explain some of the reasons why I find this theory unconvincing. First, under plausible assumptions concerning utility functions, it generates over-employment in good states, rather than under-employment in bad states. To generate unemployment for plausible assumptions concerning workers' utility functions requires that firms be risk averse (in marked contrast to traditional implicit contract theory where the function of the contract was to transfer risk from the workers to the firms). Its informational assumptions require both more and less information than seems plausibly available: to enforce these contracts, employment levels of the firm have to be observable, which means that the firm cannot contract out for labour services. (It also requires that the firm not be able to transfer some of its capital to another firm, or a subsidiary, thereby effectively avoiding the constraint on its employment.) On the other hand, there are variables, like industry sales, profits, unemployment rates, etc., which, though not perfect indicators of the state of nature, clearly convey information; if the central problem were that of the lack of information concerning the state of nature, surely this information should be employed much more extensively than it seems to be. Thirdly, these contracts are one period contracts, again, in marked contrast to traditional implicit contract theory which focused on long term contracts. While reputation may be an effective method of enforcing long term contracts, one period contracts can only be enforced if they are explicit; but few if any explicit contracts are of the form postulated by the theory. The threat of the withdrawal of current labour services may provide an effective enforcement device, but to the extent that this is the mechanism by which the contract is enforced, these theories become but a version of the efficiency wage contract theories. Moreover, these theories fail to explain why firms lay off workers, rather than engaging in work sharing. (The puzzle is particularly greater in the United States, where the lack of experience rating provides a strong incentive for rotating jobs when otherwise layoffs would extend over 26 weeks. The efficiency wage hypothesis does provide an explanation of lay-offs). Finally, they do not explain why other firms do not hire the workers who are layed off. (A theory of unemployment must explain both.)

The final theory of unemployment which I wish to mention is predicated on the assumption that the economy faces numerous disturbances which make it efficient for workers to shift from one firm to another, and that there are costs associated with this movement (specific training costs, moving costs, and search). Individuals are risk averse, and are less able to bear these risks than firms. On the other hand, if it is costly to monitor search, if individuals are guaranteed a wage, they will have no incentive to move, to seek out firms where their productivity is higher. (Indeed, in the traditional theory, this is precisely the function which wage differentials serve: to induce individuals to move from jobs where their productivity is low to jobs where their productivity is high.) The problem is a standard moral hazard problem, of the kind we discussed earlier. The solution is the usual compromise: partial insurance. Wages are not perfectly flexible, but they respond somewhat, to provide some incentive for workers to search. But more to our present point, the optimal contract entails lay-offs. (See Arnott *et al.* 1983.)

Concluding Remarks

The world-views which emerge from the alternative approaches presented in this paper are, I think, markedly different from those of the conventional theories which were prevalent until recently. The fact that both the assumptions of the analysis and the conclusions which it reaches seem more in accord with common sense seems a virtue, not a vice.

I concluded my lecture ten years ago by saying this new perspective would require a reassessment of our views of competition, equilibrium, and optimality. I went on to say,

'Although I know I have not gone very far in this lecture towards accomplishing this task, what I hope I have done is to communicate to you some of the perspective which the economics of information brings to these questions and to share with you some of the excitement that I feel as at last we begin to explore systematically an area, the potential importance of which has long been felt but whose full implications we are only now beginning to grasp.'

Most of what I said then is still true: We have made great progress, but new areas of research, new applications of this general perspective, have opened up

40 THE ECONOMIC JOURNAL

as fast as results were obtained on long standing issues. The sense of excitement is still there: diminishing returns has not yet set in. Perhaps this too is simply a reflection of the Fundamental Non-concavity in the value of information.

Princeton University and Hoover Institution, Stanford

REFERENCES

Akerlof, George. (1984). 'Gift exchange and efficiency wage theory: four views'. *American Economic Review Proceedings*.
Arnott, R. and Hosios, A. and Stiglitz, J. (1983). 'Implicit contracts, labour mobility and unemployment'. mimeo. Princeton University. (revised version of a paper presented at NBER-NSF conference, Dec. 1980).
——and Stiglitz, Joseph E. (1984). 'Moral hazard and the existence of equilibrium in competitive insurance markets', forthcoming, *Quarterly Journal of Economics*.
Azariadis, C. and Stiglitz, J. E. (1983). 'Implicit contracts and fixed price equilibria', *Quarterly Journal of Economics Supplement*.
Butters, Gerald R. (1977). 'Equilibrium distribution of sales and advertising prices', *Review of Economic Studies*, (October), pp. 465–91.
Greenwald, Bruce and Stiglitz, Joseph E. (1984). 'Pecuniary and markets mediated externalities: towards a general theory of the welfare economics of economies with imperfect information and incomplete markets', NBER Working Paper 1304.
Grossman, S., and Hart, O. (1980). 'Take-over bids, The free rider problem and the theory of the corporation', *Bell Journal of Economics*, Vol. 11 (Spring), pp. 42–64.
——and Stiglitz, Joseph E. (1976). 'Information and competitive price systems', *American Economic Review*, Vol. 66, No. 2, (May), pp. 246–53.
——and ——(1980). 'On the impossibility of informationally efficient markets', *American Economic Review*, Vol. 70, No. 3, (June), pp. 393–408.
Hart, O. (1983). 'Optimal labour contracts under asymmetric information: an introduction'. *Review of Economic Studies*. Vol. 50. pp. 3–36.
Nalebuff, B. and Stiglitz, Joseph E. (1983a). 'Information competition and markets', *American Economic Review*, May, pp. 278–84.
——and ——(1983b), 'Prizes and incentives: towards a general theory of compensation and competition', *Bell Journal*, (Spring) Vol. 14, pp. 21–43.
Ross, S. (1973). 'The economic theory of agency: the principal's problem', *American Econnomic Review*, (May) pp. 134–9.
Rothschild, Michael, and Stiglitz, Joseph E. (1976). 'Equilibrium in competitive insurance markets: an essay on the economics of imperfect information', *Quarterly Journal of Economics*, November, Vol. 90 (4), pp. 629–49.
Sah, R. K. and Stiglitz, J. E. (1984). 'The architecture of economic systems: hierarches and polyarchies', mimeo. Princeton University.
Salop, Steven (1977). 'The noisy monopolist: imperfect information price dispersion and price discrimination', *Review of Economic Studies*, (October), pp. 393–406.
——(1979). 'A model of the natural rate of unemployment'. *American Economic Review*. Vol. 69. pp. 117–25.
——and Stiglitz, Joseph E. (1977). 'Bargains and ripoffs: a model of monopolistically competitive price dispersions', *Review of Economic Studies*, Vol. 44, (October), pp. 493–510.
——and ——(1982). 'The theory of sales: a simple model of equilibrium price dispersion with identical agents', *American Economic Review*, December, pp. 1121–30.
Shapiro, C. and Stiglitz, Joseph E. (1984). 'Equilibrium unemployment as a worker discipline device', *American Economic Review*, (June), Vol. 73, no. 3, pp. 433–45.
Stiglitz, J. E. (1974). 'Incentives and risk sharing in sharecropping', *Review of Economic Studies*, (April), pp. 219–55.
——(1975). 'Information and economic analysis', in *Current Economic Problems*. J. M. Parkin and A. R. Nobay, (eds). Cambridge: Cambridge University Press, pp. 27–52. (Proceedings of the Association of University Teachers of Economics, Manchester, April, 1974.)
——(1979). 'Equilibrium in product markets with imperfect information', *American Economic Review*, Vol. 69, No. 2, (May), pp. 339–45.
——(1982a), 'Information and the capital market', in *Financial Economics: Essays in Honor of Paul Cootner*, William F. Sharpe and Cathryn Cootner (eds.), Englewood Cliffs, New Jersey: Prentice Hall, pp. 118–58.

——(1982*b*). 'Ownership, control, and efficient markets: some paradoxes in the theory of capital markets', *Economic Regulation: Essays in Honor of James R. Nelson*. Kenneth D. Boyer and William C. Shepherd, (eds.), Ann Arbor, Michigan: Michigan State University Press, pp. 311–41.

——(1983). 'Duopolies are more competitive than atomistic markets', Princeton University, mimeo, (October).

Weiss, A. and Stiglitz, Joseph E. (1981). 'Credit rationing in markets with imperfect information', *American Economic Review*, Vol. 71, No. 3, (June), pp. 393–410.

——and——(1983). 'Incentive effects of terminations: applications to the credit and labor markets', *American Economic Review*, (December), Vol. 73, pp. 912–27.

Wilson, C. A. (1977). 'A model of insurance markets with incomplete information', *Journal of Economic Theory*, (December), Vol. 16(2), pp. 167–207.

Winter, C. (1964). 'Economic "natural selection" and the theory of the firm', *Yale Economic Essays*, Spring, pp. 224–72.

[34]

JOURNAL OF ENVIRONMENTAL ECONOMICS AND MANAGEMENT 17, 266–283 (1989)

Measuring Welfare Effects of Product Contamination with Consumer Uncertainty[1]

WILLIAM FOSTER

Department of Agricultural and Resource Economics, University of California at Berkeley, Berkeley, California 94720

AND

RICHARD E. JUST

Department of Agricultural and Resource Economics, University of Maryland, College Park, Maryland 20742

Received September 17, 1987; revised July 1, 1988

A methodology is developed for measuring consumer welfare loss from market demand due to contamination when information is imperfect. Comparison of behavior before and after awareness permits calculation of the "cost of ignorance" which occurs when news of contamination is withheld or undiscovered for a time as well as when excessive reporting and exaggeration cause overreaction. Avoidance costs are also calculated for consumers who consume less than they would with perfect information due to risk aversion. The methodology is applied to analyzing the heptachlor crisis which reduced milk consumption in Hawaii by over 80%. © 1989 Academic Press, Inc.

Cases of accidental chemical contamination of food sources present difficult problems for measurement of consumer welfare effects. Direct consumer question-naires have been criticized because of a perceived reluctance by respondents to assign meaningful or valid values to "goods" that involve hypothetical or uncertain safety. On the other hand, estimating actual ex post losses is a tentative approach because estimates regarding the number of affected people (e.g., contracting cancer) are inaccurate and approaches to estimating loss per affected person (implicit value of life from other comparisons, cost of treatment, and value of work time lost) produce conflicting results [9]. Weinstein and Quinn [18] argue that these values of health risk are context dependent because ex post measures of consumer loss ignore the welfare loss associated with uncertainty, e.g., the psychological costs of worrying about the possibility of contracting cancer, defective childbirth, etc. As in the case of production under uncertainty, uncertainty about health effects has a distinct welfare effect whether or not the worst fears are realized because (1) decisions are consciously altered to avoid uncertainty, (2) psychological costs of uncertainty may be incurred even if consumer awareness occurs only after consumption of a contaminated good, and (3) an individual may prefer a more certain situation in lieu of the uncertain alternative even if he must give up something to obtain it [7].

This paper develops an ex post approach for measurement of consumer welfare loss from contamination that includes effects of uncertainty and imperfect informa-tion. Ex post analysis of supply has proven useful in evaluating contamination

[1] This research was supported by a grant from the Environmental Protection Agency.

266

effects for producers (e.g., Mjelde, Adams, Dixon, and Garcia [11]). Two recent studies have begun to develop an ex post methodology for estimating consumer losses due to specific chemically related health risks. Shulstad and Stoevener [13], who investigate the problem of mercury contamination of Oregon pheasants, provide an extension of previous environmental literature by recognizing that individuals change their behavior in response to information (as measured by newspaper accounts) to avoid pollution and that avoidance reflects a social cost. Swartz and Strand [16], who use an index of newspaper articles about kepone pollution of Virginia's James River to account for perceptions of product quality, further recognize that information may be imperfect. However, neither of these approaches provides a means of assessing the welfare effects of consumer uncertainty that prevail particularly during the initial period of public exposure, and neither provides a way to measure consumer welfare losses due to consumption after contamination has begun but before consumer awareness occurs.

Consideration of uncertainty is complicated by consumers' limited information about true health risks imposed by various types of contamination [18]. Excessive coverage in news media when information about contamination first surfaces may lead to a consumer "scare" and, thus, cause unnecessary "avoidance costs" for consumers who consume less of the contaminated good than they would with perfect information. In the Shulstad–Stoevener framework, an additional newspaper story reduces welfare regardless of whether the story is correct or incorrect and regardless of whether it suggests more or less contamination than previous stories. Thus, if news were simply not released, consumers would incur no "measured" welfare loss even though consumers may be consuming excessive mercury levels. Alternatively, in the Swartz–Strand analysis, if information incorrectly shows contamination and it is withheld until after most consumer decisions are made, then little welfare loss occurs. A desirable framework should provide an appropriate way of calculating welfare losses to consumers in the common case where news of contamination is withheld or undiscovered for some time. If a consumer attaches a given discount for uncertainty to a contaminated good, then he will presumably incur an associated loss (worrying, as well as any real health loss) even if he only learns that the good was contaminated after consumption.

Furthermore, once consumers become aware of a problem, consumption may return to normal levels only slowly even after a product is pronounced safe. For example, Smith, van Ravenswaay, and Thompson [14], in a study of the same empirical problem addressed here, found that they were unable to "explain" this very slow return to normal consumption patterns after restoration of product safety because consumer uncertainty tends to persist once confidence in a product is lost. Since this uncertainty affects consumer budget allocations, it can cause consumer welfare effects beyond the time when contamination problems are corrected.

The purpose of this paper is to develop an approach appropriate for estimating consumer welfare effects when consumer uncertainty and inappropriate information affect consumer decisions. The approach considers consumer decision making under uncertainty using an exact welfare calculation based on the expenditure function. The first section develops a model of consumer response to changes in a perceived probability distribution of contamination. The second section compares appropriate welfare measures with the classical Marshallian surplus. The third section develops welfare measures that reflect consumer loss with different types of imperfections in information—withheld information about contamination, excessive reporting on contamination, etc. Finally, an application of the framework to the 1982 heptachlor crisis of milk in Hawaii is presented. News of milk contamination by heptachlor—a pesticide used in pineapple production—was released in March, 1982, and caused monthly milk consumption on the island of Oahu to decline by over 80% the following month.

I. A MODEL OF CONSUMER RESPONSE TO CONTAMINATION UNCERTAINTY

To make the issues clear, one must distinguish between two concepts of ex ante and ex post evaluation; one relates to the probability distribution of health effects of consumption and the other relates to information. The measures in this paper are ex ante measures with respect to the probability distribution of effects but ex post with respect to information. For example, in a typical contamination problem, four distinct stages can be identified: (1) contamination and continued consumption in ignorance, (2) dissemination of information about contamination possibly involving an initial "scare" but eventually leading to consumer adjustment to correct current information, (3) worry and concern about the ultimate effects of consumption (including that undertaken in ignorance), and (4) adverse health effects on a portion of the population associated with the mortality rate of the contaminant. This paper considers the third stage as the pertinent one for economic welfare analysis. One should keep in mind, however, that welfare measures in the third stage will reflect perceived economic effects across all four stages.

The actual probability distribution of mortality is not known until the fourth stage; therefore, consumers must estimate the distribution in an ex ante sense in the third stage. This accounts for the importance of uncertainty as it affects consumer decisions and valuations. In the fourth stage, the consumer may discover the exact effects of consumption, but suffers in the third stage the psychological costs of worry and concern regarding the possibility of future health problems. Furthermore, these costs are based in part on what may have been consumed in ignorance. Actual choices reveal only preferences for what the consumer thinks he consumes at the time of choice. By the third stage, however, the consumer realizes that earlier choices were made in ignorance and now faces potential mortality. These are the effects that have political ramifications for policymakers and, thus, are of greatest interest in welfare analysis of alternative policies.

In order to examine the change in consumers' welfare associated with product contamination at this stage, consider first the behavior of an individual consumer. Suppose a representative consumer is faced with the problem of allocating a given income between a contaminated good and all other goods. Suppose some quality characteristic associated with each unit of the contaminated good determines the utility the consumer derives from its consumption, but the quality level is not certain. For purposes of discussion, quality may represent either the level of contamination or the health effect of consumption.

Let the quality level of the contaminated good be represented by q and suppose q has a probability distribution with a vector of parameters, θ. Suppose, further, that the consumer's utility function can be represented by $U(x, q, y)$ where x is consumption of the contaminated good and y is consumption of other goods. Plausible assumptions include $U_x > 0$, $U_y > 0$, $U_q > 0$, $U_{xq} > 0$, $U_{yq} = 0$, $U_{xqq} < 0$, and concavity of U in x and y for each q.[2] In addition to the standard assumptions of utility theory, these relationships imply that utility increases with quality; that marginal utility of the contaminated good increases with quality at a decreasing rate; and that marginal utility of other goods is not affected by quality of the contaminated good. The latter assumption can be relaxed (e.g., $U_{yq} \leqslant 0$, $U_{yqq} \geqslant 0$) but at the expense of requiring more discussion.[3]

The consumer's expected utility maximization problem is

$$\max_{x, y} E_\theta \{ U(x, q, y) \} \tag{1}$$

subject to the budget constraint $px + y = m$, where E_θ is an expectation with respect to the quality distribution, p is the price of x relative to the price of other goods, and m is income relative to the price of other goods. On substitution of the budget constraint, the problem becomes

$$\max_x \overline{U}(x, m, \theta) \equiv \max_x E_\theta [\tilde{U}(x, m)],$$

where $\tilde{U}(x, m) \equiv U(x, q, m - px)$, for which the first-order condition is

$$\overline{U}_x = E_\theta (U_x - pU_y) = 0, \tag{2}$$

assuming this condition is solved by some positive x and $y = m - px$.

To consider the comparative static behavior of the consumer in this framework, suppose quality is a random variable represented by $q = \mu + \sigma \epsilon$, where $\mu = E_\theta(q)$, σ represents a mean-preserving spread parameter [12], and the distribution of ϵ represents other parameters in θ. Then total differentiation of (2) can reveal the effects of a change in the distribution of quality as represented by the mean, μ, and the uncertainty or dispersion, σ. First, $dx/d\mu = -\overline{U}_{x\mu}/\overline{U}_{xx}$. From concavity of the utility function, the second-order condition of the fixed quality problem, $\tilde{U}_{xx} < 0$, must hold for all quality levels. Thus, the second-order condition for (1), $\overline{U}_{xx} = E_\theta(\tilde{U}_{xx}) < 0$, must hold. Also, using assumptions above, $\overline{U}_{x\mu} = E_\theta(U_{xq} - pU_{yq}) = E_\theta(U_{xq}) > 0$. Thus, $dx/d\mu > 0$ so consumption responds positively to an increase in the mean of the distribution of quality.

Similarly, the effect of a change in quality uncertainty can be found by examining $dx/d\sigma = -\overline{U}_{x\sigma}/\overline{U}_{xx}$. Noting that $\overline{U}_{x\sigma} = \partial E_\theta(\tilde{U}_x)/\partial\sigma$, Jensen's inequality yields $\overline{U}_{x\sigma} < 0$ since

$$\tilde{U}_{xqq} = U_{xqq} - pU_{yqq} = U_{xqq} < 0;$$

i.e., for some function $f(q)$, $\partial E_\theta[f(q)]/\partial\sigma < 0$ if $f_{qq} < 0$. Thus, $dx/d\sigma < 0$ so an increase in quality uncertainty causes a decrease in consumption when the mean of the quality distribution remains fixed.

---

[2] For the derivation of this section only, the contaminated good is assumed to be a good rather than a bad for all levels of quality for simplicity. This is not inconsistent with observed behavior of zero consumption if price is positive. However, the framework can easily be expanded to consider $U_x < 0$ for low q if a restriction $x \geqslant 0$ is added.

[3] Since q is not a choice variable, concavity of the objective criteria in q is not needed to assure an internal solution. However, the alternative qualitative effects of the quality variable would complicate the discussion of comparative static effects below.

These results imply that the mean and the variance of the quality distribution have distinct qualitative effects on consumer demand. Contamination information on consumption cannot be reflected through a single information variable (such as column inches of newspaper articles or numbers of articles). That is, when an initial "scare" leads to consumer uncertainty that declines only gradually while the subjective mean quality first decreases and then increases, data on information must be at least two-dimensional, representing both the expected contamination level and uncertainty about the level.[4]

To understand these effects one must distinguish between the quality distribution that affects consumer decisions and the one that ultimately determines consumer welfare. For example, consumption of a given quantity of a carcinogen may cause various degrees of cancer with different probabilities. This probability distribution of outcomes is conceptually induced by the probability distribution of quality q. That is, q is a random variable that determines the specific health effect of a given quantity of consumption. The specific health effect is not known at the time of consumption because not all of those consuming given amounts are affected in the same way.

The framework used here follows Bayesian decision theory in the sense that decisions are made on the basis of the subjective quality distribution held by the consumer at the time of decision making. However, the framework also assumes that the consumer's subjective distribution is improved within a fairly short time frame (during the sample period) while the harmful effects of consumption are realized only over a relatively long time horizon.[5] For example, after a consumer scare, consumer perceptions about the probability of various levels of health loss may become reasonably accurate over a period of months or a few years. On the other hand, the ill effects may take 10 to 20 years to manifest themselves. If so, then essentially all of the true ill effects of consumption (including the psychological costs of uncertainty) will be experienced even though consumption may have been undertaken initially in ignorance or with a poor subjective evaluation of potential effects. Thus, while decisions are based on subjective quality distributions held at the time of decision making, the welfare effects also depend on the true or objective quality distribution that is eventually realized.

II. EVALUATION OF WELFARE EFFECTS OF PERCEIVED QUALITY CHANGES

The most widely applied measure of change in consumer welfare brought about by a change in price or quality is "willingness to pay"—sometimes called "willingness to accept" or "willingness to sell" in the case of a detrimental change.

---

[4]This does not imply that every contamination problem requires a multidimensional measure of information. For example, a referee points out that a product warning may cause a change only in the subjective mean quality while a product ban more clearly causes a change in the subjective variance as well and, finally, that product recall may change the subjective variance without changing the subjective mean.

[5]Note that Graham [2] has shown that state dependent (quality dependent) utility functions can be estimated only if individuals can be observed both before receiving information when choices do not affect known probabilities and after receiving information when choices can be altered to affect probabilities.

Compensating variation measures a consumer's willingness to move to a new situation to which he attaches a different subjective distribution of quality when he is free to adjust his consumption bundle. When information which would have induced a correct assessment of the quality distribution (and, thus, an appropriate allocation of income) is withheld or transmitted imperfectly, however, the appropriate measure of willingness to pay is the compensating surplus [7]. For the compensating variation, the exact approach offered by Hausmann [4] to determine exact measures of consumer welfare effects can be employed. For the compensating surplus, this approach can be extended as in the next section to make further use of the consumer's response to prices.

Suppose the solution to the consumer's problem in (1) is represented by $x^* = x(p, m, \theta)$, a function of prices, income, and distribution parameters in θ. The expected utility evaluation at optimal consumption levels x^* can be represented by the indirect expected utility function, $V(p, m, \theta) \equiv E_\theta[U(x^*, q, y^*)]$, where $y^* \equiv y(p, m, \theta) \equiv m - px^*$. The dual approach to this problem considers the expenditure function, $e(p, \overline{U}, \theta) \equiv \{\min(px + y); E_\theta[\overline{U}(x, q, y)] \geqslant \overline{U}\}$, which minimizes the cost of attaining a given level of expected utility U and by differentiation yields the Hicksian demand curve,

$$h(p, \overline{U}, \theta) = \frac{\partial e(p, \overline{U}, \theta)}{\partial p}. \tag{3}$$

The willingness to accept a new situation with a different probability distribution of quality can be represented using either the indirect utility function or the expenditure function. Consider a detrimental change in the subjective quality distribution indicated by a change from θ_0 to θ_1. In terms of the indirect expected utility function, the compensating variation, CV, is defined by

$$V(p_0, m_0 + \text{CV}, \theta_1) = V(p_0, m_0, \theta_0) = U_0,$$

where U_0 is the initial utility level or, in terms of the expenditure function,

$$\text{CV} = e(p_0, U_0, \theta_1) - e(p_0, U_0, \theta_0) = e(p_0, U_0, \theta_1) - m_0 \tag{4}$$

[7]. This measure of consumer loss (gain) is equal to the change in area under the compensated demand curve at the initial utility level. Thus, the compensating variation is a willingness to sell the original quality distribution as revealed by actual behavior or demand choices. That is, defining $\hat{p}(\theta)$ as the lowest price where the compensated demand curve meets the price axis, i.e., $h(\hat{p}, U_0, \theta) = 0$ (infinity if it does not), one finds from (2) and (3) that

$$\text{CV} = \int_{p_0}^{\hat{p}(\theta_0)} h_1(p, U_0, \theta_0)\, dp - \int_{p_0}^{\hat{p}(\theta_1)} h_1(p, U_0, \theta_1)\, dp,$$

assuming no externalities. Thus the compensating variation is given by the area under the initial Hicksian demand less the area under the new Hicksian demand. Note that a change in quality does not affect utility if consumption is zero [7].

III. THE COST OF IGNORANCE AND THE ROLE OF INFORMATION

Compensating variation is appropriate for evaluation of the welfare change due to changes in consumer information regarding quality or health risk when consumers are free to adjust to the correct or objective quality distribution. However, when consumers are not given correct information that would alter their behavior or are given incorrect information that alters their behavior, then their subjective quality distribution is incorrect and they have no opportunity to avoid possible welfare losses or take advantage of additional gains by changing budgetary allocations appropriately. For example, if consumers purchase a product they believe to be safe (because adverse information is withheld) and then find out after consumption that it will cause cancer, then they experience essentially the same adverse effects as if they were forced to consume the product with perfect information (with a correct or objective quality distribution). Consumers thus incur a cost of ignorance beyond the loss they would experience if free to adjust. The appropriate willingness-to-pay measure for evaluating a welfare change relative to the initial situation when consumption quantities are not free to adjust is the compensating surplus.[6]

To consider measurement of compensating surplus using observed demand behavior, define the restricted expenditure function,

$$\tilde{e}(p, U_0, \theta, x_0) \equiv \{\min(px + y); x = x_0, E_\theta[U(x_0, q, y)] \geq U_0\}.$$

The compensating surplus is then defined by

$$CS = \tilde{e}(p_0, U_0, \theta_1, x_0) - \tilde{e}(p_0, U_0, \theta_0, x_0) = \tilde{e}(p_0, U_0, \theta_1, x_0) - m_0,$$

where θ_0 represents the subjective distribution of quality that incorrectly reflects precontamination safety and θ_1 represents the objective distribution of quality with contamination.

Two notes are in order concerning use of the compensating surplus for cases where information is withheld. First, the compensating surplus measure assumes the consumer does not remain in ignorance. Following the old cliche, "ignorance is bliss," if the consumer never learns of the contamination problem (and *never experiences the adverse effects* that are possible), then the same welfare loss is not realized. The assumption here, however, is that improved information materializes in the sample period even though the observation period is not long enough to determine whether a particular consumer will experience the worst possible effects (e.g., contract cancer). Thus, essentially the same worry, concern, and uncertainty—in addition to real costs in the case of adverse consequences—are incurred as if consumption were forced with improved information. With these considerations in mind, welfare effects must ultimately be valued with correct information where the

---

[6] Here, compensating surplus is defined as the amount of money (possibly negative) required to be added to income in order to keep the consumer as well off after the change as in the initial state if he is not free to adjust consumption quantities other than of the numeraire. In the case of the model in this paper, the numeraire is good y. This somewhat unusual definition of compensating surplus is made necessary by the fact that welfare measurements here concern quality change rather than the usual price change. If good y serves as the numeraire, a change in y is equivalent to a change in income; thus, the welfare effect can be measured equivalently by either a change in y or a change in income.

subjective distribution of quality becomes equal to the objective distribution. This resolves what some might consider a paradox whereby the consumer has a negative willingness to pay for information that reveals he is worse off than he thought.

A second consideration is that the consumer may not make a change simply from a state of no information to either perfect information or continued ignorance. When news of contamination breaks, it may be over- or understated initially. For example, contaminating industries or government agencies may (consciously or not) downplay the extent or significance of contamination, while news coverage may overstate its extent or significance. Suppose that initial information is correct and implies a distribution of quality characterized by θ_0, that information changes so that the consumer's subjective distribution of quality is reflected by θ_1, and that correct information would yield a distribution of quality represented by θ_1^*. Then the consumer is influenced to adjust only to the quality distribution with parameters θ_1; thus, he consumes the associated quantity of the contaminated good rather than what he would consume with correct information, i.e., x_1 is consumed voluntarily at (p_0, U_0, θ_1). The associated welfare effect compared to the initial state (assuming the consumer eventually obtains correct information with which to evaluate his well-being) is, thus,

$$\tilde{e}(p_0, U_0, \theta_1^*, x_1) - \tilde{e}(p_0, U_0, \theta_1, x_1) + e(p_0, U_0, \theta_1) - e(p_0, U_0, \theta_0)$$
$$= \tilde{e}(p_0, U_0, \theta_1^*, x_1) - e(p_0, U_0, \theta_0),$$

since $\tilde{e}(p_0, U_0, \theta_1, x_1) = e(p_0, U_0, \theta_1)$.

IV. MEASURING WELFARE CHANGES FROM MARKET DATA

Data regarding changes in perceived probabilities of quality levels are usually not available in cases where unexpected changes have occurred in consumers' environments. Available data are typically observations on consumer incomes and prices and quantities of goods exchanged. In addition, some variables may be available that reflect information by which consumers form their subjective probabilities. This section considers how changes in welfare can be evaluated using observed demand schedules before and after changes in the environment or in information. Marshallian surpluses can be calculated directly from econometrically estimated demand curves. Alternatively, duality can be used to derive exact estimates of compensating or equivalent variation by use of market demands (aside from statistical error).

First, following Hausmann [4], note that the Marshallian demand curve for a good satisfies Roy's identity. Maintaining utility at a constant level (remaining on an indifference curve), price and income must thus satisfy

$$\frac{\partial V[p(t), m(t), \theta]}{\partial p(t)} \cdot \frac{dp(t)}{dt} + \frac{\partial V[p(t), m(t), \theta]}{\partial m(t)} \cdot \frac{dm(t)}{dt} = 0.$$

Therefore, income can be expressed as a function of the changing price,

$$\frac{dm(p)}{dp} = x(p, m, \theta),$$

which is a differential equation and can be solved to obtain the expenditure function

$$m(p) = g(p, \theta, k) = e(p, U, \theta),$$

where k is a constant of integration that need not be known to calculate the differences in expenditure functions required for the welfare evaluation. Without loss of generality for welfare purposes, one can thus set $k = V(p, m, \theta)$; and the indirect expected utility function immediately follows from the estimated demand. Using the expenditure function derived from the observable Marshallian demand, an exact measure of compensating variation can be derived following (4). This method of deriving the expenditure function offers only a local solution but suffices, since only point estimates of the expenditure function are needed. The point estimate at θ_0 is sufficient to solve for compensating variation while the point estimate at θ_1 facilitates solution for the equivalent variation.

One of the major advantages of beginning with or retrieving a representation of the indirect expected utility function underlying the observed market demand schedule is the added ability to measure the costs associated with the absence of information relevant to consumer behavior. As discussed in the previous section, the compensating surplus can be evaluated using an expenditure function restricted such that consumption of the contaminated good is fixed. Such a restricted expenditure function cannot be derived directly from a Marshallian demand. Nevertheless, the value of the compensating surplus can be determined indirectly once the unrestricted expenditure function is recovered.

The procedure for obtaining the compensating surplus can be illustrated for the two-good case as follows. Suppose prices, income, and information are at initial levels and a change in the environment occurs represented by a shift in the subjective distribution parameters from θ_0 to θ_1. Then consider finding a price, p_1, such that the compensated demand at that price and with quality distribution parameters θ_1 is equal to the initial level of consumption, x_0; that is, $h(p_1, U_0, \theta_1) = x_0$. The compensating surplus can then be calculated following

$$\mathrm{CS} = [e(p_1, U_0, \theta_1) - p_1 x_0] - [e(p_0, U_0, \theta_0) - p_0 x_0]$$
$$= e(p_1, U_0, \theta_1) - m_0 + (p_0 - p_1) x_0$$

since the only difference in the subsequent situation with p_1 versus p_0 is the difference in expenditure required to purchase x_0. The cost of ignorance is thus

$$\mathrm{CI} = \mathrm{CS} - \mathrm{CV} = e(p_1, U_0, \theta_1) + (p_0 - p_1) x_0 - e(p_0, U_0, \theta_1).$$

The price difference, $p_0 - p_1$, can be regarded as a measure of the substitutability between goods x and y at the initial levels of utility and consumption but with new information. As p_1 approaches p_0, the cost of ignorance approaches zero.

V. AN APPLICATION TO THE HEPTACHLOR CONTAMINATION OF MILK IN HAWAII

Heptachlor is a highly toxic pesticide and carcinogen used by pineapple producers on the island of Oahu. Dairies use pineapple leaves and stems as a cheap substitute for cattle feed imported from the mainland. Prior to 1982, the residues of heptachlor thus consumed by dairy cattle were passed on to humans through the consumption of local dairy products. Essentially the entire population of Oahu (approximately 800,000) was exposed to heptachlor-contaminated milk since no fluid milk was imported. The Department of Health of the State of Hawaii has estimated that dairy products contained 15 times the official acceptable level of the pesticide for adults.

The public first became aware of the contamination problem on March 18, 1982, when the state's Health Department announced preparation to confront the rise in pesticide levels in milk. Throughout the next several months, the press followed the contamination crisis, offering consumers spectacular and troubling headlines and sometimes bewildering information on the safety of available milk supplies. Daily milk consumption dropped from 32,259 gallons in February to 5,405 gallons in April (Fig. 1).

By the beginning of May, however, the number of headlines in Honolulu's two major newspapers regarding the contamination of available supplies had declined from approximately 20 per week (immediately following the first disclosure) to approximately four per week. After May, 1982, little or no information was found in newspapers suggesting continued contamination of milk on store shelves. Indeed, the reports were encouraging and indicated that available milk was safe and that quality restrictions had been tightened [Honolulu Star-Bulletin, 5-20-82, p. A1; Honolulu Advertiser, 9-24-82, p. A1]. Consumers, however, remained wary throughout the balance of 1982 and consumption returned only slowly to normal levels (Fig. 1). By the end of August, 1982, the Honolulu Advertiser reported that 40% of the residents of Oahu were still uncertain about the quality of milk available.

One of the more disturbing aspects of this episode is the evident hesitance of state authorities to disclose information before the public became aware of the possibility of contamination. The state's Senate Committee on Health criticized the Department of Health for delaying the release of information to consumers [Honolulu Advertiser, 4-1-82, p. A1]. Substantial political acrimony arose over this issue after the initial public reports of contamination [Honolulu Advertiser, 7-24-82, p. A3; Honolulu Star-Bulletin, 7-29-82, p. A3, and 8-5-82, p. A1].

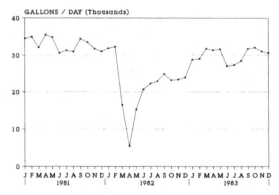

FIG. 1. Monthly consumption of fresh milk in Oahu, Hawaii. Source; State of Hawaii, Department of Agriculture, Division of Milk Control (1977–1983) [15].

To examine the consumer welfare effects of these developments, we estimate the Hawaii milk demand curve using monthly data on income, prices, and milk consumption in Hawaii. The estimated demand parameters are used in calculating compensating and equivalent variations for several months following the first disclosure of contamination. The Marshallian estimates of consumer surplus are also presented for comparison. Finally, the magnitude of monthly losses due to the withholding of information prior to March, 1982, are estimated. Although consumption in the months of March and April, 1982, was affected by Department of Health recalls, the statistics reported below assume that recalls are consistent with voluntary choices consumers would have made with the same information. Nevertheless, this assumption only affects loss estimates for these two months.

Specification of quality dependent demands for empirical purpose has presented a considerable problem in the literature. This literature, which has its roots in the quality models of Lancaster [8], Houthakker [5], and Theil [17], encounters problems in moving between demand and indirect utility specifications for purposes of consumer welfare calculations. Even taking q to be a non-stochastic measure of the quality of good x, very few specifications have been proposed that permit the plausible relations $\partial V/\partial q > 0$, $\partial V/\partial y > 0$, $\partial V/\partial p < 0$, $\partial X/\partial p < 0$, and $\partial X/\partial q > 0$ without further restricting the price or income elasticity (see Hanemann [3] for a review).[7]

The case of uncertain quality, where several parameters must be used to define the distribution of quality, presents further problems in function specification. One useful simplication is to assume the parameters, θ_t, of the distribution are weakly separable from prices, p_t, and income, m_t. That is, assume the indirect utility function is of the form

$$V(p_t, m_t, \theta_t) = \tilde{V}[p_t, m_t, f(\theta_t)],$$

where $f(\theta_t)$ is a single-valued function or index summarizing the influence of the subjective distribution of quality. One important consequence of this specification is that sets of parameters in θ_t associated with the same level of utility are associated with the same level of market demand. For example, a change in consumption brought about by a change in θ_t, *ceteris paribus*, necessarily implies a change in the underlying utility level.[8]

For the purpose of specifying an empirical demand function, theory implies that perceptions of declining expected quality or of increasing uncertainty have a decreasing effect on milk demand and consumer welfare. In terms of the index f, this is satisfied by $\partial V/\partial f > 0$, $\partial f/\partial \mu > 0$, and $\partial f/\partial \sigma < 0$. Moreover, no additional losses in expected utility occur with further declines in expected quality or increases in uncertainty if consumption is zero. That is, f and x satisfy weak

---

[7]For example, with indirect utility of the form $V(p, m, \theta) = f(\theta)g(p) + h(m)$, a log-linear specification of g implies demand must be price elastic while a log-linear specification of h implies demand cannot be income elastic. If $g(p) = 1 - \exp(-\alpha/p)$, then the law of demand is not satisfied for low prices.

[8]To reformulate in a more familiar manner, consider the subjective mean and variance of quality. Iso-utility curves in $\mu - \sigma^2$ space define indifference sets such that all pairs of mean and variance in a given set yield the same level of utility, *ceteris paribus*. Weak separability of the distribution parameters from price and income implies that, if two pairs of mean and variance are associated with the same utility level, then they assure the same level of demand. This assumption is restrictive but not implausible.

complementarity [9].[9] Also, common sense indicates that the compensated demand curve is affected by perceptions of quality in the same qualitative manner as the market demand. The popular semilog demand specification has these properties. Thus, let demand be represented by a function of the form

$$x_t = x(p_t, m_t, \theta_t) = f(\theta_t)e^{\gamma m_t - \alpha p_t}, \tag{5}$$

where $f(\theta_t) > 0$ is a function of the parameters of the subjective quality distribution and the t subscript is added to index observations.[10]

The indirect expected utility associated with this demand (aside from inconsequential multiplicative constants) is of the form

$$V(p_t, m_t, \theta_t) = \frac{1}{\alpha}f(\theta_t)e^{-\alpha p_t} + K - \frac{1}{\gamma}e^{-\gamma m_t} \tag{6}$$

for some constant K from which the expenditure function is

$$e(p_t, U_t, \theta_t) = -\frac{1}{\gamma}\ln\left\{\gamma\left[\frac{1}{\alpha}f(\theta_t)e^{-\alpha p_t} + K - U_t\right]\right\}. \tag{7}$$

Note that the effect of the index of quality parameters θ_t on expenditures decreases as p_t increases as long as $\alpha > 0$. Also, as the relative price ratio, p_t, approaches infinity (quantity approaches zero), the expenditure function approaches $-(1/\gamma)\ln \gamma(K - U_t)$, which is not dependent upon θ_t. Another advantage of this specification over many previous specifications is that the quality response is not tied directly to the price or income elasticity. For example, the indirect utility function $V[p - f(\theta), m]$ used by Willig [19] ties the quality elasticity proportionally to the price elasticity of demand while the translations $V[p, m + pf(\theta)]$ or $V[p, m + f(\theta)]$ popularized by Gorman [1] tie the quality elasticity to the income elasticity.

Finally, consider specification of $f(\theta_t)$ to account for changes in perceptions of uncertain quality that followed the initial announcements of heptachlor contamination and apparently persisted after milk was pronounced safe. Two major alternatives exist for specifying $f(\theta_t)$ to model changing information. The first involves treating $f(\theta_t)$ as a time varying parameter. In this case, one can simply include a dummy variable for each time period in which contamination information changes.

---

[9] Here we assume that Maler's [10] concept of weak complementarity holds, i.e., if $x = 0$ then $\partial U/\partial f = 0$, and that V is strongly separable in m and p. Using Hotelling's lemma, weak complementarity implies $\partial V/\partial f = 0$ if $\partial V/\partial p = 0$, which together with strong separability is sufficient to identify V up to multiplicative and additive constants. Thus, the compensating and equivalent variations are uniquely determined. While the weak complementarity assumption is plausible for the application of this paper, its plausibility should be considered in applying the methodology of this paper to other problems. For example, if a contaminant has a long half-life and affects wildlife survival or resource use by future generations, then imposing weak complementarity may lead to underestimating damages by foregone existence values.

[10] While the semilog specification is a restrictive functional form, most other common functional forms do not satisfy the theoretical properties outlined above. A few other forms that admitted plausible theoretical properties a priori were rejected due to implausible empirical estimates.

The second involves specifying $f(\theta_t)$ as a function of the moments of the subjective quality distribution and then specifying each moment as a function of actual data on contamination observed by the consumer. For example, if consumers' observations can be represented by a quantitative measurement such as a reported contamination level, then a subjective mean function might follow an adaptive expectation scheme with subjective variance following an adaptive variance specification. See Just [6] for a detailed specification used in a different decision making context.

In either case, however, information must be recognized as a multidimensional variable if new but conflicting information on contamination can lead to changes in uncertainty as well as a change in average quality perceptions. With the dummy variable approach, the dimensionality of θ_t is not limited since changes in information are estimated as changes in f, but errors in estimating other parameters of demand (and, thus, attributing remaining variation to changes in information) occur if information changes in too many observations of the sample (because of identification problems that occur with too many dummy variables). While the moment function approach does not suffer from these problems, the number of moments of the subjective quality distribution for which changes can be estimated is limited by data availability; data may not be sufficient to identify all the parameters of moment functions (which specify how moments depend on consumer-observed information variables) unless a sufficient number of observations reflect changes in these variables. Also, problems may be encountered in obtaining data on all sources of information that may be affecting consumer perceptions.

Because a relatively small proportion of the observations in the data set used here reflect changes in the subjective quality distribution, the dummy variable approach is selected. Specifically, following the semilog form used for other variables, $f(\theta_t)$ is of the form

$$f(\theta_t) = A \exp\left\{ \delta d_t + \sum_{\tau=0}^{T} a_\tau D_{t\tau} + b(1 + t)^{-c} D_t^* \right\},$$

where $d_t = 1$ if school is in session and $d_t = 0$ otherwise; $D_{t\tau} = 1$ if the observation represents month τ where the quality distribution changes, and $D_{t\tau} = 0$ otherwise; $D_t^* = 1$ if the observation represents any month following disclosure (any month following April 1982) and $D_t^* = 0$ otherwise; and A, γ, δ, a_t, b, and c are unknown parameters. That is, t indexes months in 1982 with $t = 0$ in May, $t = 1$ in June, etc. News of contamination was released essentially only in March and April, 1982. Newspaper reports indicated that milk supplies on store shelves were safe after April, 1982; and no other evidence suggests that milk was actually unhealthy after that time. Presumably, a large decrease in consumption occurred initially due to the changes in expected quality while the uncertainty supposedly declined over time once news releases indicated safe heptachlor levels in milk. The latter term in brackets is included to represent this decline since $b(1 + t)^{-c} \to 0$ as $t \to \infty$ if $c > 0$.

The data used to estimate the parameters of milk demand are per capita monthly consumption of fluid milk in half gallons; monthly price indices for milk and fruit nectar products in the Honolulu area (dollars per half gallon; fruit nectar represents other goods with which milk competes); and per capita income for Hawaii (dollars per month).[11] Since dairy production is essentially predetermined on a monthly basis by numbers of cows and breeding cycles, estimation of demand by nonlinear least squares does not suffer the otherwise familiar problem of simultaneous equations bias. The estimated coefficients of demand, using monthly data from January, 1978, to July, 1983, are as follows (t statistics are in parentheses):

$$\ln x_t = \quad .871 + .000565m_t - .325p_t + .106d_t - \quad .762 \text{ March}$$
$$\quad (12.59) \quad (2.14) \quad\quad (-2.44) \quad (8.28) \quad (-15.84)$$
$$\quad - 1.84 \text{ April} - .779D_t^*(1+t)^{-.573} \quad R^2 = .97.$$
$$\quad (-37.82) \quad (-17.19) \quad\quad\quad (-12.08)$$

Here the names of the specific months are used to represent the D_{tr} dummy variables, p_t is the price of milk relative to fruit nectar, and m_t is income relative to the price of fruit nectar following the earlier theoretical specification.

The results of the regression are intuitively plausible. The price elasticity of milk is approximately -0.41. The income elasticity is approximately 0.37. Both of these elasticities are reasonably consistent with other studies of milk demand. The long-run coefficients on the contamination months are negative, as are the coefficients on the uncertainty function, which is consistent with theoretical considerations.

Using (5), (6), and (7), the compensating variation for a change from θ_0 to θ_1 can be represented as

$$CV = e(p_0, U_0, \theta_1) - e(p_0, U_0, \theta_0)$$
$$= -m_0 - \frac{1}{\gamma}\ln\left\{\gamma\left[\frac{1}{\alpha}f(\theta_1)e^{-\alpha p_0} - \frac{1}{\alpha}f(\theta_0)e^{-\alpha p_0} + \frac{1}{\gamma}e^{-\gamma m_0}\right]\right\}$$
$$= \frac{1}{\gamma}\ln\left[\frac{\gamma}{\alpha}(x_1 - x_0) + 1\right],$$

where

$$x_t = f(\theta_t)e^{\gamma m_0 - \alpha p_0}, \quad t = 0, 1,$$

and

$$U_0 = \frac{1}{\alpha}f(\theta_0)e^{-\alpha p_0} + K - \frac{1}{\gamma}e^{-\gamma m_0}.$$

[11] The data are from the Hawaii department of Agriculture [15] for milk consumption, from the Hawaii Department of Agriculture and the *Honolulu Advertiser* for milk price, from the U.S. Department of Commerce, *CPI Detailed Report*, for fruit nectar price, and from the U.S. Department of commerce, *Survey of Current Business*, and Hawaii Department of Planning and Economic Development, *State of Hawaii Data Book 1983*, for income. Aside from scaling, the data are the same as used previously by Smith, van Ravenswaay, and Thompson [14], who argue convincingly that fruit nectar is by far the most important substitute for milk in the Hawaiian tropical climate. Mean monthly per-capita milk consumption over the period January, 1978, to July, 1983, was 0.87 half-gallon units at a mean price of $0.62 (1967 dollars). Monthly per-capita income averaged $660.35, and fruit nectar averaged $0.56 per half-gallon (again in 1967 dollars).

TABLE I
Per Capita Consumer Welfare Losses, March, 1982–September, 1982

Month	Compensating Variation	Equivalent Variation	Marshallian Consumer Surplus Change
		Dollars per month	
March	5.9421	5.9277	5.9350
April	9.3356	9.2992	9.3174
May	5.6514	5.7686	5.7755
June	3.2479	3.2420	3.2449
July	3.6016	3.5965	3.5992
August	3.2018	3.1978	3.1999
September	2.9223	2.9188	2.9204

Note: Source: computed.

For comparison, the change in the Marshallian consumer surplus is given by

$$\Delta S = \int_{p_0}^{\infty} f(\theta_0) e^{\gamma m_0 - \alpha p} \, dp - \int_{p_0}^{\infty} f(\theta_1) e^{\gamma m_0 - \alpha p} \, dp$$

$$= \frac{1}{\alpha}(x_0 - x_1).$$

These two measures of consumer welfare loss along with the equivalent variation (the additive inverse of the compensating variation of reverting back to original safety perceptions) are computed for March, 1982, through September, 1982, based on the estimated equation above (see Table I). The estimates compare the actual contamination that occurred assuming correct consumer subjective assessments of quality with the hypothetical possibility of no contamination (and no news of contamination) for each month.

The estimates are striking in several ways. First, the magnitude of loss is very high —higher than the value of milk normally consumed in April, 1982 (milk prices in Hawaii were typically nearly twice as high as mainland prices). This is possible and plausible, however, since Hicksian demands are more inelastic than Marshallian demands, since the Marshallian demands are highly inelastic, and since consumption fell by such a large amount. Thus, the change in area under the Hicksian demand and above price can be larger than the area below price and left of the initial quantity. A second striking result, which is to be expected, is the very sharp increase in consumer losses initially and then the rather rapid and, finally, more prolonged decline in losses (Table I).

While the above results give some important information regarding the magnitude of consumer losses after information of contamination became available, one of the greatest and most controllable losses may have occurred prior to public awareness. For example, some reports indicate that public officials may have been aware of the contamination problem as early as April, 1981—11 months before the public was informed. Individuals who consumed milk from April, 1981, to March, 1982, still face essentially the same risks from heptachlor consumption as if they had been forced to consume normal amounts of milk with knowledge of heptachlor contamination. Thus, the associated welfare loss from contamination can be measured by the compensating surplus, and the welfare loss associated with withholding the information can be measured by the cost of ignorance measure defined above.

To illustrate these concepts, suppose that appropriate information in, say, February, 1982 (the month before the news release), would have led to the same subjective distribution of quality that existed in April, 1982 (the month after the release). To do this, let θ_0 represent perceptions based on actual information in February (dummy variables in the estimated equation are all zero) and let θ_1 represent the subjective distribution under the hypothetical true information in February as reflected by the actual information in April (dummy variables at April levels). Following the methodology above, a hypothetical price p_1 can be found such that

$$\frac{\partial e(p_1, U_0, \theta_1)}{\partial p_1} = \frac{f(\theta_1)e^{-\alpha p_1}}{\gamma\left[\frac{1}{\alpha}f(\theta_1)e^{-\alpha p_1} + K - U_0\right]} = x_0.$$

While this equation must be solved by numerical methods for many demand specifications, it can be solved explicitly in this case by using (5) and (6) to obtain

$$p_1 = p_0 + \frac{1}{\alpha}\left[\ln f(\theta_1) - \ln f(\theta_0)\right].$$

Then the compensating surplus (which compares to releasing correct information with no chance to adjust to information of contamination) is

$$CS = e(p_1, U_0, \theta_1) - m_0 + (p_0 - p_1)x_0$$
$$= \frac{x_0}{\alpha}\left[\ln f(\theta_0) - \ln f(\theta_1)\right].$$

This yields a compensating surplus of $18.21 per person per month. This large effect is consistent with the estimated hypothetical price of $-$2.28 per half gallon which indicates that, to induce consumers to continue normal consumption given contamination, consumers would have to *be paid* more than they normally pay to consume milk.

As one would expect, this implies a larger welfare loss per month prior to release of information than after consumers are free to adjust and avoid some of the contaminated milk. The welfare loss (compensating variation) in April, for example, when consumers could make more informed decisions, was $9.33 per person per month by comparison and, according to the estimated model, would have been $8.33 in February if consumers could have responded to true information. Thus, the cost of ignorance was $9.88 per person per month for each month public officials withheld information.

VI. CONCLUSIONS

This paper has developed an approach for measurement of consumer welfare losses associated with health risks from chemical contamination. The importance of the approach is its ability to identify the cost to consumers of misinformed perceptions and uncertainty that affect consumption decisions but are ultimately of interest in the political climate surrounding a contamination crisis. Estimated actual cost criteria used elsewhere (value of life lost, productivity foregone, or cost of treatment) ignore the effects of inherent risk and uncertainty that enter into consumer evaluations of well-being whether or not actual costs are incurred [18]. The sizeable effects of consumer uncertainty are illustrated by the rapid decline in welfare effects in Table I that continued for some time after milk supplies were pronounced safe. These effects are captured through direct estimation of willingness-to-pay criteria from revealed preferences (actual demand data) for cases where sufficiently varied consumer circumstances can be observed [2]. Moreover, this paper demonstrates how these problems can be accommodated in estimating consumer losses from unannounced contamination using data both before and after release of information.

Returning to the four stage characterization of Section I, the welfare costs of contamination in the first stage must be evaluated by compensating surplus. At the time of policy relevance in the third stage, the consumer's first-stage consumption choices must be reevaluated because the goods he consumed were not what he thought he was consuming; this evaluation must explicitly recognize that he cannot now alter those consumption choices. On the other hand, the welfare cost of contamination in the third stage must be evaluated by compensating variation because the consumer is free to adjust his third-stage consumption choices to correct information. Thus, fourth-stage costs are reflected subjectively in third-stage consumption choices. While the first-stage compensating surplus cannot be calculated directly from estimated market demand, it is calculated indirectly by solving a related differential equation to find the expenditure function and finding a hypothetical equivalent price.

Adding these welfare effects over the entire period of a contamination problem (with appropriate discounting) gives the overall consumer welfare effect of contamination (i.e., what the consumer would be willing to pay as of the third stage to relive life without a contamination problem). This overall welfare effect is useful for addressing questions of what compensation is appropriate for a consumer, or how much should be spent by government to avoid contamination.

Other important questions relate to timing of information release; for example, what is the cost of withholding information of a contamination problem? This question, which is answered by the cost of ignorance computed here, may be appropriate for determining fines for companies that withhold information about contamination or for deciding how much should be spent by government to ensure rapid information dissemination. Results here show that consumer losses from contamination when information is withheld can be greater than after information is released. In particular, estimates for the Hawaiian heptachlor crisis show that consumer losses prior to consumer awareness in March, 1982, may have exceeded the losses incurred since, and that about half of the losses incurred before consumer awareness may be due to withholding of information by public officials.

For the empirical study of this paper, the second stage of the contamination problem (dissemination of information on contamination) was assumed to occur instantaneously since almost all of the available information surfaced within a single time period. Alternatively, the approach of this paper can be extended to evaluation of welfare effects over an extended second stage in which initial information is incorrect and choices are made in partial ignorance as information is gradually corrected. Suppose available initial information is translated by the consumer into quality distribution moments θ_0, correct initial information yields moments θ_0^*, available subsequent information yields θ_1, and correct subsequent information θ_1^*. Then the measure of welfare change must take account of errors in the initial allocation of income as well as the subsequent allocation of income. The appropriate measure of welfare compared to the initial situation is then

$$\tilde{e}(p_0, U_0, \theta_1^*, x_1) - \tilde{e}(p_0, U_0, \theta_0^*, x_0).$$

With this generalization, one can address questions of whether news of contamination should be released earlier with less accuracy (and, thus, more consumer uncertainty) or should be held until more information is accumulated and can be regarded as more accurate. This question presents an interesting trade off between the welfare effects of consumer uncertainty (including foregone consumption during a consumer scare) and the cost of continued consumption in ignorance. With this generalization and application of the moment-based specification of demand, the methodology of this paper can be applied not only to short-run food contamination problems but also to continuing contamination problems of various air and water resources that affect the quality of consumer goods such as housing, recreation, and fisheries products.

REFERENCES

1. W. M. Gorman, Tricks with utility functions, *in* "Essays in Economic Analysis" (M. Artis and R. Nobay, Eds.), Cambridge Univ. Press, Cambridge (1976).
2. D. A. Graham, Estimating the 'state dependent' utility function, *Natural Res. J.* **23**, 649–656 (1983).
3. W. M. Hanemann, Quality and demand analysis, *in* "New Directions in Econometric Modeling and Forecasting in U.S. Agriculture" (G. C. Rausser, Ed.), Elsevier/North-Holland, New York (1982).
4. J. A. Hausmann, Exact consumer's surplus and deadweight loss, *Amer. Econom. Rev.* **71**, 662–676 (1981).
5. H. Houthakker, Compensated changes in quantities and qualities consumed, *Rev. Econom. Stud.* **19**, 155–164 (1951–52).
6. R. E. Just, Estimation of an adaptive expectations model, *Int. Econom. Rev.* **18**, 3, 629–644.
7. R. E. Just, D. L. Hueth, and A. Schmitz, "Applied Welfare Economics and Public Policy," Prentice-Hall, Englewood Cliffs, NJ (1982).
8. K. Lancaster, A new approach to consumer theory, *J. Polit. Econom.* **74**, 132–157 (1966).
9. J. Linnerooth, The value of human life: A review of the models, *Econom. Inquiry* **17**, 52–74 (1979).
10. K. G. Maler, "Environmental Economics: A Theoretical Inquiry," Johns Hopkins Press for Resources for the Future, Baltimore, MD (1974).
11. J. W. Mjelde, R. M. Adams, B. L. Dixon, and P. Garcia, Using farmers' actions to measure crop loss due to air pollution, *J. Air Pollut. Control Assoc.* **31**, 360–364 (1984).
12. A. Sandmo, Competitive firm under price uncertainty, *Amer. Econom. Rev.* **56**, 65–73 (1971).
13. Shulstad and H. Stoevener, The effects of mercury contamination in pheasants on the value of pheasant hunting in Oregon, *Land Econom.* **54**, 39–49 (1978).
14. M. E. Smith, E. O. van Ravenswaay, and S. R. Thompson, The economic consequences of food contamination: A case study of heptachlor contamination of Oahu milk, Agricultural Economics Report No. 449, Michigan State University, June 1984.
15. State of Hawaii, Department of Agriculture, Division of Milk Control, "Statistical Reports," January 1977–July 1983.
16. D. G. Swartz and I. E. Strand, Avoidance costs associated with imperfect information: The case of kepone." *Land Econom.* **57**, 139–150 91981).
17. H. Theil, Qualities, prices and budget enquiries, *Rev. Econom. Stud.* **19**, 129–147 (1951–52).
18. M. O. Weinstein and R. J. Quinn, Psychological considerations in valuing health risk reductions, *Natural. Res. J.* **23**, 659–673 (1983).
19. R. D. Willig, Incremental consumer's surplus and hedonic price adjustment, *J. Econom. Theory* **17**, 227–253 (1978).

[35]

A SIMPLE THEORY OF ADVERTISING AS A GOOD OR BAD*

GARY S. BECKER AND KEVIN M. MURPHY

Our analysis treats advertisements and the goods advertised as complements in stable metautility functions, and generates new results for advertising by building on and extending the general analysis of complements. By assimilating the theory of advertising into the theory of complements, we avoid the special approaches to advertising found in many studies that place obstacles in the way of understanding the effects of advertising. We also use this approach to evaluate advertising from a welfare perspective. Whether there is excessive or too little advertising depends on several variables: the effects on consumer utility, the degree of competition in the market for advertised goods, the induced changes in prices and outputs of advertised goods, and whether advertising is sold to consumers.

I. INTRODUCTION AND SUMMARY

Most economists and other intellectuals have not liked advertisements that provide little information. Noninformative advertising is claimed to create wants and to change and distort tastes. Although we agree that many ads create wants without producing information, we do not agree that they change tastes. Our approach may at first blush appear strange: we include advertisements as one of the goods that enter the fixed preferences of consumers.

The usual definition of a "good" is something consumers are willing to pay for, and a "bad" is something consumers pay to have removed or must be compensated to accept. Both goods and bads are part of given utility functions. For example, horror movies are "goods" for the many people who pay to be frightened out of their wits, and garbage is a "bad" because people are willing to pay to have it removed.

These straightforward definitions of goods and bads suggest that noninformative advertisements are "goods" in utility functions if people are willing to pay for them—they need not actually pay in equilibrium—and such advertisements are "bads" if people must be paid to accept them. If advertisements are considered

*We benefited from useful comments by William Comanor, David Friedman, Paul Milgrom, Richard Posner, Sherwin Rosen, Andrei Shleifer, George Stigler, and two excellent referees, from the discussion at an Economic and Legal Organization Workshop of the University of Chicago, and from research assistance by David Meltzer and M. Rebecca Kilburn. Our research has been supported by the Lynde and Harry Bradley Foundation through the Center for the Study of the Economy and the State.

utility and "taste shifters" rather than goods, why aren't horror movies, cars, opera, and many other things that consumers buy?

To be sure, consumers may respond to the social and psychological pressures generated by advertisements. But they also respond to such pressures when considering dinners at prestige restaurants, ownership of Mercedes cars, and many other goods.

Advertisements "give favorable notice" to other goods, such as Pepsi-Cola or cornflakes, and raise the demand for these goods. In consumer theory, goods that favorably affect the demand for other goods are usually treated as complements to those other goods, not as shifters of utility functions. There is no reason to claim that advertisements change tastes just because they affect the demand for other goods.

Our analysis treats advertisements and the goods advertised as complements in stable metautility functions, and generates new results for advertising by building on and extending the general analysis of complements. By assimilating the theory of advertising into the theory of complements, we avoid the special approaches to advertising found in many studies that place obstacles in the way of understanding the effects of advertising. By removing these obstacles, a clearer picture of these effects emerges.

Clearly, very few advertisements are sold separately and directly to consumers. Ads may be given away, as those in direct mail and billboard advertisements, or they may be sold jointly with programs, newspaper articles, comics, sports pages, etc. The special properties of advertising markets are responsible for important differences between the positive and normative analysis of advertisements and that of many other complements.

Section II sets out the basic model that treats advertisements with the theory of the demand and supply of goods (or bads) that are complements to consumers. We emphasize two cases: either advertisements are given away free and rationed to consumers; or they are sold to consumers, possibly jointly with other ads and goods, and possibly at subsidized, even negative, prices. This section contrasts our approach with the traditional one that treats advertisements as shifting tastes. Ours has the major advantage that it readily incorporates the demand for advertising into the theory of rational consumer choice, and has the usual implications of utility theory concerning symmetry conditions and negatively inclined demand functions.

Section III discusses the relation between advertising and industrial structure. The well-known theorem [Dorfman and

Steiner, 1954] that the incentive to advertise rises as the elasticity of demand for the advertised good falls is shown to be highly misleading, for the incentive to advertise may rise, not fall, as a market becomes more competitive. The reason is that the effect of advertising on the price of the good advertised may rise as the elasticity of demand for this good increased. Section III also demonstrates that advertising tends to raise elasticities of demand for goods advertised by lifting the demands of marginal consumers.

Section IV uses our approach to evaluate advertising from a welfare perspective. Whether there is excessive or too little advertising depends on several variables: the effects on consumer utility, the degree of competition in the market for advertised goods, the induced changes in prices and outputs of advertised goods, and whether advertising is sold to consumers. We show that treating advertising as shifting tastes prejudices a welfare analysis toward the conclusion that advertising is excessive. We avoid that prejudice without implying that firms supply the socially optimal amount.

Section V considers the properties of radio and television, and shows that advertisements attracted to these media tend to lower the utility of viewers. This may also be true of some advertisements that use other media. Advertisers provide utility-raising programs to compensate viewers for exposing themselves to the ads. Even when the programs compensate viewers fully, we reach the strange-sounding conclusion that advertisers would profit from utility-reducing ads that sufficiently raise marginal demands for the goods advertised.

Many implications of a model of advertisements as goods in stable utility functions are similar to the implications of models where advertising provides information or lies about the goods advertised (see, e.g., Grossman and Shapiro [1984]). But there are differences: for example, the information approach to advertising has trouble explaining advertisements that lower consumer utility (see Section V).

Moreover, it is also "obvious" that many ads provide essentially no information. Rather, they entertain, create favorable associations between sexual allure and the products advertised, instill discomfort in people not consuming products popular with athletes, beauties, and other elites, and in other ways induce people to want the products. Table I gives the U. S. companies with the ten largest ratios of advertising expenditures to sales in the first quarter of 1988. Chewing gum, cereal, beer, or cola ads, to take a

TABLE I

TEN COMPANIES WITH LARGEST ADVERTISING TO SALES RATIOS AMONG MAJOR
NATIONAL ADVERTISERS

	Advertising sales	Primary business
1. Noxell Corporation	0.18	Toiletries
2. William Wrigley, Jr. Co.	0.17	Food
3. Kellogg Company	0.13	Food
4. Warner-Lambert Company	0.10	Pharmaceuticals
5. Alberto-Culver Company	0.10	Toiletries
6. Adolph Coors Company	0.10	Beer
7. Hasbro, Inc.	0.09	Toys
8. Schering-Plough Corp.	0.09	Pharmaceuticals
9. Coca-Cola Company	0.07	Soft drinks
10. Proctor and Gamble Co.	0.07	Soaps and cleaners

Source. Advertising Age, August 22, 1988
Advertising/sales is for first quarter, 1988.
From set of "100 leading national advertisers."

few of the ads produced by companies on the list, surely usually convey very little information.

Some recent literature agrees that much advertising provides little *direct* information about the goods advertised, but they are said to provide information to consumers *indirectly* by signaling the quality of the goods advertised (Nelson's [1974] study pioneered this approach; also see Kihlstrom and Riordan [1984] and Horstmann and MacDonald [1987]). We do not believe that the intensive advertising for Miller beer, Chevrolet cars, or Marlboro cigarettes, to take a few examples,[15] is signaling exceptionally high product quality. But we shall not try to compare systematically the implications of our model of advertising as a good with a signaling model, beyond pointing out that in the signaling approach, demand can be affected by advertising even when consumers are not exposed to the content of the ads, whereas in our approach demand can be affected only through exposure. Moreover, the pure signaling interpretation implies that companies should advertise how much they spend on advertising, yet almost no companies do that.

Our study builds on important work by others. Dixit and Norman [1978] provide the best formulation of the taste-shifting approach. Telser [1962, 1964] gives a pioneering analysis that includes advertisements as part of given consumer preferences; also see the comment on Dixit and Norman by Fisher and McGowan [1979]. The discussion of advertising in Ehrlich and

Fisher [1982] stresses the importance of advertising in economizing on time. Kaldor [1949–50] has a good early analysis of advertising that discusses both positive and normative economic issues. Comanor and Wilson [1974, Chapter 2] and Barnett [1966] briefly mention that advertisements on radio and television may be "bads." Stigler and Becker [1977] show why perfectly competitive firms may advertise. Analytically, our discussion of the complementarity between advertising and goods advertised is closely related in several respects to Spence's [1976] important analysis of product quality; also see Tirole [1988] and Shapiro [1982].

Although some of our discussion can be found in this earlier literature, apparently no one has worked out the many positive and normative implications of treating advertisements as part of the stable preference structure of consumers. This is the goal of our paper.

II. A MODEL OF ADVERTISING

a. Modeling Considerations

Consider a single-period utility function that depends on goods x and y, and A, advertisements for x:

$$(1) \qquad\qquad U = U(x,y,A).$$

By definition, advertising gives "favorable notice" to the good advertised, so that an increase in A raises the relative marginal utility of x. We assume that regardless of market structure, consumers can buy all they want of x and y at fixed prices. But this may not be an appropriate assumption for advertisements. Indeed, most discussions of advertising in the economics literature simply assume without much justification that advertisements are given away rather than sold to consumers. They produce revenue indirectly by raising the demand for the good advertised. Therefore, only producers of that good would be willing to pay for the advertisements since they are the only ones who benefit. Producers who give away advertisements want to limit quantities to consumers since they balance the indirect revenue in the market for the good advertised with the cost of supplying additional ads.

Consequently, the dominant model of advertising assumes both that advertisements are given away to consumers, and that quantities are controlled by producers of the goods advertised. This view is so imbedded in thinking about advertising that activities which violate either of these conditions are simply not considered "advertisements," even when they obviously give "favorable notice" about other goods and services. For example, sports columns in newspapers provide plenty of notice about local professional teams, even though sports sections are not free to readers, and team owners do not pay for the columns. The strike of Pittsburgh's two newspapers in mid-May 1992 was said to have reduced sales to games of the Pittsburgh Pirates baseball team by 3000 to 4000 tickets a game [Klein, 1992].

In this example, sport analysis and description are produced jointly with advertising for teams. In other cases, firms help advertise certain goods because of complementarities between the goods advertised and the goods supplied by these firms. But whatever the reason, there are many examples of advertising that violate one or the other of the two standard assumptions of advertising models.

The assumption that producers choose the quantity of advertising to consumers is intrinsically tied to the approach that assumes advertising shifts tastes. For such an approach has no way of determining how consumers make their choices about advertising. It resolves what otherwise would be a serious dilemma by assuming that producers determine the quantity of advertising available to consumers at a zero price. By contrast, when advertising is part of stable metapreferences, consumer demand for advertising is a straightforward implication of utility maximization (see equation (6)), and it is no longer necessary to assume that advertising is free and that producers control its quantity.

The usual model with a zero price of advertising and quantities controlled by advertisers does apply to direct mail advertisements, although consumers can discard these mailings without looking at what is inside. But it is doubtful how well it explains newspaper ads or those on radio and television.

For example, the quantity of newspaper ads available to consumers is not rationed, and these ads are not necessarily free to readers. The implicit price for these ads is measured by the difference between the actual cost of newspapers to consumers and what it would be if papers did not have the ads.

The implicit price of advertisements in newspapers or on broadcast media may be negative, even if advertisements are part of consumers' stable utility functions. Advertisers could not charge a positive price for ads that yield zero or negative marginal utility, and consumers are usually indirectly paid to listen to radio ads and to watch those on television (see Section V).

Of course, the price charged for advertisements would be much more transparent if they were sold separately, the way oranges and fish are. But technological constraints and transactions costs often make it too expensive to sell ads separately. Prior to pay television, ads on radio or television could not be sold directly since there was no way to charge the audience for what they heard or watched. Ads in print could technically be sold on small pieces of paper, but transaction costs are greatly reduced by selling printed ads together in newspapers, along with information and entertainment.

A special problem arises when consumers are paid to take ads. It might not be profitable to allow them to take all they want at a fixed (negative) price per unit. For they might "buy" a large number and ignore as many as possible, as when remote controls are used to switch off ads on television. The difficulties of monitoring these consumers have led advertisers to control the supply as well as the prices of ads with negative prices.

Therefore, transactions costs and technological constraints in some, but far from all, cases support the usual assumption that advertisers rather than consumers determine the amount of advertising. Our discussion in this and the next section treats two polar situations: either advertisements are given away and the quantity is controlled by producers, or they are sold at a fixed (implicit) price per unit to consumers who can buy all they want. Section V considers the case where consumers must be paid to accept certain advertisements.

The production of advertisements is generally a very competitive industry, where advertisers hire agencies to prepare copy for them. Competition implies that the marginal cost to advertisers of a unit of advertising would equal the marginal cost of preparing it (c_a).

We start the systematic discussion with the conventional case, where advertisements are given away, with the quantity controlled by producers. A firm that determines x and A to maximize net profits $p_x(A)x - c_x x - c_a A = p_x x(A) - c_x x(A) - c_a A$ must satisfy

$$(2) \qquad\qquad p_x(1 - 1/\epsilon_x) = c_x,$$

and

$$(3) \qquad \frac{\partial p_x}{\partial A} x = \frac{\partial x}{\partial A}(p_x - c_x) = c_a,$$

where c_x is the unit cost of x, ϵ_x is the elasticity of demand for x,

$\partial p_x/\partial A$ holds x constant as p_x changes, and $\partial x/\partial A$ holds p_x as x changes. Equation (3) assumes that consumers are willing to accept the quantity of A given away by producers because the marginal utility of A is not negative (see equation (6)).

The first condition is the usual one when firms produce a single product (x). Since A is given away, the choice of x does not depend on the price of A, but, of course, it does depend on the quantity of A. The second condition shows that the entire value of A that is given away comes from its effect on the price and quantity of x. Although A's market price is zero, it has a shadow price to each consumer that equals the money value of the marginal utility of an additional advertisement (see equation (6)).

If instead of giving advertisements away, firms allow consumers to buy all they want at a fixed price p_a, the first-order conditions for x and A become

(4)
$$p_x \left(1 - \frac{1}{\epsilon_x}\right) + \frac{\partial p_a}{\partial x} A = c_x$$

(5)
$$p_a \left(1 - \frac{1}{\epsilon_a}\right) + \frac{\partial p_x}{\partial A} x = c_a,$$

where $\partial p_a/\partial x$ holds A constant, $\partial p_x/\partial A$ holds x constant, and ϵ_a is the elasticity of demand for A. See the relation between $\partial p_x/\partial A x$ and $\partial x/\partial A$ $(p_x - c_x)$ in equation (3). If A raises the demand for x, the marginal revenue from an increase in A is partly due to an induced increase in p_x at a given x. Equation (5) shows that if $\partial p_x/\partial A$ is large, then the optimal value of A could be sufficiently large to lower p_a below c_a. Advertising would be sold below cost, even when it could be sold at a profit, if its complementary with the good advertised is sufficiently strong. The complementary is obvious with beer advertising on television during football games since many people drink beer as they watch a televised game.

A utility-maximizing consumer satisfies the following inequality both when advertising is sold and when it is not:

(6)
$$U_A \geq p_a,$$

where U_A is the marginal utility of advertising. If advertising is rationed, then $>$ holds; if it is also given away, $p_a = 0$, and $U_A > 0$. If consumers can buy all the ads they would at fixed prices, then equality holds.

When A is sold at a fixed price, nothing formally distinguishes advertising from an analysis of multiproduct firms, where the products are complements in consumption. For example, x and A

could also refer to cars and repair services or personal computers and software.

Since in our formulation advertising enters the consumer's utility function along with other goods, rational choice implies that advertising satisfies the symmetry conditions and other implications of utility theory. Therefore, this analysis implies that if advertisements are complements to goods advertised, those goods are complements to the advertisements. That is, greater consumption of advertised goods would raise the marginal utility from, and the demand for, advertising. This is a crucial implication of our approach, although some readers may be dubious about its validity.

We know of little evidence on this implication, but a study by several psychologists did find that people who have recently purchased a new car were more likely to read ads for the same type of car than for other types (see Ehrlich, Guttman, Schönbach, and Mills [1957]). The authors interpret these findings as evidence of cognitive dissonance, but our treatment of advertisements as complements to the goods advertised can explain them, perhaps including the finding that people who owned their cars for a while did not show more interest in ads for their type.

The positive implications of our approach differ in substance and not only in language from a more traditional approach that treats advertising as shifting tastes. Firm behavior is the same, once firms know the demand for advertising and how advertising affects demand for the goods advertised. But since the taste-shifting approach has no theory of consumer choice, it does not imply the various implications of consumer theory, and cannot explain how consumers choose among different ads that require time, money, or other scarce resources. In particular, this approach lacks the equivalent of equation (6), which is a first-order condition for consumers that determines their demand for advertising. It does not seem possible even conceptually for the taste-shifting approach to incorporate advertising into the theory of rational consumer choices.

By contrast, when advertisements are treated as part of given metatastes, consumer demand for advertising is subject to the same rules of behavior as their demand for other goods. These rules include consistent choices over time, symmetry between cross price effects, results about the effects of rationing on the demand for substitutes and complements, and so forth. Section IV makes clear that because the theories about behavior are so different, the welfare implications of the taste-shifting and stable tastes approaches to advertising are also very different.

b. Advertising and Consumer Surplus

A firm that rations the ads it gives away (so $p_a = 0$ and $\geq$ holds in equation (6)) can collect the marginal value of A to consumers only through the effect of the ads on the demand for x. Therefore, if the firm also charges for advertising, it might collect *more* than the value of A to consumers because the direct revenue from selling A ($p_a A$) is added to the indirect revenue in the market for x. Indeed, if the firm is setting market prices that clear the market for both x and A, it can collect twice for a small increase in A: once directly in the market for A and once in the market for x.

The source of the paradox is the effects of advertising on the ability of firms to extract consumer surplus in the market for the advertised goods. If greater advertising raises the demand for x by a constant amount, the entire increase in consumer surplus from the higher A accrues to the firm through the higher price for x, assuming that the quantity of x is held fixed (see Figure I). Additional revenue from the direct sale of A takes away some of the initial surplus. This conclusion about consumer surplus is not unique to advertising and applies to any complements produced by a firm (such as computers and their software) as long as increased quantities of one of them raises by a constant amount the negatively sloped downward curve for the other.

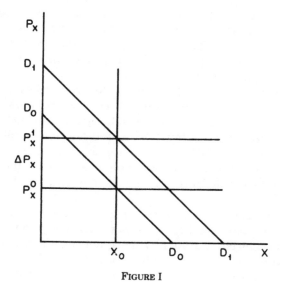

FIGURE I

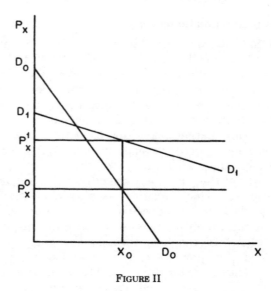

FIGURE II

If the effect of higher A on the marginal utility of x is not constant but is larger when x is bigger (compare D_1 and D_0 in Figure II), the greater revenue in the x market from an increase in A exceeds the increase in consumer surplus. Direct revenue from the sale of A only adds to the surplus extracted from consumers. This case shows that what counts to producers is the effect of advertising on the utility from *marginal* units of x. The effect on marginal units determines the effect on profits through its effect on the price and quantity of x.

Therefore, a firm that is unable to price discriminate in a market where it has monopoly power may be able to use a complementary product to extract additional consumer surplus. Even if the complement must be sold below its average cost of production—perhaps because its marginal value to consumers is less than the average cost—the complement may increase the firm's profits by sufficiently raising the demand for the monopolized good.

Since the analysis of advertising has much in common with an analysis of product quality, it is not surprising that the same emphasis on marginal units and marginal consumers is found in the literature on product quality (see Spence [1976], Shapiro [1982], and Tirole [1988]) and retail price maintenance (see Klein and Murphy [1988] and Comanor [1985]). For example, the presale services sometimes encouraged by price maintenance may well be valued most by marginal consumers because they know less about the product.

III. Advertising, Competition, and the Elasticity of Demand

a. Advertising and Competition

Seventy-three years ago, Pigou [1920] already argued that competitive firms do not advertise because they can more or less sell all they want at a given price even without advertising. This conclusion is repeated often (see, e.g., Kaldor [1949–50], or Scherer [1980, p. 387]).

That firms with elastic demand curves do not want to provide free advertising appears to be supported by the first-order profit-maximizing conditions in equations (2) and (3). The middle term in equation (3) seems to indicate that marginal revenue from advertising is low for competitive producers of x since $p_x - c_x$ is close to zero for these producers. If equation (2) is substituted into this middle term, one gets an expression that relates the marginal revenue from advertising directly to the elasticity of demand for x:

$$(7) \qquad MR_A = \frac{p_x}{\epsilon_x} \frac{dx}{dA}.$$

Therefore, *if the price of the product (p_x) and the increase in demand due to advertising (dx/dA) are held fixed,* the marginal revenue from advertising declines as the elasticity of demand for x (ϵ_x) increases. This is the famous theorem of Dorfman and Steiner [1954] that less competitive firms have more incentive to advertise.

Despite the continued reliance on their result,[1] we claim that it is highly misleading. For one thing, the theorem proves too much, for it applies not only to advertising, but to all complements produced by the same firm. If x is quantity of output and A measures quality, the theorem says that producers with more monopoly power have a greater incentive to upgrade their quality. Hence the unreasonable conclusion from the theorem that monopolistic producers make better quality products than competitive producers.

---

1. Among the numerous favorable references, see Hurwitz and Caves's recent discussion of advertising by pharmaceutical companies [1988] and Tirole's [1988, p. 103] excellent book on modern industrial organization theory.

The proof of this theorem crucially depends on the assumption that dx/dA does not change as ϵ_x increases. What happens to dx/dA depends on why ϵ_x changes, and often it would increase as ϵ_x did. For example, the elasticity of demand for the soap industry is much smaller than that for individual soap companies. And the effect of advertising on the quantity demanded at a given price is presumably also much greater when one company alone advertises than when all companies (the industry) do, since advertising by one company attracts customers from competitors. In this example, therefore, the effect of advertising on the quantity demanded of the advertised good is positively related to, not independent of, the elasticity of demand for the product advertised.

It is far more reasonable to assume that dp_x/dA is approximately constant for a given x as ϵ_x changes than that dx/dA is constant for a given p_x. The difference between these assumptions may seem minor, but actually they have very different implications. In particular, if dp_x/dA is held constant, there is no presumption that the incentive to advertise falls as ϵ_x increases. For the left-hand side of equation (3) indicates that the marginal revenue from advertising can be written not only as in equation (7) but also as

$$(8) \qquad\qquad MR_A = x\,\frac{\partial p_x}{\partial A}\,.$$

Given the output of the product advertised (x), the marginal revenue from advertising is greater when the increase in price is greater. A change in the elasticity of demand for the product advertised *has no effect whatsoever* on the marginal revenue from advertising when x and $\partial p_x/\partial A$ are held constant.

It is easy to reconcile the different implications of equations (7) and (8). When the effect of A on x is held fixed as ϵ_x increases, the effect of A on p_x falls,[2] which explains why the marginal revenue of

2. If

$$x = a(A)p_x^{-\epsilon_x}, \quad \frac{d\log x}{dA} = \frac{a'}{a} \text{ (for a given } p_x).$$

Since

$$\frac{d\log p_x}{dA} = \frac{1}{\epsilon_x}\frac{a'}{a} \text{ (for a given } x),$$

an increase in ϵ_x reduces the effect of A on p_x when a'/a (and thus $(d\log x)/da$) is held fixed.

advertising then also falls. Similarly, when the effect of A on p_x is held fixed as ϵ_x increases, the effect of A on x rises.

The value of highlighting the effect of advertising on the price of the good advertised is that the marginal revenue from advertising is then directly related to the higher marginal utility from consuming a given amount of the advertised good, as in equation (6). By contrast, the effect of advertising on the quantity demanded at a given price has no ready interpretation in terms of marginal utilities. If the effect of advertising on the marginal utility from consuming a given quantity of the good advertised is unrelated to its elasticity of demand, the effect on price and the incentive to advertise would also be unrelated to this elasticity.

For example, it is plausible to assume that the effects of advertising by one soap company on the price and marginal utility of its soap is similar to the effects of advertising by the industry on the average price of all soap. For the effect of advertising on price depends on the sensitivity of marginal demand. This sensitivity may not be very different when one soap company attracts consumers from competing companies through its advertising than when the industry attracts consumers from competing products.

The presumption that oligopolistic industries usually advertise more than monopolistic industries is based on the assumption that demand for an oligopolistic firm's product is more elastic, *and hence more sensitive to advertising,* than is demand for a monopoly's product. Such reasoning contradicts that behind the Dorfman-Steiner result, although it is fully consistent with our approach.

A different argument for why competitive firms have no incentive to advertise is that many close competitors could free ride on the advertising (see, e.g., Comanor and Wilson [1974, p. 20]). Advertising by a wheat farmer may raise slightly the demand for all wheat, but it is unlikely to raise much the demand for this farmer's wheat relative to that of others.

Of course, firms do not advertise when they cannot differentiate their products from many competing products. Yet the fact is that companies in highly competitive situations often do a lot of advertising. Perdue chickens closely compete with other chickens, Chiquita bananas with other bananas, and Jaffa oranges with other oranges. Yet all these brands have been extensively adver-

---

The discussion in Tirole [1988, pp. 100–03] is revealing. Immediately after a good analysis of product quality that uses the effect of quality on the price consumers are willing to pay for a given quantity, he analyzes advertising through its effect on the quantity demanded at a given price.

tised because say Perdue advertisements convince consumers that a pound of its chickens is worth more than a pound of other chickens. Whether advertising succeeds in differentiating further the product advertised from that of substitutes may be related empirically to the number and closeness of substitutes, but there is no strict analytical connection.

b. Advertising and Prices of Advertised Goods

That advertising raises the price of the good advertised for a *given* quantity does not in general imply that it raises the *equilibrium* price. Equations (2) and (4) show that advertising tends to raise or lower the equilibrium price as it lowers or raises the elasticity of demand for the advertised good. Advertising is often said to lower this elasticity because firms expand their monopoly power by differentiating further their products from others. However, we have shown that advertising is profitable not because it lowers the elasticity of demand for the advertised good, but because it raises the level of demand.

We believe that the presumption in fact goes the other way, that advertising tends to *raise* the elasticity of demand at the initial equilibrium quantity of the advertised good. The reason is that firms try to tailor their advertising to bring up the demands of marginal consumers since these drag down the equilibrium price paid by inframarginal consumers: again the analysis is related to discussions of product quality by Spence [1976] and others. In lieu of explicit price discrimination, advertising may help price a good *effectively* lower to marginal consumers.

Assume two classes of consumers, C and D, where each C is willing to pay $10, and each D is willing to pay only $5, for a single unit of x that costs $2 to produce. Suppose that $10 is the profit-maximizing price without price discrimination and advertising, so that only C buys x at this price. Introduce an advertising campaign aimed at D, the marginal consumers, and assume it costs $7 to raise each D's reservation price for x to $10. Although the advertising costs more than the increase in D's reservation price, advertising is profitable because it enables the firm to collect also the initial reservation price ($5) of the D consumers.

This example illustrates why advertising tends to increase the market elasticity of demand for the goods advertised in the vicinity of the initial equilibrium quantity. In the example, advertising is a way to price discriminate that is inferior to free explicit discrimination but may be superior to feasible alternatives.

The early ads for low calorie beer were targeted to women because their weak demand for beer lowered the equilibrium price of beer. Such advertising could pay even if it reduced demand by inframarginal males. Similarly, a political candidate's promises are often targeted to undecided voters even when that lowers the backing of his strong supporters, because he is likely to get their votes, and he needs undecided votes to win.

The claim that advertising raises prices of the goods advertised is often supported by evidence that advertised goods are more expensive than "similar" unadvertised goods (see the review of this evidence in Scherer [1980, pp. 381–88]). But advertised goods may have good qualities that are not observed by econometricians, as implied by the signaling literature.

Better evidence comes from the consequences of advertising regulations. Several studies find that states which permit advertising for particular goods have lower prices than states which ban the advertising (see Benham's [1972] well-known study of eyeglasses and Bond's [1980] discussion of advertising in the professions). These studies may be exceptional cases; however, perhaps they only illustrate that advertising raises elasticities of demand for advertised goods.

IV. ADVERTISING AND WELFARE

Economists have long been opposed to advertising (see, e.g., Pigou [1920, p. 199]; or Galbraith [1958, pp. 155–56]), yet they have been unable to use standard welfare analysis to show that advertising is excessive because of the peculiar attitude toward how advertising affects consumers. A major analytical advantage of our approach that treats advertising as part of given preferences rather than as shifting tastes is that the standard welfare analysis becomes directly applicable. Indeed, the following discussion is similar to the welfare analysis of product quality by Spence [1976]; also see Tirole [1988]. Some differences between the analysis of advertising and quality are considered at the end.

We use the sum of consumer and producer surplus (S) to evaluate the welfare effects of advertising by a firm:

$$(9) \qquad V(A,p_x,T) + \Pi(A,p_x,T) = S,$$

where V is the money value of the consumer's utility, Π is the surplus to the firm producing the advertising (A) and the product advertised (x), p_x is the price of x, and T is any revenue from the sale of A. Whether advertising is socially optimal after including induced changes in the output of the good advertised is found by totally differentiating equation (9) with respect to A:

(10) $$\frac{dS}{dA} = V_A + V_{p_x}\frac{dp_x}{dA} + V_T\frac{dT}{dA} + \frac{d\Pi}{dA}\left(= \Pi_A + \Pi_{p_x}\frac{dp_x}{dA} + \Pi_T\frac{dT}{dA}\right).$$

It is clear that

(11) $V_T = -1$, $V_{p_x} = -x$, $\Pi_{p_x} = x$, $\Pi_T = 1$,

$$\text{and } \Pi_A \ (p_x - c_x)\frac{dx}{dA} - c_a,$$

where c_a and c_x are the marginal costs of A and x, respectively. Note that dp_x/dA and dx/dA are the equilibrium changes in p_x and x after taking account of changes in all variables, whereas $\partial p_x/\partial A$ and $\partial x/\partial A$ in the profit-maximizing first-order condition in equation (3) are partial changes, holding x or p_x constant. The term V_A gives the marginal utility to consumers from advertisements for x, net of any reduction induced by these ads in the utility from other goods.

By substituting (11) into (10), we see that advertising is excessive, optimal, or underproduced:

(12) $$\frac{dS}{dA} \gtreqless 0 \quad \text{as } V_A + (p_x - c_x)\frac{dx}{dA} \gtreqless c_a.$$

Since a firm maximizes producer surplus, $d\pi/dA = 0$, and equation (10) also simplifies to

(13) $$\frac{dS}{dA} \gtreqless 0 \quad \text{as } V_A - x\frac{dp_x}{dA} - \frac{dT}{dA} \gtreqless 0.$$

When consumers voluntarily expose themselves to advertisements, V_A has to be ≥ 0 unless consumers are compensated for any loss in utility from the ads. That is, unless dT/dA is sufficiently ≤ 0.

Advertising has been said to be excessive when its price is less than marginal cost (see Kaldor [1949–50, p. 3] and Comanor and Wilson [1974, p. 20]). But if producers ration advertisements to consumers, the relevant price is not the price charged, but the shadow price to consumers which is measured by V_A. Equation (12) shows that the difference between the shadow price and marginal cost of advertising (c_a) does help determine whether or not advertising is socially excessive.

If the advertised good is perfectly competitive, with price equal to marginal cost ($p_x = c_x$), equation (12) gives the usual first-best criterion for welfare maximization; that is, the marginal cost of producing advertisements equals its shadow price to consumers. If x is imperfectly competitive ($p_x > c_x$), advertising also has a "second-best" aspect, for it may change the distortion in the market for the advertised good by raising or lowering output. A second-best incentive to subsidize advertising would appear to exist if advertising stimulates the demand for x, for then ($p_x - c_x$) $dx/dA > 0$. But firms do take this effect into account when they choose their advertising since profits depend on ($p_x - c_x$)dx/dA (see equation (3)). Whether firms produce too much or too little advertising from a social perspective depends on the effect of advertising on demand for the advertised good.

Equation (6) indicates that $V_a \geq p_a$; hence, $dT/dA \leq p_a \leq V_a$ because marginal revenue is not above price. Substitution of this inequality into equation (13) gives that $dS/dA \geq 0$ if $dp_x/dA \leq 0$. Therefore, no matter how advertising changes demand, equation (13) and the consumer first-order condition to maximize utility imply that the amount of advertising is insufficient if the equilibrium price of the advertised product falls. For if it falls, producers fail to include the higher amount consumers are willing to pay for the product advertised in their estimate of the gain from additional advertising.

Whether advertising lowers price of the product advertised is a remarkably simple test that can be applied in practice to determine whether there is too little advertising. And this criterion follows from the usual welfare analysis and consumer utility maximization without special assumptions about how advertising affects either demand for the product or consumer utility. In particular, it applies to the case where advertising is rationed and given away as well as when it is sold at a fixed price in whatever quantities consumers want; the case where advertising has negative marginal utility as well as when it has positive utility; and to advertising by competitive firms as well as by monopolists. This is a major implication of our approach that treats advertising as part of given metatastes, but it cannot be derived from a model where advertising shifts tastes.

Most discussions of advertising assume that it is given away to consumers ($dT/dA = 0$), and that advertisements do not directly provide utility ($V_A = 0$). Equation (13) then implies that advertising is excessive, optimal, or insufficient as it raises, does not change, or lowers the equilibrium price of the advertised good. This explains why Dixit and Norman [1978] conclude that advertising is generally excessive, for they essentially assume that $V_A = 0$, that advertising is not sold, and that advertising usually raises the price of advertised goods.

These assumptions are dubious, for advertising does affect the utility of consumers, and it is often sold—sometimes at a negative price. Therefore, with reasonable assumptions an increase in the equilibrium price does not necessarily imply that advertising is excessive. Our criterion, that advertising is insufficient if the equilibrium price *falls* does not require any special assumptions about the advertising market or the effect of advertising on consumer utility.

The surplus criterion can be generalized beyond the effects of advertising on the product advertised by including induced changes in the consumers' and producers' surplus in other markets. Equation (12) becomes

$$(14) \qquad \frac{d\left(\Sigma_{j=1}^{m}\right) S_j}{dA_1} \gtreqless 0 \quad \text{as } V_{A_1} + (p_1 - c_1)\frac{dx_1}{dA_1}$$

$$+ \sum_{i=2}^{m} (p_i - c_i)\frac{dx_i}{dA_1} \gtreqless c_{a_1},$$

where S_j is the total surplus in the jth market, x_1 is the good advertised, x_i, $i = 2, \ldots, m$ are the other products affected by advertising for x_1, p_j, and c_j are the price and marginal cost of x_j, and dx_i/dA_1 is the equilibrium change in x_i induced by an increase in A_1. If the other products affected are perfectly competitive ($p_i = c_i$), equation (14) reduces to equation (12), and the previous discussion is fully applicable.

However, if the good advertised expands partly through substitution for a monopolized good, x_2, where $p_2 > c_2$ and $dx_2 < 0$, the advantage of expanding x_1 is partly negated by the disadvantage of contracting a monopolized substitute. A full analysis of the social optimality of advertising includes induced changes in the outputs of substitutes and complements as well as changes in the output of the advertised good.

One interesting application is to competitive advertising of brands, where advertising expands output of a brand partly or wholly at the expense of competing brands. From early discussions to more recent treatments (see, e.g., Pigou [1920, pp. 197–99], Solow [1967, p. 165], and Scherer [1980, p. 389]), economists have generally agreed that brand advertising is largely worthless to society if it does not increase aggregate consumption of the brands.

But our analysis shows that even this seemingly plausible conclusion does not necessarily follow from a consumer surplus analysis.

If $p_i - c_i = p_1 - c_1$, $i = 2, \ldots, m$, equation (14) differs from equation (12) simply by substituting the total change in outputs of all brands (dX) for the change in the good advertised. If the total change $dX = 0$, then the criterion for excessive or insufficient advertising reduces simply to whether $V_{A_1} \lessgtr c_{a_1}$; i.e., whether the marginal value to consumers of the advertising exceeds or is less than its marginal cost. The relation between these marginal values and cost depends on whether advertising is sold, and how it shifts demand for the brand advertised.

If the total output of all brands is unaffected, equation (14) implies that advertising is excessive if the marginal utility of advertising is negative. For then, $V_{A_1} < 0 < c_{a_1}$. If the direct marginal revenue from advertising equals the marginal utility of the advertising (if $dT_1/dA_1 = V_{A_1}$), advertising by a firm is excessive under the frequently realized condition that the increased quantity demanded for its product exceed the increased demand for all brands. For then $V_{A_1} + dX/dA_1(p_x - c_x) < c_{a_1}$ (see equations (14) and (5) and the first two terms on the left-hand side of equation (3)). However, with the usual assumption that advertising is rationed and is given away, the amount of advertising is insufficient when total brand output is unchanged as long as $V_{A_1} > x_1 \partial p_1/\partial A_1 = c_{a_1}$ (see equation (3)); that is, if the increased utility from advertising by a firm exceeds the *marginal* increase in the demand for its product.

Our welfare analysis of advertising applies also to government efforts to persuade consumers to change behavior. Suppose that the government wants consumers to bring used bottles and cans to recycling centers. It produces advertisements that are complements in consumer utility functions with a more favorable attitude toward recycling. Even if these ads directly lower utility, and hence consumers must be compensated to accept them, they would indirectly raise utility if the externalities from throwing away bottles and cans are sufficiently strong. In equation (12), x refers to proper disposal $(dx/dA > 0)$, $p_x - c_x > 0$ because the cost to consumers of proper disposal is less than the social gain (measured by p_x), and V could be <0. If $p_x - c_x$ is sufficiently positive, government efforts at persuasion could raise utility even when $V_A < 0$, and c_a is not negligible.

As we indicated, the welfare analysis of advertising is similar to the welfare analysis of product quality and other complements, but there are some differences. Since advertisements are physically distinct from the products advertised, while quality is embodied in products, firms can more easily charge separately for advertisements than for quality, although the charge for ads is usually implicit in the cost of a package that includes other goods. For the same reason, advertisements are not likely to affect the marginal cost of the good advertised, whereas improvements in the quality of a product usually do raise the marginal cost of a larger quantity.

Although these and similar differences between advertising and quality are important, they do not explain the hostility to advertising. We believe the explanation is that economists are willing to abandon the principle of consumer sovereignty when evaluating advertising but not when discussing quality, although a few studies have criticized changes in quality (see, e.g., the well-known paper by Fisher, Griliches, and Kaysen [1962]. The taste-change interpretation of advertising abandons consumer sovereignty by ignoring the utility from advertising when evaluating its welfare effects. We have shown that respect for consumer sovereignty does not imply that the amount of advertising by profit-maximizing firms is necessarily welfare-maximizing, but it does cast doubt on most discussions of the welfare effects.

V. Negative Utility from Advertising on Radio and Television

"Free" radio and television do not charge audiences either for advertisements or programs. Advertisers usually pay for both the cost of preparing and using their ads, and for programming costs. Since radio and television could provide advertisements without programming, why do advertisers go to the expense of including costly programs?

There are several possible reasons, but we believe the main one is that utility from programs compensates the audience for tuning in and becoming exposed to the ads. Since consumers do not have to be compensated for utility-raising services, the inference must be that most ads on radio and television lower the utility of marginal viewers, after netting out the value of the time spent watching and listening. As it were, advertisers throw in free programming to generate the audience for utility-reducing ads. One can say either that advertising pays for the programming— the usual interpretation—or that programming compensates for the advertising, which is our preferred interpretation.

Advertisements that lower utility are less likely to be placed in newspapers, magazines, and other print media because readers can more easily ignore advertisements than can listeners or viewers. Therefore, the presumption is that the print media have a larger fraction of utility-raising ads, including those providing information, than do radio and television.

Although plausible, it is not true that advertisements must raise consumer utility if they increase demand for the goods advertised. For the effect of advertising on demand depends on the cross derivative in the utility function between advertising and advertised goods, while the effect on utility depends on the first derivative with respect to advertising.

Still, it may seem unlikely that most radio and television ads reduce utility since these ads constitute an important fraction of all advertising expenditures. But utility is necessarily reduced only to marginal viewers, and only after netting out the value of time spent viewing ads. And just as death, divorce, unemployment, and similar utility-reducing events often induce greater drinking, smoking, overeating, and similar changes in consumption, we believe so too do many advertisements lower utility and yet raise demand for the advertised goods. These ads produce anxiety and depression, stir up envious feelings toward the success and happiness of others, or arouse guilt toward parents or children (see Marchand [1985]).

Indeed, in some ways the assumption that many ads lower utility is easier to reconcile with consumer behavior than is the assumption that they raise utility. For consumers often do not appear to look forward to consuming advertisements, and rational consumers would not seek out even free advertising if it lowers their utility.

It may seem strange that firms can profit from advertisements that lower utility even when they have to fully compensate consumers for their loss, perhaps by including utility-raising programs along with the advertising. But suppose that advertising raises the marginal utility of the advertised good at the initial equilibrium quantity, reduces the marginal utility of the advertised good at some lower quantities, and possibly also lowers utility independently of consumption of that good. Such advertising may reduce utility overall, but the reduction could be small compared with the revenue from the higher price for the good due to the increase in marginal utilities. Essentially, such advertising would be profitable because it allows a firm to collect more of the consumer surplus from the advertised good (see the example in Becker and Murphy [1990, p. 37]).

UNIVERSITY OF CHICAGO

REFERENCES

Barnett, Harold J., Comment on "Supply and Demand for Advertising Messages," by Lester Telser; both in *American Economic Review Proceedings*, LVI (1966), 457–66, 467–70.
Becker, Gary S., and Kevin M. Murphy, "A Simple Theory of Advertising as a Good," Center for the Study of the Economy and the State Working Paper No. 58, University of Chicago, February 1990.
Benham, Lee, "The Effect of Advertising on the Price of Eyeglasses," *Journal of Law and Economics*, XV (1972), 337–52.
Bond, Ronald S., et al., "Effects of Restrictions on Advertising and Commercial Practices in the Professions," Staff Report, Federal Trade Commission, Washington, DC, September 1980.
Comanor, William S., "Vertical Price-Fixing, Vertical Market Restrictions, and the New Antitrust Policy," *Harvard Law Review*, XCVIII (1985), 983–1002.
Comanor, William S., and Thomas A. Wilson, *Advertising and Market Power* (Cambridge, MA: Harvard University Press, 1974).
Dixit, Avinash, and Victor Norman, "Advertising and Welfare," *Bell Journal of Economics*, IX (1978), 1–17.
Dorfman, Robert, and Peter O. Steiner, "Optimal Advertising and Optimal Quality," *American Economic Review*, XLIV (1954), 826–36.
Ehrlich, D., I. Guttman, P. Schönbach, and J. Mills, "Postdecision Exposure to Relevant Information," *Journal of Abnormal Psychology*, LIV (1957), 98–102.
Ehrlich, Isaac, and Lawrence Fisher, "The Derived Demand for Advertising: A Theoretical and Empirical Investigation," *American Economic Review*, LXXII (1982), 366–88.
Fisher, Franklin M., Zvi Griliches, and Carl Kaysen, "The Costs of Automobile Model Changes since 1949," *Journal of Political Economy*, LXX (1962), 433–51.
Fisher, Franklin M., and John J. McGowan, "Advertising and Welfare: Comment," *Bell Journal of Economics*, X (1979). 726–27.
Galbraith, John K., *The Affluent Society* (Boston, MA: Houghton-Mifflin Company, 1958).
Grossman, Gene M., and Carl Shapiro, "Informative Advertising with Differentiated Products," *Review of Economic Studies*, LI (1984), 63–81.
Horstmann, Ignatius J., and Glenn MacDonald, "Recurrent Advertising," No. 87-11, Economic Research Center/NORC Discussion Paper Series, September 1987.
Hurwitz, Mark A., and Richard E. Caves, "Persuasion or Information? Promotion and the Shares of Brand Name and Generic Pharmaceuticals," *Journal of Law and Economics*, XXXI (1988), 299–320.
Kaldor, Nicolas V., "The Economic Aspects of Advertising," *Review of Economic Studies*, XVIII (1949–50), 1–27.
Kihlstrom, R., and M. Riordan, "Advertising as a Signal," *Journal of Political Economy*, LXXXI (1984), 427–50.
Klein, Ben, and Kevin M. Murphy, "Vertical Restraints as Contract Reinforcement Mechanism," *Journal of Law and Economics*, XXXI (1988), 265–97.
Klein, Frederick C., "Two New Pitchers Put Reds on a Roll," *Wall Street Journal*, July 7, 1992, p. A8.
Marchand, Roland, *Advertising the American Dream: Making Way for Modernity 1920–1940* (Berkeley: University of California Press, 1985).
Nelson, Phillip, "Advertising as Information," *Journal of Political Economy*, LXXXII (1974), 729–54.
Pigou, M. A., *The Economics of Welfare* (London: Macmillan and Company, 1920).
Scherer, F. M., *Industrial Market Structure and Economic Performance*, 2nd edition (Boston, MA: Houghton Mifflin, 1980).

Shapiro, Carl, "Consumer Information, Product Quality, and Seller Reputation,"
    Bell Journal of Economics, XIII (1982), 20–35.
Solow, Robert M., "The New Industrial State or Son of Affluence," *Public Interest*,
    IX (1967), 100–08.
Spence, Michael, "Product Selection, Fixed Costs, and Monopolistic Competition,"
    Review of Economic Studies, XLIII (1976), 217–35.
Stigler, George J., and Gary S. Becker, "De Gustibus Non Est Disputandum,"
    American Economic Review, LXVII (1977), 76–90.
Telser, Lester G., "Advertising and Cigarettes," *Journal of Political Economy*, LXX
    (1962), 471–99.
——, "Advertising and Competition," *Journal of Political Economy*, LXXII (1964),
    537–62.
Tirole, Jean, *The Theory of Industrial Organizations* (Cambridge, MA: MIT Press,
    1988).

E
Non-market Welfare Measurement

[36]

THE UNIVERSITY OF NORTH CAROLINA
INSTITUTE OF STATISTICS
CHAPEL HILL
DEPARTMENT OF MATHEMATICAL STATISTICS

June 18, 1947

Mr. Newton B. Drury, Director
National Park Service
Department of the Interior
Washington 25, D.C.

Dear Mr. Drury:

After a letter from Mr. A. E. Demaray, and a conference with Dr. Roy A. Pruitt of the National Park Service, I am convinced that it is possible to set up appropriate measures for evaluating, with a reasonable degree of accuracy, the service of national parks to the public.

The development of criteria for evaluating benefits to the public has been a long-term interest of mine. Following the example set a hundred years ago by the French engineer, Jules Dupuit, who wrote formulae for the benefits of roads, bridges, and canals, I have worked out more general formulae for benefits from wider and more complicated classes of public services.

These formulae, of course, involve coefficients which must, in each case, be determined by factual statistical studies. The development of such studies I believe to be possible through several modes of attack which Dr. Pruitt and I discussed. One of these, of whose feasibility I am confident, and which might be pursued further, is as follows:

Let concentric zones be defined around each park so that the cost of travel to the park from all points in one of these zones is approximately constant. The persons entering the park in a year, or a suitably chosen sample of them, are to be listed

217

according to the zone from which they come. The fact that they come means that they presume the service of the park is at least worth the cost, and this cost can probably be estimated with fair accuracy. If we assume that the benefits are the same no matter what the distance, we have, for those living near the park, a consumers' surplus consisting of the differences in transportation costs. The comparison of the cost of coming from a zone with the number of people who do come from it, together with a count of the population of the zone, enables us to plot one point for each zone on a demand curve for the service of the park. By a judicious process of fitting it should be possible to get a good enough approximation to this demand curve to provide, through integration, a measure of the consumers' surplus resulting from the availability of the park. It is this consumers' surplus cost (calculated by the above process with deduction for the cost of operating the park) which measures the benefits to the public in the particular year. This, of course, might be compared directly with the estimated annual benefits on the hypothesis that the park area was used for some alternate purpose.

The problem of relations between different parks can be treated along the same lines, though in a slightly more complicated manner, provided people entering the park will be asked which other national parks they have visited that year. In place of a demand curve, we have as a result of such an inquiry, a set of demand functions. The consumer surplus still has a defining meaning, as I have shown in various published articles, and may be used to evaluate the benefits from the park system.

This approach through travel costs is one of several possible modes of attack on this problem. There are also others, which should be examined, though I think the method outlined above looks the most promising.

Very sincerely,

Harold Hotelling

[37]

Econometrica, Vol. 39, No. 5 (September, 1971)

ESTIMATION OF NET SOCIAL BENEFITS FROM OUTDOOR RECREATION

By Oscar R. Burt and Durward Brewer[1]

An economic framework is presented for measurement of the net social benefits that can be attributed to development of a new outdoor recreation site, taking into consideration the influence that existing recreation developments have on the demand for services from the newly developed site. Methods are given for statistically estimating the empirical measures needed to apply the model, and an application is made to water-oriented outdoor recreation in Missouri. Results of the application suggest that investments in outdoor recreation can be evaluated under an objective economic decision criterion.

1. INTRODUCTION

INCREASED INCOME and leisure, combined with advances in transportation technology, have made outdoor recreation an important consumption commodity in the United States, much of which is provided by the public sector of the economy. The need for objective, quantitative criteria to evaluate investments in outdoor recreation is acute and recognized by most public agencies delegated responsibility for allocation of public funds among such investments. Appropriations will be made and specific projects chosen for development whether good decision criteria are available or not, and it would appear that decisions made under current methods are very costly in terms of poor allocations. The objective of this paper is to provide an economic framework and operational model for estimation of net social benefits associated with outdoor recreation.

Difficulties encountered in social valuation of outdoor recreation are unique since often the recreation is resource-oriented, with transportation costs incurred by participants constituting a major part of the costs of consumption. In other words, the consumer is transported to the commodity for consumption to take place instead of vice versa. This attribute of outdoor recreation is advantageous for statistical estimation of demand equations because the costs that must be incurred to consume the recreational services provide surrogate prices with more variation in a sample than would usually be generated by market phenomena observed either over time or space. In fact, the surrogate prices derived from transportation costs can be viewed as the analogue of market prices in a cross-section, where there is large price variation across space as a result of high transportation costs.

Harold Hotelling in 1947 was apparently the first to recognize the opportunity of using travel costs as surrogates for prices, and of applying more or less conventional economic analysis to the problem [5]. The seed of Hotelling's suggestion

[1] This research was conducted under a cooperative agreement between the University of Missouri Agricultural Experiment Station and the Natural Resources Division of the Economic Research Service, U.S. Department of Agriculture. Missouri Agricultural Experiment Station Journal Series No. 7192. The authors wish to thank Sam Chase, William Green, Irving Hock, and Jack Knetsch for their helpful comments on an earlier draft of this paper, but, of course, the remaining errors and deficiencies are the authors' responsibility.

814   O. R. BURT AND D. BREWER

for measuring social benefits from outdoor recreation, however, can be found in his 1938 article [4, p. 247] where he describes a procedure for evaluating investment in a bridge. The sequel is primarily a refinement and adaptation of Hotelling's approach to social valuation of investments.

We first present a model for measuring social benefits associated with a newly developed recreation site, under the assumption that a system of demand equations for interrelated outdoor recreation sites is known. Then problems of empirically estimating this system of demand equations are considered. The paper finishes with an application to water-oriented outdoor recreation in the state of Missouri.

2. SOCIAL VALUE MEASUREMENT

Regardless of the fact that most theorems of welfare economics can be derived without assuming cardinal measurement of utility, the frequent and complex choices that must be made in public investment decisions dictate some compromise cardinal measure of social value for comparison of alternatives. It is not argued that such a measure is utility per se, but that it provides a useful approximation for making comparisons among small changes from a specified situation. Any acceptance of benefit-cost analysis in general requires the assumption that current dollar values have some close relation to social value.

The usual defense for using market value as a measure of social value is linked to an assumption of pure competition and its implication of Pareto optimality in the absence of externalities. Goods and services flowing from a public investment are estimated and evaluated at market price for comparison with the market value of factors absorbed by the investment (costs are amortized or the flow of benefits discounted). Under Pareto optimality, market value of factors is a measure of the social sacrifice, if rates of use of the various factors remain close to their original equilibrium levels; and likewise, market value of goods and services emanating from the investment are acceptable measures of social value if individual quantities are not changed "too far" from the old equilibrium.[2]

We run into two difficulties in outdoor recreation economics: (i) absence of even a semblance of competitive prices for the recreation services, and (ii) the fact that a single investment often moves the quantity of recreation services consumed a substantial distance from the old level. Both of these complexities arise from high transportation costs associated with outdoor recreation, and in particular the necessity of having consumers travel to the recreation site.

We now present a method for estimating social value from investments in outdoor recreation that is commensurable with market value utilized in traditional benefit-cost analysis. The method reduces to market value in the special case where quantities consumed in a market are changed only infinitesimally by an investment.

---

[2] The many difficulties encountered in using this approach to measurement of social value in practice, where Pareto optimality obviously does not hold, are surveyed by Krutilla [8] and related to theoretical welfare economics. The particular problem of estimating factor cost under immobility constraints is taken up by Krutilla and Haveman [9].

Outdoor recreation sites are grouped into a small number of relatively homogeneous categories, and services from each are viewed as a separate commodity. A geographic region is delineated as the potential market area for services from a contemplated investment to develop a particular recreation site. Development of the site will change the minimum distance (price) that some of the population must travel (pay) in order to consume services from the category of sites in which the development fits. Thus an investment in outdoor recreation will change the price vector faced by at least some of the population.

The relevant geographic region is denoted by R and is approximated by an area on a geometric plane. Each point (x, y) of the plane is viewed as a separate market since in general there will be a separate price vector associated with each point. Let $z_i = D_i(x, y)$ be the minimum distance from the point (x, y) to a recreation site in the ith category. We define $c_i(z_i)$ as the cost (price) associated with consumption of one unit of the ith commodity, which makes the coordinates x and y implicitly arguments of the cost function c_i. We define $P(x, y)$ to be a vector function with ith component $c_i(D_i(x, y))$, and it will be referred to as the price vector at the point (x, y).

A system of per capita demand equations is assumed known,

$$(1) \qquad q_k = g_k(p_1, p_2, \ldots, p_m) \qquad\qquad (k = 1, 2, \ldots, m),$$

where q_i and p_i are quantities and prices, respectively, of the ith recreation commodity. These are conventional demand equations that specify money income and prices of all commodities outside the system to be fixed. For a given price vector $P(x, y)$, there is an associated per capita quantity vector $Q(x, y)$ implied by the system of demand equations (1).

We denote the price vector for the existing set of outdoor recreation facilities by $P_0(x, y)$, and for the situation that would prevail after a specific investment, we have the price vector $P_1(x, y)$. Corresponding to $P_0(x, y)$ and $P_1(x, y)$ are the quantity vectors $Q_0(x, y)$ and $Q_1(x, y)$. Since the situation associated with $P_1(x, y)$ implies existence of an additional recreation site available to the population as compared to the old situation associated with $P_0(x, y)$, we have the inequality,

$$(2) \qquad P_1(x, y) \leqslant P_0(x, y).$$

The basic measurement problem that confronts us is to estimate a social value that can be attributed to the change in prices from $P_0(x, y)$ to $P_1(x, y)$ or, equivalently, the change in quantities from $Q_0(x, y)$ to $Q_1(x, y)$. A relatively small area of the consumer's utility surface is represented by variations on the arguments, $p_1, p_2, \ldots, p_m$ (or, equivalently, the quantities, $q_1, q_2, \ldots, q_m$), holding money income and all other prices (quantities) constant. This assertion is supported by the relatively small proportion of a consumer's budget that is spent on outdoor recreation. Therefore, it seems reasonable to assume that this limited area of the utility surface can be approximated by a simple algebraic relation, namely, a quadratic function.

The relatively small budget proportion in conjunction with hypothesized close substitution among outdoor recreation commodities permits us to appeal to

Wold's theorem [**14**, p. 112] to invoke the symmetry conditions of Hotelling [**3, 4**],

(3) $\partial q_i/\partial p_j = \partial q_j/\partial p_i$ $(i, j = 1, 2, \ldots, m)$.

Let it be clear that we are not assuming (3) to hold for all commodities within the consumer's budget, *but to hold only approximately among the outdoor recreation commodities, ceteris paribus*. If income elasticities among the outdoor recreation commodities are relatively close in magnitude, the approximation to (3) will also be improved.

With (3) approximately met, errors resulting from its imposition on the system of demand equations should be relatively small. When the equations of (1) satisfy (3), we have a unique multi-commodity generalization of area under a demand curve, viz., the line integral of the demand equations which was proposed by Hotelling [**4**] as a measure of social value. Thus, a system of linear demand equations with a symmetric coefficient matrix would yield a quadratic approximation to the utility function in the region of price variation for the recreation commodities.

Probably the most intuitive definition of the line integral is obtained by taking the inverse of the system of demand equations in (1), that is,

(4) $p_k = f_k(q_1, q_2, \ldots, q_m)$ $(k = 1, 2, \ldots, m)$.

Then we are concerned with the social value of a movement from $Q_0(x, y)$ to $Q_1(x, y)$. *Gross* value to the representative consumer at the point (x, y) is the line integral

(5) $G(x, y) = \int_{Q_0}^{Q_1} \sum f_k \, dq_k$,

where Q_0 and Q_1 are implicitly functions of x and y.

Assuming that the resources used by consumers to participate in outdoor recreation are paid their marginal value to society,[3] social cost associated with the movement from Q_0 to Q_1, is the difference in vector inner products,

(6) $C(x, y) = P_1 \cdot Q_1 - P_0 \cdot Q_0$.

Net social value per capita at the point (x, y) is the difference between (5) and (6),

(7) $N(x, y) = G(x, y) - C(x, y)$.

If we define the population density function[4] on the region of the plane R, by $\phi(x, y)$, total net social value attributable to the new investment is

(8) $V = \int\int_R \phi(x, y) N(x, y) \, dx \, dy$.

---

[3] This assumption is reasonable with the exception of one factor, viz., land at the recreation site. Opportunity cost of land at a developed recreation site is usually far less than its market value. Therefore, these economic rents that are captured by the market from consumers cannot be treated as social costs and must be estimated by separate analysis [7]. Consumers pay the economic rent in their expenses associated with visits to the recreation site.

[4] Population density function, as used here, has no reference to the probability distribution. It is the density of people in the region R, and thus has the property that the integral of $\phi(x, y)$ over R is total population in the region.

The use of "net social value" is not completely accurate because variable costs of operating the new recreation site have not been subtracted from (8); nor have we considered amortized cost of the investment itself. The measure defined by (8) is net value only in the sense that consumption costs have been deducted.

To put our net social value functions on a basis commensurable with market value, we would partition $\phi(x, y)$ and $N(x, y)$ by income classes (or introduce income as an additional argument in the functions) and sum the separate social values by income groups. In other words, we have made a simplification for expository convenience by not explicitly including personal income in the system of demand Equations (1) and (4). The simplified model with each individual's income, taken at the mean for the population and not treated explicitly, can be thought of as an approximation to the more complete specification.

The social value measurements being discussed are values per unit of time, say, a year. For purposes of investment decision, these annual values are discounted over the life of the investment to arrive at a present value measure of the benefit flows. Projections of population and income in each year can be used to derive separate population density and benefit functions, i.e., the functions $\phi(x,y)$ and $N(x, y)$ are changing from year to year in the general case, which makes value of benefits, V, also a function of time. Space does not permit going into the details of investment decision criteria. Our concern is to provide a methodology to estimate the change in benefit flows associated with a particular modification in the set of developed outdoor recreation sites available within a specific region.

We note in passing that the same methodology can be used to evaluate the increased benefits from outdoor recreation that are attributable to improvements in transportation within the region. An improvement in transportation, such as building a new road, will change the price vector from $P_0(x, y)$ to $P_1(x, y)$ just as development of a new recreation site would.

In applications, the usual procedure would be to divide the region R into a set of finite spaces (cities, towns, and counties excluding cities and towns, for example) and assign a single point to each area. Letting the point for the ith area be (x_i, y_i), the integral of (8) would be replaced by

$$(9) \qquad V = \sum_i \phi(x_i, y_i) N(x_i, y_i),$$

where $\phi(x_i, y_i)$ is the entire population of the ith area.

An alternative expression for (7) is given by a line integral in price-space, as opposed to quantity-space:

$$(10) \qquad N(x, y) = \int_{P_1}^{P_0} \sum g_k \, dp_k.$$

In this form, the line integral is a net measure with social cost taken into account; the analysis is a straightforward generalization from changing axes in the single commodity case.

Research thus far in recreation economics has only considered the contribution to social value of a single, independent recreation site, e.g., [1, 6, 10]. In that case,

818   O. R. BURT AND D. BREWER

the line integral of (5) reduces to the simple integral

(11) $$G(x, y) = \int_0^{q(x,y)} f(q)\, dq,$$

where $q(x, y)$ is now a scalar and $f(q)$ is the single demand equation. If we were to assume costs were equal for a given distance in any direction from the recreation site, the functions $G(x, y)$ and $q(x, y)$ could be replaced by $G(r)$ and $q(r)$, where r is the radius of the circle centered on the site, and (11) becomes

(12) $$G(r) = \int_0^{q(r)} f(q)\, dq.$$

Similarly, costs can be written $c(r) = p(r)q(r)$ and the population density function redefined $\phi(r)$. Therefore, total net benefits can be written in this simplified case as

(13) $$V = \int_0^\infty \phi(r)\left[\int_0^{q(r)} f(q)\, dq - p(r)q(r)\right] dr.$$

   An approximation to (13), using areas lying between concentric circles to replace the differential dr, is essentially the method used by Clawson [1] and later by Knetsch [6]. Their approach, however, was to translate geometrically the quantity axis up from the origin by the distance $p(r_i)$, where r_i is average distance to the recreation site from the ith area enclosed between two concentric circles. Then the second step was to form a new aggregate demand equation by summing the products of implied quantities and population across distance zones for a given price. Area under this aggregate demand relation was taken as a measure of social value. It is easily shown that their method yields the same result as

(14) $$V = \sum_i \phi(r_i)\left[\int_0^{q(r_i)} f(q)\, dq - p(r_i)q(r_i)\right],$$

which is an approximation to (13). This identity between the method of Clawson and Knetsch and Equation (14) has apparently been overlooked.
   The proof consists of stating (13) in the alternative form

(15) $$V = \int_0^\infty \phi(r)\left[\int_{p(r)}^\infty g(p)\, dp\right] dr,$$

which uses the demand equation with price as the independent variable. Then we can reverse the order of integration, yielding

(16) $$V = \int_{p(0)}^\infty dp \int_0^{\psi(p)} \phi(r)g(p)\, dr$$

where $\psi(p)$ is the inverse function of $p(r)$. The product $\phi(r)g(p)$ is total quantity for given p and r, and the integral on r is the aggregate quantity for a given price.

Therefore, the integral

$$\int_0^{\psi(p)} \phi(r)g(p)\,dr$$

is Clawson's aggregate demand equation with price as the independent variable.

A single, independent recreation site is rarely found, and applications have merely assumed independence to permit estimation of a value for the development. If services emanating from various outdoor recreation sites are competitive among one another in an aggregate sense, such applications will yield estimated values that are biased upwards. One would expect the bias to be great when closely substitutable sources of recreation are near the recreation site being evaluated.

3. STATISTICAL ESTIMATION OF DEMAND EQUATIONS

Direct interview of households is about the only feasible way to obtain data necessary for estimation of the demand equations. The first step is to classify all outdoor recreation sites within the sampling region, and those reasonably close to the sampled population, into specific categories where services from a given category are viewed as an ordinary economic good. Any excluded sites are tacitly assumed independent of those included as far as demand characteristics are concerned.

The critical information required on the interview schedule is: (i) number of days the household spent at each category of recreation sites, inclusive of travel time;[5] this information will almost certainly be collected trip by trip and the site classified by the analyst; (ii) expenditures incurred that were specific to each trip (excluding auto expenses which are estimated separately by mileage); (iii) mileage driven on each trip (could be estimated by the analyst if each site were identifiable on a map); and (iv) family income.

Items (ii) and (iii) are required to estimate surrogate prices as a function of distance. Item (i) forms the basis of quantity measures for estimating the demand equations, and (iv) is used to estimate the influence of income on consumption. The above information will have large variances if based entirely on recall at the time of interview. Therefore, the sampling process should ideally be comprised of more than one contact with the respondent; the first (probably by mail) would be to solicit cooperation in keeping a record of the necessary information.

Since a limited number of schedules is to be collected at considerable cost, there are some decisions to make in the sampling process. The obvious choice of a simple random sample (usually modified somewhat by using clusters) has the advantage of avoiding the possibility of bias. Success of estimation, however, is partially dependent on obtaining large variations on surrogate prices, and geographic dispersion of the observations increases these variances. Thus, one may wish to take chances on some bias in order to reduce standard errors on parameter estimators.

[5] See the Appendix for a discussion of the unit of measure in outdoor recreation analysis.

Linear equations are convenient in many respects, but linearity is almost a necessity in the imposition of constraints (3). The demand equations in (1) are now written as linear equations,

(17) $Q = a + BP,$

where Q, P, and a are m-component column vectors for quantity, price, and the intercept, respectively, and B is an m-dimensional symmetric matrix. The symmetry of B follows from constraints (3).

An appropriate statistical model would appear to be

(18) $q_{ij} = \alpha_j + \sum_{k=1}^{m} \beta_{jk} p_{ik} + \delta_j y_i + \varepsilon_{ij}$ $(i = 1, 2, \ldots, n; j = 1, 2, \ldots, m),$

where the subscripts i and j denote sample unit and commodity, respectively; y is family income; α_j and β_{jk} are population parameters corresponding to elements of a and B in (17), and ε_{ij} is a random disturbance with zero expectation. The symmetry of B implies the constraints $\beta_{jk} = \beta_{kj}$, $j, k = 1, 2, \ldots, m$. A first inclination would be to specify

$$\text{cov}(\varepsilon_{ij}, \varepsilon_{hk}) = \sigma_{jk}, \qquad i = h,$$
(19)
$$= 0, \qquad i \neq h, j \neq k,$$
$$= \sigma_{jj}, \qquad i \neq h, j = k,$$

which gives a block-diagonal covariance matrix for the error vector. The methods presented by Zellner and Lee [15] for applying generalized least squares are almost directly applicable to this model. The symmetry constraint is readily introduced into the Zellner-Lee approach, and single equation analyses without the constraints imposed yield estimates of the $\{\sigma_{jk}\}$ for application of generalized least squares.

However, one is likely to encounter a couple of problems. First, the number of "observations" in the generalized least squares model will be so large as to prohibit direct application of a three-stage least squares algorithm. The number of "observations" is mn and will most likely be several thousand. This difficulty is overcome by using a transformation of variables to reduce the generalized least squares problem to that of simple least squares [11, p. 20].

The second difficulty emanates from a large proportion of zero values in the $\{q_{ij}\}$ which tends to introduce heteroscedasticity across households for a given commodity. The problems discussed by Goldberger [2, p. 252], in regard to limited dependent variables, are directly related to heteroscedasticity, although the difficulties are undoubtedly aggravated by the unrealistic assumption of linearity over the entire domain of the regression equation. The above described transformations in the application of generalized least squares can be thought of as the first step in an iterative procedure, where this first step eliminates nonzero convariances and heteroscedasticity among commodities for a given household. We are then faced with heteroscedasticity which stems from a high frequency of zeros in the dependent variable.

From this point, the following heuristic approach is suggested which seemed to work quite well in application. The hypothesis is that the standard deviation of the residual is correlated with the mean of the dependent variable. Therefore, a sequence of regressions is made to estimate iteratively this relationship and to reduce the correlation with each iteration by a transformation. Let $\hat{q}_k$ and $\hat{e}_k$ be the predicted mean and residual of a regression equation for the kth observation, $k = 1, 2, \ldots, mn$. Then fit $|\hat{e}_k|$ to $\hat{q}_k$ in a polynomial regression which yields an estimate of the relation between the standard deviation of the residuals and the mean of the linear model. This polynomial regression provides an estimate of the standard deviation specific to each observation, which we denote $\hat{\sigma}_k$. The next step is to divide the kth observation equation by $\hat{\sigma}_k$ and use simple least squares on the transformed data to obtain improved parameter estimates. The process just described is repeated until the relationship between $|\hat{e}_k|$ and $\hat{q}_k$ is statistically insignificant.

The authors' experience in their application of the method, however, suggests that compromises might be necessary. Convergence was rapid for three iterations and then became erratic. Linear through fifth degree polynomials were fit at each iteration, but the fourth degree was used in computing the $\{\hat{\sigma}_k\}$. The F-statistic for all the different degree polynomials declined the first three iterations, but from there the improved fit was specific to the particular degree of polynomial used to compute the $\{\hat{\sigma}_k\}$. Nevertheless, the F-statistic on the fourth degree polynomial was reduced from 108 to less than 4 in three iterations, and the improvement was comparable for the other polynomials. This experience suggests that the specific relationship between the standard deviation and the mean of the dependent variable can be approximated by polynomials, but convergence cannot be expected to continue when the statistical relationship becomes relatively weak.

4. AN APPLICATION TO WATER BASED RECREATION

The sampling region was the state of Missouri, but water-based recreation sites in adjacent states were included in defining the alternative prices that users faced within the sampling region. This extended area was particularly important in Missouri with the two major cities of St. Louis and Kansas City being located on the state boundaries. Since the application focused on water-based recreation, the model was reduced to manageable size by excluding all recreation sites that were not associated with lakes, reservoirs, or streams. These three sources of water recreation were initially classified into twelve categories, but later reduced to six by deletions and aggregation when estimation problems were encountered.

The six groupings were: (a) Lake of the Ozarks which was considered relatively unique in its physical and institutional properties; (b) Table Rock Lake and adjoining lakes on the Arkansas border which were also viewed as somewhat unusual; (c) other large lakes constructed by the Army Corps of Engineers; these lakes all have common restrictions imposed by the Corps and are relatively large lakes; (d) other lakes greater than 200 acres; (e) other lakes between 60 and

200 acres; and (f) rivers of the Ozark Mountains area (excluding Mississippi and Missouri Rivers).

A cluster random sample of households was taken by direct interview in the autumn of 1966 and 2,031 usable schedules were collected. Information was obtained on the four critical factors listed earlier, together with many additional socio-economic factors that might affect household demand for water-based recreation. These other factors proved to be of little help as concommitant variables to improve statistical estimation of the demand equations in the three crucial variables of quantity, price, and income.

Minimum direct distances were measured from the center of each cluster of respondents to each recreation site category by using maps, and these direct distances were converted to road miles by an inflation factor estimated from a sample of measurements on road and direct distances. Road miles were then converted to costs, specific to each category of recreation sites, by regression analysis of cost data (exclusive of direct transportation cost) from the interview schedules. This cost was then increased by 5.5 cents per mile, an estimated variable cost per mile of auto travel. The final cost equation was

(20) $c = 4.57 + .1422d$

where d is one-way road miles and costs are in dollars. However, separate intercepts were estimated for groups (a) and (b) and were 10.09 and 7.67, respectively. Income and several other variables were used in the original regression, but these variables were then set at mean values in the sample and the equation reduced to the above.

Demand was defined on a per household basis and linear demand equations were estimated by the methodology outlined in the last section. Final estimates of parameters are given in Table I. The first group of lakes, 60–200 acres in size, was very weakly related to the other site categories and estimated independently in the last analysis. The parameter estimates were obtained by the iterative scheme described earlier to cope with heteroscedasticity, and the standard errors given with these estimates can be assumed to be only approximate.

A statistical test was made of the hypothesized symmetry of the matrix of price coefficients for the five interrelated recreation groups. This test was carried out using the generalized least-squares model that recognized the covariance structure in (18), but ignored the possibility of an overall problem of heteroscedasticity. Separate regressions were run on the transformed data at this stage, one with symmetry imposed and the other without. The F-statistic (at least approximately distributed as such) was computed from the residuals of the two regressions and was equal to 0.87. In the absence of specification error, the F-statistic will exceed 0.87 more than fifty per cent of the time under the hypothesis of symmetry (degrees of freedom are 10 and 10,130 for the numerator and denominator, respectively). Although the power of this test would be expected low upon examination of the standard errors, which are a little greater on the average than those in Table I, we have some empirical support for invoking the symmetry conditions on the system of demand equations.

OUTDOOR RECREATION 823

TABLE I

ESTIMATED DEMAND EQUATIONS[a]

Equation	P₁	Linear Coefficients[b] P₂	P₃	P₄	P₅	P₆	Income ($1,000)	Intercept
60–200 Acre Lakes[c]	.0046 (.0034)						.0067 (.0036)	.3310 (.0449)
Over 200 Acre Lakes (general category)		−.0355 (.0107)	.0130 (.0059)	−.0222 (.0078)	−.0097 (.0049)	.0251 (.0055)	.0181 (.0097)	.5366 (.2302)
Lake of the Ozarks		.0130 (.0059)	−.0388 (.0179)	.0301 (.0091)	.0108 (.0053)	−.0120 (.0063)	.0780 (.0484)	.7218 (.7013)
Typical Corps Lakes		−.0222 (.0078)	.0301 (.0091)	−.0775 (.0178)	.0170 (.0063)	.0210 (.0068)	.0104 (.0176)	.3193 (.2926)
Table Rock Complex of Lakes		−.0097 (.0049)	.0108 (.0053)	.0170 (.0063)	−.0368 (.0103)	.0062 (.0038)	.1024 (.0231)	.9742 (.2895)
Ozark Mountain Rivers		.0251 (.0055)	−.0120 (.0063)	.0210 (.0068)	.0062 (.0038)	−.0292 (.0059)	.0369 (.0183)	.4677 (.2933)

[a] Standard errors are given in parentheses below each estimated value of the parameter.

[b] Prices are numbered consecutively in the same order as the equations are listed, e.g., P_3 is the price corresponding to Lake of the Ozarks.

[c] Missing coefficients were specified at zero on the basis of an F-statistic of 0.27 with 5 and 12,153 degrees of freedom.

Elasticities were computed for the prices and incomes at mean levels and are presented in Table II. The standard errors reported are conditional (predicted quantities taken as given), and are consequently smaller than actual standard errors, but they at least give an indication of relative precision among the elasticities.

Thus far, the basis has been developed for the ultimate objective in the application which is to evaluate alternative investments in water-based outdoor recreation. We now present an application of the estimated system of demand equations to the evaluation, for recreation purposes, of a system of three lakes that have been proposed for construction by the U.S. Army Corps of Engineers. The proposed lakes would be near the metropolitan area of St. Louis, south of the Missouri River and west of the city between 35 and 55 miles (direct, not road miles). These lakes fit the general category of "typical corps lakes" and are assumed perfect competitors with existing lakes placed in this category.[6]

The last five equations of Table I constitute the system of interrelated demand equations used for valuation of benefits associated with the proposed lakes. Let this system of five equations, with modified intercepts computed by setting family

[6] The specific reservoirs were designated by the Corps of Engineers as Union, Meramec Park, and Pine Ford [13].

824   O. R. BURT AND D. BREWER

TABLE II

ELASTICITIES AT MEAN PRICES AND INCOME[a]

Equation	P_1	P_2	P_3	Variable[b] P_4	P_5	P_6	Income	Predicted Quantity
60–200 Acre Lakes	−.17 (.13)						.14 (.073)	.32
Over 200 Acre Lakes		−.69 (.21)	.75 (.34)	−.91 (.32)	.70 (.35)	1.44 (.32)	.20 (.11)	.59
Lake of the Ozarks		.18 (.08)	−1.58 (.73)	.86 (.26)	.55 (.27)	−.48 (.25)	.61 (.38)	.84
Typical Corps Lakes		−.35 (.12)	1.41 (.43)	−2.56 (.59)	1.00 (.37)	.98 (.32)	.093 (.157)	.73
Table Rock Complex of Lakes		−.12 (.06)	.39 (.19)	.43 (.16)	−1.67 (.47)	.22 (.14)	.71 (.16)	.94
Ozark Mountain Rivers		.78 (.17)	−1.10 (.58)	1.37 (.44)	.72 (.44)	−2.67 (.54)	.65 (.32)	.37
Mean Values (Dollars)	11.95	11.48	34.03	24.07	42.71	33.84	6.508[c]	

[a] Conditional standard errors (given the ratio of mean price to predicted quantity) are given in parentheses. Actual standard errors would be larger since predicted quantity is a random variable dependent on all other parameter estimates in the equation.
[b] Prices are numbered consecutively in the same order as the equations are listed.
[c] In units of $1,000.

income at its mean value, be denoted by the vector equation (17). We now examine the computation of net benefits that would be received by the population of a specific subarea in the region surrounding the proposed lakes. Subareas used were cities over 5,000 population and counties with these cities excluded. A single point was chosen in each county from which all prices were estimated, and the center of each city was used as the reference point.

The first step is to get a measure of benefits per household and then multiply by the subarea population to get total benefits. Equation (17) is now defined as demand per household. Let P_0 and P_1 be the price vector before and after construction of the proposed lakes. A common theorem on line integrals tells us that the line integral on (17) between initial point P_1 and terminal point P_0 can be obtained by

$$(21) \qquad \tfrac{1}{2}P_0'BP_0 + a'P_0 - [\tfrac{1}{2}P_1'BP_1 + a'P_1]$$

if the function

$$(22) \qquad \tfrac{1}{2}P'BP + a'P$$

is single valued on the region containing P_0, P_1, and the curve used as the path of integration [**12**, *p.* 437]. Since (22) is a quadratic form, there is the question of whether it is single valued on the specified region. If (22) can be assumed single valued on the region of interest, Equation (21) is an estimate of net benefits associated with the proposed lakes (per household and for the particular subarea with which P_0 and P_1 are associated).

The vector Q of (17) is the gradient of Equation (22), and theoretically must be nonnegative, which would restrict the function (22) to a region where it is single valued. However, the statistically estimated equations have this property on a region that is difficult to delineate; and if it were known in detail, we still face the problem of what to do with a subarea when P_0 or P_1 yields some negative components in the quantity vector.

An attempt was made to improve on (21) by substituting zeros for negative components of Q_0 and Q_1, which are the quantity vectors computed from (17) for P equal to P_0 and P_1, respectively. These nonnegative quantity vectors were then used as the limits of a line integral of the demand equations in quantity-space, viz., Equation (7) defined for linear demand equations. Only three negative components were encountered out of about fifty subareas, and in each of these cases, only one component out of the five was negative.

Minimum distance to any one of three proposed lakes was used to derive a price for all subareas except those comprising metropolitan St. Louis. For the latter subareas, population is so large that the nearest lake would be badly overcrowded if all visitors used only it. Therefore, weighted average distances to all three lakes were used for the metropolitan subareas, with surface area of the lakes as weights.

Estimated annual net benefits that can be attributed to outdoor recreation at the three lakes are 8.5 million dollars and predicted household-visit-days are 1.1 million. Mean size of household parties making recreation trips was 3.2, which makes a predicted total of 3.5 million visitor-days at the three lakes. Total surface area of the three lakes is 22,900 acres which combined with predicted visitor-days implies 153 visitor-days per acre per year. This level of visits would appear not to cause serious crowding when compared to experienced visitor-days at comparable lakes.

A sensitivity analysis was performed on the social benefit calculation by re-estimating benefits with two other sets of demand equations. The set of demand estimates obtained by assuming homoscedastic disturbances (actually the initial set used in the iterative process to deal with heteroscedasticity) yielded estimated benefits of 8.8 million dollars, about 3.5 per cent more than that estimate considered best. Another set of equations fitted directly to the raw data, without even a transformation to adjust for nonzero covariances, gave estimated benefits of 9.1 million dollars, which is seven per cent greater than the best estimate of 8.5 million.

Needless to say, the stability experienced in the estimated benefits was encouraging. Estimated parameters in the system of demand equations were not particularly stable when viewed individually, but there was apparently a systematic change in the parameter estimates that gave the observed stability in benefits.

Each improvement in the estimation method for the set of demand equations (based on statistical theory) had a tendency to increase the cross-price-quantity coefficients relative to the direct-price-quantity coefficients (in absolute values). That is, improved estimation appeared to elicit the interdependencies among the various categories of recreation sites.

Initial cost of the three reservoirs was estimated by the Corps to be 95.4 million dollars (1965 revised estimate [13]). Flood control benefits are about 1.9 million dollars and annual operation and maintenance costs are estimated at $871,000 [13]. Taking 8.5 million dollars as the estimated annual net benefits from recreation,[7] the rate of return on the investment is ten per cent. The annual operation and maintenance costs include replacement charges amortized at an interest rate of 3.125 per cent, but the estimated life of the major investment components is one hundred years which makes the influence of replacement costs almost nil in the rate of return calculation. The ten per cent rate of return, with recreation benefits comprising over eighty per cent of the total annual benefits, illustrates the relevance of objective economic criteria for investment decisions in outdoor recreation.

Montana State University
and
University of Missouri, Columbia

Manuscript received April, 1969; revision received November, 1969.

APPENDIX

THE UNIT OF MEASURE FOR OUTDOOR RECREATION CONSUMPTION

Quantities of outdoor recreation services are measured in units of visitor-days (or alternatively in units of the counterpart for households instead of individuals). The literature on outdoor recreation economics abounds with discussions of the cost in time and inconvenience of traveling to the source of recreation services [1]. Since these costs are extremely nebulous to quantify, there is considerable advantage in defining the recreation unit in a way that avoids this indirect cost. We define the unit as total number of days at the recreation site *plus* travel time required to make the visit. Travel time can be a pleasure or a cost, depending on the scenery, road, traffic congestion, etc.; but it is an inseparable part of the recreation trip. In other words, travel time and the recreation experience itself are a package of commodities in the usual economic sense, and the consumer has no alternative to the particular package presented to him by his spatial location.

The situation is analogous to a consumer being refused a price quotation on a commodity that he wishes to purchase, but instead, he is quoted a price per unit of that commodity taken with so many units of another commodity. The second commodity may have either a positive or negative marginal utility to the consumer. As long as purchases have to be made in this fixed proportion, all value inferences can be made from the aggregate commodity.

This method of handling travel time in consumption of outdoor recreation services requires an assumption that the entire population faces comparable conditions of travel for a given distance. This assumption can be relaxed if the varied conditions are quantifiable and incorporated in the demand equations. For example, highway congestion in weekend travel might be introduced as a concommitant variable in the demand equation.

---

[7] The figure of 8.5 million dollars is biased downward somewhat by the problem with economic rents from land mentioned in footnote 3.

OUTDOOR RECREATION 827

REFERENCES

[1] CLAWSON, MARION: *Methods of Measuring the Demand for and Value of Outdoor Recreation.* Washington, D.C.: Resources for the Future, Inc., February, 1959.
[2] GOLDBERGER, ARTHUR S.: *Econometric Theory.* New York: Wiley, 1964.
[3] HOTELLING, HAROLD: "Edgeworth's Taxation Paradox and the Nature of Demand and Supply Functions," *Journal of Political Economy*, 40 (1932), 577–616.
[4] ——: "The General Welfare in Relation to Problems of Taxation and of Railway and Utility Rates," *Econometrica*, 6 (1938), 242–269.
[5] ——: A letter quoted by Roy E. Prewitt, *An Economic Study of the Monetary Evaluation of Recreation in the National Parks.* Washington: U.S. Department of Interior, National Park Service, 1949. (Quoted letter dated June 18, 1947.)
[6] KNETSCH, JACK L.: "Economics of Including Recreation as a Purpose of Eastern Water Projects," *Journal of Farm Economics*, 46 (1964), 1148–57.
[7] ——: "The Influence of Reservoir Projects on Land Values," *Journal of Farm Economics*, 46 (1964), 231–243.
[8] KRUTILLA, JOHN V.: "Welfare Aspects of Benefit-Cost Analysis," *Journal of Political Economy*, 69 (1961), 226–235.
[9] KRUTILLA, JOHN V., AND ROBERT H. HAVEMAN: "Unemployment, Excess Capacity, and Benefit Cost Investment Criteria," *Review of Economics and Statistics*, 47 (1967).
[10] MEREWITZ, LEONARD: "Recreational Benefits of Water Resource Development," *Water Resources Research*, 2 (1966), 625–640.
[11] SCHEFFE, HENRY: *The Analysis of Variance.* New York: Wiley, 1959.
[12] TAYLOR, ANGUS.: *Advanced Calculus.* New York: Ginn and Company, 1955.
[13] U.S. ARMY CORPS OF ENGINEERS: *Meramec River, Missouri: Comprehensive Basin Study.* U.S. Army Engineer District, St. Louis, Missouri, June, 1965.
[14] WOLD, HERMAN, AND LARS JUREEN: *Demand Analysis.* New York: Wiley, 1953.
[15] ZELLNER, ARNOLD, AND TONG HUN LEE: "Joint Estimation of Relationships Involving Discrete Random Variables," *Econometrica*, 33 (1965), 382–394.

[38]

A METHOD OF ESTIMATING SOCIAL BENEFITS FROM POLLUTION CONTROL

*Karl-Göran Mäler**

The Stockholm School of Economics, Stockholm, Sweden

I. Introduction

In an article in *Water Resources Research*, 1966 [3], Joe B. Stevens tried to estimate direct recreational benefits from water pollution control by using market demand curves for a sport fishery. The quality of the fishery was represented by the angling success per unit of effort. Water pollution would cause a deterioration in the quality, i.e. would decrease angling success. By estimating a demand function for the sport fishery, both as a function of the price of using the fishery and as a function of the quality variable, Stevens thought he could calculate the recreational benefits or the willingness to pay for maintaining constant quality, from various areas under the demand curves.

Stevens' idea, although a very sound one, was not developed in a rigorous way and his conclusions were therefore vague. The aim of this article is to develop a theory which can lend support to calculations such as those presented by Stevens.

The ideas in this article will first be presented intuitively in a non-rigorous way. Then Section III includes a brief review of elements from demand analysis and a statement of the marginal conditions for Pareto-optimality in an economy with public goods. A theoretical framework is developed in Section IV which enables derivation of the willingness to pay for public goods in certain cases on the basis of information on demand functions for private goods.

II. Intuitive Presentation of the Main Idea

It is natural to assume that if it is known that a public good is complementary to a private good, then it should be possible to calculate the demand for the public good if the demand for the private good is known. And if a public good is a perfect substitute for a private one, the consumers' preferences for the public good can be derived from the revealed preferences on the market.

A systematic study of the *a priori* conditions with regard to the preferences for a public good, obtained from complementariness and substitutability is

* I am very grateful to Professors P. Bohm, Clark Reynolds and Robert Solow for valuable comments and suggestions. This project was supported by the Ford Foundation and Stiftelsen Riksbankens Jubileumsfond.

122   K.-G. Mäler

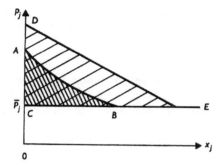

Fig. 1

required. We will not undertake this kind of study here, but instead discuss a single condition which seems realistic in some cases.

Consider a private good x_j, which can be produced in different qualities Y_k, but in only one quality at a time. The use of a fishery, for example, can be regarded as a private good. The quality of the fishery measured in terms of the catch of fish per unit of fishing time or the oxygen dissolved is a public good in the sense that all consumers using the fishery meet with the same quality. Those who do not use the fishery will generally be indifferent to quality changes. A single consumer will be indifferent to quality changes if the price of the corresponding private good is high enough to prevent him from using the fishery. This idea, simple as it is, provides an additional condition which can used for calculating the demand price for quality changes. (Note that if the private good can be supplied in different qualities at the same time, the quality ceases to be a public good. In this case we do not have one private good but many, each characterized by a certain quality.)

The condition can be stated mathematically in the following way: There exists a private good x_j and a public good Y_k such that

$$\frac{\partial u^h(x_1, \ldots, x_{j-1}, 0, x_{j+1}, \ldots, x_n, Y_1, \ldots, Y_m)}{\partial Y_k} = 0 \tag{1}$$

where u^h is the utility function of consumer h.

Assumption (1) implies that the demand price for Y_k can be calculated from the demand function for x_j. This can be observed intuitively as follows.

Consider the compensated demand curve AB for good j in Fig. 1. At the price $p_j = \bar{p}_j$, the consumer demands $\bar{x}_j$ and the consumer surplus is the cross-shaded area ABC. The consumer is thus willing to pay ABC in order to prevent a fall in the supply from $\bar{x}_j$ to zero.

Now consider a change in Y_k. This will cause the compensated demand curve to shift to DE. The new consumer surplus becomes the area CDE

(provided the price does not change). How much is the consumer willing to pay for the change in Y_k, that is how much is he willing to pay for the induced movement from B to E?

This movement can be divided into three steps:

(a) a change in p_j from C to D. In order not to put the consumer in a worse position, he has to be compensated by ABC.

(b) a change in Y_k. If we apply assumption (1), this change will not cause any need for compensation.

(c) a change in p_j from D to E. In order not to put the consumer in a beter position, he has to pay the amount CDE.

The net result is $CDE-ABC$ or the area $BADE$. The amount the consumer is willing to pay to obtain the change in Y_k is thus $BADE$.

Note that this calculation is impossible without assumption (1). If (1) is not applicable, the appropriate transfer in step (b) cannot be estimated. If the consumer is willing to offer something in order to improve the quality of x_j even if he does not consume x_j, then nothing can be said about his willingness to pay for a change on quality on the basis of his demand curve for x_j.

III. Summary of Results from Demand Analysis

This section contains a brief review of some elementary parts of demand analysis which are relevant to this study.

We assume that there are H consumers, each equipped with a utility function

$$u^h(x^h, Y) \quad h = 1, ..., H$$

where x^h is the vector of net demand for private goods (there are n private goods in the economy) and Y is the vector of public goods supplied (there are m public goods and each public good is characterized by the condition that an increase in the supply of the public good for one person means an identical increase in the supply to all other persons). In this context environmental quality is interpreted as a public good because the quality of the water in a stream is the same for everyone.

We assume that $u^h(x^h, Y)$ is twice continuously differentiable and that u^h is quasi concave. We denote the partial derivatives by subscripts:

$$\frac{\partial u^h}{\partial x_i} = u_i^h$$

$$\frac{\partial u^h}{\partial Y_k} = u_k^h.$$

124 *K.-G. Mäler*

Given the lump sum income I^h and the price vector $p \in R^n$, the budget set for the h:th consumer is defined by

$$M^h = \{x^h \mid p^T x^h \leqslant I^h, x^h \geqslant 0\}.^1$$

We can now study the two "dual" problems

$$\max\ u^h(x^h, Y)$$

s.t. $x^h \in M^h$

and

$$\min\ m^h = p^T x^h$$

s.t. $u^h(x^h, Y) \geqslant \bar{u}^n$.

The first order conditions for the problems are

$$u_i^h = \lambda^h p_i \quad i = 1, ..., n \tag{2}$$

and

$$\alpha^h u_i^h = p_i \quad i = 1, ..., n \tag{3}$$

where λ^h and α^h, respectively, are Lagrange multipliers for the two problems.

Solving the first order conditions for the first problem yields:

$$x^h = x^h(p, I^h, Y)$$
$$u^h = u^h(x^h(p, I^h, Y), Y) = v^h(p, I^h, Y)$$

and for the second problem

$$x^h = x^{h+}(p, \bar{u}^h, Y)$$
$$m^h = p^T x^{h+}(p, \bar{u}^h, Y) = m^h(p, \bar{u}^h, Y).$$

x^h is the usual Marshallian demand function and v^h is called the indirect utility function. x^h is the Hicksian compensated demand function and m^h is called the expenditure function.

We need the following results (for proofs see e.g. Karlin, Ch. 8 [1])

(a) m^h is a concave function in p

(b) $x^h(p, m^h(p, \bar{u}^h, Y), Y) = x^{h+}(p, \bar{u}^h, Y)$, that is, if income is varied so that the consumer is always on the same indifference curve, then the compensated demand functions are obtained from the Marshallian demand functions.

---

[1] A vector x is interpreted as a column vector and transposition of a vector to a row vector will be denoted by the symbol $\top$. We use the following conventions for vector inequalities:
$x \geqslant 0$ if $x_i \geqslant 0$ for all components x_i
$x \geqslant 0$ if $x \geqslant 0$ and $x \neq 0$
$x > 0$ if $x_i > 0$ for all components x_i.

(c) the Slutsky equations:

$$\frac{\partial^2 m^h}{\partial p_i \partial p_j} - \frac{\partial x_i^h}{\partial I^h}\frac{\partial m^h}{\partial p_j} - \frac{\partial x_i^h}{\partial p_j} = 0, \quad i,j = 1,...,n. \tag{4}$$

The Slutsky equations give the expenditure function as a solution to a system of (not independent) differential equations. The boundary conditions are

$$m^h(\bar{p}, \bar{u}^h, \overline{Y}) = I^h$$

$$\frac{\partial m^h(\bar{p}, \bar{u}^h, \overline{Y})}{\partial p_i} = x_i^h(\bar{p}, I^h, \overline{Y}) \quad i = 1,...,n$$

where $\bar{u}^h = v^h(\bar{p}, I^h, \overline{Y})$ and $\bar{p}, \overline{Y}$ are the prices and the supply of public goods in the initial situation.

If the Marshallian demand function $x^h(p, I^h, Y)$ are known, we can solve the Slutsky equations and determine m as a function of p. But without further assumptions m as a function of Y cannot be determined.

Let us now turn to the problem of aggregation of expenditure functions. The demand functions for consumer h are

$$x^h(p, I^h, Y).$$

The aggregate demand functions are

$$X(p, I^1,...,I^H, Y) = \sum_{h=1}^{H} x^h(p, I^h, Y).$$

A necessary and sufficient condition for writing this aggregate demand function as a function of the aggregate income $I = \Sigma_{h=1}^{H} I^h$, instead of the individual incomes for arbitrary variations in income, is that all individuals have the same marginal propensity to demand out of income. Let us therefore assume that the individual demand functions are of the form

$$x_i^h = x_i^h(p, I^h, Y), \qquad \frac{\partial x_i^h}{\partial I^h} = \frac{\partial x_i^k}{\partial I^k} = \beta_i; \quad h, k = 1,...,H, \quad i = 1,...,n.$$

We can then aggregate to

$$X_i = X_i(p, I, Y)$$

where

$$I = \sum_{h=1}^{H} I^h, \qquad \frac{\partial X_i}{\partial I} = \beta_i.$$

Let us now define the aggregate expenditure function m as

$$m = \sum_{h=1}^{H} m^h.$$

126   K.-G. Mäler

Then

$$\frac{\partial m}{\partial p_i} = \sum_{h=1}^{H} \frac{\partial m^h}{\partial p_i}$$

and

$$\frac{\partial^2 m}{\partial p_i \partial p_j} = \sum_{h=1}^{H} \frac{\partial^2 m^h}{\partial p_i \partial p_j} = \sum_{h=1}^{H} \left\{ \frac{\partial x_i^h}{\partial I^h} \frac{\partial m^h}{\partial p_j} + \frac{\partial x_i^h}{\partial p_j} \right\} = \sum_{h=1}^{H} \left\{ \beta_i \frac{\partial m^h}{\partial p_j} + \frac{\partial x_i^h}{\partial p_j} \right\} = \beta_i \frac{\partial m}{\partial p_j} + \frac{\partial X_i}{\partial p_j}$$

and the aggregate expenditure function also satisfies the differential equations (4). Thus the condition for consistent aggregation of demand fumctions for arbitrary variations in individual incomes is also the conditions for consistent aggregation of expenditure functions. From now on it is assumed that this condition is fulfilled.

Samuelson [2] has shown that for a Pareto optimum in an economy with public goods, the following condition must be satisfied:

$$\sum_{h=1}^{H} \frac{\partial u^h}{\partial Y_k} \Big/ \frac{\partial u^h}{\partial x_i^h} = MC_k^i$$

where MC_k^i is the social marginal opportunity cost of producing the public good Y_k in terms of production of the private good x_i.

Let the price of commodity 1 be p_1 and put

$$\delta_k^h = p_1 \frac{\partial u^h}{\partial Y_k} \Big/ \frac{\partial u^h}{\partial x_1^h}.$$

∂_k^h will be interpreted as consumer h's demand price for the public good k. The purpose of this paper is to discuss one way of estimating the total demand price

$$\delta_k = \sum_{h=1}^{H} \delta_k^h$$

for the public good k.

Obviously, the total demand price will be a function of the price vector p, the incomes $I^1, \ldots, I^H$ and the vector of public goods supplied Y:

$$\delta_k = \sum_{h=1}^{H} \delta_k^h = \sum_{h=1}^{H} g_k^h(p, I^h, Y).$$

The expenditure function for consumer h is

$$m^h(p, \bar{u}^h, Y) = p^T x^{h+}.$$

If we differentiate the condition $u^h = \bar{u}^h$ with respect to Y_k we have

$$\sum_{i=1}^{n} u_i^h \frac{\partial x_i}{\partial Y_k} + \frac{\partial u^h}{\partial Y_k} = 0.$$

We also know that $\alpha^h u_i^h = p_i$ so that

$$\frac{\partial m^h}{\partial Y_k} = \sum_{i=1}^n p_i \frac{\partial x_i^{h+}}{\partial Y_k} = \alpha^h \sum_{i=1}^n u_i^h \frac{\partial x_i^{h+}}{\partial Y_k} = -\alpha^h \frac{\partial u^h}{\partial Y_k} = -p_1 \frac{\partial u^h}{\partial Y_k} \bigg/ \frac{\partial u^h}{\partial x_1^h} = -\delta_k^h.$$

The same relation holds for the total demand price

$$\frac{\partial m}{\partial Y_k} = -\delta_k.$$

The marginal willingness to pay or the demand price for the public good can therefore be estimated by estimating the expenditure function as a function of Y. But it was noted above that this is impossible if the only information we have consists of the demand functions for private goods. Thus further assumptions have to be added in order to solve our problem.

IV. Estimating Demand Prices for Public Goods

Note that assumption (1) is invariant for monotonic transformations of the utility function. In fact, let F be any monotonic increasing function. Then

$$\frac{\partial F(u^h(x_1, ..., 0, ..., x_n, Y))}{\partial Y_k} = F' \frac{\partial u^h(x_1, ..., 0, ..., x_n, Y)}{\partial Y_k}.$$

Note also that (1) is equivalent to

$$\frac{\partial m(p', \bar{u}, Y)}{\partial Y_k} = 0 \tag{5}$$

where p' is the price vector which causes a zero compensated demand for x_j, that is $x_j^+ = 0$ (for simplicity the superscript h is dropped).

Assume that there is a pair x_j, Y_k such that (1) is true. Let us now aggregate all other private goods to a composite good z with a price p_z and denote x_j by x. As the supply of all public goods except Y_k is going to be held constant, we can drop the corresponding variables and denote Y_k by Y.

The demand function for x can then be written

$$x = x(p_x, p_z, I, Y).$$

Consider the first equation in (3):

$$\frac{\partial^2 m}{\partial p_x^2} - \frac{\partial x(p_x, p_z, m, Y)}{\partial I} \frac{\partial m}{\partial p_x} - \frac{\partial x(p_x, p_z, m, Y)}{\partial p_x} = 0.$$

The general solution to this equation will have the form

$$m = \psi(p_x, p_z, Y, \varphi_1, \varphi_2) \tag{6}$$

128   *K.-G. Mäler*

where φ_1 and φ_2 are functions of p_z and Y.

The initial conditions are

$$\psi(\bar{p}_z, \bar{p}_z, \overline{Y}, \varphi_1, \varphi_2) = I$$

$$\frac{\partial \psi(\bar{p}_z, \bar{v}_z, \overline{Y}, \varphi_1, \varphi_2)}{\partial p_z} = x(\bar{p}_z, \bar{p}_z, I, \overline{Y})$$

where $\bar{p}_z$, $\bar{p}_z$, Y are the prices and supply of the public good in the initial situation. By solving the initial conditions the values of φ_1 and φ_2 in the initial situation can be obtained.

Note that the compensated demand function for x is given by

$$x^+ = \frac{\partial m}{\partial p_z} = \varkappa(p_z, p_z, Y, \varphi_1, \varphi_2).$$

Denote the inverse function by

$$p_z = h_z(x^+, p_z, Y, \varphi_1, \varphi_2).$$

Because the substitution effect is always negative, we know that this function always exists.

This function enables us to find those prices for which x^+ is zero:

$$p_z \geqslant p_z' = h_z(0, p_z, Y, \varphi_1, \varphi_2).$$

If we substitute this in (6) we obtain

$$m(p_z, p_z, Y) = m(p_z', p_z, Y) = \psi(h_z(0, p_z, Y, \psi_1, \varphi_2)) p_z, Y, \varphi_1, \varphi_2) \qquad (7)$$

for $p_z \geqslant p_z'$.

Assumption (5) can now be applied. If assumption (1) or (5) holds, then the derivative of (7) with respect to Y is zero:

$$\frac{dm}{dY} = \frac{\partial \psi}{\partial p_z} \frac{\partial h_z}{\partial Y} + \frac{\partial \psi}{\partial Y} + \frac{\partial \psi}{\partial \varphi_1} \frac{\partial \varphi_1}{\partial Y} + \frac{\partial \psi}{\partial \varphi_2} \frac{\partial \varphi_2}{\partial Y} = 0. \qquad (8)$$

This is a differential equation in the two unknown functions φ_1 and φ_2 .But (8) is an identity in p_z which implies that (8) can be differentiated with respect to p_z so as to obtain one more equation.

We thus have two differential equations in the two unknowns $\varphi_1(Y)$ and $\varphi_2(Y)$. By solving these two equations, m is determined wholly as function of p_z and Y. By utilizing standard theorems on the existence and uniqueness of solutions to differential equations we see that the solution obtained is the desired expenditure function.

This analysis has, however, been carried out under one implicit assumption, i.e. that the demand function for x has Y as an argument. If this is not the case, the differential equation (8) cannot be established. Later on it will be shown that this is an exception which is not likely to occur.

The following simple example will be used to clarify the procedure outlined above.

Suppose we have obtained estimates of the demand functions

$$x = I/2p_x - aY/2$$

$$z = I/2p_z + p_x aY/2p_z$$

where a is some positive constant.

The differential equations (3) become

$$\frac{\partial^2 m}{\partial p_x^2} - \frac{1}{2p_x}\frac{\partial m}{\partial p_x} + \frac{m}{2p_x^2} = 0$$

$$\frac{\partial^2 m}{\partial p_x \partial p_z} - \frac{1}{2p_z}\frac{\partial m}{\partial p_x} = \frac{aY}{2p_z}.$$

By substitution we see that

$$m = \varphi_1(p_z, Y) p_x^{\frac{1}{2}} + \varphi_2(p_z, Y) p_x$$

is a solution to the first equation. If this expression is substituted for m in the second equation, we obtain

$$\frac{1}{2}\frac{\partial \varphi_1}{\partial p_z} p_x^{-\frac{1}{2}} + \frac{\partial \varphi_2}{\partial p_z} - \frac{1}{4p_z}\varphi_1 p_x^{-\frac{1}{2}} - \frac{1}{2p_z}\varphi_2 = \frac{aY}{2p_z}.$$

Because both φ_1 and φ_2 are indepedent of p_x, this yields two equations

$$\frac{\partial \varphi_1}{\partial p_z} - \frac{1}{2p_z}\varphi_1 = 0$$

and

$$\frac{\partial \varphi_2}{\partial p_z} - \frac{1}{2p_z}\varphi_2 = \frac{aY}{2p_z}.$$

The solutions are

$$\varphi_1 = f(Y) p_z^{\frac{1}{2}}$$

$$\varphi_2 = C(Y) p_z^{\frac{1}{2}} - aY$$

where $f(Y)$ and $C(Y)$ are undetermined functions. However, if assumption (5) is applied, these functions can be determined.

The expenditure function is

$$m = f p_z^{\frac{1}{2}} p_x^{\frac{1}{2}} + C p_z p_x^{\frac{1}{2}} - a p_x Y$$

and the compensated demand function for x is

$$x^+ = \frac{\partial m}{\partial p_x} = \frac{1}{2} f p_x^{-\frac{1}{2}} p_z^{\frac{1}{2}} + C p_z^{\frac{1}{2}} - aY.$$

130   *K.-G. Måler*

The compensated demand for x is zero when

$$p_z \geqslant p_z' = \frac{1}{4} \frac{f^2}{Y^2} \frac{p_z}{(a - p_z^{\frac{1}{2}} C/Y)^2}.$$

For $p_z \geqslant p_z'$ the expenditure function becomes

$$m(p_x, p_z, Y) = m(p_x', p_z, Y) = \frac{1}{2} \frac{f^2}{Y} \frac{p_z}{(a - p_z^{\frac{1}{2}} C/Y)}$$

$$+ \frac{1}{4} \frac{f^2}{Y} \frac{p_z}{(a - p_z^{\frac{1}{2}} C/Y)^2} \frac{C}{Y} p_z^{\frac{1}{2}} - \frac{1}{4} \frac{f^2}{Y} \frac{p_z}{(a - p_z^{\frac{1}{2}} C/Y)} a = \frac{1}{2} \frac{f^2}{Y} \frac{p_z}{(a - p_z^{\frac{1}{2}} C/Y)}.$$

If assumption (5) is true, then $m(p_x, p_z, Y)$ with $p_x \geqslant p_x'$, has to be independent of Y for all p_z. This can only be true if

$$f(Y) = A Y^{\frac{1}{2}}$$

and

$$C(Y) = BY$$

This means that the expenditure function becomes

$$m = A \sqrt{p_x p_z Y} + (B \sqrt{p_z} - a) p_z Y.$$

The constants A and B can be determined from the initial conditions. If this is done, we find that

$$A = \frac{I + \bar{p}_z \bar{Y}}{\sqrt{\bar{p}_x \bar{p}_z \bar{Y}}}$$

$$B = 0$$

and

$$m = A \sqrt{p_x p_z Y} - a p_z Y.$$

It can easily be proved that A is the indirect utility function. Then

$$\frac{\partial A}{\partial I} = \frac{1}{\sqrt{\bar{p}_x \bar{p}_z \bar{Y}}} = \lambda$$

$$\frac{\partial A}{\partial p_x} = \frac{1}{\sqrt{\bar{p}_x \bar{p}_z \bar{Y}}} \left[\frac{I}{2\bar{p}_x} - \frac{aY}{2} \right] = -\lambda x$$

$$\frac{\partial A}{\partial p_z} = \frac{1}{\sqrt{\bar{p}_x \bar{p}_z \bar{Y}}} \left[\frac{I}{2\bar{p}_z} + \frac{a\bar{p}_x \bar{Y}}{2\bar{p}_z} \right] = -\lambda z$$

A method of estimating social benefits from pollution control 131

(where λ is the Lagrange multiplier in (2)) can be used to solve for $\bar{p}_x$, $\bar{p}_z$ and I in terms of x, z, λ and $\bar{Y}$:

$$\bar{p}_x = \frac{1}{\lambda} z^{\frac{1}{2}} Y^{-\frac{1}{2}} (x + aY)^{-\frac{1}{2}}$$

$$\bar{p}_z = \frac{1}{\lambda} z^{-\frac{1}{2}} Y^{-\frac{1}{2}} (x + aY)^{\frac{1}{2}}$$

$$I = (2x + aY) \frac{1}{\lambda} z^{\frac{1}{2}} Y^{-\frac{1}{2}} (x + aY)^{-\frac{1}{2}}.$$

By substituting these expressions back into A, the original utility function is obtained (if the demand functions are those of a single individual):

$$u = 2(x + aY)^{\frac{1}{2}} z^{\frac{1}{2}} Y^{-\frac{1}{2}}.$$

The utility function has thus been derived on the basis of the demand functions for private goods by only assuming (5).

This example illustrates the technique of using assumption (5) to derive the expenditure function as a function of the public good Y. But the method fails if the differential equations (3) cannot be established. If the demand for x is a function of Y, then we have shown that (8) can be obtained by means of a routine calculation. The theorems on uniqueness of solutions to differential equations guarantee that the expenditure function ultimately derived is the correct one. But in the case where x is not a function of Y, (8) cannot be established and there is no possible way of deriving the expenditure function as a function of Y. But I will argue here that when the utility function is such that x does not depend on Y, assumption (5) is not likely to be realistic.

First, let us investigate the conditions under which the demand for a commodity does not depend on the amount of the public good.

Differentiating the optimality conditions (2) with respect to Y yields

$$u_{11} \frac{\partial x}{\partial Y} + u_{12} \frac{\partial z}{\partial Y} - p_x \frac{\partial \lambda}{\partial Y} = -u_{13}$$

$$u_{21} \frac{\partial x}{\partial Y} + u_{22} \frac{\partial z}{\partial Y} - p_z \frac{\partial \lambda}{\partial Y} = -u_{23}$$

$$-p_x \frac{\partial x}{\partial Y} - p_z \frac{\partial z}{\partial Y} = 0.$$

Let D be the determinant of coefficients in this equation system. Then the solutions for $\partial x / \partial Y$ and $\partial z / \partial Y$ are

$$\frac{\partial x}{\partial Y} = \frac{p_z}{D} (p_z u_{13} - p_x u_{23})$$

$$\frac{\partial z}{\partial Y} = -\frac{p_x}{D} (p_z u_{13} - p_x u_{23}).$$

132   *K.-G. Mäler*

The condition for $\partial x/\partial Y = \partial z/\partial Y = 0$ is

$p_z u_{13} - p_x u_{23} = 0.$

Due to (2) and because this is an identity, it can be written as

$$\frac{u_1}{u_{13}} = \frac{u_2}{u_{23}}$$

or

$$\frac{\partial}{\partial Y} \log u_1 = \frac{\partial}{\partial Y} \log u_2$$

which gives us

$\log u_1 = \log (B(x, z)u_2)$

where $B(x, z)$ is an arbitrary function of x and z.

This equation is equivalent to

$u_1 - B(x, z) u_2 = 0$

which is a partial differential equation of the first order, the characteristic of which is given by

$$dx + \frac{dz}{B(x,z)} = 0.$$

If B is differentiable, this equation has a solution which is given by

$\varphi(x, z) = C$

where C is an arbitrary integration constant.

The general solution to the partial differential equation can now be written

$u = f(\varphi(x, z), Y)$

where φ satisfies

$$\frac{\partial z}{\partial x} = -B(x, z).$$

If assumption (1) is now applied we find that

$f_2(\varphi(0, z), Y) = 0.$

Since this relation holds for all z, by differentiating with respect to z we find that

$f_{21} \varphi_2(0, z) = 0.$

Swed. J. of Economics 1971

A method of estimating social benefits from pollution control 133

$f_{21} = 0$ is not a property which is invariant for monotone increasing transformations, so (if we want to stick to an ordinal approach)

$$\varphi_2(0, z) = 0$$

or

$$\frac{\partial}{\partial z} u(0, z, Y) = \frac{\partial}{\partial Y} u(0, z, Y) = 0.$$

This relation shows that if consumption of x is zero, then the consumer is indifferent to how much of the composite commodity z he consumes. This is a very strong statement about a certain complementariness between x and z. The assumption that the demand for private goods does not depend on the supply of the public good combined with (1) therefore yields a conclusion which is not likely to be realistic.

With respect to the type of analysis discussed here, cases where the demand for private goods does not depend on the supply of the public good can be disregarded with a high degree of confidence.

References

1. Karlin, S.: *Mathematical Methods and Theory in Games, Programming, and Economics*, Vol. I. Addison-Wesley, 1959.
2. Samuelson, P.: The pure theory of public expenditure. *Review of Economics and Statistics XXXVI*, no. 4, November, 1954.
3. Stevens, J.: Recreation benefits from water pollution control. *Water Resources Research*, Vol. 2, Second Quarter, 1966.

[39]

Welfare Measurement in the Household Production Framework

By NANCY E. BOCKSTAEL AND KENNETH E. MCCONNELL*

The household production approach to consumer behavior, developed from the work of Gary Becker, William Gorman, and Kelvin Lancaster, has considerable descriptive appeal in modelling the decisions of households. The approach derives from the observation that households frequently purchase market goods that do not yield utility directly, but are combined to produce commodity service flows which the household values. Thus observed behavior is determined by household production technology as well as by tastes. The advantage of this distinction is that we can pose reasonable hypotheses about characteristics of technology, though we rarely possess useful a priori information regarding tastes.

The putative advantages of the household production approach are questioned on empirical and conceptual grounds by Robert Pollak and Michael Wachter (1975). They show that jointness in production or nonconstant returns to scale cause implicit commodity prices to depend on both tastes and technology, raising serious econometric difficulties in the estimation of commodity demand functions. In addition, since commodity prices become functions of the commodity bundle consumed, the analogy to traditional demand theory breaks down.

Joint production occurs when a good enters several production processes simultaneously, or, equivalently, when a good in one production process also enters directly into the individual's utility function. The most common example is time, which provides the

context for all production processes and is often associated with the production of several commodities simultaneously. Since joint production in the household is likely to be pervasive, the critique by Pollak and Wachter cannot be ignored. In response to the comment by William Barnett, Pollak and Wachter (1977) suggest dispensing with the notion of commodity prices and treating the demand for commodities as a function of goods prices. This approach confounds tastes and technology, but it eliminates the troublesome concept of commodity prices as parameters when, in fact, they are likely to be endogenous.

In this paper we show that results from positive analysis, such as the critique by Pollak and Wachter, have implications for the use of the household production framework for welfare analysis. The household production function approach has had considerable appeal for measuring welfare effects of public actions in the environmental and natural resource areas (Gardner Brown, John Charbonneau, and Michael Hay; Elizabeth Wilman). Yet traditional approaches to welfare measurement are frequently inapplicable. We argue that welfare measurement in this framework is complicated by the difficulties of unravelling tastes and technology.

We extend Pollak and Wachter's results by demonstrating that Marshallian demand functions for commodities cannot be uniquely defined. Thus Marshallian functions cannot be used to derive exact compensated functions in the manner of Jerry Hausman, and of George McKenzie and I. F. Pearce, nor can compensating and equivalent variation measures be bounded by Marshallian consumer's surplus estimates following Robert Willig. In fact, duality results that normally allow us to move between Marshallian and Hicksian functions are not

*Assistant and Associate Professors, respectively, Department of Agricultural and Resource Economics, University of Maryland, College Park, MD 20742. This paper is Scientific Article No. A3404, Contribution No. 6476, of the Maryland Agricultural Experiment Station. We wish to thank Darrell Hueth, James Opaluch, V. Kerry Smith, and Elizabeth Wilman for comments on an earlier draft.

applicable for commodities in the household production framework.

Because Marshallian demand functions for household produced commodities are not unique, we are forced to develop welfare measures from observations on purchases of goods; that is, inputs into the household's production process. We show that under appropriate conditions, changes in the area under the demand curve for goods can serve as welfare measures for changes in the quantities of public goods. This finding is related to Hajime Hori's result that when all technology is known, the demand for public goods can be inferred from the purchases of private goods. However we develop a basis for measuring the value of public goods which, unlike Hori's measure, does not require that we know a priori the household technology. All the information that is required will be embodied in the derived demand for goods. Thus we show that the goods market is the only market which provides an indirect means of valuing changes in public goods.

The following three sections provide the three principal results of the paper. In Section I, we show that traditionally conceived Marshallian demands are not uniquely defined in this approach. In Section II, we show, in contrast, that utility-constant marginal value functions that are dependent only on preferences and not technology do exist and have the usual normative interpretation. Regardless of joint production or nonconstant returns to scale, the area behind the marginal value and marginal cost curves measures economic surplus. Changes in this area measure welfare effects associated with changes in the individual's economic environment. In Section III, we show that equivalent measures of welfare change can often be obtained in the market for goods which serve as inputs into the household production process. This result is analogous to the work by Richard Just, Darrell Hueth, and Andrew Schmitz, and by Just and Hueth, who show that in competitive markets, welfare changes can be measured in the markets for inputs or outputs. Additionally, we are able to obtain these measures of welfare without assuming that technology is known. Thus we provide a new conceptual basis for welfare measurement of nonmarket goods.

I. Positive Economics and the Household Production Function

An economic model is a useful positive tool if it implies theorems about behavior which can be tested. We argue that very little structure and a paucity of testable hypotheses emerge from the household production function. This argument is consonant with the results of Pollak and Wachter, who argue that commodity demand as a function of commodity price is not a meaningful concept. We expand their arguments by demonstrating that a unique Marshallian demand curve, as traditionally conceived, cannot be derived for commodities produced in the household production framework. In addition, we argue that commodity demands as a function of goods prices provide few qualitatively predictable results.

To characterize the household production approach, suppose that the consumer enjoys an m-dimensional bundle of commodities z which enters the quasi-concave preference function $u(z)$. Goods, denoted $x = (x_1, \ldots, x_n)$, are purchased at market prices, denoted $r = (r_1, \ldots, r_n)$, and are combined to produce the commodities according to the production process $t(z, x) = 0$. One of the x's will typically be time and can take some function of the wage rate as its price. Joint production occurs when the technology implied by $t(z, x)$ cannot be expressed in terms of separate production functions. We do not rule out joint production nor the possibility of nonconstant returns to scale.

Positive analysis derives from the solution to the representative household's income-constrained problem

$$(1) \qquad \max u(z),$$

subject to $C(z, r) - y = 0,$

where the joint cost function $C(z, r) = \min_x \{ r \cdot x | t(z, x) = 0 \}$ and y is money income. In general, the budget constraint will be nonlinear in the z's, and the marginal costs of commodities will be functions of the commodity bundle chosen.

Because the Marshallian demand curve has held such a central position in comparative statics and normative analysis, there have been strenuous efforts to derive this concept from the first-order conditions of problem (1). In its traditional formulation, the Marshallian demand function relates the quantity of a commodity purchased to the price of the commodity, with money income, prices of other commodities, and all other relevant variables assumed constant. The demand curve is traced out by recording the amount of the commodity the consumer would be willing to purchase at each price.

In the household production formulation, the marginal cost of producing the commodity is analogous to price in the traditional case. The marginal cost of producing a commodity is not in general constant, however, and as such does not encode all the necessary information required to ensure that all first-order conditions, including the budget constraint, will be satisfied. Holding income and other marginal cost functions constant, we attempt to trace out a Marshallian demand curve for a commodity by altering the cost of the final unit consumed of that commodity. This approach, however, cannot uniquely define the quantity consumed unless it incorporates knowledge of the entire cost function (and thus technology) or specific assumptions about how the cost function changes with changes in marginal costs.

By way of demonstration, consider the following expression for the cost function. Suppose that when no commodities are produced, costs are zero, $C(0, r) = 0$. Then there exists a θ in the unit interval such that

$$(2) \quad C(z, r) = \sum_i C_i(z, r) z_i$$
$$- \sum_i \sum_j C_{ij}(z(1 - \theta), r) z_i z_j / 2.$$

From this relationship, the first-order conditions of problem (1) become

$$(3) \quad u_i(z) - \lambda C_i(z, r) = 0 \ \forall i,$$
$$y - \sum_i C_i(z, r) z_i$$
$$+ \sum_i \sum_j C_{ij}(z(1 - \theta), r) z_i z_j / 2 = 0,$$

where λ is the multiplier associated with the budget constraint. Unless the production function is nonjoint and homogeneous of degree one, the C_{ij} in (3) will be nonzero.

Now suppose we attempt to trace out a Marshallian demand curve by asking the question: how much will be purchased at different levels of marginal cost (C_i)? If the hypothetical changes in marginal cost are generated by changes in input (goods) prices or other parameters of the cost function, they will, except in special instances, alter C_{ij} terms as well as other marginal cost functions through changes in the z vector. Changes in these additional terms in the budget constraint will make it impossible to define uniquely, at each marginal cost, a level of demand for which the income constraint holds.

A related and equally debilitating aspect of the household production function is that few qualitative comparative statics results are generated. In general, the decision function for a choice variable is obtained by differentiating the decision maker's indirect objective function with respect to an economic parameter. In such cases, appealing to second-order conditions (specifically, the curvature properties of the utility-constant expenditure function) allows us to sign the change in the choice variable with a change in the parameter.

In the household production approach, however, the expenditure function, defined as

$$m(r, u^0) = \min_z \{C(z, r) | u(z) = u^0\},$$

fails to yield comparative static results. The joint cost function $C(z, r)$ will not in general be linearly homogeneous in z. Thus, there will be no parameter β such that $\partial m / \partial \beta = z_k$ and ordinary envelope theorem derivations will not follow. As a consequence there are no a priori expectations on the sign of any $\partial z_i / \partial r_k$. Pollak and Wachter's suggestion that the demand for commodities be analyzed in terms of goods prices rather than commodity prices will yield constructs which are useful for prediction but which provide no hypotheses regarding the signs of any coefficients in commodity demand functions.

The nonlinearity of the cost function also prevents the Cournot and Engel aggregations from providing useful restrictions on demand systems. Analogous to these "adding-up" theorems, we can derive the following from the constraint $C(z, r) - y = 0$ and from the fact that $C(z, r) = r \cdot x$:

$$\sum_{i=1}^{m} z_i C_i \eta_i / y = 1$$

and $$\sum_{k=1}^{n} \sum_{i=1}^{m} z_i C_i \varepsilon_{ik} / y = -1,$$

where $\varepsilon_{ik} = \partial \log z_i / \partial \log r_k$ and $\eta_i = \partial \log z_i / \partial \log y$. Unlike the standard neoclassical case with fixed prices, the ratios $z_i C_i / y$ depend on technology, do not in general sum to one, and do not possess the useful interpretation of budget shares. Only the homogeneity restrictions $\sum_{k=1}^{n} \varepsilon_{ik} = -\eta_i$ are retained.

Thus two conclusions arise in the positive economics setting. First, a unique Marshallian demand curve for commodities does not exist. Second, theory fails to provide useful prior restrictions on any function which relates consumption of the z's to parameters in the system.

II. Welfare Analysis in the Commodity Market

Pollak recognized that economists may wish to "use a household production framework to analyze the harm done by air pollution or the benefits of an outdoor recreation or child health project..." (1978, p. 286). This approach, depending as it does on the distinction between purchased goods and consumed commodities, has particular appeal for measuring nonmarket benefits derived from public goods (see, for example, Hori and Wilman). However the conceptual limitations discussed above preclude the straightforward application of well-known welfare measurement techniques in the household production framework.

Work by Willig, Hausman, and others employs duality results to demonstrate that, because of the link through the expenditure and utility functions, the unobserved compensated demand function can always be derived from knowledge of the observable Marshallian function. In the household production function approach, the fact that Marshallian demands are not unique prevents us from using duality to derive the compensated demand function. It also suggests that the compensated function may be undefined.

In this section we demonstrate three results. First, we argue that unlike Marshallian demand curves, compensated demand curves which reflect households' marginal valuations of the commodity do exist, independent of the cost function for producing commodities. Second, we derive a measure of surplus associated with a commodity as the area between the marginal cost and marginal value curves in commodity space. Finally, we demonstrate that the well-established conditions for measuring the compensating variation of a change in an exogenous (for example, publicly supplied) factor are applicable in this framework.

When the household is viewed as minimizing the cost of obtaining a given utility level, independent marginal value and marginal cost functions are identifiable. Consider the utility-constrained, cost-minimization problem

$$\min_{z} \{ C(z, r) | u^0 = u(z) \}$$

which produces the first-order conditions

$$C_i(z, r) - \mu u_i(z) = 0 \forall i,$$

$$u^0 - u(z) = 0,$$

where μ is the multiplier associated with the constraint on utility. These first-order conditions could be solved for reduced-form demand functions for the z's as functions of goods prices, and technological and preference parameters. They also, however, allow for the determination of independent marginal cost and value functions. To see this, we need only recognize that the above problem is equivalent to one where an imaginary market with fixed parameter prices intervenes between the production and consumption activities of the household. Since the budget constraint is not required to hold along the compensated demand curve, the system of compensated curves is not dependent on the total cost function. Consequently the circumstances which cause the Marshallian curve to be ambiguous in this framework do not directly affect the compensated demand curve.

We are prevented from deriving the Marshallian curve from the compensated curve by the absence of exogenous prices. Both the utility and expenditure functions exist, but the absence of prices prevents the use of Roy's Identity to derive the Marshallian curve from the indirect utility function. Also, it is impossible to move from a compensated demand function to a unique expenditure function because of the nonlinearity of the cost function. Several different cost functions (generated by different technologies), and thus different expenditure functions, can be associated with the same values of marginal costs.

Nonetheless, theoretical welfare measures can be derived in commodity space but in a way which differs from the traditional approach. For simplicity we focus on a measure for z_1, though any z_i could be chosen. Partition the commodities such that $z = (z_1, \bar{z})$ where $\bar{z} = (z_2, \ldots, z_n)$. Derive an expenditure function conditional on the level of z_1 (as though z_1 were temporarily fixed) such that

$$(4) \quad E(z_1, r, u^0)$$
$$= \min_{\bar{z}} \{ C(z_1, \bar{z}, r) | u^0 = u(z_1, \bar{z}) \}.$$

By the envelope theorem,

$$(5) \quad \partial E(z_1, r, u^0) / \partial z_1$$
$$= -\left(\mu u_1(z_1, \bar{z}^*, u^0) - C_1(z_1, \bar{z}^*, r) \right),$$

where $\bar{z}^* = \bar{z}^*(z_1, r, u^0)$ are adjusted optimally as z_1, r, and u^0 change. The first term on the right is the compensated marginal value function for z_1.[1] The second term is the

marginal cost of producing z_1. Since expression (5) reflects the change in expenditures necessary to maintain utility level u^0 as z_1 increases, this expression will be negative for $z_1 < z_1^*$, the optimal quantity of z_1. Note that when z_1 is adjusted optimally, expression (5) equals zero and the conditional expenditure function in (4) reduces to the traditional expenditure function, since

$$(6) \quad E(z_1^*(r, u^0), r, u^0) = m(r, u^0).$$

Using the function $E(z_1, r, u^0)$, we can compute the compensating variation associated with consuming z_1^*. This measure reflects the change in income which would keep the consumer at his initial utility level, a situation with no access to z_1, if he were subsequently given the opportunity to consume z_1^* at input prices, r, and given technology. The measure is calculated by integrating (5) from 0 to z_1^* yielding

$$(7) \quad \int_0^{z_1^*} \left[\partial E(z_1, r, u^0) / \partial z_1 \right] dz_1$$
$$= E(z_1^*, r, u^0) - E(0, r, u^0).$$

This expression is the negative of the area between the compensated marginal value and marginal cost functions for z_1, where that area can be expressed as

$$(8) \quad A = \int_0^{z_1^*} \left[\mu u_1(z_1, \bar{z}^*, u^0) \right.$$
$$\left. - C_1(z_1, \bar{z}^*, r) \right] dz_1.$$

Thus graphical measures of welfare exist in concept in the commodity market.

---

[1] It might be argued that one can integrate this inverse compensated demand function back to the distance function and then use the distance function to derive the Marshallian marginal value function (see, for example, Angus Deaton and John Muellbauer, ch. 2). Consider the distance function $d(z, u^0)$. Then

$$\partial d(z, u^0) / \partial z_i = MV_i(z, u^0),$$

where MV_i is the normalized marginal value function for z_i, i.e., the proportion of income one is willing to pay for

another unit of z_i. By letting $u^0 = u(z)$, we have

$$MV_i(z, u^0) = MV_i(z, u(z)).$$

The term MV_i changes with z_j as

$$dMV_i(z, u(z)) / dz_j = MV_{ij}(z, u^0) + MV_{iu} u_j.$$

This equation is an Antonelli decomposition for price-dependent demand equations. The right-hand side is composed of a utility constant slope and real income effect. Note, however, that in the household production framework, $u_j = \lambda C_j(z, r)$, so that the decomposition implies

$$dMV_i(z, u(z)) / dz_j = MV_{ij}(z, u^0) + MV_{iu} \lambda C_j(z, r).$$

Thus, each cost function $C(z, r)$ implies a different slope for the Marshallian demand function.

The ultimate task of this section is to evaluate a change in an exogenous factor in the household production framework. In our illustration, let the exogenous factor be a publicly supplied or regulated good, α, that affects the production or consumption of a household commodity. In keeping with standard welfare analysis, we interpret the compensation necessary to keep an individual at a given utility level after a change in α as a money measure of the associated welfare change.

Suppose that α is an environmental good, such as the water quality of a lake. Then it will enter the utility function directly and be complementary with some commodity which we shall denote z_1, such as lake recreation. In this case, utility will be a function of α and z. Alternatively, if α is a public health project or child care facility, it may be more appropriately viewed as an input into the production of some z_1, such as family health or child quality. Now α will enter the transformation function (i.e., $t(z, x)$ becomes $t(z, x, \alpha)$). In either case, the household's expenditure function will depend on α.

When u^0 is the initial welfare level, the compensating variation of a change in the parameter vector from α^0 to α' is given by

$$(9) \quad CV = m(r, u^0, \alpha') - m(r, u^0, \alpha^0).$$

Compensating variation is negative for an increase in α and positive for a decrease, when α is a desirable public good. Since the measure in (9) is not directly observable, we seek a means of evaluating the welfare effects of the changes in α from information on the production and consumption of the associated commodity z_1. The equivalence between compensating variation measures of z_1^* and areas in commodity space suggests a useful approach. From the results above, we know that the difference in the areas between the marginal value and marginal cost functions evaluated for α^0 and α' will be equivalent to

$$(10) \quad \int_0^{z_1^*(\alpha')} \left[\partial E(z_1, r, u^0, \alpha') / \partial z_1 \right] dz_1$$
$$- \int_0^{z_1^\dagger(\alpha^0)} \left[\partial E(z_1, r, u^0, \alpha^0) / \partial z_1 \right] dz_1.$$

Expression (10) can be written as

$$(11) \quad E\left(z_1^*(\alpha'), r, u^0, \alpha'\right) - E(0, r, u^0, \alpha')$$
$$- E\left(z_1^*(\alpha^0), r, u^0, \alpha^0\right) + E(0, r, u^0, \alpha^0).$$

However, analogous to equation (6), the conditional expenditure function $E(\cdot)$ evaluated at the optimal value of z_1 is equivalent to the usual expenditure function $m(\cdot)$, so that (11) becomes

$$(12) \quad m(r, u^0, \alpha') - m(r, u^0, \alpha^0)$$
$$- E(0, r, u^0, \alpha') + E(0, r, u^0, \alpha^0).$$

Thus when

$$(13) \quad E(0, r, u^0, \alpha') = E(0, r, u^0, \alpha^0),$$

the compensating variation associated with a change in α can be measured by changes in the area behind compensated demand and marginal cost curves for z_1. That is, expression (12) which equals this area collapses to the correct measure of welfare change given by expression (9).

When α enters the household's preference function directly, a sufficient condition for (13) to hold is that α be weakly complementary to z_1. Karl-Göran Mäler has defined weak complementary as follows: "If the demand for a private good is zero, then the demand for some environmental service [public good] will also be zero" (p. 183). Thus weak complementarity is consistent with the condition $\partial u(0, \bar{z}, \alpha) / \partial \alpha = 0$, which implies that the individual is indifferent to varying levels of the exogenous good when he does not consume z_1. Alternatively, when α serves as an input into the production process, condition (13) will hold automatically if α is only an input in the production of z_1.

This section demonstrates that the compensated marginal value and marginal cost functions generated by the household production approach have normative significance and can be used to capture the welfare effects resulting from a change in exogenous factors affecting either tastes or technology. However, these results are of minimal value if there is no means of observing utility-constant marginal value functions. The usual approximation by means of consumer's surplus as well as the possibility of deriving exact measures of compensating variation from the Marshallian demand curve are precluded as well since that curve is not uniquely defined.

III. Welfare Analysis in the Goods Market

While the commodity space of the household production framework provides conceptually valid welfare measures, our inability to observe Marshallian approximations of these measures makes normative analysis difficult. In this section we use goods space to derive equivalent and conceptually valid, but empirically feasible, measures of welfare change.

Recall that the expenditure function can be derived as

$$m(r, u^0, \alpha) = \min_x \{r \cdot x | u^0 = u(z, \alpha)\}$$

where z for any x vector satisfies $t(z, x, \alpha) = 0$ and $m(r, u^0, \alpha') - m(r, u^0, \alpha^0)$ is a money measure of the welfare effects of a change in α. Since expenditures are linear in x's, the compensated demand for some input x_1 is the derivative of the expenditure function with respect to r_1:

$$\partial m(r, u^0, \alpha) / \partial r_1 = x_1(r, u^0, \alpha).$$

Define $\tilde{r}_1(\bar{r}, u^0, \alpha)$, where $\bar{r} = (r_2, \ldots, r_n)$, as the price that induces zero-compensated demand for x_1; that is, $x_1(\tilde{r}_1, \bar{r}, u^0, \alpha) = 0$. Note that $\tilde{r}_1$ depends on the utility level u^0, the level of the public good α, and prices $\bar{r}$, although these arguments will be supressed for simplicity. The area under the compensated demand curve for x_1 is therefore

$$(14) \quad A = \int_{r_1^0}^{\tilde{r}_1} x_1(r, u^0, \alpha) \, dr_1,$$

$$= m(\tilde{r}_1, \bar{r}, u^0, \alpha) - m(r_1^0, \bar{r}, u^0, \alpha),$$

where $(r_1^0, \bar{r})$ is the prevailing price vector.

By definition, compensating variation for a change in α is given by expression (9), but this expression is not directly observable.

Our task is to demonstrate the conditions under which expression (9) can be derived from the area in the goods market given by (14), an area which if not observable can be approximated from its Marshallian counterpart. The change in the area behind the compensated demand function for some x_1 caused by a change in α from α^0 to α' can be expressed as

$$(15) \quad \Delta A = \int_{r_1^0}^{\tilde{r}_1} x_1(r, u^0, \alpha') \, dr_1$$

$$- \int_{r_1^0}^{\tilde{r}_1} x_1(r, u^0, \alpha^0) \, dr_1.$$

If

$$(16) \quad m(\tilde{r}_1, \bar{r}, u^0, \alpha') = m(\tilde{r}_1, \bar{r}, u^0, \alpha),$$

then $\Delta A = m(r, u^0, \alpha') - m(r, u^0, \alpha^0)$.

Thus when (16) holds, the welfare effect of a change in α can be measured exactly in the goods market.

Expression (16) requires that the individual be indifferent among different levels of the public good when x_1 is not purchased. Sufficient conditions for (16) to hold are that

(i) α is complementary to a subset of z denoted z_A such that $\partial u / \partial \alpha = 0$ if $z_i = 0$, for all i in A;

(ii) x_1 is an essential input in the production of all z_i, for all i in A. Writing the transformation as a generalized production function for z_i implies $z_i = t^*(\bar{z}, x)$, where $\bar{z}$ is the vector of all other z's. The essentiality of x_1 implies $0 = t^*(\bar{z}, 0, x_2, \ldots, x_n)$ for all $\bar{z}$.

The intuition of condition (i) is that when the price vector induces no units of x_1 to be purchased, z_i cannot be produced, and with no z_i, the individual is indifferent among different levels of α. If α enters the preference function, condition (i) implies weak complementarity between α and z_i. If, instead, α enters the production function only, condition (i) holds trivially.

In addition, x_1 must be an essential input into the production of the z_i. Expression (16) can hold even when x_1 is nonessential in the production of commodities which are unrelated to α. However the measure is incomplete if α is related to commodities, either through production or consumption, for which x_1 is nonessential. Consequently if we can conceptually measure the change in some commodity space, we can measure it in goods space as well, as long as an essential input to that commodity can be identified.

Welfare measurement in the household production framework gives further insight into the concept of weak complementarity which has played a crucial role in measuring the demand for public goods from market data. V. Kerry Smith argues that since weak complementarity describes a link between arguments of the preference function, it must be assumed and cannot be tested. He observes that behavior that appears to be consistent with weak complementarity between a public and a private good may instead be the result of technical links between these goods. However, in the household production framework, Smith's distinction between links of technology and tastes is unnecessary. Both technology and tastes affect the household's decisions regarding z and thus both affect demand for goods as inputs into the production of z. Conditions (i) and (ii) demonstrate that it does not matter whether the link between the public good and the produced commodity is through the preference or production function, as long as the public good is of no value when the commodity is not produced.

This approach represents an advancement in the art of valuing public goods in the household production framework on two counts. First, by focusing on goods rather than commodities, it avoids the ill-defined Marshallian commodity demands. Second, it does not require that technology be known as Hori's approach does. All information about technology necessary to derive the value of a public input is embodied in the derived demand functions for goods.

This section demonstrates that when certain conditions are met, the welfare changes resulting from the change in an exogenous variable can be measured as areas behind Hicksian demand curves for goods. This result is an important corollary to the general results of Just and Hueth, and of Just, Hueth, and Schmitz, who demonstrate the duality of

surpluses in factor and product markets for competitive firms. The equivalence of welfare measures in alternative markets depends on the input or output in question being "necessary." That is, when prices are such that the input is not hired or the output is not produced, the firm must be assumed to shut down. We show that parallel conditions on the essentiality of goods as inputs in the household technology allow us to value changes in public goods in the household production framework.

IV. Conclusion

This paper develops an approach for welfare measurement in the household production function framework. While the household production function offers almost no testable hypotheses involving the production and consumption of commodities, welfare measures in commodity space do exist. However because the Marshallian demand curve is not well defined, it is not possible to estimate this demand curve. As a consequence, the practice of approximating welfare changes as the area under Marshallian demand curves is precluded. Hence, welfare measurement using commodity demand functions is not feasible in the household production framework.

The use of purchased goods in the production of commodities provides an opportunity for measuring welfare changes. When a good is essential in the production of a commodity, and a publicly controlled resource is complementary to the commodity, changes in the area under the Hicksian demand curve for that good can be interpreted as welfare measures of changes in the public resource. Thus an alternative and feasible means of measuring welfare change is provided for the household production function framework.

REFERENCES

Barnett, William A., "Pollak and Wachter on the Household Production Function Approach," *Journal of Political Economy*, October 1977, *85*, 1073–82.

Becker, Gary S., "A Theory of the Allocation

of Time," *Economic Journal*, September 1965, *75*, 493–517.

Brown, Gardner, Jr., Charbonneau, John and Hay, Michael, "The Value of Wildlife Estimated by the Hedonic Approach," Working Paper No. 6, U. S. Department of Interior, Fish and Wildlife Service, 1978.

Deaton, Angus and Muellbauer, John, *Economics and Consumer Behavior*, Cambridge: Cambridge University Press, 1980.

Gorman, W. H., "A Possible Preference for Analysing Quality Differentials in the Egg Market," mimeo., 1956; reissued as Discussion Paper No. B4, London School of Economics Econometrics Program, 1976.

Hausman, Jerry A., "Exact Consumer's Surplus and Deadweight Loss," *American Economic Review*, September 1981, *71*, 662–76.

Hori, Hajime, "Revealed Preference for Public Goods," *American Economic Review*, December 1975, *65*, 978–91.

Just, Richard and Hueth, Darrell, "Welfare Measures in a Multimarket Framework," *American Economic Review*, December 1979, *69*, 947–54.

_____, _____, and Schmitz, Andrew, *Applied Welfare Economics and Public Policy*, Englewood Cliffs: Prentice-Hall, 1982.

Lancaster, Kelvin, J., "A New Approach to Consumer Theory," *Journal of Political Economy*, April 1966, *74*, 132–57.

McKenzie, George W. and Pearce, I. F., "Welfare Measurement—A Synthesis," *American Economic Review*, September 1982, *72*, 669–82.

Mäler, Karl-Göran, *Environmental Economics: A Theoretical Inquiry*, Baltimore: John Hopkins Press, 1974.

Pollak, Robert A., "Welfare Evaluation and the Cost-of-Living Index in the Household Production Model," *American Economic Review*, June 1978, *68*, 285–99.

_____ and Wachter, Michael, "The Relevance of the Household Production Function and Its Implications for the Allocation of Time," *Journal of Political Economy*, April 1975, *83*, 255–77.

_____ and _____, "Reply: Pollak and Wachter on the Household Production Function Approach," *Journal of Political Economy*, October 1977, *85*, 1083–86.

Smith, V. Kerry, "Introduction to Advances in Applied Microeconomics and Some Perspectives on Volume I," in his *Advances in Applied Micro-Economics*, Vol. 1, Greenwich: JAI Press, 1981.

Willig, Robert D., "Consumer's Surplus Without Apology," *American Economic Review*, September 1976, *66*, 589–97.

Wilman, Elizabeth, A., "Hedonic Prices and Beach Recreational Values," in V. K. Smith, ed., *Advances in Applied Micro-Economics*, Vol. 1, Greenwich: JAI Press, 1981.

[40]

Valuing Environmental Quality: Weak Complementarity with Sets of Goods

Nancy E. Bockstael and Catherine L. Kling

In practice, it is frequently impossible to identify a single good which is a weak complement to an environmental amenity for which welfare measures are desired. However, a set of goods exhibiting this property sometimes exists, e.g., water-related recreational activities when the nonmarket good to be valued is water quality. A set of weak complements is defined and implications for welfare measurement presented. The proper welfare measure now involves evaluation of a line integral and simple additions of areas under demand curves will not always be correct. However, under certain econometric circumstances, approximate welfare measures can be obtained from estimated functions.

Key words: benefit estimation, environmental quality, recreation demand, weak complementarity.

Weak complementarity has played a critical role in the valuation of environmental amenities. Feenberg and Mills recognized its considerable importance: "The basic result about weak complements is that if there exists a commodity, say x_1, that is a weak complement with E (environmental quality), then the benefits from improvements in E can be measured approximately from the demand equation for x_1. The result is remarkable. It opens the door to estimation of environmental benefits from market data, even though no markets exist for environmental quality" (p. 64).

Perhaps the earliest clear statement of weak complementarity between environmental quality and a private good is by Mäler, who defined the principle mathematically in two equivalent ways

$$(1) \qquad \left.\frac{\partial U(x, q)}{\partial q}\right|_{x_i=0} = 0, \text{ or}$$

$$\frac{\partial m(\bar{p}_i(q), \bar{p}, q, u)}{\partial q} = 0,$$

where x is a vector of private goods, q is environmental quality, $\bar{p}_i$ is the price at which x_i ceases to be consumed, $\bar{p}$ is the vector of other prices, u is a fixed level of utility which the expenditure function $m(\cdot)$ depends upon, and $u(\cdot)$ is the direct utility function. In words, when the demand for the weak complement is zero, the marginal value of the environmental service is zero.

Mäler's results have been recapitulated by many, and have served as the basis for valuing quality changes in the travel cost model (Freeman) and in the household production framework (Bockstael and McConnell). While failing to use the term directly, Willig provides one of the best expositions of weak complementarity in his 1978 paper on hedonic price adjustments and price-quality substitution.

For resource economists involved in environmental policy, the concept has become indispensable. It is of particular importance in obtaining environmental benefit estimates from the commonly used travel cost models. One technique for assessing the benefits of improvements in environmental quality involves estimating the demand for a good which is a weak complement to the environmental amenity and then evaluating the change in the area beneath this demand function induced by a change in quality. Weak complementarity is a necessary condition for

Nancy E. Bockstael is a professor of agricultural economics, University of Maryland; Catherine L. Kling is an assistant professor, Department of Agricultural Economics, University of California, Davis.

The research was partially funded by EPA Cooperative Agreement CR-811043-01-1. The research was conducted at the University of California, Davis.

The authors wish to thank Myrick Freeman and an anonymous reviewer for helpful comments.

the change in this area to measure the entire welfare effect of a quality change. The validity of the approach hinges on the validity of the assumption that the good for which demand is estimated is weakly complementary to the environmental quality change being evaluated.

Suppose, however, that no obvious good qualifies as a weak complement to the environmental amenity, q. Even though x_i is related to the amenity, introspection or direct questioning may indicate that when x_i is zero, individuals are still likely to care about the level of q. While much has been written about weak complementarity, little has been said about situations where weak complementarity does not exist. Strictly speaking, all we know is that evaluating the quality-induced change in the area beneath the demand function for x_i misses something. One reason something might be missed, that is one cause for $\partial u/\partial q|_{x=0}$ to be nonzero, is existence value (Madariaga and McConnell). A second is that other goods besides x_i are related to q.[1]

The potential importance of the second explanation is shown by Freeman's example of weak complementarity. The environmental amenity is water quality, and "the marginal value of water quality in a particular lake could be assumed to be zero for those persons who did not use the lake for recreation" (p. 73). As reasonable as this appears, problems may arise in its application. Consider the possible recreational uses of this lake: swimming, fishing, boating, picnicking along the shore, etc. While recreational use may exhibit weak complementarity to the lake's quality, there may be no single empirical counterpart to the notion of "recreational use" but several recreational activities, with at least some individuals participating in more than one.

Empirical examples are found in several recent attempts to value water quality improvements using recreation demand models. Sutherland recognized the importance of four water-based recreational activities in evaluating improvements in water quality to a level consistent with the fishable/swimmable goal of the clean water amendments. Caulkins, Bishop, and Bouwes identified both swimming

and fishing as important recreational activities in their Wisconsin lake recreation study. Similarly, Smith, Desvousges, and McGivney found that Monongahela River users included both fishermen and power boaters. Two recent EPA-sponsored studies (Vaughan et al.; Bockstael, McConnell, and Strand) encountered multiple recreational activities in evaluating water quality improvements. The latter identified swimming, sportfishing and boating as key benefits to recreation from improvements in Chesapeake Bay water quality.

In such circumstances a set of goods may be weakly complementary to the environmental amenity. If an individual does not consume any of the goods, then a change in the environmental good does not matter to him. Conversely, he is affected by the environmental good if he consumes any one (or more) of the goods in the set.

Faced with an array of recreational goods, no one of which is a weak complement to water quality, researchers attempting to value changes in the environmental amenity have taken one of two routes. The first is to agglomerate all recreational activities into a single good. The second is to estimate separate demands for each activity and add the welfare measures across the activities without considering whether this is the correct procedure or not.

The first part of this article develops the correct rules for measuring the welfare effects of an environmental quality change given a set of weakly complementary private goods. The answer involves a line integral. Because the demands are compensated, the integrand of the line integral is an exact differential, and one need only choose a path of integration to evaluate it. However, in the usual empirical situations where data are often limited, obvious paths of integration are precluded. In the second part of the article, typical empirical circumstances are described and the nature of the resulting biases in welfare measures is discussed. The paper concludes with the interesting result that when the prices of the set of weak complements are highly correlated, naive welfare measurement techniques may give quite accurate answers.

To extend the results to marshallian demand curves and ordinary surpluses, some fairly restrictive conditions are needed; however, they are no more restrictive than those required in the single weak complement case. The same conditions explained in Bockstael

---

[1] It is difficult practically, and perhaps even conceptually, to distinguish between existence value and the presence of an infinitely large number of goods related to the environmental quality. This article addresses the case in which a small number of goods is related to q in a well-defined way. This does not exhaust all cases in which weak complementarity of a single good fails to hold.

656 *August 1988*

Amer. J. Agr. Econ.

and McConnell (1987) for the single-good case apply here. The results are empirically relevant when (*a*) the compensated demand functions can be recovered or (*b*) the restrictive conditions hold such that differences in ordinary surpluses are at least bounded by compensating and equivalent variation.

Theory

Before addressing a set of weakly complementary goods, it is useful to review the remarkable results of which Feenberg and Mills speak. The compensating variation of a quality change in environmental amenity, q, from q^0 to q^1 is defined as

$$(2) \quad CV(\Delta q) = m(p, q^0, u) - m(p, q^1, u),$$

where p is a vector of prices and u is the original utility level of the individual. The task is to obtain this value from information on behavior which can be observed and estimated.

If a particular x_i were both nonessential and weakly complementary to q, then $CV(\Delta q)$ could be obtained by measuring the change in the area behind the hicksian demand for x_i induced by the quality change. This is true because the change in this area can be written as

$$(3) \quad \int_{p_i^0}^{\bar{p}_i(q^1)} g_i(p, q^1, u)dp_i - \int_{p_i^0}^{\bar{p}_i(q^0)} g_i(p, q^0, u)dp_i,$$

where $g_i(\cdot)$ is the compensated demand function, p_i^0 is the current price of x_i and $\bar{p}_i$ is the price at which demand equals zero (guaranteed by nonessentiality to be finite, at least in the limit as $x \to 0$). This expression can be rewritten as

$$(4) \quad m(\bar{p}_i(q^1), \bar{p}, q^1, u) - m(p_i^0, \bar{p}, q^1, u)$$
$$- m(\bar{p}_i(q^0), \bar{p}, q^0, u) + m(p_i^0, \bar{p}, q^0, u),$$

where $\bar{p}$ is the vector of all other prices. This expression equals $CV(\Delta q)$ in (2) if

$$(5) \quad m(\bar{p}_i(q^1), \bar{p}, q^1, u)$$
$$- m(\bar{p}_i(q^0), \bar{p}, q^0, u) = 0,$$

and this will be true, by definition (1), if x_i is a weak complement to q.

Despite the familiarity of this proof, it is worth noting the two features which make it work. One is the property that the integrand

in (3), the hicksian demand for x_i, is the derivative of the expenditure function with respect to the price of x_i. Thus, integrating the hicksian demand over price gives back the expenditure function (except for a constant of integration which is not a function of p_i). The second is that weak complementarity of x_i to q ensures that the expenditure function will be stationary with respect to q when it is evaluated at $p_i \geq \bar{p}_i$.

Now consider a set of goods that is weakly complementary to q. In this case, compensating variation is still given by (2), but is this value manifested in areas under demand curves?

Suppose that two such goods are designated x_1 and x_2. If the individual does not consume either x_1 or x_2, then he will not be affected by a change in the level of q. However, neither good on its own is a weak complement to q. Even if an individual does not consume x_1, for example, changes in q will matter if he is participating in the x_2 market, and vice versa.

To determine whether, in this case, compensating variation can still be measured as areas under compensated demand curves, recall the elements which make the single weak complement case work. The price derivative of the expenditure function is integrated from the actual price to the price at which the expenditure function became stationary with respect to q. Now that a set of goods (x_1, x_2) is weakly complementary to q, the expenditure function will be stationary in q only when both $p_1 \geq \bar{p}_1(q)$ and $p_2 \geq \bar{p}_2(q)$ hold. Analogous to the single good case, the relevant integrand will now be the differential of the expenditure function with respect to p_1 and p_2 and the range of integration will now be from (p_1^0, p_2^0) to $(\bar{p}_1(q), \bar{p}_2(q))$. This defines the following line integral (e.g., Goodman):

$$(6) \quad \int_C g_1(p_1, p_2, q)dt + g_2(p_1, p_2, q)dt,$$

where p_1 and p_2 are both functions of t defined by the path of integration, C, from (p_1^0, p_2^0) to $(\bar{p}_1(q), \bar{p}_2(q))$.

Because the integrand of (6) is an exact differential of the expenditure function, the line integral will be path independent. Expression (6) will have the same value irrespective of the path of price changes chosen between (p_1^0, p_2^0) and $(\bar{p}_1, \bar{p}_2)$. The reward for choosing a specific path is simplification of the line integral to a sum of single integrals. Consider the path $(p_1^0, p_2^0) \to (\bar{p}_1, p_2^0) \to (\bar{p}_1, \bar{p}_2)$ and examine the results. Expression (6) can now be rewritten as

(7) $\quad \int_{p_1^0}^{\bar{p}_1(q)} g_1(p_1, p_2^0, q)dp_1$

$$+ \int_{p_2^0}^{\bar{p}_2(q)} g_2(\bar{p}_1(q), p_2, q)dp_2.$$

If the analogy holds, evaluating (7) at q^1 and subtracting (7) evaluated at q^0 should yield the compensating variation of a quality change when the set of goods (x_1, x_2) is weakly complementary to q. This difference gives

(8) $\quad \int_{p_1^0}^{\bar{p}_1(q^1)} g_1(p_1, p_2^0, q^1)dp_1$

$$- \int_{p_1^0}^{\bar{p}_1(q^0)} g_1(p_1, p_2^0, q^0)dp_1$$

$$+ \int_{p_2^0}^{\bar{p}_2(q^1)} g_2(\bar{p}_1(q^1), p_2, q^1)dp_2$$

$$- \int_{p_2^0}^{\bar{p}_2(q^0)} g_2(\bar{p}_1(q^0), p_2, q^0)dp_2.$$

It seems likely that expression (8) is equal to the compensating variation of a quality change because (8) was derived in a way analogous to the single weak complement case. To prove this, note that (8) can be rewritten as

$m(\bar{p}_1(q^1), p_2^0, q^1) - m(p_1^0, p_2^0, q^1)$
$\quad - m(\bar{p}_1(q^0), p_2^0, q^0) + m(p_1^0, p_2^0, q^0)$
$\quad\quad + m(\bar{p}_1(q^1), \bar{p}_2(q^1), q^1)$
$\quad - m(\bar{p}_1(q^1), p_2^0, q^1) - m(\bar{p}_1(q^0), \bar{p}_2(q^0), q^0)$
$\quad\quad + m(\bar{p}_1(q^0), p_2^0, q^0).$

The two $m(\bar{p}_1(q^0), p_2^0, q^0)$ terms cancel, as do the two $m(\bar{p}_1(q^1), p_2^0, q^1)$ terms. The above expression simplifies to

$- m(p_1^0, p_2^0, q^1) + m(p_1^0, p_2^0, q^0)$
$\quad + m(\bar{p}_1(q^1), \bar{p}_2(q^1), q^1)$
$\quad\quad - m(\bar{p}_1(q^0), \bar{p}_2(q^0), q^0).$

This is equal to the compensating variation of the quality change, given by

(9) $\quad CV(\Delta q) = m(p_1^0, p_2^0, \bar{p}, q^0, u)$
$$- m(p_1^0, p_2^0, \bar{p}, q^1, u)$$

only if

(10) $\quad m(\bar{p}_1(q^0), \bar{p}_2(q^0), q^0)$
$$- m(\bar{p}_1(q^1), \bar{p}_2(q^1), q^1) = 0.$$

The set of goods, x_1 and x_2, is weakly complementary to q by assumption, which means that if the individual faces prices for both goods sufficiently high to drive him out of both

markets, then a change in q is of no value to him. Thus, weak complementarity in this context implies that (10) must hold. As a consequence, the compensating variation of the quality change, given by (9), can be captured as the (sum) of areas between the demand curves for x_1 and x_2, as given by expression (8).

These results have one very important feature. As expression (8) indicates, compensating variation is captured by the change in the area under the demand curve for good one conditioned on good two's price being p_2^0, plus the change in the area under the demand curve for good two conditioned on good one's price being high enough to cause x_1 not to be consumed. Thus, the area between the compensated demand curves for x_1 at q^1 and q^0 is evaluated at the prevailing price of x_2, while the area between the compensated demand curves for x_2 at q^1 and q^0 is evaluated at the choke price of x_1. Of course, because of path independence, the same answer would result if we conditioned x_2's demand on p_1^0 and x_1's demand on $\bar{p}_2$. However, conditioning each of the demands for x_1 and x_2 on the initial price of the other good would be incorrect since this does not correspond to a legitimate price path.[2]

This "sequencing" phenomenon is similar in spirit to the procedure for evaluating multiple price (Just, Hueth, and Schmitz) changes. For multiple price changes, one needs to choose a path of price changes and evaluate these changes sequentially across markets. The interesting finding for the weakly complementary set of goods is that, even though a single quality change is being evaluated, it must be done by sequencing price changes.

In Practice

At first blush, the above procedure for evaluating the benefits of a quality change appears straightforward. Granted, we normally have marshallian not hicksian demand functions to work with, but, since no new problem is involved, the conditions necessary for the marshallian measures of quality changes to reasonably approximate the hicksian ones are met (Bockstael and McConnell 1987). The procedure is to estimate the demands for both

[2] Feenberg and Mills examine related issues. Their analysis is based on indirect utility functions, and they do not consider the empirical implications of their results.

658   *August 1988*   *Amer. J. Agr. Econ.*

goods as functions of both prices and the quality characteristic; then simply integrate as indicated in expression (8), being sure to condition the demand functions on sequential price changes.

The difficulty is not in the thinking but in the doing. Consider what is likely to happen in practice. First, not all of the goods which are in the weak complement set may be known. And, even if they are known, data may be insufficient to estimate demands for all of them. In this case it will not be possible to estimate all of the necessary demand functions, and the resulting welfare measure will be an underestimate.

Additionally, the form of the data may make it difficult to implement the procedure described above. Often the data on multiple activities will come from different sources. Demand functions for boaters, for example, are often estimated from data collected from a survey of registered boat owners, while a data set on swimming behavior may be obtained from beach interviews. Survey design and inherent sample selection characteristics frequently will prevent data collection on a wide range of activities simultaneously. This problem is inherent in many of the periodic government surveys of recreational use as well because they are activity oriented (e.g., the National Marine Fisheries Service sportfishing survey). When data on multiple activities are not collected simultaneously, it will be difficult to condition the estimated demand for one activity on the prices of the other activities in the weak complement set.

Even with ideal data, there may still be problems because the "prices" of the recreational activities enjoyed at the same site often vary together. The major portion of the cost of each activity likely is the travel cost to the site, which by definition is exactly equal for each activity. Even if other major expenses affect one activity and not the others, the portion of the costs which vary most over individuals is probably the travel cost. Suppose the cost of swimming is the travel cost to the site, but the cost of fishing is the travel cost plus a boat rental fee. Even if the boat rental fee is extremely large relative to travel costs, multicollinearity across costs will still arise if the rental fee is the same for all individuals.

It likely is the rule rather than the exception for limited data or multicollinearity to prevent the estimation of demands for each activity as functions of the prices of all activities. In such

cases knowledge of the correct sequencing procedures is of little practical use. The remainder of the article considers what might be salvaged when the information necessary to perform the analysis in (8) cannot be obtained.

For simplicity, the weak complement set is limited to two goods, x_1 and x_2, although extension to more goods is straightforward. Consider the typical case when either limited data or multicollinearity prevent estimation of the demand for x_i ($i = 1, 2$) as a function of p_j ($j \neq i$). The consequences of this misspecification will depend on the relationship between p_1 and p_2. Two polar cases are considered—no correlation over the sample between p_1 and p_2 and (near) perfect correlation. Assume throughout that no systematic relationship exists across the data set (i.e., across individual observations) between the site quality variable and either own or substitute price. This is plausible because the quality variable does not change over individuals, only over sites, while travel cost varies considerably over both individuals and sites.

Before examining the implications of misspecification for welfare measurement, it is first necessary to consider the econometric consequences. With no correlation among prices, omission of p_j in the demand for x_i will not cause a bias in the estimated coefficients of this function. The effect of changes in p_j will be relegated to the error term and the mean effect will be captured in the constant. Thus if the true model were, for example,

$$(11) \quad x_{in} = \beta_0 + \beta_1 p_{in} + \beta_2 p_{jn} + \beta_3 q_n + u_n$$
$$i, j = 1, 2$$
$$i \neq j,$$

for all individuals $n = 1, \ldots, N$, then the estimated function would be

$$(12) \quad x_{in} = \hat{\beta}_0 + \hat{\beta}_1 p_{in} + \hat{\beta}_3 q_n + v_n$$
$$i = 1, 2,$$

where $E[\hat{\beta}_1] = \beta_1$, $E[\hat{\beta}_3] = \beta_3$, and $E[\hat{\beta}_0] = \beta_0 + \beta_2 \bar{p}_j^0$, where $\bar{p}_j^0$ is the mean substitute price over the sample and v_n is the regression residual. Thus, the expected value of the estimated model is

$$(13) \quad E[x_i] = (\beta_0 + \beta_2 \bar{p}_j^0) + \beta_1 p_i + \beta_3 q.$$

Alternatively, if p_1 and p_2 are perfectly correlated and (11) is the true model, then the omission of substitute price leads to different results. To give these results specific form, assume that

$$p_2 = \alpha_0 + \alpha_1 p_1.$$

(Perhaps p_1 is travel cost to the site, the relevant cost for swimming, and p_2 is the cost of fishing or boating which is the same as p_1 except for a fixed rental fee of α_0. In this example and probably in many empirical situations, α_1 takes the value of 1.) Estimation of (12) when (11) is the true model produces coefficients with the following properties: $E[\hat{\beta}_0] = \beta_0 + \beta_2\alpha_0$ and $E[\hat{\beta}_1] = \beta_1 + \beta_2\alpha_1$. Thus, the expected value of the estimated model is

(14) $E(x_i) = \beta_0 + \alpha_0\beta_2$

$$+ (\beta_1 + \alpha_1\beta_2)p_1 + \beta_3 q,$$

when $p_2 = \alpha_0 + \alpha_1 p_1$.

Although a simple linear function is used here for demonstration, the nature of these results holds more generally. The key point is that the effect of the omitted price is different depending on whether that price is correlated with the included variable or not. When it is not correlated, the average omitted price will affect the constant term in the estimated equation. (This may have complicating consequences in sample selection models where nonzero values are precluded and a large proportion of the population is likely to have a zero demand). If the omitted substitute price is (nearly) perfectly correlated with own price, the estimated coefficient associated with an own-price variable (however transformed) will reflect the effect of both own and substitute price. While (13) and (14) reflect the linear case, the key features of these results, as well as the subsequent discussion, hold for many commonly estimated functional forms.

Returning to the task at hand, can the welfare measure of a quality change be obtained from the misspecified demand function? It is still possible to integrate over each demand function and obtain the change in the area under each demand as quality changes. However, these demand functions are not explicit functions of substitute price, precluding the sequencing of price changes. In the two good case the result is

(15) $C\hat{V}(\Delta q) = \displaystyle\int_{p_1^0}^{\bar{p}_1(q^1)} \hat{g}_1(p_1, q^1)dp_1$

$$- \int_{p_1^0}^{\bar{p}_1(q^0)} \hat{g}_1(p_1, q^0)dp_1 + \int_{p_2^0}^{\bar{p}_2(q^1)} \hat{g}_2(p_2, q^1)dp_2$$

$$- \int_{p_2^0}^{\bar{p}_2(q^0)} \hat{g}_2(p_2, q^0)dp_2,$$

where $\hat{g}_i$ denotes the estimated demand function for good x_i.

Consider first the case when p_1 and p_2 are independent. Each demand function is implicitly conditioned on the mean prevailing substitute price which is captured in the estimated constant term. Thus, the integral of the demand function over own price is also conditioned on mean substitute price. The consequences of calculating (15) when prices are independent can be expressed explicitly. For any individual (where the individual's subscript is suppressed for simplicity), the measure thus obtained is equivalent to

(16)

$$C\hat{V}(\Delta q) = \int_{p_1^0}^{\bar{p}_1(q^1)} g_1(p_1, \bar{p}_2^0, q^1)dp_1$$

$$- \int_{p_1^0}^{\bar{p}_1(q^0)} g_1(p_1, \bar{p}_2^0, q^0)dp_1$$

$$+ \int_{p_2^0}^{\bar{p}_2(q^1)} g_2(\bar{p}_1^0, p_2, q^1)dp_2$$

$$- \int_{p_2^0}^{\bar{p}_2(q^0)} g_2(\bar{p}_1^0, p_2, q^0)dp_2$$

$$= m(\bar{p}_1(q^1), \bar{p}_2^0, q^1) - m(p_1^0, \bar{p}_2^0, q^1)$$
$$- m(\bar{p}_1(q^0), \bar{p}_2^0, q^0) + m(p_1^0, \bar{p}_2^0, q^0)$$
$$+ m(\bar{p}_1^0, \bar{p}_2(q^1), q^1) - m(\bar{p}_1^0, p_2^0, q^1)$$
$$- m(\bar{p}_1^0, \bar{p}_2(q^0), q^0) + m(\bar{p}_1^0, p_2^0, q^0).$$

Expression (16) is not equivalent to the line integral in (6) for two reasons. First, the expressions in (16) are functions of the average substitute price in the sample $(\bar{p}_j^0)$ rather than the individual's substitute price. Second, even if $\bar{p}_j^0$ were replaced by the price the individual faces, the expression would not reflect a price change path from (p_1^0, p_2^0) to $(\bar{p}_1, \bar{p}_2)$.

There are, therefore, two components to the bias produced by the welfare measure in (16). The first is the difference between (16) and the same expression when $\bar{p}_j$ is replaced by p_j:

$Bias_1 = m(\bar{p}_1(q^1), \bar{p}_2^0, q^1) - m(p_1^0, \bar{p}_2^0, q^1)$
$$- m(\bar{p}_1(q^0), \bar{p}_2^0, q^0) + m(p_1^0, \bar{p}_2^0, q^0)$$
$$+ m(\bar{p}_1^0, \bar{p}_2(q^1), q^1) - m(\bar{p}_1^0, p_2^0, q^1)$$
$$- m(\bar{p}_1^0, \bar{p}_2^0(q^0), q^0) + m(\bar{p}_1^0, p_2^0, q^0)$$
$$- m(\bar{p}_1(q^1), p_2^0, q^1) + m(p_1^0, p_2^0, q^1)$$
$$+ m(\bar{p}_1(q^0), p_2^0, q^0) - m(p_1^0, p_2^0, q^0)$$
$$- m(p_1^0, \bar{p}_2(q^1), q^1) + m(p_1^0, p_2^0, q^1)$$
$$+ m(p_1^0, \bar{p}_2(q^0), q^0) - m(p_1^0, p_2^0, q^0).$$

Unfortunately, it is not possible to determine the sign of this expression even in the aggregate. Knowing that the expenditure function is concave in a price (i.e., $\partial^2 m/\partial p_j{}^2$) merely determines that $m(\cdot, \bar{p}, \cdot) > \bar{m}(\cdot, p, \cdot)$, where $\bar{m}$ is the mean expenditure function over the sample. It does not allow us to sign differences in the expenditure function. In order to sign the average $Bias_1$, we must determine the sign of $\partial^3 m/\partial p_i \partial p_j{}^2$ and $\partial^3 m/\partial q \partial p_j{}^2$.

Similarly, the sign of the bias associated with the incorrect path of integration is indeterminate. To examine this bias, rewrite (16) as a function of p_j instead of $\bar{p}_j$, $j = 1, 2$, and subtract the true compensating variation as given in (9)

$$
\begin{aligned}
Bias_2 = \; & m(\bar{p}_1(q^1), p_2^0, q^1) - m(p_1^0, p_2^0, q^1) \\
& - m(\bar{p}_1(q^0), p_2^0, q^0) + m(p_1^0, p_2^0, q^0) \\
& + m(p_1^0, \bar{p}_2(q^1), q^1) - m(p_1^0, p_2^0, q^1) \\
& - m(p_1^0, \bar{p}_2(q^0), q^0) + m(p_1^0, p_2^0, q^0) \\
& + m(p_1^0, p_2^0, q^1) - m(p_1^0, p_2^0, q^0).
\end{aligned}
$$

Canceling like terms, rearranging, and adding the term $m(\bar{p}_1, \bar{p}_2, q^0) - m(\bar{p}_1, \bar{p}_2, q^1)$, which by definition of the weak complement set equals zero, yields

$$
\begin{aligned}
(17) \quad Bias_2 = \; & [m(p_1^0, \bar{p}_2(q^1), q^1) \\
& - m(p_1^0, p_2^0, q^1) \\
& - m(p_1^0, \bar{p}_2(q^0), q^0) \\
& + m(p_1^0, p_2^0, q^0)] \\
& - [m(\bar{p}_1(q^1), \bar{p}_2(q^1), q^1) \\
& - m(\bar{p}_1(q^1), p_2^0, q^1) \\
& - m(\bar{p}_1(q^0), \bar{p}_2(q^0), q^0) \\
& + m(\bar{p}_1(q^0), p_2^0, q^0)].
\end{aligned}
$$

Each of the two bracketed terms represents the area between the hicksian demand curves for x_2 evaluated at the two levels of quality. The only difference between the two terms, and the only reason that they do not cancel, is that the first set of hicksian demands is evaluated at the original level of p_1 and the second is evaluated at the p_1 choke price.

Once again, the sign of the bias depends on properties of the expenditure function for which there are no definitive results. To determine the sign of the bias, it is necessary to know how quality changes affect the demand for one good as the price of a related good increases. This is the sign of $\partial^2 x_1/\partial q \partial p_j$ or $\partial^3 m/\partial p_i \partial q \partial p_j$. No properties of the expenditure function will yield an unambiguous sign for this term.

The conditions under which the bias is likely to be small can be determined. Clearly, with little variation in substitute price over the sample, $Bias_1$ will be small. However, this property is unlikely and it would cause other estimation problems. If p_1^0 is large and close to the choke price, $\bar{p}_1$, then there will be little difference between the demand curve evaluated at these two prices and $Bias_2$ will be small. Again, this will not occur frequently in the sample if the substitute activity is frequently enjoyed by individuals in the sample. Of more practical use is the result that if the cross-price derivative, $\partial g_2/\partial p_1$, is small, the hicksian demand function evaluated at the original price and at the choke price do not differ by much, and both biases are small. In the extreme, if the cross-price derivative is zero, there is no need to consider sequencing, and no bias occurs.[3]

Now consider the second case in which the two prices are perfectly correlated. The estimated (misspecified) demand equation is not conditioned on a value for substitute price but on the parameters which describe the relationship between own and substitute price. Consequently, integrating demand functions over own price [i.e., evaluating (15)] does not produce the same result as when prices are independent. If there is a relationship between prices such as described earlier, then the expected value of the estimated equation is given by (13). In this situation, p_2 implicitly changes as the demand for x_1 is integrated over p_1. Thus, the integral of the estimated demand for x_1 over p_1 is equivalent to the line integral

$$
\int_C g_1(p_1, p_2, q)dt,
$$

where the implicit price change path, C, is $p_1 = t$ and $p_2 = \alpha_0 + \alpha_1 t$. Similarly, the simple integral of the estimated demand for x_2 over p_2 will imply the line integral

$$
\int_C g_2(p_1, p_2, q)dt.
$$

Evaluating the difference in these integrals at q_0 and q_1 and summing them over goods in the weak complement set gives the line integral in (6).

---

[3] This case may actually occur with some frequency in recreation, as one reviewer noted. An individual's demand for boating, for example, may be independent of the "price" of swimming access.

These are rather startling results. They suggest that when prices are perfectly correlated, demand functions which are misspecified by omitting a substitute price can be used to produce correct welfare measures. In this case, the correct measure is obtained by addition of the quality-induced changes in the areas beneath estimated demands for each of the goods in the weak complement set. Intuitively, when the prices are perfectly correlated, the coefficient on the included price captures the effects of changes in both the included and omitted prices. Thus, the effect on demand as the included price is changed will actually capture the effect of a simultaneous change in included and omitted prices, and this simultaneous change represents one legitimate path of integration.

Concluding Comments

Weak complementarity forms the foundation of the theory of welfare measurement of environmental quality changes. Little thought, however, has been given to what happens in the absence of weak complementarity. Frequently, when a single good which is weakly complementary to the environmental amenity of interest cannot be identified, a set of goods together exhibits this property. While not all problems can be handled in this way (i.e., there may be existence value or a plethora of goods related to environmental quality), the notion of a set of weak complements has considerable empirical relevance. In this article, weak complementarity with respect to a set of goods is defined and its implications for welfare measurement associated with a quality change are presented.

When environmental quality is a weak complement to a set of goods, the proper measure of compensating variation depends on the evaluation of a line integral over the relevant demands between initial and choke prices of these goods. The line integral is evaluated by choosing a path of integration. An example in the two-good case involves integrating the demand for one good over the range of its price, holding the second good's price at its original level, and adding that to the integral over the second good's demand, holding the first good's price at its choke price. With this price path, prices change sequentially, from (p_1^0, p_2^0) to $(\bar{p}_1, p_2^0)$ and finally to $(\bar{p}_1, \bar{p}_2)$.

While this is an obvious price path to choose, it is not always possible to implement. Evaluating integrals sequentially requires a demand estimate for each good in the weak complement set as a function of the prices of all goods in the set. Data limitations and/or severe multicollinearity in prices may prohibit this.

When demands cannot be estimated as functions of substitute prices, simple addition of quality-induced changes in areas under demand curves will produce different results depending on the empirical relationships among prices. If the prices of the goods in the weak complement set are not correlated, then simple addition of quality-induced changes in areas will produce incorrect measures. In general, the bias will be smaller the smaller the cross-price elasticities and the closer the original price is to the choke price.

If the prices of the goods are perfectly correlated, simple addition of areas yields correct welfare measures because an implicit path of integration is defined by the relationship between the prices; prices move from their original level to their choke price simultaneously. In this case, despite the omission of substitute prices in estimated demand functions, the welfare estimate resulting from adding the welfare changes in each market yields the correct welfare measure of the quality change.

[*Received August 1987; final revision received December 1987.*]

References

Bockstael, Nancy E., and Kenneth E. McConnell. "Welfare Effects of Changes in Quality: A Synthesis." Dep. Agr. and Resour. Econ. Work. Pap., University of Maryland, 1987, under review.

———. "Welfare Measurement in the Household Production Framework." *Amer. Econ. Rev.* 73(1983):806–14.

Bockstael, Nancy E., Kenneth E. McConnell, and Ivar E. Strand. *Benefits from Improvements in Chesapeake Bay Water Quality.* Washington DC: Environmental Protection Agency Cooperative Agreement No. CR-811043-01-0, 1987.

Caulkins, Peter, Richard Bishop, and Nicolaas Bouwes. "The Travel Cost Model for Lake Recreation: A Comparison of Two Methods for Incorporating Site Quality and Substitution Effects." *Amer. J. Agr. Econ.* 68(1986):291–97.

662   *August 1988*   *Amer. J. Agr. Econ.*

Feenberg, Daniel, and Edwin Mills. *Measuring the Benefits of Water Pollution Abatement.* New York: Academic Press, 1980.

Freeman, A. Myrick. *The Benefits of Environmental Improvement.* Baltimore MD: Johns Hopkins University Press for Resources for the Future, 1979.

Goodman, A. W. *Analytic Geometry and the Calculus.* New York: Macmillan Co., 1980.

Just, Richard, Darrell Hueth, and Andrew Schmitz. *Applied Welfare Economics and Public Policy.* Englewood Cliffs NJ: Prentice-Hall, 1982.

Madariaga, Bruce, and Kenneth E. McConnell. "Exploring Existence Value." *Water Resour. Res.* 23(1987): 936–42.

Mäler, Karl-Goran. *Environmental Economics: A Theo-* retical Inquiry. Baltimore MD: Johns Hopkins University Press for Resources for the Future, 1974.

Smith, V. Kerry, William H. Desvousges, and Matthew P. McGivney. "Estimating Water Quality Benefits: An Economic Analysis." *S. Econ. J.* 50(1983):422–37.

Sutherland, R. J. "A Regional Approach to Estimating Benefits of Improved Water Quality." *J. Environ. Econ. and Manage.* 8(1981):27–44.

Vaughan, W., J. Mullahy, J. Hewitt, M. Hazilla, and C. Russell. *Aggregation Problems in Benefits Estimation.* Washington DC: Environmental Protection Agency Cooperative Agreement No. 810466-01, 1986.

Willig, Robert D. "Incremental Consumer's Surplus and Hedonic Price Adjustment." *J. Econ. Theory* 17 (1978):227–53.

[41]

Measuring the Benefits of Amenity Improvements in Hedonic Price Models

Timothy J. Bartik

Many economists have examined the relationship between property values and the benefits of improvements in amenities (public goods that vary spatially). This literature has made special assumptions that limit these models' usefulness for benefit-cost analysis.

One strand of the literature examines the *ex post* relationship between amenity improvements and property value changes (Rothenberg 1965; Strotz 1968; Lind 1973; Pines and Weiss 1976; Starrett 1981). This *ex post* approach does not allow an evaluation of projects before they are undertaken. Before the improvements, one could estimate the hedonic price function (Rosen 1974) describing the equilibrium relationship between amenities and property values. But this function cannot be used for prediction because improvements will shift it (Freeman 1971; Polinsky and Shavell 1976; Polinsky and Rubenfeld 1977).

A second strand of the literature analyzes the benefits of amenity improvements in a small area open to migration (Polinsky and Shavell 1976; Freeman 1979). If the area is small and moving costs are zero, amenity improvements cannot affect consumer utility. All benefits accrue to landowners in the improved area in property value increases.[1] The old hedonic price function can predict these property value increases because the function will not shift after a change in a small area. *Ex ante* benefit evaluation is feasible.

A third strand of the literature examines the benefits of marginal improvements in amenities over a large area. These benefits equal the sum of the marginal willingness to pay (WTP) for the amenity of the housing consumers who originally chose each improved location

(Freeman 1974; Small 1975; Pines and Weiss 1976). The hedonic rent function shifts because of the improvements, but these rent changes are pecuniary effects. Furthermore, adjustments by consumers and producers can be ignored for marginal improvements because of the envelope theorem. An *ex ante* benefit evaluation is feasible because the marginal WTP of consumers for the amenity equals its marginal price.

This article analyzes the more general case of non-marginal amenity improvements that affect the hedonic price function and hence consumer utility. In examining non-marginal amenity improvements, most analysts assume that benefits are the sum over improved locations of the WTP for the amenity improvement of the consumer originally choosing each location (Freeman 1974, 1979; Harrison and Rubinfeld 1978; Nelson 1978; Bender, Gronberg, and Hwang 1980; Blomquist and Worley 1981; Brookshire et al. 1982; Polinsky and Rubinfeld 1977.)[2]

Assistant professor of economics, Vanderbilt University. The author has benefitted greatly from several conversations with Kerry Smith, and from excellent comments by two referees (particularly from one referee whose comments caused the author to clarify the distinction between stage 1 and stage 2 profit increases in section 4). Portions of this research were funded by the EPA.

[1] This is true even if both wages and housing prices adjust, and we have an intercity hedonic model. A change in one city, in a model without moving costs, will not affect the intercity hedonic wage or housing price functions, and can not affect household utility or firm profits. Only landowners in the affected area gain. As Freeman (1979) points out, the benefit measure should include property value increases in non-residential as well as residential property.

[2] Exceptions to this assumption are three papers by Parsons (1986), Palmquist (forthcoming), and Scotchmer (1985) that take quite different approaches from this paper. Parsons assumes a linear hedonic price function, and examines benefits of amenity improvements. The upper and lower bounds derived in the present article

Land Economics Vol 64. No. 2, May 1988
0023-7639/00/-0001 $1.50/0
©1988 by the Board of Regents
of the University of Wisconsin System

But this benefit measure ignores adjustment. The amenity improvements shift the hedonic price function. Consumers and producers may adjust their location and their supply decisions. Adjustments increase benefits, and the usual benefit measure will be an underestimate. The first goal of this article is to justify this intuition more formally.

The second goal is to develop an upper bound to the benefits of amenity improvements. This article shows that the property value increases due to amenity improvements predicted by the original hedonic property value function will generally overestimate benefits. This result allows *ex ante* calculation of an upper bound for benefits. If consumer WTP for amenities is estimable, a lower bound is also calculable. But estimating consumer WTP is difficult, so the more easily estimable upper bound will often be the best available benefit measure.

This upper bound result is not the same as the well-known result that predicted changes in property values from a hedonic must be greater than WTP. True benefits of amenity improvements are also greater than WTP; hence, it is not obvious that the hedonic-predicted changes in property values must be greater than true benefits.

I. The True Benefit Measure Can Be Described, But Is Difficult To Implement

This section sets up the basic hedonic model (Rosen 1974) and derives the true benefit measure for non-marginal amenity improvements. This true benefits measure is used in subsequent sections that derive lower and upper bounds. The discussion will seem less abstract if the reader thinks of a specific amenity as the one being improved, such as: air quality; safety from crime; school quality; neighborhood physical infrastructure such as sidewalks, parks, and streetlights.

The amenity improvements take place within a city closed to migration from the rest of the world, but with costless migration within the city; section V considers intraurban moving costs. The model's economic agents are renters and landlords. Homeowners are implicitly treated as landlords who rent from themselves.

Renter households choose a vector A of amenities, a vector Z of pure housing characteristics (number of bedrooms, lot-size, house quality), and a value x of expenditure on nonhousing goods, by choosing a housing unit. Households face the constraints of income (y), and the hedonic price function for housing, $p(Z, A)$, which describes the equilibrium relationship between housing rents and Z and A. Household utility maximization is the following problem:

$$\text{Max}_{Z,A,x} U(Z,A,x) \text{ s.t.} \quad p(Z,A) + x \le y \quad [1]$$

The first-order conditions are

$$\partial p/\partial Z = (\partial U/\partial Z)/(\partial U/\partial x)$$
$$\partial p/\partial A = (\partial U/\partial A)/(\partial U/\partial x) \quad [2]$$

or the household equates its marginal WTP to the (nonconstant) marginal price for each characteristic.

Landlords own parcels of land and choose a vector of housing characteristics to supply and a number of units M to supply. Landlords are constrained by the hedonic price function and a cost function, $C(M,Z,A)$, which may depend on site amenities.[3] For simplicity, landlord location is assumed fixed.[4] The landlord's profit-maximization problem is

$$\text{Max}_{Z,M} \pi = Mp(Z,A) - C(M,Z,A) \quad [3]$$

The first-order conditions are

---

could be shown to apply to the linear case. Palmquist uses a pseudo-expenditure function to examine benefits. As he notes, this methodology often requires forecasting the new hedonic function, unlike the bounds developed here. Palmquist also mentions that WTP is a lower bound. Scotchmer assumes a particular preference structure and zero unobserved tastes; these assumptions allow identification of amenity preferences using single-market data, and a calculation of general equilibrium adjustments to amenity changes. Finally, Polinsky and Rubinfeld (1977) briefly note the problems in assuming away adjustment.

[3] Costs will also depend on input prices, but these price terms are suppressed because input prices are assumed exogenous.

[4] This assumption is reasonable if all landlords would face the same cost function at a given location, which implies that the equilibrium hedonic will ensure landlord indifference between locations.

$$\partial p/\partial Z = (\partial C/\partial Z)/M \qquad p = \partial C/\partial M \qquad [4]$$

or the supplied Z equates marginal characteristic price and cost, while the number of units equates marginal unit price and cost.

The equilibrium hedonic price function matches demand and supply for each housing type. The equilibrium hedonic thus may shift due to any factor shifting demand or supply, such as changes in population, income, costs, or amenities.

The amenity improvements analyzed are assumed to be exogenous to the housing market; i.e., amenities are unaffected by household and landlord choices. The amenity improvements can be of any size or pattern. For example, the amenity improvements could be uniform across the city, or amenities could increase in only half the city.

Before analyzing benefits, let us consider the effects of the amenity improvements on rents, location choices, and housing supply. First, the greater supply of high amenity locations would reduce the hedonic price differential between high and low amenity locations. Because the amenity supply has gone up, one would expect the rent for any given amenity level to decline, but by relatively more for high amenity locations. Thus, sites whose amenities improved relatively little would probably experience rent declines. Sites with large amenity improvements would probably go up in rent; the rent increase associated with an amenity improvement within any hedonic would likely offset the shift in the hedonic.

Second, households will respond to lower marginal amenity prices by choosing larger amenity levels. The effect on housing expenditures is uncertain. If the hedonic were linear, the expenditure effect would depend on the price elasticity of amenity demand, but demand behavior is harder to describe with a nonlinear hedonic.

Third, the increase in each household's chosen amenity level implies that any given amenity level will attract households of lower income. Lower income households probably have lower demands for housing characteristics. Locations that improved more than the average location will attract higher income households, and these households generally

have higher demands for housing characteristics.

Fourth, the increase in amenities will decrease demand for housing characteristics that are amenity substitutes (for example, a private garden), and increase demand for housing characteristics that are amenity complements. The overall effect on the demand for a housing characteristic at a location depends on the combination of these substitution or complementarity effects with the effects of changes in the income of households choosing that location. If the income of households choosing a location changes a great deal, this author would expect the income effect to usually dominate in determining housing characteristic demand. For example, at locations that improved much more than average and thus attracted households with much higher incomes, demand would probably increase for most housing characteristics, with the exception of very strong amenity substitutes.

Finally, landlord's supply will respond to these shifts in amenities, housing demand and rents. At a given amenity level, one would expect some decline in the landlord's chosen Z, and chosen M, in response to the lower demand of low-income households for most Z, and the decline in the rent for a given A, respectively. At locations where amenities are greatly improved, higher prices and higher demands for many housing characteristics will induce more production of units and an upgrading in unit quality, with the exception that housing characteristics that are substitutes for amenities may be downgraded. The net effect on overall housing quality or quantity is ambiguous.

Turning now to the benefits and costs resulting from the amenity improvements, the discussion will ignore the costs of causing these amenity improvements, for example, the costs to industrial firms of pollution standards, or to taxpayers of public services. Calculating these costs is straightforward; the difficult task is identifying the benefits and costs that result from the effects of the amenity improvements on the housing market. The discussion also ignores the benefits of amenity improvements to visitors who travel by the improved area.

The benefits resulting from the amenity improvements are the sum of the WTP of all households and landlords for the changes that occur because of the amenity improvements. Households and landlords are directly affected if amenities changed at their original location. But households and landlords whose original location is unimproved will be indirectly affected by the shifts in the hedonic.

The benefits to households can be described using the concept of a bid function. The net benefits to household i (BH_i) of the improvements can be written as:

$$BH_i = [W(A_{ni}^a, Z_{ni}^a, v_i) - W(A_{oi}^b, Z_{oi}^b, v_i)]$$
$$- [p^a(A_{ni}^a, Z_{ni}^a) - p^b(A_{oi}^b, Z_{oi}^b)] \qquad [5]$$

Equation [5] uses the following notation: $W(\ )$ is the household's bid function, that is the rent it is willing to pay for a given housing unit at a particular utility level;[5] and v_i is the utility level. The subscripts "ni" and "oi" on the A and Z variables indicate the level of A or Z for household i at its new and old locations. The superscripts "a" and "b" on A and Z indicate the level of amenities and housing characteristics at a location after and before the amenity improvement and housing adjustments. $p^a(\ )$ and $p^b(\ )$ are the equilibrium hedonic price functions after and before the amenity improvements.

Equation [5] is a compensating variation measure if v_i is the household's original utility, and an equivalent variation measure if v_i is the household's final utility. Equation [5] says the household's benefits equal its willingness to pay for the change in housing unit characteristics minus the change in rent.

Equation [5] applies to all households in the market: households who stay in improved areas, households who stay in unimproved areas, households who move out of or into improved areas. As equation [5] implies, households may be affected by amenity improvements for several reasons: their original location's amenities may change; their original landlord may alter the housing unit supply; their rent may change; they may choose to move due to shifts in the hedonic or the other changes.

Landlord's profits change after the amenity improvement for four reasons. First, amenity improvements may affect landlord costs (e.g.,

lower crime may reduce vandalism). Second, if amenities at their site change, rents change even if the overall hedonic did not shift. Third, the shift in the hedonic function affects rent received by all landlords, even those whose sites did not experience amenity improvements. Finally, landlords may respond to these changes by choosing a different housing supply. Taking all four factors together, the resulting change in landlord j's profits (BL_j) is given by

$$BL_j = [M_j^a p^a (A_j^a, Z_j^a) - C(A_j^a, Z_j^a, M_j^a)]$$
$$- [M_j^b p^b (A_j^b, Z_j^b) - C(A_j^b, Z_j^b, M_j^b)] \qquad [6]$$

Equation [6] uses similar notation to equation [5], but only a j subscript is needed because landlords do not change locations.

Total social benefits (TSB) of the amenity improvement are derived by summing equations [5] and [6] over all households and landlords, both in and out of the improved area, to get

$$TSB = \sum_i BH_i + \sum_j BL_j \qquad [7]$$

The problem with this social benefit measure is that it is almost impossible to calculate. This measure requires knowledge of exactly how the equilibrium hedonic price function is affected by amenity improvements, and how household and landlord choices change.

This problem of finding the equilibrium hedonic function is not generally susceptible to analytic solution. Some beginning attempts have been made to solve this problem by general equilibrium simulation methods (Cropper et al. 1985). But any simulation solution requires a great deal of information that is often unavailable. Furthermore, the results of general equilibrium simulation models often depend on untestable assumptions about consumer preferences and supplier behavior.

II. The Usual Benefit Measure Is An Underestimate of True Benefits

The difficulties in estimating the true benefit measure justify examining simpler benefit

---

[5] The bid function is the function $W(A, Z, y, v_i)$ solving $U(Z, A, y - W) = v_i$. The text suppresses income because it is unchanged.

measures. This section shows that the usual benefit measure, household WTP for amenity improvements at their original location, underestimates true benefits. This result is shown by a decomposition of the effects of amenity improvements into three imaginary stages. These stages help in analyzing benefits, but are not meant to describe a realistic sequence of events. Table 1 provides formulas for the benefits accruing to households, landlords, and society during each of the three stages described below.[6]

During stage 1, the amenity improvements take place. We assume that all rent changes, and household and landlord adjustments are postponed to later stages. Given this assumption, only households and landlords at improved sites are affected. The benefit to these households is their WTP for the amenity improvement at their original site, as we have prevented any change in their rent or location. Because of our constraint on rents and adjustment, landlords are only affected if the amenity directly affects their costs. Most amenity improvements do not directly affect landlord costs (e.g., higher school quality); amenity improvements that directly affect landlord costs probably lower them (e.g., crime).

During stage 2, the hedonic rent function shifts to its final form. However, households and landlords are still constrained to their original location and supply choices. I again emphasize that this is an artificial constraint for analytic purposes, as households and landlords will want to make adjustments. Whatever the pattern of rent changes at stage 2, these rent changes are pecuniary transfers between landlords and tenants, and represent zero efficiency benefits.

During stage 3, we allow households to move and landlords to alter their housing supply. Because we are removing constraints, the new landlord and household choices can only make households and landlords better off compared to their situation at the end of stage 2. This adjustment benefit occurs for households and landlords at all sites, both improved and unimproved. The benefits received during stage 3 do not imply that everyone gains from all three stages. For example, landlords at unimproved sites probably lose profits after the

amenity improvements because of the likely rent decline; however, adjustment can only increase their profits compared to no adjustment.

This three-stage decomposition shows that the WTP for the improvements of households originally at improved sites will underestimate benefits. True benefits equal this WTP plus three non-negative values: cost-savings of landlords at stage 1; landlord profit gains at stage 3; household utility gains at stage 3. The WTP measure underestimates benefits because it ignores adjustment, which can only improve efficiency, and all other effects are pecuniary.

The three-stage decomposition also shows that the WTP benefit measure is accurate if amenities do not affect landlord costs, and no household or landlord adjustments take place. Assuming small cost effects is plausible for many amenities. An assumption of no household or landlord adjustment is plausible in the short run. Thus, the WTP measure is most accurate when used as a short-run benefit measure.

III. The Property Value Increases Predicted By The Original Hedonic Function Due To Amenity Improvements Will Usually Overestimate True Benefits

While the WTP measure is simpler to estimate than true social benefits, the literature suggests that multimarket data is needed to estimate household WTP for amenities (Brown 1981; Bartik 1987a, 1987b; Diamond and Smith 1985).[7] Furthermore, the WTP measure is only a lower bound to benefits. This section develops an easier to estimate upper bound to benefits: the property value increase due to amenity improvements that are projected from a hedonic property value function estimated before the improvements take

[6] The reader should recall that costs of causing amenity improvements are not analyzed by this paper, and are not included in Table 1.

[7] One would also need to be careful to estimate the correct compensated or equivalent variation measure of WTP rather than the Marshallian measure. For details, see Horowitz (1984).

TABLE 1

A DECOMPOSITION OF THE BENEFITS OF AMENITY CHANGE INTO HOUSEHOLD
WILLINGNESS TO PAY AND A NON-NEGATIVE QUANTITY

	Benefits at Various Stages to:		
	Households	Landlords	Net Efficiency Benefits
Stage 1: Amenity changes, no adjustment or rent change	$\sum_i W(A^a_{oi}, Z^b_{oi}, v_i) - W(A^b_{oi}, Z^b_{oi}, v_i)$ Household willingness to pay (WTP) at original location: zero for unimproved sites, positive for improved sites.	$\sum_j - [C(A^a_j, Z^b_j, M^b_j) - C(A^b_j, Z^b_j, M^b_j)]$ Landlord cost savings: assumed non-negative for improved sites; zero for unimproved sites	Sum of all household WTP plus all landlords' cost-savings.
Stage 2: Rent change	$\sum_i - [p^a(A^a_{oi}, Z^b_{oi}) - p^b(A^a_{oi}, Z^b_{oi})]$ Rent change at both improved and unimproved sites	$\sum_j [M^b_j \, p^a(A^a_j, Z^b_j) - M^b_j \, p^b(A^b_j, Z^b_j)]$ Rent change at both improved and unimproved sites.	Zero efficiency benefits; pecuniary transfer between households and landlords.
Stage 3: Adjustment	$\sum_i W(A^a_{ni}, Z^a_{ni}, v_i) - p^a(A^a_{ni}, Z^a_{ni}) -$ $[W(A^a_{oi}, Z^b_{oi}, v_i) - p^a(A^a_{oi}, Z^b_{oi})]$ Measure of household utility increase from adjustment, for households originally at both improved and unimproved sites.	$\sum_j M^a_j \, p^a(A^a_j, Z^a_j) - C(A^a_j, Z^a_j, M^a_j) -$ $[M^b_j \, p^a(A^a_j, Z^b_j) - C(A^a_j, Z^b_j, M^b_j)]$ Landlord profit increase from adjustment to new hedonic; applies to landlords at all sites.	Net gain from adjustment must be non-negative for all.
Sum of Three Stages	$\sum_i W(A^a_{ni}, Z^a_{ni}, v_i) - W(A^b_{oi}, Z^b_{oi}, v_i)$ $- [p^a(A^a_{ni}, Z^a_{ni}) - p^b(A^b_{oi}, Z^b_{oi})]$ Net household gain; sum over all households of Eq. [5] in text.	$\sum_j M^a_j \, p^a(A^a_j, Z^a_j) - C(A^a_j, Z^a_j, M^a_j) -$ $[M^b_j \, p^b(A^b_j, Z^b_j) - C(A^b_j, Z^b_j, M^b_j)]$ Net landlord gain, sum over all j of Eq. [6] in text.	Sum of 1st and 2nd columns is same as Eq. [7] in text = household WTP at original location plus non-negative quantity.

place. These projected property value increases are not the same as the actual property value changes that occur, because the hedonic property value function will shift. This upper bound result has previously been hypothesized by Anderson and Bishop (1986), although without a proof.

This section's result is not the same as the well-known result that household WTP for an increase in a characteristic above its chosen level must be bounded from above by the hedonic rent increase. This result has been used, for example, by Brookshire et al. (1982), who regarded a hedonic measure being greater than the contingent valuation (CV) measure of WTP as supporting the CV approach to estimating WTP. This relationship between WTP and the hedonic must hold for the household's original choice to be optimal; if the household is willing to pay more than the market cost for

an amenity increase above its chosen level, then the household should have chosen that higher level. But section II showed that benefits from amenity improvements exceed the WTP of the original households. Hence, while the hedonic measure clearly is an upper bound to the WTP measure, it is by no means obvious whether the hedonic is an upper or lower bound to benefits.

A. Derivation and measurement of the upper bound. This upper bound measure will be derived by a decomposition of the effects of the amenity improvement into four imaginary stages. Table 2 provides formulas for the benefits and costs of the four stages.

During stage 1, the amenity improvements occur. The hedonic rent function is constrained to remain unchanged; hence households and landlords at unimproved sites are unaffected during stage 1 because nothing

TABLE 2

A DECOMPOSITION OF THE BENEFITS OF AMENITY IMPROVEMENTS INTO THE
PROPERTY VALUE INCREASE ALONG THE ORIGINAL HEDONIC, PLUS OTHER EFFECTS

	Benefits at Various Stages to:		
	Households	Landlords	Net Efficiency Benefits
Stage 1: Amenity changes, hedonic price function unchanged, no adjustment allowed	$\sum_i W(A_{oi}^a, Z_{oi}^b, v_i) - p^b(A_{oi}^a, Z_{oi}^b)$ $- [W(A_{oi}^b, Z_{oi, w}^b) - p^b(A_{oi}^b, Z_{oi}^b)]$ Households must lose utility as hedonic unchanged, but forced to choose different A. Only affects households at improved sites.	$\sum_j M_j^b p^b(A_j^a, Z_j^b) - C(A_j^a, Z_j^b, M_j^b)$ $- [M_j^b p^b(A_j^b, Z_j^b) - C(A_j^b, Z_j^b, M_j^b)]$ Landlord increase in profits due to amenity change, without allowing for adjustment or shifts in hedonic. Can be measured by ordinary hedonic methods: see text. Only affects landlords at improved sites.	Increase in landlord profits from direct effects of amenity change, plus artificial household disequilibrium.
Stage 2: Landlord partially adjusts, households arbitrarily assigned to available sites.	Formula depends on assignment. But households still must be worse off than before stage 1 given that hedonic has not changed. Only affects households at improved sites because nothing changes at unimproved sites.	$\sum_j M_j^* p^b(A_j^a, Z_j^*) - C(A_j^a, Z_j^*, M_j^*) -$ $[M_j^b p^b(A_j^a, Z_j^b) - C(A_j^a, Z_j^b, M_j^b)]$ Effect on landlord profits of adjustment, keeping hedonic fixed: must be non-negative. Z^* and M^* are new profit-maximizing choices. Only affects landlords at improved sites.	Increase in landlord profits from adjustment under old hedonic plus continued household disequilibrium.
Stage 3: Landlord's supply adjusted to final level; households moved to final location.	$\sum_i W(A_{ni}^a, Z_{ni}^a, v_i) - p^b(A_{ni}^a, Z_{ni}^a) -$ $[W(A_{oi}^b, Z_{oi}^b, v_i) - p^b(A_{oi}^b, Z_{oi}^b)]$ This is a formula for household benefits from the beginning of stage 1. Must be negative because hedonic is unchanged, (Z, A) consumed has changed. Affects households at all locations because all households adjust.	$\sum_j M_j^a p^b(A_j^a, Z_j^a) - C(A_j^a, Z_j^a, M_j^a) -$ $[M_j^* p^b(A_j^a, Z_j^*) - C(A_j^a, Z_j^*, M_j^*)]$ Landlords lose profits because of change away from equilibrium Z^*, M^*, given A^a and old hedonic. Affects landlords at all locations because all landlords adjust.	Net effect of stage 1, 2, and 3 is increase in landlord profits at stage 1 and 2 plus disequilibrium losses.
Stage 4: Hedonic changes	$\sum_i - [p^a(A_{ni}^a, Z_{ni}^a) - p^b(A_{ni}^a, Z_{ni}^a)]$ Rent change	$\sum_j M_j^a [p^a(A_j^a, Z_j^a) - p^b(A_j^a, Z_j^a)]$ Rent change	Pecuniary transfer; zero efficiency benefits.
Sum of Four Stages	$\sum_i W(A_{ni}^a, Z_{ni}^a, v_i) - W(A_{oi}^b, Z_{oi}^b, v_i)$ $- [p^a(A_{ni}^a, Z_{ni}^a) - p^b(A_{oi}^b, Z_{oi}^b)]$ Same as sum over i of Eq. [5] in text	$\sum_j M_j^a p^a(A_j^a, Z_j^a) - C(A_j^a, Z_j^a, M_j^a) -$ $[M_j^b p^b(A_j^b, Z_j^b) - C(A_j^b, Z_j^b, M_j^b)]$ Same as sum over j of Eq. [6] in text	Same as text Eq. [7] = Increase in landlord profits at stage 1 and 2 plus non-positive quantity.

changes at these sites. Although the hedonic rent function does not change, rents increase at improved sites because the amenity improvements upgrade these sites along a fixed hedonic function. Landlords and households are prevented from adjusting supply or location choices at stage 1. Landlords will be better off because amenity improvements increase rent receipts, and probably reduce costs

or leave costs unchanged. Households are worse off because we have imposed a different amenity level, but the hedonic is unchanged.

During stage 2, the hedonic remains unchanged, but landlords in the improved area are allowed to optimally adjust their housing supply. Allowing landlord adjustment must increase profits. Households in the improved area are assigned to fill the available housing

units in the improved area.[8] Because the hedonic rent function is unchanged, no assignment can increase household utility above
what the household received before stage 1,
when the household was making an optimal
choice.

During stage 3, all landlords and households are assigned to the housing supply and
location that they will choose after the hedonic
has shifted. The hedonic rent function is still
constrained to stay the same, although actual
rents paid at a given site or by a given household may change, along the fixed hedonic
function, as the bundle supplied or consumed
is changed. Because the hedonic has not
changed, the housing supply assignment must
reduce landlord profits compared to when
their choice was unconstrained, at the end of
stage 2. Similarly, the new locations assigned
to households must reduce utility compared to
when their choice was unconstrained, before
stage 1 began.

During stage 4, rents at each location
change to reflect the new hedonic rent function. Whatever rent changes occur during
stage 4, the landlord's loss (gain) is matched
by the household's gain (loss). The stage 4
rent changes are a pecuniary transfer from
landlords to households or vice versa, and imply zero efficiency benefits during stage 4.

The net efficiency benefits from all four
stages are equal to the first-stage and second-
stage increases in landlord profits, plus the
disequilibrium profit loss imposed on landlords during stage 3, plus the disequilibrium
utility loss imposed on households during
stages 1 through 3. The first-stage and second-
stage increase in landlord profits is thus an
upper bound to the efficiency benefits resulting from these amenity improvements. Unfortunately, this upper bound is difficult to implement because it requires estimating how
landlords' supply choices adjust as amenities
improve, and how amenities and housing
characteristics affect landlord's costs.

But we can show that the first stage increase in landlord profits is readily measurable, and is usually an upper bound to benefits. One way to measure this first-stage profit
increase would require estimating an ordinary
hedonic property value function, with property values a function of amenities and hous-

ing characteristics, using data from the
pre-improvement cross-section. This estimated property value function could be used
to project property value increases resulting
from the amenity improvements, holding constant the hedonic rent function and housing
characteristics. These projected property
value increases would be the capitalized value
of the profit increases occurring in stage 1. An
alternative way to measure this first-stage
profit increase would require estimating a hedonic rent function using pre-improvement
cross-section data. Suppose, as seems reasonable, that amenities do not greatly affect landlord costs. Then the projected rent increases
caused by amenity improvements, projected
using this original hedonic rent function,
would measure the first-stge increase in annual profits.

For this first-stage profit increase to be an
upper bound to benefits, the second-stage
profit increase must be smaller in absolute
value than the losses imposed on landlords in
stage 3, and on households in stages 1 though
3. There are two reasons to suspect that this
will frequently be the case. First, many housing characteristics are difficult to alter. Small
adjustments in housing characteristics imply
that the second-stage profit increase is small.

Second, the market will cause the equilibrium housing rent function to closely reflect
differences in housing costs, and this reduces
the profit gain from even large adjustments in
housing characteristics. Suppose that in equilibrium a given neighborhood with a particular vector of amenities is associated with a variety of housing types (we often observe this
phenomenon); one explanation is that households with the same amenity demand may
have different housing characteristic demands. Suppose further that different landlords facing the same amenity vector have the
same cost function. Then the equilibrium hedonic rent function will ensure equal profits
for all the landlords in the neighborhood, de-

---

[8] There may be too few or too many households for
the available housing units in the improved area. This
problem is solved by assigning households to share units,
or rent more than one unit. The key point remains: households must be worse off from a different assignment,
given that the hedonic is unchanged.

spite the differences in housing characteristics supplied, by perfectly reflecting housing production costs. An improvement in amenities, holding the hedonic rent function constant, will then cause some landlords to adjust their housing supply as the mix of household demands changes in the improved neighborhood. But, if the neighborhood retains a variety of housing types, this landlord adjustment will have equal and opposite effects on rents and costs, and hence zero effect on profits.

A final point is that this first-stage profit increase, if not an upper bound, will probably be a better lower bound to true benefits than the conventional WTP measure. Suppose again that amenities do not affect landlord costs. Then this first-stage profit increase is simply the amenity-induced increase in rents along the original hedonic. As mentioned before, we know by revealed preference arguments that this rent increase is greater than household WTP. Thus, in the unlikely event that this first-stage profit increase is a lower bound to benefits, it will be greater than the alternative lower bound, the WTP measure, as well as being easier to estimate.

B. Intuitive rationale for the upper bound. An intuitive explanation of the upper bound can be developed from the literature on benefits of marginal amenity improvements. This literature showed that benefits of marginal amenity improvements equal the marginal WTP (equals hedonic marginal price) of the household originally choosing each location. To get the benefits of non-marginal improvements, this marginal benefit measure can be integrated, allowing for the change in the hedonic price function that takes place after each marginal amenity change. A convenient notation is to consider the change in amenities at all improved locations, as well as the change in the hedonic and housing characteristics, to be functions of a variable k that changes from k_0 to k_1. The true benefits of non-marginal amenity improvements can be written as

$$TSB = \sum_{j=1}^{N} \int_{k_0}^{k_1} \frac{\partial p^k}{\partial A_j} [A_j(k), Z(k)] \, dk \qquad [8]$$

$j = 1, \ldots, N$ are the N improved sites.[9] Note that the hedonic function is assumed to change

continuously as k changes, as signified by the k superscript on the hedonic marginal price.

Ignoring any amenity effect on costs, the profit increases that result during stages 1 and 2 of the model can also be written as the integral of a particular set of marginal price changes. A marginal amenity improvement's effects on profits is given by its direct effect on rents; the optimal supply adjustment can be ignored because of the envelope theorem. Integrating over these marginal profit changes gives the total profit change due to the amenity, or

Total Profit Increase

$$= \sum_{j=1}^{N} \int_{k_0}^{k_1} \frac{\partial p^b}{\partial A_j} (A_j(k), Z(k)) \, dk \qquad [9]$$

The main difference between equation [8] and [9] is that [9] uses the original hedonic rent function. A large amenity increase will probably decrease hedonic marginal prices of A from those predicted by the original hedonic rent function. Thus, the first- and second-stage profit increases, which assume a continued high market valuation of amenities, will be greater than true efficiency benefits, which can be seen as allowing for a decline in the market's valuation of amenities.

C. Closeness of the proposed upper bound to true benefits. The hedonic property value and rent measures of benefits are likely to be quite close upper bounds to benefits if either of two conditions holds: the amenity improvements at most sites are small; the amenity-induced shifts in the hedonic functions are small. If amenity improvements are small, then it would usually be assumed by hedonic analysts that the original households' WTP for the improvements are close to the rent increases predicted by the original hedonic due to the improvements; small amenity improvements are close to being marginal, and hedonic theory holds that household marginal WTP exactly equals the marginal price paid. Suppose we accept the arguments of section A

---

[9]This measure is proposed in a paper by Scotchmer (1985) in a very different model. This measure is not empirically feasible without a general equilibrium model that allows shifts in the hedonic function to be predicted.

that the second-stage increase in landlord profits is likely to be small, and hence the first-stage increase in landlord profits is a valid upper bound. Suppose further that the amenities' effects on landlord costs are negligible, and thus this upper bound can be measured by the original hedonic rent function. Then, for small amenity improvements, the lower bound to benefits (the original households' WTP) will be close to the upper bound (the original hedonic's projected increase in housing prices using either rents or property values). Both bounds will thus be close to true benefits.

To explain the second result, that the proposed upper bound will be close if the hedonic does not change too much, consider an analysis of the losses caused by reversing the amenity improvements. A four-stage decomposition identical to that in section A can be used to show that the property value decrease, projected by the hedonic property value function that prevails with the improvements in place, will usually be less in absolute value than the net loss caused by reversing the improvements.[10] This net loss is the negative of the net benefits caused by the improvements. Thus, true benefits are bounded from below by the property value increases due to amenities that would be predicted by the post-improvement hedonic property value function. If the market's valuation of amenity improvement does not change too much when the hedonic shifts, then this lower bound will be close to the upper bound, and both will be close to true benefits.

Exactly how close the upper bound is to true benefits depends on the case at hand. I suspect it would be unusual for the difference between the upper bound and true benefits to be as great as 50 percent. As the above discussion indicates, for the upper bound to be in error by 50 percent, the improvements must lead to a decline in the relative price of high amenity versus low amenity locations of somewhat more than 50 percent. Such an error also implies that the rent increases along the original hedonic for the improvements, which must be less than some households' WTP for the improvements, would be somewhat more than twice the WTP of the households originally choosing lower amenity levels. These large changes in relative prices, and large discrepancies between market and household valuations, would require a quite large increase in the average amenity supply in the city. An empirical study by this author (Bartik 1986) suggests that the change in amenity supply would have to be quite large for the upper bound to be substantially in error. For a large (one standard deviation) change in the amenity "neighborhood physical condition," the WTP of the original residents was only one-third less than the hedonic rent increase. The implied error in the upper bound would be somewhat less than one-third.

An error of up to 50 percent may be significant for some purposes. But the researcher should recognize that other errors, such as errors in measuring the amenities or mispecification of the hedonic, may be greater in magnitude than the error in the upper bound, and these other errors may be easier to correct.

IV. Implications of Moving Costs For The Model

This section considers modifications to the model to allow for moving and search costs. Household moving costs could include financial costs, search costs, and psychological costs from losing a familiar neighborhood. Landlords may have search costs in finding a reliable tenant to replace their current tenant.

The presence of moving costs does not require any modification to the conclusion that the WTP measure is a lower bound to benefits. In the three-stage decomposition of section II, no moving costs are incurred until households and landlords are allowed to optimally adjust at stage 3. But even with moving costs, adjustment can only add to benefits; moving costs simply imply that optimal adjustment is less likely to involve moving. Thus, because benefits are still positive during stage 3, the WTP benefits that occur during stage 1 will still be a lower bound to the net total benefits that occur from all three stages.

---

[10] As with the upper bound result, this lower bound result depends on the assumption that one can ignore the profit increases that result from landlord adjustment, holding the hedonic function fixed (i.e., the second-stage profit increase in Table 2).

Moving costs do increase the likelihood that the property value measure of section III is not always an upper bound to benefits. In the four-stage decomposition of section III, it was assumed at stage 1 that an increase in amenities, holding the hedonic rent function constant, must decrease household utility because the household originally chose its optimal amenity level. But with moving costs, the household will not always adjust amenity consumption so that household marginal benefit (MB) from the amenity equals the hedonic marginal price (MP). The household will stay at its location even if the amenity changes from the level at which MB = MP, as long as the loss from not adjusting location is less than moving costs. As shown in Bartik (1986), if amenities at a given site are below their "optimal" level (the level at which MB = MP), then amenity improvements, holding the original hedonic function constant, may increase household utility. Thus, the increase in landlord profits at stage one now overlooks this possible stage 1 increase in household utility, and is less likely to be an upper bound to true benefits. On the other hand, if amenities were originally above their optimal level, then households will lose even more utility at stage 1 due to amenity improvement, and it becomes more likely that the first-stage profit increase is an upper bound to benefits.

Despite this modification, the property value measure remains extremely useful. In many cases, a benefit analyst will be able to determine whether households in improved areas were originally below or above their optimal amenity level, and thus can tell whether the upper bound result is still likely to hold. As discussed in Bartik (1986), most households in a city neighborhood would probably be below (above) their optimal amenity level if the amenities in that neighborhood have recently decreased (increased). Furthermore, the possible household gain during stage 1 is bounded by the size of moving costs, because if the initial "disequilibrium" had been larger than moving costs, the household would have already moved. Thus, moving costs are unlikely to cause the property value measure to be too much less than true benefits.

V. Conclusion

This paper shows that the usual measure of the benefits of amenity improvements, the willingness to pay of households originally at the improved sites, underestimates benefits because this measure ignores adjustments by housing demanders and suppliers. The intuition behind this result is that it is inconsistent to use the hedonic model, in which household and landlord adjustment establishes the equilibrium hedonic rent function, and then ignore adjustment in measuring benefits.

The paper suggests that a more easily estimable benefit measure, the property value increases from the amenity improvements projected by the original hedonic, will often be close to benefits. The property value benefit measure is analogous to using real GNP to measure the welfare gain from some policy. In both cases, the analyst is using base period prices to value a quantity change. Using base period prices is less accurate than compensating or equivalent variation measures, but requires less data and statistical assumptions.

Future research on this topic should focus on two issues. First, simulation methods and empirical data should be used to examine how close the property value measure and WTP measure are to true benefits under a variety of assumptions. Second, the model should be extended to the intercity case, with costly mobility, and amenity improvements that shift the intercity hedonic functions.

References

Anderson, Glen D., and Richard C. Bishop. 1986. "The Valuation Problem." In *Natural Resource Economics: Policy Problems and Contemporary Analysis,* ed. Daniel Bromley. Hingham, MA: Kluwer-Nijhoff.

Bartik, T. 1987a. "The Estimation of Demand Parameters in Hedonic Price Models." *Journal of Political Economy* 95(1):81–88.

———— 1987b. "Estimating Hedonic Demand Parameters Using Single Market Data: The Problems Caused by Unobserved Tastes." *Review of Economics and Statistics* 69:178–80.

———— 1986. "Neighborhood Revitalization's Effects on Tenants and the Benefit-Cost Analysis of Government Neighborhood Programs." *Journal of Urban Economics* 19:234–48.

Bender, B., T. Gronberg, and H. S. Hwang. 1980. "Choice of Functional Form and the Demand for Air Quality." *Review of Economics and Statistics* 62:638–43.

Blomquist, G., and L. Worley. 1981. "Hedonic Prices, Demands for Urban Housing Amenities, and Benefit Estimates." *Journal of Urban Economics* 9:212–21.

Brookshire, D., M. Thayer, W. Schulze, and R. d'Arge. 1982. "Valuing Public Goods: A Comparison of Survey and Hedonic Approaches." *American Economic Review* 72:165–78.

Brown, J. 1981. "Structural Estimation in Implicit Markets." In *The Measurement of Labor Costs*, ed. J. E. Triplett. NBER Studies in Income and Wealth, No. 48: University of Chicago Press.

Cropper, M., L. Deck, K. McConnell, and T. Phipps. 1985. "Should the Rosen Model Be Used to Value Environmental Amenities?" Working paper, Department of Economics, University of Maryland.

Diamond, D., and B. Smith. 1985. "Simultaneity in the Market for Housing Characteristics." *Journal of Urban Economics* 17:280–92.

Freeman, A. M. 1971. "Air Pollution and Property Values: A Methodological Comment." *Review of Economics and Statistics* 53:415–16.

Freeman, A. M. 1974. "On Estimating Air Pollution Control Benefits from Land Value Studies." *Journal of Environmental Economics and Management* 1:74–83.

Freeman, A. M. 1979. *The Benefits of Environmental Improvement*. Baltimore: Johns Hopkins Press.

Harrison, D., and D. Rubinfeld. 1978. "Hedonic Housing Prices and the Demand for Clean Air." *Journal of Environmental Economics and Management* 5:81–102.

Horowitz, Joel L. 1984. "Estimating Compensating and Equivalent Income Variations from Hedonic Price Models." *Economic Letters* 14:303–8.

Lind, R. C. 1973. "Spatial Equilibrium, the Theory of Rents, and the Measurement of Ben-

efits from Public Programs." *Quarterly Journal of Economics* 87:188–207.

Nelson, J. 1978. "Residential Choice, Hedonic Prices, and the Demand for Urban Air Quality." *Journal of Urban Economics* 5:357–69.

Palmquist, R. Forthcoming. "Welfare Measurement with Nonlinear Budget Constraints." *Journal of Environmental Economics and Management*.

Parsons, G. 1986. "An Almost Ideal Demand System for Housing Attributes." *Southern Economic Journal* 53(2):347–63.

Pines, D., and Y. Weiss. 1976. "Land Improvement Projects and Land Values." *Journal of Urban Economics* 3:1–13.

Polinsky, A. M., and D. Rubinfeld. 1977. "Property Values and the Benefits of Environmental Improvements: Theory and Measurement." In *Public Economics and the Quality of Life*, eds. L. Wingo and A. Evans. Baltimore: Johns Hopkins Press.

Polinsky, A. M., and S. Shavell. 1976. "Amenities and Property Values in a Model of an Urban Area." *Journal of Public Economics* 5:119–29.

Rosen, S. 1976. "Hedonic Prices and Implicit Markets: Product Differentiation in Pure Competition." *Journal of Political Economy* 82:34–55.

Rothenberg, J. 1967. *Economic Evaluation of Urban Renewal*. Washington, DC: Brookings Institution.

Scotchmer, Suzanne. 1985. "The Short Run and Long Run Benefits of Environmental Improvement." Discussion Paper 1135, Department of Economics, Harvard University.

Small, K. 1975. "Air Pollution and Property Values: Further Comment." *Review of Economics and Statistics* 57:105–7.

Starrett, D. 1981. "Land Value Capitalization in Local Public Finance." *Journal of Political Economy* 89:306–27.

Strotz, R. H. 1968. "The Use of Land Rent Changes to Measure the Welfare Benefits of Land Improvement." In *The New Economics of Regulated Industries*, ed. J. Haring. Los Angeles: Economic Resource Center, Occidental College.

[42]

JOURNAL OF ENVIRONMENTAL ECONOMICS AND MANAGEMENT 1, 132–149 (1974)

Bidding Games for Valuation of Aesthetic Environmental Improvements[1]

ALAN RANDALL

Department of Agricultural Economics, University of Kentucky, Lexington, Kentucky 40506

AND

BERRY IVES AND CLYDE EASTMAN

Department of Agricultural Economics and Agricultural Business, New Mexico State University, Las Cruces, New Mexico 88003

Received March 19, 1974

An empirical case study of the benefits of abatement of aesthetic environmental damage associated with the Four Corners power plant and Navajo mine using the bidding game technique is presented. Bidding games were carefully designed to avoid the potential problems inherent in that technique. The results indicate the existence of substantial benefits from abatement of this aesthetic environmental damage. Aggregate bid curves, marginal bid curves, and estimates of the income elasticity of bid are presented. The effectiveness of the bidding game technique is discussed.

It has proved a difficult and often forbidding task to ascribe economic values to environmental improvements. Yet, rational and informed social decision making requires, among other things, a consideration of the economic costs and benefits of environmental improvements. The difficulties in economic evaluation are compounded in the case of environmental improvements of an aesthetic nature. This article discusses the problems inherent in the valuation of aesthetic environmental improvements and presents a case study in which bidding games were used as the valuation technique.

THE THEORY

Aesthetic damage to an outdoor environment, to the extent that it diminishes the utility of some individuals, is a discommodity and its abatement is a commodity. Abatement of this kind of external diseconomy is both a nonmarket good, since it is nonexclusive, and a public good in the sense of Davis and Whinston [6], since it is inexhaustible at least over a very substantial range. That is, additional consumers of this kind of aesthetic environmental improvement can be added without diminishing the visibility or scenic beauty available to each (at least, until crowding occurs). Additional users can be added at near zero marginal cost, over a substantial range.

Bradford [2] has presented a theoretical framework for the valuation of public goods. Traditional demand curves are inappropriate for the analysis of demand for

[1] Journal Article 506, New Mexico State University, Agricultural Experiment Station, Las Cruces. The authors are grateful for helpful comments from Ralph d'Arge and two anonymous reviewers.

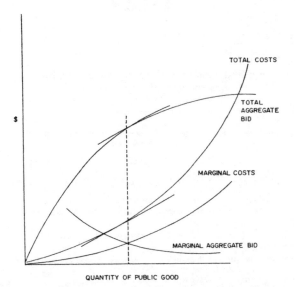

TOTAL COSTS

TOTAL
AGGREGATE
BID

$

MARGINAL COSTS

MARGINAL AGGREGATE BID

QUANTITY OF PUBLIC GOOD

FIG. 1. Collective optimization of the quantity of public good provided.

public goods, since the situation is not one of individuals responding to a parametric price per unit by choosing an appropriate number of units. Rather, the individual directly arrives at the total value to himself of various given packages. In the case of a public good, the individual is unable to exercise any choice over the quantity provided him, except as a member of the collective which makes a collective choice. Further, the nature of a public good such as aesthetic environmental improvements is such that increases in the quantity provided are not purely quantitative increases, but are more in the nature of improvements in quality. Thus, the individual values alternative packages of a public good, which may differ in quantity and quality.

Bradford proposes the concept of an aggregate bid curve for public goods. Individual bid curves are simply indifference curves passing through a given initial state, with the numeraire good (which can be dollars) on the vertical axis and the public good on the horizontal axis.[2] The aggregate bid curve is the algebraic (or vertical, in diagrammatic analyses) summation of individual bids over the relevant population.

The aggregate bid curve is an aggregate benefit curve, as it measures precisely what an accurate benefit-cost analysis of provision of a public good would measure as benefits. Using the approach of methodological collectivism, efficiency in the provision of a public good can be achieved by maximizing the excess of aggregate bid over total cost, or equating the first derivative of aggregate bid (i.e., marginal bid)

[2] If different packages of a public good represented continuous quantitative increases, the individual bid curve would be smooth and would exhibit decreasing marginal utility of increasing quantities of the public good. However, Bradford's concept of different packages differing in quantity and quality logically implies that individual bid curves need be neither smooth nor of continually decreasing slope. Bradford insists that, *a priori*, nothing can be said about the slope of the "demand," or marginal bid curve, for a public good of this nature.

with the marginal cost of provision.[3] Figure 1 shows the efficient level of provision of a public good.[4]

THE BIDDING GAME TECHNIQUE

It is possible to conceive of a number of techniques for estimating the aggregate bid curve for environmental improvements. Two general classes of techniques, direct costing techniques and revealed demand techniques, have been suggested in the literature and applied in empirical studies. Each of these has its difficulties, especially when adapted for valuation of aesthetic environmental improvements. These techniques will be briefly discussed below. Then, a third type of technique, bidding games, will be proposed. Bidding game techniques are themselves not without difficulties, but we will argue that there may be applications for which they are the preferable or even the only feasible method for empirical studies. Methods of maximizing the reliability of bidding games will be discussed and an empirical study using bidding games will be presented.

Direct costing methods. Implicit in the concept of a "marginal value of damage avoided by abatement" curve, as proposed by Kneese and Bower [12], is the idea of estimating the benefits of abatement of environmental damage by directly estimating the costs attributable to that damage. Several workers have made progress along these lines. For example, Lave and Seskin [13] have had some success in relating the costs of impairment of human health to levels of air pollution. If all relevant costs of a particular incidence of environmental damage can be identified, evaluated and summed, a curve relating the value of damage avoided to levels of environmental improvements can be fitted. The first derivative of this curve is the "M.V.D.A." curve of Kneese and Bower [12].

These costing techniques are theoretically sound and may often be feasible in practice. However, difficulties may be introduced by the unavailability of information and the pricing and accounting problems inherent in this type of analysis. These techniques will have limited application in valuation of aesthetic environmental improvements, since the costs of aesthetic damages may seldom be directly reflected in the market.

Revealed demand techniques. Revealed demand techniques have been widely used for estimation of the demand for outdoor recreation, often a nonmarket good.[5] A number of applications to valuation of the benefits of air pollution abatement have been made [1, 11, 14, 16, 18]. The principle is as follows. The benefits of provision of a nonmarket good are inferred from the revealed demand for some suitable proxy. In the case of air pollution abatement, the revealed demand for residential land is related by regression analysis to air pollution concentrations. In metropolitan areas, it is possible to obtain information on the concentration of specific air pollutants in different parts of the city. If all other variables relevant to the valuation of urban residential land can be identified[6] and measured, it ought to be possible to determine by

[3] In the approach of methodological individualism, Pareto-efficiency is still not achieved since the price to the individual cannot equal the marginal cost to the individual (which is zero) and allow collection of sufficient funds to cover the total cost of provision.

[4] In Fig. 1, the aggregate and marginal bid curves are drawn as smooth curves consistent with diminishing marginal utility. As pointed out in footnote 2, this need not be even the typical case.

[5] See [4].

[6] Some appropriate variables are size and value of structures on the land, distance from places where services and employment opportunities are concentrated, proportion of park land and open space in the neighborhood, density of population, proportion of various racial and ethnic minorities in the immediate vicinity, and the incidence of violent crimes.

regression analysis the extent to which air pollution concentrations affect observed land values. In this way, a proxy measure of the benefits of air pollution abatement is obtained.

There are a number of difficulties with this type of analysis. Since the value ascribed to air pollution control is derived directly from the regression coefficient of the pollution concentration variable, accurate results require perfect and complete specification of the regression equation. In an interesting recent study, Wieand [17] claims that when such regression models are completely specified, the regression coefficient of the pollution concentration variable may not be significantly different from zero. Another difficulty, researchers in the field agree, lies in interpretation of the results. Are all of the benefits of air pollution abatement captured in residential land values? Most think not. For our purposes, the other side of that coin is of interest: Surely some benefits in addition to the aesthetic benefits are captured. Which additional benefits?

In the case study reported below, the geographical area affected by environmental damage includes urban areas, but also rural and agricultural areas, and substantial areas of Indian reservation and National Park, Monument, and Forest lands (which are typically not exchanged in the market). Thus, those revealed demand techniques currently available would seem to be inapplicable to the situation faced in our study.

Bidding games. In analysis of the demand for outdoor recreation, Davis [7] pioneered in the use of bidding games. During personal interviews, the enumerator follows on iterative questioning procedure to elicit responses which enable the fitting of a demand curve for the services offered by a recreation area. Respondents are asked to answer "yes" or "no" to the question: Would you continue to use this recreation area if the cost to you was to increase by X dollars? The amount is varied up or down in repetitive questions, and the highest positive response is recorded. Individual responses may then be aggregated to generate a demand curve for the recreation services provided by the area.

It seems reasonable that bidding games may be adapted to the estimation of the benefits from provision of an inexhaustible nonmarket good such as abatement of aesthetic environmental damage. Bidding games would seem to be the most direct method of estimating Bradford's aggregate benefit curve, which is derived from vertical summation of individual bid curves. The difficulties of interpretation which are inherent in the revealed demand techniques developed thus far do not occur when the bidding game technique is used. The data obtained with bidding games are not cost observations but individuals' perceptions of value. Thus, bidding games can be used in situations where direct costing techniques are ineffective for lack of data. These advantages of bidding games over revealed demand and direct costing techniques seem sufficient to justify attempts to adapt the bidding game technique for use in valuation of aesthetic environmental improvements.

Some General Considerations in the Design of Bidding Games

Bidding games are designed to elicit information on the hypothetical behavior of respondents when faced with hypothetical situations. In the case study presented below, the purpose of bidding games is to provide a measure of the benefits of aesthetic environmental improvements by measuring the willingness of a sample of respondents to pay for such improvements. The efficacy of bidding games used for this purpose depends on the reliability with which stated hypothetical behavior is converted to action, should the hypothetical situation posited in the game arise in actuality.

Willingness to pay is the behavioral dimension of an underlying attitude: concern for environmental quality.[7] Sociologists and public opinion researchers have built up a substantial body of literature which considers ways in which survey techniques of measuring attitudes and their behavioral component can be made as reliable as possible. Some desirable characteristics of such surveys have been identified [5, 9]. The hypothetical situation presented should be realistic and credible to respondents. Realism and credibility can be achieved by satisfying the following criteria for survey instrument design: Test items must have properties similar to those in the actual situation; situations posited must be concrete rather than symbolic; and test items should involve institutionalized or routinized behavior, where role expectations of respondents are well defined. Where the behavioral predisposition under study are affected by attitudes about a number of different things, the test instrument must be designed to focus upon those attitudes which are relevant. An example may be helpful. In the case study reported here, willingness to pay additional taxes to achieve aesthetic environmental improvement is affected by attitudes toward environmental quality, but also by attitudes toward the current tax burden and attitudes toward the idea of receptors of pollutants paying to obtain abatement of emissions. If the survey is carried out for the purpose of measuring the benefits of abatement, the test instrument must be designed to take cognizance of the various diverse attitudes which affect willingness to pay and to allow isolation of the relevant attitudinal dimensions.

Since abatement of aesthetic environmental damage is an inexhaustible, public good, bidding games intended to provide data for valuation of that good must be designed to avoid the effects of the freeloader problem, which encourages nonrevelation of preferences. One method would be to design games in which each respondent is told that all consumers of the good would pay for it on a similar basis, thus eliminating the possibility of freeloading.

With careful design of bidding games to ensure that the responses recorded are predictive of behavior, it should be possible to use the bidding technique to estimate the benefits of environmental improvements with reasonable accuracy.

AN EMPIRICAL APPLICATION:

ESTIMATION OF THE BENEFITS OF ABATEMENT OF AESTHETIC ENVIRONMENTAL DAMAGES ASSOCIATED WITH THE FOUR CORNERS STEAM ELECTRIC GENERATING PLANT

At New Mexico State University, research is under way to examine the socio-economic impacts of development of the rapidly expanding coal strip-mining and steam electric generation industry in the Four Corners Region (southwestern United States), and to predict the impacts of alternative policies with respect to environmental management and economic development, as such policies would affect the industry. One facet of this research required estimation of the benefits of abatement of aesthetic environmental damage associated with the Four Corners power plant at Fruitland, NM, and the Navajo mine which provides its raw energy source—low energy, low sulfur, high ash, sub-bituminous coal.[8]

---

[7] Three dimensions of attitudes are recognized [8]: (1) a cognitive dimension, (2) an affectual dimension, and (3) a behavioral dimension.

[8] The following facts may provide some idea of the magnitude of this operation and its attendant environmental problems. In 1970, the power plant had a capacity of 2,080 MW. The mine provides

Applied Welfare Economics

The mine–power plant complex causes several kinds of aesthetic environmental damage. Particulates, sulfur oxides and nitrous oxides are emitted into the air. The adverse effects of particulate pollutants on visibility is considered the most important aesthetic impact of the complex. The strip-mining process will create some aesthetic damage. Although the soil banks will be leveled, reclamation in the sense of re-establishing a viable plant and animal eco-system is uncertain. Transmission lines radiate from the plant in several directions, passing through the Navajo Reservation and bringing the paraphernalia of development to a landscape which is in some places very beautiful and otherwise untouched.[9]

It was decided to use bidding games to measure the benefits of abatement of the aesthetic environmental damage associated with the Four Corners power plant and the Navajo mine.[10] Considerable attention was devoted to the design and development of bidding games which provide a reliable estimator of these benefits.

Questionnaire Design

The bidding games were part of prepared schedules designed for use in a personal interview survey of samples of users of the Four Corners Interstate Air Quality Control Region environment (i.e., residents and recreational visitors to the region). In preparation for the bidding games, respondents were asked a series of questions about environmental matters, to focus their attention on that topic. Then, the subject of the coal–electricity complex in the Four Corners area was explicitly raised. The respondents were shown three sets of photographs depicting three levels of environmental damage around the Four Corners Power Plant, near Fruitland, NM.

Set A showed the plant circa 1969, prior to installation of some additional emissions control equipment, producing its historical maximum emissions of air pollutants. Another photograph depicted the spoil banks as they appear following strip-mining, but prior to leveling. A third photograph showed electricity transmission lines marring the landscape. Set A depicted the highest level of environmental damage, and accurately represented the actual situation in the early years of operation of the plant.

Set B showed an intermediate level of damage. One photograph showed the plant circa 1972, after additional controls had reduced particulate emissions (i.e., the type of emissions most destructive of visibility). Another showed the spoil banks leveled but not revegetated; a third showed the transmission lines placed less obtrusively (i.e., at some distance from major roads).

Set C was intended to depict a situation where the industries continued to operate,

---

coal at a rate of 8.5 millions tons annually. Over the 40 year projected life span of the mine, 31,000 acres will be stripped. In 1970, approximately 550 people were employed in the mine and power plant, total value of sales of electricity was $146 million, and 96,000 tons of particulates, 73,000 tons of sulfur oxides and 66,000 tons of nitrous oxides were emitted annually.

[9] To place this aesthetic environmental damage in perspective, it may be useful to point out that the Four Corners Interstate Air Quality Control Region includes the greatest concentration of National Parks and Monuments in the United States and a number of Indian reservations, the largest of which are the Navajo and Hopi reservations. The value of the region for tourism and recreation depends largely on its bizarre and unusual landscapes, the enjoyment of which requires excellent long distance visibility and depth and color perception. There exists a substantial minority of "traditional" Native Americans who have strong religious and cultural attachments to nature, and who resent the air pollution, strip-mining, and transmission lines; witness the prolonged litigation about location of the Tucson Gas and Electric Company transmission line from the San Juan power plant, which is under construction about 9 miles from the Four Corners plant.

[10] In that part of the overall study which deals with nonaesthetic environmental damage, direct costing techniques are used.

but with minimal environmental damage. One photograph showed the plant with visible emissions reduced to zero.[11] A second photograph showed a section of arid land in its natural state; it was intended to depict a situation where the transmission lines were placed underground and the strip-mined land completely reclaimed.

The interviewers pointed out the salient features of each set of photographs to each respondent. For most of the respondents (with the exception of many recreationists), the situations were rooted in real experience: the residents of the region were familiar with the plant and mine, and their operation for the previous eight years. Most remembered situation A well, for that was exactly how it was only a few years earlier. Situation B was a fairly good approximation of the real situation at the time of the interviews. With the help of the photographs, situation C would be readily visualized.

Since the fitting of bid or benefit curves requires an expression of willingness to pay for abatement of aesthetic damages, it was necessary to design games based upon appropriate vehicles of payment. The vehicles for payment were chosen so as to maximize the realism and credibility of the hypothetical situation posited to respondents. As will be discussed below, it was necessary to design and use a series of bidding games, because no one vehicle of payment was appropriate for use with all of the subpopulations sampled. First, the general format applicable to all games is discussed. Then, the particular games used for particular subpopulations are discussed.

For each bidding game played, respondents were asked to consider situation A, the highest level of environmental damage, as the starting point. The bidding games were designed to elicit the highest amount of money which the respondent, an adult speaking for his or her household, was willing to pay in order to improve the aesthetic environment to situation C, and to situation B. Answers were elicited in terms of "yes" or "no" to questions expressed in the form "would you pay amount X . . . ?" A "yes" answer would lead the enumerator to raise the amount and repeat the question, maybe several times, until a "no" answer was obtained. A "no" answer would lead the enumerator to reduce the amount until a "yes" answer was obtained. The amount which elicited the highest "yes" answer was recorded as the amount the respondent was willing to pay.

It was emphasized that the respondent was to assume that the vehicle for payment used in a particular game was the only possible way in which environmental improvements could be obtained. This stipulation was designed to minimize the incidence of zero bids as protests against either the zero liability rule implicit in "willingness to pay" games or the particular method of payment used in a particular game. If a respondent indicated that he was willing to pay nothing at all, he was asked a series of questions to find out why. A respondent indicating that he did not consider his household to be harmed in any way by the environmental damage and, therefore, saw no reason to pay for environmental improvements was recorded as bidding zero. If a respondent indicated that his zero bid was in protest against the game, his answer was analyzed as a nonresponse to the bidding game, since he had refused to play the game by the stated rules.[12]

---

[11] This feat was accomplished by photographing the plant on a day when all units were shut down.

[12] For the purpose of estimating the benefits of abatement, the treatment of "protest bids" as non-responses is legitimate. By definition, a "protest bid" recognizes that positive benefits from abatement exist, but registers a protest against a particular method of financing abatement. We recognize that the elimination of "protest bids" from analyses aimed at estimating the benefits of abatement fails to remove all downward bias from the responses to particular games: some respondents may bid low (i.e., underestimate the benefits to themselves of abatement) in conscious or subconscious protest against the method of financing assumed in a game.

The selection of appropriate vehicles for payment provided a challenge. People are not accustomed to paying for abatement of air pollution and strip-mining damage. However, they are accustomed to paying for many other types of useful goods and services, many of which, such as parks and highway beautification, have aesthetic or "quality of life" components. So selection of realistic vehicles for payment was not impossible. However, the heterogeneous nature of the affected population meant that no single vehicle was suitable for data collection among all groups. In the Four Corners Region, the affected population can be divided into three broad groups: (1) the residents of Indian reservations, primarily Navajos, but also including members of several other tribes; (2) the residents of the nonreservation sections of the region, primarily Anglo-Americans, but with a sprinkling of Spanish-Americans, Native Americans living off the reservations, and other minorities; and (3) the tourists and recreationists who visit the area to enjoy its unique natural, historical and cultural attractions. Different versions of the questionnaire, using bidding games based on different vehicles for payment, were constructed for use with the three different sub-populations of the affected population.

The particular bidding games used are described below.

The sales tax game. Members of all three subpopulations are familiar with the practice of paying sales taxes. For most, this is a frequent occurrence. It is also understood by most that income collected in sales taxes is used to provide useful public services. It does not require much imagination to conceive of a public agency collecting a sales tax from residents of the affected region and using the income to finance environmental improvements.

The sales tax bidding game was used for both the resident samples. It was not used with the recreationist sample, since that group often purchased only a few items in the region, bringing most of their equipment and supplies with them. This would make a regional sales tax largely irrelevant for that group.

Respondents were asked to assume that a regional sales tax was collected on all purchases in the Four Corners Interstate Air Quality Control Region for the purpose of financing environmental improvements.[13] All revenue from the additional tax would be used for abatement of aesthetic environmental damage associated with the power plant and mine, and all citizens would be required to pay the tax. Recreational visitors to the region would contribute to environmental improvement through payment of additional users fees for facilities.

The electricity bill game. The monthly electricity bill seemed to be a suitable vehicle for measurement of willingness to pay. It is the production of electricity which causes the environmental damage, and most people can readily comprehend that reduction of the damage may raise the cost of operating the industry and that passing these additional costs on to consumers of electricity is a not unlikely outcome. For the residents of those sections of the region outside the Indian reservations, payment of a monthly electricity bill is a routinized behavior. Therefore, a bidding game based upon the monthly electricity bill was played with the nonreservation resident sample.

This game was unsuitable for use with the other two samples. Many residents of

---

"Protest bids" were recorded and used in some other types of analyses. For example, the incidence of "protest bids" is an indicator of the relative political acceptability of various methods of financing abatement.

[13] The regional sales tax would be additional to current state and local sales taxes and would be charged on all commodities subject to existing state and local sales taxes.

Indian reservations do not have electricity available in their homes. Recreationists do not pay monthly electricity bills while vacationing away from home.

The respondent was first asked the amount of his monthly household electricity bill. He was then asked to imagine that an additional charge was added to his electricity bill, and the electricity bills of everyone who uses electricity produced in the Four Corners Region, even people as far away as southern California. All of the additional money collected would be used to repair the aesthetic environmental damage caused as a result of electricity production and transmission in the Four Corners region.

The user fees game. Measuring recreationists' willingness to pay for environmental improvements raised problems which prevented use of the electricity bill and sales tax games. For the recreationists, a satisfactory game would need to focus upon (1) the activities associated with vacationing, and (2) the collection of payments while they are in the region and using the regional environment. The payment of user fees for recreation services (i.e., campsite, utilities hook-up, boat launching), seemed to be a promising vehicle for a bidding game for the recreationists. If visitors were concerned about environmental quality in the places where they vacation, the payment of an additional sum along with their usual daily user fees would provide a suitable way to express that concern.

A sample of recreationists in the national parks, monuments and forests and state parks in the region played a bidding game based on user fees. Only recreationists who were not residents of the region were included. They were first asked the total sum of user fees they paid daily. They were then asked to suppose user fees in all the recreation areas in the Four Corners area were increased. All the additional money collected would be spent on environmental improvements. All recreators would pay and the year-round residents would pay, too, through additional regional sales taxes.

The Conduct of the Survey

The bidding games, as described above, were included in prepared schedules which also served as the instrument for collection of data for socioeconomic analysis of citizen environmental concern. Personal interviews were conducted by enumerators who were closely supervised and who had been carefully trained in formal sessions and in two separate field pre-tests of the questionnaire. Interviews were conducted during the summer of 1972.

Usable questionnaires were completed by 526 residents of nonreservation sections of the Four Corners Interstate Air Quality Control Region, 71 residents of Indian reservations and 150 recreators and tourists from outside the region who were using recreation sites within the region. The ratio of reservation residents to nonreservation residents sampled was proportional to their total numbers in the regional population; the size of the recreationist sample was chosen arbitrarily. Respondents from each subpopulation were selected by stratified random sampling. Stratification was based on concentration of air pollutants above the respondent's home or recreation site, as estimated by an atmospheric diffusion model developed as part of the larger research project. The population in higher pollution concentration zones was sampled more heavily.

Analysis and Results

For the *determination of three points on the aggregate bid curve*, corresponding to the situations, A, B, and C, the bidding game results were aggregated by methods appro-

TABLE I

AGGREGATE BIDS FOR ABATEMENT OF AESTHETIC ENVIRONMENTAL DAMAGE
ASSOCIATED WITH THE FOUR CORNERS POWER PLANT, 1972

Item	Situation		
	A	B	C
Emissions (tons of particulates per year)	96,000	26,000	0
Level of abatement (tons of particulates per year)	0	70,000	96,000
Estimated regional aggregate bid ($ millions per year)	0	15.54	24.57
Standard error ($ millions per year)	—	1.24	1.52
95% Confidence limits ($ millions per year)	—	±2.43	±2.97
Estimated consumer aggregate bid ($ millions per year)	0	11.25	19.31
Standard error ($ millions per year)	—	0.68	0.98
95% Confidence limits ($ millions per year)	—	±1.33	±1.92

priate to the stratified random sampling technique used, to provide estimates of the total bid for the relevant population. Two methods of aggregation were used, to generate two different aggregate bid curves.

(1) The results of the sales tax game with area residents (reservation and non-reservation) were added to the results of user fee games played by recreators to estimate a total regional willingness to pay for three levels of environmental improvement.

(2) The results of the electricity bill game were extrapolated over all consumers of power from the Four Corners plant to estimate consumer willingness to pay. This latter procedure involved the ethical premise that, since the production of electricity causes environmental damage, all citizens who consume Four Corners power ought to be willing to pay as much in additional electricity charges for environmental improvements as those who live in the region which suffers the damage. However appealing this ethical premise may be, our survey did not include people outside the region. Thus the consumer bid cannot be interpreted as an estimate of true "willingness to pay." It would be interesting to extend this research to include bidding games for these consumers of Four Corners electricity who do not live or recreate in the affected environment.

While both the regional and consumer aggregate bids are of interest, the authors believe that more faith may be placed in the regional bid since that bid was derived from samples of all segments of its relevant population.

Table I presents the estimated aggregate bids, standard errors, and 95% confidence limits at points A, B, and C. Regional and consumer bids are presented.

Using the estimated aggregate bids (Table I), a *regional aggregate bid curve* and a *consumer aggregate bid curve* were fitted. To fit two-dimensional aggregate bid curves, it was necessary to select a single independent variable to serve as a proxy for the total package of aesthetic environmental improvements under consideration. Situations A, B, and C were defined so that all three forms of aesthetic damage (air pollution, strip-mining, and transmission lines) were successively reduced together from their most obtrusive in situation A to virtual elimination in C. Of the three forms of damage, reduced visibility due to particulate air pollution was considered by respondents to be far and away the most serious. So, abatement of particulate air pollutant emissions (measured as the difference, in tons per year, between the level at A and the levels at

TABLE II

TESTS OF HYPOTHESES CONCERNING THE SLOPES OF THE AGGREGATE BID CURVES

Hypothesis	Confidence of rejecting H_0	
	Regional aggregate bid curve (%)	Consumer aggregate bid curve (%)
1. The aggregate bid curve is of linear positive slope[a]	99.9	99.9
2. The aggregate bid for situation B is one half of that for C[b]	99.9	94.5

[a] Rejection implies that the aggregate bid curve is of increasing positive slope.
[b] Rejection implies that the aggregate bid for B exceeds one half of that for C.

B and C, respectively) was arbitrarily chosen to serve as a single independent variable for graphical analyses.[14]

The form of the curve requires some discussion. It has already been noted [footnote 2] that the usual restraints placed on the slope of demand curves are inappropriate for the first derivatives of aggregate bid curves for public goods, due to the impossibility of separating quantity and quality factors. Here we have a case in point. It seems resonable that "consumers" of abatement of particulate emissions desire the attribute, visibility. Given the reasonable assumption that marginal utility of additional visibility is diminishing, one would expect the first derivative of the aggregate bid curve for visibility to be of negative slope.

Meteorologists have established that an inverse relationship exists between visibility and concentration of particulate pollutants. Visibility increases at an increasing rate as particulate pollution (measured in terms of weight) is abated [3, 10]. Therefore, the slope of the marginal aggregate bid curve for abatement of emissions (in tons per year) is *a priori* unpredictable, since the diminishing marginal utility of visibility and the increasing marginal visibility resulting from additional abatement influence that slope in opposite ways.

In terms of visibility, the aggregate bid curve form which provided the best fit of the three data points was

$$B = c \ln (v),$$

where B = aggregate bid in dollars, c = a constant, and v = visibility.

In terms of abatement of particulate air pollutants (measured in tons per year), the appropriate curve form was

$$B(q) = c \ln \frac{k}{k - q},$$

[14] In the case study at hand, we recognize the inelegance introduced by this procedure. We do not believe it does serious violence to the truth, since most of the aesthetic environmental damage occurring is, in fact, due to particulate air pollutants. We emphasize, however, that this problem should not typically occur in the use of aggregate bid methodology and bidding game techniques. Rather, its occurrence here was a special case and is attributable to our need to value a package of different aesthetic environmental improvements within the following constraints: (1) a limited research budget, which confined us to one personal interview survey, and (2) the need to limit the length of each interview, to avoid exhausting the patience of respondents.

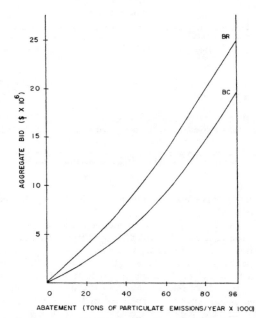

FIG. 2. Estimated aggregate bid curves for abatement of aesthetic environmental damage, Four Corners power plant, 1972. BR, Regional aggregate bid; BC, Consumer aggregate bid.

where k = a parameter relating visibility to emissions, which is determined behaviorally, and q = tons of particulate emissions abated annually.

The aggregate bid curve fitted using this equation form passes through the origin, as logically it must, given that rational citizens would bid zero for zero abatement. The first derivative of the aggregate bid curve is of positive slope.[15] Statistical tests (Table II) resulted in rejection of the hypotheses (1) that the aggregate bid curve was linear, or of decreasing positive slope, and (2) that the aggregate bid at point B was simply one-half of that at C. Regional and consumer aggregate bid curves are presented (Fig. 2).

[15] It must be emphasized that the curve form used provided the best fit, given the three data points available. It would have been desirable to have collected information adequate to generate more data points. The decision to collect data for only three points was made in recognition of limits to the patience of respondents. The multipurpose schedule was already quite lengthy, given the need to collect data relevant to the situation of the respondent, play the bidding games, and collect socio-economic, sociological and attitudinal data.

It is recognized that, if more data points had been available, a different curve form may have been appropriate. The possibility of a sigmoid aggregate bid curve is logically appealing. Such a curve would have a segment of increasing slope, where the increasing marginal visibility from particulate abatement dominates the decreasing marginal utility of additional visibility then, as complete abatement is approached (i.e., somewhere to the right of our point B), the slope may become decreasing as the diminishing marginal utility of visibility becomes dominant. Such a curve form would be consistent with theoretical considerations and with the three data points available.

144 RANDALL, IVES AND EASTMAN

The fitted aggregate bid curves were:

$$B_r = \$29,175,840 \ln \frac{168,890}{168,890 - q}, \quad \text{for the regional aggregate bid curve, and}$$

$$B_c = \$15,396,700 \ln \frac{134,490}{134,490 - q}, \quad \text{for the consumer aggregate bid curve.}$$

Marginal aggregate bid curves, or *price curves,* were generated by taking the first derivatives of the aggregate bid curves (Fig. 3). The derived price curves were:

$$P_r = \$\frac{29,175,840}{168,890 - q}, \quad \text{derived from the regional aggregate bid curve, and}$$

$$P_c = \$\frac{15,396,700}{134,490 - q}, \quad \text{derived from the consumer aggregate bid curve.}$$

These derived price curves are very useful for public policy analyses with respect to optimal environmental management policies. In Fig. 4, a hypothetical derived price curve is presented, along with a hypothetical marginal cost of abatement curve. In this hypothetical example, the optimal level of abatement is S. A standard allowing maxi-

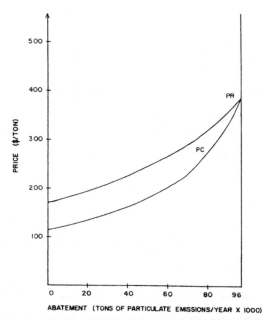

FIG. 3. Derived price curves for abatement of aesthetic environmental damage, Four Corners power plant, 1972. PR, price curve derived from regional aggregate bid; PC, price curve derived from consumer aggregate bid.

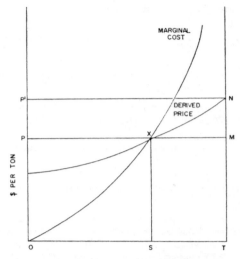

FIG. 4. Optimal standards, penalties and per unit taxes on emissions, given hypothetical marginal cost and price curves.

mum annual emissions of $(T–S)$ tons of particulates would be appropriate, and the penalty for violation of that standard should be set sufficiently high that the polluter's expected penalty per ton of emissions in excess of the standard would be at least P. An alternative institutional framework would call for a fine or tax per ton of particulate emissions. The fine ought to be set at least as high as P per ton. At the level P, the optimal level of abatement would be achieved. A fixed fine per ton of remaining emissions would result in collection of the amount $XMTS$. However, since the derived price curve is of positive slope, the sum of the fines collected would be insufficient to compensate the receptors of the pollutants for their loss in welfare. The necessary amount would be $XNTS$. This amount could be collected, if full compensation were the accepted policy,[16] by using a sliding scale of fines, ranging from P' for the first ton of emissions down to P for all emissions in excess of $T–S$.

If the marginal costs of abatement of aesthetic environmental damage associated with the Four Corners power plant were known,[17] the derived price curves presented

[16] Under a full compensation policy, a derived price curve generated from bidding games based on the concept of willingness to pay (which implicitly places the liability with the receptor of damages) would underestimate both the optimal level of abatement and the appropriate level of fines or taxes. Randall [15] and others have demonstrated that the demand for abatement of an external diseconomy is greater in the full liability situation than in the zero liability situation implicit in willingness to pay games.

[17] We are not yet in a position to present a complete benefit/cost analysis of the abatement of the aesthetic environmental damage associated with the Four Corners power plant and Navajo mine. Preliminary and tentative calculations indicate that, *if our attribution of most of the benefits reported here to abatement of particulate air pollutants is reasonable,* 99.7% abatement of particulate emissions (the current New Mexico standard for 1975) is economically justified on the basis of aesthetic considerations alone. Some additional abatement beyond the 1975 standard may be justified. The economic benefits from that abatement which has already taken place appear to far exceed the costs.

TABLE III

INCOME ELASTICITY OF BID FOR ABATEMENT OF AESTHETIC DAMAGES
ASSOCIATED WITH THE FOUR CORNERS POWER PLANT, 1972

Subpopulation	Game	Level of abatement	Income elasticity of bid	Standard error	Significantly greater than zero[a] ?
Nonreservation residents	Sales tax	B	0.65	0.10	Yes
		C	0.65	0.08	Yes
Reservation residents	Sales tax	B	0.23	0.18	No
		C	0.24	0.18	No
Nonreservation residents	Electricity bill	B	0.54	0.09	Yes
		C	0.39	0.06	Yes
Recreators	Users fees	B	0.09	0.15	No
		C	0.16	0.11	No

[a] At the 95% level of confidence.

in Fig. 3 could be used to perform policy analyses similar to those in the hypothetical example above.

The *relationship between willingness to pay and household income* is of interest. However, the concept of income elasticity of demand is inappropriate to the public good under study. The calculation of an income elasticity of quantity of abatement demanded would require consideration of the relationship between income and quantity of homogeneous units of abatement demanded at a constant price per unit. However, in this study there were no explicit unit prices for abatement; neither were there individual variations in quantity of abatement demanded, as the quantities were fixed as defined in situations A, B, and C. These conditions result from the inherent non-exclusive nature of abatement of aesthetic environmental damage: Everyone obtains the same quantity and there is no explicit price. This situation is the inverse of the market situation for private goods; dollar bids are the response to a quantity which is given.

Since there existed no market price at which to calculate the income elasticity of demand, an "income elasticity of bid" was estimated. The income elasticity of bid was defined as:

$$e_Y = \frac{dB}{dY} \frac{Y}{B} = b_1 \frac{Y}{B},$$

where Y = household income, and B = the individual's total annual bid. A linear regression model was used to determine the statistic b_1. The mean value of Y and B were used, and the calculation was made at each level of abatement.

Calculated income elasticities of bid for the various subpopulations and bidding games are presented in Table III. In all cases, income elasticity of bid was greater than zero, indicating that higher income households were willing to pay a greater amount than lower income households to achieve the same level of abatement of aesthetic damages. For the non-reservation residents, calculated income elasticity of bid

This conclusion is extremely tentative and subject to revision. It is presented in this footnote (at the request of an anonymous reviewer) to provide a "ball park" indication of the conclusions which may arise from our research.

ranged from 0.39 to 0.65, depending on the game and the level of abatement. Income elasticity of bid was significantly greater than zero at the 95% level of confidence. For the residents of Indian reservations and the recreational visitors to the region, lower positive income elasticities were recorded. These were not significantly greater than zero, at the 95% level of confidence.[18]

It was also found that willingness to pay an additional charge in the electricity bill for a particular level of abatement increased as the size of the electricity bill increased. Electric bill elasticity of bid, as defined as

$$e_b = \frac{dB}{d\text{Bill}} \frac{\text{Bill}}{B},$$

was calculated (for the nonreservation resident sample) to be 0.30 for situation B and 0.25 for situation C; at both points, it was significantly greater than zero at the 95% level of confidence. These estimates indicate that willingness to pay for a given level of environmental improvements increased as the size of the electricity bill increased, but at a lesser rate.

The Reliability of the Results

In the statistical sense, our estimates of the aggregate benefits from abatement of aesthetic environmental damage would seem to be of a high order of reliability. The 95% confidence limits of the aggregate bids are quite narrow, compared with the size of the estimated aggregate bids. Statistical estimates of the confidence which may be placed in these estimated aggregate bids are based upon the variance of the responses of the samples, and indicate the confidence with which sample results may be extrapolated to the whole population. These statistics, *per se*, are unable to give any indication of the reliability with which predispositions to behave, as measured by the bidding games, would be transmitted to actions should the hypothetical situation arise.

We argue, nevertheless, that our estimates of the benefits of abatement of aesthetic environmental damages associated with the Four Corners power plant are of a reasonable order of magnitude and, if anything, conservative. (1) We believe the design of the bidding games allows confidence in their efficacy. (2) The individual household bid for abatement, on average, is of the same order of magnitude as the estimates of the value of particulate pollution abatement obtained in revealed demand studies [1], when the latter are converted to a comparable basis. Mean individual household willingness to pay for abatement, measured by the sales tax game played with the nonreservation resident sample, was about $50 annually to achieve situation B and $85 annually to achieve situation C. (3) The estimated aggregate bids for abatement are relatively small given the scale of the operation at Four Corners, as indicated by its 1970 emissions rate and its total annual sales of $146 million [footnote 5]. (4) Theoretical analyses indicate that the demand for abatement of an externality will

---

[18] The estimates of income elasticity obtained with the nonreservation resident sample may be more reliable, for two reasons. First, the nonreservation sample was considerably larger than either of the other two samples. Second, the range of incomes encountered in the nonreservation resident sample more nearly approached that of society as a whole. The reservation resident sample was representative of its underlying population, in which incomes are concentrated at the extreme lower end of the national range. The visiting recreators had a mean household income about fifty per cent greater than the national average; very few recreators had incomes in the lower half of the national range.

148   RANDALL, IVES AND EASTMAN

be lower under a zero liability rule than under intermediate or full liability rules [15]. The bidding games used were based on zero liability rules, and they should be expected to yield conservative estimates of the benefits of abatement.

It is recognized that three data points provide an inadequate basis on which to draw conclusions with respect to the shapes and slopes of the aggregate bid curves and their first derivatives. However, it is consistent with theoretical considerations and with the limited data available that the aggregate bid curves may have at least a segment with increasing slope.

It would seem that the income elasticity of bid and the electric bill elasticity of bid fall in the range from zero to -1. This result was consistent with our prior expectations.

CONCLUDING COMMENTS

In the case study reported, bidding games were used to estimate the benefits which would accrue from abatement of the aesthetic environmental damages associated with the Four Corners power plant and the Navajo mine. The problem situation was not amenable to the use of direct costing nor revealed demand techniques.

This study has revealed that substantial benefits may be gained from abatement of aesthetic environmental damage associated with the Four Corners power plant and Navajo mine. These potential benefits have not been revealed or realized in the market place. However, the process of political and institutional change has led to the imposition of increasingly rigorous control standards for particulate emissions from the plant, indicating a recognition, in some broad sense, that benefits may be gained from emissions controls. Our contribution has been to attempt a quantification of these benefits.

We believe that the use of bidding game techniques was successful in meeting the objective, valuation of these benefits. Bidding game techniques seem amenable to use as a research tool for valuation of a wide variety of nonmarket goods. It must be understood, however, that bidding games measure the hypothetical responses of individuals faced with hypothetical situations. Thus, considerable care must be exercised in the design of bidding games and the conduct of surveys for data collection, to ensure that the results obtained are as reliable as possible.

REFERENCES

1. R. J. Anderson, Jr. and T. D. Crocker, Air pollution and housing: Some findings, Paper No. 264, Institute for Research in the Behavioral, Economic and Management Sciences (January 1970).
2. D. F. Bradford, Benefit-cost analysis and demand curves for public goods, *Kyklos* 23, 775–91 (1970).
3. R. J. Charlson, N. C. Ahlquist, and H. Horvath, On the generality of correlation of atmospheric aerosol mass concentration and light scatter, *Atmos. Environ.* 2, 455–464 (1968).
4. M. Clawson and J. L. Knetsch, "Economics of Outdoor Recreation," Johns Hopkins Press, Baltimore (1966).
5. I. Crespi, What kinds of attitude measures are predictive of behavior? *Pub. Opin. Quart.* 35, 327–34 (1971).
6. O. A. Davis and A. B. Whinston, On the Distinction Between Public and Private Goods. *Amer. Econ. Rev.* 57, 360–373 (1967).
7. R. K. Davis, Recreation planning as a economic problem, *Natural Res. J.* 3, 239–249 (1963).
8. J. F. Engel, D. T. Kollat, and R. D. Blackwell, Attitude formation and structure, *in* "Consumer Behavior," Holt, Rinehart, and Winston, New York (1968).
9. H. Erskine, The polls: Pollution and its costs, *Pub. Opin. Quart.* 36, 120–135 (1972).
10. H. Ettinger and G. W. Roger, Particle size, visibility and mass concentration in a nonurban environment, Los Alamos Scientific Laboratory, LA-DC-12197 (1971).

11. J. A. Jaksch and H. H. Stoevener, Effects of air pollution on residential property values in Toledo, Oregon, Agricultural Experiment Station Special Report 304, Oregon State University, Corvallis (1970).
12. A. V. Kneese and B. Bower, "Managing Water Quality: Economics, Technology and Institutions," Johns Hopkins Press, Baltimore (1972).
13. L. Lave and E. Seskin, Air Pollution and Human Health, *Science* 169, 723–732 (1970).
14. H. O. Nourse, The effect of air pollution on house values, *Land Econ.* 43, 181–189 (1967).
15. A. Randall, On the theory of market solutions to externality problems, Agricultural Experiment Station Special Report 351, Oregon State University, Corvallis (1972).
16. R. G. Ridker and J. A. Henning, The determination of residential property values with special reference to air pollution (St. Louis, Missouri), *Rev. Econ. Stat.* 49, 246–257 (1967).
17. K. F. Weiand, Air pollution and property values: A study of the St. Louis area, *J. Reg. Sci.* 13 91–95 (1973).
18. R. O. Zerbe, Jr., The economics of air pollution: A cost-benefit approach, Ontario Dept. of Public Health, Toronto (1969).

[43]

Welfare Analysis with Discrete Choice Models[*]

W. Michael Hanemann

2.1   INTRODUCTION

A major accomplishment in recent years has been the development of statistical models suitable for the analysis of discrete dependent variables. This has enabled economists to study behavioral relationships involving purely qualitative variables that are not amenable to conventional regression techniques. In Amemiya's (1981) terminology, the multi-response qualitative response (MRQR) model involves a dependent variable taking N distinct values, $\tilde{y} = 1, 2,\ldots,$ or N , which is related to vectors of independent variables, W_j, and parameters, β_j , by some functions of the general form[1]

$$\pi_j \equiv \Pr\{\tilde{y} = j\} = H_j(W_1\beta_1,\ldots,W_N\beta_N) \qquad j = 1,\ldots,N. \qquad (2.1)$$

Specific examples are the polychotomous probit model (Daganzo, 1979),

$$\pi_1 = \int_{-\infty}^{\infty}\int_{-\infty}^{W_1\beta_1 - W_2\beta_2 + \varepsilon_1} \cdots \int_{-\infty}^{W_1\beta_1 - W_N\beta_N + \varepsilon_1} n(\varepsilon_1,\ldots,\varepsilon_N;0,\Sigma)d\varepsilon_1,\ldots,d\varepsilon_N \qquad (2.2)$$

where $n(\cdot)$ is a multivariate normal density with zero mean and covariance matrix Σ, and the generalized logit (GEV) model (McFadden, 1978, 1981),

$$\pi_j = \frac{\exp(W_j\beta_j)G_j\left[\exp(W_1\beta_1),\ldots,\exp(W_N\beta_N)\right]}{G\left[\exp(W_1\beta_1),\ldots,\exp(W_N\beta_N)\right]} \qquad j = 1,\ldots,N \qquad (2.3)$$

---

[*] This chapter appeared earlier as Hanemann (1985); it extends research initiated in Hanemann (1982).

[1] Throughout the paper a tilde will be used to denote random variables.

where G is a positive, linear homogeneous function, and G_j denotes its partial derivative with respect to the jth argument.[2]

These statistical models have been used to analyze many types of economic behavior. Aitchison and Bennett (1970) and McFadden (1974) have offered a theoretical derivation of these models which applies whenever the events whose probabilities are given by (2.1) represent the outcome of a decision by a maximizing agent. Suppose an agent is choosing among N courses of action and π_j = Pr{jth act chosen}. Assume that the payoff or utility associated with the jth act, $\tilde{u}_j$, is a random variable with mean $W_j\beta_j$. Equivalently, $\tilde{u}_j = W_j\beta_j + \tilde{\varepsilon}_j$, where $\tilde{\varepsilon}_j$ is a random variable with zero mean. The agent chooses that act which has the highest utility. This yields a MRQR model of the form (2.1):

$$\pi_j = \Pr\{W_j\beta_j + \tilde{\varepsilon}_j \geq W_i\beta_i + \tilde{\varepsilon}_i, \forall i\} \equiv H_j(W_1\beta_1,...,W_N\beta_N)$$
$$j = 1,...,N. \quad (2.4)$$

Let $\tilde{\eta}_{(j)} = (\tilde{\eta}_{1j}, \ ..., \ \tilde{\eta}_{j-1,j}, \tilde{\eta}_{j+1,j}, ..., \tilde{\eta}_{Nj})$ where $\tilde{\eta}_{ij} \equiv \tilde{\varepsilon}_i - \tilde{\varepsilon}_j$. It follows from (2.4) that

$$H_j(W_1\beta_1,...,W_N\beta_N) = F_{(j)}(W_j\beta_j - W_1\beta_1,..,W_j\beta_j - W_N\beta_N)$$
$$j = 1,...,N, \quad (2.5)$$

where $F_{(j)}$ is an $(N-1)$ dimensional joint cumulative distribution function associated with the random vector $\tilde{\eta}_{(j)}$. As Daly and Zachary (1970) have shown, the converse is also true. Any MRQR model (2.1) in which the probability functions $H_j(\cdot)$ can be cast in the form of an $(N-1)$ dimensional joint cumulative distribution function as in (2.5) is derivable from a utility maximization choice model such as (2.4). For this reason, a MRQR model satisfying (2.5) is said to be a random utility maximization (RUM) model.

This link between statistical models for discrete dependent variables and the economic concept of utility maximization is potentially very valuable because it raises the possibility of applying the conventional apparatus of welfare theory to empirical models of purely qualitative choice. Suppose the statistical model satisfies (2.5) and some subset of the variables in W_j represents attributes of the jth discrete choice. Can one derive from the fitted model an estimate of the effect on the agent's welfare of a change in these attributes analogous to the compensating and equivalent variation measures of conventional utility theory?

---

[2] The standard independent logit model (McFadden, 1974) is a special case where

$$G(t_1,...,t_N) \equiv \sum t_j, \text{ and } \pi_j = \exp(W_j\beta_j)\left[\sum \exp(W_i\beta_i)\right]^{-1}.$$

This issue was first raised in connection with RUM models of transportation mode choice by Domenich and McFadden (1975), Williams (1977), and Daly and Zachary (1978) but, until recently, it has received relatively little attention in other branches of applied economics. An exception is the papers by McFadden (1981) and Small and Rosen (1981) which explore the relationship between RUM models and conventional deterministic models of consumer behavior. However, both of these papers impose special restrictions on the underlying random utility function which have the effect that the discrete choice probabilities are independent of the consumer's income. Not only does this limit the applicability of their analysis, but it also obscures some important distinctions between alternative approaches to welfare measurement in the random utility context that happen to vanish when there are no income effects. When income effects *are* present, there are at least three distinct ways to formulate measures of compensating variation for RUM models (and three ways to formulate measures of equivalent variation) that can differ significantly in numerical value. In this paper I explain these different approaches to welfare measurement and analyze the relationships among them. I also provide formulas for computing the welfare measures, together with some numerical examples. Furthermore, I show that the same approaches to welfare measurement carry over to RUM models involving *mixed* discrete/continuous choices of the type analyzed by Dubin and McFadden (1984) and Hanemann (1984).

The paper is organized as follows. Sections 2.2 and 2.3 focus on the most common type of logit and probit models involving what I will call an additively random utility function and purely discrete, budget-constrained choices. In section 2.2, I analyze the relationship between this type of RUM model and the more conventional, deterministic model of consumer choice. In section 2.3, I explain the alternative approaches to measuring welfare changes in the random utility setting and investigate the relationships among them. In section 2.4, this analysis is extended to other forms of RUM models including those with a more general stochastic structure and those involving mixed discrete/continuous choices. Section 2.5 deals with the practical problems of calculating the welfare measures and analyzes their properties in the case of some simple price/quality changes.

2.2   BUDGET-CONSTRAINED DISCRETE CHOICE

2.2.1   Deterministic Utility Models

The general setup of a purely discrete choice model is as follows. An individual consumer has a quasi-concave, increasing utility function defined over the commodities $x_1,...,x_N$, and z, where z is taken as the numeraire. In addition, the

36 *Valuing Recreation and the Environment*

individual's utility may depend on some other variables, $q_1,...,q_N$, which he takes as exogenous; these are, for example, quality attributes of the nonumeraire goods.[3] He chooses (x, z) so as to maximize

$$u = u(x_1, \ ..., \ x_N, q_1, \ ..., \ q_N, z) \tag{2.6}$$

subject to a budget constraint,

$$\Sigma p_j x_j + z = y, \tag{2.7}$$

and two other constraints which introduce an element of discreteness into his choice. First, for logical or institutional reasons, the x_j's are mutually exclusive in consumption,

$$x_i x_j = 0 \qquad all \quad i \ne j. \tag{2.8}$$

Secondly, the x_j's can only be purchased in fixed quantities,

$$x_j = \bar{x}_j \ or \ 0 \qquad j = 1, \ ..., \ N. \tag{2.9}$$

An example might be where the x_j's are different brands of an indivisible durable good, and the consumer needs only one of these brands. Since the quantities of the x_j's are limited by (2.9), the choice among them is a qualitative choice. Moreover, although the numeraire is inherently a divisible good, once one of the x_j's has been selected the quantity of z is fixed by the budget constraint (2.7).[4] Thus, the model (2.6)–(2.9) represents a purely discrete utility-maximizing choice.

To obtain the demand functions implied by this model, first suppose that the individual has selected good j. His utility conditional on this decision, denoted by u_j, is

$$\begin{aligned} u_j &= u(0,...,0,\bar{x}_j,0,...,0,q_1,...,q_N,...,y - p_j\bar{x}_j) \\ &\equiv v_j(q_1,...,q_N,y - p_j\bar{x}_j) \end{aligned} \tag{2.10}$$

where v_j is increasing in $(y - p_j\bar{x}_j)$. I will refer to the $v_j(\cdot)$'s as conditional indirect utility functions. At this point it is common to make an additional

---

[3] For simplicity, I treat the q_j's as scalars, but they could be vectors.
[4] I assume that $y \ge \max[p_j, \bar{x}_j]$, so that $z \ge 0$.

assumption about the utility function (2.6) that the consumer does *not* care about the attributes of a good unless he actually consumes that good, i.e.,

$$x_j = 0 \Rightarrow \frac{\partial u}{\partial q_j} = 0 \qquad j = 1, \ldots, N. \tag{2.11}$$

This assumption was introduced by Mäler (1974), who named it "weak complementarity." Given (2.11), the conditional indirect utility functions (2.10) take the special form[5]

$$u_j = v_j(q_j, y - p_j \bar{x}_j) \qquad j = 1, \ldots, N. \tag{2.12}$$

The solution to the consumer's problem can be represented by a set of binary-valued indices, $\delta_1, \ldots, \delta_N$, where $\delta_j \equiv 1$ if $x_j > 0$ and $\delta_j \equiv 0$ if $x_j = 0$. These indices are related to the conditional indirect utility functions by

$$\delta_j(p, q, y) = \begin{cases} 1 & \text{if } v_j(q_j, y - p_j \bar{x}_j) \geq v_i(q_i, y - p_i \bar{x}_i) \quad \forall i \\ 0 & \text{otherwise.} \end{cases} \tag{2.13}$$

Accordingly, the unconditional ordinary demand functions associated with the utility model (2.6)–(2.9) can be expressed as

$$x_j(p, q, y) = \delta_j(p, q, y) \, \bar{x}_j \qquad j = 1, \ldots, N. \tag{2.14}$$

Substitution of these demand functions into the direct utility function (2.6) yields the unconditional indirect utility function,

$$v(p, q, y) = \max [v_1(q_1, y - p_1 \bar{x}_1), \ldots, v_N(q_N, y - p_N \bar{x}_N)]. \tag{2.15}$$

This purely discrete choice model may be compared with the conventional utility maximization model where (2.6) is maximized subject only to the budget constraint (2.7) and a nonnegativity constraint on x and z that is assumed not to be binding. The point to be emphasized is that all the constructs of conventional, continuous choice models—the ordinary demand functions, the indirect utility function, and consumer's surplus—carry over to the discrete

---

[5] If and only if $u(\cdot)$ is increasing in q_j, then $v_j(\cdot)$ in (2.10) and (2.12) is increasing in q_j.

choice model. Duality relationships also carry over, including Roy's Identity (see Small and Rosen, 1981) and the duality between expenditure minimization and utility maximization (see below). The discrete choice model serves to provide a theoretical underpinning for the statistical MRQR model. However, in order to generate the statistical model, it is necessary to add a stochastic element and introduce the notion of random utility.

2.2.2   Random Utility Models

A random utility model arises when one assumes that, although an individual's utility function is deterministic for *him*, it contains some components which are unobservable to the econometric investigator and are treated by the investigator as random variables. This combines two notions which have a long history in economics—the idea of a variation in tastes among individuals in a population and the idea of unobserved variables in econometric models. These components of the utility function will be denoted by the random vector $\tilde{\varepsilon}$, and the utility function will be written $\tilde{u} = u(x, q, z, \tilde{\varepsilon})$. More specifically, throughout the remainder of this section I assume that the random elements enter additively as follows:[6,7]

$$u(x, q, z, \ \tilde{\varepsilon}) = u(x, q, z) + \Sigma \zeta(x_j) \ \tilde{\varepsilon}_j \qquad (2.6')$$

where $\zeta(x_j) = 1$ if $x_j > 0$ and $\zeta(x_j) = 0$ otherwise. For the individual consumer $\tilde{\varepsilon}_1, \ldots, \tilde{\varepsilon}_N$ is a set of fixed constants (or functions); but for the investigator, it is a set of random variables with some joint cumulative distribution function, $F_\varepsilon(\varepsilon_1, \ldots, \varepsilon_N)$, which induces a distribution on $\tilde{u}$.

In the budget-constrained random utility discrete choice model, the individual is assumed to maximize (2.6′) subject to the constraints (2.7)–(2.9). In addition, I will assume that the nonstochastic component of (2.6′) satisfies (2.11). This maximization yields a set of ordinary demand functions and an indirect utility function which parallel those developed above except that they now involve a random component from the point of view of the econometric investigator. Suppose that the individual has selected good *j*. Conditional on this decision, his utility is $\tilde{u}_j$ where, from (2.6′), (2.7), (2.8), (2.9), and (2.11),[8]

---

[6] This additive specification is employed by Domenich and McFadden (1975), Williams (1977), Daly and Zachary (1978), McFadden (1981), Small and Rosen (1981), and many others. More general formulations of $u(x,q,z,\tilde{\varepsilon})$ will be considered in section 2.4.1.

[7] With no loss of generality, I assume that $E\{\varepsilon_j\} = 1$, $\forall j$.

[8] It follows from the weak complementarity assumption, (2.11), that the elements of W_j include the attributes and price of good *j* but not those of the other goods. Without this assumption, $\tilde{u}_j = v_j(q_1, \ldots, q_N, y - p\bar{x}_j) + \tilde{\varepsilon}_j$, and the vector W_j includes $q_i, i \neq j$. In the case of the inde-

$$\tilde{u}_j = v_j(q_j, y - p_j \bar{x}_j) + \tilde{\varepsilon}_j \qquad j = 1, \dots, N, \qquad (2.12')$$

the nonstochastic component being identical to (2.12). The discrete choice indices,

$$\tilde{\delta}_j = \delta_j(p, q, y, \tilde{\varepsilon}) = \begin{cases} 1 & \text{if } v_j(q_j, y - p_j \bar{x}_j) + \tilde{\varepsilon}_j \\ & \geq v_i(q_i, y - p_i \bar{x}_i) + \tilde{\varepsilon}_i \ \forall i \quad (2.13') \\ 0 & \text{otherwise,} \end{cases}$$

are now random variables. Their mean, $E\{\delta_j\} \equiv \pi_j$, is given by

$$\begin{aligned} \pi_j &= \Pr\{v_j(q_j, y - p_j \bar{x}_j) + \tilde{\varepsilon}_j > v_i(q_i, y - p_i \bar{x}_i) + \tilde{\varepsilon}_i \ \forall i\} \\ &= F_{(j)}[v_j(q_j, y - p_j \bar{x}_j) - v_1(q_1, y - p_1 \bar{x}_1), \\ &\qquad \dots, v_j(q_j, y - p_j \bar{x}_j) - v_N(q_N, y - p_N \bar{x}_N)], \qquad (2.16) \end{aligned}$$

where $F_{(j)}$ is the joint cumulative distribution function of the (N-1) differences $\tilde{\eta}_{ij} = \tilde{\varepsilon}_i - \tilde{\varepsilon}_j$. When $v_j(\cdot)$ can be cast in the form $v_j = W_j \beta_j$, (2.16) constitutes a RUM as defined in (2.5). I refer to it as a budget-constrained discrete choice RUM because of the restrictions on the regressors W_j and coefficients β_j implied by (2.12'), namely, that the variables y and p_j enter in the form $(y - p_j \bar{x}_j)$ and that v_j is increasing in this term.

The requirement that the arguments of $F_{(j)}$ in (2.16) take the form of utility differences may be regarded as the analog of the integrability conditions in conventional demand theory. It provides a criterion for determining whether a given statistical MRQR model is compatible with the economic hypothesis of utility maximization. In addition, it offers a practical procedure for specifying a statistical model in empirical applications: First postulate some parametric function for $v_j(q_j, y - p_j x_j), j = 1, \dots, N,$ and then form the differences

---

pendent logit model where the $\tilde{\varepsilon}_j$'s are independent extreme value variables, the resulting discrete choice possibilities,

$$\pi_j = \frac{\exp[v_j(q_1, \dots, q_N, y - p_j \bar{x}_j)]}{\sum \exp[v_i(q_1, \dots, q_N, y - p_i \bar{x}_i)]}$$

do not possess the Independence of Irrelevant Alternatives (IIA) property. (This is a version of what McFadden (1981) calls the "universal logit" model.) Thus, there is some connection between weak complementarity and the IIA property.

$v_j - v_1, \ldots, v_j - v_N$ and substitute these into $F_{(j)}$. Another analog with conventional demand theory is worth mentioning. Suppose that the utility function (2.6′) is replaced by some monotonic transformation, $\hat{u}(x, q, z, \tilde{\varepsilon}) \equiv T[u(x, q, z) + \Sigma \zeta_j \tilde{\varepsilon}_j], T' > 0$. The discrete choices indices (2.13′) and, hence, the discrete choice probabilities (2.16) are invariant with respect to this transformation since

$$v_j(q_j, y - p_j \bar{x}_x) + \tilde{\varepsilon}_j \geq v_i(q_i, y - p_i \bar{x}_i) + \tilde{\varepsilon}_i$$
$$\Leftrightarrow T[v_j(q_j, y - p_j \bar{x}_j) + \tilde{\varepsilon}_j] \geq T[v_i(q_i, y - p_i \bar{x}_i) + \tilde{\varepsilon}_i]. \qquad (2.17)$$

Thus, when one estimates the MRQR model (2.16), he recovers the underlying utility function (2.6′) only up to an arbitrary monotonic, increasing transformation.

The unconditional ordinary demand functions associated with the budget-constrained discrete choice RUM model are

$$\tilde{x}_j = x_j(p, q, y, \tilde{\varepsilon}) = \delta_j(p, q, y, \tilde{\varepsilon}) \bar{x}_j \qquad j = 1, \ldots, N, \qquad (2.14′)$$

and the expected quantity demanded is $E\{\tilde{x}_j\} = \pi_j \bar{x}_j$. Substituting the demand functions (2.14′) into the discrete utility function (2.6′) yields the unconditional indirect utility function

$$\tilde{u} = v(p, q, y, \tilde{\varepsilon}) \equiv \max[v_1(q_1, \bar{y} - p_1 x_1) + \tilde{\varepsilon}_1, \ldots, v_N(q_N, y - p_N \bar{x}_N) + \tilde{\varepsilon}_N]. (2.15′)$$

Recall that $v(\cdot)$ gives the utility attained by the individual maximizing consumer when confronted with the choice set (p, q, y). This is a known number for the consumer; but for the econometric investigator, it is a random variable with a cumulative distribution function $F_v(\omega) \equiv \Pr\{v(p, q, y, \tilde{\varepsilon}) \leq \omega\}$ derived from the assumed distribution $F_\varepsilon(\cdot)$ by a change of variables

$$F_v(\omega) = F_\varepsilon(\omega - v_1, \ldots, \omega - v_N). \qquad (2.18)$$

In section 2.3, I show how the unconditional utility function is used to measure the welfare effects of a change in p or q. But first I identify a special family of utility models in which this welfare analysis is considerably simplified.

2.2.3   The Case of No Income Effects

Dual to the above utility maximization is an expenditure minimization problem: minimize $\sum p_i x_i + z$ subject to (2.6′), (2.8), and (2.9). This generates a set of compensated demand functions and an expenditure function which, like the ordinary demand functions and the indirect utility function, involve a random component from the econometrician's viewpoint. Suppose that the individual has selected good j. Assuming that his utility function satisfies the weak complementarity condition (2.11), his expenditure conditional on this decision is $\tilde{e}_j = g_j(q_j, u - \varepsilon_j) + p_j \bar{x}_j$, where $g_j(\cdot)$ is the inverse of $v_j(\cdot)$ in (2.12′), i.e., $g_j[q_j, v_j(q_j, t)] \equiv t$. The unconditional compensated demand functions can be written as $x_j(p, q, u, \tilde{\varepsilon}) = \delta_j(p, q, u, \tilde{\varepsilon}) \bar{x}_j$, where

$$\delta_j(p, q, u, \tilde{\varepsilon}) \equiv \begin{cases} 1 & \text{if } g_j(q_j, u - \tilde{\varepsilon}_j) + p_j \bar{x}_j \\ & \leq g_i(q_i, u - \tilde{\varepsilon}_i) + p_i \bar{x}_i \quad \forall i \\ 0 & \text{otherwise,} \end{cases} \tag{2.19}$$

and the unconditional function is

$$\begin{aligned} \tilde{e} &= e(p, q, u, \tilde{\varepsilon}) \\ &= \min \left[g_1(q_1, u - \tilde{\varepsilon}_1) + p_1 \bar{x}_1, \ldots, g_N(q_N, u - \tilde{\varepsilon}_N) + p_N \bar{x}_N \right]. \end{aligned} \tag{2.20}$$

An important class of utility models, to which Small and Rosen (1981) and McFadden (1981) have drawn attention, is that for which the unconditional ordinary and compensated demand functions coincide. In the Appendix the following result characterizing this class of utility models is proved:

PROPOSITION. The unconditional ordinary and conditional demand functions coincide if the direct utility function (2.6′) is some monotonic transformation of

$$\tilde{u} = h(x, q) + \gamma z + \Sigma \zeta(x_j) \tilde{\varepsilon}_j \tag{2.21a}$$

for some function $h(\cdot)$ and positive constant g. Assuming that $h(\cdot)$ satisfies (2.11), the corresponding form of the conditional indirect utility function is

$$\tilde{u}_j = h_j(q_j) + \gamma y - \gamma p_j \bar{x}_j + \tilde{\varepsilon}_j, \qquad j = 1, \ldots, N, \tag{2.21b}$$

42 Valuing Recreation and the Environment

where $h_j(q_j) \equiv h(0, \ldots, \overline{x}_j, 0, \ldots, 0, q)$.

In order to motivate the proof of this proposition, it is useful to introduce an alternative method of representing the unconditional ordinary and compensated demand functions. Consider the demand for the first good. Given $(p_2, \ldots, p_N, q, y)$, one can write the ordinary demand function as a step function

$$x_1(p, q, y, \widetilde{\varepsilon}) = \begin{cases} 0 & \text{if } p_1 \geq \widetilde{p}_1^* \\ \overline{x}_1 & \text{otherwise,} \end{cases} \tag{2.22}$$

where the switch price, $\widetilde{p}_1^*$, is a function of $(p_2, \ldots, p_N, q, y, \widetilde{\varepsilon})$. Suppose that the actual price of the good is p_1^0; accordingly, the utility attained by the consumer is $\widetilde{u}^0 = v(p_1^0, p_2, \ldots, p_N, q, y, \widetilde{\varepsilon})$. The compensated demand function evaluated at $\widetilde{u}^0$ is also a step function

$$x_1(p, q, \widetilde{u}^0, \widetilde{\varepsilon}) = \begin{cases} 0 & \text{if } p_1 \geq \widetilde{p}_1^{**} \\ \overline{x}_1 & \text{otherwise,} \end{cases} \tag{2.23}$$

where the switch price, $\widetilde{p}_1^{**}$, is a function of $(p_2, \ldots, p_N, q, \widetilde{u}^0, \widetilde{\varepsilon})$.

By construction $x_1(p_1^0, p_2, \ldots, p_N, q, y, \widetilde{\varepsilon}) \equiv x_1(p_1^0, p_2, \ldots, p_N, q, \widetilde{u}^0, \widetilde{\varepsilon})$. However, the entire graphs of the two demand functions coincide, $x_1(p_1, p_2, \ldots, p_N, q, y, \widetilde{\varepsilon}) \equiv x_1(p_1, p_2, \ldots, p_N, q, \widetilde{u}^0, \widetilde{\varepsilon})$ for *all* p_1, if and only if $\widetilde{p}_1^* = \widetilde{p}_1^{**}$. In the appendix, I show that this occurs nontrivially only when the direct utility function takes the form in (2.21a). The assertion about the conditional indirect utility functions (2.21b) follows directly from (2.21a) by application of (2.10).

There is an important corollary to this proposition which enables one to test whether an empirical MRQR model satisfies (2.21). Observe from (2.21a) that the income variable drops out of the utility differences

$$\widetilde{u}_j - \widetilde{u}_i = h_j(q_j) - h_i(q_i) - \gamma \ (p_j \overline{x}_j - p_i \overline{x}_i) + \widetilde{\varepsilon}_j - \widetilde{\varepsilon}_i. \tag{2.24}$$

Since it is these utility differences that enter into the formula for the discrete choice probabilities (2.16), it follows that the choice probabilities are *independent* of the consumer's income when the utility function satisfies (2.21)—there are no income effects.[9]

---

[9] The marginal utility of income, γ, can still be estimated because it appears as the coefficient of the price difference term in (2.24). The point is that income itself cannot appear as an explicit variable in a MRQR model satisfying (2.21).

The utility function in (2.21a) satisfies the quasilinearity property that one finds when there are no income effects in conventional, continuous choice models—for example, see Katzner (1970, p. 93). As will be shown in the next section, it has the same implications for welfare analysis in discrete choice RUM models as in conventional, continuous choice models, namely, that the compensating and equivalent variations coincide and can be measured by areas under ordinary demand functions.

2.3   COMPENSATION MEASURES

In this section I show how one can perform welfare evaluations with statistical MRQR models that satisfy the integrability condition (2.16) and, hence, are derivable from the utility maximization model (2.6')–(2.9). Suppose that the set of prices and qualities available to the individual changes from $\left(p^{o}, q^{o}\right)$ to $\left(p^{1}, q^{1}\right)$. Thus his utility changes from $\tilde{u}^{o} \equiv v(p^{o}, q^{o}, y, \tilde{\varepsilon})$ to $\tilde{u}^{1} \equiv v(p^{1}, q^{1}, y, \tilde{\varepsilon})$. By analogy with welfare analysis in conventional, continuous choice models, this utility change could be measured in money units by the quantity $\tilde{C}$ which satisfies

$$v(p^{1}, q^{1}, y - \tilde{C}, \tilde{\varepsilon}) = v(p^{o}, q^{o}, y, \tilde{\varepsilon}) \qquad (2.25)$$

or the quantity $\tilde{E}$ which satisfies

$$v(p^{1}, q^{1}, y, \tilde{\varepsilon}) = v(p^{o}, q^{o}, y + \tilde{E}, \tilde{\varepsilon}). \qquad (2.26)$$

The problem in the RUM context is that $\tilde{C}$ and $\tilde{E}$ are random variables since they depend on $\tilde{\varepsilon}$. Although the compensation required to offset the price/ quality change is a fixed number for the individual consumer, for the econometric investigator it is a random variable since the individual's utility function is known only up to a random component. How, then, to obtain a single number representing the compensating or equivalent variation for the price/quality change?

In fact, the existing literature contains hints of up to three different approaches to welfare evaluation in the random utility context, but the conceptual distinction between these approaches does not appear to have been recognized. One approach is to derive the probability distribution of the quantity $\tilde{C}$ and calculate its mean, $C^{*} \equiv E\{\tilde{C}\}$. As shown below, this calculation is sometimes difficult because of the complexity of the distribution of $\tilde{C}$. A second approach

44 *Valuing Recreation and the Environment*

is to employ the expectation of the individual's indirect utility function, $V(p, q, y) \equiv E\{v(p, q, y, \tilde{\varepsilon})\}$ and define the compensating variation in terms of this function.[10] The resulting welfare measure, $C^{\cdot}$, satisfies

$$V(p', q', y - C^{\cdot}) = V(p^0, q^0, y). \qquad (2.27)$$

The distinction between $C^{\cdot}$ and $C^{\cdot}$ is subtle but important. $C^{\cdot}$ is the observer's expectation of the maximum amount of money that the individual could pay after the change and still be as well off as he was before it. By contrast, $C^{\cdot}$ is the maximum amount of money that the individual could pay after the change and still be as well off, in terms of the observer's expectation of his utility, as he was before it. The third welfare measure is derived as follows. One might want to know the amount of money such that the individual is just at the point of indifference between paying the money and securing the change or paying nothing and foregoing the change. For the observer, this could be taken as the quantity C^* such that

$$\Pr\{v(p', q', y - C^*, \tilde{\varepsilon}) \geq v(p^0, q^0, y, \tilde{\varepsilon})\} = 0.5, \qquad (2.28)$$

i.e., there is no more than a 50:50 chance that the individual would be willing to pay C^* for the change.

Although these three welfare measures are conceptually distinct, several relationships can be established among them. First, it is simple to show that, while $C^{\cdot}$ is the *mean* of the distribution of the true but random compensation $\tilde{C}$, C^* is the *median* of this distribution.[11] Thus, if the distribution were symmetric, $C^{\cdot}$ and C^* would coincide. In practice, however, this may not occur: the distribution of $\tilde{C}$ may be highly skewed, and its mean, $C^{\cdot}$, may differ by an order of magnitude from its median, C^*. Some circumstances in which this can occur are described in Section 2.5.

The second point is that, whereas $C^{\cdot}$ and C^* are both invariant with respect to a transformation of the utility function, the welfare measure $C^{\cdot}$ is *not* invariant. As noted earlier, the statistical MRQR model allows one to recover the underlying utility function (2.6') only up to an arbitrary monotone transformation. Consider the transformation $\hat{u}(x, q, z, \tilde{\varepsilon}) \equiv T[u(x, q, z, \tilde{\varepsilon})], T > 0,$

---

[10] Table 2.1 provides formulas for calculating $V(\cdot)$ for the GEV model, (2.3), the independent logit model, and binary and trichotomous probit models.

[11] The median of the distribution of $\tilde{C}$, C_M, has the property that $\Pr\{\tilde{C} \geq C_M\} = 0.5$. But, since $v(p, q, y, \tilde{\varepsilon})$ is increasing in y,

$\tilde{C} \geq C_M \Rightarrow v(p', q', y - C_M, \tilde{\varepsilon}) \geq v(p', q', y - \tilde{C}, \tilde{\varepsilon}) = v(p^0, q^0, y, \tilde{\varepsilon})$ from (2.28), $C^* = C_M$.

introduced in connection with (2.17), and let $\hat{v}(p, q, y, \widetilde{\varepsilon}) \equiv T[v(p, q, y, \widetilde{\varepsilon})]$. Then

$$v(p^1, q^1, y - \widetilde{C}, \widetilde{\varepsilon}) = v(p^0, q^0, y, \widetilde{\varepsilon})$$
$$\Leftrightarrow \hat{v}(p^1, q^1, y - \widetilde{C}, \widetilde{\varepsilon}) = \hat{v}(p^0, q^0, y, \widetilde{\varepsilon}). \tag{2.29}$$

It follows that $\widetilde{C}$ and therefore, both C^+ and C^* are unaffected by the utility transformation. This is not true for $C^\cdot$ because, if one defines $\hat{C}^\cdot$ by

$$E\{\hat{v}(p^1, q^1, y - \hat{C}^\cdot, \widetilde{\varepsilon})\} = E\{\hat{v}(q^0, q^0, y, \widetilde{\varepsilon})\}. \tag{2.30}$$

In general $\hat{C}^\cdot$ does not satisfy (2.27). Thus, $\hat{C}^\cdot \neq C^\cdot$. In effect, the welfare measure $C^\cdot$ implies a cardinal concept of utility.

This general result notwithstanding, there *are* some circumstances in which $C^\cdot$ is invariant with respect to a utility transformation. The most important is when there are no income effects. In this case, from (2.21b) the unconditional indirect utility function takes the following form:

$$v(p, q, y, \widetilde{\varepsilon}) = \gamma y + \max[h_1(q_1) - \gamma p_1 \bar{x}_1 + \widetilde{\varepsilon}_1, \dots, h_N(q_N) - \gamma p_N \bar{x}_N + \widetilde{\varepsilon}_N]$$
$$\equiv \gamma y + s(p, q, \widetilde{\varepsilon}). \tag{2.31}$$

Hence

$$V(p, q, y) = \gamma y + E\{s(p, q, \widetilde{\varepsilon})\} \equiv \gamma y + S(p, q), \tag{2.32}$$

and from (2.27)[12]

---

[12] $S(p, q)$ can be constructed from the formulas given in Table 2.1. For example, with the GEV model one obtains

$$C = \frac{1}{\gamma} \left\{ \ln G[\exp(v_1^1), \dots, \exp(v_N^1)] - \ln G[\exp(v_1^0), \dots, \exp(v_N^0)] \right\}$$

while, with the binary independent probit model where Σ is diagonal and normalized so that $\sigma = 1$, one obtains

$$C = \frac{1}{\gamma} \left\{ \Delta^0 \Phi(\Delta^0) + v_2^0 + \phi(\Delta^0) - \Delta^1 \Phi(\Delta^1) - v_2^1 - \phi(\Delta^1) \right\}$$

where $v_j^t \equiv v_j(q_j^t, y - p_j^t \bar{x}_j) = h_j(q_j^t) + \gamma(y - p_j^t \bar{x}_j)$ and $\Delta^t \equiv v_1^t - v_2^t, t = 0,1$.

46 Valuing Recreation and the Environment

$$C^* = \frac{1}{\gamma}[S(p^1, q^1) - S(p^0, q^0)].$$ (2.33)

However, on substituting (2.31) into (2.25), one obtains

$$\tilde{C} = [s(p^1, \ q^1, \tilde{\varepsilon}) - s(p^0, q^0, \tilde{\varepsilon})]/\gamma.$$ (2.34)

It follows, therefore, that when there are no income effects [13]

$$C^+ \equiv E\{\tilde{C}\} = C^*.$$ (2.35)

What about measures of equivalent variation? By working with (2.26) rather than (2.25), one obtains three alternative measures of equivalent variation, which I denote E^+, E^*, and E^*.[14] These are related to one another in the same ways as C^+, C^*, and C^*. Moreover, it follows directly from (2.31) and (2.32) that, when there are no income effects, $E^+ = C^+$, $E^* = C^*$, and $E^* = C^*$. When there *are* income effects, however, the corresponding equivalent and compensating variations differ. The similarity with welfare analysis in conventional, continuous choice models is evident.

Another result that carries over from conventional, continuous choice models is the relationship between compensation measures and areas under ordinary demand curves when there are no income effects. To show this, I need to employ the following result about $V(\cdot)$, which applies regardless of whether or not there are income effects[15]

$$\frac{\partial V}{\partial v_j} \equiv \frac{\partial E\{\max[v_1 + \tilde{\varepsilon}_1, ..., v_N + \tilde{\varepsilon}_N]\}}{\partial v_j} = \pi_j \qquad j = 1, ..., N. \quad (2.36)$$

Now suppose that there are no income effects and, for simplicity, the only change is in p_1 and q_1, with $p_2, ..., p_N$ and $q_2, ..., q_N$ remaining constant. In this case, using (2.36),

---

[13] When there are no income effects, C^* satisfies:
$$\Pr\{s(p^1, q^1, \tilde{\varepsilon}) - s(p^0, q^0, \tilde{\varepsilon}) \geq \gamma C^*\} = 0.5.$$

[14] The equivalent variation for a change from (p^a, q^a) to (p^b, q^b) is equal to the negative of the corresponding compensating variation measure for the change from (p^b, q^b) to (p^a, q^a).

[15] This is proved by Williams (1977), Daly and Zachary (1978), and Sheffi and Daganzo (1978).

Welfare Analysis with Discrete Choice Models 47

$$C^{\cdot} = \frac{1}{\gamma}[V(p^{1},q^{1},y) - V(p^{0},q^{0},y)]$$

$$= \frac{1}{\gamma}\int_{v_{1}^{0}}^{v_{1}^{1}}\frac{\partial V}{\partial v_{1}}dv_{1} \tag{2.37}$$

or

$$C^{\cdot} = \frac{1}{\gamma}\int_{v_{1}^{0}}^{v_{1}^{1}}\pi_{1}(v_{1},\ldots,v_{N})dv_{1} \tag{2.38}$$

In particular, if only p_{1} changes, (2.38) becomes[16]

$$C^{\cdot} = \frac{1}{\gamma}\int_{p_{1}^{0}}^{p_{1}^{1}}\frac{\partial V}{\partial v_{1}}\frac{\partial v_{1}}{\partial p_{1}}dp_{1}$$

$$= -\bar{x}_{1}\int_{p_{1}^{0}}^{p_{1}^{1}}\pi_{1}(p_{1})dp_{1}$$

$$= -\int_{p_{1}^{0}}^{p_{1}^{1}}E\{x_{1}(p,q,y,\tilde{\varepsilon})\}dp_{1}. \tag{2.39}$$

Thus, when there are no income effects, the expected compensating variation for a price change is given by the area under the expected ordinary demand function.

It may be useful to relate the foregoing analysis to the papers by McFadden (1981) and Small and Rosen (1981), which also deal with welfare evaluations in RUM models. Both of these papers focus on the case where there are no income effects and employ the welfare measure $C^{\cdot}$.[17] Thus they do not consider the distinction between $C^{\cdot}$ and the other two welfare measures introduced above. McFadden derives the formula for $C^{\cdot}$ in (2.37) from the utility function (2.21)[18], and in his Theorem 5.1 he proves the converse: if the formula for $C^{\cdot}$

---

[16] The second line follows from the fact that $\partial v / \partial p_{1} = -\gamma \bar{x}_{1}$ using (2.21b). The third line follows from the fact that $E\{\bar{x}_{1}\} = \bar{x}_{1}\pi_{1}$.

[17] McFadden (1981) and Small and Rosen (1981) interpret $V(\cdot)$ as the average indirect utility function over a population of individuals and $C^{\cdot}$ as the average compensation. I interpret $V(\cdot)$ and $C^{\cdot}$ as the observer's expectation of a single individual's utility function and compensation. I would calculate $C^{\cdot}$ (or C^{+}, or C^{*}) for each individual separately and then aggregate over the entire population, perhaps using weights derived from some social welfare function.

[18] McFadden (1981) actually derived (2.37) for a more general additively random RUM model involving continuous as well as discrete choices. This type of model is discussed further in section 2.2.

is given by (2.37), the utility function is (2.21).[18] Small and Rosen obtain the formula for C^* in (2.39) but with some additional assumptions. However, their analysis appears to be defective: given the additively random utility specification, the no-income-effects utility function (2.21) is both necessary and sufficient for (2.39) to hold.[19]

2.4   OTHER RANDOM UTILITY MAXIMIZATION MODELS

2.4.1   Random Coefficients Models

In the discrete choice model studied in sections 2.2 and 2.3, the random element representing differences in tastes among individuals and/or unobserved variables was introduced in a very specific way, namely, additively as in (2.1'). In some circumstances, however, this may seem unduly restrictive, and one may prefer to introduce the random element in a different manner. For example, one may wish to specify the no-income-effects utility model (2.21a, b) as

$$u(x, q, z, \widetilde{\varepsilon}) = h(x, q) + \widetilde{\gamma} z + \Sigma \xi(x_j) \, \widetilde{\varepsilon}_j \qquad (2.40a)$$

$$\widetilde{u}_j = h_j(q_j) + \widetilde{\gamma} y - \widetilde{\gamma} p_j \bar{x}_j + \widetilde{\varepsilon}_j, \qquad (2.40b)$$

where $\widetilde{\gamma}$ is now a random variable, uncorrelated with $\widetilde{\varepsilon}_1, ..., \widetilde{\varepsilon}_N$, with a mean of $\bar{\gamma}$ and a variance of σ_r^2. Equivalently, $\widetilde{\gamma} = \bar{\gamma} + \widetilde{\varepsilon}_o$ where $E\{\widetilde{\varepsilon}_o\} = 0$ and var $\{\widetilde{\varepsilon}_o\} = \sigma_r^2$. An interpretation of this formulation could be that consumers vary in the weight they place on the numeraire good, z, relative to the x's; in addition, because of (our) errors of measurement or observation in the attributes of the discrete choices, consumers appear to vary in their preferences for individual x's. I will refer to any RUM model such as (2.40) where the random element enters nonadditively via the slope coefficients as a "random coefficients" model. This type of model was introduced into the MRQR literature by Hausman and Wise (1978).[20]

---

[19] Besides assuming that there are no income effects, Small and Rosen (1981) make two additional assumptions: (1) $\partial v_j / \partial y$ is independent of p_j and q_j and (2) $\partial v_j / \partial q_j \to 0$ as $p_j \to \infty$. It can be shown that (2.21) implies (1) but precludes (2).

[20] It has generally been restricted to probit rather than logit models because the normal distribution is closed under addition, unlike the extreme value distribution. This is less of a consideration if the discrete alternative-specific random terms, $\varepsilon_1, ..., \varepsilon_N$, are omitted from the model, leaving only the random slope coefficients(s).

Much of the analysis in sections 2.2 and 2.3 carries over to random coefficients models. Given some direct utility function $u(x,q,z,\tilde{\varepsilon})$, the conditional indirect utility functions are

$$\tilde{u}_j = u(0,\ldots,0,\overline{x}_j,0,\ldots,0,q,y-p_j\overline{x}_j,\tilde{\varepsilon}) \equiv v_j(q_j,y-p_j\overline{x}_j,\tilde{\varepsilon}). \quad (2.41)$$

The discrete choice indices are

$$
\begin{aligned}
\tilde{\delta}_j &= \delta_j(p,q,y,\tilde{\varepsilon}) \\
&= \begin{cases} 1 & \text{if } v_j(q_j,y-p_j\overline{x}_j,\tilde{\varepsilon}) \geq v_i(q_i,y-p_i\overline{x}_i,\tilde{\varepsilon}) \ \forall i \\ 0 & \text{otherwise,} \end{cases}
\end{aligned}
\quad (2.42)
$$

and the discrete choice probabilities are

$$\pi_j = \Pr \{v_j(q_j,y-p_j\overline{x}_j,\tilde{\varepsilon}) \geq v_i(q_i,y-p_i\overline{x}_i,\tilde{\varepsilon}) \text{ all } i\}. \quad (2.43)$$

Similarly, the unconditional indirect utility function is

$$v(p,q,y,\tilde{\varepsilon}) = \max [v_1(q_1,y-p_1\overline{x}_1,\tilde{\varepsilon}),\ldots,v_N(q_N,y-p_N\overline{x}_N,\tilde{\varepsilon})]. \quad (2.44)$$

Using this function, the welfare measures C^+, C^*, and $C^\cdot$, or E^+, E^*, and $E^\cdot$ can be constructed along the lines indicated above for the additively random utility model.

However, depending on the precise form of the random coefficients specification, some of the relationships among these welfare measures may no longer hold. In particular, it is not necessarily true that $C^+ = C^\cdot$ when there are no income effects. In the case of the model (2.40), the discrete choice probabilities are independent of the consumer's income since they take the form

$$\pi_j = \Pr \{h_j(q_j)-\overline{\gamma}\,p_j\overline{x}_j + \tilde{\omega}_j \geq h_i(q_i)-\overline{\gamma}\,p_i\overline{x}_i + \tilde{\omega}_i \text{ all } i\} \quad (2.45)$$

where $\tilde{\omega}_j \equiv \tilde{\varepsilon}_j - \tilde{\varepsilon}_0 p_j \overline{x}_j$, $j = 1,\ldots,N$. But, from (2.40b),

$$
\begin{aligned}
v(p,q,y,\tilde{\varepsilon}) &= (\overline{\gamma}+\tilde{\varepsilon}_0)y \\
&\quad + \max[h_1(q_1)-\overline{\gamma}p_1\overline{x}_1 + \tilde{\omega}_1,\ldots,h_N(q_N)-\overline{\gamma}p_N\overline{x}_N + \tilde{\omega}_N] \\
&\equiv (\overline{\gamma}+\tilde{\varepsilon}_0)y + s(p,q,\tilde{\omega});
\end{aligned}
\quad (2.46)
$$

50 Valuing Recreation and the Environment

hence,

$$C^* = E\left\{\frac{s(p^1, q^1, \tilde{\omega}^1) - s(p^0, q^0, \tilde{\omega}^0)}{\bar{\gamma} + \tilde{\varepsilon}_0}\right\} \tag{2.47}$$

while

$$C^* = \frac{E\{s(p^1, q^1, \tilde{\omega}^1) - s(p^0, q^0, \tilde{\omega}^0)\}}{\bar{\gamma}} \tag{2.48}$$

where $\tilde{\omega}'_j \equiv \tilde{\varepsilon}_j - \tilde{\varepsilon}_0 p'_j \bar{x}_j$, $t = 0,1$. Thus, $C^* \neq C^*$. Similarly, although the relationships in (2.37) and (2.38) still apply to C^*, the relationship in (2.39) no longer holds. Nevertheless, it still follows from (2.46) that $E^* = C^*$, $E^* = C^*$, and $E^* = C^*$ in the random coefficients, no-income-effects model.

2.4.2 Nonbudget-Constrained and Mixed Discrete/Continuous Choices

The budget-constrained discrete choice RUM model implies that the conditional indirect utility functions have the form given in (2.12′) or (2.41). This imposes substantive restrictions on the manner in which the price and income variables enter the formula for the discrete choice probabilities. However, the literature contains many empirical examples of logit or probit models of consumer choices that violate these restrictions. For example, one finds MRQR models based on conditional indirect utility functions of the form

$$\bar{u}_j = h_j(q_j) - \beta_j p_j + \gamma_j y + \tilde{\varepsilon}_j, \quad \beta_j \neq \gamma_j \quad j = 1, \ldots, N \tag{2.49}$$

or

$$\bar{u}_j = h_j(q_j) - \beta p_j + \gamma y p_j + \tilde{\varepsilon}_j \quad j = 1, \ldots, N, \tag{2.50}$$

which are clearly inconsistent with (2.12′) or (2.41). How can such models occur?

One possible explanation is that the consumer is not actually making a purely discrete choice but rather what might be called a "mixed discrete/continuous" choice. In this case, the utility maximization is *not* constrained by (2.9); instead, the x's can vary continuously, subject to a nonnegativity constraint. However, there is an element of discreteness in the consumer's choices which arises either because the x's are mutually exclusive—i.e., the constraint (2.8) applies—or because the consumer's preferences force a corner solution in which some of the x's are not consumed (in effect, the various x's are perfect substitutes). Thus, the consumer faces both a discrete choice—which of the x's to select—and a continuous choice—how much to consume if he selects x_j. The discrete choice may lead to a statistical MRQR model which satisfies (2.5), but the structure of the conditional indirect utility functions is now different; they no longer satisfy (2.12') or (2.41).

Since these models are described in detail in Hanemann (1984), my discussion here will be brief. They typically involve a random coefficients specification of the utility function rather than the additive formulation in (2.6'). Suppose the consumer has selected good j. Maximization of $u_j(x_j, q_j, z, \widetilde{\varepsilon}) \equiv u(0, \ldots, 0, x_j, 0, \ldots, 0, q, z, \widetilde{\varepsilon})$ with respect to x_j (now freely variable) and z subject to a budget constraint, $p_j x_j + z = y$, yields a conditional ordinary demand function $x_j(p_j, q_j, y, \widetilde{\varepsilon})$, and a conditional indirect utility function, $v_j(p_j, q_j, y, \widetilde{\varepsilon})$. The latter is quasi-convex and decreasing in p_j and increasing in y, but it does not have the same structure as (2.41)—the coefficient of p_j is no longer equal to minus the coefficient of y. Allowing for this difference, the consumer's discrete choice indices are defined as in (2.42), and the discrete choice probabilities are defined as in (2.43). Instead of (2.14'), the unconditional ordinary demand function for the jth good takes the form: $x_j(p, q, y, \widetilde{\varepsilon}) = \delta_j(p, q, y, \widetilde{\varepsilon}) x_j(p_j, q_j, y, \widetilde{\varepsilon})$. Thus, the probability that one observes an individual who selects, say, the first brand and consumes three units is

$$\Pr\{x_1(p, q, y, \widetilde{\varepsilon}) = 3 \text{ and } x_i(p, q, y, \widetilde{\varepsilon}) = 0, \ \forall i \geq 2\}$$
$$= \Pr\{x_1(p_1, q_1, y, \widetilde{\varepsilon}) = 3 | v_1(p_1, q_1, y, \widetilde{\varepsilon}) \geq v_i(p_i, q_i, y, \widetilde{\varepsilon}) \ \forall i\}$$
$$\times \ \Pr\{v_1(p_1, q_1, y, \widetilde{\varepsilon}) \geq v_i(p_i, q_i, y, \widetilde{\varepsilon}) \ \forall i\}. \tag{2.51}$$

Substituting the unconditional ordinary demand functions into the direct utility function yields the unconditional direct utility function which also can be defined as in (2.44). From this, the welfare measures C^+, C^*, and $C^\cdot$ can be constructed in the same manner as for purely discrete choices. [21]

Thus, mixed discrete/continuous choices can give rise to formulas for the discrete choice probabilities involving conditional indirect utility functions that violate the restrictions implied in (2.12') or (2.41)—c.f., the second probability statement on the right-hand side of (2.51). However, precisely because there is

---

[21] An example of an application of welfare analysis in a mixed discrete/continuous choice RUM model is given in Hanemann (1984).

52 *Valuing Recreation and the Environment*

also a continuous choice in these models, it is inefficient to estimate the parameters of the utility model from data on the discrete choices alone: the continuous choices contain information about the individual's preferences that should not be overlooked. Accordingly, if one really is dealing with a mixed discrete/continuous choice, the estimation should be based on (2.51) rather than on (2.41) as in conventional MRQR models. Once the model has been estimated, the three approaches to welfare evaluation described in section 2.3 carry over directly.

Another explanation for MRQR models which violate the restrictions in (2.12') or (2.41) is that the individual genuinely faces a purely discrete choice but one that is not bound by the budget constraint (2.7). An example where this occurs is discrete choices among actions with uncertain consequences by a von Neumann–Morgenstern expected-utility-maximizing individual. Suppose an individual has wealth y and a utility-of-wealth function whose nonstochastic component is denoted by $\psi(y)$. The individual must choose among N actions whose consequences depend on the state of the world, $s = 1, \ldots, S$. Associated with act j are a vector of state probabilities, $\rho_j = \left(\rho_{j1}, \ldots, \rho_{jS}\right)$, and a vector of monetary consequences, $z_j = \left(z_{j1}, \ldots, z_{jS}\right)$. Using an additively random formulation, the individual's utility conditional on the choice of act j is

$$\tilde{u}_j = \sum_s \rho_{js} \, \psi(y + z_{js}) + \tilde{\varepsilon}_j, \tag{2.52}$$

and the discrete choice probabilities are

$$\pi_j = \Pr\{\Sigma\rho_{js}\psi(y + z_{js}) + \tilde{\varepsilon}_j \geq \Sigma\rho_{is}\psi(y + z_{is}) + \tilde{\varepsilon}_i, \; \forall i\} \quad j = 1, \ldots, N, \tag{2.53}$$

which is a statistical MRQR model that differs from (2.12'). Given that the individual has chosen optimally, his utility is $v(\rho, z, y, \tilde{\varepsilon}) \equiv \max[\tilde{u}_1, \ldots, \tilde{u}_N]$. Suppose that the state probabilities and/or payoffs change from $\left(\rho^0, z^0\right)$ to $\left(\rho^1, z^1\right)$. In order to measure the welfare effects of this change, the quantities C^+, C^*, and $C^\cdot$, or E^+, E^*, and $E^\cdot$ can be constructed from $v(p, z, y, \tilde{\varepsilon})$ along the lines indicated above. For example, $C^+ = E\{\tilde{C}\}$ where $\tilde{C}$ satisfies $v(\rho^1, z^1, y - \tilde{C}, \tilde{\varepsilon}) = v(\rho^0, z^0, y, \tilde{\varepsilon})$ and, similarly, with the other welfare measures.[22]

---

[22] In Hanemann (1979) this type of discrete choice model is employed to infer the value of life (i.e., the value of changes in mortality probabilities) from data on individual risk-taking behavior.

2.5   APPLICATIONS

In this section I show how one actually computes the welfare measures once the parameters of the RUM model have been estimated. For simplicity, I deal with measures of compensating variation; but, with appropriate changes, everything carries over to measures of equivalent variation. I will concentrate mainly on the calculation of C^* and C^{**}: the formulas in Table 2.1 should usually suffice for calculating the expected indirect utility function, $V(\cdot)$, from which C^* can be obtained via (2.27). If there are no income effects, one obtains a closed-form expression for C^* [see (2.38) and (2.48)]. If there are income effects, however, numerical techniques, such as Newton's method, will be required to solve (2.27).[23]

In order to cover both additively random and random coefficient specifications, I write the conditional indirect utility functions as $v_j\left(p_j, q_j, y, \varepsilon\right)$, $j = 1$, ..., N, where ε is a vector of *all* the random elements in the model, with joint density function $f_\varepsilon(\cdot)$. I focus on the special case where there is a change in the prices and/or quality attributes of only *one* good, say x_1. Furthermore, I assume that the change is unambiguously an improvement, i.e., $\tilde{u}_1^1 \equiv v_1(p_1^1, q_1^1, y, \tilde{\varepsilon}) > \tilde{u}_1^0 \equiv v_1(p_1^0, q_1^0, y, \tilde{\varepsilon})$. In addition to presenting computational formulas, I will develop some bounds on the magnitudes of C^* and C^{**} and identify the circumstances in which $C^* \lessgtr C^{**}$. When there are more complex price/quality changes, the analysis becomes more complicated, but it follows the same basic logic as that presented here.

To simplify the exposition, it is convenient to present the formulas for the case when $N = 3$; however, with appropriate changes everything carries over to the case of an arbitrary $N \geq 2$. Define $\tilde{u}_i \equiv v_i(p_i, q_i, y, \tilde{\varepsilon})$ $i = 2, 3$, $\tilde{u}^{0\theta} \equiv \max[\tilde{u}_1^0, \tilde{u}_2, \tilde{u}_3]$, and $\tilde{u}^1 \equiv \max[\tilde{u}_1^1, \tilde{u}_2, \tilde{u}_3]$. The trick in computing C^* in this case is to recognize that there are five possible events which partition the domain of $f_\varepsilon(\cdot)$ into five disjoint regions. I denote these events (1/1), (2/1), (2/2), (3/1), and (3/3) and the corresponding regions A(1/1), A(2/1), etc. The events are as follows. The event (1/1) is that the individual originally chose good 1; since good 1 improves while there is no change in goods 2 and 3, it follows that he continues to prefer good 1. Another possibility is that the individual originally chose good 2 and, after the change, he either still prefers good 2 (2/2) or switches to good 1 (2/1). The last two events are that the individual originally chose good 3 and either still prefers that good after the change (3/3), or switches to good 1 (3/1). The corresponding regions of ε-space are

---

[23] Some formulas for approximating C^{**} were presented in Hanemann (1982, 1983).

54 Valuing Recreation and the Environment

$$A(1/1) = \{\tilde{\varepsilon}|\tilde{u}_i \leq \tilde{u}_1^o, i = 2,3\}$$
$$A(2/2) = \{\tilde{\varepsilon}|\tilde{u}_1^1 \leq \tilde{u}_2 \text{ and } \tilde{u}_3 \leq \tilde{u}_2\}$$
$$A(2/1) = \{\tilde{\varepsilon}|\tilde{u}_3 \leq \tilde{u}_2 \text{ and } \tilde{u}_1^o \leq \tilde{u}_2 \leq \tilde{u}_1^1\}$$
$$A(3/3) = \{\tilde{\varepsilon}|\tilde{u}_1^1 \leq \tilde{u}_3 \text{ and } \tilde{u}_2 \leq \tilde{u}_3\}$$
$$A(3/1) = \{\tilde{\varepsilon}|\tilde{u}_2 \leq \tilde{u}_3 \text{ and } \tilde{u}_1^o \leq \tilde{u}_3 \leq \tilde{u}_1^1\}.$$

The probabilities of the events are

$$Pr\{1/1\} = \pi_1^o$$
$$Pr\{2/2\} = \pi_2^1$$
$$Pr\{2/1\} = \pi_2^o - \pi_2^1 \qquad\qquad (2.54)$$
$$Pr\{3/3\} = \pi_3^1$$
$$Pr\{3/1\} = \pi_3^o - \pi_3^1$$

where π_i^t is the probability that the individual chooses the ith good either before the change ($t = 0$) or after it ($t = 1$).

Observe that, if events (2/2) or (3/3) occur, the individual does *not* gain from the improvement in good 1 because it is still dominated by some other good; if events (1/1), (2/1), or (3/1) occur, he *does* gain, and the improvement in his welfare can be measured in money by the quantities $\tilde{C}(1/1)$, $\tilde{C}(2/1)$, or $\tilde{C}(3/1)$ where

$$v_1[p_1^1, q_1^1, y - \tilde{C}(1/1), \tilde{\varepsilon}] = \tilde{u}_1^o \qquad\qquad (2.55a)$$

$$v_1[p_1^1, q_1^1, y - \tilde{C}(2/1), \tilde{\varepsilon}] = \tilde{u}_2 \qquad\qquad (2.55b)$$

$$v_1[p_1^1, q_1^1, y - \tilde{C}(3/1), \tilde{\varepsilon}] = \tilde{u}_3 . \qquad\qquad (2.55c)$$

Thus, the compensation $\tilde{C}$ defined in (2.25) is given by

$$\tilde{C} = \begin{cases} 0 & \text{if } \tilde{\varepsilon} \in A(2/2) \text{ or } \tilde{\varepsilon} \in A(3/3) \\ \tilde{C}(1/1) & \text{if } \tilde{\varepsilon} \in A(1/1) \\ \tilde{C}(2/1) & \text{if } \tilde{\varepsilon} \in A(2/1) \\ \tilde{C}(3/1) & \text{if } \tilde{\varepsilon} \in A(3/1). \end{cases} \qquad (2.56)$$

Welfare Analysis with Discrete Choice Models 55

Hence

$$C^* = \int_{A(1/1)} \tilde{C}(1/1)f_\varepsilon(\varepsilon)d\varepsilon + \int_{A(2/1)} \tilde{C}(2/1)f_\varepsilon(e)d\varepsilon + \int_{A(3/1)} \tilde{C}(3/1)f_\varepsilon(\varepsilon)d\varepsilon. \quad (2.57)$$

By virtue of the assumption that the change in (p_1, q_1) is unambiguously an improvement,

$$\tilde{C}(1/1) > 0. \qquad (2.58)$$

When the event (2/1) occurs, since $\tilde{u}_1^0 \le \tilde{u}_2 \le \tilde{u}_1^1$, from (2.55) one has

$$v_1[p_1', q_1', y - \tilde{C}(1/1), \tilde{\varepsilon}] \le v_1[p_1', q_1', y - \tilde{C}(2/1), \tilde{\varepsilon}] \le v_1(p_1', q_1', y, \tilde{\varepsilon}).$$

Because $v_1(\cdot)$ is increasing in y, this implies that, over the region where $\tilde{C} = \tilde{C}(2/1)$, $0 \le \tilde{C}(2/1) \le \tilde{C}(1/1)$. Similarly, over the region where $\tilde{C} = \tilde{C}(3/1)$, $0 \le \tilde{C}(3/1) \le \tilde{C}(1/1)$. Hence, from (2.56),

$$0 \le \tilde{C} \le \tilde{C}(1/1). \qquad (2.59)$$

Since $\tilde{C} > 0$ with positive probability (as long as $\pi_1^0 > 0$), and also $\pi_j = \exp(W_j \beta_j) G_j[\exp(W_1 \beta_1), \dots, \exp(W_N \beta_N)] G[\exp(W_1 \beta_1), \dots, \exp(W_N \beta_N)]^{-1}$ with positive probability (as long as $\pi_2^1 + \pi_3^1 > 0$), it may be deduced that

$$0 < C^* \equiv E\{\tilde{C}\} < E\{\tilde{C}(1/1)\}. \qquad (2.60)$$

What about the welfare measure C^*? It follows from (2.26), (2.54), and (2.56) that if $\pi_2^1 + \pi_3^1 = (1 - \pi_1^1) \ge 0.5$, i.e., if $\pi_1^1 \le 0.5$, then $C^* = 0$. If $\pi_1^1 > 0.5$, C^* can be determined in the following manner. Given any constant C^*, define $\tilde{u}_1^*(C) \equiv v_1(p_1', q_1', y - C, \tilde{\varepsilon})$, $\tilde{u}_i^*(C) \equiv v_i(p_i, q_i, y - C, \tilde{\varepsilon})$, $i = 2, 3$, and $\pi^*(C) \equiv \Pr\{\tilde{u}^*(C) \ge \tilde{u}^0\}$. Then, the welfare measure C^* solves

$$0.5 = \pi^*(C^*)$$

$$= \Pr\{\tilde{u}^*(C^*) \ge \tilde{u}_1^0 \text{ and } \tilde{u}_1^*(C^*) \ge \tilde{u}_1^0\}$$

$$= \Pr\{\tilde{u}_2 \le \tilde{u}_1^0, \tilde{u}_3 \le \tilde{u}_1^0 \text{ and } \tilde{u}_1^0 \le \tilde{u}_1^*(C^*)\}$$

$$+ \Pr\{\tilde{u}_3 \le \tilde{u}_2 \text{ and } \tilde{u}_1^0 \le \tilde{u}_2 \le \tilde{u}_1^*(C^*)\}$$

$$+ \Pr\{\tilde{u}_2 \le \tilde{u}_3 \text{ and } \tilde{u}_1^0 \le \tilde{u}_3 \le \tilde{u}_1^*(C^*)\}. \qquad (2.61)$$

56 Valuing Recreation and the Environment

These results apply to *any* RUM model. They can be sharpened somewhat if one focuses specifically on additively random models in which $v_j(p_j, q_j, y, \widetilde{\varepsilon}) = v_j(p_j, q_j, y) + \widetilde{\varepsilon}_j$, $j = 1, 2, 3$.

In that case (2.55a) becomes $v_1[p_1^1, q_1^1, y - \widetilde{C}(1/1)] + \widetilde{\varepsilon}_1 = v_1(p_1^0, q_1^0, y) + \widetilde{\varepsilon}_1$, or, canceling out $\widetilde{\varepsilon}_1$, $v_1[p_1^1, q_1^1, y - C(1/1)] = v_1(p_1^0, q_1^0, y)$, i.e., $C(1/1)$ is nonstochastic.[24] Accordingly (2.57) becomes

$$C^* = C(1/1)\pi_1^0 + \int_{A(2/1)} \widetilde{C}(2/1)f_\varepsilon(\varepsilon)d\varepsilon + \int_{A(3/1)} \widetilde{C}(3/1)f_\varepsilon(\varepsilon)d\varepsilon. \qquad (2.57')$$

Now, the quantity $C(1/1)$ is the compensation measure that one might calculate if he disregarded the random elements in the utility function. For example, Feenberg and Mills [1980] used $C(1/1)$ to measure the benefits from an improvement in the quality of a site after they estimated an additively random logit model of discrete choices among recreation sites. If one knew for sure that an individual would select good 1, then $C(1/1)$ would indeed be the appropriate welfare measure. In the random utility context, however, two adjustments must be made: $C(1/1)$ must be multiplied by $\pi_1^0 < 1$, and the other terms on the right-hand side of (5.57') must be added which measure the gain to the individual if he originally selected some other good and then switched to good 1. The net effect is that $C(1/1)$ *overestimates* the value of C^* since, with $C(1/1)$ nonstochastic, (2.60) yields[25]

$$0 < C^* < C(1/1). \qquad (2.60')$$

As for C^*, it was already noted that, if $\pi_1^1 \le 0.5$, $C^* = 0$. Similarly, from (2.55) and (2.56), if $\pi_1^0 \ge 0.5$, then $C^+ = C(1/1)$. If $\pi_1^0 < 0.5 < \pi_1^1$, C^+ can be obtained by solving (2.61) which, in this case, may be simplified to

$$
\begin{aligned}
0.5 &= \pi^*(C^*) \\
&= \Pr\{\widetilde{u}_2 \le \widetilde{u}_1^0 \text{ and } \widetilde{u}_3 \le \widetilde{u}_1^0\} + \Pr\{\widetilde{u}_3 \le \widetilde{u}_2 \text{ and } \widetilde{u}_1^0 \le \widetilde{u}_2 \le \widetilde{u}_1^*(C^*)\} \\
&\quad + \Pr\{\widetilde{u}_2 \le \widetilde{u}_3 \text{ and } \widetilde{u}_1^0 \le \widetilde{u}_3 \le \widetilde{u}_1^*(C^*)\} \\
&= \pi_1^0 + (\pi_2^0 - \pi_2^*) + (\pi_3^0 - \pi_3^*) \\
&= 1 - (\pi_2^* + \pi_3^*) \\
&= \pi_1^*
\end{aligned}
\qquad (2.61')
$$

---

[24] Equivalently, $C(1/1)$ satisfies $E\{v_1[p_1^1, q_1^1, y - C(1/1)] + \widetilde{\varepsilon}_1\} = E\{v_1[p_1^0, q_1^0, y] + \widetilde{\varepsilon}_1\}$.

[25] A similar conclusion is reached in Hanemann (1983) where Feenberg and Mills' (1980) welfare measure is compared with C^*.

where

$$\pi_1^* \equiv \Pr\left\{\tilde{u}_2 \leq \tilde{u}_1^*\left(C^*\right) \text{ and } \tilde{u}_3 \leq \tilde{u}_1^*\left(C^*\right)\right\},$$

$$\pi_2^* \equiv \Pr\left\{\tilde{u}_1^*\left(C^*\right) \leq \tilde{u}_2 \text{ and } \tilde{u}_3 \leq \tilde{u}_2\right\}, \text{ and}$$

$$\pi_3^* \equiv \Pr\left\{\tilde{u}_1^*\left(C^*\right) \leq \tilde{u}_3 \text{ and } \tilde{u}_2 \leq u_3\right\}.$$

As an illustration, consider the additively random model derived from the conditional indirect utility functions

$$\tilde{u}_j = \psi_j(p_j, q_j) + \gamma_j(p_j, q_j) y + \tilde{\varepsilon}_j \equiv v_j + \tilde{\varepsilon}_j \qquad j = 1, 2, 3, \qquad (2.62)$$

where $\gamma_j(\cdot) > 0$, which is a generalization of (2.49) and (2.50). Applying (2.55a–c), one obtains

$$C(1/1) = \frac{[\psi_1^1 - \psi_1^0 + y(\gamma_1^1 - \gamma_1^0)]}{\gamma_1^1} \equiv \frac{v_1^1 - v_1^0}{\gamma_1^1} \qquad (2.63a)$$

$$\tilde{C}(2/1) = \frac{[\psi_1^1 - \psi_2 + y(\gamma_1^1 - \gamma_2) + \tilde{\varepsilon}_1 - \tilde{\varepsilon}_2]}{\gamma_1^1} \equiv \frac{v_1^1 - v_2 + \tilde{\varepsilon}_1 - \tilde{\varepsilon}_2}{\gamma_1^1} \qquad (2.63b)$$

$$\tilde{C}(3/1) = \frac{[\psi_1^1 - \psi_3 + y(\gamma_1^1 - \gamma_3) + \tilde{\varepsilon}_1 - \tilde{\varepsilon}_3]}{\gamma_1^1} \equiv \frac{v_1^1 - v_3 + \tilde{\varepsilon}_1 - \tilde{\varepsilon}_3}{\gamma_1^1} \qquad (2.63c)$$

where $\psi_1^t \equiv \psi_1(p_1^t, q_1^t), \gamma_1^t \equiv \gamma_1(p_1^t, q_1^t)$, and $v_1^t \equiv \psi_1^t + \gamma_1^t y$, $t = 0, 1$. By assumption, $v_1^1 > v_1^0$. Then, C^* is given by (2.57') where, for $i = 2, 3$,

$$\int_{A(i/1)} \tilde{C}(i/1) f(\varepsilon) d\varepsilon = \left(\frac{v_1^1 - v_i}{\gamma_1^1}\right)\left(\pi_i^0 - \pi_i^1\right) + \int_{\eta_1 - \eta_1^0}^{\eta_1 - \eta_1^0} \int_{-\infty}^{\eta_1 - v_i} \frac{\eta_1}{\gamma_1^1} f_\eta(\eta_1, \eta_2) d\eta_1 d\eta_2 \quad (2.64)$$

where $\tilde{\eta}_1 \equiv \tilde{\varepsilon}_1 - \tilde{\varepsilon}_i, \tilde{\eta}_2 \equiv \tilde{\varepsilon}_j - \tilde{\varepsilon}_i, j \neq 1, j \neq i$, and $f_\eta(\cdot)$ is the bivariate density of $(\tilde{\eta}_1, \tilde{\eta}_2)$. Similarly, assuming that $\pi_1^0 < 0.5 < \pi_1^1$, C^* solves

58 Valuing Recreation and the Environment

$$0.5 = \int_{-\infty}^{\infty} \int_{-\infty}^{v_1^1 - \gamma_1^1 C - v_2 + \varepsilon_1} \int_{-\infty}^{v_1^1 - \gamma_1^1 C - v_3 + \varepsilon_1} f(\varepsilon_1, \varepsilon_2, \varepsilon_3) \, d\varepsilon_1 \, d\varepsilon_2 \, d\varepsilon_3. \qquad (2.65)$$

Suppose, specifically, that $f_\varepsilon(\cdot)$ is the extreme value density, so that this is a standard logit model. The integral in (2.64) can readily be evaluated and, on substituting into (2.57′) and simplifying, one obtains

$$C^+ = \frac{1}{\gamma_1^1} \ln \left(\frac{e^{v_1^1} + e^{v_2} + e^{v_3}}{e^{v_1^0} + e^{v_2} + e^{v_3}} \right). \qquad (2.66)$$

The corresponding forumula for C^* is

$$C^* = \begin{cases} 0 & \text{if } v_1^1 \leq \ln\left[\exp(v_2) + \exp(v_3)\right] \\[2mm] \dfrac{v_1^1 - \ln\left[\exp(v_2) + \exp(v_3)\right]}{\gamma_1^1} & \text{if } v_1^0 \leq \ln\left[\exp(v_2) + \exp(v_3)\right] \leq v_1^1 \quad (2.67) \\[2mm] \dfrac{\left(v_1^1 - v_1^0\right)}{\gamma_1^1} & \text{if } v_1^0 \geq \ln\left[\exp(v_2) + \exp(v_3)\right] \end{cases}$$

Hence,

$$C^* \underset{<}{\overset{>}{=}} C^+ \text{ as } \frac{v_1^1 + v_1^0}{2} \underset{<}{\overset{>}{=}} \ln\left[\exp(v_2) + \exp(v_3)\right]. \qquad (2.68)$$

Observe from (2.66) that C^* satisfies

$$\ln\left[\exp(v_1^1 - \gamma_1^1 C^+) + \exp(v_2 - \gamma_1^1 C^+) + \exp(v_3 - \gamma_1^1 C^+)\right]$$
$$= \ln\left[\exp(v_1^0) + \exp(v_2) + \exp(v_3)\right]. \qquad (2.69)$$

By contrast, using (2.27) and the formula in Table 2.1, the welfare measure C^* satisfies

$$\ln\left[\exp(v_1^1 - \gamma_1^1 C^*) + \exp(v_2 - \gamma_1^1 C^*) + \exp(v_3 - \gamma_1^1 C^*)\right]$$
$$= \ln\left[\exp(v_1^0) + \exp(v_2) + \exp(v_3)\right]. \qquad (2.70)$$

Table 2.1 Formulas for $V \equiv E\{\max[v_1 + \tilde{\varepsilon}_1, ..., v_N + \tilde{\varepsilon}_N]\}$

1. Generalized extreme value

$$F_\varepsilon(\varepsilon_1, ..., \varepsilon_N) = \exp\{-G[\exp(-\varepsilon_1), ..., \exp(-\varepsilon_N)]\}$$

$$V = \ln\{G[\exp(v_1), ..., \exp(v_N)]\} + 0.57722$$

2. Independent logit

$$F_\varepsilon(\varepsilon_1, ..., \varepsilon_N) = \exp[-\Sigma \exp(-\varepsilon_j)]$$

$$V = \ln \Sigma \exp(v_j) + 0.57722$$

3. Probit[3]

$$F_\varepsilon(\varepsilon_1, ..., \varepsilon_N) = N(0, \Sigma), \quad \Sigma = \{\sigma_{ij}^2\}$$

   a. Binary probit, $N = 2$

$$V_2 = (v_1 - v_2)\Phi\left(\frac{v_1 - v_2}{\kappa_2}\right) + v_2 + \kappa_2\phi\left(\frac{v_1 - v_2}{\kappa_2}\right),$$

$$\kappa_2 \equiv \left(\sigma_{11}^2 + \sigma_{22}^2 - 2\sigma_{12}^2\right)^{1/2}$$

   b. Trichotomous probit, $N = 3$[b]

$$V_3 \approx (V_2 - v_3)\,\Phi\left(\frac{V_2 - v_3}{\kappa_3}\right) + v_3 + \kappa_3\,\phi\left(\frac{V_2 - v_3}{\kappa_3}\right)$$

$$\kappa_3 \equiv \left(\sigma_{33}^2 + S_2^2 - 2S_{2,3}^2\right)^{1/2}$$

$$S_{2,3}^2 \equiv \sigma_{23}^2 + \left(\sigma_{13}^2 - \sigma_{23}^2\right)\Phi\left(\frac{v_1 - v_2}{\kappa_2}\right)$$

$$S_2^2 \equiv v_2^2 + \sigma_{22}^2 + \left(v_1^2 + \sigma_{11}^2 - v_2 - \sigma_{22}^2\right)\Phi\left(\frac{v_1 - v_2}{\kappa_2}\right)$$

$$+ (v_1 + v_2)\kappa_2\left(\frac{v_1 - v_2}{\kappa_2}\right) - V_2^2$$

---

[a] ϕ and Φ are, respectively, the standard univariate normal probability density function (p.d.f.) and cumulative distribution function (c.d.f.).

[b] Using Clark's (1961) approximation.

Table 2.2 Welfare Calculations for the Logit Model (2.62)

Case	π_j^o	π_i^1	$C(1/1)$	C^*	$\hat{C}^*$	C^*	$\pi_i^o \cdot C(1/1)$
i	0.06338	0.33333	2	0	0.33999	0.35018	0.12676
ii	0.33333	0.78699	2	1.31	1.14093	1.17827	0.66667
iii	0.78699	0.96466	2	2	1.79643	1.81183	1.57397

Thus, $C^* < C^+$ if $\gamma_1^1 < \min(\gamma_2, \gamma_3)$, and $C^* > C^+$ if $\gamma_1^1 > \max(\gamma_2, \gamma_3)$, while $C^* = C^+$ if $\gamma_1^1 = \gamma_2 = \gamma_3$; the last case corresponds to the no-income effects utility model (2.21).

In order to get a feel for these formulas, it may be helpful to resort to a numerical example. Suppose that $v_2 = v_3 = 0$, $\gamma_1^1 = 1, \gamma_2 = 0.5$, and $\gamma_3 = 1.5$. I consider three sets of values for v_1^0 and v_1^1: (i) $v_1^0 = -2$, $v_1^1 = 0$; (ii) $v_1^0 = 0$, (iii) $v_1^1 = 2$, $v_1^0 = 2, v_1^1 = 4$. Thus, in each case $C(1/1) = 2$. In the first case, $\pi_1^1 < 0.5$ so that $C^* = 0$, while in the third case $\pi_1^0 > 0.5$, so that $C^* = C(1/1)$. The corresponding values of C^+ and C^* are presented in Table 2.2. It will be seen that C^+ and C^* are close in value but they both differ from C^*. As one would expect, in the first two cases the quantity $C(1/1)$ significantly over-estimates all three welfare measures. The last column in the table gives the value of $\pi_1^0 \cdot C(1/1)$, the first term in the formula for C^+ (2.57′). It can be seen that this yields a very crude approximation of the value of C^+, the quality of the approximation becoming worse as π_1^0 gets lower.

To what extent can these formulas be generalized? If $N > 3$ in the logit model (2.62), the term $\left[\exp(v_2) + \exp(v_3)\right]$ in (2.66)–(2.70) is replaced by

$$\sum_{j=2}^{N} \exp(v_j).$$

This is when the change is restricted to good 1. When one is dealing with a more complex change, the formulas are different but they can readily be developed by following the steps that lead to (2.66)–(2.70). For example, if there is an improvement in good 1 combined with a deterioration in good 2, there are now *six* possible events which partition $\widetilde{\varepsilon}$ – space —(1/1), (2/2), (2/1), (3/3), (3/1), and (2/3)—and

$$\widetilde{C} \begin{cases} < 0 & \text{if } \widetilde{\varepsilon} \in A(2/2) \\ = 0 & \text{if } \widetilde{\varepsilon} \in A(3/3) \\ > 0 & \text{otherwise.} \end{cases}$$

Alternatively, suppose the only change is in good 1 and the utility function is given by (2.62), but this is now a GEV (generalized logit) or multivariate probit model. In the GEV case, the appropriate formulas are a straightforward extension of (2.66)–(2.70). In the probit case, however, numerical techniques would be required to evaluate the integrals in the formulas for C^+ and C^*, (2.64) and (2.65). If the RUM model is additively random but *not* linear in y, unlike (2.62), this affects the formulas for $\widetilde{C}(1/1)$, $\widetilde{C}(2/1)$, and $\widetilde{C}(3/1)$ in (2.63) as well as

62 Valuing Recreation and the Environment

(2.64) and (2.65). Finally, if the RUM model is not additively random, one has to work directly with (2.55), (2.57), and (2.61), and numerical evaluation may well be required.

APPENDIX: PROOF OF PROPOSITION

Here I prove that the consumer's preferences have the form given in (2.21a) if the switch prices $\tilde{p}_1^*$ in (2.22) and $\tilde{p}_1^{**}$ in (2.23) coincide. With no loss of generality, I shall assume that $N = 2$ and $\bar{x}_1 = \bar{x}_2 = 1$. The switch price $\tilde{p}_1 = p_1^*(p_2, q_1, q_2, y, \tilde{\varepsilon})$ is defined implicitly by

$$u(1, 0, q_1, q_2, y - \tilde{p}_1^*) + \tilde{\varepsilon}_1 = u(0, 1, q_1, q_2, y - p_2) + \tilde{\varepsilon}_2. \tag{A.1}$$

Suppose that the actual price of good 1 is p_1^0. By virtue of (A.1), one can write

$$\tilde{p}_1^* = p_1^0 - \tilde{A}^*, \tag{A.2}$$

where $\tilde{A}^*$ is defined by

$$u(1, 0, q_1, q_2, y - p_1^0 + \tilde{A}^*) + \tilde{\varepsilon}_1 = u(0, 1, q_1, q_2, y - p_2) + \tilde{\varepsilon}_1. \tag{A.3}$$

The switch price $\tilde{p}_1^{**} = p_1^{**}(p_2, q_1, q_2, \tilde{u}, \tilde{\varepsilon})$ is defined by

$$g_1(q_1, \tilde{u}^0 - \tilde{\varepsilon}_1) + \tilde{p}_1^{**} = g_2(q_2, \tilde{u}^0 - \tilde{\varepsilon}_2) + p_2 \tag{A.4}$$

or

$$\tilde{p}_1^{**} = p_2 + u^{-1}(\tilde{u}^0 - \tilde{\varepsilon}_2 | 0, 1, q_1, q_2) - u^{-1}(\tilde{u}^0 - \tilde{\varepsilon}_1 | 1, 0, q_1, q_2), \tag{A.5}$$

where $u^{-1}(u | x_1, x_2, q_1, q_2)$ is the inverse of $u(x_1, x_2, q_1, q_2, z)$ with respect to its last argument.

Observe that $\tilde{p}_1^* = \tilde{p}_1^{**}$ trivially when $p_1^0 \geq \tilde{p}_1^*$; then $x_1 = 0$ from (2.22), $\tilde{u}^0 = u(0, 1, q_1, q_2, y - p_2) + \tilde{\varepsilon}_2$, and so

$$u^{-1}(\tilde{u}^0 - \tilde{\varepsilon}_2 | 0, 1, q_1, q_2) = y - p_2. \tag{A.6}$$

Substituting this into (A.5) yields

$$\tilde{p}_1^{**} = y - u^{-1}(\tilde{u}^0 - \tilde{\varepsilon}_1 | 1, 0, q_1, q_2). \tag{A.7}$$

The last two equations together imply

$$u(1, 0, q_1, q_2, y - \tilde{p}_1^{**}) + \tilde{\varepsilon}_1 = u(0, 1, q_1, q_2, y - p_2) + \tilde{\varepsilon}_2, \tag{A.8}$$

and a comparison with (A.1) shows that $\tilde{p}_1^* = \tilde{p}_1^{**}$.

Accordingly, I focus on the nontrivial case where $p_1^0 < \tilde{p}_1^*$. In this case, $\tilde{u}^0 = u(1, 0, q_1, q_2, y - p_1^0) + \tilde{\varepsilon}_1$ and, in general, $\tilde{p}_1^* \neq \tilde{p}_1^{**}$. Since

$$u^{-1}(\tilde{u}^0 - \tilde{\varepsilon}_1 | 1, 0, q_1, q_2) = y - p_1^0, \tag{A.9}$$

(A.5) may be written as

$$\tilde{p}_1^{**} = p_1^0 - \tilde{A}^{**}, \tag{A.10}$$

where

$$\tilde{A}^{**} \equiv y - p_2 - u^{-1}(\tilde{u}^0 - \tilde{\varepsilon}_2 | 0, 1, q_1, q_2). \tag{A.11}$$

It follows from (A.2) and (A.10) that $\tilde{p}_1^* = \tilde{p}_1^{**}$ iff $\tilde{A}^* = \tilde{A}^{**}$. However, (A.1) implies that

$$u(1, 0, q_1, q_2, y - p_1^0) + \tilde{\varepsilon}_1 = u(0, 1, q_1, q_2, y - p_2 + \tilde{A}^{**}) + \tilde{\varepsilon}_2. \tag{A.12}$$

From (A.3) and (A.12), $\tilde{A}^* = \tilde{A}^{**}$ independently of $(p_1^0, p_2, q_1, q_2, y)$ if and only if the utility function has the quasilinear form given in (2.21a).

REFERENCES

Aitchison, J. and Bennett, J. (1970), "Polychotomous Quantal Response by Maximal Indicant," *Biometrika*, 57, pp. 253–62.

Amemiya, T. (1981), "Qualitative Response Models: A Survey." *Journal of Economic Literature*, 19, pp. 1483–536.

Clark, C.E. (1961), "The Greatest of Finite Set of Random Variables," *Operation Research*, 9, 145–62.

Daganzo, C. (1979), *Multinomial Probit*. New York: Academic Press.

64 Valuing Recreation and the Environment

Daly, A. and Zachary, S. (1978), "Improved Multiple Choice Models." In *Determinants of Travel Choice*, ed. by D.A. Hensher and M.Q. Dalvi. Farnborough, England: Saxon House.

Domenich, T.A. and McFadden, D. (1975), *Urban Travel Demand: A Behavioral Analysis*. Amsterdam: North-Holland.

Dubin, J.A. and McFadden, D.L. (1984), "An Econometric Analysis of Residential Electric Appliance Holdings and Consumption," *Econometrica*, 52, No. 2, pp. 345–62.

Feenberg, D. and Mills, E.S. (1980), *Measuring the Benefits of Water Pollution Abatement*. New York: Academic Press.

Hanemann, W.M. (1979), "The Value of Lifesaving Reconsidered." University of California, Agricultural and Resource Economics, Giannini Foundation Working paper no. 113, August.

Hanemann, W.M. (1982), "Applied Welfare Analysis with Qualitative Response Models," University of California, Agricultural and Resource Economics, Giannini Foundation Working paper no. 241.

Hanemann, W.M. (1983), "Marginal Welfare Measures for Discrete Choice Models." *Economics Letters*, 13, pp. 129–36.

Hanemann, W.M. (1984), "Discrete/Continuous Models of Consumer Demand." *Econometrica*, Vol. 52, pp. 541–61.

Hanemann, W.M. (1985), "Welfare Analysis with Discrete Choice Models," University of California, Agricultural and Resource Economics, Giannini Foundation Working paper.

Hausman, J.A. and Wise, D.A. (1978), "A Conditional Probit Model for Qualitative Choice: Discrete Decisions Recognizing Interdependence and Heterogeneous Preferences." *Econometrica*, 14, pp. 403–26.

Katzner, D.W. (1970), *Static Demand Theory*. New York: Macmillan.

Mäler, K. (1974), *Environmental Economics*. Baltimore: Johns Hopkins University Press.

McFadden, D. (1974), "Conditional Logit Analysis of Qualitative Choice Behavior." In *Frontiers of Econometrics*, ed. by P. Zarembka. New York: Academic Press.

McFadden, D. (1978), "Modelling the Choice of Residential Location." In *Spatial Interaction Theory and Planning Models*, ed. by A. Karlquist, L. Lundquist, F. Snickars, and J.L. Weibull. Amsterdam: North-Holland.

McFadden, D. (1981), "Econometric Models of Probabilistic Choice." In *Structural Analysis of Discrete Data*, ed. by C.F. Manski and D. McFadden. Cambridge, MA: MIT Press.

Sheffi, Y. and Daganzo, C.F. (1978), "Another Paradox of Traffic Flow," *Transportation Research*, 12, pp. 43–46.

Small, K.A. and Rosen, H.S. (1981), "Applied Welfare Economics with Discrete Choice Models." *Econometrica*, 49, pp. 105–30.

Williams, H. (1977), "On the Formation of Travel Demand Models and Economic Evaluation Measures of User Benefit." *Environment and Planning*, 9, pp.285–344.

Part VI
Reflections

[44]

JOURNAL OF ENVIRONMENTAL ECONOMICS AND MANAGEMENT 8, 1–10 (1981)

Reflections of an Applied Welfare Economist

Presidential Address Presented at the Annual Meeting of the Association
of Environmental and Resource Economists September 6, 1980,
Denver, Colorado

JOHN V. KRUTILLA

Resources for the Future, Washington, D.C. 20036

Received August 1980

I. INTRODUCTION

Someone embarking on a serious study of economics forty years ago enjoyed numerous advantages. Although rear guard opposition to the Keynesian Revolution had not yet subsided, the young, energetic, and more reform-oriented group of young adults could be readily convinced of the power of a three-equation system to control macroeconomic events. This persisted for some time. Indeed, Larry Lau confided somewhat ruefully to me much later that he abandoned physics for economics because of the higher level of certitude in the latter—a conclusion to which he felt entitled as a result of his macroeconomics course as an undergraduate. Not only did we feel we enjoyed the power of complete control over the economy with only three or four levers, but those of us who wanted to tinker normatively at the micro level received much comfort from the Keynesian sanction to employ fiscal measures in part to justify expenditures for public sector capital improvements—and from the works of Lange [14] and Lerner, particularly Lerner's *Economics of Control* [15]. The latter, illustrating principles of welfare economics, showed us precisely how to do this efficiently. Indeed, Keynes probably did as much to popularize Pigou's welfare economics [22] as he did to divert attention from Pigou's rare lapses from reality regarding full employment. Economics, and particularly applied welfare economics, did not attract the professionally meek—it attracted, if not the power hungry, at least those who wanted to control events, not just to comment objectively on the state of things.

But there were more senior members of the profession who were motivated to comment precisely on the objective state of things. One of the most troublesome of these was Lionel Robbins. In his *Nature and Significance of Economic Science* [26] he not only vexed successive generations of applied welfare economists by successfully asserting the absence of any objective validity for comparing the welfare of different individuals; he also provoked an astonishing army of gifted students and camp followers to elaborate the theoretical implications of this challenge to the orthodox rationale underlying the progressive income tax, minimum wage legislation, and other policy prescriptions largely in the field of public finance since the time of Wicksell [33], if not earlier.

The assault on the rationale for applying postulates of welfare economics following Robbins' 1935 challenge was indeed formidable, though the battle was

1

0095-0696/81/010001-10$02.00/0

2   JOHN V. KRUTILLA

joined by such notables as Harold Hotelling [10], John R. Hicks [9], Nicholas Kaldor [11], and even, arguably, I. M. D. Little [17]. For someone entering the field as a practitioner at the end of the decade, the intellectual buffeting that one had to survive certainly merited recognition for service in a combat theater. Let me then first review: (1) the nature of the criticism advanced to justify the low esteem welfare economics was accorded at about the time some of us were entering the field, (2) the more or less weak formal response to the weight of theoretical criticism, (3) the unaccountably robust growth of applied welfare economics in the face of severe theoretical criticism, and (4) finally, why and where applied welfare economics flourished despite the assault on its theoretical underpinnings.

II. THE CHALLENGE TO PIGOUVIAN WELFARE ECONOMICS

Lionel Robbins' surfacing the interpersonal comparison issue really implied three distributional facets of the problem. The first, which was not explicitly addressed by him, touches on the question of the normative properties of the *initial* distribution of income and hence the normative significance of the configuration of relative prices that we have to use in measuring the social cost and gains resulting from any collective action. The second, more directly relevant to Robbins' criticism of interpersonal utility comparisons, dealt with the redistributional effects of any welfare improving action by public authority—whether tax or transfer—or expenditure for capital improvements. The third was more technical and was referred to as the Scitovsky paradox [29]. This involved the effect of the income redistribution on the ex post configuration of relative prices. Scitovsky raised the possibility that a welfare-improving action as evaluated under the initial distribution of income might be subject to improvement by moving back to the original condition under the new set of relative prices. This paradox is basically an index number problem arising out of the different weights represented by the pre- and postevent distributions. Scitovsky thus argued that the prospective improvement must meet the test of remaining superior with both ex ante and ex post income distributions. Not to let the matter rest, Samuelson, in his "Evaluation of Real National Income" [27], implied that this double criterion attributed unwarranted normative significance to just those two distributions of income and that since neither distribution necessarily enjoys a social sanction, the proposed action would need to result in a welfare improvement for all possible distributions of income.[1]

Well, then, how did those who were inclined to defend public intervention respond to this criticism? Since Robbins' critique introduced an indisputable need for the Pareto criterion of welfare improvement (namely, that at least one individual must gain from a collective action without *anyone* losing) for welfare to be unambiguously improved—and the universe of such opportunities did not provide sufficient scope for the active reformers—the Hicks–Kaldor compensation principle was advanced [9, 11], along with a rationale involving dynamic considerations and repeated events. Here we were encouraged to feel that welfare could be

---

[1] Not only did Samuelson raise the issue of the normative significance of the initial distribution of income, he introduced an equally disturbing issue about the efficiency of the initial allocation of resources—i.e., a pervasive second-best problem which I prefer to treat in connection with the Lipsey–Lancaster characterization of the issue.

improved if the gainers could compensate the losers, even if the gainers did not actually do so, provided that there was more or less pervasive collective action with the gainers and losers distributed randomly over an unending sequence of actions. Hotelling was similarly associated with this viewpoint [10], although it did not receive adequate theoretical attention before Polinsky's treatment in 1972 [23].

I doubtless should include here I. M. D. Little's constructive position despite the title of his very practical volume, *A Critique of Welfare Economics* [17]. Indeed, Little's book could be termed the bible of the applied welfare economists because he addressed the practical problem of what might guide practicing economists' professional behavior in the areas to which welfare economics addressed itself. Little made two essential points in the context of my theme. One was that while there was no objective validity for comparisons of interpersonal welfare, there was scope for value judgements (presumably embracing a widely accepted social, rather than a highly personalized, ethic). This led to the prescription that first, gainers must be *able* to compensate the losers, whether they do so or not, and that second, the resulting distribution should be "good"—that is, consistent with the predominant community ethic. (Parenthetically, Meade, in his *Trade and Welfare* [20], further advanced Little's position.)

The second basic point that Little argued was that the necessary conditions for a welfare optimum were not interesting; that instead, conditions sufficient for a welfare improvement should guide the work of applied welfare economists. As a future applied welfare economist, I would have appreciated this sensible dispensation, but with the scant time devoted to welfare economics at graduate school, we somehow missed completely Little's message. Indeed, severe criticism of the utility of welfare economics was the common currency at Harvard in my graduate days and continued to appear in the literature both in the work of Lipsey and Lancaster ("The General Theory of the Second Best") [16] and in the work of Graaff (*Theoretical Welfare Economics*) [8] extending beyond the publication of Little's constructive contribution.

Although most of the discussion questioning the normative significance of welfare propositions centered on distributional issues throughout this period, at this same time, Samuelson questioned in passing the initial allocative conditions as well as the initial income distribution. Baumol, in his *Welfare Economics and the Theory of the State* [1], added to the literature raising some profound questions (especially in Chapter V) addressing fundamental issues that attend the initial allocative conditions. On the whole, however, I confess to having received a great deal more encouragement, as an applied welfare economist, from Baumol's monograph than Baumol ever intended. For this as well as for other expositional reasons, I want to address the questions regarding initial allocative conditions in the manner in which Lipsey and Lancaster presented them.

You will recall that one of the issues they discussed was piecemeal welfare economics—the practical strategy advanced by Little. Their conclusions seemed to undermine Little's position that in a practical sense the necessary conditions for a welfare optimum are not very useful. For example, when a policy maker asks for a recommendation on a substantially circumscribed problem, is that recommendation also required to be consistent with a general welfare maximum? Little's message for practicing economists was that criteria sufficient for achieving a welfare improvement rather than necessary for a welfare optimum should govern. But in their general theory of the second best, Lipsey and Lancaster countered with

4   JOHN V. KRUTILLA

in a general equilibrium situation there will be no conditions which in general are sufficient
for an increase in welfare without also being necessary for a welfare maximum. [16, p. 17]

And, as they maintained, if Pareto optimal initial conditions are not met everywhere other than in the area targeted for public intervention, the pricing policies
derived from welfare economics cannot be applied in the target area either.

Placing Lipsey and Lancaster's work into perspective was some time in coming.
Eventually Davis and Whinston [4, 5] ingeniously formulated the problem in a way
that made it possible to distinguish those cases where unrelated constraints on
allocative efficiency were not sufficiently important to warrant departures from the
necessary Pareto conditions in the target area from those in which departures
would be indicated. Further work by Rees [25] which summarized such second-best
pricing rules for public undertakings and discriminated more finely among different classes of constraints, combined to make another significant step toward
rehabilitating piecemeal welfare economics consistent with Little's recommendation.

It must be acknowledged, however, that if one is concerned with rapidly
achieving an *overall* allocatively efficient condition, *with consistent relative prices,*
then indeed all of the difficulties presented in the literature of the second best are
likely to be encountered. But if one is concerned, as were Little and the bulk of the
practitioners of applied welfare economics, in making piecemeal Pareto improvements, then undertaking activities where prices (or nonpriced benefits) exceed
opportunity costs will indeed lead to piecemeal Pareto improvements, and the
second-best discussion is largely an irrelevant complication. The complicated
first-order conditions in the second-best literature merely arise out of the complicated dependencies, and they should not obscure the fact that small step-wise
Pareto moves can be inferred from observable market information. The appropriate inference to draw from the discussion of the general theory of the second
best, addressing the initial allocative conditions, is that one cannot expect to
achieve a welfare optimum by blindly setting price equal to marginal cost. But one
is usually correct if incremental changes are based on the rule that marginal
benefits exceed marginal opportunity costs.

III. CONCURRENT ROBUST GROWTH OF APPLIED WELFARE ECONOMICS

Considering the substantial theoretical controversy over the normative significance of welfare propositions that continued for three decades following Robbins'
initial assault, did we observe—as we might expect—hesitancy in using welfare
economics in the applied area? Quite the contrary. Applied welfare economics
flourished throughout this period *as though* (if not *actually*) innocent of the
controversy over its theoretical underpinnings. There were three main sources of
the exploding application of welfare economics.

The coincidence of the Flood Control Act of 1936 with all of the kinds of direct
interdependencies in the water resource field which give rise to departures between
private and social costs and gains, motivated implementing in a practical way what
old-fashioned Pigouvian welfare economics could tell us regarding public expenditure and investment criteria. Moreover, the Flood Control Act of 1936 said, among
other things, that the benefits from water resource development projects must

exceed the costs "to whomsoever they may accrue" (Section 701a). It thus simultaneously required the estimation of benefits and costs, and provided *legal sanction* for a Hicks–Kaldor-like compensation principle *even before* interpersonal utility comparisons had become an issue in theoretical welfare economics.

A second line of development, which occurred if not simultaneously, then certainly shortly after the impetus the 1936 water resources legislation gave to applied welfare economics, came through the introduction of economics into operations research, primarily through the economics division at the Rand Corporation during the 1950s. Here the problem had a somewhat different character. It dealt with the attempt to achieve a given set of military performance standards with different weapons systems in the most economical way. That is, the matter of evaluating the benefit of a given level of national security was properly left to the political or collective decision making apparatus, but the problem of determining resource-allocative efficiency within the target area once the goals were established politically was restricted to searching for the combination of systems that would provide the most cost-effective result. Hence the emergence of the companion nomenclature in applied welfare economics; namely, cost-effectiveness analysis.

The growing, albeit brief, ascendancy of economics in the postwar period was in part attributable to the advent of the "efficiency in government" movement following installation of the first Republican administration in two decades [19]. Moreover, this persisted into the 1960s with the infiltration of the national government—mainly the Department of Defense and the Office of Management and Budget's predecessor agency, the Bureau of the Budget—by a contingent from the Rand Corporation marching to the beat of McNamara's band. If cost effectiveness was a desirable objective in the design and procurement of military capability, it was thought to be equally so in other departments of the government where expenditures were made on behalf of beneficiaries who were not subject to a direct test of "willingness to pay." Such programs involved either essentially income redistributive objectives for which willingness to pay was inappropriate, or the provision of public goods like national defense for which efficient markets cannot be established. While the Program Planning Budgeting System (PPBS) encountered spirited opposition in the bureaucracy—and by some accounts suffered an unlamented death—reports of its demise were premature. Evidence of this is the series begun by the Aldine Publishing Company in 1971 which, for a time, reprinted annually a selection of the best benefit-cost and policy analyses published during the year. Similarly, in 1973 the Joint Economic Committee published a volume of papers entitled *Benefit-Cost Analysis of Federal Programs* [32].

In addition to the water resources field and the extension of the use of cost effectiveness in analysis of programs where expenditure levels are established by political decisions, there was a third area in which applied welfare analysis flourished—perhaps in part prompted by Little and Mirrless's work, which has come out in its most complete form in the 1974 edition of *Project Appraisal and Planning for Developing Countries* [18]. Essentially, project appraisal preparatory to funding was a major activity of the World Bank, and we see in connection with this practical need substantial attention devoted to the problem of benefit-cost analysis throughout this entire period addressing the somewhat special circumstances in the developing countries.

It may be noted in passing that the theoretical criticism of "old-fashioned" Pigouvian welfare economics beginning with Lionel Robbins and perhaps most

6   JOHN V. KRUTILLA

pessimistically advanced by Graaf was deeply rooted in the implications of wealth redistribution associated with changes in basic policy and the traditional acceptance of interpersonal utility comparisons. The fact that applied welfare economics flourished throughout this period in the face of unremitting criticism of its theoretical bases may be attributable to the fact that initially, at least, it was customarily used in connection with *project evaluation* rather than *policy choice*, whereas the theoretical discussion often focused on the unsuccessful attempt to develop a value-free policy analysis for public decisions. Used to evaluate actions that result in large shifts in the distribution of income, as may occur from basic changes in policy, benefit-cost analysis may indeed encounter even the kinds of measurement problems surfaced by Scitovsky. But the analysis of projects, particularly in developed countries, where redistributive consequences are unlikely to have appreciable effects on the configuration of relative prices [13] are not likely to encounter that problem. And, as mentioned previously, provisions of the legislation that ushered in benefit-cost analysis for project evaluation in the United States sanctioned the use of the Hicks–Kaldor compensation principle. Accordingly, the objectives and aspirations of applied welfare economics were modest, and their very modesty permitted the application of welfare principles defined either as the measurement of benefits and costs with a legislatively sanctioned directive to ignore the redistributional considerations in benefit-cost estimates, or as the minimization of costs through comparing different ways of achieving a given legislatively stipulated objective.

When one considers the application of welfare economics above the project level, here too the aspirations have come to be much more modest than implied in the literature of the mid-thirties through the mid-sixties. It is true that given the general acceptance of the need for community governance and collective action [21], decisions regarding the necessary revenue and expenditure of public bodies need to be rationalized. We see this explicitly stated very early in, for example, the Vermont constitution and certainly implied in the Gallatin report [24]. Thus, despite the perforated rationale when viewed in terms of the objectives of the theoretical fraternity, the corpus of welfare economics does address the issues that are relevant for public fiscal and economic decisions. The normative content for policy prescription may be severely qualified—but this is no longer seen as the most productive use of welfare economics. Making explicit the value judgements implicit in any given prescription—the service which theoretical welfare economics performed—can be expected to provide more discriminating bases for policy than innocence of the value judgements involved in any event when public decisions are being made.

IV. APPLIED WELFARE AND ENVIRONMENTAL AND RESOURCE ECONOMICS

Even one who finds this background of some interest might be excused for wondering what the relationship between applied welfare and environmental and resource economics is held to be. Having observed the application of welfare propositions, whether explicitly or implicitly, in the discussions of investment and operating criteria for well over a third of a century in the publicly managed resources sector—and more recently in the analysis of environmental problems—it is not difficult to claim that environmental and resource economics have been a most effective vehicle for the creative application of what is useful that we have learned from welfare economics. Recall that Pigou highlighted the problem which externalities posed for efficient resource allocation and provided the rudiments of a rationale for public intervention in the workings of a predominantly market-driven economy.

While the profession suffered some unease over its failure to find measureable evidence of externalities to deposit in Edgeworth's "empty economic boxes," the tangible evidence was nevertheless readily at hand. Any perceptive member of the earth or life sciences and their associated applied areas—for example, sanitary engineering and public health; or hydrology, soil mechanics, and stream morphology—could have supplied, and is still able to supply, pertinent information of this kind, were the barriers to communication effectively reduced. Indeed, while Tibor Scitovsky in his "Two Concepts of External Economies" [28] tended to discount the quantitative significance of static external economies—having to find "bucolic" examples (orchards and bees) with which to certify their existence—what was not readily perceived was that these examples were representative of a significant class of cases; namely, those provided by nature whether we elect to address them in the context of natural resources or natural environments.

It is in the natural ambience viewed as backdrop for resource extraction, transportation, and conversion that we find all of the examples of Pigou's divergences between net private and social product. It is here where the direct interdependence among production functions, between production and utility functions and among utility functions—abounds in profusion. The fact that examples appear partly in bucolic settings does not diminish their importance for economy-wide efficient resource allocation.

The fact that welfare economics found its application in the water resources earlier and more widely than elsewhere in the resource management field is perhaps more a historical accident than a matter of inherent differences among resource sectors. Even so the water resource area exhibits all of the stuff of which theoretical discussion in political economy is made. There are not only externalities. There are also problems involving significant irreversibilities. Moreover, we find indivisibilities in production leading to the problem Dupuit [6] originally addressed (and further to the natural monopoly problem) as well as in consumption, the latter leading to the problem involving efficient provision of public goods.

Indeed, the problem concerning the revelation of preferences for public goods—made with great clarity by Samuelson [28]—was confronted in one of its more tractable forms in the valuation of flood stage reduction services obtained from storage reservoirs, and happily was solved even before the publication of Samuelson's seminal paper. Faced with a legislative mandate to estimate the benefits and costs of flood management facilities, the practitioners made use of what Myrick Freeman [7] has observed to be complementary and substitute relationships among public and private goods, to estimate the value of a public good. Admittedly, this was a special tractable case, but one nonetheless representative of a significant class of cases. To appreciate this we need only acknowledge the work of Trice and Wood [31], Clawson and Knetsch [3], and perhaps most ingeniously performed by Cicchetti *et al.* [2]. This work addressed problems of increasing complexity, where use of the relationship between a private and a public good can be employed to reveal preference for the latter from the economic behavior of consumers of such nonpriced resource services. Indeed, for applied welfare analysis, there is no absence of challenge in the natural resource field, a field where misallocation

8   JOHN V. KRUTILLA

would otherwise result because of direct interdependencies on the one hand and collective consumption attributes of various resource services on the other. Under such conditions the market would not provide adequate incentives for private entrepreneurs to undertake more socially efficient economic activities.

Although the widest application of welfare economics was first made in the water resources field as a matter of historical accident, it was nonetheless a happy one, for it fostered early development of the initial serious economic analysis of environmental issues [12]. Indeed, the substance of environmental economics deals with competition among rival users and uses of open-access common property resources, and the Riparian Doctrine governing the use of water treated a stream as if it provided Samuelson's type of public goods. Recall that under the doctrine, a riparian is entitled to use of the waters of a stream so long as he does not diminish the stream in either quantity or quality. This has all the attributes attending the consumption of a public good and did characterize the earlier uses of streams for water power and navigation. When the concept of use was extended to accommodate transporting municipal and industrial effluents, and damming streams that damaged anadromous fisheries, however, the previous public goods character of the use was compromised. But out of this grew the line of work that characterized a significant part of environmental economics; i.e., economic analysis of the externalities which arise from the use of common property resources as transport media for the effluents associated with the transportation, conversion, and consumption of private property resources. Environmental economics was largely the extension of resource economics into previously neglected areas involving rival demands for common property resources. This is equally true of that area of environmental economics that has as its main concern the diminution of welfare suffered through progressive landscape degradation and reduction of the capacity of environmental resources to continue to provide nonpriced common property resources services.

V. PARTING THOUGHTS

In concluding, let me now suggest that the earlier, more limited, roles that the practitioners of welfare economics played insulated them substantially from many of the problems which theoretical welfare economists exposed. But there are growing and more pervasive problems falling within the domain of resource and environmental economics that will certainly demand our attention, and these may not be the kind of lower-level concerns previous "workers in the trenches" encountered. I have in mind two areas of concern for the profession which have become increasingly fashionable and will demand a great deal of responsible analysis. One deals with the question of excessive regulation; the other deals with the issue of declining productivity. Both touch on areas of interest to most members of the Association of Environmental & Resource Economists.

It is perhaps quite true that there is an excess of regulation and that ill-conceived, nonproductive features of regulations should be eliminated by every practicable means. It does not mean, however, that much of the regulation was motivated initially without reason. Regulation of child labor, occupational conditions affecting health and safety, and many other areas involving the ambient environment, is essential to the welfare of a civilized community. We should remain mindful of this. What is called for is perceptive discrimination between regulations that have taken on a life of their own after the need for them has ceased (for example, CAB airlines rate regulation), and those that are well conceived to promote the welfare of the community. Possibly what is required of those of us who find both the Pigouvian divergences between private and social product and cost on the one hand, and an intolerable dead weight burden in perhaps clumsy attempts to reduce this welfare loss on the other—is a dedication to the improvement of the regulatory process where it is needed rather than the indiscriminate reduction or even wholesale elimination of regulations. Association members, I would expect, could address this issue with greater sensitivity and sophistication than other branches of the economics discipline are likely to do.

The second matter we have to address responsibly is that of the relevant concepts and measures of productivity changes. We need to distinguish between measured, but spurious, productivity gains, and unmeasured but real productivity changes. I have in mind part of the past large gains in productivity as revealed by conventional concepts and measures which we presumed to have experienced, when only private goods and private property entered the calculus while increasing social costs were being borne by the neglected degradation of open access common property resources. The apparent widespread contamination of ground water aquifers on which a large part of the urban population draws for its water, as an example, represents a deferred heavy social cost or unmeasured productivity loss caused by the absence of effective regulation of toxic chemical disposal. Similarly, efforts to protect the life support contribution of common property resources through legally required "nonproductive" capital expenditures and operating costs will not be reflected as investment in productive capacity—but only as unrequited capital expenditures—unless we address the problem with greater sophistication and commitment to meaningful analysis. To do this, however, will require a humble recognition of the growing interdependence among economists on the one hand and the earth and life scientists on the other.

The responsible analysis of regulations with the objective of eliminating excess burdens while maintaining protection of the community, and the challenge to develop a more meaningful characterization of inputs and outputs—and hence more accurate indicators of changes in productivity—are worthy problems for the applied economist to address. These are certainly worthy of the vigor and the mettle of those who will be embarking on a serious study of environmental and resource economics in the 1980s.

REFERENCES

1. W. J. Baumol, "Welfare Economics and the Theory of the State," Harvard Univ. Press, Cambridge (1952).
2. C. J. Cichetti, A. C. Fisher, and V. K. Smith. An econometric evaluation of a generalized consumer surplus measure: The mineral king controversy, *Econometrica* (1976).
3. M. Clawson and J. L. Knetsch "Economics of Outdoor Recreation," The Johns Hopkins University Press for Resources for the Future, Baltimore (1966).
4. O. A. Davis and A. B. Whinston, Welfare economics and the theory of the second best, *Rev. Econ. Studies* 32, 1–14 (1965).
5. O. A. Davis and A. B. Whinston, Piecemeal policy in the theory of second best, *Rev. Econ. Studies* 34, 323–331 (1967).
6. J. Dupuit, De la mesure d'utilite des travaux publics, *in* "Annales des Ponts et Chaussees," 1844, reprinted under the heading" De l'Utilite et de sa Mesure," *La Riforma* (Turin, 1932).
7. A. M. Freeman, III, "The Benefits of Environmental Improvement: Theory and Practice," Johns Hopkins Press for Resources for the Future, Baltimore (1979).

10 JOHN V. KRUTILLA

8. J. de V. Graaff, "Theoretical Welfare Economics," Cambridge Univ. Press, Cambridge (1957).

9. J. R. Hicks, Foundations of welfare economics, *Econ. J.* **49**, 696–712 (1939).

10. H. Hotelling, The general welfare in relation to problems of taxation and of railway and utility rates, *Econometrica* **6**, 242–269 (1938).

11. N. Kaldor, Welfare propositions of economics and interpersonal comparisons of utility, *Econ. J.* **49**, 549–552 (1939).

12. A. V. Kneese, "The Economics of Regional Water Quality Management," Johns Hopkins Press for Resources for the Future, Baltimore (1964).

13. J. V. Krutilla and O. Eckstein, "Multiple Purpose River Development: Studies in Applied Economic Analysis," Johns Hopkins Press for Resources for the Future, Baltimore (1958).

14. O. Lange, "On the Economic Theory of Socialism" (B. E. Lippincott, Ed.), University of Minnesota Press, Minneapolis (1938).

15. A. P. Lerner, "The Economics of Control: Principles of Welfare Economics," Macmillan Co., New York (1947).

16. R. G. Lipsey and R. K. Lancaster, The general theory of the second best, *Rev. Econ. Studies* **24**, 11–32 (1956–57).

17. I. M. D. Little, "A Critique of Welfare Economics," Oxford Univ. Press (Clarendon), London (1950).

18. I. M. D. Little and J. A. Mirrless, "Project Appraisal and Planning for the Developing Countries," Heinemann Educational Books, London (1974).

19. R. McKean, "Efficiency in Government through Systems Analysis, with Emphasis on Water Resource Development," Wiley, New York (1958).

20. J. E. Meade, "The Theory of International Economic Policy: Volume II: Trade and Welfare," Oxford Univ. Press, New York (1954).

21. M. Olson, Jr., "The Logic of Collective Action," Harvard Univ. Press, Cambridge, Mass. (1965).

22. A. C. Pigou, "The Economics of Welfare," Macmillan & Co., London (1920). Originally published as "Wealth and Welfare," London (1912).

23. A. M. Polinsky, Probabilistic compensation criteria, *Quart. J. Econ.* **86**, 407–425 (1972).

24. Report from the Secretary of the Treasury, No. 250, to the first session of the 10th Congress, April 6, 1808, *in* "American State Papers: Class X, Miscellaneous," Vol. I (W. Lowrie and W. Franklin, Eds.) pp. 724–921, Gales & Seaton, Washington, D.C. (1834).

25. R. Rees, Second best rules for public enterprise pricing, *Econometrica* 260–273 (1968).

26. L. Robbins, "The Nature and Significance of Economic Science," St. Martin's Press, New York (1935).

27. P. A. Samuelson, Evaluation of real national income, *Oxford Econ. Papers*, *N.S.* **2**, 1–29 (1950).

28. P. A. Samuelson, Pure theory of public expenditure, *Rev. Econ. Statist.* **36**, 387–389 (1954).

29. T. Scitovsky, A note on welfare propositions in economics, *Rev. Econ. Studies* **9**, 77–88 (1941).

30. T. Scitovsky, Two concepts of external economies, *J. Pol. Econ.* **62** No. 2, 143–151 (1954).

31. A. H. Trice, and S. E. Wood, Measurement of recreation benefits, *Land Econ.* **34**, 195–207 (1958).

32. U.S. Congress, Joint Economic Committee, Subcommittee on Priorities and Economy in Government Benefit Cost Analysis of Federal Programs. 92nd Congress, 2nd Session (1973).

33. K. Wicksell, "Lectures in Political Economy," Vol. I, Robbins' edition, 1934.

[45]

Preface

W. MICHAEL HANEMANN, DEPARTMENT OF AGRICULTURAL &
RESOURCE ECONOMICS UNIVERSITY OF CALIFORNIA, BERKELEY

Until recently, it could have been said with some accuracy, if no little chauvinism, that placing an economic value on the natural environment was the pastime of a few rich countries – especially the United States. Like some other topics in microeconomics, the economics of environmental valuation might have been seen as exemplifying a typically American tendency to quantify that which is best left unquantified. Among many American economists, environmental valuation was perceived as something of primarily methodological interest – it was an extension of existing benefit-cost techniques to value a rather novel public good, namely, the natural environment. For their part, environmental policy makers generally had relatively little interest in economics: they felt that they could function perfectly well without the benefit of advice from economists.

Within less than a decade, all of this has begun to change. The protection of the environment has moved to the forefront of the political scene in America, Europe, and many other parts of the world. Within the European Community, for example, there has recently been a wave of environmental policymaking as part of the effort to harmonize domestic policies by 1992. In Eastern Europe, since the fall of communism in 1989 it has been recognized that massive degradation of the environment may be one of its most enduring legacies. Longstanding concerns about the harmful environmental side-effects of economic growth are finally receiving attention from international development agencies. The Earth Summit in Rio is, indeed, a testament to the global nature of the concern to protect the environment.

However, a corollary to this heightened sense of concern is that the economic aspects of environmental protection will become correspondingly more important: pollution control is not necessarily cheap, and the resources devoted to it must be allocated wisely. In the US, for example, the Environmental Protection Agency has recently estimated that, by the end of this decade, almost 3 % of the

GNP will be spent on pollution control, either by the private sector or by the federal and state governments. With expenditures on that scale, it will be hard to avoid economic questions such as whether the benefits in particular cases are sufficient to justify the cost.

Hence, this volume dealing with the economic valuation of the natural environment is most timely. Its focus on Europe is particularly useful because of the rapid pace of change there. Moreover, it provides an important corrective to the existing published literature, which mostly deals with the US.

For European readers, however, it may be helpful to give a brief description of how environmental valuation evolved in the US, and to comment on some of the lessons to be learned from this experience. The first point to be made is that environmental valuation grew out of cost-benefit analysis, which itself first emerged as a practical tool of government decisionmaking in the US in the early part of this century. The history since then can be divided roughly into four phases. The first phase lasts through World War II; the second phase is the early post-war era through about 1964; the third phase is from 1965 to about 1980, and the fourth phase is from then to the present.

In the first phase, cost-benefit analysis emerged, in Hammond's [1960] words, as "an administrative device owing nothing to economic theory." It was conceived as a tool for managing the activities of the U.S. Army Corps Engineers. The 1902 River andd Harbor Act created a Board of Engineers to review navigation projects and required the Board, in conducting its review, to consider the commercial benefits from such projects in relation to their costs. The River and Harbor Act of 1920 further required the separate reporting of special, or local, benefits as opposed to general, or national, benefits, for the purposes of ensuring appropriate local cost-sharing. During the New Deal, there was a call to broaden project evaluation in order to recognize larger social concerns, especially unemployment, In 1934, the National Resources Board appointed a Water Resources Committee to consider "the development of an equitable system of distributing the cost of water resource projects, which should include not only private but social accounting." Its report spoke of the need to study "the part played by intangible factors" in assessing the equities, benefits and costs of public-works programs. Some of the Committee's recommendations were embodied in the Flood Control Act of 1936, which added flood control – previously seen as a responsibility of state and local government – to the Corps' mandate and permitted it to participate in such projects "if the benefits to whomsoever they may accrue are in excess of the estimated costs, and if the lives and social security of people are otherwise adversely affected." Hammond comments that, given the political and economic climate of 1936, these words were an open invitation to discover new types of benefits that might justify public works projects.

Over the next decade, other federal agencies rose to this challenge adopting, as they did so, the practice of benefit-cost analysis, and expanding its scope in two ways. First, agencies sought to identify intangible factors that could be counted among the project benefits, such as national defense, saving human lives, or aesthetic or recreational impacts. Second, some agencies – notably the Bureau of Reclamation – attempted, in Hammond's words, "to travel down the chain of economic causation and evoke *secondary* or *indirect* benefits and costs: not content with crediting the dam with the value of the wheat grown on the land it was going to irrigate, they would add the net value of the bread that might be baked from the wheat." Moreover, each agency developed its own approach. There were no attempts at standardization until the late 1940's, which marks the second phase in the history of benefit-cost analysis – a period of consolidation, systematization and, for the first time, academic engagement.

In 1946, the Fedral Inter-Agency River Basin Committee appointed a Subcommittee on Benefits and Costs to investigate the practices of the various federal agencies that engaged in the evaluation of water resources projects and to formulate some "mutually acceptable principles and procedures" which could serve as a common approach. The Subcommittee's review of current practices was presented in interim reports issued in 1947, 1948 and 1949. Then, it turned to the task of developing "a systematic, consistent, and theoretically sound framework for the economic analysis of river basin projects." The resulting report, published in May 1950 and known as the "Green Book", received widespread attention. As Hammond says, for the first time in an official publication it applied the language of conventional welfare economics to the analysis of federal policy. It covered most aspects of project evaluation, including measurement of benefits and costs, correct definition of secondary impacts forecasting future price levels, choice of a discount rate, period of analysis, allowances for risk, treatment of taxes, and cost-allocation for multipurpose projects. With regard to the benefit measurement, it characterized the issue thus: "The ultimate aim of river basin development, in common with all productive activity, is to satisfy human needs and desires. The problem of evaluating, from a public viewpoint, the extent to which a project accomplishes this aim presents a major difficulty ... because there are no common terms in which all effects of a project are normally expressed. All objects and activities which have the power of satisfying human wants ... are referred to ... as "goods and services." The values placed on goods and services through the exchange process afford one means of measuring the degree of want-satisfying power attached to those goods and services by those who participate in the exchange. Most of the effects of projects involve goods and services which are readily evaluated in terms of market prices. Some effects of a project, however, such as improvement of health and enjoyment of recreation, have not been customarily evaluated in the monetary terms used in the market system."

For valuing project effects, the Green Book recommended a tripartite solution. First, use market prices wherever possible. Failing this, use values "derived or estimated indirectly from prices established in the market for similar or analogous [outputs] or ... derived from the most economical cost of producing similar effects by an alternate means." Second, "projects effects which are ordinarily evaluated incompletely or not at all in actual exchange processes should be given, insofar as possible, an adjusted or estimated market value in monetary terms." For example, "for the purpose of establishing a greater comparability among the benefit-cost analyses of the various agencies, a human life might be given, as a minimum, the same economic value as would be payable for a life lost during project construction under compensation arrangements which are normally included in estimates of project costs." Alternatively, "on a broader basis the value might approximate the average ... amount paid for accidental loss of life in court awards." With regard to recreational impacts, "since market prices are not available to express the value of this increase in monetary terms, an estimated or derived value comparable to market value may be used for this purpose. Under one procedure ... the value of recreational benefit to an individual is assumed to be equal to the sum of expenditures by the recreationist for such items as gasoline, food, lodging, and sporting equipment ... This method, however, provides a measure of gross rather than net values and from the project standpoint does not measure benefits creditable to the project." As an alternative, the Green Book suggested measuring recreational benefits on the basis of "informed estimates of the average value of these recreational facilities to prospective users. In estimating or deriving these tangible values, consideration should be given to all pertinent factors, including the charges which the recreationalists who may be expected to use the facilities would be willing to pay and to any actual charges being paid by users for comparble facilities in other areas." The third type of effects was intangibles, i.e, "effects which it is considered impossible or undersirable to express in monetary terms." Examples include "the loss of a scenic or historic site" or "the strengthening of national security and the national economy." The Green Book held that these effects "need to be described with care and should not be overlooked or minimized merely because they do not yield to dollar evaluation." Rather, they should be "considered and described in such a way that their importance and influence on project formulation and selection can be clearly indicated."

Although the Green Book was recognized as a landmark in the application of microeceonomics to policy analysis, its impact was muted in two ways. First, its recommendations were advisory not mandatory: the participating agencies were still free to continue with their existing practices, and some did. Hence, fierce battles continued to be waged during the 1950's – both among rival federal agencies and between the agencies and their outside, especially academic, critics – regarding issues such as the Bureau of Reclamation's treatment of secondary impacts or its choice of a discount rate. Second, while some parts of its economic analysis were of enduring value, other parts were quickly overtaken by contemporaneous developments in welfare economics. The "new welfare economics" created in the late 1930's and 1940's by Bergson, Hicks, Hotelling, Kaldor and Lerner was consolidated and synthesized in such works as Little (1950), Baumol (1952) and Graff (1957) which employed a more technically advanced mode of analysis than that found in the Green Book. Perhaps because of this – and perhaps because of interest aroused by controversies over water projects – benefit-cost analysis quickly became an attractive area for academic research on applied welfare economics, generating an extensive literature in the 1950's and early 1960's, including six major books in as many years, four coming out of Harvard University's Water Program – Eckstein (1958), Krutilla and Eckstein (1958), Maass et al. (1962), and Marglin (1963) – and two from the Rand Corporation – McKean (1958) and Hirshleifer et al. (1960).

Much of the conceptual framework for valuing project outputs came ultimately from Hotelling (1938), who had rediscovered for the Anglo-Saxon world Dupuit's (1844) classic analysis of marginal cost pricing and had reformulated it in modern, welfare-theoretic terms. An important implication was that, while market prices can safely be used to value marginal changes in the supply of market commodities, for non-marginal changes one needs to measure the impact in terms of the change in producer's plus consumer's surplus and this, in turn, requires knowledge not of market prices but of the underlying demand and supply curves. The detailed application of these principles to specific water project outputs, such as irrigation supply, hydropower generation, navigation and flood control, was elucidated in the works of Eckstein and the others. In this respect, to be sure, their analysis represented a significant advance over that presented in the Green Book, with its simplistic emphasis on market prices.

But not in other respects. For, whereas the Green Book emphasized all three kinds of project output – marketed commodities, those non-marketed commodities which still could be given an estimated monetary value, and intangibles – the newer treatments, especially those emanating from Harvard, were far more disposed to write off the latter two categories, preferring to concentrate on a more rigorous analysis of the former. For example, Eckstein's core analysis of recreation reads, in its entirety, as follows: "There have been many attempts to measure the benefits of recreation. Since people actually hire the use of recreational facilities one might expect that one could find prices that would measure willingness to pay. When a dam creates a lake, agencies look to the total expenditures which people make on swimming and fishing. but these expenditures are for travel, equipment, lodging, and so forth, and are not expenditures for the lake. A proper measure of benefit would be to indicate how much managers of the lake could collect in the form of user charges; since there are no charges for use of reservoirs or comparable bodies of water elsewhere, appropriate prices cannot be found. Such purposes as recreation must therefore be judged on other criteria, for the use of benefit-cost analysis for them not only is invalid, but casts general doubt and suspicion on procedures which can effectively serve a high purpose where they are appropriate. ... To assure proper consideration of such immeasurable outputs, an analysis of intangibles should be part of every project report. Verbal discussion of the intangible benefits and costs will communicatae the facts to Congress more clearly than invalid benefit estimates. Relevant figures may be submitted without forcing them into the benefit-cost framework; for example, recreation benefits of a project can be described in terms of expected use."

Eckstein's attitude towards the valuation of recreation in monetary terms might be characterized as: "it can't be done, and you shouldn't try." By contrast, the Green Book had at least said "try." Moreover, there was some reason to believe that it *could* be done. The source was no less than Hotelling. This came about in the following manner. In June 1947, the directorate of the National Park Service

(NPS) was casting about for some way to place an economic value on the services provided by national parks in order to justify the federal government's expenditures on them. Their problem was compounded by the fact that, at that time, there were no entrance fees for visiting the national parks. Hence, the parks generated no revenues: they were a pure drain on the federal budget. The project was assigned to an economist in the Planning Division, Roy Prewitt, and he conceived the idea of sending a letter to 10 distinguished experts soliciting their advice. Almost all of them responded negatively – they counselled that it would be impossible to measure recreational values in monetary terms. The chief exception was Harold Hotelling, then a professor of mathematical statistics at the University of North Carolina. He saw that, from a conceptual standpoint, the question was identical to that considered by Dupuit. Dupuit had sought a criterion for determining the value of social overhead capital such as a road or a bridge and had pointed out that the total value was *more* than the aggregate revenues collected, since many people would be willing, if necessary, to pay more than they actually did for the use of the bridge – an extreme case would be where the bridge was free, but people valued it at some positive amount. Dupuit, and Hotelling following him, argued that the social value of the bridge was measured by the area under people's demand curve for its use. The practical problem was to measure this demand curve. It certainly existed – with a high toll, there would be a low demand to use the bridge while, with a low toll, the demand would undoubtedly be higher – but it was latent: only a single point on the curve was observed, corresponding to the particular price being charged (perhaps zero), and from this nothing could be inferred about the position of the *rest* of the curve. For that, there would have to be some variation in price. Hotelling saw that valuing a national park or a lake was conceptually the same as valuing Dupuit's bridge. But, there was one possible difference which worked in the park's favor, namely that there were other inputs associated with the use of the park, such as travel, equipment or lodging, which could provide the necessary price variation. Eckstein had dismissed these items as "not expenditures for the lake" but they *were* – the costs of travelling to the lake or the park were as much a part of the cost of enjoying its recreational services as an entrance fee: they were not captured by the NPS, but they set a price on visiting the site. Moreover, this price would vary among potential visitors residing at different distances. If this price could be measured, one could construct a demand function for visits to the recreation site, from which its value could be determined.

Prewitt went along with the majority opinion of the other consultants and concluded that "recreational values cannot be measured in
dollar terms." The consultants responses and this analysis were
published in an NPS report in 1949. Hotelling's response was included in the report but received no attention. It remained buried in obscurity for almost a decade, while the NPS turned to other methods
of assigning "judgment values" to outdoor recreation. In 1950, the
NPS adopted a policy of assuming, for planning purposes, that
primary recreation benefits were approximately equal in value to the
costs of providing and maintaining recreation sites, and that secondary recreation benefits were approximately equal to primary benefits; "thus, benefits are always twice as great as costs in NPS calculations." This practice was not without its critics – including Eckstein
– and it was abandoned in 1957. In that year Senator Robert Kerr
held hearings before his subcommittee on Public Works regarding
the evaluation of recreation benefits from reservoirs. Testimony was
presented that "failure properly to estimate recreational potentials of
reservoir projects had led to dangerous overcrowding with, in many
cases, actual recreational use in the first year far exceeding facilities
provided." Remedial action was recommended. As a result, both the
Corps of Engineers and the NPS decided to adopt a dollar value –
initially, $1.60 per visitor day – for the purpose of valuing recreation
benefits. This figure was based on a previous study of entrance
charges and other costs at several hundred private recreation areas;
it was intended as judgment estimate of the consumer's surplus for
at typical visitor at a national park – i.e. of the amount that a discriminating monopolist could capture through entrance fees. As the
earlier quote indicates, Eckstein did not think much of this method
either.

It was just at this time, however, that Hotelling's idea finally resur-
faced – ironically, almost simultaneously with the publication of
Eckstein's book. In 1956 the State of California was planning the
Feather River Project and it retained an economic consulting company to quantify the recreational benefits associated with the project's reservoirs. This company became aware of Hotelling's idea
through Harold Ellis, a professor of economics at the University of
California, Berkely and fellow consultant to the NPS in 1947, and
decided to try it out. Accordingly, a survey of visitors was conducted
at several sites in the Sierras during 1956 to obtain information about
where they had come from and how much they had spent. On the
basis of these data, a rough demand curve was traced out and an
approximate estimate of consumer's surplus was constructed. This
analysis appeared in Trice and Wood (1958), which is the first pub-

lished application of what subsequently became known as the "travel-cost" method of estimating the economic value of recreation. The second appeared only a few months later. In 1957, Marion Clawson had initiated a research project at Resources for the Future to collect data on visitation at Yosemite and other major national parks for the purpose of applying the Hotelling method. His preliminary estimates of consumer's surplus based on these data were published in Clawson (1959), which stated as its premise "that it is both theoretically possible and practically manageable to put monetary value on outdoor recreation. The conceptual and theoretical problems, while somewhat novel, are not insurmountable nor perhaps unusually difficult; the problem of getting accurate and dependable data is serious but still manageable." Putting the travel coost method on the map was Clawson's goal, and with this in mind he was soon joined at RFF by Jack Knetsch; their joint work was first circulated in draft form in 1961, and subsequently published as a book, Clawson and Knetsch (1966). Meanwhile, other papers applying the travel cost method were published by Lerner (1962), Ullman and Volk (1962), Knetsch (1963), Brown et al. (1964) and Wennergren (1964).

Two related developments should be mentioned. In 1958, the U.S. Outdoor Recreation Review Commission was appointed to examine the future needs for outdoor recreation resources. As one of several studies, it sponsored a national household survey on outdoor recreation participation in 1960–61. The Commission's report was published in 1962, and it led to the creation of a Bureau of Outdoor Recreation within the Department of Interior for the purpose of planning and coordinating the development of outdoor recreation facilities at the national level. The Bureau sponsored a second national survey of outdoor recreation in 1965; an analysis of the data from the two surveys was subsequently published in Cicchetti, Seneca and Davidson (1969). Secondly, in 1962 recreation was given official status as a primary purpose of federal water projects, alongside navigation, flood control, hydropower, and irrigation, U.S. Senate (1962). The procedures for valuing recreation benefits were promulgated in U.S. Senate (1964); they were based on an updated and expanded version of the 1957 unit-day values.

By this time, it was apparent that benefit-cost analysis had become established as both a legitimate branch of welfare economics and a standard tool for the analysis of government expenditures. In 1960, it had been introduced by Robert McNamara to the Department of Defense in the form of Program Planning and Budgeting (PPB) and, in 1965, President Johnson directed all federal agencies to start using PPB. The range of applications covered in the literature had by now

18　PREFACE

widened from water resource projects to other facets of government activity such as road and rail transportation, [Mohring (1961), Mohring and Harwitz (1962), Foster and Beesley (1963), and Winch (1963)], health care [Weisbrod (1960), Mushkin (1962), Klarman (1965)], education and job training [Bowman (1962), Hansen (1963), Becker (1964) and Blaug (1965)], and urban renewal [Rothenberg (1965)]. The first major academic assessments of this new vintage were publishehd in Dorfman (1965) and Prest and Turvey (1965). Like the contemporaneous work on recreation, it valued non-marginal impacts in terms of changes in consumer's plus producer's surplus derived from underlying demand and supply functions and, in order to deal with the demand for an intangible such as health, it found a surrogate in the observed demand correlated marketed commodities such as expenditures on averting or preventative behavior.

With regard to water resources project evaluation, developments since 1965 can be subdivided into two periods: from 1965 to about 1980, and from then to the present. During the first of these periods, much academic attention was focused on refining the travel-cost approach to valuing recreation. In terms of both statistical methodology and consistency with the economic theory of futility-maximizing choice. As a crude index of the growth of this research, while about 5 papers on travel cost were published between 1960 and 1964, about 15 were published between 1965 and 1969 and about 35 between 1970 and 1976. Furthermore, the publication in 1974 of Karl-Goran Maler's treatise on environmental economics represented a landmark in showing how changes in the quality of market goods, and quasi-market goods such as recreation, could be treated rigorously within the framework of utility theory. In reflection of its maturation, when the federal governement's principles and standards for evaluating water projects were revised in 1973 they now listed the travel-cost method as an approved procedure, although they still permitted the use of unit-day values as an interim measure.

The major innovation during this period concerned the valuation of what the Green Book had called intangibles, although these would now be defined as items for which there was no direct market demand function nor could one be inferred, as in the travel-cost method, from the demand for surrogate market commodities. For those items a different approach was required: one would have to interview people and ask them directly for their monetary evaluation. In fact, this approach, known as contingent valuation (CV), had first been suggested in 1947, the same year that Hotelling proposed the travel cost method. It was suggested by S. V. Ciriacy-Wantrup (1947), a professor in the Department of Agricultural Economics at the University of California, Berkeley, in the context of a discussion of measuring the benefits from soil conservation practices, some of which were collective, extra-market goods – his phrase – such as reduced siltation of reservoirs or reduced impairment of scenic resources. He characterized the essential problem as being how to obtain a demand schedule for such goods, and suggested the following solution: "Individuals of a sample or of a social group as a whole may be asked how much money they are willing to pay for successive additional quantities of a collective extra-market good. The choices offered relate to quantities consumed by all members of a social group. If the group interrogated is only a sample ... the modal schedule of the sample is obtained, and each point on this schedule is then multiplied by the number of individuals in the whole social group being investigated." What was thus obtained could be taken as the analog of a market demand schedule for the collective good. Ciriacy-Wantrup went on to consider some possible objections to this evaluation procedure, including the objection that "expectations of the incidence of costs in the form of taxes will bias the responses to interrogation." However, he was confident that "through proper education and proper design of questionnaires or interviews it would seem possible to keep this potential bias small." The same suggestion was repeated in Ciriacy-Wantrup's 1952 book on resource economics. Both times, however, it fell on deaf ears.

Nevertheless, there was considerable intuitive appeal to this notion of surveying people and asking them directly what they would be willing to pay. Thus, when the first applications of CV occurred, the authors conceived the idea independently and were unaware that it had been suggested earlier by Ciriacy-Wantrup. The first such application appears to have been in 1958 at the bequest of none other than the NPS. The circumstances are described by Mack and Myers (1965): "In a survey of the outdoor recreational activities and preferences of persons living in the Delaware River Basin area, respondents were qestioned about their willingness to pay entrance fees. They expressed a general willingness to pay entrance fees for 'satisfactory publicly owned outdoor recreational areas' for day trips. ... The median average amount they said they would consider a reasonable fee was 50 cents per person." To this, Mack and Myers added the following qualification: "The interviewers noted, however, that this finding must be interpreted with some caution because people often express a willingness to pay before the fact, but are much less willing when the time comes. But those respondents who are puffing up their status by indicating a willingness to pay a fee are undoubtedly balanced by others who hesitate to admit such willing-nesss lest officials might be moved to institute or raise fees. Such con-flicting biases fatally weaken interpretations that might be drawn from the data. But this does not necessarily signify that the approach itself is barren; rather, it may argue for a more searching methodo-logy ... [One] technique entails the selection of three or four similar large sample groups who would be told that a proposed service or facility would cost a different price long an ascending scale. For example, one group might be told the admission charge was 50 cents, the next group that it was 75 cents, and so on. Each would be asked to indicate on a "reaction scale" the statement that best reflects their own attitude towards this price. The resulting data could indicate when a sizable "resistance point" is reached. "This actually fore-shadows a later development in contingent valuation. Mack and Myers conclude with the assessment that "the approach is worth exploring more fully."

The second application of CV occurred in 1961 when Robert K. Davis (1963) interviewed a sample of hunters and other visitors to the Maine woods for his Harvard Ph. D. dissertation on the benefits of outdoor recreation, and asked them how much they would have been willing to pay (WTP) to engage in these activities. Four years elapsed before the next application. In 1965, influenced by Davis, Ridker (1967) included some WTP question in two surveys that he conduct-ed on attitudes to air pollution in Philadelphia and Syracuse. In 1969, Hammack and Brown (1974) surveyed duck hunters in several western states to elicit both their maximum WTP for the right to hunt waterfowl and their minimum willingness to accept to surrender this right. In 1970, Cicchetti and Smith (1973) surveyed hikers in wilder-ness areas for their WTP to reduce crowding in these areas, and Acton (1973) conducted a CB survey to value health programs which reduced the risk of dying from heart attacks. In 1972, Darling (1973) conducted a CV study on the valuation of amenities at urban parks in California, Alan Randall and colleagues initiated a series of CV studies to value visibility in the Four Corners Area [Randall, Ives and Eastman (1974)]. Indeed, when Hanemann (1978) was conduct-ing a survey of Boston area households in 1974 to collect data for a travel cost model of beach recreation, CV seemed sufficiently well established and a sufficiently obvious thing to do that he included a CV component in his questionnaire. More than a dozen other CV studies were conducted in the US during the next few years. By the end of the decade, this number was growing exponentially. In 1979, official recognition was given to CV when the Water Resources Coun-cil revised the Principles and Standards for water project evaluation:

the new edition included travel cost, CV, and unit day values as the three recommended methods of valuation.

The other important innovations during the period 1965–1980 concerned the conceptual foundations of non-market valuation and grew out of two seminar papers by Burton Weisbrod (1964) and John Krutilla (1967). Both papers started from the premise that the natural environment is not a conventional type of economic commodity, and that some of people's motives for valuing it may differ from those for valuing private market goods. In particular, people may value the natural environment – at least in part – out of considerations unrelated to their own immediate and direct use of it. Weisbrod focused on uncertainty and what became known as "option value": some people who do not now visit a national park, say, may still be wiling to pay money to protect it from destruction or irreversible damage because they want to preserve their option of visiting it in the future. Krutilla focused on what became known as "bequest value" and "existence" or "non-use" value. Some people would be willing to pay because they want to preserve the park for future generations. And, others would be willing to pay even if they knew that neither they nor their children would ever visit it because, as Krutilla put it, they "obtain satisfaction from mere knowledge that part of the wilderness in North America remains, even though they would be appalled by the prospect of being exposed to it." All of these are legitimate sources of value, Krutilla and Weisbrod felt, but they would not be captured by conventional demand analysis, nor would they be respected by private managers of the resource. These arguments have become widely accepted. However, because both authors employed a largely non-mathematical mode of exposition, there was some ambiguity as to the precise definition of the concepts that they were describing. A substantial literature was generated before those issues were largely resolved during the 1980's. A key implication of the consensus definition which has emerged is that non-use value can *only* be measured by the CV method: it cannot be measured through the travel cost or similar methods that rely on the demand for surrogate market goods because it reflects a value placed on the natural environment from quite separate motives.

The other distinctive characteristic of this period was the relatively limited interaction between federal agencies and the academic research community. During the 1950's many of the leading researchers had worked quite closely with the agencies and were personally interested in improving project evaluation practices. The new generation of researchers who became active in the late 1960's and the 1970's were, on the whole, more concerned with benefit-cost analysis as an academic field and had little interest in – perhaps, even some disdain for – what the governement agencies did.

This began to change in the late 1970's. The period since about 1980 has been marked by a heightened level of interaction between the academic community and government agencies, and a renewed interest on the part of the agencies in employing more up-to-date and sophisticated measurement techniques for public decisionmaking. During this period, environmental valuation came of age. As it did so, it has emerged from the academy into the rough and tumble of the outside world.

One of the important influences in this regard was the 1979 Revision of the Principles & Guidelines, but there are many others. For example, in preparation for the 1980 Resource Planning Assessment (RPA), the Forest Service launched a large-scale effort to collect data on the economic values associated with recreational uses of forest lands, in order to balance these against timber production and other uses. This research effort was expanded for the 1985 and 1990 RPAs. Another example is what has become known in the electric utility industry as environmental costing. At the federal level, the Electric Consumers Protection Act of 1986 required the Federal Electric Utility Commission to take account of environmental impacts when issuing licenses for new hydro facilities or relicensing existing ones. At about the same time, some state Public Utility Commissions (PUCs), which regulate the pricing and investment behavior of investor-owned utilities, started becoming interested in the same concept. One of the pioneers was the New York State Energy Research & Development Authority which in 1988, inspired by Hohmeyer's (1988) study of externality costs in Germany, commissioned the first major US study of the environmental costs of electricity generation [Pace (1991)]. Since then, 29 PUCs have required, or are now considering, the incorporation of environmental externality costs in electricity supply planning and resource selection procedures.

However, the greatest impetus to the diffusion of environmental valuation in the US over the past decade has come from Executive Order (EO) 12291 and from CERCLA. EO 12291 was issued by President Reagan a few weeks after he took office in 1981 with the aim of controlling what he regarded as excessive government regulation. In pursuit of this goal, he required all federal agencies to prepare a Regulatory Impact Analysis (RIA) before undertaking any major regulatory action, including both the promulgation of new regulations and the review or revision of existing ones. The RIAs had to be submitted to the Office of Management and Budget (OMB) for review and approval. OMB was given the power both to define what constituted a major regulatory action (and to waive the requirement of a regulatory review, if it so chose) and to specify the procedures to be followed in conducting a RIA. Grubb et al. (1984) reviewed the accomplishments of EO 12291 after two years and found them to be modest. The RIAs that had been conducted were highly variable in quality. For the most part, they were based on off-the-shelf information and very few resources were devoted to their preparation. At worst, they were uninformative and misleading. Moreover, there were obvious signs of bias in their coverage: OMB tended to require a RIA for actions involving more regulation but to waive the RIA for actions involving deregulation or the granting of exemptions from regulation. Besides issuing a vacuous, five-page leaflet, OMB had done nothing to promote consistency in the RIAs or improve their quality. Nevertheless, Grubb et al. concluded, "more important than the absolute number of high-quality analyses under EO 12291 – which is small by any standard – is the fact that benefit-cost analysis seems to be taking its place in the routine procedures associated with the regulatory process. The consciousness that costs and benefits need to be analyzed rather than assumed, that alternatives need to be considered, that information is uncertain and may require sensitivity analyses, that the claims of external interest groups need to be independently checked – all these views are implicit in EO 12291 and are present in the best RIAs that have been performed so far." Almost a decade later, the same conclusion still holds.

While EO 12291 applied to tall federal regulations, its impact fell somewhat disproportionately on environmental regulations. This is partly because of the bias noted above, but also because the EPA responded to it more openly than some of the other agencies. As Andrews (1984) noted, during most of the 1970's the EPA's economic analysis had focused largely on the costs of pollution control as "a flank-protection strategy against potential business attacks;" it did relatively less on the benefits side until the late 1970's, when the growing pressure from the regulatory reform movement forced it to pay more sustained attention to the balancing of benefits against costs. Thus, after the apperance of EO 12291, EPA was one of only two agencies to prepare its own manual on benefit-cost analysis (the other was the Department of Transportation). Moreover, it adopted a strategy of funding basic and applied research on various aspects of benefits analysis. Among the work funded in this way was the research by Smith and Desvousges (1986) on applying the travel cost and CV methods to measure the use and non-use benefits associated with improving water in the Monogahela River, the work by Bockstael, McConnell and Strand (1988) on applying the travel cost and hedonic methods to value improved water quality in Chesapeake Bay, and the 1984 Palo Alto conference assessing the state-of-the-art of the CV method.

A feature of that assessment was the involvement of a review panel of eminent economists and psychologists, including Nobel laureate Kenneth Arrow. At the conference, many leading researchers offered their views about CV's potential as a means of valuing environmental goods [the proceedings were subsequently published in Cummings et al. (1986)]. The lead authors' conclusion was that, while the method showed promise, some real challenges remained. In particular, more focused research was needed on the methodological foundations of CV, including the theory of individual behavior in contingent market settings, the question of incentive compatibility, and the specification of "reference operating conditions" for the accuracy of CV measures. Around the time of the conference there was a quantum leap of interest in CV, and some of the new work addressed in various ways the issues raised at the conference. For example, researchers began to move away from the open-ended questioning that had been the hallmark of the early CV studies to closed-ended questions in which respondents were offered a single dollar amount of payment, to which they could respond "yes" or "no." This format had been mentioned by Mack and Myers (1965) and had first been implemented by Bishop and Heberlein (1979). It was found to be more incentive compatible and, since it could be cast in the form of a referendum, it tended to make the WTP question more realistic for respondents. The new research was also marked by a greater attention to the utility-theoretic interpretation of CV responses and, in many cases for the first time, a heightened sensitivity to the survey research aspects of the CV method. The new point of view was fully reflected in Robert Mitchell and Richard Carson's treatise on CV, published in 1989. This work sought to place CV in a broader context as a technique of social science research, involving elements of economics, sociology, psychology and survey research, and having strong links to public opinion polling and market research. It drew on the literature from all of these fields in order to define what it would take to obtain reliable and valid CV measures. Through its scope it set a new standard for the field.

Compared to EO 12291, CERCLA's impact on environmental valutaion was slower to develop, but ultimately far more dramatic. The term is an acronym for the Comprehensive Environmental Response, Compensation and Liability Act, passed by Congress in December 1980 primarily in response to the notorious case of dioxin contamination at Love Canal, NY that had come to light in 1978.

CERCLA contained two main sets of provisions. By far the better known – at least until recently – were those providing for the creation of Superfund to finance the remedial clean-up of existing hazardous waste sites. The other provisions established a liability on the potentially responsible parties (PRPs) to pay damages for the injuries to natural resources resulting from the spill or release of hazardous substances, in addition to the costs of clean-up, removal, remediation, and any other necessary response costs including the costs of the damage assessment. In order to exercise these liabilities and recover these damages, CERCLA created the legal concept of a resource trustee. The federal and state governments would be the trustees for the natural resources owned or controlled by the federal, state or local governments; in this capacity, they would conduct an assessment of the natural resource damages and then take appropriate steps to recover the damages from the PRPs. How were these damages to be assessed? CERCLA required that, within two years, the President promulgate regulations which would identify the "best available procedures" for determining natural resource damages. Congress almost certainly was thinking of something analogous to the Principle & Guidelines for water projects. It stipulated that the regulations would specify both "(A) standard procedures for simplified assessments requiring minimal field observation, including establishing measures of damage based on units of discharge or release or units of affected area, and (B) alternative protocols for conducting assessments in individual cases to determine the type and extent ... of loss." The Type A assessment, as it became known, would be like using off-the-shelf unit day values, whereas the Type B assessment would be a investigatiion tailored to the specifics to the particular incident: the trustees would decide which type to perform. Finally, CERCLA stipulated that the President review the regulations every two years and revise them as appropriate.

The new Reagan administration was less than enthusiastic about the damage liability provisions of CERCLA and did not hurry to implement them, beyond designating the Department of the Interior (DOI) as the agency responsible for promulgating the regulations. In 1984 several states sued DOI for its failure to issue regulations and obtained a court order compelling action. Drafts of the regulations were published in 1985, and the final regulations were issued in August 1986 (Type B) and March 1987 (Type A). The final Type B regulations contained at least two distinctive features. The first was the "lesser-of" rule: the DOI regulations made the measure of damages either replacement/restoration costs or lost use value, *whichever was the lesser.* The second was the "hierarchy of assessment methods." The regulations specified that the diminution in market price should be used to estimate the damages if there existed a reasonably competitive market for the injured resource. Alternatively, if market prices were not appropriate, the damage estimate should be based on the loss in appraised value using commercial appraisal techniques. Only if the trustee had determined that neither the market price nor the appraisal methodologies were appropriate could non-market valuation methods be used, including travel cost, hedonic pricing, unit day values, and CV. Here, too, there was a hierarchy: the use of CV to measure existence or option value was permitted only if no use values could be ascertained. Thus, both CV and non-use values were firmly relegated to an inferior status. While the lesser-of rule was a standard application of economic principles, the hierarchy of methods was nothing short of bizarre within this context of assessing the public (as opposed to private) losses from injuries to natural resources. As permitted by Congress, appeals were filed against these and other aspects of the regulations with the District of Columbia Circuit of the US Court of Appeals: some state governments and environmental groups attacked the rules for being too narrow, while some industrial groups representing potential PRPs attacked them for being too broad – in particular for being too liberal in permitting the use of CV. The DC Court of Appeals issued its *ruling on* what became known as the case of *Ohio v. US Department of the Interior* on Bastille Day in 1989. On the main issues concering environmental valuation it sided firmly with the states. It threw out the lesser-of rule and held that the Congressional intent was to make restoration costs the proper measure of damages, unless they were "grossly disproportionate" to the lost use values. Moreover, it held that Congress had intended lost use values to *include* non-use values: "option and existence values may represent 'passive use,'" the Court wrote, "but they nonetheless reflect utility derived by humans from a resource, and thus prima facie ought to be included in a damage assessment." In the same vein, the Court struck down the hierarchy of assessment methods as "not a reasonable interpretation of the statute." It directed DOI to permit trustees to derive values for natural resource damages "by summing up all reliably caluculated use values, however measured, so long as the trustee does not double count." Lastly, it dealt with the industry petitioners' objections to the use of CV. They had argued that CV could not possible qualify as a "best available procedure" because of the unreliability of CV responses. The court examined this argument at some length and rejected it in no uncertain terms. For example, in response to the argument that "respondents do not actually pay money, and likely will overstate their willingness to pay" the Court replied that "the simple and obvious safeguard against overstatement ... is more sophisticated questioning." It found that CV was a best available procedure and it sustained DOI in its conclusion that CV could be utilized as a "valid, proven technique ... when properly structured and professionally applied." DOI was directed to revise its regulations in line with all these findings.

By the time of the *Ohio* ruling these issues were of more than academic interest: after a slow start caused by the novelty of the concept as well as by DOI's delays in issuing the regulations, litigation over natural resource damages had by now become a reality. The first suits for natural resource damages were brought by the state of Colorado in connection with the pollution of groundwater and surface water by mining operations at the Eagle Mine near Gilman and the Idarado Mine near Telluride. During 1985 and 1986 the state conducted something like Type B assessments (this was before the DOI regulations had been issued) that included estimates of lost recreation based on unit-day values and estimates of both use and non-use values based on a CV study. In each case, the defendants countered by presenting estimates of lost use value derived from a travel cost analysis intended to account for the presence of substitute sites [a penetrating analysis of the economic tactics in these cases is provided by Kopp and Smith (1989)]. Although these cases involved the first court test of the CV method, the outcome was inconclusive – the Eagle Mine case was settled without a court decision, and the Idarado case is still in process. In 1983, the fedral government brought its first natural resources damage action in connection with PCB contamination of New Bedford Harbor in Massachusetts. The government's damage assessment was conducted in 1986 and involved travel cost analysis and hedonic property value analysis, but not CV; the defendant conducted similar analyses in 1987. These were not tested in open court, however, and the case was settled in 1990–91. The pace of events quickened in 1988. In April, there was a spill at the Shell Oil refinery near San Francisco and the state of California initiated a natural resources damage action; a CV study was contemplated, but this was not followed up and the damages were estimated on the basis of off-the-shelf information (the case was settled the next year – details on this and other cases are provided in Ward and Duffield (1992). In June, Resources for the Future held a conference on natural resource damage assessment which brought the subject to the attention of many environmental economists for the first time [the proceedings are being published in Kopp and Smith (forthcoming)]. In the fall, the state of Montana announced its intention to initiate a natural resources damage action in connection with mining pollution of the Clark Fork Basin. At the end of December, the barge *Nestucca* ruptured off the coast of state of Washington, and oil killed birds and soiled beaches in Washington and British Columbia. The state of Washington and the Canadian government subsequently brought suit and conducted a CV study at the end of 1990 to measure the damages [Rowe, Shaw and Schulze (1992)].

Then, on March 24, 1989, the tanker *Exxon Valdez* ran aground and spilled 11 million gallons of crude oil into the waters of Prince William Sound, a remote and pristine part of Alaska. This was the largest oil spill in U.S. history: it caused substantial environmental damage and attracted worldwide attention. Within a short period of time the state and federal governments, on the one hand, and Exxon, on the other, retained many prominent environmental economists with a view to the natural resource damages litigation that was likely to follow. This was clearly going to involve natural resource damages that were an order of magnitude larger than in any previous case, and non-use values were likely to play a major role. The *Ohio* ruling, coming a few months later, could not have been more timely!

While the *Exxon Valdez* dominated the scene, it was not the only natural resource damage case under way. In addition to those already mentioned, there were several more oil spills on the East Coast later in 1989 and one on the West Coast in 1990 which genereated actions for natural resource damages . In addition, in March 1990 the federal government announced its intention to bring several suits for PCB or DDT contamination of harbors in California and Washington. All of these cases involved some degree of non-use values and some possibility of CV. Moreover, there was action in Congress: in response to the *Exxon Valdez,* an Oil Pollution Act was passed in August 1990 which superseded CERCLA with respect to oil spills (but not other hazardous releases); this act kept many of the elements off CERCLA, including the notion of the fedral and state governments as trustees for injured natural resources, but it substantially extended the scope of recoverable damages and it strongly reaffirmed the elements of the *Ohio* ruling dealing with the lesser-of rule and non-use values. As a sign of Congressional dissatisfaction with DOI, the responsibility for promulgating the regulations for the assessment of natural resource damages under the new act was handed to the Department of Commerce's National Oceanic & Atmospheric Administration (NOAA).

During 1989 and 1990, the state and federal governments worked on separate natural resource damage assessments for the *Exxon Valdez.* Appraently, both included some work on CV. Then, in mid-

March 1991, it was announced that the state and federal governments were ready to settle with Exxon on payment of $100 million in criminal fines and $900 million in natural resource damages, the latter to be paid over 11 years without interest. According to some newspaper accounts, the notion of a $1 billion settlement had originated with Governor-elect Hickel of Alaska in December 1990, a month before he took office. However it was conceived, it bore no known relationship to the findings of the natural resource damage assessments; several newspaper accounts suggested that they put the damages at several billions of dollars. At the request of the Hickel administration, the economic components of both the federal and state damage assessments were not publicly released. At the end of April the settlement was rejected by a federal judge in Alaska as financially inadequate relative to the magnitude of the damages. However, the judge apparently had a change of heart, for he accepted a virtually identical settlement at a hearing on October 8, 1991.

While there are still some private lawsuits by Alaskan recreationists claiming lost consumer's surplus, the settlement ended the bulk of the natural resource damage litigation. But, at least for some of the economists on both sides, the argument continued in other forums. The first grew out of DOI's revision of its regulations, as mandated by the *Ohio* ruling. In September 1989, DOI solicited comments from the public on some aspects of the revisions. The majority of comments came from economists associated with potential industrial PRPs. Most of them argued that CV was unreliable and that the estimation of non-use values should be restricted to a limited class of cases – long-lasting or irreversible damage to unique, well-known resources. In both respects, their position was effectively that the *Ohio* ruling had been wrong. Eighteen months later, in April 1991, DOI issued its new version of the regulations for public comment. These followed the *Ohio* ruling faithfully with respect to the lesser-of rule, but somewhat reluctantly with respect to the hierarchy of methods, CV, and non-use values. The preamble – but not the main text of the regulations – suggested that non-use values be limited along the lines proposed by the PRPs. With regard to the choice of methodologies, DOI remarked that «generally the use value-marketed valuation methodologies are more reliable than the use value-nonmarketed valuation methodologies, which in turn are more reliable than the non-use value-contingent valuation methodology.» Moreover, while in the preamble DOI agreed that CV was the *only* method for assessing non-use values, in the main text it opined that, when used to determine non-use values, CV was the least reliable method. To the untrained eye, these statements might seem incon-

30   PREFACE

sistent and at variance with the *Ohio* ruling. However, as before, the majority of the public comments came from the PRP side and either supported the regulatins or urged a more restrictive position with regard to to CV and non-use values.

DOI was supposed to have issued its final regulations this spring – but that was overtaken by other events. Starting in April 1991, at the time the settlement was first proposed, Exxon's economic consultants conducted a series of theoretical and empirical studies on CV for public release. That came a year later, on April 2–3 1992, when Exxon held what it described as a seminar in Washington, DC, to which it invited several hundred attorneys and government officials, along with economists who had been involved on both sides of the *Exxon Valdez* case. This was more of a public relations exercise than a conventional seminar: the only speakers were Exxon's consultants, their oral presentations were polished but light on the details, the written papers were more detailed but were not to be distributed until after the seminar was over, and questions from the floor were tightly controlled. The thrust of all the papers, which are to be published in Hausman (forthcoming), was that CV does not measure an economic value that conforms with the economic theory of preferences, that CV is biased and does not provide reliable estimates for non-use values, and that, because of the impossibility of measuring them accurately, non-use values should be omitted from natural resource damages. This seemed strongly reminiscent of Eckstein's attitude towards the travel cost method 35 years earlier: it can't be done, and you shouldn't even try. Since Exxon has not yet released the data used in the empirical studies, there has been no independent verification of whether they show what the authors claim; some questions to this effect have been raised by Carson and Hanemann (1992) based on inconsistencies in the published papers. The surveys used in these studies seem to have been conducted in a hurried manner and contain obvious potential for error. Moreover, there appear to be some problems with the theoritical analysis of non-use value. Clearly, these are matters which will be debated for a long time to come.

At the same time that Exxon was preparing for this conference, it was also vigorously lobbying the Bush administration to intervene both in DOI's damage regulations and in the regulations that NOAA would start to develop in 1992 for oil spills. The pressure on NOAA grew particularly intense. In response, the week after the Exxon seminar. NOAA's General Counsel announced that he was convening a blue-ribbon panel to advise him on the use of CV in natural resource damage assessments for oil spills. The panel is headed by two Nobel laureats – Kenneth Arrow, who had been retained by Exxon but was not on the program at the April seminar, and Robert Solow, who had been retained by the state of Alaska. The other members are the economists Edward Leamer, Paul Portney and Roy Radner, and the sociologist and survey research expert Howard Schuman. The panel has identified three questions for consideration: "(1) Can constructed market methodologies, including CV, be implemented reliably ... to calculate non-use values for natural resources? If so, under what circumstances and under what guidance? (2) If constructed market methodologies cannot be implemented to reliably calculate non-use values, what additional work or studies should be conducted to refine constructed market methodologies so they can reliably determine non-use values of natural resources? (3) What are the alternatives, if any, to the use of constructed market methodologies to reliably calculate non-use values?" The panel is receiving written testimony on these issues through October 1, 1992, It is expected to deliver its report some time in the fall. Pending its report, both NOAA and DOI have put their rule writing process on hold.

In the U.S., then, this is a somewhat exciting time for those engaged in environmental valuation. CV, in particular, faces a crucial challenge, from which it surely will emerge as a stronger tool. A recent bibliography by Carson et al. (1992) lists almost one thousand CV studies throughout the world. Much as some might wish this, it seems unlikely to vanish overnight. The concern that due weight be given to what were once known as intangibles and are now called non-use values goes back to the very beginnings of benefit-cost analysis in the US in the 1930's. This is no less valid today. It was recognized in the 1960's that benefit-cost analysis may always attract some controversy because of the crucial importance of distributional considerations. Of course, this also applies to the benefit-cost analysis of environmental projects. But, there is a sense in which non-use value plays the same role within environmental valuation that income distribution has played within conventional benefit-cost analysis: it is an indicator of the maturity of the discipline, in that the ability of economics to render an adequate accounting of it becomes the hallmark for judging its success as a social science.

References

Jan P. Acton, *Evaluating Public Programs to Save Lives: The Case of Heart Attacks* Research Report R-73-02, Rand Corporation, Santa Monica, CA, 1973.

Richard N. L. Andrews, "Economics and Environmental Decisions, Past and Present," in V. Kerry Smith (ed.) *Environmental Policy Under Reagan's Executive Order: The Role of Benefit-Cost Analysis* Chapel Hill: University of North Carolina Press. 1984.

K. J. Arrow, *social Choice and Individual Values* New York: John Wiley, 1951.

F. M. Bator, "The Simple Analytics of Welfare Maximization," *American Economic Review* 1957.

W. J. Baumol, *Welfare Economics and the Theory of the State* London: Longmans, 1952.

G. S. Becker, *Human Capital* New York: Columbia University Press, 1964.

Richard C. Bishop and Thomas A. Heberlein, "Measuring Values of Extra-Market Goods: Are Indirect Measures Biased?" *American Journal of Agricultural Economics* 61 (1979) pp. 926–30.

M. Blaug, "The Rate of Return on Investment in Education in Great Britain," *The Manchester School,* Vol. XXXIII, 3, September 1965.

Nancy E. Bockstael, Kenneth E. McConnell, and Ivar E. Strand, *Benefits from Improvements in Chesapeake Bay Water Quality* Report for USEPA Cooperative Agreement CR-811043-01-0, Washington, D. C.: US Environmental Protection Agency, 1988.

Mary J. Bowman, "Social Returns to Education," *International Social Science Journal,* Vol. XIV, No. 4, 1962.

W. G. Brown, E. N. Castle and A. Singh, *An Economic Evaluation of the Oregon Salmon and Steelhead Sport Fishery* Oregon Agricultural Experiment Station Technical Bulletin No. 78, Corvallis, 1964.

R. T. Carson, N. C. Conaway, A. Albelrini, N. Flores, K. Riggs, J. Vencil and J. Winsen, *A Bibliography of Contingent Valuation Studies and Papers* NRDA Inc, La Jolla, CA June, 1992.

Richard T. Carson and W. Michael Hanemann, "A Critique of the Exxon Papers on CV," Working paper, UC Berkeley Department of Agricultural & Resource Economics, presented at the AAEA Annual Meetings, Baltimore MD, August 10, 1992.

C. J. Cicchetti, J. Seneca, and P. Davidson, *The Demand and Supply of Outdoor Recreation.* Washington: D.C.: U.S. Bureau of Outdoor Recreation, June 1969.

Charles J. Cicchetti and V. Kerry Smith, "Congestion, Quality Deterioration, and Optimal Use: Wilderness Recreation in the Spanish Peaks Primitive Area," *Social Science Research* Vol. 2 (1973), pp. 15–30.

S. V. Ciriacy-Wantrup, "Capital Returns from Soil-Conservation Practices," *Journal of Farm Economics* 29 (1947) pp. 1181–1196.

S. V. Ciriacy-Wantrup, *Resource Conservation: Economics and Policies.* Berkeley: University of California Press, 1952.

Marion Clawson, *Methods of Measuring the Demand for and Value of Outdoor Recreation.* Reprint No. 10, Resources for the Future, Inc., Washington, 1959.

Marion Clawson and J. L. Knetsch, *Economics of Outdoor Recreation* Baltimore: Johns Hopkins Press, 1966.

R. G. Cummings, D. S. Brookshire and W. D. Schulze, *Valuing Environmental Goods: An Assessment of the Contingent Valuation Method.* New Jersey: Rowman & Allanheld, 1986.

Arthur H. Darling, "Measuring Benefits Generated by Urban Water Parks," *Land Economics* Vol. 49, No. 1 (1973) pp. 22–34.

Robert K. Davis, *The Value of Outdoor Recreation: An Economic Study of the Maine Woods* Ph.D. Dissertation, Harvard University Department of Economics, 1963.

Robert Dorfman (ed.) *Measuring Benefits of Government Investments* Washington, D. C.: The Brookings Institution, 1965.

Jules Dupuit, "De la Mesure de l'Utilite des Travaux Publics." *Annales des Ponts et Chaussees,* 2nd series, 8 (1944). Reprinted in translation as "On the Measurement of the Utility of Public Works" in *International Economic Papers,* 2 (1952) pp. 83–110.

Otto Eckstein, *Water-Resource Development: The Economics of Project Evaluation* Cambridge: Harvard University Press, 1958.

C. D. Foster and M. E. Beesley, "Estimating the Social Benefit of Constructing an Underground Railway in London," *Journal of the Royal Statistical Society,* Vol. 126, Part 1, 1963.

J. de V. Graff, *Theoretical Welfare Economics* Cambridge: Cambridge University Press, 1957.

W, Norton Grubb, Dale Whittington, and Michael Humphries, "The Ambiguities of Benefit-Cost Analysis: An Evaluation of Regulatory Impact Analyses under Executive Order 12291," in V. Kerry Smith (ed.) *Environmental Policy Under Reagan's Executive Order: The Role of Benefit-Cost Analysis* Chapel Hill: University of North Carolina Press, 1984.

Judd Hammack and Gardner Mallard Brown Jr., *Waterfowl and Wetlands: Toward Bioeconomic Analysis* Baltimore: The Johns Hopkins University Press for Resources for the Future, 1974.

R. J. Hammond, *Benefit-Cost Analysis and Water-Pollution Control* Food Research Institute, Standford University Press, 1960.

W. Michael Hanemann, *A Methodological and Empirical Study of the Recreation Benefits from Water Quality Improvement* Ph. D. Dissertation, Harvard University Department of Economics, 1978.

W. L. Hansen, "Total and Private Returns to Investment in Schooling," *Journal of Political Economy* Vol. LXXI, April 1963.

Jerry A. Hausman (ed) *Contingent Valuation: A Critical Assessment* New York: North-Holland, forthcoming.

Jack Hirshleifer, James C. de Haven, Jerome W. Milliman, *Water Supply: Economics, Technology and Policy* Chicago: University of Chicago Press, 1960.

Olav Hohmeyer, *Social Costs of Energy Consumption: External Effects of Electricity Generation in the Federal Republic of Germany* Berlin: Springer-Verlag, 1988.

Harold Hotelling, "The General Welfare in Relation to Problems of Taxation and of Railway and Utility Rates." *Econometrica* 6 (1938) pp. 242–69.

Inter-Agency River Basin Committee (Sub-Committee on Costs and Budgets), *Proposed Practices for Economic Analysis of River Basin Projects."* Washington, D. C., May 1950.

Herbert E. Klarman, "Syphilis Control Programs," in Robert Dorfman (ed.) *Measuring Benefits of Government Investments* Washington, D. C.: The Brookings Institution, 1965.

Jack L. Knetsch, "Outdoor Recreation Demands and Benefits." *Land Economics* 39 (November 1963)

Raymond J. Kopp and V. Kerry Smith, "Benefit Estimation Goes to Court: The Case of Natural Resource Damage Assessments," *Journal of Policy Analysis and Management* 8 (1989) pp. 593–612.

R. J. Kopp and V. K. Smith (eds.) *Valuing Natural Assets: The Economics of Natural Resource Damage Assessment* Washington, DC: Resources for the Future, forthcoming.

34   PREFACE

John V. Krutilla, "Conservation Reconsidered," *American Economic Review* Vol. 57, No. 4, September 1967, pp. 777–786.

John V. Krutilla and Otto Eckstein, *Multiple Purpose River Development: Studies in Applied Economics* Baltimore: Johns Hopkins Press, 1958.

Lionel J. Lerner, *Quantitative Indices of Recreational Values,* University of Nevada, Conference Proceedings of the Committee on the Economics of Water Resource Development, Report No. 11, Reno, 1962.

I. M. D. Little, *A Critique of Welfare Economics* Oxford: Oxford University Press, 1950.

Ruth P. Mack and Sumner Myers, "Outdoor Recreation," in Robert Dorfman (ed.) *Measuring Benefits of Government Investments* Washington, D. C.: The Brookings Institution, 1965.

Arthur Maass et al,, *Design of Water-Resource Systems* Cambridge, MA: Harvard University Press, 1962.

Karl-Goran Maler, *Environmental Economics: A Theoretical Inquiry* Baltimore: The Johns Hopkins University Press for Resources for the Future, 1974

Stepen A. Marglin, *Approaches to Dynamic Investment Planning* Amsterdam: North Holland, 1963.

Roland N. McKean, *Efficiency in Government Through Systems Analysis* New York: John Wiley & Sons, 1958.

Robert Cameron Mitchell and Richard T. Carson, *Using Surveys to Value Public Goods: The Contingent Valuation Method* Washington, D. C.: Resources for the Future, 1989.

H. Mohring, "Land Values and the Measurement of Highway Benefits," *Journal of Political Economy,* Vol. LXIX (June, 1961).

H. Mohring and N. Harwitz, *Highway Benefits: An Analytical Framework* North-Western University Press, 1962.

Selma J. Mushkin, "Health as an Investment," *Journal of Political Economy,* Vol. LXX (Supplement), October 1962.

Outdoor Recreation Resources Commission, *Outdoor Recreation for America: A Report to the President and the Congress.* Washington: U. S. Government Printing Office, 1962

Pace University Center for Environmental Legal Studies, *Environmental Costs of Electricty* New York: Oceana Publications, 1991.

A. R. Prest and R. Turvey, "Cost-Benefit Analysis: A Survey. *Economic Journal* December 1965.

Robert D. Rowe, W. Douglas Shaw, and William Schulze, "Nestucca Oil Spill" in Kevin M. Ward and John W. Duffield, *Natural Resource Damages: Law and Economics* New York: John Wiley, 1992.

V. Kerry Smith and William H. Desvousges, *Measuring Water Quality Benefits* Boston: Kluwer Nijhoff, 1986.

A. H. Trice and S. E. Wood, "Measurement of Recreation Benefits," *Land Economics* XXXIV (August, 1958).

Edward L. Ullman & Donald J. Volk, "An Operational Model for Predicting Reservoir Attendance and Benefits: Implications of a Location Approach to Water Recreation," *Papers of the Michigan Academy of Arts and Letters,* Vol. XLVII, 1962, pp. 473–484.

U. S. National Park Service, *The Economics of Public Recreation: An Economic Study of the Monetary Evaluation of Recreation in the National Parks.* Washington DC, 1949.

U. S. Congress, Senate. *Policies, Standards and Procedures in the Formulation, Evaluation, and Review of Plans for Use and Development of Water and Related Land Resources.* Senate Document No. 97, 87th Cong., 2d sess., 1962.

U. S. Congress, Senate. *Evaluating Standard for Primary Outdoor Recreation Benefits* Supplement No. 1, June, 1964.

Kevin M. Ward and John W. Duffield, *Natural Resource Damages: Law and Economics* New York: John Wiley, 1992.

Burton A. Weisbrod, *Economics of Public Health: Measuring the Economic Impact of Diseases* Philadelphia: University of Pennsylvania Press, 1960.

Burton A. Weisbrod, "Collective Consumption Services of Individual-Consumption Goods," *Quarterly Journal of Economics* Vol. 78, No. 3, 1964, pp. 471-7.

E. B. Wennergren, "Valuing Non-Market Priced Recreational Resources," *Land Economics,* Vol. XL, NO. 3 August, 1964.

D. M. Winch, *The Economics of Highway Planning* Toronto: University of Toronto Press, 1963.

[46]

Int Tax Public Finance (2007) 14: 349–364
DOI 10.1007/s10797-007-9036-x

Reflections on the general theory of second best at its golden jubilee

Richard G. Lipsey

Published online: 13 June 2007
© Springer Science+Business Media, LLC 2007

Abstract The origin of the second best article is described and criticisms assessed. Distortions making impossible the achievement of either first or second best optima are outlined. Attempts to establish the applicability of first best rules are criticised, as are general rules for making piecemeal efficiency improvements. Both often use models containing empirically invalid assumptions and a selected few of the full set of distortions. Practical policy advice requires more parochial objective functions than community welfare; must rely on formal and appreciative theory, empirical evidence, and large doses of judgment; and should concentrate on making piecemeal improvements in context-specific situations.

Keywords Second best · Piecemeal policies · Context-specific policies · Distortions · Efficiency conditions · Optimality conditions

JEL Classification D60

1 Formal and appreciative theorising

We begin by noting two approaches to theorising and policy advising. *Formal theories* are expressed mathematically, while *appreciative theories* are developed rigorously in verbal terms. The contrast between the two can be seen by considering two types of argument justifying the market economy.

This paper is a revised version of a Key Note Address
Presented to the 62nd Congress of the International Institute of Public Finance.
I am indebted to Robin Boadway, Mark Blaug, Avinash Dixit, and Curtis Eaton for criticisms and suggestions.

R.G. Lipsey (✉)
Simon Fraser University, RR#1 Q70, Bowen Island, BC, V0N 1G0 Canada
e-mail: rlipsey@sfu.ca

The first is the formal proof of the "two fundamental theorems of welfare economics." The important proposition for what follows is that the perfectly competitive idealisation of the market economy leads in equilibrium to an *efficient* allocation of resources and, given sufficient value judgements (e.g., a social welfare function can be assumed, and theoretical compensation is a valid criterion for judging social gains), to an *optimal* allocation.[1]

Although the proof of the efficiency and optimality of the perfectly competitive market is an intellectual triumph, it raises practical problems because the required assumptions do not mirror reality. So, economists must rely on their subjective judgements about the relevance of these theorems to policy. Here opinions vary from 'highly relevant' to 'totally irrelevant'—surely a most unsatisfactory situation.[2]

The second argument uses appreciative theorising. Two key propositions are (1) the market system co-ordinates economic activity better than any known alternative— not optimally, just better than the alternatives and (2) markets do this *relatively* efficiently by producing prices that are influenced (but not solely determined) by relative scarcities.[3]

Those who rely on the formal defence typically seek to give policy advice that is derived 'scientifically' from theories containing neither value judgements nor guesswork. Those who rely on the informal defence typically deny this possibility, seeking instead to base advice on a combination of formal models, appreciative theorising, empirical knowledge, and a large dose of judgement.[4] In what follows, examples of each approach are discussed and arguments are advanced for the practicality of the latter alternative.

2 The genesis of the general theory of second best

During my first term as a PhD student at the LSE, I attended a lecture by Dr. Helen Makower on Viner's *Theory of Customs Unions* (1950). Although the concepts of

---

[1] In public economics, much is made of the distinction between the purely positive concept of a Pareto efficient allocation and the normative one of an optimum allocation, which requires the value judgements referred to in the text. Most of what is mentioned in this paper is applicable to both concepts.

[2] Blaug (2007) refers to the differences in views over the practical applicability of the welfare theorems as economists' "intellectual schizophrenia" and goes on to contrast the judgement of Baumol and Akerlof on the real-world inapplicability of the theorems with statements such as Starr's (1997:151) that they provide "...a significant defence of the market's resource allocation mechanism" and Mas-Colell et al. (1995: 556) that they offer "...a strong conceptual affirmation of the use of competitive markets, even for dealing with distributional issues."

[3] This justification uses two other well-known propositions: compared to its alternatives, a well-functioning market economy with the necessary institutional underpinnings (i) has fewer concentrations of power, involves less coercion, and fewer opportunities for corruption (not 'none' just 'less' and 'fewer') and (ii) is more conducive to growth. Some readers have suggested that the informal justification must have some formal theory behind it. To the contrary, it has been based on a long line of appreciative theorising running from Adam Smith to Milton Freedman and Thomas Schelling and many others who have expounded these four propositions verbally.

[4] For example, Baumol (2002: 143) calls the second theorem a "fairy tale" that should be discarded, or as Mark Blaug (1997: 255) puts it: "...these beautiful theorems are mental exercises without the slightest possibility of ever being practically relevant...".

trade creation and trade diversion seemed insightful, I thought they neglected the demand side. That night in a flurry of excitement, I developed the proof that the demand side benefits could outweigh the supply side losses of trade diversion, a proof that I subsequently published in Lipsey (1957). Over the next two years, 1953–1955, I worked on customs union theory. My PhD dissertation was accepted in 1958 and subsequently published (Lipsey 1970).[5]

During my first year on the staff, 1955–1956, it occurred to me while reading an article on customs unions by Andrew Ozga (1955) that many economists, myself included, were discovering the same result in different contexts but not recognising its generality. When Kelvin Lancaster entered my room, we discussed my insight. He said it had occurred to him, when reading Samuelson's *Foundations* (1947), that there was no justification for piecemeal policies establishing first best conditions when the fully efficient allocation was not attainable.[6] Later that day, I expounded my insight to Harry Johnson who encouraged me to develop it. Kelvin invented a proof of the main proposition that afternoon and submitted it to *The Review of Economic Studies*. Harry, who was one of its editors, suggested that Kelvin and I should join forces. He argued that Kelvin's bare proof would probably go unnoticed and to have an impact we must relate our proposition to the existing literature.[7] He provided several references unknown to me. So the form in which the article finally appeared owed much to Harry.[8]

2.1 What was new?

What I should have known was that James Meade covered many second best issues in his *Trade and Welfare*. But as explained in detail in Lipsey (1997: Introduction), I had neither attended his lectures nor seen the proofs of *Trade and Welfare* that my fellow graduate student, Max Cordon, was reading in 1953–1954. Nonetheless, it may have been in the air where I picked it up unconsciously—in a not unfamiliar story concerning originality.

Neither did I know of the many precursors to my 'original' idea. In the *Palgrave Dictionary* (1987: 280), Peter Bohm states: "This state of affairs in 1956 was somewhat puzzling considering that the Lipsey–Lancaster conclusion was not entirely novel." He notes that both Pareto and Samuelson had observed that if some of the optimum conditions could not be fulfilled, there was no presumption that fulfilling others would improve efficiency or welfare.

---

[5] I have told the surrounding story in more detail in Lipsey (1997: Introduction: An Intellectual Autobiography).

[6] This is not something I could have done at the time because I had arrived at the LSE to do my PhD totally innocent of anything beyond high-school mathematics and had to teach myself the calculus that I needed for my thesis.

[7] Of the articles subsequently cited in Lipsey and Lancaster (1956), I had read at that time: Viner (1950), Corlett and Hague (1953–1954), Ozga (1955) and Little (1951). I am indebted to Robin Boadway for pointing out the importance in this context of Ramsey's paper on optimal taxes and Hotelling's on monopoly pricing, a precursor of optimal tax theory.

[8] As originally published, the article had an embarrassingly large number of slips in the formal manipulations, particularly in the sections on the nationalised industry and the general proof of the main theorem. I corrected these when the article was reprinted in Lipsey (1997) (although the section numbers were for some unaccountable reason, omitted from that reprint).

🖄 Springer

All I do know is that in my office that morning in 1954, I got the insight in a blinding flash.

2.2 Some terminology

Factors preventing attaining an efficient resource allocation are variously called 'constraints' or 'distortions.' Since neither of these terms cover everything that follows, I use the term "sources of divergence," *sources* for short. I define these as anything that if introduced on its own would prevent the achievement of a perfectly competitive, price-taking equilibrium that was Pareto efficient and otherwise attainable.

Some confusion was caused by our use of terms. A 'second best situation' referred to *any* situation in which the first best was unachievable. The 'second best optimum setting' for any *source* referred to the setting of that *source* that maximises the value of the objective function, given settings on all the other existing sources. I follow those usages here.

2.3 What we thought it said

Bohm (1987: 281) says L&L "...tried to formulate a constraint which would cover most of what the literature had observed as obstacles to achieving a first best Pareto optimum." We clearly did not think deeply enough about the kinds and origins of our *sources*. But we did believe that their ubiquity made it impossible to fulfil most first-best conditions and that the issues that resulted would be revealed by any *source* that made a first best unattainable.[9] So our one irremovable *source* stood for the vast number of *sources* that could not be removed in given circumstances. Some criticisms seemed to miss that point.

- Athanasiou (1966) argued that our constraint of a monopolist charging k times marginal cost was unrealistic because the profit maximising relation between marginal cost and price changes as the demand curve shifts. We agree. But the k rule was meant illustratively not realistically.
- The theory lacks generality because it is inapplicable where the economy is separable, for example, no externalities and a subset of traded goods that are neither complements or substitutes[10] (Davis and Whinston 1965). Agreed, if two parts of the economy do not communicate with each other, there can be no second best inter-relations between them. This is what L&L meant to rule out when we assumed a "general equilibrium"—everything depended on everything else. I do not, however agree that this qualification has the effect of "narrowing the domain of the second best conditions... [making] the application of second best rules appear manageable..." (McKee and West 1981: 439) since I know of few, if any, empirically demonstrated cases of separability.

---

[9]Indeed most of the then-existing books on welfare economics devoted much space to showing the how impossible it would be to fulfil the efficiency conditions in real world. See, for example, Little (1957) and de Graff (1957).

[10]The latter condition requires that the good has a unit elasticity of demand and be additively separable from all other goods in the utility function.

- The theory has been characterised as "...having as its aim, the recommendation of a particular policy to some existing government..." (McKee and West: 441) and has been criticised for positing a benevolent policy maker (Hoff 2001). But our proof says nothing about the motivation of policymakers. It only predicts the outcome of policies adopted in second best situations for any reason.
- "...the policy recommendations depend on the taste/technology specifications of the model and the latter are difficult to assess empirically" (Hoff 2001). We believed that second best conditions would be far too complex to provide realistic policy guides. Hoff's point reinforces this, as does Athanasiou (1966: 85) when he writes: "...it is hard to see how any of the imperfections current at a time will be so enduring and stiff as to justify an adjustment of the whole system to them." Indeed, governments do not attempt to achieve either first or second best optima, nor do they often attempt to remove the source of the "distortion;" instead they often attempt to influence its consequences.

2.4 An illustration of what it said

For illustrative purposes in what follows, I summarise the example in Lipsey and Lancaster (1956: Sect. V). Let there be a small country specialised in the production of commodity X and importing commodities Y and Z at fixed prices. Initially assume an equal ad valorem tariff on the imports and no other sources of 'distortion.' In this situation, there will be too much consumption of the domestic good X and too little of both imports Y and Z compared with the first best optimum. To consider a customs union, I asked: given that consumption of the domestic good is untaxed while imports of Z are subject to a fixed duty, t_z, what is the second best import duty, t_y, on commodity Y? What I proved was that for a second best optimum (i) $t_y > t_z$, (ii) $0 < t_y < t_z$, (iii) $t_y < 0$ (a subsidy), according as in consumption Y is (i) complementary with X, (ii) a substitute for both X and Z (iii) complementary with Z.

3 First and second best resource allocations

Next, I argue that the set of realistic policy goals does not include achieving either an economy-wide, Pareto efficient allocation of resources or an economy-wide second best setting for any one *source*.

3.1 Types of *sources*

L&L did not give enough consideration to the nature of *sources*. Some are created by private agents, some are created by the state and some are given exogenously and cannot be altered by policy. It is often argued that exogenously given constraints become part of the first best solution and so can be ignored, leaving only policy-created *sources* to be the subject of second best theory. Although such things as the budget and resource constraints are not *sources*, other exogenous constraints are. For example, because information is costly to acquire, agents remain 'rationally ignorant' when the cost of acquisition exceeds its value to the agent. But the state can rationally acquire the information and provide it to agents at a cost-covering price that is a fraction of each agent's private acquisition cost (assuming that the state's cost is less than the sum of individual agents costs). This example illustrates the important proposition that *sources* that are in the nature of things can lead to inefficient allocations so that there is scope for policy intervention to improve efficiency as long as some of the consequences can be altered. So not all *sources* are policy created, something that is denied by many writers who seek to restore first best conditions as guides for piecemeal policy (e.g., Faith and Thompson 1981; McKee and West 1981 and Hoff 2001).

Next, consider some of the most important real-world *sources, many of which are not policy created* .

3.2 Static considerations[11]

1. Market structures are rarely competitive enough to make marginal cost equal to price: oligopoly, monopolistic competition and monopoly vastly outnumber cases where firms are price takers. Some price setting behaviour occurs because of technologically determined factors such as scale economies, some because of firm-determined entry barriers and product characteristics[12] and some because of policy.
2. Since most products are differentiated, fixed costs that create significant non-convexities are ubiquitous: entry costs to establish distribution networks, product development costs, and advertising needed to introduce new products.
3. Location in space creates overlapping oligopolies where neither monopolistic nor perfect competition is typically possible (Eaton and Lipsey 1989 and 1997: Introductory Essay). Fixed costs ensure that space is inhabited by "lumpy" firms located at distinct points in space. This implies that free entry will not drive profits to zero (Eaton and Lipsey 1978). Furthermore, the Nash equilibrium under free entry produces a pattern of rectangular markets rather than the efficient pattern of Löschian hexagons (Eaton and Lipsey 1976).
4. Many labour markets are not auction markets. Wages are often payments on implicit long term economic contracts, varying with age. Wages are often signalling devices. Labour markets are often internal, employers promoting existing employees rather than searching outside for better candidates. Even where these, and many other similar forms of behaviour, are efficient responses to non-perfectly competitive circumstances, they upset the Paretian conditions in labour markets.
5. Governments intervene in many markets with such things as rules, regulations quantity restrictions, taxes and subsidies, import tariffs and non-tariff barriers.
6. Incomplete and asymmetric information abounds.

---

[11]No doubt, there is some overlap among these items and if I were writing a text book, I would strive to remove them. For present purposes, however, the extent and variety of *sources* is what matters so that any overlap among *sources* does not detract from the general argument.

[12]There is no impersonal market in which the price of a generic version of differentiated products, such as refrigerators, is determined. Individual manufacturers must administer their own prices and take externally determined sales as their market signals. For discussion of the effect of product differentiation on the competitive model see Eaton and Lipsey (1989).

7. Positive and negative externalities are attached to many economic activities.
8. There are many missing markets.
9. One of the foundations of welfare economics, the maximisation of utility functions in which the only arguments are the commodities consumed by the agent in question, is currently being challenged (Layard 2005). Modern research confirms that individuals are social animals and what others do enters into their utility functions in myriad ways. This greatly alters the set of policy changes that can increase welfare.

3.3 Dynamic considerations: endogenous technological change[13]

Innovation typically involves Knightian uncertainty (Knight 1921). Risky events have well-defined probability distributions and expected values. Uncertain events have neither. In a risky situation, two agents desiring the same objective, having the same information, and choosing among the same alternative actions, will make the same choice—the one that maximises the expected value of the outcome. In uncertain situations, however, these two agents may make different choices, neither of which can be shown *ex ante* to be better than the other.

Because firms make R&D choices under uncertainty, there is no unique line of behaviour that maximises their expected profits—if there were, all equally well-informed competing firms seeking the same breakthrough would be doing identical R&D.[14] Thus, firms are better seen as groping into an uncertain future in a profit-seeking manner, rather than maximising the present value of expected future profits. Such groping behaviour makes technological trajectories path dependent and non-unique. An important implication is that the conditions for an efficient allocation of resources cannot even be defined when technology is changing endogenously under conditions of uncertainty—we do not know what allocation will produce the best results, however defined, until *after* the results are in. From this follows that there does not exist a set of scientifically determined optimal public policies with respect any variable such as taxes, subsidies, tariffs, commercial and industrial policy, that influence R&D directly or indirectly.

3.4 Conclusion

We do not have a GE model of an institutionless, fully free market economy with the mix of market forms and that characterises a typical industrialised economy. Thus, there is no compelling theory or evidence to suggest that such economies are statically efficient and many government policies reveal the judgement that the allocation achieved by such markets can be improved. Furthermore, we do not have a model that incorporates the other static *sources* mentioned above. Finally, once we allow for endogenous technological change accomplished under uncertainty, we cannot even define the conditions for an efficient allocation of resources. The upshot is that in

---

[13]The material in this section is based on Lipsey et al. (2005: Chaps. 2 and 4).

[14]Compelling illustrations of the consequences of choice made under uncertainty are seen when competing Japanese and American firms make different R&D decisions although both are searching for the next advance in some product over which they compete. For examples, see Dertouzos et al. (1989).

practical situations, as opposed to theoretical models, we do not know the necessary and sufficient conditions for achieving an economy-wide, first-best allocation of resources.

Achieving an economy-wide second best optimum allocation looks even more difficult than achieving the first best. Without a model of the general equilibrium that contains most let alone all of the above *sources*, we cannot specify the existing situation formally and so cannot calculate the second best optimum setting for any one *source* that is subject to policy change.[15] This is an important point since much of the literature that is critical of second best theory assumes that economists know a distortion when they see one and know that the ideal policy is to remove the distortion directly, something that is necessarily welfare improving only in the imaginary one-distortion world.

This leaves us with two questions: (1) Can we find general conditions for piecemeal improvements in welfare? (2) Can we make piecemeal improvements in specific situations? I consider these questions in Sects. 5 and 6. But first, I must consider some issues that arose from our article but which I could not critique without the material just covered.

4 Subsequent developments

Boadway (1997a: 3) points out, the large literature on optimal taxes, as well as several other issues in public economics, address second best problems. However, I find that when graduate students trained in general theory are asked for policy advice with respect to a taxed market, they typically suggest removing the 'distortion' with no consideration of possible second best ramifications.

As discussed by Davis and Whinston (1965 and 1967), two interpretations of second best theory were advanced soon after our article. One, advocated by authors such as McManus (1958–1959) and Bohm (1967), argued that "...all relevant economic problems must be solved within the context of a general equilibrium model (Davis and Whinston 1967: 324)." The other, championed by D&W, was that "...it is not helpful (and probably not feasible) to view all economic problems within the context of a general equilibrium model (Davis and Whinston 1967: 324)." D&W investigate conditions under which piecemeal policy can apply second best rules to a sub-set of the economy while ignoring the remainder. Lancaster and I saw the message of our article as being close to D&W's interpretation. However, because of the existence of a wide range of *sources*, most of which are not even considered in existing models, we believed that for all practical purposes global second best maxima were unobtainable and also that the piecemeal application of first best rules, where they could be imposed, had no guarantee of improving efficiency. So what remained for policy was to make piecemeal changes.

There is insufficient space to consider all of the many attempts to show that piecemeal policy based on establishing first best conditions is still relevant. I consider three very different arguments each of which has been widely quoted with approval.

---

[15] Indeed, Boadway reports that "Stiglitz general account of conditions for welfare improvements in multi-consumer situations are technical and not easy to interpret." And this is in a model that ignores virtually all of the *sources* listed above!

Faith and Thompson (1981) introduce a monopoly as the single 'distortion' and argue: "While much of the applied literature appealing to "second best" arguments suggests all sorts of informational limitations on government decisions makers, this is hardly reasonable given that the decision maker must know the $U[t]$ and $T[t]$ functions in order to ascertain the second best policy."[16] So the only plausible reason for not attacking a distortion directly is that voters do not trust policy makers to adopt the correct policy of a per unit subsidy and a lump sum tax. But a second best set of taxes on the rest of the economy designed to increase the monopolist's output to the competitive level would also increase its profits, causing a paradox between what was not allowed directly but was allowed through a second best back door. The paradox is removed by adopting a set of taxes and subsidies in the rest of the economy that leaves the monopoly unaffected. This, not surprisingly, calls for zero taxes. So the paradox is removed by applying first best elsewhere, leaving the monopoly unaffected.

My objections are as follows. First, the argument that the only source of persistent 'distortion' is fear of perverse behaviour on the part of government requires the unjustified belief that governments understand the general equilibrium of the entire economy. This understanding is required if, as F&T assume, governments can design a global second best policy. If as I argue, policy makers lack the required knowledge, monopolies may be tolerated for reasons other than fear. Second, policy makers are faced with many *sources*, that are not policy induced. When in a many-*source* economy they seek to alter the behaviour of a monopoly, they do so in a second best setting where making marginal cost equal price (whether by acting directly on the firm or indirectly by altering things that impinge on its decision) is not necessarily the optimal policy.

The second example alleges that "The Lipsey–Lancaster formulation . . . begs the question of why the distortion that makes the economy second best is out of bounds for policy makers. . ." (Hoff 2001). "Bohm (1967) recognised that if the distortion were escapable, that is accessible to direct policy action, the second best policy would, by definition, vanish" (McKee and West 1981: 442).[17] In a world of many *sources* of various kinds, attacking all *sources* directly is not a feasible policy and removing some does raise second best issues. The same comment applies to Bhagwati (1971: 77) who argues that optimal policy is to attack the source of the distortion directly.

Anther argument for a presumption in favour of first best policies has been advanced by Ng (1977) and quoted favourably by several authors (e.g., Hoff 2001; Bohm 1987).[18] He assumes a parametric 'constraint,' c_p, and one that can be varied by policy, c_v, plus a welfare function that is concave plotted against the degree of

---

[16]This argument puts Faith and Thompson in the same camp as McManus and Bohm in holding that second best policies consist of solving the GE of the entire economy to produce the second best optimum.

[17]Space limitations prevent me from considering in detail McKee and West's (1981) critique of second best. They are in the camp who believes that all relevant distortions must be policy induced and they develop a critique based on the idea that many of these are optimal outcomes of the political market place. Possibly, but many sources are not policy induced and of those at least some are welfare reducing.

[18]Ng calls a situation in which the second best optimum cannot be achieved and small improvements in welfare are sought "third best." We call this piecemeal second best policy (as opposed to optimum second best polices) but as long as we know what is being done, the words used to describe it are immaterial.

departure from the first best rule by either constraint because "... it is reasonable to expect that as we diverge more and more from the first-best rule, the marginal damage increases" (Ng 1977: 2–3). First, establish a first best by setting both constraints at zero. Then, set the parametric constraint at a non-zero level. This shifts the welfare function $W = W(\bar{c}_p, c_v)$ but the policy makers do not know which way it has shifted. If altering c_v moves the economy towards its second best optimum, the absolute value of the welfare gain is less, by the convexity assumption, than the absolute value of the welfare loss if the alteration moves the economy away from its second best optimum. So the expected value of the utility function is maximised by holding to the first best rule, $c_v = 0$.

Ng takes as "reasonable" the convexity of the welfare function plotted against the degree of departure from the first best solution. But this is by no means necessary. As an illustration, consider the example outlined in Sect. 2.4 above with the addition of a Cobb Douglas utility function as analysed in Lipsey (1970), $U = X^\alpha Y^\beta Z^\gamma$. The implied welfare function $W = W(t_y, t_z)$ is maximised for $t_y = t_z = 0$.[19] However, the function $W = W(t_y, \overline{t_z})$ is not everywhere convex. While its first derivative is everywhere negative, its second derivative shifts from negative to positive as t_y increases beyond a point of inflection. This should not be surprising since it is impossible to drive welfare to zero with any finite level of tax given these tastes. So while as t_y is increased over some range starting from zero the W function does get steeper, eventually its steepness begins to decrease. Hence for this case Ng's argument is correct for some small enough values of $\overline{t_z}$ but is reversed for larger values since the expected value of a small increase in t_y from zero is then positive.

5 Are there general policy rules for piecemeal improvements?

My answer to the question posed in the heading is "no". As Boadway (1997b: 756–657) puts it: "...though duality theory operationalised second-best theory, the results were not encouraging: simple piecemeal policy rules do not hold in a distorted, second-best world except under extremely unlikely combinations of taste and technology." And this is said without taking into account most of the *sources* that I outlined in Sect. 3.

Nonetheless, some economists have tried to develop useful *general rules* for making piecemeal improvements. To consider these, I first look at Harberger's classic 1971 article, where he argues that second best policies are easier to establish than L&L maintained. In a space for the set of all (economic) activities he plots the subset of those that are affected by significant 'distortions' and the subset of activities that would be affected if public policy alters one of these. He argues that the intersection of these sets is all that matters for small changes in public policy because a marginal policy-induced change in any non-distorted activity has no significant effect on welfare. He states that the area of this intersection is small enough "...to dispel

---

[19]For the case of $\alpha = \beta = \gamma = 1/3$, the welfare function is $U = [\frac{A^3 i^2 j^2}{p_y p_z (ij+i+j)^3}]^{1/3}$ (Lipsey 1970: page 46, (1)) where the $i = (t_x + 1)$, $j = (t_z + 1)$, A is the country's endowment of X and p_y and p_z are the prices of the two imports the domestic good, p_x being the numeraire.

any thoughts that the job of incorporating general-equilibrium aspects is so big as to be effectively hopeless." (791) My response is twofold. First, the material in Sect. 3 makes me sceptical of Harberger's judgement that the proportion of the total space affected by 'distortions' (my *sources*) is small. As a first approximation, I would say it was close to 100%. Second, I know of no evidence that the space of activities that is significantly affected by the typical new policy is small. After all, sectors everywhere can be affected by a 'distortion' anywhere and to say that only a few markets will be affected by changing a *source* in one is an empirical judgement whose substantiation requires evidence gathered case by case.

I now consider some specific generalisations. Most of these, as well as the three more general arguments that I criticised in the previous section, are subject to three types of objection.

Type 1 objections: Only one type of *source* is considered, such as taxes, and then usually only two items from this *source*, one that is given and one that can be varied by policy. No one knows if the results will stand in models with more items from the one type of *source* plus items from other *sources*.

Type 2 objections: Many of the propositions are based on restrictive assumptions not found in reality and so provide no obvious guide for practical policy.

Type 3 objections: The possible effect on technological change is ignored—a serious shortcoming since small induced changes in the growth rate can have large cumulative effects on GDP.

Many of the specific generalisations that follow are corollaries of the one proposition stated in Sect. 2.4 above: when all goods are substitutes for each other and are subject to a set of indirect taxes, the second best value of any one tax, given fixed values of all the others, is lower than the highest tax and higher than the lowest tax. We use this example in what follows

1. *Lowering the highest distortion must be welfare increasing.* In the three commodity case if $t_y > t_z$ reducing t_y will necessarily increase welfare only if Y and X are substitutes in consumption. If they are complementary, reducing the value of t_y in the neighbourhood of the value of t_z will necessarily reduce welfare.
2. *Two small distortions are better than one large one.* This is not necessarily true on its own terms (ignoring all three types of objections, which also apply). We saw when discussing Ng, that if the utility function is Cobb–Douglas, the function showing how welfare changes with the variable constraint goes through a point of inflection. It follows that for some high enough tax rates, situation 1 in which $(t_{y_1} = t_{z_1} > 0)$ will yield less welfare than situation 2 in which $(t_{y_2} = 2t_{y_1}, t_z = 0)$.[20]
3. *The optimal level of a policy reduced distortion will fall short of correcting the distortion fully.*[21] Again this is not true if Y and Z are complementary in consumption, in which case not only is each reduction of the tariff on Y down to zero welfare improving, the second best optimum requires $t_y < 0$.

---

[20]For example for the utility function given in the previous footnote the utility associated with a uniform 50% tariff on Y and Z is less than the utility associated with a 100% tariff on Y and a zero tariff on Z.

[21]Hoff (2001) attributes this to Bhagwati (1971). Hoff does not mention the qualification that the goods must be substitutes while Bhagwati does.

4. *A small dose of a policy that has some effect on the distorted margin is better than no policy at all, because the initial marginal gain from mitigating the distorted market is of first order while the initial welfare cost from introducing the new distortion is of second order.* Bhagwati et al. (1969: 1009) This applies only to the case where the policy introduces a distortion that was previously zero. Given the *sources* discussed in the previous section, it is hard to identify a real world market that does not already contain some *sources* such as marginal cost does not equal price.

5. *Starting from an arbitrary set of tax rates and reducing the highest and raising the lowest will be welfare increasing if tax receipts rise in both markets and if both goods are substitutes for the aggregate of all goods.* (Hatta 1986: 105) This theorem not only requires the conditions stated in point 4 but also that there are no other types of taxes (and no other *sources* since their possible effects on the theorem are not investigated).

6. *Starting from a tax-distorted situation, a proportional reduction in the size of all distortions will generally raise welfare.* (Atkinson and Stiglitz 1976 as quoted by Boadway 1997a: 11)

All of these, and virtually all other similar propositions in public economics, are open to type 1 objections in that all types of *sources* other than the one being considered are ignored. For example in point 6, how do we measure an "equal reduction" in each of the many items in each of the types of *sources*?

Almost all of these generalisations are open to type 2 objections in that all but number 6 require restrictive assumptions about substitutability. Other generalisation not listed here are also open to type 2 objections in that they make empirically unsupported assumptions about separability in the utility function.

All the generalisations are also subject to type 3 objections. For example, with respect number 2, two monopolistically competitive firms, each with only a small divergence between marginal cost and price may not be better than one oligopoly with a large divergence yielding high profits used to finance R&D?

6 Context specific piecemeal policies

Can we use welfare economics to derive useful policies that are not open to the objections already stated? It is more obviously useful where the objectives are more parochial than maximising the welfare of the whole society, the objective function is clearly specified, spillovers may not matter (or can be roughly taken into account), partial equilibrium analysis is useful and both direct and the most obvious indirect effects can be measured.

Harberger seems to agree when he writes (1971: 795) that rather than telling how to reach global second or first best optima "[t]he practitioner...is more likely to be asked which of two alternative agricultural programs is better, or what resource-allocation costs a given tax increases involves, or whether a certain bridge is worth its cost." Here are further examples.

Let the task be to reduce noxious emissions by a given amount at the least cost. There may be indirect effects, but either these do not matter to policy makers or

 Springer

they can be roughly estimated. Unlike theories that predict how to maximise society's welfare, the predictions of these theories concerning the relative advantages of alternatives can be tested against direct measurements of the results.

For years Ontario Hydro insisted on pricing electricity at the average cost of production by low-cost hydro electric, high-cost coal fired and medium-cost atomic energy. New plants all produced at costs higher than this average but were built whenever there was excess demand at the going price although customers were unwilling to pay the marginal cost of producing electricity with them.

Many principal agent problems are fairly contained. The principal is interested in getting good work from his agents. Theories about alternative methods of doing this can be tested against observable results. There may be second best side effects but that is not the issue. The economist's brief is to get what the principal wants at the least cost.

In these and most similar cases, policy advisers need a good knowledge of 'Harberger rectangles,' the theory related to such things as pollution permits, and a general understanding of second best issues as a caution, while highly sophisticated formal GE theory adds little value to the tool kit. When such non-GE methods can be used and how many indirect effects to consider are a judgements based on appreciative theorising—not something that can be established conclusively through formal modelling.

But although there can be few if any valid general *policies,* much of the useful work emanating from second best theory has been to develop scientific *approaches* that can be generally useful when adapted to local circumstances. For example, cost-benefit analysis is an area where scientific principles based on second-best analysis have been widely and successfully applied. The notion of shadow pricing of project inputs and outputs to take account of market 'distortions' is a general principle. Nonetheless, because these techniques do not take account of all *sources,* a large element of judgement is needed whenever they are used to derive specific policy advice.

7 Conclusion

In all practical circumstances, economists investigate policy issues using methods that omit a potentially significant subset of *sources.* Thus, we must of necessity make personal judgements about the applicability of such models when predicting where piecemeal, second-best improvements are possible. This is one of the many reasons why policy advice must use a mixture of formal modelling, appreciative theorising, relevant evidence and an inevitable amount of judgement—and why it must be context specific (i.e., there are few practical generalisations that apply to each and every set of items in each and every *source*). The task is easier if the objective function is more circumscribed than the whole society's welfare. Although this may be obvious to economists with policy experience, it is not a warning typically emphasised in public economics texts. These mainly give students rigorous proofs of propositions that appear to be policy relevant and universally applicable, but are open to the types of objections stated earlier. Much of the literature that I have surveyed (and there is

 Springer

much more than I have had space to review) directly objects to these second best conclusions arguing that scientifically derived first best conditions are applicable to real policy situations.

Finally, I offer two replies to the allegation that second best theory provides justification for just about any crazy interventionist policy.

First best theory is also often used perversely as when it is used to justify the one-size-fits-all policy advice that often does more harm than good. For example, it is counter productive to advise a developing country to remove its "distorting" subsides on sugar production when the result is the elimination of its sugar industry by subsidised US production while its former workers remain unemployed.[22] The best response to these one-size-fits-all policy advisors is to observe that they are operating in a second best situation and that, since the specific *sources* vary temporally and spatially, the policies needed for piecemeal improvements also vary.

My second reply is that the 'anything goes' implication seems persuasive because it is viewed from the aspect of the formal defence of the price system and the scientific approach to policy advice. When the intuitive appreciative approach is used, both to defend the market economy and to assess policies, it is easier to spot counter productive advice. According to the appreciative approach, since the competitive market economy is the best known method of allocating resources, departures from it through either public policy or private behaviour, are regarded as *prima facie* undesirable, unless justified by well-reasoned and persuasive arguments. This is sufficient to rule out the kinds of massive tariffs that used to be found in many developing countries, but not to rule out carefully designed, administered and sunsetted infant industry tariffs. It also rules out private sector actions in restraint of competition, again unless there are very good reasons for them. Highly elaborate theory is not necessary in these cases and many others like them. What is needed is a good appreciative understanding of how the price system works, as well as understanding the cautionary warning from second best theory that any policy may have unexpected and undesirable consequences in apparently unrelated parts of the economy that need to be watched for and mitigated where necessary. Useful piecemeal policy advising is not impossible; neither can it be determined purely scientifically; instead it is an art, assisted by good economics, both theoretical and empirical.

References

Athanasiou, L. (1966). Some notes on the theory of second best. *Oxford Economic Papers*, *18*(1), 83–87, March.

Atkinson, A. B., & Stiglitz, J. E. (1976). The design of the tax structure: direct versus indirect taxation. *Journal of Public Economics*, 6, 55–75.

Baumol, W. J. (2002). *The free market innovation machine*. Princeton: Princeton University Press.

Bhagwati, J. N. (1971). The generalized theory of distortions and welfare. In J. N. Bhagwati, R. W. Jones, R. Mundell, & J. Vanek (Eds.), *Trade, balance of payments and growth: papers in international economics in honor of V. Charles P. Kindleberger* (pp. 69–90). Amsterdam: North-Holland.

Bhagwati, J. N., Ramaswami, V. K., & Srinivasan, T. N. (1969). Domestic distortions, tariffs, and the theory of optimum subsidy: some further results. *Journal of Political Economy*, 77, 1005–1019.

---

[22] For examples of this sort of misguided policy see Griffiths (2003).

Blaug, M. (1997). Competition as an end-state and competition as a process. In *Trade technology and economics: essays in honour of Richard G. Lipsey* (pp. 241–261). Cheltenham: Edward Elgar.

Blaug, M. (2007). The fundamental theorems of modern welfare economics, historically contemplated. *History of Political Economy*, *32*(2), 186–207.

Boadway, R. (1997a). The role of second-best theory in public economics. In B. C. Eaton, & R. G. Harris (Eds.), *Trade, technology and economics essays in honour of Richard G. Lipsey* (pp. 3–25). Cheltenham: Edward Elgar.

Boadway, R. (1997b). Public economics and the theory of public policy. *The Canadian Journal of Economics*, *30*, 753–772.

Bohm, P. (1967). On the theory of 'second best'. *Review of Economic Studies*, *34*, 301–314.

Bohm, P. (1987). Second best. In J. Eatwell, M. Milgate, & P. Newman (Eds.), *The new palgrave, a dictionary of economics* (pp. 280–283). London: Macmillan.

Corlett, W. J., & Hague, D. C. (1953–1954). Complementarity and the excess burden of taxation. *The Review of Economic Studies*, *21*, 21–30.

Davis, O. A., & Whinston, A. B. (1965). Welfare economics and the theory of second best. *Review of Economic Studies*, *32*, 1–14.

Davis, O. A., & Whinston, A. B. (1967). Piecemeal policy in the theory of second best. *Review of Economic Studies*, *34*, 323–331.

de Graff, J. (1957). *Theoretical welfare economics*. Cambridge: Cambridge University Press.

Dertouzos, M. L., Lester, R., & Solow, R. (1989). *Made in America: regaining the productive edge*. London: MIT Press.

Eaton, B. C., & Lipsey, R. G. (1976). The non-uniqueness of equilibrium in the Loschian model of spatial location. *American Economic Review*, *66*, 77–93.

Eaton, B. C., & Lipsey, R. G. (1978). Freedom of entry and the existence of pure profit. *Economic Journal*, *88*, 455–469.

Eaton, B. C., & Lipsey, R. G. (1989). Product differentiation. In R. Schmalensee, & R. Willig (Eds.), *Handbook of industrial organization* (pp. 725–768). Amsterdam: North Holland.

Eaton, B. C., & Lipsey, R. G. (1997). *On the foundations of monopolistic competition and economic geography: the selected essays of B. Curtis Eaton and Richard G. Lipsey*. Cheltenham: Edward Elgar.

Faith, R. L., & Thompson, E. A. (1981). A paradox in the theory of second best. *Economic Inquiry*, *XIX*, 235–244.

Griffiths, P. (2003). *The economist's tale: a consultant encounters hunger and the World Bank*. New York: ZED Books.

Harberger, A. C. (1971). Three basic postulates for applied welfare economics: an interpretive essay. *Journal of Economic Literature*, *9*, 785–797.

Hatta, T. (1986). Welfare effects of changing commodity tax rates towards uniformity. *Journal of Public Economics*, *29*, 99–112.

Hoff, K. (2001). Second and third best theories. In J. Michie (Ed.), *Reader's guide to the social sciences*. London: Fitzroy Dearborn.

Knight, F. H. (1921). *Risk, uncertainty and profit*. New York: Houghton Mifflin Co.

Layard, R. (2005). *Happiness: lessons for a new science*. London: Penguin Books.

Lipsey, R. G. (1957). The theory of customs unions: trade diversion and welfare. *Economica*, *24*, 40–46, February.

Lipsey, R. G. (1970). *The theory of customs unions: a general equilibrium analysis*. London: Weidenfeld & Nicolson. A late publication of the 1957 Ph.D. thesis by the same name.

Lipsey, R. G. (1997). *The selected essays of Richard Lipsey: Volume I: microeconomics, growth and political economy*. Cheltenham: Edward Elgar.

Lipsey, R. G., & Lancaster, K. (1956). The general theory of second best. *The Review of Economic Studies*, *24*, 11–32. Reprinted with errors corrected in Lipsey 1997.

Lipsey, R. G., Carlaw, K. I., & Bekar, C. (2005). *Economic transformations: general purpose technologies and long-term economic growth*. Oxford: Oxford University Press.

Little, I. M. D. (1951). Direct versus indirect taxes. *The Economic Journal*, *61*(243), 577–584, September.

Little, I. M. D. (1957). *A critique of welfare economics* (2nd ed.). Oxford: Clarendon Press.

Mas-Colell, A., Whinston, M.D., & Green, R.J. (1995). *Microeconomic theory*. New York: Oxford University Press.

McKee, M., & West, E. G. (1981). The theory of second best: a solution in search of a problem. *Economic Inquiry*, *XIX*, 436–448.

McManus, M. (1958–1959). Comments on the general theory of second best. *Review of Economic Studies*, *26*, 209–224.

 Springer

Ng, Y.-K. (1977). Towards a theory of third-best. *Public Finance, 32*(1), 1–13.
Ozga, S. A. (1955). An essay in the theory of tariffs. *Journal of Political Economy, 63*, 489–499, December.
Samuelson, P. A. (1947). *Foundations of economic analysis*. Cambridge: Harvard University Press.
Starr, R. M. (1997). *General equilibrium theory: an introduction*. Cambridge: Cambridge University Press.
Viner, J. (1950). *The customs union issue*. New York: Carnegie Endowment of International Peace.

 Springer

Name Index

The International Library of Critical Writings in Economics